# the genocide studies reader

"*The Genocide Studies Reader* is a very useful introduction to the many acts of genocide all over the world as well as to the genocide studies field in general. Analyzing legal and sociological definitions and discussions, this book is an essential synthesis of the works produced in English on the subject."
—**Dr. Daniel Feierstein**, Director, Center of Genocide Studies, Universidad Nacional de Tres de Febrero, República Argentina

"This reader provides an excellent introduction to the field of genocide studies. Ranging far and wide, the volume includes foundational essays and covers key topics such as issues of definition, sexual violence, prevention, legal redress, intervention, and denial. It is a great resource both for classroom use and for scholars, students, and anyone interested in genocide."
—**Alex Hinton**, Center for the Study of Genocide and Human Rights, Rutgers, Newark

"It is no longer the historical occurrence of genocide that preoccupies social scientists, rather its disturbing recurrence in recent times despite the international conventions drawn up to protect human rights. To address this new reality, this instructive reader on the subject of genocide goes beyond the challenges of definition, theory, and history, and looks at the promise of intervention, prosecution, and prevention. All aspects of the problem of genocide are explored with particular attention to the issue of sovereignty and adjudication in the face of the hurdles of the claims of immunity and denials of responsibility. This collection of authoritative voices addressing this most serious crime against humanity brings new focus to the conflict between national and international interests and between standards of legality and the claims of state authority, and underscores no less the importance of studying the problem as much as developing the instruments to restrain mass violence."
—**Dr. Rouben Adalian**, Director, Armenian National Institute

This thorough overview of all aspects of the field of genocide studies brings together for the first time classic and contemporary writings from some of the most noted scholars writing on genocide in the fields of genocide studies, political science, history, and sociology. The *Reader* covers key aspects of a host of complex and thor... ... such as the definition of genocide, theories of genocide, prevention and intervention, and its c... ... collection of writings is essential reading for anyone who... understand this most atro... ... form of political violence that has plagued human history.

**Samuel Totten** is a Profes... ... at the University... ... ... founding editor of *Genocide Studies and Pre*... ... ... An... ... ... ... Fellow at the Centre for Conflict Mana... ... ... National University, Rwanda.

**Paul R. Bartrop** is an honorary fellow at... ... ... ... ... ... Australia, head of the dep... ... of history at Bialik College, Melbourne, and a past president of the Australian Association of Jewish Studies.

# the genocide studies reader

EDITED BY Samuel Totten
*University of Arkansas, Fayetteville*

Paul R. Bartrop
*Deakin University and Bialik College,
Melbourne, Victoria, Australia*

Routledge
Taylor & Francis Group

NEW YORK AND LONDON

## Dedication

Samuel Totten dedicates this book to both the pioneers of genocide studies and those scholars who follow in their footsteps, and does so with the hope that the primary goal of all those in the field is the effective prevention and intervention of genocide.

Paul R. Bartrop dedicates this book to Genia Janover, whose ongoing commitment to teaching about the Holocaust, genocide and human rights represents both development and continuity, and serves as a model for all educators.

First published 2009
by Routledge
270 Madison Ave, New York, NY 10016

Simultaneously published in the UK
by Routledge
2 Park Square, Milton Park, Abingdon, Oxon OX14 4RN

*Routledge is an imprint of the Taylor & Francis Group, an informa business*

© 2009 Taylor & Francis

Typeset in Minion by
RefineCatch Limited, Bungay, Suffolk
Printed and bound in the United States of America on acid-free paper by
Sheridan Books, Inc.

*Library of Congress Cataloging in Publication Data*
The genocide studies reader / edited by Samuel Totten and Paul R. Bartrop.
        p. cm.
    Includes bibliographical references and index.
    1. Genocide. 2. Genocide—Case studies. 3. Genocide—Prevention. I. Totten, Samuel. II. Bartrop, Paul R. (Paul Robert), 1955–
    HV6322.7.G4565 2008
    304.6′63—dc22
    2008026188

ISBN10: 0–415–95394–4 (hbk)
ISBN10: 0–415–95395–2 (pbk)

ISBN13: 978–0–415–95394–8 (hbk)
ISBN13: 978–0–415–95395–5 (pbk)

# Contents

Introduction     ix

## Part I    Definitions of Genocide

### 1    *The Origin of the Term Genocide and the Definition Used in the UN Convention on the Prevention and Punishment of the Crime of Genocide*    *3*

1.1   Raphael Lemkin, "Genocide: A Modern Crime"    6

1.2   Lawrence J. LeBlanc, "Development of the Rule on Genocide"    11

1.3   Morten Bergsmo, "Intent"    22

1.4   The United Nations Convention on the Prevention and Punishment of the Crime of Genocide    30

### 2    *Alternative Definitions*    *34*

2.1   Israel W. Charny, "The Definition of Genocide"    36

2.2   Roger W. Smith, "Human Destructiveness and Politics: The Twentieth Century as an Age of Genocide"    40

2.3   Helen Fein, "Defining Genocide as a Sociological Concept"    44

### 3    *Related Terms*    *57*

3.1   Andrew Bell-Fialkoff, "A Typology of Cleansing"    60

3.2   Michael Mann, "Explaining Ethnic Cleansing"    63

3.3   Barbara Harff, "Recognizing Genocides and Politicides"    71

3.4   William Schabas, "Crimes Against Humanity"    78

3.5   Jacques Semelin, "Massacres"    86

# Part II    Theories and Causes of Genocide

## 4    *Theories of Genocide*                                                      *95*

    4.1  Ervin Staub, "The Origins of Genocide and Mass Killing: Core Concepts"                                                         97

    4.2  Barbara Harff, "The Etiology of Genocides"                       108

    4.3  Roger W. Smith, "Scarcity and Genocide"                          120

    4.4  Gregory H. Stanton, "The Eight Stages of Genocide"               127

# Part III    Genocidal Crimes

## 5    *Cases of Genocide*                                                        *133*

    5.1  Paul R. Bartrop and Samuel Totten, "The History of Genocide: An Overview"                                                        135

    5.2  Donald L. Niewyk, "Holocaust: The Genocide of the Jews"          157

    5.3  Lisa Sharlach, "State Rape: Sexual Violence as Genocide"         180

    5.4  Jan Willem Honig, "Srebrenica"                                   192

    5.5  Samuel Totten, "The Darfur Genocide"                             194

## 6    *Comparative Studies of Various Cases of Genocide*                         *231*

    6.1  Robert F. Melson, "The Armenian Genocide as Precursor and Prototype of Twentieth-Century Genocide"                           234

    6.2  Ben Kiernan, "Twentieth-Century Genocides: Underlying Ideological Themes from Armenia to East Timor"                       243

    6.3  Mark Levene, "Connecting Threads: Rwanda, the Holocaust, and the Pattern of Contemporary Genocide"                          258

# Part IV    The Complexities of the Prevention and Intervention of Genocide

## 7    *The Issues of Sovereignty and Political Will*                             *287*

    7.1  M. Cherif Bassiouni, "Realpolitik"                               288

    7.2  Jackson Nyamuya Maogoto, "The Concept of State Sovereignty and the Development of International Law"                         290

    7.3  Bruce W. Jentleson, "The Dilemma of Political Will: How Fixed, How Malleable the Domestic Constraints?"                           293

7.4 The Responsibility to Protect: Report of the International Commission on Intervention and State Sovereignty 298

**8 The Prevention of Genocide** 316

8.1 Gregory H. Stanton, "Early Warning" 317

8.2 Helen Fein, "The Three P's of Genocide Prevention: With Application to a Genocide Foretold—Rwanda" 320

8.3 Interview: General Romeo Dallaire 338

**9 Intervention** 361

9.1 Thomas G. Weiss and Cindy Collins, "Policies of Militarized Humanitarian Intervention" 363

9.2 George A. Lopez, "Economic Sanctions and Genocide: Too Little, Too Late, and Sometimes Too Much" 378

9.3 Francis Kofi Abiew, "The East Pakistan (Bangladesh) Intervention of 1971" 390

9.4 Francis Kofi Abiew, "Vietnam's Intervention in Cambodia (Kampuchea), 1978" 395

9.5 James Cotton, "Against the Grain: The East Timor Intervention" 397

9.6 Nicholas J. Wheeler, "Reflections on the Legality and Legitimacy of NATO'S Intervention in Kosovo" 409

**Part V  Prosecution of Crimes against Humanity and Genocide**

**10 Setting a Precedent: The Nuremberg Trials** 425

10.1 Howard Ball, "The Path to Nuremberg: 1944–1945" 427

**11 The International Criminal Tribunal for the Former Yugoslavia** 439

11.1 Payam Akhavan and Mora Johnson, "International Criminal Tribunal for the Former Yugoslavia" 441

11.2 "Radislav Krstic Becomes the First Person to Be Convicted of Genocide at the ICTY and Is Sentenced to 46 Years Imprisonment" 452

**12   The International Criminal Tribunal for Rwanda**                    **463**

    12.1  Peter Uvin and Charles Mironko, "The International Criminal
    Tribunal for Rwanda"                                                   465

    12.2  Howard Ball, "Formation of the ICTR"                           468

    12.3  Michelle S. Lyon and Mark A. Drumbl, "International Criminal
    Tribunal for Rwanda"                                                   473

    12.4  "Historic Judgement Finds Akayesu Guilty of Genocide"         482

**13   Trials in National Courts**                                         **485**

    13.1  Jennifer Balint, "National Trials in Rwanda"                  487

**14   The International Criminal Court (ICC)**                             **491**

    14.1  Howard Ball, "Nuremberg's Legacy: Adoption of the
    Rome Statute"                                                          493

**Part VI   Denial of Genocide**

**15   Denial of Genocide**                                                **517**

    15.1  Israel W. Charny, "A Classification of Denials of the Holocaust
    and Other Genocides"                                                   518

    Permissions Acknowledgements                                          538

    Index                                                                  542

# Introduction

The day after he accepted the Nobel Peace Prize in 1986, celebrated author and Holocaust survivor Elie Wiesel referred to the incredulity experienced by his generation at the state of the world four decades after Europe's liberation from Nazism: "If someone had told us in 1945 that in our lifetime religious wars would rage on virtually every continent, that thousands of children would once again be dying of starvation, we would not have believed it. Or that racism and fanaticism would flourish once again."[1] Wiesel' major concern was that in the decades since the end of World War II nothing substantial seemed to have been learned as a result of that terrible conflict. All the cries of "Never Again!" so frequently uttered at the time of the liberation of the Nazi concentration and death camps had amounted to little more than hot air. No one these days seemed to care about the suffering of others; everyone, it appeared, was out for themselves at the expense of their fellow human beings. While none of this was new to Wiesel, it saddened him to look at the world and constantly be forced to draw the same depressing conclusion. Everyone, he believed, should be looking out for everyone else, but in a later statement, Wiesel was forced to ask: "How can I expect a man to have compassion for humanity if he has none for the individual who lives alongside him?"[2]

Wiesel's despair in 1986 was diametrically opposite to the feelings of many in 1945. The world that had been fought for by the democracies had been safeguarded, and with Nazism destroyed in Europe optimism for the future underwent a rebirth. The euphoria would, of course, be short-lived, but there was reason to hope that the post-war world would bring with it the realization of all the best ideals that liberal democracy saw as worthwhile.

One of several measures adopted by the newly established United Nations to bring this about was an agreement in 1948 to prevent and punish the crime of genocide. The word itself was then of only recent invention: in 1944 a Polish-Jewish jurist, Raphael Lemkin, coined the term by linking the Greek word *genos* (tribe, nation) with the Latin-based suffix—*cide* (killing). For Lemkin, the Nazi assault in Europe was cause for a great deal of serious reflection about the state of humanity in the modern world, and about its future. Accordingly, he wrote, "New conceptions require new terms. By 'genocide' we mean the destruction of a nation or ethnic group. . . . It is intended . . . to signify a coordinated plan of different actions aiming at the destruction of essential foundations of life of national groups, with the aim of annihilating the groups themselves."[3]

The enormous range and variety of outbreaks that have been termed genocide throughout history have since led to a multiplicity of theories that have attempted to explain it. From Lemkin's invention, a full scholarship of genocide has emerged, as reflected in the range of articles, ideas, and concepts reproduced in the current volume.

Defining genocide is not, in itself, a difficult matter. The end point of any genocidal act is always the same, namely, the intentional destruction, in whole or in part, of a specific group of people. It is a matter of some debate, however, as to how these aims are to be achieved, and for some scholars this determines the extent to which an act may or may not be deemed genocidal. Raphael Lemkin tried to construct as wide a definition as possible when determining what could be included within the framework of genocide. He incorporated such matters as the dismantling of nationhood, forced disintegration of political and social institutions, and destruction of culture, language, religion, and economic existence. According to Lemkin, genocide could also involve the destruction of the lives of individuals belonging to the targeted group; possibly because of the horrors of the past century, it is frequently only through this last feature that many contemporary commentators give credence to the term.

While the development of different theories about genocide may employ numerous approaches-historical, social, political, psychological, economic, environmental, religious, ideological, military, cultural, and so on—invariably a great deal of genocide theory proceeds from (and all too often, gets bogged down by) discussions relating to definitional matters. Whereas Lemkin's original conception began with the statement that genocide means "the destruction of a nation or ethnic group," many others have built their discussions around definitions that diverge from this. Other forms of destruction that do not fit comfortably into the concept of genocide have led scholars to devise even newer terms: hence, in addition to genocide we are often required to now also address ideas such as ethnocide, autogenocide, politicide, democide, omnicide, and gendercide, among others. But while these notions are often useful in creating models to help approach specific issues, it could be argued that a full appreciation of genocide itself, in all its guises, has yet to be exhausted.

Quite clearly, precision is needed when applying the term; we need to know what it *is* and what it *is not*. If anything can be incorporated or rejected as genocide according to individual preferences, there is no certainty that we will ever be able to bring the intellectual rigor to the topic that serious academic scholarship demands. In a formal, almost scientific, sense, we have to know when to apply the term and when not to do so.

Ever since the term "genocide" was first coined by Lemkin, there have been ongoing disputes within academe over how the concept should, once and for all, be defined and interpreted. While these disputes have been vigorous and, at times, even acrimonious, they have led to substantial and significant misuse of the term. For some, genocide equates directly with war; for others, with language extinction; for yet others, with colonialist occupation; and for some, with population collapse caused through natural famine or disease. In certain quarters, arguments for "accidental" genocide have been posited where a population's numbers are reduced despite the best efforts of others to stop such reduction. Elsewhere, genocide has been misapplied when conflated into other examples of inhumanity or gross human rights violations, such as slavery or political incarceration. The popularization of the term has extended into the realms of education and journalism. As a result, all too often it appears as though any definition or understanding of the term is seemingly just as legitimate as any other.

On a different note, the term genocide has been misapplied in a variety of ways. More specifically, all of the following scenarios have, at one time or another, been referred to as genocide: "race-mixing" (the integration of blacks and non-blacks); the practice of forced birth control and abortions among Third World peoples; sterilizations and so-called "Mississippi appendectomies" (tubal ligations and hysterectomies); the closing of synagogues in the Soviet Union; a lack of support for research into AIDS; the adoption of black children by whites; the human genome project collecting DNA samples from peoples around the globe; respective United States governments' policies regarding illicit drugs (which purportedly allowed the rampant sale of drugs in the inner cities of the USA); and even abortions.

In 1945, as Lemkin was attempting to popularize his new concept in the academic, legal, and governmental spheres, there seemed to be no difficulty in people identifying it for what it was. A vast number of Europeans, in particular, already instinctively knew about genocide, even if the term was not yet in wide usage. In Allied capitals around the world, reports through both official channels and the media had already been conveying for some time the realities of the Nazi Holocaust, as evidence of the worst expressions of inhumanity was uncovered by liberating forces.

Genocide is a crime that has been committed throughout the ages. A new name for a very old practice, as a legal term it was accepted and absorbed by the United Nations in order to describe the intentional destruction, in whole or in part, of a specific group of people. This was clearly delineated in the United Nations Convention on the Prevention and Punishment of the Crime of Genocide 1948 (UNCG).

The initial design of the UNGC was in large part drafted by Lemkin himself, though substantial redrafting at committee stage by United Nations member states saw it changed considerably from what had originally been envisaged. The main areas of contention in the final document, both then and now, are located in its Article 2, as follows:

> In the present Convention, genocide means any of the following acts committed with intent to destroy, in whole or in part, a national, ethnical, racial or religious group, as such:
>
> (a) Killing members of the group;
> (b) Causing serious bodily or mental harm to members of the group;
> (c) Deliberately inflicting on the group conditions of life calculated to bring about its physical destruction in whole or in part;
> (d) Imposing measures intended to prevent births within the group;
> (e) Forcibly transferring children of the group to another group.

A few key points can be noted by way of summarizing the content of Article 2:

1 For a successful charge of genocide to be brought, the notion of *intent* on the part of the perpetrators must be demonstrated, though how such intent is to be proven is not spelled out. Given this, intent can be inferred from the actions of those charged with the crime; neither written not verbal orders need not be extant in order to prove intent.
2 Destruction can be "in whole" or "in part," though just how many individuals constitute "in part" is not spelled out.
3 Four possible groups are listed as the only acceptable targets for genocide. Thus, if other groups of people are persecuted—for example, as a result of political affiliation, social origin, cultural background, or sexual preference—this is not protected within the UN's definition of genocide.
4 While the popular view generally holds that genocide equates with killing, the UNCG shows that killing is not the only means to commit genocide; four other activities, in which lives are not necessarily taken, can also constitute genocide. As a result, a much broader range of actions than mass murder is included under the acts than can be termed "genocide," and, as a result, the UNCG, though far from perfect, is nonetheless useful in that it casts a wider net than if it focused only on killing.

To address various perceived weaknesses and/or gaps in the UNCG's definition of genocide, some scholars have developed structures whereby genocides can be classified and categorized. Helen Fein, for instance, has created four overall categories of genocide:

1 *developmental genocide* (where perpetrators clear an area of its inhabitants prior to colonization);
2 *despotic genocide* (where destruction happens so as to clear the way for new regimes to come to power);
3 *retributive genocide* (where peoples are targeted for reasons based around social dominance and struggle); and
4 *ideological genocide* (where a population is defined doctrinally as undeserving of life).[4]

In other areas, scholars have sought to broaden the range of categories, such as adding war-related genocides, or to find ways of gathering together all instances of massacre, area bombing, state-directed killing of large numbers of people, or mass destruction caused by other agencies or individuals.

Locating such actions within a taxonomy of genocide can be useful, but only if an acceptable definition has also been agreed upon. And herein lies a problem; grouping genocides for the purpose of plotting, prediction, or planning is a worthwhile task only if scholars can first agree on precisely what it is they are studying. And other than the definition in the UNCG, there are no other universally accepted definitions of genocide prevailing today. Grouping examples of mass killing and human rights violations together within a matrix of genocide may be a means to break the impasse, but it has only a limited value in law. Even though conceptually it provides assistance to scholars, such classification can only be applied narrowly for lawyers and courts.

It is largely in order to rise above this chaos that one should be wary about straying too far from the UNCG, imperfect though it is. Moreover, if the quest to understand genocide is to be more than just an abstract scholarly enterprise, we must face one essential fact: it is *only* through the United Nations, at least in today's world, that the countries of the world will ever apply themselves seriously to the question of confronting genocide. For now, the international community has only one definition with which to work, and does not recognize any other. Therefore, we are stuck with the UN definition, and have to operate accordingly. This is the main reason why we should be concerned to ensure respect for the UNCG; not because it is the best, but rather because, in the eyes of the international community, it is the *only one* likely to bring prosecutions that can lead to the punishment of perpetrators, and, thereby, to act as a deterrent.

For these reasons, as well as others, we need to consider the root cause behind the establishment of international legislation designed to confront genocide. Quite simply, the trend over the course of the past century has been towards greater killing, greater targeting of civilians, and a greater likelihood than ever before that groups are being singled out for destruction. In the enormous death toll of World War I, the vast majority were military deaths; our best estimates tell us that on average, 5,600 soldiers were killed per day, every day, for four-and-a-quarter years.[5] Only five percent of all deaths in combat zones during World War I numbered civilians.[6] After that conflict, however, the rate of civilian deaths in wartime increased enormously. By the time of World War II, civilians could be calculated at 66 per cent of all war-related deaths; into the 1970s and 1980s, this figure moved inexorably towards 80 per cent.[7] The vast majority of such deaths by now can be put down to an accumulation of massacres (some predetermined, some spontaneous) and genocide (by definition deliberate, intended, and justified).

A word on the relationship between war and genocide is needed here, as many people tend to equate the two as synonymous. In the popular consciousness, the first thing that can come to mind is the idea of killing on a vast scale. Genocide is almost always seen as having something to do with death, brutal death, massive of type and uncompromising in its choice of victim. And, more often than not, armies in war are seen as the major agents through which this killing takes place. Many people have tried to make sense of the twentieth century by reference to its warlike character, as if to suggest that genocidal devastation can only surface during such times rather than during periods of peace. Yet not all the wars of the twentieth century took on a genocidal character, even though obviously some were extremely violent and destructive. Moreover, there can be little doubt that war contains within it the potential for a genocidal regime to realize its aims, and probably more easily than in the absence of war.

But war does not have to be present for genocide to occur. One of the fundamental lessons of the twentieth century was that living in a peacetime environment does not safeguard immunity from mass and horrific atrocity. The point is, genocide does not equate with war, and the two terms should not be employed interchangeably, for although in some cases there is a relationship of interdependence between the two, this is by no means a given in every situation.

Genocide is a criminal act. Its criminal nature must be emphasized, and emphasized *yet again*; it became the twentieth century's greatest man-made catastrophe. It is, arguably, a worse disaster than war, with which it is often linked but from which it can be separated. Genocide speaks of human dreams (perverse or as perverted as they can be); it addresses questions of how people perceive one another, and influences their behavior when they interact. Above all, it conceives of humanity's future in light of how some people view themselves—superior, intelligent, vibrant, and perfectible. To attain that future, so-called "surplus humans"—to use U.S. theologian Richard L. Rubenstein's term—have had to be sacrificed, and as regimes around the world have tried to achieve their version of the dream innumerable mass murders have been undertaken. Rubenstein identified in modernity the existence of populations "that for any reason can find no viable role in the society in which [they are] domiciled."[7] This horrible reality had for many centuries already been played out, but it was not until the massive carnage of World War I that this thinking resulted in the idea that a "surplus population" could simply be eliminated through just killing it off, and thereafter imagine—falsely, of course—that the group had never existed. After 1918, people knew that millions of human beings could be killed by other human beings. A psychological limit was breached, from which the boundaries of the human mind would never again be the same. There is nothing on the horizon to suggest that, so long as the vision prevails of a perfectible world built on the bodies of so-called "imperfect" human beings, the killing will stop.

The disaster of Bosnia-Herzegovina, for instance, dominated international news for much of the early 1990s; not only was it the first genocide (in Srebrenica, in 1995) to take place in Europe since the Holocaust, but a term from the past—"ethnic cleansing"—had been introduced into the mix. Unfortunately, as often happens, the larger situation in the former Yugoslavia got bogged down, in part, at least, in a debate over whether what was transpiring in different parts of the region constituted ethnic cleansing or genocide. Often the talk added to the confusion over what to do and how to do it.

Almost as an acknowledgment of a guilty conscience owing to its failure to act effectively in Bosnia, in March 1999 NATO forces attacked Serbia with the intention of compelling that country's government to stop its persecution of the ethnic Albanian population living in the Serbian province of Kosovo. Regardless of whatever underlying motives may have conditioned NATO leaders' actions, this was the first occasion on which a war was fought for the avowed purpose of stopping genocide before its worst horrors took place. Under international law, the attack was illegal; it was neither called for nor approved by the United Nations. Nonetheless, it was successful in that it stopped a potential genocide—even though it resulted in a disaster that allowed the Serbs to ethnically cleanse substantial expanses of territory, forcibly removing hundreds of thousands of people, and murdering many thousands of others in the process. The Serbian regime of Slobodan Milosevic, after a lengthy and intensive NATO bombing campaign, pulled its troops out of Kosovo, allowed for a UN peacekeeping presence in the province, and permitted nearly one million persecuted Kosovars, who had been expelled from the country in a huge outbreak of "ethnic cleansing," to return home.

The international community's guilty conscience, if indeed one existed, had not helped the Tutsi population of the tiny African country of Rwanda in 1994. The Rwanda genocide tells us much about the nature and priorities of the international system in the 1990s, and offers lessons of which all citizens of democratic nations should take note. This was an eruption of violence that saw possibly up to one million people murdered in the space of a hundred days. The then head of the UN Department of Peacekeeping Operations, Kofi Annan, was shaken by the experience. When he became UN Secretary-General three years later he was determined to do something about injecting the world organization with some of the political will that had been so dramatically lacking during the Rwandan genocide. With a sense of personal shame and responsibility for his failures and those of others in the UN Security Council in 1994, Annan's new-found resolve on the matter culminated in the launch by Annan on April 7, 2004 of an Action Plan to Prevent Genocide, accompanied by an announcement of the future appointment of a Special Adviser on Genocide Prevention. The new initiatives could not have come at a more appropriate time, as a twenty-first century test case of the Secretary-General's new initiative appeared—seemingly out of the blue—in the western Darfur region of Sudan. Despite Annan's avowed determination for the UN to appear proactive in stemming the tide of genocide, next to nothing happened in the years that followed. The disaster of Darfur, still being played out in 2009, was yet another example of a UN peacekeeping fiasco that was effectively useless in bringing genocide to an end.

For a number of reasons it is possible that serious interventionist action will have to occur in Darfur, Sudan, even though the Sudanese government has stated that it will resist with force any such intervention. If intervention does take place, it will be an indication of how far the international community has come since Rwanda. However, the same dilemmas will remain, most notably the question of the point at which such action was taken, and, once decided, why it wasn't taken earlier.

The history of genocide in the modern world would appear to show that evil people are much more dedicated toward evil than good people are toward good. The major questions that some scholars have spent a lifetime trying to resolve—what are we to do? and do we need to change the world?—have been asked many times before. Some think it can be done through adherence to the law; others have tried to convince the world that only through democracy and the freedoms it guarantees can nations and peoples see that state violence is contrary to their own self-interest. It is within the context of such thinking that we can perhaps appreciate where more recent international developments, such as forced regime change and unilateral military action, can lead if backed up by an effective degree of political will at the highest levels. So far, however, attention has been drawn in other directions, and recent U.S.-led debacles in Iraq and Afghanistan have led governments around the world to adopt a much more wary approach to international involvement based on some greater good that has little direct impact on perceived national interest.

Combating genocide on a global scale has not assumed the importance it should. It would seem natural that we should try to build the means of ensuring that the twenty-first century will not go the way of the twentieth (the perpetration of genocide in each of its decades), but of course, that is no easy task. Internationally, the range of legal instruments related to human rights since 1948 has expanded beyond anything previously envisaged by even the most farsighted of activists—but despite this, the number of genocidal eruptions has actually *increased* during this time. There is, unfortunately, no ready-made answer to the question of what to do. Despite the legal and institutional processes that have been instituted against it, genocide still exists. It is, sadly, both a defining characteristic of our time, and a social problem of the first magnitude. Genocide has been described as the crime of crimes. If it is true that the last century was the Century of Genocide, we need to ask not only why this was so, but also whether or not this has had a permanently destructive impact on world civilization.

During the 1930s, when Hitler's expansionist policies were threatening the security of Europe and human rights were being trampled on everywhere, a man of immense learning, the Chassidic rabbi of the Hungarian town of Berbest, asked a simple question for which there was, at the time, no answer: "When a person is a murderer, the state will arrest and punish him; but when the state is the murderer, who will arrest and punish it?"[8] Since 1945, and owing to the worldwide concern expressed over the destruction of vast numbers of the Berbester Rebbe's people, we now know that there are ways in which this can be achieved, and the UNCG is, for all its faults, the most appropriate instrument to do so if backed up by an accompanying political will.

We are faced with the question of how all this is to be interpreted: the question, perhaps, of "whether again?" rather than "never again." If the trend over the course of the past century has been towards greater killing, greater targeting of civilians, and a greater likelihood than ever before that groups are being singled out for destruction, what hope does this offer those with a commitment to peace and the sanctity of life?

Again, there is no ready-made answer to this question. Genocide still exists, despite the legal processes that have been instituted against it.

If we are to develop a satisfactory appreciation of the lessons of the Century of Genocide for humanity today—indeed, if genocide studies is not to become simply another branch of intellectual endeavor about which movies are made—we must all stand back, have a look at the facts of the situation, and ask ourselves "what does this mean to *me*?" At the moment of our asking, we are automatically confronted with our understanding of where we stand in relation to the rest of society—to what our responsibilities and obligations should be towards that society and towards the state which claims to represent its interests. Ultimately, we might even find ourselves approaching the ultimate question: "How should I have behaved in the same situation?"—a question that carries much greater weight for our present and our future than the unanswerable, hit-or-miss, and highly irrelevant "How *would* I have behaved?"

All in all, understanding genocide can help us appreciate that massive evil exists in the world, and that the onus is on all of us to ensure that it be resisted before it gets out of hand. It is to our advantage to realize that living in a peaceful environment does not necessarily safeguard immunity. Just because genocides have usually happened in lands that could be described as "over there" does not mean they cannot happen "over here" as well. In this sense, it is worth remembering that it was only a very few years between the Sarajevo Olympics and the siege of Sarajevo, or between Cambodia as a peaceable tourist destination and Cambodia as a hell on earth.

\* \* \*

*The Genocide Studies Reader,* comprised of a wide array of articles by some of the most noted scholars addressing the issue of genocide, provides a relatively succinct but solid overview of the burgeoning area of genocide studies. This compilation of articles, along with the introductions to each section, addresses a host of significant issues regarding key aspects of genocide (for example, from definitional concerns to theories of genocide, and from cases of genocide to issues relating to genocide prevention and intervention).

*The Genocide Studies Reader* does not (and could not), of course, include every seminal document available on genocide, let alone a piece by every noted scholar, activist, or government or intergovernmental official who has done significant work related to the issue. In light of the fact that scholarship on genocide has increased exponentially over the past two decades, it would be virtually impossible to include every article that is worthy of note in a work such as this. In that regard, *The Genocide Studies Reader* constitutes a solid reference tool that addresses some of the more weighty issues to confront society as it continues to wrestle with how to prevent genocide or, once it has broken out, to stanch it quickly and effectively.

The selection of articles involved a lengthy process of weighing the merits (or lack thereof) of literally hundreds of articles, book chapters, and reports. Prior to examining potential articles for inclusion in *The Genocide Studies Reader*, a tentative table of contents was created. Subsequently—and again, prior to the selection of any articles—that initial table of contents was revised close to a dozen times.

Once the table of contents was more or less firmly in place, scores of books and articles in journals by noted scholars in a variety of fields (including, though not limited to, genocide studies, political science, psychology, history, and sociology), and book chapters and articles on an array of topics (e.g., debates about the definition of genocide and related terms, theories of genocide, specific genocides, prevention of genocide, intervention in genocide, punishment of perpetrators) were combed for pieces that were highly informative. Numerous articles addressing the same topic were examined and then selected based on the following criteria: significance of the information presented, depth of information, clarity of the writing, and, of course, accuracy of the information presented. Concomitantly, the more thought-provoking an article was the more likely it was to be selected for inclusion in the book. Articles were also selected, in part, for their brevity (that is, the shorter they were the better, as that allowed the inclusion of more articles in the book). Finally, once all the articles had been selected, they were read again to make sure that there was as little redundancy as possible between the various pieces. Any article that may have been too close in content to another was cut (being sure to retain the stronger of the two pieces).

## Notes

1  Elie Wiesel, *From the Kingdom of Memory: Reminiscences.* New York: Summit Books, 1990, p. 246.
2  Elie Wiesel with Michael de Saint Cheron, *Evil and Exile.* 2nd edition. South Bend, IN: University of Notre Dame Press, 1990, p. 138.
3  Raphael Lemkin, *Axis Rule in Occupied Europe: Laws of Occupation, Analysis of Government, Proposals for Redress.* Washington, D.C.: Carnegie Endowment for International Peace, 1944, p. 79.
4  See this summary of Fein's conclusions in Israel W. Charny (Editor-in-Chief), *Encyclopedia of Genocide.* Vol. 1. Santa Barbara, CA: ABC-Clio, 1999, p. 5.
5  Martin Gilbert, *First World War.* London: Weidenfeld and Nicolson, 1994, p. 541.
6  Eric Markusen and David Kopf, *The Holocaust and Strategic Bombing: Genocide and Total War in the Twentieth Century.* Boulder, CO: Westview Press, 1995, p. 244.
7  Richard L. Rubenstein, *The Age of Triage: Fear and Hope in an Overcrowded World.* Boston, MA: Beacon, 1983, p. 1.
8  David Weiss Halivni, *The Book and the Sword: A Life of Learning in the Shadow of Destruction.* New York: Farrar, Straus and Giroux, 1996, p. 51.

# Part I

*Definitions of Genocide*

# 1

# The Origin of the Term Genocide and the Definition Used in the UN Convention on the Prevention and Punishment of the Crime of Genocide

In 1944, Raphael Lemkin, a Polish-Jewish jurist, coined the term "genocide." He did so by combining the Greek *genos* for kin, clan, race, or tribe, and the Latin suffix *-cide* for kill or murder. As it has been noted repeatedly, Lemkin created a term for a practice that had been perpetrated through the ages.

As a youth, Lemkin heard and learned songs and poetry about how the innocent, poor, and voiceless were often ill-treated throughout history, and the stories inherent in such accounts resonated with him. As he grew older, he became a voracious reader and gravitated to works about the persecution of groups due to their religious beliefs, race, or characteristics and/or for other reasons. He was particularly moved by Henryk Sienkiewicz's *Quo Vadis*, which told the story of Nero's destruction of the Christians. He became indignant, he said, when he also learned about the French king who watched impassively as Huguenots were hanged.

Later still, Lemkin was extremely disturbed when he heard that a pogrom had been perpetrated in the city of Bialystok, during which mobs slit open the stomachs of their victims. Not much later, he read that the perpetrators of the slaughter of the Armenians (1915–1923) were arrested for the alleged crimes they had perpetrated, only to be released subsequently. Writing in his unpublished autobiography, *Totally Unofficial Man*, Lemkin said: "I was shocked. A nation that killed and the guilty persons were set free. Why is a man punished when he kills another man? When is the killing of a million a lesser crime than the killing of a single individual? I didn't know all the answers, but I felt that a law against this type of racial or religious murder must be adopted by the world" (Lemkin, 2002, p. 371).

Following the Nazi invasion of Poland in September 1939, Lemkin fled Europe, ultimately immigrating to the United States. His parents and a bevy of other relatives, however, remained in Poland, 49 of whom perished at the hands of the Nazis.

Consumed with the conflagration engulfing Europe as a result of Hitler's and the Nazis' hatred of those they deemed less than human, Lemkin, in 1944, coined the term and concept of genocide. (Interestingly, in October 1933, Lemkin had already wrestled with the concept, formulating two crimes he entitled "the crimes of barbarity and the crimes of vandalism.")

Approximately six months before the outset of the Nuremberg Tribunal to try alleged Nazi criminals for crimes against peace, crimes against humanity, and war crimes, Lemkin published several articles on genocide, including one in the *American Scholar*. Subsequently, he wrote a draft resolution, initially asking the UN to study genocide with an eye to establishing it as an international crime. Working indefatigably over a number of years, Lemkin gave his all to nurturing relationships with those diplomats considering the possibility of establishing a convention on genocide, traveling from one venue to another in an attempt to educate various nations' representatives about the significance of and the need for such a convention. Indeed, he carried out a one-man crusade to see that genocide became a crime under international law.

From the outset, the development of the UN Convention on the Prevention and Punishment of Genocide was plagued by great difficulty and controversy. Nations with diverse philosophies, culture, "historical experiences, and sensitivities to human suffering" (Kuper, 1985, p. 10) presented different interpretations as to what constituted genocide and argued in favor of a definition and wording that were in accord with their particular perspectives.

On December 11, 1946, the United Nations General Assembly passed this initial resolution (96–1):

> Genocide is a denial of the right of existence of entire human groups, as homicide is the denial of the right to life of individual human beings. . . . Many instances of such crimes of genocide have occurred, when racial, religious, political, and other groups have been destroyed entirely or in part.
>
> The General Assembly Therefore, Affirms that genocide is a crime under international law which the civilized world condemns, for the commission of which principals and accomplices—whether private individuals, public officials or statesmen, and whether the crimes is committed on religious, racial, political or any other grounds—are punishable.

There was unanimous acceptance of this resolution. Of the utmost significance is that the initial resolution included "political or any other groups." However, a controversy erupted when the Soviet Union, Poland, and other nations argued against the inclusion of political groups. The Soviet representatives argued that the inclusion of political groups would not conform "with the scientific definition of genocide and would, in practice, distort the perspective in which the crime should be viewed and impair the efficacy of the Convention." Similarly, the Poles added that "the inclusion of provisions relating to political groups, which because of their mutability and lack of distinguishing characteristics did not lend themselves to definitions, would weaken and blur the whole Convention."

Another argument put forth against the inclusion of political groups was that unlike national, racial, or religious groups, membership in political groups was voluntary. However, in a later session, the French representative argued that "whereas in the past crimes of genocide had been committed on racial or religious grounds it was clear that in the future they would be committed mainly on political grounds." Representatives of many other nations concurred with this position and offered strong support in favor of its recognition.

A particularly moving argument put forth against the exclusion of political groups was that "those who committed the crime of genocide might use the pretext of the political opinion of a racial or religious group to persecute and destroy it, without becoming liable to international sanctions."

In 1981, Leo Kuper reported that

> Political groups survived for many sessions and seemed securely ensconced in the Convention, but on 29 November 1948, the issue was reopened in the Legal Committee on a motion by the delegations of Iran, Egypt, and Uruguay. A compromise seems to have been reached behind the scenes. The United States delegation, though still committed to the principle of extending protection to political groups, was conciliatory. It feared nonratification of the Convention, and rejection of the proposal for an international tribunal, if political groups were included. On a vote, political groups were expunged (Kuper, 1981, p 29).

Ultimately, the UN Convention on the Prevention and Punishment of the Crime of Genocide (UNCG), which was approved by the General Assembly of the United Nations on December 9, 1948, defined genocide in the following manner:

> In the present Convention, genocide means any of the following acts committed with the intent to destroy, in whole or in part, a national, ethnical, racial, or religious group, as such:
>   (a) Killing members of the group;
>   (b) Causing serious bodily or mental harm to members of the group;
>   (c) Deliberately inflicting on the group conditions of life calculated to bring about its physical destruction in whole or in part;
>   (d) Imposing measures intended to prevent births within the group;
>   (e) Forcibly transferring children of the group to another group.

The arguments and counter-arguments resulted in what can best be described as a "compromise definition." Many scholars have roundly criticized the exclusion of political and social groups from the UN Convention. It is worth noting that in 1973, the International Commission of Jurists recommended that the definition of genocide be revised so that it would include political groups. In 1985, Ben Whitaker, UN Rapporteur on Genocide, made a similar recommendation in his much heralded *Revised and Updated Report on the Question of the Prevention and Punishment of the Crime of Genocide.* (Even earlier, in 1959, Pieter N. Drost, a Dutch law professor, ardently argued that the United Nations needed to redefine genocide as "the deliberate destruction of physical life of individual human beings by reason of their membership of any human collectivity as such," p. 125.)

Section 1 of *The Genocide Studies Reader* includes four pieces. In the first, "Genocide: A Modern Crime," Lemkin discusses why he coined the concept of and term "genocide," and why genocide should be considered a crime under international law and the ramifications of the latter. The second piece in this section, "Development of the Rule on Genocide" by Lawrence J. LeBlanc, discusses Lemkin's definition of genocide, Lemkin's effort to see the UNCG ratified by the United States (and his failure to do so and why this was), the role of the UN in defining genocide, the process of drafting the UNCG and the ensuing battles, and, finally, the basic elements of genocide. In "Intent," Morten Bergsmo discusses the sticky issue of "intent" *vis-à-vis* the definition of the UNCG. It is sticky for without evidence of "intent" by the perpetrators to destroy a particular group (protected under the UNCG), in whole or in part, the crimes perpetrated do not constitute genocide. In doing so, he discusses, among other issues, the international treaty law on degree or quality of genocidal intent and international case law on degree or quality of intent *vis-à-vis* cases tried at the International Criminal Tribunal for the former Yugoslavia and the International Criminal Tribunal for Rwanda. The section concludes with a copy of the UNCG itself.

# References

Drost, Pieter, N. (1959). *The Crime of State* (vol. 2). Leyden: A. W. Sythoff.

Kuper, Leo (1981). *Genocide: Its Political Use in the Twentieth Century.* New Haven, CT: Yale University Press.

Kuper, Leo (1985). *The Prevention of Genocide.* New Haven, CT: Yale University Press.

Lemkin, Raphael (2002). "Totally Unofficial Man," pp. 365–399. In Samuel Totten and Steven Leonard Jacobs (Eds.) *Pioneers of Genocide Studies.* New Brunswick, NJ: Transaction Publishers.

Whitaker, Benjamin (1985). Revised and Updated Report on the Question of the Prevention and Punishment of the Crime of Genocide. (E/CN.4/Sub.2/1985/6, 2 July 1985).

# 1.1    Raphael Lemkin, "Genocide: A Modern Crime"
April 1945

This article first appeared during World War II in the April 1945 issue of *Free World*—"A Non-Partisan Magazine devoted to the United Nations and Democracy," published in five languages. [*Free World*, Vol. 4 (April 1945), pp. 39–43]

The article summarized for a popular audience the concepts Lemkin originally presented in Chapter 9 of *Axis Rule in Occupied Europe*, published by the Carnegie Endowment for International Peace in November 1944.

*"International premeditated murder, as planned and practiced against the peoples of Europe by Hitler, must be brought within the scope and jurisdiction of future international law. This is a major problem facing the coming world."*

"One of the great mistakes of 1918 was to spare the civil life of the enemy countries, for it is necessary for us Germans to be always at least double the numbers of the peoples of the contiguous countries. We are therefore obliged to destroy at least a third of their inhabitants. The only means is organized underfeeding which in this case is better than machine guns."

The speaker was Marshal von Rundstedt addressing the Reich War Academy in Berlin in 1943. He was only aping the Fuhrer who had said, "Natural instincts bid all living human beings not merely conquer their enemies but also destroy them. In former days it was the victor's prerogative to destroy tribes, entire peoples."

Hitler was right. The crime of the Reich in wantonly and deliberately wiping out whole peoples is not utterly new in the world. It is only new in the civilized world as we have come to think of it. It is so new in the traditions of civilized man that he has no name for it.

It is for this reason that I took the liberty of inventing the word, "genocide." The term is from the Greek word *genos* meaning tribe or race and the Latin *cide* meaning killing. Genocide tragically enough must take its place in the dictionary of the future beside other tragic words like homicide and infanticide. As Von Rundstedt has suggested the term does not necessarily signify mass killings although it may mean that.

More often it refers to a coordinated plan aimed at destruction of the essential foundations of the life of national groups so that these groups wither and die like plants that have suffered a blight. The end may be accomplished by the forced disintegration of political and social institutions, of the culture of the people, of their language, their national feelings and their religion. It may be accomplished by wiping out all basis of personal security, liberty, health and dignity. When these means fail the machine gun can always be utilized as a last resort. Genocide is directed against a national group as an entity and the attack on individuals is only secondary to the annihilation of the national group to which they belong.

Such terms as "denationalization" or "Germanization" which have been used till now do not adequately convey the full force of the new phenomenon of genocide. They signify only the substitution of the national pattern of the oppressor for the original national pattern but not the destruction of the biological and physical structure of the oppressed group.

## Philosophy of Genocide

Germany has transformed an ancient barbarity into a principle of government by dignifying genocide as a sacred purpose of the German people. National Socialism is the doctrine of the biological superiority of the German people. Long before the war nazi leaders were unblushinghly announcing to the world and propagandizing to the Germans themselves the program of genocide they had elaborated. Like Hitler and Von Rundstedt, the official nazi philosopher Alfred Rosenberg declared "History and the mission of the future no longer mean the struggle of class against class, the struggle of church dogma against dogma, but the clash between blood and blood, race and race, people and people." As the German war machine placed more and more defeated nations under the full control of nazi authorities, their civilian populations found themselves exposed to the bloodthirsty and methodical application of the German program of genocide.

A hierarchy of racial values determined the ultimate fate of the many peoples that fell under German domination. Jews were to be completely annihilated. The Poles, the Slovenes, the Czechs, the Russians, and all other inferior Slav peoples were to be kept on the lowest social levels. Those felt to be related by blood, the Dutch, the Norwegian, the Alsatians, etc., were to have the alternatives of entering the German community by espousing "Germanism" or of sharing the fate of the inferior peoples.

## Techniques of Genocide

All aspects of nationhood were exposed to the attacks of the genocidal policy.

### Political

The political cohesion of the conquered countries was intended to be weakened by dividing them into more or less self-contained and hermetically enclosed zones, as in the four zones of France, the ten zones of Yugoslavia, the five zones of Greece; by partitioning their territories to create puppet states, like Croatia and Slovakia; by detaching territory for incorporation in the Greater Reich, as was done with western Poland, Alsace-Lorraine, Luxembourg, Slovenia. Artificial boundaries were created to prevent communication and mutual assistance by the national groups involved.

In the incorporated areas of western land, Luxembourg, Alsace-Lorraine, Eupen, Malmedy, Moresnet, local administrations were replaced by German administrative organization. The legal system was recast on the German model. Special Commissioners for the strengthening of Germanism, attached to each administration, coordinated the activities designed to foster and promote Germanism. They were assisted by local inhabitants of German origin. These, duly registered and accredited, served as a nucleus of Germanism and enjoyed special privileges in respect to food rations, employment and position.

National allegiances were impaired by creating puppet governments, as in Greece, Norway and France, and by supporting national nazi parties. Where the people, such as the Poles, could not achieve the dignity of embracing Germanism, they were expelled from the area and their territory (western Poland) was to be Germanized by colonization.

### Social

The social structure of a nation is vital to its national development. Therefore the German occupant endeavored to bring about changes that weakened national spiritual resources. The focal point of this attack has been the intelligentsia, because this group largely provides leadership. In Poland and Slovenia the intellectuals and the clergy were to a large extent either murdered or removed for forced labor in Germany. Intellectuals and resistants of all occupied countries were marked for execution. Even among the blood-related Dutch some 23,000 were killed, the greater number of them being leading members of their communities.

### Cultural

The Germans sought to obliterate every reminder of former cultural patterns. In the incorporated areas the local language, place names, personal names, public signs and inscriptions were supplanted by German inscriptions. German was to be the language of the courts, of the schools, of the government and of the street. In Alsace-Lorraine and Luxembourg, French was not even permitted as a language to be studied in primary schools. The function of the schools was to preserve and strengthen nazism. Attendance at a German school was compulsory through the primary grades and three years of secondary school.

In Poland, although Poles could receive vocational training, they were denied any liberal arts training since that might stimulate independent national thinking. To prohibit artistic expression of a national culture, rigid controls were established. Not only were the radio, the press, and the cities closely supervised, but every painter, musician, architect, sculptor, writer, actor and theatrical producer required a license to continue his artistic activities.

## Religious
Wherever religion represented a vital influence in the national life, the spiritual power of the Church was undermined by various means. In Luxembourg children over 14 were protected by law against criticism if they should renounce their religious affiliations for membership in nazi youth organizations. In the puppet state of Croatia an independent, but German-dominated Orthodox Church was created for Serbs, in order to destroy forever the spiritual ties with the Patriarch at Belgrade. With the special violence and thoroughness reserved for Poles and Jews, Polish church property was pillaged and despoiled and the clergy subjected to constant persecution.

## Moral
Hand in hand with the undermining of religious influence went devices for the moral debasement of national groups. Pornographic publications and movies were foisted upon the Poles. Alcohol was kept cheap although food became increasingly dear, and peasants were legally bound to accept spirits for agricultural produce. Although under Polish law gambling houses had been prohibited, German authorities not only permitted them to come into existence, but relaxed the otherwise severe curfew law.

## Economic
The genocidal purpose of destroying or degrading the economic foundations of national groups was to lower the standards of living and to sharpen the struggle for existence, that no energies might remain for a cultural or national life. Jews were immediately deprived of the elemental means of existence by expropriation and by forbidding them the right to work. Polish property in western incorporated Poland was confiscated and Poles denied licenses to practice trades or handicrafts, thus reserving trade to the Germans. The Post Office Savings Bank in western Poland taken over by the occupying authorities, assured the financial superiority of Germans by repaying deposits only to certificated Germans. In Slovenia the financial cooperatives and agricultural associations were liquidated. Among the blood-related peoples (Luxembourgers, Alsatians) the acceptance of Germanism was the criterion by which participation in the economic life was determined.

## Biological
The genocidal policy was far-sighted as well as immediate in its objectives. On the one hand an increase in the birth rate, legitimate or illegitimate, was encouraged within Germany and among Volksdeutsche in the occupied countries. Subsidies were offered for children begotten by German military men by women of related blood such as Dutch and Norwegian. On the other hand, every means to decrease the birth rate among "racial inferiors" was used. Millions of war prisoners and forced laborers from all the conquered countries of Europe were kept from contact with their wives. Poles in incorporated Poland met obstacles in trying to marry among themselves. Chronic undernourishment, deliberately created by the occupant, tended

not only to discourage the birth rate but also to an increase in infant mortality. Coming generations in Europe were thus planned to be predominantly of German blood, capable of overwhelming all other races by sheer numbers.

## Physical

The most direct and drastic of the techniques of genocide is simply murder. It may be the slow and scientific murder by mass starvation or the swift but no less scientific murder by mass extermination in gas chambers, wholesale executions or exposure to disease and exhaustion. Food rations of all territory under German domination were established on racial principles, ranging in 1943 from 93 per cent of its pre-war diet for the German inhabitants to 20 per cent of its pre-war diet for the Jewish population. A carefully graduated scale allowed protein rations of 97 per cent to Germans, 95 per cent to the Dutch, 71 per cent to the French, 38 per cent to the Greeks and 20 per cent to the Jews. For fats, where there was the greatest shortage, the rations were 77 per cent to the Germans, 65 per cent to the Dutch, 40 per cent to the French and 0.32 per cent to the Jews. Specific vitamin deficiencies were created on a scientific basis.

The rise in the death rate among the various groups reflects this feeding program. The death rate in the Netherlands was 10 per thousand; Belgium 14 per thousand; Bohemia and Moravia 13.4 per thousand. The mortality in Warsaw was 2,160 Aryans in September 1941 as compared to 800 in September 1938, and for the Jews in Warsaw 7,000 in September 1941 as against 306 in September 1938.

Such elementary necessities of life as warm clothing, blankets and firewood in winter were either withheld or requisitioned from Poles and Jews. Beginning with the winter of 1940–1941 the Jews in the Warsaw Ghetto received no fuel at all. Even God's clean air was denied—the Jews in the overcrowded ghettos were forbidden the use of public parks. The authoritative report of the War Refugee Board published in November 1944, and the overwhelming new evidence that appears daily of the brutal mass killings that have taken place in such notorious "death camps" as Maidanek and Oswiecim are sufficient indication of the scope of the German program.

In Birkenau alone between April 1942 and April 1944 approximately 1,765,000 Jews were gassed. Some 5,600,000 Jews and around 2,000,000 Poles have been murdered or died as a result of the extermination policies. Whole communities have been exterminated. It is estimated, for instance, that of the 140,000 Dutch Jews who lived in the Netherlands before occupation, only some 7,000 now survive, the rest being transferred to Poland for slaughter.

## International Implications

Why should genocide be recognized as an international problem? Why not treat it as an internal problem of every country, if committed in time of peace, or as a problem between belligerents, if committed in time of war?

The practices of genocide anywhere affect the vital interests of all civilized people. Its consequences can neither be isolated nor localized. Tolerating genocide is an admission of the principle that one national group has the right to attack another because of its supposed racial superiority. This principle invites an expansion of such practices beyond the borders of the offending state, and that means wars of aggression.

The disease of criminality if left unchecked is contagious. Minorities of one sort or another exist in all countries, protected by the constitutional order of the state. If persecution of any minority by any country is tolerated anywhere, the very moral and legal foundations of constitutional government may be shaken.

International trade depends on the confidence in the ability of individuals participating in the interchange of goods to fulfill their obligations. Arbitrary and wholesale confiscations of the properties and economic rights of whole groups of citizens of one state deprives them of the possibilities of discharging their obligations to citizens of other states, who thereby are penalized.

A source of international friction is created by unilateral withdrawal of citizen rights and even by expulsion of whole minority groups to other countries. The expulsion of law-abiding residents from Germany before this war has created friction with the neighboring countries to which these people were expelled. Moreover mass persecutions force mass flight. Thus the normal migration between countries assumes pathological dimensions.

Our whole cultural heritage is a product of the contributions of all peoples. We can best understand this if we realize how impoverished our culture would be if the so-called inferior peoples doomed by Germany, such as the Jews, had not been permitted to create the Bible or to give birth to an Einstein, a Spinosa; if the Poles had not had the opportunity to give to the world a Copernicus, a Chopin, a Curie, the Czechs a Huss, and a Dvorak; the Greeks a Plato and a Socrates; the Russians, a Tolstoy and a Shostakovich.

## Safeguards and Remedies

The significance of a policy of genocide to the world order and to human culture is so great as to make it imperative that a system of safeguards be devised. The principle of the international protection of minorities was proclaimed by post-Versailles minority treaties.

These treaties, however, were inadequate because they were limited to a few newly created countries. They were established mainly with the aim of protecting political and civil rights, rather than the biological structure of the groups involved; the machinery of enforcement of such political rights was as incomplete as that of the League of Nations.

Under such conditions the genocide policy begun by Germany on its own Jewish citizens in 1933 was considered as an internal problem which the German state, as a sovereign power, should handle without interference by other states.

Although the Hague Regulations were concerned with the protection of civilians under control of military occupants, they did not foresee all the ingenious and scientific methods developed by Germany in this war.

Genocide is too disastrous a phenomenon to be left to fragmentary regulation. There must be an adequate mechanism for international cooperation in the punishment of the offenders.

The crime of genocide includes the following elements:

- The intent of the offenders is to destroy or degrade an entire national, religious or racial group by attacking the individual members of that group.
- This attack is a serious threat either to life, liberty, health, economic existence or to all of them.
- The offenders may be representatives of the state or of organized political or social groups.
- Liability should be fixed upon individuals both as to those who give the orders and to those who execute the orders.
- The offender, should be precluded from invoking as his defense the plea that he had been acting under the law of his country, since acts of genocide should be declared contrary to international law and morality.
- Since the consequences of genocide are international in their implications, the repression of genocide should be internationalized. The culprit should be liable not only in the country in which the crime was committed, but in the country where he might be apprehended. The country where he is found may itself try him or extradite him.
- Since a country which makes a policy of genocide cannot be trusted to try its own offenders, such offenders should be subject to trial by an international court.

Eventually, there should be established a special chamber within the framework of the International Court of Justice.

- The crime of genocide should be incorporated into the penal codes of all states by international treaty, giving them a legal basis upon which they could act.
- It is also proposed that the Hague Regulations be modified to extend to captive nations the controls provided for the treatment of war prisoners by the Convention of July 1929. Attempts to rescue or alleviate the suffering of captive nations have been hampered by lack of accurate information.

Germany has reminded us that our science and our civilization have not expunged barbarism from the human animal. They have merely armed it with more efficient instruments. We must call upon the resources of all our social and legal institutions to protect our civilization against the onslaught of this wanton barbarism in generations to come.

# 1.2   Lawrence J. LeBlanc, "Development of the Rule on Genocide"

*[I]t is clear that the Genocide Convention is a moral document. It is a call for a higher standard of human conduct. It is not a panacea for injustice, [but it will] make an important step toward civilizing the afairs of nations.*

—Senator William Proxmire, 1977 Senate hearings

What is genocide? For most people, the word calls to mind the atrocities committed against the Jews, Poles, Gypsies, and other groups before and during World War II. For some, the word also calls to mind the Turks' slaughter of hundreds of thousands of Armenians during World War I. In fact, these two cases are generally regarded as constituting the modern historical paradigms of genocide. But there is also substantial confusion regarding the meaning of the term. It is often perceived of simply as mass murder, though the Genocide Convention makes it clear that genocide is more than that, or as a crime against humanity, though it is not, strange as it may seem, regarded as such under the terms of the convention. It has been applied, or alleged to apply, to circumstances so different from one another that it is clear that those who make the accusations have different conceptions of the crime. As the Senate Committee on Foreign Relations has often indicated in its reports, the word "genocide" has been loosely bandied about in recent years. Let us look, then, at how the author of the word "genocide" defined it and how it came to be defined the way it is in the Genocide Convention.

## Raphael Lemkin's Definition of Genocide

Raphael Lemkin, a Polish jurist of Jewish origin, coined the word "genocide" in *Axis Rule in Occupied Europe* (1944). He derived the term from a combination of the Greek word *genos*, which means "race" or "tribe," and the Latin word *cide*, which means "killing."[1] He noted that the word "ethnocide," a combination of the Greek word *ethnos*, which means "nation," and the Latin word *cide*, would convey the same idea as genocide.[2] In fact, it is noteworthy that Lemkin did not adopt "ethnocide" rather than "genocide" to identify the crime he had in mind, because, as we shall see, he liberally used the words "nations" and "national groups" in his definition. Be that as it may, the important point is that Lemkin conceived of genocide in broader terms than simply killing members of groups; rather, he thought of it as the *destruction* of groups which could be brought about by a variety of means including, but not limited to, outright killing of their members.

> Generally speaking, genocide does not necessarily mean the immediate destruction of a nation, except when accomplished by mass killing of all members of a nation. It is intended rather to signify a coordinated plan of different actions aiming at the destruction of essential foundations of the life of national groups, with the aim of annihilating the groups themselves. The objective of such a plan would be disintegration of the political and social institutions, of culture, language, national feelings, religion, and the economic existence of national groups, and the destruction of the personal security, liberty, health, dignity, and the lives of the individuals belonging to such groups. Genocide is directed against the national group as an entity, and the actions involved are directed against individuals, not in their individual capacity but as members of the national group.[3]

According to Lemkin, there are two main stages in this genocidal process: in the first stage, the oppressor seeks to destroy the "national pattern" of the oppressed group; in the second stage, the oppressor seeks to impose its own national pattern on the oppressed group.[4]

The passages quoted above suggest that Lemkin was concerned solely with the destruction of national groups. At another point in his work, however, he tells of his concern as early as 1933 over actions aimed at the "destruction and oppression of populations," and that he had proposed then that two offenses, which he called "barbarity" and "vandalism," be made crimes under international law. He defined the crime of barbarity as "oppressive and destructive actions directed against individuals as members of a national, religious, or racial group," and the crime of vandalism as "malicious destruction of works of art and culture because they represent the specific creation of the genius of such groups."[5] Since Lemkin believed that these two crimes, taken together, amounted to what he would later call genocide, it would seem that he had in mind groups other than national groups as possible victims of genocide.[6] While he failed to provide a clear and consistent definition, his work provides insight into the nature of the crime.

Lemkin fled Poland in the wake of the Nazi invasion in 1939. By 1941 he had emigrated to the United States, and subsequently he served on the faculties of several law schools, including Duke and Yale. During World War II he served the government of the United States in various capacities, including a stint as a staff member at the Nuremberg War Crimes Trials. He had begun to collect evidence of Nazi atrocities against the Jews, Poles, Gypsies, and other groups while he was still in Europe, and this documentary evidence later formed part of his major work on the subject of genocide, *Axis Rule in Occupied Europe*.[7]

After World War II Lemkin became an outspoken advocate of the conclusion and adoption of a convention on genocide by the United Nations. By then, according to some accounts, he displayed such devotion to the cause that he had become known as a "dreamer" and "fanatic."[8] Still, he was able to persuade enough UN delegates to support the idea of drafting a convention that the General Assembly adopted a resolution in 1946 (to which we shall return shortly) that set in motion the work on what eventually became the Genocide Convention. Lemkin served as a consultant to the UN Secretariat when it prepared the first draft of the convention. Many of his ideas were incorporated into that draft, but it proved unacceptable to many states for various reasons, and the definition of genocide eventually adopted for the convention fell short of what Lemkin seemed to have in mind in his work.[9]

## Lemkin and the Ratification Effort in the United States

Whatever shortcomings Lemkin might have thought the Genocide Convention possessed, he became an indefatigable champion of it, and he lobbied aggressively for its ratification by the United States in the late 1940s and early 1950s. In the process he became something of an issue himself. He had apparently lobbied too aggressively, annoying a number of prominent and influential senators. Consequently, despite his prominence in the field, Lemkin was not called to testify when a subcommittee of the Senate Committee on Foreign Relations held the first hearings on the convention in 1950. When he died in 1959, the question of whether or not the United States should ratify the Genocide Convention was not even under active consideration in the Senate.

Remarks made during the 1950 hearings revealed the extent of some senators' displeasure with Lemkin's lobbying tactics. The remarks were so critical of him personally that it is not surprising that their publication was suppressed for nearly twenty-five years, finally being released in a compilation of executive sessions of the Senate Committee on Foreign Relations in 1976. In 1950 one committee member, Senator H. Alexander Smith (R., New Jersey), observed that he and others were troubled by the definition of the "new idea" of genocide. Moreover, he could not understand why the "biggest propagandist" for the Genocide Convention should be "a man who comes from a foreign country who . . . speaks broken English."[10] Smith claimed that he knew of "many people who have been irritated no end by this fellow running around." Although he was "sympathetic with the Jewish people," Smith believed that "they ought not to be the ones who are propagandizing [the convention], and they are."[11] Adrian Fisher, legal adviser to the State Department at the time, pointed out that Lemkin was a private citizen doing what he thought he should do. But Smith still believed that "having a man talking broken English in the forefront" of the ratification movement was a "mistake psychologically," and that many other senators were irritated by Lemkin's lobbying activities.

Even senators who supported ratification in 1950 had mixed emotions about Lemkin. Senator Henry Cabot Lodge, Jr. (R., Massachusetts), for example, suggested during the hearings that Lemkin had "done his own cause a great deal of harm" and that he should be notified of that fact.[12] Even the strongest supporters of ratification, such as Senators Brien McMahon (D., Connecticut) and Theodore Francis Green (D., Rhode Island), felt that if Lemkin was not the "biggest minus quantity" in the struggle over ratification, he was the "least plus quantity."[13]

The remarks at the 1950 hearings suggest that Lemkin had become regarded as a dreamer and fanatic on the subject of genocide as much by senators as he was by UN diplomats and personnel. Different life experiences and the "realities" of politics undoubtedly had much to do with the different perspectives of Lemkin and his detractors. Lemkin had lost all of his family in the Holocaust, and he had come to believe deeply in the utility of international law in the prevention and punishment of genocide.[14] In fact, as noted earlier, Lemkin had agitated for the development of international legal standards in this field as far back as the early 1930s. But the senators had no similar life experiences. Moreover, as we shall see, some of them were profoundly skeptical about, and even hostile to, the notion of assuming an international legal obligation on genocide. The subcommittee of the Committee on Foreign Relations that held the hearings in 1950 recommended ratification, but the full committee failed to report the convention to the Senate. As a result, it languished in committee until President Nixon resurrected it in 1970.

There is nothing on the subsequent record that approaches the criticisms of Lemkin made during the 1950 hearings, at least not by senators. On occasion, however, such criticisms were made by representatives of extremely conservative fringe groups. At the 1985 hearings of the Committee on Foreign Relations, for example, Trisha Katson, legislative director of Liberty Lobby, an organization that never found any redeeming features in the Genocide Convention, got Senator Jesse Helms to agree to have printed in the hearings the conclusion of a book by James Martin titled *The Man Who Invented "Genocide": The Public Career and Consequences of Raphael Lemkin*.[15] Martin attacked Lemkin on many grounds, including his failure to display "the faintest concern for majorities anywhere."[16] He also criticized *Axis Rule in Occupied Europe* as a flimsy effort to document Nazi atrocities: "Since he did not witness anything he included in his book, Lemkin essentially is passing on the substance of sources hostile to the Germans, much of it inflammatory rhetoric from various conduits of anti-Axis opinion-making, incapable of confirmation then and little of it since, with more than a dollop of ordinary mendacity."[17]

In essence, Martin's book seems to be a diatribe against Jews, Zionists, and Communists, and it undoubtedly appeals only to fringe groups such as Liberty Lobby. Katson herself evidently thinks highly of the book and agrees with its central line of reasoning, as she indicated at the 1985 hearings:

> As a believer in our constitutional republic, I am opposed to any alien political philosophy that would undermine it, be it Marxism, communism, socialism, national socialism or Nazism, or Zionism.
>
> For the purposes of my testimony, it is important that I point out that Zionism is not synonymous with Judaism. Zionism is a political movement while Judaism is a religion. I know Jews who are anti-Zionist. Also I know Zionist Christians.
>
> I am concerned with how pro-Zionist forces have aided in America's having a one-sided foreign policy in the Middle East. I would like to at this point note that every witness that spoke here today and also at Senator Hatch's Subcommittee on the Constitution last week mentioned different horrendous acts of genocide and holocausts that have occurred in the past, and while it was alluded to that Israel might be accused by the Arabs of committing genocide, there has never been a word said on the record that they possibly might be guilty of it.
>
> I would like to take this time to speak on behalf of the Palestinian people who have been victimized by acts of genocide on the part of the Zionist-controlled government of Israel.[18]

During the 1970s and 1980s Lemkin was sometimes recognized and praised for his work on genocide and the Genocide Convention. Nonetheless, the attacks against him during the 1950 Senate hearings, and Trisha Katson's testimony at the 1985 hearings, provide some insight into the pettiness that has sometimes characterized the ratification debate. They also provide some insight into the thinly veiled, and not-so-thinly veiled, anti-Semitism that has sometimes been expressed. For very obvious reasons Jews have had a deep and long-standing interest in the ratification movement. As one might expect, organized Jewish groups repeatedly endorsed ratification of the convention, and prominent Jewish individuals such as Arthur Goldberg, and Jewish senators such as Jacob Javits (R., New York), worked hard to secure ratification. At the same time, these individuals and groups, as well as tireless proponents of ratification such as Senator William Proxmire, always took pains to rebut the notion that the issue of ratification was a "Jewish issue." For Proxmire, in particular, ratification of the convention was a moral imperative and therefore an issue for everyone. Moreover, he saw ratification as good foreign policy because the failure of the United States to ratify undermined its leadership role in the field of international action on human rights. Yet, as we shall see throughout this book, critics of the convention have been all too willing to use any argument, however base or petty, to defeat the ratification movement.

## The Role of the United Nations in Defining Genocide

Although Raphael Lemkin coined the word "genocide," it was up to the United Nations to adopt the official "rule," or definition of the crime. The organization was involved in this process of rule creation for about two years, from 1946 to 1948. Its work began when the delegations from Cuba, India, and Panama took the initiative and proposed that the subject of genocide be placed on the agenda of the first regular session of the General Assembly in 1946. After some discussion of a draft resolution in committee, the assembly unanimously and without debate adopted Resolution 96 (I) on genocide on December 11, 1946. That resolution created the "norm" on genocide. Specifically, it elaborated basic standards that were to be incorporated into the more important convention on genocide that the General Assembly resolved to conclude. As such, it was a necessary first step on the way to the adoption of the Genocide Convention. For this reason it is quoted in full.

> Genocide is a denial of the right of existence of entire human groups, as homicide is the denial of the right to live of individual human beings; such denial of the right of existence shocks the conscience of mankind, results in great losses to humanity in the form of cultural and other contributions represented by these groups, and is contrary to moral law and to the spirit and aims of the United Nations.
>
> Many instances of such crimes of genocide have occurred when racial, religious, political and other groups have been destroyed, entirely or in part.
>
> The punishment of the crime of genocide is a matter of international concern.
>
> The General Assembly therefore,
>
> Affirms that genocide is a crime under international law which the civilized world condemns, and for the commission of which principals and accomplices—whether private individuals, public officials or statesmen, and whether the crime is committed on religious, racial, political or any other grounds—are punishable;
>
> Invites the Member States to enact the necessary legislation for the prevention and punishment of this crime;
>
> Recommends that international cooperation be organized between States with a view to facilitating the speedy prevention and punishment of the crime of genocide, and, to this end,
>
> Requests the Economic and Social Council to undertake the necessary studies, with a view to drawing up a draft convention on the crime of genocide to be submitted to the next regular session of the General Assembly.

Resolution 96(I) addressed three important matters: first, it provided the essential rationale for a convention on genocide; second, it set in motion the process through which such a convention was to be drafted; and, third, it outlined in general terms the basic elements of the rule on genocide that would be affirmed in that convention. Let us consider each of these points.

## Why a Convention on Genocide Was Believed Necessary

The origins of the Genocide Convention lie in the atrocities that were committed against the Jews, Poles, Gypsies, and other groups by the Nazis during World War II. However, Resolution 96 (I) does not refer to this particular episode of genocide. Rather, it refers to the crime in a broader historical perspective, which is arguably one of its main strengths. Clearly, the resolution is not grounded in any particular historical experience, which gives it a timeless quality. It refers to "many instances" of genocide that resulted in "great losses to humanity." It asserts that "punishment of the crime of genocide is a matter of international concern," and it goes on to affirm that the crime is a "crime under international law."

The reason why a convention on genocide was believed necessary is implied in these basic principles. Its instigators aimed to establish genocide as a crime whenever it occurs. A convention establishing genocide as a crime whenever it occurs would overcome a major problem that had arisen as a result of the Nuremberg War Crimes Tribunal's interpretation of its own charter. The tribunal, which was established by the Allied powers at the close of World War II to try high-ranking Nazi war criminals, was empowered by its charter to try persons for crimes against humanity such as murder, extermination, and deportation of civilian populations. As we will discuss in chapter 5, some of these acts later fell within the meaning of genocide as it is defined in Article II of the Genocide Convention.

But the tribunal had interpreted its charter as meaning that persons could be convicted of committing crimes against humanity only if they had committed those crimes in execution of

or in connection with an aggressive war. This interpretation had important practical implications. It meant that any crimes against humanity that were committed prior to September 1,
1939, the date of the opening of the war against Poland, did not fall within the purview of the
tribunal.[19] Many activists, including Raphael Lemkin, believed that this interpretation created
an undesirable and dangerous loophole that could be closed only through the adoption of a
convention that would make genocide a crime whenever it occurs. Article I of the Genocide
Convention effectively does this by stating that genocide is a crime under international law
"whether committed in time of peace or in time of war." In this respect, therefore, the
convention not only reiterates what Resolution 96 (I) had to say about the issue but states it
with greater clarity and force.

It is arguable that if the Genocide Convention had been made applicable only to crimes
committed during times of war, there would have been no need for it. Such a narrow construction would have had devastating consequences regarding many of the allegations of
genocide that have been made since World War II. Genocide is alleged to have occurred, for
example, during periods of acute domestic strife in Rwanda in the late 1950s and early 1960s,
and in Burundi in the early 1970s.[20] In other instances, genocide is alleged to have occurred
during periods of no domestic strife, such as the atrocities committed against the Aché
Indians in Paraguay.[21] In none of these instances could it be said that a state of war existed,
yet it may very well be that genocide did occur.

Genocide is also alleged to have occurred during periods that might be reasonably characterized as wars; for example, during the struggle over the creation of Pakistan in the late 1940s
and Bangladesh in the early 1970s.[22] In addition, as we will see in chapter 3, there were
widespread charges that the United States was waging a genocidal war in Vietnam during the
1960s and 1970s, and the so-called Russell Tribunal found the United States and powers allied
with it "guilty" of the charges. The charges, as well as the judgment of the tribunal, have been
the subject of a great deal of debate. As far as many critics of the convention in the United
States were concerned, it did not matter that the Russell Tribunal was an unofficial body.
What mattered was simply that the charges were made and that they were fairly widespread.
At one point the government of North Vietnam cited the massacre of civilians at My Lai as
proof that the United States was waging a genocidal war.[23]

Without rendering a judgment on any of these episodes, since such judgments properly
belong to courts, it is important to note that genocide is alleged to have occurred in a great
variety of circumstances since World War II. Some scholars and human rights activists are
concerned that minorities throughout the world remain exposed to genocide and genocide-
like acts. In retrospect, therefore, the General Assembly very wisely aimed to conclude a
convention that would apply whenever the crime of genocide occurred. The fact that the
drafters followed through on this objective has made the Genocide Convention potentially
applicable to many of the cases that have arisen in the post–World War II period.

## The Process of Drafting the Convention

The last paragraph of Resolution 96 (1) indicates that the General Assembly expected to act
on a convention on genocide at its second regular session in 1947. To this end, it charged the
Economic and Social Council (ECOSOC) with undertaking the necessary studies that would
culminate in the preparation of a draft convention. The ECOSOC turned to the UN Secretariat
for assistance in this matter. Specifically, it asked the Secretariat to prepare a draft convention.
The Secretariat, using experts in international and criminal law such as Raphael Lemkin as
consultants, prepared a draft convention by June 1947. However, the process of preparing a
final draft that the General Assembly could adopt began to slow down. The UN Secretariat
submitted its draft to the Committee on the Progressive Development of International Law
and Its Codification, but the committee declined to make any comments on it since the

member states of the United Nations had not yet done so. The secretary general then requested the member states to submit such comments, but very few of them replied. Consequently, when the ECOSOC met in July 1947, it deemed any action on the draft convention inappropriate and referred the matter back to the General Assembly.[24]

Important philosophical disagreements arose in the General Assembly. Some delegates took the position that Resolution 96 (1) should be fundamentally altered; that is, that the ECOSOC should be charged with studying the question of whether or not a convention on genocide was desirable and necessary. Others insisted that the assembly had already decided that the conclusion of a convention was a worthy and important goal, and that instead of changing course it should reaffirm Resolution 96 (1). The assembly endorsed the latter viewpoint. It adopted another resolution, Resolution 180 (II), in which it reaffirmed Resolution 96 (I) and requested that the ECOSOC "continue the work" it had begun and "proceed with the completion of a convention" on genocide. The assembly now hoped to consider a draft convention at its third regular session in 1948. While Resolution 180 (II) brought about the desired result, it was not adopted with as much enthusiasm as Resolution 96 (I) had been. The vote on Resolution 180 (II) was thirty-eight in favor, none against, and fourteen abstentions.[25] Apparently no one could vote *against* a resolution on genocide (as no one would later vote against the adoption of the convention itself), but some were having second thoughts; a genocide convention was not an urgent matter on their agenda.

What explains the change in attitude? The official records indicate substantial displeasure among some representatives at the United Nations with the content of the Secretariat's draft convention. But their displeasure with the provisions of the draft reflected the deeper philosophical reservations they had begun to develop regarding the question of whether or not a convention was truly necessary or desirable. Undoubtedly these problems were made worse by the emergence of the cold war between the United States and the Soviet Union, which seemed to make many of the UN representatives considerably more cautious about the possibility of international cooperation in the further development and strengthening of international law.

These issues came to the forefront when the ECOSOC, in keeping with Resolution 180 (II), began to work on a draft convention at meetings in February and March 1948. It examined the Secretariat's draft, which reflected a very liberal construction of the guidelines laid down in Resolution 96 (I). The draft aimed to protect "racial, national, linguistic, religious, or political groups." In sweeping terms it branded as criminal many physical and biological acts aimed at the destruction of such groups in whole or in part, or of "preventing [their] preservation or development."[26] It specified acts that would be punishable, including attempt to commit genocide, participation in genocide, conspiracy to commit genocide, and engaging in a variety of "preparatory" acts such as developing techniques of genocide and setting up installations. It called for punishment of "all forms of public propaganda tending by their systematic and hateful character to provoke genocide, or tending to make it appear as a necessary, legitimate, or excusable act." It called for the creation of an international criminal court to try offenders in cases when states were unwilling either to try them or to extradite them to another country for trial.

The representatives of states with divergent political, economic, and social systems expressed dissatisfaction with the terms of the Secretariat's draft convention at meetings of the ECOSOC. The Venezuelan representative, for example, criticized the breadth of coverage of the draft, arguing that the ECOSOC was concerned with "a very delicate matter, which required careful, unhurried, and profound study. The question of the sovereignty of states was involved."[27] The Australian representative stressed that "while speed was essential, it was even more important to ensure that the convention . . . be based on solid legal and moral principles which would command universal respect and would be enforced" by all member states.[28] The Brazilian representative expressed the view that the convention had to "be considered in two aspects, the political and the legal."[29] A number of representatives, the French and Polish among them, stressed "political" aspects of the convention which they felt the ECOSOC should resolve before beginning work on drafting a convention.[30] The representative of the United Kingdom was perhaps the most pessimistic about the outcome. He argued that it was not clear that anything beyond what the General Assembly had already done in Resolution 96 (I) was either necessary or desirable. The resolution had branded genocide a crime under international law. What further sanctions could the proposed convention provide? He feared that, "on the contrary, it might have the reverse effect and only serve to weaken the force of international law."[31]

Although the comments varied in substance, most representatives on the ECOSOC seemed to be concerned about the same thing—the Secretariat's draft convention "lacked realism."[32] As the Soviet representative put it, the definition of genocide contained in the draft was "much too wide."[33] In brief, most representatives on the ECOSOC seemed to think that they were more attuned to "political realities" than were Secretariat personnel and experts such as Raphael Lemkin. The experts could concern themselves with developing the best possible rule on genocide, but the representatives of states had to consider what their governments would accept. The ECOSOC therefore resolved to create an ad hoc committee consisting of representatives of seven states (China, France, Lebanon, Poland, USA, USSR, and Venezuela). It met during April and May 1948 and took into account mainly the technical provisions of the Secretariat's draft in preparing its own.[34] The ad hoc committee's draft then became *the* draft convention that was discussed and revised by the Sixth (Legal) Committee of the General Assembly.

The Sixth Committee of the General Assembly debated the terms of the Genocide Convention during meetings it held from September through November 1948, and its final draft was adopted without alterations at a plenary meeting of the General Assembly in December 1948. The commitee's deliberations were marked by sharp differences of opinion among the delegates on matters of principle as well as details of specific provisions of the convention. In fact, the attitudes expressed in the ECOSOC on the Secretariat's draft convention provided a good indication of the sort of debate that would occur again in the assembly. Many provisions of the Genocide Convention were heavily influenced by political and ideological considerations. This is not to say that the convention is flawed as a result; the drafters managed to produce a good instrument that was surely more acceptable to states than the Secretariat's draft would have been. Nor is it to say that there was anything unusual in the fact that political considerations influenced the outcome, for it is hard to imagine any law, domestic or international, that is not influenced by political considerations. Nonetheless, it is important to bear in mind that the drafters were diplomats who represented states, and these states had different interests so far as specific provisions of the convention were concerned. At the same time, as diplomats, the drafters had to find ways to produce an instrument that would be acceptable to a large number of states. In fact, the question of what would be acceptable to states was at all times a matter of great concern to the drafters. Achieving that goal meant that compromises of various sorts had to be reached, and these compromises did not always reflect the best possible choice among competing principles and ideas, but rather the most acceptable choice.

## The Basic Elements of the Rule on Genocide

The political compromises that the drafters of the Genocide Convention had to make are apparent in many of its provisions, including those that pertain to the basic elements of the rule on genocide. Although Resolution 96 (I) provided the drafters with some guidance on what the General Assembly expected the convention to say with regard to the rule, in some crucial respects the resolution was vague and even contradictory. Consequently, while the drafters were able to adhere to the provisions of Resolution 96 (I) in some cases, in others they found it either necessary or desirable to exercise discretion.

One issue on which the drafters were able to adhere rather closely to Resolution 96 (I) was the question of who could be convicted of committing genocide. Significantly, the resolution does not say that the active backing or connivance of a government is necessary in the commission of genocide. Rather, it refers to the punishment of "principals and accomplices—whether private individuals, public officials or statesmen." The drafters of the Genocide Convention discussed this formula at length, especially in connection with Article IV of the convention. Some representatives on the Sixth Committee believed that Article IV should make it clear that genocide is "committed, encouraged, or tolerated by the rulers of a State."[35] This position was understandable in light of the historical context in which the convention was being drafted: it was obvious to everyone concerned that Hitler's government had committed, encouraged, and tolerated the commission of genocide. Nonetheless, a formal proposal to include a provision in Article IV to the effect that government complicity was necessary in cases of genocide was overwhelmingly rejected by a vote of forty against, two in favor, and one abstention.[36] Those who argued against the proposal maintained that genocide could be committed without the active backing of a government—for example, by terrorist organizations or even private individuals—and that in some instances governments might be unable to prevent the commission of genocide.[37]

While the drafters of the convention took the same position as the General Assembly on the issue of government complicity, they had more difficulty endorsing the precise categories of persons who could be punished for committing the crime. Resolution 96 (I) refers to "principals and accomplices—whether private individuals, public officials, or statesmen." The drafters of the convention had some difficulty with these categories. Those most concerned about them were the representatives of states with monarchies, such as the United Kingdom, Thailand, Sweden, and the Netherlands. They pointed out that their kings could not be brought to trial, and that the words "heads of State," which some drafters wanted to use in Article IV, could not be used without creating serious constitutional problems for them. Various alternative combinations of words and phrases that were proposed—"agents of State," "rulers," and so on—were also deemed inappropriate by most drafters because they created, or seemed to create, undesirable exemptions, depending on the language into which they were being translated. Therefore, after extensive negotiations the drafters settled on the words "constitutionally responsible rulers, public officials, or private individuals" for Article IV.[38] The clause "constitutionally responsible rulers" was intended to create an exemption for monarchs who cannot be brought to trial.

Critics of the convention in the United States have never expressed any serious concern about the exemption that Article IV creates. But they have often criticized the convention's failure to require government involvement or connivance in the commission of genocide. These critics usually cited the Nazi case, and, of course, Stalinism, and insisted that genocide was inconceivable without at least the connivance of a government. The issue was repeatedly raised, especially during the 1970s and 1980s. At the 1971 hearings of the Senate Committee on Foreign Relations, for example, Eberhard Deutsch, testifying on behalf of the American Bar Association, which at the time opposed ratification of the convention, maintained that "for genocide to be an international crime, and accordingly a matter of international concern appropriately the subject of a treaty with other nations under the Constitution of the United States, it must, by definition, be committed with the complicity of the government concerned—not merely by individuals."[39] During the 1980s Senator Jesse Helms, ever prepared with statements intended to clarify—or confuse, as the case might be—provisions of the convention, proposed that if the United States should ratify the convention, it should be with an understanding that "complicity of government" is an "essential element" of the crime of genocide.[40]

The problem with Senator Helms's proposal, as with Eberhard Deutsch's earlier argument, was that it would have rewritten the Genocide Convention in a very fundamental way. The understanding was therefore more on the order of an amendment, which would have required the renegotiation of the convention before the United States could become a party to it. The understanding would surely have made the convention inapplicable in all cases of, say, racially motivated lynchings that were not committed with the backing of the government, and probably was proposed precisely to eliminate charges of genocide in such cases. But the arguments involving this issue, carried to their logical conclusions, could have extremely undesirable consequences that one supposes—or hopes—even Senator Helms would not like. They would mean that no treaty could be concluded on, say, terrorism or hijacking if such a treaty aimed to punish individuals who act without the backing of a government. Presumably no one would want to reach this conclusion. In fact, one of the positive features of the Genocide Convention is that it recognizes the international responsibility of individuals for criminal acts, an issue that was dealt with at Nuremberg. In its judgment the Nuremberg Tribunal expressed the dictum: "Crimes against international law are committed by men, not by abstract entities, and only by punishing individuals who commit such crimes can the provisions of international law be enforced."[41]

Supporters of ratification successfully rebuffed attempts to rewrite the convention to require the complicity of government in the commission of genocide. Apart from the highly undesirable consequences of such proposals, those who defended the convention as written pointed out that it does deal with both individuals and states[42] inasmuch as it specifies that the parties may call upon the United Nations to take appropriate action under the UN Charter to prevent and suppress genocide (under Article VIII). Moreover, under Article IX, the parties can bring disputes concerning the interpretation, application, or fulfillment of the convention, including those relating to state responsibility for genocide, to the International Court of Justice.[43] (We shall return to this point in chapter 9.)

Although the drafters were able to follow through on the terms of Resolution 96 (I) regarding individual responsibility for genocide, other aspects of the rule on genocide were more problematic. The resolution is vague, even contradictory, regarding some key points that had to be addressed in the convention. For example, it states that genocide is "a denial of the right of existence of entire human groups, as homicide is the denial of the right to live of individual human beings"; it then refers to past instances of genocide when "racial, religious, political, and other groups" had been destroyed "entirely or in part." But by what acts or techniques could a denial of the right of existence be effected? Would only killing members of the groups constitute genocide? Or would other acts, such as Lemkin's "barbarity" and "vandalism" also constitute genocide? Was it necessary for entire groups to be destroyed, or could genocide be committed against parts of groups? To what groups should the convention extend protection? Religious, racial, and political groups are expressly mentioned in Resolution 96 (I): did this mean that the convention must cover all of them? What "other groups" did the General Assembly have in mind?

These questions illustrate in broad strokes the difficulties the drafters of the convention faced in elaborating the rule on genocide. Resolution 96 (I) could be invoked—and was invoked, especially during debates in the Sixth Committee—whenever its terms supported a particular position that one or another delegate wished to take. In fact, the drafters were able to exercise considerable discretion on key points. As a result, they inserted in Article II of the convention, the core article, some of the ideas and statements expressed in Resolution 96 (I); in other important instances they altered the resolution's terms.

In view of the importance of Article II, it is not surprising that it was the most controversial article when the convention was drafted. It subsequently became exceedingly controversial in the United States in the struggle over ratification. Article II is quoted in full below to facilitate discussion of the various issues involved.

In the present Convention, genocide means any of the following acts committed with intent to destroy, in whole or in part, a national, ethnical, racial or religious group, as such:

(a) Killing members of the group;
(b) Causing serious bodily or mental harm to members of the group;
(c) Deliberately inflicting on the group conditions of life calculated to bring about its physical destruction in whole or in part;
(d) Imposing measures intended to prevent births within the group;
(e) Forcibly transferring children of the group to another group.

This article makes it clear that genocide is a crime committed against groups of human beings. Beyond that, it identifies certain elements crucial to the definition of the crime, including (1) the notion of the intent to destroy groups, (2) the types of groups to which the convention extends protection, and (3) the kinds of acts considered genocidal. All of these elements became major issues in their own right during the drafting stage and, later, in debates over ratification of the convention by the United States. In fact, specific aspects of some of these elements became so controversial in the United States that the opponents of ratification insisted on framing statements in the Lugar-Helms-Hatch Sovereignty Package indicating what the United States understands them to mean.

As understandings, the statements presumably were intended to explain or clarify the meaning of certain words and phrases in Article II, and not to exclude or vary their legal effect, as would reservations. But under the international rules of treaty law, other parties to the Genocide Convention have a voice in determining the appropriateness of the labels used by the United States in the Sovereignty Package; they could also object to the conditions if they should find them incompatible with the object and purpose of the convention. The other parties, of course, may be reluctant to raise objections to the U.S. conditions, especially if they are in some important way dependent upon the United States. Be that as it may, the possibility that objections could be raised exists.

## Notes

1. R. Lemkin, *Axis Rule in Occupied Europe* 79 (1944).
2. *Ibid.*
3. *Ibid.*
4. *Ibid.* See also M. Lippman, *The Drafting of the 1948 Convention on the Prevention and Punishment of the Crime of Genocide*, 3 Boston U. Int'l L. J. 2–3 (1984).
5. *Ibid.*, at 91.
6. *Ibid.*
7. *Current Biography* 336 (1950).
8. *Ibid.*, at 337.
9. The Secretariat's draft convention is reproduced in N. Robinson, *The Genocide Convention: A Commentary* 122–30 (1960).
10. 2 Executive Sessions of the Senate Foreign Relations Committee, *Historical Series* 645 (1976).
11. *Ibid.*
12. *Ibid.*
13. *Ibid.*, at 645–46.
14. *Current Biography* 337 (1950).
15. *Hearing on the Genocide Convention Before the Senate Comm. on Foreign Relations*, 99th Cong., 1st sess. 132–46 (1985) [hereinafter cited as *1985 Senate Hearings*].
16. *Ibid.*, at 132.
17. *Ibid.*, at 137.
18. *Ibid.*, at 116.
19. Perlman, *The Genocide Convention*, 30 Neb. L. R. 1–2 (1950); see also testimony of Ambassador Rita Hauser, *Hearings on the Genocide Convention Before a Subcomm. of the Senate Comm. on Foreign Relations*, 91st Cong., 2d sess. 39 (1970).

20. In Rwanda, Hutus are alleged to have slaughtered Tutsis; and in Burundi, Tutsis are accused of having slaughtered Hutus. See L. Kuper, *The Pity of It All* 170–208 (1977); T. Melady, *Burundi: The Tragic Years* (1974).

21. *Genocide in Paraguay* (R. Arens, ed., 1976).

22. Emerson, *The Fate of Human Rights in the Third World*, 27 World Politics (1975); K. Chaudhuri, *Genocide in Bangladesh* (1972); L. Kuper, *The Prevention of Genocide* 44–61 (1985); Paust and Blaustein, *War Crimes Jurisdiction and Due Process: The Bangladesh Experience*, 11 Vand. J. Trans. L. (1978).

23. *Hearing on the Genocide Convention Before a Subcomm. of the Senate Comm. on Foreign Relations*, 92d Cong., 1st sess. 53 (1971) [hereinafter cited as *1971 Senate Hearings*].

24. Robinson, *supra* note 9, at 18–19.

25. *Ibid.*, at 22; see also Lippman, *supra* note 4, at 20–25.

26. *Supra* note 9.

27. 3 UN ESCOR, Doc. E/447–623, at 139–40 (1948).

28. *Ibid.*, at 141.

29. *Ibid.*, at 143.

30. *Ibid.*, at 141–42.

31. *Ibid.*, at 145.

32. *Ibid.*, at 146.

33. *Ibid.*, at 147.

34. *Report of the Ad Hoc Committee on Genocide*, 3 UN ESCOR Supp. 6, UN Doc. E/794 (1948) [hereinafter cited as *Report of the Ad Hoc Committee on Genocide*.]

35. 3 UN GAOR C.6 (78th mtg) at 145 (1948).

36. 3 UN GAOR C.6 (80th mtg) at 170 (1948).

37. 3 UN GAOR C.6 (79th mtg) at 153–61 (1948).

38. The matter was debated in the Ad Hoc Committee of the ECOSOC (*Report of the Ad Hoc Committee on Genocide, supra* note 34, at 9) and in the Sixth Committee (3 UN GAOR C.6 [92d mtg] at 303–4, [95th mtg] at 340, 358, and [128th mtg] at 660 [1948]).

39. *1971 Senate Hearings, supra* note 23, at 17–18, 100.

40. *1985 Senate Hearings, supra* note 15, at 14–15.

41. R. Woetzel, *The Nuremberg Trials in International Law* 96 (1962).

42. See testimony of Ambassador Richard Gardner in *Hearings on the Genocide Convention Before a Subcomm. of the Senate Comm. on Foreign Relations*, 91st Cong., 2d sess. 116–17 (1970).

43. *Hearing on the Genocide Convention Before the Senate Comm. on Foreign Relations*, 97th Cong., 1st sess. 25 (1981).

# 1.3   Morten Bergsmo, "Intent"

The anatomies of international crimes tend to include material elements (relevant to conduct), mental elements (relevant to state of mind) and contextual or circumstantial elements (relevant to the context or pattern within which the criminal conduct occurs). Each of these elements must be established beyond a reasonable doubt—within the context of international criminal jurisdictions—if a criminal conviction is to be sustained. In addition, one must establish beyond a reasonable doubt the appropriate mode of liability or form of participation by the accused in the relevant crime, such as individual perpetration, superior responsibility, complicity, or common purpose. Legal definitions of modes of liability have both subjective and objective requirements.

*Intent* describes a specific state of mind, proof of whose existence is required in the establishment of some of the abovementioned mental elements of crime. The distinction between the scope and degree or quality of requisite intent is valuable in international criminal law in the same way as it is in many national jurisdictions. There is a logical distinction to be made between the intensity of intent (i.e., its degree or quality) and the result, consequence, or other factor that such intent is alleged to have engendered (i.e., its scope). Intent may be described in relative terms, as lesser in degree (at the level of premeditation) or greater in degree (rising to the level of recklessness, or *dolus eventualis*).

This article examines the degree or quality of intent that is requisite to a finding of guilt with regard to the international crime of genocide. The definition of genocide in international law includes specific intent (*dolus specialis*) as a distinctive mental element of the crime; namely, the intent to destroy, in whole or in part, a national, ethnical, racial, or religious group, as such. However, the degree of that specific intent is not articulated explicitly in the relevant international treaties. Thus, a close analysis of case law coming out of the two ad hoc international criminal tribunals—the International Criminal Tribunal for the Former Yugoslavia (ICTY) and the International Criminal Tribunal for Rwanda (ICTR)—is in order. Also relevant are other sources of international criminal law (including the work of the United Nations (UN) International Law Commission), national case law, and commentaries by some publicists in the field. The state of international criminal law is critically appraised, with particular reference made to the Judgment of the ICTY Appeals Chamber in *Prosecutor v. Goran Jelisić* and other related cases.

## International Treaty Law on Degree or Quality of Genocidal Intent

International treaty law does not define the degree or quality of intent that is requisite to the international crime of genocide more precisely than is provided by its use of the word *intent*. The 1948 UN Convention on the Prevention and Punishment of the Crime of Genocide (Genocide Convention) simply states that the genocidal conduct must have been committed "with intent to destroy, in whole or in part, a national, ethnical, racial or religious group, as such." This definition is, in the words of the International Law Commission, "widely accepted and generally recognized as the authoritative definition of this crime." The same wording is used in the Statutes of the ICTY, the ICTR, and the International Criminal Court (ICC). The chapeaux of Article 4, paragraph 2, of the ICTY Statute and Article 2, paragraph 2, of the ICTR Statute reiterate a portion of Article II of the Genocide Convention. Article 6 of the ICC does the same. This minimalist formulation of the requisite degree or quality of intent may have been of practical value to the declaratory function of the Genocide Convention and to national counterparts of the Convention, but it has proven to be somewhat vague, to the point where appellate litigation in the ICTY has been needed. *Prosecutor v. Goran Jelisić* provides an appropriate window on the problem.

## International Case Law on Degree or Quality of Genocidal Intent

### ICTY
The Judgement of the ICTY Appeals Chamber in *Prosecutor v. Goran Jelisić* sets forth the prevailing legal standard on the degree or quality of intent that must accompany the crime of genocide. In this case, the Prosecution appealed the Trial Chamber Judgment on the grounds that it "is ambiguous in terms of the degree or quality of the mens rea required under Article 4 for reasons articulated by the Trial Chamber itself." In its brief for the Appeals Chamber the Prosecution stated that the

> Trial Chamber erred in law to the extent it is proposing that the definition of the requisite mental state for genocide in Article 4 of the Statute only includes the *dolus specialis* standard, and not the broader notion of general intent [. . .].

The expression "to the extent it is proposing" suggests a caution or conditionality in this declaration of the grounds for the appeal; indeed, its written Appeals submission had suggested that the Trial Judgment was far from clear, left open the question of degree of intent, and used inconsistent terminology.

The Appeals Chamber astutely ruled, without any detailed discussion, that in order to convict an accused of the crime of genocide, he or she must have sought to destroy a group entitled to the protections of the Genocide Convention, in whole or in part. The mental state that corresponds to having sought the destruction of a group is referred to as *specific intent*:

> The specific intent requires that the perpetrator, by one of the prohibited acts enumerated in Article 4 of the Statute, seeks to achieve the destruction, in whole or in part, of a national, ethnical, racial or religious group, as such.

The Appeals Chamber went beyond setting aside the arguments of the Prosecution. It stated that the Prosecution had based its appeal on a misunderstanding of the Trial Judgment. The Appeals Chamber stated that a "question of interpretation of the Trial Chamber's Judgment is involved," and that

> the question with which the Judgment was concerned in referring to dolus specialis was whether destruction of a group was intended. The Appeals Chamber finds that the Trial Chamber only used the Latin phrase to express specific intent as defined above [. . .].

In other words, because the Prosecution was judged to have misunderstood the Trial Chamber's singular use of the term *dolus specialis* in the Trial Judgment, the Appeals Chamber did not consider it necessary to take on the substance of the Prosecution's submissions. Rather, the Appeals Chamber ruled that the term *intent* (as it appears in the definition of genocide that is used in international law) means "specific intent," which again must be understood as an intent to seek the destruction of a group. The Prosecution's attempt to advance a broader interpretation of the term was dismissed as a mere misunderstanding of the Trial Chamber's Judgment.

The Appeals Chamber affirmed that insofar as its preferred term, specific intent, is concerned, it "does not attribute to this term any meaning it might carry in a national jurisdiction." In making this statement the Appeals Chamber could be seen to have characterized comparative analysis of domestic criminal law as having little significance in the development of ad hoc tribunal case law relating to the requisite quality or degree of genocidal intent.

The *Jelisić* Appeals Judgment was rendered on July 5, 2001. Less than five weeks later, in *Prosecutor v. Radislav Krstić*, an ICTY Trial Chamber—in a Judgment dated August 2, 2001— convicted General Krstić of genocide for his participation in genocidal acts following the fall of the "safe area" of Srebrenica in July 1995. The *Krstić* Trial Judgment is in keeping with the *Jelisić* Appeals Judgment with respect to the mental state requirement for the establishment of guilt for the crime of genocide:

> For the purpose of this case, the Chamber will therefore adhere to the characterization of genocide which encompasses only acts committed with the goal of destroying all or part of a group.

> The Trial Chamber stated that it is aware that it must interpret the Convention with due regard for the principle of *nullum crimen sine lege*. It therefore recognizes that, despite recent developments, customary international law limits the definition of genocide to those acts *seeking* [italics added] the physical or biological destruction of all or part of the group.

However, the *Krstić* Trial Chamber did not exclude the possibility that the definition of genocide is a portion of the international law on genocide that is evolving. The Judgment provides that "[s]ome legal commentators further contend that genocide embraces those acts whose foreseeable or probable consequence is the total or partial destruction of the group without any necessity of showing that destruction was the goal of the act."

On the whole, in *Prosecutor v. Radislav Krstić*, the Trial Chamber's discussion of genocidal intent was unusually event-dependent. The discussion of the elements of genocide never strayed from the facts of the case. (In this way a Trial Chamber may try to shelter its legal findings and prevent them from being over-turned on appeal.) The Trial Judgment did, however, give more space to its finding on the mental state requisite to the crime of genocide than the corresponding (and very brief) discussion in the *Jelisić* Appeals Judgment. The *Krstić* Appeals Chamber held that the Trial Chamber "correctly identified the governing legal principle" and "correctly stated the law," but "erred in applying it."

The *Jelisić* Appeals Chamber standard (with respect to genocidal intent), as reinforced by the *Krstić* Trial Chamber, has been upheld by later decisions of the ad hoc tribunals.

ICTY Trial Chamber III, in *Prosecutor v. Duško Sikirica et al.*, issued a "Judgment on Defense Motions to Acquit" (September 3, 2001), in which it engaged in an elaborate and frank discussion of the law of genocide. The Prosecution's response to the half-time challenges submitted by the Defense, as well as the oral hearing before the *Sikirica* Trial Chamber, predated the *Jelisić* Appeals Judgment. In other words, the Prosecution had not adjusted its statements on the question of intent so as to encompass the *Jelisić* Appeals Judgment. It had, however, formulated these statements so as to be in line with the revised position advanced by the Prosecution during the oral argument in the *Jelisić* appeal.

Hence, the Prosecution proposed that three different mental state standards be part of the mental state requirement of the genocide provision in the ICTY Statute (Article 4):

1. The accused consciously desired the genocidal acts to result in the destruction, in whole or in part, of the group, as such;
2. The accused, having committed his or her genocidal acts consciously and with will to act, knew that the genocidal acts were actually destroying, in whole or in part, the group, as such; or
3. The accused, being an aider and abettor to a manifest, ongoing genocide, knowing that there was such an ongoing genocide and that his or her conduct of aiding and abetting was part of that ongoing genocide, knew that the likely consequence of his or her conduct would be to destroy, in whole or in part, the group, as such.

The Trial Chamber's response to this proposition is, although cursory, unmistakably clear. The Chamber stated that Article 4 of the ICTY Statute, "expressly identifies and explains the intent that is needed to establish the crime of genocide. This approach follows the 1948 Genocide Convention and is also consistent with the ICC Statute. [. . .]." The Chamber also noted that, "[a]n examination of theories of intent is unnecessary in construing the requirement of intent in Article 4(2). What is needed is an empirical assessment of all the evidence to ascertain whether the very specific intent required by Article 4(2) is established."

The Trial Chamber adopted a purely textual approach in its interpretation of genocidal intent, and refused to "indulge in the exercise of choosing one of the three standards identified by the Prosecution"—because, in its opinion, the wording of the ICTY Statute (and hence, the Genocide Convention) expressly provides and explains the applicable standard. The fact that the word *intent* does not reveal the degree of intent that is required suggests that the Trial Chamber wished to defuse the notion of quality or degree of intent (as opposed to its scope) in the context of the international crime of genocide.

The half-time Decision in *Prosecutor v. Milomir Stakić* provides some clarification. It was a Decision pursuant to a Defense challenge to dismiss the Prosecution's case on the grounds that there was insufficient evidence to sustain a conviction prior to the Defense's presentation of its evidence (in accordance with Rule 98*bis* of the ICTY Rules of Procedure and Evidence).

The *Stakić* Trial Chamber had observed that genocide is "characterized and distinguished by the aforementioned surplus intent." Genocidal conduct, it held, is only elevated to the crime of genocide.

> when it is proved that the perpetrator not only wanted to commit those acts but also intended to destroy the targeted group in whole or in part as a separate and distinct entity. The level of this specific intent is the dolus specialis. The Trial Chamber observes that there seems to be no dispute between the parties on this issue.

At the time of this Decision (October 2002), the ad hoc tribunal Prosecution had for more than one year accepted the mental state requirement as set forth in the *Jelisić* Appeals Judgement and the subsequent *Krstić* Trial Judgement. The emphasis of the *Stakić* Rule 98*bis* Decision was therefore not the quality or degree of genocidal intent, but rather the mental state requirement for accomplices. The *Stakić* Trial Judgement, not surprisingly, confirmed *Jelisić* and *Krstić* and its own half-time Decision. The Trial Chamber observed that the crime of genocide is "characterized and distinguished by a surplus of intent." The perpetrator must not only have "wanted to commit those acts but also intended to destroy the targeted group in whole or in part as a separate and distinct entity. The level of this intent is the *dolus specialis* or *specific intent*—terms that can be used interchangeably."

## ICTR

Several decisions of the ICTR in effect confirm that there is a specific intent requirement for the international crime of genocide. In *Prosecutor v. Jean-Paul Akayesu* the Trial Judgement clearly states that a "specific intention" is required, a dolus specialis; however, the Judgement is rather unclear when it attempts to describe what this means. The Judgement suggests that the significance of this "specific intention" is that the perpetrator "clearly seeks to produce the act charged." Accordingly, the object of the seeking is "the act charged," and not the complete or partial destruction of the group, as such. In other words, the ordinary meaning of the formulation used in the Judgment would suggest that the "specific intention" referred to by the *Akayesu* Trial Chamber actually concerns the genocidal conduct or *actus reus*, and not the aim of destruction.

Furthermore, in *Prosecutor v. Clément Kayishema and Obed Ruzindana*, the Trial Judgment states that a "distinguishing aspect of the crime of genocide is the specific intent (dolus specialis) to destroy a group in whole or in part." The Trial Chamber then opined that, "for the crime of genocide to occur, the mens rea must be formed prior to the commission of the genocidal acts. The individual acts themselves, however, do not require premeditation; the only consideration is that the act should be done in furtherance of the genocidal intent."

The expression "done in furtherance of the genocidal intent" is to a certain extent helpful in addressing the relationship between the genocidal conduct and the genocidal intent. The genocidal conduct must be undertaken in the service of the broader intent to destroy a group in whole or in part. The expression suggests the presence of both a cognitive component and volition as part of the mental state. It is difficult to imagine how one can do something to further the realization of an intention without knowing about and wanting the intended result. Doing something in furtherance of a specific intent would seem to imply a conscious desire.

*Prosecutor v. Alfred Musema* also includes a consideration of genocidal intent. In this case, the Trial Chamber stated that the crime of genocide is distinct from other crimes "because it requires a dolus specialis, a special intent." The Trial Chamber then tried to elucidate what it meant by dolus specialis by positing that the "special intent of a crime is the specific intention which, as an element of the crime, requires that the perpetrator clearly intended the result charged." This language expressly identifies result as the object of the perpetrator's intent or mental state. The specific intent does not refer to the conduct of destroying, but rather the result of at least partial destruction of the group. In this sense, it may be illustrative to use the term *subjective surplus* (of intent).

However, the *Musema* Trial Judgment refers to the result "charged." Identifying the result of destruction as pivotal (in the assignment of guilt), rather than the conduct that contributes to or brings about that destruction, would seem to be based on the assumption that the result of destruction is an integral part of the crime of genocide. Regrettably, paragraph 166 of the *Musema* Trial Judgment reinforces this assumption:

> The dolus specialis as a key element of an intentional offense is characterized by a psychological nexus between the physical result and the mental state of the perpetrator.

The word *nexus* is not particularly descriptive in this context; neither is the reference to physical result. The very notion of subjective surplus presupposes a broader intent that goes beyond the actus reus and includes a further objective result or factor that does not correspond to any objective element of crime. That is why this intent requirement amounts to a "surplus." International case law suggests that there has been no recognition of an objective contextual element (such as actual physical destruction) for genocide in international treaty law. It is certainly difficult to locate such an objective contextual element in the wording of the Genocide Convention.

The Musema decision draws on the earlier *Rutaganda* Trial Judgment (*Prosecutor v. Georges Anderson Nderubumwe Rutaganda*). The latter asserts that the distinguishing feature of the crime of genocide is the requirement of "dolus specialis, a special intent." It also uses the expression "clearly intended the result charged"—as well as "encompass the realization of the ulterior purpose to destroy"—both of which have been discussed in preceding paragraphs.

Finally, the International Court of Justice itself *insisted* (borrowing the word of the *Krstić* Trial Judgment), in its Advisory Opinion on the Legality of the Threat or Use of Nuclear Weapons, that specific intent to destroy is required for the international crime of genocide, and it indicated that "the prohibition of genocide would be pertinent in this case [possession of nuclear weapons] if the recourse to nuclear weapons did indeed entail the element of intent, towards a group as such, required by the provision quoted above." The *Krstić* Trial Chamber noted that some of the dissenting opinions critized the Advisory Opinion "by holding that an act whose foreseeable result was the destruction of a group as such and which did indeed cause the destruction of the group did constitute genocide."

## Other Relevant Sources on the Requisite Quality or Degree of Genocidal Intent

Even if international case law were unequivocal vis-à-vis the question of the requisite quality or degree of genocidal intent, it is also useful to consider additional sources of international law.

### International Law Commission

Notably, the International Law Commission stated in its commentary on the 1996 Draft Code of Crimes Against the Peace and Security of Mankind that "the definition of the crime of genocide requires a specific intent which is the distinguishing characteristic of this particular crime under international law." The Commission further observed that

> [a] general intent to commit one of the enumerated acts combined with a general awareness of the probable consequences of such an act with respect to the immediate victim or victims is not sufficient for the crime of genocide. The definition of this crime requires a particular state of mind or a specific intent with respect to the overall consequences of the prohibited act."

Caution should be observed in relying on the *travaux préparatoires* (preparatory work, or works) of the Genocide Convention, insofar as it is often difficult to establish the prevailing thinking of the negotiating states at the time. One can find support for widely differing positions on the same issues in the preparatory work. However, the *Krstić* Trial Judgment invoked the preparatory work for its position, claiming that it "clearly shows that the drafters envisaged genocide as an enterprise whose goal, or objective, was to destroy a human group, in whole or in part." The Chamber continued:

> The draft Convention prepared by the Secretary-General presented genocide as a criminal act which aims to destroy a group, in whole or in part, and specified that this definition excluded certain acts, which may result in the total or partial destruction of a group, but are committed in the absence of an intent to destroy the group.

### National Case Law

A few recent cases presented in German courts may be relevant to this discussion (although there is little evidence of other relevant national case-law). The Federal Supreme Court of Germany observed in its review of a 2001 case that genocidal acts "only receive their imprint of particular wrong by their combination with the intent [Absicht] required by section 220a(1) to destroy, in whole or in part, a group protected by this norm as such, keeping in mind that the desired goal, i.e., the complete or partial destruction of this group, does not have to be accomplished." The German term *Absicht* signifies *dolus directus* in the first degree—or, in more familiar terminology, conscious desire. The Court added, with an encouraging degree of precision:

> However, this goal has to be included within the perpetrator's intent as a subjective element of the crime that does not have an objective counterpart in the actus reus. This intent, which really characterizes the crime of genocide and distinguishes it, presupposes that it is the objective of the perpetrator, in the sense of a will directed towards a specific goal, to destroy, in whole or in part, the group protected by section 220a.

In another case that went before the German Federal Supreme Court, the judges provided further elaboration of the same conscious desire standard that was upheld by the *Jelisić* Appeals Chamber:

> The desired result, i.e., the complete or partial destruction of the group as such, does not have to be accomplished; it suffices that this result is comprised within the perpetrators intent [Absicht]. It is through this subjective element that, figuratively speaking, "anticipates" the desired outcome in the subjective sphere, that the crime of genocide [...] as such and thus its full wrong is determined.

### Commentaries

Antonio Cassese, a widely recognized authority on international criminal law, observes that genocidal intent "amounts to dolus specialis, that is, to an aggravated criminal intention, required in addition to the criminal intent accompanying the underlying offense [...]." He states that it "logically follows that other categories of mental element are excluded: recklessness (or dolus eventualis) and gross negligence." He correctly points out the ad hoc tribunals have contributed greatly to the elucidation of the subjective element of genocide.

William A. Schabas, an expert on the law of genocide, commenting on Article 6 (concerning genocide) of the ICC Statute, mentions "the special or specific intent requirement," "this rigorous definition," and the "very high intent requirement" without describing what the standard set out in the Genocide Convention and the ICC Statute actually is. It would seem that Schabas does not recognize the concept of degree or quality of mental state. He reiterates that the "offender must also be proven to have a 'specific intent' or dolus specialis," but without elaboration of what this phrase or the language of the intent formulation in the

Genocide Convention actually means. He does observe that a "specific intent offense requires performance of the actus reus but in association with an intent or purpose that goes beyond the mere performance of the act." He also suggests that the chapeau of Article II of the Genocide Convention actually defines the specific intent via the formulation "with intent to destroy, in whole or in part."

German legal scholar Albin Eser's brief but sophisticated treatment of specific intent in a contribution to Cassese's three-volume commentary on the Rome Statute of the ICC is instructive. He observes that "with special intent particular emphasis is put on the volitional element." Or, more specifically on genocide:

> In a similar way, it would suffice for the general intent of genocidal killing according to Article 6(a) of the ICC Statute that the perpetrator, though not striving for the death of his victim, would approve of this result, whereas his special "intent to destroy" in whole or in part the protected group must want to effect this outcome.

This overview of the positions taken by leading specialists on the issue of degree or quality of genocidal intent shows that there are no significant discrepancies between principal and secondary sources of international law with respect to the requisite degree or quality of intent for the international crime of genocide.

## The Nature of the Prosecution's Third Ground of Appeal in *Prosecutor v. Goran Jelisić*

Against the background of such strong and consistent arguments coming out of primary and secondary sources of international criminal law, it is necessary to inquire whether the Prosecution's third ground of appeal (pertaining to genocidal intent) in the *Jelisić* case was completely without merit, and whether it was misinterpreted by the Appeals Chamber.

The essence of the Prosecution's argument was: (1) that the Trial Chamber had erroneously held that the requisite quality or degree of intent for genocide is dolus specialis; (2) that the Trial Chamber had erroneously construed dolus specialis as being confined to consciously desiring complete or partial destruction; and (3) that the Trial Chamber had erred in not including the following two mental states in the scope of the requisite genocidal intent: knowledge that one's acts were destroying, in whole or in part, the group, as such; and that described by the case in which an aider and abettor commits acts knowing that there is an ongoing genocide which his acts form part of, and that the likely consequence of his conduct would be to destroy, in whole or in part, the group as such.

The Appeals Chamber held that the Prosecution's first assertion in the foregoing sequence was wrong and based on a misunderstanding, and that as a consequence it was rejecting the Prosecution's third ground of appeal. The Appeals Chamber proceeded to interpret the word *intent* as requiring that the perpetrator was seeking the result of destruction, which in reality amounts to a requirement of conscious desire. In other words, the Appeals Chamber did not address whether the Trial Chamber had held that the genocide provision of the ICTY Statute requires conscious desire (the Prosecution's second assertion in the foregoing sequence), but the Appeals Chamber itself held that conscious desire in the form of seeking the destruction of the group is required under the Statute. The concern that underlay the Prosecution's third ground of appeal was of course the level of the requisite intent, not whether or not it was called dolus specialis.

The Prosecution had advanced the two additional mental states (described above) that it claimed fell within the scope of the requisite genocidal intent—the first referring to the perpetrator of genocidal conduct, the second referring exclusively to accomplice liability. By insisting that the point of departure of the Prosecution's argument had been based on a misunderstanding, the Appeals Chamber chose not to discuss the merits of the Prosecution's second and third assertions with respect to the Trial Chamber's putative failings. As a consequence, there does not seem to be a recorded consideration by the Appeals Chamber of the possible merit of the Prosecution's material propositions.

This omission is noteworthy, not only against the background of the extensive briefing on this issue by the parties in the *Jelisić* appeal, but also in light of recent case law coming out of the same ad hoc tribunal.

## Concluding Considerations

The relevant sources in international criminal law provide a firm legal basis for the conclusion that conscious desire is the special intent requirement for the international crime of genocide.

It would seem that findings by the ICTY *Jelisić* Appeals Chamber and the *Krstić* Trial Chamber of the requisite quality or degree of genocidal intent remain sound. It is difficult to see how one can avoid requiring that the perpetrator of genocide has sought at least partial destruction of the group, or had such destruction as the goal of the genocidal conduct. It is reasonable to assert that the mental state must be composed both of a cognitive and emotive or volitional component. The perpetrator consciously desires the result of destructive action if that is what he or she seeks or harbors as the goal. The idea that one can seek a result with a mind bereft of volition as regards this result seems to be an abstraction not in conformity with practical reality. Consciousness of the result of action undertaken to further the destruction of the group, of the process leading to the destruction of the group, or of how one's conduct is an integral part of this process is not the same as wanting, desiring, or hoping for the destruction to occur. Desiring the destruction itself, with no awareness of a process to bring it about, of one's own contribution to such a process, or of the ability of one's conduct to bring about partial destruction would amount to a mental state that lacks the resolve that characterizes the intent to undertake action with a view to that action's ensuring at least the partial destruction of the targeted group.

It is unlikely that the state of the law will evolve significantly in the milieu of the ad hoc Tribunals, which are expected to be in operation until sometime between 2008 and 2010. The ICTY Appeals Chamber did not leave sufficient room for the Trial Chambers to attempt to expand the scope of the applicable standard for genocidal intent. The *Krstić* Trial Judgment is courageous in this respect, insofar as it suggests that customary international law could have moved on this question but had not done so by 1995.

# 1.4   The United Nations Convention on the Prevention and Punishment of the Crime of Genocide

Approved and proposed for signature and ratification or accession by General Assembly resolution 260 A (III) of 9 December 1948

*entry into force* 12 January 1951, in accordance with article XIII

## The Contracting Parties

Having considered the declaration made by the General Assembly of the United Nations in its resolution 96 (I) dated 11 December 1946 that genocide is a crime under international law, contrary to the spirit and aims of the United Nations and condemned by the civilized world,

Recognizing that at all periods of history genocide has inflicted great losses on humanity, and

Being convinced that, in order to liberate mankind from such an odious scourge, international co-operation is required,

Hereby agree as hereinafter provided:

## Article 1
The Contracting Parties confirm that genocide, whether committed in time of peace or in time of war, is a crime under international law which they undertake to prevent and to punish.

## Article 2
In the present Convention, genocide means any of the following acts committed with intent to destroy, in whole or in part, a national, ethnical, racial or religious group, as such:

(a) Killing members of the group;

(b) Causing serious bodily or mental harm to members of the group;

(c) Deliberately inflicting on the group conditions of life calculated to bring about its physical destruction in whole or in part;

(d) Imposing measures intended to prevent births within the group;

(e) Forcibly transferring children of the group to another group.

## Article 3
The following acts shall be punishable:

(a) Genocide;

(b) Conspiracy to commit genocide;

(c) Direct and public incitement to commit genocide;

(d) Attempt to commit genocide;

(e) Complicity in genocide.

## Article 4
Persons committing genocide or any of the other acts enumerated in article III shall be punished, whether they are constitutionally responsible rulers, public officials or private individuals.

## Article 5
The Contracting Parties undertake to enact, in accordance with their respective Constitutions, the necessary legislation to give effect to the provisions of the present Convention, and, in particular, to provide effective penalties for persons guilty of genocide or any of the other acts enumerated in article III.

## Article 6
Persons charged with genocide or any of the other acts enumerated in article III shall be tried by a competent tribunal of the State in the territory of which the act was committed, or by such international penal tribunal as may have jurisdiction with respect to those Contracting Parties which shall have accepted its jurisdiction.

## Article 7
Genocide and the other acts enumerated in article III shall not be considered as political crimes for the purpose of extradition.

The Contracting Parties pledge themselves in such cases to grant extradition in accordance with their laws and treaties in force.

*Article 8*
Any Contracting Party may call upon the competent organs of the United Nations to take such action under the Charter of the United Nations as they consider appropriate for the prevention and suppression of acts of genocide or any of the other acts enumerated in article III.

*Article 9*
Disputes between the Contracting Parties relating to the interpretation, application or fulfil-ment of the present Convention, including those relating to the responsibility of a State for genocide or for any of the other acts enumerated in article III, shall be submitted to the International Court of Justice at the request of any of the parties to the dispute.

*Article 10*
The present Convention, of which the Chinese, English, French, Russian and Spanish texts are equally authentic, shall bear the date of 9 December 1948.

*Article 11*
The present Convention shall be open until 31 December 1949 for signature on behalf of any Member of the United Nations and of any nonmember State to which an invitation to sign has been addressed by the General Assembly.

The present Convention shall be ratified, and the instruments of ratification shall be deposited with the Secretary-General of the United Nations.

After 1 January 1950, the present Convention may be acceded to on behalf of any Member of the United Nations and of any non-member State which has received an invitation as aforesaid. Instruments of accession shall be deposited with the Secretary-General of the United Nations.

*Article 12*
Any Contracting Party may at any time, by notification addressed to the Secretary-General of the United Nations, extend the application of the present Convention to all or any of the territories for the conduct of whose foreign relations that Contracting Party is responsible.

*Article 13*
On the day when the first twenty instruments of ratification or accession have been deposited, the Secretary-General shall draw up a proces-verbal and transmit a copy thereof to each Member of the United Nations and to each of the non-member States contemplated in article 11.

The present Convention shall come into force on the ninetieth day following the date of deposit of the twentieth instrument of ratification or accession.

Any ratification or accession effected subsequent to the latter date shall become effective on the ninetieth day following the deposit of the instrument of ratification or accession.

*Article 14*
The present Convention shall remain in effect for a period of ten years as from the date of its coming into force.

It shall thereafter remain in force for successive periods of five years for such Contracting Parties as have not denounced it at least six months before the expiration of the current period.

Denunciation shall be effected by a written notification addressed to the Secretary-General of the United Nations.

## Article 15

If, as a result of denunciations, the number of Parties to the present Convention should become less than sixteen, the Convention shall cease to be in force as from the date on which the last of these denunciations shall become effective.

## Article 16

A request for the revision of the present Convention may be made at any time by any Contracting Party by means of a notification in writing addressed to the Secretary-General.

The General Assembly shall decide upon the steps, if any, to be taken in respect of such request.

## Article 17

The Secretary-General of the United Nations shall notify all Members of the United Nations and the non-member States contemplated in article XI of the following:

(a) Signatures, ratifications and accessions received in accordance with article 11;

(b) Notifications received in accordance with article 12;

(c) The date upon which the present Convention comes into force in accordance with article 13;

(d) Denunciations received in accordance with article 14;

(e) The abrogation of the Convention in accordance with article 15;

(f) Notifications received in accordance with article 16.

## Article 18

The original of the present Convention shall be deposited in the archives of the United Nations.

A certified copy of the Convention shall be transmitted to each Member of the United Nations and to each of the non-member States contemplated in article 11.

## Article 19

The present Convention shall be registered by the Secretary-General of the United Nations on the date of its coming into force.

# 2

# Alternative Definitions

The definition of genocide settled upon for inclusion in the United Nations Convention on the Prevention and Punishment of Genocide (UNCG) has come to be commonly referred to as a "compromise definition"—a definition that was worked out in committees comprised of actors representing the interests of their particular nations. Thus, while some states were in favor of including, for example, political groups as one of those protected under the UNCG, others did not. The same was true of social groups. Following a great deal of debate and give and take, protection under the UNCG was granted to national, religious, racial, and ethnic groups, but not political, social, or gender groups. In the years since 1948, a host of scholars interested in and concerned about genocide have developed their own definitions of genocide and offered them as an alternative to the one used in the UNCG.

The exclusion of certain groups was not the only matter that scholars were concerned about in regard to the wording of the definition of genocide in the UNCG. There was, and is, as the debate continues to this day, the issue of the meaning of the words/phrases "intent," "in whole or in part," and "as such." With regard to the issue of intent, scholars have debated over exactly what should constitute "intent" when it comes to trying to ascertain whether or not perpetrators intend to destroy, in whole or in part, a specific group of people. That is, scholars (and lawyers and judges, for that matter) have engaged in long discussions and debates as to whether "intent" means that there must be clear evidence such as a document (e.g., a directive, report, letter), copy of a broadcast over radio or television, or testimony from one or more planners attesting to the fact that either plans and/or orders were given to destroy in whole or in part a particular group of people. This is a critical issue, for, in more cases than not, the sticking point in debates over whether or not a situation constitutes genocide revolves around the issue of the intent of the perpetrator and the evidence of such intent. As a result of case law in the *ad hoc* tribunals for the former Yugoslavia (ICTY) and Rwanda (ICTR), international law now allows the issue of "intent" to be inferred from the actions on the ground, so to speak, as distinct from a particular document or oral statement. Concomitantly, according to the Report of the Preparatory Commission for the International Criminal Court (PCICC), the International Criminal Court may infer such from "conduct [that] took place in the context of a manifest pattern of similar conduct directed against that group or was conduct that could itself effect such destruction" (Article 6a), including "the initial acts in an emerging pattern" (Article 6, Introduction).

With regard to the issue of "in whole or in part," scholars have debated over what that means in actuality. The "in whole," of course, is self-explanatory. The fact is, though, no genocide in recent times has ever resulted the complete extermination of a group of people. The Nazis, of course, intended to exterminate every single Jew on the face of the earth, but the Allies won the war thus shutting down the Nazis' industrial-like killing of those they deemed unworthy of life. Furthermore, it is not impossible, of course, for a group, particularly a small indigenous group, to be wiped out "in whole," but to date, at least as far as anyone knows, no group has been destroyed in whole.

That still leaves the meaning of the words "in part." Does that mean, scholars have asked, a major part of the group, a large percentage of the total population, or the targeting of a specific part of the group (e.g., the educated people, the leaders, male members), or something else altogether? R. J. Rummel (2002), a political scientist, has asserted that "in part" means that "there is no *lower limit* to the number of people on which these acts may be committed. It is genocide even [if] any of the Acts (a)–(e) are on *one person* with the intent described." Corroborating the latter but providing additional insights into the meaning of "in part," Gregory Stanton, a lawyer, professor, and geno-cide scholar, states that "Most authorities require intent to destroy a substantial number of group members—mass murder. But an individual criminal may be guilty of genocide even if he kills only one person, so long as he knew he was participating in a larger plan to destroy the group. . . . Destruction of only part of a group (such as its educated members, or members living in one region) is also genocide." On the latter point, "if a specific part of a group is emblematic of the overall group, or is essential to its survival, that may support a finding that the part qualifies as substantial within the meaning of Article 4" (ICTY, 2004, p. 1).

With regard to the wording "as such," it refers to the fact that specific groups are intentionally targeted for destruction, and that the destruction of such groups is not a result of an accident, side effect, or offshoot of another effort (e.g., "collateral damage").

But the debates do not end there. There has also been ample discussion over whether and/or when such actions as the following constitute genocide: causing serious bodily or mental harm to members of the group; deliberately inflicting on the group conditions of life calculated to bring about its physical destruction in whole or in part; and, forcibly transferring children of the group to another group. As might be expected, scholars with different backgrounds and perspectives have different takes on the feasibility of including each of the aforementioned actions under the rubric of genocide.

In developing alternative definitions, scholars have attempted to overcome what they perceive as weaknesses or gaps in the UNCG definition. In some cases, the alternative definitions developed by scholars are, in some respects, stronger than that found in the UNCG, but in other respects they are weaker, and instead of adding clarity to an already murky situation, they only muddy the waters.

It is important to note that scholars can develop all of the alternative definitions they wish, and while such may be useful for scholarly endeavors, at this point in time, one and only one definition—that found in the UNCG—is used by courts of law, *ad hoc* tribunals, and the ICC.

In this section, three articles are included that address the issue of the weaknesses and gaps in the UNCG's definition of genocide and various ways in which such weak-nesses and gaps may be overcome. In "The Definition of Genocide," Israel W. Charny succinctly discusses the focus of the definition of genocide found in the UNCG and offers what he refers to as his "more humanistic definition." It is a definition that is all-inclusive. Charny argues that no group should be excluded from protection under the UNCG and while his notion is heartfelt, he has been taken to task by many scholars for creating a definition that is so broad and inclusive that it is not a tenable definition and one that certainly could not be of any value in a court of law.

Roger Smith, in "Human Destructiveness and Politics: The Twentieth Century as an Age of Genocide," considers a number of ways in which genocides can be classified according to the nature of their target victims, the motives of the perpetrators, and the outcomes thereby achieved.

In one of the longer articles ("Defining Genocide as a Sociological Concept") included in *The Genocide Studies Reader*, Helen Fein, a pioneer of genocide studies, provides a detailed analysis of a host of alternative definitions developed by genocide scholars from such fields as psychology, political science, sociology and history. In doing so, she provides a razor-sharp critique of each definition, noting what she perceives as their strengths, weaknesses, and gaps. She concludes by offering her own definition and a rationale for its wording and conceptual make-up.

## References

ICTR (1998). Judgement and Sentence of Jean-Paul Akayesu (ICTR-96-4-T). September 2 and October 2, 1998, respectively. Accessed at: www.un.org/ictr/

Rummel, R. J. (2002). "Genocide." Accessed at: www.hawaii.edu/powerkills/GENOCIDE/ENCY.htm

Stanton, Gregory (2004). "Definition of Genocide." Prevent Genocide International Website. Accessed at: www.preventgenocide.org/genocide/officialtext.htm

# 2.1   Israel W. Charny, "The Definition of Genocide"

Lemkin (1944, p. 79) saw genocide as the effort to destroy the "essential foundations of the life of national groups" whose objectives "would be the disintegration of the political and social institutions of culture, language, national feelings, religion, and the economic existence of national groups, and the destruction of the personal security, liberty, health, dignity, and even the lives of the individuals belonging to such groups."

Notwithstanding the above emphasis on the elimination of the continuity of a people even more than the fact of mass murder itself, for most lay people the central, immediately understood meaning of genocide is mass destruction of any target people. However, many legal and political authorities continue to insist on a definition of genocide as deriving from a distinct intention to obliterate the continuity of an ethnic, racial or religious group, in whole or in part. This definition would mean that even an overwhelming event of mass murder which did not aim to destroy the identity of the victim people would *not* be considered genocide. Thus, the atom-bombing of Nagasaki by the U.S.A. would not be considered genocide—even if it were agreed that military needs did not justify dropping the second bomb, and even if it were agreed that insufficient warnings were given the victims—not only because it was an act of "war," but *because* the U.S.A. did not intend to exterminate the Japanese people as such. Of course, it cannot be emphasized too much that whatever one's opinions about the U.S. atomic bombings of Japan, it is clear that nuclear weapons figure prominently in the potential for even more terrible mass murders in the future.

The U.N. Convention on Genocide confirmed that genocide was a crime under international law. It defined the crime to include the killing of members of any national, ethnic, racial or religious entity. Conspicuously omitted, as a result of political pressures at the time of the formulation of the Convention, are instances of killing political enemies, and there is also no coverage of the mass murder of a country's own nationals. The case of Stalin's murders of "enemies" of the Soviet regime is a good example of both exclusions; the case of Pol Pot's regime in Cambodia murder of 1 to 3 million of its own nationals is another instance. [If only to mitigate the absurdity and injustice that such events do not qualify as genocide, scholars seek nonetheless to prove that among the target population there were distinct national or religious entities earmarked for extermination because of their identity, hence some of these mass killings would also constitute genocide. *See* Letgers (1984) on the case of Stalin's killing of 20 million Soviets, and Hawk's (1984) research of the mass murder of Cambodians.]

Genocide may also take the form of an artificial introduction of famine or the deliberate withholding of aid to famine-ridden areas. During 1932–33, the Soviet Union created a famine in the Ukraine with as many as 6 million people reported dead. From the point of view of definitional issues, Mace (1984) and Conquest (1970) argue that this famine was intended not only to crush the peasants' resistance to collectivization, but also to undermine Ukrainian nationalism—which would qualify the killing as genocidal.

Helen Fein (1984, p. 4) has proposed an all-encompassing definition of genocide: "I believe one underlying explanation can encompass all types. Genocide is the calculated murder of a segment or all of a group defined outside the universe of obligation of the perpetrator by a government, elite, staff or crowd representing the perpetrator in response to a crisis or opportunity perceived to be caused by or impeded by the victim."

Fein has distinguished between four overall categories of genocide: *developmental genocide*, where the perpetrators clear the way for their colonization of an area inhabited by an indigenous people; *despotic genocide*, where the perpetrators clear away the opposition to their power as for example in a political revolution; *retributive genocide*, where peoples are locked into ethnic and other stratifications of order and dominance-submission struggles; and *ideological genocide*. She has created an outstanding teaching as well as research tool by projecting these types of genocide in a series of "fictional" scenarios where she removes the actual identifying names and places of actual events of genocide in the past, and thus creates a series of templates for possible situations in which genocides can be expected in the future.

Most major scholars of genocide have called for a broadening of the definition. Leo Kuper (1985) makes the point that "political affiliation can be as permanent and as immutable as racial origin" (p. 16), and further emphasizes that in many cases "it is impossible to disentangle the political component from the ethnic, racial or religious" (p. 100). Others also call for inclusion of sexual groups, such as homosexuals—the objects of Nazi extermination in the Holocaust (Porter, 1982)—or any other real group, such as the retarded and mentally ill, who were executed by the Nazis, or city dwellers, who were killed by the Cambodians, and even a "pseudo-group" such as "demonic enemies" or witches or enemies of the people according to whichever ruler's definition.

Some authors suggest using closely related terms like "genocidal massacres" (Kuper, 1981) or "genocidal killing" to cover instances that do not qualify technically as genocide under the existing Convention. Charny (1985) has proposed what he calls a *humanistic* definition of genocide, namely "the *wanton* murder of human beings on the basis of any identity what-soever that they share—national, ethnic, racial, religious, political, geographical, ideological." He argues: "I reject out of hand that there can ever be any identity process that in itself will justify the murder of men, women and children 'because' they are 'anti' some 'ism' or because their physical characteristics are high- or low-cheekboned, short- or long-eared, or green- or orange-colored" (p. 448).

An authoritative U.N. study on genocide submitted by Special Rapporteur Ben Whitaker in 1985 seeks to maintain the gravity of the concept of genocide and calls for consideration of both the proportionate scale and the total number of victims in deciding what constitutes genocide. At the same time, the report calls for an extension of the definition under the Convention to include genocide of one's own group, and sexual groups, and also points to the desirability of including political genocide. Furthermore, the report (p. 13) also recommends further study of the possibilities of including cultural genocide or "ethnocide," as well as "ecocide."

## When Does Genocide Take Place?

Although genocide is omnipresent in human history, it nonetheless occurs with a certain regularity under predictable conditions. Porter (1982) noted that genocide is most prevalent in times of war, colonization, and tribal conflict. Kuper (1981, 1985) provides a classification of genocide which is similar to that of Fein, and specifies some of the conditions under which genocide is more frequent:

1. Genocide against indigenous peoples (e.g. the murder of Indians in South American countries such as Paraguay).
2. Genocide following decolonization of a two-tier structure of domination (e.g. the Hutu in genocidal massacres by the Tutsi in Rwanda and Burundi).
3. Genocide in the process of struggles for power by ethnic or racial or religious groups, or struggles for greater autonomy or for secession (e.g. Bangladesh in 1971).
4. Genocide against hostage or scapegoat groups (e.g. the Armenians by the Turks in 1915, and the persecution of the Jews by the Nazis in the Holocaust).

Kuper further notes that "domestic" genocides, that is, genocides which arise on the basis of cleavages within a society, are a phenomenon of plural societies, in which there are sharp cleavages between ethnic, racial or religious groups. They arise under a variety of circumstances: struggles for power, consolidations of despotic regimes, annihilation of hostage groups in situations of crisis for host societies, economic expansion into areas inhabited by hunting and gathering groups, and under the facilitating conditions of international war.

Sociologist Horowitz (1980; *see* Horowitz, 1976) places emphasis on defining the nature of societies in which genocide takes place. Genocide is not a random or sporadic event, but a special sort of mass destruction that requires the approval of the State, which uses genocide as a technique for national solidarity. He proposes an analytical framework of eight types of society:

1. Genocidal societies—the State takes the lives of people who are deviant or people whose behaviour is dissident.
2. Deportation or incarceration societies—the State removes certain individuals or prevents them from interacting with a larger body politic.
3. Torture societies—peoples are victimized short of death and returned as living evidence of the risks of deviance.
4. Harassment societies—people are constantly picked up, searched, seized and held.
5. Traditional-shame societies—participation and collective will is generated through instilling a sense of disapproval and isolation.
6. Guilt societies—these internalize a sense of wrongdoing in the individual in addition to the shame mechanism previously described.
7. Tolerant societies—norms are well articulated and well understood; deviance is not celebrated, but it is not destroyed.
8. Permissive societies—norms are questioned and the community defines the normative rather than the State.

Porter (1982) undertook to formulate the clustering of characteristics that predict the occurrence of genocide, and also the contrasting convergence of characteristics that predict the reduced likelihood of genocide (Table 1).

Fein (1984) has also especially emphasized the objective powerlessness of the victim. She notes the following facilitating conditions of genocide:

1. Lack of visibility of the genocidal action.

*Table 1* Genocide Prediction

| Predict genocide | Predict genocide unlikely |
| --- | --- |
| Minority group is considered an outsider | Pervasive tolerance for minorities |
| Racist ideology | Strong minority with ready access to legal and human rights |
| Strong dependence on military | Temperate attitude to military |
| Power exclusion of political parties | Democratic political structure |
| Leadership has strong territorial ambitions | Weak territorial and imperial ambitions |
| Power of the State has been reduced by defeat and war or internal strife | No such precipitant events |
| Possibility of retaliation for genocide from some source is at minimum | Possibility of retaliation or interference by outside nations is considerable |

2. Inability of the bystanders and third parties to apprehend the pattern of the crime.
3. Objective powerlessness of the victims and/or their stigmatization as not so innocent.
4. Inability of the victims to prosecute their victimizers.
5. Lack of sanctions by third parties and/or lack of will of other states to use their sanctions.

Fein also notes that once genocide has taken place, the most common way for the perpetrator to account for genocide is to deny that it ever happened. Another way is to declare that the actions were justified as defensive responses to attacks by the victims on the perpetrator.

Charny (1982), together with his collaborator Rapaport, propose that we look at how societies are organized both around forces that promote human life and forces that move towards the destruction of life long before an actual genocide event emerges. They suggest that all societies are characterized by both types of process, and under certain circumstances, which they believe can be analyzed and eventually taken as a basis for prediction of genocidal dangers, the balance is titled in favor of societal processes that authorize mass destruction of another people. Charny and Rapaport's analytic schema is a unique effort to relate macroso-cietal processes that culminate in genocide to the principles of psychology of the individual, and the behaviors of individuals in the family, groups, and society. Their analysis generates what they call a series of *genocide early warning processes*, which are systematic exaggerations and distortions of what are originally normal life experience processes. They suggest that looking at the unfolding process of genocide in this way gives us new possibilities for understanding how, some day, genocide can be prevented insofar as human beings, as individuals and as societal groups, can learn to cope with normal life experience processes more constructively and not allow violence to gain the upper hand.

They too note that once genocide has taken place, there are a considerable number of "experience-denying mechanisms" that are intended to make it possible to deny the very facts of the brutal murders that are being or have been committed—denials on the level of the individuals in the murdering society that enable them to go on with their everyday lives as if nothing untoward has taken place, as well as denials on the larger governmental and collective cultural level that are intended first to conceal and then cynically to wipe out the record of the murders.

## References

Charny, Israel (1982) *How Can We Commit the Unthinkable? Genocide, The Human Cancer.* In collaboration with Chanan Rapaport. Boulder, CO: Westview Press.

Charny, Israel (1985), "Genocide, the Ultimate Human Rights Problem," pp. 448–452. *Social Education.* In Special Issue on Human Rights edited by Samuel Totten, 49(6):448–452.

Conquest, Robert (1970). *The Nation Killers.* New York: Macmillan.

Fein, Helen (1984). "Scenarios of Genocide: Models of Genocide and Critical Responses," pp. 3–31. In Israel Charny (Ed.) *Toward the Understanding and Prevention of Genocide: Proceedings of the International Conference on the Holocaust and Genocide.* Boulder, CO: Westview Press.

Hawk, David (1984). "Pol Pot's Cambodia: Was it Genocide?" pp. 51–59. In Israel Charny (Ed.) *Toward the Understanding and Prevention of Genocide: Proceedings of the International Conference on the Holocaust and Genocide.* Boulder, CO: Westview Press

Horowitz, Irving Louis (1976). *Genocide: State Power and Mass Murder.* New Brunswick, NJ: Transaction Publishers.

Horowitz, Irving Louis (1980). *Taking Lives.* Revised version of *Genocide: State Power and Mass Murder.* New Brunswick, NJ: Transaction Publishers.

Kuper, Leo (1981). *Genocide: Its Political Use in the Twentieth Century.* London: Penguin Books; New Haven, CT: Yale University Press.

Kuper, Leo (1985). *The Prevention of Genocide.* New Haven, CT: Yale University Press.

Lemkin, Raphael (1944). *Axis Rule in Occupied Europe.* Washington, D.C.: Carnegie Endowment for World Peace.

Letgers, Lyman (1984). "The Soviet Gulag: Is It Genocide?" pp. 60–66. In Israel Charny (Ed.) *Toward the Understanding and Prevention of Genocide: Proceedings of the International Conference on the Holocaust and Genocide.* Boulder, CO: Westview Press.

Mace, James E. (1984). "The Man-made Famine of 1933 in the Soviet Ukraine: What Happened and Why?" In Israel Charny (Ed.). *Toward the Understanding and Prevention of Genocide: Proceedings of the International Conference on the Holocaust and Genocide.* Boulder, CO: Westview Press.

Porter, Jack (1982). "What Is Genocide? Notes Toward a Definition," pp. 2–33. In Jack Porter (Ed.) *Genocide and Human Rights: A Global Anthology.* Washington, D.C.: University Press of America.

Whitaker, Ben (1985). *Revised and Updated Report on the Question of the Prevention and Punishment of Genocide.* 62 pp. (E/CN.4/Sub.2/1985/6, 2 July 1985).

# 2.2   Roger W. Smith, "Human Destructiveness and Politics: The Twentieth Century as an Age of Genocide"

Genocide is almost always a premeditated act calculated to achieve the ends of its perpetrators through mass murder. Sometimes, however, genocidal consequences precede any conscious decision to destroy innocent groups to satisfy one's aims. This is most often the case in the early phases of colonial domination, where through violence, disease, and relentless pressure indigenous peoples are pushed toward extinction. With the recognition of the consequences of one's acts, however, the issue is changed: to persist is to intend the death of a people. This pattern of pressure, recognition, and persistence is typically what happened in the nineteenth century. Today, however, when indigenous groups come under pressure, the intention to destroy them is present from the outset; there are few illusions about the likely outcome. The distinction, then, between premeditated and unpremeditated genocide is not decisive, for sooner or later the *genocidal* is transformed into *genocide.*

Rather than being simply an expression of passion, genocide is a rational instrument to achieve an end. While these ends have varied from perpetrator to perpetrator and, to a large extent, by historical period, they have typically included the following: revenge, conquest, gain, power, and purification/salvation. From these we can construct a grammar of motives which, in effect, asks the perpetrator: What are you trying to do and why is it so important that you are willing to sacrifice thousands, even millions of lives (including those of children) to achieve it? Formal, but nevertheless useful, answers to these questions are contained in the different types of genocide, arranged in terms of the grammar of motives. Classified in this manner, the pure types of genocide are retributive, institutional, utilitarian, monopolistic, and ideological.[1]

## Retributive Genocide

Retribution may play a role in all genocide, but it does so mainly as a rationalization: it is a way of blaming the victim. Though it draws from the vocabulary of justice and of judicially administered punishment, genocide destroys persons most often for what they are rather than for anything they have done. In this sense, retribution flows from the dehumanization that has been fastened to the victims before they are attacked. As a principal motive in genocide, retribution is rare, but it does seem to figure prominently in accounts of conquerors like Chingis-khan (Genghis Khan).[2] Nevertheless, it is difficult to see how the "Conqueror of the World," as he called himself, differed in his actions when inspired by revenge than he and others did when they engaged in the institutional genocide associated with warfare until about the fifteenth century.

## Institutional Genocide

Institutional genocide was the major source of politically sanctioned mass murder in the ancient and medieval worlds. The massacre of men, the enslavement of women and children, and, often, the razing of towns and the destruction of the surrounding countryside, were universal aspects of conquest: genocide was embedded in the very notion of warfare.[3] As such, no explicit decision had to be made to commit genocide—it had become routinized. In part, institutional genocide was motivated by the desire to create terror, to display one's power, and to remove the possibility of future retaliation. But it was also due to a failure of political imagination: genocide was a substitute for politics. Instead of ruling a city or territory, extracting tribute from it, and perhaps even incorporating it into one's own system of power and authority, the society was devastated. By the late medieval period this practice had largely ended in the West (indeed, it had begun to change with the Romans, who understood that only through politics could one build an empire), yet it became a prominent part of the Crusades and was made all the more deadly because of religious passion.[4] In any case, institutional genocide continued in the East with figures like Timur Lenk until the fifteenth century. For some 500 years thereafter, the genocide of conquest disappeared. It is possible, however, that both guerrilla warfare and the use of nuclear weapons signify a revival of this early form of genocide. If the means are different, the motives seem not that dissimilar, and the consequences include both widespread devastation and the massive taking of innocent life by those in authority.

## Utilitarian Genocide

If utility played a role in institutional genocide, it became particularly prominent in the genocide of the sixteenth and nineteenth centuries, when colonial domination and exploitation of indigenous peoples in the Americas, Australia, Tasmania, parts of Africa, and elsewhere became pronounced. It has continued in the twentieth century, especially in Latin America, where Indians have been subjected to genocidal attacks in the name of progress and development. Apart from the more sadistic aspects of this kind of destruction, the object has been Indian land—for the timber it contains, the minerals that can be extracted, and the cattle it can feed—and, at the turn of the century, Indian labor to harvest, under conditions of forced labor, the sap of the rubber tree.[5]

Richard Rubenstein has recently argued that development leads to a population "surplus," which in turn leads to programs to eliminate the superfluous population.[6] What is happening with the remaining indigenous population of Latin America, and what was the fate of millions in various areas of the world earlier, has nothing, however, to do with a surplus population (whatever that is, for Rubenstein never defines his basic term). They are being killed, were killed, because of a combination of ethnocentrism and simple greed. The basic proposition contained in utilitarian genocide is that some persons must die so that others can live well. If that proposition no longer claims a large number of lives, it is because the previous genocide was so effective and the remaining tribes so small, with at most a few thousand members each. Yet precisely because of the tenacity of the assaults against them, and the small size of the groups, utilitarian genocide, although somewhat rare in the twentieth century, tends to be *total*.

## Monopolistic Genocide

Most genocide prior to the twentieth century was external—it was exacted of groups that lived outside one's territorial boundaries. There are some important exceptions—most of which are connected with religious persecution—but for the most part genocide was directed outward: its goals were conquest and colonial exploitation. Today almost all genocide is domestic—groups within one's borders are destroyed. Again there are exceptions—Hitler committed both domestic and external genocide—but most examples of genocide in the twentieth century have been directed inward. Issues that were not at stake in external genocide are central today: who belongs, who is to have a voice in the society, what is to be the basic shape of the community, what should its purposes be?

While these questions obviously lend themselves to ideological solutions, the genocide that has emerged as a means of shaping the basic structure and design of the state and society has been more inclusive than that. Examples of such attempts come from those that are ideologically motivated (Cambodia), those that are not (Pakistan), and those that combine elements of both (Armenia). In fact, whatever the shape of the regime, the most frequent source of genocide in the twentieth century has been the struggle for the monopolization of power. While issues of international dominance, of the distribution of power, of who rules can be raised in any political system, they have been crucial to conflicts that have emerged in Pakistan, Burundi, Nigeria, and other societies that have pervasive cleavages between racial, religious, and ethnic groups. These plural societies are in large part a legacy of nineteenth-century colonialism, but their genocidal struggles take place today within the framework of self-determination.[7] Having been subjected to colonial exploitation and genocide, these societies now butcher themselves.

## Ideological Genocide

Most genocide in the twentieth century has not been ideological but, where it has, the results have been catastrophic: ideology under modern conditions tends toward holocaust.[8] Most genocide in the past was also not ideological: it was an instrument not for the restructuring of society according to some blueprint of the mind, but for gaining, on the ideal plane, revenge, and on the more tangible one, booty, women, territory, public slaves, or the exploitation of "native" labor and resources. Ideology, in the form of religion, did contribute to human destructiveness—it provided rationalization to the Spanish for conquering and enslaving Indians, it formed the background for repeated attacks on Jews, and was one, but only one, ingredient in the so-called wars of religion in the sixteenth and seventeenth centuries. On the other hand, the Inquisition, which is sometimes cited as an example of genocide, was nothing of the kind: cruel as it was, the Inquisition took the form of a judicial inquiry, with those suspected of either heresy or of insincere belief receiving scrutiny; those convicted (and not all were) were burned en masse, but they were tried as individuals.[9] Nevertheless, some genocide before the twentieth century certainly was ideological: the destruction of unholy cities in ancient Israel and of the Albigensians in the thirteenth century. The Crusades also to some extent had a religious basis, though many other elements (political ambition, desire for material acquisitions) became entangled in it. In all these cases, however, the aim was essentially conservative: genocide was used to protect and defend a particular religious faith, not as contemporary ideology is, to transform society. With us the attempt has been to eradicate whole races, classes, and ethnic groups—whatever the particular ideology specifies—in order to produce a brave new world free of offensive human material.

At the heart of contemporary ideology is what Camus called a "metaphysical revolt" against the very conditions of human existence: plurality, mortality, finitude, and spontaneity.[10] It is, as it were, an attempt to re-establish the Creation, providing for an order, justice, and humanity that are thought to be lacking. At the same time that it strives for a kind of salvation, it is often motivated by a profound desire to eliminate all that it perceives as being impure—be it race, class, or even, in the case of the Khmer Rouge, cities. The revolt is metaphysical, but it is also deeply moral in an ancient way: the rejection of the unclean, the fear of contamination. How else explain the constant references in Nazism to purification and the Cambodian references to the cleansing of the people? When one attempts to bring about a "perfect" society, much of the human material must be jettisoned; and since humans are going to be killed for what they are rather than for what they have done, the most primitive, but still basic, moral category surfaces, that of the unclean, the impure. Indeed, one contemporary philosopher suggests that the "dread of the impure and rites of purification are in the background of all our feelings and all our behavior relating to fault."[11] When defilement is understood ideologically, it is literally true, as Paul Ricoeur notes in a different context, that "we enter into the reign of Terror."[12] Yet it is possible to substitute one symbol of evil for another, in the Soviet Union the idea of guilt, especially the objective guilt of class origins, assumes the role played elsewhere by defilement. At bottom, ideology turns politics into a variety of the sacred. Yet holocausts are born, not in the name of God, but of biology, history, and peasant simplicity.

Tendencies, however, are not necessarily results; holocaust is not a matter of deduction. Ideology seldom exists in a pure form: its relationship to culture is of particular importance. Does the culture reinforce the ideology, as in Nazi Germany and the Soviet Union, or does it come into conflict with it, as in Italy and Cuba? That culture can humanize and restrain ideology gives hope; that it does not always succeed and may even buttress ideology is part of the contemporary uncertainty about the future of genocide in its most extreme form, holocaust.

## Notes

1. For other types of classifications, see Vahakn N. Dadrian, "A Typology of Genocide," *International Review of Modern Sociology* 5 (1975), pp. 201–12, and Leo Kuper, *International Action Against Genocide* (London: Minority Rights Group Report No. 53, 1982), pp. 5–9.
2. René Grousset, *Conqueror of the World: The Life of Chingis-Khan*, trans. Marion McKellar and Denis Sinor (New York: Viking Press, 1972).
3. Cf. Thomas Alfred Walker, *A History of the Law of Nations*, Vol. 1 (Cambridge, England: Cambridge University Press, 1899).
4. Antony Bridge, *The Crusades* (New York: Franklin Watts, 1982).

5.  Arens, *Genocide in Paraguay*; Shelton H. Davis, *Victims of the Miracle: Development and the Indians of Brazil* (Cambridge, England: Cambridge University Press, 1977); and an older, but important account, W. E. Hardenburg, *The Putumayo/The Devil's Paradise* (London: Unwin, 1912).
6.  Richard L. Rubenstein, *The Age of Triage: Fear and Hope in an Overcrowded World* (Boston: Beacon Press, 1983).
7.  Kuper, *Genocide*, Chap. 4.
8.  If this is the tendency, it may not, for reasons suggested later, always be the result. Yet, with one partial exception, all holocausts have been associated with deeply ideological regimes. The Armenian holocaust was motivated in equal parts by ideology and the quest for dominance, but retribution and even utility played important roles, especially at the local level. I am uncertain whether a holocaust could ever come about wholly apart from ideology, but it may be that a strong convergence of motives could produce such a result.
9.  Cf. Kuper, *Genocide*, p. 13. A. S. Turberville, *The Spanish Inquisition* (Oxford: Oxford University Press, 1932), provides an excellent factual account.
10. Albert Camus, *The Rebel*, trans. Anthony Bower (New York: Vintage Books, 1956).
11. Paul Ricoeur, *The Symbolism of Evil*, trans. Emerson Buchanan (Boston: Beacon Press, 1969), p. 25.
12. Ibid.

# 2.3   Helen Fein, "Defining Genocide as a Sociological Concept"

For the last decade, social scientists considering genocide have devised varying definitions and typologies, often reflecting consensus on evaluation of specific cases but dissensus on the borderlines of genocide. Controversy continues not only because genocide is hard to differentiate categorically but because most definers have normative or prescriptive agendas; we are activated by what we feel genocide should encompass—often not wishing to exclude any victims.

Debates recur about the identity of the target group, the scope of acts deemed genocidal, the identity of the perpetrator, the distinction among types of genocide, and whether or how to distinguish intent. This problem has been complicated lately by the convergence of interests linking researchers of genocide and state terror; the latter concentrate more on explanations of state behavior than of the choice of the victim group. Although this may prove to be a much-needed intellectual opening, it can also confound explanations when diverse objectives and behaviors are aggregated.

Because genocide itself occurs in the context of diverse social relations, it is useful to clarify how the term evolved in order to return to the underlying assumptions behind the concept; then I shall suggest a more generic concept, appropriate for sociological usage, paralleling the terms of the UNGC.

## Lemkin's Conception and the UNGC Definition

Lemkin's conception (1944, 79) emerged from an attempt to explain and indict German population policy. Later study has shown that Lemkin overidentified commonalities and implied a coherent and common objective in different countries. In fact, Hitler's objectives varied and were not always premeditated. However, Lemkin recognized that Hitler had different population policies and aims in the occupied east and the west: 'Germanization' or coerced denationalization and assimilation was not the same as 'genocide.' According to Lemkin (1944),

genocide does not necessarily mean the immediate destruction of a nation, except when accomplished by mass killings of all members of a nation. It is intended rather to signify a coordinated plan of different actions aiming at the destruction of essential foundations of the life of national groups, with the aim of annihilating the groups themselves. (79). . . .

Hitler's conception of genocide is based not upon cultural but only biological patterns. . . . Some groups—such as the Jews—are to be destroyed completely. A distinction is made between peoples considered to be related by blood to the German people (such as Dutchmen, Norwegians, Flemings, Luxembourgers), and peoples not thus related by blood (such as the Poles, Slovenes, Serbs). The populations of the first group are deemed worthy of being Germanized. With respect to the Poles particularly, Hitler expressed the view that it is their soil alone which *can and should be profitably Germanized* (81–82). . . .

In the occupied countries of 'people of non-related blood,' a policy of depopulation is pursued. Foremost among the methods employed for the purpose is the adoption of measures calculated to decrease the birthrate of the national groups of non-related blood, while at the same time steps are taken to encourage the birthrate of the *Volksdeutsche* living in these countries (86). The physical debilitation and even annihilation of national groups in occupied countries is carried out mainly in the following ways:

1. *Racial discrimination in Feeding . . .*
2. *Endangering of Health . . .*
3. *Mass Killings . . .* (87–8)

First, we note, the object of genocide was always the defeated national group except for the Jews, conceived by the Nazis as a race or anti-race—non-human, superhuman and menacing. Political groups and classes within the nation who were killed and incarcerated by the German occupiers were conceived as members of a national group. Second, Lemkin conceived of genocide as a set of coordinated tactics or means. *Cultural genocide* was not a term used by Lemkin: cultural discrimination may be a tactic to assimilate or to destroy a group. The objective of genocide was both the social disintegration and the biological destruction of the group. Third, Lemkin recognized grades of genocide: some groups were to be immediately and wholly annihilated (the Jews); others (especially the Poles) were to be slowly destroyed by other means to decimate their numbers and decapitate their leadership. The victims might be observed by contemporaries as destroyed in whole or in part. Members of other occupied nations would be allowed to survive as individuals but their national institutions, culture and group organization would be destroyed and they would become Germanized. Such coerced assimilation without killing or the interruption of procreation and parenting was not cited by Lemkin as genocide. The deliberate destruction of the culture of a distinct group without physical annihilation of its members is most often termed *ethnocide* now.

The United Nations committees that framed the UNGC both further specified the protected groups and delimited the connotations of genocide to 1) biological destruction and serious injury (see Art. II, a, b, and c) and 2) indirect sociobiological destruction by restricting the biological reproduction of group members and breaking the linkage between reproduction and socialization (d and e).

Article II: 'In the present Convention, genocide means any of the following acts committed with intent to destroy, in whole or in part, a national, ethnical, racial or religious group as such: (a) Killing members of the group: (b) Causing serious bodily or mental harm to members of the group; (c) Deliberately inflicting on the group conditions of life calculated to bring about its physical destruction in whole or in part; (d) Imposing measures intended to prevent births within the group; (e) Forcibly transferring children of the group to another group.'

Three problems are repeatedly noted by critics of the Convention: 1) the gaps in groups covered; 2) the ambiguity of *intent to destroy a group 'as such'* and 3) the inability of non-state parties to invoke the Convention and the failure to set up an independent enforcement body. Since the first two problems bear on the definition (an essential for research), I will concentrate on this criticism. Furthermore, I will argue that the second problem—the question of intent—can be resolved by discriminating intent from motive; intent is purpose-ful action.

The Convention has been repeatedly criticized for omission of political groups and social classes as target groups; a recent report commissioned by the UN Human Rights Commission recommended its extension to political and sexual groups (Whitaker 1985, 16–19). Drost, an early critic, made these incisive objections:

> Man lives not alone but in groups. He belongs to a group either by birth or from choice. . . . By leaving political and other groups beyond the purported protection the authors of the Convention also left a wide and dangerous loophole for any government to escape the human duties under the Convention by putting genocide into practice under the cover of executive measures against political or other groups for reasons of security, public order or any other reason of state. . . . A convention on genocide cannot effectively contribute to the protection of certain, described minorities when it is limited to particular defined groups. . . . It serves no purpose to restrict international legal protection to some groups firstly because the protected members always belong at the same time to other, unprotected groups. . . . (1951, Vol. 2, 122–123).

LeBlanc, on the other hand, believes the exclusion of political groups was wise because of the 'difficulty inherent in selecting criteria for determining what constitutes a political group,' their instability over time, the right of the state to protect itself, and the potential misuses of genocide—labelling of antagonists in war and political conflict (1988, 292–294). He refers to a proposal by Jordan Paust for a new draft convention criminalizing the 'Crime of Politicide.'

The first draft of the UNGC in the UN Ad Hoc Committee on Genocide extended protection to political groups, groups which were never considered by Lemkin as subjects of genocide. Such inclusion was opposed not only by Soviet bloc states but by other states, an often-overlooked point (LeBlanc 1988, 273–276). That draft also criminalized 'cultural genocide' (intentional acts destroying language, religion and culture)—a proviso opposed by western states—although Lemkin had never distinguished cultural genocide.

This instigated vigorous debate on the roots and rationale of genocides. Some states expressed fears that the inclusion of political groups would impede the ratification of the Convention because states might anticipate that suppression of subversive elements and disorders could instigate external intervention—states might be called to account. Finally, committee members arrived at an accommodation, deleting both cultural genocide and polit-ical groups (Kuper 1981, 24–29). The US accepted the deletion of political groups in exchange for a clause allowing the establishment of an international criminal tribunal (LeBlanc 1988, 277–278). The exclusion of political groups was one of the charges against the UNGC which critics used to prevent its ratification by the US Senate for forty years.

The unpublished work of Lemkin shows that he was fully cognizant that the nature of groups which might be targets changed as forms of social organization and historical situ-ations changed. His examples of genocide or genocidal situations include: Albigensians, American Indians, Assyrians in Iraq, Belgian Congo, Christians in Japan, French in Sicily (c. 1282), Hereros, Huguenots, Incas, Mongols, the Soviet Union/Ukraine, Tasmania. Appar-ently, Lemkin did not consider political groups as targets. In a description of an abstract for a book he intended to write, 'Introduction to the Study of Genocide,' he observed: 'The philosophy of the Genocide Convention is based on the formula of the human cosmos. This cosmos consists of four basic groups: national, racial, religious and ethnic. The groups are protected not only by reasons of human compassion but also to prevent draining the spiritual resources of mankind.'

## Some Sociological Definitions and Issues

Many social scientists have accepted the UNGC definition of genocide explicitly or implicitly (Fein 1979b, Kuper 1981, Porter 1982, 12; Harff and Gurr 1987) or a broadened version thereof, including political and social groups (Horowitz 1976, 18, 42; Chalk and Jonassohn 1990; Tal 1979). Charny proposes 'what he calls a *humanistic* definition . . .: the *wanton* murder of human beings on the basis of any identity whatsoever that they share' (1988, 4). Legters, who says he generally favors a strict construction of genocide excluding political groups, argues for the inclusion of social classes as class is the unit of social organization in socialist societies (1984, 65).

Those who accept the UNGC definition usually acknowledge that mass killings of political groups show similarities in their causes, organization and motives: some authors refer to these as 'genocidal massacres' (Kuper 1981), 'ideological massacres' (Fein 1984) or 'politicides' (Harff and Gurr 1987).

Virtually everyone acknowledges that genocide is primarily a crime of state. Chalk and Jonassohn refer to the 'state or other authority' as perpetrators, encompassing settlers acting in the name of the nation-state (1990, 23). Although there is little disagreement over this, heuristically it seems preferable to me to omit variable terms as criteria in a definition: marginal situations in which genocide or genocidal massacres not authorized by the state occur include colonization, civil wars, and the transfer of powers during decolonization. Actors who may have committed genocide without state authorization include soldiers, settlers, and missionaries.

Dadrian (1975), attempting to offer a general explanation encompassing the Armenian genocide, was the first sociologist known to propose a definition—actually an explanation sketch—of genocide. He states:

> Genocide is the successful attempt by a dominant group, vested with formal authority and with preponderant access to the overall resources of power, to reduce by coercion or lethal violence the number of a minority group whose ultimate extermination is held desirable and useful and whose respective vulnerability is a major factor contributing to the decision for genocide (1975, 123).

Here explanation has usurped definition; furthermore, it is not clear what is to be observed and classed as genocide except that the perpetrator is a representative of the dominant group and the victims are a minority group. This elementary distinction was later outmoded by the Khmer Rouge genocide in Kampuchea.

Chalk and Jonassohn, beginning to teach a course on the history and sociology of genocide in the 1980s—some may have seen earlier editions of their (1990) book—advanced a singular and straight-forward definition which is essentially similar to one they have employed since 1984:

> *Genocide* is a form of one-sided mass killing in which a state or other authority intends to destroy a group, as that group and membership in it are defined by the perpetrators (1990, 23).

There are several problems with this definition:

1) The limitation of the perpetrator to 'a state or other authority.' Chalk argues that if settler murders go unpunished, it is because states do not try to stop them or prosecute them; hence the state is responsible for condoning them (1988, 7). It seems to me this confuses the question of who is the perpetrator (in definition) with who—what organization or persons—is responsible for prevention and prosecution.
2) The specification of 'one-sided mass killing' implies a numeric threshold or ratio of victims which may obscure recognition of the earlier stages of genocide. Their emphasis on mass killing also omits other forms of intentional biological destruction

(see earlier discussion of Lemkin). 'One-sided' killing is also problematic; it is unclear whether or when this includes mass killings of groups which may have an armed party or sub-group either defending themselves or attacking a party or elite of the dominant group.

3) The definition of the group is open-ended, implying that an endless number of groups can be constructed, including groups constructed from the paranoid imagination of despots—'wreckers' in Stalin's time. This is in accord with the assumptions of labelling theory (although the authors do not explicitly draw on this) which posits that the construction (and destruction) of enemies depends on their labeling by the powerful. Chalk and Jonassohn explain that their definition follows 'W. I. Thomas' famous dictum that if people define a situation as real it is real in its consequences' (1990, 25). But, like all dicta, this has to be examined to determine how, when, and why it applies.

The definition of Chalk and Jonassohn has served their goal of casting a wide net, exploring a range of situations in which people are victimized by definition or at random—'witches' (the witch-hunt is considered a precursor of genocide), the Knights Templar, the victims of Shaka's and Stalin's terror. It points the way toward an emerging theory of terror—murder, torture and intimidation—and genocide. But to get there, we need to distinguish both processes. Indeed, Chalk and Jonassohn reflected in an earlier paper on the different functions served by torture and genocide: torture is a means to control people whom state agents expect to remain as members of the state; genocide is a means to eliminate a group or people from the state (1983, 13–14). The study of terror should include the explanation of victims created by definition—conspiracies of witches and wreckers. When and why do states manufacture victims by labeling them with fictive identities and accusing them of nonexistent crimes? The labelling perspective is most suggestive for studies of manufactured deviance for social control.

However, the victims of genocide are generally members of real groups, whether conceived of as collectivities, races or classes, who acknowledge their existence, although there may be administrative designation of their membership as German authorities designated Jews for 'the Final Solution,' including some people of Jewish lineage who no longer considered themselves Jews (and did not register voluntarily with the Jewish community) or were members of other religious communities (converts and their children). Had there not been an actual Jewish community with its own institutions, German authorities could not have defined and enumerated Jews, for there was no objective indicator of their alleged criteria of Jewishness—race—which divided 'Jews' and 'Aryans' categorically.

Harff and Gurr (1987) distinguish genocides (using an abbreviated version of the UNGC) from 'politicides'—massacres of political groups in opposition, including groups in rebellion. Thus, Harff and Gurr's universe of politicide includes many cases Chalk and Jonassohn label as genocide; however, other cases included in the Harff and Gurr universe of politicides are excluded from Chalk and Jonassohn's universe of genocide because they include bilateral killing.

## Intent and Extent—Recalling Some Frontiers

A major issue in the study of genocide is that of *intent*. This is most often problematic when killings occur during war and colonization.

At times, the charge of genocide has been raised by scholars studying the decimation of indigenous populations whose numbers have gravely declined during colonial occupations through direct and indirect causes related to the occupier's political economy: disease, usurpation of land rights and destruction of the indigenes' economy, starvation, warfare, massacre, and malign neglect. Nietschmann (1987), studying contemporary cases, asserts the prevalence of genocide in contemporary wars and occupations by which the 'Third World' states subjugate the unrepresented 'Fourth World' nations. Barta (1987, 239–240) argues that genocide was a systemic function of the settlement of Australia (and by implication of other white settler-societies). Chalk and Jonassohn observe that ethnocide, the failure to protect indigenous peoples in the Americas from famine, and genocide were usually not unforeseeable or unintended (1990, 195–203).

Wallimann and Dobkowski challenge the adequacy of restricting the concept of genocide to intentional or planned mass destruction, given the pervasiveness of structural violence and the bureaucratization and anonymity of modern political and economic organization (1987, xvi–xviii). Yet they do not propose an alternate definition or propose to exonerate individual perpetrators, indicating some ambivalence about the implications of their position.

To avoid the whole question of inference of intent, both Barta (1987), Huttenbach (1988) and Thompson and Quets (1987, 1990) propose that we simply eliminate intent as a criterion. Churchill proposes a new legal definition of genocide, similar to that of homicide, discriminating grades of intent: genocide in the first degree, second degree (intent unclear), third degree ('intent is probably lacking'), fourth degree (corresponding to manslaughter) (1986, 416–417). Since this is avowedly a legal resolution—and one not likely to be taken up although it is a creative one—I will focus on the social-scientific definitions that purport to have more general uses.

Huttenbach proposes the criteria be whether the action threatens the continued existence of the group but does not distinguish between premeditated and accidental deaths (e.g. Bhopal 1984, Chernobyl 1986) or deaths resulting from poor industrial or national planning. Thus, genocide becomes a rubric for all bad things that can endanger peoples, a concept lacking all but rhetorical use for scholars or social activists: it does not indicate either common causes or similar solutions.

Barta argues for 'a conception of genocide which embraces *relations* of destruction and removes from the word the emphasis on policy and intention which brought it into being' (1987, 238) but seems to overlook the authorization and effects of the most rationalized genocide of the century, disagreeing with Irving Louis Horowitz who,

> misleadingly in my view calls Germany 'a genocidal society' because during one terrible period of *political* aberration the 'state bureaucratic apparatus' was used for 'a structural and systematic destruction of innocent people.' My conception of a genocidal *society*—as distinct from a genocidal state—is one in which the whole bureaucratic apparatus might officially be directed to protect innocent people but in which a whole race is nevertheless subject to remorseless pressures of destruction (239–240).

This opposition and segregation of state from society appears very arbitrary in the 20th century and excludes, rather than uncovers, clues to their relationship. Substantively, Barta does not clarify the process of destruction of indigenous peoples and ignores major genocides. As Chalk puts it,

> In Barta's configuration, Australian society is genocidal for taking the lives of over 20,000 aborigines, but German society, whose victims number in the millions, is not. Barta makes no attempt to explain the significance for his analysis of Germany's devastation of the Herero people of South West Africa in the years from 1904 to 1907 (1988, 11).

Thompson and Quets suggest eliminating the question of intent and the objectives of the perpetrators, proposing

> A sociological definition of genocide as a continuous multidimensional variable. . . . Genocide is the extent of destruction of a social collectivity by purposive action, and has a theoretical range

*from none to total. . . . Genocide is the extent of destruction of a social collectivity by whatever agents, with whatever intentions, by purposive actions which fall outside the recognized conventions of legitimate warfare* (1987, 1, 11).

This definition is severely flawed by 1) the omission (in the first) of a perpetrator and 2) the lack of boundaries due to their omission of intent, allowing the inclusion of accidents, ecological and environmental damage; it is unclear why Thompson and Quets exempt war and war crimes given the boundlessness of their definition. Further, they confuse the definition of genocide and the scale of measurement; whether genocide has occurred is a different question from its effects—e.g. the percentage of the targetted population killed. Moreover, they extend the connotations of genocide to cover all kinds of acts undermining collectivities as a result of social policy—'sociocide,' 'linguicide,' 'cultural genocide'—so that genocide becomes not only unbounded but banal, an everyday occurrence. If both the US and France (states which do uniformally promote or tolerate bilingual education) are in the same class (of perpetrators) as Nazi Germany and the USSR, we have a construct good for nothing.

In practice, Thompson and Quets have conceptually aggregated cases of genocide and collective violence—pogroms, lynchings, certain kinds of race riots—collective terrorism and homicides which are intended to destroy members of 'a national, ethnical, racial or religious group as such.' Certainly collective violence could be defined and measured on a continuum of state authorization and continuity as I suggested (Fein 1977, 186)—see Figure 1.[1]

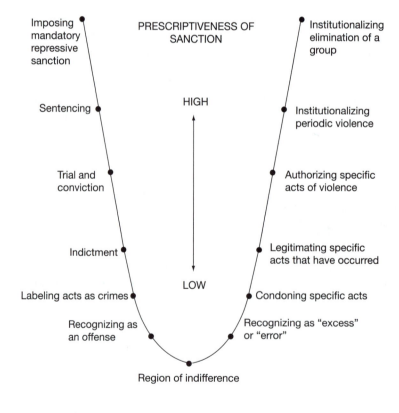

*Figure 1* Stages in the sanctioning of collective violence

Source: Fein (1977: 186)

Modern collective terrorism, organized acts in which the victims are picked by their membership in a collectivity in conflict with that of the victimizer—perpetrated recently in the Punjab, Sri Lanka, Turkey, Northern Ireland—could fit under the definition of genocide of the UNGC: '. . . acts [killing members of the group] committed with intent to destroy, in whole or in part, a national, ethnical, racial or religious group as such.' The definition does not prescribe a minimal threshold. Some may assume that terrorists who strike group members episodically aim not to kill them but kill for an instrumental political purpose. But, in most cases, the acts speak for themselves: the victims are picked because of who they are— Hindu and Buddhist bus riders, Jews praying in an Istanbul synagogue, Irish Protestants and Catholics drinking in a pub or shopping. The perpetrators do not ask anything of the victims or the bystanders as the price to spare them; the victims are seldom used as hostages for bargaining.

We are not inhibited from labeling such acts as genocide by the definition of genocide but by an unexplicated assumption of scale and continuous action: we assume that the victimizers do not have the capacity to kill a significant part of the group and that such acts are likely to be episodic rather than continuous.

One solution to this problem of scale is to label such events as *genocidal massacres*, giving recognition to the intent inherent in the selection of victims, as many have labeled large-scale and semi-organized communal massacres (e.g. India before and during partition) as genocidal massacres. Genocidal massacres—pogroms, collective terrorism, some race riots—may be clues or predecessors of future genocide. But the universe of genocidal massacres is much wider than that of genocides, indicating the operation of control and authorization by the state and other authorities.

## Intent Re-examined

One contribution of Thompson and Quets has been to substitute purposive action for intent in definition, a term many of us confuse but is clear in law. As sociologists, immersed in the distinctions between 'manifest' and 'latent' function as a paradigm of intended and unintended action (Merton 1957, 31), we have needlessly confused the meaning of intent. Intent or purposeful action—or inaction—is not the same in law or every-day language as either motive or function. An actor performs an act, we say, with intent if there are foreseeable ends or consequences: for what purpose is different from why or for what motive is the act designed.

Two teams of scholars/lawyers/activists discuss this issue in arguing for the finding of genocide in Cambodia and Afghanistan. The key concept of Art. 2 of the UNGC—'[specified] acts committed with intent to destroy, in whole or in part, a national, ethnical, racial, or religious *group as such* [my italics]' is illuminated by referring back to the UN debate.

> a Venezuelan amendment eventually adopted substituted the phrase 'as such' for this specific listing of motives. . . . Mr Perez Perozo (Venezuela) recalled that he had already stated . . . that *an enumeration of motives* was useless and even dangerous, as such a restrictive enumeration *would be a powerful weapon in the hands of the guilty parties and would help them to avoid being charged with genocide.* . . . *The aim of the amendment was to give wider powers of discretion to the judges who would be called upon to deal with cases of genocide.* . . .

As some attempt to make a case under the Convention (not, so far, instigating the UN to act) we can see that the Convention has greater flexibility than understood by some.

> The 'intent' required by the Convention as a necessary constituent element of the crime of genocide cannot be confused with, or interpreted to mean, 'motive.' . . . The 'intent' clause of

article II of the Genocide Convention requires only that the various destructive acts—killings, causing mental and physical harm, deliberately inflicted conditions of life, etc.—have a purposeful or deliberate character as opposed to an accidental or unintentional character (Hannum and Hawk 1986, 140–146).

Hannum and Hawk documented mass killings in Kampuchea—as well as the deliberate targetting of minority ethnic groups and Buddhist priests—authorized by the Khmer Rouge, arguing that such mass killing—often called 'autogenocide'—is proscribed under the Convention because the Khmer Rouge aimed to destroy a significant part of the majority Khmer people (Hannum and Hawk, 1986). This was (despite the fact that their brief had no legal effect) a remarkable innovation because it made the case that genocide could be committed by perpetrators of the same ethnicity who justified their murders by an ideology which reclassified and labelled the victims, discriminating their collaborators and those to be saved as a new kind of people.

Reisman and Norchi (1988) argued that the Soviet destruction of the Afghan people through depopulation, massacre, mass bombardment and bombing of refugees (which led to the killing of about 10 percent of them in eight years) and the forced removal of children demonstrated Soviet and Afghan government intent to destroy the Afghan people as a people—an intent which could be masked or explained by political and social motives. However, intent, they argue, should be simply construed as deliberate or repeated acts with foreseeable results rather than motive. Thus, the sociological concept of purposeful action is the bridge paralleling the legal concept of intent in the Genocide Convention; this lies between legal guilt (an external judgment) and the perpetrator's construction of an account or motive (a psychological variable).

## War and Genocide

Since much killing of unarmed civilians is a foreseeable consequence of war—conventional or nuclear—and several cases have been presented of genocides during wars, one may ask whether wars—or certain wars—are inherently genocidal. Should nuclear or massive aerial bombardment of civilians in war be construed as intrinsically genocidal? Both Chalk and Jonassohn (1990) and Thompson and Quets (1987) exclude such killings. Kuper, in contrast, repeatedly refers to nuclear and conventional bombings of Hiroshima and Nagasaki, Dresden, and Vietnam as genocidal massacres (1981: 14, 17, 34–5, 45–6, 50, 55, 91–2, 102, 139, 174). Dadrian (1975) labeled deaths from such causes as 'latent genocide.'

Markusen (1987), surveying the definitions and attributes of 'total war' and of genocide, concludes that these state-sanctioned mass killings have several significant similarities: dehumanization of the enemy, mass killing of civilians, bureaucratic organization and the use of technology distancing the perpetrators from the victims. But Markusen fails to note that both distancing and bureaucracy are very variable attributes of modern genocide. Nor does Markusen note the dissimilarities: the selection of victims for genocide is not based on where they are but who they are; were the victims during war to surrender, their killing should cease (assuming adherence to the war convention) but the surrender of victims in genocidal situations does not avoid their mass murder but expedites it.

Changes in the norms and technology of war are evident over time but they are contradictory; some expanded and others diminished the scope of killing of innocent civilians. Chalk and Jonassohn concluded that the first genocides in history arose from attempts in antiquity of imperial powers to destroy their recurrent enemies; best known of these is the destruction of Carthage (1990, 32–35).

Surveying such wars in antiquity, Lerner infers slavery arose from the successful separation of conquered peoples, slaughtering the males and incorporating the females into the nation of the conqueror (1986, 9, 78–81). Changes in sex roles and the patriarchal organization of society now make women more vulnerable to genocide than ever before, Smith observes (1989b). In premodern times, women belonging to enemies defeated in war were enslaved and raped as they were valued for their reproductive power and could be incorporated in a new society, isolated from social participation and power. But women in the twentieth century have been both perpetrators and victims of genocide.

The social relationships between antagonists and types of war also seem to condition the likelihood of observing the war convention. Wright has recorded the rise of conventions of war in many different civilizations and also observed how states are much less likely to adhere to these in civil wars and in colonial wars involving antagonists of different races and civilizations (1942, 2: 810–812). Walzer, considering how the war convention—based on the premise that fighters must respect the immunity of civilians—has evolved, observes how war crimes and the use of terror emerge in different situations—anti-guerrilla warfare, total war—and the moral questions posed by the escalating technology of warfare (1977).

We can not yet conclude there is any simple or linear relation between genocide and historical trends in destructiveness in the conduct of wars; both may be curvilinear, diminishing as European states regulated warfare, confining fighting to a specialized force, and enlarging as modern war becomes more total, involving mobilization of whole populations.

Taylor observes that a

> very basic characteristic of the laws of war and war crimes is that, as these names indicate, they concern only conduct which is directly related to *war*—to hostilities in progress between organized belligerent forces. When the Nazis killed or assaulted German Jews in Germany, that may have been a crime, but it was not a war crime. . . . today [such atrocities] would no doubt be covered by the international treaty defining and condemning genocide . . . (1971, 30–31).

The question of whether killings of civilians in war are war crimes, consequences of acts of war admissable under the war convention, or instances of genocide has been clouded by the fact that genocide-labeling of wars today is often a rhetorical strategem for political delegitimation of specific wars which the labeler opposes.

Genocide was charged by several influential critics of the U.S. war in Vietnam, principally Sartre (1968) and Falk: but Daniel Ellsberg dissented from this, saying: 'I have misgivings about the use of the word "genocide" in the context of the Vietnam war . . . An escalation of rhetoric can blind us to the fact that Vietnam is . . . no more brutal than other wars in the past' (in Knoll and McFadden 1970, 81–82). Bedau concluded, after careful conceptual and legal analysis, that the charge was 'Not proven, not quite' (Bedau 1974, 46). Similarly, Bassiouni concluded the three essential elements of genocide were absent: 1) the opposing parties were not separate national or ethnic groups; 2) US actions 'could [not] be classified as part of a coordinated plan to destroy in whole or in part any particular national, ethnical, racial or religious group' and 3) 'American activities in Vietnam were not conducted with sufficient intent to support a charge of "genocide" (1979, 174–176). But Hannum and Hawk's brief on the Khmer Rouge genocide (1986) implicitly rejects Bassiouni's first criteria.

Both Reisman and Norchi (1988), in their (previously discussed) analysis of Soviet (and Afghan) government actions in Afghanistan and Goodwin (1988) assert there has been genocide in Afghanistan. Yet there has been almost no serious discussion of their charges. No antiwar movement developed in the Soviet Union or in the west on the scale of the anti-Vietnam War movement. Even the opponents of the Soviet Union's intervention have often overlooked the character of the war. This again illustrates the highly variable concern with genocide: the likelihood a case will be recognized and labelled as genocide arises both from the biases and organization of protesters.

Journalists and scholars examining how little response there was to the initial news of the

Khmer Rouge genocide have made the same point; it was generally not recognized by the media or opinion-leaders because it challenged our biases, confirming the communist blood-bath theory (Shawcross 1984; DeMarco 1988; Adams and Joblove 1980). Similarly, Mace has shown how prominent western journalists denied the existence of the famine that Stalin created in the Ukraine in 1932–1933—a famine estimated to have killed five to seven million Ukrainians—from ideological and opportunistic motives (1988).

## A Sociological Definition Proposed

I believe that the UNGC definition of genocide can be reconciled with an expanded—but bounded—sociological definition if we focus on how the core concepts are related. From the root of *genus* we may infer that the protected groups were conceived (by Lemkin and the UN framers) as basic kinds, classes, or subfamilies of humanity, persisting units of society. What is distinctive sociologically is that such groups are usually ascriptive—based on birth rather than by choice—and often inspire enduring particularistic loyalties. They are sources of identity and value; they are the seed-bed of social movements, voluntary associations, congregations and families; in brief, they are *collectivities*.

Further, these collectivities endure as their members tend to reproduce their own kind (to the extent in-group marriage is the norm). But collectivities need not be self-reproducing to be cohesive over a given span in time.

The UNGC implies a universalistic norm: each group has a right to exist and develop its own culture, assuming neither their aim or methods are criminal; all collectivities should be protected from such crimes against humanity. One can also argue that political, sexual, and class-denominated status groups or collectivities, just like ethnic and religious collectivities, are basic continuing elements of the community. (Whitaker (1985) made a similar argument for extension of the UNGC.)

There is no categorical line, in fact, between the enduring character of ascribed (heritable) identities and elected or achieved identities: both may be constructed or passed on genera-tionally. Being an Italian working-class Communist Party member may be just as heritable a characteristic as being an Italian church-going Roman Catholic. Indeed, church and party could be regarded as counter-congregations or counter-cultures. Both affiliations may be outcomes of election or ascription, conscience or inheritance.

A new sociological definition should include the following elements: a) it should clearly denote the object and processes under study and discriminate the latter from related pro-cesses; b) it should stipulate constructs which can be transformed operationally to indicate real-world observable events; and c) the specification of groups covered should be consistent with our sociological knowledge of both the persistence and construction of group identities in society, the variations in class, ethnic/racial, gender, class/political consciousness and the multiplicity and interaction of peoples' identities and statuses in daily life. Further, d) it should conform to the implicit universalistic norm and a sense of justice, embracing the right of all non-violent groups to co-exist.

Briefly put,

**Genocide is sustained purposeful action by a perpetrator to physically destroy a collectivity directly or indirectly, through interdiction of the biological and social repro-duction of group members, sustained regardless of the surrender or lack of threat offered by the victim.**

To expand on this sociological definition, one can also show how it encompasses the legal definition [terms of the UNGC are noted in these brackets]:

**Genocide is sustained purposeful action** [thus excluding single massacres, pogroms, accidental deaths] **by a perpetrator** (assuming an actor organized over a period) **to physically destroy a collectivity** ['acts committed with intent to destroy, in whole or in part a national/ethnical/racial or religious group:' Art. 2]] **directly** (through mass or selective murders and calculable physical destruction—e.g. imposed starvation and poisoning of food, water, and air—[see Art. 2, a–c]) **or through interdiction of the biological and social reproduction of group members** (preventing births [Art. 2, d] and ['forcibly transferring children of the group to another group' Art. 2, e], systematically breaking the linkage between reproduction and socialization of children in the family or group of origin.

This definition would cover the sustained destruction of nonviolent political groups and social classes as parts of a national (or ethnic/religious/racial) group but does not cover the killing of members of military and paramilitary organizations—the SA, the Aryan Nations, and armed guerrillas.

Documenting *genocide* or **genocide** demands (at the very least) identifying a perpetrator(s), the target group attacked as a collectivity, assessing its numbers and victims, and recognizing a pattern of repeated actions from which we infer the intent of purposeful action to eliminate them. Such inference is easiest to draw when we can cite both pre-existent plans or statements of intent and the military or bureaucratic organization of a death machine; seldom do we have both kinds of evidence.

## Note

1. By collective violence, I refer to all violation of victims chosen by one collectivity because of membership in another racial, religious, tribal, or ethnic collectivity; this includes group punishment, random punishment and exemplary punishments. It is similar to Janowitz's use (1969) of communal violence and to Tilly's early use of primitive violence (1969) but both Janowitz and Tilly use collective violence to refer to what others call mass or political violence.

## References

Adams, William, and Joblove, Michael (1980). "The Unnewsworthy Holocaust." *Policy Review*, 11:59–67.

Barta, Tony (1987). "Relations of Genocide: Land and Lives in the Colonization of Australia," pp. 237–252. In I. Wallimann and M. Dobkowski (Eds.) *Genocide and the Modern Age: Etiology and Case Studies of Mass Death*. Westport, CT: Greenwood Publishers.

Bassiouni, M. Cherif (1979). "International Law and the Holocaust," pp. 146–181. In B. L. Sherwin and S. Ament's *Encountering the Holocaust: An Interdisciplinary Survey*. Chicago, IL; Impact Press.

Bedau, Hugo A. (1974). "Genocide in Vietnam?" pp. 5–46. In V. Held, S. Morgenbesser and E. Nagel's *Philosophy, Morality and International Affairs*. New York: Oxford University Press.

Chalk, Frank, and Jonassohn, Kurt (1990). *The History and Sociology of Genocide: Analyses and Case Studies*. New Haven, CT: Yale University Press.

Charny Israel W. (1982) *How Can We Commit the Unthinkable?: Genocide, The Human Cancer*. In collaboration with Chanan Rapaport. Boulder, CO: Westview Press.

Charny Israel, W. (1988). *Genocide: A Critical Bibliographic Review*. New York: Facts on File.

Churchill, Ward (1986) "Genocide: Toward a Functional Definition." *Alternatives* 11: 403–430.

Dadrian, Vahakn (1975). "A Typology of Genocide." *International Review of Modern Sociology*, 5:201–212.

DeMarco, Edward A. Jr. (1988). "Asian Holocaust: Coverage of the Khmer Rouge by Three US News Organizations [MA Thesis]" in *Masters Abstracts*, 27(01).

Drost, Pieter N. (1959). The Crimes of the State. Leyden: A. W. Sythoff.

Fein, Helen (1977). *Imperial Crime and Punishment: The Massacre at Jallianwalla Bagh and British Judgment, 1919–1920*. Honolulu: University Press of Hawaii.

Fein, Helen. *Accounting for Genocide: National Responses and Jewish Victimization During the Holocaust*. New York, Free Press, 1979. Comparative study which primarily asks what explains the relative success of the Holocaust in different states (the per cent of Jews seized), using historical, quantitative and qualitative methods to probe explanations.

Fein, Helen (1984). "Scenarios of Genocide: Models of Genocide and Critical Responses," pp. 3–31. In

Israel Charny (Ed.) *Toward the Understanding and Prevention of Genocide: Proceedings of the International Conference on the Holocaust and Genocide*. Boulder, CO: Westview Press.

Goodwin, Jan (1988). "The Media Ignore Genocide in Afghanistan." *ISG Newsletter*, 1(1):2.

Hannum, Hurst, and Hawk, David (1986). *The Case Against the Standing Committee of the Communist Party of Kampuchea*. New York: Cambodia Documentation Commission.

Harff, Barbara, and Gurr, Ted R. (1987). "Genocides and Politicides Since 1945: Evidence and Anticipation." *Internet on the Holocaust and Genocide*, 13:1–7.

Hawk, David (1984). "Pol Pot's Cambodia: Was it Genocide?" pp. 51–59. In Israel Charny (Ed.) *Toward the Understanding and Prevention of Genocide: Proceedings of the International Conference on the Holocaust and Genocide*. Boulder, CO: Westview Press.

Horowitz, Irving Louis (1976). *Genocide: State Power and Mass Murder*. New Brunswick, NJ: Transaction.

Huttenbach, Henry (1988). "Locating the Holocaust on the Genocide Spectrum." *Holocaust and Genocide Studies*, 3(3):289–304.

Knoll, Erwin, and McFadden, Judith N. (Eds.) (1970). *War Crimes and the American Conscience*. New York: Holt, Rinehart and Winston.

Kuper, Leo (1981). *Genocide: Its Political Use in the Twentieth Century*. London: Penguin Books; New Haven, CT: Yale University Press.

LeBlanc, Lawrence J. (1988). "The United Nations Genocide Convention and Political Groups: Should the United States Propose an Amendment?" *Yale Journal of International Law*, 13(2): 268–294.

Legters, Lyman H. (1984). "The Soviet Gulag: Is It Genocide?" pp. 60–66. In Israel Charny (Ed.) *Toward the Understanding and Prevention of Genocide: Proceedings of the International Conference on the Holocaust and Genocide*. Boulder, CO: Westview Press.

Lemkin, Raphael (1944). *Axis Rule in Occupied Europe*. Washington, D.C.: Carnegie Endowment for World Peace.

Lerner, Gerda (1986). *The Creation of Patriarchy*. New York: Oxford University Press.

Mace, James (1988). "Genocide in the USSR," pp. 116–136. In I. W. Charny (Ed.) *Genocide: A Critical Bibliographic Review*. New York: Facts on File.

Markusen, Eric (1987). "Genocide and Total War: A Preliminary Comparison," pp. 97–125. In I. Wallimann and M. Dobkowski (Eds.) *Genocide and the Modern Age: Etiology and Case Studies of Mass Death*. Westport, CT: Greenwood Publishers.

Merton, Robert K. (1957). *Social Theory and Social Structure*. New York: Free Press.

Porter, Jack N. (1982). "What Is Genocide? Notes Toward a Definition," pp. 2–33. In Jack N. Porter (Ed.) *Genocide and Human Rights: A Global Anthology*. Washington, D.C.: University Press of America.

Reisman, W. Michael, and Norchi, Charles H. (1988). "Genocide and the Soviet Occupation of Afghanistan." *ISG Newsletter*, 1(1):4–6.

Sartre, Jean-Paul (1968). *On Genocide*. Boston, MA: Beacon Press.

Shawcross, William (1984). *The Quality of Mercy: Cambodia, Holocaust and Modern Conscience*. New York: Simon and Schuster.

Smith, Roger (1989). "Fantasy, Purity, Destruction: Norman Cohn's Complex Witness to the Holocaust." A paper prepared for presentation at the 19th Annual Scholars Conference on the Holocaust, Philadelphia, 5–7 March 1989.

Tal, Uriel (1979). "On the Study of the Holocaust and Genocide." *Yad Vashem Studies*, 13:7–52.

Taylor, Telford (1971). *Nuremberg and Vietnam*. New York: New York Times Book.

Thompson, John L., and Quets, Gail A. (1987). "Redefining the Moral Order: Towards a Normative Theory of Genocide." New York: Columbia University (mimeograph).

Thompson, John and Quets, Gail A. (1990) "Genocide and Social Conflict: A Partial Theory and Comparison." In Louis Kriesberg (ed.), *Research in Social Movements, Conflicts and Change*. Vol. 12. Greenwood, CN: JAI Press.

Wallimann, I, and Dobkowski, M. N. (Eds.) (1987) *Genocide and the Modern Age: Etiology and Case Studies of Mass Death*. Westport, CT: Greenwood Publishers.

Walzer, Michael (1977). *Just and Unjust Wars: A Moral Argument with Historical Illustrations*. New York: Basic Books.

Whitaker, Ben (1985). *Revised and Updated Report on the Question of the Prevention and Punishment of Genocide*. 62 pp. (E/CN.4/Sub.2/1985/6, 2 July 1985).

Wright, Quincy (1942). *A Study of War*. 2 Volumes. Chicago, IL: University of Chicago Press.

# 3

# Related Terms

In addition to the word "genocide," numerous other terms and concepts have been developed to describe what was once referred to as "man's inhumanity to man." Recently, one of these, "ethnic cleansing," has even become synonymous with genocide within the popular consciousness. Many incorrectly assume that the term is of recent vintage, but in fact it reaches back at least to World War II. During the latter period of that conflict, the Nazi-backed Croats used "ethnic cleansing" to refer to their brutal actions against the Serbs. The Nazis also used the term "*Säuberung*" to denote the "cleansing" of Jews from occupied countries, towns, and territories. That said, "ethnic cleansing" gained wide currency during the 1990s to explain actions carried out in the former Yugoslavia, during which various sides in the four wars (Slovenia, 1991; Croatia, 1991; Bosnia-Herzegovina, 1992–1995; Kosovo, 1998–1999) purposely and systematically forced entire groups of people from villages and towns in an effort to "cleanse" the areas they coveted of rival ethnic and/or religious groups. Ethnic cleansing in the former Yugoslavia was undertaken *via* various means, including, though not limited to: arbitrary arrest and detention; vile mistreatment of both civilian prisoners and prisoners of war; attacks on hospitals; extrajudicial executions; military attacks or threats of attacks against civilians and civilian centers; murder; mass murder; rape and others types of sexual assault; torture; the ransacking of homes; and the utter destruction of property, including religious and cultural edifices such as mosques, libraries, and monuments. In its essence, ethnic cleansing came to mean the forced removal of one group of people, by another, from a region or territory and the subsequent occupation of that region or territory by members of the perpetrator group as though the target group had never existed there.

It is this that causes the greatest degree of confusion for observers of the phenomenon of ethnic cleansing in the modern world. In the eyes of many, genocide and ethnic cleansing equate directly with each other, but a closer look at the two terms reveals that such is not the case. Genocide, a crime in international law defined by United Nations statute and incorporated precisely into the legal codes of a majority of the world's nation states, is a very precise category of crime. Ethnic cleansing, on the other hand, is the name given to a form of behavior embracing a number of crimes that fall within other groupings: war crimes, crimes against humanity (both of which, it should be emphasized, are *categories* of crimes, rather than crimes *per se*), and, on occasion, the crime of genocide itself.

Consequently, there is no universally recognized definition of ethnic cleansing, nor is there a specific crime in international law that outlaws it—even though elements of the practice are banned under other legislation (for example, murder, deportation, torture, rape, persecution on political, racial, and religious grounds, and genocide). Andrew

Bell-Fialkoff, conscious of this shortcoming in international legislation, has, in his essay "A Typology of Cleansing," attempted to create both an appropriate taxonomy for recognizing ethnic cleansing where it takes place, and a set of historical precedents that can help to illustrate it. He shows, further, that ethnic cleansing need not be a permanent act; it can also, he points out, be a temporary measure designed to achieve limited aims within a particular time-frame.

On the other hand, as Michael Mann shows in "Explaining Ethnic Cleansing"—an argument that is at once controversial and original—ethnic cleansing is a complicated affair that, although an old practice, is nonetheless very much grounded within the modern dynamics of nation, state, ethnicity, and democracy. For Mann, ethnic cleansing and genocide are thus very closely related; indeed, it might well be argued in support of Mann that there are times when they are indistinguishable, at least with regard to the same techniques (if not motivations).

When Raphael Lemkin introduced the term genocide in 1944, he wrote about the destruction of a nation or ethnic group. The means to achieve such destruction, as he saw it, did not include deportation or forced removal of populations from a territory; these acts are not necessarily aimed at destroying the group, just at moving it away from a designated piece of land. Then, when the United Nations enacted the Convention on the Prevention and Punishment of the Crime of Genocide (UNCG), on December 9, 1948, its key definitional term was "intent to destroy"—not "intent to remove." All of the ways in which this could be achieved, as outlined in Article 2 of the Convention, are the means by which the United Nations considers that group destruction can take place. Removal of a group in order to obtain coveted land, according to which the group may retain its existence in another place—that is, ethnic cleansing—is not of itself group destruction occasioning genocide.

That having been said, genocide *can* be employed, of course, to clear territory of an unwanted population, but when this happens we find that we have to interrogate the perpetrators as to their primary goal: acquisition of "cleansed" territory, or destruction of a targeted group? Which is the priority? Is one simply a means to an end? And, ultimately, why should the distinction matter?

Looking at the issue of other terms related to genocide, we must also bear in mind that the UNCG deliberately omitted certain groups from within its definition. The most striking, in this regard, are political groups, social groups, cultural groups, and groups identified according to sexual or sexual-preference criteria. In part due to the fact that political groups are not specifically protected under the UNCG, U.S. political scientist Barbara Harff coined and developed the term "politicide" in order to refer to those groups victimized primarily because of their political opposition to a particular regime. In her essay "Recognizing Genocides and Politicides," Harff shows that politicide, like ethnic cleansing, does not have legal credibility within international statutes. She argues, further, that a case could be put that such a covenant or agreement is needed in the modern world—the more so as political affiliation, throughout the past century, has increasingly been a standard by which a person's "guilt" or "innocence," in the eyes of genocidal regimes, has been measured. The same is most definitely true where a person's social status and cultural background are concerned.

The term "crimes against humanity" is another kindred concept to genocide that seems not to be clearly understood where gross human rights violations are involved. As William Schabas delineates and discusses in his article, "Crimes Against Humanity," the notion of crimes against humanity is an omnibus legal category within international law that identifies punishable offenses for substantial violations of human rights, atrocities, and mass murder of non-combatant civilians. Such offenses are a relatively new category, largely the product of international human rights legislation enacted during the twentieth century. Often, crimes against humanity are bracketed alongside of war crimes, though they differ from the latter in that they are not, for the most part, violations of the laws and practices of war; indeed, crimes against humanity need not occur in wartime at all. A lengthy list of acts that can be considered as crimes against humanity include, but are not confined to, the following: murder, extermination, enslavement, deportation, imprisonment, torture, rape, and persecutions on political, racial, and religious grounds. Other unspecified inhumane acts can also be included, rendering crimes against humanity as an evolutionary category over which international (or, less likely, national) courts have some degree of discretion. There is no generally accepted definition of crimes against humanity, and, to date, no universal international legislation covering such crimes exists. Several groundbreaking initiatives have, however, placed the category of crimes against humanity in the forefront of major international humanitarian issues requiring attention. Important case-law precedents were created through the International Military Tribunal at Nuremberg in 1946, when the category of crimes against humanity was actually listed as one of the four counts facing the accused Nazi leaders. Since then, the category has been included in the Articles establishing the International Criminal Tribunals for the Former Yugoslavia and Rwanda (ICTY and ICTR, respectively). On July 1, 2002, the International Criminal Court (ICC) was established at The Hague, and it incorporated a lengthy list of acts that constitute crimes against humanity. The category is, generally speaking, a useful one for covering acts which are not considered "genocide" according to the UNCG. Such crimes do not have to include proof of intent to destroy a group, as with genocide, nor does the category of crimes against humanity even specify which groups can and cannot be included as target victims—which, of course, the UNCG does. Given that there is no universally recognized or binding definition of crimes against humanity, and that the term is therefore legally imprecise, heinous acts that cannot be prosecuted as genocide can be prosecuted as crimes against humanity. But the two categories are not interchangeable, and genocide is now usually considered to be a crime of greater magnitude. While genocide is a single crime, crimes against humanity is a category embracing a number of crimes.

Where the annihilation of a section of a group in a localized context—for example, in the wiping out of a whole village of men, women, and children—contains some of the elements of a genocide, the notion of genocidal massacre is particularly helpful as a way to describe the events without devaluing them. In "Massacres," French scholar Jacques Semelin describes the general concept of massacre within the context of genocide and crimes against humanity. As he shows, the notion is disputed in some quarters, primarily as it has undergone changes in application over the centuries. It is, however, generally held that massacre is a means to "remove" an unwanted population, whether this is as part of a genocidal campaign or something more local. The concept is especially useful in describing colonial situations, as the large number of massacres accompanying colonial acquisition can often point clearly to an affinity between colonialism and genocide. Moreover, while even an aggregation of massacres need not necessarily connote a policy of genocide, the motives which underlay such massacres can, in their time-and-place circumstances, be motivated by a genocidal intent. The notion of massacre, therefore, while not equating with genocide, can be employed for explaining the many examples of destruction that take place during territorial acquisition, maintenance, and decolonization.

# 3.1   Andrew Bell-Fialkoff, "A Typology of Cleansing"

It will be useful to set forth a short typology of cleansing. First, to classify is to understand. By listing major kinds of cleansing we will be able to understand the phenomenon better. Second, classification will enable us to explore the complex interrelationships between various types of cleansing. It will help us to trace its evolution. Ultimately, a typology may clarify trends in cleansing, for classification often has a predictive value. And prediction takes us halfway to prevention.

Building a typology of cleansing is complicated by the fact that the group's view of itself may differ from the way others view it. It is the difference between ascription and self-ascription, and the two do not always match. For example, there were hundreds of thousands of Jewish converts to Christianity all over Europe in the 1930s. In Hungary alone their number reached about 100,000. They regarded themselves as Christians, but when the Germans occupied Hungary the converts were reclassified as racially Jewish, and many of them perished along with other Jews.

Even where the difference in ascription and self-ascription is absent the motivation of the cleanser is not always clear. We cannot say, for example, whether Armenians were cleansed for their ethnicity or religion. Both aspects of their collective identity were fused together and separating them is impossible. One thing is certain: the Turkish government and most ethnic Turks perceived Armenians, both as Christians and non-Turks, as a major threat to their collectivity and state, a threat that had to be eliminated.

Another complicating factor is the diachronic changes in ascription and self-ascription. Jews, for example, in their long history in the diaspora, changed from a religious minority in medieval Europe to an ethnic group in the nineteenth century central and eastern Europe to, of all things, a racial contaminant in Nazi ideology.

At the same time, Jewish self-ascription has also changed significantly. Actually, there was not one but many self-ascriptions, since Orthodox Jews, assimilated Jews, Zionists, and all other ideological strands in between view "the Jew" differently. The oldest self-ascription, and also the one with the most continuity, is that of the Orthodox Jews, who see themselves as a people united by their covenant with God and separated, by the same covenant, from all other people. Although cleansing affected all kinds of Jews the criteria applied to cleansing changed from one epoch to another.

An overview of cleansing reveals that historically cleansing went through three phases. In antiquity it was used as a political tool to ensure control over alien, recently conquered, populations and as a source of slaves. It was the economic aspect of cleansing that was probably the most salient characteristic of that period. The conqueror not only weakened the enemy and diminished the likelihood of future resistance, he could also make a profit and procure a steady supply of manpower for the economy back home. Cleansing was thus virtually devoid of any ideological component (inasmuch as ideology is an abstract system of belief in the modern sense rather than something that is implied in the pattern of one's culture).

During the Middle Ages cleansing acquired a mostly religious character although ethnic and political cleansing did not entirely disappear. But economic cleansing had virtually died out since money could no longer be made off slavery. Uprooted serfs from an enemy state could be resettled on a conqueror's land if there was a labor shortage, but that kind of settlement was sporadic. Even on the German-Slav frontier in the twelfth and thirteenth centuries peasants from as far away as Flanders were usually invited, not forced, to settle. They were often enticed by wide-ranging privileges. Slavery continued to flourish in the Middle East, through capture of Christians from the northern shores of the Mediterranean and Africans, but this was a purely for-profit exercise, like the later trade in African slaves, not cleansing as defined in this book.

In the early modern period cleansing gradually lost its religious character and acquired the ethnic orientation we are familiar with today. It was superseded by colonial cleansing of indigenous peoples carried out by European settlers. Finally, in this century we have witnessed a proliferation of various types of cleansing—ideological, postcolonial, and, of course, purely ethnic—which, I believe, shows the accumulation of different types of collective identities. This accumulation is manifested in the addition of "outer rings" or boundary maintenance mechanisms to the existing core.

Geographically, cleansing in the Old World differed from cleansing in the New World. The first kind was practiced by states, often empires, in their struggle for territorial control and/or expansion. The second type comprised a slow push-back of the indigenous populations by colonial powers in the Americas and Australia. The difference was partly determined by the absence of political structures that could organize effective resistance in most new territories of the New World and Australia. Another factor was the profound difference in technological development of the autochthonous peoples and the invading Europeans, which made the conquest easy and the subsequent mass immigration and settlement possible.

In addition to historical and geographical divisions, there is also what I would call, for lack of a better term, paradigmatic cleansing: cleansing based on certain (undesirable) character-istics of a segment of the population. This is a varied collection.

First, there is cleansing by physical characteristics. This type includes cleansing by race, which occurs when a certain group is cleansed because of its genetic makeup. Such was the cleansing of Indians in the Americas, Aborigines in Australia, Whites in Haiti, and Asians in Uganda. Racial cleansing was often presented as a civilizational imperative due to the incompatibility of two civilizations and the impossibility of their peaceful coexistence. There is also what I would call a pseudoracial cleansing, such as the cleansing of Jews by the Nazis, who conceived it as a racial cleansing even though Jews do not constitute a distinct race and are, in fact, often indistinguishable from the general population among whom they live.

A rare variety of this type of cleansing is the elimination of people with physical deform-ities. Such was the murder of weaklings and malformed babies in Sparta. Perhaps, in this instance we should call it preemptive cleansing. I would classify it as a borderline case since deformed babies did not constitute a group or a population. But the desire to weed out a certain kind of people in a given population—to cleanse—was definitely there.

Probably the most common kind of cleansing is that by cultural markers, which has proliferated in the last 200 years. Here we have ethnic cleansing based on culture, language, and ascription. Examples include the mass expulsion of Germans from Eastern Europe in 1945–47 and that of the Salvadorans from Honduras. Another subdivision is religious cleans-ing, which was prevalent in the Middle Ages. It has by no means disappeared in our time although it is now usually combined with ethnicity. In this century alone, Armenians and Greeks in Turkey, Hindus and Muslims in the Indian subcontinent and, right before our eyes, Christians of various denominations and Muslims in Bosnia and Croatia, all provide examples of religious and ethnoreligious cleansing. Where ethnicity and religion are fused we may call a cleansing civilizational, since the adversaries often represent two distinct civilizations.

As civilizations became more complex, new social categories were created, and this in turn resulted in new forms of what may be called ideological cleansing. Thus, the introduction of the concept of class led to the cleansing of undesirable classes in Marxist states. Here Soviet Russia was the pioneer, later followed by other Communist states in Europe and Asia. Class cleansing affected the bourgeoisie, the aristocracy, and, in Russia and China, rural bourgeoisie known in Russian as the kulaks. Class cleansing was a characteristic of early Communist societies: by the time they reached maturity all "parasitic" classes slated for annihilation had been eliminated.

Another variety of ideological cleansing is political cleansing directed against political opponents and, on occasion, against politically unreliable populations as a whole. Like so many other phenomena, political cleansing originated in the poleis of preclassical Greece in the eighth to sixth centuries B.C. during a period of acute political struggle between the monarchy and "democracy."

Such cleansing was merely a matter of expediency. As a clearly enunciated political principle, the modern variety grew out of religious cleansing. As a political principle it was first formulated by the Peace of Augsburg in 1555.

Strategic cleansing is often closely linked with political persecution. To distinguish the two we must keep in mind that strategic cleansing is more limited in scope and is usually applied to sensitive military areas.

Here we can also distinguish two subvarieties: first, external cleansing directed against alien populations or opponents in the newly acquired territories, and second, internal cleansing, or self-cleansing, focused on the elimination of internal political opponents. This kind of cleansing is often practiced against political foes, especially after a civil war (in which case it falls into the category of political cleansing). For example, the suppression of the Paris Commune in 1871 led to the shooting of 20,000 to 25,000 communards and the deportation of about 5,000 to New Caledonia. Seventy years later, in the Spanish civil war of 1936–39, the Republicans killed about 20,000 opponents while the Nationalists eliminated about 400,000. Tellingly, the mass executions were called *limpia* (cleanup).

To this category we may add (political) refugees who fled in anticipation of persecution based on certain characteristics. The Russian civil war of 1919–22 generated 1.5 million White refugees, the Spanish war of 1936–39 about 300,000 Republicans. Or the flow can be generated by a politically motivated invasion, such as the suppression of the Hungarian revolution in 1956, which sent some 200,000 political refugees from Hungary, or the invasion of Czechoslovakia in 1968, which generated an outflow of over 120,000. But this type of anticipatory self-cleansing is hard to distinguish from flight under pressure or forced emigration. It is another borderline case.

An altogether different kind of cleansing is a cleansing whose goal is making a profit. This type can be called economic cleansing. It was particularly widespread in antiquity, when selling newly enslaved populations could bring enormous profits to slave traders. However, we must distinguish between this type of enslavement as an instrument of cleansing and simple enslavement for profit only, which was common in Africa in the sixteenth to nineteenth centuries. (This refers to the slave trade practiced by Europeans; slavery by Arab traders had been going on much longer. Both were purely economic enterprises.) Only when enslavement was directed at the population of a given polity, as in Thebes, and was combined with political goals can we speak of an economic cleansing. In other words, this kind of cleansing does not exist independently; it must include political goals, such as destruction of the adversary's political power and demographic base.

A much rarer type is cleansing by gender, as when the entire male population of a conquered tribe was slaughtered or enslaved, or when young women were taken by conquerors as concubines. Here we should apply the same test that we applied to economic cleansing: if the elimination of the male or female population was done expressly for the purpose of destroying the community then it would qualify as cleansing. Otherwise, it will simply be a matter of greed, status, and lust. The recent rape of thousands of mostly Muslim women in Bosnia had clear ideological overtones and thus can serve as an example of cleansing by gender. The perpetrators were aiming at destroying the honor and integrity of the Muslim population (they actually dishonored themselves, but that is another matter).

Even rarer is cleansing by sexual preference. We know of several attempts to suppress (male) homosexuality in Byzantium. In most civilizations such campaigns were extremely rare, partly because not every civilization regarded homosexuality as a sin, partly because homosexuals were not regarded as a community (a homosexual was acting as an individual, to be punished on an individual basis), and partly because gays were usually closeted and led a clandestine existence that attracted little attention. Only the totalitarian states of the twentieth century, especially Nazi Germany and Soviet Russia (although Soviet Russia does not seem to have practiced it on the same scale) put cleansing by sexual preference on the map.

Cleansing by age is also very rare. We know of the cleansing of babies ordered by Herod. Sparta killed weak and malformed babies as a matter of course, but this was an elimination of individuals, not a population cleansing per se. Still, such babies were weeded out as a class of individuals, and the goal was to make sure that Sparta's population stayed healthy.

At the other end of the age spectrum we have cleansing by old age. In some technologically primitive societies old people past a certain age were abandoned to the elements, particularly in lean years. However, this was not a regular occurrence and, as with babies, the elimination was carried out on an individual basis rather than as a campaign affecting the whole community. In neither case was the destruction of a population pursued as a goal. So, cleansing by age is another borderline case.

There are several more categories of elimination and persecution that defy easy definition. One such was the burning of witches in medieval Europe. Like the cleansing of the aged or gays, it was usually applied to individuals; on the other hand, the elimination of the entire witch population, presumed in existence, was clearly the aim. The fact that the witch population was probably an "imagined community" does not invalidate the elimination of this category as cleansing. So this would be yet another borderline case.

Other types include the killing of approximately 70,000 mentally ill patients in Nazi Germany in 1939, soon discontinued; the mass removal of prostitutes occasionally practiced by various states in different epochs; and the elimination of beggars in medieval Wallachia by Vlad the Dracul. The last probably qualifies as social cleansing although this was a bizarre and isolated incident.

Finally, virtually all types of cleansing can be either permanent (as is usually the case) or temporary (such as the internment of the Japanese in the United States during World War II). Temporary cleansing is often practiced in strategically sensitive military areas (the expulsion of some 600,000 Jews from the Russian frontier zone in 1914–15, for example) although examples of permanent expulsions in these areas are also fairly well known (such as the resettlement of approximately 60,000 Armenian families from Old Jolfa in Isfahan in 1604).

# 3.2   Michael Mann, "Explaining Ethnic Cleansing"

74-year-old Batisha Hoxha was sitting in her kitchen with her 77-year-old husband, Izet, staying warm by the stove. They had heard explosions but did not realize that Serbian troops had already entered the town. The next thing she knew, five or six soldiers had burst through the front door and were demanding "Where are your children?" The soldiers began beating Izet, "so hard that he fell to the floor," she said. While they were kicking him, the soldiers demanded money and information on the whereabouts of the couple's sons. Then, while Izet was still on the floor looking up at them, they killed him. "They shot him three times in the chest," recalled Batisha. With her husband dying before her, the soldiers pulled the wedding ring off her finger.

"I can still feel the pain," she said. They fired shots . . . and finally they kicked Batisha and a 10-year-old boy who was staying with them and told them to get out.

"I was not even outside the gate when they burned it." . . . Her husband's body was in the flames. In that moment she was paralyzed. She was standing on the street in the rain with no house, no husband, no possessions but the clothes she was wearing. Finally, strangers passed in a tractor and bundled her into their wagon. Batisha's daughter later found her in a refugee camp in northern Albania.

Looking tenderly at her one photograph of herself and Izet, Batisha murmurs: "Nobody understands what we have seen and what we have suffered. Only God knows."[1]

This is how murderous ethnic cleansing was wreaked on one household in the village of Belanica in Kosovo in the very last year of the 20th century. The perpetrators were Serbs, using murder and mayhem to terrify the local Albanians into flight. Then the land could be occupied by Serbs, as was "our historic right," they said. Now the Kosovo boot is on the other foot. Since 1999 Albanians have been kicking out Serbs. Kosovo is now cleansed, not of Albanians but of almost all its Serbs.

Change the names of the people and places and the incident could have occurred almost anywhere in the world over the past few centuries—in Australia, Indonesia, India, Russia, Germany, Ireland, the United States, Brazil. Ethnic cleansing is one of the main evils of modern times. We now know that the Holocaust of the Jews—though unique in important ways—is not unique as a case of genocide. The world's genocides remain thankfully few, but they are flanked by more numerous cases of less severe but nonetheless murderous cleansing.

For the sake of clarity, I lay it out up front now, in the form of eight general theses. These proceed from the very general to the particular, from the macro to the micro, successively adding parts of an overall explanation.

1. My first thesis concerns the broad historical era in which murderous cleansing became common. *Murderous cleansing is modern, because it is the dark side of democracy.* Let me make clear at the outset that I do not claim that democracies routinely commit murderous cleansing. Very few have done so. Nor do I reject democracy as an ideal—I endorse that ideal. Yet democracy has always carried with it the possibility that the majority might tyrannize minorities, and this possibility carries more ominous consequences in certain types of multiethnic environments.

This thesis has two parts, concerning modernity and democracy. Ethnic cleansing is essentially modern. Though not unknown in previous history (and probably common among the very small groups who dominated prehistory), it became more frequent and deadly in modern times. The 20th-century death toll through ethnic conflict amounted to somewhere over 70 million, dwarfing that of previous centuries. Additionally, conventional warfare increasingly targeted entire peoples as the enemy. Whereas civilians accounted for less than 10 percent of deaths in World War I, they rocketed to over half in World War II and to somewhat above 80 percent in wars fought in the 1990s. Civil wars, mostly ethnic in nature, were now taking over from interstate wars as the main killers. Perhaps 20 million have died in them, though it is impossible to be precise (figures have been hazarded by Chesterman, 2001: 2; Fearon & Laitin, 2003; Gurr, 1993, 2000; Harff, 2003; Markusen & Kopf, 1995: 27–34).

Ethnic and religious conflicts continue to simmer as I write in 2003—in Northern Ireland, the Basque Country, Cyprus, Bosnia, Kosovo, Macedonia, Algeria, Turkey, Israel, Iraq, Chechnya, Azerbaijan, Afghanistan, Pakistan, India, Sri Lanka, Kashmir, Burma, Tibet, Chinese Xinjiang, Fiji, the southern Philippines, various islands of Indonesia, Bolivia, Peru, Mexico, the Sudan, Somalia, Senegal, Uganda, Sierra Leone, Liberia, Nigeria, Congo, Rwanda, and Burundi. Over half of these cases involve substantial killing. As you read these words, one ethnic crisis probably will be exploding into violence on your television screen or newspaper, while several other explosions will not be deemed newsworthy. The 20th century was bad enough. Perhaps the 21st will be even worse.

The mayhem committed on September 11, 2001, and the "war against terrorism" that it triggered, have imprinted the horror of murderous ethnic and religious strife on the consciousness of the entire world. It has especially struck home in the prosperous countries of the North, shielded from such things over the past half-century. Neither the attack of September 11 nor the retaliatory attacks on Afghanistan and Iraq had as their intent ethnic cleansing, but they promptly became entwined with ethnic-religious conflicts involving cleansing between Israelis and Palestinians, Sunni and Shi'ite Muslims, Iraqis and Kurds, Russians and Chechens, Kashmiri Muslims and Hindus, and various Afghan tribes. In fact, some seem to be leading by the nose the foreign policies of the Great Powers.

Thus, unfortunately for us, murderous ethnic cleansing is not primitive or alien. It belongs to our own civilization and to us. Most say this is due to the rise of nationalism in the world, and this is true. But nationalism becomes very dangerous only when it is politicized, when it represents the perversion of modern aspirations to democracy in the nation-state. Democracy means rule by the people. But in modern times *the people* has come to mean two things. The first is what the Greeks meant by their word *demos*. This means the ordinary people, the mass of the population. So democracy is rule by the ordinary people, the masses. But in our civilization the people also means "nation" or another Greek term, *ethnos*, an ethnic group—a people that shares a common culture and sense of heritage, distinct from other peoples. But if the people is to rule in its own nation-state, and if the people is defined in ethnic terms, then its ethnic unity may outweigh the kind of citizen diversity that is central to democracy. If such a people is to rule, what is to happen to those of different ethnicity? Answers have often been unpleasant—especially when one ethnic group forms a majority, for then it can rule "democratically" but also tyrannically. As Wimmer (2002) argues, modernity is structured by ethnic and nationalist principles because the institutions of citizenship, democracy, and welfare are tied to ethnic and national forms of exclusion. I concede that some other features of modernity play more subsidiary roles in the upsurge of cleansing. We will see that some modern professional militaries have been tempted toward wars of annihilation of the enemy, while modern ideologies like fascism and communism have been similarly ruthless. But underlying all this is the notion that the enemy to be annihilated is a whole people.

I clarify this first thesis with some subtheses.

1a.  Murderous ethnic cleansing is a hazard of the age of democracy since amid multiethnicity the ideal of rule by the people began to entwine the *demos* with the dominant *ethnos*, generating organic conceptions of the nation and the state that encouraged the cleansing of minorities. Later, socialist ideals of democracy also became perverted as the *demos* became entwined with the term *proletariat*, the working class, creating pressures to cleanse other classes. These have been the most general ways in which democratic ideals were transmuted into murderous cleansing.

1b.  In modern colonies, settler democracies in certain contexts have been truly murderous, more so than more authoritarian colonial governments. The more settlers controlled colonial institutions, the more murderous the cleansing. It is the most direct relationship I have found between democratic regimes and mass murder.

1c.  Regimes newly embarked upon democratization are more likely to commit murderous ethnic cleansing than are stable authoritarian regimes (Chua, 2004, also makes this argument). When authoritarian regimes weaken in multiethnic environments, *demos* and *ethnos* are most likely to become entwined. In contrast, stable authoritarian regimes in such contexts tend to govern by divide-and-rule. This leads them to seek to balance the demands of powerful groups, including ethnic ones. However, a few highly authoritarian regimes deviate. They mobilize majoritarian groups into a mass party-state mobilizing the people against "enemy" minorities. The Nazi and Communist regimes were dictatorships, not democracies, though they did emerge out of would-be democratizing contexts, which they then exploited. They mobilized the people as *ethnos* or proletariat. They are partial exceptions to this subthesis.

1d.  Stably institutionalized democracies are less likely than either democratizing or authoritarian regimes to commit murderous cleansing. They have entrenched not only elections and rule by the majority, but also constitutional guarantees for minorities. But their past was not so virtuous. Most of them committed sufficient ethnic cleansing to produce an essentially mono-ethnic citizen body in the present. In their past, cleansing and democratization proceeded hand in hand. Liberal democracies were built on top of ethnic cleansing, though outside of the colonies this took the form of institutionalized coercion, not mass murder.

1e. Regimes that are actually perpetrating murderous cleansing are never democratic, since that would be a contradiction in terms. These subtheses therefore apply beforehand, to the earlier phases of escalation of ethnic conflict. Indeed, as escalation proceeds, all perpetrating regimes become less and less democratic. The dark side of democracy is the perversion through time of either liberal or socialist ideals of democracy.

In view of these complex relations, we will not find any simple overall relationship in the world today between democracy and ethnic cleansing—as Fearon and Laitin (2003) confirm in their quantitative study of recent civil (mostly ethnic) wars. But mine is not a static comparative analysis. It is historical and dynamic: murderous cleansing has been moving across the world as it has modernized and democratized. Its past lay mainly among Europeans, who invented the democratic nation-state. The countries inhabited by Europeans are now safely democratic, but most have also been ethnically cleansed (as in thesis 1d). Now the epicenter of cleansing has moved into the South of the world. Unless humanity takes evasive action, it will continue to spread until democracies—hopefully, not ethnically cleansed ones—rule the world. Then it will ease. But if we wish to ease it more quickly from the world, we now have to face squarely up to the dark side of democracy.

2. *Ethnic hostility rises where ethnicity trumps class as the main form of social stratification, in the process capturing and channeling classlike sentiments toward ethnonationalism.* Cleansing was rare in the past because most big historic societies were class-divided. Aristocracies or other small oligarchies dominated them, and they rarely shared a common culture or ethnic identity with the common people. In fact they despised the people, often considering them barely human. The people did not exist across class lines—class trumped ethnicity.

Even the first modern societies were dominated by the politics of class. Liberal representative states first emerged as a way of compromising class conflict, giving them a plural sense of people and nation. They tolerated some ethnic diversity. But where the modern struggle for democracy involved a whole people struggling against rulers defined as foreign, an ethnic sense of the people arose, often capturing class resentments. The people was seen as a proletarian nation asserting fundamental democratic rights against upperclass imperial nations, which retorted that they were bringing civilization to their backward peoples. Today the Palestinian cause is decidedly proletarian in its tone, seeing its oppressor as an exploiting and colonial Israel—backed up by American imperialism—while Israelis and Americans claim they are defending civilization against primitive terrorists. The arguments are similar to those of class enemies of former times.

Ethnic differences entwine with other social differences—especially of class, region, and gender. Ethnonationalism is strongest where it can capture other senses of exploitation. The most serious defect of recent writing on ethnonationalism has been its almost complete neglect of class relations (as in Brubaker, 1996; Hutchinson, 1994; Smith, 2001). Others wrongly see class as materialistic, ethnicity as emotional (Connor, 1994: 144–64; Horowitz, 1985: 105–35). This simply inverts the defect of previous generations of writers who believed that class conflict dominated while ignoring ethnicity. Now the reverse is true, and not only among scholars. Our media are dominated by ethnic strife while largely ignoring class struggles. Yet in actuality these two types of conflict infuse each other. Palestinians, Dayaks, Hutus, and so on believe they are being materially exploited. Bolsheviks and Maoists believed that landlord and Kulak classes were exploiting the nation. To neglect either ethnicity or class is mistaken. Sometimes one or the other may come to dominate, but this will involve the capturing and channeling of the other. The same can be said of gender and regional sentiments.

Indeed, murderous cleansing does not occur among rival ethnic groups who are separate but equal. Mere difference is not enough to generate much conflict. It is not Christians against Muslims that causes problems, but contexts in which Muslims feel oppressed by Christians (or vice versa). If South Africa had actually lived up to its own apartheid claim to produce separate but equal development of the races, Africans would not have revolted. They revolted because apartheid was a sham, involving racial exploitation of Africans by whites. For serious ethnic conflict to develop, one ethnic group must be seen as exploiting the other. And in turn, the imperial oppressor will react in righteous outrage against the threat of having its "civilization" overwhelmed by "primitivism"—just as upper classes do when threatened with revolution.

3. *The danger zone of murderous cleansing is reached when (a) movements claiming to represent two fairly old ethnic groups both lay claim to their own state over all or part of the same territory and (b) this claim seems to them to have substantial legitimacy and some plausible chance of being implemented.* Almost all dangerous cases are bi-ethnic ones, where both groups are quite powerful and where rival claims to political sovereignty are laid on top of quite old senses of ethnic difference—though not on what are generally called *ancient hatreds*. Ethnic differences are worsened to serious hatreds, and to dangerous levels of cleansing, by persistent rival claims to political sovereignty. I characteristically identify four major sources of power in societies: ideological, economic, military, and political. Murderous ethnic conflict concerns primarily *political power relations*, though as it develops it also involves ideological, economic, and finally military power relations too. Mine is essentially a political explanation of ethnic cleansing.

4. *The brink of murderous cleansing is reached when one of two alternative scenarios plays out. (4a). The less powerful side is bolstered to fight rather than to submit* (for submission reduces the deadliness of the conflict) *by believing that aid will be forthcoming from outside*— usually from a neighboring state, perhaps its ethnic homeland state (as in Brubaker's, 1996, model). In this scenario both sides are laying political claim to the same territory, and both believe they have the resources to achieve it. This was so in the Yugoslav, Rwandan, Kashmiri, and Chechen cases, for example. The current U.S. war against terrorism aims at eliminating such outside support, labeling it *terrorism. (4b) The stronger side believes it has such over-whelming military power and ideological legitimacy that it can force through its own cleansed state at little physical or moral risk to itself.* This is so in colonial settler cases, as in the North American, Australian, and Circassian cases considered later. The Armenian and Jewish cases mixed these two scenarios together, since the dominant Turkish and German sides believed they had to strike first in order to prevent the weaker Armenian and Jewish sides from allying with far more threatening outsiders. All these terrible eventualities were produced by inter-action between the two sides. We cannot explain such escalation merely in terms of the actions or beliefs of the perpetrators. We need to examine the interactions between the perpetrator and victim groups—and usually with other groups as well. For few even bi-ethnic situations lead to murderous cleansing. One or both sides must first decide to fight rather than conciliate or manipulate, and that choice is unusual.

5. *Going over the brink into the perpetration of murderous cleansing occurs where the state exercising sovereignty over the contested territory has been factionalized and radicalized amid an unstable geopolitical environment that usually leads to war.* Out of such political and geo-political crises radicals emerge calling for tougher treatment of perceived ethnic enemies. In fact, where ethnic conflict between rival groups is quite old, it is usually somewhat ritualized, cyclical, and manageable. Truly murderous cleansing, in contrast, is unexpected, originally unintended, emerging out of unrelated crises like war. Conversely, in cases where states and geopolitics remain stable, even severe ethnic tensions and violence tend to be cyclical and manageable at lesser levels of violence. But where political institutions are unstable and affected by war, violence may lead to mass murder—as Harff's (2003) study of political cleansings across the world confirms.

There are different forms of political instability. Some states were fragmenting and factionalizing (like the Hutu state of Rwanda); others had been seized and were being newly consolidated, determinedly repressing dissidents and factionalism (like the Nazi state). In some brand-new states, consolidation was very uneven (as in the new Bosnian and Croatian states). But these were not stable and cohesive states, whether democratic or authoritarian. Nor were they often the failed states that political science researchers have shown are most likely to generate civil wars (the Congo at the beginning of the 21st century is an exception). Ethnic cleansings are in their most murderous phases usually directed by states, and this requires some state coherence and capacity.

6. *Murderous cleansing is rarely the initial intent of perpetrators.* It is rare to find evil geniuses plotting mass murder from the very beginning. Not even Hitler did so. Murderous cleansing typically emerges as a kind of Plan C, developed only after the first two responses to a perceived ethnic threat fail. Plan A typically envisages a carefully planned solution in terms of either compromise or straightforward repression. Plan B is a more radically repressive adaptation to the failure of Plan A, more hastily conceived amid rising violence and some political destabilization. When these both fail, some of the planners radicalize further. To understand the outcome, we must analyze the unintended consequences of a series of inter-actions yielding escalation. These successive Plans may contain both logical and more contin-gent escalations. The perpetrators may be ideologically determined from quite early on to rid themselves of the ethnic out-group, and when milder methods fail, they almost logically seem to escalate with resolute determination to overcome all obstacles by more and more radical means. This was true of Hitler and his myrmidons: the Final Solution of the Jewish question seems much less of an accident than the logical escalation of an ideology ruthlessly overcom-ing all obstacles in its path. For the Young Turks, however, the final solution to the Armenian problem seems much more contingent, flowing out of what they saw as their suddenly desperate situation in 1915.

To downplay intentionality like this is morally uncomfortable, often involving me in argu-ing against those who speak in the name of the victims. Genocide of the Jews, the Armenians, the Tutsis, of some colonized native peoples, and of others was deliberately accomplished. The evidence is overwhelming. But surviving victims like to emphasize premeditation by their oppressors. This probably derives mostly from their need to find meaning in their sufferings. What could be worse than to regard such extreme suffering as accidental? In *King Lear*, Edgar says of his sufferings: "Like flies to wanton boys are we to the gods." I find that a tempting theory of human society, but I doubt many victims do. I am not actually arguing that murderous cleansing is accidental, only that it is far more complex and contingent than blame-centered theories allow. It is eventually perpetrated deliberately, but the route to deliberation is usually a circuitous one.

7. *There are three main levels of perpetrator: (a) radical elites running party-states; (b) bands of militants forming violent paramilitaries; and (c) core constituencies providing mass though not majority popular support.* Elites, militants, and core constituencies are all normally necessary for murderous cleansing to ensue. We cannot simply blame malevolent leaders or ethnic groups en masse. That would be to credit leaders with truly magical powers of manipulation or whole peoples with truly remarkable single-mindedness. Both assumptions are at odds with everything sociologists know about the nature of human societies. In all my cases particular elites, militants, and core constituencies are linked together in quite complex ways, forming social movements that (like other social movements) embody mundane power rela-tions. Power is exercised in three distinct ways: top-down by elites, bottom-up by popular pressures, and coercively sideways by paramilitaries. These pressures interact and so generate mundane relations like those found in all social movements—especially of hierarchy, comradeship, and career. This has a big impact on perpetrators' motives, as we will see in a moment.

The notion of core constituencies reveals that murderous cleansing resonates more in environments favoring combinations of nationalism, statism, and violence. The main core constituencies are ethnic refugees and people from threatened border districts; those more dependent on the state for their subsistence and values; those living and working outside of the main sectors of the economy that generate class conflict (who are more likely to favor class over ethnonationalist models of conflict); those socialized into acceptance of physical violence as a way of solving social problems or achieving personal advancement—like soldiers, policemen, criminals, hooligans, and athletes; and those attracted to machismo ideology—young males striving to assert themselves in the world, often led by older males who were socialized as youths in an earlier phase of violence. So the main axes of stratification involved in cleansing movements are region, economic sector, gender, and age. Radical ethnonationalist movements tend to contain a normal class structure: leaders come from the upper and middle classes, the rank-and-file from lower down—with the real dirty work often performed by the working class. I explore all these groups' motivations, careers, and interactions.

8.  Finally, *ordinary people are brought by normal social structures into committing murderous ethnic cleansing*, and their motives are much more mundane. To understand ethnic cleansing, we need a sociology of power more than a special psychology of perpetrators as disturbed or psychotic people—though some may be. As the psychologist Charny (1986: 144) observes, "the mass killers of humankind are largely everyday human beings—what we have called normal people according to currently accepted definitions by the mental health profession."

Placed in comparable situations and similar social constituencies, you or I might also commit murderous ethnic cleansing. No ethnic group or nation is invulnerable. Many Americans and Australians committed murderous cleansing in the past; some Jews and Armenians—the most victimized peoples of the 20th century—have perpetrated recent atrocities against Palestinians and Azeris (and, in turn, some of these victim groups are also perpetrators). There are no virtuous peoples. Religions tend to stress the presence in all humans of original sin, the human capacity for evil. Indeed, placed in the right circumstances and core constituencies, we are almost all capable of such evil—perhaps even of enjoying it. But original sin would be an insufficient explanation for this. In the case of cleansing, these circumstances are less primitive or ancient than modern. There is something in modernity releasing this particular evil on a mass scale.

Given the messiness and uniqueness of societies, my theses cannot be scientific laws. They do not even fit perfectly all my case studies. For example, Nazi genocide does not fit neatly into thesis 3, since Jews were not claiming sovereignty over any part of Germany. Mass murder has been ubiquitous if uncommon throughout most of human history. But murder in order to remove ("cleanse") a people was rare in earlier centuries. Things became more dangerous with the rise of salvation religions and then with the rise of rule by the people.

## Defining Terms: Ethnicity, Nation, Ethnic Cleansing

Ethnicity is not objective. Ethnic groups are normally defined as groups sharing a common culture and common descent. Yet culture is vague and descent usually fictitious. A common culture may refer to a relatively precise characteristic, like a shared religion or language. But it may merely refer to a claim to share a way of life—which cannot be precisely defined. Common descent is mythical for any group larger than a clan or a lineage (what I call a *micro-ethnicity*). The future use of DNA analysis will probably reveal that relatively immobile populations share substantial common heredity, but this will not be so for most large groups claiming ethnic commonality. People who define themselves as Serbs or Germans or Scots actually descend from many smaller descent groups who have moved around and intermarried with their neighbors. Claims to commonality among large groups actually aggregate together numerous descent groups. None of the ethnic conflicts considered here are natural or primordial. They and their conflicts are socially created.

They are created in diverse ways. A common language is important in uniting Germans but not Serbs (their language is shared with Croats and Bosniaks). Religion is important for Serbs (their orthodox Christianity distinguishes them from Croats, Bosniaks, and Albanians) but not Germans (divided into Catholics and Protestants). Theories of civilization and race helped give Europeans a common sense of being civilized and then white, in contrast to their colonial subjects. Economic dominance or subordination can form identities, and so can military power. Imperial conquerors often create macro-ethnicities by allocating particular roles to groups they define as belonging to a single people or tribe. Finally, a shared political history as an independent state or province is of ubiquitous importance—as it is for Scots, not distinct in language or religion from the English but with a distinct political history. Given this diversity, it is safer to define ethnicities subjectively, in terms they themselves and/or their neighbors use.

An *ethnicity* is a group that defines itself or is defined by others as sharing common descent and culture. So *ethnic cleansing* is the removal by members of one such group of another such group from a locality they define as their own. A *nation* is such a group that also has political consciousness, claiming collective political rights in a given territory. A *nation-state* results where such a group has its own sovereign state. Not all self-conscious nations possess or desire nation-states. Some claim only local autonomy or entrenched rights within a broader multi-ethnic state.

Ethnic groups treat each other in many ways, most of which do not involve murder. Since the advent of global news media, the few cases involving mass murder have been imprinted upon our consciousness. But thankfully, they are rare. The continent of Africa figures mostly in the Western media only for really bad news. But there are only a few African cases of murderous ethnic cleansing—in a continent in which all states are multiethnic. Fearon and Laitin (1996) estimate all the cases of serious ethnic violence as less than 1 percent of all the multiethnic environments found in Africa.

## Note

1. We know too—thanks to *Los Angeles Times* reporter John Daniszewski, whose graphic report on Belanica appeared on April 25, 1999.

## References

Brubaker, R. (1996). *Nationalism Reframed: Nationhood and the National Question in the New Europe.* Cambridge: Cambridge University Press.

Charny, Israel W. (1986). "Genocide and Mass Destruction: Doing Harm to Others as a Missing Dimension in Psychopathology." *Psychiatry*, Volume 49.

Chesterman, S. (2001). *Civilians in War.* Boulder, CO: Lynne Rienner.

Chua, A. (2004) *World on Fire: How Exporting Free Market Democracy Breeds Ethnic Hatred and Global Instability.* New York: Anchor Books.

Connor, W. (1994). *Ethnonationalism: The Quest for Understanding.* Princeton, NJ: Princeton University Press.

Fearon, J., and Laitin, D. (1996). "Explaining Interethnic Cooperation." *American Political Science Review.* Volume 90.

Fearon, J., and Laitin, D. (2003) "Ethnicity, Insurgency and Civil War." *American Political Science Review.* Volume 97.

Gurr, Ted (1993). *Minorities at Risk: A Global View of Ethnopolitical Conflicts.* Washington, D.C.: United States Institute of Peace.

Gurr, T. (2000) *People versus States: Minorities at Risk in the New Century.* Washington, D.C.: United States Institute of Peace.

Harff, Barbara (2003). "No Lessons Learned from the Holocaust? Assessing Risks of Genocide and Political Mass Murdre Since 1955. *American Political Science Review*, Volume 97.

Horowitz, D. (1985). *Ethnic Groups in Conflict.* Berkeley and Los Angeles: University of California Press.

Hutchinson, J. (1994). *Modern Nationalism.* London: Fontana.

Markusen, Eric, and Kopf, David (1995). *The Holocaust and Strategic Bombing: Genocide and Total War in the Twentieth Century.* New York: Oxford University Press.

Smith, A. (2001). *Nationalism.* Oxford: Polity.

Wimmer, A. (2002). *Nationalist Exclusion and Ethnic Conflict: Shadows of Modernity.* Cambridge: Cambridge University Press.

# 3.3   Barbara Harff, "Recognizing Genocides and Politicides"

In genocides the victimized groups are defined primarily in terms of their communal characteristics. In politicides, by contrast, groups are defined primarily in terms of their political opposition to the regime and dominant group.

The term *genocide* is fraught with ambiguities, possibly because it became a catchphrase for the dispossessed. It is often used indiscriminately to describe any and all kinds of social policies and alleged injuries caused by states; many such acts bear little resemblance to the crime of genocide as defined in the U.N. Genocide Convention. The literal meaning refers to the killing of a race or kind (*genos*). Lemkin coined the term to describe the systematic destruction of peoples in Europe during the Nazi reign, foremost among them Jews, Gypsies, and Slavic people.[1]

Genocide, according to Article II of the U.N. Genocide Convention, refers to "acts committed with intent to destroy, in whole or part, a national, ethnical, racial, or religious group." The article refers to killing members of a group; points c, d, and e specifically refer to conditions whose cumulative effects are conducive to the destruction of a group. These points are (c) "deliberately inflicting on the group conditions of life calculated to bring about its physical destruction in whole or in part"; (d) "imposing measures intended to prevent births within the group"; and (e) "forcibly transferring children of the group to another group." Point b, however, which refers to acts "causing serious bodily or mental harm to members of the group," is problematic, for it has given rise to innumerable claims of victimization. For example, the World Council of Churches made such a claim on behalf of Australian aborigines during the early 1980s, at a time when the Australian federal government was making concerted efforts to improve aboriginal welfare. Other claims have referred to acts of repression in which governments disrupted or tried to destroy the cultural life of a group. In rare cases such acts have led to isolated massacres, which then became the cause célèbre of beleaguered minorities claiming the advent of a genocide or a holocaust. The exclusion of this problematic point would delimit the crime of genocide to those acts that endanger the *physical* life of group members and thus would eradicate some confusion. Geno/politicides are unfortunately not uncommon, and if we were to extend the usage of the term to all forms of repression that incur death, we would be unable to distinguish between serious and frivolous claims.

I think of genocide as standing in a similar relationship to ecocide (the destruction of the environment) or ethnocide (the destruction of a culture) as premeditated homicide stands to intentional rape. In the case of homicide the perpetrator clearly attempts to destroy the whole person, whereas in the case of rape the objective is to harm, alter, or use the victim. Those who injure the environment or deny groups the ability to propagate their culture are far less likely to plan a genocide than are revolutionaries and despots such as Adolf Hitler, Joseph Stalin, Pol

Pot, and Idi Amin—their intentions were obvious. Armed with ideologies that excluded certain groups from the public conscience, these men succeeded in making the victimized groups easy scapegoats.

During the empirical phase of my research, I generated a cross-national data set that identifies episodes of mass murder by governments, and I began to differentiate between genocide and what I identified as politicide. Politicides are events in which the victims are defined primarily in terms of their political position—their class, political beliefs, or organized opposition to the state and the dominant group. In genocides people are defined primarily by their membership in a particular ethnic, religious, national, or racial group. Both are types of extreme state repression, in which coherent policies by a ruling elite result in the deaths of a substantial portion of the targeted group. The difference usually is readily apparent. In genocides the victims share ascriptive traits; in politicides that may or may not be the case. In politicides victims are always engaged in some oppositional activity deemed undesirable by those in power; in genocides that may not be so.

The empirical phase of my research concentrates on cases since World War II. The rationale for concentrating on post-Holocaust cases is simple. First, I want to show that genocides and politicides are recurrent phenomena. Second, I leave to historians those earlier cases for which empirical evidence is not readily available or for which a substantial literature already exists. But as much as I have tried to avoid the fruitless debate on whether or not the Holocaust was unique and should therefore be treated somewhat differently, it has been impossible to do so, given the comparative nature of my research. Empirical research relies on comparison to explain the origins and consequences of political behavior. All cases have unique properties but also share some discernible patterns with others, from which social scientists can identify some common sequences and outcomes. Evidence shows that the systematic killing of individuals because of their ethnic, religious, or racial traits, or because they share certain political beliefs, has not ceased since 1945. Obviously elites, ability, willingness, and opportunity to kill groups of unwanted people have not disappeared since the Holocaust became part of public memory. If we want to keep alive the memories of all victims of senseless death, we need to recount all of them and identify their killers. We must also develop the ability to monitor ongoing events so that eventually we will be able to forewarn of genocides in the making.

## How to Detect a Genocide

Although "body counts" in principle do not enter the definition of genocide, in practice the destruction of small groups often is not detected until after the fact. As long as one can identify victims as members of a deliberately targeted group whose existence or survival is at stake, numbers of victims are irrelevant. For purposes of identifying cases, however, I count only episodes that last six months, on the ground that it takes time to plan and execute the destruction of a group. Thus, isolated massacres are excluded unless we see some continuity in the form of intermittent but repeated reprisals against such groups; the Iraqi government's treatment of Kurds is a case in point. But the threshold between massacres and an episode of geno/politicide is one of inherent uncertainty.

How does one evaluate a situation to determine whether a genocide is in the making? Ideally, all persecuted minority groups or repressed majorities should be monitored on an ongoing basis, but in practice this is impossible. Thus, we often recognize a situation only after a number of people are already dead. On the other hand, the literature abounds with information identifying minorities or majorities that are at risk in various countries. I especially call attention to the "Minorities at Risk" data set of Ted Robert Gurr, which assesses the civil and political rights at the societal and national level of 237 minorities in 126 countries.[2] His key indicator of whether an ethnic or racial group is at risk of human rights violations is the existence of systematic differential treatment by the larger society. Gurr and I have published an article comparing forty-four episodes of geno/politicides (see Table 1) with such groups at risk, which enables us to identify the groups that are the most probable targets of extreme repression in the future.[3] Genocides and politicides do not develop overnight and without warning. We often know that specific coercive violations of rights have taken place.

Sometimes during periods of national emergency basic political rights are curbed with the intent of protecting rather than punishing peoples. This can be appropriate in situations in which the victimized groups espouse hate propaganda and are themselves engaged in violent activities—the Tamil Tigers in Sri Lanka are a case in point. This is different from situations in which groups have endured officially sanctioned discrimination for some time and then are subjected to the declaration of a state of emergency, a situation that provides the climate for further curtailments of rights and abuse. The British-Malayan treatment of ethnic Chinese in Malaya (1948–1956) may illustrate this point.[4]

*Table 1* Victims of Genocides and Politicides since World War II[a]

| Country | Type, Dates of Episodes[b] | Communal Victims | Political Victims | Numbers of Victims[c] |
|---|---|---|---|---|
| USSR[d] | P 1943–47 | | Repatriated Soviet nationals | 500–1100 |
| USSR[d] | G 11/43–1/57 | Chechens, Ingushi, Karachai, Balkars | | 230 |
| USSR[d] | G 5/44–1968 | Meskhetians, Crimean Tatars | | 57–175 |
| China | PG 2/47–12/47 | Taiwanese nationalists | | 10–40 |
| USSR[d] | P 10/47–? | Ukrainian nationalists | | ? |
| Madagascar | P 4/47–12/48 | Malagasy nationalists | | 10–80 |
| People's Republic of China | P 1950–51 | | Kuomintang cadre, landlords, rich peasants | 800–3000 |
| N. Vietnam | P 1953–54 | | Catholic landlords, rich and middle peasants | 15 |
| Sudan[e] | P 1952–72 | Southern nationalists | | 100–500 |
| Pakistan[e] | PG 1958–74 | Baluchi tribesmen | | |
| People's Republic of China | GP 1959 | Tibetan Buddhists, landowners | | 65 |
| Iraq[e] | PG 1959–75 | Kurdish nationalists | | ? |
| Angola | P 5/61–1962 | Kongo | Assimilados | 40 |
| Algeria | P 7–12/62 | | Harkis (French-Muslim troops), OAS supporters | 12–60 |
| Paraguay | G 1962–72 | Ache Indians | | 0.9 |
| Rwanda | PG 1963–64 | Tutsi ruling class | | 5–14 |
| Laos | PG 1963–? | Meo tribesmen | | 18–20 |
| Zaire[f] | P 2/64–1/65 | Europeans, missionaries | Educated Congolese | 1–10 |

(*Continued overleaf*)

*Table 1* Continued

| Country | Type, Dates of Episodes[b] | Communal Victims | Political Victims | Numbers of Victims[c] |
|---|---|---|---|---|
| S. Vietnam | P 1965–72 | | Civilians in NLF areas | 475 |
| Indonesia | GP 10/65–1966 | Chinese | Communists | 500–1000 |
| Burundi[e] | PG 1965–73 | Hutu leaders, peasants | | 103–205 |
| Nigeria | G 5/10/66 | Ibos living in the North | | 9–30 |
| People's Republic of China | P 5/66–1975 | | Cultural Revolution victims | 400–850 |
| Guatemala | P 1966–84 | Indians | Leftists | 30–63 |
| India | P 1968–82 | | Naxalites | 1–3 |
| Philippines | PG 1968–85 | Moro (Muslim) nationalists | | 10–100 |
| Equatorial Guinea | GP 3/69–1979 | Bubi tribe | Political opponents of Macias | 1–50 |
| Uganda | GP 2/71–1979 | Karamojong, Acholi, Lango; Catholic clergy | Political opponents of Idi Amin | 100–500 |
| Pakistan | PG 3–12/71 | Bengali nationalists | | 1250–3000 |
| Chile | P 9/73–1976 | | Leftists | 2–30 |
| Ethiopia | P 1974–79 | | Political opposition | 30 |
| Kampuchea | GP 1975–79 | Muslim Cham | Old regime supporters, urban people, disloyal cadre | 800–3000 |
| Indonesia | PG 12/75–present | East Timorese nationalists | | 60–200 |
| Argentina | P 1976–80 | | Leftists | 9–30 |
| Zaire[e] | P 1977–? | Tribal opponents | Political opponents of Mobutu | 3–4 |
| Burma | G 1978 | Muslims in border region | | ? |
| Afghanistan | P 1978–89 | | Supporters of old regime, rural supporters of rebels | 1000 |
| Uganda | GP 1979–1/86 | Karamojong, Nilotic tribes, Bagandans | Supporters of Amin regime | 50–100 |
| El Salvador | P 1980–present | | Leftists | 20–70 |
| Iran | GP 1981–? | Kurds, Baha | Mujahedeen | 10–20 |
| Syria | P 4/81–2/82 | | Muslim Brotherhood | 5–25 |
| Sri Lanka | PG 1983–8/87 | Tamil nationalists | | 2–10 |
| Ethiopia | PG 1984–85+ | Victims of forced resettlement | | ? |
| Somalia | PG 5/88–1989 | Issak clan (Northerners) | | ? |

*Source:* This is an updated version of a table that appeared in the *International Review of Victimology* 1, no. 1 (1989).

a. Episodes of mass murder carried out by or with the complicity of political authorities, directed at distinct communal (ethnic, national, religious) or politically defined groups. Politically organized communal groups, placed in the table between the two column headings, share both kinds of defining traits.

b. This code is based on a more precise categorization of types of genocide and politicide as follows: G = genocide, victims defined communally; P = politicide, victims defined politically; PG = politicides against politically active communal groups; GP = episodes with mixed communal and political victims. [*Continued opposite*

An example of a situation that has the potential of developing into a politicide is the practice of tolerating private militias that kill innocent civilians. Such a situation exists at present in the Philippines, where the privileged class and the government are trying simultaneously to preserve the status quo and to fight a Communist insurgency. Militias can easily evolve into killing squads that are not only accepted but often endorsed by governing authorities, as, for example, in El Salvador.

In most conflict analyses participants are assumed to behave rationally. Yet to an outside observer genocide appears irrational. This is especially true of genocides carried out in the service of an ideological doctrine. The annihilation of Jews in Nazi Germany, where even during all-out war the death camps were working to capacity, shows how pure hate can lead to self-defeating behavior. If winning the war was the foremost goal of the Germans, then a well-treated, albeit subjugated, people could have served the war effort by working in war-related jobs. Apparently the foremost goal was the annihilation of European Jewry and the Gypsies and the enslavement of Slavic peoples. Similar irrational policies led to the annihilation of the intelligentsia in Kampuchea in an effort to institute a utopian self-contained peasant society.

How does one begin to explain irrational behavior? In these cases normal standards of behavior cease to have meaning. Does irrational behavior follow some internal logic similar to that of rational behavior? One can start by tracing less bizarre aspects of coercion to the onset of a genocide or politicide. Obviously, the assumption here is that recurrent episodes of discrimination and denial of rights sometimes lead to more severe forms of coercion.

One condition that may predict that genocide is in the making is the practice of denying groups access to political and/or economic positions. In Germany prior to Nazi rule, the Jews were only marginally integrated politically. Economically Jews were overrepresented in the professions, but traditionally had been excluded from the guilds and civil service. The anti-Semitism that denied Jews access to political office, education, and the professions eroded slowly during the nineteenth century, only to reemerge at the end of the century. Prior discrimination and prejudice made the Jews a convenient target for Nazi ideologues.

In the case of Kampuchea, a tiny elite made up of ethnic Chinese merchants, foreign-educated bureaucrats, and traditional groups surrounding the court enjoyed privileges,

---

Notes to Table 1—continued

c. Estimates in thousands. The victims include all civilians reported to have died as a direct consequence of regime action, including victims of starvation, disease, and exposure as well as those executed, massacred, bombed, shelled, or otherwise murdered. Numbers of victims are seldom known with any exactitude, and sometimes no reliable estimates of any kind are available. The numbers shown here represent the ranges in which the best estimates or guesses lie.

d. The first three Soviet episodes all began during and as a consequence of World War II but continued well past the war's end; hence they are regarded as postwar episodes. The second, third, and fourth Soviet episodes all involved the rapid, forced deportation of national groups to remote areas under conditions in which many died of malnourishment, disease, and exposure. Few of these victims were deliberately murdered. The terminal dates for the second and third cases represent the dates on which rights of citizenship were restored to the survivors. Estimates of deaths vary widely, as in most other episodes. Our coding of deaths is based on the more direct and detailed analysis of A. M. Nekrich in *The Punished People: The Deportation and Fate of Soviet Minorities at the End of the Second World War* (New York: W. W. Norton, 1978) rather than the demographic projections of J. G. Dyadkin in *Unnatural Deaths in the U.S.S.R., 1928–1954* (New Brunswick, N.J.: Transaction Books, 1983).

e. These episodes are discontinuous, including two or more distinct periods of mass murder, typically initiated in response to renewed resistance by the victim group.

f. Killings by the short-lived Congolese People's Republic between February 1964 and the recapture of its Stanleyville capital in January 1965.

although short-lived in the case of the Chinese merchants, which aroused the envy of the peasants. This envy was a pliable tool in the hands of the zealous ideologues of the Khmer Rouge. The Khmer Rouge's early successes in attracting support were a result of foreign intervention, Khmer Rouge's ideology, rampant internal corruption, and widespread poverty, among other factors. Peasant envy of indigenous and minority elites made these groups natural targets for Khmer Rouge fury against all their enemies.

How do we infer that governments deliberately plan and execute genocides or politicides? If the killings are carried out by military or quasi-military groups or death squads, then it follows that decisions to do so have been made at a high level. Unfortunately many people may die before we can decide whether this is a genocide. Even more difficult is the case of civil war, in which there is no effective central authority. Who is responsible the the killings? Pogroms, however, are distinct from genocides: they are short-lived outbursts by mobs, which, although often condoned by authorities, rarely persist.

What other factors distinguish genocide from lesser forms of repression? Genocidal policies require planning and preparation. Therefore we should look for evidence of official deliberations in which comprehensive plans are laid for controlling/relocating/eliminating categories of people. Similarly, the early stages of genocidal policies are likely to include campaigns of hate propaganda and the issuance of directives and laws that provide justifications and instructions for acting against target groups. Intermediate phases may include campaigns of deception during which a resistant public is lulled by an apparent let-up in persecution or by official denials of wrong-doing. During the implementation phase, the institution of new agencies or bureaucracies may give us a clue about what to expect. The final phase frequently includes a systematization of ongoing forms of persecution, which we may be able to observe by tracing the establishment of special forces, the fortification of labor camps, and an increased emphasis not on the final objective (killing people) but on the means of destruction. An example is the Wannsee conference in Nazi Germany on January 20, 1942, which systematized Nazi policies of extermination that were already well underway: it accelerated the construction of new facilities and the fortification of former labor camps into full-fledged extermination centers and routinized the mass deportation of Jews from the occupied states of Europe.

Evidence suggests that the type and organization of a government also play a role in determining the scale of a genocide. Democracies are the least likely to use systematic repression; totalitarian and authoritarian governments are the most likely to do so. But regardless of the political form, bureaucratically developed structures are best equipped to execute a genocide on the scale and in the manner of the Holocaust.

## Death War and Genocide: The Means and Ends of Destruction

During war civilians get killed, sometimes by the thousands. How do we differentiate between a genocide and deaths incidental to combat? International wars are fought between states, whereas perpetrators of genocide rarely cross boundaries unless they occupy other countries. Most civilized states adhere to the rules of war, which proscribe the intentional killing of civilians during war. These principles rarely are applied fully, but the intent nonetheless is to avoid killing noncombatants.

During a nuclear war, the distinction between combat soldiers and civilians becomes irrelevant. The nature of total warfare changes the equation. Most nuclear strategists stress the irrationality of total war because it ensures mutually assured destruction. Few are willing to admit that nuclear weapons will ever be used in a "limited" war. Yet, strategies designed to knock out the opponent's nuclear arsenal may make massive civilian casualties unavoidable. Thus, some scholars see total war as a genocide because it is likely to result in the annihilation of a large percentage of the world's population. Nevertheless, nuclear war is not genocide.

Whether or not nuclear strikes are genocidal depends on the intent of those who order them. Limited and defensive uses of nuclear weapons are not inherently genocidal, even if they have the unwanted consequences of massive civilian deaths. This is not to say, however, that genocides cannot take place during a war.

Another type of war in which many civilian members of a specific national group are likely to be killed is guerrilla war. What are the differences between civilian victims of such a war and victims of genocide? Let's examine a worst-case scenario: a village woman carrying a child conceals a hand grenade, which she throws in the midst of a group of soldiers. Three are killed, and the woman and child are shot on the spot. If the officer in charge now orders the whole village demolished and the villagers killed, this is a massacre, a war crime. If such excesses become a regular occurrence with superiors doing little to prevent them, we have a case of criminal war: war crimes are committed and tolerated with regularity. If, however, the authorities order the killing of a whole group or class of people in a larger area because some of them are suspected of resistance, we have a genocide or politicide. In other words, we need to know who is killed, by whom, and with what intent. An example is the 1904–1906 genocide against the Hereros in southwest Africa. The German commander, Lothar von Trotha, said, to justify reprisals, "The nation as such must be annihilated or if this is not possible from a military standpoint, then they must be driven from the land."[5] Seldom do we have such clear-cut declarations of the intentions of perpetrators, but often there are other telling clues about their objective.

Such scenarios have been played out repeatedly in situations of guerrilla and revolutionary wars as well as by occupying forces in interstate wars. It is even more difficult to make distinctions in cases of civil war where there is no effective central authority, responsibility for order is in the hands of warring factions, and civilians are killed routinely as a strategy to weaken the opponent. Here we have to look closely at the speeches and declarations of those in charge of each faction to assess intent.

Finally, we need to consider the means by which a genocide is implemented. Have the means changed since enlightened people embarked upon efforts to break down the barriers of ignorance and prejudice? The lesson of the Holocaust tells a different story: medieval torture methods coexisted with the techno-death of millions. Unfortunately, neither the Holocaust nor the active efforts of international agencies—private and public—have eliminated extreme brutality, though they seem to have banished it to the fringes of the third world. Kampuchea is a case in point. I interviewed refugees in Thailand in 1981, who told me abhorrent tales of mayhem and murder with clubs and knives and of children ordered to kill their parents. The worst cases are little different from the barbarism of Timur Lenk, whose mountains of skulls were the legacy of a pillaging conqueror. Today's perpetrators are more likely to burn or bury the dead. Is it because they realize that they have committed a crime against humanity?

## Notes

1. Raphael Lemkin, *Axis Rule in Occupied Europe* (Washington, D.C.: Carnegie Endowment for International Peace, 1944).
2. Ted Robert Gurr and James R. Scarritt, "Minorities' Rights at Risk: A Global Survey," *Human Rights Quarterly* 11 (August 1989): 375–405.
3. Barbara Harff and Ted Robert Gurr, "Victims of the State: Genocides, Politicides and Group Repression since 1945," *International Review of Victimology* 1, no. 1 (1989): 23–41.
4. See Geoffrey Fairbairn, *Revolutionary Guerrilla Warfare: The Countryside Version* (Harmondsworth, Middlesex: Penguin Books, 1974).
5. Jon M. Bridgman, *The Revolt of the Hereros* (Berkeley and Los Angeles: University of California Press, 1981), 128.

# 3.4   William Schabas, "Crimes Against Humanity"

Crimes against humanity is a category of international crime usually associated with the related concepts of genocide and war crimes. Although international law contains several different definitions of crimes against humanity, they generally involve acts of physical violence or persecution committed against vulnerable groups of civilians. The Tel-Aviv District Court, in a 1952 judgment, said a crime against humanity "must be one of serious character and likely to embitter the life of a human person, to degrade him and cause him great physical or moral suffering." The United Nations (UN) Secretary-General has described them as "inhumane acts of a very serious nature."

Crimes against humanity are closely related to the crime of genocide, yet broader in scope, in that they encompass attacks on a wide range of civilian populations, whereas the crime of genocide is confined to national, ethnic, racial, or religious groups. Moreover, they do not require the physical destruction of the victims. Unlike war crimes, crimes against humanity may be committed in time of peace. It may be convenient to view crimes against humanity as being broadly analogous to serious violations of human rights. In the case of breaches of international human rights law, it is the state that is held responsible, whereas in the case of crimes against humanity, individuals are the perpetrators and they are the ones who are held criminally responsible. The consequence of a serious violation of human rights may be an order to cease the impugned act or to compensate the victim, whereas the consequence of a crime against humanity will generally be a significant term of imprisonment.

Because crimes against humanity are designated as an international crime, they are viewed as an exception to the general rule that it is the sovereign right of states to prosecute crimes committed within their own borders or by their own citizens. Crimes against humanity may be punished by courts of countries other than where the crime took place, and by international courts, such as the International Criminal Tribunals for the Former Yugoslavia (ICTY) and Rwanda (ICTR) or the International Criminal Court (ICC).

## History of the Term *Crimes Against Humanity*

Perhaps the first use of the expression *crimes against humanity* was by the French revolutionary Maximilien Robespierre, who described the deposed King Louis XVI as a *criminel envers l'humanité* (criminal against humanity). He argued that for this reason King Louis XVI should be executed, although Robespierre had earlier fought for the abolition of capital punishment in the French National Assembly. A century later journalist George Washington Williams wrote to the U.S. Secretary of State, informing him that King Leopold's regime in the Congo Free States was responsible for "crimes against humanity."

The preamble to the important Hague Conventions of 1899 and 1907, in what is known as the Martens clause, spoke of "the usages established between civilized nations, from the laws." But the concept of crimes against humanity in international law made its first formal appearance in the declaration made by the governments of France, Great Britain, and Russia, dated May 24, 1915, directed at the Turkish massacres of the minority Armenian population, that "[i]n the presence of these new crimes of Turkey against humanity and civilization, the allied Governments publicly inform the Sublime Porte that they will hold personally responsible for the said crimes all members of the Ottoman Government as well as those of its agents who are found to be involved in such massacres." The United States did not joint in the denunciation, with U.S. Secretary of State Robert Lansing explaining this by referring to what he called the "more or less justifiable" right of the Turkish government to deport the Armenians to the extent that they lived "within the zone of military operations."

After the war the victorious Allies attempted to prosecute Turkish officials for what were called "deportations and massacres" of the Armenians. The Turkish authorities actually arrested and detained scores of their leaders, later releasing many as a result of public demonstrations and other pressure. But Turkey refused to ratify the Treaty of Sèvres, signed on August 10, 1920, which imposed an obligation to surrender those who were deemed responsible for the persecutions of the Armenians. It also contemplated the establishment of a tribunal by the League of Nations with jurisdiction to punish those charged. The Treaty of Sèvres was eventually replaced by the Treaty of Lausanne of July 24, 1923. Rather than call for prosecution, it included a "declaration of amnesty" for all offenses committed between August 1, 1914, and November 20, 1922.

The essence of the controversy surrounding the Turkish prosecutions was whether or not atrocities, persecution, and deportations committed by a sovereign government against its own civilian population, including ethnic or national minorities established on its territory, should be subject to international law at all. As outrageous as the crimes against the Armenian minority were, the major victorious powers were nervous about a principle that might return to challenge their own treatment of vulnerable minorities within their own territories and especially their colonial empires. The debate resurfaced in the early 1940s, as work began to prepare the post-World War II Nazi prosecutions.

As early as 1943 the Allies proclaimed their intention to hold Nazi leaders accountable for war crimes. The United Nations War Crimes Commission was established to prepare the groundwork for postwar prosecutions. Meeting in London, it initially agreed to use the list of offenses that had been drafted by the Responsibilities Commission of the Paris Peace Conference in 1919 as the basis for its prosecutions. The enumeration consisted of a variety of war crimes, already recognized for the purposes of international prosecution, which had been agreed to by Italy and Japan and, at least, tacitly accepted without objection by Germany. These crimes addressed the means and methods of the conduct of warfare, and various acts of persecution committed against civilians in occupied territories.

Nevertheless, from an early stage in its work, efforts were made to extend the jurisdiction of the Commission to civilian atrocities committed against ethnic groups not only within occupied territories but also those within Germany itself. Serving on the Legal Committee of the Commission, the U.S. representative Herbert C. Pell used the term *crimes against humanity* to describe offenses "committed against stateless persons or against any persons because of their race or religion." But the idea that international criminal law extended to atrocities perpetrated against civilians by their own governments remained controversial, and there was ongoing resistance from the British and American governments because of the implications this might have for their own treatment of minorities. Jewish groups and other nongovernmental organizations (NGOs) lobbied members of the Commission to ensure that the postwar trials would not be confined to traditional war crimes, one of the first examples of the influence of NGOs and contributions to law-making in this area.

Within weeks of the end of the war in Europe, the four victorious major powers, the United Kingdom, France, the Soviet Union, and the United States, convened the London Conference, whose purpose was the organization of the postwar trials. In addition to war crimes, the draft treaty on which they worked included a category with as yet no generic name, which was labeled "atrocities, persecutions, and deportations on political, racial or religious grounds." As the Conference concluded, the U.S. delegate, Robert Jackson, suggested the category be given the title "crimes against humanity." Article VI of the Charter of the Nuremberg Tribunal, adopted by the London Conference on August 8, 1945, defined three categories of crimes over which the Tribunal would exercise jurisdiction: war crimes, crimes against peace, and crimes against humanity. Crimes against humanity were defined as follows:

> Murder, extermination, enslavement, deportation, and other inhumane acts committed against any civilian population, before or during the war, or persecutions on political, racial or religious grounds in execution of or in connection with any crime within the jurisdiction of the Tribunal, whether or not in violation of the domestic law of the court where perpetrated.

Crimes against humanity are comprised of two categories of specific punishable behavior. The first, such as murder, extermination, enslavement, and inhumane acts, correspond generally to crimes under virtually all domestic criminal law systems, and cover such offenses as killing, assault, rape, and kidnapping or forcible confinement. The second, persecutions on discriminatory grounds, run afoul of antidiscrimination laws in many countries but fall short of criminal behavior. What elevates these acts to crimes against humanity, as held by the courts, is their commission as part of a widespread or systematic attack on a civilian population, although this is not stated explicitly in the Nuremberg Tribunal's definition.

In late 1945, acting in their role as the occupying government of Germany, the Allies enacted criminal legislation that made crimes against humanity a crime within German law. Although similar to the Nuremberg Charter definition, it was somewhat broader:

> Atrocities and offenses, including but not limited to murder, extermination, enslavement, deportation, imprisonment, torture, rape, or other inhumane acts committed against any civilian population, or persecutions on political, racial or religious grounds whether or not in violation of the domestic laws of the country where perpetrated.

Known as Control Council Law No. 10, it extended to all atrocities and offenses. Moreover, unlike the Nuremberg Charter, it did not require that crimes against humanity be committed "in execution of or in connection with any crime within the jurisdiction of the Tribunal."

## Nexus with Aggressive War

The condition in the Nuremberg Charter that crimes against humanity be committed "in execution of or in connection with any crime within the jurisdiction of the Tribunal" is often referred to as the nexus. The Nuremberg Tribunal interpreted this phrase to mean that atrocities and persecution committed prior to the outbreak of the war, in September 1939, were not punishable as an international crime. It acknowledged that "political opponents were murdered in Germany before the war, and that many of them were kept in concentration camps in circumstances of great horror and cruelty. . . . The persecution of Jews during the same period is established beyond all doubt."

According to the judges at Nuremberg, to constitute a crime against humanity the acts had to be committed in pursuit of an aggressive war. This interpretation would appear to be consistent with what was intended by those who established the Nuremberg Tribunal. At the London Conference, the U.S. delegate, Jackson, spoke of "some regrettable circumstances at times in our own country in which minorities are unfairly treated," and of the concern of his government that such acts might now fall within the scope of crimes against humanity. The way to deal with his concern was to include, as an element of crimes against humanity, this nexus with aggressive war.

There was controversy about the nexus virtually from the day the Nuremberg judgment was issued. Frustrated by this limitation, other countries seized the occasion of the first session of the UN General Assembly to propose that the UN recognize and codify yet another international crime, to be named "genocide," that would not be confined to a link with aggressive war. The Convention on the Prevention and Punishment of the Crime of Genocide, adopted by the General Assembly on December 9, 1948, affirmed that genocide could be committed "in time of peace or in time of war" precisely in order to distinguish it from crimes against humanity. The price of this important concession was a definition of genocide that was confined to the destruction of a national, ethnic, racial, or religious group, in other words, to a much narrower class of atrocities than what was covered by the existing definition of crimes against humanity.

Over the years much debate and lingering uncertainty surrounded the link or nexus between crimes against humanity and aggressive war. In 1968 the Convention on the Non-Applicability of Statutory Limitations to War Crimes and Crimes Against Humanity referred to crimes against humanity "whether committed in time of war or in time of peace." Five years later the International Convention on the Suppression and Punishment of the Crime of Apartheid defined apartheid, which was clearly a practice not limited to wartime, as a crime against humanity. But confusion persisted when the Security Council, in establishing the ICTY in May 1993, reaffirmed that crimes against humanity should be punishable only when committed "in armed conflict." In the first major judgment of the ICTY, issued in October 1995, the Appeals Chamber dismissed the significance of these words, saying they were incompatible with customary international law. The issue was rather definitively resolved in 1998, in the Rome Statute of the ICC, which imposes no requirement of a nexus between crimes against humanity and aggressive war, although it does not explicitly state that crimes against humanity may be committed in time of peace as well as in time of war. Thus, for the future, little doubt can exist about this matter, although to the extent that there are prosecutions for crimes against humanity committed between 1945 and 1998, lawyers will continue to argue both sides of the question.

## Contextual Elements of Crimes Against Humanity

Because the punishable acts falling within the rubric of crimes against humanity are either punishable as ordinary crimes under national laws or, in the case of persecution-type acts, often not punishable at all, it is fundamental that crimes against humanity be committed within a context of widespread or systematic attacks on a civilian population. If there were no such limitation on the scope of crimes against humanity, states would never accept the right of the courts of other states, or of international tribunals, to prosecute such acts when committed on their own territory. In other words, it is only when murder, extermination, and persecution reach a threshold of great seriousness and broad scale that states are prepared to let down the curtain of sovereignty that traditionally gives them the sole right to criminalize behavior committed within their borders. These additional constraints on the definition of *crimes against humanity* lie at the core of the entire concept and are often referred to as the "contextual elements."

Crimes against humanity originally derived from a need to prosecute Nazis for acts committed against German nationals within Germany itself. Until 1945 international law clearly protected Jewish civilians within the occupied lands of Europe, such as Poland, Russia, Hungary, France, and the Netherlands, but the same could not be said of the German Jews. To some extent, the acts of persecution committed against the Germany Jews were legal under national legislation and even mandated by German laws. This explains the section of the Nuremberg Charter that states crimes against humanity were punishable "whether or not in violation of the domestic law of the court where perpetrated."

As a result, it may be said that crimes against humanity involve organized persecution that is either directed by a state and carried out in pursuance of laws, or tolerated by the state and tacitly condoned or encouraged. Although this is probably an accurate statement of the law in a historical sense, a marked evolution has occurred over the years to weaken the requirement of state policy or plan in the commission of crimes against humanity.

One authoritative body, the International Law Commission, stated in 1996 that crimes against humanity are inhumane acts "instigated or directed by a Government or by any organization or group." This matter was the subject of considerable debate when the Rome Statute of the ICC was being adopted in the 1990s. The Rome Statute's definition of *crimes against humanity* requires that they be committed as part of a "widespread or systematic attack on a civilian population," and that this attack be "pursuant to or in furtherance of a State or organizational policy to commit such attack." This definition is large enough to encompass what are sometimes called "non-State actors," and it certainly applies to statelike entities that exercise de facto control over a given territory and fulfill the functions of government.

It is somewhat less clear whether crimes against humanity may also be committed pursuant to a plan or policy of a terrorist organization, which operates without any formal link to a state and often with no obvious ambition to take power. The terrorist attacks of September 11, 2001, were described by many observers, including the United Nations High Commissioner for Human Rights, as crimes against humanity. But in extending the scope of crimes against humanity to terrorist organizations, it becomes increasingly difficult to distinguish them from ordinary crimes punishable under domestic law. While it may seem only logical and proportionate to describe acts such as those committed on September 11 as crimes against humanity, because of their sheer scale and horror, the choice of terminology is far less evident when the crimes are committed on a smaller scale. Indeed, if terrorist groups responsible for atrocities can be held accountable for crimes against humanity, why not organized crime families, motorcycle gangs, and individual serial killers? The distinctions become increasingly difficult to make once the context of a plan or policy of a state or statelike organization is removed from the definition of crimes against humanity. Yet this is precisely what the ICTY has done in its judgments subsequent to adoption of the Rome Statute, suggesting that it considers the Rome Statute requirements to be narrower than what should apply as a matter of customary international law.

The other factor serving to distinguish crimes against humanity as an international crime from ordinary crimes that fall within the scope of national laws is the element of discrimination. The definition in the Nuremberg Charter refers to "persecutions on political, racial or religious grounds," although it does not seem to make the same requirement with respect to other acts, such as murder and extermination. This aspect of crimes against humanity is even more explicit in the definition found in the ICTR Statute, adopted by the Security Council in November 1994:

> The International Tribunal for Rwanda shall have the power to prosecute persons responsible for the following crimes when committed as part of a widespread or systematic attack against any civilian population on *national, political, ethnic, racial or religious grounds.*

This requirement suggests that a racist or otherwise discriminatory motive must exist for the crime. Therefore, when a defendant charged with crimes against humanity can suggest that a widespread or systematic attack was conducted on grounds that did not involve racial discrimination and that the motive was, for example, to achieve a military victory, the act might not qualify as a crime against humanity. This argument might be submitted, for instance, to counter claims that the atomic bombing of Hiroshima and Nagasaki in August 1945 was a crime against humanity.

Recent case law from the ICTY and ICTR has established that a discriminatory motive is not generally an element of crimes against humanity. This is a relief to prosecutors, for whom proof of motive is a daunting challenge. Exceptionally, discriminatory motive remains an element of the crime against humanity of persecution. This is because persecution-type crimes against humanity may involve acts that are actually authorized by national laws, such as measures preventing intermarriage with persons from specific ethnic groups, as was the case in Nazi Germany.

## Punishable Acts

The lists of punishable acts of crimes against humanity are not the same in the various definitions of crimes against humanity. They have at their core the enumeration found in the Nuremberg Charter: murder, extermination, enslavement, deportation, other inhumane acts and persecution. The definition in Control Council Law No. 10, adopted in December 1945, added imprisonment, torture, and rape to the list. The definition was updated to take account of recent developments in international law when the Rome Statute of the ICC added apartheid and the forced disappearance of persons. But the Rome Conference rejected attempts to recognize other new acts of crimes against humanity, such as economic embargo, terrorism, and mass starvation.

The crime of murder is well defined in national legal systems and poses little difficulty within the context of crimes against humanity. Although there has been some disagreement about this in cases, it is now well established that the murder need not be premeditated.

Extermination as a crime against humanity refers to acts intended to bring about the death of a large number of victims. Evidence must exist that a particular population was targeted and that its members were killed or otherwise subjected to conditions of life calculated to bring about the destruction of a numerically significant part of the population.

Enslavement was widely practiced by the Nazis, who took hundreds of thousands of Jews, other minorities, and foreign nationals conscripted in various parts of their conquered territories, and forced them to work in factories making munitions and rockets and meeting other needs of their military machine. As the Nuremberg judgment pointed out, one of the perverse features of the Nazi slave labor policy was that "useless eaters"—the elderly and infirm, and the disabled—were systematically murdered precisely because they could not be enslaved. In the early twenty-first century international law recognizes various contemporary forms of slavery. The related practice of trafficking in persons, particularly women and children, is associated with modern crimes against humanity of slavery.

The act of deportation involves the forcible expulsion of populations across international borders. The Rome Statute of the ICC added the words "forcible transfer of population" to deportation, thereby recognizing in its condemnation what in recent years has been known as "ethnic cleansing," particularly when this has occurred within a country's own borders. It should be borne in mind that the Allies themselves following their victory in 1945, indulged in the forced transfer of ethnic Germans from parts of Eastern Europe. To this day some policy makers still entertain the suggestion that population transfer is an effective technique for dealing with ethnic conflict.

Imprisonment is, of course, a normal act of states carried out in the enforcement of criminal justice. For it to rise to the level of a crime against humanity, imprisonment must amount to the deprivation of physical liberty that is in violation of the fundamental rules of international law. Holding captured prisoners indefinitely, while denying them access to ordinary legal remedies, could fit within the parameters of this crime against humanity.

Torture was not explicitly listed in the Nuremberg Charter as a crime against humanity, although it clearly falls within the catch-all term *other inhumane acts*. A substantial body of international law now exists that addresses the issue of torture, including the UN Convention Against Torture and Other Cruel, Inhuman and Degrading Treatment or Punishment. According to the Rome Statute, *torture* means "the intentional infliction of severe pain or suffering, whether physical or mental, upon a person in the custody or under the control of the accused; except that torture shall not include pain or suffering arising only from, inherent in or incidental to, lawful sanctions." Human rights law requires that state officials perpetrate torture, but this is because human rights law governs the relationship between the individual and the state. In the case of crimes against humanity, there is no such requirement.

The most dramatic enlargement of the scope of crimes against humanity in recent years has taken place in the now very significant list of gender crimes that complement the more traditional reference to rape. In fact, the Nuremberg Charter did not even recognize rape as a form of crime against humanity, although it would have fallen under "other inhumane acts." In any event, the oversight was corrected some months later in Control Council Law No. 10. Building on the word *rape*, the 1998 Rome Statute enumerates several other related acts, namely "sexual slavery, enforced prostitution, forced pregnancy, enforced sterilization, or another form of sexual violence of comparable gravity." Forced pregnancy means the unlawful confinement of a woman forcibly made pregnant, with the intent of affecting the ethnic composition of any population or carrying out other grave violations of international law.

The crime of apartheid was first defined to describe the racist regime in South Africa during much of the second half of the twentieth century. According to the Rome Statute, it refers to inhumane acts "of a character similar to" other crimes against humanity, when "committed in the context of an institutionalized regime of systematic oppression and domination by one racial group over any other racial group or groups and committed with the intention of maintaining that regime." Here, then, the involvement of a state in the commission of crimes against humanity is quite explicit.

Enforced disappearance of persons is a phenomenon that became widespread under repressive regimes in Latin America during the 1970s and 1980s. It was first recognized as a crime against humanity by the General Assembly in a 1992 resolution. In the ICC's Rome Statute, the term refers to the

> Arrest, detention or abduction of persons by, or with the authorization, support or acquiescence of, a State or a political organization, followed by a refusal to acknowledge that deprivation of freedom or to give information on the fate or whereabouts of those persons, with the intention of removing them from the protection of the law for a prolonged period of time.

Most of the lists of crimes against humanity conclude with the term *other inhumane acts*. Its scope is quite obviously vague, and for this reason some national attempts to introduce crimes against humanity have eliminated the reference. Even judges of international criminal tribunals have indicated their discomfort with applying criminal law whose meaning is not sufficiently certain. Reflecting these concerns, the Rome Statute declares that such "other inhumane acts" must not only be similar to those in the list of acts qualifying as crimes against humanity, but must also intentionally cause great suffering, or serious injury to body or to mental or physical health.

Finally, the crime against humanity of persecution comprises acts that are motivated by discrimination against an identifiable group. In the Nuremberg Charter, discrimination was limited to political, racial, or religious grounds, but more recent definitions, such as that of the Rome Statute, enlarge the concept to include nationality, ethnicity, culture, and gender as prohibited forms of discrimination. Moreover, they also extend the definition to "other grounds that are universally recognized as impermissible under international law," thereby allowing for the further evolution of this concept. Perhaps sometime in the near future, it will be unquestioned that the crime against humanity of persecution may also be committed against the disabled, or against persons identified by their sexual orientation.

The case law of international criminal tribunals provides several examples of the crime against humanity of persecution: in general, destruction of property or means of subsistence, destruction and damage of religious or educational institutions, unlawful detention of civilians, harassment, humiliation and psychological abuse, violations of political, social and economic rights violations. At the same time, these tribunals have rejected the argument that acts such as encouraging and promoting hatred on political grounds, or dismissing and removing members of a specific ethnic group from government, amount to persecution.

## Statutory Limitations

Many legal systems provide that after a certain period of time has expired, offenses may no longer be prosecuted. This is known as statutory limitation or, sometimes, "prescription." It reflects a number of concerns, including the fact that with the passage of time prosecution becomes much more difficult because of the unavailability of witnesses and other evidence, as well as the interest of the state in prompt repression of crime, in order to deter the individual offender as well as others. Although these concerns may be relevant for many crimes, they are highly questionable in the context of the seriousness and horror of international crimes.

In the 1960s, when it appeared that some Nazi war criminals who had not yet been caught and prosecuted might escape justice, international law was extended to prohibit statutory limitations for crimes against humanity as well as war crimes. Countries whose laws contained statutory limitations were required to make amendments. Before an international criminal tribunal, no defendant can invoke the passage of time as a defense to a charge. This is stated explicitly in the Rome Statute of the ICC.

There are many examples of prosecutions of persons alleged to be responsible for crimes against humanity many decades after the acts transpired. In the late 1990s French courts convicted Maurice Papon for atrocities committed in occupied France during World War II. Papon was almost ninety years old at the time, but he was found guilty and sentenced to a term of imprisonment.

## Prosecution of Crimes Against Humanity

The first prosecutions for crimes against humanity were held at the Nuremberg Tribunal. Most of the leading Nazi defendants were convicted of crimes against humanity, as well as other crimes punishable by the Tribunal. One of the defendants, Julius Streicher, was convicted only of crimes against humanity. He was executed for his role as propagandist in the Nazi persecution of Jews within Germany.

Crimes against humanity were also very much part of the prosecution at the other international tribunal, in Tokyo, and in a range of other postwar trials held by national military tribunals. After the late 1940s no international prosecutions for crimes against humanity occurred until the establishment of the ICTY and ICTR in 1993 and 1994, respectively.

Many national legal systems have introduced the concept of crimes against humanity into their own criminal legislation. Although neither required nor authorized by any international treaties, these jurisdictions have established that prosecution for crimes against humanity may be conducted even if the crime was committed outside the territory of the state and by a noncitizen. Although this principle of "universal jurisdiction" is increasingly recognized in national laws, it is in practice used rather rarely. Two such important trials were held in Israel: those of former Nazi mastermind Adolf Eichmann and John Demjanjuk, purported to have been a sadistic guard at the Treblinka death camp. In the late 1980s Canada prosecuted a Hungarian Nazi official, Imre Finta, for crimes against humanity committed forty-five years earlier. Of these three prosecutions, two led to acquittals. The difficulties in prosecuting crimes committed elsewhere, and usually many years earlier, pose great challenges to national justice systems and largely explain the reluctance to use the principle of universal jurisdiction on a large scale.

## Distinguishing Genocide and Crimes Against Humanity

Two categories of international crime, genocide and crimes against humanity, both emerged in the 1940s as a response to the Nazi atrocities committed before and during World War II. Nervous about the implications that a broad concept of crimes against humanity might have for their own administrations, the great powers confined crimes against humanity to acts committed in the context of aggressive war. Unhappy with such a restriction, other states pushed for recognition of a cognate, genocide, which would require no such connection with armed conflict. As a result, for many decades, in their efforts to condemn and prosecute atrocities, international human rights lawyers attempted to rely on genocide rather than the considerably broader notion of crimes against humanity out of concerns that the acts were perpetrated in peacetime.

The nexus between crimes against humanity and aggressive war no longer exists. As a result, aside from some minor and insignificant technical distinctions, all acts of genocide are subsumed within the definition of crimes against humanity. Genocide can be usefully viewed as the most extreme form of crimes against humanity. The ad hoc tribunals for the former Yugoslavia and Rwanda have christened it "the crime of crimes." But if the distinction is no longer particularly consequential with respect to criminal prosecution, it remains important because there is no real equivalent to the Genocide Convention for crimes against humanity, The Genocide Convention imposes obligations on states to prevent the commission of genocide. It might be argued that this duty also exists with respect to crimes against humanity. However, the Convention, in addition, recognizes the jurisdiction of the International Court of Justice (ICJ) to adjudicate disputes between states with respect to their treaty obligations concerning genocide, and several such lawsuits have in fact been filed. No similar right to litigate crimes against humanity before the ICJ exists.

### Bibliography

Cherif Bassiouni, M. (1999). *Crimes Against Humanity*, 2nd edition. Dordrecht, Netherlands: Kluwer.

Clark, Roger S. (1990). "Crimes Against Humanity at Nuremberg." In *The Nuremberg Trial and International Law*, ed. G. Ginsburgs and V. N. Kudriavstsev. Dordrecht, Netherlands: Martinus Nijhoff.

Robinson, Darryl (1999). "Defining 'Crimes Against Humanity' at the Rome Conference." *American Journal of International Law* 93:43.

Schwelb, Egon (1946). "Crimes Against Humanity," *British Yearbook of International Law* 23:178.

# 3.5   Jacques Semelin, "Massacres"

The term *massacre* can be defined as a form of action, usually collective, aimed at the elimination of civilians or non-combatants including men, women, children or elderly people unable to defend themselves. The definition may also include the killing of soldiers who have been disarmed. One of the most notorious European examples of the latter was when Soviet troops massacred Polish officers in Katyn in February 1940. There are various definitional problems inherent in the notion of "massacre." For instance, there are divergent interpretations between adversaries, such as can be seen in the Israeli-Palestinian dispute over the tragic events at Jenin in April 2002. The Palestinians labeled the event a massacre, a charge that Israel denied. The Palestinian charge was further undercut by a report from the Secretary General of the United Nations, which challenged the Palestinian claim of hundreds of dead, substituting instead the much lower estimate of about fifty-five. This brings up an additional problem regarding the determination of a massacre based on victim tallies. After the Guatemalan Civil War, a UN commission conducting an inquiry on human rights violations stated that a massacre implies at least three murders, while certain experts consider this number to be "very low."

## Debates Surrounding the Notion

Another debate surrounds the practices attached to the term *massacre*. Etymologically, the word derives from the popular Latin *matteuca*, meaning "bludgeon." The word contains the sense of butchery, designating both the abattoir and the butcher's shop. In Europe from the eleventh century on, *massacre* became synonymous with the putting to death both of animals and human beings. Massacre has historically presupposed a situation where the perpetrator and his victim are face-to-face, since it is based on the practice of slitting the throat—the technique used to slaughter animals for market. This technique was used in massacres such as the civil wars fought in Algeria or Greece. However, if the concept of massacre implies a type of one-on-one interaction, must we conclude that technologies of murder exercised from a distance cannot be considered massacres? What then of the modern technique of air bombing? If we retain such a limited definition, we ignore the evolution of the technologies of war and the political motivation of the practice. Military forces that employ air strikes to create a climate of terror in order to force a town or country to surrender exemplify this phenomenon. In that regard, it makes sense to distinguish between local massacres (face-to-face encounters) and long-distance massacres (aerial bombings).

The connection between war and massacres poses another problem, because it is easy to assume that massacres only happen within the context of war. However various historical examples show that massacres can be perpetrated in relatively peaceful times. For instance, in Nazi Germany the Crystal Night (*Kristallnacht*) pogrom against the Jewish community took place on November 9, 1938), and in Indonesia, an even larger massacre was directed against all suspected communist partisans from October 1965 to June 1966. It is also possible to consider famine as a type of slow, "soft" massacre. If we do, we can cite the Ukraine famine that was essentially willed by Stalin from 1932 to 1933. Nevertheless, the context of war can without a doubt generate various practices of massacre, since war provokes a radical social polarization into the dialectic pair "friend vs. foe."

A massacre can then be one of several types. It can be integrated into the act of war when it is an extension of war. Such was the case of the massacre at Oradoursur-Glane in France by a division of the SS on June 10, 1944. In this massacre, the military killed the whole population of this village just to intimidate the so-called terrorists in the area. Alternatively, a massacre can be deeply associated with the objectives of a war. Thus, for example, when a nationalistic power wants to force a given population to flee, one of the most efficient means is to massacre this population. As a result, the flow of refugees generated by this killing is not the consequence of the war but is, rather, its very goal. This was the case in the ethnic cleansing operations within the former Yugoslavia during the 1990s. Finally, a massacre may be quasi-autonomous with regard to war. This happens when practices of massacre tend to be detached from the battlefield and grow on their own. One such case is the genocide of European Jews during the Holocaust. The logic of war seemed to contrast with the logic of massacre in this instance. Indeed, soldiers or trains were employed to destroy civilian populations instead of being deployed on the front, where they could be more useful from a military standpoint.

This leads to another problem: how can we differentiate between the notions of massacre and genocide? Some authors do not make any distinction between the two, and even go so far as to include within the concepts such industrial catastrophes as the Chernobyl nuclear disaster in 1986. Other experts consider it crucial to distinguish between the notions of massacre and genocide. These experts believe the term *massacre* refers to the deliberate but unsustained killing of unarmed human beings within a relatively short period of time and in a relatively small geographic area. According to this definition, neither the Saint Bartholomew massacre in France (August 24, 1572) that was perpetrated by Catholics against important members of the Protestant community; the Kishinev pogrom in Russia (April 19–20, 1903), when Moldavian Christians killed dozens of Jews in the city; nor the Amritsar massacre in Punjab (April 13, 1919), perpetrated by British general Reginald Dyer against Indian demonstrators, can be considered genocides. Nevertheless, sometimes a variety of massacres tend to evolve in a genocidal process, in which case certain authors use the expression "genocidal massacre." One of the key issues in genocide studies is to explain why and how this particular framework of violence can pass—slowly or suddenly—from massacre to genocide. The answer to this question presupposes developing our understanding of the logics of massacre operations.

## Delusional Rationality

When a massacre is committed and is made known by the press, journalists are inclined to stress its apparent irrationality. Why attack children, women, and the elderly? Details of atrocities are also given in such reports. The appalling aspects of massacres must not, however, prevent us from examining the question of the perpetrators' rationale, their operating techniques, their objectives, and their perceptions of the enemy. Beyond the horror, it must be acknowledged that they are pursuing very specific aims, which may include amassing wealth, controlling territory, gaining power, destabilizing a political system, or other goals.

Envisaging the notion of massacre thus means attempting to understand both its rationality and its irrationality. This means taking into account the human capacity for both cold calculation and folly, in sum, for delusional rationality. The term *delusional* relates to two mental phenomena. The first is psychosis. In this context, the psychotic element of the aggressor's behavior toward the victim or victims stems from the belief that the victim can and must be destroyed. The aggressor in effect denies the humanity of the victims, perceiving them as "other," as "barbarians."

However, *delusional* can also signify a paranoid image of this "other" (the victim) who is perceived as constituting a threat or even as the embodiment of evil. The particularity and dangerousness of a paranoid syndrome and the conviction that one is dealing with an evildoer are so strong that they create the risk of acting out against the perceived enemy. In a massacre, the "good vs. evil" and "friend vs. foe" binary polarization is at its peak, as is also true in war. Massacre is therefore always compatible with war and, if there is no actual war, it is experienced as an act of war.

Hence massacres are not irrational in the eyes of those who perpetrate them, because they are part of one or more dynamics of war. In this respect, those who commit massacres attribute specific political or strategic aims to them. These aims can, however, change with the course of the action, the international context, the victims' reactions, or other variables. The diversity of historical situations in which massacres occur leads us to distinguish between at least two fundamental types of objectives linked to the processes of partial and even total destruction of a community: its subjugation and its eradication.

## Destruction in Order to Subjugate

The aim here is to bring about the death of civilians with a view to partially destroying a community in order to subjugate what remains of it. The destruction process is partial by definition, but it is intended to have an impact on the total community because those responsible for the deed rely on the effect of terror in order to impose their political domination on the survivors. The act of massacre is particularly suited to such a strategy. The slaughter need not be wholesale; it only has to become widely known so that its terrorizing effect spreads throughout the population.

Since the dawn of time, this form of massacre has been associated with warfare. The civilian destruction-and-subjugation dynamic can in fact be fully incorporated within a military operation to precipitate an adversary's surrender, speed up the conquest of its territory, and facilitate the subjugation of its people. Massacres can be found in most wars, both ancient to modern, and not merely as excesses of war but as part of its actual dimensions. However, such types of destruction sometimes turn "mad." This occurred during the Japanese invasion of China, when Japanese soldiers, apparently free to pursue their will, raped, slaughtered, and pillaged the Chinese people of Nanking for six weeks from December 1937 to January 1938. What could have been justified as an awful but rational practice of war by some realist strategists became completely irrational in this case, particularly due to the impunity of the invading soldiers.

Such destruction-and-subjugation methods can also be found in contemporary civil warfare, where the distinction is no longer made between combatants and non-combatants. Even if the women and children of a village are unarmed, they can be suspected of supporting enemy forces by furnishing them with supplies. They therefore become potential targets that must be destroyed. Many examples of this phenomenon can be found in certain past conflicts (e.g., Lebanon, Vietnam, Guatemala, and Sierra Leone) or in ongoing conflicts (e.g., Colombia and Algeria).

These destruction-and-subjugation practices can also extend to the ways in which people are governed. A war of conquest, which may have been conducted by massacre, might give way to the economic exploitation of the conquered population, with further recourse to the murder of some of its members if necessary. That was the essential attitude of the Conquistadors toward Native Americans, whom they perceived as worthless beings existing to do their (Spanish) masters' bidding. History offers other political variants of the shift of the destruction-and-subjugation strategy from a means of warfare to a tool of governance. In this instance, Clausewitz's formula ("War is the continuation of politics by other means") could be reversed. Instead, politics becomes the means of pursuing war against civilians.

Those who win a civil war are logically drawn into this power-building dynamic, as illustrated to some extent by the example of revolutionary France. There, the "*Colones infernales*" slaughtered large segments of the Vendean population in 1793. The Bolsheviks in Lenin's Russia after 1917 and the Khmers Rouges in Pol Pot's Cambodia (1975–1978) illustrate this phenomenon even more radically than the case of the French Revolution. The perpetration of extreme violence that builds up in the course of a civil war tends to be transferred to a power-building phase.

Whether in the case of civil wars or not, this process dates back a long time. Torture and killing to "set an example" constitute one of the standard techniques of the tyrant seeking to quash an internal rebellion. A more recent example was the tactic of hostage execution employed in Europe by the Nazis, who executed one hundred civilians for every German killed in a bid to overcome armed resistance groups. Sometimes dictatorial powers do not hesitate to kill nonviolent demonstrators, as the racist South African regime did in Sharspeville on March 21, 1960 against black opponents. In this case the massacre was committed in order to deter any kind of resistance. Other regimes developed more sophisticated techniques, such as the "disappearance" method implemented by various Latin American dictatorships in the 1970s.

## Destroy in Order to Eradicate

The destruction-and-eradication dynamic is quite different. Its aim is not the actual subjugation of a populace, but rather the utter elimination of a fairly extensive community. This involves "cleansing" or "purifying" the area where the targeted group (which is deemed undesirable or dangerous) is present. This concept of *eradication* is particularly relevant here because the word's etymology conveys the idea of "severing roots" or "removing from the earth," in short "uprooting," as one would root out a harmful weed.

This identity-based process of destruction and eradication can also be connected with wars of conquest. The massacre process, combined with rape and pillage, is the means by which one group makes its intentions clear and consequently hastens the departure of another group, either because that group is deemed undesirable or because it occupies territory that the attacking group wants for its own use. The partial destruction of the victimized group and the resulting terror bring about and accelerate such departure. This was the practice employed by European settlers in North America against Native American peoples, who were driven further and further west, beyond the Mississippi River. In the Balkans, the forced movement of populations from a territory has been termed *ethnic cleansing*, in particular to describe the operations conducted mainly by Serbia and Croatia in the early 1990s. However the methods used (e.g., slaughtering people, burning villages, and destroying religious buildings) can be linked to earlier practices in that region. Since at least the nineteenth century, similar practices occurred in the context of the rise of nationalism and the decline of the Ottoman Empire.

These practices of massacre aimed at chasing away undesirable populations are genuinely universal. Regimes often used militias to do their work. These militias could usually rely on the support of conventional armed forces, however, even though the latter might prefer to remain in the background. One example of this situation is the Sabra and Shatila massacre in Lebanon (September 18, 1982), in which more than 1,000 Palestinians were killed by the Christian Lebanese militia with the support of the Israeli army. The goal was to terrorize the Palestinians and chase them out of Lebanon. This episode can be related to massacres that were perpetrated in 1948 by Israel in an attempt to chase Palestinians out of the territory claimed by the newly formed Israeli state. Numerous other such examples can also be found dating to the eighteenth century, when state building began to imply a homogeneous population. Achieving this homogeneity entailed the forced departure of populations that did not share in the same cultural, ethnic, or religious heritage. If war makes the State to the same extent as the State makes war, as historian Charles Tilly put it, the same could be said of massacres.

Once again, the processes at work in warfare can be reemployed in terms of the internal governance of a destroyed people. This is the case across the spectrum of ethnic and religious nationalistic conflicts, which include the riots between Muslims and Hindus in India since at least the late 1940s. Generally speaking, these types of conflicts involve the instrumental use of ethnic or religious criteria for the purposes of a group's political domination over an entire community. Recourse to killing is justified by the appeal to homogeneity in order to resolve a seemingly insoluble problem.

This process can, however, take on an even more radical form, such as the total elimination of a targeted community whose members are not even given the chance to flee. In such circumstances, the aim is to capture all of the individuals belonging to the targeted community, with the goal of eradicating them. The notion of a territory to be cleansed becomes secondary to the idea of actual extermination. Some colonial massacres were probably perpetrated with this in mind, such as the slaughter of the Herero population in 1904 by the German colonial army in Namibia. We still know far too little about colonial massacres, including those perpetrated by England, France, and Belgium in their conquest of African territories in the nineteenth and early twentieth centuries.

The leaders of Nazi Germany went further than any others in the planned total destruction of a community. Their systematic extermination of European Jews between 1941 and 1945, which followed the partial elimination of mentally sick Germans, is the prototypical example of this eradication process taken to the extreme. In very different historical contexts, the same can be said of the extermination of the Armenians within the Ottoman Empire in 1915 and 1916, and that of the Rwandan Tutsis in 1994. In each of these cases, the objective was not to scatter a people across other territories, but rather, in the words of Hannah Arendt, "to cause it to disappear not just from *its* own land, but from *the* land."

It is at this final stage of the eradication process that the concept of genocide can be introduced as a notion in social science. In general, the public at large sees genocide as a form of large-scale massacre. In the popular view, whenever the death toll reaches several hundred thousand, it becomes possible to refer to a genocide. This kind of intuitive criteria, based on a large number of victims, is not, however, adequate to describe genocidal behavior. Moreover, no expert could effectively set a minimum number of deaths as the necessary criterion for declaring that genocide has occurred. A qualitative criterion *combined* with a quantitative criterion, however, could offer a more reliable definition of genocide. For instance, most experts would agree that widespread killing combined with the implicit or express desire for the total eradication of a community qualifies for the label of "genocide."

Genocide thus fits within the same destructivity continuum as ethnic cleansing, but is essentially distinguishable from it. Their respective dynamics are both aimed at eradication; however, in the case of ethnic cleansing the departure or flight of the targeted population is still possible, whereas in the case of genocide, escape is futile or impossible. In this regard, genocide can be defined as the process of specific civilian destruction directed at the total eradication of a community, for which the perpetrator determines the criteria.

However, such reasoning is necessarily further complicated by the fact that the destruction-and-subjugation and destruction-for-eradication processes can coexist and even overlap within the same historical situation by targeting different groups. In general, one is the dominant process and the other is secondary. In 1994, Rwanda saw the attempted eradication of the Tutsi population (which can therefore be classified as a genocide) occurring simultaneously with the killing of Hutu opponents of the government (which constitutes a destruction-and-subjugation process. Conversely, the mass killing in Cambodia clearly constituted a destruction-and-subjugation process because Pol Pot never sought to destroy all the Khmers, but that process included certain eradication offensives directed at specific groups, particularly the Cham Muslim minority. Identifying these different dynamics of violence is often a very complex task, because they may not only overlap, but also change over time, shifting, for example, from subjugation to eradication.

# Part II

Theories and Causes of Genocide

# 4

# Theories of Genocide

One of the major problems associated with applying the term genocide to an event or cluster of events relates not only to how genocide may be defined, but also to which groups should be included. Article 2 of the 1948 United Nations Convention on the Prevention and Punishment of the Crime of Genocide (UNCG) states the following: "Genocide means any of the following acts committed with intent to destroy, in whole or in part, a national, ethnical, racial or religious group, as such:

- (a) Killing members of the group;
- (b) Causing serious bodily or mental harm to members of the group;
- (c) Deliberately inflicting on the group conditions of life calculated to bring about its physical destruction in whole or in part;
- (d) Imposing measures intended to prevent births within the group;
- (e) Forcibly transferring children of the group to another group.

The two main groups omitted from the above are political and social groups, an omission that was the result of compromise between the states developing the UNCG in the post-World War II years, leading up to the final version of the document settled on by the UN General Assembly. (Other groups were also not addressed, for example, sexual and sexual preference groups.) Much scholarly debate has taken place since 1948 over the UNCG definition of genocide: in certain cases, in an attempt to clarify what the world community understands by genocide, and in other cases, to expand the definition of genocide in order to provide protection to a greater number of groups.

The enormous range and variety of outbreaks throughout history that have been termed genocide have led to a multiplicity of theories attempting to explain it as a human phenomenon. From the time the word was first coined in 1944 by Raphael Lemkin, the development of genocide as a field of scholarly study has emerged. For many, theorizing about the nature of genocide has become a major intellectual activity; for others, doing so is irrelevant other than to acknowledge that it is a crime (for some, the crime of crimes), and that as such little theorizing is needed beyond the legislation that has established its criminality—that is, the UNCG.

As the field of genocide studies becomes more sophisticated and gains ever-increasing attention from scholars from a wide array of backgrounds and experiences, theories of genocide not only grow in number but in breadth of approach (e.g., cultural, economic, environmental, historical, ideological, political, social). This is true of any vibrant field; and in light of that, one can readily assume that over the next fifty or more years the theories are bound to grow in number and, hopefully, become more useful in both the study and the prevention of genocide.

To this day, though, and unfortunately, theorizing about genocide often gets muddied —versus gaining clarity—from so-called "definitional debates" over what exactly constitutes genocide. Even those who adhere to the "legal definition" of genocide—that found in the United Nations Convention on the Prevention and Punishment of the Crime of Genocide (UNCG)—get caught up in splitting fine hairs that often result in vehement disagreement, if not acrimonious debate.

In light of these ongoing and heated debates, it is not surprising that various scholars have coined new concepts and terms in an attempt to describe events that either appear to verge or actually verge on constituting genocide but are not protected under the the the UNCG. Among such terms and concepts are autogenocide, democide, ethnocide, gendercide, libricide, politicide, and omnicide. Some of the terms have become widely accepted (which is certainly the case with regard, for example, to the concept of politicide) while some have engendered great debate over their value (e.g., autogenocide and gendercide). In light of the fact that the field of genocide studies is still in its infancy, it is highly likely that additional terms and concepts will be created in the future.

Among various governments, moreover, there has been added confusion. The terminology of the UNCG states that "The Contracting Parties confirm that genocide, whether committed in time of peace or in time of war, is a crime under international law which they undertake to prevent and to punish," though what this undertaking obliges states to do has not yet been put to the test. Hence, although some states may recognize or deem an act to be genocide, there is, more often than not, little to no concrete follow-up.

Genocide has become such a popular term that it is now used by many (everyone from educators to social activists and from journalists to the so-called common man and woman on the street) who wish to emphasize the seriousness of an event or incident. The result sees a constant misuse of the term. Ironically, such overuse (and even, all too frequently, abuse) contributes to watering down the effectiveness of the correct usage of the term/concept.

Even those who believe they are using the term correctly but have not done so contribute to conceptual confusion. For example, human rights violations that are serious in their own right (e.g., ethnic cleansing short of mass murder) but are incorrectly deemed genocide also result in the blurring of facts, concepts and, ultimately, real understanding.

So what are the activities in which theorists of genocide engage? What can be termed justifiable scholarly discussion? As one example of many, we can take the issue of what has become known as "multiple genocide:" that is, the targeting of a number of victim groups simultaneously during the course of genocide taking place. It has been concluded by some psychoanalysts that once the psychological limit or awe surrounding the killing of large numbers of human beings has been broken, it is easier to kill again. It is the first genocide that is the hardest for regimes to condition their populations to commit, just as it is for a regime itself to get to that position. Once there, however, both governments and peoples can make the jump from killing one population to targeting and killing another. Hence, those committing genocides can develop a disposition for murderous destruction beyond their initial brief, once they realize they are capable of carrying out acts they might otherwise not normally have considered possible. The notion of "multiple genocide" is therefore the kind of issue with which theorists of genocide wrestle. They seek to learn of the inspirations, impulses, justifications, and techniques employed by those committing genocide; to ascertain, in short, what drives génocidaires to engage in activities leading to the destruction of entire groups of people.

This is precisely the interest of Ervin Staub, whose article, "The Origins of Genocide and Mass Killing: Core Concepts," seeks to ascertain the origins of genocide within the human psyche—and, just as importantly, the social psyche. Genocide, in his view, is a phenomenon that is carried out as a social activity. Why, he wants to know, do some people become killers, while others remain bystanders? What motivations drive certain societies toward genocide, and how are those motivations given practical form?

Perhaps, when it comes right down to it, the truth lies with the *choices* governments and individuals make; because, when all is said and done, genocide is a policy option that is consciously chosen from a number of alternatives. It does not have a life of its own; it must be adopted as a course of action *consciously*. This is one of the matters that concerns Barbara Harff, in her essay entitled "The Etiology of Genocides." The fundamental issue she tries to address relates to how genocides are caused—indeed, the very issue of why some situations develop into genocide while others do not. Through the use of historical case studies, Harff shows that genocide can take place when a change, or attempted change, to the existing structure of power within a society is "justified" by the perpetrator through the identification of a group from which real or perceived opponents will emerge. While it is true that not all revolutionary regimes will try to intentionally destroy a group, some do; being able to identify where (and why) this is the case, Harff suggests, is an important step on the road to genocide prevention—though, all too frequently, reasons have been given by international organizations for why preventive action cannot be taken, rather than why it can.

It could be suggested, therefore, that a way is needed to convince the nations of the world that genocide prevention is in their own self-interest. This would seem to be uppermost in the thinking of Roger W. Smith, who argues in "Scarcity and Genocide" that in the future it will be scarcity that will serve as one of the handmaidens of genocide. Competition for fresh water, food, agricultural land, fuel, resources, and living areas will, as Smith points out, likely result in human, social, and political catastrophes in the future from which few will be immune. While a doomsday scenario such as this might be challenged by some, a consensus is nonetheless forming that suggests that Smith may be right. Where government is concerned, Smith contends, ways can and must be found in which cooperation will take place to find solutions to the problems generated by scarcity. The most important of these, in his view, is for governments to redefine the concept of national interest in such a way that genocide prevention forms a necessary part of that designation.

Finally, genocide scholar Gregory Stanton has attempted to both summarize and codify much earlier theorizing through the creation of a taxonomy of genocide classification. In "The Eight Stages of Genocide," Stanton lists a number of progressive steps that lead to genocide. While in his view they build upon each other, they are not inexorable; at each stage, he argues, preventive measures can be introduced to prevent its progress to the next.

# 4.1   Ervin Staub, "The Origins of Genocide and Mass Killing: Core Concepts"

I believe that tragically human beings have the capacity to come to experience killing other people as nothing extraordinary. Some perpetrators may feel sick and disgusted when killing large numbers of people, as they might feel in slaughtering animals, but even they will proceed to kill for a "good" reason, for a "higher" cause. How do they come to this? In essence, difficult life conditions and certain cultural characteristics may generate psychological processes and motives that lead a group to turn against another group. The perpetrators change, as individuals and as a group, as they progress along a continuum of destruction that ends in genocide. The behavior of bystanders can inhibit or facilitate this evolution.[*]

# A Conception of the Origins of Genocide and Mass Killing

## Difficult Life Conditions

Human beings often face hard times as individuals or as members of a group. Sometimes a whole society or substantial and potentially influential segments of society face serious problems that have a powerful impact and result in powerful motivations.

Economic conditions at the extreme can result in starvation or threat to life. Less extreme economic problems can result in prolonged deprivation, deterioration of material well-being, or at least the frustration of expectations for improved well-being. Hostility and violence threaten and endanger life, whether political violence between internal groups or war with an external enemy. Political violence threatens the security even of people who are uninvolved. Widespread criminal violence also threatens life and security. War threatens the life of at least some individuals and affects many aspects of the life of a society. Rapid changes in culture and society—for example, rapid technological change and the attendant changes in work and social customs—also have the psychological impact of difficult life conditions. They overturn set patterns of life and lead to disorganization.

The meaning assigned to life problems, the intensity of their impact, and the way groups of people try to deal with them are greatly affected by the characteristics of cultures and social organizations. By themselves, difficult life conditions will not lead to genocide. They carry the potential, the motive force; culture and social organization determine whether the potential is realized by giving rise to devaluation and hostility toward a subgroup (or a nation).

Difficulties of life vary in nature, magnitude, persistence, and the accompanying disorganization and chaos in society. As a result, the impact also varies: the threat may be to life, to security, to well-being, to self-concept, or to world view. In all four cases I discuss, political violence, civil war, or external war was involved. Political violence may create a new political system that changes traditional ways of life and values; this has the impact of difficult life conditions. The new system can further cultural and social characteristics that contribute to genocide. In all four cases I will examine, changes in political systems preceded genocides and mass killings by less than a decade.

One important cultural characteristic is the rigidity or the adaptability of a society. Monolithic societies, with a limited set of acceptable values and ways of life, may be more disturbed by change. For example, the disruptive changes in technology, ways of life, and values under the shah probably contributed to the intensity of Islamic fundamentalism in Iran. Rigidity and flexibility partly depend on societal self-concept, the way a group and its members define themselves. Greater rigidity makes the difficulties of life more stressful.

## Psychological Consequences: Needs and Goals

Difficult life conditions give rise to powerful needs and goals demanding satisfaction. People need to cope with the psychological effects of difficult life conditions, the more so when they cannot change the conditions or alleviate the physical effects. Hard times make people feel threatened and frustrated.[†] Threats to the physical self are important, but so are threats to the psychological self. All human beings strive for a coherent and positive self-concept, a self-definition that provides continuity and guides one's life. Difficult conditions threaten the self-concept as people cannot care for themselves and their families or control the circumstances of their lives.

Powerful self-protective motives then arise: the motive to defend the physical self (one's life and safety) and the motive to defend the psychological self (one's self-concept, values, and ways of life). There is a need both to protect self-esteem and to protect values and traditions. There is also a need to elevate a diminished self.

Disruption in customary ways of life, the resulting chaos, and changing mores can profoundly threaten people's assumptions about the world and their comprehension of reality.

Because understanding the world is essential, people will be powerfully motivated to seek a new world view and gain a renewed comprehension of reality. Without such comprehension life is filled with uncertainty and anxiety.

When their group is functioning poorly and not providing protection and well-being, people's respect for and valuing of the group diminish; their societal self-concept is harmed. Because people define themselves to a significant degree by their membership in a group, for most people a positive view of their group is essential to individual self-esteem—especially in difficult times. The need to protect and improve societal self-concept or to find a new group to identify with will be powerful.

Persistent difficulties of life also disrupt the relationships among members of the group. They disrupt human connections. People focus on their own needs, compete with others for material goods, and feel endangered by others. The need for connection, enhanced by suffering, will be powerful.

These psychological reactions and motivations are natural and often adaptive. People are energized by a sense of personal value and significance, connection to other people, the feeling of mutual support, and a view of the world that generates hope. However, when these motivations are very intense and fulfilled in certain ways, they become likely origins of destruction.

Threats and frustrations give rise to hostility and the desire to harm others. The appropriate targets of this hostility are, of course, the people who caused the problems, but usually they cannot be identified. Often no one is to blame; the causes are complex and impersonal. At other times those responsible are too powerful, or they are leaders with whom people identify too much to focus their hostility on them. The hostility is therefore displaced and directed toward substitute targets. Hostility is especially likely to arise if people regard their suffering as unjust, as they often do, and especially if some others are not similarly affected.

### Ways of Coping and Fulfilling Needs and Goals

Constructive actions have beneficial, practical effects and also help a person cope with the psychological consequences of life conditions. Unfortunately, it is often difficult to find and to follow a practically beneficial course of action. When this is the case, it is easy for psychological processes to occur that lead people to turn against others. The psychological needs must be controlled, or satisfied in other ways. People must unite without creating a shared enemy or an ideology that identifies enemies. Wisdom, vision, the capacity to gain trust, and effective institutions are needed to strike out on a constructive course of action.

Certain ways of seeing and evaluating events and people require no physical action (and any actions that follow from them usually do not change life conditions), but they help people satisfy at least the psychological needs and goals that arise from difficult life conditions. Some of these internal processes are basic psychological tendencies common to all human beings: differentiation of ingroup and outgroup, "us" and "them"; devaluation of those defined as members of an outgroup; just-world thinking, which is the tendency to believe that people who suffer, especially already devalued, must deserve their suffering as a result of their deeds or their characters; and scapegoating, or blaming others for one's problems. Individuals differ in such psychological tendencies depending on their socialization and experience and resulting personality; societies differ depending on their history and the resulting culture.

Blaming others, scapegoating, diminishes our own responsibility. By pointing to a cause of the problems, it offers understanding, which, although false, has great psychological usefulness. It promises a solution to problems by action against the scapegoat. And it allows people to feel connected as they join to scapegoat others. Devaluation of a subgroup helps to raise low self-esteem. Adopting an ideology provides a new world view and a vision of a better society that gives hope. Joining a group enables people to give up a burdensome self, adopt a new social identity, and gain a connection to other people. This requires action, but it is frequently not constructive action.

Often all these tendencies work together. The groups that are attractive in hard times often provide an ideological blueprint for a better world and an enemy who must be destroyed to fulfill the ideology. Sometimes having a scapegoat is the glue in the formation of the group. But even if the ideology does not begin by identifying an enemy, one is likely to appear when fulfillment of the ideological program proves difficult. Thus these psychological tendencies have violent potentials. They can bring to power a violent group with a violent ideology, as in Germany, or shape an ideology, as they probably did in the case of the Pol Pot group that led the Khmer Rouge to genocide in Cambodia.

## The Continum of Destruction

Genocide and mass killing do not directly arise from difficult life conditions and their psychological effects. There is a progression along a continuum of destruction. People learn and change by doing, by participation, as a consequence of their own actions. Small, seemingly insignificant acts can involve a person with a destructive system: for example, accepting benefits provided by the system or even using a required greeting, such as "Heil Hitler." Initial acts that cause limited harm result in psychological changes that make further destructive actions possible. Victims are further devalued; for example, just-world thinking may lead people to believe that suffering is deserved. Perpetrators change and become more able and willing to act against victims. In the end people develop powerful commitment to genocide or to an ideology that supports it.

Deeply ingrained, socially developed feelings of responsibility for others' welfare and inhibitions against killing are gradually lost. Often the leaders assume responsibility, and accountability is further diminished by compartmentalization of functions and the denial of reality. The most terrible human capacity is that of profoundly devaluing others who are merely different. Often there is a reversal of morality, and killing them comes to be seen as good, right, and desirable. In the course of all this, new group norms evolve, and institutions are established in the service of genocide or mass killing. The progression may occur in a short time, although often intense devaluation has already developed by the time those who become the perpetrators of genocide appear on the scene.

Some people become perpetrators as a result of their personality; they are "self-selected" or selected by their society for the role. But even they evolve along the continuum of destruction. Others who were initially bystanders become involved with the destructive system and become perpetrators. Even bystanders who do not become perpetrators, if they passively observe as innocent people are victimized, will come to devalue the victims and justify their own passivity.

There are usually some people whose values or other personal characteristics make them oppose the treatment of the victims. Most such people, if they are to remain opposed, need support from others. With that support, some may come to resist the killing or the system that perpetrates it. Small initial acts can start a progression on a continuum that leads them to heroic resistance and to risking their lives to help the victims.

## Cultural-Societal Characteristics

The characteristics of one's culture and society determine not only the consequences of difficult life conditions and the choice of avenues to satisfy needs, but also whether reactions to initial acts of mistreatment occur that might inhibit further steps along the continuum of destruction. Most cultures have some predisposing characteristics for group violence, and certain cultures possess a constant potential for it. Also, when life problems are more intense, a weaker pattern of cultural-societal preconditions will make group violence probable.

The cultural self-concept of a people greatly influences the need to protect the collective psychological self. A sense of superiority, of being better than others and having the right to rule over them, intensifies this need. Collective self-doubt is another motivation for psychological self-defense. When a sense of superiority combines with an underlying (and often unacknowledged) self-doubt, their contribution to the potential for genocide and mass killing can be especially high.

Nationalism arises partly from this combination of superiority and self-doubt. One form of nationalism is the desire to enlarge the nation's territory or to extend the influence of its values and belief system. Another form is the desire for purity or "cleansing." Nationalism is often strengthened under the influence of difficult life conditions. Strong nationalism sometimes originates in the experiences of shared trauma, suffering, and humiliation, which are sources of self-doubt.[1]

Societal values can embody a positive or negative evaluation of human beings and human well-being. But even in societies that do value human welfare, an outgroup may be excluded from the moral domain.

"Us"–"them" differentiation is a basic human potential for which we even carry "genetic building blocks". It is one source of cultural devaluation. Negative stereotypes and negative images of a group can become deeply ingrained in a culture. The needs I have described are often fulfilled by turning against such a "preselected" group. Its members are scapegoated and identified as the enemy of the dominant group's well-being, safety, and even survival, or as an obstacle to the realization of its ideological blueprint.

Strong respect for authority and strong inclination to obedience are other predisposing characteristics for mass killing and genocide. They make it more likely that responsibility will be relinquished and leaders will be followed unquestioningly. People who have always been led by strong authorities are often unable to stand on their own in difficult times. Their intense need for support will incline them to give themselves over to a group and its leaders.

A monolithic, in contrast to a pluralistic, culture or society is another important precondition. In a monolithic culture there is limited variation in values and perspectives on life. In a monolithic society strong authority or totalitarian rule enforces uniformity. The authorities have great power to define reality and shape the people's perception of the victims. Societies with strong respect for authority also tend to be monolithic, and this combination makes adjustment to social change especially difficult.

In a pluralistic society with varied conceptions of reality and greater individual self-reliance, people will find it easier to change and gain new perspectives and accept new customs and mores. Reactions against initial harmful acts are more likely to occur and to inhibit the progression along the continuum of destruction.

As I have noted, an ideology with a destructive potential can become a guiding force, overriding contrary elements in culture or society. However, an ideology has to fit the culture if it is to be adopted by the people.

Partly but not entirely as a result of the above characteristics, societies vary in aggressiveness. Some have a long history of violence: aggression has become an accepted mode of dealing with conflict, even valued and idealized. Institutions that serve as the machinery for destruction may already exist.

Even more important than the current tendencies of a society is its deep structure. In the late nineteenth century, France might have seemed as likely as Germany to turn on the Jews. Anti-Semitism, as expressed in the Dreyfus affair, was widespread and racial ideologies attracted sympathetic interest. But the deep structure of anti-Semitism was stronger in Germany; for example, the medieval persecution of Jews was especially intense and cruel there.[2] There was also a long authoritarian tradition, as opposed to the celebration of individual freedom and rights by the French Revolution.[3] A deeply embedded anti-Semitism joined with other cultural characteristics and with difficult life conditions to create the conditions for genocide.

Why was there no Holocaust in Russia, where anti-Semitism was intense, the government was despotic, and life conditions near the end of World War I were difficult? Normally, there are a number of potential enemies. The Soviet leaders had an ideology that identified the wealthy as the enemy. This built on deep-seated class divisions in society. The ideology justified violence for the sake of the better world that the Communist Party and the new state were going to create. Eventually, it too led to the deaths of many millions under Stalin.

## The Role of Bystanders

Another important factor is the role of bystanders, those members of society who are neither perpetrators nor victims, or outside individuals, organizations, and nations. In most societies there are some who are prepared to turn against other groups. It is the population as a whole that provides or denies support for this. The people's support, opposition, or indifference largely shapes the course of events.[‡] Opposition from bystanders, whether based on moral or other grounds, can change the perspective of perpetrators and other bystanders, especially if the bystanders act at an early point on the continuum of destruction. They may cause the perpetrators to question the morality of their violent acts or become concerned about the consequences for themselves. Internal opposition from bystanders may require great courage. Other nations are often passive, even though attempts to exert influence may require little courage or real sacrifice from them.

## The Role of Motivation

My conception of the origins of genocides and mass killings (see Table 1) is based on a theory of motivation and action, *personal goal theory*, that I have developed in other publications.[4] According to this theory, both individual human beings and cultures possess a hierarchy of motives. Individuals and cultures do not always act on their most important motives. Circumstances can activate motives lower in the hierarchy. For example, the need for self-defense and the need for connection to other people can be important or relatively unimportant motives. The lower a motive is in an individual's or culture's hierarchy, the more extreme the life conditions needed to make it active and dominant.

Whether a motive is expressed in behavior depends on the skills and competencies of individuals, or on the social institutions. Even the intention to commit genocide cannot fully evolve without a machinery of destruction. Personal goal theory describes how individuals and cultures select goals to actively pursue and suggests ways to determine when it is likely that they will act to fulfill them.

This is a probabilistic conception. The combination of difficult life conditions and certain cultural preconditions makes it probable that motives will arise that turn a group against another. This combination makes it probable that initial acts of harm-doing will be followed by further steps along the continuum of destruction. The behavior of bystanders can faciliate or inhibit this progression. Genocide arises from a pattern, or gestalt, rather than from any single source.

The outcome of this evolution and the immediate cause of the genocide is that perpetrators come to believe either that the victims have something they want or (more likely) stand in the way of something they want. In Germany the victims threatened an imagined racial purity and superiority and stood in the way of the nation's (and humanity's) improvement. In Turkey the victims seemed to threaten a pure national identity and a return to past greatness. In Cambodia the victims were seen as class enemies or judged incapable of helping to create a particular type of communist society. In Argentina the victims were seen as threatening national security, a way of life, and religious ideals, as well as the perpetrators' own safety.

## Leadership and Followership

The genocide of the Jews could hardly have occurred without Hitler, but that does not mean the accident of his presence was responsible. There will always be individuals with extreme

*Table 1* The origins and motivational sources of mistreatment

| Environmental and cultural origins[a] → | Motivational consequences | Psychological and behavioral means of fulfilling motives |
|---|---|---|
| **A. Difficult life conditions** Economic problems (inflation, depression, etc.); political, criminal, or other widespread violence, including war; rapid changes in technology, social institutions, values, ways of life; social disorganization. ↓ Experience of attack on or threat to life, physical safety, material well-being; to the fulfillment of goals and expectations; to the psychological self, ways of life, and values; to world view and comprehension of reality | 1. Retaliation and harmdoing (hostile aggression) 2. Defense of the physical self 3. Motivation to overcome obstacles, to fulfill expectations and goals 4. Defense or elevation of psychological self (self-concept, values, ways of life); desire to relinquish burdensome identity 5. Desire for a feeling of efficacy, control, power | Mistreatment, aggression Escape, nonaggressive self-defense, aggression; submission or giving up Instrumental aggression, constructive (individual and/or communal) actions[b] Devaluating, scapegoating; diminishing others by mistreatment or aggression; giving up self to new group or leader; adopting an ideology; acting constructively for change Same as no. 4 |
| **B. Cultural and personal preconditions** Self-concept, goals and aims, value orientations; ingroup–outgroup differentiation, devaluation; orientation to authority; monolithic (vs. pluralistic) culture; emerging ideology; cultural aggressiveness; and others | 6. Motivation to protect and elevate social identity (societal self-concept) 7. Motivation to gain renewed comprehension of the world and of the self in the world | Protecting and elevating one's group, partly by diminishing other groups; adopting new group; see also means listed under no. 4. Adopting ideology; joining new group; acting to elevate and protect old group |
| **C. Societal-political organization** Authoritarian or totalitarian system; social institutions discriminating (vs. promoting harmony, cooperation, and altruism); institutions capable of carrying out mistreatment | 8. Motivation to regain hope 9. Need for feeling connected to other human beings 10. Obedience to authority | Giving up self to new group or leader; adopting an ideology; acting constructively for change Joining group; promoting joint cause; creating strong ingroup by scapegoating; creating an experience of threat to the group Submission to authority, an agentic state |

*a* The difficult life conditions, cultural and personal characteristics (preconditions), and organization of society shown in column one join to create the motives listed in column two. Especially the last two components also influence the methods employed (shown in column three) to fulfill these motives.

*b* Other results can be giving up or succumbing to feelings of hopelessness and depression.

views, radical ideologies, and the willingness to use violence who offer themselves as leaders. Cultural preconditions, combined with difficult life conditions, make it probable that they will be heard and accepted as leaders. Hitler's ideology and mode of leadership fitted important characteristics of German culture, tradition, and society.

Leaders also vary in personal characteristics, charisma, organizational ability, and the like. But even here culture has a role. Non-Germans always had trouble comprehending

Hitler's personal appeal.[5] Leadership is crucial to move people and give them direction, but it is a transactional process, a relationship between group and leader. Because of shared culture, what a leader offers often naturally fulfills cultural requirements. Leaders also intentionally adjust their style and vision to the group. Hitler's authoritarian leadership was effective in Germany (in the United States, for example, appeal to individualism seems required of a leader).

If difficult life conditions persist and the existing leadership and societal institutions do not help people cope at least with the psychological effects, the people are likely to turn to radical leadership. In general, our capacity to predict what kinds of leaders emerge and where they lead is limited. However, conditions conducive to genocide and mass killing are likely to give rise to the kind of leadership that plans and promotes these acts. If Hitler had not existed, Germans would probably still have directed violence against some subgroup or nation; the environmental and cultural preconditions were both present. But even in Germany, leaders might conceivably have emerged who provided more peaceful and coopera-tive solutions. Conversely, if Hitler had lived in a country with fewer of the cultural precondi-tions for genocide, he would have been much less likely to gain power. And if the society were not facing severe life problems, his capacity to influence would have been further reduced.

## The Individual and the System

Genocide is usually organized and executed by those in power, by a government or ruling elite. Governments will commit genocide if the way of thinking and motivations out of which genocide evolves are already consistent with the culture or if they become so under the influence of the government. What is the relationship between the characteristics of indi-viduals and those of the system to which they belong? What is the relative contribution of each to cruelty (or kindness)?

Human beings have genetic propensities for both altruism and aggression. Which of these propensities evolves more depends on individual socialization and experience. A child in a family that is highly aggressive and antisocial will usually grow up aggressive and antisocial. In a family that prohibits the expression of anger (or joy) children will learn that it is wrong to express and even to feel anger (or joy).

Effective socialization of the young will create individuals whose personal values and conduct accord with those of the system. It is unlikely that Roman soldiers who killed enemies defeated in battle experienced remorse: their socialization and experience made killing defeated enemies and enslaving women and children normal operating procedures. In some societies violence against people seen as outsiders is a way of life. We do not assume that members of such a society should have resisted a way of life integral to their social-cultural system. We do not blame individual Mundurucú headhunters, because being a Mundurucú male meant being a headhunter.[6] When a long cultural continuity of this type exists, which creates synchrony between the characteristics of the individual and the group, the social organization, not the individual, is responsible. In the modern world, however, even violence-prone societies or subsystems of societies, such as the Argentine military, usually also hold and transmit moral and social values that prohibit violence. This creates individual responsibility. Usually person and system each carry a share of the responsibility.

Socialization and experience in most modern societies result in a wide range of personal characteristics, so there will be people whose values, sympathies, self-interest, and current needs suit a violent and inhumane system and others who are opposed to such a system. The degree of opposition and conformity to a new social order depends on the nature of the preceding society. But human malleability continues through life. People not initially involved in creating the new system often undergo *resocialization*. This can be slow or fast and may affect a smaller or larger segment of the population. The speed and amount of change depend on the degree to which the original culture and therefore personal characteristics are at variance with the new system, how effective the new system is at resocialization, and the magnitude of life problems and resulting needs.

When we ask how people could do this, we must not judge only by universal moral standards that represent our ideals but must also appreciate how people are influenced by systems. Ultimately, we must ask how to create cultures and social systems that minimize harm-doing and promote human welfare, in part by how they shape individuals.

## The Roots of Evil

*Evil* is not a scientific concept with an agreed meaning, but the idea of evil is part of a broadly shared human cultural heritage. The essence of evil is the destruction of human beings. This includes not only killing but the creation of conditions that materially or psychologically destroy or diminish people's dignity, happiness, and capacity to fulfill basic material needs.

By evil I mean *actions* that have such consequences. We cannot judge evil by conscious intentions, because psychological distortions tend to hide even from the perpetrators themselves their true intentions. They are unaware, for example, of their own unconscious hostility or that they are scapegoating others. Frequently, their intention is to create a "better world," but in the course of doing so they disregard the welfare and destroy the lives of human beings. Perpetrators of evil often intend to make people suffer but see their actions as necessary or serving a higher good. In addition, people tend to hide their negative intentions from others and justify negative actions by higher ideals or the victims' evil nature.

Most of us would not regard it as evil to kill to defend one's own life or the life of one's family, or to protect others' lives. In contrast, most of us would regard terrorist violence against civilians (who are not responsible for the suffering of either the terrorists or those whose interests they claim to represent) as evil.

But any kind of group violence has evil potential. It is rarely directed only at people who cause suffering. Its aim is rarely just to protect people or alleviate their suffering. And its intensity and the circle of its victims tend to increase over time, as our discussion of genocide and mass killing will show. This is also evident in the history of torture. In the Middle Ages, when torture was part of the legal system, the circle of victims expanded over time. Starting with low-status members of society accused of a crime, progressively higher-status defendants and then witnesses were tortured in order to extract evidence from them.[7]

Ordinary psychological processes and normal, common human motivations and certain basic but not inevitable tendencies in human thought and feeling (such as the devaluation of others) are the primary sources of evil. Frequently, the perpetrators' own insecurity and suffering cause them to turn against others and begin a process of increasing destructiveness.

But the same needs and motivations that cause evil can be fulfilled, and probably more completely, by joining others. This may be a more advanced level of functioning, requiring more prior individual and cultural evolution toward caring and connection. The tendency to pull together as an ingroup and turn against an outgroup is probably more basic or primitive. Threats and stress tend to evoke more primitive functioning.

There are alternative views of the roots of evil, of course. Some believe that because power and self-interest are strong human motives, human beings are basically unconcerned about others' welfare and will therefore do anything to satisfy their own interests. Thomas Hobbes developed this view most fully, and Freud's thinking is congenial to it.

According to Hobbes, people must be controlled externally, by society and the state, to prevent them from harming others in fulfilling their own interests. According to Freud they must acquire a conscience through socialization, which then controls them from within. However, assumptions about human nature cover a wide range. Some regard humans as basically good but corrupted by society (Rousseau). Others regard them as good but capable of being shaped by experience with parents and other significant people in such a way that they become unloving and unconcerned about others (the psychologist Carl Rogers).

Human beings have varied genetic potentials, and the way they develop is profoundly shaped by experience. Human infants have a strong genetic propensity to develop powerful emotional attachment to their primary caretakers. However, the quality of attachment varies greatly. One widely used classification system differentiates between infants who are "securely attached" (who are secure and comfortable in their relationship to caretakers), those whose attachment is anxious/conflictful, and those whose attachment is avoidant.[8] Infants with secure attachment to their parents or caregivers develop more successful relationships with peers in preschool and early school years.[9]

Moreover, the behavior of the caretaker seems to powerfully affect the quality of attachment. Greater responsiveness to the infant's needs, more eye contact, and more touching and holding are associated with secure attachment.[10] While the infant's own temperament and actions are likely to influence—evoke or diminish—such caretaking behaviors, their principal determinant is the caretaker. Once a certain quality of attachment appears, it is still changeable. More or less stress in the life of the mother can change the quality of the infant's attachment, presumably because the mother's behavior changes.[11]

We have the potential to be either altruistic or aggressive. Security, the fulfillment of basic needs, the propagation of one's genes, and satisfaction in life can be ensured as much by connection to other people as by wealth and power. But feelings of connection to many or all human beings require a reasonably secure and trustworthy world or society.

Differences in socialization and experience result in different personal characteristics, psychological processes, and modes of behavior. Some people develop dispositions that make them more likely to act violently and do harm, especially in response to threat. At the extreme, the desire to diminish, harm, and destroy others can become a persistent characteristic of a person (or group). People may also learn to be highly differentiated, good in relation to some while evil in relation to other humans.

## Groups as Evil or Good

Reinhold Niebuhr regarded human beings as capable of goodness and morality, but considered groups to be inherently selfish and uncaring.[12] It is a prevalent view that nation-states are only concerned with power and self-interest. Only fear prevents them from disregarding human consequences in pursuing power and self-interest.

I see evil in groups as similar, though not identical, to evil in individuals. It arises from ordinary motivations and psychological processes. Like individuals, groups can develop characteristics that create a great and persistent potential for evil. But they can also develop values, institutions, and practices that promote caring and connection.

Moral constraints are less powerful in groups than in individuals. Groups are traditionally seen as serving the interests of their members and the group as a whole, without moral constraints or moral obligations to others. There is a diffusion of responsibility in groups.[13] Members often relinquish authority and guidance to the group and its leaders. They abandon themselves to the group and develop a commitment that enables them to sacrifice even their lives for it.[14] This can lead to altruistic self-sacrifice or to joining those who turn against another group. Combined with the group's power to repress dissent, abandoning the self enhances the potential for evil.

But in both individuals and groups the organization of characteristics and psychological processes is not static but dynamic. As a result, very rarely are either evil or good immutable.

Influences acting on persons and groups can change their thoughts, feelings, motivations, and actions.

The more predisposing characteristics a society possesses and the more it progresses along the continuum of destruction—the more the motivation for genocide and the associated institutions and practices develop—the less potential there is to influence the society peacefully. Here my view converges with that of Hobbes: there is a point at which only inducing fear by the use of power will stop perpetrators from destruction. At times not even that will work, because fanaticism overcomes the desire for self-preservation. Single individuals with a strong potential for evil might be checked by the social group. But who is to inhibit groups? Powerful nations or the community of nations have not customarily assumed this responsibility, perhaps because of the tradition that nations are not morally responsible.

## Notes

\* *Psychological processes* include the thoughts and feelings of individuals, the meanings they perceive in events. *Culture* includes the thoughts, feelings, and ways of perceiving and evaluating events and people shared by members of a group—the shared meanings. Specific aspects of culture are shared rules, norms, values, customs, and life-styles. Culture is coded, maintained, and expressed in the "products" of a group: its literature, art, rituals, the contents of its mass media, and the behavior of its members. A result of shared culture is similarity in psychological reactions to culturally relevant events. *Society*, as I use the term, means the institutions and organizations of the group. These express the culture, embodying shared meanings that guide the life of the group. Thus, while devaluation of a group is a cultural characteristic, discrimination is embodied in social institutions such as schools or a military that segregates members of a group or uses them only for labor and does not give them weapons (as was the case with the Armenians in Turkey before the genocide). Society also includes political organizations and institutions. Occasionally culture and social organization can be discrepant, as when a repressive dictatorial system emerges in a democratic culture. But a truly great discrepancy of this kind is probably rare. In both Germany and the Soviet Union, the two great totalitarian states, the culture supported authoritarian rule or at least made it acceptable.

† I will several motivational concepts, some in part interchangeably. *Motivation* designates an active psychological state that makes an outcome or end desirable, whether eating to diminish hunger or killing to feel powerful or avenge real or imagined harm. A *motive* is a characteristic of the individual or culture out of which active motivation arises. There are different kinds of motives. *Needs* are more intense and have a more imperative quality. They push an organism to action, either because they are required for survival or because they are essential to the wholeness and functioning of an individual or culture. *Goals* have desired outcomes that are self-enhancing and are sources of satisfaction. The more deeply a goal (acquisition of wealth, writing a great book, making a contribution to humanity) comes to be an important aspect of self-definition, the more imperative it becomes. Essential, unfilled goals thus become needlike in character. I will sometimes use the word *aim* to designate the outcomes that individuals desire as a result of the active motivation arising from their needs and characteristic (personal) goals.

  Frustration is an emotion that results from interference with fulfilling a motive or from the failure to fulfill it. The emotional consequences are greater when the motive is more important. Difficult life conditions often frustrate basic goals, and needs.

‡ In 1985, during the trials of the Argentine military leaders for their role in the disappearances, many voices expressed dismay about the silence in Argentina at the time of the disappearances—a silence that expressed not just fear but acceptance.

1. Berlin, I. (1979). Nationalism: Past neglect and present power. *Partisan Review, 46.* Mack, J. (1983). Nationalism and the self. *Psychohistory Review, 2,* nos. 2–3, 47–69.

2. Dimont, M. I. (1962). *Jews, God and history.* New York: New American Library. Po-chia Hsia, R. (1988). The myth of ritual murder: Jews and magic in Reformation Germany. New Haven: Yale University Press.

3. Craig, G. A. (1982). *The Germans.* New York: New American Library.

4.  Staub, E. (1978). *Positive social behavior and morality.* Vol. 1, *Social and personal influences.* New York: Academic Press.

Idem. (1980). Social and prosocial behavior: Personal and situational influences and their interactions. In E. Staub (Ed.), *Personality: Basic aspects and current research.* Englewood Cliffs, N.J.: Prentice-Hall.

Idem. (1984). Steps toward a comprehensive theory of moral conduct: Goal orientation, social behavior, kindness and cruelty. In J. L. Gewirtz & W. M. Kurtines (Eds.), *Morality, moral behavior, and moral development.* New York: Wiley-Interscience.

Idem. (1986). A conception of the determinants and development of altruism and aggression: Motives, the self, and the environment. In C. Zahn-Waxler, E. M. Cummings, & R. Iannotti (Eds.), *Altruism and aggression: Social and biological origins.* New York: Cambridge University Press.

Idem. (Forthcoming). *Social behavior and moral conduct: A personal goal theory account of altruism and aggression.* Century Series. Englewood Cliffs, N. J.: Prentice-Hall.

5.  Craig, *The Germans.*

6.  Wilson, E. O. (1978). *On human nature.* New York: Bantam Books.

7.  Peters, E. (1985). *Torture.* New York & Oxford: Basil Blackwell.

8.  Ainsworth, M. D. S. (1979). Infant-mother attachment. *American Psychologist, 34,* 932–7.

9.  Sroufe, L. A. (1979). The coherence of individual development: Early care, attachment and subsequent developmental issues. *American Psychologist, 34,* 834–42.

Bertherton, I., & Waters, E. (Eds.). (1985). *Growing points of attachment theory and research.* Monographs of the Society of Research in Child Development, vol. 34, nos. 1–2. Chicago: University of Chicago Press.

10.  Bertherton and Waters, *Growing points.*

Shaffer, D. R. (1979). *Social and personality development.* Monterey, Calif: Brooks-Cole.

11.  Sroufe, Coherence of individual development.

12.  Niebuhr, R. [1932] (1960). *Moral man and immoral society: A study in ethics and politics.* Reprint. New York: Charles Scribner's Sons.

13.  There is much evidence for this from the observation of group behavior, and there is also evidence from psychological research:

Wallach, M. A., Kogan, N., & Bem, D. J. (1962). Group influences on individual risk taking. *Journal of Abnormal and Social Psychology, 65,* 75–86.

Latane, B., & Darley, J. M. (1970). *The unresponsive bystander: Why doesn't he help?* New York: Appleton Century Crofts.

Mynatt, C., & Sherman, S. J. (1975). Responsibility attribution in groups and individuals: A direct test of the diffusion of responsibility hypothesis. *Journal of Personality and Social Psychology, 32,* 1111–18.

14.  Campbell, D. T. (1965). Ethnocentric and other altruistic motives. In D. Levine (Ed.), *Nebraska symposium on motivation.* Lincoln: University of Nebraska Press.

# 4.2   Barbara Harff, "The Etiology of Genocides"

One of the most enduring and abhorrent problems of the world is genocide, which is neither particular to a specific race, class, or nation, nor rooted in any one ethnocentric view of the world. Genocide concerns and potentially affects all people. Some people have found refuge in the idea that the Holocaust was particular to the inhuman Nazis. Thus, all barbarous activities perpetrated by these subhumans had to be judged by different standards. However, evidence suggests that the many who participated in the extermination of a people were not sadistically inclined.[1] Israel Charny argues that in many societies "traditions of humanitarian concerns for victims" coincide with "the role of killer . . . or of accomplice to other more vicious genociders."[2] Often democratic institutions are cited as safeguards against mass excesses. In view of the treatment of Amerindians by agents of the U.S. government, this view is unwarranted. For example, the thousands of Cherokees who died during the Trail of Tears

(Cherokee Indians were forced to march in 1838–1839 from Appalachia to Oklahoma) testify that even a democratic system may turn against its people.

It is tempting to exaggerate the role of individuals, to blame leaders for leading their citizens to genocide. But is it not the case that citizens and leaders are able to make choices? Although powerful elites in a democratic society are able to inject their political preferences into the democratic process, sometimes not consistent with the preferences endorsed by the majority, that likelihood is far greater in a totalitarian system. But the capabilities for implementing ruthless decisions are always hampered or aided by the decisions made in countless bureaucracies. Thus, all people associated with the decision-making process lend their own motives, rationalization, and legitimation to the genocidal outcome. Although most of these people are not directly involved in executing their victims, their ability to halt the process makes them equally responsible for the executions. Clearly, the decision to destroy a certain people is a product of the many involved, and although some decisionmakers are more important than others, the role of the "helpers" surely facilitates the larger choice which delivers others to death.

Throughout the course of history genocides or massacres have been directed against specific groups in the context of larger political aims. Thus, the Nazis' aim of eliminating "foreign" elements from within by targeting Jews, Gypsies, Communists, and the mentally handicapped for annihilation was advanced by stressing mystical qualities of the dominant group. Similarly, the Turkification efforts, aided by the cry for "holy war" of the Young Turks, may have led to the destruction of the Armenians. A more recent example is Kampuchea, where under the leadership of Pol Pot all potential political adversaries were eliminated, which included the children of those perceived as reactionary elements. Though some massacres could be explained as acts of violence in the course of widespread mass hysteria, most genocides are devoid of the emotional climate which is conductive to a compulsion to murder those who are perceived as enemies of the dominant interests. In contrast, murderous leaders are voted into office, are allowed to propagate their pathological ideas, and often have ample time to plan and meticulously execute genocidal policies. What environment allows for organized officially sanctioned violence? What enables individuals to shed their responsibilities and become part of the murderous machine? In the absence of that passion which sometimes kills, how do "normal" people become vicious killers of children, old and infirm people, and the many others who have died in the genocides of modern times?

The following analysis investigates the conditions under which some genocides have taken place. The theoretical framework is provided by the author's previous efforts to shed light on why states engage in genocide.[3]

## Assumptions and Propositions

Scholarly persuasion has it that the state is the ultimate obstacle to a just world order, while others see ideological identity or class solidarity as the one true path to that envisioned order. Some attempts to overcome these predominant modes of analysis in international relations, such as the Club of Rome's "doom project," have met with criticism and sometimes ridicule. It is not my purpose to assess in detail the ecologists' realists', or Marxists' contribution to the analysis of international relations. Instead, this modest effort attempts to incorporate various elements of different modes of analysis into a framework which allows for an assessment of why past genocides have occurred and why future ones will occur. Ecological challenges and the international security dilemma have greatly contributed to the erosion of the state as the central actor in the world. In contrast, the durability of the state is demonstrated through its expanding role in providing social services to its citizens. The often conflicting roles of the state as provider and entrepreneur have sometimes led to increased elite domination internally or increased military/economic adventurism abroad.[4] Here elite domination refers to people who hold the controlling positions in the state structure; in other words, they are the political elite. Under exceptional circumstances this elite domination may lead to genocide. The following identifies the conditions conducive to the occurrence of genocide in national societies. National societies are those coincidental with the emergence of the modern state system during the early seventeenth century. This does not mean that genocides are confined to modern times. But "historical" genocides are of lesser importance to my argument, which claims that the "legitimate" authority structure, i.e., the state, is the predominant culprit in genocides.

One of the emphases of my theoretical argument is on structural change as exemplified in the concept of national upheaval. National upheaval is an abrupt change in the political community, caused, for example, by the formation of a state through violent conflict, when national boundaries are reformed, or after a war is lost. Thus, lost wars and the resultant battered national pride sometimes lead to genocide against groups perceived as enemies. Post-colonial and post-revolutionary regimes are prone to internal violence during times of national consolidation, when competing groups/tribes fight for leadership positions.

Structural change is a necessary but not sufficient condition to promote the likelihood of genocide. A second factor leading to the development of genocide is the existence of sharp internal cleavages combined with a history of struggle between groups prior to the upheaval. The stronger the identification within competing groups the more likely that extreme measures will be taken to suppress the weaker groups. Polarization is usually intensified by such factors as the extent of differences in religion, values, and traditions between contending groups, and their ideological separation. There are numerous examples from past genocides in which group polarization provided the background to genocides. Gentiles versus Jews, Muslims versus Hindus, Fascists versus Communists, Germans versus Gypsies, whites against blacks and Indians—such are the genocides of Nazi Germany, Bangladesh, Uganda, German Southwest Africa, and countless others.

A third factor triggering genocide against national groups is the lack of external constraints on, or foreign support for, murderous regimes. At present, lack of international sanctions and/or interventions against massive human rights violators is the norm rather than the exception. Unless national interest combined with the ability to interfere dictates intervention, few efforts are made to ameliorate the suffering of local populations.

Who are the genociders? Here genocide is defined as public violence—by some political actor—aimed at eliminating groups of private citizens. Sometimes genociders are state officials, e.g., soldiers, police, or special *Einsatzgruppen*; sometimes genociders are less openly linked with state power, e.g., death squads. Usually genocide is the conscious choice of policymakers, one among other options for repressing (eliminating) opposition. However, the likelihood of genocide occurring is rare compared to the likelihood that officials will use sporadic violence and/or torture to repress opposition. Thus, we have to differentiate between sporadic violence used against opposition groups, i.e., state terrorism, and systematic, Draconian attempts to eliminate or annihilate them. Additional incentives to settle scores through lesser means are the avoidance of regime instability and/or sometimes the threat of regional/international sanctions or other forms of interference. Genocide is not just another policy instrument of repression; genocide is the most extreme policy option available to policymakers.

International wars are not genocides, because victims have no specific group identity and are often unintended, i.e., civilians. The crime of fighting an aggressive war, though outlawed as an instrument of international policy, is sometimes used as a coercive means to bring about structural changes in the target state, not to eliminate the total population. More difficult is the distinction between civil strife (wars) and genocides—civil wars are contributing factors to the possible occurrence of genocides but are not genocides themselves. In civil wars the legitimate authority structure is weak and is opposed by strong opposition forces. Again, as in wars, though atrocities may become a pattern on both sides, the intent to destroy the opposition in part or as a whole is the crucial variable in determining the onset of genocide. Burundi is a good example, one in which civil war eventually turned into a genocide, given an array of other contributing factors, such as previous tribal rivalries, and lack of regional and international intervention.

In addition, my definition of genocide differs from the official definition (Convention on the Prevention and Punishment of the Crime of Genocide/Declaration by the General Assembly of the United Nations, Resolution 96, dated December 11, 1946, article 2) insofar as it broadens the scope of the victims and perpetrators. Thus, political opponents are included in my definition, though they lack the formal legal protection of the Convention on Genocide. The official definition includes those acts leading to the physical destruction of the group when "such acts are committed with intent to destroy, in whole or part, a national, ethnical, racial or religious group," but says nothing about political groups. The Kampuchean mass slaughter under Pol Pot (1975) testifies to the need to include political opponents in the definition, thereby allowing the Kampuchean tragedy to be properly called genocide and thus to enjoy the unfortunately limited protection of the Convention. Political victims are not political as in contrast to religious or ethnic victims; rather, it is their *political affiliation* which singles them out as victims, not their ethnic identity. Thus, a Jew in Stalin's Russia who opposed Stalin would have been a likely victim during the murderous campaigns of the 1930s because he opposed Stalin, not because he was a Jew. Furthermore, in my conception the Holocaust is the ultimate instance of genocide, rather than a unique event defying comparison. Only through comparison with other similar or dissimilar cases of genocide can we begin to understand what triggered that monstrous episode. This is not to deny Holocaust survivors and victims their place in the conscience of humanity; rather, it is to remind us of our special responsibility to its millions of dead children, women, and men in finding ways to anticipate and eliminate future holocausts.

What follows is an analysis of information about twentieth-century governments which have engaged in genocidal activities. It describes the systemic properties, external environment, and internal conditions of states at the time of genocide. It is based on the cases listed in Table 2, a list which is by no means complete. What is attempted here is only the beginning of a systematic ordering of specific cases into categories. The cases are selected because they are relatively recent and well known, and because information is readily available about them; thus, their analysis should foster the kind of international reaction envisioned in the United Nations Charter. The cases may also make it possible to test the plausibility of my argument that national upheaval and prior internal struggle, combined with lack of constraints in the international environment, are conducive to genocide. It should be noted that the estimated numbers of victims vary greatly, often because "statistics" were not kept (with the exception of the Holocaust) or because population data were inadequate or dated. However, I do not believe that the *number* of victims makes a great difference: the important factor is that they were the victims of genocidal policies.

## Types of National Upheaval

Genocide happens in different types of political society—what types of society? The classification scheme follows from the theoretical framework and distinguishes between types of societies formed after major national upheavals. The task of differentiating among societies with ongoing fundamental political change is difficult. Obviously a successful revolution with clearly defined ideological goals is much more likely to lead to a restructuring of society than anticolonial rebellions with "reformist" goals. In other words, the greater the changes affecting society through new governments, the likelier it is that genocidal policies are implemented to insure total obedience. Thus, the extent of structural change is a major factor underlying my typology.[5]

Table 1 Some Twentieth-Century Genocides

| Country | Dates | Perpetrators | Victims' Identity | Estimated Numbers |
|---|---|---|---|---|
| German SW Africa | 1904 | German troops | Herero | 65,000[1] |
| Ottoman Empire | 1915 | Young Turks/Kurds | Armenians | 800,000–1.8 million[2] |
| Germany | 1941–45 | Germans | Jews | 5–6 million[3] |
| | | | Gypsies | 48,000 |
| Sudan | 1955–72 | Sudanese army | Southern Sudanese | 500,000[4] |
| Indonesia | 1965–67 | Vigilantes | Supposed Communists | 200,000–500,000[5] |
| Nigeria | 1967–70 | Other Nigerians | Ibos | 2–3 million[6] |
| Bangladesh | 1971 | East Pakistan army | Bengalis | 1,247,000–3 million[7] |
| Burundi | 1972 | Tutsis | Hutus | 100,000–200,000[8] |
| Paraguay | 1968–72 | Paraguayans | Guayaki Aché (Indians) | 1,000[9] |
| East Timor | 1975 | Indonesian army | Timorese | 60,000–100,000[10] |
| Kampuchea | 1975–79 | Khmer Rouge | Kampucheans | 740,800–3 million[11] |
| Uganda | 1976–78 | Sections of Ugandan army | Ugandans | 500,000[12] |

1. For an extended discussion see Jon M. Bridgman, *The Revolt of the Hereros* (Berkeley: University of California Press, 1981); Horst Drechsler, *"Let Us Die Fighting": The Struggle of the Herero and Nama against German Imperialism (1884 1915)* (London: Zed Press, 1980); Arnold Valentin Wallenkampf, "The Herero Rebellion in South West Africa, 1904–1906: A Study in German Colonialism" (Ph.D. dissertation, University of California, 1969).

2. For an extended discussion see Helen Fein, "A Formula for Genocide: Comparison of the Turkish Genocide (1915) and the German Holocaust (1939–1945)," *Comparative Studies in Sociology*, 1 (1978); A. D. Sarkissian, *Martyrdom and Rebirth* (Published by the Armenian Church of America; New York: Lydian Press, 1965); Viscount Bryce, *The Treatment of Armenians in the Ottoman Empire 1915–1916* (prepared by Arnold Toynbee; London: H.M.S.O., 1916).

3. For an extended discussion see Hannah Arendt, *The Origins of Totalitarianism* (New York: Harcourt, Brace and World, 1966); Helen Fein, *Accounting for Genocide: National Responses and Jewish Victimization During the Holocaust* (New York: The Free Press, 1979); Leo Kuper, *Genocide: Its Political Use in the Twentieth Century* (New Haven: Yale University Press, 1981).

4. For an extended discussion see Mohammed Omer Beshir, *The Southern Sudan: From Conflict to Peace* (London: C. Hurst and Co., 1975); Robert O. Collins, *The Southern Sudan in Historical Perspective* (Tel Aviv: The Shiloah Center, 1975); Cecil Eprile, *War and Peace in the Sudan 1955–1972* (London: David and Charles, 1974); Edgar O'Ballance, *The Secret War in the Sudan: 1955–1972* (London: Faber and Faber Limited, 1977).

5. Brian May, *The Indonesian Tragedy* (London: Routledge and Kegan Paul, 1978).

6. For an extended discussion see John De St. Jorre, *The Nigerian Civil War* (London: Hodder and Stoughton, 1972); Alexander A. Madiebo, *The Nigerian Revolution and the Biafran War* (Enugu, Nigeria: Fourth Dimension Publishing Co., 1980); Arthur Agwuncha Nwankwo and Samuel Udochukwu Ifejika, *The Making of a Nation Biafra* (London: C. Hurst and Company, 1969); Peter Schwab, ed., *Biafra* (New York: Facts on File, 1971).

7. Kalyan Chaudhuri, *Genocide in Bangladesh* (Bombay: Orient Longman, 1972).

8. For an extended discussion see René Lemarchand, *Rwanda and Burundi* (New York: Praeger, 1970); Norman Wingert, *No Place to Stop Killing* (Chicago: Moody Press, 1974).

9. For an extended discussion see Richard Arens, *Genocide in Paraguay* (Philadelphia: Temple University Press, 1976).

10. For an extended discussion see Jill Joliffe, *East Timor: Nationalism and Colonialism* (Australia: University of Queensland Press, 1978); Justus M. van der Kroef, *Patterns of Conflict in Eastern Indonesia* (London: The Eastern Press, 1977).

11. For an extended discussion see François Ponchaud, *Cambodia Year Zero* (Harmondsworth: Penguin Books, 1978); Michael Vickery, *Cambodia 1975–1982* (Boston: South End Press, 1984).

12. Dan Wooding and Ray Barnett, *Uganda Holocaust* (Grand Rapids, Mich.: Zondervan Publishing House, 1980).

Revolutions are a type of national upheaval. Revolutions always involve the overthrow of the ruling political elite and aim at bringing about fundamental social change.

Anticolonial rebellions, which are similar to separatist conflicts, are a type of national upheaval. Anticolonial rebellions are internal struggles with mass participation, directed against the ruling foreign power, seeking autonomy. In the case of separatist conflicts, the major struggle takes place between two movements, one trying to break away, the other to prevent it.

Coups may constitute a type of national upheaval. Coups involve the total or partial replacement of the ruling elite and lack mass participation. Thus, coups which involve the total replacement of the ruling elite are more likely to induce fundamental social change.

A special case is a takeover by duly elected or appointed political elites who endorse extreme ideologies (right-wing or left-wing). There is no abrupt structural change, but rather a move to exert total control. Such changes may lead to the creation of a climate in which people are absolved from making personal judgments and are rewarded for their total obedience to authority.

Another crucial factor in the development of genocide is the existence of sharp internal cleavages. In some societies internal violence is a way of life,[6] and some societies are preconditioned to accept political violence (coups, for example) because they frequently do occur (for example, in Bolivia). However, genocide needs more than reinforcement through societal acquiescence. Genocide is a product of state policy, with an involvement and commitment of massive resources, and is only marginally beneficial to people involved in the process.

National upheaval always intensifies internal cleavages. Depending on the preferences of policymakers, some groups may become targets of genocidal policies. Groups which are most "different" from the dominant group are more likely to become targets than those which more closely resemble the dominant group. Thus, groups different in religion, culture, wealth, education, and/or ideology have a greater chance to be singled out for genocide. Economic preponderance by some groups may be enough to induce genocidal policies against them. These cleavages usually pre-exist, but in some cases they are introduced by the new elite. Thus, for example, the targeted group may involve all those opposed to the new regime (Kampuchea), or rich peasants (Communist Russia).[7]

The structural precondition of national upheaval combined with societal receptiveness for internal violence targeted against "most different" groups may pave the path to genocide, but a third condition may ultimately provide the final incentive for the occurrence of genocide. Here we are talking about external support for either the genocider or the target group. Sometimes the genociders are foreign powers, for example, colonizers; sometimes genocidal elites enjoy support/protection from powerful neighbors. In modern times the overt or covert support of one of the superpowers is a warrant for the survival of regimes involved in repression or genocide. In other cases, states may neither condemn nor praise other states engaged in internal repression. The state in question may be too unimportant to warrant international attention, thus enjoying the kind of freedom which comes from lack of automatic sanctions in cases of extreme human rights violations.

Support of a different kind may come for the genocidal target. Thus, fellow religionists or ethnic groups may induce their governments to intervene on behalf of the potential victims. A more limited kind of support may come from international organizations in the form of protests or boycotts. In some cases irredentist movements elsewhere may lend military support.

## Common Elements in Different Genocides

The merits of this theoretical argument can be demonstrated by analysis of the characteristics of cases of genocide categorized according to their political circumstances.

### Post-War, Post-Imperial Genocides

The Holocaust is undisputably the most abominable instance of modern genocide; however, it has many structural, societal, and external similarities with lesser genocides. Hitler's rise to power, though by constitutional means, came in the wake of a worldwide depression. The post-war economic crises and the inability of the new democratic government to cope with massive unemployment and extreme currency inflation greatly strengthened the radical left and the extreme right. Fear of a Communist takeover led to the bare victory of the National Socialist Party, and the "Enabling Act" left Hitler with dictatorial powers, which he used to bar any opposition.

The emergence of the nationalist movements of the "Young Turks" came in the wake of a disintegrating Ottoman Empire. A prior rebellion in 1908, which briefly restored a constitutional monarchy, led to a coup in 1913 and the total takeover by the Young Turks under their leader, Enver Pasha. During the Balkan wars (1912–1913) the Ottoman Empire lost almost all its territory in Europe, which left the new nationalist movement with little sympathy for the national aspirations of the remaining ethnic minorities in Turkey.

Both countries—Turkey and Germany—did experience a major restructuring of their respective governments following loss of territory in war and a rapid succession of different versions of government. The German Empire was replaced by a democratic government, which lacked the strength to unite the warring factions of Communists and Monarchists. In Turkey the Sultan was briefly replaced by a constitutional Sultan, who, however, was in no position to halt the nationalist movement of the Young Turks, who tried to propel Turkey into the twentieth century with sweeping reforms. The national upheavals following the takeover by both nationalist movements had disastrous consequences for some ethnic/religious minorities in both countries—Armenians in Turkey and Jews and Gypsies in Germany.

The annihilation of Jews and Gypsies in Germany and the genocide against Armenians in Turkey followed a similar pattern. In both countries domination of the state apparatus by a tightly controlled political elite was complete. Both the Young Turks and the Nazi movement introduced a kind of myth, exalting the likeness of the dominant group, i.e., "Aryan"–Germans and Turks. Germanization and Turkification both emphasized pureness of race and common cultural/ethnic and religious values. Thus, all "real" Germans were to be Christian, Aryan, and non-Communist, as all Turks were to be Muslim, Turkoman, and pro Young Turk. Both Jews and Armenians were easy targets, for they were different in religion, "racial" heritage, and culture. The age-old division between Christians and Muslims and Christians and Jews accelerated receptiveness for a renewal of a crusade against infidels and the people of the book. The readiness to massacre Jews and Armenians was not new to either society. Sporadic violence or planned massacres had taken place prior to both genocides. But the Holocaust and the Genocide of 1915 against the Armenians were exceptional, because they were premeditated acts by policymakers to eliminate a people. Why?

I have argued that once preconditions such as structural changes, lack of external constraint, and internal cleavages combine, *the stage is set for genocide.* In both cases external constraints were either nonexistent or too late and too little to halt the slaughters of thousands of innocent victims. Neither meager German protest in 1915 (Turkey's major ally) nor an international boycott by World Jewry did much to stop impending disaster. Russian threat of intervention against Turkey was superseded by World War I, similar to Allied lack of intervention due to World War II. International sympathy for Jews was virtually nonexistent, evidenced by the refusal of other countries to grant entry permits to fleeing Jews. Armenians fared little better in the wake of competing nationalist movements elsewhere in Europe and the impending Russian Revolution, and the making of new alliances culminating in World War I.

But neither structural change nor external conditions *fully* explain why policymakers decide to eliminate or annihilate a people rather than engage in *sporadic* violence, i.e., why they resort to genocide rather than state terrorism to suppress opposition. Internal conditions may provide the final clues to why states engage in genocide. Often the strength of a new government greatly depends on its ability to mobilize mass support. Often divisions within culturally heterogeneous societies are overcome by declaring one group responsible for the other's misfortunes. Sometimes that is the case in socialist revolutions, where capitalists serve as scapegoats for the misery of the workers. Turkification and Germanification both served to unite people in their pride of belonging to a people, both inheritors of a long history, i.e., heirs of the Holy Roman Empire and the Ottoman Empire. Armenians may have been a legitimate threat to the Young Turks because they were collectively organized and demanded limited autonomy within the new state. Jews, however, were no threat to the Nazis; they were neither politically organized nor particularly visible as a group—Germany boasted a more assimilated "enlightened" (non-religious) Jewish population than most other European countries. Yet Nazi propaganda had singled out the Jew from its beginning. If Jews in Germany were at all special as a group they were so because of achievements in the professions. A disproportionate number of them were doctors, scientists, literary greats, and artists. Leading lights of Marxism/Socialism included many Jews, e.g., Karl Marx, Rosa Luxembourg, Ferdinand Lassalle, and Eduard Bernstein. Why did the Nazis single out the Jews? Anti-Semitism has long been part of European history. It was probably the single most appealing prejudicial doctrine available to the Nazis, who were trying to consolidate their power. Different groups in Germany may have had different animosities, but the Jews offered more value as scapegoats than other groups such as Gypsies or Communists. Communists were after all "genuine Germans," whereas Gypsies were too small in number and not a settled people. The successful merchant image of the Jews spelled competition for the average shopkeeper in Germany; the dominance of Jewish scientists may have caused envy among their colleagues; legendary Jewish international finance connections added to the image resented by others. The liberal image of artists residing in the capital did nothing to persuade the provincial German that the Jew was part of their world. Hitler's claim that Marxism/Communism was after all a Jewish invention thus was easily absorbed into an ideology offering an escape for many. The Jews had something for everyone, and those enlightened enough to realize the demagoguery thought that Hitler could be controlled. Once the Nazis realized the appeal of anti-Semitism, propaganda made full use of it. Nazis, once in power, fulfilled their promises to put people to work and "clean" the towns of Jews. Once the Nazis realized that the world was not eager to take "their" Jews, the "final solution" was to take care of the Jewish "problem." Who was to stop the murderous engine? In 1944 the Germans, their cities bombed, were losing the war, yet the death camps were working to full capacity.

Killing the Jewish population of Europe may have been the rational choice of the Nazis, yet the utility of doing so was utterly irrational. The costs of keeping the camps going despite the war effort were immense. Thousands of people were involved in killing Jews; trains transporting Jews had priority over those aiding the war effort.[8] The fanatic pursuit of "finishing the job" was part of the robot-like performance of those selected to serve the "higher cause" of Nazi ideology.

*Post-Colonial Genocides*
The genocides of Southern Sudan, Biafra, Bangladesh, Burundi, and East Timor all took place following massive internal rebellions. Bangladesh, Biafra, East Timor, and the Southern Sudan sought to secede—from Pakistan, Nigeria, Indonesia, and the Northern Sudan, respectively. Bangladesh was successful; Biafra, East Timor, and the Southern Sudan were not. In Burundi the Hutus tried unsuccessfully to throw off the minority rule of the Tutsis. All five genocides happened in the wake of colonial liberation. In each case euphoria over liberation soon gave way to a *reemphasis* of existing cleavages.

The Northern Sudanese, Muslims who claim Arab descent, saw their future tightly bound to the Arab world. For the Southern Sudanese, mostly Negroid, animist (though including many Christians), and multi-ethnic, the traditional societies of East Africa seemed a more likely ally. The racial division is somehow arbitrary, since many Northerners who claim to be Arabs are Negroid in appearance and many Southerners called Negroid have non-Negroid features.[9] More important, Southern economic development was grossly inferior to the North. It was no surprise that the politically and economically powerful (and more populous) North should dominate the South after independence in 1956. Thus, domination by the British was replaced with domination by the North. Even before independence came to the country the South revolted against the North, which resulted in the slaughter of many thousands of innocent people.

Nigeria after independence in 1960 was united under a federal system. But unity was fragile among the three dominant ethnic groups, the Hausa-Fulani (about 15 million), the Yoruba (about 10 million), and the Ibos (about 10 million). The three were different in language, religion, and social organization.[10] The Ibos who became the targets of genocide, were mostly Christians and animists, in contrast to the Hausa-Fulani, who were Muslim and organized in the traditional Arab way under a strong central authority. Adding to the problem was the Ibos' dominance in education and industrialization. The North, with a high illiteracy rate and a largely agrarian economy, nevertheless controlled the federation by sheer weight of numbers (the total Northern region numbered about 35 million people).[11] The Ibos who attempted to secede in 1967 capitulated to the federal government of Nigeria in 1970. During the years of warfare hundreds of thousands died either in battle, during massacres, or by starvation.

The process of decolonization in India brought the division of India and Pakistan, strongly fostered by religious cleavages. Pakistanis were largely Muslims, and most Indians were Hindus; intermingling between the two groups was prohibited because of the caste system of the Hindus. Caught between the two groups were the Sikhs, who were divided between the emerging states of India and Pakistan. Before partition the Sikhs were embroiled in a "holy war" against the Muslims. Communal strife during this time took on mass proportions as an estimated 1 million people lost their lives. Upon partition Pakistan was divided into West and East Pakistan, separated by 1,000 miles of India. As in the Sudan, one region, West Pakistan, was considerably more industrialized, whereas the East was predominantly agricultural. In addition to economic domination, political domination was secured by a bureaucracy consisting largely of West Pakistanis. Negotiations for greater autonomy for the East in 1971 ended in massive retaliations by the West Pakistani government. During the following months genocidal policies were implemented which resulted in the indiscriminate deaths of men, women, and children numbering well over 1 million.

Burundi became independent in 1962 after years of extended rebellions against Belgian authorities. The country has a majority of Hutus—about 85 percent of the population—ruled by a minority government composed of Tutsis, who make up about 15 percent of the population. This domination by a minority was over 400 years old, established when the warrior Tutsis invaded the country from Ethiopia. Three aborted coups in 1965, 1969, and 1972 against the unwanted minority government led to severe reprisals by the Tutsis and in 1972 to genocide against the Hutus which claimed about 200,000 lives.

East Timor was a Portuguese colony which was to become independent in 1978 but preempted that step in 1975 by unilaterally declaring independence. The people are largely of Malay and Papuan stock, with a majority of Christians and some Muslim minorities. Past rivalries were confined to interparty conflicts. The most popular party, FRETILIN, which enjoyed 60 percent of the popular vote, was anticolonial and anti-Indonesian and was thought to be left-leaning. Two other parties, APODETI and UDT, called for union with Indonesia. This division erupted into violence during August 1975. Indonesia immediately reacted by initiating a blockade against East Timor and subsequently invaded the country in December 1975. With the help of UDT and APODETI forces, independence was exchanged for union with Indonesia; the invasion resulted in looting, torture, and slaughter, with the result that nearly 10 percent of the population was killed.[12]

In all five cases foreign intervention significantly added to the success or failure of the secessionist movement. The intervention by India in December 1971 ended the genocidal massacres and also secured the independence of the new state of Bangladesh. Not so typical was the international support given to Nigeria/Biafra. China, France, Portugal, Israel, and South Africa supported Biafra, while Great Britain and the Soviet Union supported Nigeria. The latter "alliance" was probably due to Britain's effort to curtail growing Soviet influence in Nigeria. Biafran support came in the midst of conflicting European and big-power politics (e.g., France's oil interest in Biafra and China's tensions with Moscow), while Israel mostly confined its support to humanitarian relief efforts. The United States paid lip service to a united Nigeria. The Organization for African Unity (OAU) also supported Nigeria.[13] The Southern Sudanese enjoyed almost no support from outside sources, while Egypt, Libya, Algeria, Kuwait, East Germany, and the Soviet Union were said to have armed the North. In Burundi, no international action was taken to halt the massacres, although protests through diplomatic channels were plentiful. So, for example, the OAU supported the Burundi government, as did China, North Korea, and France. The greatest concern was shown by the former colonial power, Belgium, which early on protested against Burundi's genocidal policies. East Timor received verbal support from Australia and Portugal, and Indonesia received military support from the United States, while others claimed ignorance about accusations of genocide in East Timor. In all cases United Nations actions were confined to humanitarian relief efforts.[14]

## Post-Coup and Post-Revolutionary Genocides

The genocides of Kampuchea, Uganda, and Indonesia took place after a revolution in Kampuchea, after a coup in Uganda, and after an attempted coup in Indonesia, each conflict causing massive internal upheaval.

With the deposal of Prince Norodom Sihanouk in 1970 a relatively tranquil period ended in Cambodia. Increased involvement in the Vietnam War led to increased turmoil in the Khmer Republic. Forces of the Khmer Republic fought the Khmer Rouge in a civil war, which ended in the takeover by the Khmer Rouge Communists in 1975 and the establishment of Democratic Kampuchea. From 1975 to 1979 the Khmer Rouge expelled all foreigners and instituted one of the bloodiest regimes known in the twentieth century. Under the leadership of Pol Pot the urban population was sent to the countryside to become part of the "new" productive forces. He designated as expendable all those unable to perform the task. Pol Pot's "Marxist" revolution was but a peasant uprising against the feudal class represented by the townspeople.[15] Though his fury was mainly directed against townspeople, former collaborators including loyal peasants were also eliminated; thus, all perceived as opposing the regime were targets of genocidal policies. The failure of the regime was sealed with the invasion by Vietnamese forces in 1979; Vietnam is still occupying the country.

In January 1971 Idi Amin overthrew Milton Obote of Uganda in a coup, setting in motion a regime which ruled with unprecedented brutality. Amin, the dictator of Uganda who is often compared with Hitler, during his first three months in office was responsible for the deaths of 10,000 civilians and 2,000 soldiers. Like Pol Pot, Amin immediately chose to expel all foreigners from the country. His genocidal policies extended to all perceived as opposing his regime. His henchmen were members of his own tribe, the Kakwa, Nubians inside Uganda, and mercenaries from the Southern Sudan. In the effort to consolidate his power, Amin was responsible for the slaughter of an estimated 500,000 people. His regime ended with an invasion by Tanzanian forces in 1979, leaving behind a legacy of tyranny.[16]

On October 1, 1965, six Indonesian generals and a lieutenant were murdered in an uprising against President Sukarno. Although the truth may remain forever a secret, the events were thought to be Communist inspired and/or initiated.[17] In a predominantly Muslim society, the Communist party was something of an enigma (membership estimated at 10 million or one-quarter of the adult population). The short-lived uprising was crushed a few days later and led to the *systematic* slaughter of hundreds of thousands of Communists over a period of two years. Participating in the slaughter were soldiers and civilians trained for the purpose. Some officials of the Suharto regime later explained the slaughter as the "people's revenge," suggesting a spontaneous mass reaction to avenge the death of some of their leaders—hardly convincing in light of the fact that the slaughter continued over two years.

International support for the revolutionaries in Kampuchea came from Vietnam and China, while the regime was supported by American arms and aid. The faltering United States effort in Vietnam led to an abandonment of the pro-American Lon Nol regime, which enabled Pol Pot to take over. The subsequent fall of the Pol Pot regime was in part due to the growing antagonism between China and Vietnam, eventually leading to the invasion by the latter, whereupon Pol Pot fled to China. Uganda's Amin received full support from Libya but was criticized by the leaders of Tanzania, Zaire, and Zambia. By and large, however, the OAU remained silent about the indiscriminate killings of Ugandans. Only after Uganda invaded Tanzania did Tanzania respond with a counterinvasion. Supported by renegade Ugandan soldiers, the invasion successfully removed the murderous regime, and Amin fled to Libya. In Indonesia the coup was thought to be inspired by Peking, though no direct link with China could be detected. American sympathies went to the Suharto regime. In all cases the United Nations did little other than express its dismay and verbally condemn these flagrant violations of human rights.

*Genocides of Conquest*

During the imposition of German colonialism in what is today Namibia, the Hereros became the target of genocidal policies. In the early 1970s "the International League for the Rights of Man, joined by the Inter-American Association for Democracy and Freedom, charged the government of Paraguay with complicity in genocide against the Guayaki Indians."[18]

In the short-lived colonial history of the German Empire (ending in 1918), early efforts of peaceful colonization in Southern Africa were soon replaced by measures which reduced the indigenous people to serfdom. The Hereros, a pastoral people noted for their large cattle herds, saw themselves slowly stripped of their land by German settlers. From 1903 to 1907 they revolted against the German colonizers—with devastating results. Successful at first, the Hereros were eventually defeated by superior technology and firepower. Thousands lost their lives in the actions following the uprising. The Germans "hunted them down like wild beasts all during 1905."[19] An estimated 65,000 Hereros lost their lives.

The Guayaki (Aché) Indians, a hunting and gathering people, were targets of genocide when "modern" Paraguayans encroached upon their traditional lands. During 1974 the Paraguayan government was blamed for allowing the slaughter, torture, and enslavement of the Indians by hunters and slavetraders.

International action was negligible in the first case. Wars against native Africans warranted no attention from other colonizers. There was some international attention given to the Aché Indian case, and verbal condemnation of Paraguayan policy eventually resulted in some response by the government.

## Conclusions

In all the cases considered here genocides were preceded by some attempt to change the existing power structure. It should be obvious that any attempt to change existing power relations carries a certain amount of risk for the challenger. Though most potential revolutionaries accept the calculus of losing some lives, genocide would be an unacceptable risk to anyone.

Successful rebellions (Kampuchea, for example) more often resulted in massive internal upheavals than did failed attempts (Indonesia, for example). Moreover, unsuccessful coups often resulted in the slaughter of those affiliated with the rebelling faction, for example, in Indonesia and East Timor. Evidently governments utilize genocidal policies to eliminate the opposition in an attempt to maintain the existing power structure. In some cases these processes may extend to include attempts to annihilate a people, i.e., a holocaust. This does not mean that holocausts result in more deaths; it simply means that the pursuers seek the total destruction of a people rather than their partial destruction. The difference is especially apparent in cases where the victims belong to the political opposition—often the slaughter stops short of family members. The child of a Communist may not necessarily become one himself, but the child of a Jew cannot escape his/her Jewishness, as a result often becoming the victim of a holocaust. Utilizing genocide to eliminate political opposition thus appears to be a more rational choice than the attempt to annihilate a people. As such, policymakers sometimes make the argument that political victims are legitimate targets of governmental violence which aims to prevent further violence, e.g., future civil war. In contrast, one may argue that ethnic/religious victims are illegitimate targets of governmental violence because they have neither the means to fight back, nor do they compete with government, and thus are truly innocent of any wrongdoing. But what is at stake is not the characteristics of the victim group, but the motives of the perpetrators. The killing of a people for attempting to change the existing government structure cannot be based on the collective character of a group, simply because not everybody is involved in the struggle. The only public offense which warrants the execution of an individual is the murder of another (in some societies even murder does not result in death). Excluded from this principle are killings done in the process of war, although many people view war and the resulting human carnage as an unacceptable means of international interaction. In cases of no war and where no individual crime has taken place, any killing either done by or conspired in by public authorities against a group of people is a crime.

The theoretical argument advances the proposition that structural challenges result in upheavals, polarize existing internal cleavages, and—with external help or the lack of it to either the dominant group or the rebelling faction—sometimes lead to genocide. In all cases cited above the genocides were preceded by challenges to the dominant power strata. In all cases genocidal processes were accelerated through the polarization of internal cleavages. The most distinct cases are those of the Holocaust, the Armenian genocide, and Burundi, where the groups were targets of prior discrimination and/or random violence, and also were easily identified by differences in culture, religion, and ethnicity. The Southern Sudan, Biafra, and Bangladesh similarly saw incidences of random violence and/or repression against target groups who were culturally, ethnically, and/or religiously different. In East Timor, Kampuchea, and Indonesia the victim groups shared similar ethnic characteristics with the dominant group, but, though prior internal rivalries existed in all cases, the victims were considered enemies mainly because of their political affiliations. Uganda is something of a special case, because victims were neither clearly political enemies nor did they belong to one specific religious or ethnic group. The killings, although systematic, seemed to be instituted to consolidate the despotic power of a tyrant, similar to the "Enabling Act" which gave Hitler the license to kill. The genocides against the Hereros and the Aché Indians were policies designed to extend the control of the dominant "civilization." In the case of the former, the Germans encountered a new type of warfare in the guerrilla tactics of the Hereros, which they responded to in kind. Thus, random incidents of "savagery" by the Hereros led to their wholesale, systematic slaughter by the Germans. The Achés, although part of the same racial stock as their persecutors, were culturally separated from the dominant stratum of Paraguay. Malign neglect by the government led to their genocide, perpetrated by those acting on behalf of the dominant interest, in a march toward their version of civilization.

In all cases external support for either the dominant group or a rebellious faction added significantly to the success or failure of the undertaking. The Herero genocide is the exception, probably because the slaughter of "savages" in 1904 by the colonizers was more acceptable then. Today, the "savages" of the past are replaced by either the *Untermenschen* or enemies of the dominant group. Nowadays, the drive toward civilization is replaced by the search for a better world, in which those perceived as standing in the way of "progress" are liquidated.

If we are able to explain past genocides and thus to anticipate future genocides, the next logical step is their prevention. International organizations such as the United Nations have failed to halt the use of genocidal policies by sovereign states. Internal bickering and competing interests have prevented the effective use of international diplomacy to prevent or stop genocides. Yet, the emergence of numerous private organizations, in combination with a few U.N. efforts, gives the impression that something may yet be done.

## Notes

1. For an extended discussion see Israel W. Charny, *How Can We Commit the Unthinkable? Genocide: The Human Cancer* (Boulder, Colo.: Westview Press, 1982), and Herbert C. Kelman, "Violence Without Moral Restraint: Reflections on the Dehumanization of Victims and Victimizers," *Journal of Social Issues* 29 (1973).
2. Charny, op. cit.
3. Barbara Harff, *Genocide and Human Rights: International Legal and Political Issues* (Denver: University of Denver Monograph Series in World Affairs, 1984).
4. Richard Falk, *The End of World Order: Essays on Normative International Relations* (New York and London: Holmes and Meier, 1983).
5. D.E.H. Russell, *Rebellion, Revolution and Armed Force: A Comparative Study of Fifteen Countries with Special Emphasis on Cuba and South Africa* (New York: Academic Press, 1974).
6. Helen Fein, "A Formula for Genocide: Comparison of the Turkish Genocide (1915) and the German Holocaust (1939–1945)," *Comparative Studies in Sociology*, 1 (1978).
7. Leo Kuper, *Genocide: Its Political Use in the Twentieth Century* (New Haven: Yale University Press, 1981).
8. Fein, op. cit.
9. Cecil Eprile, *War and Peace in the Sudan 1955–1972* (London: David and Charles, 1974).
10. Peter Schwab, ed., *Biafra* (New York: Facts on File, 1971).
11. Ibid.
12. This discussion draws in part upon an unpublished paper by Christian C. Mattioli, "Invasion and Genocide in East Timor," Department of Political Science, Northwestern University, 1983.
13. Schwab, op. cit.
14. Mattioli, op. cit.
15. Michael Vickery, *Cambodia 1975–1982* (Boston: South End Press, 1984), and Kuper, op. cit.
16. Dan Wooding and Ray Barnett, *Uganda Holocaust* (Grand Rapids, Mich.: Zondervan Publishing House, 1980).
17. Kuper, op. cit., and Brian May, *The Indonesian Tragedy* (London: Routledge and Kegan Paul, 1978).
18. Kuper, op. cit., p. 33.
19. Jon M. Bridgman, *The Revolt of the Hereros* (Berkeley: University of California Press, 1981).

# 4.3   Roger W. Smith, "Scarcity and Genocide"

Genocide is not inevitable; it is a political choice. But political choices, including genocide, are effected by many different forces, internal and external. Scarcity will increasingly be one of those forces in the not-so-distant future.

The question of the relationships between scarcity and genocide is an important one, both in terms of understanding the causes of genocide and in anticipating the prospects for genocide in the twenty-first century. If current trends continue, a combination of environmental degradation, loss of agricultural land, depletion of fish stocks, dwindling of fuel resources, and a doubling of population to around 11 billion persons in the latter part of the century will lead to conditions of extreme hardship, even disaster, in many parts of the world. These areas, mainly in the Third World, are the very places where much of the genocide since 1945 has taken place.

The genocides that have occurred in Bangladesh, Burundi, Cambodia, Indonesia, and Rwanda, however, have not been brought about by material scarcity. In fact, genocide, with some exceptions to be noted later, has seldom been the result of material scarcity; on the contrary, material scarcity has often been a direct result of genocide. Nevertheless, in a world that in the twentieth century displayed an unparalleled capacity for mass slaughter, it would be surprising if severe shortages would not exacerbate existing tendencies toward resolving social and political problems through elimination of the groups thought to constitute the problem.

"Scarcity" is a concept that includes both the relative and the absolute. For those people used to affluence and abundance, a mild reduction in goods available to them will be perceived as a matter of scarcity; similarly, they may feel worse off if other persons improve their material condition while they remain at their previous level. Scarcity, in these instances, is not only relative, but also psychological: desire is confused with need. Psychological scarcity is an important facet of the "developmental" genocide that indigenous peoples have faced, and, most likely, will face. Although many philosophers have seen "desire" and its control as a crucial problem, the modern view, one that underlies ideas of progress and development, is that the expansion of desire and continual efforts to satisfy its expectations thereby created are the principal reasons for social existence. It is this artificial scarcity, a scarcity created by desire rather than need, that in large part drives the development projects that have destroyed the lives of indigenous peoples in the name of "progress." Scarcity may also be both absolute and material: without food and water for a certain period, we, of course, die.

Considered in material terms, scarcity can take at least two different forms. First, there may be a scarcity of resources—little usable land, forests that have been depleted, minerals long ago extracted from the soil. Some of these resources can be renewed, whereas others are simply no longer there. Whether resources are renewable or not is itself an important dimension of overcoming scarcity and any role it may have in prompting murderous conflict. Second, resources may be scarce because of the size of the population: even if all goods were distributed equally, there would still be generalized poverty. In order to overcome this kind of scarcity, either the material resources would have to be increased (the green revolution in agriculture, for instance) or the population would have to be decreased.

In addition to psychological scarcity and the material scarcities described, there is a kind of scarcity—political scarcity—that includes both material and political deprivation. Where political scarcity exists, there may be sufficient resources to meet everyone's needs, but the allocation of resources favors certain groups and discriminates against other groups. In practice, there will often be a scarcity of resources and an expanding population, both of which may contribute further to policies of unequal distribution of goods. Such situations frequently exist in ethnically divided ("plural") societies and help to drive demands for equal treatment, demands that may be met with repression and, if the conflict persists, with an attempt at partial or total genocide. Power sharing, protection of basic rights, and equality of treatment could go a long way in overcoming the difficulties otherwise exacerbated by deteriorating resources and expansion of population.

The relationships between genocide and scarcity fall into four broad patterns. First of all, genocide typically produces scarcity: it creates social chaos; disrupts the economy; destroys the lives of hundreds of thousands, even millions, of persons who possess skills and productive capacities; and diverts the perpetrators themselves from their role in economic life, turning them into persons who destroy rather than produce and create. In extreme cases, such as that of Rwanda, economic production may cease altogether. Moreover, in many instances, disease may sweep through the society, facilitated in part by famine, water sources contaminated by the dead, and lack of sanitation. Where the genocide occurs in the context of war, as in Bosnia, human habitations, production facilities, and the environment itself may all suffer significant damage, creating additional material scarcities.

If genocide falls most heavily upon the intended victims, the perpetrators are not immune to the scarcities it induces. In Cambodia, for example, hundreds of thousands of people whom the Khmer Rouge tried to turn into the foundation of a peasant society died from malnutrition brought about by its agricultural policies. Although humanitarian aid in the form of both food and medicine was available, the Khmer Rouge would not accept it for ideological reasons: its vision was of a self-sufficient peasant society; moreover, if food was scarce, the regime maintained it was due to sabotage by "enemies of the revolution," not any failure of the revolutionary design itself.

Perpetrators may be so intent upon destroying a group that they fail to calculate the effects that their actions will have on themselves. Or there may be a recognition of this consequence, but the calculus used to assess costs and benefits is one that stresses ideology, revenge, or power rather than the material well-being of the perpetrator group.

There is one type of genocide in which scarcity falls almost entirely upon the victims. In developmental genocide, it is the indigenous peoples' land that is taken and their sources of food eliminated. The perpetrators, on the other hand, gain land, gold, timber, or cheap electricity from the hydroelectric projects erected on the indigenous peoples' territory.

Scarcities that stem from genocide may be either short-term (a temporary shortage of food, for example) or long-lasting (where much of the existing housing is damaged or destroyed, as in Bosnia). In some cases, the damage to the economy will continue for generations: eighty-six years after the 1915 genocide of the Armenians, lands that were once highly productive lie barren in eastern Turkey.

Direct conflict over scarce resources is another recurrent theme. It is likely to occur in three situations, each of which is compatible with genocidal actions. The first is the result of migration into areas occupied by other groups. A well-known example of this occurrence is the Israelite exodus from Egypt, their migration into Canaan, and the ensuing wars over resources that the early books of the Bible invariably depict as wars of extermination. Migration may itself result from lack of adequate resources, but more commonly in the modern world from persecution, war, and genocide.

Direct conflict over material resources is also likely where resources held by indigenous peoples are slated for "development." Much of the scarcity perceived by the ones who set development into motion involves a lack of abundance rather than economic hardship. The other form of scarcity involved here is the maldistribution of resources, particularly land, within the perpetrators' territory, rather than a lack of resources. One of the reasons that development appeals to political and economic elites ("progress" is another) is that it offers a kind of safety valve to release the frustrations of the landless and the impoverished without requiring any redistribution of resources held by the elites. The costs of development will be borne instead by those people whose lands are taken. There are currently some 200 million indigenous peoples around the world, most of whom are already vulnerable to existing pressures for greater and more productive utilization of resources. Given an age of scarcity in the twenty-first century, the future of indigenous peoples would appear to be bleak.

The third basis for direct conflict over resources occurs when a state collapses, followed by fragmentation, with no group capable of gaining overall power or control. When a state fails, with the consequent breakdown of security for life and property, scarcity can be expected to increase, leading to a struggle over basic resources.

In principle, a dominant group may arise out of the "state of nature" and impose a repressive order. But it is possible that a variety of groups will sustain the low-level conflict for many years, with repeated genocidal attacks being made by all sides. Genocide, rather than being exceptional, would become part of an equilibrium of destruction. Under these conditions, life would almost certainly be "poor, nasty, brutish, and short." In this situation, any distinction between war and crime, and war and genocide, would blur or disappear.

The history of genocide also provides many examples of the act being carried out primarily through depriving the victims of food. Ancient warfare was synonymous with genocide; when a walled city offered resistance, the perpetrators would resort to siege warfare, cutting the inhabitants off from fresh supplies of food and drink. Eventually, the people within the city would starve or would capitulate and then be killed or enslaved. During the Spanish "conquest" of Mexico, Indians were forced into submission or died by starvation when their supplies of food were confiscated and their crops burned. A modern example is the Stalinist man-made famine of 1932–1933 in Soviet Ukraine that led to the death by starvation of some 5 million Ukrainians, most of them the very peasants who had produced the grain that was confiscated. A calculated policy to force peasants into collective agriculture and to crush a rising Ukrainian nationalism led, in two years, to the death of almost 20 percent of the population.

Scarcity, particularly in its psychological and political forms, has played a role in genocide for centuries; material scarcity has less rarely been a source for mass killing. Other motives have included conquest, retribution, dominance, and, where certain ideologies were involved, the total remaking of society to achieve salvation and purification. Although many of the motives and pressures for genocide that have existed from ancient times to the present will likely continue, it may be that we are entering an age in which scarcity in its various forms will increasingly contribute to the decision to resort to genocide. In this context, "scarcity" includes degradation and depletion of natural resources, fewer goods per capita due to population growth, and unequal resource distribution. It also includes the psychological and political scarcities that play a role in the genocide of indigenous peoples and minorities in plural societies. Each form of scarcity can contribute to the conditions that make genocide more likely: they include conflict over resources; population displacement and ensuing conflict between groups; allocation of resources along racial, religious, or ethnic lines, resulting in demands for autonomy or independence; and weakening of the legitimacy of the state, followed by either revolution, an attempt at secession, or a growing authoritarianism that seeks to solve social and political problems by force. New ideologies may also arise, and are likely to be formulated along lines of ethnicity or religion. In some instances, states may fragment into warring groups, with no group able to achieve dominance, but able to decimate other groups in intermittent combat. Finally, genocide itself begets new, especially material, scarcities, laying the basis for further violence in the future.

To spell out one example of the possible effects of scarcity contributing to genocide: where the legitimacy of the state or the ruling group in a plural society is challenged, it is likely that the old regime will resort to authoritarian solutions to hold onto power. But in so doing, it will further alienate the minority groups that it has previously excluded from power. This alienation will provoke further challenge to the elite's authority, which will be met with greater force, including massacres. This example is, in fact, the classic case of what leads to genocide in ethnically divided, plural societies. If there is also the problem of material scarcity, which is likely to be accentuated in the future, then increasing demands will be made on those people in power. These demands, due to lack of resources, competence, or fairness, will not be met, resulting in further erosion in the legitimacy of rule by the dominant elite. In such a situation, the tendency is to crack down on the ones making the demands, but also to allocate scarce resources even more decidedly along ethnic lines, favoring members of the dominant group. This result is in part a matter of what might be called a politics of identity, in which one favors one's own group, but also in part a strategy to reward those citizens thought to be loyal to the people in power. The end result will be that in times of scarcity, the regime will move from its usual pattern of discrimination to a policy that increases hardship and, at the extreme, leads to destitution. If the destitute have the means to resist, then this violence will in turn generate a new spiral of repression, beginning with massacres, which are a way of keeping a group in its place, and possibly ending with genocide, which attempts to eliminate the group itself.

In this scenario, a type of society (plural), a type of regime (authoritarian), a type of policy (unequal allocation of resources), a challenge to that policy (by the group that is viewed as inferior and excluded from power), and material scarcity (whatever its sources) come together in a mix that is fatal.

## Preventing Genocide

Those people who study genocide do so in order to understand why such extreme violence takes place and why it is directed at particular groups. The quest to understand, however, is a desire not only to know, but also to find ways in which that understanding can be used to prevent future acts of genocide. As previously mentioned, there is nothing inevitable about genocide; nevertheless, there are certain predisposing elements, and the likelihood of preventing genocide is enhanced if they can be overcome. The chapter will conclude with some reflections upon possible means of removing the links between genocide and scarcity.

The means fall into two broad patterns. First, there is the question of how "scarcity" can be dealt with so that it does not put pressure on regimes to commit genocide. Second, there is the more general question of how genocide can be prevented, even if such pressures cannot be wholly removed.

### *Reducing Scarcities*
As we have seen, "scarcity" takes a number of different forms: psychological, political, and material. Let us consider each in turn.

The psychological expectation of ever increasing material satisfaction is deeply embedded in the modern worldview, but instead of attempting to dominate nature, we could respect and work with it, seeing ourselves as part of nature, and dependent upon it for our very existence. Another approach would call attention to the fact that cutting down rain forests, for example, is not the best use to which they can be put, and that many large-scale development projects in indigenous areas have been failures at great cost in terms of lives, money, and damage to the environment.

Deprivation, on the other hand, is the hallmark of political scarcity. It contains three elements: deprivation in terms of power, material well-being, and respect. Plural societies often display these forms of deprivation, prompting challenges to the structure of authority, and leading in turn to repression, renewed demands for equality or autonomy, and, without outside intervention, genocide. In fact, the most frequent source of genocide in the twentieth century was that which sprang from the political scarcity imposed by domination and exclusion. The question, then, is not only of divided societies, but also of authoritarian government.

The conditions for averting genocide that arises in part from political scarcity are reasonably clear. Some form of power sharing would be necessary. The precise form it would take could vary from society to society, but it might involve, for example, federalism, a degree of autonomy, or certain offices, or a percentage of offices in the military, bureaucracy, or parliament, being reserved for members of the previously subordinate group. It would require justice in the allocation of goods. And finally, it would require some degree of acceptance of the minority group as persons, and the repudiation of stereotypes and prejudices that had served as justifications for exclusion from equal treatment.

The conditions are easily stated, but societies have their own histories, and their social arrangements are not accidental. The alternative to changing the existing arrangements is outside intervention.

The third form of scarcity is the most obvious and the most difficult to overcome. Material scarcity has two possible sources: resources either are not available or have been degraded in ways that make them less productive, and there may be fewer goods per capita due to population expansion. The solutions to resource scarcity and population explosion are both technical and political. Further, these two sources of scarcity are so entangled that it is not possible to solve one without the other.

High growth rates in population tend to occur precisely in societies that can least afford them, those places that are already resource scarce or whose government allocates resources in ways that favor some groups and deprive others. Given the existing strains in such societies, rapid population growth will lead to increased scarcity, violence, and possible genocide. The spiral of scarcity will increase both because goods now have to be divided among more people and because attempts to increase production (especially of food and shelter) often produce severe ecological damage, undermining further the capacity to meet material needs.

Populations in the past have been reduced within a specific territory by migration, disease, famine, war, and genocide. These factors may operate in the future; less apocalyptic visions, however, are possible, though they are not without their own difficulties in terms of implementation. High birthrates will tend to fall where four conditions are present: a low mortality rate, a relative improvement in earnings, the availability of family planning and birth control, and an equal status for women. Where these conditions are not met, the surge in population will most likely continue, leading both to increasing impoverishment and to long-term environmental damage.

Solutions to the problems of resource scarcity are likewise difficult to implement, but some progress can be made if the size of the population can be stabilized. Too often, however, the response to growing population has been to adopt means that may offer some temporary relief, but lead to even more resource scarcity in the future.

## Institutional and Political Means

Scarcities exacerbate the conditions that favor genocidal choices, but they do so within societies already divided along racial, religious, or ethnic lines and governed by authoritarian regimes. This realization brings us, then, to the more general question of how genocide can be prevented, even if not all of the pressures exerted by scarcities can be removed.

There are numerous steps that can be taken to prevent genocide. A carrot-and-stick approach might be adopted by states and international organizations to support social and political transformation in divided and repressive societies. Societies that are likely to resort to genocide can be identified and closely monitored. Early warning systems can be devised to forecast the likelihood of genocide, allowing governments and international bodies time to decide upon appropriate responses. Publicity and the mobilization by nongovernmental organizations of a human-rights constituency to pressure governments to act are also important in this context. International law can be strengthened through the creation of a standing, permanent tribunal to sit in judgment of those people who commit war crimes, crimes against humanity, and genocide. Also, the right of humanitarian intervention must be both recognized and made effective. At present, individual states have the capacity to intervene, and the United Nations is capable of putting together a coalition of forces, as in Bosnia and Somalia. But far more effective, and most likely a precondition for preventing genocide, is a permanent, standing international force that can be rapidly deployed. What is also crucial, for it is unlikely that the other steps will be undertaken to any extent without it, is for states to enlarge their definition of national interest to include the prevention of genocide. Here morality and realpolitik largely coincide.

## Conclusion

Many, if not all, of the strategies for preventing genocide and reducing the scarcities—psychological, political, and material—that can contribute to it could be effective, *if implemented.* The prevention of genocide, however, is less a matter of knowledge than of political will. Two related questions thus hang over the future: Will the states and international organizations of the world continue to be bystanders to genocide, looking on and doing little? Or will a human capacity to resolve political and social problems in a manner befitting humankind finally assert itself in this century?

## Ways Out

There are neither simple nor guaranteed solutions to the problems of scarcity, genocide, or the increasing likelihood that the material scarcities of the twenty-first century will exacerbate the pressures toward genocide already exerted by scarcities rooted in politics and modern expectations. But there are possible solutions, and even if not completely effective, they could mitigate or even reduce the incidence of genocide.

If scarcity contributes to the decision to commit genocide, then it is plausible to attempt to reduce scarcity. But as we have seen, there are several forms of scarcity. A reduction in material scarcity will require above all a decrease in population growth. Raising the status of women and providing family planning are crucial here. To prevent the continued assault on the lives of indigenous peoples will require a change in attitudes toward the environment, greater concern by international lending agencies for the environmental and human effects of "development," and restraint by global capitalism. Political scarcity could be reduced by power sharing and the replacement of authoritarianism by democracy. An economy adequate to meet needs is also crucial.

On the international plane, many steps could help to prevent genocide. But the most important of these methods is for governments to redefine "national interest" to include the prevention of genocide. Until there is political will to take effective steps to prevent this crime against humankind, genocide will remain a distinct possibility.

## Suggested Reading

Arens, Richard, ed. 1976. *Genocide in Paraguay.* Philadelphia: Temple Univ. Press.

Conquest, Robert. 1986. *The Harvest of Sorrow: Soviet Collectivization and the Terror-Famine.* New York: Oxford Univ. Press.

Fein, Helen. 1993. "Accounting for Genocide after 1945: Theories and Some Findings." *International Journal on Group Rights* 1: 79–106.

Hirsch, Herbert. 1995. *Genocide and the Politics of Memory: Studying Death to Preserve Life.* Chapel Hill: Univ. of North Carolina Press.

Hobbes, Thomas. 1960. *Leviathan; or, The Matter, Forme, and Power of a Commonwealth Ecclesiasticall and Civil.* 1651. Reprint. Oxford: Blackwell.

Homer-Dixon, Thomas F. 1991. "On the Threshold: Environmental Changes as Causes of Acute Conflict." *International Security* 16: 76–116.

Kuper, Leo. 1981. *Genocide: Its Political Use in the Twentieth Century.* New Haven: Yale Univ. Press.

Smith, Roger W. 1987. "Human Destructiveness and Politics: The Twentieth Century as an Age of Genocide." In *Genocide and the Modern Age: Etiology and Case Studies of Mass Death,* edited by Isidor Wallimann and Michael N. Dobkowski, 21–39. Westport, Conn.: Greenwood Press.

———. 1998. "Scarcity and Genocide." In *The Coming Age of Scarcity: Preventing Mass Death and Genocide in the Twenty-first Century*, edited by Michael Dobkowski and Isidor Wallimann, 199–219. Syracuse: Syracuse Univ. Press.

Van Crevold, Martin L. 1991. *The Transformation of War*. New York: Free Press.

# 4.4   Gregory H. Stanton, "The Eight Stages of Genocide"

Classification Symbolization Dehumanization Organization Polarization Preparation Extermination Denial

Genocide is a process that develops in eight stages that are predictable but not inexorable. At each stage, preventive measures can stop it. The later stages must be preceded by the earlier stages, though earlier stages continue to operate throughout the process.

**1. CLASSIFICATION:** All cultures have categories to distinguish people into "us and them" by ethnicity, race, religion, or nationality: German and Jew, Hutu and Tutsi. Bipolar societies that lack mixed categories, such as Rwanda and Burundi, are the most likely to have genocide. The main preventive measure at this early stage is to develop universalistic institutions that transcend ethnic or racial divisions, that actively promote tolerance and understanding, and that promote classifications that transcend the divisions. The Catholic church could have played this role in Rwanda, had it not been riven by the same ethnic cleavages as Rwandan society. Promotion of a common language in countries like Tanzania has also promoted transcendent national identity. This search for common ground is vital to early prevention of genocide.

**2. SYMBOLIZATION:** We give names or other symbols to the classifications. We name people "Jews" or "Gypsies", or distinguish them by colors or dress; and apply the symbols to members of groups. Classification and symbolization are universally human and do not necessarily result in genocide unless they lead to the next stage, dehumanization. When combined with hatred, symbols may be forced upon unwilling members of pariah groups: the yellow star for Jews under Nazi rule, the blue scarf for people from the Eastern Zone in Khmer Rouge Cambodia. To combat symbolization, hate symbols can be legally forbidden (swastikas) as can hate speech. Group marking like gang clothing or tribal scarring can be outlawed, as well. The problem is that legal limitations will fail if unsupported by popular cultural enforcement. Though Hutu and Tutsi were forbidden words in Burundi until the 1980s, code-words replaced them. If widely supported, however, denial of symbolization can be powerful, as it was in Bulgaria, where the government refused to supply enough yellow badges and at least eighty percent of Jews did not wear them, depriving the yellow star of its significance as a Nazi symbol for Jews.

**3. DEHUMANIZATION:** One group denies the humanity of the other group. Members of it are equated with animals, vermin, insects or diseases. Dehumanization overcomes the normal human revulsion against murder. At this stage, hate propaganda in print and on hate radios is used to vilify the victim group. In combating this dehumanization, incitement to genocide should not be confused with protected speech. Genocidal societies lack constitutional protection for countervailing speech, and should be treated differently than democracies. Local and international leaders should condemn the use of hate speech and make it culturally unacceptable. Leaders who incite genocide should be banned from international travel and have their foreign finances frozen. Hate radio stations should be shut down, and hate propaganda banned. Hate crimes and atrocities should be promptly punished.

**4. ORGANIZATION:** Genocide is always organized, usually by the state, often using militias to provide deniability of state responsibility (the Janjaweed in Darfur). Sometimes organization is informal (Hindu mobs led by local RSS militants) or decentralized (terrorist groups). Special army units or militias are often trained and armed. Plans are made for genocidal killings. To combat this stage, membership in these militias should be outlawed. Their leaders should be denied visas for foreign travel. The U.N. should impose arms embargoes on governments and citizens of countries involved in genocidal massacres, and create commissions to investigate violations, as was done in post-genocide Rwanda.

**5. POLARIZATION:** Extremists drive the groups apart. Hate groups broadcast polarizing propaganda. Laws may forbid intermarriage or social interaction. Extremist terrorism targets moderates, intimidating and silencing the center. Moderates from the perpetrators' own group are most able to stop genocide, so are the first to be arrested and killed. Prevention may mean security protection for moderate leaders or assistance to human rights groups. Assets of extremists may be seized, and visas for international travel denied to them. Coups d'état by extremists should be opposed by international sanctions.

**6. PREPARATION:** Victims are identified and separated out because of their ethnic or religious identity. Death lists are drawn up. Members of victim groups are forced to wear identifying symbols. Their property is expropriated. They are often segregated into ghettoes, deported into concentration camps, or confined to a famine-struck region and starved. At this stage, a Genocide Emergency must be declared. If the political will of the great powers, regional alliances, or the U.N. Security Council can be mobilized, armed international intervention should be prepared, or heavy assistance provided to the victim group to prepare for its self-defense. Otherwise, at least humanitarian assistance should be organized by the U.N. and private relief groups for the inevitable tide of refugees to come.

**7. EXTERMINATION** begins, and quickly becomes the mass killing legally called "genocide." It is "extermination" to the killers because they do not believe their victims to be fully human. When it is sponsored by the state, the armed forces often work with militias to do the killing. Sometimes the genocide results in revenge killings by groups against each other, creating the downward whirlpool-like cycle of bilateral genocide (as in Burundi). At this stage, only rapid and overwhelming armed intervention can stop genocide. Real safe areas or refugee escape corridors should be established with heavily armed international protection. (An unsafe "safe" area is worse than none at all.) The U.N. Standing High Readiness Brigade, EU Rapid Response Force, or regional forces—should be authorized to act by the U.N. Security Council if the genocide is small. For larger interventions, a multilateral force authorized by the U.N. should intervene. If the U.N. is paralyzed, regional alliances must act. It is time to recognize that the international responsibility to protect transcends the narrow interests of individual nation states. If strong nations will not provide troops to intervene directly, they should provide the airlift, equipment, and financial means necessary for regional states to intervene.

**8. DENIAL** is the eighth stage that always follows a genocide. It is among the surest indicators of further genocidal massacres. The perpetrators of genocide dig up the mass graves, burn the bodies, try to cover up the evidence and intimidate the witnesses. They deny that they committed any crimes, and often blame what happened on the victims. They block investigations of the crimes, and continue to govern until driven from power by force, when they flee into exile. There they remain with impunity, like Pol Pot or Idi Amin, unless they are captured and a tribunal is established to try them. The response to denial is punishment by an international tribunal or national courts. There the evidence can be heard, and the perpetrators punished. Tribunals like the Yugoslav or Rwanda Tribunals, or an international tribunal to try the Khmer Rouge in Cambodia, or an International Criminal Court may not deter the worst genocidal killers. But with the political will to arrest and prosecute them, some may be brought to justice.

# Part III

*Genocidal Crimes*

# 5

# Cases of Genocide

Although the concept and term of "genocide" is relatively new, the crime itself has spanned the ages, from antiquity through today. The list of genocides perpetrated by various groups against others is long and sordid. A mere fraction of the genocides perpetrated over the centuries include, for example, the following: the Athenian mass slaughter of the Melians (416 BCE); the destruction of Carthage by the Romans (146 BCE); various genocides perpetrated by the Mongols (over the course of the thirteenth century); the Puritan genocide of the Pequots (1637); the genocide of the Yuki Indians of Round Valley, California by American settlers (1851–1880); the massacre of the Cheyennes by U.S. Cavalry troops (1864); the genocide of the Hereros of Southwest Africa by German troops (1904); the Ottoman Turk genocide of the Armenians (1915–1923); the Soviet manmade famine in Ukraine (1932–1933); the Nazi genocide of the Jews, Roma, and Sinti, and the physically and mentally handicapped (1933–1945); the Khmer Rouge "autogenocide" of their fellow Cambodians (1975–1979); the Iraqi gassing of the Kurds in northern Iraq (1988); the extremist Hutu genocide of Tutsi and moderate Hutu in Rwanda (1994); the Serb massacre of Bosnian Muslim boys and men at Srebrenica (1995); and the ongoing genocide of the black Africans of Darfur by Government of Sudan troops and *Janjaweed* (Arab militia) (2003–present).

Genocide over the ages has been perpetrated for a wide variety of reasons. Among some of the many motives driving perpetrators are the following (some of which overlap): ideological, xenophobic, hegemonic, retributive, repressive, developmental, and despotic.

Tellingly, and disturbingly, the twentieth century has come to be referred to by many as "the century of genocide." That is true due to the fact that every single decade of the twentieth century was marred by at least one genocide. It is also the century that saw the introduction of modern inventions and technology to help facilitate and expedite genocide (e.g., the use of railroads to transport victims to their deaths as the Ottoman Turks and Nazis did; bureaucracy; teletype machines; the forerunner of computers such as the use of the Hollerith machine by the Nazis for the purpose of taking the census; industrial mechanization of the killing process such as the Nazis' use of gas chambers and crematoria; and the use of poison gas by the Iraqi regime of Saddam Hussein to kill Iraqi Kurds). At one and the same time, it is significant to note that not all of the mass killing perpetrated in the twentieth century relied on modern technology; indeed, in 1994, for example, the extremist Hutus in Rwanda carried out a genocide of between 500,000 and one million people (Tutsis and moderate Hutus) primarily using machetes and other farm implements.

Many of the genocides perpetrated in the twentieth century were, ironically, carried out at a time when many were speaking of the glorious progress being made *vis-à-vis* the protection of the individual's basic human rights across the globe. The latter was part and parcel of the so-called "human rights regime" that saw the creation and ratification of such notable and noble documents as the UN Declaration of Human Rights (1948) and the UN Convention on the Prevention of and Punishment of Genocide, to mention but two.

The twenty-first century has already seen its first genocide, that of the black Africans of Darfur. It is a genocide that has raged for more than half a decade (2003–present) as the United Nations, individual nations, and others have looked on and engaged in not much more than talk, talk, and more talk. Indeed, it appears that despite all of the admonitions of "Never Again" issued by politicians, statesmen, survivors of various genocides, and human rights activists, little to nothing has truly been learned in regard to the need to stanch major human rights abuses early on, before they degenerate into genocide. Or, possibly more accurately, plenty of lessons have been learned but the international community has lacked (and continues to lack) the political will to overcome its addiction to *realpolitik*.

This section comprises five articles that address various genocidal events, ranging from those perpetrated in antiquity through the ongoing genocide in Darfur today. The section begins with a detailed examination ("The History of Genocide: An Overview"), by historian Paul R. Bartrop and genocide scholar Samuel Totten, who provide an overview of genocide through the ages, addressing a range of examples of genocide that have been perpetrated over time.

Although the plight and fate of the Jews during the Holocaust years is the most well-known genocide in history, the editors still hold it important to include a chapter on that genocide in this volume. In "Holocaust: Genocide of the Jews," historian Donald Niewyk does an outstanding job of delineating the antecedents, chronology, and main events of the Holocaust in a relatively short space.

Throughout history, rape during warfare and genocidal events has been a constant. For centuries, male combatants automatically assumed that female bodies were part and parcel of what they were entitled to as they engaged in battle. Beginning in the 1990s, though, rape began to be perceived in a different light, and that was a direct result of several watershed decisions at the International Criminal Tribunal for the former Yugoslavia (ICTY) and the International Criminal Tribunal for Rwanda (ICTR). More specifically, in the case of Jean-Paul Akayesu, the first person ever to be convicted for the crime of genocide, the ICTR found that rape, under certain conditions, can and does constitute genocide (September 2, 1998). According to the evidence mounted against Akayesu, the former mayor of the commune of Taba, numerous Tutsi women who had sought sanctuary within Taba were systematically raped by local militia. Akayesu was found to have encouraged and condoned such acts by his "attitude and his utterances." The ICTR found that "sexual violence was an 'integral' part of the process of destruction of the Tutsi ethnic group. The rape of Tutsi women was systematic and was perpetrated against all Tutsi women and solely against them." In "State Rape: Sexual Violence as Genocide," Lisa Sharlach examines how rape has been (and continues to be, at least in certain cases) condoned, supported, and perpetrated by state officials and why the latter constitutes genocide under international law.

In 1995, during the course of the ongoing civil war in the former Yugoslavia, a so-called "safe area" established by the United Nations in the small Bosnian city of Srebrenica was overrun by Bosnian Serb forces under the command of General Ratko Mladic. Fleeing for their safety, seeking shelter and protection from Serbian aggression, thousands of Bosnian Muslims rushed to Potocari, where a UN contingent of Dutch troops, codenamed Dutchbat, were based. The inhabitants of Srebrenica begged the UN troops for assistance but the Serbs overran the Dutchbat posts: the women, youngest children, and eldest members of the community were bused away and the boys and men hunted down, rounded up, and slaughtered. Between 7,000 and 8,000 males were murdered in cold blood. Reminiscent of the mass murder conducted by the *Einsatzgruppen* in Poland and the Soviet Union during the Holocaust years, the Bosnian Muslim males were lined up and machine-gunned, and then buried in mass graves. The massacre was the largest single massacre in Europe since the Holocaust. The article "Srebrenica," by Jan Willem Honig, details what happened to the inhabitants of the city during that summer of 1995. In doing so, Honig addresses the following: the actors involved, the Bosnian Serb attack on the Dutchbat posts, Srebrenica's fall, the UN Security Council's response, the forced evacuation of Bosnian Muslim women, children, and the elderly, the mass killing of the Bosnian boys and men, and the aftermath of the massacre.

The last piece in this section, "Genocide in Darfur" by Samuel Totten, discusses the various causes of the Darfur crisis, the genocidal actions of the Government of Sudan and the *Janjaweed*, and the anemic reaction of the international community to the mass killing, mass rape, and massive forced dislocation of millions of people from their villages.

# 5.1   Paul R. Bartrop and Samuel Totten, "The History of Genocide: An Overview"

## Introduction

Genocide is a crime that has been committed throughout the ages. Indeed, every century of recorded history has been marred by genocidal acts. It was not until the twentieth century, though, that this particular act of mass murder was given the name "genocide." The term itself was originally coined in 1944 by Raphael Lemkin, a Polish-Jewish jurist who lost most of his family members in the maw of the Holocaust. It was a term appropriated by the fledging United Nations to describe the planned, systematic mass murder, in whole or part, of a particular group of people in its landmark convention, the United Nations Convention on the Prevention and Punishment of the Crime of Genocide (UNCG).

In this chapter, we provide an overview of the history of genocide. In doing so, we discuss, albeit briefly, the following: genocide through the ages, genocide in the twentieth century, Raphael Lemkin's efforts to staunch genocide, the development and ratification of the U.N. Convention on the Prevention and Punishment of the Crime of Genocide (1948), definitional issues, genocide during the Cold War years and the reaction of the international community, genocide in the post-Cold War years (late 1980s–2003), and the possibility and likelihood of intervening and preventing future cases of genocide.

## Genocide Through the Ages

As Chalk and Jonassohn (1988) have noted, "The first genocidal killing is lost in antiquity" (p. 41). That said, as previously noted, genocide is a new word for an ancient practice, and it has taken many forms in the past. The Hebrew Bible contains a number of important passages that refer to mass destruction of a kind which we would, today, identify as genocide. The Greeks engaged in the practice, as chronicled by Thucydides in the famous case of the island inhabitants of Melos, as did the Romans—most notably in the fate that befell the inhabitants of Rome's arch-enemy Carthage, where both the people were destroyed and the land on which they lived was despoiled. (For a detailed discussion of the history of genocide, including the earliest genocides, see Chalk & Jonassohn, 1991.)

In the aftermath of the Roman victories over the Jews of Palestine (Judaea) during the first century CE, at which time the Temple was destroyed (70 CE) and the last remnants of Jewish opposition to Roman rule under Simeon Bar Kochba were snuffed out at Betar (135 CE), the Jews were a devastated people. Over half a million had been killed in the aftermath of the wars, their cities had been laid waste (Katz, 1994, pp. 80–81), and the survivors were dispersed through slave markets across the known world (Safrai, 1976, pp. 330–335). In what was a clear case of genocide, the Jewish state was extinguished, and would not appear again for over 1,800 years.

Other cases of mass killing in the premodern period are similarly prominent, embracing a variety of locations and situations. As the Mongols under Genghis Khan swept through central Asia and eastern Europe during the thirteenth century, they wrought havoc and destruction on a massive scale. There is little doubt that this was done as a matter of deliberate policy; the more brutal the Mongols were, the more their reputation for violence spread. This, in turn, made it easier to conquer new territories and cities. The death and destruction wrought by the Mongols was a direct outcome of the need to find a practical method of ruling a large empire using limited resources.

Another example of what may be termed a premodern genocide was the persecution and eradication in the early thirteenth century of the Cathars (or Albigensians) of France, who were accused by the church of heresy. In its drive to wipe out all traces of dissent, the French church fell on the free-thinking people of the Languedoc region, destroying them utterly (O'Shea, 2001). Their example introduces the issue of doctrine (or ideology) to our under-standing of genocide. By this stage, Europe had moved far down the road toward becoming a persecuting society established on notions of religious intolerance, a frightening portent of things to come at the dawn of the modern age. The development of such attitudes, exempli-fied in the European perspective of the undesirability of "the Other," ultimately became internalized as part of European civilization, and it was this development which dominated European society just at the time Europe began to expand overseas into non-European cul-tures. This ethos of intolerance and persecution, coupled with an advanced military technol-ogy, was to have a devastating effect of the societies being invaded—though, it must be recalled, in numerous ways the Europeans were only applying to populations overseas the kind of actions they had already been doing to themselves for centuries.

The destruction of the indigenous peoples of the Americas represents one of the most extensive human catastrophes in history. The pace and magnitude of the devastation varied from region to region over the years, but it can safely be concluded that in the two-and-a-half centuries following Christopher Columbus's "discovery" of the Americas in 1492, probably 95% of the pre-Columbian population had been eradicated—by disease as well as by deliber-ate policy on the part of the Spanish, the French, the English, and, ultimately, by the American-born heirs of those colonizing nations (Stannard, 1992). It was a massive case of population collapse, sometimes intentional, sometimes not, but nonetheless effective in clear-ing the way for the European expropriation of two continents. This was a horrific case of mass human destruction, in which tens of millions of people lost their lives.

In the case of the indigenous peoples within the United States, the destruction did not stop once the people had died or been killed. Policies of population removal, dispossession of lands, forced assimilation and confinement to "reservations" meant that even the survivors were denied the opportunity to retain a sense of peoplehood.

In order to reinforce the "European-ness" of the genocidal impulse at this time, we need look no further than the fate of the Jews in eastern Poland and the Ukraine in the mid-seventeenth century. A series of massacres perpetrated by the Ukrainian Cossacks under the leadership of Bogdan Chmielnicki saw the death of up to 100,000 Jews and the destruction of perhaps 700 communities between 1648 and 1654 (though instances of anti-Jewish pogroms kept appearing for several years after this).

Religious persecution resulting in mass death was a constant throughout the early modern period, some of the most terrible examples taking place before and during the Thirty Years' War. Some areas in the lands that were later to comprise Germany were depopulated by as much as 90 percent, while in France the struggle between Catholics and Protestants (in their French variant, Huguenots) was played out after the revocation of the Edict of Nantes. On St. Bartholomew's Day (August 24, 1572) massacres of the Huguenot leadership took place all over Paris, and in the days that followed scores of thousands more were killed all over France. Up to 100,000 men, women and children were murdered as a result of these persecutions.

The pattern of European-inspired brutality that had hit the Americas from 1492, and been refined in Europe itself in the years that followed, was repeated in other lands of European colonial settlement later, particularly in Australia—after the continent had been claimed for Britain and settled as a convict colony (or rather, series of colonies) from 1788 onwards. For well over a century, for example, it was generally accepted in Australian popular wisdom that a woman named Truggernanna (sometimes spelled Truganini), of the Bruny Island people, was "the last Tasmanian," and that after her death in 1876 an entire people had been exterminated—the first "total" genocide in history. The nonsense of this myth has since been demonstrated many times over; but the story of "the last Tasmanian" has very deep roots which are still being fed today (Reynolds, 1995). This does not alter the fact, however, that the indigenous Tasmanians suffered a population collapse (largely through warfare with the encroaching settlers, through diseases, and, after the concentration and removal of the remaining tribal members to Tasmania's Flinders Island, through a pitiful longing for their lost homeland and way of life in which they simply pined away) as complete as any that had ever taken place elsewhere, and probably more than most.

The situation of the Aborigines in mainland Australia was very different, and serves as yet another dimension to the study of genocide before the modern era. The question that must be asked is straightforward: did the destruction of Aboriginal society in the century following the arrival of the First Fleet in 1788 constitute an act of genocide? (Reynolds, 2001). For some, unequivocally so; for others, the answer is nowhere near as obvious. Here, we find ourselves studying a situation in which there was no definite state-initiated plan of mass extermination; indeed, it was frequently the case that colonial governments went to great lengths to maintain Aboriginal security in the face of settler and pastoralist encroachments, and of punishments (even hangings) of those found guilty of the murder of Aborigines. Despite this, there were immense and very intensive periods of killing in the bush, accompanied by enormous population losses commensurate with those in the Americas as a result of disease and starvation.

There is no doubt that the nineteenth century saw the effective destruction of Aboriginal society by European settlement, but where genocide is concerned this must be understood against two essential facts. In the first place, there was no unified stance on the Aborigines throughout the nineteenth century, as the Australian continent was divided into six separate British colonies, mostly self-governing from the middle of the century, until federation in 1901. Secondly, no government at any time displayed the necessary intent, in word or in deed, to prove the existence of a genocidal policy. This is no way mitigates the catastrophe which destroyed the Aborigines, but neither does the history show that that tragedy was the result of what might be termed genocide.

If there is debate among some scholars concerning the question of genocide in nineteenth century Australia, there can be no doubt that one series of actions in the twentieth century fits the United Nations Genocide Convention perfectly. This relates to the forcible removal of children of part-Aboriginal descent from their parents and subsequent placement in a non-Aboriginal environment for the purpose of "breeding out the color." The policy, which was set in place by state and federal governments, was to last in various forms until the 1970s. It decimated at least two generations of Aborigines of mixed descent, and in a major federal government inquiry in the late 1990s, the allegation of genocide of these "Stolen Generations" was for the first time raised in an official capacity (Bartrop, 2001; Reynolds, 2001, pp. 162–165).

Returning to the nineteenth century, colonial expansion across the globe was the most likely scenario in which genocidal episodes took place at this point in time, and it is here that we must be very careful to distinguish between instances of death and destruction that took place in wartime—during which innocent people were killed as the by-product of conflict (what in the twentieth century would come to be called "collateral damage")—and massacres and other deliberate violations of human rights in which wanton and wholesale annihilation took place. These latter events clearly fell under a different heading from the sort of destruction that usually occurred in wartime. This must be understood clearly. There is a relationship between war and genocide, of course, but war does not have to be present for genocide to be perpetrated (Bartrop, 2002).

Genocide, though while occurring often throughout history, reached its zenith during the twentieth century, and it is to this period we now turn.


## Genocide in the Twentieth Century

The twentieth century has been deemed by some to be "the century of genocide" (Smith, 1987; Totten, Parsons, & Charny, 1997). That is due to the fact that the twentieth century was a century plagued by genocide. Indeed, genocidal acts were perpetrated in every decade of the century, and, over the course of the century, on at least four different continents (Africa, Asia, Europe, and South America)—and arguably, Australia (i.e., the "Stolen Generations"). Among such genocides were: the German-perpetrated genocide of the Herero in southwest Africa in 1904; the Ottoman Turk genocide of the Armenians between 1915 and 1918; the Soviet man-made famine in Ukraine in 1932–1933; the Holocaust (1933–1945); the Bangladesh Genocide (1971); the Khmer Rouge-perpetrated genocide in Kampuchea (Cambodia) 1975–1979; the Iraqi genocide of its Kurdish population in the late 1980s; the 1994 Rwandan genocide of the Tutsis and moderate Hutus by the extremist Hutus; and the genocide committed in the former Yugoslavia in the early to mid-1990s. There were also the almost totally unnoticed genocides of many indigenous groups across the globe.

Three major genocides were perpetrated over the course of the first half of the century: the Ottoman Turk genocide of the Armenians, the Soviet manmade famine in Ukraine, and the Holocaust.

While the history of the genocide of the Armenians by the Ottoman Turks from 1915 onward is now well known, that of the enormous massacres of Armenians between 1894 and 1896, and again in 1909, is less so. Yet it was these massacres that, in numerous ways, led the Turks to adopt a mind-set conducive to their later genocidal actions. The worst of the massacres took place in 1895, when at least 100,000 (and certainly more, possibly as high as 200,000 to 300,000) Armenian civilians were killed by Turkish mobs acting under instruction from Sultan Abdul Hamid II (a direction which gave the slaughter its name as the "Hamidian Massacres"). While these statistics were horrible enough, they were but a prelude to the even greater number of killed—at least one million, according to most accounts, though on the balance of probabilities probably closer to 1.5 million—in the genocide that was perpetrated by the Young Turks after April 1915. At that time, well after the outbreak of World War I, the Turkish nationalist revolutionary government known as the Young Turks (formally, the Committee of Union and Progress) launched a wholesale assault against the Armenian population of the empire. It was far more extensive than the earlier massacres, and saw all the relevant agencies of government directed toward the singular aim of totally eradicating the Armenian presence in Turkey. That the genocide took place under the cover of war was more than just a matter of interest; the war was in reality a crucial part of the genocide's success. By conducting deportations of Armenians in places far off the beaten track, forcing many victims (primarily women and young children, including babies) into underpopulated desert regions of the empire, the Turks were able to exploit the war situation for the purpose of achieving their genocidal aims. The eventual result was a loss of life in a very short space of time.

In Ukraine, over the course of 1932–1933, between five and seven million peasants—most of them ethnic Ukrainians—starved to death due to a Soviet manmade famine as a result of Josef Stalin's government having seized all crops and methods of food production. In this case, the huge number of deaths was the product of ideologically-driven social destruction. Purportedly, the goal was the destruction of the so-called "kulak" class: the independent peasantry who were sacrificed in Stalin's urgent desire to collectivize the agricultural sector along communist lines. In fact, anyone who supported Ukrainization (Ukrainian nationalism, freedom, and the expression of its culture) was targeted, including the poorest of the poor. Accompanying this was the forced integration of a diverse array of religious and national groups into the existing Soviet political structure, a move which took place in an environment of forced Russification. This had a catastrophic effect on Ukrainian national aspirations, hopes which had been initially dashed in the immediate aftermath of the Great War and the effective reconquest of the country by the nascent Red Army in the early 1920s.

As the Soviets swept through Ukraine, Stalin's agents pointed to the need to wage a class war for the good of the entire Soviet Union and the communist revolution. The genocide, a product of an extreme form of social engineering, transformed traditional forms of land holding and land use, and literally stripped the countryside of everything that could be consumed by the peasantry.

As mentioned above, while Stalin was committed to the destruction of the kulak class, people from a variety of classes, religions, and ethnic/national groups were victims of the deliberately-inflicted starvation policies—although, again, Ukrainians formed the majority of those who lost their lives. Despite this, by even the strictest of definitional interpretations the massive destruction wrought by the Soviet regime can be classified as genocide.

Gasting a giant shadow over the myriad positive achievements of the twentieth century is the Nazi Holocaust of the Jewish people, a genocidal event that resulted in a horrific break with all of the humanitarian traditions that had been developing in Europe over the previous thousand years. The relationship between mass death and the industrial state as manifested in the Holocaust was both intimate and interdependent.

The perpetrators of the Nazi Holocaust had but one aim in mind: the physical removal of all Jews falling under their rule and beyond. A change of status through religious conversion or naturalization was not acceptable to the Nazis. What was planned and what was intended was a total annihilation, from which none would be allowed to escape. The Nazis intended nothing less than the physical destruction, through murder, of every Jew who fell into their net.

The means the Nazis employed in order to achieve their murderous aims, especially from early 1942 onwards, was the death (or extermination) camp (*Vernichtungslager*), though earlier murderous measures such as mass shootings by mobile killing squads known as Einsatzgruppen, which accompanied the Nazi invasion of the Soviet Union in mid-1941, also played a huge role in the extermination program. So, too, did brutal treatment and deliberately-induced starvation policies in ghettos and other segregated areas, and the early use of gas vans.

The six death camps established in Poland for the mass murder of the Jews—Auschwitz-Birkenau, Belzec, Chelmno, Majdanek, Sobibor, and Treblinka—were a departure from anything previously visualized in both their design and character. With the exception of Auschwitz (which must always fit into a category of its own in any discussion of the Holocaust), these camps were institutions designed to methodically and efficiently murder millions of people. The mass murders took place in specially designed gas chambers. The death camps became the most lucid and unequivocal statement National Socialism made about itself, demonstrating beyond doubt that it was an antihuman ideology in which respect for life and moral goodness counted for nothing.

The Nazi death camps add to our knowledge of genocide in two important ways. In the first place, it shows us how a regime dedicated to mass murder mobilized all its resources for the purpose of feeding the demands of an industry that had been deliberately assigned the tasks of incarceration, degradation, and annihilation. Second, the history and fate of the camps demonstrates that genocidal regimes can be aware that their activities are of a criminal nature; just as the Turks did before them, the Nazis chose to carry out their murderous assignments in places far removed from key population centers, accompanied by an exhaustive effort to destroy as much evidence of the killing as possible prior to being overrun by the advancing Allied forces.

A number of the aforementioned genocides (meaning the long list of genocides perpetrated over the course of the twentieth century) either went undetected until the mass killing was well under way and tens of thousands or more had already been murdered; or, more commonly, they were detected by outside governments and/or the United Nations (in the latter case, after 1945), but the officials of such entities were, for various reasons, hesitant or simply unwilling to deem the actions genocide. Primarily, though, officials of governments (other than those where the genocide was being perpetrated) were cognizant of the fact that if they deemed a situation to be "genocide," not only would there be a moral imperative to attempt to prevent it, but—if their nation was a signatory to the UN Convention on Genocide—a legal imperative as well. In many cases, realpolitik also played a role in "hearing no evil, seeing no evil." And just like the officials of individual nations, the officials of the United Nations acted similarly.

The governments of individual states and officials of the United Nations, though, are not the only entities that have been tentative about deeming a series of mass murders "genocidal" or outright genocide. Indeed, many journalists, human rights activists, humanitarian personnel, and even genocide scholars have often been hesitant—most often early on, but sometimes even well into the killing period—to designate a situation "genocidal." It is important to note that some of these individuals and groups, particularly scholars, were not being circumspect for cowardly or evasive reasons—nor due to any other ulterior motive—but rather because they were (and are) intent on using the term only when it is truly applicable. Such individuals are cognizant and appreciative of the fact that the terms "genocide" and genocidal" are highly charged terms, and thus look askance at the fact that the terms are often applied to situations that are not technically genocidal (Totten, 1999, pp. 35–36). Furthermore, they appreciate the fact that a loose use of the term/concept only serves to water down its import.

Conversely, there are others—more often than not these individuals and/or groups include certain journalists, politicians, and others who are not well-versed in the field of genocide studies—who tend to assert hastily that a situation is genocidal even when there is no hard evidence to support such an assertion. Again, a fast and loose use of the term is counterproductive in that it degenerates, over time, into a situation where it loses its real value and purpose.

Unfortunately, one cannot be sanguine about ending genocidal acts in the near future. Political, racial, religious, and social conflicts are rife across the globe and seemingly will be for a long time to come. Furthermore, there is as yet no single, central, and highly effective genocide early warning mechanism in place. Concomitantly, both the United Nations and individual states are not a little tentative about providing the needed resources and personnel to halt massive human rights abuses at their outset, when a situation may be slouching toward genocide. And yet, certain progress—some of it significant—has been made in addressing the problem of genocide, its prevention, and its punishment.

## Raphael Lemkin's Efforts to Prevent Genocide

No history of genocide would be complete without acknowledgment of the significant efforts and accomplishments of Raphael Lemkin (1900–1959). Lemkin was born in what was historically known as White Russia. As he grew up, he heard stories about vicious pogroms that were being perpetrated in the region where he lived. Such stories influenced him greatly. As he states in his autobiography, *Totally Unofficial Man*, "I could not define history with my childish mind, but I saw it vividly and strongly with my eyes, as a huge torture place of the innocent" (quoted in Lemkin, 2002, p. 370). Early in life, he also became aware of the fact that Ottoman Turkey perpetrated a genocide against its Armenian population, murdering more than a million women, children, and men. He was incensed that following World War I the 150 Turkish war criminals who had been arrested and interned by the British government on the island of Malta had been released. This shocking turn of events caused him to ponder the following:

> A nation that killed and the guilty persons were set free. Why is a man punished when he kills another man? Why is the killing of a million a lesser crime than the killing of a single individual? I didn't know all the answers, but I felt that a law against this type of racial or religious murder must be adopted by the world. (Lemkin, 2002, p. 371)

Eventually, Lemkin studied international criminal law, during which he became obsessed with the then current debate about the sanctity of state sovereignty. As he relates in his autobiography:

> [My professors] evoked the argument about sovereignty of states. "But sovereignty of states," I answered, "implies conducting an independent foreign and internal policy, building of schools, construction of roads, in brief, all types of activity directed towards the welfare of people. Sovereignty," I argued, "cannot be conceived as the right to kill millions of innocent people." (Lemkin, 2002, p. 371)

In October 1933, at an international conference for the unification of Penal Law in Madrid, he put forth the notion that there was a dire need "to outlaw the destruction of national, racial, and religious groups, [and that] the crime was so big that nothing less than declaring it an international offense would be adequate. This should be done by international treaty or convention" (Lemkin, 2002, p. 372).

The draft international law he proposed along such lines was not met with any enthusiasm; and indeed, he was told that the formulation of such laws was "not necessary, because they apply to crime(s) which occur seldom in history" (Lemkin, 2002, p. 367).

In 1939, with the Nazis on the move and following the initial bombing of Warsaw where he was living, Lemkin fled Poland, first to Sweden and then the United States (where he moved to Durham, North Carolina, having taken an appointment at Duke University). At the time, he sensed that the Nazis' intentions included more than simply conquering other nations for their land and wealth: "I knew that this was more than war, that this was the beginning of genocide, on a large scale" (Lemkin, 2002, p. 367).

Throughout World War II, Lemkin continued to work at a torrid pace to convince world leaders, including U.S. President Franklin Delano Roosevelt, of the critical need to pass an international law against the perpetration of genocide, but his Herculean efforts came to nil. Throughout this period, he was obsessed with the issue of genocide, writing about it, talking to anyone and everyone about the need to establish an international convention against genocide, and attempting to figure out ways to convince government officials and others to support his efforts. During this period he wrote what is considered his magnum opus, *Axis Rule in Occupied Europe: Laws of Occupation, Analysis of*

*Government, Proposals for Redress* (1944). It was also at this time that he coined the term "genocide."

Following the war, Lemkin served as an advisor to United States Justice Robert Jackson at the International Military Tribunal at Nuremberg, Germany, hoping the Nazi war criminals would be found guilty of genocide. It was not to be. Of the Nuremberg judgment, Lemkin asserted that

> it relieved only in part the moral tensions in the world. [T]he purely juridical consequences of the trials were wholly insufficient, [i.e.] the refusal of the Nuremberg Tribunal to establish for the future a precedent against this type of international crime. In brief, the Allies decided in Nuremberg a case against a past Hitler, but refused to envisage future Hitlers, or like situations. They did not want to or could not establish a rule of international law which would prevent and punish future crimes of the same type. . . .

> The Tribunal declared that it is bound by the Statute of the International Military Tribunal which did not contain the charge of genocide. In brief, the Germans were punished only for crimes committed during or in connection with the war of aggression (Lemkin, 2002, pp. 384, 385).

Lemkin eventually turned to the newly formed United Nations. Within a couple of days of returning to the United States from Europe, he had convinced the governments of Cuba, India, and Panama to sponsor his resolution that genocide be a crime under international law, without any limitations to war or peace. The resolution he prepared also "called for the preparation of an international treaty against genocide" (Lemkin, 2002, p. 368).

Initially, the Soviet Union argued against the resolution, but in the 1946 Assembly it changed its position and argued in favor of the Convention. Initially, the Soviet Union looked askance as such legislation, arguing that it was not needed. Many scholars have argued that the latter position was likely due to the heinous acts that the U.S.S.R. committed against both its own people and those of others, and that it feared being held accountable for them. Eventually, though, diplomatic efforts by other nations convinced the U.S.S.R. to support the nascent effort to prevent and punish genocide. Ultimately, the Assembly adopted the resolution to include the issue of genocide on its agenda for discussion. Subsequently, a special subcommittee of the Legal Committee was established to prepare the text of the resolution on genocide. Lemkin wrote that "The subcommittee decided to include, in the resolution, a declaration that genocide is a crime under international law, a condemnation of this crime by all civilized nations and the decision to prepare a convention on the prevention and punishment of the crime of genocide and to present it to the next Assembly" (quoted in Lemkin, 2002, pp. 386–387). Ultimately, there was an unanimous vote by the Legal Committee to support the resolution, and several days later the resolution was, likewise, adopted unanimously by the General Assembly.

In July 1948, a discussion of the resolution was undertaken by the U.N.'s Economic and Social Council in Geneva. Lemkin traveled to Geneva to act as the spokesman for the establishment of a U.N. Convention on Genocide. Of this period, Lemkin (2002) wrote that

> There were still three weeks before the Economic and Social Council would start discussing the Genocide Convention. I felt that the issue must be made important in the eyes of the delegates. Major John A. F. Ennals (of the World Association) organized two lectures on genocide; one in the building of the United Nations to which the delegates were invited, the other in the summer school which the World Federation of the U.N. Associations was running for foreign students. After both lectures a discussion followed. Interest was aroused by my historical examples dating from antiquity through the middle ages to modern times. Then questions were asked. I did not refrain from reading aloud from my historical files in considerable detail. In such a way I conveyed the impression that genocide is not the result of a casual mood of a ruler but that it has its place in history.

What can you do to prevent such a thing from happening?

You do exactly the same as to prevent other crimes. We have to deal with this matter on two levels: national and international. Nationally, we must make it a crime in our criminal codes and punish through national courts in the same way as we punish for larceny and arson.

On the international level, I continued, we must make every nation responsible to the world community, either by bringing up cases of genocide in the World Court of Justice in the Hague to which all civilized nations belong or in all organs of the U.N. The main thing is to make the nations of the world feel that minorities and weaker nations are not chickens in the hands of a farmer, to be slaughtered, but they are groups of people of great value to themselves and to world civilization (p. 388).

On September 15, 1948, in Paris, the Legal Committee met to discuss those acts which constituted genocide. Speaking of the discussion that ensued, Lemkin (2002) reported that

> The delegates seem[ed] to be lost in an endless discussion on the motives of the crime of genocide. Erling Wikborg of the Norwegian delegation proposed to include in the definition also the destruction of a group "in part." He argued that when intellectual leaders, who provide the forces of cohesion to the group, are destroyed, then the group is destroyed as such, as a group.
>
> Finally, the following formula emerged from the discussion: "deliberately inflicting on the group conditions of life calculated to bring about its physical destruction in whole or in part." In order to avoid misapplication of this article in cases when people objectively suffer from bad conditions such as extreme poverty, unsanitary conditions and the like, which generally prevail in a country or locality, the Committee required that the intent to destroy the groups should be strengthened by the additional expression of intent such as "deliberately inflicting conditions of life calculated to bring about . . ."
>
> Two days later the representatives of twenty two nations signed the Convention. [A s]ignature meant the intention to ratify by the parliament. It is an act of government, which must be followed up later by an act of parliament, if a nation decides to ratify a treaty (pp. 392, 395).

In large part because of Lemkin's indefatigable work, the United Nations Convention on the Prevention and Punishment of the Crime of Genocide was adopted unanimously and without abstentions by the United Nations General Assembly on December 9, 1948.

Next, Lemkin began work on obtaining at least 20 ratifications, which would enable the General Assembly of 1950 to draw up the protocol for bringing the Convention into force. To do so, he focused on the small nations of Latin America, who, he considered, needed the protection of international law more than the bigger, more powerful nations. As a result, Ecuador became the first Latin American nation to ratify the Genocide Convention. Ultimately, the Convention was ratified by enough countries to go into effect on January 12, 1951 (LeBlanc, 1991, p. 1). It would take the United States almost four decades after Lemkin's death, to ratify—during the Reagan Administration—the Convention.

In the last half of the twentieth century, the Convention was applied sporadically and selectively, and remains a source of continuing debate and discussion among legal and genocide scholars the world over. To this day, however, it remains the cornerstone of international legal and moral-ethical reasoning regarding genocide and its prevention. (Lemkin's autobiography, *Totally Unofficial Man*, is now, for the first time, available in print in Totten & Jacobs, 2002.)

## United Nations Convention on the Prevention and Punishment of Genocide (1948)

In the aftermath, then, of World War II and the Nazi extermination of six million Jews and of approximately five million other people (including but not limited to the Gypsies, mentally and physically handicapped, and Slavic peoples), the United Nations adopted a resolution on

December 9, 1946, recommending that international attention and cooperation be focused on the prevention and punishment of genocide. It was, in fact, this horrific slaughter by the Nazis, along with Lemkin's continuing efforts and prodding, that prompted the member states of the United Nations to formally recognize genocide as a crime in international law.

As alluded to in the above section, from the outset the development of the U.N. Genocide Convention was plagued by great difficulty and controversy. As might be expected, nations with diverse philosophies, cultures, "historical experience[,] and sensitivities to human suffering" (Kuper, 1985, p. 10) presented different interpretations as to what constituted genocide, and argued in favor of a definition and wording in the Convention that fit their particular perspective(s).

On December 11, 1946, the United Nations General Assembly passed this initial resolution (96–I):

> Genocide is a denial of the right of existence of entire human groups, as homicide is the denial of the right to life of individual human beings. Many instances of such crimes of genocide have occurred, when racial, religious, political, and other groups have been destroyed entirely or in part. The General Assembly, Therefore, Affirms that genocide is a crime under international law which the civilized world condemns, for the commission of which principals and accomplices—whether private individuals, public officials or statesmen, and whether the crime is committed on religious, racial, political or any other grounds—are punishable. (United Nations, 1978, pp. 6–7)

Of the utmost significance here is that the initial resolution included "*political or any other grounds*" (italics added). However, a brouhaha erupted when the Soviet Union, Poland, and other nations argued against the inclusion of political groups. The Russians argued that the inclusion of political groups would not conform "with the scientific definition of genocide and would, in practice, distort the perspective in which the crime should be viewed and impair the efficacy of the Convention" (U.N. Economic and Social Council, 1948, p. 721). Similarly, the Poles added that "the inclusion of provisions relating to political groups, which because of their mutability and lack of distinguishing characteristics did not lend themselves to definition, would weaken and blur the whole Convention" (U.N. Economic and Social Council, 1948, p. 712).

Yet another argument against the inclusion of political groups was that unlike national, racial, or religious groups, membership in political groups was voluntary. However, in a later session, the French argued that "whereas in the past crimes of genocide had been committed on racial or religious grounds, it was clear that in the future they would be committed mainly on political grounds" (U.N. Economic and Social Council, 1948, p. 723). Representatives of many other nations concurred with this position and offered strong support in favor of its recognition.

A particularly moving argument put forth *against the exclusion* of political groups was that "those who committed the crime of genocide might use the pretext of the political opinions of a racial or religious group to persecute and destroy it, without becoming liable to international sanctions" (U.N. Legal Committee, October 1948, p. 100).

Ultimately,

> Political groups survived for many sessions and seemed securely ensconced in the Convention, but on 29 November 1948, the issue was reopened in the Legal Committee on a motion by the delegations of Iran, Egypt, and Uruguay. A compromise seems to have been reached behind the scenes. The United States delegation, though still committed to the principle of extending protection to political groups, was conciliatory. It feared non-ratification of the Convention, and rejection of the proposal for an international tribunal, if political groups were included. On a vote, political groups were expunged (Kuper, 1981, p. 29).

The upshot was that the United Nations Convention on the Prevention and Punishment of Genocide came to define genocide in the following manner:

> In the present Convention, genocide means any of the following acts committed with the intent to destroy, in whole or in part, a national, ethnical, racial or religious group, as such:
>
> (a) Killing members of the group;
> (b) Causing serious bodily or mental harm to members of the group;
> (c) Deliberately inflicting on the group conditions of life calculated to bring about its physical destruction in whole or in part;
> (d) Imposing measures intended to prevent births within the group;
> (e) Forcibly transferring children of the group to another group.

The aforementioned arguments and counter-arguments resulted in what can best be described as a "compromise definition."

The exclusion of political and social groups from the U.N. Convention has been roundly criticized by many scholars (Chalk, 1989; Charny, 1988a, 1988b; Drost, 1959; Hawk, 1987; Kuper, 1981, 1985; Totten, 2002; Whitaker, 1985). It is also worth noting that in 1985, Ben Whitaker, the U.N. rapporteur on genocide, made a recommendation, in his much heralded report entitled *Revised and Updated Report on the Question of the Prevention and Punishment of the Crime of Genocide*, that political groups be protected under the UNCG.

Hawk (1987), for one, asserts that "The absence of political groups from the coverage of the Genocide Convention has unfortunately had the effect of diverting discussion from what to do to deter or remedy a concrete situation of mass killings into a debilitating, confusing debate over the question of whether a situation is, legally genocide" (p. 6). In a similar but somewhat different vein, Whitaker (1988) argues that

> There are strong arguments for the addition of at least political groups to the United Nations definition. In some cases of mass crimes it is not easy to determine which of overlapping political, economic, racial, social, or religious factors was the determinant, motivating one. For example, were comparatively recent selective genocides in Burundi and Kampuchea intrinsically political or ethnic in their intent? Most genocides (including that by Nazis) have at least some political tinge, and it can be argued that to leave political and other groups beyond the protection of the [U.N. Convention on Genocide] offers a dangerous loophole that would permit any designated group to be exterminated, ostensibly under the excuse that this was for political reasons. (p. 53)

As for the controversy over the issue of cultural genocide, Kuper (1981) notes the following:

> In this controversy, the roles of the national delegations were somewhat reversed. The Soviet Bloc pressed for inclusion of cultural genocide in the Convention, the Western European democracies opposed. The issue was not whether groups should be protected against attempts to destroy their culture. . . . The issue was rather whether the protection of culture should be extended through the Convention on Genocide or in conventions on human rights and rights of minorities. This conflict was not sharply ideological, but presumably the representatives of the colonial powers would have been somewhat on the defensive, sensitive to criticism of their policies in non-self governing territories.
>
> In the result, cultural genocide was excluded from the Convention, though vestiges remain. The Convention makes special reference to the forcible transfer of children from one group to another, and the word ethnical has been added to the list of groups covered by the Convention. This would have the effect of extending protection to groups with a distinctive culture or language. (p.31)
>
> Regarding the need for the inclusion of social groups in the definition of genocide, Chalk (1989) argues that

Within living memory the governments of the Soviet Union, Germany and Kampuchea had defined class, mental and physical defects, and sexual preference as primary classifications in their societies. In the hands of rulers who claimed a monopoly on truth and of a bureaucracy which did their bidding, membership of these social categories had proven lethal to millions of human beings. It seem[s] obvious that researchers of genocide must investigate the destruction of such social groups or surrender any hope of explaining the modern world in all its complexity. (p. 151)

It is instructive to note that in 1959, Pieter N. Drost, a Dutch law professor, argued ardently that the United Nations needed to redefine genocide as "the deliberate destruction of physical life of individual human beings by reason of their membership of any human collectivity as such" (p. 125). By doing so, the definition would be more inclusive—and thus not exclude political and social groups that were targeted for annihilation.

Totten (2002) has argued that

one needs to realize and appreciate the fact that the very wording of the Convention includes the following: "in the *present* Convention" (italics added). The use of "present" denotes that the Convention, as it stands, is not set in stone for eternity. Indeed, it is possible to revise it so that it is clear in its statements and more efficacious in its reach and intent to protect people from the insidious scourge of genocide. It seems that if the world community truly cares about preventing genocide then it is reasonable to radically overhaul this remarkable yet flawed Convention in order to tighten it up, delete the ambiguity, and make it inclusive enough to ensure that all groups of people are placed under its protective umbrella. (p. 566)

All that said, the Genocide Convention, along with the United Nations Declaration on Human Rights, constitutes a major milestone in the history of international law vis-à-vis the attempt to provide protection for hundreds of millions across the globe from horrific abuse.

The hope among many was that the Convention on the Prevention and Punishment of the Crime of Genocide would put "teeth" into the cry of "Never Again." The aforementioned hope, though, was one that was not to be realized. As R. J. Rummel (2002), a political scientist and a scholar of genocide and democide studies, has trenchantly noted, "instead of 'Never Again,' the fact of the matter is, genocide reappeared in the last half of the twentieth century again, and again, and again" (p. 173).

## Definitional Issues of Genocide: the Debate Continues

The on going debate (and one must add, confusion) over the most accurate and "workable" definition of genocide has played into the hands of those who do not wish to admit to the rest of the world (e.g., the perpetrators themselves) or wish to recognize (e.g., intergovernmental organizations such as the United Nations and/or individual nations) that a genocide is in the making. In certain instances, it has also hamstrung government analysts and even scholars and activists in ascertaining whether a situation is moving toward genocide or has actually exploded into genocide.

While the United Nations and most individual governments accede to the definition used in the U.N. Convention on the Prevention and Punishment of Genocide, scholars and activists have, as noted above, debated the usefulness of the latter. Over and above the debate regarding the exclusion of social and political groups from the Convention's definition of genocide, heated debates have centered around the wording and the actual meaning of key words in the UNCG. Indeed, at the heart of the often contentious, and seemingly endless, debate over the efficacy of the UNCG's definition is the issue of "intent." (Again, in part, the definition used in the UNCG reads as follows: "In the present Convention, genocide means any of the following acts committed with *intent* to destroy, in whole or in part, a national, ethnical, racial or religious groups, as such. . . ." (italics added)). In *Genocide: Its Political Use in the Twentieth Century*, Kuper (1981) asserted that "The inclusion of intent in the definition of genocide introduces a subjective element, which would often prove difficult to establish.... In contemporary extra-judicial discussions of allegations of genocide, the question of intent has become a controversial issue, providing a ready basis for denial of guilt" (p. 33). The inclusion of the word "intent," then, seems to suggest that a situation can only be deemed genocide if, in fact, there is hard evidence that genocide was the actual intent of the perpetrator. But, as Kuper ponders, what if a perpetrator of genocide asserts that he/she never had any intent to commit genocide, and what if there is no documentation or any corroborative evidence whatsoever that there was an actual plan to commit genocide?

Tellingly, when confronted with the accusation that Paraguay committed genocide against the Achè people, the Paraguayan defense minister argued as follows: "Although there are victims and victimizer, there is not the third element necessary to establish the crime of genocide—that is 'intent.' Therefore, as there is no 'intent,' one cannot speak of 'genocide' " (cited in Alvarez, 2001, p. 52). The latter case provides a counterweight to those who claim, as some scholars do, that the debate over the definition of genocide is little more than an academic exercise. Indeed, in the case of Paraguay, not only does the Convention's definition play into the hands of deniers, but it could possibly be used (though, hopefully without success) as a defense in court against the charge of genocide.

In *The Prevention of Genocide*, Kuper (1985) further argued that "There are also problems in determining the conditions under which intention can be imputed" (p. 12). Continuing, he stated that "I will assume that intent is established if the foreseeable consequences of an act are, or seem likely to be, the destruction of a group. But this may be controversial.... [Ultimately,] it would be for a court to decide the issue in the circumstances of the particular case" (Kuper, 1985, pp. 12, 13).

Some scholars, such as Barta (1987) and Huttenbach (1988), have suggested that intent should be eliminated as a criterion, thus avoiding, altogether, the ambiguity inherent in it.

Helen Fein (1990), a sociologist and executive director of the Institute for the Study of Genocide in New York City, though, makes the following argument vis-à-vis the meaning of "intent":

> As sociologists, immersed in the distinctions between "manifest" and "latent" function as a paradigm of intended and unintended action, we have needlessly confused the meaning of intent. Intent or purposeful action—or inaction—is not the same in law or every-day language as either motive or function. An actor performs an act, we say, with intent if there are foreseeable ends or consequences ...
>
> As some attempt to make a case under the Convention (not, so far, instigating the UN to act) we can see that the Convention has greater flexibility than understood by some:
>
> > The "intent" required by the Convention as a necessary constituent element of the crime of genocide cannot be confused with, or interpreted to mean, "motive".... The "intent" clause of Article II of the Genocide Convention requires only that the various destructive acts—killings, causing mental and physical harm, deliberately inflicted conditions of life, etc.—have a purposeful or deliberate character as opposed to an accidental or unintentional character. (Hannum & Hawk, 1986, pp. 140–146, as cited in Fein, 1990, pp. 19–20)

Unfortunately, many, both inside and outside of government and the academy, do not seem to be cognizant of, or, at the least, appreciative of, the above points made by Fein. And that is a major problem for when the very wording in such a significant definition used by the international community to ascertain whether genocide is being committed or not is confusing, it constitutes a major stumbling block. Likewise, it sends the wrong message to past, current and future perpetrators of genocide who may think that they can use semantics to avoid prosecution.

Other wording in the UNCG that has caused consternation is the phrase, "in whole or in part." As Kuper (1985), again, notes: "The ambiguity lies in determining what number or what proportion would constitute a part for purpose of the definition. . . . Presumably, the Convention is intended to deal with acts against large numbers, relative to the size of the persecuted groups, and it would rest with the courts to adjudicate on this issue" (p. 12).

In light of the ambiguities in the wording of the Convention, it is plain to see why many scholars have committed great amounts of time and effort to analyzing, interpreting, and rephrasing the wording of the definition in the Convention in an attempt to strengthen it. For the same reason, many scholars have developed their own definitions of genocide. While some have been successful in developing stronger definitions, others have muddied the waters with definitions that are as ambiguous, if not more so, than that used in the UNCG. Presently, at least, such definitions are irrelevant vis-à-vis international law, for only the definition in the United Nations Convention on the Prevention and Punishment of the Crime of Genocide is used to prosecute the perpetrators of genocide. (For an informative, instructive, and detailed discussion of definitions of genocide, including their strengths and weaknesses, see Fein, 1990.)

The purpose of broaching the above issues is not to make excuses for or to "rationalize away" the fact that the international community has been agonizingly slow in recognizing actual genocides for what they are. Nor is it to excuse the totally inadequate and negligent way in which the international community has reacted to a genocide once one has been detected. Rather, it is to illustrate the complexity of the situation, even for scholars of genocide, in ascertaining that which constitutes genocide versus that which constitutes a series of sporadic massacres, war crimes or crimes against humanity in a region.

## The Cold War Years and Genocide

We move now to an examination of genocide in the post-World War II period, to a time when the world was confronted by an enormous number of bewildering stresses and strains: economic boom and bust, decolonization and wars of liberation, social protest and wide-sweeping calls for change, and the biggest threat of them all—mutually-assured total nuclear destruction (MAD). Characterizing many of these stresses were the numerous genocidal outbreaks which took place in the former colonial lands vacated (sometimes amicably, but often violently) by departing European powers in the years following 1945. Nowhere were these played out with such devastating ferocity as in Africa and Asia.

The objectives of those who shaped the post-1945 agenda increasingly became diluted as the twentieth century wore on, until the postwar cry of "Never Again!" became more and more muted; indeed, until the second half of the century began to appear as nothing other than a continual period of killing—in large wars, small wars, civil wars, and sometimes when there was no war at all. A number of these stand out as "models" of what the world became during the time that became known as the Cold War, a period approximating 1945 to 1989 (with localized variations).

The first concerns a place now often forgotten in the popular consciousness—and almost completely overlooked by genocide scholars. This is the case of a small, short-lived country in west Africa called Biafra. For many people born before the mid-1970s, the very name instantly conjures up images of babies with large staring eyes and bloated bodies, tiny stick-like limbs and a helplessness preceding death which only starvation can bring. Biafra was formed in 1967, when the Eastern State of Nigeria broke away to establish itself as an independent country. The Nigerian Civil War of 1967–1970, which followed, was the first occasion in which scenes of mass starvation were brought home to a television-dominated West, and millions throughout Europe, North America, and elsewhere were horrified by what they saw.

Less apparent was the reality which lay behind this otherwise simple case of a brutal and bloody secessionist conflict, for in the Nigerian determination to defeat the Biafran breakaway state a deliberately designed genocidal policy of enforced famine was perpetrated against the population of the newly-formed country (Kuper, 1981, pp. 75–76).

The Biafran conflict led to an eventual death toll of up to a million people, mostly of the largely Christian Ibo ethnic group. The Nigerian Federal Army, and the government which supported it, was a perpetrator of genocide through a premeditated and strictly-enforced policy of starvation, as well as the military targeting of civilians. There was little doubt as to the Nigerians' genocidal intent; Biafra existed only two-and-a-half years, until its final collapse in January 1970.

The year 1971 saw an independence struggle in which East Pakistan sought to secede from West Pakistan, a move which was resisted with staggering violence. The subsequent emergence of the independent nation of Bangladesh was accompanied by some three million dead and a quarter of a million women and girls raped, the result of a calculated policy of genocide initiated by the government of West Pakistan for the purpose of terrorizing the population into accepting a continuance of Pakistani rule over the region. Ultimately the strategy did not work, as Bangladesh achieved its independence after the involvement of India in the conflict and the consequent defeat of the Pakistani forces.

The following year, 1972, another outbreak of genocidal violence took place in the tiny central African nation of Burundi, where a Hutu-instigated uprising against Tutsi domination resulted in the army subjugation and massacre of scores of thousands of Hutu civilians over a five-month period. The final total numbered up to 150,000 people, men, women, and children, and ushered in a period of Tutsi dominance which was to last for several decades—and during which time the Hutu majority population was reduced to a position of entrenched second-class subservience (Lemarchand, 1997).

It was characteristic of the era that Burundi became a location for Cold War rivalries. The Western world, and in particular the United States, saw the catastrophe that befell the Hutu as an irrelevancy so far as the bigger picture of defeating communism was concerned. The French government saw the conflict as an opportunity to reinforce its preferred Francophone client-state, while communist countries such as China and North Korea took the opportunity to assist the Tutsi junta with arms and infrastructural support as a means to woo the regime away from the West.

A little over two years after the worst of the violence ceased in Burundi, a communist tyrant, Pol Pot, and his cronies, the Khmer Rouge, won a bloody civil war in Cambodia, and began one of the most radical attempts at remodeling an existing society the world had ever seen. In taking the Cambodian people back to the Year Zero, as Pol Pot put it, at least 1.5 million people lost their lives (Kiernan, 1995, p. 334), though the figure was almost certainly higher. This would appear to be a clear-cut case of genocidal mass murder, though some strenuously question whether or not the massive human destruction that took place can truly be deemed a case of genocide when examined under the lens of the United Nations definition. The difficulty lies in the fact that the majority of the deaths that took place under Pol Pot's Khmer Rouge were perpetrated against their own Khmer (Cambodian) people (thus the appellation, "autogenocide"). Most of the victims were not targeted for reasons related to their membership in any of the groups identified under the United Nations definition, but were rather killed for social or political reasons. That said, there were specific groups that were singled out for " 'eradication' by the leadership of the ruling Communist Party of Kampuchea because of their membership to a particular group; and these included Cambodia's preeminent religious group, the Buddhist monkhood, Cambodia's ethnic minorities, and the large portion of the Cambodian 'national group' deemed to [have been] tainted by 'feudal,' 'bourgeois' or 'foreign influences' " (Hawk, 1988, p. 138).

Ultimately, though, scholars and others are confronted with a primary definitional issue:

under what circumstances may they depart from the U.N. definition in order to apply the classification of genocide to an event of massive human destruction, and what are the implications of our doing so? Under international law, of course, no charge of genocide could stick in a case where those killed came from a political or social group. The thorny issue of "intent" could also come into play. Pol Pot intended to create a new type of communist utopia, to be sure, but did he intend to annihilate millions of his own people in order to do so—and were his victims targeted for the sole reason of their existence? The answer in regard to what took place in Cambodia is, sometimes yes, at other times no. The issues of "target group" and of "intent" are key sticking points militating against a satisfactory blanket application of the U.N. Convention in this case.

While the cataclysm of Cambodia was being played out, yet another Cold War genocide was taking place elsewhere in Asia, this time in the former Portuguese overseas territory of East Timor. In 1975, one of the political factions jockeying for power in the aftermath of Portuguese decolonization, Fretilin, declared the territory's independence; within weeks, Indonesian military forces invaded, declared East Timor to be that country's twenty-seventh state, and began a systematic campaign of human rights abuses which resulted in the mass murder, starvation, and death by torture of up to 200,000 people—about a third of the preinvasion East Timorese population (Dunn, 1997).

For many years, the international response to what was happening in East Timor was one of indifference. Indonesia's neighbor, Australia, was especially keen not to antagonize the populous nation to its north, and was the first (and for a long time, only) country to recognize the de jure incorporation of East Timor into the body of Indonesia (Aubrey, 1998). United Nations resolutions calling on Indonesia to withdraw were ignored, and the United States, anxious lest a hard-line approach toward the annexation be seen by the Indonesians as a reason to look elsewhere for support—for example, to nonaligned nations—trod very softly on the whole issue (Gunn, 1997). Only in 1999, after a long period of Indonesian oppression and the threat of another outbreak of genocidal violence (this time committed by Indonesian-backed militias and units of the Indonesian army), was East Timor freed. In 2002, the first parliament, elected by universal suffrage and guaranteed by the United Nations, took its place in the community of nations.

In sum, the Cold War had a devastating effect on post-1945 hopes that a new, nongenocidal regime could be created throughout the world. Not only were peoples and groups in conflict left to fight out their differences unimpeded; all too often, as capitalist and communist states saw the possibility of achieving an advantage through either action or inaction, those committing genocidal acts were frequently aided and abetted for the most blatant of realpolitik motives. Britain, for example, refused to assist Biafra in alleviating its distress, for to do so would further undermine Nigeria at a time when oil exploration was starting to bear fruit, and a strong Nigeria was needed to keep out Soviet influence in sub-Saharan Africa, as well as to block Francophone designs.

As long as the Cold War raged, there was little chance that the kind of pressures likely to lead to a genocidal situation would find a "release valve." The great powers played a leading role in manipulating local conflicts so as to suit their own needs, after which each side was able to serve as a proxy in the greater ideological conflicts of the time. The Cold War showed with great clarity that the world's major players paid only lip service to their postwar commitment to "never again" stand by while genocide took place.

## Post-cold War Years and Genocide: A Move Toward the Intervention and Prevention of Genocide?

Following the end of the Cold War, it appeared that a sea change was taking place in international relations regarding the willingness of nations to intervene to prevent genocide. More specifically, as Geoffrey Robertson (2000) notes in his book, *Crimes Against Humanity: The Struggle for Global Justice,*

> It was not until 1993, after the Cold War was over and as the spectre of "ethnic cleansing" returned to Europe, that there was sufficient superpower resolve to apply the *proviso* to Article 2(7) [of the United Nations Charter, which reads, in part, "Nothing contained in the present Charter shall authorize the United Nations to intervene in matters which are essentially within the domestic jurisdiction of any State ..."], namely that it could be overridden by Chapter VII. This is the chapter of the Charter which permits the Security Council to order armed intervention against any state once it has determined that such a response is necessary to restore international peace and security. Since Article 55 expressly makes the observance of human rights a condition necessary for peaceful relations, the appalling crimes against humanity [and genocide] which occurred after 1945 could have been forcibly combated by the UN under its Chapter VII power, but until the Balkan atrocities in the 1990s the Security Council never sought or even thought to invoke military action upon human rights grounds. (p. 25)

But, in fact, did a sea change occur? In actuality, the verdict is still out.

Certainly, the issue of "sovereignty" in the post-Cold War period came under closer scrutiny, if not under attack, and was no longer seen, in certain cases at least, as sacrosanct. That is, a nation committing genocide or other egregious human rights violations against its own people was no longer seen as "untouchable." Furthermore, such situations were no longer automatically deemed a matter of "internal affairs."

Be that as it may, if one were to ask if a "sea change" had actually taken place in regard to the realities on the ground every time a genocide appeared on the horizon, the answer would be an unequivocal "No!" Why? Because the international community failed, time and again, to halt various genocides in a timely and effective manner.

Still, there was a change in the air for, in certain notable cases, the international community did act in concert to stave off certain potential genocides.

The disaster of Bosnia-Herzegovina, in the former Yugoslavia, dominated international news for much of the 1990s. It was the first genocide committed within a military conflict in Europe since the Holocaust, and involved the killing and displacement of Bosnia's Muslims by both local Serbs and Serbian forces from the Yugoslav National Army. These actions were justified by the perpetrators on the grounds of ideology and the desire to acquire (or retain) territory seen as sacred by the Serbs (Cigar, 1995). The questions thrown up by the genocide were many, but of equal, if not greater, concern was the position of the bystanders. Efforts to stop the genocide while it was happening were neither quick to emerge nor effective when attempted (Gow, 1997; Power, 2002, pp. 247–327; Simms, 2001).

The genocide in Bosnia—though probably the most closely reported genocide in history (Sadkovich, 1998)—was yet another case of international inaction in the face of massive human rights violations. In Bosnia, the Western powers, led by the U.N., the European Community and the North Atlantic Treaty Organization (NATO) (and preeminently, the United States and Britain), failed consistently both to resolve the war and to stop the killing. Diplomatic efforts were subjected to ridicule by the perpetrators, and military efforts reached their lowest ebb with what was effectively a surrender by Dutch peacekeepers—while acting as part of the United Nations Protection Force (UNPROFOR)—of the so-called "safe haven" of Srebrenica. Following this surrender, up to 7,000 Muslim men and boys were hunted down and killed; it was the greatest massacre on European soil since the Second World War (Honig & Both, 1996).

Also of note is the fact that the Serbians used rape as "a weapon of war" (Rieff, 2002, p. 67) and as a means, in part, to destroy the Bosnian Muslim population.

In 1999, almost as an acknowledgment of a guilty conscience concerning their failure to act in Bosnia, the combined air forces of the United States, Great Britain, France, Germany, Italy, and the Netherlands, operating together as part of NATO, attacked Serbia with the intention of forcing the Serbs to stop their persecution of the ethnic Albanian population living in the Serbian province of Kosovo (Weymouth & Hening, 2001). It was the first occasion in which a war was fought for the express purpose of stopping a genocide before its worst horrors took place. Under international law, however, the attack was illegal; it was neither called for nor approved by the United Nations. Nonetheless, after a lengthy and intensive bombing campaign, the Serbian regime of Slobodan Milosevic pulled its troops out of Kosovo. U.N. peacekeepers moved into the province, allowing the one million persecuted Kosovars, who had been expelled from the country in a huge outbreak of so-called "ethnic cleansing," to return home.

The NATO intervention in Kosovo is an example of how a potential genocide can be addressed early on if the international will to do so is present. That said, the action was not without controversy; not only was there the issue of acting without the imprimatur of the U.N. but many innocent people were also killed as a direct result of the bombing missions. Many also assert that the use of ground troops would have likely avoided a good number of the innocent deaths that resulted from the bombings.

The international community's guilty conscience, if indeed one existed, did not help the Tutsi population of the tiny African country of Rwanda earlier in the 1990s. There, in 1994, in the space of 100 days, perhaps as many as one million people were killed in a genocide. The United Nations did practically nothing to stop the killing, and indeed the killing continued right up to the point where the extremist Hutu killers, attacking innocent Tutsi and moderate (which is to say, democratic) Hutu victims, had almost virtually exhausted their killing machine. The killings were, for the most part, done by hand, with the murderers using machetes (*pangus*) or nail-studded clubs (*masus*). This was an outbreak of savagery on a grand scale. And yet, as we now know—and as the U.N. Security Council had been warned nearly four months beforehand by a defector from those who would become the killers—the Rwanda genocide was carefully planned in advance, to such a degree that death lists of names marked for murder had been prepared long before the killing actually began.

The Rwanda genocide tells us much about the nature and priorities of the international system in the 1990s, and offers lessons of which all citizens of democratic nations should take note. To a large degree, the main players in both world and regional politics did nothing to stop the killing or intervene to rescue the survivors. The United Nations Security Council scaled back the size and scope of the peacekeeping forces already present on the ground, and worked hard to ensure that no aid of a practical nature was sent to Rwanda (Barnett, 2002). Belgium, the former mandatory power, withdrew from the Rwanda altogether, along with most other Western countries. France, after the worst of the killing had taken place, established a so-called "safe zone" in the south, but its ultimate effect was to protect the tens of thousands of Hutu killers who had poured into the area escaping the advancing Tutsi rebel army (Melvern, 2000, pp. 210–226).

In view of cases such as Bosnia and Rwanda, how can the final years of the twentieth century be interpreted? If the trend over the course of the past century has been toward greater killing, greater targeting of civilians, and a greater likelihood than ever before that groups are being singled out for destruction, what hope does this offer those with a commitment to the sanctity of life?

There is, unfortunately, no ready-made answer to this question. Genocide still exists, despite the legal processes that have been instituted against it. Genocide, one of the legacies of the twentieth century, has been described as "the crime of crimes"; and if it is true that the twentieth century was an "age of genocide," we need to ask not only why this was so, but what its impact has been on world civilization, as a whole. Furthermore, it seems natural that we should try to build the means of ensuring that the twenty-first century will not go the same way, but of course, that is no easy task.

In 1993 and 1994 two ad hoc international courts were established by the United Nations Security Council for the express purpose of trying those indicted for genocide, crimes against humanity, and war crimes, as they pertained to the former Yugoslavia and Rwanda. The International Criminal Tribunal on Yugoslavia (ICTY) and the International Criminal Tribunal on Rwanda (ICTR) have both been moderately successful (if excruciatingly slow) in bringing prosecutions, and in September 1998 the ICTR made history when it found Jean-Paul Akayesu, the former mayor of the Rwandan town of Taba, guilty of the crime of genocide. This was the first time any international court had issued such a verdict for this specific crime. Other prosecutions have followed, and case-law precedents in the law of genocide prosecutions are now growing. Quite clearly, genocide is now recognized throughout the world as a crime that is abhorrent.

It is noteworthy that during the trial of Jean-Paul Akayesu, Pierre Prosper, an African American serving as a prosecutor at the ICTR, argued ardently to convince the court that "sexual violence against women could be carried out with an intent that amounted to genocide" (Power; 2002, p. 485). As Power (2002) notes, Prosper argued that "a group could physically exist, or escape extermination, but be left so marginalized or so irrelevant to society that it was, in effect, destroyed" (p. 486). Ultimately, the ICTR found that the "systematic rape of Tutsi women in Rwanda's Taba commune was found to constitute the genocide act of 'causing serious bodily or mental harm to members of the group' " (Power, 2002, p. 486) and thus Akayesu was found guilty of genocide.

As if to demonstrate the firmness of the international community's resolve to do something about genocide—and to prove that impunity is no longer an option for those who commit it—the Rome Statute of the International Criminal Court (ICC) was adopted on July 17, 1998. The court was established by the United Nations under the aegis of the U.N. Security Council. The statute gives the court jurisdiction for the crime of genocide, crimes against humanity, and war crimes. It is both an extension of the ICTY and the ICTR, and the fulfillment of the promises first articulated in the aftermath of 1945 (Schabas, 2001, pp. 1–21). The Court became operative on July 1, 2002, after a minimum of 60 U.N. countries had ratified it. Notable among those refusing to ratify was the United States. Cognizant of the United States' intransigence, most European countries had earlier decided that the leadership of the U.S. would not be required for the purpose of establishing what was seen as a highly moral body, the purpose of which would be to assist in safeguarding the peace of the world and the lives of its citizens. The U.S. promptly sought, and received, an agreement within the U.N. that would place Americans serving in foreign postings outside the court's jurisdiction.

It is perhaps instructive to note that the ICC, after considerable debate, decided to absorb the U.N. Convention on Genocide, including its definition, directly into its charter.

## Intervention and Prevention of Genocide: is it Possible?

Since the late 1970s, an ever-increasing number of scholars—and in the mid- to late-1980s, more and more policy makers—focused attention on the development of effective methods to intervene and/or prevent genocide. Based on the fact that genocide continues to plague humanity, such efforts are, obviously, still at their most incipient stage.

The aforementioned efforts have involved a wide array of theoretical and practical components that will, hopefully, lend themselves to detecting potential situations that may lead to genocide and/or assisting in the effort to staunch genocides already under way. Among such efforts are the following: developing categories (or classifications) of genocide; defining the "nature of societies in which genocides take place" (Charny, 1988b, p. 5); developing potential predictors of genocide; developing "specified conditions of communal conflicts and the analysis of 'accelerators' " (Harff, 1994, pp. 25–30); developing of theoretical risk assessments (Gurr, 1994, pp. 20–24); developing various types of early warning systems by nongovernmental organizations, individual nations, and the United Nations; and, establishing of the ICC, which many hope will serve as a deterrent of sorts to those contemplating the perpetration of genocidal acts. (For a more detailed and technical discussion of many of the above-mentioned issues, see Gurr, 1994, and Harff, 1994. For a more general discussion of the above issues, see, Rittner, Roth, & Smith, 2002).

Possibly the thorniest issue of all is that of political will. That is, the political will of the United Nations Security Council and individual states (especially, the strongest nations, including but not limited to the United States, Germany, France, Great Britain, Russia, China) to act in a timely and effective fashion to intervene and/or prevent genocide. Driven to a large extent by realpolitik and, though to a lesser extent today, the sense that sovereignty is all but sacrosanct, many, if not most, nations are still tentative about intervening in another nation's so-called "business." Indeed, all one needs to do is look at either the record of the United Nations or the United States in regard to their efforts at intervention and prevention (Power, 2002)

Totten (2002) asserts that there are a host of additional issues and concerns that genocide scholars need to take into account as they continue to work with nongovernmental personnel, policy makers, and others in the development of effective mechanisms for the intervention and prevention of genocide, and these include, but are not limited to the following: information-gathering and analysis (including satellite observation methods, systematic gathering of information, accurate analysis of information, timely dissemination of findings to key bodies); intelligence sharing; confidence building measures in states enmeshed in conflict; preventive diplomacy; Track I diplomacy; Track II diplomacy; conflict prevention; conflict management; conflict resolution; information peacekeeping; peacekeeping; diplomatic peacekeeping; peacemaking; peace enforcement; sanctions (various types, and the purposes and efficacy of); failed states (how to deal with them in an effective manner); partitioning (the efficacy of such, and to make it more effective); temporary protection measures for refugees fleeing internal and other types of conflict; the plight of displaced persons within a state; the conceptualization of various types of policing efforts; institution building; the role of the United Nations vis-à-vis intervention and prevention efforts; and, possibly most significantly, systemic issues (e.g., endemic poverty; the shocking divide between the "haves" and "have nots"; greedy consumption by the few—and the United States of America is a primary culprit of this phenomena—to the detriment of the many; and unjust governmental systems) that cause dissension and often result in violent conflict, including genocide. To neglect to address the aforementioned issues is tantamount to groping blindly at intervention and prevention.

Ultimately, as discussed above, with the establishment of the ICC (and the success, thus far, of the ICTY and ICTR), movement, even if glacial, is being made in the direction of recognizing that individual nations have no right, morally, legally, or otherwise, to commit genocide.

## The Future?

Knowing the innate atavism of humanity and the thirst for power and revenge by some, one can safely, if sorrowfully, predict that genocide will be perpetrated again in the future—if not, again and again. On the other side of the coin, never in the history of humanity has so much been done in such a short span of time to attempt to quell, if not completely stop, genocide from being perpetrated.

The development and ratification of the U.N. Convention on the Prevention and Punishment of Genocide, the trials of the Nazi war criminals, the revitalized and vigorous scholarly and activist focus in the 1980s, 1990s, and early 2000s on the intervention and prevention of genocide, the trials conducted by the ICTR and ICTY, and the development of the ICC all bode well for the future. That said, what is now needed is a central, highly sophisticated genocide early warning system and the international resolve (i.e., political will) to quickly and effectively act early on in an attempt to prevent genocide from becoming a reality. To accomplish the latter is going to be the most difficult component, thus far, in the attempt to prevent genocide from becoming a reality, for nations are often apt to revert to realpolitik when positions, decisions, and actions are not perceived to be in their own, often selfish, interest.

## References

Alvarez, A. (2001). *Governments, citizens, and genocide: A comparative and interdisciplinary approach.* Bloomington: Indiana University Press.

Aubrey, J. (Ed.) (1998). *Free East Timor: Australia's culpability in East Timor's genocide.* Sydney: Vintage/ Random House Australia.

Barnett, M. (2002). *Eyewitness to a genocide: The United Nations and Rwanda.* Ithaca, NY: Cornell University Press.

Barta, T. (1987). Relations of genocide: Land and lives in the colonization of Australia. In I. Wallimann & M. N. Dobkowski (Eds.), *Genocide and the modern age: Etiology and case studies of mass death* (pp. 237–252). New York: Greenwood.

Bartrop, P. R. (2001). The Holocaust, the Aborigines, and the Bureaucracy of destruction: An Australian dimension of genocide. *Journal of Genocide Research, 3*(1), 75–87.

Bartrop, P. R. (2002). The relationship between war and genocide in the twentieth century: A consideration. *Journal of Genocide Research, 4*(4), 519–532.

Chalk, F. (1989). Definitions of genocide and their implications for prediction and prevention. *Holocaust and Genocide Studies, 4*(2), 149–160.

Chalk, F., & Jonassohn, C. (1988). The history and sociology of genocide. In I. W. Charny (Ed.), *Genocide: A critical bibliographic review* (pp. 39–58). New York: Facts on File.

Chalk, F., & Jonassohn, C. (1991). *The history and sociology of genocide.* New Haven, CT: Yale University Press.

Charny, I. W. (Ed.). (1988a). Intervention and prevention of genocide. In *Genocide: A critical bibliographic review* (pp. 20–38). New York: Facts on File.

Charny, I. W. (Ed.). (1988b). The study of genocide. In *Genocide: A critical bibliographic review* (pp. 1–19). New York: Facts on File.

Cigar, N. (1995). *Genocide in Bosnia: The policy of "ethnic cleansing."* College Station: Texas A & M University Press.

Drost, P. (1959). *The crimes of state* (Vol. 2). Leyden, the Netherlands: A.W. Sythoff.

Dunn, J. (1997). Genocide in East Timor: In S. Totten, W. S. Parsons, & I. W. Charny (Eds.), *Century of genocide: Eyewitness accounts and critical views* (pp. 264–290). New York: Garland.

Fein, H. (1990). Genocide: A sociological perspective. *Current Sociology, 38*(1), 1–126.

Gow, J. (1997). *Triumph of the lack of will: International diplomacy and the Yugoslav War.* New York: Columbia University Press.

Gunn, G. C. (1997). *East Timor and the United Nations: The case for intervention.* Lawrenceville, NJ: Red Sea Press.

Gurr, T. R. (1994). Testing and using a model of communal conflict for early warning. *The Journal of Ethno-Development, 4*(1), 20–24.

Harff, B. (1994). A theoretical model of genocides and politicides. *The Journal of Ethno-Development, 4*(1), 25–30.

Hawk, D. (1987, January). Quoted in the Institute of the International Conference on the Holocaust and Genocide's *Internet on the Holocaust and Genocide* (Jerusalem), Issue Eight, n. p.

Hawk, D. (1988). The Cambodian genocide. In I. W. Charny (Ed.), *Genocide: A critical bibliographic review* (pp. 137–154). New York: Facts on File.

Honig, J. W., & Both, N. (1996). *Srebrenica: Record of a war crime.* New York: Penguin Books.

Huttenbach, H. (1988). Locating the Holocaust on the genocide spectrum. *Holocaust and Genocide Studies, 3*(3), 289–304.

Katz, S. T. (1994). *The Holocaust in historical context.* New York: Oxford University Press.

Kiernan, B. (1995). The Cambodian Genocide, 1975–1979. pp. 334–371. In S. Totten, W. S. Parsons & I. W. Charny (Eds.), *Century of genocide: Eyewitness accounts and critical views*. New York: Garland.

Kuper, L. (1981). *Genocide: Its political use in the twentieth century*. New Haven, CT: Yale University Press.

Kuper, L. (1985). *The prevention of genocide*. New Haven, CT: Yale University Press.

LeBlanc, L. (1991). *The United States and the genocide convention*. Durham, NC: Duke University Press.

Lemarchand, R. (1997). The Burundi Genocide. In S. Totten, W. S. Parsons, & I. W. Charny (Eds.) *Century of genocide. Eyewitness accounts and critical views* (pp. 317–333). New York: Garland.

Lemkin, R. (1944). *Axis rule in occupied Europe: Laws of occupation, analysis of government, proposals for redress*. Washington, DC: Carnegie Endowment for International Peace.

Lemkin, R. (2002). Totally unofficial man. In S. Totten & S. Jacobs (Eds.), *Pioneers of genocide studies* (pp. 365–399). New Brunswick, NJ: Transaction.

Melvern, L. (2000). *A people betrayed: The role of the West in Rwanda's genocide*. London: Zed Books.

O'Shea, S. (2001). *The perfect heresy: The revolutionary life and death of the medieval Cathars*. London: Profile Books.

Power, S. (2002). *"A problem from hell": America and the age of genocide*. New York: Basic Books.

Reynolds, H. (1995). *Fate of a free people*. Ringwood, Victoria, Australia: Penguin Books.

Reynolds, H. (2001). *An indelible stain? The question of genocide in Australia's history*. Ringwood, Victoria, Australia: Viking/Penguin Books.

Rieff, D. (2002). Murder in the neighborhood. In N. Mills & K. Brunner (Eds.), *The new killing fields: Massacre and the politics of intervention* (pp. 55–69). New York: Basic Books.

Rittner, C., Roth, J. K., & Smith, J. M. (Eds.). (2002). *Will genocide ever end!* St. Paul, MN: Paragon House.

Robertson, G. (2000). *Crimes against humanity: The struggle for global justice*. New York: The New Press.

Rohde, D. (1997). *Endgame: The betrayal and fall of Srebrenica: Europe's worst massacre since World War II*. New York: Farrar, Straus and Giroux.

Rummel, R. J. (2002). From the study of war and revolution to democide. In S. Totten & S. L. Jacobs (Eds.), Pioneers of genocide studies (pp. 153–177). New Brunswick, NJ: Transaction.

Sadkovich, J. J. (1998). *The U.S. Media and Yugoslavia, 1991–1995*. Westport, CT: Praeger.

Safrai, S. (1976). The era of the Mishnah and Talmud (70–640). In H. H. Ben-Sasson (Ed.), *A history of the Jewish people* (pp. 307–382). London: Weiderfeld & Nicolson.

Schabas, W. A. (2001). *An Introduction to the International Criminal Court*. Cambridge: Cambridge University Press.

Simms, B. (2001). *Unfinest hour: Britain and the destruction of Bosnia*. London: Allen Lane/The Penguin Press.

Smith, R. (1987). Human destructiveness and politics: The twentieth century as an age of genocide. In I. Wallimann & M. Dobkowski (Eds.), *Genocide and the modern age: Etiology and case studies of mass death* (pp. 21–39). Westport, CT: Greenwood Press.

Stannard, D. E. (1992). *American holocaust: The conquest of the new world*. New York: Oxford University Press.

Totten, S. (1999). Technology and genocide. In I. W. Charny (Ed.), *Encyclopedia of genocide* (pp. 533–534). Santa Barbara, CA: ABC CLIO Press.

Totten, S. (2002). A matter of conscience. In S. Totten & S. Jacobs (Eds.), *Pioneers of genocide studies* (pp. 545–580). New Brunswick, NJ: Transaction.

Totten, S., Parsons, W. S., & Charny, I. W. (Eds.). (1997). *Century of genocide: Eyewitness accounts and critical views*. New York: Garland Publishers.

United Nations. (1978). *Study of the question of the prevention and punishment of the crime of genocide*. (July 4, E/CN. 4/Sub. 2/416)

United Nations Economic and Social Council. (1948). *Official records, August 26, Session 7*.

Weymouth, T., & Henig, S. (Eds.). (2001). *The Kosovo crisis: The last American war in Europe?* London: Reuters.

Whitaker, B. (1985, April). *Revised and updated report on the question of the prevention and punishment of the crime of genocide*. (E/CN.4/Sub.2/1985/6, 2 July 1985.) Submitted to the United Nations Subcommission on Prevention of Discrimination and Protection of Minorities of the Commission on Human Rights of the United Nations Economic and Social Council in Geneva.

Whitaker, B. (1988). Genocide: The ultimate crime. In P. Davies (Ed.), *Human rights* (pp. 51–56.). London and New York: Routledge.

## 5.2   Donald L. Niewyk "Holocaust: The Genocide of the Jews"

The Nazi slaughter of the Jews during World War II gave the world the idea of genocide. The Nazis themselves did not use the term, nor was this the first such mass murder. But the systematic extermination of between 5 and 6 million Jews through shootings, gassings, and forced labor was a catastrophe on a massive scale. It was, moreover, closely related to broader Nazi racial policies that led to the murder of very large numbers of Gypsies, Russian and Polish prisoners of war, East European slave laborers, and Germans who were physically disabled or mentally retarded.

### Perpetrators

Following Hitler's seizure of power in Germany in 1933, the Nazi state pursued policies designed to isolate and pauperize the 600,000 German Jews. The goal, more or less openly acknowledged, was to make the Jews despair of their future in Germany and emigrate, which many of them did. Violent attacks on Jews were uncommon, and Jews were sent to concentration camps only if they had been prominent in anti-Nazi parties. The exception to these rules was the "Crystal Night" (*Kristallnacht*) pogrom of November 9–10, 1938, when Nazi thugs physically attacked thousands of Jews and sent them to concentration camps. The latter were released only after promising to leave Germany. These actions were clearly the work of virulent anti-Semites in the Nazi Party, supported by government officials who found pogroms useful in advancing economic objectives. Most ordinary Germans ignored these atrocities out of indifference to the Jews or a sense of powerlessness to help them.

These policies aimed at forcing Jewish emigration held for more than a year after World War II began. While many Jews in the part of Poland conquered by Germany in 1939 were mistreated, the Nazi bureaucracy made plans to expel them and all other Jews in German hands farther to the east or else to the Indian Ocean island of Madagascar. Only when Hitler invaded the Soviet Union in 1941 did emigration give way to extermination. Believing that the German people would not understand such a ghastly policy, the Nazis carried out the genocide of the Jews in secrecy and under cover of war. Accordingly, responsibility for mass murder was placed in the hands of the SS (*Schutzstaffel*), Hitler's special guard of policemen and soldiers that had grown into the central agency of terror in Nazi-dominated Europe. Some of its officers were convinced anti-Semites who accepted the view that the Jews were Germany's most dangerous enemies. All of them were convinced Nazis who were sworn to obey orders without question.

Genocide was too vast a process for the SS alone. The German army cooperated in the roundup of victims. Volunteers from the conquered Eastern countries served as auxiliary police and as guards in the camps out of sympathy with the Nazis or the desire to escape some worse fate at German hands. Occasionally local mobs in Poland, the Baltic states, and the Ukraine massacred their Jewish neighbors, with German encouragement. However, unlike the Germans, none of these other groups were dedicated to the systematic slaughter of every single Jew in Europe. The point is, the Holocaust was masterminded and implemented by Hitler's elite guard, the SS.

## Genocide: Policies and Procedures

As SS leaders prepared to participate in Hitler's invasion of the Soviet Union in June 1941, they created four mobile killing squads called *Einsatzgruppen* for the purpose of liquidating Jews, Polish and Soviet intellectuals, and Communist Party officials. The 3000 members of these four squads shot and buried in mass graves between 1 and 2 million Jews during the course of the war on the Eastern Front, but their methods were considered slow and inefficient—particularly if all 11 million European Jews were to die. Hence, Hermann Goering placed the formulation of what was to become the Nazis' "Final Solution to the Jewish problem" in the hands of Reinhard Heydrich, the most powerful SS leader after Heinrich Himmler. Heydrich's plan was submitted at a conference of top Nazi officials held in the Berlin suburb of Wannsee in January 1942. It called for concentrating all the Jews under German control in Eastern European ghettos and labor camps, where those capable of doing slave labor for the Third Reich would be worked to death. Those who could not work or who were not needed would be sent to special camps for immediate extermination.

Existence for the Jews in ghettos and their nearby forced labor camps almost defies description. Overcrowded, overworked, and underfed, they could hope only that producing for the Nazi war machine would buy enough time to save at least a remnant of the Jewish people. That hope, combined with the Nazi policy of holding all the Jews of the ghetto collectively responsible for any attempt at opposition or escape, kept Jewish resistance to a minimum. In 1944, the SS shut down the last of the ghettos and sent their piteous remnants to camps in Germany or else to the extermination centers.

The six extermination centers, all of them situated on what had been Polish territory, ended the lives of 3 million Jews. Four of them—Chelmno, Belzec, Sobibor, and Treblinka—were strictly killing centers, where victims were gassed immediately following their arrival. The Nazis already possessed the technical expertise, having employed poison gas to kill more than 70,000 incurably ill Germans in a "euthanasia" program between 1939 and 1941 (see chapter 6). The remaining two extermination centers—Auschwitz and Majdanek—were both killing and slave labor camps. In them, the able-bodied were selected for work in various military industries; the rest were consigned to the gas chambers or firing squads. To be selected for work often meant only a brief reprieve, since conditions were atrocious. As the SS saw it, the victims were to die eventually anyway, and there was no reason to spare them when a steady stream of replacements kept arriving. Hence tens of thousands were literally worked to death. Others were subjected to grotesque and painful medical experiments. Survival depended on almost superhuman determination to live and often on the good fortune of securing jobs in camp kitchens, offices, or medical wards.

Auschwitz was the last of the extermination centers to be shut down as Soviet forces overran Poland late in 1944. The SS drove the survivors of the various camps to Germany, where they were dumped in already overcrowded concentration camps and their outlying slave labor centers. Deprived of even the most elementary needs in the last days of the war, thousands died of malnutrition, tuberculosis, typhus, and other diseases. The liberating Allied armies found the camps littered with unburied corpses, and many of those still alive were too far gone to be saved. Of the approximately 200,000 Jews who survived, the majority attempted to return to their former homes, while the remainder entered European displaced persons' camps and applied for permission to enter Palestine, the United States, or some other place of permanent refuge.

## Why the Jews?

Answering the question "Why the Jews?" requires an understanding of Adolf Hitler, the undeniable author of the Holocaust. His anti-Semitism dates from his youth in Austria before

World War I, where Jew-baiting was advanced by the politicians he admired and the tabloids he read. If the psychohistorians are to be believed, it may have been more deeply rooted in some early personal trauma (Binion, 1976; Waite, 1977).

Whatever its sources, Hitler's Judeophobia comprised all the wellestablished and virtually universal stereotypes: Jews were corrupt and predatory materialists, devoid of patriotism and feelings for others, and they advocated subversive ideas such as liberalism, Marxism, and cultural modernism. Hitler adopted this hackneyed litany in its most extreme, social Darwinian form that interpreted history as a struggle between superior and inferior races. By the time he began his political career in postwar Munich, he was a convinced anti-Semite.

Doubtless, Hitler's anti-Semitism, and that of many of his followers, was intensified by the Bolshevik revolution in Russia, Germany's defeat in World War I, and the abortive Spartacus Revolt by German Communists in 1919. Then Hitler and his fledgling Nazi Party began associating the Jews with the alleged "stab in the back" of the German army, the liberal Weimar Republic established in Germany after the defeat, and the Communist menace. Anti-Semitism was always one of his central teachings. Occasionally Hitler called for the emigration or deportation of the Jews, but more often he blamed problems on a Jewish world conspiracy without specifying a cure beyond inviting Germans to support his movement. Moreover, the Nazi Party tended to use anti-Jewish propaganda opportunistically, playing it up or down depending on the responses it received. Hence no one could know exactly what Hitler and his party planned to do with the Jews, and it cannot be said that the large minority of Germans who came to support him after 1930 deliberately endorsed violent anti-Semitism. Today it is far clearer than it was at the time that genocide was implicit in Hitler's ideology.

That genocidal impulse became explicit as part of the events surrounding Operation Barbarossa, the attack on the USSR in 1941. No one knows exactly when or why the Germans decided to kill all the European Jews (and not just those targeted by the *Einsatzgruppen*). Fragmentary evidence suggests that the euphoric atmosphere surrounding Germany's initial victories on the Eastern Front may have convinced Hitler that the creation of his Aryan utopia was imminent. The dictator's increasingly barbaric campaign against the Soviet Union also sharpened his hatred for what he called "Judeo-Bolshevism" at the same time as it foreclosed opportunities to resettle the Jews. By 1942, Nazi genocide was being aimed at all of European Jewry.

## The Victims

Although the Third Reich targeted all the Jews in Nazi-dominated Europe, their fate varied with local conditions. Jews were most vulnerable where German officials managed affairs directly (and did so from the beginning of the Holocaust); where the Jewish communities were large and unassimilated; and where indigenous anti-Semitism encouraged some degree of cooperation with the murderers.

All three of these elements combined to decimate the Jews of Poland, the western USSR, and the Baltic states. There Nazi rule was most openly brutal. First under the guns of the Einsatzgruppen and then in ghettos and labor and extermination camps, Jews from these areas died in numbers amounting to three quarters of the total Holocaust casualties. Very few survived. Direct German control over Serbia, the Protectorate of Bohemia and Moravia, and part of Greece meant that their Jews were deported to Poland and subjected to similar atrocities. Such was also the fate of the remaining German and Austrian Jewish communities. Only small numbers of German Jews who were of mixed race, living in mixed marriages, highly decorated war veterans, or prominent persons were spared. Hungary came under direct German rule only in March 1944, following which the SS, aided by Hungarian officials, swallowed up more than half of the large Jewish population. Doubtless the losses in Hungary would have been even greater had the Nazis taken control earlier.

Unlike Hungary, Germany's other Eastern European allies—Romania, Bulgaria, Slovakia, and Croatia—retained some measure of independence to the end of the war. Slovakia and Croatia, both satellites created by Nazi Germany, willingly established their own forced labor camps for some of the Jews and sent the rest to the extermination centers. Romania and Bulgaria, however, refused to comply with some Nazi demands. Neither was a German creation, and both were fiercely protective of their national rights. Bulgaria confiscated the property of many native-born Jews and forced some of them into slave labor, but it would not hand them over to the Germans. It did, however, deport Jews from lands newly acquired from Greece and Yugoslavia. In Romania, where (unlike Bulgaria) there was considerable anti-Semitism, tens of thousands of Jews in the newly reconquered provinces of Bessarabia and Northern Bukovina were murdered in pogroms or else deported across the Dniester River to be murdered by the Einsatzgruppen or at Auschwitz. And yet, the majority of Bulgarian and Romanian Jews survived the Holocaust.

The Jews of Western Europe, remote from the killing fields and the intense anti-Semitism of Eastern Europe, lost about 40 percent of their numbers to the Nazis. The SS gave priority to exterminating the Jews of the east, and the war ended before it could finish its work in the west. There, too, the pace of extermination varied with local conditions. In Holland, which had been placed under direct German rule, three quarters of the Jews perished because they were numerous, heavily concentrated in one place (Amsterdam), and led by passive community officials; they also had little opportunity to escape or hide in their heavily populated country. French Jews, too, perished as a result of the Vichy regime's collaboration with the Nazis. And yet, only about 20 percent of them died in the Holocaust because they seized opportunities to hide in remote villages or to flee to neutral Spain and Switzerland.

At the opposite extreme, almost all members of the very small Danish Jewish community were transported the short distance by boat to Sweden by Danes who had no sympathy with anti-Semitism. The Italians, too, although German allies, were not racists. Only after Mussolini's fall and the German takeover of the country were about 16 percent of the Italian Jews sent to their deaths, and the retreating Nazis had to do the job themselves. Hence, in certain circumstances resistance to the occupiers by local officials and private individuals saved lives. The fate of the different Jewish communities was determined by various concatenations of local attitudes, opportunities for flight or concealment, the size and location of the Jewish populations, and the nature of Nazi rule in the several countries (Fein, 1979).

## Participants and Bystanders

Direct participation in the Holocaust by SS officials, Einsatzgruppen personnel, and camp guards was required in relatively small numbers. Indirect involvement by police, civil servants, private businessmen who profited from slave labor, and the like was considerably broader. Moreover, news of the exterminations rapidly leaked out of Eastern Europe in 1942, enmeshing much of the world in the catastrophe.

German police and government bureaucrats who defined, identified, assembled, and deported the Jews to the east were not always fanatical Nazis or anti-Semites. Many were careerists and efficient professionals, dedicated to following instructions and improvising solutions to problems in the spirit of their superiors. Amorality was encouraged by specialization; each department and individual was accountable for only one small segment of the program, diffusing personal responsibility. Ordinary Germans who had nothing to do with the Holocaust might hear rumors of crimes against the Jews in Eastern Europe, but they were preoccupied with staying alive and making ends meet in an increasingly disastrous wartime situation. The Jews quite literally were out of sight and out of mind.

In occupied Western Europe, the Nazis were stretched thin and depended heavily on local authorities to deliver the Jews for deportation. Especially in France and Holland, such assistance was widespread, encouraged by careerism and fear of reprisals. Small minorities in all the Western European countries risked their lives to hide Jews or help them escape to neutral havens. Tens of thousands were saved as a result. Equally small minorities of Nazi sympathizers turned Jews and their helpers in to the authorities. The vast majority, however, were as apathetic and selfabsorbed as most Germans.

Neutral countries such as Switzerland, Sweden, Spain, and Turkey accepted limited numbers of refugees, but none wanted to antagonize Hitler while his armies seemed invincible. Once the tide turned against him, however, they became more willing to aid the Jews. The Vatican also held to its traditional neutrality. Pope Pius XII kept silent about the Holocaust, evidently fearing German reprisals and hoping to enhance his role as a mediator. Individual Catholic clerics and laymen, however, did intervene on behalf of the Jews, notably in France, Hungary, and Slovakia.

The nations allied against Hitler reacted to the genocide of the Jews in diverse ways. The Soviet Union gave refuge to large numbers of Eastern European Jews who had fled before the *Wehrmacht*, but it acknowledged no special Nazi program to kill the Jews. In contrast, Great Britain and the United States warned the Germans and their allies that they would be called to account for their acts of genocide. A key question is: Could more have been done? It has been charged that Jewish lives could have been saved if President Roosevelt had not waited until 1944 to establish the War Refugee Board; if Germany and its satellites had been pressed to release their Jews; if the Allied air forces had bombed Auschwitz and its rail approaches in 1944; and if negotiations with the Nazis to ransom the Jews had been pursued. That the measures were not taken may be explained by indifference or even covert anti-Semitism among Allied leaders.

Or it may be argued that the Allies' single-minded preoccupation with the military side of the war was responsible. As they saw it, the best way to help all the victims of fascism was to press for the quickest possible victory. Nor will everyone agree that such measures would have altered the outcome in any significant way. No one should underestimate Nazi determination to exterminate the Jews, regardless of disruptions of the killing centers and promises held out in negotiations.

## The Burden of History

A number of historical trends combined to make the Holocaust possible: anti-Semitism, racism, social Darwinism, extreme nationalism, totalitarianism, industrialism, and the nature of modern war. The absence of any one of these trends would have made the genocide of the Jews unlikely.

Anti-Semitism has a long history in most of Europe, not just in Germany. Traditional anti-Semitism arose out of Christian rejection of the Jews as deicides and deliberate misbelievers. Once it had generated pogroms, but in modern times it inspired contempt for the Jews by providing an explanation for their alleged materialism. Having rejected the saving grace of Jesus, so the argument went, they had lost their ethical standards in the pursuit of physical wealth and materialistic philosophies. Religiously based Judeophobia partially merged with newer criticisms of the Jews' role in the modern economy. Having been emancipated from special laws and restrictions only in the 19th century, the Jews were still concentrated in a few highly visible economic sectors such as banking, publishing, and the metal and clothing trades. This made them convenient targets for the victims of industrialization, some of whom blamed the Jews for economic depressions, bankruptcies, and unemployment. At the same time, the Jews' support for liberal political movements that had advocated Jewish emancipation generated anti-Semitism among conservative foes of individualism and representative government. The prominence of Jewish intellectuals such as Karl Marx and Leon Trotsky in the European socialist movements sparked criticisms of Jews for sacrificing patriotism to internationalism.

Although anti-Semitism was widespread before World War I, it was not a central issue. Most Judeophobes advocated solving the "Jewish problem" through assimilation or the restoration of special laws for the Jews, not through violent action. Only in backward Russia were there pogroms against the Jews. Racism, which implied that Jews were incapable of changing their ways, and social Darwinism, some forms of which predicted inevitable struggle between nations and races, gained adherents before 1914. But even their most radical exponents limited themselves to advocating Jewish emigration, and they were marginal figures without much influence.

World War I changed that. Anti-Semitism became entwined in the outraged nationalism of defeated Germany and in the quest for national identity in new states like Poland and Hungary and would-be states like the Ukraine and Croatia. Demagogues—such as Adolf Hitler in Germany—associated the Jews with economic hard times and the foreign oppressors. The growth of threatening Communist movements, some of them led by Jews, added grist to the anti-Jewish mill. Hitler, who had become a racial anti-Semite and social Darwinist as a young man in Vienna before 1914, advocated total solutions to Germany's staggering economic and political problems. Once in power, his totalitarian Third Reich enforced the "leadership principle" of absolute obedience to authority. Like Lenin, Hitler had learned totalitarianism from total war between 1914 and 1918. Then the belligerents had employed political centralization, economic regimentation, and thought-control to mobilize all national resources in a terrible war of attrition. The Third Reich would use them to destroy domestic rivals, to mobilize the German economy for aggressive war, and ultimately to exterminate the Jews.

All of these historical trends came together in 1941 with Hitler's war against the Soviet Union. Having identified the Jews with Communism, the dictator's crusade against "Judeo-Bolshevism" provided both cover and justification for genocide. In Hitler's name, highly specialized bureaucrats used the latest industrial technology to make war on the Jews as part of the larger national struggle for survival. The techniques of mass slaughter developed in the First World War were brought to new levels of perfection, only this time poison gas would be reserved for noncombatants.

## Post-Holocaust Victim Responses

Studies of Holocaust survivors have shown that virtually all suffered to some degree from a "survivor syndrome" that included acute anxiety, cognitive and memory disorders, depression, withdrawal, and hypochondria. Some became clinical cases, but most learned to live with their trauma and rebuild old lives or start new ones (Berger, 1988).

Nazi genocide decimated the once-thriving Jewish communities of Eastern Europe. Hundreds of thousands of Holocaust survivors, fearing Communism and renewed outbreaks of anti-Semitism, would not or could not return to their former homes. Stranded in displaced persons' camps in Germany and Austria, virtually all expected to emigrate to Palestine or the United States. The U.S. government, however, limited the entry of refugees and placed heavy pressure on Great Britain to admit large numbers of Jews to Palestine. When Britain chose instead to honor its promises to the Arab majority limiting Jewish immigration, guerrilla uprisings by militant Zionists and international pressure forced Britain to withdraw from the area. The Jewish state that emerged from the partition of Palestine by the United Nations might eventually have come into being anyway, but the creation of Israel in 1948 was greatly facilitated by the need to find a home for large numbers of Holocaust survivors and by the widespread sympathy for Zionism engendered by Hitler's murderous actions.

The genocide of the Jews also had a major impact on Jewish religious thought. For Judaism, God's covenant with the ancient Israelites bound Him and the Jewish people to the end of time. History was viewed as the expression of God's will, working out a divine plan in which the Jews occupied a special place. Judaism conceived of God as merciful, loving, and omnipotent. How, then, could the dehumanization and mass murder of God's people be explained?

For some Jewish scholars this question could not be confronted without challenging traditional Judaism. After Auschwitz, they reasoned, faith in the redeeming God of the covenant, an omnipotent and merciful deity, was no longer possible. Nor did they find it credible any longer to regard the Jews as His chosen people. Just where this reappraisal was leading remained unclear, and other Jewish theologians rushed to the defense of continuity with covenantal Judaism. One such response was to reaffirm orthodoxy by placing the Holocaust within the tradition that heard God's commanding voice in catastrophes such as the destruction of the First and Second Temples. Judaism endured then, and Jews must not hand Hitler a posthumous victory by losing faith as a result of his policies.

A second approach embraced the traditional covenant by distinguishing between God's work and man's. God, for reasons that would become evident at the end of time, voluntarily placed restraints on Himself in order to make history possible. Hence the genocide of the Jews was man's responsibility, not God's. A third line of thought accepted that the covenant had been shattered in the Holocaust but held out the possibility of renewing it by returning to the quest for redemption and redefining tradition by living authentically religious lives (Roth and Berenbaum, 1989, pp. 259–370). In all these viewpoints, the impact of genocide on Judaism and on the Jews' sense of their place in the world was unmistakable.

## Other Post-Holocaust Responses

Among Christian thinkers, the Holocaust induced a profound reappraisal of the traditional view of the Jews as living examples of what happens to those who reject Jesus. It is unlikely that those who advanced this view ever intended it to culminate in violence against the Jews, nor would it have done so by itself. And yet, there was no explaining away the contributions made by Christian anti-Semitism to the climate of opinion that made the genocide of the Jews possible in the European heartland of ostensibly Christian Western civilization.

Protestant theologians demanded a critical reappraisal of traditional Christian teachings of contempt for Judaism. They called for a reinterpretation of church Christology and eschatology to affirm the authenticity of the religion of the Jews and Christianity's vital roots in Judaism. The Catholic Church repudiated Judeophobia during the reforming pontificate of John XXIII. One of the key documents that emerged from the Second Vatican Council in 1965 recognized the common patrimony of Christianity and Judaism and denounced "hatred, persecutions, and displays of anti-Semitism, directed at Jews at any time and by anyone." In 1998, the Vatican Commission for Religious Relations with the Jews issued the document "We Remember: A Reflection on the Shoah," apologizing for the Catholic Church's failures during the Holocaust. It aroused controversy, however, because it did not link traditional Christian teachings about the Jews to Nazi genocide. German church scholars of both denominations confronted the lamentable failure of German Christians to stand up for the Jews under Hitler.

Germans as a whole, however, were slow to absorb the implications of the genocide of the Jews. Although a few called it an Allied fabrication, most repressed it and the whole memory of the now-discredited regime that had brought about their downfall. Although the new West German government in 1952 agreed to pay reparations to Jewish survivors, the West German courts were reluctant to pick up prosecutions of war criminals where the Allied jurists left off in 1949.

German consciousness of the Holocaust arose principally during the 1960s when a new generation began asking uncomfortable questions, primed by the sensational 1961 trial of SS Lieutenant Colonel Adolf Eichmann in Jerusalem. Since that time, critical examinations of the Holocaust and the regime that brought it about have entered the media and the school and university curricula. Perhaps the most concrete expression of Germany's reaction to the human rights abuses of the Nazis was its liberal postwar asylum law that up until 1993 made Germany a haven for political refugees from many lands.

The Eichmann trial also caused the Holocaust to have a delayed impact on American Jewry. Before then, little attention was paid to survivors and GI liberators of the concentration camps. The effects of the trial were intensified by the Six-Day War of 1967, which strengthened the Jews' sense of solidarity with Israel and encouraged them to encounter the agony of their coreligionists under Hitler as a means of intensifying their Jewish identity. For some American Jews that suffering imposed a special obligation to become involved in all forms of civil rights movements.

Elsewhere, the genocide of European Jewry had a much smaller impact. Austrians, who had welcomed Hitler in 1938 and perpetrated anti-Semitic outrages, hid behind the cloak of having been passive objects of Nazi aggression. Eastern Europeans, and especially Poles, saw themselves as victims of Nazism on the same level as the Jews. Until recently that view was reinforced by the refusal of Communist governments to acknowledge that the Jews had been singled out for annihilation by the Nazis.

## Debates about the Holocaust

How and when did the decision to exterminate the Jews come about? For a group of historians referred to as "intentionalists," Hitler probably planned the extermination all along and certainly gave the order no later than early 1941, when the attack on the Soviet Union was being prepared. Opposing this interpretation is the "functionalist" view that the Nazi leadership replaced resettlement schemes with genocide only after the June 1941 attack on the Soviet Union. Some functionalists explain it as a result of euphoria over early victories in the summer. Others stress Hitler's frustration over stiffening Soviet resistance and the entry of the United States into the war later in the year. Most functionalists refer to a "decision-making process" that involved two or more increasingly radical orders made over several months. Although some functionalists believe that the central decisions were made by Hitler and other top Nazi leaders, others stress initiatives by local and regional officials facing hopelessly overcrowded ghettos and believing (correctly) that Hitler would not disapprove of mass murder. Since documents have been lost and orders were often given orally (and not in writing), the evidence is incomplete. Hence these debates promise to go on indefinitely (Browning, 2000, pp. 1–57).

Some Holocaust scholars have faulted the Jews for failing to offer armed resistance to the Germans or cooperating with them to some degree (Hilberg, 1985, pp. 1030–44). Other scholars have disputed this reasoning, stressing instead the Jews' almost total vulnerability to their tormentors and demanding a broader definition of resistance that embraces all efforts to keep Jews alive. These include measures to make Jews economically useful to the Germans, to smuggle food into the ghettos and Jews out of Nazi-dominated territory, and to provide the victims with moralebuilding cultural and social support (Bauer, 1979, pp. 26–40).

What motivated the perpetrators? A popular interpretation contends that the killers were "willing executioners" because their German culture had been deeply anti-Semitic long before Hitler came to power. (Goldhagen, 1996) Another stresses the immediate impact of Nazi indoctrination and ideology on the perpetrators (Bartov, 2003). A third viewpoint holds that the killers were mostly "ordinary men" who yielded to peer pressure and deferred to authority (Browning, 1992).

Controversy also surrounds the role of Holocaust bystanders, both those in German-controlled areas and those abroad. Some scholars have criticized the Poles in particular for failing to aid the Jews and even for actively betraying their Jewish neighbors (Gutman and Krakowski, 1986). The contrary view holds that the Poles were themselves so direly persecuted by the Germans that they had few opportunities to assist the Jews (Lukas, 1986). The United States and its allies have been condemned for doing little to rescue the Jews (Wyman, 1984). Opposing this is the view that, given German determination to kill all the Jews, there was nothing more that outsiders could have done except defeat Germany as quickly as possible (Rubinstein, 1997).

## People's Perspective of the Holocaust Today

The Holocaust is perhaps the one genocide of which every educated person has heard. Especially in Israel and the United States, its memory is kept alive by schools, the mass media, and the observance of national days of remembrance. A network of Holocaust memorial centers educates the public at large, although they often come under pressure from groups that would vulgarize the genocide of the Jews by placing it at the service of their political agendas.

In the not-too-distant past, German consciousness of this genocide helped spark what has come to be called the "historians' debate." Conservative German historians suggested that their countrymen are much too mindful of past Nazi crimes. It is time, they said, to regard the Holocaust as one of many genocidal acts around the world and pay closer attention to more positive episodes in German history. These conservative scholars were strongly attacked by scholars who stressed the uniqueness of the Holocaust and the need for Germans to confront their heavy historical responsibility for it. It remains to be seen whether and how Germans' continuing preoccupation with The reunification of West and East Germany will affect their receptivity to neoconservative revisionism.

Austrians were shaken out of their historical amnesia in the 1980s by a scandal over their president, Kurt Waldheim. Although he was no war criminal, Waldheim clumsily attempted to cover up his youthful service in Hitler's armed forces; once revealed, it called attention to Austria's role in the atrocities of the Third Reich. Similarly, the 1987 trial in France of Klaus Barbie, the Gestapo "butcher of Lyon" who excelled in deporting the French to Auschwitz, raised uncomfortable questions about French complicity in Nazi crimes against the Jews. In Eastern Europe, however, the post-Communist revival of nationalism seems ill-suited to any similar reconsideration of the Holocaust.

## Lessons of the Genocide of the Jews

German history dramatizes the insidious nature of racial prejudice. Many Germans were prejudiced in varying degrees, but only a minority wanted or expected actual violence against the Jews. Although the Nazis were deliberately vague about the practical implications of their anti-Semitism, they were sufficiently bold in their propaganda against the Jews that anyone supporting Hitler had at least to condone his Judeophobia. Moderate anti-Semitism made that possible and helped deliver the German nation into the hands of one of history's most malicious leaders. The Holocaust demonstrates that there is no safe level of racism. On the contrary, it teaches that any agenda that places economic and political concerns above human rights has the potential to result in disaster. Once the genocide of the Jews began, there was little that outsiders could do to rescue them. Earlier, however, many of the victims might have been saved had other countries opened their doors to Jewish refugees. The time to aid the targets of racial bigotry is before their situation becomes untenable.

Those who were called upon to carry out the extermination process found that the modern state has effective ways of securing obedience and cooperation. Although the threat of coercion and reprisal was always present, compliance was more commonly assured by assigning each person only a single, highly specialized function, often not particularly significant in itself. Overall responsibility rested with someone else, and ultimately with Hitler. Unable or unwilling to answer for anything but their little spheres, well-educated and cultured individuals effectively placed themselves at the service of barbarism. Their participation made possible the bureaucratic organization of modern technology for mass extermination, this genocide's most characteristic feature. It challenges us all to develop sufficient moral sensitivity to take responsibility as individuals for all our fellow human beings.

## Eyewitness Accounts: Holocaust—The Jews

Although the Germans kept careful records of their genocide of the Jews, not all of those records survived the downfall of the Third Reich, and in any event they could never view events from the standpoint of the victims. Hence, oral histories of the Holocaust are indispensable sources. Fortunately, interviews of survivors and witnesses have been conducted in many countries. These interviews cover a wide range of topics, including Jewish life before the Holocaust, Nazi policies toward the Jews in many countries, ghettoization, slave labor, resistance, successful and unsuccessful attempts at escape, liberation, and efforts to start over. Naturally, Jewish survivors living in North America, Western Europe, and Israel are most heavily represented.

Among the first scholars to interview Holocaust survivors was the American psychologist David P. Boder (1949). During the summer of 1946, he wire-recorded interviews with 70 displaced persons, many of them Jews, at camps in France, Italy, Germany, and Switzerland. Eight of the interviews were translated and published in book form under the title *I Did Not Interview the Dead*. The interview that follows was conducted by Boder, but was not included in that volume.

The Holocaust can never be encapsulated in a single person's recollections. However, this interview with Nechama Epstein reveals a remarkable breadth of experiences, including survival in ghettos, slave labor camps, and extermination centers. Made soon after World War II ended, it has the advantages of freshness and immediacy. Epstein begins her story in 1941 when the 18-year-old native of Warsaw and her family were herded into the city's ghetto together with 350,000 other Jews. [Note: This interview is housed in the David Boder Collection at the Simon Wiesenthal Center in Los Angeles. Acquisition #81–992, spools 95, 96, pp. 104A/2593–2668.]

**Epstein:** When the ghettos began, among us began a great fight of hunger. . . . We began selling everything, the jewelry. . . . We finished at the last at the featherbed. . . .

**Q:** Who bought it?
**A:** People who were smuggling. They had. They were earning. Christians bought it. . . . And then we could already see that it was very bad. We had nothing to sell any more. Eight people were living on a kilo [2.2 lbs.] of beets a day. . . . With water. And every day, day by day, there remained less strength. We did not have any more strength to walk. My brother's 4-year-old child did not have anything to eat. He was begging for a small baked potato. There was none to give him. . . . And thus it lasted a year's time. Until . . . the first burned offering in my home was my father who, talking and walking, said he is fading from hunger, and died. My father was 60 years old. . . . When my father died, there began among us a still greater hunger. A kilo of bread cost 20 zlotys. . . . Every day there were other dead, small children, bigger children, older people. All died of a hunger death.

**Q:** What was done with the dead?
**A:** The dead were taken . . . if one fell on the street . . . he was covered. A stone was put on top, and thus he lay until. . . . There was not enough time to collect the dead. . . . And then people drove around with small carts. There were no funeral coaches any more, nothing. People drove around with small carts, collected the dead, loaded them up, took them to the

cemetery, and buried them—women, men, children, everybody in one grave. . . . And we . . . It had broken out, the first deportation that was in the year 1942. . . . I do not remember the exact month. In the beginning of winter [Note: *sic.* Between September 5 and 12, 1942] There came down a whole . . . a few thousand Germans had come down, with weapons, with machine guns, with cannons, and they . . . made a blockade. They surrounded from one end of the street to the other. . . . They began to chase the people out of the houses. . . . It was terrible. Many ran into the gates. They [the Germans] saw small children. They grabbed them by the legs and knocked them against the walls. . . . The mothers saw what is being done to their children. They threw themselves out of windows. . . . They [the Germans] went into a hospital, a Jewish hospital. . . . And they began taking out all the sick that were there. . . .

**Q:** Did you see it yourself?
**A:** Yes. . . . I was being led to the rail terminal. . . . The sick began jumping out the windows. So they [the Germans] ran on the roofs with machine guns and shot down at the sick. And all were shot. And we were led away to the rail terminal. There I was the whole night. That night was a terrible one. . . .

**Q:** What sort of a building was it [the rail terminal]? . . .
**A:** A school was there at one time. . . . Then a depot was made there, and the Jews of the ghetto were all concentrated there. They were led in there, and there they were a night, two nights. They led a railroad siding to the street, and in trains [Jews were] transported to Treblinka. . . . At night Germans came in, threw hand grenades. At the people. . . . There were loud screams. We had no place to go out. One lay on top of the other; we had to . . . eh . . . relieve ourselves on the spot. . . . It was a frightful experience to live through that night. . . . In the morning they began to chase us out. "Alle aus!" . . . And they began to arrange in rows of five mothers with children, men, everybody together. And whoever could not . . . walk straight, he was immediately shot on the spot. . . . We got into the railroad cars. Two hundred persons were packed into one railroad car. Riding in these wagons everyone saw death before the eyes at any instance. We lay one of top of the other. One pinched pieces from another. We were tearing pieces.

**Q:** Why?
**A:** Because everybody wanted to save oneself. Everybody wanted to catch air. One lay suffocating on top of another. . . . We could do nothing to help ourselves. And then real death began. . . . After we had traveled for four hours, it became terribly hot. But so fast did the train travel that there was nothing. . . . We began thinking, the youths, what should we do. The mothers were telling their children they should save themselves, they should jump. Maybe in spite of all they will remain alive.

**Q:** Were the doors open?
**A:** Closed, everything! There was a small window with bars.

**Q:** Then how could one jump?
**A:** Many had along with them files, knives, hammers. . . . There had begun a great thirst. It became terribly hot. Everybody undressed. . . . There were small children who began to cry terribly. "Water!" . . . So we started banging on the doors. The Germans should give water. . . . We were screaming. So they began to shoot inside, from all four sides.

**Q:** On the stations?
**A:** Not on the sta- . . . while traveling. They were sitting on the roofs. . . . where one steps down, on the steps, Germans were sitting. . . . And they began to shoot inside. When they

began to shoot inside, very many people were killed. I was sitting and looking how one gets hit by a bullet, another one gets hit by a bullet. I, too, expected to get hit in a moment. . . . And I saved myself by hiding under the dead. I lay down underneath the dead. The dead lay on top of me. The blood of the killed was flowing over me. . . . There lay a little girl of four years. She was calling to me, "Give me a little bit of water. Save me." And I could do nothing. Mothers were giving the children urine to drink. . . .

**Q:** Is it really true?

**A:** I saw it! I did it myself, but I could not drink it. I could not stand it any more. The lips were burned from thirst. . . . I thought this is it, I am going to die. . . . So I saw that the mother is doing it, and the child said, "Mama, but it is bitter. I cannot drink it." . . . So she said, "Drink, drink." And the child did not drink it, because it was bitter. And I myself imitated it, but I was not able to drink it, and I did not drink it. But what then? There were girders inside the railroad cars. . . . From the heat, perspiration was pouring from the girders. This we . . . one lifted the other one up. It was high up, and we licked the moisture off the girders. . . . It was very stifling. There was that little window, a tiny one, so we wanted to open it. Every time we opened it, they would shoot in. . . . And when we wanted to open it, not minding that they were shooting, we did. There were small children, and they were all suffocating. . . . We could not stand it any more.

**Q:** And then?

**A:** And thus I rode all night. Early in the morning—it was about 2 in the morning, maybe 3, just before dawn—my mother began crying very much. . . . She begged us to save ourselves. The boys took a saw and cut a hole—it [the door] was locked with a chain from the other side. . . . And we took the bars off the windows. . . . And we started to jump. No. What does "to jump" mean? One pushed out the other one. . . .

**Q:** Aha. Did the Germans let them?

**A:** They did not let them. They immediately started shooting on the spot. When I jumped out I fell into a ditch. . . . And I remained lying completely unconscious. And the railroad car . . . the train passed. . . . I came to. It was at night, around three in the morning, so I. . . .

**Q:** And your mother herself did not jump.

**A:** No. The mother could not. With the small child she could not jump. And a woman of 60, she could not jump. . . .

**Q:** And then? . . .

**A:** I came to. I got back my thoughts, so I went to look for my brother. . . . In the meantime there arrived some sort of a Polish militia man . . . and told me that I should quickly run away from here, because the Gestapo is all around here. I will be shot here. I should run away. He told me that I had jumped near Radzin and Lukow. . . . So he told me to go to the Miedzyrzec ghetto. There is a ghetto with Jews. . . . I began to walk on foot toward Miedzyrzec. . . . When I jumped out I met a little girl. She had also jumped. She had her entire leg completely torn open. While jumping she had caught on a piece of iron, and she tore open her leg. . . . And the two of us started to walk. Yes, after getting up I went to look for my brother. I had gone about ten feet. He lay shot. He had a bullet here in the heart. . . . I could not move away from him, but that Christian [the militia man] said that I should go away quickly. The struggle for life was stronger than anything. I left my brother on the road. I do not know what happened to his bones. And I went on. I had walked with that little girl for about three hours. Dark it was. Through woods, through fields we crawled, crawled, crawled. . . .

**Q:** That little girl was a stranger?

**A:** A strange little girl. I don't know at all that little girl. . . . She was about 14 years old. . . . And the little girl with the bleeding leg . . . for terror she did not feel the pain. . . . After having walked thus for perhaps ten kilometers, the two of us remained sitting where the road leads into a forest. And we could not walk any more. The child said that she cannot walk any more. The leg hurts her. We don't know what will be. In the meantime I had heard gentiles saying that Germans prowl on this road looking for Jews. And I saw it is bad. With the child I cannot walk. So I took the child. I did not know what to do. I carried her perhaps . . . perhaps, who knows, a kilometer or two. I myself did not have any strength. I was barefoot. My shoes had remained in the railroad car, because I had undressed. I did not have the time to put anything on. I was completely naked and barefoot. And that child remained in the field. And I went away. I could not help any more at all. The child had fallen, and I could not do anything to help any more. I went away. [A pause]

**Q:** Go on.

**A:** I had walked thus for about 20 kilometers. I do not know myself how many kilometers I had covered. I came to the Miedzyrzec ghetto. . . . I went in. It was a day after a large deportation. So I went in. . . . Entering the ghetto, it became faint before my eyes. It was at night. I did not have anywhere to go. When arriving there, I regretted very much that I had jumped off the train, because at every step, wherever I went, shot people were lying. Broken windows, all stores looted. Terrible things happened there. . . . In that ghetto I lived eight months.

**Q:** Did you . . .?

**A:** . . . in deathly fear.

**Q:** . . . register with the . . .?

**A:** There was a Jewish Community Council. I registered with the Jewish Community Council, and I [just sat there and waited]. It was not worth it. Every four weeks there were new deportations. From the small towns all around and around Jews were brought in there. And there was a sort of an assembly depot for Jews. And from there all the Jews were being sent to Treblinka. There I lived through three terrible deportations. During the first deportation I hid in an open attic and lay there for four weeks. I lived just on raw beets. . . . I did not have anything to drink. The first snow fell then, so I made a hole in the roof and pulled in the hand a little snow. And this I licked. And this I lived on.

**Q:** Were you there alone?

**A:** No. We were about . . . there were about 20 people there. There was a father with a mother with child. There were some others. . . . We had nothing to eat. Thus we lived four weeks. We found raw peas which we ate. I had pared the beets, and afterwards I gathered the rinds of the beets, because I had nothing more to eat. And thus I nourished myself for four weeks, till there was a deportation. It lasted four weeks, that deportation. After the deportation we came down from the attic. At that time a lot of Jews had also been shot. Coming down from the attic, it was a terrible thing to see. We had to . . . we were taken to work removing the dead.

**Q:** Who were the SS? Germans and who else? . . .

**A:** There were a few Ukrainians, too, but not many. . . . All the streets were splashed with blood. In every ditch Jewish blood had been poured. We went down. We had nothing to eat. We started looking for something to eat so we . . .

**Q:** Was there no council, no Community Council?

**A:** At the time the chairman had been taken away. The chairman had been shot. He was taken out first. He was the first. . . . A very fine man. He was taken out the first—with the wife, with the child. They were told to turn around, and they were shot. There were Jewish police, too. . . . Jewish policemen. So they [the Jews of the ghetto] were shot little by little. During each deportation ten, twenty were taken and also transported into the railroad cars. And they were shot, sent away. Those who escaped were shot. . . . So there was nobody to turn to. Everybody was afraid to go out. Many were lying [in hiding] there still a few weeks after the deportation. They did not know that it is already safe. . . . When we came down it was sort of peaceful for about two months. For two months time we lived on that which the Jewish Council gave to those who were strangers [from other towns and waiting for deportation]. . . . They gave them every day a kilo of potatoes and a piece of bread. The food was not important, because it was . . . every day we lived in great fear. People walking in the streets were shot at.

**Q:** Did you have relatives there? Did you know anyone?
**A:** Nobody. I was all alone. . . . Mine had all gone away. I had remained all alone. I had to support myself. By how did I support myself? I carried water.

**Q:** For whom?
**A:** For the Jews who lived there I carried water. And for that I received a few pennies. And that is how I supported myself. . . . In brief, it dragged on till winter, till the Birth of Christ.

**Q:** That is when? Christmas?
**A:** Yes. Then there was a frightful night to live through. There came down drunken Gestapo from Radzin. . . . And in the middle of the night we were asleep in a room. There were perhaps, who knows, 30 people altogether in that house where we were. . . . And they entered. I was sleeping there with two little girls. These children had also escaped from the Radzin ghetto. Two girls, little ones. One was about eight years old, and one about six years. I was sleeping with them in the room. There were other girls. In our room there were about 15 persons. In the middle of the night we hear . . . shooting. We lay in great deathly fear. And they were knocking on our door. And I did not know why they could not enter through the door. In the morning I got up. I opened the door. A shot person fell into . . . my room, into the house where we were lying. When we came in [into the other rooms] there lay shot all who were living in those rooms. Two children with a father who were sleeping in bed, everything was shot. A man lay with his stomach completely torn open, his guts outside on the ground. And later Jewish police came in. The Germans had left, and we had to clean up the blood and all that. . . . During the second deportation I was not able to hide any more. I was led away to a synagogue. There was a large synagogue. There, all the Jews were assembled. In the synagogue it was terrible. They simply came in—if they heard a cry, they shot in. They threw grenades. They beat. They struck. They did not give anything to drink. We had to relieve ourselves on the same place were we slept. I was there a whole night. I saw it was bad. I did not want to go to death. I went on fighting against it. I went over to a window. It was on the first floor. We took two towels, I and another girl. We lowered the towels from the windows, and we crawled down and escaped down into a cellar, and there we again lived through the second deport-ation. . . . Again we lived [there] a few months. During the last deportation I was not able to hide any more. I was led away into a transport. It was a beautiful summer day. . . . It was May Day. . . . We were loaded on railroad cars. We were led through the streets exactly like we had been driven to Treblinka. They shot at those who did not walk in line. Many people fell, children. [We were] running fast. I myself received from a German . . . a [rubber] hose over the head. I got a large bump. I did not pay attention to the pain, but I ran fast. . . .

**Q:** What then?
**A:** We were put into the railroad cars. It was the same as to Treblinka, shooting. We had

nothing to drink. We drove a day and a night. We were taken down to Majdanek. Many were saying that we were being taken to Treblinka, but the direction was toward Majdanek. We were taken off at the Majdanek camp. We were all lined up. There were many who were shot. They were taken down, those who were still alive. They were taken down on the square, and they were immediately shot to death. The mothers were put separately, the children separately, the men separately, the women separately. . . . Everything was separated. The women, the young women, were taken to the Majdanek camp. The men were taken to another camp. The children and the mothers were led to the crematory. All were burned. . . . We never laid eyes on them again. . . . I was in Majdanek two months. I lived through many terrible things. We had nothing to eat. We were so starved. At first we did not know yet what such a thing as a camp means. In the morning, at 6 in the morning, came in a German, an SS woman, and started to chase us with a large strap, beating everybody. We were lying on the beds, grieved, with great worries, thinking where the mothers were, where the fathers and the children were. We were crying. Then came in a German woman at 6 in the morning with a large strap and beat us over the head to go out to the inspection. At inspection it could happen that we would stand four, five hours.

**Q:** Why so long?
**A:** People were being kept so long because everybody did not know yet what . . . what this was all about. Many children of about 16 years hid in the attic. They were afraid to come out. They thought they were going to be shot. . . . And for that, that they had hidden, we stood five hours as a punishment. Later nobody hid any more. They said whoever will hide himself will be shot. And so I was in Majdanek two months.

**Q:** Did you work there?
**A:** Yes. We were sent to do garden work. We were sent to carry the shit which. . . . There were no toilets there, so we carried it in buckets. We were not given anything to eat. They were hitting us over the legs. They were beating us over the heads. The food consisted of 200 grams [7 ounces] of bread a day, and a little soup of water with [leaves of] nettles. This was the food. And I was there two month's time. The hunger there was so great that when a caldron of food was brought, we could not wait for it to be distributed, but we threw ourselves on the food, and that food would spill on the ground, and, with the mud, we ate it. After having been there two months . . . they began to select the healthy, healthy children who are able to work. . . . They tested the heart. Whoever had the smallest blemish on the body did not come out [any more] from there. Only 600 women were picked out, and I was among them. This was in. . . July. . . . I was taken away to Auschwitz. The conditions were then already a little better. Fewer were being packed into a railroad car. They were putting in already 60 to a wagon. . . . Arriving at Auschwitz, we were led into a large hall before taking us to be bathed. All the women had their hair cut off. . . .

**Q:** That was the first time you had that done?
**A:** For the first time . . . just in Auschwitz. . . . So I had my hair shorn off, and they tattooed numbers on us. . . . We had very great anguish, because we had our hair cut off. How can a woman live without hair? They took us and dressed us in long pants . . .

**Q:** Who cut off your hair?
**A:** Our hair was cut off by women who were working there.

**Q:** Yes. What then? They cut it from the whole body?
**A:** Completely. On the body, here [she points], everywhere, everywhere, everything. . . . And we were dressed in trousers and blouses. We were terribly hungry. . . .

**Q:** What did you do there? . . .

**A:** We went to work in a detail which was call the death detail. Why? This I will tell, too. . . . We went to work, the 600 women from Majdanek. It took a month, and there remained no more than 450. We died out of hunger. . . . We worked carrying stones on barrows, large stones. To eat they did not give us. We were beaten terribly. There were German women who were also prisoners [i.e., prisoner foremen]. They were imprisoned for prostitution. . . . They [the prostitutes] used to beat us terribly. They said that every day they must kill three, four Jews. And food they did not give us. . . . We carried stones on . . . barrows. We carried sand, stones. We were building a highway—women! The work was very hard. We got heavily beaten with rubber hoses over the legs from those German women overseers, those who also were imprisoned, prisoners. . . . Thus I labored for three months, until I became sick. I had gotten malaria. . . . I went around for two weeks with a 41-degree fever [about 105 degrees F]. I was afraid to go to the sick-ward. There was such a sick-ward. . . . I was afraid to go, because it was said that if one goes there one does not come back any more, one is taken away to the crematory. . . . I saw that I cannot stand it any more. The legs were buckling under me. Each day I got more and more beaten, because I did not work. I could not eat any more. . . . I would accumulate bread from one day to the next. I could not eat it any more. I gave it away to other girls. . . . I decided to go away to the sick-ward. . . . There were no medicines. I lay around for about four weeks without medicine. . . . There was a doctor, also a prisoner, a Jewess. . . . She was not able to help at all. She had no medicaments. None were given to her. And in this way I pulled through the crisis. . . .

**Q:** And then?

**A:** I lay around in such a way for four weeks. I did not have anything to drink. . . . I pleaded for a drink of water. They did not want to give it to me, because the water there was contaminated. It was rusty from the pipes. If one drank that water one became still more sick. I passed the crisis, and during that time there were three such . . . selections. They came to take sick [people] to the crematory. During each time I lived through much deathly fear. My whole method of saving myself was that I hid myself. Christian women were lying there, so I climbed over to the Christians, into their beds, and there I always had the good fortune to hide.

**Q:** Did the Christian women let you?

**A:** Yes. There was a Christian woman, a very fine one. . . . She was also very sick. She was already near death, that Christian woman.

**Q:** Why was she in the concentration camp?

**A:** She was there for political causes. . . . And . . . she was not taken. Christians were not taken to the crematory, just Jews. . . . [Note: Epstein was mistaken on this point.] They had it much better. They received aid from the Red Cross. They received packages from home, and we nothing. We had to look on how they ate. If there was one, a kind one, she would occasionally give us, the sick, something. And that is how I was going on saving myself in the sick-ward. My sickness was very terrible to describe. Complications set in afterwards. I had many boils on the body. I had neglected scabies. . . . And I had nothing with which to cure myself. At one time I lay already completely dead, that the Christian women cried . . . they made an outcry that I am already going to die. So there came up to me a doctor, and she brought some sort of an injection, and she gave it to me.

**Q:** A Jewish doctor?

**A:** Yes. . . . [Note: The SS routinely used Jewish doctors to treat fellow inmates who fell ill. This illustrates the tension that existed between the need to provide slave labor and the ultimate goal of genocide.] After that injection I became a little stronger, and I got out of bed. I nursed the other sick. Much strength I did not have, but I was already able to walk around a little. Three weeks had passed. There came an order to deliver the names of all the sick, everyone who had scabies. . . . Then one knew that he is for sure going to his death. And I had it, too. I was very worried, and I knew that now has come the moment that I have to go. . . . I did not sleep at night. I could not eat, because I knew that all my misery, all my suffering was for nothing, because now had come my end. . . . But it was not so. The same day when they had ordered to make the list of us, they came to that sickward where there were only typhus patients, and all were taken out, the entire sick-ward. Not one remained. It was on the night of Yom Kippur.

**Q:** What was done with them?

**A:** All were taken, undressed, nude, wrapped in blankets, thrown in the . . . truck like sheep, shut the trucks, and driven away in the direction of the crematory. We all went and looked, so we saw how the women [on the trucks] were singing *Kol Nidrei.* . . . They were singing the *Hatikvah.* When they said good-by, they said, "We are going to death, and you take revenge for us." . . . They are still pleading to be left. They are young. There was a girl 18 years old, and she was crying terribly. She said that she is still so young, she wants to live, they should leave her, they should give her some medicine to heal her scabies. And nothing helped. They were all taken away.

**Q:** How come you were not included? You also had scabies.

**A:** I was not yet in the line. . . . Everything went according to the line. . . .

**Q:** How many sick were taken?

**A:** Four hundred persons. An entire block. . . .

**Q:** Could the crematory be seen burning?

**A:** Of course! When we went out at night we saw the entire sky red [from] the glow of the fire. Blood was pouring on the sky. We saw everything. We knew. When we went to the shower hall we saw the clothing of the people who were not any more lying there. The clothing was still there. We recognized the clothing of the people who had left and returned no more. . . . So that we knew. It was 100 percent! We saw every night the burning crematory. And the fire was so red it was gushing forth blood towards the sky. And we could not help at all. Sometimes, when we would go out at night to relieve ourselves, we saw how illuminated . . . how transports were brought with mothers and children. The children were calling to the mothers.

**Q:** That was in Birkenau. [Note: Birkenau was the extermination division of Auschwitz.]

**A:** It was to Birkenau that they brought huge transports from Hungary, from Holland, from Greece . . . from all over Europe. . . . And all that was burned in Auschwitz. The children they burned immediately, and from a certain number of people, from thousands, a hundred might be taken out, and they were brought to the camp. . . . And the rest were burned. . . . The next morning a German doctor appeared. I became very scared. All who were in the block became scared—we were all sick from malaria—because it was said that the others were taken yesterday and us they will take today. . . . In the meantime he came with a list, and called out my name and another 12 Jewish names, and to that another 50 Christian women. . . . And he said that we who are sick with malaria, who show a positive sickness—because there were positive and non-positive. . . . Because on me was made a . . . a . . . a . . .

**Q:** A blood test?

**A:** . . . a blood test, and it showed that I had a positive malaria. So they told us that we were going to Majdanek, back to Majdanek. . . . I did not believe it. In the evening all of us were taken, 70-odd people. We were put on a truck and driven to the train. Riding on the truck all of us believed that we were going to the crematory. We had thought that it will be an open truck, and we will be able to see where we are being taken to, but ultimately it turned out to be quite different. We were taken in a closed one. But [as we were driven] past the guard we heard . . . "70-odd prisoners for Majdanek." . . . So we already knew that we were being taken to Majdanek. . . . We were put . . . on the station, we were led into a freight car, which is used for transporting cattle. We were all put in. Among [us] were many ethnic German women who had also been imprisoned there in the camp. . . .

**Q:** Because of what?
**A:** They were for prostitution.

**Q:** How did they behave, those women?
**A:** Very mean. Very mean. They beat so. They hit so. One can't at all imagine.

**Q:** [Fighting] among themselves?
**A:** No they beat us, us. . . . And upon coming into the railroad car they made such a little piece of a ghetto. They put us into a small part of the railroad car. . . . And for themselves they took the bigger part. And in our part we were squeezed one on top of another. We nearly crushed ourselves to death. En route two girls died. They were very weak. We had no food. And they were full of scabies. . . . They could not stand it any more. En route . . . they were taken down in the middle of the night in Majdanek, and they were dead. . . . We arrived there, 11 Jews. . . . When I was there the first time there were still 30,000 Jews. . . . A few days later we found out that there were Jews here. So one Jew sneaked away . . . and came to us. She wanted to see the Jews who had arrived. From them we learned about a most sad misfortune. . . . On the 3rd of November it was. At 4 in the morning there came down the entire Gestapo with many policemen, with many SS men. They surrounded the entire Majdanek camp and called out all the people. There were 23,000 people.

**Q:** Not only Jews, everybody. . . .
**A:** Just the Jews. All the Christians remained in the blocks. . . . The Jews were taken out and told to form rows of five. The music played very violently and . . .

**Q:** Was it Jewish music?
**A:** No. Polish music. German music. . . . And the people were told to go up [to the place where] the crematory had been installed. Two days before, 80 men had been taken out. And they were told to dig very large pits. And nobody knew what these pits were for. . . . Ultimately it turned out that those pits were for the people who had dug them. . . . They went up in rows of fives, children, mothers, old, young, all went up to the fifth sector [of the camp]. Coming to the graves, there stood sentries with Tommy guns and with machine guns. And they told them all to undress. Young women flung themselves at the sentries and began to plead that he should shoot them with good aim so that they should not suffer. . . . In the head . . . not in the stomach or the leg so that they should suffer. . . . And the sentries laughed at that and said, "Yes, yes. For you such a death is too good. You have to suffer a little." And not everyone was hit by the bullet. And from them were separated 300 women, those who had remained whom we had met. And these women had to clean up next morning—all those who remained— the shot. They were doused with gasoline and were burned.

**Q:** In the pits?
**A:** In the pits. And afterwards they had to take the clothes which everybody recognized

from her mother from her sister, from her children. They cried with bloody tears. They had to take those clothes and sort them. And everybody was thinking, "Why did I not go together with them? Why did we remain alive?" . . .

**Q:** How had they been selected?

**A:** They came to the square where they were standing and picked out the most beautiful women . . . the youngest, the healthiest women were separated. . . . And 55 men. . . . Those men were prisoners of war. . . .

**Q:** Were they Christians or Jews?

**A:** Jews. All Jews. . . . And these Jews had remained there, these 55 Jews who helped us very much—[we] the women who had returned from Auschwitz. . . . We were completely non-human [i.e., dehumanized]. We looked like skeletons. And they [the 55 Polish-Jewish POWs] put us on our feet. They helped us very much.

**Q:** What could they do?

**A:** They had . . . in the things that they sorted from the dead was very much gold, very many diamonds, whole bars of gold. This they gave away. There were Christians there. . . . And the Christians received food packages from home, from the Red Cross. So they [the Polish Jewish POWs] gave all that away, and they received pieces of bread, whatever one could. And with that they nourished us.

**Q:** Tell me, you were all searched. They looked and they searched, and one had to undress. How was it possible to find gold on the dead? . . .

**A:** A Jew had it sewn in their drawers. A Jew had it in the sole of the shoes. A Jew had it concealed in the hair. On a Jew they could never. . . . they searched and they searched, and they did not find. . . . With that the Jews would save themselves. They always had something on themselves. . . .

**Q:** And they did not hand it over to the Gestapo?

**A:** No. It made no difference any more. Who wanted to go to the Gestapo? We knew today we live and tomorrow we die. . . . It was already all the same. At that time we were not afraid of anything any more, because we knew that our turn was coming now and now we have to perish. . . . Later, . . . when we became healthier, we were transferred to the fifth sector and we lived together in one block with these 300 women. . . .

**Q:** You had recovered from the scabies?

**A:** Yes, I became cured, because these men took from the Christians salves which they received from the Red Cross, stole it from them and brought to us. . . .

**Q:** Why did they bring you over there? . . . To Majdanek, these who had positive malaria?

**A:** Because they . . . it was [just] a whim on their part. Thirty thousand they burned and 13 they led to life. . . . That is how it was being done by them. . . . And I had the luck that I was among these 13, and that I had been taken out. . . . And we could not believe it ourselves. . . . And we were in Majdanek also thinking any day we will be burned. There are no Jews. To the crematory we saw them bringing every day other . . . children, women. . . . They were brought and immediately burned, from Lublin, from all over, from the entire Lublin region. Christians. . . .

**Q:** They were not gassed?

**A:** Gassed first and then burned. If there was no gas, they [the SS] would shoot and then burn [them]. We even heard shots, too, because it was very near. . . . And we were there together with them and we lived together with them. The women told us about those tragedies. It was so frightful. They cried so terribly that it was. . . . They would just repeat, "Are there still Jews in the world?" We thought there were no more Jews, only we few have remained. We thought that they have already exterminated all the Jews from Europe, from all Poland. And we told them there is still a camp in Auschwitz, they are still burning Jews every day. . . .

**Q:** And then?

**A:** After having been eight months in Majdanek, the second time, an order came: These women, the 300, the women survivors of the action, must go to Auschwitz. And we, the 13, of whom had remained 11, go someplace else, because we have been tattooed, and they [are] not. They began crying very much. . . . Two days later we were led out to Plaszow. . . . Near Cracow, a [forced labor] camp. . . . They had added yet 300 women from Radom. . . . There were little children, too. Pregnant women were there, and they led us away to Plaszow. Arriving in Plaszow, they took away the small children. They took away the pregnant women. There was a famous hill. They were taken to the top and undressed nude. There were no crematories. They were shot, and afterwards we carried boards and made a fire, and they were all burned.

**Q:** You yourself carried the . . .

**A:** Yes I carried the board! We carried the boards, and we saw how they shot them. If anyone had gold teeth, they pulled the teeth out.

**Q:** You saw that yourself?

**A:** Saw myself. I had afterwards still worse [experiences]. Before leaving Plaszow. . . . It was on the Jewish cemetery. Where the cemetery was once . . . they made a camp. . . . We walked on the tombstones. With the tombstones they made streets. They [the SS] shot people every day at first. A Jew was pushing a barrow with stones. He struggled. So he [the guard] did not like the way he pushed it. He was instantly shot. . . .

**Q:** And then?

**A:** While in Plaszow, a transport was brought with small children from Krasnik. I was all alone. I had it very hard, but I remedied it a little. I went to scrub floors in the blocks. People who had [something] gave me a little piece of bread to eat. When they brought the children I took a great liking to a little girl. That little girl was from Krasnik. Her name was Chaykele Wasserman.

**Q:** How come children were brought without mothers?

**A:** The mothers had been . . . It was like this. They had liquidated the camp. The Russians were approaching Krasnik, so they liquidated the camp. And that child's mother had escaped, and she was shot. And that child had come alone, without a mother, to the lager. And many children—they were all without mothers, because the mothers were immediately taken away. And the children separately. And the children were . . . they did not have enough time to take along the mothers. They grabbed the children and ran with them. And the children were brought to Plaszow. I took that little girl. I was with that little girl for four months. That child was very dear to me. I loved it very much. That child could not go anyplace without me. I was thinking I shall live through this war. I will be very happy with such a pretty and smart little girl, because it had hurt me very much that I had lost my brother's children. And I cheered myself up a little with that child. . . .

**Q:** What did the child do there all day in the camp?

**A:** The child did nothing. The child went around . . . on the street. It was not even called to inspection. Sometimes it went to inspection, and sometimes not. . . . After a time, they [the guards] came and took away from us all the children, without exception. And that child was very clever. She had a very clever head on her.

**Q:** How old was she?

**A:** She was eight years old. . . . She hid in a latrine, that is in a privy. . . . All the children were taken away. People came and told me to go there, Chaykele is calling me, she cannot crawl out from the hole. And I went and pulled out the child. The child stank very badly. I . . . washed her up, dressed her in other clothes, and brought her to the block. And that child . . .

**Q:** You have to excuse me. When a child hides in a latrine . . . did the other people know when they went to the latrine . . .

**A:** No. When inspection was over [and] the children were taken away, women went to the latrine. This was a women's latrine. So the child began yelling they should call me and I should take her out. . . . And I was instantly called, and I pulled the child out. When I pulled her out she was overjoyed with me, and she said she was a very clever little girl. "Now I shall already remain alive." You see? . . . But, alas, it was not so. After a time we were . . . The Russians were approaching Plaszow . . . and we were again dragged away. I was the second time taken to Auschwitz. . . . We arrived in the middle of the night.

**Q:** And the child with you?

**A:** The child I took along. What will be, will be. I kept the child with me. We came there at night. All night long the child did not sleep. She did not want to eat anything. She just kept asking me, "Does gas hurt?" . . . If not, [then] she is not afraid. But I cried very much. I said, "Go, you little silly one. There is a children's home. There you will be." She says, "Yes, a children's home! You see, there is the crematory. It burns. There they will burn me." It was very painful for me. I could not stand it. I could not sleep. But suddenly the child fell asleep in my arms. I left the child lying on the ground and went over to some man who worked there in the shower-bath, and I pleaded with him. I lied to him. I said it was my sister's child, and he should see to help me save the child. So he said, "You know what? Tomorrow morning you will all be undressed nude, and you will all be led before the doctor. He will make such a selection. And the child . . . you will hide in your rags when you will undress." And that child was very clever. She did not even take off the shoes. She hid in the rags. And I was waiting thus—it was in the morning—till the evening, till the child will come out. And in the evening I saw the child all dressed up . . . When they took away all the children . . . the child got out from under the rags and came to me. The German doctor had left, and the child came to me.

**Q:** And who . . . how did she wash herself and everything?

**A:** In the shower-bath there were Jewish women, there where the bath was. She was washed. Clothes there were very plentiful, from the many children [who] had been burned there, thousands, hundreds of thousands of children. She had been dressed very nicely. And the child came to me with great joy. "See," she says, "again I have remained alive. I shall again remain alive."

**Q:** And how . . . you too were left [alive]?

**A:** I bathed and was sent out. . . . They beat badly. We were chased out. I waited. It was a huge transport of a few thousand people, so I waited till the last. Everybody had gone to the camp, to the block and I waited for the child to come out. . . . And together with the child I left for the block. . . . While being in the block, not long, a short time, three days, it was very bad. It was cold. They chased us out bare to inspection. There was nothing to eat. . . . The cold was so cutting, one could get sick. And the child, too, had to go to inspections. . . . The child was counted as a grown-up person, but that child had much grief. She was not numbered. . . . [Note: Only those who were to be kept alive were tattooed.] After the three days there came a doctor. . . . And he again selected women to be sent to Germany. I was taken away. And that child cried very much. When she saw that I was being taken, she cried very much and screamed, "You are leaving me. Who will be my mother now?" But, alas, I could not help any. I could do nothing with the German. I went away and left the child. . . .

**Q:** Did you ask them . . . they should . . .
**A:** I asked, so he said, "If you want to go to the crematory, you can go with the child. And if not, then go away from the child." . . .

**Q:** And so you don't know what happened to the child.
**A:** I don't know anything [about] what happened to the child. I know only one thing: I left. The child said good-bye to me, and I was led away to Bergen-Belsen. . . . Arriving in Bergen-Belsen, there reigned a terrible hunger. People were dying . . .

**Q:** Do you remember in which month, in what year? . . .
**A:** The last month. In the year 1944, in winter. . . . I was in Bergen- Belsen three months. The hunger was so great—a terror. We went to the garbage heap and picked the peels from the turnips that were cooked in the kitchen. And if one chanced to grab a turnip . . . I was very daring. I did everything. I fought strongly to stay alive. So I got out through the gate, where they were shooting, and grabbed a turnip. And a minute later they shot a girl who grabbed a turnip. I ran into the block.

**Q:** Did the turnip lay outside the gate?
**A:** No. Outside the gate there was located the kitchen . . . with . . . with wires so one would not be able to get near. . . . So I opened the gate and go in. I risked it. I knew that the moment I grab it the bullet may hit me, but the hunger was stronger than [the fear of] death. . . . And I went and brought such a turnip. I returned to the block. People, corpses, dead ones, assaulted me, that I should give them [some] too. I shared it with them. We rejoiced. We finished the meal and went to sleep. After having been [there] three months, a German came again, and again selected Jews. I did not know where to [turn]. But I only wanted to go on, on. It always seemed to me here it is no good, there it will be better. And again I traveled. They collected 200 Hungarian women, 300 Polish women, and we were led away to Aschersleben. . . .

**Q:** What was there?
**A:** There was an airplane factory. . . . There everything had been bombed. . . . There was a camp commander, a very mean one. There were foreigners. . . . Prisoners of war . . . Dutch, French, Yugoslavian. [Note: After about two months, the camp was evacuated on foot as American forces approached.]

**Q:** Where did you go?
**A:** Very terrible was the road. On the way many were shot, those who couldn't walk. We didn't get [anything] to eat. They dragged us from one village to another, from one town to another. We covered 60, 70 kilometers a day.

**Q:** How many people were you?
**A:** Five hundred. . . . Only women. Two hundred fell en route. . . . I stood and looked how the camp commander took out his revolver, and [to each] one who couldn't walk he said,

"Come with me," took her aside and shot her. . . . We endured all that till they dragged us as far as Theresienstadt. . . . [Note: Theresienstadt was the model Nazi ghetto, in Czechoslovakia, about 260 km. from Aschersleben.] Arriving in Theresienstadt we were completely in tatters. From the blankets we had to cover ourselves with, we made socks, we dressed ourselves. We were very dirty. We were badly treated. We were beaten. They screamed at us. "Accursed swines! You are filthy. What sort of a people are you?" . . . We were thinking how would they look if they were on our level. . . . There were only Jews, many Jews from Germany. There were very many old women who were mixed [intermarried], Germans and Jews. They had Jewish sons, SS men. . . . They were serving Hitler, and she was Jewish; the husband was a German. And that is the reason they remained alive. All old, grey women, And all the children with mothers had been transported to Auschwitz before. . . . There was very little food. And the Germans prepared a large crematory. They had heard that the front is again approaching. They prepared a large crematory, but they did not have enough time to do it. . . . [Note: Theresienstadt was liberated on May 8, 1945.] We heard the Russian tanks were here. And we didn't believe it ourselves. We went out, whoever was able. There were a lot of sick who couldn't go. We went out with great joy, with much crying. . . .

**Q:** And then?

**A:** But now there began a real death. People who had been starved for so many years. . . . The Russians had opened all the German storehouses, all the German stores, and they said, "Take whatever you want." People who had been badly starved, they shouldn't have eaten. . . . And the people began to eat, to eat too much, greedily. . . . Hundreds of people fell a day. After the liberation, two, three days after the liberation, there had fallen very many people. In about a month, half of the camp had fallen. And nothing could be done about it. . . . There were full stables full with dead. People crawled over the dead. It stank terribly. There was raging a severe typhus. And I, too, got sick. I lay four weeks in the hospital . . . Epstein recovered from typhus and returned to Warsaw where she married and made preparations to emigrate to Palestine.

## References

Bartov, Omer (2003). *Germany's War and the Holocaust*. Ithaca, NY: Cornell University Press.

Bauer, Yehuda (1979). *The Jewish Emergence from Powerlessness*. Toronto: University of Toronto Press.

Berger, Leslie (1988). "The Long-Term Psychological Consequences of the Holocaust on the Survivors and Their Offspring," pp. 175–221. In Randolph L. Braham (Ed.) *The Psychological Perspectives of the Holocaust and of its Aftermath*. Boulder, CO: Social Science Monographs.

Binion, Rudolph (1976). *Hitler Among the Germans*. New York: Elsevier.

Boder, David (1949). *I Did Not Interview the Dead*. Urbana: The University of Illinois Press.

Browning, Christopher R. (1992). *Ordinary Men: Reserve Police Battalion 101 and the Final Solution in Poland*. New York: HarperCollins.

Browning, Christopher R. (2000). *Nazi Policy, Jewish Workers, German Killers*. Cambridge: Cambridge University Press.

Fein, Helen (1979). *Accounting for Genocide: National Responses and Jewish Victimization During the Holocaust*. New York: Free Press.

Goldhagen, Daniel Jonah (1996). *Hitler's Willing Executioners*. New York: Alfred A. Knopf.

Gutman, Yisrael, and Krakowski, Shmuel (1986). *Unequal Victims: Poles and Jews During World War Two*. New York: Holocaust Library.

Hilberg, Raul (1985). *The Destruction of the European Jews*. (Three volumes). New York: Holmes and Meier.

Lukas, Richard C. (1986). *The Forgotten Holocaust: The Poles Under German Occupation, 1939–1944*. Lexington: University Press of Kentucky.

Roth, John K., and Berenbaum, Michael (1989). *Holocaust: Religious and Philosophical Implications*. New York: Paragon House.

Rubinstein, William D. (1997). *The Myth of Rescue*. London: Routledge.

Waite, Robert G. L. (1977). *The Psychopathic God, Adolf Hitler*. New York: Basic Books.

Wyman, David (1984). *The Abandonment of the Jews: America and the Holocaust, 1941–1945*. New York: Pantheon.

# 5.3   Lisa Sharlach, "State Rape: Sexual Violence as Genocide"

*There will never be a really free and enlightened State, until the State comes to recognize the individual as a higher and independent power, from which all its own power and authority are derived, and treats him [and her] accordingly.*

—Henry David Thoreau [1]

Rape is among the most traumatic and the most prevalent of human rights abuses, and it has accompanied warfare since prehistory. Nevertheless, scholars of political violence, if they address rape at all, tend to present it as a consequence of war rather than as a component of it.[2] Examination of the civil wars in Pakistan, the former Yugoslavia, and Rwanda suggests, however, that states may use rape as a policy to maintain social and political inequality. A state dominated by one sex and one ethnic group (or ethnic coalition) may encourage men of the dominant ethnic group to rape women of another ethnic group to keep the subordinate group subordinated. In the worst-case scenarios, the dominant group, frightened by what its members perceive as an onslaught of international and internal movements for democracy and socioeconomic change, harnesses the state apparatus to destroy the subordinated group altogether. This is genocide, and the overtly or covertly state-sanctioned use of sexual violence as a tactic of genocide is the focus of this chapter.

A study of ethnic warfare that omits sexual violence tells only part of the story. It ignores the full extent of the humiliation of the ethnic group through the rape of its women, the symbols of honor and vessels of culture. When a woman's honor is tarnished through illicit intercourse, even if against her will, the ethnic group is also dishonored. The aftereffects of rape—forced impregnation, psychological trauma, degradation, and demoralization—go beyond the rape victims themselves.

The shame surrounding sexual violence complicates investigation of rape's political uses. Recent efforts by human rights and international organizations to document sexual violence against women in wars across the continents provide the necessary scraps with which to quilt together the other part of the story of ethnic warfare in the final decades of the twentieth century. Few political scientists have taken advantage of the emerging resources with which to study rape in political conflict.[3] The absence of systematic study may stem from an assumption that rape is a topic that our colleagues in sociology and psychology rightfully own. Political science is, however, a promising vantage point from which to analyze sexual violence in war because of the discipline's emphasis upon power relations and the institutions that mediate them. This study therefore is of *state rape*, mass rape either perpetrated, encouraged, or tacitly approved by the institutions of the state.

The function of state rape is to inflict sexualized degradation and injury upon women who belong to a less powerful ethnic group. State rape is especially likely in societies in which dominant groups—based on gender, ethnicity, region, or religion—have disproportionate control of the coercive apparatus of the state. The trigger for a campaign of mass rape by the dominant group is the threat of transition toward political and economic equality. Thus, state rape perpetuates the dominant group's hegemony—its preponderant influence in politics and society.

## Rape as Genocide

Genocidal rape is not new, but how governments and armies use it is. In ancient times, invading conquerors killed the men and enslaved the women. The rape of the slaves lasted for generations, until the conquerors had completed the genocide through miscegenation. No longer does the conqueror assimilate the females of an ethnic group through generations of enslavement and forcible miscegenation. Since the Holocaust, almost all genocide has occurred in civil, not international, war. The level of the modern state's involvement in genocidal rape has escalated from "toleration" to "encouragement and sanction" to "institutionalization" to "instrumentalization as a tactic serving strategic war aims."[4]

The legal definition of genocide, enshrined in the 1948 *Convention on the Prevention and Punishment of the Crime of Genocide* (hereinafter the "Genocide Convention"), is as follows:

> Genocide means any of the following acts committed with intent to destroy, in whole or in part, a national, ethnic, racial or religious group, as such:
>
> (a) Killing members of the group;
> (b) Causing serious bodily or mental harm to members of the group;
> (c) Deliberately inflicting on the group conditions of life calculated to bring about its physical destruction in whole or in part;
> (d) Imposing measures intended to prevent births within the group;
> (e) Forcibly transferring children of the group to another group.[5]

Nowhere does the Genocide Convention explicitly address sexual violence. However, rape may fall under Section D of the definition above because forced impregnation of a group's women by men from outside the group results in ethnically mixed offspring. Had these women not been forcibly impregnated by outsiders, they could have delivered babies fathered by men within their own group. Additionally, rape may fit within Section B of the Genocide Convention's definition—rape causes serious physical and/or mental injury to the survivor, and may destroy the morale of her family and community.

The authors of the Genocide Convention debated whether mass killings of people on the basis of political identity—such as partisan or ideological affiliation—should constitute genocide.[6] The final version of the Genocide Convention does *not* encompass crimes against political groups.[7] Thus, it matters greatly whether a specific episode of political violence meets the criteria specified in the Genocide Convention's definition. Genocide warrants, even mandates, intervention by the international community through the auspices of the UN Security Council. Any state may prosecute crimes of genocide by another state, wherever those crimes might have transpired. States do *not* have this right of intervention in another country's internal affairs if the violence that is taking place there does not meet the legal definition of genocide. Political violence, even the slaughter of tens of thousands of people, does not merit international intervention unless the killing is motivated by an intent to destroy an ethnic, religious, or national group.

In the early 1990s news of rape as ethnic cleansing in Croatia and Bosnia-Herzegovina sparked law professor Catharine MacKinnon to denounce rape as a tactic of extermination:

> It is also rape unto death, rape as massacre, rape to kill and to make the victims wish they were dead. It is rape as an instrument of forced exile, rape to make you leave your home and never want to go back. It is rape to be seen and heard and watched and told to others: rape as spectacle. It is rape to drive a wedge through a community, to shatter a society, to destroy a people. It is rape as genocide.[8]

Other legal scholars argue that it is forced impregnation, not rape per se, that constitutes genocide.[9] Forcing females of a targeted ethnic group to conceive is genocidal because those so impregnated cannot bear the offspring of men of their own ethnic group while their wombs are so "occupied." Under this logic, anal rape, oral rape, object rape, rape of prepubescent girls, rape of postmenopausal women, and vaginal rape using a condom or without ejaculation would not constitute genocide because such rape would not result in conception of an ethnically hybrid fetus.

In 1998 the International Criminal Tribunal for Rwanda (ICTR) ended this debate. The ICTR ruled that Jean-Paul Akayesu, the former mayor of Taba Commune, was guilty of a number of crimes of genocide, including rape.[10] The ICTR's decision sidesteps entirely the issue of forced impregnation. Rape may fit within the legal definition of genocide simply because it represents the enemy's intent to destroy.

The expansion of the Genocide Convention's mandate to encompass sociopolitical groups might permit international criminal courts to deem mass rape to be genocide, intended to harm or destroy the female sex in whole or in part, regardless of whether the sexual violence had an ethnically or religiously based motivation. The Genocide Convention should be expanded to include sexual violations of girls and women, even if there is not evidence that the rapists targeted their victims on the basis of racial/ethnic, national, or religious identity. Intent to destroy people on the basis of sex should, in my analysis, merit the same status under international law as the intent to destroy people on the basis of ethnicity, nation, and religion.

## Case Studies of State Rape

Bangladesh, the former Yugoslavia, and Rwanda may appear to have little in common. The levels of economic development, the degree of religious heterogeneity, the political cultures, and the patterns of ethnic and class stratification vary tremendously. Similar to all three, however, was potential political liberalization quashed by the eruption of ethnic war. Moreover, in all three case studies, a dominant social group harnessed the coercive apparatus of the state to inflict sexual violence as one tactic in a larger strategy of humiliation, subjugation, and attempted eradication of a less powerful ethnic group.

Admittedly, the structure of this study reflects the methodological sin of selection on the dependent variable. All the cases in this chapter are of state rape; no case study is of a state that does not perpetuate or perpetrate sexual violence to influence power relations. Therefore, it must be emphasized that these three cases are *not* representative of all instances in which men have used rape as genocide. The observations drawn from these cases are not truisms.

## East Pakistan, 1971

Pakistan, an Islamic nation, formed after the bloody 1940s Partition from India. The Muslims in predominantly Hindu colonial South Asia wanted self-determination because they feared that their minority voice would not be heard in the postindependence democracy. Pakistan had two noncontiguous regions, West (now simply Pakistan) and East (now Bangladesh), both on the northern border of India. Disgruntled East Pakistanis perceived themselves as exploited by the Western half of the country, which reserved for itself most of the national development projects and the jobs in the military.[11] During 1971 East Pakistanis waged a nine-month war of independence on their territory. East Pakistani insurgents fought Pakistan's national army, which was comprised almost entirely of West Pakistani troops.

The invading West Pakistanis (and their East Pakistani sympathizers) raped between 200,000 and 400,000 women as part of a campaign to destroy East Pakistani Bengalis, an ethnic group that encompasses all castes and includes both Hindus and Muslims.[12] Approximately three million people died. Not all of the casualties were Bengalis, however. Fearing their potential complicity with West Pakistan, the Bengalis themselves killed approximately 150,000 of the five to six million non-Bengalis living in East Pakistan.[13]

The national army raped and killed civilians—men, women, infants, and children—purposefully.[14] War correspondents heard repeatedly from refugees that soldiers killed babies by throwing them in the air and catching them on their bayonets, and murdered women by raping them and then spearing them through the genitals. *Newsweek* concluded that the prevalence of these unusual techniques of homicide of children and women was an indication that the West Pakistani army was "carrying out a calculated policy of terror amounting to genocide against the whole Bengali population."[15]

There is no evidence of a directive from West Pakistan to rape, but there is evidence that senior officers were aware of, encouraged, or themselves participated in the rape warfare. For example, survivors reported that a high-ranking Pakistani officer alluded to the mass rape as a means of subjugating the enemy women. In allusion to the Bengal tigers, he referred to the rape of Bengali women as "taming the tigresses."[16] Additionally, a Bangladeshi political scientist reports that the West Pakistani officers showed pornographic films in the barracks in East Pakistan to encourage their weary soldiers to rape.[17] Moreover, when India's army intervened on behalf of East Pakistan to force the West Pakistani army to surrender, an Indian journalist notes that a West Pakistani soldier shouted:

> "*Hum ja rahe hain. Lekin beej chhor kar ja rahe hain.*" (We are going. But we are leaving our Seed Behind). He accompanied it with an appropriately coarse gesture. Behind that bald statement lies the story of one of the most savage, organized and indiscriminate orgies of rape in human history: rape by a professional army, backed by local armed collaborators. It spared no one, from elderly widows to schoolgirls not yet in their teens, from wives of high-ranking civil officers to daughters of the poorest villagers and slum dwellers. Senior officers allowed, and presumably encouraged, the forced confinement of innocent girls for months inside regimental barracks, bunks and even tanks.[18]

The rapists inflicted degradation, physical and psychological trauma, and/or death upon the Bengali women. After rape, soldiers might murder the victims by forcing a bayonet between their legs.[19] Soldiers kept some captives in their barracks.[20] Women and girls in detainment suffered gang rape and torture, such as being tied to the window bars by their hair. A captive who displeased the soldiers might be murdered—shot or speared up the vagina.[21]

The majority of the rape survivors had contracted syphilis, gonorrhea, or both.[22] These venereal diseases, left untreated, would cause many of the rape survivors to be ill and/or sterile for the remainder of their lives. Additionally, the rapes inflicted psychological harm. One survivor of sexual enslavement relates that of the six hundred women with whom she was detained in Syedpur, many developed mental illnesses.[23] Even those Bengali girls who evaded the rapist soldiers by hiding or by fleeing from place to place suffered nine months of fear. An act of such physical and psychological violence may fall within the domain of Article II, Section B of the 1948 Genocide Convention if one can demonstrate the rapist's intent to harm the victim because of her ethnic affiliation.

In addition to causing injury, the rapes were genocidal in that they caused the forced impregnation of some group members by outsiders. Twenty-five thousand pregnancies due to the 1971 raping is a standard estimate.[24] Soldiers allegedly told their victims that "They must carry loyal 'Pakistani' offsprings instead of 'bootlickers of India or the Hindus' in their wombs."[25] Moreover (and providing additional evidence of the military leaders' coordination of a rape campaign), a Pakistani major in occupied East Pakistan wrote to another, " 'I have not been astonished that Rashid has controlled and made pet the Bengali women/their next generation must have to be changed/perhaps oneday [*sic*] you or me will be found there.' "[26]

An International Commission of Jurists concluded that Pakistani officers turned a blind eye when enlisted men raped, and in some cases themselves sexually enslaved Bengali girls.[27] In sum, the rapes of 1971 were not simply the mischief of errant young soldiers, but were coordinated by some of the senior officers of the state to facilitate the defeat the secessionist Bengalis.

## Civil War in Yugoslavia

### Bosnia-Herzegovina, 1990–1995

Rape was a tactic to influence political power relations during the civil war in the former Yugoslavia. Estimates of the number of rape victims range from ten thousand to sixty thousand.[28] Most of the rapists were ethnically Serbian men; most of the victims were Muslim women.[29] The sexual violence, according to Amnesty International's monitors, "has been carried out in an organized or systematic way with the deliberate detention of women for the purpose of rape or sexual abuse."[30]

Croatia and Bosnia-Herzegovina's secessions from Yugoslavia and the war with Serbia and Montenegro that ensued have been well publicized, and need not be reiterated here. Ethnic cleansing entailed killing, raping, or abducting everyone who was not Serbian within days or hours.[31] News of mass rape in towns nearby caused entire villages to flee, thus facilitating their occupation by Serbs. The fighting in Bosnia-Herzegovina killed approximately 200,000 and displaced half of the entire population.[32] Seventeen thousand of the fatalities and 34,000 of the wounded were children.[33]

Some believe that international observers avoided using the term "genocide" so as to absolve themselves of responsibility for intervening on behalf of the victims. Those who argue that the Serb and Bosnian-Serb aggression against Muslim civilians in Bosnia-Herzegovina constituted genocide point to the fact that Serbs killed Muslims simply on the basis of their ethno-religious identity; Serbs intentionally attacked civilians, and high-level Serb officers authorized at least some of the killing. Croats and Muslims also committed war crimes during this conflict. However, there is no evidence that during the 1990s either Croats or Muslims perpetrated genocide.

In February of 2001 the ICTY (International Criminal Tribunal for the former Yugoslavia) convicted three Bosnian Serb men for gang-raping Muslim women detained in the war. For the first time an international court condemned "sexual enslavement" as a crime against humanity.[34] To understand the court's difficulty in substantiating charges of genocide, one must note that Serbian politicians during and after the war practiced what some suspect was a well-rehearsed strategy of refutation of any involvement in rape, forced expulsion, torture, or killing of Croats and Muslims. This tactic of denial at every level—from Banja Luka to Belgrade—has left international prosecutors with little evidence of the *intent* to destroy an ethnic or religious group that is necessary to meet the Genocide Convention's criteria for genocide.[35]

The Serbian nationalists' cover-up of the ethnic cleansing campaign was brazen. Serb officials called the notorious detention camp Trnopolje an "Open Reception Center" and "an El Dorado for them [the Muslims]. They think this is a guaranteed way to go abroad. Many people have closed their houses and apartments in order to come here."[36] The Serbian government, military, and Orthodox Church denied that any detention centers existed on Serbian territory, much less that rape transpired in them. The state-run television warned that anyone spreading such lies would face prosecution. When the Serb leaders could not deny that violence had taken place—the destruction of an estimated six hundred mosques in the summer of 1992, the shelling of Srebrenica at the conclusion of a peace agreement,[37] the mortar fire upon a Sarajevo market that killed sixty and wounded two hundred—the Serb leaders denied responsibility. Instead, they charged that the Muslims (or the UN) had perpetrated the violence themselves as a ploy to win international sympathy for the Muslim-Croat alliance.[38]

A skeptic might dismiss the Serb rapes in their campaign to expel the members of Bosnian and Croatian households from the region as akin to looting—an unfortunate yet inevitable fact of war. The skeptic might argue that rape is a spoil, not a strategy, of war. He or she might add that rape in war represents self-gratification for a pent-up soldier, not military policy. However, the "boys-will-be-boys" and "women-are-booty" explanations do not explain the mass rape of girls and women in the *official* detention centers. Here, interrogators might rape to torture those women they suspected of lying.[39] Some of the detention centers held only women; the survivors and refugees referred to them as "rape camps."[40] Serb forces invading Foca sent women to what had been a high school, an athletic arena, and to private residences. They interred sexual slaves in what had been taverns or restaurants, innocuously renamed "Nymph's Tresses," "Laser," "Coffeehouse Sonja," and "Fast Food Restaurant."[41] In one large arena turned "rape camp" in Doboj, soldiers allegedly detained between 2,000 and 2,500 women and girls between May and June of 1992.[42]

The apparent objective of at least some of the rape in detention was not sexual gratification alone, but impregnation. Soldiers intentionally detained some women they impregnated until abortion was no longer possible.[43] Serb forces allegedly bussed some of those visibly pregnant back to the front lines in vehicles "often painted with cynical comments about the babies to be borne."[44]

Disgrace of the victims and by proxy the men to whom they were related was another motive, one inextricable from and closely related to the tactic of impregnation by Serbs. The rapists denigrated their Muslim victims with epithets that fused images of Muslim inferiority and extinction: " 'Fuck your Turkish mother,' 'Death to all Turkish sperm,' "[45] " 'You should not bear a Balija, you should rather bear Serbs.' "[46]

Serbian leaders deny that such assaults took place, much less that they issued a directive to rape. In 1992 President Radovan Karadzic stated that his army "did not commit a single crime, rape, or attack against civilians."[47] Karadzic also said, "The lies about the organized rapes of Muslim women are shameful, lacking all basis in fact and going beyond all bounds of human decency."[48] The following year Karadzic conceded that there had been eighteen isolated incidents of rape in Serb-held territory, but he insisted that allegations of a rape policy were "propaganda" from "Muslim Mullahs."[49] In 1997 the state-run television announced that investigation of claims by Muslim women of rape by Serbs had proven that all such reports were false.[50] In 1999 the Milosevic government's official press reported that a Jewish-American lobbyist had confessed to persuading the *New York Times* to print fictional allegations of mass rape by Serbs on behalf of his clients, the president of Croatia, the leader of the Muslim-Croat alliance in Bosnia-Herzegovina, and the Kosovo Albanians.[51] In November 2000, after sixteen Bosnian-Muslim women from Foca gave testimony before the ICTY of repeated rape during their detention (lasting up to two years) in the Partizan sports hall, the lawyer for the three accused Bosnian Serbs explained that the alleged detention centers were merely "collection centers" to which the women fled for their own protection and from which they had been free to leave at any time.[52] Moreover, Serbian leaders charged that the international press overlooked the rapes perpetrated by Croat and Muslim men. Authorities, to prove that Serbian women and girls had suffered rape, released the hospital files of those raped by the enemy to foreign journalists.[53]

Nevertheless, many believe that the rape was a Serbian political strategy.[54] Indicators of a plan include: (1) in noncontiguous parts of Bosnia-Herzegovina soldiers raped educated or upper-class women first and ordered family members to commit incest; (2) the rapes happened across Bosnia-Herzegovina simultaneously and accompanied the fighting; and (3) many rapes took place within official detention centers.[55] Moreover, witnesses reported that Karadzic's advisors spoke of rape as part of the cleansing of the town of Foca.[56] Finally, Alija Delimustafic, formerly the Bosnian minster of the interior, claimed to have secretly recorded orders to rape issued by Velibor Ostojic, a minister to Karadzic.

However, prosecutors are unable to secure evidence of a Serbian government-issued rape plan that is strong enough to hold up in court. During the war crimes trials, the ICTY did establish the complicity of Foca's chief of police, Dragan Gagovic, in rape. His office was adjacent to the Partizan Sports Hall, a detention center for women, children, and the elderly. A group of detainees spoke to the chief of police to complain of rape. The next day, under the ruse of taking her statement, Gagovic orally, anally, and vaginally raped one of the complainants. In the summer of 1996 the ICTY indicted Dragan Gagovic for knowledge of the detention centers and what transpired in them.[57]

## Kosovo, 1999

Kosovo is a symbol of Serbian nationalism. In the 1990s, however, ethnic Albanians in Kosovo outnumbered Serbs nine to one.[58] Upon becoming president in 1989, Milosevic banned the Albanian language, removed Albanians from their jobs in the civil service, and dismantled the existing Albanian legislature. These moves sparked a militant Albanian insurgency, which the Serbian government tried to repress. In 1999 Serb forces killed an estimated ten thousand Kosovar Albanians and forcibly displaced over 1.5 million.[59] In early June of 1999 the United Nations Population Fund reported that Serb men were raping Albanian women fleeing Kosovo.[60] The survivors felt that commanding officers were responsible.

Rape in Kosovo was systematic and sometimes took place at the direction of commanding officers.[61] The Serb forces—official or paramilitary—trucked some women to detention centers, where rape was only one form of torture inflicted upon them. Captors released the raped and brutalized Albanian women after several hours or several days.[62] A Serbian commander in the town of Pec kept a list of the soldiers' names to ensure that each had his turn to go to the Hotel Karagac to rape the detainees there.[63]

Moreover, troops staged rapes before the victims' families or in public to shame not only the victim but also her kin and the community.[64] Investigators suspect that the troops raped in plain sight and later publicly bragged about the assaults so that news of the sexual terrorism would spread and frighten Albanian residents out of Kosovo.

Researchers believe that the nearly one hundred reports of rape obtained from survivors and direct witnesses represent only a fraction of the total.[65] Many of the Albanian women killed were probably first raped.[66] The Yugoslav authorities were aware that their paramilitaries had raped in Bosnia-Herzegovina, but they again relied upon paramilitaries in Kosovo without taking precautions to prevent sexual assault.[67]

Serb officials once again deny that any rape by their men occurred. The Serbian state-run media instead depicted the Serbs in Kosovo as victims, and blamed the fighting—and rape—upon Albanian "terrorist hordes" trained by U.S. and German instructors.[68]

## Rwanda, 1994

Rwanda had experienced several episodes of ethnic conflict between the Hutu and the Tutsi, who had been the economic and political elite before and during colonialism. The Hutu rebelled against the Tutsi in 1959 and took control of the state the following year, which caused many alarmed Tutsi to flee Rwanda. The Hutu ruling party, Parmehutu, discriminated against the Tutsi that remained in a variety of ways, such as instituting quotas for the number of university and civil service seats that Tutsi might occupy.[69] The Tutsi expatriates periodically tried to reenter Rwanda, and each such attempt caused the Rwandan Hutu to attack those Tutsi within Rwanda. In 1990 the RPF (the Rwandan Patriotic Front, the army of the Tutsi in exile) invaded Rwanda. The French and Belgians helped the Hutu government to drive the RPF away before it reached Kigali, the Rwandan capital.[70]

In the early 1990s both the international community and emerging Rwandan social movements pressured the Hutu government to find a solution to the Tutsi expatriate problem and embrace multiparty democracy.[71] The Arusha Accords that President Habyarimana reluctantly consented to in 1993 promised reconciliation with the Tutsi. Threatened, and viewing Habyarimana's action as capitulation, Hutu extremist leaders drew a plot to exterminate Rwanda's Tutsi.

The state-controlled RTLMC radio announced on April 3, 1994, that residents of Kigali were likely to hear "a little something" involving RPF weapon fire within the next three days.[72] The following day a prominent Hutu announced before a gathering that included UN representatives that the only acceptable solution to the Tutsi problem was to eliminate them from Rwanda altogether. Others well-placed in the government informed the head of an African nongovernmental organization that the RPF would kill Habyarimana before the following Friday, the swearing-in date for the new government. On April 6, 1994, near the Kigali airport, air missiles struck down a plane carrying President Ntaryamira of Burundi, President Habyarimana, and everyone else aboard. An OAU-sponsored panel of experts observed, "(R)adio station RTLMC immediately blamed the Belgians, among others, [sic] Since then, virtually every conceivable party has been accused of the deed."[73]

The death of Habyarimana was also the birth of the three months of slaughter that killed an estimated one million Rwandans, most of whom were Tutsi.[74] Few of the Hutu extremists were well-armed, and an international force, a foreign national army, or a combination of the two probably could have prevented the genocide. Belgium, France, the United States, and other world powers, however, refrained from calling the extermination of Tutsi "genocide"— perhaps to avoid an unpopular and costly intervention such as the one in Somalia. Some suggest that Western leaders did not deploy their soldiers to protect Rwandan civilians because they did not want to risk a few white lives for many black ones.

Hutu men raped Tutsi women across the country during the genocide.[75] The UN estimates that in this tiny country there were between 250,000 and 500,000 rapes.[76] Leaders ordered the informal militia known as the *interahamwe* (literally, "those who stand together") not to spare Tutsi women and children. Men often raped before they killed; some of the rape victims who survived the spring of 1994 had been left for dead.[77]

In some areas of postwar Rwanda, almost all the Tutsi women who remain from before 1994 are rape survivors.[78] One explains that a Hutu during the mass slaughter might capture an attractive Tutsi woman for what Rwandans euphemistically refer to as "marriage."[79]

Leaders planned the genocide carefully, but it is uncertain whether they planned the mass rapes. Some believe that rape in Rwanda was systematic, premeditated, and used intentionally as a weapon of ethnic conflict to destroy the Tutsi community and to render any survivors silent.[80] One survivor interviewed by the author disagreed; she said that the raping began spontaneously as recompense for those *interahamwe* who were especially prolific killers.[81]

Unlike in the former Yugoslavia, there seems to be no evidence of the Hutu men's intent to impregnate the enemy's women by rape (although pregnancy was sometimes a consequence).[82] However, a uniquely Rwandan component of rape as genocide was the deliberate transmission of HIV. According to witnesses, Hutu rapists said that they had HIV and wanted to give it to their victims so that they would die slowly and gruelingly from AIDS.[83] The majority of rape survivors do test positive for HIV.[84] In Rwanda protease inhibitors (to control HIV) are not available, and HIV left untreated for five to fifteen years almost always results in AIDS-related death. In essence, the intentional transmission of HIV is protracted genocide.[85]

One similarity to the war in the Balkans, however, is that Hutu rapists denigrated their victims because of their ethnic identity. Examples gathered by Human Rights Watch include: "You Tutsi women are too proud;" "We want to see how sweet Tutsi women are;" "You Tutsi women think you are too good for us;" "We want to see if a Tutsi woman is like a Hutu woman;" and "If there were peace, you would never accept me."[86] A survivor relates, "Before he raped me, he said that he wanted to check if Tutsi women were like other women before he took me back to the church to be burnt."[87]

The International Criminal Tribunal for Rwanda ruled in the case of Jean-Paul Akayesu, the former mayor of Taba Commune, that rape was a component of the genocide.[88] The court noted that the killers raped Rwandan women because of their ethnic identity: "The rape of Tutsi women was systematic and was perpetrated against all Tutsi women and solely against them."[89] The tribunal has also prosecuted a woman, Pauline Nyiramasuhuko, for encouraging her subordinates (including her son) to rape Tutsi women. Nyiramasuhuko, at the time of the genocide, was the Rwandan minister of family and women's affairs.[90]

## Conclusion

State rape is especially effective against groups that shame not the rapist, but the raped. In such societies, rape diminishes the social standing of the victim and her kin. Family honor may be linked with female chastity, and a raped woman brings disgrace upon her family and her community. In newly independent Bangladesh, Sheikh Muhibur Rahman tried to lesson the stigma surrounding rape victims (which was so strong that it caused husbands to leave their wives and parents to abandon their daughters). Rahman valorized the rape survivors as *biranganas* (war heroines), set up rehabilitation centers on their behalf, and offered rewards to men who would marry them. Nevertheless, few proposals were forthcoming. Some of the *biranganas* committed suicide; others fled to West Pakistan, where their shame would be a secret.[91] Similarly, the Bosnian Muslim rape survivors, in addition to coping with the rape-related injuries and trauma, face a culture in which a raped woman is forever dishonored. Muslim religious leaders there also urged bachelors to marry the rape victims, but few did.[92] Likewise, the Kosovar Albanians do not perceive raped women and girls to be innocent victims; the death of the family member defiled by rape may seem the only way to restore the family's honor.[93] A common saying is that a good woman should commit suicide if she has been raped.[94] Finally, Rwandans today also shun the rape survivors. The popular perception is that the survivors prostituted themselves to spare their own lives. In Rwanda the physiological and psychological complications of rape, that the rape victims became pariahs, and the destitution of those widowed, orphaned, or abandoned in the genocide led many rape survivors to say that they would rather have been killed.[95]

The methods of state rape vary. Soldiers may rape women before murdering them, they may attempt to dilute an ethnic community's bloodline by raping and impregnating its women, or they may intend for the mass rapes to demoralize the surviving members of a community. Rwandan Hutu men used the HIV virus as a weapon of genocide against some Tutsi women. Top-level leaders, rather than prevent or prosecute such acts, ignored them or, in the case of Yugoslavia, denied that they even happened. Neither the Pakistani, nor the Serbian, nor the Rwandan Hutu government issued a formal directive during the civil war to rape women of the insurgent ethnic group. Nevertheless, their agents—and, in some cases, commanding officers—encouraged and/or engaged in rape as part of a strategy of subjugation or eradication of a people that had attempted to upset a politically and economically inequitable status quo.

## Notes

Portions of this chapter appear in a paper presented at the 1999 meeting of the Association of Genocide Scholars and in Lisa Sharlach, *Sexual Violence as a Political Weapon: The State and Rape* (Lynne Rienner Publishers, forthcoming). The Institute on Global Conflict and Cooperation and the University of California Davis Pro Femina Research Consortium funded this research. I am indebted to Lesley Mandros Bell, Matthew Hoddie, Dave Massengale, and especially Howard Sharlach for their assistance.
  1. Henry David Thoreau, "On the Duty of Civil Disobedience," in *Social and Political Philosophy*, ed. John Somerville and Ronald E. Santoni (New York: Anchor Books, 1963), p. 301.
  2. Ruth Seifert, "The Second Front: The Logic of Sexual Violence in Wars," *Women's Studies International Forum* 19, nos. 1–2, (1996): 35–36.

3. Inger Skjelsbaek, *Sexual Violence in Times of War: An Annotated Bibliography* (Oslo, Norway: PRIO International Peace Research Institute, 1999).

4. Helen Fein, "Genocide and Gender: The Uses of Women and Group Destiny," *Journal of Genocide Research* 1, no. 1 (1999), p. 49.

5. *Convention on the Prevention and Punishment of the Crime of Genocide*, December 9, 1948, Article II.

6. Ervin Staub, *The Roots of Evil: The Origins of Genocide and Other Group Violence* (Cambridge: Cambridge University Press, 1989), pp. 7–8.

7. Frank Chalk, "Redefining Genocide," in *Genocide: Conceptual and Historical Dimensions*, ed. George Andreopoulos (Philadelphia: University of Pennsylvania Press, 1994), pp. 48–53.

8. Catharine A. MacKinnon, "Rape, Genocide, and Women's Human Rights," *Harvard Women's Law Journal* 17 (1994): pp. 11–12.

9. Siobhan K. Fisher, "Occupation of the Womb: Forced Impregnation as Genocide," *Duke Law Journal* 46 (1996): p. 125.

10. *The Prosecutor versus Jean-Paul Akayesu*, Case No. ICTR-96-4-T, September 2, 1998, Count 12.

11. R. J. Rummel, *Death by Government* (New Brunswick and London: Transaction Publishers, 1994), p. 316.

12. Rounaq Jahan, "Genocide in Bangladesh," *Century of Genocide: Eyewitness Accounts and Critical Views*, ed. Samuel Totten, William S. Parsons, and Israel W. Charny (New York and London: Garland Publishing, 1997), p. 296; R. J. Rummel (*Death by Government*, p. 329) writes that West Pakistan was guilty of genocide against Hindus and mass murder of Bengalis; P. C. C. Raja, "Pakistan's Crimes Against Humanity in Bangladesh," FBIS-NES-97-351, "India: Commentary Raps Pakistan for Crimes Against Bangladeshis," December 19, 1997 (originally broadcast by Delhi All India Radio General Overseas Service in English, December 17, 1997); Urvashi Butalia, "A Question of Silence: Partition, Women, and the State," in *Gender and Catastrophe*, ed. Ronit Lentin (London and New York: Zed Books, 1997), p. 264; Amita Malik, *The Year of the Vulture* (New Delhi, India: Orient Longman, 1972), p. 152.

13. Jahan, "Genocide in Bangladesh," p. 299; Rummel, *Death by Government*, pp. 331–35.

14. Malik, *The Year of the Vulture*, pp. 140–54.

15. *Newsweek*, June 28, 1971, in Fazlul Quaderi, *Bangladesh Genocide and the World Press* (Dacca, Bangladesh: Begum Dilafroz Quaderi, 1972), p. 158.

16. Sultana Kamal, "The 1971 Genocide in Bangladesh and Crimes Committed Against Women," in *Common Grounds: Violence Against Women in War and Armed Conflict Situations*, ed. Indai Lourdes Sajor (Quezon City, Philippines: Asian Center for Women's Human Rights, 1998), p. 272.

17. Abul Hasanat, *The Ugliest Genocide in History; Being a Resume of Inhuman Atrocities in East Pakistan, Now Bangladesh* (Dacca, Bangladesh: Muktadhara, 1974), p. 64.

18. Malik, *The Year of the Vulture*, p. 154.

19. *Newsweek*, June 28, 1971, reprinted in Quaderi, *Bangladesh Genocide*, p. 158.

20. Susan Brownmiller, *Against Our Will: Men, Women and Rape* (New York: Fawcett, 1993), p. 82.

21. Kamal, "The 1971 Genocide," p. 273.

22. Hasanat, *The Ugliest Genocide*, p. 77; Brownmiller, *Against Our Will*, p. 75.

23. Kamal, "The 1971 Genocide," p. 274.

24. Brownmiller, *Against Our Will*, pp. 79, 84.

25. Kamal, "The 1971 Genocide," p. 272.

26. In Shumi Umme Habiba, "Mass Rape and Violence in the 1971 Armed Conflict of Bangladesh: Justice and Other Issues," in *Common Grounds*, p. 260.

27. International Commission of Jurists, Secretariat, *The Events in East Pakistan, 1971* (Geneva: International Commission of Jurists, 1972), p. 40.

28. Charlotte Bunch and Niamh Reilly, *Demanding Accountability: The Global Campaign and Vienna Tribunal for Women's Human Rights* (New Jersey and New York: Center for Women's Global Leadership and the United Nations Development Fund for Women, 1994), p. 36.

29. Amnesty International, *Bosnia-Herzegovina: Rape and Sexual Abuse by Armed Forces* (New York: Amnesty International, 1993), p. 4.

30. Ibid.

31. Seada Vranic, "Mass Rape in Bosnia: Breaking the Wall of Silence," www.cco.caltech.edu/ ~bosnia/articles/serbmedia.html (January 13, 1999). Serb captors also inflicted sexual torture

upon Croatian or Muslim males. Amnesty International, *Bosnia-Herzegovina*, p. 5; J.L.M. Commission 1994, 5, 8; (J.L.M.) Commission of Experts' Final Report (S/1994/674), Parts I and II, United Nations Security Council, May 27, 1994, www.his.com:80/~cij/commxyu3.htm#II.I; Fein "Genocide and Gender," p. 55.

32. U.S. Department of State, "Background Notes: Bosnia-Herzegovina," Bureau of European Affairs, August         1999,         www.state.gov/www/background_notes/bosnia_9908_bgn.html (June 18, 2000).

33. U.S. Department of State, "1999 Country Reports on Human Rights Practices," February 25, 2000, www.state.gov/www/global/human_rights/1999_hrp_report (April 2, 2000).

34. Jerome Socolovsky, "Serbs Convicted of Rape, Torture," *Associated Press*, February 22, 2001. International law permits the prosecution of crimes against humanity even if they took place in the absence of war.

35. Norman Cigar, *Genocide in Bosnia: The Policy of "Ethnic Cleansing"* (College Station, Tex.: Texas A&M University Press, 1995), p. 87.

36. Ibid., p. 90.

37. Eric Stover and Gilles Peress, *The Graves: Srebrenica and Vukovar* (Zurich, Berlin, and New York: Scalo, 1998), p. 116.

38. In Cigar, *Genocide in Bosnia*, pp. 93–94.

39. International Criminal Tribunal for the Former Yugoslavia (Press Office), "Gang Rape, Torture and Enslavement of Muslim Women Charged in ICTY's First Indictment Dealing Specifically with Sexual Offenses," June 26, 1996, www.haverford.edu/relg/sells/indictments/gagovic.html.

40. In 1994 the author worked in Croatia for the World University Service-Austria, Zagreb Office and Unaccompanied Children in Exile.

41. Maria B. Olujic, "Women, Rape, and War: The Continued Trauma of Refugees and Displaced Persons in Croatia," originally published in *Anthropology of East Europe Review* 13, no. 1 (1995), condor.depaul.edu/~rrotenbe/aeer/aeer13_1/Olujic.html (January 14, 1999).

42. Alexandra Stiglmayer, "The Rapes in Bosnia-Herzegovina," *Mass Rape: The War Against Women in Bosnia-Herzegovina*, ed. Alexandra Stiglmayer (Lincoln, Nebr.: University of Nebraska Press, 1993), p. 118.

43. (J.L.M.) Commission of Experts' Final Report. Also Stiglmayer, "The Rapes in Bosnia-Herzegovina," pp. 134–35.

44. Ruth Seifert, "Rape in Wars: Analytical Approaches," *Minerva: Quarterly Report on Women and the Military* 5.11, no. 2 (June 30, 1993): p. 17.

45. Stiglmayer, "The Rapes in Bosnia-Herzegovina," p. 109.

46. State Commission for Gathering Facts on War Crimes in the Republic of Bosnia and Herzegovina, "War Crimes Against Women," March 1993, gopher://gopher.igc.apc.org:70/00/peace/yugo/crimes/so/38 (April 6, 2000). Bosnia-Herzegovina used to be part of the Ottoman Empire, and many of the Muslims have some Turkish ancestry. "Balija" is a derogatory reference to a Muslim.

47. In Cigar, *Genocide in Bosnia*, p. 88.

48. In Stiglmayer, "The Rapes in Bosnia-Herzegovina," p. 163.

49. Roy Gutman, "Evidence Serb Leaders in Bosnia OKd Attacks," *Newsday*, April 19, 1993, www.haverford.edu/regl/sells/rape2.html (November 8, 1999).

50. Paris AFP, "Bosnia-Herzegovina: UN Demands Airtime on Bosnian-Serb TV to Refute 'Lies,'" August 13, 1997, FBIS Transcribed Text Document Number FBIS-EEU-97-225.

51. According to the Ministry, the U.S. lobbyist disclosed, "Everything functioned perfectly, placing the Jewish organizations on the side of 'Bosnians,' that was an excellent bluff. We were in position to make the Serbs look like Nazis in public." Serbian Ministry of Information, "Media Lies, Propaganda War Against Serbs and a Warning to Jews," April 17, 1999, www.serbia-info.com/news/1999-04/17/10982.html (June 24, 2000).

52. Moreover, the defense's brief stated that the sixteen Muslim women provided testimony so coherently that "it is obvious that there are no permanent psychological and psychiatric consequences suffered by any of these witnesses." Jerome Socolovsky, "Serb Defense: Women Lied About Rape," *Associated Press*, November 21, 2000.

53. Lepa Mladjenovic, "Ethics of Difference: Working with Women War Survivors," in *Common Grounds*, ed. Sajor, p. 351.

54. Stiglmayer, "The Rapes in Bosnia-Herzegovina," pp. 148, 154; Human Rights Watch Women's Rights Project, *Human Rights Watch Global Report on Women's Human Rights* (New York: Human Rights Watch, 1995), p. 11; Amnesty International, *Bosnia-Herzegovina*, p. 4; (J.L.M.) Commission of Experts' Final Report, I.G.I; personal communication with young refugee women, Zagreb, June–July, 1994.

55. (J.L.M.) Commission of Experts' Final Report, IV. E.3, 8.

56. Roy Gutman, "Evidence Serb Leaders in Bosnia OKd Attacks," *Newsday*, April 19, 1993, www.haverford.edu/regl/sells/rape2.html (November 8, 1999).

57. International Criminal Tribunal for the Former Yugoslavia, "Gang-Rape, Torture, and Enslavement," The Hague: Netherlands, 1996.

58. *Washington Post Online*, "Kosovo: The Jerusalem of Serbia," July 1999, www .washingtonpost.com/wp-srv/inatl/longterm/balkans/overview/kosovo.htm.

59. U.S. Department of State, "Executive Summary," *Ethnic Cleansing in Kosovo: An Accounting*, December 1999, www.state.gov/www/global/human_rights/kosovoii/homepage.html (June 18, 2000).

60. Some witnesses report that there were needles in the victims' arms and froth on their mouths. OSCE (Organization for Security and Cooperation in Europe), "Kosovo/Kosova: As Seen, As Told," 1999, http://www.osce.org/kosovo/reports/hr/part1/index.htm (June 19, 2000).

61. Almost all of the rapes in Kosovo were gang rapes. Human Rights Watch, "Federal Republic of Yugoslavia: Kosovo: Rape as a Weapon of 'Ethnic Cleansing,' " 2000, www.hrw.org/reports/2000/fry/Kosov003–06.htm#TopOfPage (April 12, 2000).

62. Amy Bickers, "Kosovo/Sex Crimes," transcript of *Voice of America* broadcast No. 2-250174, June 3, 1999.

63. U.S. Department of State, "Documenting the Abuses," *Ethnic Cleansing in Kosovo: An Accounting*, December 1999, www.state.gov/www/global/human_rights/kosovoii/document.html (June 18, 2000).

64. OSCE, "Kosovo/Kosova."

65. Reports exist of rape by ethnic Albanians of Serbian, Albanian, and Roma women subsequent to the entry of NATO troops in Kosovo. Human Rights Watch, "Federal Republic"; U.S. Department of State, "Documenting."

66. OSCE, "Kosovo/Kosova."

67. Human Rights Watch, "Federal Republic."

68. Miroslav Markovic, "KFOR: U.N. Peacekeeping Mission or a New Fraud for the Serbs," Serbian Ministry of Information, June 29, 1999, www.serbia-info.com/news/1999–06/29/12974.html (June 24, 2000).

69. Alain Destexhe, *Rwanda and Genocide in the 20th Century*, trans. Alison Marschner (New York: New York University Press, 1995), p. 44.

70. Guy Vassall-Adams, *Rwanda: An Agenda for International Action* (Oxford, U.K.: Oxfam, 1994), p. 21.

71. Destexhe, *Rwanda and Genocide*, p. 29.

72. Philip Gourevitch, *We Wish To Inform You That Tomorrow We Will Be Killed With Our Families* (New York: Farrar, Strauss, and Giroux, 1998), p. 110.

73. International Panel of Eminent Personalities to Investigate the 1994 Genocide in Rwanda and the Surrounding Events, "Special Report," July 7, 2000, www.oau-oua.org/Document/ipep/report/Rwanda-e/EN-III-T.htm (December 3, 2000).

74. Felicite Umutanguha Layika, "War Crimes Against Women in Rwanda," in *Without Reservation: The Beijing Tribunal on Accountability for Women's Human Rights*, ed. Niamh Reilly (New Jersey: The Center for Women's Global Leadership, 1995), p. 38.

75. Catherine Bonnet, "Le viol des femmes survivantes du génocide au Rwanda," in *Rwanda, un génocide du XXe siécle*, ed. R. Verdier, E. Decaux, and J.-P. Chrétien (Paris: Editions L'Harmattan, 1995), p. 19; Elizabeth Royte, "The Outcasts," *New York Times Magazine*, January 19, 1997, p. 38.

76. Binaifer Nowrojee, "Shattered Lives: Sexual Violence during the Rwandan Genocide and Its Aftermath," New York: Human Rights Watch, 1996, p. 24.

77. Nowrojee, *Shattered Lives*, p. 35.

78. Layika, "War Crimes Against Women in Rwanda," p. 39.

79. Interview of anonymous survivor, AVEGA, Association des venues du genocide d'avril (Association of Widows of the April Genocide), Kigali, Rwanda, November 10, 1998.

80. Bonnet, "Le viol des femmes survivantes du génocide au Rwanda," p. 2.

81. Interview of anonymous survivor, AVEGA.

82. Interview of Alice Karekezi, Special Monitor for Women's Human Rights at the ICTR, Arusha, Butare, Rwanda, November 12, 1998.

83. Interview of Chantal Kayitesi, AVEGA, Kigali, Rwanda, November 10, 1998; United Nations High Commission on Human Rights, "Fundamental Freedoms," p. 18.

84. Interview of staff member, Rwandan Women's Net, Kigali, Rwanda, November 11, 1998. Of course, a survivor may have contracted HIV before or after being raped.

85. Layika, "War Crimes Against Women in Rwanda," p. 40; Interview of staff member, Rwandan Women's Net, Kigali, Rwanda, November 11, 1998.

86. Nowrojee, *Shattered Lives*, p. 18.

87. Ibid., p. 43.

88. Bill Berkeley, "Judgment Day," *Washington Post Magazine*, October 11, 1998, pp. 10–15.

89. UN Press Office, "Rwanda International Criminal Tribunal Pronounces Guilty Verdict in Historic Genocide Trial," Press Release AFR/94L/2895, September 2, 1998, http://www.un.org/News/Press/docs/1998/19980902.afr94.html (September 16, 1999).

90. "U.N. Charges Rwandan Woman with Rape," *Associated Press*, August 12, 1999.

91. Santi Rozario, "Disasters and Bangladeshi Women," in *Gender and Catastrophe*, ed. Lentin, p. 264.

92. Slavenka Drakulic, "The Rape of Women in Bosnia," in *Women and Violence: Realities and Responses Worldwide*, ed. Miranda Davies (London: Zed Books, 1994), p. 181.

93. Carol J. Williams, "Kosovo Rape Victims Face Society's Harsh Judgment," *The Sacramento Bee*, May 30, 1999.

94. OSCE, "Kosovo/Kosova."

95. Nowrojee, *Shattered Lives*, pp. 49–59.

# 5.4   Jan Willem Honig, "Srebrenica"

The Srebrenica massacre, in which some seven thousand Bosnian Muslim males were executed by Bosnian Serb forces in July 1995 in the Yugoslav War, is widely recognized as the worst single war crime committed in Europe since World War II. The International Criminal Tribunal for the Former Yugoslavia (ICTY) has condemned the crime as an act of genocide. Srebrenica has also become synonymous with a great failure of the international community. Neither the protection of United Nations (UN) Security Council Resolutions nor the presence of a Dutch peacekeeping battalion deterred the Bosnian Serb attack on the "safe area" or prevented the subsequent massacre. Not until June 11, 2004, did the Bosnian Serb government, responding to strong international pressure, release a forty-two-page report admitting that police and army units under its control had "participated" in the massacre, and that government forces had undertaken extensive measures to "hide the crime by removing bodies."

## The Massacre

Srebrenica is a little town in eastern Bosnia and Herzegovina that was bypassed in the Serb offensive in the opening stages of the war in March and April 1992. A renewed offensive in 1993 led to UN Security Council Resolution 819 (April 16, 1993), which declared the town and its surroundings a "safe area." Some 40,000 Muslim refugees from all over eastern Bosnia were surrounded in the isolated enclave. On July 6, 1995, as part of the attempt to "clean up the map" in preparation for ending the war, Bosnian Serb forces launched a carefully prepared attack, which led to the fall of the enclave on July 11. Approximately 15,000 Muslim men tried to break out and reach Bosnian government-held territory in central Bosnia. Thousands were captured and executed in a well-organized operation, lasting slightly more than a week. Some 25,000 people sought refuge around the main UN compound. Males were separated from women and children. While the 23,000 women and children were deported, approximately 2,000 men were taken away and executed.

The massacre reveals a pattern that was common to Serb strategy and tactics in the war. Srebrenica is a clear instance of the strategy of ethnic cleansing practiced by the Serbs since 1991. This strategy aimed to create an ethnically homogenous Serb state by forcing non-Serbs to flee as the result of acts of demonstrative atrocity against civilians. In the atrocities, men were objects of special attention. Their removal in particular was deemed to render communities incapable of further resistance and prevent the return of the surviving population to their original homes.

Nonetheless, the scale of the massacre was uncommon. Why did the Bosnian Serbs attempt to kill all the men from Srebrenica? The official Dutch investigation concluded that it was a combination of anger and frustration at the surprise escape attempt by the men, as well as of a desire to revenge the vicious attacks by Bosnian Muslims from the enclave in the previous years. A more convincing explanation, also accepted by the Appeals Chamber in the Krstic trial, is that the genocide would remove a cross-section of men from all over eastern Bosnia and thereby secure the whole region from effective Muslim irredentism. A related contentious issue is the timing of the decision to massacre the men. The official Dutch investigation claims that the decision was taken after the fall of the enclave and hence the genocide was a largely improvised action. Others argue that the decision was taken much earlier and thus the genocide was a premeditated act.

## The Aftermath

Soon after the event, the ICTY indicted prominent Bosnian Serb leaders for their crimes. In November 1995 the first individuals to be indicted were Bosnian Serb president Radovan Karadzic and the Bosnian Serb Army commander, General Ratko Mladic. Although as of mid-2004 they had avoided capture, the former Yugoslav leader, Slobodan Milosevic, appeared before the Tribunal and was accused of complicity in the genocide (although the evidence linking him with Srebrenica was slight). Many of the "second echelon" of lesser military figures with direct involvement were also tried. A member of one of the execution squads, Drazen Erdemovic, was convicted in 1996. More importantly, the commander of the Bosnian Serb Army Corps that controlled the area, General Radislav Krstic, was sentenced to forty-six years in 2001 (a sentence that was reduced to thirty-five years on appeal in 2004). A number of his subordinate officers were convicted in late 2003. The massacre was committed by relatively small numbers of troops and guided primarily by Security and Special Police personnel. The most senior officers were Colonels Ljubisa Beara and Ljubomir Borovcanin. They, like their commanding officer General Mladic, remained at large as of mid-2004.

The evidence in the trials was based on forensic proof, witness statements, and documents. This has led to the judgment that the Srebrenica massacre constituted genocide. The exhumation of bodies reveals that many thousands of Muslim men died not as the result of combat, but of large-scale executions. Moreover, the victims were not exclusively of military age, but included boys, old men, and invalids. Finding witnesses has posed a problem. Very few Muslims survived the massacres and few Serb suspects have admitted guilt. Controversially, the prosecution reverted to plea bargaining. Trial judges, however, have expressed great reservations about this practice as it suggests that individual punishment for some of the most heinous crimes possible can be avoided by testifying against others.

Documentary evidence has been critical in all trials. A key part is formed by the military archive of the Bosnian Serb armed forces that was captured by North American Treaty

Organization (NATO) troops after the war ended. This archive included, for example, the plan of attack and much administrative material that revealed which units and personnel were involved in the Srebrenica operation. A second important documentary trail involved intercepts of radio communications of Bosnian Serb forces made by Bosnian Muslim military intelligence. These intercepts played a major role in the Krstic trial as they tended to be more explicit about what actually took place than the written documents. On appeal, however, many intercepts were judged sufficiently ambiguous to allow for weaker interpretations benefiting the defendant. Hence, General Krstic's conviction for being a "principal perpetrator" of genocide was reduced to one of an "aider and abettor."

## Unsucccessful Humanitarian Intervention

Srebrenica is often regarded as the emblematic failure of the humanitarian intervention in the former Yugoslavia. The Dutch UN battalion that was there to protect the "safe area" has become a particular focus of criticism. The unit appeared to have consciously allowed itself to be reduced to the role of impotent bystander while the genocide was committed. Despite undoubted shortcomings, much of the criticism is misplaced. In the end, Srebrenica fell because of a lack of will on the part of the international community to use force in defense of human rights. The weak and ambiguous mandate of the 1993 UN Security Council Resolution that made Srebrenica a "safe area" already exemplified this. It was confirmed by a string of other actions, ranging from the unwillingness to back up the implementation of peace plans by force, if necessary, to the half-hearted attempt to use NATO air power in May and June 1995 (which resulted in extensive hostage taking by the Bosnian Serbs and a swift capitulation by the international community). Within this political context, the behavior of the Dutch troops and, more broadly, the UNPROFOR mission in the former Yugoslavia, becomes understandable. They were expected to avoid actions that led to UN casualties and might involve the international community in a shooting war. Added into this mix was a persistent disbelief that the Bosnian Serbs would dare take the whole safe area and commit genocide. The shock of Srebrenica did directly lead to the armed intervention of August and September 1995 that resulted in the Dayton Peace Agreements being signed the following November. It also led to a much firmer stance, and ultimately armed intervention, over Kosovo in 1999.

## Bibliography

Gow, James (2003). *The Serbian Project and Its Adversaries: A Strategy of War Crimes* London: Hurst.

Honig, Jan Willem, and Norbert Both (1997). *Srebrenica: Record of a War Crime*, revised edition. New York: Penguin.

Netherlands Institute for War Documentation. (April 2002). "Srebrenica, a 'Safe' Area: Reconstruction, Background, Consequences and Analyses of the Fall of a Safe Area." Available from http://www.srebrenica.nl.

Report of the Secretary-General Pursuant to General Assembly Resolution 53/55. (November 15, 1999). *The Fall of Srebrenica*. Available from: http://www.un.org/peace/srebrenica.pdf.

Wood, Nicholas (June 12, 2004). "Bosnian Serbs Admit Responsibility for the Massacre of 7,000." *The New York Times*.

# 5.5  Samuel Totten "The Darfur Genocide"

## Introduction

The mass killing of black Africans of Darfur, Sudan, by Government of Sudan troops and *Janjaweed*[1] (Arab militia) constitutes the first acknowledged genocide of the twenty-first century (2003 to present).[2] Unlike the other genocidal events addressed in *Century of Genocide*, this genocide continues unabated to this day (December 2007) against the few remaining black African villages in Darfur and against internally displaced persons camps that dot the Darfur landscape. Although the process of killing (bombings from airplanes, automatic weapons fire, stabbings, the torching of people, the poisoning of wells, and chasing the victim population out into forbidding deserts without water or food) has remained constant over the years, the "progress" of the killing has ebbed and flowed as the Government of Sudan has turned the spigot of violence on and off according to its wiles in its game of brinkmanship with the international community. To date, it is estimated that well over 250,000 people have been killed and/or perished as a result of "genocide by attrition" (meaning, via starvation, dehydration, and unattended injuries).

Darfur, a region in west Sudan, is comprised of three states (Northern Darfur, Western Darfur, and Southern Darfur). The three-state region is roughly the size of France, and shares borders with Libya, Chad, and the Central African Republic. The vast majority of the people of Darfur, both the so-called "black Africans" and the Arabs, are Muslim.

Darfur is one of the most under-developed and isolated regions of Sudan, the latter of which constitutes one of the 25 poorest countries in the world. More specifically, over 90 percent of Sudan's citizens live below the poverty line, barely eking out an existence.

While much of the Darfur region consists of large swaths of burning desert (except during the rainy season when *wadis* swell with water), it also has lush grasslands where herds graze and areas where crops are cultivated. Up until recently, the most productive land was largely occupied by sedentary farmers and cattle owners who tended to be non-Arabs. At certain times of the year, though, the pasture land was used by the nomads to graze the herds, as a result of mutual agreement between the sedentary black Africans and Arab semi-nomadic and nomadic peoples. This resulted in a symbiotic relationship of sorts; that is, while the Arabs' animals were allowed to feed and be watered, the herds fertilized the ground owned by the black Africans, thus renewing the soil for subsequent growing seasons.

When conflicts erupted in the not too distant past amongst individuals and/or groups (be it among individuals in the same village, different black African tribal groups, or between black Africans and Arabs), the disagreements were generally resolved by the intervention and mediation of local leaders (*umdas* or *sheiks*). While neither conflict nor violence were uncommon, it rarely resulted in wholesale violence that went on for months, let alone years. When called for, some sort of "blood money" was paid to the victim, be it for kin who were killed, animals stolen, or for some other transgression. The handing over of the blood money by the "guilty party" to the "victim" generally settled the grievance, and life went on as usual.

Notably, there was a certain amount of intermarriage amongst and between the various peoples of Darfur, including non-Arabs and Arabs. Thus, different groups of people cohabited as neighbors, friends, and even relatives—and not as sworn enemies due to ethnic, racial, or any other type of classification/category.

## Who Is Committing This Genocide?

Both Government of Sudan (GOS) troops and the so-called *Janjaweed* (Arab militia) are the actors carrying out the actual killing, mass and gang rape, and the wholesale destruction of black African villages. Ample evidence indicates that the vast majority of the attacks against black African villages from 2003 onward have been undertaken, in tandem, by GOS troops and the *Janjaweed*. In most cases, the attacks have involved bombings by GOS aircraft, followed by a ground attack involving hundreds of *Janjaweed* on camels and horses and four-wheel vehicles (some mounted with machine guns) carrying both GOS troops and *Janjaweed*.

The *Janjaweed* comprises semi-nomadic and nomadic Arab herders. Many had previously fought in one or more of the wars in the region, a good number serving as mercenaries.

Increasingly, it should be noted, many Arab herders have been forced—upon the threat of death to themselves and harm to their families—to join in the attacks against the black Africans. It is also significant to note, and recognize, that many Arab herders are not involved in the attacks, are not members of the *Janjaweed*, and do not necessarily support—and may, in fact, look askance at—the actions of the GOS and *Janjaweed*. In this regard, Julie Flint's (2004) observations are significant:

> It cannot be stated too often that the majority of Arab tribes in Darfur have refused to join the government war in Darfur, despite blandishments, threats and inducements that range from sacks filled with cash to cars to development programs and homes in the capital, Khartoum

In Darfur, the Rizeigat, Beni Halba, Habbaniya, Taaisha, Mahariya, Beni Hussein, Misseriya, and Maaliya tribes, to name only some of Darfur's Arab tribes, have all chose either to cast their lot in with the African neighbors or to endeavourer to remain neutral (p. 1).

The Sudanese government readily admits that its troops responded to attacks on government facilities (including military bases) by black African rebels, but it has claimed, time and again, that the *Janjaweed* is responsible for the subsequent and sustained scorched earth attacks against the black Africans and that it (the government) does not have the means to rein them in as they (the *Janjaweed*) are loose cannons. Such assertions are disingenuous, at best; again, ample evidence exists that the vast majority of the attacks on the black African villages have been carried out by both GOS troops and the *Janjaweed* (Human Rights Watch, 2004a; Physicians for Human Rights, 2005; U.S. State Department, 2004).

There is also evidence that the GOS purposely hired the *Janjaweed* to join GOS troops in carrying out the attacks because GOS military troops were already overstretched in their war in southern Sudan and thus did not have enough soldiers available to address the crisis in Darfur (Human Rights Watch, 2004b).[3] Concomitantly, since many of the soldiers in the GOS military were black African, the GOS didn't trust the latter to carry out attacks on their own people's villages.

## Who Are the Victims?

As previously mentioned, the victims of the genocide in Darfur are various black African tribal groups in Darfur. The main groups that have been attacked are the Fur, Massalit, and Zaghawa. That said, like many, if not most, of the issues surrounding the Darfur crisis, the composition of the population of Darfur is a complex one. Indeed, although "African" and "Arab" are common terms used in describing and, at least in part, explaining, the conflict, neither term does justice to the diversity of ethnic groups that make up Darfur nor to "the nuanced relationships among ethnic groups" (Human Rights Watch, 2004a, p. 1 of "The Background").

There are many, in fact, who claim that there is virtually no difference between the so-called black Africans of Darfur and the Arab population (Mamdani quoted in Sengupta, 2004, p. 1; De Waal, 2004a; De Waal, 2004c). Mamdani (2004), for example, asserts that ". . . all parties involved in the Darfur conflict—whether they are referred to as 'Arab' or as 'African'—are equally indigenous and equally black" (p. 2). He has also stated that "from the cultural point of view, one can be both African and Arab" (Mamdani, 2004, p. 2). Such individuals assert that all the people are black (and not necessarily "light" as the Arabs are sometimes purported to be), and that since all live in Africa they are all African. In this regard, Alex De Waal (2004a), an expert on Sudan, has asserted that "characcterizing the Darfur war as 'Arabs' versus 'Africans' obscures the reality. Darfur's Arabs are black, indigenous, African Muslims—just like Darfur's non Arabs, who hail from the Fur, Massalit, Zaghawa and a dozen smaller tribes" (p. 1). More specifically, De Waal (2004b) asserts that

The Zaghawa . . . are certainly indigenous, black and African: they share distant origins with the Berbers of Morocco and other ancient Saharan peoples. But the name of the "Bedeyat," the Zaghawa's close kin, should alert us to their true origins: pluralize in the more traditional manner and we have "bedeyiin" or Bedouins. Similarly, the Zaghawa's adversaries in this war, the Darfurian Arabs, are "Arabs." In the ancient sense of "Bedouin," meaning desert nomad . . ., Darfurian Arabs, too, are indigenous, black and African. In fact there are no discernible racial or religious differences between the two: all have lived there for centuries (n.p.).

Many also assert that there has been so much intermarriage between various groups (and there are scores upon scores of various tribal groups within the three-state region of Darfur) that it is almost impossible to definitively state whether a person is from one tribe (or ethnic group) or another. Some also assert that "where the vast majority of people [in Darfur] are Muslim and Arabic-speaking, the distinction between 'Arab' and 'African' is more cultural than racial" (UN Office for the Coordination of Humanitarian Affairs, 2003, n.p.; IRIN, 2007, p. 2). Mamdani has asserted that "the real roots of combat are not racial or ethnic but political and economic" (quoted in Hill, 2006). Some have also noted that certain individuals who have, over time, attained a certain amount of wealth have actually chosen to become "Arab."

That said, both the perpetrators and the victims, themselves, *do make a distinction between* those who are purportedly "Arab" and those who are purportedly "black African." One major report after another (Human Rights Watch, 2004a; Physicians for Human Rights, 2005; U.S. State Department, 2004) that includes first-person testimony by the internally placed persons (IDPs) and refugees from Darfur contains vast amounts of information in regard to the aforementioned distinctions made by the very people involved in the crisis. For example, in its report, *Darfur Destroyed*, Human Rights Watch (2004a) reports that "Especially since the beginning of the conflict in 2003, members of the Zaghawa, Fur, and Massalit communities have used these terms [black Africans and Arabs] to describe the growing racial and ethnic polarization in Darfur, perceived to result from discrimination and bias emanating from the central government" (p. 1, "The Background").

Furthermore, such testimony also includes ample evidence that the *Janjaweed* frequently scream racial epithets at their black African victims. The same is true in the scores of testimony this author has collected in interviews in refugee camps in Chad with survivors of the genocide. More specifically, one black African IDP and refugee after another has commented on how the *Janjaweed* (and, for that matter, GOS soldiers) screamed such epithets as slave, slave dogs, and *zurega* (which is roughly the equivalent of "nigger") at them during the attacks on their villages. All are considered extremely derogatory and vile by the victims.

Other comments that the perpetrators have spewed at the black Africans are: "You are not a real Sudanese, you're black. . . . We are the real Sudanese. No blacks need stay here"; "We are going to cut off your roots"; "The President of Sudan ordered us to cleanse Darfur of the dirty slaves so we can have the beginning of the Arab Union" (quoted in Totten, 2006, p. 98). Emily Wax (2004), a *Washington Post* correspondent in Africa, reported that as a 22-year old black African woman was grabbed and about to be raped by six *Janjaweed*, they spat out: "Black girl, you are too dark. You are like a dog. We want to make a light baby" (p. 1). Wax (2004) also reported that another young woman who was raped by militiamen was told, "Dog, you have sex with me. . . . The government gave me permission to rape you. This is not your land anymore, *abid* [slave], go" (p. 2).

## Why Is This Genocide Being Committed?

The causes of any genocide are extremely complex, and the Darfur genocide is no exception. No act of genocide is ever the result of a single factor; indeed, genocide results from a synergy of trends, issues, and events that influence the thinking and actions of potential perpetrators who, ultimately, intend to extirpate, in one way or another, those it perceives as enemies, dangerous and/or loathsome in some way (and thus "outside their universe of obligation"). In the case Darfur (2003–present), the issues/events that combined to make genocide possible were the following: extreme drought; increased desertification; Arab supremacism; authoritarianism; extreme nationalism; an ever-increasing bellicosity in the region (within Sudan, Darfur and beyond its borders); and the disenfranchisement of black Africans at the hands of the Sudanese government.

## Extreme Drought and Desertification

Since the early 1970s, numerous droughts (including the "great drought" of 1984–1985), resulted in ever-increasing desertification within the Darfur region. Tellingly, a result of a severe drought in the 1970s, sections of the Sahara Desert reportedly crept south by as much as 60 miles.

The desertification of the land in Darfur, accompanied by fierce stand storms, resulted in a dramatic decline in the yield of produce, loss of pastureland, and a loss of livestock. All of the latter, along with famine (some caused by nature, some by man—and some lasting much longer than those of the past), increased tensions over land usage and access to water and, ultimately, resulted in ever-increasing conflict and violence between the nomadic/semi-nomadic Arab groups and the sedentary/farming group of non-Arabs. .

Exacerbating the situation was the fact that drought affected other countries in the region as well, and nomads from Chad and Libya migrated to Darfur in extremely large numbers in search of grazing land, which put further pressure on the scant resources available.

Not only did nature force nomadic groups to sweep lower south to locate sustenance for their herds, it also resulted in their grazing their herds for longer than usual. At one and the same time, farmers became evermore protective of their land. Some even resorted to putting up fences and establishing fees for land and water usage. What constituted protective efforts by the sedentary peoples/farmers were perceived by the nomads as being stingy and unfair.

## Arab Supremacism

Arab supremacism is an ideology that preaches, promotes, and sustains—in certain situations, at all cost—the notion that Arab beliefs and way of life are superior to all others. In that regard, it is an ideology that perceives all those who are not Arab as inferior. In Sudan, this has led to both the demonization and disenfranchisement of certain groups. Essentially, and, ultimately, it calls for Arab dominance in all aspects of life—culturally, politically, economically, judicially, and socially.

The origins of Arab supremacism "lay in the Libya of Colonel Gaddafi in the 1970s" and "the politics of the Sahara" (Flint and De Waal, 2005, p. 50). Gaddafi, in fact, fantasized about establishing an "Arab belt" across Africa. To accomplish this goal, he created, with his oil riches, various mechanisms, including the *Faliq al Islamiyya* (Islamic Legion), which recruited Bedouins from Mauritania to Sudan; the *Munazamat Daʾawa al Islamiyya* (Organization of the Islamic Call), which fostered Islamic philanthropy and evangelization; and sponsored the Sudanese opposition National Front, including the Muslim Brothers (or Muslim Brotherhood) and the *Ansar* (the *umma*'s military wing).

Any mention of Arab supremacism and Sudan is incomplete if it neglects to comment on the role of Hassan Abd al Turabi—an Islamist, former law professor at the University of Khartoum, and a government official under Jaafar Nimeiri and then Omar al Bashir. Turabi was a major figure for decades in the Muslim Brotherhood, which originated in Eygpt and had been active in Sudan since 1949. The group's primary goal in Sudan was to "institutionalize Islamic law" (Mertz, 1991, n.p.). In 1964, Turabi became the Secretary-General of the

Muslim Brotherhood, which was the year that the Brotherhood established its first political party. Turabi was closely involved with the Islamic Charter Front, which proposed that Sudan adopt an Islamic Constitution. The latter basically established that those Sudanese who were not Muslim would, from that point forward, be considered and, treated, as second-class citizens.

Over time, the Brotherhood established a close relationship with young Darfurians, convincing the latter that the Brotherhood's headlong push for the establishment of Islamic law was positive and that, as an organization, it was bereft of the prejudice and discrimination that was so rife within the Sudanese government when it came to ethnic and tribal differences. Understandably, these same young people came to trust and support Turabi.

Beginning as a peaceful civilian movement, the Brotherhood gradually morphed into a powerful and radical rebel group. More specifically, following a *coup d'état* in 1969, in which Colonel Jaafar Nimeiri became prime minister of Sudan, Turabi's Islamist Party was dissolved. Immediately, though, the Islamists began planning its own rebellion. The planned rebellion, however, was quashed by the Sudanese military in March 1970. The combined effort of the Sudanese air force and ground troops resulted in the deaths of hundreds of Islamists fighters. Many survivors sought exile in Libya, where they established military-like camps in preparation for a later attempt to dislodge the Nimeiri (who eventually became president) government. As Flint and De Waal (2005) note, "Their [the Islamists'] plan [while undergoing training] was an armed invasion of Sudan from bases in Libya, crossing Darfur and Kordofan to storm the capital. [Ultimately,] in July 1976, the Ansar-Islamist alliance very nearly succeeded . . . but the army counterattacked and the rebels were defeated" (pp. 22–23).

Turabi, a master at Machiavellian politics, found a way to disassociate himself from the failed invasion and to ingratiate himself with Nimeiri. In fact, Turabi became so close to Nimeiri that he became his attorney-general in 1977. At one and the same time, in his quest to establish an Islamic state, "[Turabi] infiltrated Islamist cadres into the armed forces, including elite units such as the air force" (Flint and De Waal, 2005, p. 23).

Always intent on imposing his Islamist vision on Sudan, Turabi, in 1983, led the way in implementing *shari?a* (Islamic law) in Sudan. The imposition of *shari?a* resulted in a slew of amputations and hangings. Due to a combination of disgust and fear at the brutality meted out by the government as a result of its *shari?a*-induced legislation and actions, Nimeiri was overthrown in 1985. Parliamentary rule was subsequently reinstated. Almost immediately, Turabi helped to establish the National Islamic Front (NIF), a political party that was controlled by the Muslim Brotherhood.

For a short while, Sudan returned to parliamentary rule. However, in 1989, with Turabi in the shadows but playing an integral role as a power broker, the military overthrew the elected government, and Omar al Bashir was installed as president of Sudan. As Sudan entered a period of increased turbulence, Turabi is said to have virtually served as the real power behind the scenes.

In the early 1990s, the Sudanese Islamists began to inculcate Islamist thought throughout Sudan. At the forefront of the effort were Turabi and Ali Osman Mohamed Taha, an ardent Islamist and an on again, off again government figure. As part and parcel of this effort, Turabi, in 1990, had established the Popular Arab Islamic Conference (PAIC), which was basically a regional organization for political Islamist militants. In his position as secretary-general of PAIC, Turabi induced the Sudan government to create "an-open door policy for Arabs, including Turabi's Islamist associate Osama bin Laden, who made his base in Sudan in 1990–1996" (Human Rights Watch, 2002, p. 1). In order to accomplish their goals, "Islamist cadres were dispatched to foment a new Islamist consciousness in every village. Islamist philanthropic agencies were mobilized to open schools and clinics, and to support the Popular Defence Forces. A raft of programmes aimed at building an Islamic Republic was launched" (Flint and De Waal, 2005, p. 28). Ultimately, though, Turabi concluded that if he was to succeed in gaining power through the elective process, he needed to part ways with the Brotherhood. That was true, for the Brotherhood perceived Islamism and Arabism as one and the same, and many of those residing in Darfur were not Arab; and since Turabi believed he needed the votes of those in the West who were not Arab, he, calculatingly, cut his ties with the Brotherhood.

In 1999, Turabi set out to become the major power in Sudan. But, once again, his grand plans came to naught. Not only did Ali Osman break with Turabi as a result of looking askance at Turabi's ploys, schemes, and intrigues, but al Bashir—not about to be pushed aside—announced a state of emergency and removed Turabi from office (thus, wiping out Turabi's powerbase within the government). The ramifications were immense for Darfur: "The Bashir-Turabi split lost Darfur for the government, but made it possible to make peace in the South" (Flint and De Waal, 2005, p. 41).

## Authoritarianism

For nearly twenty years (1989–present), Sudan has been under the authoritarian rule of Omar al Bashir. His government controls virtually every aspect of Sudanese life. And when al Turabi was a power behind the scenes, it meant that the Islamists were, like puppeteers, largely directing all aspects of Sudanese life. Those living in what is commonly referred to as the "peripheries" in Sudan (that is, those areas far from Khartoum, the "center" or powerbase in Sudan), were (and are) perceived and treated as second class citizens.

As soon as the new al Bashir government, with its Islamist focus, took power in 1989, it began dictating what was and was not acceptable in the way of behavior, dress, speech, and assembly (or association) with others. Furthermore, individuals were arrested for any and all dissent, people "disappeared" into secret prisons, torture was meted out regularly and viciously, and the judicial system answered only to al Bashir and his cronies.

## Disenfranchisement

First, it is important to note that Darfur is not only one of the poorest regions in Sudan but one of the poorest regions in all of Africa. Second, a single region of Sudan, the North (where Khartoum, the capital, is located), which comprises just over five percent of the population of the country, virtually controls all of Sudan. Put another way, it controls the wealth of the nation and it controls the politics of the nation. Almost all of those who hold major posts within the country have come from the North. Indeed, all of the presidents and prime ministers have come from the North, along with the vast majority of those who head-up important positions dealing with development, the infrastructure of the country, and banking. It is also the seat of advanced education in the nation Third, for years on end, the black Africans of Darfur have requested the establishment of more schools, medical facilities, and roads—all of which are minimal in number, sorely under-funded, or, as is true in the case of roads, largely nonexistent. Fourth, most, if not all, of the black Africans' requests for assistance and largely fell on deaf ears in Khartoum.

For many years, the black Africans of Darfur decried the hegemony of the North, as well as the fact that they (those residing in the West) have suffered prejudice, discrimination, and disenfranchisement. Numerous examples of such disenfranchisement could be cited, but three shall suffice. First, "infant mortality in the West (at 122.5 boys and 104.2 girls dying per 1000 births) is strikingly different from infant mortality in the North (100.1 boys and 88.8 girls per thousand births)" (Cobham, 2005, n.p.). This difference is undoubtedly due in large part to the fact that adequate medical facilities and qualified medical personnel are available in the North but not in the West. According to the Justice and Equality Movement

(2000), a rebel group that issued the so-called *Black Book* that delineated the facts of disenfranchisement in Darfur, "The entire State of Western Darfur has two medical specialists in the field of obstetrics and gynaeology, one in Geneina and the other in Zalengay. They are to serve a population of 1,650,000 aided by [a] few medical students who visit the area for training and for escaping mandatory military service" (p. 53).

Second, "water development is currently reserved for the ever-expanding capital Khartoum. The rest of the country is left out, dying of thirst as well as diseases like malaria, kalazar, bilharsiasis, and other water-borne diseases" (Justice and Equality Movement, 2000, p. 41).

Third, the development of the country (the construction of roads, bridges, water systems, hospitals, schools) is largely limited to the North. Even those other areas that have seen development largely benefit those who are from the North. As for the West, "the entire Western region now lacks a single developmental scheme which could support one province for a single week" (Justice and Equality Movement, 2000, p. 5).

In May 2000, *The Black Book* (whose complete title is *The Black Book: Imbalance of Power and Wealth in Sudan*) mysteriously appeared in Khartoum. Copies were handed out outside major mosques following Friday prayers. Many are said to have even been placed, brazenly, on the desks of key Sudanese officials, including that of al Bashir. As photocopies of the book were "spontaneously" produced, *The Black Book* began to appear throughout the country and abroad. *The Black Book*, was dedicated, in part, to ". . . the Sudanese people who have endured oppression, injustice and tyranny."

*The Black Book* argues that ever since Sudan's independence those who control the political and economic power within the Sudanese government (frequently referred to as "the elite," or, variously, "the ruling elite"), and by extension, the entire country, are from northern Sudan. More specifically, it asserts that the vast majority of posts in the government, the judiciary, the military, and the police all come from the North (and primarily from three tribal groups, the Shaygiyya, Ja?aliyiin and Danagla), and/or are appointed by the "centre" or the ruling elite. It also states that the "peripheries" of the country (those in the West, South and East) have been purposely denied fair representation in the government, and have been forced to lead a life of impoverishment. In the authors' introduction, it is asserted that at the turn of the millennium, Sudan remains "steeped in poverty, illiteracy, disease and lack of development" (Justice and Equality Movement, 2000, p. 1).

De Waal (2004b) argues that *The Black Book* essentially "condemned the Islamist promise to Darfur as a sham. *The Black Book* was a key step in the polarization of the country along politically constructed 'racial' rather than religious lines, and it laid the basis for a coalition between Darfur's radicals, who formed the SLA, and its Islamists, who formed the other rebel organization, the Justice and Equality Movement" (p. 8). *The Black Book* may have constituted a key step in the polarization of the country along politically constructed "racial" lines, but it was hardly the first or *the* major step. In light of the ongoing attacks since the early 1990s by various Arab groups (nomads, semi-nomads and then, collaboratively, by Arab herders and GOS troops) against black African villages, it seems obvious that the "racial divide" was certainly evident, and being acted up, many years prior to the appearance of *The Black Book*. In that regard, it seems that *The Black Book* was more the messenger versus the instigator of the polarization along "racial lines."

## Ever-Increasing Insecurity and Bellicosity in the Darfur Region

Beginning in the early to mid-1990s, Arab herders began carrying out attacks against entire villages of sedentary black African farmers. Over time, such attacks began to involve both GOS troops and the Arab herders working in tandem. While vicious, such attacks were certainly not as systematic as the scorched-earth attacks that became increasingly common in 2003 and beyond. Such attacks have ebbed and flowed over the years, up to today.

The initial increase in violent conflict within the region was due to a host of issues. For example, in the 1980s, the GOS, under President Nimeiri, abruptly replaced the tribal councils, the traditional bodies that helped solve and bring an end to conflicts, with government oversight of the region. Nimeiri, however, failed to provide adequate resources to the regional government offices in order to carry out their work, and, as a result, the offices and expected services largely became hollow shells

Making matters even more volatile, since riverine Arabs held the vast majority of positions in the government posts (including those as police and court officials), the black Africans of Darfur were automatically put at a distinct disadvantage. That is, disputes that were once dealt with, for the most part fairly and equitably, by traditional authorities and/or a combination of the latter and governmental authorities, were now handled by officials partial to the Arab sector of the population.

Furthermore, as certain groups of nomads increasingly bought into the beliefs of Arab Supremacism, they began to act as if they were superior to the black Africans.[4] Along with the huge influx of weapons into Darfur (resulting, in part, due to the various wars in the region, three of which were the Libya/Chad conflict, the prolonged war in southern Sudan, and the Eritrean separatist war with Ethiopia (1961–1993)), more and more herders began carrying weapons. This was likely done as a means of protection, but also because they had become accustomed to carrying them as a result of their having fought in one or more of the violent conflicts in the region. Ultimately, the GOS also provided such groups with weapons with the expectation that the Arab herders would, in various cases, serve as their proxies in dealing with the black Africans. As the Arab herders increasingly engaged in conflicts with the black Africans over land and water usage, they (the Arabs) made it known that they were ready and willing to use their weapons. Thus, with the difficulties presented by the droughts and desertification of pasture land, the influence of Arab Supremacism, and the Arab herders' experiences as mercenaries, it is not surprising that many of the Arab nomadic groups became increasingly cavalier and aggressive in their use of the sedentary people's lands in the early to mid-1990s.

Not only did the Arab nomads purposely neglect to seek permission to use the land, but they refused to apologize for trespassing when confronted by the black African farmers. And when confronted by the farmers, it was not uncommon for the nomads to threaten the lives of the farmers—and, in many cases, they carried out their threats.

Out of fear and anger over the constant assaults and attacks on their villages and a lack of protection from local and regional governmental authorities, along with the gradual realization that the Arab marauders had tacit approval from the local government officials to do as they wished, the black Africans began to form self-defense groups "on a tribal basis as opposed to based on local communities" (Fadul and Tanner, 2007, p. 301).[5]

## The Initial Rebel Attacks and the Response by the Government of Sudan

By the early 1990s, traditional dispute resolution approaches were proving to be inadequate. Arab nomadic attacks against black Africans were becoming more brazen, more frequent, more vicious and more costly in terms of lost lives and destroyed villages, farm land, and orchards. In August 1995, for example, Arab raiders attacked and burned the non-Arab village of Mejmeri in West Darfur, stealing 40,000 cattle and massacring twenty-three civilians. By late 1998, more than 100,000 non-Arab Massalit had fled to Chad to escape the violent attacks (Flint and De Waal, 2005, p. 69).

A great many of the attacks on villages were not one-time affairs. In fact, in the early to late 1990s, some villages were attacked up to three to four and more times. In certain cases, African villages were partially burned down by the marauders; in others, villages were utterly destroyed. Almost always, the villages were pillaged and then the black Africans' herds were stolen. Black Africans were often forced out of their villages only to be chased down in the desert and beaten and/or killed.

Desirous of remaining on their land, the black Africans more often than not returned to their villages once the marauders had left, rebuilt those sections destroyed, and carried on with life. However, as these attacks continued unabated, the black Africans began to look askance at the government. In light of the way the black Africans were being treated (a frustrating combination of being ignored and/or ill-treated by the government), it is not surprising that the following statement/critique of the Sudanese government made it into *The Black Book*:

> *Conditions for accepting the authority of the ruler/ governing power*. The authority must demonstrate its commitment to maintain sovereignty of land against foreign intruders; treat its citizens equally; afford them peace and protection; guarantee dignified life; spread freedom and dignity, and must enable its citizens to fully participate in conducting their public affairs. All that is to take place within an environment that is conducive for participation of all without religious, ethnic, skin colour and gender discrimination.

The state authority cannot implement that without commitment to its national laws that regulate and divide powers among different state organs. Most important here is the separation between state powers, and in particular the political, the judicial and the legislative (Justice and Equality Movement, 2000, p. 6).

In 2001 and 2002, before the current conflict became widely known to the outside world, a rebel movement comprising non-Arabs in Darfur emerged. The first rebel group to appear called itself the Sudanese Liberation Movement/Army (SLM/A), and on March 14, 2003, it issued the following political declaration: "The brutal oppression, ethnic cleansing and genocide sponsored by the Khartoum government left the people of Darfur with no other option but to resort to popular political and military resistance for purposes of survival. This popular resistance has now coalesced into a political movement known as the Sudan Liberation Movement and its military wing, the Sudan Liberation Army (SLM/SLA)" (The Sudan Liberation Movement and Sudan Liberation Army, 2003, pp. 1–2). Within a relatively short period of time, the group splintered, and from the split emerged a rebel group that called itself the Justice and Equality Movement (JEM). According to Flint and De Waal (2005), within JEM there are "two main tendencies that dwarf all others: one is tribal, the other Islamic" (p. 89).

In addition to providing local security for the black African villagers of Darfur, the two rebel groups issued protests against the economic and political marginalization of Darfur. The aforementioned *Black Book*, the brainchild of the leaders of JEM, was one such protest; indeed, it constituted the most detailed critique of the government to date, as well as the protest that reached the greatest and most diverse audience (from the top officials of the country all the way to the illiterate population who learned about the contents of *The Black Book* as a result of having it read to them). Members of both rebel groups came primarily (but by no means exclusively) from three non-Arab tribes—the Fur, Massalit, and Zaghawa—that had been attacked for years by nomadic Arab groups and GOS troops.

By late 2003, a flood of black Africans had either been forced from their homes as a result of GOS and *Janjaweed* attacks or had left out of sheer fear. By September 2003, the United Nations (UN) reported that some 65,000 refugees from Darfur had fled to Chad.[6] By December 9, 2003, the United Nations estimated that there were up to 600,000 internally displaced people (IDP) in Darfur as a result of the attacks on the black Africans' villages. In November 2004, *Médecins Sans Frontières* (Doctors Without Borders) estimated that some 1.8 million Darfurians had been displaced from their homes, with 200,000 of them in refugee camps in Chad (*Médecins Sans Frontières*, 2004, p. 1).

At one and the same time, the leaders of both rebel groups seemingly followed the ongoing peace negotiations between the GOS and the rebel groups in southern Sudan and realized that armed insurrection in the south had eventually led to important concessions by the GOS, including power-sharing and access to major economic resources. Whether such knowledge was the catalyst or trigger for the rebel initial attacks against the government only the leaders of SLM/A know for sure.

Popular account has it that the GOS, alarmed by the rebel attacks and with its own military forces stretched thin by the north–south civil war, decided to recruit, train, and equip Arab militias (the so-called *Janjaweed*) to help suppress what it purportedly perceived as a black African rebellion in Darfur.[7] Any government whose military bases and/or other government facilities are attacked is going to retaliate and attempt to suppress future attacks. Governments will either arrest the perpetrators or, if the situation degenerates into violence, shoot and then apprehend them, or, kill them outright. What the GOS did, however, was something vastly different and, ultimately, criminal. Using the argument that it believed that black African villagers were harboring rebels, the GOS (along with the *Janjaweed*) began attacking village after village after village of black Africans. Thus, instead of solely tracking down and attacking the black African rebel groups, the GOS and *Janjaweed* began carrying out a widespread and systematic scorched earth policy against non-Arab villagers. In doing so, the GOS troops and the *Janjaweed* slaughtered men and boys (including infants), raped, mutilated and often killed females, looted household goods and animals, and then burned the homes and villages to the ground (Physicians for Human Rights, 2005; UN Commission of Inquiry into Darfur, 2005; U.S. State Department, 2004). The attacks comprised bombings by aircraft, helicopter gunships, and four wheel vehicles with *dushkas* (mounted machine guns), as well as hundreds of *Janjaweed* on camels and horses. In a report of its findings, the UN Commission of Inquiry on Darfur (2005) stated that ". . . the large majority of attacks on villages conducted by the [*Janjaweed*] militia have been undertaken with the acquiescence of State officials" (paragraph 125). As previously mentioned, the attacks led to the forcible displacement of, at first, tens of thousands, then hundreds of thousands and, ultimately (or at least through today, December 2007) over two-and-a-half million people in Darfur alone (and more than another 250,000 in Chad). All constituted early warning signals that something was vastly wrong in Darfur.

As early as spring 2002 (May 1, to be exact), a group of Fur politicians complained to Sudanese President Omar al Bashir that 181 villages had been attacked by Arab militias, with hundreds of people killed and thousands of animals stolen (Flint and De Waal, 2005, pp. 77–78).

In what Flint and De Waal call a "pivotal point" in the conflict between the black African rebels and the GOS troops, the SLA and JEM forces struck the government air force base at el Fasher on April 25, 2003. In doing so, they killed at least 75 people, destroyed several airplanes and bombers, and captured the base's commander (Flint and De Waal, 2005, pp. 99–100). In quick succession, numerous other attacks were carried out. In fact, "The rebels were winning almost every encounter—34 out of 38 in the middle months of 2003. [At this point in time, the GOS purportedly] feared it would lose the whole of Darfur . . ." (Flint and De Waal, 2005, p. 101).

Between 2003 and today, the GOS has repeatedly denied that its troops have taken part in the scorched earth actions against the black Africans of Darfur. Furthermore, while the rest of the world asserts that at least over 250,000 have been killed in Darfur over the past four years (with certain activist organizations claiming that the number is closer to 400,000 or more), the GOS asserts that just 9,000 have been killed, mostly as a result of rebel actions. Ample evidence, though, from a broad array of sources (e.g., the black African survivors of the attacks, African Union troops deployed in Darfur as monitors, numerous humanitarian organizations working in the IDP camps, numerous human rights organizations, including

Human Rights Watch, Physicians for Human Rights, and Amnesty International, and the investigations conducted by the United States in 2004 and the UN in 2004 and 2005 respectively) have provided evidence that clearly and definitively refutes the GOS' denials.

By late 2003, various NGOs (nongovernmental organizations) and the UN scrambled to help the IDPs and the refugees flooding across the Sudan/Chad border, and began getting the word out about the escalating carnage in Darfur. Finally, in December 2003, Jan Egeland, UN Under-Secretary for Humanitarian Affairs, asserted that the Darfur crisis was possibly the "worst [crisis] in the world today" (United Nations, 2004, p. 1). That same month, Tom Vraalsen, the UN Security General's Special Envoy for Humanitarian Affairs for Sudan, claimed that the situation in Darfur was "nothing less than the 'organized' destruction of sedentary African agriculturalists—the Fur, the Massaleit and the Zaghawa" (quoted in Reeves, 2003, p. 1).

In early 2004, one activist organization after another in the United States, Canada, and Europe began rallying around the Darfur issue, variously decrying the lack of action to halt the atrocities against the black Africans of Darfur, preparing and issuing reports, calling on the United Nations, the U.S. Government and/or the European Union to be proactive in addressing the crisis, and issuing calls for citizen action. On June 24, 2004, the United States Holocaust Memorial Museum (USHMM) took the extraordinary measure of shutting down normal operations for 30 minutes to focus attention on the ongoing crisis in Darfur. U.S. Senators Sam Brownback and Jon Corzine, U.S. House of Representative Donald Payne, as well as a Holocaust survivor and a member of the Darfurian community-in-exile, came together in a special program in the USHMM's Hall of Witness to highlight and discuss the unfolding conflict in Darfur. On the same day, the U.S. House of Representatives unanimously declared that the situation in Darfur constituted genocide.

On June 30, 2004, U.S. Secretary of State Colin Powell visited a refugee camp for IDP camps and a refugee camp in Chad. While visiting the IDP camp, Abu Shouk, where malnutrition was rife among the 40,000 or so black Africans, Powell said: "We see indicators and elements that would start to move you toward a genocide conclusion but we're not there yet" (quoted by the BBC, 2004, p. 2).

In July and August 2004, the United States—in a joint effort involving the U.S. State Department, the Coalition of International Justice (CIJ), and the United States Agency for International Aid (USAID)—sent a team (the Atrocities Documentation Team or ADT) of twenty-four investigators to Chad to conduct interviews with Sudanese refugees from the Darfur region of Sudan for the express purpose of collecting evidence to help ascertain whether genocide had been perpetrated by the GOS and the *Janjaweed*. The ADT, which was the first ever official field investigation of a suspected genocide by one sovereign nation into another sovereign nation's actions while the killing was underway, conducted more than one thousand interviews with Darfurian refugees in camps and settlements on the Chad side of the border with Sudan. Evidence collected by the ADT led U.S. Secretary of State Colin Powell, on September 9, 2004, in a hearing before the U.S. Senate's Foreign Relations Committee, to publicly accuse the GOS of genocide. This was the first time that a government ever accused another government of genocide during an ongoing conflict.

Ultimately, the U.S. State Department presented the findings of the ADT in an eight-page report, "Documenting Atrocities in Darfur." The analysis of the data collected in the 1,136 interviews by the ADT revealed "a consistent and widespread pattern of atrocities in the Darfur region of western Sudan" (U.S. State Department, 2004, p. 1). The data also suggested a "close coordination between GOS [Government of Sudan] forces and Arab militia elements, commonly known as the Jingaweit [*Janjaweed*]" (U.S. State Department, 2004, p. 2). Furthermore, the data indicated that there was a clear "pattern of abuse against members of Darfur's non-Arab communities, including murder, rape, beatings, ethnic humiliation, and destruction of property and basic necessities" (U.S. State Department, 2004, p. 3).

Sixteen percent of the respondents witnessed or experienced rape. Significantly, the report suggests that the rapes are probably "under-reported because of the social stigma attached to acknowledging such violations of female members of the family" (U.S. State Department, 2004, p. 7). What makes the under-reporting even more probable is the fact that all of the interpreters and half of the investigators on the team were males, and that many female victims were not inclined to mention such assaults in the company of males (strangers or otherwise).

During the course of his report on the ADP findings to the Senate Foreign Relations Committee on September 9, 2004, Powell remarked that the findings did not mean that the United States needed to do anything other than what it had already done. What that meant was this: while the U.S. had called on the GOS to cease and desist its ongoing attacks, submitted and supported various resolutions at the UN Security Council, applied sanctions against Darfur, and provided hundreds of millions of dollars for humanitarian aid and material/resource assistance to the African Union contingent on the ground in Darfur, it was not about to carry out an intervention in Darfur.

With that said, under Chapter VII of the UN Charter, the United States referred the Darfur matter to the United Nations. Subsequently, on September 18, 2004, the UN established the UN Commission of Inquiry into Darfur (COI), whose express purpose, as outlined in UN Security Council Resolution 1564, was to conduct its own investigation into the Darfur crisis. The COI conducted its inquiry in December 2004 and January 2005, and submitted its report to the Security Council in late January 2005. In its final section, "Conclusions and Recommendations," the COI report states: ". . . the Commission concludes that the Government of the Sudan and the *Janjaweed* are responsible for a number of violations of international human rights and humanitarian law. Some of these violations are very likely to amount to war crimes, and given the systematic and widespread pattern of many of the violations, they would also amount to crimes against humanity" (UN, 2005, para 603). While many scholars agreed with the conclusions of the COI, others were taken aback that—based on the COI's own findings—it had not concluded that genocide had been perpetrated (see, for example, Fowler, 2006, pp. 127–139; Stanton, 2006, pp. 181–188; Totten, 2006, pp. 199–222).

## Talk, Talk and More Talk by the International Community

Between 2004 and today, the UN Security Council issued over twenty resolutions vis-à-vis the ongoing crisis in Darfur. The resolutions addressed a host of issues, including but not limited to the following: the need by the GOS to halt the ongoing indiscriminate attacks on black African civilians and the forced displacement of hundreds of thousands of the latter; the need for the perpetrators of the atrocities in Darfur to be brought to justice without delay; concern over the GOS' failure to meet its obligations in ensuring the security of the civilian population of Darfur; disappointment regarding the constant cease-fire violations by all actors; the threat to issue various types of sanctions; the issuance of actual sanctions, including the freezing of certain actors' assets (including those of GOS officials, *Janjaweed* leaders, and a leader of a rebel group); and the referral of the Darfur conflict to the International Criminal Court (ICC), along with the names of alleged perpetrators of various atrocities.

The results of the resolutions were, at best, mixed. Some were acted on, but most were not. Various resolutions were revised time and again, along with ever-increasing threats, but largely to no avail due to a dearth of action. Tellingly, in July 2006, a senior Sudanese government official was quoted as saying that "The United Nations Security Council has threatened us so many times, we no longer take it seriously" (cited in Nathan, 2007, p. 249).

After considerable debate, compromise, and dithering, the United States and the UN Security Council finally imposed some sanctions on Sudan. For example, on April 25, 2006, the UN Security Council passed a resolution imposing sanctions against four Sudanese individuals, all of whom have been accused of war crimes in Darfur. Those sanctioned: were Gaffar Mohamed Elhassan, an ex Sudan air force commander; Sheikh Musa Hilal, a *Janjaweed* militia leader; Adam Yacub Shant, a rebel SLA commander; and Gabril Abdul Kareem Badri, a rebel National Movement for Reform and Development field commander. All four were to be subject to a ban on foreign travel, and any assets they had in banks abroad were to be frozen.

As for the United States, in May 2007, President George W. Bush ordered the imposition of sanctions that prevents 31 Sudanese companies (many of them oil related) and three individuals (two high-level government leaders and a black African rebel leader) from doing business in the United States or with U.S. companies.

*Realpolitik* was at the center of the dithering, the watering down of certain sanctions, and the decision not to follow through on numerous resolutions and threatened sanctions. More specifically, various members of the Permanent Five in the UN Security Council (the United States, Great Britain, France, the Russian Federation and China) have vested interests in Sudan and wanted to protect them.[8] China, for example, has an enormous petroleum deal with Sudan, and engages in significant weapons sales to it; Russia also has a major arms deal with Sudan; and the United States has, off and on, taken advantage of GOS' offers to help shut down terrorist cells within Sudan and prevent potential terrorists from traveling through Sudan on their way to Afghanistan and Iraq to battle the United States in the latter's efforts to, respectively, capture Osama Bin Laden (terrorist mastermind of the September 11, 2001 attacks on the World Trade Center in New York City and the Pentagon in Washington, D.C.) and to stabilize Iraq following the U.S.'s overthrow of dictator Saddam Hussein, which resulted in internecine conflict that has ripped the fabric of Iraq apart. Already engaged in two separate wars in two Muslim states, Afghanistan and Iraq, the United States was not about to intervene in another Muslim state, Sudan, especially when the latter issued warning after warning that any and all interveners not invited in by the GOS would face an all-out war.

In June 2004, Sudan allowed the African Union (AU) to deploy a small ceasefire monitoring team in Darfur comprised of representatives from the AU, the GOS, two (later, three) rebel groups, along with the European Union, the UN and the U.S. From a tiny force of 300 troops, the force slowly increased to—and eventually leveled off at (up through December 2007)—about 7,000 troops. "As violence against civilians continued, the African Union Mission in Sudan (AMIS) force's mandate was expanded in October 2004 to protecting 'civilians whom it encounters under imminent threat and in the immediate vicinity, within resources and capability' " (Human Rights Watch, 2007a, p. 5). The new mandate, though, for all intents and purposes constituted little more than a paper tiger. The AU had neither the resources nor the capability to truly protect anyone, let alone themselves.

Between 2003 and the end of 2007, the international community worked in various, though hardly effective, ways to bring the Darfur crisis to a close; and as it did, it continually decried the GOS troops' and *Janjaweed*'s attacks on innocent civilians and the GOS' support of the *Janjaweed* and its murderous behavior, and called on the GOS to reign in the *Janjaweed*. As previously stated, the GOS vigorously and disingenuously protested the validity of the accusations made by the international community, but, periodically, also made lukewarm promises to bring the situation under control. Such promises, though, were quickly broken. In most cases, however, the GOS blithely ignored the international community's requests, demands and threats.

When it became obvious that the AU troops were outmanned and outgunned, various calls were issued by various actors to insert UN troops into Darfur. Initially, the AU adamantly rejected the offer, asserting that it wanted to operate an all-African operation. As for Sudanese President Omar al Bashir, he was vociferous in his rejection of the suggestion. Time and again, he asserted that any force that entered Sudanese territory without an invitation from the Government of Sudan would not only be a violation of Sudan's sovereignty, but would be perceived and treated as an enemy invasion. On February 26, 2006, for example, al Bashir asserted, and then warned, that "We are strongly opposed to any foreign intervention in Sudan and Darfur will be a graveyard for any foreign troops venturing to enter" (quoted in *Sudan Tribune*, 2006, p. 1).

Finally, after immense international pressure, Sudan, in mid-June 2007, agreed to allow the deployment of a special force into Darfur, the UN/AU Hybrid (UNAMID) force. Ultimately, that was followed, on July 31, 2007, by the passage of UN Security Council Resolution 1769 which authorized a combined AU/UN Hybrid force for deployment in Darfur. The resolution called for "the immediate deployment of the United Nations Light and Heavy Support packages to the African Union Mission in the Sudan (AMIS) and a [AU/UN] Hybrid operation in Darfur [UNAMID], for which back-stopping and command and control structures will be provided by the United Nations. . . . [The] UNAMID . . . shall consist of up to 19,555 military personnel, including 360 military observers and liaison officers, and an appropriate civilian component including up to 3,772 police personnel and 19 police units comprising up to 140 personnel each." In addressing the mandate of the UNAMID, the resolution asserted that: "Acting under Chapter VII of the Charter of the United Nations: . . . UNAMID is authorized to take the necessary action, in the areas of deployment of its forces and as it deems within its capabilities, in order to: (i) protect its personnel, facilities, installations and equipment, and to ensure the security and freedom of movement of its own personnel and humanitarian workers; (ii) support early and effective implementation of the Darfur Peace Agreement, prevent the disruption of its implementation and armed attacks, and protect civilians, without prejudice to the responsibility of the Government of Sudan." Although the hybrid force is tentatively scheduled for deployment in December 2007/January 2008, as late as December 2007 there were reports that few nations had committed troops to the new hybrid force and few countries had offered support in the way of providing needed vehicles, planes, and other materiel, let alone the resources (gas and oil) to help maintain such.

## Talk, Talk and More Talk About Peace

In early September 2007, U.N. Secretary General Ban Ki-moon asserted that a new round of peace talks, which were to begin on October 27, 2007, in Libya, must be "a final settlement of this issue" (quoted in the *International Herald Tribune*, 2007, p. 1). At best, that seemed wishful thinking. As the *International Herald Tribune* (2007) noted, "Darfur has a history of peace talks—their sheer numbers a testimony to their lack of success. . . . Since fighting began in 2003 between ethnic African rebels and the Arab-dominated Sudanese government, there have been over half a dozen cease-fires or peace deals of various formats—all quickly breached by both sides" (p. 1).

In fact, beginning in 2004 and continuing through today, peace talks between the GOS and various rebel groups have been on and off affairs, with agreements often being broken by various and/or both sides within days, if not hours, of signing the agreements. In various cases and at various points in time, the intransigence of the GOS and/or rebel groups has placed one barrier after another in the way of finding a workable solution to the crisis in Darfur. The GOS has broken agreements both blatantly (attacking black African villages with Antonov bombers, helicopter gun ships and GOS troops and *Janjaweed*) and surreptitiously (whitewashing planes, attaching UN insignias to the wings and sides of the planes, and using the planes to transport weapons and personnel into Darfur). Various black African rebel groups have not only reneged on agreements, but purposely prevented other rebel factions from taking part in the peace talks. Throughout parts of 2007, some of the many rebel groups even began to treat their counterparts as enemies and engaged in battles with them. Not only that, but the various factions—currently, the UN estimates that there are up to 28 declared rebel factions (Gettleman, 2007, p. A6)—have even shot and killed civilians, raped black

African women and girls, attacked and killed AU troops, and harmed and killed humanitarian aid workers.

Each rebel faction is eager to be involved in the peace talks and each no doubt has its own motives for doing so. Undoubtedly, many, if not most, are anxious to have their say regarding the fate of Darfur. And, as previously mentioned, all are undoubtedly cognizant of the new-found wealth and power that those residing in the south garnered upon the signing of the Comprehensive Peace Agreement, which finally brought to an end the twenty year war between north and southern Sudan.[9]

A peace agreement in Darfur was finalized in May 2006 (see details below), but it was signed by only one of three negotiating rebel groups—the SLA faction led by Minni Arkoy Minawi. Over time, and particularly from mid-2007 onwards, the lay of the land has gotten even more dangerous in Darfur. This is true for numerous reasons: the *Janjaweed* not only continue to attack black Africans but have began fighting amongst and between themselves; the various rebel groups continue to battle GOS troops and *Janjaweed* but have also begun fighting between and amongst themselves and attacking black African people in their villages and IDP camps; and roaming the region are bandits who continue to attack anyone and everyone, including IDPs and humanitarian workers. Disturbingly, and tellingly, a report entitled *Chaos by Design: Peacekeeping Challenges for AMIS and UNAMID*, Human Rights Watch (2007a) asserted that "the [GOS] continues to stoke the chaos, and, in some areas, exploit intercommunal tensions that escalate into open hostilities, apparently in an effort to 'divide and rule' and maintain military and political dominance over the [Darfur] region" (p. 1).

## The Darfur Peace Agreement (DPA)

Following seven rounds of contentious negotiations, a peace accord, the Darfur Peace Agreement (DPA), was signed in May 2006. However, as Fadul and Tanner (2007) aptly put it, the peace agreement was "stillborn" (p. 284). While the DPA was signed by GOS and the Minni Arkoy Minawi faction of the SLA, it was not signed by the SLA faction led by Abdel Wahid Mohamed al Nur nor by the Justice and Equality Movement led by Khail Ibrahim. Within a short time following the signing of the DPA, battles broke out between the non-signatories and the "government coalition," which included the SLA faction headed by Minni Arkoy Minawi.[10] Even greater violence was perpetrated by GOS troops and the *Janjaweed* against both black African rebel groups and black African civilians. As the attacks by the latter increased in number, there was a surge in the rape of girls and women, the murder of black African civilians, and thousands fled their villages seeking sanctuary in internally displaced persons camps or refugee camps in Chad. The most current attacks (those in mid- to late 2006 and all of 2007) have centered on both the relatively few remaining black African villages in Darfur as well as the IDP camps. Out of fear of being murdered should they venture outside the IDP camps, black African men insist that girls and women scavenge for wood needed to build fires to cook food even if it means (as it often does) that the females will be raped by GOS soldiers and *Janjaweed*.

Due to the ongoing violence which contributed to their ongoing insecurity, black African Darfurian civilians understandably looked askance at the DPA. As Fadul and Tanner (2007) note, there were other issues in regard to why the black Africans found the DPA a dubious proposition, and they included the lack of attention to: ". . . compensation [for the destruction of their villages and homes and the theft of their worldly goods], the rehabilitation of infrastructure, basic services, and reconciliation" (p. 286). The caveat, though, in regard to the latter statement was that "people always stressed these [compensation, rehabilitation of the infrastructure, reconciliation, et al] were secondary to security" (p. 286).

As the violence continued unabated month after month in the aftermath of the signing of the DPA, many black African Darfurians began asserting that "there could be no peace unless it was forced on the government militarily. In other words, peace depended on one of two things, a non-consensual deployment of Western troops or a rebel military victory—or both" (Fadul and Tanner, 2007, pp. 287, 288). Continuing, Fadul and Tanner (2007) observed that

> [a]s late as 2004, many Darfurian intellectuals criticized the decision to take up arms against the government. The brutality of Khartoum's reaction was predictable, they argued, and the violence had cast the region back many decades. By late 2006, it was striking to hear many of those same individuals say they believed armed rebellion was the only solution to Darfur's problems, despite disenchantment with the shortcomings and human rights abuses by rebel groups on the ground (p. 288).

In early December 2007, the UN Under Secretary General for Humanitarian Affairs, John Holmes, informed the UN Security Council that "280,000 people had been forced to flee the violence in Darfur this year [2007], that attacks on aid workers and their convoys had reached 'unprecedented levels' and that national authorities were closing off access to areas 'where there are tens of thousands of civilians in severe need' " (quoted in Hoge, 2007b, p. A10). The Human Rights Council in Geneva reported that "from June 20 to mid-November [2007], at least 15 land and air attacks were carried out against civilian centers in Darfur by government troops and their affiliated militias and one faction of the rebel Sudanese Liberation Army" (Hoge, 2007b, p. A10).

During the summer of 2006, the rebel groups who had not signed the DPA won a series of battles against the GOS, the *Janjaweed*, and Minni's SLA faction. This not only caused great consternation amongst GOS officials, but emboldened the rebel non-signatory groups.

As a result of the ongoing fighting and massive displacement of civilians, a vast number of black African Darfurians began to look askance at the efforts and credibility of the African Union mission (AMIS) in Darfur. More specifically,

Not only was AMIS weak but it was increasingly seen as partisan. The AU's role in imposing the DPA on the non-signatories compromised its neutrality in the eyes of those groups. In August, when the AU expelled the non-signatories from the AU-chaired Ceasefire Commission and AMIS was seen providing logistics to the forces of SLA-Minni amid escalating violence, many Darfurians concluded that the AU had taken sides (Fadul and Tanner, 2007, p. 308).

Such concern and doubts underscored for many the perceived need for the deployment of an international force in Darfur. The GOS, however, was not so sanguine about the idea. Although it repeatedly agreed to the deployment of an international force, it also repeatedly withdrew such agreements. Only incessant pressure from the international community finally forced the GOS' hand.

## Late 2007 and Early 2008

The deployment of the AU/UN hybrid force has met one barrier after another. Well into December 2007, the GOS resisted the inclusion of non-African military personnel into the new force, the latter of whom were considered critical to the mission. The GOS also refused to provide land to the hybrid force, which was needed for supplying and housing troops. Likewise, the GOS refused to ease visa and travel restrictions, and was "blocking support staff and materials from the area through bureaucratic maneuvers" (Hoge, 2007a, p. A5). Additionally, the GOS asserted its right to "close down the [hybrid] force's communications when its own army was operating in the areas and was refusing to give United Nations planes clearances to fly at night" (Hoge, 2007a, p. A5). In effect, the GOS was making a mockery of its so-called promises to allow the deployment of the hybrid force and it was drastically impeding the international community's intention to provide African Darfurians with protection around the clock.

If the above was not enough of a hindrance to the deployment of the AU/UN hybrid force, in November 2007, UN Secretary General Ban Ki-moon complained vehemently that not a single country had donated helicopters for the hybrid force, which was restricting the mobility and transportation of the force.

## Is There Agreement of Disagreement Among Legitimate Scholars as to the Interpretation of this Particular Genocide?

Various scholars, activists, politicians, individual governments, and others hold a wide-range of views in regard to whether the GOS and *Janjaweed* attacks on the black Africans constitute genocide or not. In mid-2004, various U.S.-based activists and some U.S. politicians declared that genocide had been perpetrated in Sudan. For example, in July 2004, the United States Holocaust Memorial Museum's Committee on Conscience, which uses "graduated categories of urgency" (e.g., "watch," "warning," and "emergency") to warn of potential genocidal situations, signaled an "emergency" (e.g., "acts of genocide or related crimes against human-ity are occurring or immediately threatened"). On July 22, 2004, both chambers of the U.S. Congress adopted concurrent resolutions (House Concurrent Resolution 467 and Senate Concurrent Resolution 133) in which they condemned the atrocities in Darfur as "genocide." Then, as previously mentioned, following a U.S. State Department-sponsored investigation, on September 9, 2004, U.S. Secretary of State Colin Powell declared that genocide had been perpetrated and was possibly still being perpetrated in Darfur.

Also, as previously mentioned, a subsequent investigation (December 2004/January 2005), conducted by the UN Commission of Inquiry into Darfur concluded that "crimes against humanity," not genocide, had been perpetrated in Darfur. The UN left the door open that upon subsequent study of the crisis and/or additional investigations by other bodies (presumably the International Criminal Court), it was possible that genocide might be found to have been perpetrated. (For a discussion of the ADT and COI findings, see Samuel Totten, 2006.)

In a May 7, 2004 report ("Sudan: Government Commits Ethnic Cleansing in Darfur") and later, in October 2007, in a paper ("Q & A: Crisis in Darfur"), Human Rights Watch declared that the GOS had committed both ethnic cleansings and crimes against humanity in Darfur. Amnesty International, another major human rights organization, has deemed the killings cases of crimes against humanity and war crimes, but has not taken a stand in regard to whether the atrocities amount to genocide or not. Following two on-the-ground investiga-tions in Darfur (2004 and 2005) and an in-depth analysis of the data collected in such investigations (see, respectively, *Assault on Survival: A Call for Security, Justice and Restitution*, and *Destroyed Livelihoods: A Case Study of Furawiya Village, Darfur*), Physicians for Human Rights declared that the GOS had carried out a genocide in Darfur.

Among those scholars who assert that the atrocities perpetrated in Darfur do not constitute genocide are, for example: Mahmood Mamdami (2007), who argues in an article entitled "The Politics of Naming Genocide: Genocide, Civil War, Insurgency" that the situation in Darfur appears to be more a case of insurgency and counter-insurgency versus genocide; Alex De Waal (see *Newsweek*, 2007), who sees the crisis in Darfur as basically a war and not genocide; and Gerard Prunier (2005 and 2007), who wavers between calling the crisis in Darfur "an ambiguous genocide" (2004), and in a later article, both a genocide and a case of ethnic cleansing (2007).

On the other hand, such scholars as Kelly Dawn Askin (2006), Gerald Caplan (2006), Stephen Kostas (2006), Eric Markusen (2006), and Samuel Totten (2004 and 2006) assert that the crisis in Darfur constitutes genocide. Furthermore, such noted anti-genocide activists as

Jerry Fowler (2006) and Gregory Stanton (2006), both of whom are lawyers (Stanford Law School and Yale Law Schools, respectively), have also concluded that the atrocities committed in Darfur constitute genocide.

To establish whether a crisis/event is genocide or not, it is imperative to use the language of the UNCG as the means for examining the facts. Among the most critical words, phrases and conditions set out in the UNCG there are located in Article II:

In the present Convention, genocide means any of the following acts committed with intent to destroy, in whole or in part, a national, ethnical, racial or religious group, as such:

(a)  Killing members of the group;
(b)  Causing serious bodily or mental harm to members of the group;
(c)  Deliberately inflicting on the group conditions of life calculated to bring about its physical destruction in whole or in part;
(d)  Imposing measures intended to prevent births within the group;
(e)  Forcibly transferring children of the group to another group.

In asserting that the crisis in Darfur constitutes a genocide, many scholars argue that there is ample evidence that the attacks by the GOS and *Janjaweed* have clearly resulted in a through c of Article II of the UNCG. The group that is under attack, they have argued, constitutes a racial group, and the issue of intent can be inferred from the events on the ground (e.g., what has taken place during the course of the attacks on the black African villages). More specifically, the aforementioned individuals provide analysis/rationales vis-à-vis their assertions that genocide has been perpetrated in Darfur by the GOS and the *Janjaweed*.

Stephen Kostas (2006), an International Bar Association Fellow at the Appeals Chamber of the International Criminal Tribunal for the former Yugoslavia, discussing Colin Powell's finding of genocide based on the analysis of the data collected by the U.S. State Department's Atrocities Documentation Project (ADP), writes as follows:

First, they [Powell and Pierre Prosper, former U.S. Ambassador-at-Large for War Crimes, among others in the U.S. Government] noted that villages of Africans were being destroyed and neighboring Arab villages were not. Large numbers of men were killed and women raped. Livestock was killed and water polluted. In IDP camps, the GOS was preventing medicines and humanitarian assistance from going in despite persistent international calls for access. Examining these factors, they concluded there was a deliberate targeting of the group with the intent to destroy it.

Prosper recalls the group examining the concepts of unlawful killing, causing of serious bodily and mental harm, and "the real one that got us, . . . was the deliberate infliction of conditions of life calculated to destroy the group in whole, or in part." Looking at the IDP camps, Prosper and Powell could not find any "logical explanation for why the Sudan government was preventing humanitarian assistance and medicine" into the camps "other than to destroy the group." The GOS was seen as offering unbelievable excuses, leading Powell to conclude that there was a clearly intentional effort to destroy the people in the camps who were known to be almost exclusively black African (pp. 121–122).

Gregory Stanton (2006), a Yale Law School graduate and a genocide scholar, asks and then asserts, "Was the killing [in Darfur by the GOS and *Janjaweed*] 'intentional'? Yes. According to the elements of crimes defined by the Statute of the International Criminal Court, genocide must be the result of a policy, which may be proved by direct orders or evidenced by systematic organization. Was the killing in Darfur systematically organized by the al-Bashir regime using government-armed *Janjaweed* militias, bombers, and helicopter gunships? Yes. Were the victims chosen because of their ethnic and racial identity? Yes. Fur, Massalit, and Zaghawa black African villages were destroyed, while Arab villages nearby were left untouched. . . .

Does this conclusion constitute the intentional destruction, in part, of ethnic and racial groups? Yes. In short, the violence in Darfur is genocide, and it continues" (pp. 182–183).

Jerry Fowler (2006), a Stanford Law School graduate and Director of the United States Holocaust Memorial Museum's Committee of Conscience, argues the following regarding the issue of intent as it relates to the GOS and *Janjaweed's* actions in Darfur: "U.S. Secretary of State Colin Powell concluded that intent could be inferred from the Sudanese Government's deliberate conduct. Inferring intent from conduct in the absence of direct evidence is widely accepted. The International Criminal Tribunal for Rwanda (ICTR) has delineated numerous circumstances that are relevant to determining 'intent' to destroy, many of which are present in the case of Darfur:

- "The general context of the perpetration of other culpable acts systematically directed against the same groups"
- "The scale of atrocities committed"
- "The 'general nature' of the atrocity"
- "Deliberately and systematically targeting members of some groups [black Africans] but not others [Arabs]"
- "Attacks on (or perceived by the perpetrators to be attacks on) the foundations of the group" [especially, the rape of the girls and woman, thus creating "Arab babies" and resulting in girls and women being considered "damaged goods" by their families and thus ostracized, which, in turn, generally, and automatically, precludes them from having children with their husbands or, if single, from even getting married and having children]
- "The use of derogatory language toward members of the targeted groups"
- "The systematic manner of killing"
- "The relative proportionate scale of the actual or attempted destruction of a group" (International Criminal Tribunal for Rwanda, 1998, paras. 523–524; International Criminal Tribunal for Rwanda, 2000, para. 166) (Fowler, 2006, p. 131).

Kelly Dawn Askin (2006) notes the following: "Rape as an instrument of genocide most often invokes subarticle (b) [of the UNCG] intending to 'destroy a protected group by causing serious bodily or mental harm to members of that group,' and (d) 'imposing measures intended to prevent births within a group'. . . . The Akayesu Judgment of the ICTR [International Criminal Tribunal for Rwanda] is the seminal decision recognizing rape as an instrument of genocide" (p. 150). Continuing, she argues that "There is every indication that the official policy of the GOS and *Janjaweed* forces is to wage, jointly or separate, concentrated and strategic attacks against black Darfurians by a variety of means, including through killing, raping, pillaging, burning and displacement. Various forms of sexual violence regularly formed part of these attacks. . . . Rape crimes have been documented in dozens of villages [now, in 2008, it is more like scores, and probably hundreds] throughout Darfur and committed in similar patterns, indicating that rape itself is both widespread and systematic" (p. 150).

Askin (2006) also comments on the epithets made by the attackers during the course of the rapes, which indicates, in various ways, a desire to "deliberately inflict on the group conditions of life calculated to bring about its physical destruction in whole or in part"; and "impose measures intended to prevent births within the group": "We want to change the color. Every woman will deliver red. Arabs are the husbands of those women" (quoted on p. 147); and "We will take your women and make them ours. We will change the race" (quoted on p. 147).

That which is delineated above is only a fraction of each individual's argument vis-à-vis why the Darfur crisis constitutes genocide.

## Do People Care About This Genocide Today? If So, How Is That Concern Manifested?

Since 2003, the issue of Darfur has generated astonishing attention and concern among journalists, scholars, activists, university and high school students, church people, movie stars, film makers and others. Numerous journalists have written about the crisis in Darfur, and some have consistently done so. Most notably, Nicholas D. Kristof of *The New York Times* has made at least half a dozen trips to Darfur and the refugee camps in Chad, and has written extremely powerful and thought-provoking articles about what he witnessed, heard, and experienced. For his efforts, Kristof was awarded a Pulitzer Prize in 2006 for his series of articles on Darfur. Equally deserving of a Pulitzer Prize for her reporting on Darfur is Emily Wax, a journalist with the *Washington Post*. Her columns, too, over the years, have been extremely powerful and thought provoking. A less well-known but equally committed journalist to the Darfur cause is George Arnold, editorial writer for the *Arkansas Democrat Gazette*. Arnold has written at least half a dozen articles (and at least four or five editorials) on Darfur, all in an effort to educate and cajole his readership to begin to care about the ongoing genocide in Darfur.

A whole host of organizations and sub-organizations have arisen over the years that address the Darfur genocide. Among the most active are Save Darfur and STAND: A Student Anti-Genocide Coalition. The Save Darfur Coalition comprises "over 180 faith-based, advocacy and humanitarian organizations." The former claims that "the Save Darfur Coalition's member organizations represent 130 million people of all ages, races, religions and political affiliations united together to help the people of Darfur." The express purpose of The Save Darfur Coalition "is to raise public awareness about the ongoing genocide in Darfur and to mobilize a unified response to the atrocities that threaten the lives of two million people in the Darfur region."

Students Taking Action Now: Darfur (which has changed its name to STAND: A Student Anti-Genocide Coalition, and thus enlarged its focus) is comprised of student chapters in universities and high schools across the United States. The first U.S.-based STAND chapter was established at Georgetown University in Washington D.C. in 2004, shortly after President George W. Bush called Darfur "genocide." The students had attended a conference on Darfur at the United States Holocaust Memorial Museum and walked away thinking they had to do something to bring the issue of the Darfur genocide to the attention of the nation's students and beyond. That initial effort has expanded into an international network of student activism and now comprises more than 700 STAND chapters around the globe.

STAND has been active on numerous fronts, including the following: In January 2006, STAND initiated its Power to Protect campaign, which collected over one million postcards calling on President Bush to undertake more effective action vis-à-vis Darfur. In April 2006, STAND and the Genocide Intervention Network collaborated to bring more than 800 students from around the country to Washington, DC to lobby their elected officials. During the 2006–2007 school year, STAND students held six regional conferences at schools around the country, raised hundreds of thousands of dollars for civilian protection in Darfur, and was instrumental in getting more than 20 states and over 50 universities to divest funds connected in any way to Sudan. Additionally, STAND groups have held hundreds of awareness-raising events in cities around the world.

Among the most noted movie stars involved in bringing attention to the Darfur crisis are George Clooney, Mia Farrow, Don Cheadle, Matt Damon and, to a lesser degree, Brad Pitt. They have loaned their names to various efforts, have spoken at major rallies, helped to fundraise, and, in the case of Cheadle, helped to produce a documentary and co-author a book on Darfur. Essentially, their "star power" has drawn immense attention to the crisis and in doing so have brought the issue to the consciousness of untold numbers of people.

Finally, over the past three years, numerous documentary films have been produced about the Darfur crisis, including but not limited to the following: "All About Darfur" (2005); "Darfur Diaries" (2006); "Darfur Now" (2007); and "The Devil Came on Horseback" (2007).

At a minimum, all of the aforementioned efforts have helped to educate people about Darfur, keep the Darfur crisis front and center in people's (including politicians') minds, and not allowed the international community to totally ignore the plight of the victim population. It hasn't though, at least thus far, resulted in pushing the international community to provide real protection for the black Africans of Darfur. That said, one has to pause and ponder whether many more black Africans would have been killed had there not been such a clamour made over the atrocities carried out by the GOS and *Janjaweed*. There is no doubt that the killing by the GOS and *Janjaweed* has waxed and waned, and the latter is likely, at least in part, due to the fact that the international community has focused fairly sustained attention on the ongoing crisis in Darfur.

## What Does This Genocide Teach Us If We Wish to Protect Others from Such Horrors?

The genocide in Darfur has taught humanity, once again, as if it really needed another lesson along this line, the following: that the international community is more wedded to *realpolitik* than it is saving the lives of innocents; the UN Security Council is a group of disparate members whose primary focus is their own particular wants and needs and, as a body, it has no conscience to speak of; the UN Security Council's Permanent Five wield the power of life and death with their vetoes, but that doesn't constrain individual members from using their veto even when it will mean certain death to groups facing horrific atrocities, be they crimes against humanity or genocide; that individual nations and leaders talk a good game but at one and the same time, and more often than not, lack the political will to act when it counts (be it due to *realpolitik*, politics at home, or simply a lack of concern or a dearth of real care); that the time to act to save people from genocide is before genocide is found to have been committed (that is, early on when threats of and/or actual human rights violations far short of genocide are being carried out against a particular group); that all of the good intentions and efforts of activists can move many to action on the behalf of beleaguered others facing genocide but far too often, at least in today's world, they are overpowered by the *realpolitik* and the power of veto practiced by one or more of the Permanent Five members of the UN Security Council.

## Conclusion

As the international community dithers, innocent people in Darfur continue to either be murdered, perish as a result of malnutrition, dehydration and lack of medication attention, and/or suffer rape at the hands of the GOS troops and *Janjaweed* (and increasingly, members of some of the rebel groups). Four long years have gone by since the start of the crisis in Darfur, and the international community continues to engage in talk over real action in an "effort" to ameliorate the problems that beset Darfur. Unfortunately, Darfur is a stark reminder that the world is no closer to solving, halting, let alone, preventing genocide than it was during the Ottoman Turk genocide of the Armenians (1915–1923), the man-made famine in Ukraine (1933), and the Holocaust perpetrated by the Nazis (1933–1945). The same is true, unfortunately, in regard to sexual assaults against girls and women during periods of violent conflict.

## First-Person Accounts by Survivors

*The respondent [name has been deleted for sake of confidentialty] was born in 1972 in Andukeria, near Genenia in West Darfur. He is a Massaleit and had seven years of schooling. He first worked as a tailor and then a trader in produce.*

*This interview/oral history was conducted by Samuel Totten on 6/10/2007. It was conducted in the Gaga Refugee Camp in Eastern Chad. It was conducted under a lean-to within a larger compound with the respondent, interviewer and interpreter sitting on multicolored rugs.*

I lived in Goker during the attacks. Goker is between Habilia and Geneina. Its population was about 2,600. I left Goker about one month ago.

The trouble in Darfur started long ago, in Darfur in 1994 and in Goker in 1995. Before, there were not a lot of camels in our area and then in 1995 more than 20,000 camels arrived. These camels, when they come along, they destroy everything. These camels were looked after by Arab people and the camels eat the plants that are growing and the Arabs say you can't do anything about it. When this happens, the people go and report it to the police and the police go and see the Arabs and the police come back and say, "These people are our people and we won't do anything to them." Because the head of the police are Arabs, and they have a program [an agreement] with the Arabs to destroy us. All of the farms were destroyed, including mine. They [the camels] ate all of the grain and plants.

After the rainy season, the farms was destroyed and the war between the Arabs and us began. In my own family, two of my cousins, both were farmers, were killed. They went to the market and they were returning and Arabs killed them, Arabs who had camels. The Arabs would stay in between villages and when our people visited friends or family members, the Arabs would rob and kill our people. They were criminals. This was the beginning of the *Janjaweed* [Arab militia who have conducted attacks, largely in conjunction with the troops of the Government of Sudan, on the villages of black Africans].

Because my cousins and others were killed at this time, all of our tribe members came together and fought the Arabs for six days and chased them way. Many of our people died and a lot of Arabs were killed. From our people, 190 were killed. All were fighters.

I, too, fought with those. We had no real weapons but we got weapons when we fought them. They had horses and camels and Kalashnikovs and Gems [shorter rifles than Kalashnikovs]. We fought in villages of a Massaleit and ate there and did not return home.

I was injured in the hand by a bullet. At the time I just salted the wound and bandaged it. I still do not have feeling in my thumb.

When we fought, the Arabs told us this country [Sudan] was not to be inhabited by slaves. When the Arabs were being beat, some started to run and others called out, "Don't run away from the slaves" and "This is a jihad against the slaves!"

After the battle, the government tried to help the Arabs and gave them horses, camels and money and weapons. And soon after, about one month, more Arabs came and attacked again. They came from different areas in Darfur, and Chad, and even Abeche [a major town in Eastern Chad, and which the Gaga Refugee camp is located near]. And the fighting continued through 2000. There was no solution unless you fought. There was no security.

We would set up ambushes because we knew the Arabs would attack us again. So, we were ready. Mothers of fighters would often come out to where we were fighting and beg their children to return. Most of us, though, would tell our mothers we were going to a meeting and not tell them we were actually going to fight. We knew the Arabs would attack us in the village if we didn't ambush them and we didn't want that. The Arabs come from as far away as Libya, Mauritania, and Egypt and some are even Palestinians.

As for my mother, she told me "You must fight even if you die because you are defending your people." Everyone knew if something wasn't done the Arabs would sneak up and attack and kill everyone. Of course, my mother feared that I would die.

In 2000, General Mohammed Ahmed Mustafa Deby came to meet with representatives of Massalit and Arabs and said he was a representative of the President of Sudan, al Bashir. In the meeting the representatives of the Massalit told the general that we were here before the Arabs came to Africa and all the tribes came to our areas and they lived peacefully but the Arabs came and started killing our people and so we fought them. The general said he was there to make a peace between us and the Arabs but he was deceiving us. Two months after this agreement, the Arabs started killing the leaders of the Massalit, and even some of the politicians inside Genenia.

After this, the Arabs started eliminating the educated people. There was a man named Ahmed Abdouffrag—an engineer and he went to Khartoum to ask the government to build roads in the Massalit area and he was killed in his home upon his return. This was in 2000. Some Arab people drove up to his home, called him out and shot and killed him.

Others who were killed were Ibrahim Darfouri, who was head of the legislative body in Genenia. His was wife was head of the Women's Union in Genenia. They were both killed the same day. They shot and killed them both. This, too, was in 2000.

People outside Genenia, leaders of other villages, were also killed. Saleh Dakoro, *umda* of Morley, was killed in 2001. He went to Genenia and on his way back some *Janjaweed* shot and killed him.

Yacoub Congor, another *umda*, was also eliminated in 2001. He was in the *suq* in Habilia and about 35 *Janjaweed* came into the suq, searched for him and one shot and killed him.

In 2002, the Arabs established their own villages in our areas. When our people were killed by the Arabs and went to the police, they said, "That's a tribal problem and we have nothing to do with it." But if a Massaleit killed even one Arab, the police would collect other police from other areas and even call the army and then come and attack the village [of the Massalit] where the Arab was killed.

The police would also go to other villages and arrest Massaleit [in retaliation for the one killing]. The police have a weapon called Fang, which is a rocket propelled grenade [RPG] and they would take the powder out of the shell and put it on the head of people and set it on fire and it would explode like diesel [gasoline]. I saw this with my own eyes.

You should know, all those people who were in Darfur and worked for the police, the army and security were all taken out of Darfur and moved away to other parts of Sudan and they were all replaced by *Janjaweed*.

They had another weapon where they would tie you to two vehicles—your arms to one and your legs to another—and they would drive off in separate directions, pulling our body apart.

And many people were arrested and taken to the security office, and many of those people have never been heard from again. And it's the *Janjaweed* who run the security office. All were red people.

Possibly around May 2002, Arabs from different nationalities were brought into Idelganim to train them [the local Arabs] to help them establish a state comprised of Darfur, Chad and the Republic of Central Africa. al Bashir visited the camp and changed the name from Idelganim to Idelfoursan. He changed the meaning of the location, the camp, from "where goats live" to "where brave men with horses live."

Massalit from our tribe who are red like Arabs went into the training camps and posed as Arabs. Seven days after Omar Bashir visited the camp, Osama Bin Laden gave them [the Arabs] camels as presents. This place is east of Nyala in a village called Idelganim, near Korodfan. When these groups began moving about in Darfur, they were referred to as *gowat alsalam* (Peace Force). When they attacked, they would come in with 400 to 500 men on horses, surround the village and destroy it. And this was how our village was destroyed.

This day, about seven in the morning, in some villages near us, we saw horses, I cannot say the number, and three vehicles and helicopters. When the people were fighting at this time, the helicopters would land and take off but I don't know what they were doing. And we saw planes, all gray, Antonovs, come and go and we heard the dropping of bombs.

I left our village before it was attacked. We all fled right away, and I went to the police station and military in Goker [the regional headquarters of Goker]. The village was burned down and I could see that as I was fleeing. We, many, many villagers, people from over

40 villages, about 6,000 people, stayed there [the aforementioned regional headquarters in Goker]. I stayed there from that time until one month ago, when I came here [Gaga camp in Eastern Chad]. Some organizations came there and helped us—such organizations as Red Cross and Oxfam.

I never returned to my village. There was nothing I could do there. The huts were built of grass and thus nothing remained after the fire.

In the village, there were about 700 cows, nine camels, and more than 2,000 goats, and 19 horses. I personally lost 28 cows and 61 goats.

So, from November 2003 to last month [June 2007] I was in an internally displaced camp. While our IDP [internally displaced persons] camp was not attacked, it was not peaceful. For example, women could not go out to collect firewood. If a woman went outside the camp, the *Janjaweed* would rape them. If they stayed inside, the government did not help provide wood for cooking. A man can't go out because if you go out yourself you'll receive one bullet [meaning, a man will be shot and killed]. The government also interferes with the distribution of food. There are many different types of food handed out by relief groups and the *Janjaweed* tells them not to give us certain food just to make us angry.

The African Union troops had an office in the IDP camp but there were very few men— only about thirteen. But when there was, for example, a crime, such as the rape of a woman, we'd tell them and they would say they would look for the criminals but always came back and said they couldn't find them.

I think some of the African Union (AU) troops are on the side of the *Janjaweed* and the government of Sudan. I say this because the *Janjaweed* bring the troops sheep and milk. We can see with our own eyes they bring such things. What else they may bring we do not know.

It is also true, some of the African Union troops truly help us. For example, the Rwandese soldiers are very good and helped us. So did troops from Eritrea. But troops from Nigeria, Chad, Cameroon, Egypt, and Libya are working for their own benefit, not the benefit of Darfur.

So, again, for example, if a person like you comes to speak to me [in Darfur] during the day, the *Janjaweed*, GOS troops and members of the AU will come at night and take me and kill me. And if something happens to you [meaning, black Africans], the Egyptian troops will even laugh.

Another time, in Mistere, where there are a lot of AU soldiers, the *suq* was attacked and two people, two traders, were killed and the market was looted, all by the *Janjaweed*, and all the AU soldiers did was take photographs during the attacks and nothing else.

One time, a journalist spoke to a person in our camp and that night some people—I'm not sure if it was *Janjaweed* or security people in the camp—went to his house. The man, though, thought there might be trouble so he had left his hut, but only after placing materials in his bed to make it appear he was sleeping there. Men burst into his room and fired four shots into the bed. The next morning we went to the African Union to report this, and the African Union soldiers went and got more soldiers, from all different countries, plus a man from a rebel group, JEM, to go to the man's house. When the soldier, who was from Egypt, saw the bullets he smiled. We told the one Rwandese soldier who was there that the killers would be back that night and asked him to take the man who was in danger to Genenia. The Rwandese soldier agreed but the Egyptian said no. We took the Rwandese soldier to the man who was hiding and when the soldier was about to take him to Genenia, the Egyptian said, "No, he is not to be taken there." The Rwandese soldier said, "Yes, he will be. It's our job to protect people." So, the Rwandese soldier took him to Genenia and the Egyptian just stood there and allowed him to do so.

The problem is truly worse than before—that is, worse with the African Union troops. Before they came, everyone knew there was ethnic cleansing (*tathir irgi*) and mass killing (*ibada jamia*) but after the AU came, because they insisted on coming in order to show they were doing something to help, [but,] all they do is take photographs and talk. And the violence continues. So, it's worse now, because there was hope there'd be real help but there's not. The situation is the same but the hope is gone.

We stayed in the camp for a long time, and we hoped that with the African Union the situation would be better but it never was so we decided to leave and come to Chad.

Several small villages between Genenia and Mornei were attacked at 6:00 in the morning and I saw a lot of horses and dust and vehicles, Toyota Landcruisers. The people who were being attacked flew toward our village. Many rode horses and many came on foot. And the enemy, the *Janjaweed* and the GOS, was chasing them, and we, too, fled—with all of us were donkeys and they were running.

As we were fleeing the *Janjaweed* would halt women with babies and force the women to show whether their children were boys or girls. And when the enemy caught a man, the man was killed. And if they caught a woman and she had a child, if the baby was a boy, they would kill him. They would take the baby boy and throw him on the ground and step on his throat and kill him. In other cases, they would throw the baby boys into the fire to burn alive. If the baby was a girl, they would leave them. The same for little girls. But if the girls were 13, 14, 15 or older, they often took them away for three or four days, and they [the girls] would often come back. But some never came back and we still don't know what happened to them.

Not from our village but others, people I know were taken and made slaves. The attackers would say in front of the people, "You, I am taking as a slave!" They would force such people to watch their animals as herders. They don't take big people [adults] but young boys about eight or nine years old.

The last days before I came to Gaga, there was interference by the government [of Sudan] in the work of the international organizations. What I mean is that one organization was formed by the Sudanese government and when they distributed food to us they told us we wouldn't get any food unless we went back to where we came from. This began two months before we came here [Gaga camp in Chad]. Then, when you went to your village, they would come and take pictures and pass them around and say, "Everything is alright." They would bring food once or twice, but then the *Janjaweed* would come and kill you. I refused to go back, as did my friends.

When we refused to return to our villages, for 50 days we did not receive any food. And there were no other organizations providing food for any of us. The only way we were able to eat is that we knew the future could be worse so while we received three meals a day, we only ate two meals; and when we started receiving no food, we began to eat only once a day.

And during this time, just by accident, some journalists passed (three men and one woman) by our camp, and we told these journalists we had no food for 50 days and the journalists reported this to a human rights organization. A human rights organization came to see us after seven days and when we told them our problem, they reported it to the Red Cross, brought us food, and three days later, the other organization [the Sudanese organization] packed up all their food and left and never came back.

This is my daughter [indicating a little girl sitting in his lap], and I named her Condoleezza Rice. Her complete name is Condoleezza Mahjoub Oumar. I want to give Condoleezza Rice [the U.S. Secretary of State] this girl, my daughter, who is two years [old]. Because Condoleezza Rice came to visit us in Darfur when we were in a very bad situation. I have no means to contact Condoleezza Rice to tell her that I want to give her my child, and I wish I did.

Many people work for Darfur—the African Union, the United Nations, Kofi Annan (at one point, however, he gave the *Janjaweed* three months to turn in their weapons; can you imagine how many people could be killed in that time?)—Condoleezza Rice and Colin Powell [the former U.S. Secretary of state] worked more than all these others to help us. So, we do not forget people who help us, who help Africa. I wish I had a boy and a girl, because then I would give the boy to Colin Powell and the girl to Condoleezza Rice. I also know that Condoleezza Rice has no child and thus I would like her to have my child.

*The respondent [name has been deleted for sake of confidentialty] is about 30 years old (not sure of her date of birth, it is a guess). She was born in the village of Tolos in West Darfur, which is near the larger town of Mornei. She is a Massaleit.*

*This interview/oral history was conducted by Samuel Totten on 6/10/2007. It was conducted in the Gaga Refugee Camp in Eastern Chad. It was conducted under a lean-to on which the interviewee, interviewer and interpreter sat. Approximately ten to fifteen family members (e.g., her children, mother, sister, nieces and nephews and others) sat and stood on the periphery listening in on the interview session.*

When our village, Tolos, was attacked I was living with eight people in my home, my six children, me and my husband. Our village was attacked four years ago. I can't remember the month but it was about two months after Ramadan.

In the morning, early, we were taking breakfast, and we heard the planes. They are too loud, from far you can hear them.

The planes came first, then the trucks, and then the horses and camels. Some [*Janjaweed*] were on foot. The planes, Antonovs, flew over the village. They [the planes] were all white and the sides were red. They [three or four of them] dropped big things like *binil* [barrels], and they made fire. Everything caught fire, buildings, animals, people.

The planes dropped the big things and about 20 minutes after the Landcruisers came. Some were green color, some were black and green [camouflaged]. There were many, I don't know how many because at the time I was scared, but it might have been about 100. They came from all directions.

When we heard the big things falling and hitting, we ran out of the house but we didn't know where to go. The big things caused big holes, like wells.

Driving the cars were Sudaense soldiers. Most *Janjaweed* rode horses, camels and were on foot. On the trucks, they have a big gun [she is most likely referring to what are called *doskas*], and the soldiers held big guns, some red and some black [Bilgic, possibly of Italian make]. There were also *modra* [tanks] with men inside but you can't see them. Outside there is a big gun and everything was colored black and green. There were about ten *modra*. The camels and horses and Landcruisers were more than 400. They were crying louding as they came in, calling out "Nuba! Nuba!"

At that time, we were ten persons and we began running. I was with three of my sisters, my sister-in-law, my father's two sisters, and three were my neighbors. All of my children had run in fear and I didn't know where they were. My husband, too [was gone and she still does not know his whereabouts].

We ran outside the village to the West. There was a lot of shooting but none of us were hit.

I was so frightened, I left the village without my two babies and little four year old daughter who were inside our hut. I later found them because someone had grabbed them and run out with them.

As we were running I saw men from our village shot. They killed 27 men. They [the soldiers and *Janjaweed*] aimed at the men. I saw two of my fathers [her father's two brothers; in other words, her uncles, who are generally referred to as "fathers" by the black Africans] killed. We didn't have any guns in our village and they [the Government of Sudan troops and the *Janjaweed*] did all of the shooting.

I was looking and crying and running but what can I do? I was so fearful, didn't stop running and I was hysterical, crying and running. After the attack, we came back to our village and we found the dead bodies.

We ran for three days, to Habila. No food and no water.

Not for 23 days did I find my one son [name withheld for the sake of confidentiality], in Mornei on the way out in the bush. On the way out, we came across my husband who had two of our other sons in the bush. Then we went to Habila. We had nothing. Sometimes we went to the bush for firewood but we were attacked by the *Janjaweed*.

We returned to our village after ten days. We returned because it was safe. When we made it back, we did not find anything but bodies. There were about seven dead bodies.

Our animals, our cows, our sorghum, our millet, our clothes, nothing was left. Nothing. It was all burnt, destroyed. The whole village was destroyed.

We found three who were injured in a small valley, in different places. All three had been shot—one man in both arms and both legs and the other man in one leg and the other one in his hand.

We took the injured to Mornei on donkey and then they [the injured] were taken in automobile to Zallingi, east of Genenia. The people with the cars were black but I don't know if they were an organization or not. They were Sudanese, but I don't know where they were from. There was no hospital in Mornei and so they took them to Zallingi. The three are still living and one is here [in Gaga camp] in Block 7 and two are in Mornei.

When we left the village to return to Habila, we came across the *Janjaweed* again, out in the bush. The *Janjaweed* were shooting guns and we began running. Because we are far away we could not hear what they were yelling at us. They followed us, but not too closely and then left.

In Habila, we stayed without any work; sometimes we went into the bush to get firewood that we sold to buy food. We stayed there for two years, in an internally displaced persons camp.

Life was not good in the camp. There was not enough food and if you left the camp, the *Janjaweed* would sometimes beat us. There was not freedom.

I was attacked by the *Janjaweed*. We, men and women, were cutting firewood and they stopped us and beat us. They beat us with sticks for two hours. One person was injured very badly from the beating and he had head injures that left him feeling unwell.

Another time I was also out with five women and three girls (13 years old, 14 years old, and 15 years old) gathering firewood and the *Janjaweed* raped the three girls and a woman. We were about two hours from the camp, and we were on foot. When we first arrived at the area with the wood the *Janjaweed*, about twenty of them, were on camels and horses and came up on us very quickly. Some of them said, "We already took your land, why are you around here? We use your land and now we are going to use you."

We all started running away and four of us got captured, three girls and one woman. One girl who was captured was my sister's daughter, who was thirteen years old. From the morning until the evening the *Janjaweed* kept the girls and the woman.

When we reached the camp we told the mothers of the daughters about the capture of their daughters and the mothers went out and brought their daughters back on donkeys and took them to the hospital in Habila. The four were badly injured because of the rape and the woman spent five days in the hospital and the girls were in for ten days. The girls were raped by many men, some by five, some by ten.

From the four girls, one got pregnant and had the baby. She was the one who was fifteen years. She is still in Habila with the baby from the *Janjaweed*. When the girl's father heard about the baby from the *Janjaweed*, he got very angry and sick from his anger and died [possibly from a heart attack]. He was 50. He was not sick before that, but when he heard what happened he died.

We came to Gaga camp about one year ago. When we were in Habila, there was no way you could go out without trouble from the *Janjaweed*. When we were in the Habila camp, the *Janjaweed* came three times at night and attacked the camp. One time, they killed four guards, all [of whom] were Massaleit. So, it was not safe to stay there.

From Habilia, we, sixteen of us (me, my mother, my mother's sister, my own sister, my husband, my father, my six children, my husband's sisters, my husband's brothers) went to Genenia and from Genenia to Adre, and from Adre [in Chad, along the Chad/Sudan border] to Gaga. In the *suq* in Habilia we found a car to take us to Genenia. We stayed for two days in Genenia, in the station of cars. Already we were forced out of Sudan [Habilia] and Genenia is in Sudan so we did not want to stay. From Genenia we found a direct car to Adre in Chad. In Adre we stayed for two days. In Adre there is no camp or organization to help so we did not want to stay there. We reached Gaga by car we hired.

In Gaga, it took one month and ten days to get a tent. At that time, we lived outside the camp. Because there are many Massaleit in this camp, they would come out to see us and give us food.

The life in camp [the UNCHR camp in Gaga] is very difficult, but what can we do? There is no other way. When we first arrived, everything was fine, but now there is not enough food, not enough water, and not enough medicine.

With my husband and I live our four children and my mother. Before we got food every two weeks then it went to one month and now we have not had food for two months. So, now we have to go outside of the camp and work for Chadian people and they give us money and with it we buy millet. Sometimes, we buy sugar and sometimes okra and sometimes meat for our soup. We have had meat one time in months. We buy sugar more often because we like tea, so if we have money we can buy it every day, if not, then we don't. If we have money we also buy okra every day, if not we don't.

One day we get water and the next we don't. It's not regular. We don't know why this is so.

If we don't get water in the camp, we have to walk one hour on foot to get water out of the well. We get one *baka* [jerry can] of water from the well. I am the one who goes for the water and the *baka* with the water is very heavy so I can only carry one.

My baby [a little girl with a huge extended stomach], one and a half years, has had diarhoea for one year and we have seen a doctor here in Gaga ten times and he gave us medicine but it didn't do any good. We told the doctor and he gives more medicine and it doesn't do anything.

And when I make water [urinates] I feel very hot inside. This has gone on for three months. In Habilia I went to the doctor and got medicine for it and I felt better but here I go to the doctor and the medicine he gave me makes me feel no better

I don't have a lot of hope. If the Americans bring peace to Darfur and bring security then maybe life will get better, but here, I don't think so. If the UN [peace force] goes to Darfur, we'd like to go back to our country.

*The respondent [name has been deleted for sake of confidentialty] is 17 years old and resides in the Gaga Refugee Camp in Eastern Chad. She is a Massalit.*

*This interview/oral history was conducted by Samuel Totten on 6/10/2007 It was conducted on a rug sitting in front of a UNCHR-issued tent with the sun beating down. A small makeshift fence made of tree branches surrounded the small, mostly dusty area which this woman and her family called home.*

I was born during Ramadan but I don't know the day, month or year. I studied only one year in school. It was last year, here in Gaga.

I came to Gaga with my mother and my two sisters. One sister is 32 years and one is 20 years. In Masteri I lived with my mother and father and two sisters until three years ago. I met my husband, who is now 23, here in Gaga. I live with my husband and a baby girl, who is three months [old].

The government [of Sudan] used planes and trucks to attack us and the *Janjaweed* came on horse and camels and on foot. They came in the early morning just before sunrise and I was asleep. I first knew there was an attack because I heard the sound of weapons from the planes and the trucks. As soon as I heard the sounds I got up and ran from the hut. As we ran I heard some *Janjaweed* scream "Nuba *afnine*" [Nuba shit"]. I don't know how many *Janjaweed* and soldiers there were but maybe it was around 200. So many I can't count. Maybe 20 green and black [camouflaged] Landcruisers and hundreds of horses and camels.

The soldiers and *Janjaweed* chased us and they kept shooting men and boys. Many were killed. They also caught men and slashed them with long knives on the legs and arms, cutting off their arms and legs, and sometimes both on men—and sometimes both arms. Some who had their legs cut off were able to move, some could not. Those who survived were later given a new leg and a stick [crutch]. But those who had different sides of their bodies cut off [such as a right arm and a left leg] could not continue on. They could not walk. All of the attackers were wearing black and green and white [camouflaged].

At such times you do not look around for other persons, you take care of yourself. We (my mother and my two sisters) made it to Goagor in one day. But for three months we did not see my father. He went another way and we did not know it. He went to Tabrie in Chad, and then he came to find us in Goagor.

In my village, the *Janjaweed* and soldiers killed my second "father" [uncle] and his two sons. The two were older than me, but I don't know how old they were. They were all shot and killed. My second father was shot and as we, my two sisters and I, were running we saw him. He had just been shot in the side of his body and his insides came out the other side. We picked him up and placed him under a tree. We were very young then and very frightened and so we left him and rushed off.

Later, some people went back to the village and they saw my second father under the tree, dead. And at this time they also found the two sons of my second father, dead.

We stayed in Goagor for two years. We stayed with the people in the village there. There were about 200 people from Darfur, from different villages. When we were there we asked to farm but they said "How could you farm, you are refugees and have no land." And then when we went to go to the well, the Chadians caused us problems and told us we could not get water before them because we are refugees. So, we had to wait until every Chadian got water before trying to get some ourselves. We stayed there because we had no other place to go.

We finally decided to leave Goagor because many other refugees were going to Hajar Hadid and Gaga and since we were refugees we decided to go, too.

From Goagor we went to Gaga. We wanted to go to Hajar Hadid but we were told that there was no room for new refugees at Hajar Hadid and so we came to Gaga.

Gaga is [a] bad life because there is not enough food or water. I hope life will get better, but I don't know. The food [though] is not the important thing; the important thing is that we get our country back.

## Mohammed Abdullah Arbab

*The respondent was born on June 15, 1977 in Baouda, West of Congo Haraza-Beida in West Darfur. He completed school through the eleventh year. He is Massaleit. He is the umda of the UNCHR refugee camp, Farchana.*

*This interview was conducted by Samuel Totten on July 12, 2007 inside the tent of the respondent in the UNCHR camp of Farchana. Sitting in the crowded tent, which contained all of the interviewee's earthly possessions, were the interviewee, the interviewer and the interpreter. The initial interview lasted for just over two hours. At 4:50pm the interview had to be terminated for the day since there was a regulation that all non-residents had to be out of the camp by no later than 5:00pm. It was agreed that the interviewer and interpreter would meet the interviewee back at the same place, the interviewee's tent, the next morning at 8:00 to resume the interview. Unfortunately, an emergency arose in which the interviewee needed to assist someone who had become sick in the middle of the night and had to be taken to the camp hospital. Since the interviewer and interpreter had arranged to be taken to a different camp the next day this remarkable interview was never completed. As it stands, though, it contains insightful and important information on a broad array of issues.*

Before the first attacks on our area in May 2002, the relationship with Arabs and black Africans was very good. There was even intermarriage.

We had no rebel groups in our village. The rebels at that time were in the north.

We heard about attacks on other Massalit prior to the attack on our village—about two months before we were attacked. Many villages in our areas were attacked before ours was attacked. We had nothing to help with—nothing. The Government of Sudan had Antonovs and the *Janjaweed* had weapons and horses, and all we could do to assist was go and help bury the dead bodies.

Beginning with the first attacks on our area, the Sudanese government gave Hamid Dawai weapons, vehicles, and equipment for communication. Brought in to work with Hamid Dawai was Jamal (with *Shurta*, the the Sudanese National Police) and Yasir (with the Sudanese Army), both with the rank of lieutenant. Then after this they attacked the first village, Kassia, on July 27, 2002. Thirteen huts were burned down and two villagers (Shiekha Dardama and Arbab Abou Koik) were killed. The attack was carried out in the early evening by both the *Jesh* (Sudanese Army) and the *Janjaweed.*

That night the dark came and the attackers returned to Beida. The villagers stayed in their homes for two days and then on Thursday the *Jesh* and *Janjaweed* attacked Kassia again. This time they killed seventeen people, destroyed the entire village by burning it down, stole all of the animals, and took the zinc roof of the school. Hamid Dawai's brother, Hasballa Dawai, was stabbed in the neck with a spear by a villager and killed. That was on Thursday, and then on Friday, three villages (Toucou/Toucoul, Migmesi, and Conga) were burned, totally burned down. In Toucou/Toucoul seven villagers were killed and in Migmesi one person was killed. The iman's brother was shot in the upper arm.

After the three villages were attacked and burned down, all of the villagers crossed the border into Chad, into such places as Amliona, Abassana, Matabano, Aboy, Sesi, and Berkangi. Then, on Monday, the *Janjaweed* and *Jesh* burned down villages called Andrig, Ajabani, Mermta, Temblei, Haraza, Bouta, Gobe, and Dim. The villagers from these villages could not go directly to Chad because right between their villages and Chad is a place, Aun Rado, where the *Janjaweed* are trained by the *Jesh.* So, the people, thousands, went to Kango Haraza in Darfur. They settled there for some days and the *Janjaweed* and the government returned and the area was burned down, and all the animals were stolen. And on the same day, several other villages, Awikar, Boukerei, Ararah, Megalo, and Kassedo were burned down. Out of this entire area, which is very big, only two villages remained—including Baouda, my village.

During many of these attacks, people were kidnapped and forced to work as guides to lead the *Jesh* and *Janjaweed* to important people.

In December 2002, they came and attacked Baouda and 25 people were killed. In Baouda, the attack was at 4:30 in the morning. The *Janjaweed* surrounded the village and before they started shooting they put fire on the houses, in the east part of the village. We didn't realize the *Janjaweed* had attacked the village, we just thought the village had caught fire. The houses were built of grass and we went to support and help the people with the fire. We heard about the fire because the owners were screaming. And when a man appeared to help with the fire the *Janjaweed* would shoot him. And when others heard the shooting they knew it was the *Janjaweed.* They were shooting with Kalashnikovs and Gem 4s. All the people rushed to their house to get their wives and children.

Everyone began to run towards Chad and as people ran, the *Janjaweed* shot them. The *Janjaweed* and *Jesh* wanted to kill them all, but Chad was only one kilometer away. The government also brought more soldiers in government vehicles, Landcruisers, gray military Landcruisers, and all had *doskas* [large mounted automatic weapons] and they also had *animoks* [a big truck] that carries soldiers—up to 100 men. They chased people until they reached the *wadi*, which is at the border between Sudan and Chad. Then they [the soldiers and *Janjaweed*] returned and looted the village.

There were a lot of people who had sought refuge in our village from the other villages that had been destroyed, and many, many people were killed, so we don't know the number and since that day we have not returned to Sudan or our village.

I was on my way to help with the fire when I heard the sound of the shooting. The sound was very loud, and the *doskas* were firing, and the camels and horses were running into the village.

I returned to my house, got my wife and children (two girls, one two years and one four years), packed up my cart with a bag of clothes and some rugs to sleep on, hitched up my donkey, and when we were leaving the village, a leader of the *Janjaweed* called out to me. It was Algali Haron and he shot at me several times but the bullets didn't hit me. While on his horse, he grabbed me by the collar of my *gelabiah* and pulled me down from my cart and another *Janjaweed* called Salih Dardamo caught me from the back and held me as the other one stabbed me twice with a knife in the middle of the chest, just below the lungs. When he's stabbing me, my wife camde up behind Algali Haron and hit him with an axe handle in the neck and knocked him down and my mother and my grandmother ran towards me and may father-in-law came to help me but he was shot by Salih Dardamo in the upper chest. (My father-in-law is now OK and is in Breidjing camp He has two wives so you can find him in Breidjing and Triendi camps.)

Salih Dardamo, who was all alone and surrounded by my family members, ran to his vehicle and raced off. I then put my father-in-law on the cart. We then crossed the wadi into Chad. Many of the people didn't make it as they were shot and killed.

Another one of my uncles was slashed by a bayonet and he was so bloody we thought he was dead so we didn't pick him up. But somehow he managed to get on his knees and made it to Chad.

Across the wadi was a Chadian garrison and some of the soldiers helped to fight off the *Janjaweed* and *Jesh* and were killed. This was inside Chad. The commander of the soldiers, Battalion Commander Tadjedin, was shot and killed inside Chad.

The dress of *Jesh* and *Janjaweed* were exactly the same—camouflague shirts and pants. The only difference is the *Jesh* had insignias showing rank and the *Janjaweed* had none. The *Jesh* and police also had something over their pockets, but I could not see what it was as I was not close enough.

The *Janjaweed* and *Jesh* were screaming at the villagers, *Abid* [Arabic for "slave"] and *amby* [Arabic meaning, "You have no religion"].

We settled across the *wadi* in Naclouta for one month. While there, the Chadian government tried by all means to protect us. But when people went to the *wadi* to get water or went to get their animals, the *Janjaweed* killed them. Sometimes the *Janjaweed* also stole our animals.

As we were escaping, I saw my cousin's husband, Alamin Idris, killed. He was shot in the *wadi*. There were many, many people who were killed. And nobody buried them, nobody returned there and thus they remained unburied. Some of them may have been carried away by the *wadi*, some may be buried by the sand, but many others have never been buried.

Other people in Kassia had tried to return and bury their dead and they were attacked by *Jesh* and *Janjaweed*. There, my father's brother, Khamiss Roy, was killed trying to do so.

After one month, the UNCHR came and picked us up in vehicles and took us to Farchana camp. When we arrived there were four blocks only and now there are 26. The first people arrived here on January 17, 2003, and we arrived in April 2003. Then in the beginning of 2004 I was selected to be *umda* of Farchana by the sheiks. The sheiks themselves nominated and elected me.

Before I was *umda* I was working with *Médécin Sans Frontières* in community service. I told the sheiks I didn't want to be *umda* but they insisted. At that time, we needed a person who could speak English and serve as a translator and they selected me as I know how to write and read. The most difficult aspect of the job is to make the people behave honestly.

The food we receive is not enough here [in the UNCHR refugee camp, Farchana], and there is a problem with water in April, May, and June; that is, there is a shortage. They give us a ration of twelve kilos of sorghum a month per person, but that is not enough. And we've never received meat. We have asked them to bring sardines [meaning fish in a can, not actual sardines] if they cannot provide us with meat, but they have not given us that either. They bring us sorghum only, every month. It's not ready to eat and and so we have to bring it to the flour mill and when you take it there they take half of it because you have no money to have it milled. So, you end upwith six kilos.

Nothing special is provided for the babies, the infants. And those at one year and above only get sorghum as well.

We all wonder if there is no solution. The United Nations, the Security Council, and the Secretary General, they all make resolutions but fail to force the Sudanese government to obey. Some people are shocked by this, when the decisions are continually reversed. It makes people lose hope.

## Notes

1. Colloquially, according to the black Africans of Darfur, *Janjaweed* means, variously, "hordes," "ruffians," and "men or devils on horseback."

2. The phrase "the first acknowledged genocide" is used here for it is possible that other genocides were and are being perpetrated in the early part of the twenty-first century but not detected yet by the international community. In fact, various scholars and political pundits have suggested that genocide could be underway in such places as the Democratic Republic of the Congo, and in far-flung areas across the globe where indigenous groups reside.

3. Civil war broke out in southern Sudan in 1983 and ended in 2005 as a result of a complex and prolonged international effort to bring the civil war to a close. It is estimated that some two million were killed during that twenty year period and another four million people were displaced. In fact, over the course of the war, at one time or another, about 80 percent of southern Sudan's people experienced displacement. The war began when the GOS implemented Islamic Sharia law through-out the country. Both Christian and animist peoples residing in the south were adamantly against such a law, and made their disenchantment known. Ultimately, the GOS and rebel groups from the south (comprised of individuals from the Christian and animist groups) engaged in the lengthy and deadly fight—the rebels to wrest the south from the GOS in the north and the GOS to regain control of the south and to banish the Christian and animists from their homes and land. As one journalist put it, "When government plane are not bombing [the] homes, churches, and schools [of the people in the south in the areas controlled by the Sudan Peoples Liberation Army or SPLA], armed Arab militias on horseback spread terror throughout the villages, killing men, raping women and taking way their domestic animals. The conflict in Sudan is one in which all known rules of war have constantly been violated" (Achieng, 2000, p. 1). A December 1998 report issued by the United States Committee for Refugees asserted that "Sudan's civil war has been characterized by an incremental ferocity that has left untouched practically no one in southern Sudan.... The government has systematically blocked food supplies to the south, attacked villages and driven large groups of people to areas where they could not survive.... It's a very deliberate strategy on the part of the government of Sudan to depopulate large parts of southern Sudan" (quoted in BBC News, 1998, pp. 1, 2)

4. Arab nomadic groups were, and are not, of course, of a single mind and thus should not be painted as a monolithic group or movement.

5. In regard to the establishment of the self-defense groups by non-Arabs in Darfur, Fadul and Tanner (2007) comment as follows:

From the 1980s onwards, in Darfur and elsewhere, successive governments in Khartoum mobilized and armed Arab groups to do their bidding, mostly to attack and subdue populations considered hostile. The NIF [National Islamic Front] government furthered the tribal militia policy with the passage of the Popular Defense Act of 1989, making the PDF official. The government entrenched the policy in local government by elevating Arab traditional administrators above non-Arabs in the native Administration. . . . The Arab groups of western Sudan, Darfur, and Kordofan have been militarized for over two decades. By contrast, non-Arab communities mobilized along far more local lines, resorting to community-level strategies to try to ensure their protection. One such response was the establishment of self-defense committees. In the late 1980s and early 1990s, as Arab violence against non-Arab communities mounted, especially in western Darfur, and the state did not intervene, some of these communities started arming themselves. . . . These groups were poorly equipped and ill-coordinated, despite isolated attempts in the late 1980s and early 1990s to organize them. . . . They sold government sugar rations and livestock, and bought light weapons and ammunition from the Chadian military on the border.

. . . The important point here is that the locus of these groups was the village and its outlying homesteads. There was little if any tactical cooperation among the self defense groups; if Arab militias attacked one village, the self defense force in the next village would most often just stay put until it in turn was attacked (p. 302).

6. In October 2006, the London-based Minority Rights Group International issued a report that asserted that United Nations' authorities were warned of ethnic tensions in Darfur as early as 2001 but chose to ignore the facts: "As early as 2001, the UN Commission on Human Rights' Special Rapporteur for Human Rights in Sudan began paying particular attention to Darfur, visiting the region in early 2002. His August 2002 report highlighted the violence in Darfur and noted Masalit claims that 'the depopulation of villages, displacement and changes in land ownership are allegedly part of government strategy to alter the demography of the region.' Despite his concerns, the 2003 Commission on Human Rights removed Sudan from its watch-list and ended the mandate of the Special Rapporteur" (Srinivasan, 2006, p. 6). Many argue that the international community was so intent on bringing the 20-year Sudanese civil war in the south to a close that it believed attention directed at Darfur might result in "a peace spoiler."

7. Tellingly, in interviews with black African Darfurian refugees in Gaga and Forchana refugee camps in eastern Chad during the summer of 2007, this author was told that Arab nomads had been provided with weapons and trained by the GOS as early as the mid-1990s. Furthermore, the so-called *Janjaweed* had been used by the Sudanese leadership since the late 1980s to supplement government troops in the fight against southern rebels (Prunier, 2005, p. 97), and it is certainly possible, if not highly probable, that many of them had roamed throughout Darfur and even joined nomadic groups as the latter herded livestock.

8. Each member of the Permanent Five of the UN Security Council can, alone, with a vote of "no" on any resolution defeat any motion or vote on an issue. The Permanent Five are the only members of the UN Security Council with such power.

9. Following a series of complex talks during 2002 and 2003, a Comprehensive Peace Agreement (CPA) was signed in Nairobi on January 9, 2005. The CPA provided for the sharing of power between the Government of Sudan (GOS) and leaders of the SPLM and determined that the main rebel leader, John Garang, would become the First Vice-President of Sudan. (Shortly after Garang became first vice-president, he died when his helicopter crashed during a storm.) An important provision of the CPA called for the sharing of revenues from oil, which had begun to be pumped in 1999, between the north and the south of the nation. Six years after the signing of the CPA, the south will be permitted to hold a referendum for self-determination and essential independence.

10. The signing of the DPA by Minni Arkoy Minawi did not bode well for him or his faction. Not only did his faction lose battle after battle with the rebel groups that refused to sign the DPA, but his men began to defect to the other side. By September 2006, it was estimated that up to 75 percent of

his men had joined the non-signatory rebel groups. Furthermore, and understandably, many Darfurians began to look askance at Minni's collaboration with GOS troops and the *Janjaweed*.

## References

Achieng, Judith (2000). "Sudan's Protracted War." *ICG News Desk*. August 25. Accessed at www.hartford-hwp.com/archives/33/137.html.

Amnesty International (2004). *Darfur: Rape as a Weapon of War: Sexual Violence and its Consequences.* London: Author. Accessed at: http://web.amnesty.org/library

Anonymous (2000). *The Black Book: The Imbalance of Power and Wealth in Sudan.* Khartoum: Author(s).

Apiku, Simon (2007). "African Darfur Troops Must Meet UN Standards—Adada." *Reuters*, August 16. Accessed at: www.reuters.com/resources/archive/us/20070816.html

Askin, Kelly Dawn (2006). "Prosecuting Gender Crimes Committed in Darfur: Holding Leaders Accountable for Sexual Violence." In Samuel Totten and Eric Markusen (Eds.) *Genocide in Darfur: Investigating Atrocities in the Sudan*, pp. 141–160. New York: Routledge.

Baldauf, Scott (2007). "Sudan: Climate Change Escalates Darfur Crisis." *The Christian Science Monitor.* July 27. Accessed at: www.cscomonitor.com/2007/0727/p01s04-woaf.html

BBC (2005). "UN Accuses Sudan Over Darfur Rape." July 29, n.p. Accessed at: http://news.bbc.co.uk/2/hi/Africa/4728231.stm

BBC News (UK Edition) (2004). "Sudanese Refugees Welcome Powell." June 30, 4 pp. Accessed http://news/bbc.co.uk

BBC Online Network (1998). "Millions Dead in Sudan Civil War." December 11. Accessed at: http://news/bbc.co.uk/1/hi/world/Africa/232803.stm

Cobham, Alex (2005). "Causes of Conflict in Sudan: Testing the *Black Book.*" *Queen Elizabeth House, University of Oxford, Working Paper Series.* Oxford: University of Oxford. Accessed at: ideas.re-pec.org/p/qeh/qehw.ps/qehw.ps

De Waal, Alex (2004a). "Darfur's Deep Grievances Defy All Hopes for an Easy Solution." *The Observer* (London). July 25, p. 1. Accessed at: www.guardian.co.uk/sudan/story/0,14658,1268773.00.html

De Waal, Alex (2004b). *Famine That Kills: Darfur, Sudan.* New York: Oxford University Press.

De Waal, Alex (2004c). "Tragedy in Darfur: On Understanding and Ending the Horror." *Boston Review: A Poltical and Literary Forum.* October/November, n.p. Accessed at boston-review.net/BR29.5/dewaal.html

Fadul, Abdul-Jabbar, and Tanner, Victor (2007). "Darfur After Abuja: A View from the Ground." In Alex de Waal (Ed.) *War in Darfur and the Search for Peace*, pp. 284–313. London and Cambridge, MA: Global Equity Initiative, Harvard University, and Justice Africa respectively.

Flint, Julie (2004). "A Year On, Darfur's Desapir Deepens." *The Daily Star* (Regional, Lebanon). December 30, p. 1. Accessed at: www.dailystar.com.lb/article.asp?edition_id=10&categ_id=5&article_id=11388

Flint, Julie, and De Waal, Alex (2005). *Darfur: A Short History of a Long War.* New York: Zed Books.

Fowler, Jerry (2006). "A New Chapter of Irony: The Legal Defintion of Genocide and the Implication of Powell's Determination." In Samuel Totten and Eric Markusen (Eds.) *Genocide in Darfur: Documenting Atrocities in the Sudan*, pp. 127–139. New York: Routledge.

Gettleman, Jeffrey (2007). "At the Darfur Talks in Libya, Rebel Unity Is as Scarce as the Rebels Themselves." *The New Times*, October 31, p. A6.

Global News Monitor (2004). "Genocide Emergency in the Darfur Region of Sudan." July 28, p. 2. http://www.preventgenocide.org

The Guardian (2006). "The Rape of Darfur. Special Reports." *Guardian Unlimited*, January 18, n.p. Accessible at: www.guardian.co.uk/sudan

Hoge, Warren (2007a). "U.N. Official Criticizes Sudan for Resisting Peace Force in Darfur." *The New York Times*, November 28, p. A5.

Hoge, Warren (2007b). "Lack of Donated Copters Harms Darfur Effort, U.N. Leader Says." *The New York Times*, December 7, p. A10.

Human Rights Watch (2002). "Biography of Hassan al Turabi." New York: Author. Accessed at: www.hrw.org/press/2002/03/turabi-bio.htm

Human Rights Watch (2004a). *Darfur Destroyed: Ethnic Cleansing by Government and Militia Forces in Western Sudan.* New York: Author. Accessed at: hrw.org/reports/2004/sudan0504/

Human Rights Watch (2004b). "Darfur Documents Confirm Government Policy of Militia Support: A Human Rights Watch Briefing Paper." New York: Author. July 20. Accessed at: hrw.org/English/docs/2004/07/19/darfur9096

Human Rights Watch (2004c). *Sudan: Government Commits "Ethnic Cleansing" in Darfur.* New York: Author.

Human Rights Watch (2007a). *Chaos by Design: Peacekeeping Challenges for AMIS and UNAMID.* New York: Author.

Human Rights Watch (2007b). "Q & A: Crisis in Darfur." New York: Author. Accessed at: www.hrw.org/english/docs/2004/05/05/darfur8536.htm

International Herald Tribune (2007). "Success Uncertain for New, U.N.-Sponsored Darfur Peace Talks." September 12. Accessed at www.iht.com/articles/ap/2007/09/12/africa/AF-GEN-Darfur-Peace-Talks.php

Kevane, Michael (2005). "Was the *Black Book* Correct? Regional Equality in Sudan." Santa Clara, CA: Santa Clara University, Department of Economics. Unpublished paper. Accessed at: understanding-sudan.org/darfur/Was%20the%black%book%correct.doc

Kinnock, Glenys (2006). "The Rape of Darfur." *Guardian Unlimited*, January 18. Accessed at: www.guardian.co.uk/sudan

Kostas, Stephen A. (2006). "Making the Determination of Genocide in Darfur." In Samuel Totten and Eric Markusen (Eds.) *Genocide in Darfur: Investigating Atrocities in the Sudan*, pp. 111–126. New York: Routledge.

Lumeya, Fidele (2004). *Rape, Islam, and Darfur's Women Refugees and War-Displaced.* Washington, D.C.: Refugees International. Accessed at: www.refugeesinternational.org/content/article

Mamdani, Mahmood (2004). "How Can We Name the Darfur Crisis? Some Preliminary Thoughts." *Black Commentary*, p. 2. Accessed at: www.neravt.com/left/pointers.html

Mamdani, Mahmood (2007). "The Politics of Naming: Genocide, Civil War, Insurgency." *London Review of Books*, March 8. Accessed at: www.wespac.org/WESPACCommunity/DiscussionMessages/tabid/124/forumid/7/postid/408

Malan, Mark (2007). "Africom: A Wolf in Sheep's Clothing?" Testimony Before the Subcommittee on African Affairs, Committee on Foreign Relations, U.S. Senate, August 1. Accessed at: www.senate.gov-foreign/testimoy/2007/MalanTestimony070801/pdf

Mariner, Joanne (2004). *Rape in Darfur.* FindLaw's Writ—Mariner: October 27. Accessed at: writ.news.-findlaw.com/mariner/20041027.html

Médecins Sans Frontières (2005). *The Crushing Burden of Rape and Sexual Violence in Darfur.* March 8. Paris: Author.

Médecins Sans Frontières (2005). "Persecution, Intimidation and Failure of Assistance in Darfur." *MSF Reports.* November 1. Paris: Author. Accessed at: www.msf.org/msfinternationa/invoke.cfm?objectid

Nathan, Laurie (2007). "The Making and Unmaking of the Darfur Peace Agreement." In Alex De Waal (Ed.) *War in Darfur: And the Search for Peace*, pp. 245–266. Cambridge, MA and London: Global Equity Initiative, Harvard University, and Justice Africa, respectively.

Newsweek (2007). "Dueling Over Darfur: A Human Rights Activist and an African Scholar Disagree—Vehemently—on the Best Way to Help Sudan." *Newsweek Web Exclusive*, November 8. Accessed at: www.newsweek.com/id/69004/output

Nieuwoudt, Stephanie (2006). "No Justice for Darfur Rape Victims." *Darfur Daily News.* October, n.p. Accessed at: iwpr.net/?p=acr&s=f&o=324842&apc_state=henpacr

Payne, Donald M. (2004). "Rep. Payne Urges Action at Congressional Black Caucus Press Conference on the Crisis in Darfur, Sudan"—Press Release, June 23, p. 1. Washington, D.C: U.S. Representative Donald M. Payne's Office.

Physicians for Human Rights (2006). *Assault on Survival: A Call for Security, Justice and Restitution.* Cambridge, MA: Author. Accessed at: physiciansforhumanrights.org/library/report-sudan-2006.html

Physicians for Human Rights (2005). *Destroyed Livelihoods: A Case Study of Furawiya Village, Darfur*. Cambridge, MA: Author. Accessed at: physiciansforhumanrights.org/sudan/news

Powell, Colin (2004). "Darfur." *Wall Street Journal*, August 5, p. 1.

Reeves, Eric (2007). "Darfur Betrayed Again: The UN/AU 'Hybrid' Force Steadily Weakens." August 24. Accessed at: www/sudanreeves/org/Article182.html

Reeves, Eric (2003). " 'Ethnic Cleansing' in Darfur: Systematic, Ethnically Based Denial of Humanitarian Aid Is No Context for a Sustainable Agreement in Sudan." SPLMToday.com, the official website of the SPLM/A, December 30, p. 1.

Refugees International (2007). *Laws Without Justice: An Assessment of Sudanese Laws Affecting Survivors of Rape*. Washington, D.C.

Stanton, Gregory H. (2006). "Proving Genocide in Darfur: The Atrocities Documentation Project and Resistance to Its Findings." In Samuel Totten and Eric Markusen (Eds.) *Genocide in Darfur: Investigating Atrocities in the Sudan*, pp. 181–188. New York: Routledge.

Sengupta, Somini (2004). "In Sudan, No Clear Difference Between Arab and African." *The New York Times, Week in Review*, October 3, p. 1. Accessed at: www.nytimes.com/2004/10/03/weekinreview/03seng

Srinivasan, Sharath (2006). *Minority Rights, Early Warning and Conflict Prevention: Lessons from Darfur*. London: Minority Rights Group International.

The Sudan Liberation Movement and Sudan Liberation Army (SLM/SLA) (2003). "Political Declaration." March 14. 4 pages. Accessed at: http://www.sudan.net/news/press/postedr/214.shtml

Sudan Tribune (2006). " 'Darfur Will be Foreign Troops' Graveyard'—Bashir." *Sudan Tribune*, February 27, p. 1. Accessed at: www.sudantribune.com/spip.ph?

Totten, Samuel (2006). "The U.S. Investigation into the Darfur Crisis and Its Determination of Genocide: An Analysis." In Samuel Totten and Eric Markusen (Eds.) *Genocide in Darfur: Investigating Atrocities in the Sudan*, pp. 199–222. New York: Routledge.

United Nations (2004). "Sudan: World's Worst Humanitarian Crisis"—Press Release, March 22. New York: Author, p. 2

United Nations Commission of Inquiry (2005). *UN Commission of Inquiry: Darfur Conflict*. New York: Author.

UN News Centre (2003). "As Refugees Pour into Chad from Sudan, UN Announces Plans for Safer Camps." *UN News Centre*. December 23. New York: United Nations. 2 pp.

U.S. State Department (September 9, 2004). *Documenting Atrocities in Darfur*. State Publication 11182. Washington, D.C.: Author. 4 pp.

Wax, Emily (2004). " 'We Want to Make a Light Baby': Arab Militiamen in Sudan Said to Use Rape as Weapon of Ethnic Cleansing." *The Washington Post*, June 20, pp. A01–02. Accessed at www.washingtonpost.com/wp-dyn/articles/A16001-2004Jun29.html

# 6

# Comparative Studies of Various Cases of Genocide

Comparative analysis is one of the most difficult scholarly pursuits in which to engage. Where the concept of genocide is concerned, this is especially true, owing to a multiplicity of case studies, languages, cultures, unique events, and variables that need to be taken into account if sense is to be made of the study being undertaken. One of the most significant questions that needs to be examined is just when a given situation might properly be considered genocide, and what general lessons can be derived from that appreciation.

Those seeking to understand genocide from a comparative perspective are required to undertake a variety of tasks in order to be successful. They must recognize and define the many different interpretations given to the term "genocide"; understand the text of the United Nations Convention on the Prevention and Punishment of the Crime of Genocide 1948 (UNCG); account for the historical development of the term since it was first coined in 1944; identify how the preconditions for the occurrence of genocide emerge; consider how it is that modern society has created a population of "surplus people," who form a target for entrenched interest groups committed to retaining a position of privilege; and, finally, appreciate the more important trends that have taken place in the development of the literature of genocide, which explains some of the reasons why scholars have come to differing interpretations when defining the term.

Accounting for genocide is not an easy task. We all think we have an understanding of what genocide means, but once one thinks long and hard about the term we find that it involves more than simply killing people. Moreover, comparative analysis of genocide shows that the phenomenon does not simply emerge out of nowhere. The violence required to achieve it might be sudden, but in every case there are always a number of preliminary steps on the road to a regime's ultimate "solution" of a "problem." Such steps invariably involve—prior to the introduction of the decisive stage of the target group's removal—processes of identification, alienation, isolation, and oppression. The twentieth century saw the continued development of such processes, processes that were refined by the Nazis and developed throughout the rest of the century, right up to the 1990s in the former Yugoslavia and Rwanda. In the twenty-first century the issue has been developed further, through the campaigns of the Government of Sudan (GoS) and the *Janjaweed* militia it supports, in the Darfur region of that country.

Comparative analysis provides researchers with other insights. We learn, for example, that all cases of genocide stem from a long-standing obsession on the part of the perpetrators with the physical, political, social, psychological, religious, or cultural differences of the victim group—differences ostensibly so great and irreconcilable that the perpetrators can see no other solution than elimination of the "other," by killing or some other means. In addition, comparative analysis can help to explain some of the ways in which conquered, occupied, and/or disempowered peoples have been exposed to genocidal forms of destruction, and what that means for contemporary society.

Through a close analysis of a range of case studies, we can look for patterns and similarities regarding a number of important issues relating to the very essence of humanity: the nature of evil, and how it can be explained; the limitations of language to explain it; the nature of power, and how it is used and abused; the implications for humanity and the international community of a society that violates civil and human rights; and the role and responsibilities of individuals, groups, and nations when confronting human rights violations and genocidal acts. Examining these issues can broaden our understanding of concepts that are the building blocks of responsible citizenship: concepts such as prejudice, discrimination, obedience, loyalty, conflict, and conflict resolution, decision making, justice, prevention, and survival. While these can all be explored *via* single case studies, the comparative approach brings such matters into much sharper relief, and is therefore an attractive tool for scholars seeking a closer understanding of the issues in question.

The study of genocide from a comparative perspective can best be explained as a multifactoral phenomenon, and this has to happen through considering a wide variety of motives, actions, and circumstances. In view of this, it must be borne in mind that there are, of course, a massive number of issues to be canvassed in any study if it is to be effective. Three can be considered briefly here, summarized as scope, language, and audience.

The first, "scope," concerns the impossibility of studying all cases of genocide. Even though reference can be made to numerous examples, clearly it is untenable to study everything, and it is thus vital that researchers have a solid understanding of why certain examples, studied in detail, have been chosen in preference to others. In this respect it is thus vital that there is an unambiguous appreciation of why certain victim groups are being studied, and not others—and to what end such study is undertaken. Scholars of comparative genocide must continually question why they are doing what that are doing, and sincerely attempt to maintain their focus once they have commenced their analysis.

The second issue to be discussed, "language," is also important when studying genocide from a comparative perspective. A succession of terrible events is not studied in isolation; these genocides are studied side by side in order to compare and contrast the role of the perpetrators, the collaborators, the bystanders, and those who either attempted to assist and protect the victims or to fight against the perpetrators. The victims, too, are studied, to inquire after their mechanisms of survival, their capacity (or incapacity) to withstand persecution, as well as the nature of that persecution. That said, comparative analysis of genocide should in no way be misconstrued as the study of relative suffering, where scholars balance the qualities and quantities of pain experienced by different peoples at different times. There can be no pecking order or hierarchy of suffering among victim peoples; rather, comparative analysis looks at relative similarities and differences between genocides, with regard to their antecedents, early warning signals, processes, the actions and reactions of the actors involved, and the response (or lack of response) of the international community, among many other variables. No more disastrous or sordid situation can occur than if perceptions of comparative suffering only serve to pit one injured people against another.

This leads directly to a third issue, that of "audience." There is a certain numbing that can take place when confronted by massive numbers of death statistics. How can scholars, perhaps accustomed to studying a single case of genocide, get behind the horror of one in order to expand their field of interest to two or more genocides? Another issue that needs to be borne in mind is that those studying the phenomenon of genocide are only human themselves; much of what they see in these hideous outbreaks of anti-human behavior is utterly distasteful, sickening, and depressing. How does one get around such things?

The study of genocide is more than just the study of acts of brutality and mass killing, and as a consequence such study has to be more than a vehicle for observing horror personified. Looking at genocidal outcomes should be only one part of the task; comparative analysis also enables scholars to explore in considerable depth the *process* of destruction, and what can be done to stop it. Miss this, and we miss the enormity of what genocide actually is, how it occurs, and how to recognize its early warning signs. Along the way, scholars of genocide must of necessity be exposed to images of the violence perpetrated in those truly genocidal situations, lest perspective be lost with a consequent failure to see the fundamental differences between genocidal killings and other forms of persecution. Comparative analysis enables scholars to discern, for example, the difference between a genocidal *society* and a genocidal *regime*, and arrange such reflections within a framework that is both historical and truly comparative. When all is said and done, genocide is all about devaluing people to the point where either their continued existence is regarded as being of no consequence or they are actively destroyed, and comparative analysis, in the view of many, is one of the best ways to seek an understanding of why this human phenomenon takes place.

Among the numerous efforts of genocide scholars to achieve worthwhile comparative analysis, a number are noteworthy and are reproduced in the current collection. Taking the theme of revolution and genocide, for instance, the scholar who has done the most in this area, Robert F. Melson, looks at the case study of the Armenian Genocide of 1915–1923 as a precursor to other genocides that followed in the twentieth century. In his chapter "The Armenian Genocide as Precursor and Prototype of Twentieth-Century Genocide," Melson writes about how revolution and war have served, in various situations, as key factors in creating contexts that lend themselves to the creation of genocidal policies in order to create a new society. In doing so, he highlights a number of ways in which the revolutionary situation in the Ottoman Empire in the first decades of the twentieth century provided a model of sorts as to how, later in time and in other countries, violent conflict degenerated into genocide. One of the important qualifications he makes, however, is that the Armenian Genocide, while a precursor to later genocides such as the Holocaust, was not an archetype; comparative analysis, he rightly points out, does not provide exact templates.

Ben Kiernan, in an excellent summary of the subject ("Twentieth Century Genocides: Underlying Ideological Themes from Armenia to East Timor"), takes comparative analysis into a different realm—that of motive. Considering such issues as race, religion, physical expansion, and what he calls "cultivation"—that is, social engineering according to a dogmatic program—Kiernan shows that their radicalization and combination can create environments favorable to genocidal eruptions. In a wide-ranging discussion that takes in almost the entire twentieth century, Kiernan's essay is a masterful example of comparative analysis at its finest. Painting with very broad brush-strokes, he concludes that race, religion, expansion, and cultivation, taken singly, can often be benign; but that the historical record shows that when combined they can produce deadly results.

A final example of comparative analysis in the current collection is an essay by Mark Levene. In his "Connecting Threads: Rwanda, the Holocaust, and the Pattern of Contemporary Genocide," he examines both the Holocaust and the Rwandan Genocide in order to draw general conclusions about the nature of mass killing. His attempt, like those of Kiernan and Melson, is based on a comprehensive discussion of a number of themes relating to more than a single genocide; in fact, he introduces additional cases beyond his two major examples in order to illustrate the general points he seeks to make. Through comparative analysis, he is able to draw a conclusion essential to all comparative studies of genocide: namely, that genocide is the most direct consequence of a regime's pursuit of social and/or racial perfection—the ultimate expression of perverted science and thought.

## 6.1   Robert F. Melson, "The Armenian Genocide as Precursor and Prototype of Twentieth-Century Genocide"

### Twentieth-Century Genocide

During this century, the world has experienced four tidal waves of national and ethnic conflict and genocide in the wake of collapsing states and empires. These were punctuated by the First and Second World Wars and by the postcolonial and post-Communist eras. During the First World War and its aftermath the Ottoman empire collapsed, and it committed the first total genocide of the twentieth century against its Armenian minority.[1] In the same period, the disintegration of the German and Austro-Hungarian empires set off *Volkisch*, nationalist and fascist movements that repressed minorities and precipitated the Second World War. In the context of that war, the Nazis attempted to exterminate the Jews and Gypsies and committed partial genocide against other peoples. Following the Second World War, as former European colonial empires—notably Britain and France—withdrew from their possessions, they left behind fragile regimes that lacked legitimacy. Such "Third World" governments frequently ruled over culturally plural societies and tried to impose the hegemony of one ethnic group over the rest. In reaction, minorities rebelled and sought self-determination. This led to ethnic wars and genocide in places like Indonesia, Burundi, Sri Lanka, Nigeria, Pakistan, Ethiopia, Sudan, and Iraq. In the wake of the recent collapse of Communist regimes in the Soviet Union and former Yugoslavia, we are experiencing the fourth wave of nationalist upsurge, ethnic conflicts, and genocide. Meanwhile, as in contemporary Rwanda, it should be noted that the third wave of postcolonial genocide has not yet spent its force.

This chapter puts forth the position that the Armenian genocide was not only the first total genocide of the twentieth century but that it also served as the prototype for genocides that came after. In particular, the Armenian genocide approximates the Holocaust; but at the same time its territorial and national aspects, which distinguish it from the Holocaust, make it an archetype for ethnic and national genocides in the Third World, as well as in the post-Communist states.

This chapter offers a brief historical overview of the Armenian genocide, then compares that event first to the Holocaust and also to the Nigerian and Yugoslav genocides. The second set of cases represents contemporary instances of genocide in the Third World and the post-Communist states, respectively. The chapter concludes by raising a number of questions about the Armenian genocide and about genocide in general.

### The Armenian Genocide

In traditional Ottoman society, Armenians—like other Christians and Jews—were defined as a *dhimmi millet*, a non-Muslim religious community of the empire. Their actual treatment by the state varied to some extent with the military fortunes of the empire, with the religious passions of its elites, and with the encroachment upon their land of Muslim refugees from the Balkans and the Caucasus and of Kurdish pastoralists.

Although by and large *dhimmis* (religious minorities) were free to practice their religion, they were considered to be distinctively inferior in status to Muslims.[2] However, in the nineteenth century, the Armenians challenged the traditional hierarchy of Ottoman society as they became better educated, wealthier, and more urban. In response, despite attempts at reforms, the empire became more repressive, and Armenians, more than any other Christian minority, bore the brunt of persecution.[3]

Throughout the nineteenth century, the Ottoman sultans were caught in the vise between great power pressures on the one hand and the demand for self-determination among their minorities on the other. By the time Abdul Hamid II came to power in 1876, he had set a course of political and social repression and technological modernization. Nevertheless, he could not halt the military and political disintegration of his regime, and he was replaced in 1908 by a political revolution of Young Turks with new and radical ideas of how to address the Ottoman crisis.

In the first instance, the Committee of Union and Progress (CUP), the political organization formed by the Young Turks, attempted radically to transform the regime following liberal and democratic principles that had been embodied in the earlier constitution of 1876. They hoped for the support of the Great Powers for their reforms, but neither the European powers nor the minorities reduced their pressures. On the contrary, they took the opportunity of internal Ottoman disarray and revolutionary transformation to press their demands, and between 1908 and 1912 they succeeded in reducing the size of Ottoman territory by 40 percent and its population by 20 percent.[4]

Concluding that their liberal experiment had been a failure, CUP leaders turned to Pan-Turkism, a xenophobic and chauvinistic brand of nationalism that sought to create a new empire based on Islam and Turkish ethnicity. This new empire, stretching from Anatolia to western China, would exclude minorities or grant them nominal rights unless they became Turks by nationality and Muslim by religion.

This dramatic shift in ideology and identity, from Ottoman pluralism to an integral form of Turkish nationalism, had profound implications for the emergence of modern Turkey.[5] At the same time, Pan-Turkism had tragic consequences for Ottoman minorities, most of all for the Armenians. From being once viewed as a constituent *millet* of the Ottoman regime, they suddenly were stereotyped as an alien nationality. Their situation became especially dangerous because of their territorial concentration in eastern Anatolia on the border with Russia, Turkey's traditional enemy. Thus, the Armenians, at one and the same time, were accused of being in league with Russia against Turkey and of claiming Anatolia, the heartland of the projected Pan-Turkic state.

This was the situation even before the First World War. When war broke out, however, the Young Turks, led by Talaat Pasha, the minister of interior, and Enver Pasha, the minister of war, joined the German side in an anti-Russian alliance that would allow Turkey to expand at Russia's expense. It was in this context of revolutionary and ideological transformation and war that the fateful decision to destroy the Armenians was taken.

By February 1915, Armenians serving in the Ottoman army were turned into labor battalions and were either worked to death or killed. By April, the remaining civilians were deported from eastern Anatolia and Cilicia toward the deserts near Aleppo in an early form of ethnic cleansing. The lines of Armenian deportees were set upon again and again by Turkish and Kurdish villagers who were often incited and led by specially designated killing squads, *Teshkilat-i Makhsusiye*. These units had been organized for their murderous purposes at the highest levels of the CUP.[6] Those Armenians who escaped massacre were very likely to perish of famine on the way. In this manner, between 1915 and the armistice in 1918, some 1 million people—out of a population of 2 million—were killed. Later, a half-million more Armenians perished as Turkey sought to free itself of foreign occupation and to expel minorities. Thus, between 1915 and 1923 approximately one-half to three-quarters of the Armenian population was destroyed in the Ottoman empire.

## The Armenian Genocide and the Holocaust

The Armenian genocide and the Holocaust are the principal instances of total domestic genocide in the twentieth century. In both cases, a deliberate attempt was made by the government of the day to destroy in whole an ethno-religious community of ancient provenance. When one compares the situation and history of the Armenians in the Ottoman empire to the Jews in Europe, a pattern leading to genocide becomes apparent. It is a pattern that also reveals some significant differences, and it is those differences that link the Armenian genocide not only to the Holocaust but to contemporary instances of that crime. Let us first consider the similarities between the Armenian genocide and the Holocaust:

1. Under the prerevolutionary regimes in the Ottoman empire and Germany, Armenians and Jews were ethno-religious minorities of inferior status that had experienced rapid social progress and mobilization in the nineteenth century. These circumstances helped to create what came to be known as the "Armenian question" and the "Jewish problem." Armenians raised a "question" and Jews created a "problem," because neither the Muslim Ottoman empire nor Christian Europe were prepared to deal with low-status religious minorities that had become increasingly assertive and successful in the modern world.

2. Under the prerevolutionary regimes, Armenians may have suffered massacres, and Jews may have experienced discrimination in Germany as well as pogroms in Russia; but in none of these cases was a policy of total destruction formulated or implemented to resolve "questions" or to solve "problems." Genocide followed in the wake of revolutions in the Ottoman empire and Germany.

3. Following the reversals of 1908–1912, the CUP rejected Pan-Islam and Ottomanism as legitimating ideologies linking state to society and turned to Turkish nationalism and Pan-Turkism. The CUP identified the Turkish ethnic group as the authentic political community on which the Turkish state could and should rely, and by implication it excluded the Armenians from the Turkish nation.

   The Armenians were in danger of being conceived as enemies of Turkey and of the Turkish revolution once Ottoman Turks came to view themselves not in religious terms but in ethnic terms. What made the Armenian situation significantly more dangerous than that of other minorities was the Armenian *millet*'s concentration in eastern Anatolia, an area that Turkish nationalists claimed to be the heartland of the Turkish nation. Moreover, the eastern *vilayets* (provinces) of Anatolia were on the Russian border, Turkey's traditional enemy, casting the Armenian presence in a sinister light.

   In a similar fashion, a revolutionary situation in Germany allowed the Nazis to recast German identity and ideology. The German revolution destroyed the Weimar Republic, undermined democratic and socialist conceptions of legitimacy, and enabled the Nazis to come to power. Once the Nazis controlled the apparatus of the state, they set about recasting German political identity in terms of their racial and antisemitic ideology. They did this by excluding and expelling those whom they defined as "non-Aryans" and "Jews" from the newly valued and invented "Aryan" community.

4. When the First World War broke out, the CUP enthusiastically joined the Ottoman empire to the Germans against the Russians. This permitted Talaat and Enver to claim that the internal Armenian enemy was in league with the external Russian foe. Wartime circumstances then were used to justify the deportation and destruction of the Armenian community.

Similarly, the Nazis launched the Second World War in order to carve out an empire for

Germany, and it was under wartime circumstances that they implemented their policies of partial genocide against Poles, Russians, and others and their extermination against the Jews. In particular, they viewed the Soviet Union as their principal foreign foe, and they assumed that it was ruled by a "world Jewish conspiracy." Thus, in 1941, at the same time that they invaded the Soviet Union, they launched the "Final Solution."

Thus did ideological vanguards use the opportunities created by revolution and war to destroy ancient communities that had been judged to be "problematic" under the prerevolutionary regimes and "enemies" under revolutionary and wartime circumstances. These elements—the prerevolutionary statuses of the victims and revolutionary and wartime circumstances—may be said to account for some of the essential similarities between the two genocides. There were, however, significant differences as well.

The perpetrators of the Armenian genocide were motivated by a variant of nationalist ideology, the victims were a territorial ethnic group that had sought autonomy, and the methods of destruction included massacre, forced deportation, and starvation. In contrast, the perpetrators of the Holocaust were motivated by racism and antisemitism and ideologies of global scope; the victims were not a territorial group, and so, for the most part, they had sought integration and assimilation instead of autonomy, and the death camp was the characteristic method of destruction. A word needs to be said about these factors that differentiate the Armenian genocide from the Holocaust. It will be shown, however, that it is precisely these differences that link the Armenian genocide to contemporary events.

## Differences Between the Armenian Genocide and the Holocaust

Like these similarities, the differences between the Armenian genocide and the Holocaust may be plotted along the same dimensions: Jews and Armenians differed in status in the two empires; Nazi racist antisemitism differed significantly from the Pan-Turkist nationalism of the Young Turks; and the killers of the Armenians relied mostly on massacre and starvation rather than the death camps.

Like the Armenians in the Ottoman empire, the Jews were an ethno-religious community of low status in Christian Europe. Unlike the Armenians, however, who were the subject of contempt for being non-Muslims, the Jews of feudal Europe became a pariah caste stigmatized as "killers of the Son of God." Thus, Jews were not only despised in most parts of Europe, they were also hated and feared in a way the Armenians in the Ottoman empire were not.

In the nineteenth century, to the extent that the state became bureaucratic, the society meritocratic, and the economy capitalistic, Armenians and Jews began to advance in status and wealth. Indeed, it has been suggested that Armenian and Jewish progress was viewed as illegitimate and subversive, which precipitated antagonistic reactions both in the Ottoman empire and in imperial Germany.[7]

Here at least two variations may be noted. Whereas Armenians were a territorial group that increasingly made known its demands for greater autonomy and self-administration within the Ottoman system, Jews were geographically dispersed and thus, with the exception of the Zionists who sought a Jewish state in Palestine, most made no territorial demands on the larger societies in which they lived.[8] Instead, to the extent that they accepted the modern world, most Jews sought assimilation to the culture and integration into the wider society.

The reaction against Jewish progress, assimilation, and attempts at integration became a wide movement of European antisemitism, a form of racism that set up unbridgeable obstacles to Jewish inclusion. According to antisemites, Eugen Dühring, for example, not even conversion would allow Jews to become the equals of Germans or other Europeans. Already in 1881, he wrote:

A Jewish question would still exist, even if every Jew were to turn his back on his religion and join one of our major churches. Yes, I maintain that in that case, the struggle between us and the Jews would make itself felt as ever more urgent ... It is precisely the baptized Jews who infiltrate furthest, unhindered in all sectors of society and political life.[9]

According to Wilhelm Marr (another nineteenth-century antisemite), for example, Jews were not only an alien race, they constituted an international conspiracy whose aim was the domination of Germany, Europe, indeed, the whole world. Thus, antisemites founded not only a movement that opposed Jewish progress and assimilation, they formulated a far-reaching ideology that helped them to explain the vacillations and crises of the modern world. It was an ideology that came to rival liberalism and socialism in its mass appeal.

By way of contrast, no such ideology of anti-Armenianism developed in the Ottoman empire. Armenians may have been popularly despised for being *dhimmis*, or *Gavur* (infidels), and later, under the Young Turks, they may have been feared as an alien nation supposedly making claims to Anatolia, the heartland of the newly valued "Turkey." However, even Pan-Turkism left the door open to conversion and assimilation of minorities, something that racism and antisemitism explicitly rejected.

Moreover, though the Young Turks may have claimed that the Armenians were in league with their international enemies, especially the Russians, there was no equivalent in the Pan-Turkish view of the Armenians to the Nazis' hysterical struggle against the "Jewish spirit" that was said to linger in Germany and Europe even after most of the Jews had been murdered. Saul Friedländer has noted:

> It was the absolutely uncompromising aspect of the exterminatory drive against the Jews, as well as the frantic extirpation of any elements actually or supposedly linked to the Jews or to the "Jewish Spirit" ... which fundamentally distinguished the anti-Jewish actions of the Nazis from their attitude toward another group.[10]

Thus, the Holocaust became centered not only in Germany but evolved into an international policy of mass murder and cultural destruction that included Europe and even the whole world. Finally, the death camp, a conception of the Nazi state, was an extraordinary organization, not seen before or since. It was a factory managed by the SS but staffed at all levels by the inmates themselves. Its primary aim was to dehumanize and kill its prisoners after confiscating their property and making use of their labor. Although Jews, like Armenians, perished in massacres and by starvation, the use of the death camp as a method of extermination differentiates the Holocaust from the Armenian genocide.

At the same time that these differences—the nationalist ideology of the perpetrators, the territoriality of the victims, and the methodology of destruction, especially expulsion and starvation—differentiate the Armenian genocide from the Holocaust, they link that earlier genocide to contemporary destructions in the Third World and in the post-Communist states. In that sense, as has already been noted, the Armenian genocide predates and partly encompasses both kinds of genocide and is, thereby, a prototype for genocide in our time. We now turn to an examination of the Nigerian and Yugoslav genocides and to their comparison to the Armenian prototype.

## Nigeria

Genocide has been committed throughout the Third World. Following are a few examples: Indonesia, Burundi, Rwanda, Sudan, East Pakistan, and Iraq. In all of these instances, a shaky and hardly legitimate postcolonial state ruling over a culturally plural society attempted to establish the hegemony of a leading ethnic group over other ethnic segments of society. This attempt at domination provoked movements of resistance and self-determination, which the postcolonial state then tried to halt by force, including massacre and partial genocide.

Nigeria gained its independence from Great Britain in 1960. It was organized as a federation of three states, each centering on a major ethnic group. The northern state was dominated by the Hausa-Fulani, the western by the Yoruba, and the eastern by the Ibos. The major ethnic groups jockeyed for power at the federal level, but each had its "minorities" that felt discriminated against at the state level of the federation. The postindependence government, dominated by Hausa-Fulani Muslims, was resisted by southern, largely non-Muslim groups, especially the Ibos. In 1966, after a failed military coup, thousands of Ibos were massacred in northern Nigeria. In 1967, a year after the massacres, the Ibos tried to secede. They called eastern Nigeria "Biafra" and fought a war of self-determination until 1970, when their secession attempt collapsed.

During the war, over 1 million Biafrans starved to death as a result of the deliberate Nigerian policy of blockade and disruption of agricultural life. Thus, between 1966 and 1970, a "genocide-in-part" occurred in Nigeria, following the United Nations (UN) definition. It is important, however, to recall that what happened in Biafra differed from the Holocaust and the Armenian genocide in that the policies of the Nigerian Federal Military Government (FGM) did not include extermination of the Ibos.

## Yugoslavia

A definitive history of the recent conflict in former Yugoslavia does not yet exist, but it is possible to render a provisional sketch. The Yugoslav disaster stems from the failure of the Communist regime to establish legitimate political institutions, a viable economy, and a compelling political culture. After Marshal Tito's death in 1980, ethnically based nationalist movements started to mobilize and to demand greater autonomy if not yet self-determination. The process of dissolution and disintegration was drastically accelerated with the rise of Slobodan Milosevic, who articulated an integral form of Serbian nationalism and irredentism that called for the creation of a Yugoslavia dominated by Serbia such as had existed after the First World War. This frightened the other nationalities and encouraged intransigent elements.

Milosevic's integral Serbian nationalism, in a context of Yugoslav and Communist institutional decay and insecurity, helped to sharpen ethnic enmities, strengthen centrifugal forces throughout the federation, and accelerate the processes of disintegration. Thus, on September 27, 1989, the parliament of Slovenia adopted amendments to its constitution giving the republic the right to secede from Yugoslavia. Thousands of Serbs demonstrated in Novi Sad, fearing for their status in an independent Slovenia. On July 3, 1990, the Slovenian parliament declared that the laws of the republic took precedence over those of Yugoslavia; on December 22, 1990, Slovenia reported that 95 percent of the voters supported a plebiscite on independence; and on June 25, 1991, Slovenia declared its independence from Yugoslavia.

A similar march of events occurred in Croatia, which declared its independence on the same day. The big difference between Slovenia and Croatia, however, was the presence of a large Serbian minority in the latter. Moreover, no sooner was independence declared in Croatia than the Franjo Tudjman regime launched an anti-Serb campaign that would have alarmed the Serbs, even if nationalist elements among them had not been earlier mobilized by Milosevic. Now that their kin were being threatened in Croatia, Milosevic and other Serbian nationalists could call forth the terrible history of the Ustasha genocide of the Second World War to mobilize the Serbs against Croatian independence and in support of Serbian irredenta.

After June 25, 1991, when Slovenia and Croatia, in declaring their independence, thereby created Serbian minorities—especially in Croatia—the Serb radicals, using the cover of the Yugoslav army, launched an attack intended to incorporate Serbian-populated Croatian territory. To this end, Serbian forces not only initiated hostilities but set out on a path of terrorism and massacre in order to drive Croats out of areas that they desired to incorporate into Greater Serbia.

This policy of terrorism and ethnic cleansing accelerated with even greater ferocity against Bosnia when it declared independence on March 3, 1992. Indeed, in time, both Serb and Croat forces descended on Bosnia with the clear intention of carving up and destroying a state that initially had tried to stand aside from ethnic nationalism and had opted for a pluralist society. However, both Serb and Croat nationalists were intent on either carving up and destroying Bosnia or making it a rump state that would in time collapse. To this end, the Bosnian Serbs, led by their leader, Radovan Karadzic, a psychiatrist of Montenegrin origin, especially practiced massacre, ethnic cleansing, and cultural destruction against those they called the "Turks." Taken together, such policies of destruction on a wide scale are called genocide.[11]

Keeping Nigeria and Yugoslavia in mind, it is also important to note the great fear and insecurity that possess everyone when a government is challenged and a state begins to disintegrate. This great fear, especially in culturally plural societies, leads people to seek the shelter of families and kin and persuades various groups to band together for protection and to view one another as potential enemies.

Indeed, before a culturally plural state like Nigeria or Yugoslavia disintegrates, its politics may revolve about various ethnic issues of group status and the distribution of scarce goods; but once a state crashes, for whatever reasons, ethnic groups begin to fear for their lives, as well they should. Once a political order disintegrates, who can guarantee an ethnic group that its mortal enemies won't come to power and try to dominate it or even destroy it? It is this great fear that has seized all the groups in Yugoslavia, including those Serbs who are the main perpetrators of partial genocide.

## The Armenian and Nigerian Genocides

In both the Nigerian and Bosnian cases, we can see some parallels to the Armenian genocide. A dominant ethnic group in a culturally plural society attempted to establish its hegemony. It was resisted by minorities that attempted to gain some form of autonomy or self-determination. In reaction, the dominant group perpetrated repression and genocide. Yet there are significant differences that may be even more instructive.

The crucial difference between a total domestic genocide, as occurred in the Armenian case, and a partial one, as occurred in Nigeria, can also be seen by comparing the two. Unlike the Armenians, once Biafra was defeated and the danger of secession passed, the Ibos were not massacred or further expelled from Nigeria. On the contrary, there was a genuine attempt to reintegrate the Ibo population into Nigeria when the war ended.

This difference may be due to two reasons. First, although the FGM was dominated by Hausa-Fulani elements, it included minorities in its leadership; indeed, General Yakubu Gowon, its commander, was a Christian from the north. Thus, the FGM never developed an ideology of "northernization" or "Muslimization" the way the Young Turks relied on Turkification and sought to create an ethnically homogeneous Turkey.

Second, the territorial issue, a crucial element in the Armenian case, was present in the Biafran case, but it worked in favor of the Ibos. The Ibos of the north were "strangers" and not "sons of the soil"; thus, they could not make a legitimate claim to northern territory.[12] Moreover, it is significant that the Ibos had their own area, which, except for its oil, the north did not covet. Once the Ibos were driven from the north back into their space and the Biafran secession was defeated, the northern elements in the army and elsewhere had succeeded in their major aims. Further massacre and starvation of the Ibos was unnecessary for ideological, territorial, or any other reasons, and the partial genocide ceased.

The Biafran state was never claimed as the "homeland" of the Hausa-Fulani in the manner that Anatolia had been staked out by the Turks. Thus, a federal solution to ethnic conflict could be implemented in Nigeria the way it could not in the Ottoman empire. The Armenians could not be driven back to "their" lands, since their lands were claimed to be the heartland of Turkey. Indeed, it may be suggested that this Turkish claim to Armenian lands was a major reason why the Armenian genocide, unlike the mass death of Biafra, became total in the manner of the Holocaust.

## The Armenian and Bosnian Genocides

Two major similarities between the Armenian genocide and the partial genocide occurring in Bosnia should be apparent. Like the Young Turks, the Serbian—and to some extent the Croat—nationalists are also dreaming of a large state that would include their peoples and exclude other ethnic and national groups. Like the Armenians, the Bosnian Muslims, an ethno-religious community making claims to land, were being massacred and driven out by Serb and Croat nationalist movements that sought to incorporate their lands, "cleanse" the area of their presence, and destroy their culture.[13]

However, the status of Bosnia as an independent state recognized by the international community marks a significant difference between the situations of Ibos in Nigeria and of Armenians in the Ottoman empire. Neither Armenians nor Biafrans were widely recognized as members of independent states while their destructions were in process.[14]

Armenians were largely abandoned to their fate, in part because the genocide occurred in the midst of a world war. During the cold war, both the Eastern and Western blocs discouraged movements of self-determination, fearing superpower involvement; and the African states did the same, fearing their own disintegration along ethnic lines. This may explain, in part, why Ibos, like Armenians, were also abandoned, except for some humanitarian relief.

That "partial" and not "total" genocide occurred in Bosnia, unlike Armenia, should be very cold comfort for the world community. Eighty years after the Armenian genocide and fifty years after the Holocaust, a European state practiced genocide while Europe, the United States, and the United Nations seemed unable or unwilling to halt the slaughter. If genocide cannot be halted in Europe, it cannot be stopped or prevented anywhere else, certainly not in places like Rwanda or Burundi. This, then, is the "New World Order" we face as we stand at the threshold of the third millennium.

## Conclusion

The Armenian genocide was a precursor and prototype for the Holocaust in that a minority of traditionally low status that had successfully begun to enter the modern world was set upon and nearly destroyed in the context of revolution and war. However, the Holocaust was not an identical replay of the Armenian genocide. The Armenian case differed from the Holocaust in three dimensions: First, the Young Turks were largely motivated by an ideology of nationalism, whereas the Nazis were moved by an ideology heavily influenced by social Darwinism and racism. Second, the Armenians were a territorial group concentrated in the eastern *vilayets* of the empire, and they had historical claims to the land. In contrast, the Jews were not a territorial group. To destroy the Jews, the Nazis had to formulate a policy of genocide that transcended Germany and even Europe. Lastly, the method of destruction of the Armenians centered on their deportation, shooting, and starvation, whereas in the Holocaust the majority of Nazi victims perished in death camps. This is not to deny that a large percentage of Nazi victims also perished by shootings and starvation in the manner of their Armenian predecessors.

It should be noted, however, that it is precisely these differences that enable the Armenian genocide to be a precursor and prototype for contemporary genocide. Indeed, one conclusion we can draw from this analysis is that the Armenian genocide is a more accurate archetype than is the Holocaust for current mass murders in the postcolonial Third World and in the contemporary post-Communist world. In Nigeria and Yugoslavia, for example, as in the Armenian case and unlike the Holocaust, the perpetrators were driven by a variant of nationalism, the victims were territorial ethnic groups aiming at some form of autonomy or self-determination, and the methods of destruction involved massacre and starvation.

I have tried to show that the Armenian genocide was a precursor and prototype both for the Holocaust and for contemporary nationalist genocides. In no case was it an exact template for later genocides, nor were these duplicates of the Armenian case; nevertheless, the Armenian pattern of destruction set a terrible precedent for our century and for the future.

## Notes

This chapter was first delivered as a paper at "The Armenian Genocide: An Eighty Year Perspective, 1915–1995," a conference held at the University of California–Los Angeles, April 7–8, 1995. An earlier version of this paper was presented at "Remembering for the Future International Conference on the Holocaust," held at Berlin, Germany, March 13–17, 1994.

1. On the basis of the United Nations definition, it is possible to distinguish between "genocide-in-whole" and "genocide-in-part." In this chapter, a "total domestic genocide" is a genocide-in-whole directed against a group of a state's own society, whereas "partial" genocide is a genocide-in-part. Total genocide implies extermination and/or massive death of such order that a group ceases to continue as a distinct culture and collectivity. Partial genocide stops at extermination and the annihilation of culture. For further discussion concerning these distinctions, see Robert F. Melson, *Revolution and Genocide: On the Origins of the Armenian Genocide and the Holocaust* (Chicago: University of Chicago Press, 1992), pp. 22–30.

2. See Roderic H. Davison, "Turkish Attitudes Concerning Christian-Muslim Equality in the Nineteenth Century," *American Historical Review* 4 (1954):844–864.

3. See Melson, *Revolution and Genocide*, pp. 43–69.

4. See Feroz Ahmad, *The Young Turks* (Oxford: Clarendon Press, 1969), p. 153.

5. See Bernard Lewis, *The Emergence of Modern Turkey* (New York: Oxford University Press, 1961).

6. See Vahakn N. Dadrian, "Genocide as a Problem of National and International Law: The World War I Armenian Case and Its Contemporary Legal Ramifications," *Yale Journal of International Law* 2 (Summer 1989):221–334.

7. See Melson, *Revolution and Genocide*, p. 137.

8. For discussions of the ideological crosscurrents that affected Jews in this period, see Jonathan Frankel, *Prophesy and Politics: Socialism, Nationalism, and the Russian Jews, 1862–1917* (Cambridge: Cambridge University Press, 1981), and Ezra Mendelsohn, *The Jews of East Central Europe Between the World Wars* (Bloomington: Indiana University Press, 1983).

9. Cited in Paul R. Mendes-Flohr and Jehuda Reinharz, *The Jews in the Modern World: A Documentary History* (New York: Oxford University Press, 1980), p. 273.

10. See Saul Friedlander, "On the Possibility of the Holocaust: An Approach to a Historical Synthesis," in *The Holocaust as Historical Experience*, ed. Yehuda Bauer and Nathan Rotenstreich (New York: Holmes and Meier, 1981), p. 2.

11. According to a Helsinki Watch *Report*, genocide is taking place in Bosnia and other former areas of Yugoslavia. Although all sides have been accused of atrocities, it is the Serbian side, especially in Bosnia, that is charged with genocide. See *War Crimes in Bosnia-Hercegovina* (New York: Human Rights Watch, 1992), p. 1.

12. See Donald L. Horowitz, *Ethnic Groups in Conflict* (Berkeley: University of California Press, 1985), for discussions of how groups validate their claims to status and power. A basic distinction lies between those who have historically dominated an area and migrants who are new arrivals. The first, the "sons-of-the-soil," make their claims on the basis of ancestral privilege; the second cannot. Thus, Armenians in Anatolia could make a claim to the land, the way Ibos in the north could not.

13. As of this writing (January 1996), Bosnian Muslims and Croats are part of a shaky confederation. In the recent past, however, Croat and Bosnian Croat troops, like their Serbian counterparts, were

equally intent on dismembering Bosnia and expelling Muslim populations from territories they claimed for Croatia.

14. See Richard G. Hovannisian, *Armenia on the Road to Independence* (Berkeley: University of California Press, 1967), and John J. Stremlau, *The International Politics of the Nigerian Civil War* (Princeton: Princeton University Press, 1977).

## 6.2   Ben Kiernan, "Twentieth-Century Genocides: Underlying Ideological Themes from Armenia to East Timor"

The perpetrators of the 1915 Armenian genocide, the Holocaust during World War II, and the Cambodian genocide of 1975–79 were, respectively, militarists, Nazis, and communists. All three events were unique in important ways. Yet racism—Turkish, German, and Khmer—was a key component of the ideology of each regime. Racism was also conflated with religion. Although all three regimes were atheistic, each particularly targeted religious minorities (Christians, Jews, and Muslims). All three regimes also attempted to expand their territories into a contiguous heartland ("Turkestan," "Lebensraum," and "Kampuchea Krom"), mobilizing primordial racial rights and connections to the land. Consistent with this, all three regimes idealized their ethnic peasantry as the true "national" class, the ethnic soil from which the new state grew.

These ideological elements—race, religion, expansion, and cultivation—make an explosive mixture. Most also appear, in different colors and compounds, in the chemistry of other cases of genocide, including the Indonesian massacres of Communists in 1965–66 and in East Timor from 1975 to 1999, and also in the Bosnian and Rwandan genocides of the early 1990s.

### Religion and Race

In colonial genocides, racial divisions are usually clear-cut, overriding even religious fraternity. The first genocide of the twentieth century pitted the German military machine against the Herero and Nama peoples of South West Africa, whose leaders were mostly Christian-educated.[1] Two days after issuing his 1904 "extermination order" against the Herero, General Lothar von Trotha wrote to the Berlin General Staff: "My knowledge of many central African peoples, Bantu and others, convinces me that the Negro will never submit to a treaty but only to naked force. . . . This uprising is and remains the beginning of a racial war."[2]

In other cases, race and religion have played important, intertwined roles. The Young Turk ideologue Yusuf Akçura asserted in 1904 that "the Turks within the Ottoman realms would unify quite tightly with both religious and racial bonds—more tightly than with just religious ones." He added: "The great majority of those Turks whose union is possible are Muslim. . . . Islam could be an important element in the formation of a great Turkish nationality." But because "the general trend of our era involves races," for Islam "to perform this service in the unification of Turks it must change in a manner that accepts the emergence of nations within it. . . . Therefore, it is only through the union of religions, with race, and through religions as buttressing and even serving ethnic groups, that they can preserve their political and societal importance." Akçura rejected multinational Ottomanism and argued that Pan-Islamism "would split into Turkish and non-Turkish components." Looking to "a world of Turkishness," Akçura praised "the brotherhood born of race."[3] The Armenian genocide, which coincided with Turkish massacres of Greeks, can be portrayed in part as an attempt to eliminate Christian non-Turks from a newly defined Turkish Muslim nation, but the racial element is significant.

Pol Pot's Cambodia perpetrated genocide against several ethnic groups, systematically dispersed national minorities by force, and forbade the use of minority and foreign languages.[4] It also banned the practice of religion. The Khmer Rouge repressed Islam, Christianity, and Buddhism, but its fiercest extermination campaign was directed at the ethnic Cham Muslim minority.[5]

In the German case, Saul Friedlander argues, antisemitism "gives Nazism its *sui generis* character . . . the Jewish problem was at the center, the very essence of the system."[6] In the words of Hitler's October 1941 proclamation; "The Jewish question takes priority over all other matters." Gerald Fleming notes Hitler's "unlimited and pathological hatred for the Jews, the very core of the dictator's *Weltanschauung*."[7] But he also makes a distinction between two different aspects of Hitler's hatred—"the one a traditionally inspired and instinctively affirmed anti-Semitism that due to its racialist/biological component took a particularly rigid form; and the other *a flexible, goal-oriented* anti-Semitism that was pragmatically superimposed on the first."[8]

## Genocidal Pragmatism

This political flexibility is a feature of other cases too. Genocidal regimes, radical and often unstable, need to make pragmatic as well as ideological decisions, in order to maintain or secure their grip on power. Genocidal power often proves deadly to dissenters, even those of the supposedly privileged or protected race. This was not true in the case of the Armenian genocide, given the small number of civilian victims from the Turkish ethnic majority. However, the Serb perpetrators of the Bosnian genocide regarded dissident fellow Serbs as a special threat, and treated them with the same brutality as the more numerous Muslim victims.[9] In Rwanda, too, the first victims of "Hutu Power" in 1994 were the Hutu moderate politicians, and thousands of Hutu in the south of the country were killed for lacking zeal to exterminate Tutsi.[10] In absolute numbers, most of the victims of the Khmer Rouge regime were from Cambodia's ethnic Khmer majority, though minorities, again, were disproportionately targeted. Under Nazism, Jews were the largest single group to be exterminated, but the numerous other victims were not limited to "non-Aryans" such as Gypsies and Slavs. Hitler also targeted German homosexuals, communists, liberals, trade unionists, and other oppositionists. In the Nazi purge of German culture, books and paintings were burned, literary and film criticism abolished, and modern music banned.[11] The day after the *Kristallnacht* pogrom, Hitler speculated that "he might one day exterminate the intellectual classes in Germany if they no longer proved to be of use."[12] Intellectuals of the Khmer and Hutu majorities were also targeted in both Cambodia and Rwanda.[13] The "rejection of the individual in favour of the race"[14] did not privilege individuals for their membership of a preferred race but on the contrary it made them vulnerable to measures to "protect" it.

## Defining Race

Nazi "eugenics" also eliminated 70,000 Germans with hereditary illnesses.[15] The late George L. Mosse pointed out the close link, spanning the races, between this euthanasia and the destruction of Jews: "Putting euthanasia into practice meant that the Nazis took the idea of 'unworthy' life seriously, and a life so defined was characterized by lack of productivity and degenerate outward appearance," while similar "ideas of unproductivity and physical appearance were both constantly applied to Jews."[16] Richard Evans adds, "It was not these people's racial identity that marked them out for elimination, but their supposed biological inferiority, irrespective of race."[17] By the same token, Gypsies, although defined in 1935 as "alien to the

German species," were in the early years of the war "not persecuted on 'racial' grounds, but on the basis of an 'asocial and criminal past' and a security threat." Some of the more assimilated, known as Sinti, "even served in the armed forces until the order came in 1942 that all Gypsies must be sent to Auschwitz."[18]

"One can see how confused Nazi racism was," Yehuda Bauer comments, "when Jewish grandparents were defined by religion rather than so-called racial criteria."[19] The November 14, 1935, "Nuremberg law" defined a "mixed-blood" Jew (*Mischling*) as "anyone who is descended from one or two grandparents who are fully Jewish as regards race. . . . A grandparent is deemed fully Jewish without further ado, if he has belonged to the Jewish religious community." Raul Hilberg adds that "a person was to be considered Jewish if he had three or four Jewish grandparents. . . . If an individual had two Jewish grandparents, he would be classified as Jewish only if he himself belonged to the Jewish religion [or] was married to a Jewish person. The critical factor in every case was in the first instance the religion of the grandparents."[20]

In Cambodia, Khmer Rouge racism was even more inconsistent.[21] There was no attempt at "scientific" precision, but biological metaphors abounded. The Khmer Rouge considered its captive urban populations "subhuman" (*anoupracheachun*), the same term the Nazis had used for conquered Slavic *Untermenschen*.[22] Democratic Kampuchea referred to its enemies as "microbes," "pests buried within," and traitors "boring in."[23] The Germans had talked of "vermin" and "lice."[24] Pol Pot considered his revolution the only "clean" one in history, just as the Nazis "cleaned" occupied areas of Jews. Both regimes were obsessed with the concept of racial "purity"[25] Pol Pot called himself the "Original Khmer,"[26] but his preoccupations had precedents. And they prefigured biological depictions by Bosnian Serbs of the "malignant disease" of Islam threatening to "infect" Europe,[27] and by the Hutu Power regime in Rwanda, which described Tutsi as "cockroaches" (*inyenzi*), requiring a "big clean-up."[28]

## Territorial Expansionism

Genocidal regimes often proclaim a need to "purify" not only a race but a territory. Prior to World War I, the Young Turks dreamed of a "Pan-Turanian" empire of all Turkic-speaking peoples. They initially chose to name their country "Turkestan," with its irredentist Central Asian connotations. In 1904 Yusuf Akçura questioned whether "the true power of the Ottoman state" lay "in preserving its current geographical shape." He instead called for "the unification of the Turks—who share language, race, customs, and even for the most part, religion, and who are spread throughout the majority of Asia and Eastern Europe." This meant "the Turks' formation of a vast political nationality . . . from the peoples of the great race" encompassing Central Asian Turks and Mongols "from Peking to Montenegro."[29]

This goal was shelved for a time, but in 1917–18 the collapse of the opposing tsarist armies in the Caucasus allowed a revival of Pan-Turanianism. Young Turk armies pushed into Russian Armenia where 300,000 survivors of the 1915 genocide had taken refuge, "extending the genocide of Ottoman Armenians to the Russian Armenians."[30] In the words of the allied German military attaché von Lossow, this involved "the total extermination of the Armenians in Transcaucasia also," in what he called the Young Turks' attempt "to destroy all Armenians, not only in Turkey, but also outside Turkey." After the defeat and fall of the Young Turk regime, Kemalist forces again invaded the fledgling Republic of Armenia in 1920. The minister of foreign affairs in Ankara instructed the commander in chief of the Eastern Front Army: "It is indispensable that Armenia be annihilated politically and physically."[31] Purification and expansion went hand in hand.

In *Mein Kampf*, Hitler proclaimed that "for Germany . . . the only possibility of carrying out a healthy territorial policy lay in the acquisition of new land in Europe itself . . . it could be obtained by and large only at the expense of Russia, and this meant that the new Reich must again set itself on the march along the road of the Teutonic knights of old, to obtain by the German sword sod for the German plow and daily bread for the nation. . . . We take up where we broke off six hundred years ago."[32] Holocaust historian Christopher Browning has pointed out that, as with the expansionism accompanying the Armenian genocide, the Nazi "achievement of *Lebensraum* through the invasion of Russia and the Final Solution to the Jewish Question through systematic mass murder were intimately connected."[33] Hitler initially envisaged "three belts of population—German, Polish and Jewish—from west to east." Pragmatic considerations gave first priority to deporting rural Poles to make way for German settlers, before expelling or exterminating Jews.[34]

Hitler's deputy Heinrich Himmler wrote in his diary in 1919, at the age of nineteen: "I work for my ideal of German womanhood with whom, some day, I will live my life in the east and fight my battles as a German far from beautiful Germany."[35] According to Rudolf Hoess, in 1930 Himmler again "spoke of the forcible conquest of large sections of the East."[36] Hoess recalled: "Himmler considered his true life's work to be the spread of the continued existence of the German people, secured by a superior peasantry on a healthy economic basis and provided with a sufficient amount of land. All his plans for settlements, even long before the assumption of power, were directed to this objective. He never made a secret of the fact that this could be accomplished only if land was seized by force in the East."[37]

In 1977–78 the Khmer Rouge regime launched attacks against all three of Cambodia's neighbors: Vietnam, Laos, and Thailand. The Pol Pot leadership harbored irredentist ambitions to reunite Cambodia with ancient Khmer-speaking areas that had formed part of the medieval Angkor empire.[38] On the sea border with Vietnam, the Khmer Rouge regime unilaterally declared a new expanded frontier line to which Hanoi objected. Internal Khmer Rouge documents also reveal a demand for "changes at some points in the present [land] border line." In speeches in various parts of Cambodia throughout 1977–78, as all Vietnamese residents were being hunted down for extermination, numerous Khmer Rouge officials announced their ambition to "retake Kampuchea Krom," Vietnam's Mekong Delta.[39]

The 1986 "Serbian Memorandum," which prepared much of the ideological basis for the genocide in Bosnia, urged "the establishment of the full national integrity of the Serbian people, regardless of which republic or province it inhabits." Five years later Slobodan Milosevic warned that "it is always the powerful who dictate what the borders will be, never the weak. Thus, we must be powerful." Just as Hitler in 1939 had threatened the Jews with annihilation if war broke out, Bosnian Serb leader Radovan Karadzic asserted in 1991 that Bosnia's Muslim community would "disappear from the face of the Earth" if it decided to "opt for war" by choosing an independent Bosnia-Herzegovina. He added later that "Muslims are the most threatened, . . . not only in the physical sense . . . rather, this is also the beginning of the end of their existence as a nation" Karadzic added in 1992: "The time has come for the Serbian people to organize itself as a totality, without regard to the administrative [existing] borders." The next year, the speaker of the Bosnian Serb parliament proclaimed the need "to grasp our ethnic space," while Belgrade's army chief of staff referred to "our *lebensraum* in Bosnia."[40] Again we see genocide and expansionism marching hand in hand.

For their part, the Hutu chauvinist leaders in Rwanda advocated a "final solution to the ethnic problem" there.[41] For years their world view had also focused on territorial issues. The genocidal *akazu*, or "little house," was a secret clanlike network of extremist Hutu officials from the northwest of Rwanda, mostly from the Bushiru region incorporated into the kingdom of Rwanda ("Tutsified") only in the 1920s.[42] The 1973 coup by Juvénal Habyarimana, married to a Bushiru princess, initially brought "northern revenge" by "marginalised, fiercely Hutu, anti-royalist Rwanda" over the more liberal and tolerant Hutu communities of southern Rwanda.[43] After Habyarimana's death in a plane crash on April 6, 1994, these *akazu* chauvinists conducted the genocide of Tutsi, until their overthrow four months later. Gérard Prunier describes them as " 'the real northwesterners,' the representatives of the 'small

Rwanda' which had conquered the big one."[44] Their campaign against the Tutsi and more pluralist southern Hutu suggests that they aimed to extend throughout Rwanda the ethnic Hutu purity of the defunct northwest kingdom of Bushiru. After the regime's overthrow in July 1994, the genocidal Interahamwe forces "not only continued to kill Tutsis in Rwanda but also targeted Banyarwanda Tutsis living in Eastern Congo." These Hutu militias ranged across Kivu province of Congo, massacred the local Tutsi cattle herders known as Banyamulenge, and also "sent elements into the Masisi plateau to gain support amongst the Banyamasisi Hutu and to eliminate the Banyamasisi Tutsi."[45] Prunier explains that in this way the Interahamwe could also "carve out for themselves a kind of 'Hutuland' which could be either a base for the reconquest of Rwanda or, if that failed, a new Rwanda outside the old one."[46] Meanwhile, Hutu forces from Rwanda joined those in Burundi, and "increasingly operated together against the common ethnic enemy," the Tutsi, who did likewise.[47] Again, a genocidal conflict became an international one.

## Narratives of Territorial Decline

Real or perceived geographic diminution is often the backdrop to aggressive expansionism accompanied by genocide. The decline of the Ottoman Empire from the sixteenth century made fear of further territorial diminution a political preoccupation. By 1625 an Ottoman official warned that without defensive action, "the Europeans will rule over the lands of Islam." An Ottoman official cautioned in 1822: "Let us . . . not cede an inch of our territory."[48] But financial collapse in 1874 begat uprisings in Bosnia and Herzegovina, and by Bulgarians, Serbs, and Montenegrins in 1876; the Russo-Turkish War followed in 1877–78, the British and French replaced Turkish overlordship in Egypt in 1879, and in 1896 the Cretan insurrection and Greco-Turkish war led to the Turkish evacuation of Crete in 1898. Yusuf Akçura wrote in 1904: "Russia was in pursuit of possessing the Bosphorus Straits, Anatolia and Iraq, Istanbul, the Balkans and the Holy Land . . . [renewing] the age-old competition between Russia and England for [control of] the Islamic collective and the sacred Islamic lands."[49] As historian James Reid puts it, "the collapse of the Ottoman Empire deprived the ruling elite of any security it once had and created a condition of paranoia."[50] This same period saw the first major massacres of Armenians, in which 100,000 to 200,000 perished in Anatolia in 1894–96. The Ottoman collapse accelerated with the Austrian annexation of Bosnia and Herzegovina in 1908, the declaration of Bulgarian independence in 1909 and revolts in Albania in 1910–12, the Italian seizure of Tripoli in 1911–12, and the Balkan Wars of 1912–13. Now "only the Armenians and Arabs" remained as Ottoman subject nationalities.[51] At the outbreak of World War I, the empire comprised little more than Anatolia and the Arab countries directly to its south. In 1915 the Young Turks launched the genocide of Armenians.

For his part, Hitler projected himself as the ruler of a constricted country as a result of World War I. In an extraordinary speech in August 1939, he described Germany and Poland "with rifles cocked": "We are faced with the harsh alternative of striking now or of *certain annihilation sooner or later*." "I have taken risks," he went on, "in occupying the Rhineland when the generals wanted me to pull back, in taking Austria, the Sudetenland, and the rest of Czechoslovakia."[52] Thus, even as he recited his list of territorial gains, Hitler was still proclaiming the threat of Germany's "certain annihilation." This was much less rational than the Ottoman fears. Striking is Hitler's tactical assumption that German *territorial* stability was unachievable. Failure to expand meant annihilation. Actual expansion was denied or dismissed as insufficient to deter enemies.

Pol Pot's regime, too, saw Cambodia's post-Angkorean geographic decline as a millennial theme, uninterrupted by the twentieth-century fact of territorial recovery.[53] The Khmer Rouge view of the past simply stressed "2,000 years of exploitation," in which "royal and feudal authorities" sold off the national territory to foreigners.[54] In his major public speech in

1977, Pol Pot urged his people to "prevent the constant loss of Cambodia's territory."[55] This required both "tempering" (*lot dam*) the country's population to become hardened purveyors of violence and reconquering long-lost territory from Vietnam, such as "Kampuchea Krom."[56] The next year, Khmer Rouge radio exhorted its listeners not only to "purify" the "masses of the people" of Cambodia, but also to kill thirty Vietnamese for every fallen Cambodian, thus sacrificing "only 2 million troops to crush the 50 million Vietnamese, and we would still have 6 million people left."[57]

The leaders of the Young Turks, Nazis, and Khmer Rouge came disproportionately from "lost" territories beyond the shrinking homeland. The Young Turks' four ideological leaders included a Russian Tatar and a Kurd (Yusuf Akçura and Ziya Gokalp) and two Azeris; political leaders Talaat and Enver were from Bulgaria and Albania, while Dr. Nazim and two others came from "obscure Balkan origins." In the Nazi leadership, *Volksdeutsch* from Austria and central Europe were disproportionately represented, including Hitler, Rosenberg, Hess, Röhm, Goering, and Kaltenbrunner.[58] Of the top three Khmer Rouge leaders, Pol Pot's deputy Nuon Chea grew up in Thai-occupied Battambang province, and Ieng Sary was a Khmer Krom born in southern Vietnam—as was Khmer Rouge defense and security chief Son Sen.[59] These leaders likely heightened the sense of territorial threat faced by their regimes.

The Bosnian Serb military commander, General Ratko Mladic, also complained that Serbs were threatened with extinction. In 1992–93, he claimed that German, Croatian, and Muslim goals included "the complete annihilation of the Serbian people." Mladic added: "We Serbs always wait until it reaches our throats. Only then do we retaliate.... In the thirteenth century, we were more numerous than the Germans. Now, there are just over twelve million of us, while they have grown to one hundred fifty million."[60] The Serbian governor of Herzegovina promised to "correct the injustice with regard to the borders which Josip Broz [Tito] drew with his dirty finger. He gave Serbian lands cheaply to the Croatians and Muslims." It would be "pure Serbian masochism to keep Broz's borders." The Serb response, then, was mere self-defense, in Mladic's words: "I have not conquered anything in this war. I only liberated that which was always Serbian, although I am far from liberating all that is really Serbian.... Even Trieste [Italy] is an old Serbian city."[61]

## Idealization of Cultivation

The myth of racial victimization and territorial diminution are not the only metaphysical preoccupations of the genocidal world view. Idealization of the peasant cultivator has been another key element. Enver Pasha claimed that his Young Turk army had drawn "all its strength from the rural class," adding that "all, who seek to enrich those who do not work should be destroyed."[62] Before World War I the word "Turk" itself, while meaning "Muslim" in the West, had a connotation in Turkey of "rural" or "mountain people." The Ottoman cities of Istanbul and Izmir, on the other hand, comprised majorities—56 and 62 percent respectively—of non-Turks: Armenians, Greeks, and Jews.[63] In 1920–21, Enver Pasha briefly flirted with Bolshevism; it is possible that he had long seen such urban ethnic communities as capitalist parasites on the Turkish peasant body.

The leading Young Turk ideologue, Yusuf Akçura, considered the peasantry "the basic matter of the Turkish nation" and the group requiring greatest assistance,[64] a view he combined with his ethnic-based Turkism and his Pan-Turkist territorial irredentism.[65] The leading organizer of the 1915 genocide, Talaat Pasha, became first honorary president of the farmers' association in 1914–16.[66] According to Feroz Ahmad, "in their first flush of glory and while they were at their most radical," the Young Turk leaders had proposed "measures intended to lighten the burden of the peasant," including land distribution, low-interest loans, tithe reductions, agricultural schools, and a cadastral system, and "promised to encourage the development of agriculture in every way possible." It was considered "vital to save the peasant from the feudal lords." Stressing "the importance of the small farmer," Young Turk intellectuals also urged cooperativization.[67] However, the political leadership quickly encountered the stranglehold of the notables in rural areas; the top 5 percent of landowners owned 65 percent of the land. The Young Turks then "took the path of least resistance," accommodating landlord power for "the salvation of the empire" and pursuing only modest reforms to modernize and commercialize agriculture. They promoted "ambitious irrigation projects" including creation of "another Egypt" in Cilicia, and even envisaged eventual "nationalization of agriculture and the joint cultivation of the soil."[68] Dr. Nazim, an architect of the Armenian genocide, boasted in 1917 that "our peasants, who made fortunes through the unwarranted rise in food prices, can pay three liras for a pair of stockings for their daughters." In fact, most peasants suffered increased forced labor and land expropriations under the Young Turks, but the regime's ideological claim to foster the peasantry and cultivation is clear.[69]

In Germany, National Socialism's precursor, the *völkisch* tradition, was "essentially a product of late eighteenth-century romanticism."[70] Nazi nationalism sprang directly from the concept of "blood and soil" (*Blut und Boden*). This sought strength for the *Herrenvolk* (master race) in "the sacredness of the German soil ... which could not be confined by artificial boundaries." And in peasant virtues. Hitler declared the farmer "the most important participant" in the Nazi revolution.[71] In *Mein Kampf*, he linked German peasant farmland with German racial characteristics, adding: "A firm stock of small and middle peasants has been at all times the best protection against social evils." He urged that "Industry and commerce retreat from their unhealthy leading position," to become "no longer the basis for feeding the nation, but only a help in this"—to the peasant sector.[72]

In the late 1920s the future Nazi peasant leader Richard Walther Darré took up government contracts in the field of animal breeding. He forged a reputation with his publications on selective breeding, "which became the basis of his subsequent racist anthropological theoretisation."[73] Darré authored the Nazi doctrine of *Blut und Boden*, becoming "the main theoretician of eastward continental expansion and agricultural settlement."[74] According to Richard Breitman, Darré helped to convince Heinrich Himmler of "the need for a new racial-German aristocracy."[75] In Munich, Himmler had studied agriculture "intensely for several years" and was "an impassioned agriculturalist," according to Rudolf Hoess, the man he later placed in command at Auschwitz.[76] In 1930 Himmler headed the Bavarian branch of the Artamanen, a sect advocating return to a Teutonic rural life-style. Hoess, who had fought in the German army in Turkey during the Armenian genocide[77] and was also a member of the Artamanen, later recalled: "It was the objective of the Artaman society to induce and aid ideal healthy young Germans of every party and ideology who, because of widespread unemployment, were without proper occupation, to return to the countryside and to settle there once again."[78] Himmler's ideal was "the primeval German peasant warrior and farmer."[79] The editor of the SS newspaper *Das Schwarze Korps*, Gunter d'Alquen, later described Himmler as "a theoretical agriculturalist with an academic education" that influenced "his character formation and its consequences," including "[m]any of the practices he enlarged on subsequently with regard to breeding, selection, and perhaps even what he understood by extermination of vermin."[80] Himmler also used an agricultural metaphor to order that homosexuals be "entirely eliminated ... root and branch."[81] Breitman adds: "He thought he could apply the principles and methods of agriculture to human society ... Darré, like Himmler, had studied agronomy and the two men knew all about the breeding of livestock." Himmler, whom Breitman calls the "architect" of the Holocaust, appointed Darré the first head of the SS Race and Settlement Office; "until they quarreled in the late 1930s the two men both tried to turn the SS into their new stock."[82] When Poland fell, Himmler toured the conquered land with his amanuensis, who wrote: "And so we stood there like prehistoric farmers and laughed. ... All of this was now once more German soil! Here the German plough will soon change the picture. Here trees and bushes will soon be planted. Hedges will grow, and weasel and hedgehog, buzzard and hawk will prevent the destruction of half the harvest by mice and other vermin."[83] As Himmler put it, "The yeoman of his own acre is the backbone of the German people's strength and character."[84]

Martin Bormann, head of the Nazi Party chancellery and an old friend and assistant of Himmler, was another "passionate agriculturalist."[85] Many Nazis believed in "the superior virtue of rural life."[86] *Blut und Boden* became the title of a film made for use in Nazi Party meetings, subtitled "Foundation of the New Reich." Historian David Welch asserts that "the peasant provides the constant culture hero for National Socialism."[87] Hitler's minister of agriculture saw the issue in a way that Pol Pot himself could have put it: "Neither princes, nor the Church, nor the cities have created the German man. Rather, the German man emerged from the German peasantry. . . . [The] German peasantry, with an unparalleled tenacity, knew how to preserve its unique character and its customs against every attempt to wipe them out. . . . One can say that the blood of a people digs its roots deep into the homeland earth."[88] Goebbels commissioned at least seven feature films on the topic of "blood and soil."

Another semi-documentary, *The Eternal Forest* (*Ewiger Wald*) expressed "anti-urban, anti-intellectual sentiments," and "idolatry" of the woods: "Our ancestors were a forest people. . . . No people can live without forest, and people who are guilty of deforesting will sink into oblivion. . . . However, Germany in its new awakening has returned to the woods." The film depicts "a pure German race, in which the peasant represents the primordial image of the Volk—a Master Race whose roots lie in the sacred soil fertilized for centuries by the richness of their blood."[89]

This view is related to the Nazis' antisemitism. Historian Jeffrey Richards writes: "The Jew was characterized as materialist and thus the enemy of Volkist spiritualism, as a rootless wanderer and therefore the opposite of Volkist rootedness, and as the epitome of finance, industry and the town and thus alien to the agrarian peasant ideal of the Volk."[90] Hitler proclaimed that "a nation can exist without cities, but . . . a nation cannot exist without farmers."[91] He described modern industrial cities as "abscesses on the body of the folk [*Volkskörper*], in which all vices, bad habits and sicknesses seem to unite. They are above all hotbeds of miscegnation and bastardization."[92] Himmler agreed: "Cowards are born in towns. Heroes in the country."[93]

Himmler projected Auschwitz itself as "*the* agricultural research station for the eastern territories." He instructed Hoess in 1940: "All essential agricultural research must be carried out there. Huge laboratories and plant nurseries were to be set out. All kinds of stockbreeding was to be pursued there." Early the next year, Hoess wrote, Himmler visited Auschwitz with plans for "the prisoner-of-war camp for 100,000 prisoners." But he added: "In addition there will be the agricultural research station and farms!" In mid-1942 Himmler observed "the whole process of destruction of a transport of Jews," and ordered: "The gypsies are to be destroyed. The Jews who are unfit to work are to be destroyed. . . . Armaments factories will also be built. . . . The agricultural experiments will be intensively pursued, for the results are urgently needed."[94] The German peasant warrior must destroy his ethnic foes.

As in the case of the Young Turks, once in power the Nazis' peasant policy came up against "the requirements of a powerful war economy, necessarily based on industry." But as Barrington Moore adds, "a few starts were made here and there"[95]—including at Auschwitz.

The Khmer Rouge took all this much further, emptying Cambodia's cities and seeing "only the peasants" as allies in their revolution.[96] A Khmer Rouge journal announced: "We have evacuated the people from the cities which is our class struggle."[97] These unorthodox communists wrote: "There is a worker class which has some kind of stand. We have not focused on it yet."[98] "We do not use old workers. . . . We do not want to tangle ourselves with old things."[99] The entire population of Cambodia became an unpaid agricultural labor force, and the economy a vast plantation. In their violent repression of enemies, the Khmer Rouge regularly used metaphors such as "pull up the grass, dig up the roots," and proclaimed that the bodies of city people and other victims would be used for "fertilizer."[100]

The Young Turks, the Nazis, and the Khmer Rouge all had to contend with other ethnic groups occupying the land they coveted. Armenian peasants inhabited large areas of eastern Anatolia, straddling the route to "Turkestan." Poles and Russians were obstructive occupants of the eastern territory on which the Nazis planned to settle Aryan farmers. Touring Poland with Himmler in 1939, his amanuensis Johst dismissed it as "not a state-building nation. . . . A country which has so little feeling for systematic settlement, that is not even up to dealing with the style of a village, . . . is a colonial country!"[101] The Nazis considered Slavic *Untermenschen* to be in conflict with the German peasantry in a different way from archetypal urban Jewry. In Cambodia from 1975 to 1979, the Khmer Rouge demonization of ethnic Vietnamese encompassed both these ideological features: some were considered exploitative city dwellers, workers and shopkeepers consuming rural production without benefiting the peasantry in return, and others, rice farmers occupying land that the Pol Pot regime saw as belonging to the authentic homeland of the Khmer.

Other genocidal regimes have also portrayed themselves as protectors of peasant life against urbanites and rural rivals. The perpetrators of the Bosnian genocide of 1992–94 saw their Muslim victims as city dwellers, in contrast to the rural Serb peasantry.[102] In Rwanda, too, the Tutsi were seen either as urban dwellers or as cattle-raising pastoralists, not hardy peasant cultivators like the idealized Hutu. Belgian scholar Philip Verwimp has noted that the protogenocidal regime of Juvenal Habyarimana in Rwanda (1973–94) shared some of the characteristic features of idealization of the peasantry. Habyarimana's justification of his coup d'etat was "to ban once and for all, the spirit of intrigue and the feudal mentality . . . to give back to labor and individual yield its real value . . . the one who refuses to work is harmful to society." "We want to fight this form of intellectual bourgeoisie and give all kinds of physical labor its value back." "Our food strategy gives absolute priority to our peasants," Habyarimana announced; "the government always takes care of the peasant families, . . . the essential productive forces of our country."[103] Verwimp considers Habyarimana to have been influenced (like the Pol Pot group) by physiocratic economic theories, but he also notes reports that literature about Nazism was found in Habyarimana's home after his death. Verwimp adds: "The dictator considered cities a place of immorality, theft and prostitution . . . [and that] Rwanda is a peasant economy and should remain one."[104]

During the 1992 pregenocidal massacres of Tutsis, Prunier adds, "There was a 'rural' banalisation of crime. Killings were *umuganda*, collective work, chopping up men was 'bush clearing' and slaughtering women and children was 'pulling out the roots of the bad weeds.' The vocabulary of 'peasant-centered agricultural development' came into play, with a horrible double meaning."[105] In Verwimp's view, the subsequent genocide "was indeed a 'final solution,' to get rid of the Tutsis once and for all, and to establish a pure peasant society."[106]

## From Mass Murder to Genocide: Indonesian Expansion into East Timor

In one recent case, territorial aggression made the difference between mass murder and genocide. In the 1960s, the Indonesian regime of President Suharto compiled a record of murderous repression of domestic political opponents but not of genocidal racism or territorial expansion. In the 1970s, however, Indonesia's attempted conquest of the former territory of Portuguese Timor brought about a genocide.

In October 1965 General Suharto came to power in a military takeover in Jakarta.[107] A massacre of the communist opposition, members of the Partai Kommunis Indonesia (PKI), immediately began. Suharto later recalled: "I had to organize pursuit, cleansing, and crushing."[108] He ordered an "absolutely essential cleaning out" of the PKI and its sympathizers from the government. As his paratroops moved into Central Java, General Nasution reportedly said that "All of their followers and sympathizers should be eliminated" and ordered the party's extinction "down to its very roots."[109] In a few months, half a million to a million communists were slaughtered.[110]

In legal terms, this was not genocide.[111] There was no particular ethnic or racial bias against the victims. The number of ethnic Chinese killed, for instance, was comparatively small, and limited to two regions of the country.[112] Most victims were Javanese peasants, usually only nominal Muslims. Fervent Muslim youth groups did much of the killing, instigated by the army to massacre suspected PKI supporters. The killings were political, concentrated in areas like Java and Bali where the PKI had won large numbers of votes in elections in the 1950s.[113] Paratroop commander Sarwo Edhie reportedly conceded that in Java "we had to egg the people on to kill Communists."[114] In his study of Bali, Geoffrey Robinson states that the armed forces ensured "that only PKI forces were killed and that they were killed systematically."[115]

Ten years later, the Indonesian armed forces launched another slaughter, this time of genocidal proportions. The victims now were of a different nationality and religion, in a territory outside Indonesia's borders, and they specifically included the Chinese ethnic minority. Jakarta's troops invaded East Timor, a small neighboring Portuguese colony about to become independent. The East Timorese were not Muslims, but Catholics and animists. Indonesia, which had never claimed the territory, now planned to destroy the popular leftist anticolonial movement known as Fretilin, which had won local elections in the Timorese villages,[116] and then won a brief civil war. By November 1975 Fretilin had consolidated power in East Timor after the Portuguese withdrawal. Indonesia's December seizure of the capital, Dili, was bloody and successful. But unlike the PKI a decade before, Fretilin waged continued resistance and held sway in much of the mountainous hinterland of the island.[117]

Although its anticommunist political motives remained similar, this time the Suharto regime could not destroy what it termed the "gangs of security disruptors" (GPK).[118] Fretilin was politically predominant in East Timor, and despite massive losses it continued to harass the occupying forces. In its effort to wipe out this resistance, Indonesia now became embroiled in a genocidal campaign to suppress the Timorese people. Of the 1975 population of 650,000, approximately 150,000 people disappeared in the next four years.[119] Among the first victims were Timor's 20,000-strong ethnic Chinese minority, who were singled out for "selective killings." Indonesian troops murdered 500 Chinese in Dili on the first day of the December 1975 invasion. Soon afterward, "In Maubara and Liquica, on the northwest coast, the entire Chinese population was killed." Surviving Chinese in East Timor numbered only "a few thousand."[120]

An Indonesian census in October 1978 produced a population estimate of only 329,000. Possibly 200,000 more may have been living in Fretilin-held areas in the hills.[121] In the strongly pro-Fretilin eastern third of the territory, for instance, Indonesian officials secretly acknowledged that "a large part of the population in this region fled to the mountains and only came down to the new villages at the beginning of 1979." Moreover, "as a result of all the unrest, many village heads have been replaced, whilst many new villages have emerged."[122] The experience of two eastern villages is instructive: "With the upheavals," an Indonesian commander acknowledged, the inhabitants "fled into the bush," returning in May 1979, when they were "resettled" in a district town. "But this led to their being unable to grow food on their own land, so that food shortages have occurred."[123] In fact, famine ravaged East Timor in 1979. Indonesian aerial bombardment of homes and cultivated gardens in the hill areas had forced many Timorese to surrender in the lowlands, but food was scarce there. As Indonesian control eventually expanded, counts of the Timorese population rose to as many as 522,000 in mid-1979.[124]

The new racism against the Chinese was thus only part of a broader targeting of the Timorese majority in a determined counterinsurgency campaign. While insisting that "God is on our side," Indonesian intelligence and military commanders in Dili acknowledged confidentially in 1982 that "despite the heavy pressure and the disadvantageous conditions under which they operate, the GPK [Fretilin] has nevertheless been able to hold out in the bush," and can still deploy "a very sizeable concentration of forces in one place." After seven years of occupation, Fretilin "support networks" still existed "in all settlements, the villages as well as the towns." Thus, "threats and disturbances are likely to occur in the towns as well as in the resettlement areas."[125] Indonesian commanders still aimed "to obliterate the classic GPK areas" and "to crush the GPK remnants to their roots and to prevent their re-emergence," so that the conquered territory would "eventually be completely clean of the influence and presence of the guerrillas."[126] Deportations continued; in one sector of the East, thirty villages were resettled in 1982.[127] Two years later, a new territory-wide military campaign attempted what one commander called the obliteration of Fretilin "to the fourth generation."[128]

Traditional swidden agriculture on dispersed hill fields did not favor Indonesian control. The population of each village had to be closely controlled. The military commander of the province ordered local officials to "suspect everyone in the community."[129] He hoped to uncover and block "every attempt by inhabitants or the GPK to set up gardens to provide logistical support for the GPK."[130] Thus, the intelligence commander ordered officials to "Re-arrange the location of gardens and fields of the population":

(a) There should be no gardens or fields of the people located far from the settlement or village.
(b) No garden or field of anyone in the village should be isolated (situated far from the others). Arrange preferably for all the gardens and fields to be close to each other.
(c) When people go to their gardens or fields, no-one should go alone; they should go and return together.[131]

The overriding motive for such measures was military. But the result resembled the ideological inspiration of the close-knit, communal Javanese village. Beginning in 1980, Indonesia also established new "transmigration" villages in Timor for 500 families of Javanese and Balinese peasants, who were much easier to control.[132] Jakarta considered the Timorese agriculturally backward: the first group of 50 Balinese transmigrants were given the task to "train East Timorese farmers in the skills of irrigated farming." John Taylor comments that the Indonesians overlooked the long tradition of irrigation agriculture in their area of settlement, making the impact "largely symbolic."[133] Here too, glorification of an imagined superior cultivation trumped Timorese reality. In September 1981 an eyewitness reports that after his unit had massacred 400 Timorese civilians near Lacluta, an Indonesian soldier uttered a remark "which was considered to be part of the wisdom of Java. He said: 'When you clean your field, don't you kill all the snakes, the small and large alike?' "[134]

In early 1999, as a long-awaited UN-sponsored referendum finally approached, Indonesian military and militia commanders threatened to "liquidate . . . all the pro-independence people, parents, sons, daughters, and grandchildren."[135] Jakarta's governor of the territory ordered that "priests and nuns should be killed."[136] The Indonesian military commander in Dili warned: "[I]f the pro-independents do win . . . all will be destroyed. It will be worse than 23 years ago."[137] In May 1999 an Indonesian army document ordered that "massacres should be carried out from village to village after the announcement of the ballot if the pro-independence supporters win." The East Timorese independence movement "should be eliminated from its leadership down to its roots." The forced deportation of hundreds of thousands was also planned.[138] It was implemented, along with a new wave of mass killing, immediately after the UN's announcement of the result of the August 30 ballot, in which 79 percent of Timorese voted for independence from Indonesia. The killing was halted only after the UN took over the territory itself.

As in other cases of mass murder, the Suharto regime's territorial expansionist project transformed earlier repression—domestic political slaughter of communists—from mass murder into genocide of the Timorese. Thus from 1975 unprecedented massacres of the Chinese racial minority complemented the more widespread violent assault on the East Timorese national group.[139] As in the Armenian genocide, the Holocaust, Cambodia, Bosnia, and Rwanda, the tragedy of East Timor demonstrates the virulent, violent mix of racism, religious prejudice, expansionism, and idealization of cultivation. Each of those factors is, of course, often a relatively harmless component of nationalist ideology. Taken singly, none is a sufficient condition even for mass murder. But their deadly combination is a persistent feature of twentieth-century genocide.

## Notes

1. Mark Cocker, *Rivers of Gold, Rivers of Blood: Europe's Conquest of Indigenous Peoples* (New York, 1998), 304, 314–15, 335.
2. Jon Bridgman and Leslie J. Worley, "Genocide of the Hereros," in Samuel Totten, William S. Parsons, and Israel W. Charny (eds.), *Century of Genocide* (New York, 1995), 18–19.
3. Yusuf Akçura, *Uç Tarz-I Siyaset* (Three kinds of politics) (Istanbul, 1911). Barak Salmoni kindly provided a copy of his English translation and preface.
4. United Nations, AS, General Assembly, Security Council, A/53/850, S/1999/231, March 16, 1999, Annex, *Report of the Group of Experts for Cambodia Established Pursuant to General Assembly Resolution 52/135*; Ben Kiernan, "The Ethnic Element in the Cambodian Genocide," in Daniel Chirot and Martin E. P. Seligman (eds.), *Ethnopolitical Warfare: Causes, Consequences, and Possible Solutions* (Washington, D.C., 2001), 83–91.
5. See Ben Kiernan, *The Pol Pot Regime: Race, Power and Genocide in Cambodia under the Khmer Rouge, 1975–1979* (New Haven, 1996), 251–88, 427–31.
6. Introduction to Gerald Fleming, *Hitler and the Final Solution* (Berkeley, 1984), xxxii.
7. Ibid., 31, 69.
8. Ibid., 29 (emphasis added).
9. Norman Cigar, *Genocide in Bosnia: The Policy of "Ethnic Cleansing"* (College Station, Tex., 1985), 83–85.
10. Gérard Prunier, *The Rwanda Crisis: History of a Genocide* (New York, 1997), 231, 249–50; Alison Des Forges, *"Leave None to Tell the Story": Genocide in Rwanda* (New York, 1999), 19.
11. Jeffrey Richards, *Visions of Yesterday* (London, 1973), 292.
12. Richard Evans, *In Hitler's Shadow* (New York, 1989), 81, citing Ernst Nolte.
13. Prunier, *The Rwanda Crisis*, 249–50.
14. Richards, *Visions of Yesterday*, 289.
15. "The euthanasia program killed some 70,000 people . . .," quotation from George L. Mosse, *Towards the Final Solution: A History of European Racism* (Madison, 1987), 218, reprinted as "Eugenics and Nazi Race Theory in Practice," in Frank Chalk and Kurt Jonassohn (eds.), *The History and Sociology of Genocide: Analyses and Case Studies* (New Haven, 1990), 356. See also Henry Friedlander, *The Origins of Nazi Genocide: From Euthanasia to the Final Solution* (Chapel Hill, 1995).
16. Mosse, "Eugenics and Nazi Race Theory in Practice," 356.
17. Evans, *In Hitler's Shadow*, 79.
18. Gabrielle Tyrnauer, " 'Mastering the Past': Germans and Gypsies," in Chalk and Jonassohn, *The History and Sociology of Genocide*, 366–77, at 368, 376, 377.
19. Y. Bauer, "The Evolution of Nazi Jewish Policy, 1933–1938," in Chalk and Jonassohn, *The History and Sociology of Genocide*, 345.
20. See "The Anatomy of the Holocaust," in Chalk and Jonassohn, *The History and Sociology of Genocide*, 348, 358–66, at 360–61.
21. See Kiernan, "The Ethnic Element in the Cambodian Genocide," 83–91.
22. François Ponchaud, *Cambodia Year Zero* (London, 1978), 109 (*anoupracheachun*); on the Nazi term *Untermenschen*, see, e.g., Hélène Carrère D'Encausse, *Stalin: Order through Terror* (New York, 1981), 91.

23. D. P. Chandler, "A Revolution in Full Spate: Communist Party Policy in Democratic Kampuchea, December 1976," in D. Ablin and M. Hood (eds.), *The Cambodian Agony* (Armonk, N.Y., 1987), 129; and *Ieng Sary's Regime: A Diary of the Khmer Rouge Foreign Ministry, 1976–79,* translated by Phat Kosal and Ben Kiernan, Cambodian Genocide Program, Yale University and Documentation Center of Cambodia (1998), 30 <www.yale.edu/cgp>.

24. Fleming, *Hitler and the Final Solution,* xxxv, quoting Ernst Nolte.

25. The Law for the Protection of German Blood and German Honor, passed on September 15, 1935, claims that "the purity of German blood is a prerequisite for the continued existence of the German people." Quoted by Bauer, "The Evolution of Nazi Jewish Policy, 1933–1938," 348. The horrendous 1978 massacres in Cambodia's Eastern Zone were launched with the call to "purify the masses of the people." An earlier example is in *Tung Padevat* 9–10 (September–October 1976), noting the need for a rural cooperative to be "purified."

26. *Khemara Nisit* (Paris), no. 14 (August 1952).

27. Cigar, *Genocide in Bosnia,* 31, 100.

28. Prunier, *The Rwanda Crisis,* 54, 171, 188, 200; Des Forges, "*Leave None to Tell the Story,*" 51, 249–51, 405–6. See also Scott Strauss, "Organic Purity and the Role of Anthropology in Cambodia and Rwanda," *Patterns of Prejudice* 35, 2 (2001): 47–62.

29. Akçura, *Uç Tarz-I Siyaset.*

30. Vahakn N. Dadrian, *The History of the Armenian Genocide* (Oxford, 1995; rev. ed., 1997), 349.

31. Ibid., 349, 358.

32. Adolf Hitler, *Mein Kampf* (Boston, 1943), 139f., 654, quoted in Deborah Dwork and Robert Jan van Pelt, *Auschwitz: 1270 to the Present* (New York, 1996), 82.

33. Christopher R. Browning, *The Path to Genocide: Essays on Launching the Final Solution* (New York, 1992), 26. For valuable further discussion, see Michael Burleigh, *Germany Turns Eastwards: A Study of Ostforschung in the Third Reich* (Cambridge, 1988), and Klaus Hildebrand, *The Foreign Policy of the Third Reich* (Berkeley, 1973).

34. Browning, *The Path to Genocide,* 8–9, 12–13, 22.

35. Quoted in Peter Padfield, *Himmler* (London, 1990), 13.

36. Rudolf Hoess Aufzeichnungen, Institut für Zeitgeschichte, Munich, F 13/5, p. 279/283. Himmler returned to this theme nine years later in a speech to SS leaders a month after the invasion of Poland, where ethnic German warrior-settlers would hold off "Slavdom." Michael Burleigh, *The Third Reich: A New History* (New York, 2000), 446–47. See also Nicholas Goodrick-Clarke, *The Occult Roots of Nazism* (New York, 1992), ch. 14.

37. Rudolf Hoess Aufzeichnungen, Institut für Zeitgeschichte, Munich, F 13/5, p. 295.

38. See Kiernan, *The Pol Pot Regime,* 102–25, 357–69, 386–90. For evidence of Khmer Rouge irredentism against Thailand and Laos, see ibid., 366–69.

39. Ibid., 360–66.

40. Cigar, *Genocide in Bosnia,* 23, 40, 42, 63, 79.

41. Prunier, *The Rwanda Crisis,* 200–1, 221–22.

42. Des Forges, "*Leave None to Tell the Story,*" 44; Prunier, *The Rwanda Crisis,* 19, 86.

43. Prunier, *The Rwanda Crisis,* 86, 124.

44. Ibid., 222, 167–68.

45. LTC Rick Orth, "Rwanda's Hutu Extremist Genocidal Insurgency: An Eyewitness Perspective," 41pp., unpublished manuscript (2000), 15, also citing Jeff Drumtra, "Where the Ethnic Cleansing Goes Unchecked," *Washington Post,* weekly edition, July 22–28, 1996, 22.

46. Prunier, *The Rwanda Crisis,* 381.

47. Ibid., 378–79.

48. Bernard Lewis, *The Emergence of Modern Turkey* (Oxford, 1968), 25–38, 325, 332.

49. Akçura, *Uç Tarz-I Siyaset.*

50. James J. Reid, "Philosphy of State-Subject Relations, Ottoman Concepts of Tyranny, and the Demonization of Subjects: Conservative Ottomanism as a Source of Genocidal Behaviour, 1821–1918," in L. Chorbajian and G. Shirinian (eds.), *Studies in Comparative Genocide* (London, 1999), 75–78.

51. Feroz Ahmad, *The Young Turks* (Oxford, 1969), 154, quoted in Dadrian, *History,* 192.

52. Anthony Read and David Fisher, *The Deadly Embrace: Hitler, Stalin, and the Nazi-Soviet Pact,*

*1939–1941* (New York, 1988), 241–42 (emphasis added). For an explanation of the psychology of the Nazi belief in "total annihilation," see Elizabeth Wirth Marvick (ed.), *Psychopolitical Analysis: Selected Writings of Nathan Leites* (New York, 1977), 284–85.

53. See Ben Kiernan, "Myth, Nationalism, and Genocide," *Journal of Genocide Research* 3, 2 (June 2001): 187–206; Anthony Barnett, "Cambodia Will Never Disappear," *New Left Review* 180 (1990): 101–25.

54. Kiernan, *The Pol Pot Regime*, 360.

55. Pol Pot's September 27, 1977, speech.

56. See Kiernan, *The Pol Pot Regime*, 103–5, 357–69, 425–27.

57. BBC, *Summary of World Broadcasts*, FE/5813/A3/2, May 15, 1978, Phnom Penh Radio, May 10, 1978.

58. R. Hrair Dekmejian, "Determinants of Genocide: Armenians and Jews as Case Studies," in Richard G. Hovannisian (ed.), *The Armenian Genocide in Perspective* (New Brunswick, N.J., 1986), 92–93.

59. Kiernan, "Myth, Nationalism and Genocide," 187–206.

60. Cigar, *Genocide in Bosnia*, 78. Cigar comments aptly: "This dualistic self-view of superiority and accompanying vulnerability bordering on paranoia can be a particularly explosive mix."

61. Ibid., 81, 43–44.

62. Gregor Alexinsky, "Bolshevism and the Turks," *Quarterly Review* 239 (1923): 183–97, at 185–86.

63. Ronald Grigor Suny, "Ideology or Social Ecology: Rethinking the Armenian Genocide," paper presented to the conference on State-Organized Terror, Michigan State University, Lansing, November 1988, 24.

64. *Turk Yurdu*, xii, 1333/1917, p. 3521, quoted in Feroz Ahmad, "The Agrarian Policy of the Young Turks, 1908–1918," in *Economie et sociétés dans l'empire Ottoman*, Editions CNRS, *Colloques internationaux* no. 601 (Paris, 1983), 287–88.

65. Akçura, *Uç Tarz-I Siyaset.*

66. Ahmad, "The Agrarian Policy of the Young Turks," 284 n. 34.

67. Ibid., 276, 278, 286.

68. Ibid., 279, 282–83, 286.

69. Ibid., 286–87.

70. David Welch, *Propaganda and the German Cinema, 1933–1945* (Oxford, 1983), introduction.

71. Ibid., 96–97, 102.

72. Adolf Hitler, *Mein Kampf*, 141st ed. (Munich, 1935), 151–52, quoted in Barrington Moore Jr., *Social Origins of Dictatorship and Democracy* (Harmondsworth, 1973), 450.

73. Gustavo Corni, "Richard Walther Darré: The Blood and Soil Ideologue," in Ronald Smelser and Rainer Zitelmann (eds.), *The Nazi Elite* (New York, 1993), 19.

74. Woodruff D. Smith, *The Ideological Origins of Nazi Imperialism* (New York, 1986), 243.

75. Richard Breitman, *The Architect of Genocide: Himmler and the Final Solution* (New York, 1991), 34.

76. In 1934 Hoess had "wanted to settle on the land," but Himmler recruited him to the active SS and had him posted initially to Dachau. Rudolf Hoess, *Commandant of Auschwitz*, trans. Constantine Fitzgibbon (New York, 1960), 227. See also Dwork and van Pelt, *Auschwitz*, 189–90, 207.

77. Vahakn N. Dadrian, *German Responsibility in the Armeniàn Genocide* (Cambridge, Mass., 1996), 202.

78. Rudolf Hoess Aufzeichnungen, Institut für Zeitgeschichte, Munich, F 13/5, p. 279/283.

79. Breitman, *The Architect of Genocide*, 35.

80. Gunther d'Alquen Unterredung, Institut für Zeitgeschichte, Munich, ZS 2, March 13–14, 1951, 95.

81. Quoted in Peter Tatchell, "Survivors of a Forgotten Holocaust," *London Independent*, June 12, 2001

82. Breitman, *The Architect of Genocide*, 12–13, 34–35.

83. Burleigh, *The Third Reich*, 447–48.

84. Heinrich Himmler, quoted in BBC documentary series, *The Nazis* (1997), part 1, "Helped into Power."

85. Rudolf Hoess Aufzeichnungen, Institut für Zeitgeschichte, Munich, F 13/5, p. 286. See also Joche von Lang, "Martin Bormann: Hitler's Secretary," in Smelser and Zitelmann, *The Nazi Elite*, 8, 12.

86. David Schoenbaum, *Hitler's Social Revolution* (London, 1967), 161, quoted in Welch, *Propaganda*, 9.

87. Welch, *Propaganda*, 97, 101, 103.

88. Ibid., 101–2.

89. Ibid., 108.

90. Richards, *Visions of Yesterday*, 288.

91. Smith, *The Ideological Origins of Nazi Imperialism*, 242.

92. Quoted in Henry A. Turner Jr., "Fascism and Modernization," in *Reappraisals of Fascism* (New York, 1975), 117–39, at 136 n. 12.

93. Heinrich Himmler, quoted in BBC documentary series, *The Nazis* (1997), pt. 1, "Helped into Power."

94. Hoess, *Commandant of Auschwitz*, 230, 232, 234, 238.

95. Moore, *Social Origins of Dictatorship and Democracy*, 450.

96. David P. Chandler, Ben Kiernan, and Chanthou Boua (eds.), *Pol Pot Plans the Future: Confidential Leadership Documents from Democratic Kampuchea, 1976–77* (New Haven, 1988), 219. The full quotation reads: "Concretely, we did not rely on the forces of the workers. The workers were the overt vanguard, but in concrete fact they did not become the vanguard. In concrete fact there were only the peasants. Therefore we did not copy anyone."

97. Communist Party of Kampuchea, *Tung Padevat*, special issue 9–10 (September–October 1976): 40. See Ben Kiernan, "Kampuchea and Stalinism," in Colin Mackerras and Nick Knight (eds.), *Marxism in Asia* (London, 1985), 232–50.

98. *Tung Padevat*, special issue 9–10 (September–October 1976): 52.

99. Democratic Kampuchea, *Kumrung pankar buon chhnam Sangkumniym krup phnaek rebos pak, 1977–80* (The Party's Four-Year Plan to build socialism in all fields, 1977–80) (July–August 1976), 110 pp., at 52.

100. For use of the "fertiliser" metaphor during the genocide of the Aborigines, see Raymond Evans and Bill Thorpe, "Indigenocide and the Massacre of Australian History," *Overland* 163 (2001): 21–39 at 29.

101. Burleigh, *The Third Reich*, 447.

102. Cigar, *Genocide in Bosnia*, 119.

103. These speeches by Habyarimana are dated, respectively, October 14, 1973; May 1, 1974; July 5, 1983; and July 5, 1984. For references, see Philip Verwimp, *Development Ideology, the Peasantry, and Genocide: Rwanda Represented in Habyarimana's Speeches*, Genocide Studies Program Working Paper no. 13 (New Haven, 1999), 18ff.

104. Verwimp, *Development Ideology, the Peasantry, and Genocide*, 18–21.

105. Prunier, *The Rwanda Crisis*, 139–42.

106. Verwimp, *Development Ideology, the Peasantry, and Genocide*, 45. See also Philip Verwimp, *A Quantitative Analysis of Genocide in Kibuye Prefecture, Rwanda*, Center for Economic Studies, Discussion Paper Series DPS 01.10, Departement Economie, Katholieke Universiteit Leuven, May 2001, 54 pp.

107. For recent discussion, see Benedict Anderson, "Petrus Dadi Ratu," *Indonesia* 70 (October 2000): 1–7; R. E. Elson, *Suharto: A Political Biography* (Cambridge, 2001), chs. 5–6.

108. Elson, *Suharto*, 125.

109. Suharto's formal order was signed on November 15, 1965. Arnold C. Brackman, *The Communist Collapse in Indonesia* (Singapore, 1969), 118–19, quoted in Charles Coppel, "The Indonesian Mass Killings, 1965–66," paper presented at the colloquium on Comparative Famines and Political Killings, Genocide Studies Program, Yale University/Department of History, Melbourne University, August 1999.

110. Robert Cribb (ed.), *The Indonesian Killings, 1965–1966: Studies from Java and Bali* (Clayton, Australia, 1990).

111. Robert Cribb, "Genocide in Indonesia, 1965–66," *Journal of Genocide Research* 3, 2 (June 2001): 219–39.

112. Charles Coppel writes that the number of Chinese killed in 1965–66 "cannot have exceeded about two thousand, in other words disproportionately low when compared to their percentage of the total population." *Indonesian Chinese in Crisis* (Kuala Lumpur, 1983), 58–61.

113. See, e.g., Iwan Gardono Sujatmiko, "The Destruction of the Indonesian Communist Party (PKI): A Comparative Analysis of East Java and Bali," Ph.D. diss., Harvard University, 1992; M. C. Ricklefs, *A History of Modern Indonesia* (London, 1981), 238, 248; and Herbert Feith, *The Indonesian Elections of 1955* (Ithaca, 1957).

114. John Hughes, *The End of Sukarno* (London, 1968), 181. Sarwo Edhie added, "In Bali we have to

restrain them, make sure they don't go too far." But Coppel comments: "Although political tension was high and some violence had occurred before the arrival of the paratroops, the worst of the violence occurred afterwards."

115. Geoffrey Robinson, *The Dark Side of Paradise* (1995), 295–97, quoted in Coppel, "The Indonesian Mass Killings."

116. James Dunn, *Timor: A People Betrayed* (Milton, 1983), 100.

117. For a map of the areas still reportedly occupied by Fretilin in August 1976, see Carmel Budiardjo and Liem Soei Liong, *The War against East Timor* (London, 1984), 23.

118. Ibid., 82.

119. At a meeting in London on November 12, 1979, Indonesia's foreign minister Mochtar Kusumaatmadja gave a figure of 120,000 Timorese dead from 1975 to November 1979. See John Taylor, *East Timor: The Price of Freedom* (London, 1999), 203.

120. Ibid., 68–70, 164, 207, citing *Far Eastern Economic Review* 8 (September 1985).

121. Taylor, *East Timor*, 89–90.

122. Budiardjo and Liong, *The War against East Timor*, 201, 243.

123. Ibid., 212–13.

124. Taylor, *East Timor*, 98.

125. Indonesian documents translated in Budiardjo and Liong, *The War against East Timor*, 182, 215, 222, 227, 194–96, 216, 184.

126. Ibid., 242, 193, 228, 241.

127. Ibid., 243, 213.

128. Taylor, *East Timor*, 151.

129. Budiardjo and Liong, *The War against East Timor*, 212, 214, 218–19, 229.

130. Ibid., 205.

131. Ibid., 220.

132. Jakarta aimed not only to reduce the overpopulation of Java and Bali, but also, as Taylor writes, " 'Minority populations' are to be assimilated into national development plans because this will make them easier to control, and because the movement of the population to outer island areas will create pools of cheap labour." Taylor, *East Timor*, 124–25.

133. Ibid., 124–25. For another contemporary case, see Robin Osborne, *Indonesia's Secret War: The Guerrilla Struggle in Irian Jaya* (Sydney, 1985).

134. Quoted in Taylor, *East Timor*, 102.

135. Andrew Fowler, "The Ties That Bind," Australian Broadcasting Corporation, February 14, 2000, quoted in Noam Chomsky, *A New Generation Draws the Line: East Timor, Kosovo, and the Standards of the West* (London, 2000), 72; for further details see Annemarie Evans, "Revealed: The Plot to Crush Timor," *South China Morning Post*, September 16, 1999.

136. Evans, "Revealed: The Plot to Crush Timor."

137. Brian Toohey, "Dangers of Timorese Whispers Capital Idea," *Australian Financial Review*, August 14, 1999; John Aglionby et al., "Revealed: Army's Plot," *Observer*, September 12, 1999; and other sources quoted in Chomsky, *A New Generation Draws the Line*, 72–76.

138. Chomsky, *A New Generation Draws the Line*, 74.

139. See also Dunn, *Timor: A People Betrayed*, 283–86. Further research might usefully examine whether the killings of Chinese in Timor expressed antiurban as well as xenophobic prejudices.

# 6.3   Mark Levene, "Connecting Threads: Rwanda, the Holocaust, and the Pattern of Contemporary Genocide"[1]

The starting point for this essay is to make two propositions. The first is that the scale, scope and intensity of the genocide in Rwanda in 1994 invites comparison with the Holocaust. The second is that the two events share the same historical space. These are bald, admittedly tendentious, statements which require explanation. Even if one disagrees with the argument of Steven Katz, to the effect that the Holocaust (as taken specifically to mean the Nazi 'final solution of the Jewish question') is in a category of its own as the only 'true' genocide[2] and would go on from this to accept that what happened in Rwanda also requires the same appelation, this is not in itself sufficient grounds for comparison. It could, for instance, be argued that each example of genocide can be explained within a matrix of socio-economic, political, cultural and environmental relationships that is specific to itself. Thereby, one is different from the next, and that next different from a third, the only commonality being an outcome of extermination or attempted extermination of some defined population group. And again, even if some genocides are comparable as has been suggested by Helen Fein, Vahakn Dadrian, Florence Mazian, or, most recently and comprehensively, by Robert Melson[3] in regard to the Holocaust and the destruction of the Ottoman Armenians in the First World War, it still does not necessarily follow that additional comparisons are relevant or available. On the other hand, as Charles Maier has properly noted, "To compare two events does not entail claiming that one caused the other. Comparison is a dual process that scrutinizes two or more systems to learn what elements they have in common, and what elements distinguish them. It does not assert identity: it does not deny unique components."[4]

In seeking a further comparison between Rwanda and the Holocaust, this essay follows a well-trodden path in its assertion that the latter has specific characteristics both in terms of motivation and mechanism which have not yet been replicated elsewhere. If this makes for a Holocaust singularity, it does not follow that none of its critical features are observable in the case of Rwanda or other genocides. On the contrary, the aim here is to argue that not only do modern examples of genocide, including the Holocaust, have characteristics in common, but these may amount to common threads. This is not to argue, as Ernest Nolte has attempted to do with regard to the Soviet Gulag system and the Holocaust,[5] that one genocide is necessarily a precedent for, or even causes another, though there may be instances where this directly or indirectly occur. It is to assert, however, that there might be, if not a single pattern of genocide, then, at the very least, patterns of genocide in the modern world, and that these patterns tell us not only something about the nature of genocide itself but, more importantly, something about the nature of contemporary history and society.

It is in this sense that I propose that Rwanda and the Holocaust share the same historical space. Though spatially and temporally removed from one another by a continent and half a century, their broadest relevance lies not just in what they tell us about domestic social and political arrangements in National Socialist Germany or a Rwanda led by the National Revolutionary Movement for Development[6] but about the place of these two nation-states within an emerging twentieth century international system of nation-states. Thus, it is only by examining the historical- and current- space in which states operate and attempt to function in the modern world, namely within the boundaries of a global economic and political community, and of the actual as well as perceived relationships and discourses between these states and this broader international system, that we can fully attempt to appreciate the growing incidence of genocide.[7] Conversely, by looking at each genocide's domestic preconditions, formation, scope and scale, we might also achieve a vantage point that will allow us to understand more about the direction of the contemporary world.

The first part of this analysis, then, aims to suggest points of comparison between the Holocaust and Rwanda. The second, joins up the dots, so to speak, by suggesting how the Holocaust and Rwanda fall within a broader and growing pattern of genocide.

## II

Suggesting connections between the Holocaust and Rwanda may superficially appear a not highly rewarding exercise, at least not to a Western public. What shocks or mortifies so many people brought up in this culture, about the former, is the alleged inversion and perversion of a great European Enlightenment project of which Germany was a central part. How frequently has the question been asked how could it happen 'here,' in the land of Beethoven, Goethe and Schiller, where Kantian philosophers and university professors inculcated generations in the virtues of Bildung and humanism and where politicians, state jurists and teachers sincerely laboured to create an authentic civil society in a new, modern, technologically advanced, civilised and cultured Rechtstaat?

Comparison with the latter in these terms is inadmissible because Rwanda, culturally as well as infrastructurally, might just as well be on another planet. For what is Rwanda of the late-twentieth century by comparison with Weimar, or even Wilhelmine, Germany, but an underdeveloped, stunningly poor, post-colonial backwater, a liliput of a state somewhere 'out there,' so obscure and so far outside the main thoroughfares of commerce that few Westerners before 1994 could have placed it on a cognitive, let alone an actual map. A society moreover whose deserved obscurity is compounded by its supposedly 'tribal' (sic) black inhabitants, who, existing hardly removed from a state of Hobbesian barbarity, cannot but commit violence and killing as if it were not abnormal but of life's very essence. The typecasting is, of course, utterly skewed. It does, however, serve the purpose of confirming and concretising the way Rwanda has been and continues to be distanced from the Holocaust.[8]

What happened in 1994, in this narrative, was thus an episodic outburst if not of tribal, then of ethnic hatred, a hatred so intense that frenzied gangs of youths, the Interahamwe, set about indiscriminately attacking men, women and children and then mutilating before killing them in a nation-wide orgy of violence and atrocity. At the end of it all, the hillsides, rivers and lakes were so littered with decaying, decapitated corpses that in neighbouring Uganda it sparked off an environmental health scare.[9] How far removed was this passionate, inchoate but necessarily labour intensive killing process from the cold, calculating planned system which culminated in Auschwitz?

Later I shall be commenting more on this 'primitive black man' version of genocide compared with the 'industrialised, streamlined modernity' thesis which has come to be strongly associated with the Holocaust.[10] Suffice to say, at this that both versions only provide garbled truths, while, nevertheless, reinforcing 'our' cultural preconceptions or, perhaps more accurately, misconceptions about the disjuncture between a 'civilised' genocide and a 'third world' one. Such apparent dissimilarities, however, have not prevented Robert Melson from drawing analogies between the Armenian genocide and the Holocaust.[11] In offering a contextual comparison of the pre-1914 Ottoman Empire with post-1918 Germany, he has shown how state collapse accompanied by acute societal dislocation provided critical preconditions for potential genocide. In particular, Melson argues, these conditions enabled untried, politically inexperienced, but nevertheless 'revolutionary' elites to 'seize' the apparatus of the residual state with a view to the implementation of ideologically-driven agendas intended both to reassert state power and resolve its societal crisis. In each instance, this ultimately involved a conscious lurch into another war. These renewed crisis circumstances in turn stimulated the elites' project to meld the nation together as one in the face of a common danger while providing justification and cover for the attempted physical elimination of a communal group who, allegedly, in its very existence, represented the primary challenge to the nation's historic existence as well as future hopes of redemption. If Melson's thesis for a correlation between revolution, war and preconditions for a 'total' genocide can be worked backwards from a mid-century Holocaust to early century Armenia, could we not argue in similar fashion for a forward comparison with another 'total genocide,' in an end-of-century Rwanda?

An outline of Rwanda's recent history would provide us with most, if not all, of Melson's critical ingredients. Located in East Central Africa, Rwanda belonged to an already existent if still consolidating group of pre-modern state kingdoms, notably alongside Burundi, Buganda and, most dramatically Ethiopia, whose contact with, and then subordination to, the European colonial powers occurred towards the very end of the late-nineteenth century 'scramble for Africa.' This determined that the period of colonial rule was a relatively short interregnum. But it also signalled that the period from full colonisation to decolonisation, literally no more than two to three generations, would be one of even more speeded up 'hothouse' social transformation than perhaps happened elsewhere in the continent. More-over, though colonial divide and rule was practiced by Europeans throughout the continent, the original German colonisers in the mini-kingdoms of Rwanda and Burundi specifically employed racial terminology to both explain and justify it. The pre-existing social hierarchies with crown at apex, mostly Tutsi overlords and Hutu peasantry, were upheld and concretised as the natural outcome of the arrival in the region, in previous centuries, of the allegedly more intelligent, physically superior Tutsi, of Hamitic ancestry, possibly with a strain of Aryan, who had conquered the inferior, physically less presupposing but majority Hutu population.[12] In pursuing the bureaucratic modernisation of the colonies, German officials and missionary-educators, followed by their post-First World War Belgian successors, used this Tutsi equals 'superior,' Hutu 'inferior,' dichotomy as a basis for administrative practice and educational policy. Not only were identity cards introduced to categorise people according to whether they were Hutu or Tutsi but the latter were overtly encouraged and Westernised as first collaborators in colonial rule and then, in the 1950s, as potential stewards in the event of evolution to some form of notional independent statehood.[13] If all this flew in the face of the common cultural and social relationships which made the Rwandese one people—the Banyarwanda—while at the same time exacerbating the position of those identified as Hutu, Rwanda's potential for combustibility only became fully apparent when the Belgians began 'bringing on' Hutu elements too. On the cusp of independence, in the late 1950s, the colonial power found itself in Rwanda, if not initially so forcefully in Burundi, caught very much on the horns of its own making, with two groups of competing elites, both vying for control of the apparatus of state and with competing, potentially ethnocentric versions of what consti-tuted the Rwandese nation.[14] The fact that the Tutsi were very much the minority element in demographic terms, constituting perhaps no more than 14% of the population[15] may have catalysed the Belgian authorities to attempt a quick switching of horses at this point to the majority Hutu 'side.' If this, however, was intended as a last-ditch effort to faciliate a peaceful transfer of power, it clearly came too late.

Events which followed not only involved the rapid evacuation of the Belgians but the eviction of the Tutsi-led feudal monarchy. The revolutionary credentials of these develop-ments was clearly evident for some observers, in the composition of the new Hutu elite now in power and of the popular movement of the country's Hutu *menu peuple*[16] which they successfully mobilised against former Tutsi masters and rural overlords. In a matter of four to five years, from 1959 to 1964, long-standing social, economic and political relationships, in which the Tutsi had for centuries been the dominant factor, were swept away in favour of what appeared to be a new republican order representing the demographic majority. Yet the achievement of the new order did not in itself make for stability. Not only had the revolution involved near-genocidal massacres of thousands of Rwanda's Tutsi inhabitants[17] but thou-sands more had fled to neighbouring countries, notably to Burundi where, in exact contrast to Rwanda, Tutsi hegemony over the Hutu majority was in the process of being confirmed and consolidated. From here a series of attempted counter-invasions had been launched, most seriously in 1963. These had been defeated ensuring that the Tutsi remaining in Rwanda were henceforth politically isolated and emasculated.[18]

Nevertheless, Rwanda's leadership could hardly settle to being complete masters in their own house. If on one level, revolution had ostensibly delevered political power, land and a potential resource base for development and modernisation to their new Hutu-led order, it also conferred on it a heightened sense of *angst* and insecurity. Its leadership might now seek to favour the peasantry and thereby bind them to a new consciously revolutionary regime, at the expense of those—the Tutsi—who it was perceived, under the colonial administration, had had the good education, the jobs, the status and the money, but it could not shake off the ghost of the 1959–64 years. Everything that it did henceforth would be done with reference back to that watershed. The history of Rwanda would now be written as a struggle between its authentic indigenous people and 'alien' invaders, whose arrival had heralded generations of oppression and servitude. To defend the revolution signified being in a constant state of alert against another such invasion. And with many of the *inyenzi*—the Tutsi insurrectionists of the early 1960s—or their children, still at large in Burundi or Uganda, it was not difficult for a new breed of Hutu academics and opinion-formers to construct an entirely demonic, as well as racial, picture of this adversary, biding his time, waiting for the moment to lead another general Tutsi insurrection to strike a mortal blow at the Hutu 'nation' and, in so doing, wreak some apocalyptic vengeance for all the Tutsi fields and families lost in the early 1960s.[19]

The removal in 1973 of the original revolutionary leadership in favour of the military-led dictatorship of Juvenal Habyarimana, ostensibly offered the possibility of national reconciliation which would transcend the Hutu-Tutsi divide. It in fact took Habyarimana's MRND regime nearly twenty further years to begin moves toward a pluralistic, multi-party democracy. By this time, however, it was too late. Not only had the regime continued to freeze out the vast majority of Tutsi from higher education, the army and civil positions, it had also failed to deliver to its own avowed Hutu constituency. Export earnings, largely dependent on the international market price of Rwanda's primary cash crop, coffee, had crashed with its global overproduction in the second half of the 1980s. The subsequent demands of Western donors for 'structural readjustment,' not only struck at an already impoverished peasantry but also threatened hundreds of thousands of government employees in an historically *dirigiste*, bureaucratic top-heavy administration.[20] If Rwanda was thus teetering on the brink, with or without the spectre of Tutsi invasion, this was, nevertheless, provided by developments in neighbouring Uganda. Here the victory of Yoweri Museveni's National Resistance Army (NRA) against the dictator Milton Obote, in 1986 after many years of fighting from the bush, had been won with a substantial input from second generation Rwandese Tutsi exiles. Himself a Hima, an ethnic grouping with some historical ties with the Tutsi,[21] Museveni was widely held to have been sympathetic to, and given logistical support for, the largely Tutsi Rwandese Patriotic Front, when it crossed the border in 1990 to begin military operations in northern Rwanda.

Whether the RFP wanted simply to overthrow Habyarimana's government in favour of its own 'ethnic' interest or, alternatively, to use its military leverage as a basis for power-sharing in a newly reorganised, reunited and democratic Rwanda is a matter of some debate.[22] What is known is that while the United Nations, neighbouring states, as well as many Rwandese politicians and active citizens, both Hutu and Tutsi, strove for an internationally-agreed accommodation, a countervailing tendency, made up of a number of political parties and factions both within and outside the MRND government, coalesced to defend it against what they saw as a repeat of 1963.[23] This time however, said the leaders of Hutu-Power, as they came to call themselves,[24] there would be no second chance for the Tutsi 'enemy,' no basis upon which the external 'threat' to the Hutu 'social revolution' of more than thirty years standing would be allowed to work its contagion into the fabric of Rwandese society, no turning the clock back, no Burundi in Rwanda. Contingency plans were drawn up, black lists of Rwandese Tutsi as well as moderate Hutu *ibyitso* (alleged RFP collaborators) prepared, and quasi-covert but nationwide militia armed, trained, and put in a state of readiness.[25]

The self-proclaimed carriers of the authentic vision of the Hutu state awaited their signal. It came on 6 April 1994. Habyarimana's private plane conveying him and his Burundi counterpart from another bout of peace talks in Dar-es-Salaam—where the vacillating Rwandese president had been under presure from other East African heads of state to implement the

Arusha peace accords he had already signed the previous August—was shot out of the sky close to Kigali airport. In view of what happened thereafter responsibility for who carried out the attack is ultimately immaterial.[26] What matters is that in the succeeding days of chaos, Hutu-Power wrested full control of the government from those elements still loyal to the Arusha arrangements. With the assistance of the Presidental Guard, it immediately began to carry out its nationwide contingency plans. In Kigali, the Tutsi elite as well as Hutu government and opposition party adversaries were slaughtered. So too were human rights activists, schoolteachers and businessmen. If this suggests an orchestrated campaign of selective massacre, the escalation of the killings thereafter begs the question whether Hutu-Power had always intended to kill every last Tutsi in Rwanda. The incessant inflammatory broadcasts from the ostensibly 'independent' Radio-Television Libre des Mille Collines and from the pages of the journal *Kangura*,[27] seem to suggest an answer in the affirmative. Moreover, a renewed RPF offensive towards Kigali launched *after* the events of 6 April seemed to provide retrospective justification for an urgent and uncompromising Hutu-Power response.[28] Here was an emergency government which under the cover of war had found its pretext to eliminate *in toto* the communal body, which, it argued, had threatened the integrity of the modern Rwandese state and its agenda since its founding. And any other opponents too. Yet here was also a government too weak to defend either the integrity of its territorial borders or a terrified Hutu population convinced by that government that it was they who would be butchered by the RPF. This almost schizophrenic tension surely compounded and radicalised the killing process. As the RPF advanced and the Hutu government retreated, so the possibility, even the probability, of ultimate state destruction stared its ministers in the face. With the RPF hurricane threatening to engulf them, there could be no holding back. All Tutsi would be killed, those who were friends, those given sanctuary by the church, women, children, across the country, even if it meant turning Rwanda into a wasteland in the process; even if it meant a veritable Rwandese Gotterdammerung.

These apocalyptic events, beginning in April 1994, bring to mind other strikingly similar genocidal scenarios, in particular, in Indonesia, almost thirty years earlier. In 1965 a botched coup in which a number of senior generals were killed, and for which the Communist Party of Indonesia (PKI) was blamed and widely held responsible, provided the pretext for a massive army-led extermination of perhaps half a million communists, sympathisers and their families.[29] As in Rwanda, so here, large elements of the population were mobilised to participate in this archipelago-wide manhunt, though the supposed executive power, President Sukarno, played no role whatsoever. He had in effect been eliminated as an active political player both by the rapidity of events and by politically motivated generals who had stepped into the breach in what they claimed to be a national emergency mortally threatening the integrity of state and society.

But where does all this assist comparison with the Holocaust? In Indonesia, as in Rwanda, one may be able to differentiate between 'perpetrators' and 'victims' but one can also without much difficulty discern a plausible, tangible dynamic between the two. The communist 'threat' was not entirely a figment of General Nasuntion and Suharto's imagination, anymore than the RPF was entirely blameless for the explosion of violence in April 1994. Moreover, in neighbouring Burundi, the situation was genuinely reversed. Here it was Tutsi, though in population terms a minority, who controlled the apparatus of state and state-violence and who had unequivocally been primary perpetrators in the genocide of the Hutu in 1972, and to a lesser degree in the series of inter-ethnic massacres of 1988, 1993, and 1995.[30] This does not mean that the vast majority of Tutsi men, women and children in Rwanda, or the families of PKI affiliates in Indonesia, were anything than innocent 'victims' when the killings began. What it does mean is that, at least on one level, there was in these countries a genuine struggle for power between two (or more) definable sides. By contrast, the most striking thing about the countdown to the Holocaust is how utterly and totally it was a one-sided affair.

There can be no question of any genuine dynamic in which Jews as a group even remotely threatened Nazi power or state authority. Nazis were 'absolute' perpetrators, Jews, 'absolute' victims.

Yet, paradoxically, even here there *was* a dynamic of genocide. For many Germans there did exist in the 1920s and 1930s a genuine, real struggle between themselves and the Jews.[31] It may have all been a function of an entirely distorted, even paranoid mindset, but it did not make it any the less 'real' for those who believed it. And as with Rwanda, so here there was a given historical moment which gave definition to the 'struggle.' "They should not have staged 9 November 1918 with impunity" raged Hitler to the Czech foreign minister, Chvalkovsky, more than twenty years later in January, 1939.[32] The 'they' was the Jews and their sin was supposed responsibility for the insurrectionary movement on the streets of Germany which, popular opinion believed, had forced Germany to sign the armistice and accept defeat in the First World War. 'Every German knows,' stated a book written in 1922 that was popular among university students, that 'Prussianism and heroism go together. Judaism and defeatism go together.'[33] Revolution on the streets of Germany, the collapse of the Reich, the abdication and flight of the Kaiser were the proof for anybody who doubted it: Germany had not been defeated in the war, she had had victory snatched away from her by a filthy conspiracy which had stabbed her in the back. The conspiracy was led and run by international Jewry. Their purpose was to destroy the Reich and turn it into a Bolshevik satrapy run by themselves. Its internal agents were Jewish-Bolsheviks, who had opposed the war and who were now going to undermine and sweep away everything for which respectable, *echt* Germans stood. If the seeds of Rwanda's 1994 genocide can be traced back to 1959 and the 'national' trauma associated with the collapse of colonialism which led to five further years of revolution, civil war, and massive societal dislocation, so too can the seeds of the Holocaust be found in a not dissimilar sequence, between late 1918 and 1923. As with Rwanda, these were for Germans *anni horribili*. And coming to terms with a largely self-inflicted mutilation was for many Germans psychologically too hard to bear. An explanation that pointed the finger at some supra-powerful but malevolent force made much more sense.[34] That this bore no relationship to Jews qua Jews was beside the point. In their frenzied liquidation of the soviets in Berlin, Munich, and elsewhere, the armed and self-styled *Trutz und Schutzbund* had added two and two together to make five. The threat to Germany was a Jewish threat. Golo Mann has asserted of these years that antisemitic passions were much more intense and violent than they were either in the period 1930–33 or 1933–1945.[35] It was certainly Hitler's reference point. 9 November 1918, he concluded in his speech to the Czech foreign minister, "shall be avenged . . . the Jews shall be annihilated in our land."[36]

But if the supposed direct Jewish threat—in the form of the soviets—had been physically defeated, anxiety about them no more evaporated than it did with Rwanda's *inyenzi*. German Jews, though actually a small, highly integrated religious minority, continued to be noted for their conspicious attachment to and involvement in the social and cultural life of the new, if for many ordinary Germans, nationally adulterated and debased, Weimar republic just as in Rwanda, despite the supposed quotas on their advancement, the Tutsi still seemed, prior to 1994, to occupy most of the more prestigious and attractive posts in embassies and international aid projects.[37] In post-1918 Germany, the Jews were similarly *perceived* by many not only to have ridden the economic disasters of inflation and then mass unemploy-ment, but to have actually done so at their expense, 'taking over' in the process, the good jobs, the money, the status.[38] Hitler's populist mobilisation of the masses, in the run-up to the *Machtergreifung* of 1933, carried with it implicit as well as explicit messages about the Jews. The new order would restore true Germans to the dignity and freedom which they deserved. A newly reconstituted *Volksgemeinschaft* would have no place for those who were not its authentic members. Like the Tutsi in Rwanda, the Jews would not only be occupationally frozen out but even more dramatically and completely divorced and isolated from the country's national life. And this would be given respectability in a country full of universities and research institutes, by academics, scientists, doctors and other opinion formers who flocked to endorse publicly the Nazi message that the Jews were an 'alien' race without any historic connection with the authentic Germany, whose very physical presence contaminated its people's racial health and collective hygiene.[39] Yet, despite German Jewry's increasing economic and social marginalisation under the Nazis, the mental fixation of the regime remained unyielding. As an SS training pamphlet stated in 1936: "The Jew is the German people's most dangerous enemy."[40]

It was this entirely 'constructed' Manichean adversary, who in his Jewish-Communist malevolence, posed the real, long-term threat; biding his time, waiting for the right moment of German weakness to once again strike at the nation's heart, not only from 'inside' Hitler's brave, new Reich but also from the outside, from the United States, Britain, Leon Blum-led France and above all supposedly Jew-led Soviet Russia. Forcing actual Jews to leave what had become by spring 1939 a Greater Germany embracing Austria and the truncated Czech republic, thus far from alleviating the threat, only served to exacerbate it by encouraging Jews to find refuge elsewhere. Further, invading Poland in September 1939 turned completely on its head Germany's *judenfrei* intentions by hugely increasing its captive Jewish population. If under cover of a wider European conflict the Nazis might, however, at last find an opportunity to deal with this demographic nightmare as well as organise a final settling of accounts with ubiquitous Jewish 'power,' all well and good. On the other hand, the very visionary agenda of Hitler's war, geared as it was not to some limited goal à la Clausewitz, but to an all-or-nothing struggle, the ultimate prize of which was the destruction and conquest of Soviet Russia, posed the potential consequences of failure. A sense of invincible strength mixed with euphoria may well have been the Nazi self-appraisal in the first weeks of Operation Barbarossa, in late June and July 1941. But as the summer wore on, it became clear that what Germany was actually engaged in was indeed of a life and death nature. Failure to keep to Barbarossa's timetable, failure to smash the Soviet military machine, all pointed not to strength but to ultimate vulnerability.[41] The spectre of 1919 was returning with a vengeance. And unless desperate measures were taken to skotch it, Judeo-Bolshevism would simply turn the tables to wreak ultimate destruction on the Reich. It was this searing tension between, on the one hand, the opportunity to enact a 'final solution of the Jewish question,' and on the other, a horrified realisation that they, the Nazis, themselves had possibly engineered Germany's own special road to oblivion that acted as trigger in the high summer and early autumn of 1941 to the beginnings of full-blown, systematic genocide.[42]

But just as the 'primitive black man' narrative is belied by the tightly centralised and bureaucratic nature of the Rwandese state, whose compilation of district by district lists of inhabitants, ensured a very modern systematisation to the process of mass killing, so, obversely, one can overplay the streamlined, routinised efficiency thesis associated with the Holocaust. The killings in the East perpetrated by Einsatz, Wehrmacht and Axis allies in 1941 bear many of the hallmarks of frenzied, mass revenge killings we might otherwise associate with those perpetrated by the Rwandese army, gendarmerie and death squads. True, they were ultimately superseded by the conveyor belt mode of liquidation, fixed industrial systems, the ultimate model for which were the gas chambers and crematoria at Auschwitz-Birkenau. These technological innovations, certainly made possible the disposal of thousands of people on a daily basis and in so doing psychologically, as well as physically, did create distance between perpetrators who were 'functionaries' and victims who were simply 'cargo.' Yet while all this was going on, daily face to face mass killing by ordinary German conscripts and policemen as well as by Einsatzgruppen and 'native' auxiliaries continued into 1942 and 1943 on the Eastern Front, in the Balkans and nearer to the Reich heartlands, in the process of deportation to the death camps.[43] The numbers killed in these bloody, messy and increasingly brutal operations were immense reminding us, as do the seven to eight weeks of the Rwandan apocalypse, that state of the art technology is not in itself a precondition for, or indeed necessary for, the perpetration of an efficient genocide.[44]

The purpose of this exercise, however, has not been to draw exact parallels between the Holocaust and Rwanda. There are clear variations in time-frame and political context. Rwanda's initial national trauma associated with decolonisation produced a radical Hutu regime almost immediately, which then gradually became institutionalised before a final crisis revitalised its most extreme tendencies. A radical response to Germany's post-First World War crisis only emerged after a lengthy hiatus. Its subsequent lurch towards further war and genocide were played out on a full European stage over a protracted period, making Rwanda's war and genocide seem by comparison a parochial and transient affair. Moreover, cultural disjunctures, as well as obvious dissimilarities in available weaponry, may account for the fact that despite the grisliness of the Einsatz and other 'hands on' killings, there was little in the way of mutilation, disemboweling, or mass rape of the victims as there was in Rwanda.[45] Above all, for all the demonisation of the Tutsi, there was at least a kernel of truth in the Hutu fear of them. The Nazi *projection* of threat, by contrast, remains entirely in the realms of fantasy, one so charged and pathological that it made a supposed collective Jewry all-powerful, when not only was the premise of collectivity false, but the power non-existent.[46] The intensity of this projection may indeed be in inverse relation to the entirely exceptional lengths to which the Nazis went to try and eradicate all Jews.

But if this confirms the Holocaust *par excellence*, similarities with Rwanda are too salient simply to be dismissed. In both instances, the victim groups were not only represented in monolithic terms by the perpetrators but as some people-obstacle which threatened the integrity of an agenda for national survival and/or regeneration. That in itself suggests the particular circumstances in which this role was fashioned and developed. For the Hutu in Rwanda, Tutsi may have for generations been viewed as an alien grouping feeding on the body of Hutu society, though it is doubtful that there ever existed a hatred of loathing as intense or religiously informed as pre-modern Europe felt towards its Jews.[47] However, in both cases, though in quite different ways, what held these antipathies largely in check was a series of social, cultural and economic markers which delineated the exact position of each group within the broader society, reinforced in turn by political-legal restraints against boundary transgression.[48] These restraints were neither fair nor equitable. They were not intended to be, but rather were strictly hierarchical with the expressed intention of preserving one group's political and/or economic power or prerogatives at the expense of the other—Tutsi over Hutu in the Rwandese case, Christians over Jews in the European one.

This situation only began to properly, and paradoxically, dangerously unravel with the emergence of the idea of the modern nation-state. Paradoxically, because this carried with it a liberal theory of citizenship which posited that all of a country's inhabitants owed not only allegiance to, but together, held a common national identity which bound them to that state, and gave them equal rights within it, regardless of their ethnic or religious origins. In both pre-1871 Germany and pre-1959 Belgian colonial Rwanda this formulation, on paper, represented a clearer opportunity to create a public domain which discarded distinctions between Jew and Christian, Hutu and Tutsi. In practice, the idea in our two cases had quite the opposite effect. In circumstances of rapid economic and social change[49] in which many Jews and Tutsi were at its high profile cutting-edge, exacerbated traditional antipathies and encouraged an alternative conceptualisation of the nation, which focused more closely on its avowed historic origins, and made claims as to its authenticity based exclusively on ethnicity. In this view, Tutsi or Jewish rights to inclusion were illegitimate. A traditional, but containable, hate model was in danger of being transformed into a highly active and volatile one. All that was needed was a genuine crisis of state to crystallise and embed in popular consciousness the charge that Tutsi and Jews were not only outsiders, but dangerous outsiders.[50]

For Rwanda, the crisis came out of a messy, confused and largely unexpected decolonisation process, in 1959, in which efforts by Tutsi to hold onto the new state, and failing that foment their own revolutionary seizure of it, were defeated. For Germany, the crisis was engendered out of the largely unexpected defeat in the Great War and an aftermath, in 1919, of acute chaos and dislocation in which revolutionary groups, many of which had leaders or cadres of Jewish background, attempted to seize control of the apparatus of the new state, but were defeated. It is important to emphasise that, in both instances, the revolutionary groups were not instantly identifiable with the traditional communal attributes of either Tutsi or Jews. Indeed, the groups themselves were responses to modernity and in the latter case involved individuals who, though of Jewish birth, were vociferous in their repudiation of that connection.[51] In both cases, however, these complexities were largely ignored in favour of an emerging myth of a Tutsi or Jewish threat to nation and state. If the myth was challenged by many who did not accept its logic, it was, nevertheless, amplified by others willing, or psychologically needing, to have the crisis explained as the outcome of subterfuge and trickery worked by secret, outside forces bent on malevolent ends. The myth of Jewish international conspiracy powerfully provided answers for many ordinary Germans in the wake of defeat and revolution.[52] But the Rwandan Tutsi, by dint of their diaspora and broad African connections, were also perceived by the more radical and conspiratorially-minded of their haters, as an internationally powerful and demonic force, to the extent that a 1990 Rwandan government pamphlet could postulate a Tutsi-Hima 'takeover' of Rwanda, led by a Hitler-like Museveni,[53] with lurking in the wings to rubber stamp the takeover, if not the entire international community, then at the very least its 'Anglo-Saxon' elements.[54]

Here we see, then, an intense psychopathological projection onto the Tutsi, as we indeed see in all perpetrator/victim relationships. But this projection in itself does not explain how a genocide of this nature happens. Genocide requires a political will which can only come from a state apparatus which is willing to carry the mythic input into the inner workings of its state policy and agenda. What is thus telling about MRND Rwanda and Nazi Germany is not simply that both regimes had been shaped by myth, but could locate an actual historic moment (i.e. 1919/1959) when the myth became incontestable reality. Indeed, twenty years on for the Nazis, more than thirty years on for Hutu-Power, they carried in their heads not only memory of this moment, but their own perpetrators version of a 'Never Again' response to it. Never again would the Jews be allowed to foist a pernicious Bolshevism onto Germany. Never again would the *inyenzi* be allowed to foist a racial Tutsi tutelage onto Rwanda.[55] The myth became central to what the new regimes were striving to transcend but also in a sense underscored their weakness and vulnerability. Their agendas were postulated on the idea that a new homogenous monoculture could be created, exclusive of either Tutsi or Jews. But there were also equally important parallel assumptions that national regeneration and wellbeing were achievable without the existence of such people.

But what if the political and social route towards these goals simply engendered another crisis or crises? The running jump at political and societal transformation—through war, specifically war with an allegely Jew-led Soviet Russia—underscored the ultimate fragility of the whole Nazi experiment. Once Operation Barbarossa started going wrong, genocide became not simply a spasm response but paralleled and became closely enmeshed with Germany's life and death war struggle. In the process, many other groups who were outside the Nazi 'universe of obligation,' to use Helen Fein's language, notably Roma (gypsies), were also marked down for elimination as were political opponents, both close to and in opposition to the state. The killing thus escalated as the struggle became more bitter and final.[56] Similarly, Hutu-Power conflict with the RPF posed not so much the probability of victory but a much greater likelihood of defeat and destruction. As the Hutu state strove to meet the challenge, it unleashed genocide against the Tutsi population as well as its political opponents. But as its edifice came crashing down, so the scope and scale of its killing intensified, embracing a further Rwandese ethnic group, the Twa, very much like the European Roma in that historically it was outside the 'universe of obligation,' as well as literally anybody who might be suspected of dissenting from its purpose.[57] In both our cases, therefore, the momentum towards total genocide was carried forward in the knowledge that the state itself was on the brink of destruction. And though in reality, it was self-destruction, it was for Nazis, as for Hutu-Power, the victim's fault.

## III

The total genocides of Rwanda and Germany have, then, striking characteristics in common, compounded ultimately by the fact that both involved dual elements, destruction and self-destruction, genocide and national suicide. At the end of the day Germany reached Year Zero, a state which was non-existent, a society in complete ruins. Exactly the same could be said for post-genocide Rwanda.[58] But if some total genocides, such as that perpetrated by the Khmer Rouge regime in Cambodia between 1975 and 1979, produced this result, others, notably the Turkish destruction of the Armenians during the First World War, did not. Turkey's creation and indeed flourishing as a nation-state was, in a very particular sense, predicated on its genocidal actions both during and after the 1914–18 war.[59]

If ultimate results may not be a precise guide, where then do we search for an explanatory historical framework which would link Armenia to Cambodia, the Holocaust to Rwanda? Certainly, in all these cases, we are dealing with perpetrator regimes which in some sense were revolutionary, though one might add that Rwanda had moved a long way from its revolutionary moment back in the 1960s. Is revolution then, or revolution linked to war, as Robert Melson has suggested with reference to Armenia and the Holocaust, the key to genocide? There have been many twentieth century revolutions, obscure as well as famous, but not all have produced this result, Cuba being one obvious example. War linked to revolution or vice-versa would seem to narrow down the exceptions. Looking at an earlier century, however, one would not associate the American revolutionary war with the phenomenon, though interestingly one might if one were looking at the French revolutionary wars a decade later.[60] And what of genocides which happen in peacetime; Stalin's destruction of the kulaks, for instance?[61] Or of states which do not claim revolutionary credentials, yet which, as in the case of Indonesia, have busily engaged in genocide, most notably against the East Timoreans, since the later 1970s?[62]

If there is a pattern here, it is not obviously discernible by direct reference to a type of society or regime.[63] To say that 'totalitarian' or ideologically driven regimes may be more likely to commit genocide may correlate closely to some of the available data,[64] though it may beg the question whether Rwanda is, or has been, more 'totalitarian' than some of her Central African neighbours, or whether a genocide-prone Communist China has been more ideologically-driven than a not noticeably genocidal Communist East Germany. Nor, in any of this, is there a way of explaining why some genocides carry through to destruction of a group in toto compared with others which, at some stage, break off the engagement.

Yet the growing incidence of genocide in recent decades, in all hemispheres,[65] surely does demand explanation. If both the Holocaust and Rwanda are part of a bigger pattern, an unravelling sequence of contemporary history rather than simply spasmodic and otherwise unrelated aberrations, where should we turn for an answer? Historical writing which is itself ideologically-driven is not helpful. The Great Soviet Encyclopedia which, in the wake of the Nazi defeat, defined genocide as 'as an offshoot of decaying capitalism,'[66] rather conveniently ignores the fact that Communist Russia itself, closely followed by other putative Marxist states, China, Cambodia, possibly Ethiopia, have been in the vanguard of its operation. Some genocides, in the era of the Cold War, may have originated in the interstices of the contest between the communist and the capitalist world. Tibet in 1959, Indonesia in 1965, the 'dirty war' in Argentina in the late 1970s (arguably a political genocide), or Guatemala in 1983, all had something of this quality. But if now, as American guru, Francis Fukuyama assures us, the collapse of communism and the end of the Soviet system have brought not only an end to these sorts of struggles but to history itself,[67] how—and where—do we locate Rwanda's catastrophe?

To be fair to Fukuyama, he has not argued that conflict in many parts of the globe would not continue, but rather that this would not be part of the greater scheme of things. This analysis, however, would argue the converse to be true by focusing on the emergence of the very international system with which Fukuyama is so enamoured: capitalism. Fukuyama argues that capitalism, combined with the liberal ideology of the West, is the goal toward which all humankind is striving. But it is a truism to note that its historical development can be traced to a very small number of Western European countries in the early modern period and that the primary infrastructural arrangement which made for success was their formation and consolidation as nation-states.[68] These early nation-states were prototypal in the sense that nothing of the sort had previously been attempted. They consequently began with no coherent blueprint or agenda for social change or economic development. Yet their growing international clout, including political and economic penetration into all corners of the globe, as well as the export of ideas, ensured that other societies, which either wished to emulate their power or not be 'taken over' by them, would pay considerable attention to the model. It was during this embryonic stage in the formation of a Western dominated international system, that this select group of nation-states set and determined the ground-rules for 'progress' and 'development,' most particularly associated with the market-place accumulation of capital.[69] It is noteworthy, however, that this did not prevent these states themselves from breaking the rules whenever it was considered to be in their 'national interest.'

There were a variety of short-cuts to nation-state building and expansion. These included hyper-exploitation through slavery, commercial as well as outright warfare, and the ethnic cleansing, deportation, or elimination of peoples who stood in the way of national and territorial consolidation, settlement and/or control of economic or actual resources, either within the state's home boundaries or in its increasing colonies overseas. Most usually, though not always, these genocidal acts against perceived people-obstacles to the 'national interest' were initiated at crisis moments under the cover, or in the aftermath, of war.[70] Nevertheless, by a combination of mainstream accumulation and the short-cut, 'a new world order' was already emerging in the eighteenth and nineteenth centuries, or more accurately a 'new world pecking order.'[71] There were strong states at its front, weaker states behind them. The race was on to modernise, everything depended on that. The price of failure would be political and/or economic subjugation: eternal weakness.

What is remarkable about this race is the lengths so many polities have gone to in order to catch up. Japan provides perhaps the example *par excellence*. Here was a traditional state which at break-neck speed completely transformed its social and economic arrangements with a view to becoming modern and so meeting the Western challenge. What is equally remarkable about this, is that it did so, albeit with considerable upheaval and bloodletting, without anything we could specifically call genocide. Perhaps, simplistically, one could surmise that this was because it was already largely nationally and culturally homogenous, and succeeded in what it was attempting to do. It became a coherent capitalist society with a large industrial, including initially, military-industrial base, within the dominant Western system.[72] But this, of course, is only half the picture. With the race for position perpetual, what thus remained so frustrating for a state like Japan, even though by the early twentieth century it was clearly in the first rank, was that it felt itself held back and restrained by the other key global players. Resort to a war of expansion to regain its economic and political position was ultimately perceived as its only available option. There is a problem, however, with this sort of short-cut. The higher the stakes, the greater the gamble, the more probable the whole enterprise might come tumbling down around you like a pack of cards. This is what happened to Japan in 1945. But it had already happened to Germany a global war earlier.

Like Japan, Germany was an already modernised and advanced nation-state when its political and military elites eagerly resorted to war in 1914—'a war of illusions' as Fritz Fischer has so cogently called it[73]—in order to assert a position from which it perceived it had been consistently thwarted by the other dominant Great Powers. The perception in this was at least as important as the reality. A latecomer to nation-statehood and to the colonial scramble, late Wilhelmine Germany was self-consciously aware that despite its rapid industrialisation and increasing European dominance, it would still have to make up considerable lost ground in order to gain parity with its key rivals. In its belated colonial advance it was prepared, therefore, to be utterly ruthless. Resistance from people-obstacles in Southwest and east African colonies were dealt with in genocidal fashion.[74] Yet at the end of the day, its striving for European and possibly broader hegemony collapsed in national exhaustion and revolutionary chaos. Phase one of Germany's attempts to 'realise the unrealisable'[75] culminated in an internationally imposed peace of national humiliation. The Weimar interregnum culminated in a further bout of almost total economic collapse. 'Mainstream' routes to domestic economic and political cohesion and international Great Power status had been tried and exhausted. The ensuing massive social and economic dislocation thus paved the way for an entirely radicalised approach, one which on the micro-level did not accept classic Western liberal universalist views about what constituted either society or indeed social reality, and on the macro-level repudiated the official rules which were supposed to govern relations between states. Nazism in this sense represented an ambitious and audacious programme of 'alternative' development.[76] National regeneration would be achieved through a racially informed and determined homogenisation and cohesion of its people. The alleged extraneous elements —'criminal, 'asocial,' the physically and mentally ill, Jews, Gypsies and other racial *Untermenschen*—would not be incorporated in this *Gleichshaltung* but physically expelled or expunged.[77] Deriving strength from its social transformation and a new found, allegedly historic, sense of national unity and community, the agenda would move not simply to reassert Germany's independence, but to transform the very fabric of international relations. Through the instrument of total war, a new German dominated European, even world order, would be fashioned.

If, however, the Nazi experiment (phase two of Germany's efforts to 'realise the unrealisable') represents the most extreme example of an attempt to buck the system in which its specific attributes were entirely *sui generis*, it is noteworthy that the major dictatorships of the inter-war years were all, in their often highly individualistic ways, willing to tear up the rule book of traditional and accepted means of incremental growth and opt instead for high risk strategies of alternative development.[78] And these in turn became models for development elsewhere. If Fascism and Kemalism fell by the wayside, or were replaced in the post-1945 world by more modern, supposedly streamlined ideologies, Stalinist 'socialism in one country' certainly provided the model for many third world revolutionary elites who were attempting to transcend Western dependency in favour of an authentic independence. The parallels between many of these new post-colonial states and the Germany of 1933, the Russia of 1917, or the Ottoman Empire of 1908, are quite striking. The Rwanda of 1959, like the Germany of 1933, was led literally by a bunch of 'nobodys,'[79] who were in effect in power only by dint of the fact that the old regime, through crisis-laden circumstances, had proved itself discredited and bankrupt. In 'normal' circumstances the 'nobodys' agenda would be dismissed as eccentric or downright lunatic. In order to fashion a new legitimacy for themselves, it thus became incumbent upon them to deliver development, well-being and prosperity in double-quick time. For the Rwandan revolutionary programme this entailed its very own short-cut: removal of the traditional landowning (more specifically, cattle-wealthy) and governing class in favour of the Hutu masses. If genocide was not actively intended in this programme, the programme certainly contained the potential. If on a much less grand scale than Germany in 1933, it assumed steam-rolling over any political, social or communal interests which did not fit into the programme or actively resisted it. Nevertheless, the actuality of full-blown genocide only came considerably later, at a crisis moment when the state, in a belated attempt to transcend fully these limitations, exposed its inherent vulnerability and weakness.

If, however, Germany and Rwanda are among a handful of states where a particular set of historic and actual convergences have provided for the resolution of self-inflicted crisis through total genocide, these circumstances are not so utterly dissimilar from a score of modern states which have in recent decades either experienced less intense forms of the phenomenon or have the potential to be arenas for enactment. The reasons why this is so have already been outlined. The international nation-state system which did not emerge fully until the 1960s and 1970s, with the ebb of European imperialism, demanded of all its members participation in a global economic and political community. Not being a level playing field but, on the contrary, one where an advanced group of Western states dictated the rules of the game, the onus was on less developed, even very poor, new states to compete. The further behind states have perceived themselves to be, the more urgent the perceived need to catch up, to maximise their resource potential, rapidly modernise and become strong. Hence the need for short-cuts.

Not all states who, in the process have committed genocide, have opted for a path overtly antagonistic to the dominant Western players. Countries like Indonesia and Guatemala, for instance, have cemented their place in the capitalist system by exterminating both those who have resisted and those who have actively sought power in order to pursue alternative—communist or socialist—agendas.[80] By contrast, on occasions, communism has itself been used as a vehicle for an entirely radicalised and overtly anti-Western approach. Cambodia between 1975 and 1979 represents the most dramatic example of this 'third way' to date.[81] If, however, the extremity of this case would seem to bring us back to a combination of revolution and the radicalised ideology of the revolutionary party in power, as preconditions for total genocide, a note of caution may be in order. Regimes which began with revolution as their justification, and ideology as their apparent guide, may in the longer term be propelled by nothing more complex than a *Wille zu Macht* determined, in the minds of the leaders, by one enduring and constant theme, the need to assert genuine state independence within the international system. Saddam Hussein's odyssey of short-cuts involving war, more war, and genocide as a by-product, was not ultimately impelled by Ba'athist pan-Arabism, but by a naked determination to make and keep the Iraqi nation-state strong.[82] And while Saddam's Ba'athist rhetoric is a facade for popular consumption only, both Slobodan Milosevic in Serbia and Franco Tudjman in Croatia have attempted people mobilisation by adroitly changing their spots from communist to nationalist.[83] Yet their resort, or their Bosnia or Krajina proxies, to wars of territorial aggrandisement—in which ethnic cleansing and sub-genocide have been conscious by-products—is driven by simple state-building imperatives, albeit founded on perceived historic missions to create and consolidate enlarged but homogeneous versions of their respective states.

Of critical note here is the response of the international community in the guise of the United Nations to such ventures. True, both Iraq and Serbia (though, not Croatia), through isolation and quarantine, have been effectively turned into pariahs in the international state system. This was not, however, for enacting genocide, but rather for violating the system's first rule, namely invading and attempting to annex other recognised and notionally independent nation-states.[84] Nobody is talking of dismantling either state as a result. On the contrary, in time they will be duly reintegrated within the system of which they are an integral part. Their international reprobation and censure has been, in other words, for attempting to bring the official ground-rules which govern relations between nation-states into disrepute, not for what they have done to populations under their rule. Leo Kuper, an authoritative and sober observer, focuses precisely on this reality when he states that "the United Nations, for all practical purposes defends the right of the sovereign territorial state . . . as an integral part of its sovereignty . . . to commit genocide."[85] If MRND (or for that matter Hutu-Power) Rwanda were still in existence, we could be sanguine about its continued representation at the UN, the political and military backing it would receive from key Western governments, the economic assistance it would seek and most probably obtain from the IMF and other donors.[86] But would not the same approximate contours also have been valid if Nazi Germany, instead of going down to total defeat, in 1942 or 1943 had crushed the Soviet Union at Stalingrad or Kursk, forcing the Western Powers to come to terms with the Nazi new order as part of the international system?

## IV

If MRND Rwanda, writ-small, and Nazi Germany, writ-large, were both ultimately swept away by the overload or over-reach implicit in their efforts to 'realise the unrealisable,' what then does this tell us about the pattern and/or incidence of genocide in the future? This essay has argued that modern genocide[87] is closely bound up with the efforts of nation-states to operate independently and effectively within an international nation-state system. In order to achieve this, regimes which are the legacy of previous failure have undertaken radicalised, or forced pace, or 'alternative,' programmes for development which have involved by-passing or avoiding the accepted 'official' ground-rules and conventions of the system. This may not in itself lead to genocide. However, when a regime encounters, or perceives itself to encounter, serious obstacles which seem to threaten not only the achievement of this agenda but the integrity of the state itself, the potentiality for it 'taking it out' on some 'scapegoat' group or groups is greatly magnified.[88] Total genocide, as in Armenia, the Holocaust, or Rwanda, has been the end-result where specific 'insider/outsider' groups have, through the regime's pro-jection, been endowed with a supposedly historic, yet powerful malevolence, to both itself and its interpretation of the authentic state/society. Only the complete destruction of the group, as a group, is thus posited as enabling the state to overcome its crisis and breakthrough to the successful completion of its programme.

Yet, while these psychosocial dimensions are clearly instructive, if not critical, it is the structural framework, the imperative to modernise and compete within the capitalist world system which, in giving the nation-state its *raison d'etre*, also provides the primary well-springs and motor for the perpetration of genocide. This presupposes that all modern states have and will continue to have the potential for genocide. Yet it is obvious that this is not carried in equal degrees. The most genocidally-prone states in the contemporary world are those caught in a dilemma of perception and self-perception; the states, in short, who most intensely perceive themselves to be weak, yet feel that they *ought* to be strong, and who in order to be so are prepared to go to the greatest lengths to remedy their perceived shortcomings.

With this formulation in mind, it might be possible to suggest which states in the near future are likely to be the most high-risk ones and which the least. This, of course, carries with it the obvious imponderables as well as one huge assumption as to the persistence of the current, overarching, international nation-state system. Yet this essay is predicated on the persistence of an emerging pattern of contemporary history, in some ways linked to Wallerstein's categorisation of core, semi-peripheral and peripheral elements. If interactions between these elements may undoubtedly lead to key transformations, and if, in particular, the nation-states within the core may in time possibly integrate into larger political-cum-economic units prefigured in Nafta or the European Union, either cooperating or competing[89] with one another, nevertheless, it is assumed here that this core, whatever shape or form it takes, will continue to command and control the essential terms of the global economic system well into the next millenium. It is on this assumption that I would propose a *three tier hierachy*, within which we can locate the greatest potentiality for genocide.

Tier one includes all the leading industrial nation-states of what used to be called the 'free world,' in other words, Wallerstein's core. It is likely that there will be little or no genocide committed in this tier in the immediate future, at least not by states within their own territorial domains. Liberal institutions, democratic checks and balances and the civil society which characterise the political culture of this tier are, however, likely to pay only a minimal role in that genocide-avoidance.[90] Indeed, the states of tier one will continue to have direct responsibility for much of the genocidal and other mass killing perpetrated in tiers two and three, through the political and economic aid, including military logistical and training support, they will continue to provide.[91] Not only, in other words, is tier one's non-genocidal rating in no way exemplary, or related to its institutional framework, its position at the top of the global economic hierarchy acts as the very stimulus to the genocidal-prone actions of regimes lower down the rung. Though the internal coherence of states in this tier is now itself questionable, leading to a future of increasing insecurity, disorder and societal breakdown,[92] domestic genocidal tendencies are only likely to emerge if their political-economic predominance in the global system is seriously challenged by others.

If tier one, thus, will safeguard itself from genocide by being ahead of the international race, tier three, paradoxically, will witness little or no genocide by dint of being out of the race altogether. Currently, there are very few recognised nation-states that would unquestionably fit this category. Candidates, however, would include the very poorest, weakest and most underdeveloped countries in the international system, embracing much, if not all, of sub-Sahara Africa, as well as possibly large chunks of Central Asia. Here economic and societal breakdown is already so acute and widespread that the continued existence of *effective*, infrastructurally cohesive states may only require time and the termination of Western, international aid to cease altogether. Forced-pace, state-driven modernisation in previous decades, with a view to competing within the international system, bears considerable responsibility for this potential outcome. Far from enabling these states, it has served only to underscore the massive overload implicit in the attempt. The major manifestations of this overload, particularly in terms of economic debt and linked environmental degradation, mean that these are now not simply falling by the wayside in the international race, but beginning to fall apart at the seams.[93] Indeed, doubly paradoxical in this may be the retrospective realisation that the genocide in Rwanda possibly represented the last gasp of such a polity attempting to maintain its coherence and status as a fully-fledged entity within the system.[94]

This should emphasise a singular (even idiosyncratic) aspect of the origins of the Rwandan genocide. Rwanda was able to buck the terms of the international state system for thirty odd years only by acute and total dependence upon it. The aim of the Hutu revolutionaries at the outset, may, in Lemarchand's words, have been to undertake a "fundamental transformation of the economic and social structure of society,"[95] but this quickly gave way in practice to a self-perpetuating and corrupt regime whose survival and integrity was premised not so much on creating conditions for change, but on getting as much aid out of the international community as possible.[96] Rural poverty and rapid population growth certainly enabled the MRND government to play the aid card in this way, though whether these factors, alongside attendant environmental pressures on land and habitat helped, in 1994, to precipitate Rwanda over the edge, is debatable.[97] What is noteworthy, however, is that its strong centralised, administrative infrastructure, founded both on its colonial, and equally importantly, pre-colonial coherence, marked it off from many other, often much larger but in practice acutely fragmented sub-Saharan entities, while its economic performance—thanks again, largely to Western economic aid—confirmed that, until the mid-1980s, Rwanda could not be classed as a typical example of post-colonial African disaster, but relatively speaking, as a success story with encouraging indices for economic growth, as well as for educational and health care development.[98]

It was the radical, yet also entirely desperate, Hutu response to what it saw as a direct Tutsi threat to the very integrity of these achievements, aspired and worked for on the rhetorical, if not actual, behalf of the country's masses, which catapulted Rwanda into a genocide, the consequences of which may finally and possibly irreversibly confirm its tier three position. With chances of its post-apocalypse recovery very slim or non-existent, the paradox lies in the possibility that the future Rwandese state may simply not be capable or sufficiently viable to commit systematic genocide. This does not signify, however, that its future status will be associated with the diminution of violence or the absence of mass killings. Its post-genocide experience, from the massive hemorrhage of its majority Hutu population, in the wake of the RPF victory, into Burundi, Tanzania and Zaire, through to the continuing massacres by both sides, as the surviving refugees have returned, should be sufficient evidence of that. Moreover, the unravelling of events in Zaire (Congo), in particular, in large part as a direct result of the export there of Rwanda's inter-communal tensions, poses the degree to which states already precipitously close to internal breakdown can be pushed over the abyss by the actions of their neighbours.[99] What we could thus be witnessing in the heart of Africa, as indeed in other parts of the continent already, is the emergence of a quite different pattern of killing than where the state organises and directs genocide through identifiable perpetrators in *its* army, *its* militia, *its* gendarmerie. With the state little more than a shell, and an ideology relevant to state-building largely redundant, petty warlords are likely to be the only authority able to maintain a semblance of local order. Yet if parts of Africa, Central Asia and elsewhere fragment in this way, possibly, though not necessarily, along historic tribal or ethnic lines, their rivalries and standoffs are likely to give rise to large zones of acute lawlessness. If in recent decades there have been zones of genocides,[100] these new zones of endemic instability and warfare are likely to be fueled by near-total environmental collapse, mass movements of refugees, famine, and the one remaining commodity super-abundantly available: advanced modern weaponry.

If thus genocide in tier three is in the process of being replaced by more diverse and less easily chartable patterns of mass killing, in the remaining tier two, it is likely to hold its own, very possibly proliferating to the nth degree. Tier two consists of a broad band of states, in all hemispheres, who still perceive of themselves as nation-state players in the international system's race. Some of these players, particularly the 'Tigers' and 'Little Tigers' of the Pacific Rim, through programmes of rapid modernisation and exponential economic growth, are relatively strong states and conscious, despite the recent and continuing disastrous economic recession in the region, of their ability to narrow the gap between themselves and the economic giants of the West. What the recession has done, however, is highlight the degree to which the accelerated efforts to challenge the latter's technological edge, market lead and resources control is limited by the factors that have also beset tier three states, notably massive environmental degradation and demographic explosion as well as by fierce economic competition, both with each other and the industrial giants themselves. Under increasingly crisis conditions, with the collapse of the strongly Western-backed Suharto regime in Indonesia as the most prominent causality, these factors are likely to ensure that states of this type will continue to be governed by authoritarian or 'hard' regimes, usually of a military or quasi-military hue, who attempting a draconian mix of 'national-socialist' measures, will stop at nothing to fulfill their state building agendas.[101]

This again need not necessarily lead to genocide. But the temptation to overleap the limiting factors by short-cuts, even one 'great leap forward,' will be very great, especially as the race, and, thus, the crisis conditions heat up. War and territorial conquest could well be likely consequences as will be the consolidation of residual frontier regions or disputed territories in the interests of maximised resource control and settlement. That the most obvious victims of these trends are likely to be indigenous peoples who straddle such regions or territories is indeed clearly observable in Indonesia's persistent (and Western-backed) genocidal actions in West Papua and East Timor.[102]

But it is not just the most muscular and powerful of these states that will commit these 'developmental' genocides. Much weaker states, quite literally at the bottom of the pile of tier two, such as Bangladesh, have on a smaller scale also been recent perpetrators.[103] Their determination to keep in the race against the odds, and out of tier three, will fuel increasingly desperate programmes of resource consolidation, social engineering, including population resettlement, and change. While any alleged threat to such programmes from native peoples is clearly going to be more imaginary than real, there may, however, be cases where there is genuine dynamic, where tangible resistance to the state's agenda, involving possibly secession-ist or neo-secessionist opposition,[104] may precipitate a lurch into the actuality of genocide without the fullblown symptoms of 'enemy' projection noted in Armenia, the Holocaust or Rwanda.

Ideologically-driven regimes, unwaveringly convinced of the absolute correctness of their view of social reality and utterly committed to their own special path to the achievement of state and society as 'it ought to be,' have certainly provided some of the foremost candidates for total genocide in the twentieth century. The ideological goals of a Nazi Germany or a Hutu-Power Rwanda, combined with an equally angst-laden fear of a supposed mythic enemy seeking to overthrow their state, provide a lethal concoction for which there have been few contenders to date. But on another level, these have simply been extreme, more complete examples of what so many states, attempting to short-cut, or otherwise circumvent the arrangements of the international nation-state system, have perpetrated. The terms of the system demand acceptance of the global market-place. The consolidation of these terms with the collapse of communism may, for Fukuyama, herald the end of history. Unfortunately, they also provide the best recipe for the continuation of genocide. As the demands of the system intensify, the drive of the relatively weaker states to more rapid, fast-speed development will also intensify; so in turn will the limiting factors, economic competition, demographic explosion, resource scarcity and massive ecological degradation, conspire to wreck their ambition. Genocide in the future is likely to become a function and all too regular by-product of attempts to attain the unattainable.

## Notes

1. A shortened version of this paper was originally given at the Conference of the Association of Genocide Scholars at Williamsburg, Virginia in June 1995 with financial assistance from the British Academy and University of Warwick. It was thus written before the publication of either Daniel Goldhagen's *Hitler's Willing Executioners* or Gerard Prunier's *The Rwanda Crisis* both of which contain arguments which mirror some aspects of this thesis. Where appropriate I have made changes or additions, which make reference to their work, particularly Prunier's masterly account and analysis which also makes some significant and astute points of comparison with the Holocaust. Thanks also to Anne Mackintosh (Oxfam representative in Kigali, April 1933–1994) for her comments and suggested emendations and Betty Levene for providing many of the relevant newspaper cuttings.

2. Steven T. Katz, The Holocaust in Historical Context: *Volume 1: The Holocoust and Mass Death before the Modern Age* (New York and Oxford, 1994). See also his comparative essays in *Historicism, the Holocaust and Zionism, Critical Studies in Modern Jewish Thought and History* (New York, 1992).

3. Helen Fein, "A Formula for Genocide: Comparisons of the Turkish Genocide (1915) and the German Holocaust (1939–1945)," *Comparative Studies in Sociology*, 1 (1978), pp. 271–293; Vahakn N. Dadrian, "Towards a Theory of Genocide incorporating the Instance of the Holocaust," *Holocaust and Genocide Studies*, 5 (1990, pp. 129–43; Florence Mazian, *Why Genocide? The*

*Armenian and Jewish Experiences in Perspective* (Ames, Iowa, 1990); Robert F. Melson, *Revolution and Genocide: On the Origins of the Armenian Genocide and the Holocaust* (Chicago, 1992).

4. Charles S. Maier, *The Unmasterable Past: History, Holocaust and German National Identity* (Cambridge, Mass., 1998), p. 69.

5. Ernst Nolte, *Der europäische Burgerkreig. Nationasozialismus und Bolschevismus* (Frankfort am Main, 1987). See also Maier's comments in *The Unmasterable Past*, pp. 67–69. For the heat generated by Nolte's highly suspect standpoint, see Peter Baldwin, ed., *Reworking the Past: Hitler, the Holocaust and the Historians Debate* (Boston, Mass., 1990).

6. In 1991 MRND changed its name to the National Republican Movement for Democracy and Development while retaining its original initials. MRND was itself, via a military coup, the successor to the original post-colonial PARMEHUTU regime. See African Rights, *Rwanda: Death, Despair and Defiance* (London, 1994), p. 29. However, given that the genocide of post-6 April 1994 was perpetrated by an emergency post-MRND coalition regime, calling it the work of MRND is both somewhat inaccurate and inappropriate. A descriptive tag for the perpetrators of the Rwandese genocide remains problematic. I have plumped for the term 'Hutu Power', which Gerard Prunier describes as an 'informal club-like network' of individuals from various parties, as well as from the presidential circle. Its existence dates back to at least the summer of 1993 when plans for a genocidal solution were first being seriously considered. After 6 April, its members were key elements in the new regime and thus the primary initiators and organisers of the genocide. See Gerard Prunier, *The Rwanda Crisis: History of a Genocide, 1959–1994* (London, 1995), p. 188.

7. Identified as an average of almost one a year since 1945 in the research findings of Barbara Harff and Ted Robert Gurr, "Toward Empirical Theory of Genocides and Politicides: Identification and Measurement of Cases since 1945," *International Studies Quarterly* (1988), pp. 359–371. See also their "Victims of the State: Genocides, Politicides and Group Repression from 1945 to 1995," in Albert J. Jongman, ed., *Contemporary Genocides: Causes, Cases, Consequences* (Den Haag, 1996), 33–58.

8. At the time of the Auschwitz fiftieth anniversary commemoration in January 1995, when the British media was full of Holocaust reports and broadcasts, I came across only one piece which made more than passing comment on connections with Rwanda. See Robert Block, "Never Again obviously doesn't apply to Rwanda," *The Independent*, 28 January 1995. See also my "The Holocaust: After Rwanda," *Jewish Quarterly* (Winter 1994/5), pp. 15–21.

9. Mwambu Wanendeya, "Rwanda's deadly tide pollutes Lake Victoria," *The Sunday Times*, 22 May 1994.

10. See David Dabydeen, "The Black Body in the Bush," *Rwanda Stories*, Broadcast BBC 2, October 11, 1994 for a short critique of Westernocentric 'primitive black man' versions of the Rwanda genocide. For the modernity thesis, see Zygmunt Bauman, *Modernity and the Holocaust* (Oxford, 1989), notably the following comment, p. 89: "Like everything else done in the modern-rational, planned, scientifically informed, expert, efficiently managed, coordinated way, the Holocaust left behind and put to shame all its pre-modern equivalents, exposing them as primitive, wasteful and ineffective by comparison."

11. Melson, *Revolution and Genocide*, especially "Introduction," pp. 1–39.

12. See Jaques J. Macquet, *The Premise of Inequality in Ruanda* (Oxford, 1961) for the pre-colonial political-social stratification. It should be noted that this Tutsi-Hutu divide was much more pronounced in Rwanda than in Burundi. See also, Prunier, *Rwanda Crisis*, pp. 5–11 and Edith Sanders, " 'The Hamitic Hypothesis': its Origin and Functions in Time Perspective," *Journal of African History*, 10 (1969), pp. 521–32, for European racial theorising.

13. For racial terms of reference as an instrument of colonial policy, see Ian Linden, *Church and Revolution in Rwanda* (Manchester, 1977) and Catherine Newbury, *The Cohesion of Oppression: Clientship and Ethnicity in Rwanda, 1860–1960* (New York, 1988).

14. See René Lemarchand, *Rwanda and Burundi* (New York and London, 1970), pp. 145–196, for developments leading to ethnically-based political parties and independence.

15. The official Tutsi population before the 1994 genocide was 9% but was intentionally underestimated as such by the MRND regime. See, Africa Rights, *Rwanda*, p. 20.

16. See especially Lemarchand's vocabulary for these events: the land takeovers a series of jacquerie, the political Hutu leaders, self-conscious Jacobins. *Rwanda and Burundi*, pp. 141, 159–169, 254–263.

17. Bertrand Russell publicly called the killings "the most horrible and systematic human massacre we have had occasion to witness since the extermination of the Jews by the Nazis," a view echoed almost word for word by Vatican radio when knowledge of Rwandese events reached the rest of the world in February, 1964. Quoted in Stanley Meisler, "Holocaust in Burundi, 1972," in Willem A. Veehoven, ed., *Case Studies on Human Rights and Fundamental Freedoms: A World Survey* (Hague, 1976), vol. 5, pp. 227–232. See also Lemarchand, *Rwanda and Burundi*, pp. 216–227.

18. The special representative of the UN Secretary-General reported that a quarter of a million Tutsi were still living in Rwanda after 1963. See Learthen Dorsey, *Historical Dictionary of Rwanda* (Metuchen, NJ. and London, 1994), pp. 90–91.

19. Ferdinand Nahimana is the most notable example of a respected, indeed highly regarded, university academic and opinion-former to become an active advocate of anti-Tutsi genocide. See Prunier, *Rwanda Crisis*, p. 37. See also Alex de Waal, "The genocidal state," *Times Literary Supplement*, July 1, 1994, p. 3. For the flip-side of this, in neighbouring Tutsi-dominated Burundi, see Rene Lemarchand, "Burundi: The Politics of Ethnic Amnesia," in Helen Fein, ed., *Genocide Watch* (New Haven and London, 1992), pp. 70–86. For the chronology of the next serious but abortive invasion in 1966, see Dorsey, *Historical Dictionary*, p. 93.

20. See Africa Rights, *Rwanda*, pp. 12–30. Prunier, *Rwanda Crisis*, pp. 84, 159–160, for the policies and problems of the Habyarimana regime.

21. More specifically, Museveni is a member of the Banyankole grouping which is divided, not unlike the Rwandan Banyarwanda, into high caste Bahima and low-caste Baiuru. On Museveni's complicated relations with the RFP, see Prunier, *Rwanda Crisis*, pp. 67–74.

22. Africa Rights, *Rwanda*, pp. 27–30 gives an essentially sympathetic and positive view of the RFP. Prunier, *Rwanda Crisis*, pp. 151–158 is both more cautious and convincing.

23. Prunier, *Rwanda Crisis*, chapter 5 and Africa Rights, *Rwanda*, pp. 32–34, for the attempted Arusha accords and pp. 20–22 and 28–29, for the groupings which gathered around the Akazu, the self-interested clique close to President Habyarimana's wife and family who exercised most of the powers of Rwanda state patronage and who had most to lose in the event of the implementation of the Arusha accords.

24. See note 6. Also Chris McGreal, "Blood on their hands," *The Guardian* (Weekend), December 3, 1994 for an early journalistic reference to Hutu-Power.

25. For the radicals committed to a clean sweep, all Tutsi living in Rwanda were by definition fifth-columnists and *ibyitso*, i.e. traitors. Their fate had already been graphically and chillingly foretold in an infamous speech by the MRND radical Leon Mugesera in November 1992: "What are we waiting for? . . . And what about those accomplices (*ibyitso*) who are sending their children to the RPF? . . . Why are we waiting to get rid of these families? . . . We have to take responsibility into our own hands and wipe out these hoodlums . . . The fatal mistake we made in 1959 was to let them (the Tutsi) get out . . . We have to act. Wipe them all out!" Quoted in Prunier, *Rwanda Crisis*, pp. 172–173. By 1994 it is noteworthy that the term ibyitso had also come to embrace Hutu moderates willing to negotiate a deal with the RPF. Prunier, *Rwanda Crisis*, p. 367. See also Africa Rights, *Rwanda*, pp. 42–86 on the detailed preparations for genocide.

26. The post-6 April government naturally blamed the RPF. Prunier, *Rwanda Crisis*, pp. 213–226, makes it blindingly obvious that the Hutu-Power conspirators were to blame. See also African Rights, *Rwanda*, pp. 86–92.

27. Africa Rights, *Rwanda*, pp. 35–41, 64–67.

28. One of Melson's favourite 'academic' bogeys, which he has sought to explode, is the 'provocation thesis,' namely that responsibility for the Armenian genocide could be laid firmly at the door of the Armenians themselves. See *Revolution and Genocide*, pp. 152–159. It is therefore interesting to note that a crop of similar charges against the (Tutsi) RPF surfaced soon after the Rwandese genocide. See, for example, Jean-Luc Vellut, "Ethnicity and Genocide in Rwanda," *Times Literary Supplement*, July 15, 1994.

29. See Harold Crouch, *The Army and Politics in Indonesia* (Ithaca, 1978) and Robert Cribb, ed., *The Indonesian Killings 1965–1966* (Clayton, Victoria, 1990).

30. René Lemarchand and David Martin, *Selective Genocide in Burundi*, Minority Rights Report No. 20 (London, 1974) and Lemarchand, "Burundi in Comparative Perspective, Dimensions of Ethnic Conflict," in John McGarry and Brendan O'Leary, eds., *The Politics of Ethnic Conflict*

*Regulation. Case Studies of Protracted Ethnic Conflicts* (New York and London, 1993), pp. 151–171. The Burundi events did have a direct knock-on effect in Rwanda, particularly the 1993 army killings which helped crystallise the hardline Hutu position against an RPF deal. See Prunier, *Rwanda Crisis*, pp. 198–206.

31. I participated in a high school conference on Nazi Germany, organised by the Imperial War Museum, at which a perfectly well-intentioned German war veteran reminded his young audience of 'the struggle' between Jews and Germans. See also Maier, *The Unmasterable Past*, pp. 67–68 on Nolte's supposedly scholarly treatment of this 'struggle'.

32. Quoted in Gerald Fleming, *Hitler and the Final Solution* (Oxford, 1986), pp. 14–15.

33. Hans Bluher, *Secessio Judaica, Philosophical Foundations of the Historical Situation of Judaism and the Anti-Semitic Tradition* (1922), quoted in L. Poliakov, *History of Anti-Semitism, vol. IV, Suicidal Europe, 1870–1933* (Oxford, 1985), p. 325.

34. Norman Cohn, *Warrant for Genocide: The Myth of Jewish World Conspiracy and the Protocols of the Elders of Zion* (London, 1967) for the classic study of 'explanation' through projection. See also the commentary by Roger W. Smith, "Fantasy, Purity, Destruction: Norman Cohn's Complex Witness to the Holocaust," in Alan L. Berger, ed., *Bearing Witness to the Holocaust 1939–1989* (Lewiston, Queenston and Lampeter, 1991), pp. 115–124.

35. Mann, quoted in Poliakov, *History of Anti-Semitism*, vol. IV, pp. 326–327.

36. Fleming, *Hitler and the Final Solution*, pp. 14–15.

37. Prunier, *Rwanda Crisis*, pp. 75–76.

38. Michael H. Kater, "Everyday Anti-semitism in Pre-War Nazi Germany, the Popular Bases," in Michael Marrus, ed., *The Nazi Holocaust*, vol. 5 (Westport and London, 1985), pp. 151–181. Daniel Jonah Goldhagen, *Hitler's Willing Executioners: Ordinary Germans and the Holocaust* (London, 1996) takes this line of reasoning much further by arguing that antisemitism was inbuilt into historic German culture and was indeed 'eliminationist' long before the arrival of Nazism.

39. See Michael Burleigh and Wolfgang Wipperman, *The Racial State, Germany 1933–1945* (Cambridge, 1991).

40. Quoted in Uriel Tal, "On the Study of the Holocaust and Genocide," *Yad Vashem Studies*, 13 (1979), pp. 7–52.

41. The point at which the leadership of the German state recognised this is, of course, a controversial one. Recent scholarship, notably Klaus Reinhardt, *Moscow, The Turning Point? The Failure of Hitler's Strategy in the Winter of 1941–2* (Oxford and Washington, 1992) would suggest it was from relatively early on in the Russian campaign. Note also the intriguing comment of Alfred Jodl, chief of Hitler's general staff from the vantage point of defeat, in 1946: "Long before anyone else in the world, Hitler suspected or knew that the war was lost." Quoted in Percy Ernst Schramm, *Hitler, The Man and the Military Leader* (Chicago, 1971), p. 204.

42. My own broader comparative research leads me to conclude that the lurch into genocide is often precipitated by the realisation that a particular risky course of military or political action far from ensuring the enhanced security and strengthening of the state will instead lead to its nemesis. See Mark Levene, "The Frontiers of Genocide: Jews in the Eastern War Zones, 1914–20 and 1941," in Panikos Panayi, ed., *Minorities in Wartime* (Berg, 1993), pp. 83–117, a view endorsed in Phillipe Burrin, *Hitler et les Juifs, Genèse d'une Génocide* (Paris, 1989) and more controversially in Arno Mayer, *Why did the Heavens Not Darken? The Final Solution in History* (New York, 1988). However, a number of historians would disagree, most notably Christopher Browning who in *Fateful Months: Essays on the Emergence of the Final Solution* (New York, 1985) argues that it was success and elation, not a premonition of disaster which precipitated the 'final solution'. This debate is not about the mass executions begun by the Einsatzgruppen at the outset of Barbarossa, but the radicalisation of the killing process from selected adult male targets to the extermination of whole communities, beginning in the high summer of 1941. See also Jurgen Forster, "The Wehrmacht and the War of Extermination against the Soviet Union," *Vad Vashem Studies*, 14 (1981), pp. 7–34 and Christian Streit, "The German Army and the Policies of Genocide," in Gerhard Hirschfeld, ed., *The Policies of Genocide* (London, 1986), pp. 1–14.

43. See Christopher Browning, *Ordinary Men: Reserve Police Battalion 101 and the Final Solution in Poland* (New York, 1992), Omer Bartov, *The Eastern Front, 1941–45: German Troops and the*

*Barbarisation of Warfare* (London, 1985), and Mark Mazower, *Inside Hitler's Greece, The Experience of Occupation, 1941–1944* (London, 1993).

44. Reserve Police Battalion 101 operating in central Poland was, according to Browning, alone responsible for a minimum of 38,000 deaths, nearly all Jews, between 1942 and 1943. Browning, *Ordinary Men*, Appendix, p. 191. Also Goldhagen, *Hitler's Willing Executioners*, p. 111. Such killings, implicitly if not explicitly, raise questions about Bauman's modernity thesis. See, on this score, the critiques of Jonathan Steinberg, "The Holocaust, Society, and Ourselves," *The Jewish Quarterly*, 153 (Spring, 1994), pp. 46–50 and Michael Freeman, "Genocide, civilisation and modernity," *The British Journal of Sociology*, 46 (1995), pp 207–223.

45. See on this aspect, Roger W. Smith, "Women and Genocide: Notes on an Unwritten History," *Holocaust and Genocide Studies*, 8 (1994), pp. 315–334. Lindsey Hilsum, "Rwanda's time of rape returns to haunt thousands," *The Observer*, 26 February 1995. Also Richard Dowden, "The graves of the Tutsis are only half full—we must complete the task," *The Independent*, 24 May 1994 for a careful but graphic report on the nature of the Rwandan killings.

46. See Cohn, *Warrant for Genocide*, especially chapters 8 and 9. On Hitler's Jewish conspiracy-laden Weltanschauung, see Robert G. L. Waite, *The Psychopathic God, Adolph Hitler* (New York, 1977).

47. Hutu antipathy to Tutsi overlordship seems to have been particularly persistent in regions which were most recently incorporated into the Nyiginya kingdom sometimes with the assistance of the Europeans, though as Prunier, *Rwanda Crisis*, p. 21, crucially points out, this was primarily "a centre versus periphery affair and not one of Tutsi versus Hutu." Prunier indeed avers (p. 39) that "although Rwanda was definitely not a land of peace and bucolic harmony before the arrival of the Europeans, there is no trace in its precolonial history of systematic violence between Tutsi and Hutu as such."

48. Bauman's chapter on 'Modernity, Racism, Extermination', in his *Modernity and the Holocaust*, is particulary good at examining the contrast between pre-modern Jewish-Gentile relationships and modern ones. Even in modern circumstances, ethnic or religious hate requires a particular socio-political context, as well as a catalyst or catalysts for it to be converted into genocide. Note Wladyslaw Bartoszewski's succinct comment on this score: "A large number of people can be antagonistic towards another national group but it does not mean there has to be some ultimate reckoning." Quoted in Antony Polonsky, ed., *My Brother's Keeper, Recent Polish Debates on the Holocaust* (London, 1990), p. 227. This conforms with my argument that ethnic, religious and racial prejudices or hatreds per se, though possibly critical background ingredients, do not in themselves explain a lurch into genocide or its increasing incidence.

49. Melson, *Revolution and Genocide*, pp. 61–69, 84–100, particularly notes the social and economic mobility of 'modernising' Armenians and Jews in the Ottoman Empire and Wilhelmine/Weimar Germany as factors precipitating increasing social and political tensions. See also Stephen Astourian's important essay, "Genocidal Process: Reflections on the Armeno-Turkish Polarization," in Richard G. Hovannisian, ed., *The Armenian Genocide: History, Politics, Ethics* (London and New York, 1992), pp. 53–79, as well as Lemarchand, *Rwanda and Burundi*, p. 491, on the specific ethnic contradictions inherent in Rwanda's attempt to build and modernise a nation-state.

50. A major weakness of the Goldhagen thesis is in his assumption that German eliminationist anti-semitism was constant and unwavering throughout recent centuries. Lacking historical context, the criticality of the collapse of Germany at the end of 1918 providing the essential and crucial moment for the transformation of latent tendencies into a widely popular and politically manipulable judeophobia is missed.

51. The most famous perhaps being Rosa Luxemburg, who baldly stated to a friend: "Why do you come with your particular Jewish sorrows . . . I have no separate corner in my heart for the ghetto: I feel at home in the entire world wherever there are clouds and birds and human tears." Quoted in Paul R. Mendes-Flohr and Jehuda Reinharz, *The Jew in the Modern World, A Documentary History* (New York and Oxford, 1980), p. 225.

52. Most fully examined in Cohn, *Warrant for Genocide*.

53. De Waal, "Genocidal State," p. 3, Africa Rights, *Rwanda*, p. 38.

54. This provides a sobering reminder that not only little nation-states themselves may be obsessed with conspiracy but some quite big ones too. In this instance, Prunier, *Rwanda in Crisis*, pp. 102–107, provides a telling narrative which confirms that behind the francophone MRND

regime's fears of an RPF invasion, or power-sharing via Arusha, was a French government equally obsessed that what they were witnessing was the potentiality of an Anglo-Saxon takeover in their African 'patch' via another Fashoda.

55. It is interesting to note that the 'Never Again' syndrome also provided 'mythic' justification for the army perpetrators of the Indonesian genocide in 1965, the referral point being the defeated leftist-Communist revolt staged at Madiun in 1948. Not only was this characterised by the Indonesian army chief of staff, Nasution, as "a case of being stabbed in the back" but led to his call, after the assassination of the army generals in 1965, for the extermination of the PKI "down to its very roots so there will be no third Madiun." Quoted in Julie Southwood and Patrick Flanagan, *Indonesia, Law, Propaganda and Terror* (London, 1983), p. 68.

56. See Michael Berenbaum, ed., *A Mosaic of Victims* (New York, 1990), Hirschfeld, *Policies of Genocide*. Specifically on Roma, see Donald Kenrick and Grattan Puxon, *Gypsies under the Swastika* (Hatfield, 1995). Also Sybil Milton, "Nazi policies towards Roma and Sinti, 1933–1945," *Journal of the Gypsy Lore Society*, 5th series, 2 (1992), pp. 1–18, and Ian F. Hancock, "Uniqueness, Gypsies and Jews," in Ronnie Landau, ed., *Remembering for the Future* (Oxford, 1988), pp. 2017–2025.

57. On Rwandese political opponents, Africa Rights, *Rwanda*, pp. 131–183. On the Twa, Evan Prentice, "Rwandan pgymies disappear amid butchery of civil war," *The Times*, 30 May 1995. See also Charles Uwiragiye, 'The Forgotten people,' *Survival International Newsletter*, 34 (1995), p. 12. The term 'outside the universe of obligation' comes from Helen Fein's *Accounting for Genocide* (New York, 1979). See also Fein, 'Scenarios of Genocide; Models of Genocide and Critical Responses,' in Israel W. Charny, ed., *Toward the Understanding and Prevention of Genocide: Proceedings of the International Conference on the Holocaust and Genocide* (Boulder and London, 1984), pp. 3–31.

58. Recent UN estimates suggest that in addition to the up to one million dead in the eight weeks of genocide or about 14% of the population, a further five million people, or 70% of the population, have been displaced either inside or beyond Rwanda's borders. In comparative terms, its losses are thus equivalent to that of the whole British empire during World War One, or put another way, if Britain had suffered a proportionate catastrophe, it would have lost seven million people. See Peter Hall and Andrew Carney, "Politics by Genocide," *Peace and Society* (Summer 1995), p. 22.

59. Note the following assessment of the Armenian genocide by an American professor: "By 1918 with the definitive excision of the total Armenian Christian population from Anatolia and the Straits area ... the hitherto largely peaceful process of Turkification and Moslemization had advanced in one great surge by the use of force ... Had Turkification and Moslemization not been accelerated by the use of force, there certainly would not today exist a Turkish Republic, a Republic owing its strength and stability in no small measure to the homogeneity of its population, a state which is now a valued associate of the United States." Lewis V. Thomas, in Thomas and Richard N. Frye, *The United States and Turkey and Iran* (Cambridge, MA, 1951), p. 61. I refer in great detail to Prof. Lewis's comments in "Creating a Modern Zone of Genocide: The Impact of Nation and State Formation on Eastern Anatolia, 1878–1923" (forthcoming, *Holocaust and Genocide Studies*, Winter 1998).

60. See Reynauld Secher, *Le Génocide franco-français, La Vendée-Venge* (Paris, 1986) has caused controversy with his thesis of a genocide committed by Frenchmen against Frenchmen. So, too, has his estimate of 117,000 genocide-related deaths. Yet an older, more conservative study by Peter Paret, *Internal War and Pacification; The Vendee 1789–1796* (Princeton, 1961), p. 68, argues for 130,000 direct deaths or 15% of a pre-revoution population of 800,000.

61. See Roger W. Smith's review of Melson's Revolution and Genocide, *The ISG Newsletter*, 10 (Spring, 1993) pp. 15, 17.

62. Carmel Budiardjo and Liem Soei, *The War against East Timor* (London, 1984), John Taylor, *Indonesia's forgotten war: The hidden history of East Timor* (London, 1991), Hugh O'Shaughnessy, "Secret Killing of a Nation," *The Observer*, 7 April 1991, and "East Timor, The Silence and the Betrayal," *New Internationalist*, No. 253, March 1994.

63. Irving Lois Horowitz, *Taking Lives, Genocide and State Power* (New Brunswick, NJ., 1980) argues that societies can be classified as genocidal or non-genocidal depending on where they are on a spectrum running from repressive and totalitarian at one end to permissive and pluralist at the other. The Horowitz model is certainly valuable, but does not address processes of historical

change or crisis in which a society might pass from being non-genocidal to genocidal, or vice-versa.

64. See Helen Fein, "Accounting for Genocide after 1945: Theories and Some Findings," *International Journal on Group Rights*, 1 (1993), pp. 79–106.

65. Harff and Gurr, "Toward Empirical Theory."

66. Quoted in Frank Chalk and Kurt Jonassohn, "The History and Sociology of Genocidal Killings," in Israel W. Charny, ed., *Genocide: A Critical Bibliographical Review* (London, 1988), p. 57.

67. Francis Fukuyama, *The End of History and the Last Man* (London, 1992).

68. See Charles Tilly, ed., *The Formation of National States in Western Europe* (Princeton, 1975) and Paul Kennedy, *The Rise and Fall of the Great Powers: Economic Change and Military Conflict from 1500 to 2000* (New York, 1988).

69. In this analysis, readers will recognise some of the arguments of Immanuel Wallerstein, *The Capitalist World-Economy* (Cambridge, 1979) and *The Modern World System*, three volumes (New York, 1974–1988), Alexander Gerschenkron, *Economic Backwardness in Historical Perspective* (Cambridge, Mass., 1966), and Anthony Giddens, *The Nation-State and Violence* (Cambridge, 1985).

70. Key events in the 'national' consolidation of the British state, for example, might include the Cromwellian subjugation of Ireland in the early 1650s and the subsequent Scottish 'Highland Clearances' in the aftermath of the failed Jacobite rising in 1745. Both involved elements of genocide. On Ireland, see Peter Berresford Ellis, *Hell or Connaught! The Cromwellian Colonisation of Ireland 1652–1660* (London, 1975) and more recently Ian Gentles, *The New Model Army in England, Ireland and Scotland 1645–1653* (Oxford, 1992), pp. 357–364, who argues for a systematic scorched policy in the aftermath of the extirpation of Irish resistance, directly responsible for a population collapse of an estimated 1.5 million of 1641 to only 850,000 in 1652. Post-Culloden events again were not genocide per se, but involved enough of the ingredients to be remembered in Scottish folk history as such. For a fine measured account, see Bruce Lenman, *The Jacobite Risings in Britain 1689–1746* (London, 1980), especially the penultimate chapter, "The Aftermath of the '45," pp. 260–282.

71. The term is borrowed from Misha Glenny's BBC broadcast, "All Fall Down," Radio 4, 31 March 1995.

72. On Japan's emergence into the Western system, see Jon Halliday, *A Political History of Japanese Capitalism* (New York and London, 1978) and Takafusa Nakamura, *Economic Growth in Pre-War Japan* (New Haven, 1983).

73. Fritz Fischer, *War of Illusions, German Politics from 1911 to 1914* (London and New York, 1975).

74. See Horst Dreschsler, *Let Us Die Fighting, The Struggle of the Herero and Nama against German Imperialism 1884–1915* (London, 1980) and Tilman Dedering, "A Certain Rigorous Treatment of all Parts of the Nation: The Annihilation of the Herero in German South West Africa, 1904," in Mark Levene and Penny Roberts, ed., *The Massacre in History* (Oxford, forthcoming). An estimated 60% of the tribal population was liquidated between 1904 and 1907. On the subjugation of the Maji-Maji revolt in East Africa, of which much less has been written, see Thomas Pakenham, *The Scramble for Africa* (New York, 1971), pp. 616–628.

75. The term comes from Ronald Aronson, *The Dialectics of Disaster, A Preface to Hope* (London, 1983), p. 169.

76. See Horst Matzerath and Heinrich Volkmann, "Modernisierungtheorie und Nationalsozialismus," in Jurgen Kocka, ed., *Theorien in der Praxis des Historkiers* (Göttingen, 1977), pp. 90–109 for their interpretation of the Nazi special 'third way' route to development.

77. See Michael Burleigh, *Death and Deliverance, 'Euthanasia' in Germany 1900–1945* (Cambridge, 1994), Burleigh and Wipperman, *The Racial State*, Benno Muller-Hall, *Murderous Science. Elimination by Scientific Selection of Jews, Gypsies and Others: Germany 1933–1945* (Oxford, 1988), Henry Friedlander, *The Origins of the Nazi Genocide: From Euthanasia to the Final Solution* (Chapel Hill and London, 1995), Jeremy Noakes, "Social Outcasts in the Third Reich," in Richard Bessel, ed., *Life in the Third Reich* (Oxford, 1987), pp. 83–96.

78. See A. James Gregor, *Italian Fascism and Developmental Dictatorship* (Princeton, 1979), especially the chapter on "Fascism and Development in Comparative Perspective;" Ali Kazancigil and Ergun Ozbudun, eds., *Atatürk, Founder of the Modern State* (London, 1981), notably the Ahmad Feroz

article, "The political economy of Kemalism;" Caglar Keyder, *State and Class in Turkey, A Study in Capitalist Development* (London, 1987); Alec Nove, *An Economic History of the U.S.S.R.* (London, revised ed., 1976), chapter on "The Great Leap Forward, 1. Collectivisation," and Robert Bidelux, *Communism and Development* (London, 1985), especially chapter on "Socialist forced industrialisation strategies."

79. See Lemarchand, *Rwanda and Burundi*, p. 141 on the 'outsider' status of the Hutu revolutionaries and their psychological insecurity in a society traditionally ruled and run by Tutsi. On the relationship between new 'outsider' elites and genocide more generally, see R. Hrair Dekmejian, "Determinants of Genocide: Armenians and Jews as Case Studies," in Richard Hovannisian, ed., *The Armenian Genocide in Perspective* (New Brunswick, N.J., 1986), pp. 85–96.

80. It should be emphasised, moreover, that both Guatemala and Indonesia have had the full, if not always loudly publicised, support of the leading players in the system for their genocidal campaigns. To this should be added the logistical assistance, military training and materiel supplied, particularly by the United States. See Noam Chomsky's writings, especially *Turning the Tide: US Involvement in Central America and the Struggle for Peace* (London, 1985), *Deterring Democracy* (London, 1991) and with Edward Herman, *The Washington Connection and Third World Fascism: The Political Economy of Human Rights* (Montreal, 1979). Also, Michael McClintock, *The American Connection, State Terror and Popular Resistance in Guatemala* (London, 1985), Rudolf Mrazek, "The United States and the Indonesian Military, 1945–1965," *Dissertationes Orientales*, 39 (1978), pp. 1–2, Helen Fein, "Revolutionary and Antirevolutionary Genocides: A Comparison of State Murders in Democratic Kampuchea, 1975–1979, and Indonesia, 1965 to 1966," *Society for Comparative Study of Society and History* (1993), pp. 796–823.

81. See Ben Kiernan, *The Pol Pot Regime: Race, Power and Genocide* (New Haven and London, 1996) and Michael Vickery, *Cambodia 1975–1982* (Boston, 1984) for markedly different interpretations of Khmer Rouge Cambodia. See also Karl D. Jackson, ed., *Cambodia, 1975–1978, Rendezvous with Death* (Princeton, 1989).

82. This reading of Saddam derives from Samir al-Khalil, *Republic of Fear, Saddam's Iraq* (London, 1989).

83. The way Milosevic used the six hundredth anniversary of the disasterous but to Serbs, mythic, battle of Kosovo in 1389, as the historical lynchpin for his own version of 'Never Again,' directed, implicitly and explicitly, against the majority Albanian population of the province, springs immediately to mind. See Noel Malcolm, *Bosnia: A Short History* (London, 1994), p. 213.

84. In this context, it will be interesting to see what will be the eventual outcome of the UN War Crimes Tribunal indictments against named Serbian leaders. The Turkish (as opposed to Nazi) precedent, in the form of post-1918 Allied charges against Ittihadist leaders responsible for the Armenian genocide, is not promising, having been unceremoniously dropped when Kemalist Turkey reentered the international state system. See Richard G. Hovannisian, "Historical Dimensions," in Hovannisian, ed., *The Armenian Genocide in Perspective*. Note also the defence of the Khmer Rouge regime as the recognised government of Cambodia, long after it was driven out of Phnom Penh by the Vietnamese. At the thirty-fourth session of the General Assembly of the UN in September 1979, Western and ASEAN delegates were successful in pointing out "that the United Nations charter is based on the principle of non-interference and that UN membership has never been granted or withheld on the basis of respect for human rights. If it were, a large proportion of the governments presently there would have to leave." Quoted in William Shawcross, *The Quality of Mercy: Cambodia, Holocaust and Modern Conscience* (London, 1984), p. 138. More recently, while Serb massacres of possibly 8000 Bosnian Muslims around Srebrenica in July 1995 led to Western public outrage which helped catalyse a Nato military response, the Croat capture of Serb-held Krajina the following month, leading to the ethnic cleansing of some 200,000 of its inhabitants (the largest single movement of its kind in Europe since the Second World War) accompanied by atrocities, led to no international censure against Croatia. On the contrary, comments such as the following were commonplace: "Croatia is far too important geopolitically at the moment for the UN to make a fuss." Western diplomatic source, quoted in Charlotte Eager, "Future Bosnia shot to pieces," *The Observer*, 8 October 1995, or "I think that at the end of the day there's enough of an understanding with Croatia to let sleeping dogs lie." Quoted in Julian Borger, "EU accuses Croatia of atrocities," *The Guardian*, 30 September 1995.

85. Leo Kuper, *Genocide: Its Political Use in the Twentieth Century* (New Haven, 1982), p. 161.

86. John Pilger and Anthony Barnett, *Aftermath: The Struggle for Cambodia and Vietnam* (Manchester, 1982) and Shawcross, *Quality of Mercy*, for the post-1979 international aid and Western diplomatic support that the Khmer Rouge regime continued to receive. My verdict on MRND Rwanda, should it have survived, is moreover in complete agreement with that of Prunier, *Rwanda Crisis*, pp. 228–229: "After the genocide, there would have been a period of shocked reprobation: then possibly a UN-sanctioned (partial) economic boycott: then many violations of the boycott, some probably discreetly organised from Paris: then renewed relations with some non-respectable countries such as Serbia, China or Iran … then arguing on the basis of their 'traditional' ties with the French, the Belgians and possibly the Germans would have come back too. After all, Hutu power, genocidal or not, presents no threat to European interests."

87. See Frank Chalk and Kurt Jonassohn, *The History and Sociology of Genocide* (New Haven, 1990), pp. 27–40, for arguments as to the prevalence of genocide throughout human history. I do not disagree that the phenomenon of mass extermination is an ancient as well as common one, nor that there are linkages between the old and the new. What I am proposing, however, is that it has been radically reshaped, not necessarily in terms of form, but rather in terms of the framework within which it takes place, and that this should be the starting point and key to our understanding of modern genocide.

88. See Mark Levene, "Is the Holocaust simply another example of Genocide?," *Patterns of Prejudice*, 28 (1994), p. 10.

89. This analysis has not space to pursue these much broader lines of inquiry. See Mary Kaldor's still highly prophetic *The Disintegrating West* (London, 1978) on the increasingly fraught competition between the three great contemporary capitalist power blocs. See also Mathew Horsman and Andrew Marshall, *After the Nation-State: Citizens, Tribalism and the New World Disorder* (London, 1995) for possible prospects.

90. This view thus disputes the central significance of political system as explanation for genocide, as outlined in Horowitz, *Taking Lives* and in the work of R. J. Rummel who postulates democracy to be both bulwark against, and antidote to, mass killing by states. See his "Democide in Totalitarian States: Mortocracies and Megamurders," in Israel W. Charny, ed., *The Widening Circle of Genocide*, vol. 3 of *Genocide: A Critical Bibliographic Review* (New Brunswick and London, 1994), pp. 3–39.

91. The French role, for instance, in assisting the Hutu-Power perpetrators of genocide, including after their RPF defeat, is now well known. Prunier, *Rwanda Crisis*, provides damning evidence throughout, but see especially chapter 8 on 'Operation Turquoise.' See also "Rwanda—The Bloody Tricolor" (Panorama special programme) broadcast BBC-2, 20 August 1995, which focused on French involvement in the training of the army and militias, and Chris McGreal, "French accused of protecting killers," *The Guardian*, 27 August 1994.

92. The phenomenon of armed enclaves, including drug baronages beyond the rule of law and thereby beyond the nation-state's monopoly of violence, may be one critical feature of this breakdown in Western states, as elsewhere. See "Pulp Future" (Panorama report), broadcast BBC1, 20 March 1995 and "The New Middle Ages," broadcast BBC2, 3 April 1995.

93. See Robert D. Kaplan, "The Coming Anarchy," *Atlantic Monthly*, February 1994, pp. 44–74.

94. A UN official has described post-genocide Rwanda "as a basket case for years." See David Beresford, "Who is guilty for Africa's holocaust?," *The Guardian*, 30 July 1994 and Alison des Forges' comments in "An Interview with Alison des Forges: Genocide in Rwanda was foreseen and could have been deterred," in Helen Fein, ed., *The Prevention of Genocide: Rwanda and Yugoslavia Reconsidered* (ISG Working Paper, 1994), pp. 24–25 and 30, on the initial refusal of the World Bank to release funds designated for RPF-led Rwanda until interest arrears had been paid, and the blocking by France of European Union aid to the RPF government. The RPF search for international aid has fared better as it has come to be recognised as the de jure government of Rwanda.

95. Lemarchand, *Rwanda and Burundi*, p. 285.

96. See Africa Rights, *Rwanda*, pp. 15–21.

97. The neo-Malthusian argument advanced by Richard L. Rubenstein in *The Age of Triage* (Boston, 1983) that genocide is a governmental response to surplus population, though interesting, seems to me to be grossly insufficient and inadequate to explain Rwanda's genocide, in spite of its acute rural overpopulation. But this does not mean that the interaction between population, land and

other resources may not be of relevance. See Thomas Fraser Homer-Dixon, "On the Theshold: Environmental Changes as Causes of Acute Conflict," *International Security*, 16 (Fall 1991), pp. 76–116.

98.  Prunier, *Rwanda Crisis*, pp. 77–79.
99.  In these terms Richard Dowden's terrifying forecast in "A wound at the heart of Africa," *The Independent*, 11 May 1994, has proved prophetic.
100. A swath of the Horn and East Central Africa including the interlacustrine states of Rwanda and Burundi, plus Uganda, Ethiopia and Southern Sudan could, over the last twenty to thirty years, be characterised as such a zone. But conflicts, involving civil war and secession in this area, have also led to massive civilian causalties. These have not been the outcome of state-sponsored genocide. Nor have the 'tier three' mass killings in Somalia.
101. See "Unmasked: The East Asian Economic Miracle," *New Internationalist*, No. 263, January 1995.
102. See note 62 for East Timor. There is less data on West Papua. See TAPOL, *West Papua, The Obliteration of a People* (London, 1994).
103. On the 'creeping' genocide in the Chittagong Hill Tracts, see Anti-Slavery Society, Report No. 2, *The Chittagong Hill Tracts, Militarisation, Oppression and the Hill Tribes* (London, 1984) and Amnesty International, *Bangladesh, Unlawful Killings and Torture in the Chittagong Hill Tracts* (London, 1986). Also Survival *Bulletins*, May 1992 and January 1994.
104. See especially Fein, "Accounting for Genocide after 1945."

# Part IV

*The Complexities of the Prevention and Intervention of Genocide*

# 7

# The Issues of Sovereignty and Political Will

Ever since the signing of the Treaty of Westphalia in 1648, a common belief is that a sovereign state's border is inviolate. As a result, for several centuries the so-called internal affairs of states were, for the most part, considered sacrosanct, and not the business of others. In other words, no matter what individual states did domestically—short of aggression against another state, that is—they were considered entities unto themselves that could (and largely did—and, in many ways, still do) act with impunity.

Over time, as various conventions (e.g., the Geneva Conventions and their Additional Protocols [1864, 1929, 1949, 1977] and the UN Convention on the Prevention of the Crime and Punishment of Genocide [1948]), various tribunals and their findings (for example, the Nuremberg Tribunal), and human rights declarations (the Universal Declaration of Human Rights 1948 being the most notable) became part and parcel of international law, the so-called sanctity of sovereignty began to erode. That is, grievous human rights violations committed by state actors and their proxies were slowly but surely beginning to be looked askance at, and such actors were not granted impunity from prosecution.

Even more recently, with the establishment of the International Criminal Tribunal for the former Yugoslavia (ICTY) and the International Tribunal for Rwanda (ICTR), state sovereignty has eroded just that much more. The latter have resulted in tribunal personnel crossing states' boundaries to interview witnesses and victims, to collect or photograph records, and in the tribunals issuing indictments against citizens of various states and demanding their extradition to The Hague or Arusha, Tanzania. With the even more recent establishment of the International Criminal Court (ICC), such activities will become more common as investigators and others traverse national borders to carry out their work.

As a direct result of the unleashing of horrific ethnic violence and the perpetration of crimes against humanity and genocide across the globe throughout the 1990s, various members of the international community perceived the need to attempt to prevent such atrocities and crimes, and devised a new concept referred to as "the responsibility to protect." The concept of the "responsibility to protect" purports that a government is responsible for protecting its own citizens against major human rights infractions, and if it fails to do so then the international community has the "right to protect" those individuals who are in danger of egregious harm.

In light of this new concept, the mandate and work of the ICTY and ICTR, and the establishment of the ICC, some scholars and intergovernmental and nongovernmental organizations whose focus is the protection of international human rights argue that the world is moving toward the gradual emergence of a customary law of humanitarian intervention. Such a position is not uncontested, though, and the debate and battle over the issue is far from over.

In "Realpolitk," noted jurist M. Cherif Bassouni succinctly delineates why he believes *realpolitik* constitutes "criminal law's biggest challenge." In "The Concept of Sovereignty and the Development of International Law," Jackson Nyamuya Maogoto, a senior lecturer in international law at University of Newcastle (Australia), provides an equally succinct and cogent discussion of the concept of sovereignty and in doing so provides a brief history of how the notion of sovereignty has played out over the centuries.

Time and again when the international community and/or individual nations neglect to act to stanch major human rights violations, be they crimes against humanity or genocide, journalists, scholars, and others decry the inaction as a lack of political will. That may be true, but it is just as likely to be a classic case of *realpolitik* or simply a lack of care about "those others" in distant lands. In "The Dilemma of Political Will: How Fixed, How Malleable the Domestic Constraints?" Duke University political scientist Bruce W. Jentleson examines the "conventional wisdom" regarding the issue of political will, and discusses the impact of such issues as "the Vietnam trauma," "the Somalia trauma," the U.S. response to the situation in Bosnia, Rwanda, and Kosovo, and the so-called "CNN factor" *vis-à-vis* the willingness of nations to act or not act in the face of a potential or actual genocide.

The last piece in this section is taken directly from the original "Responsibility to Protect" document prepared in Canada by the International Commission on Intervention and State Security in 2001.

# 7.1   M. Cherif Bassiouni, "Realpolitik"

*Realpolitik* is international criminal law's biggest challenge. It reflects narrow state interests carried out in state policies and practices. The *realpolitik* I refer to encompasses the broader meaning of the political realists' school of thought in international relations, which essentially sees these relations as anarchical, and based on power and states' interests. Thus, it excludes the notion that there is an international community, and that it has commonly-shared values and collective interests. The realists' starting point is an absolutist approach to sovereignty. Among sovereigns, however, some states are more sovereign than others because of their power, be it military or economic.

At a time when the world's states were clearly identified by geography, separated by seas, rivers and mountains, where distances translated in time, and where contacts between peoples could only be done physically, absolute sovereignty made sense. With the emergence of new factors which have radically changed inter-state and inter-peoples' relations, absolute sovereignty makes no sense.

In 1648, the treaty of Westphalia reflected a *weltanschauung* of a world made of different units, consisting of equal sovereign states. But an agglomeration of states does not a community of states make. In time, however, states developed a commonality of interests and shared common values. This brought about what we call, among other terms, the international community. The changing political configuration of the world through new discoveries, colonialism, the end of colonialism, the breakdown of nation-states and their fragmentation into many new states, the emergence of intergovernmental and private transnational organizations, and the revolution of communications and transportation means, changed this historic *weltanschauung*.

In the era of globalization, mostly characterized by the fact that both time and space are collapsed through instant communications, by rapid transportation, and the massive and relatively free flow of people, goods, and money across state boundaries, the concept of absolute sovereignty no longer exists. Though many of these historical barriers have disappeared, others survived, mostly of a political nature. On occasion, one can even detect efforts by some states to revert back to the traditional concept of absolute sovereignty when it suits their political purposes.

Few people today stop and think that by placing a national stamp on an envelope, a letter can reach across many states, with its ultimate destination across the globe, and without any state raising the issue of sovereignty. In 1962, the USSR shot down an American U-2 spy plane 15 miles above its territory, because it had violated its sovereign airspace, and an international crisis ensued. Today, the so-called sovereign air space of states is limited to the reach of aircrafts, with right of innocent passage, though not absolute. Hardly anyone thinks that orbiting communications satellites violate the sovereignty of the states over which they circulate. No one claims that the taking of photographs by these satellites or their relaying of communications, or transmitting sound and images into a state, constitutes a violation of state sovereignty. Similarly, no one claims that the millions of daily electronic communications through which the world's financial movements transit, constitute a violation of state sovereignty.

Yet curiously, when it comes to international criminal justice, states re-discover sovereignty, and jealously defend it, not on the grounds that they have priority in the exercise of criminal jurisdiction, but as a bar to justice, whether be it exercised by a national or international institution. In some respect, this means that the values of international criminal justice have not yet been absorbed in the values of globalization, and states' interests trump the values of international criminal justice and the collective interests of the international community in achieving accountability for international crimes.

In short, state sovereignty remains an obstacle to international criminal justice, not because of the inherent nature of sovereignty, or its exigencies, but because it is interpreted and used as a means of achieving goals that contradict those of international criminal justice.

With respect to international criminal justice, state sovereignty could be interpreted as a neutral concept in which national criminal jurisdiction has primacy for crimes committed on its territory, and by extraterritorial extension, when the crime is committed by a national, or against a national of that state, or when it is committed by non-nationals of that state outside the territory of that state, but with an intangible or tangible impact upon the national state.

The relationship between different sovereigns and their respective national criminal jurisdictions is thus simply an allocation of competences between the different sovereign units of the international community. Indeed, if each one of these sovereign units fulfilled its obligations of prosecution or extradition, there would be no need for another state to attempt to do so, nor would there be a need to establish supranational or inter-national entities with criminal jurisdictional competence to carry out that task. The type of state sovereignty which carriers out its legal responsibilities under national and international law can and should be respected. But when sovereign states fail to carry out their national and international legal obligations deriving from the maxim *aut dedere aut judicare*, the substantive norms and enforcement mechanisms of international criminal law must supercede national sovereignty.

International criminal law's penetration and then superceding of national law developed gradually. It first emerged with the formulation of substantive norms, such as the 1899 First Hague Convention on the regulation of international armed conflicts and others, and then after WWI, in the efforts to establish international criminal prosecutions. The failure of that effort nevertheless became a precedent to the International Military Tribunal at Nuremberg and the International Military Tribunal for the Far East in Tokyo. In the wake of these two international tribunals, came some national prosecutions.

The post-WWII period was mostly marked by United Nations efforts to codify parts of international criminal law through the codification of "Offences Against the Peace and Security of Mankind." But even after more than half a century, because of political reasons, that effort failed. In a parallel effort, the United Nations started in 1951 working on a statute for an international criminal court, and as a result of different factors, this United Nations effort came to fruition in 1998.

In the meantime, the world community remained unaffected by the needs for international criminal justice, even though some 250 conflicts have occurred since WWII, producing at the minimum, more than 70 million casualties. Yet most of the perpetrators of these crimes which fall in the categories of genocide, crimes against humanity, and war crimes, have benefited from impunity. For a long time, this situation was attributed to the politics of the "Cold War," but in 1992, the Security Council ended its long silence on international criminal justice by establishing the Commission of Experts to Investigate Violations of International Humanitarian Law in the former Yugoslavia, which led to the establishment of the International Tribunal for the former Yugoslavia, and ultimately the International Criminal Tribunal for Rwanda.

These two tribunals were established by the Security Council and that was the first time in history that this body exercised its supra-national authority over sovereign states in respect to international criminal justice. Thus, the psychological iron curtain was lifted, and the United Nations, with the support of many states and international civil society, proceeded to establish in 1998 the International Criminal Court. Today, that institution is in existence with 90 states-parties. Unlike the ICTY and ICTR, it is not a supra-national entity, but an inter-national one, as it is created by treaty, and not pursuant to the Security Council's supranational authority in respect to matters involving peace and security.

# 7.2   Jackson Nyamuya Maogoto, "The Concept of State Sovereignty and the Development of International Law"

The modern independent Nation-State is founded on a reverence of sovereignty emanating from the Peace of Westphalia of 1648, which ended the wars of religion between the Protestant and Catholic States. The treaty completed a process that began towards the end of the Middle Ages which focused upon the establishment of single overriding authorities in the growing national areas of Europe. Westphalian sovereignty enshrined the internal and external autonomy of the State. The accompanying sovereign tenets of political independence and territorial supremacy enshrined the State's freedom of action and unlimited use of power internally, forbidding an exercise of jurisdiction by any State over issues and individuals within another State's territorial boundaries thus precluding external interference and unsolicited intervention. Consistently reinforced by early international law, internal and external supremacy of the State strengthened the importance of complete autonomy of the sovereign State in managing its own internal affairs and its international capacity to determine the nature of its obligations.

The intention of the Peace of Westphalia in interpreting sovereignty as it did was the termination of conflicts between private and public jurisdictions as well as the more general conflict all over Europe between ecclesiastical and secular claims for the citizenry's obedience and allegiance. We now know, of course, that despite the promise of the Westphalian Peace, the advent of the sovereign independent Nation-State did not usher in a new era of peace and stability. If anything nation statehood has been characterised by conflict resulting in widespread death and destruction. Post-Westphalia international law, such as it was, imposed no effective restraints on Nation-States and their leaders in starting and carrying out aggressive wars. This was a world in which there were minimal constraints on national leaders in relations with other States and even fewer constraints on the treatment by a State of its own nationals. This was a world in which leaders of Nation-States were not accountable for any alleged violations of international law and in which the strongest States—militarily, economically and politically—prevailed.

World War I was a watershed conflagration. Apart from inaugurating total war, the end of the war saw an unsuccessful attempt to prise open the iron curtain of Westphalian sovereignty by individualising criminal responsibility for violations of the emerging law of war. The punishment provisions of the peace treaties of Versailles and Sevres sought to limit the scope of the principle of sovereign immunity by punishing military and civilian officials, while at the same time extending universal jurisdiction to cover war crimes and crimes against humanity. These treaties were seen by some as contrary to the general nationalistic, statist and positivistic philosophies generally ascendant in the 19th century and early part of the 20th century. Largely due to their seemingly radical innovation of individual criminal responsibility and disregard for sovereign immunity, the provisions of the treaties dealing with individual criminal responsibility were never implemented. In the end, the anticipated international penal process yielded to the demands of national sovereignty leading to sham national trials in Germany and Turkey after a major revision and scaling down of the defendant list in both countries. Political considerations woven around the mantle of sovereignty prevailed over the efforts to prosecute war criminals rendering the war time atrocities impervious to both prevention and punishment. While the envisaged international efforts to secure international criminal liability failed to materialise, important principles were established. The 1919 Commission on the Responsibilities of the Authors of War and on Enforcement of Penalties articulated crimes against humanity, and attempted to limit the previously solid conception of sovereign immunity that shielded Heads of State as well as officials from the reach of international law. Importantly too, for the first time, the idea that the State did not hold exclusive criminal jurisdiction was challenged. The efforts to extend international criminal jurisdiction beyond national frontiers in a bid to enforce international criminal law norms presented a challenge to the traditional scope of national sovereignty which precluded an extension of international norms into the domestic sphere absent a State's consent. Importantly too, the recognition of the need of international penal institutions to repress violations of international criminal law in the face of State recalcitrance questioned the State's exclusive right to legal competence over management of its affairs.

It however took another round of State orchestrated carnage about two decades later to spur States into giving international criminal law life and vitality. The resultant economic and political chaos of World War II, reinforced by increasing moral disquiet over the idea that States had a right to go to war whenever they wanted to provided the basis for focusing on international accountability through penal process. It was at Nuremberg (and later at Tokyo) that the iron curtain of sovereignty was dramatically drawn back. Nuremberg was designed to change the anarchic context in which nations and peoples of the world related to one another. The rejection of "obedience to superior orders," "acts of State" and "sovereign immunity" for the first time exposed the State to inquiry into its freedom of action and law-making competence. Nuremberg demonstrated that national leaders could be held responsible for their actions as Heads of State under international law. It held that individuals had rights under international law as well as obligations, independent of Nation-State recognition. By establishing individual accountability for violations of international law, the Nuremberg and Tokyo judgments explicitly rejected the argument that State sovereignty was an acceptable defence for unconscionable violations of human rights—from this fountainhead sprung up many important developments including the extension of universal jurisdiction to cover war crimes and crimes against peace, the start of the internationalisation of the human being as a subject of international law as well as the restriction of the State's law-making competence.

The post-World War II international trials revealed the enforceability of international norms governing the conduct of armed conflict and represented a watershed for the Westphalian notion of national sovereignty. By establishing individual accountability for violations of international law, the Nuremberg and Tokyo judgments explicitly rejected the argument that State sovereignty was an acceptable defence for unconscionable violations of international criminal law. The previously conflicting demands of sovereignty and global order that crippled the post-World War I attempts at international penal process were overcome by the viability of individual accountability. Henceforth, citizens were firmly a concern of international regulation instead of internal State prerogatives, and the State's law-making competence in certain aspects was to be limited by the requirements of international law. Even more significantly, the trials constituted an unprecedented inroad into the great barrier of sovereignty—exclusive territorial and national jurisdiction—and set a lasting precedent in relation to the extension of international criminal jurisdiction beyond national frontiers, previously an impossibility in view of the iron curtain cast by the Westphalian notion of sovereignty. The mantle of legal protection against the worst forms of violent abuse was to be a central feature in the drive to clip State sovereignty, by subjecting the State to external restraints and controls. But the precedent set at Nuremberg, and amplified at Tokyo, pointing to a restrained State disciplined by international law norms was to run into a storm as the world's third hegemonic struggle in the 20th century—the Cold War—commenced even before the ashes of World War II had cooled.

The Cold War largely put an end to the spurt of international judicial activity inaugurated at Nuremberg and Tokyo and contributed to the preservation of a statist international order. Many States were reluctant to enthusiastically embrace any form of international penal process and displayed a great deal of ambivalence in the normal conduct of their foreign affairs. With lack of State cooperation, the blood-soaked Cold War era was characterised by impunity. The bipolar politics of the era effectively scuttled any possibility of international efforts to address numerous atrocities despite major advances in the enaction of numerous treaties covering human rights and humanitarian law. Statism was taken particularly seriously in the newly independent and fragile countries of the developing world, where even if the State acted unjustly or genocidally against its own people, the prevailing wisdom was that this was not an affair for outside powers. But even amidst the dominant ideological rivalry of the Cold War, the United Nations was beginning to move, tentatively but assuredly, from mere standard-setting to considerations of implementation of those standards. The Cold War era involved mixed blessings for international penal process. Tremendous advances were made in the codification and broadening of international criminal law, but East-West rivalries effectively prevented any enforcement at the international level. Bipolar politics rendered the United Nations powerless to deal with many of the humanitarian crises accompanied by gross human rights violations. At the municipal level, States ever wary of the implications to sovereignty that a viable international justice regime entailed did not do much in enshrining norms of international criminal law or developing its jurisprudence.

Though a series of conflicts in the Cold War era set the arena for violations of international criminal law, the lack of a systematic international enforcement regime contributed to the lack of respect for the legitimacy of the international justice and even to a degree of cynicism about it. The *ad hoc* international criminal tribunals in the 1990s represented an international effort to put in place an international enforcement regime, the lack of which had helped ensure impunity during the Cold War era. The war crimes and crimes against humanity counts at Nuremberg were the forerunners at the heart of the United Nations Security resolutions of the 1990s which created the two *ad hoc* international criminal tribunals with jurisdiction over international crimes committed in the former Yugoslavia and Rwanda. Not without controversy, the international community, with the Security Council at its helm, decided that the establishment of *ad hoc* international criminal tribunals empowered to prosecute persons responsible for serious violations of international criminal law committed in the territories of the former Yugoslavia and Rwanda was a worthy precedent to set, worthy even to the extent of subjugating the sovereignty of the State involved directly as well as that of other States by placing binding legal obligations on them as well. Hot on the heels of the *ad hoc* international criminal tribunals, the international community finally voted in the summer of 1998 to adopt the *Rome Statute* for an International Criminal Court, tearing away a large chunk from the Westphailian veil, through tacit acceptance that States do not posses unlimited power and authority over their territory.

Though classic ideas about sovereignty die hard, the difficult and often bitter struggle waged in the 20th century against the edifice of the State, in a bid to curb both its power and freedom of action through the concept of international accountability by penal process, has had its moments of triumph which have played a large part in clipping State sovereignty. The moments of triumph have not simply been events in history, but rather the building blocks of a legacy that reached its zenith with the adoption of the *Rome Statute*, a legacy that has seen the acceptance (whether tacit or reluctant) that the State (through its organs and officials) operates within a framework of international rules and norms, to which it is not only answerable but to which it can be held accountable through international penal process. Insofar as sovereignty conceives of the State as quintessentially a structure exercising absolute power and authority in society, practical and normative limits to the exercise of sovereignty have been imposed by international penal process through enforcement of international criminal law.

Though the international community has consistently recognised sovereignty as the most fundamental right a nation can assert, complete autonomy of the sovereign State in managing its own internal affairs and its freedom from outside interference and unsolicited intervention has changed over time. Although State sovereignty in its international context continues to play a vital role, the powers, immunities, and privileges of sovereignty are now subjected to increased limitations. These limitations are the result of the need to balance the recognised rights of sovereign States against the greater need for international justice spawned by a concern for humanitarian norms—a trend evident from the *ad hoc* international penal processes of the 20th century.

# 7.3 Bruce W. Jentleson, "The Dilemma of Political Will: How Fixed, How Malleable the Domestic Constraints?"

Almost every study of conflict prevention concludes that when all is said and done, the main obstacle is the lack of political will. As an explanatory statement this is largely true. The United States and other governments have not acted because they have not had the political will to do so. If the domestic constraints that make this so are unchangeable and fixed, then that would be the end of the story. Prevention would continue to be sporadic and mostly too little, too late. There is reason to argue, though, that the domestic constraints are not necessarily all that fixed, that they have greater potential malleability than typically is presumed. I focus on the U.S. case, focusing particularly on public opinion and its ostensible "casualty phobia," with some analysis also of the role of the media and the CNN effect as well as the role of Congress.

## The "Pretty Prudent Public": Questioning the Conventional Wisdom about Casualty Phobia

It is conventional wisdom that the American public will not support commitments that risk casualties, and that even if initial support exists it will collapse under the weight of the first casualties incurred. This is attributed to the continuing hangover of the "Vietnam trauma" as reinforced by the "Somalia trauma." Key decisions made in numerous cases in the 1990s (for example, Bosnia, Rwanda, Kosovo, East Timor) on whether or not to use U.S. military force, and if so what strategy that action should follow, took the American public's casualty aversion as a hard and fast premise. Although no belief is more ingrained these days, it is a highly simplistic and inaccurate one.

We need to start with a clear understanding of the "Vietnam trauma" from which the American public has been said to have suffered for so long. From the late 1940s to the late 1960s the Cold War consensus largely defined American public opinion. Internationalism prevailed over isolationism—65 percent to 8 percent in a typical poll. Support for NATO was 80 percent. Containment was ranked number two among all national objectives, domestic policy included. And when the United States first sent troops to Vietnam in 1965, only 24 percent considered this a mistake. The experience in Vietnam dramatically changed this pattern. By 1971, 61 percent considered the Vietnam War a mistake. More generally, the public had become much less internationalist and much more isolationist. Its ranking of the importance of containment as a national objective dropped from second to seventh. The percentage of people willing to use American troops to defend Western Europe—a solemn commitment we made in signing the NATO treaty—plummeted from 80 percent to 39 percent. Support for troops to fight a communist revolution in our own hemisphere was even lower, down from 73 percent to 31 percent.

The term "trauma" implies severe reaction, even clinically so. Although this characterization was true in certain ways, it was misleading in two respects. First, it hardly was irrational or precipitous for the American public to stop supporting a war that was going as badly as Vietnam, and about which its leaders from both parties and over more than one administration had been so duplicitous and dishonest. "It was difficult to fault the American people," as one American military officer later wrote, "when, after that long a period of active engagement, the Joint Chiefs of Staff could only offer more of same for an indefinite period with no assurance of eventual success."[1]

Second, although the sense of trauma did last for some years immediately after Vietnam, by the early 1980s it was beginning to wear off. Opinion poll data show the beginning of a "post post-Vietnam" period and the emergence of what elsewhere I have called the "pretty prudent public," a pattern in public opinion of supporting some uses of force but opposing others, neither as trigger-happy as some would have liked nor as gun-shy as some feared.[2] The pattern was based on a distinction between two types of principal policy objectives for which force was being used: restraining aggression and remaking governments. To the extent that the American people perceived the principal objective of coercion as restraining aggressors who were threatening the United States, its interests, or its allies, they were more likely to support the use of force than when the principal objective was to engineer internal political change, as in many Third World interventions during the Cold War.[3] The underlying albeit usually unarticulated logic was that the antiaggression objective both had a greater sense of international legitimacy and was one for which military force was more likely to be efficacious.

It was not that casualties ever were taken lightly but that the willingness to accept casualties varied with the principal objective for which force was being used. This differentiated pattern held true for a number of limited-force cases in the 1980s, and was especially strong for the 1990–91 Gulf War. Nor was support for the Gulf War strictly a function of the low casualties actually incurred. Initial support at 78 percent was higher than support for Vietnam ever was (that is, pre-body bag levels) and despite what were very grave concerns about the risks of sending two hundred thousand troops to such a volatile region as the Middle East and against an enemy such as Saddam Hussein. Yet one poll on the eve of the ground war showed support being sustained at very high levels even in anticipation of as many as five thousand casualties.[4]

A follow-on study I did of 1990s cases, now including humanitarian intervention cases as well, showed the public to be "still pretty prudent."[5] Humanitarian interventions actually started with extraordinarily high levels of support, as seen in the early stages of the Somalia case. Although these interventions fell precipitously because of the Somalia debacle, as with Vietnam, there was nothing irrational or unstably reactive about not supporting a policy when it appeared that the nation's leaders lacked a strategy. Some studies argue that had President Clinton responded to the Mogadishu debacle with a firm and determined retaliatory strategy, public support would have been there.[6] Be that as it may, we did see in ensuing cases such as Rwanda that while never rising back to the 70 percent-plus levels accorded to the early Somalia mission, support did rebound somewhat from its Somalia-trauma lows as the public wrestled with the implications of inaction in the face of genocide. In a poll taken shortly after the eighteen U.S. soldiers were killed in Mogadishu, 90 percent of respondents agreed that "we can never hope to solve the Somalis' political problems for them and so should 'bring our boys home.'" Yet in the Rwanda crisis, just six months later, while still reluctant to make a troop commitment, 56 percent favored finding a way to do something.

Around the same time the crisis with North Korea over its development of nuclear weapons was coming dangerously close to war. If casualty phobia was as chronic as it is so often said to be, and given memories of the Korean War and images of the North Korean leadership, public opinion should have been even less supportive of military action than in Somalia and Rwanda. But polls showed an average plurality supportive of the use of force (47 to 45 percent). Forty-seven percent is not all that high in absolute terms, but it was achieved even though President Clinton never explicitly advocated taking military action and thus lacked the 5–10 percent "bump" that usually comes from presidential cues and the rally-round-the-flag effect. The key was that this case very much fit the objective of restraining aggression.

In the case of Bosnia, support fluctuated greatly. Support for air strikes averaged 45 to 50 percent in early 1993 but declined over time, in part because of fallout from Somalia and in part because of the dissensus in Washington as to whether the mission was doable or even in the U.S. interest. Even then there were some spikes in support in response to events, as after the February 1994 Sarajevo market massacre. Some fluctuation also was a function of how polling questions were phrased. This Bosnia case was very mixed in that all three types of objectives—restraining aggression, promoting internal political change, and rendering humanitarian assistance—were involved. One of the interesting subpatterns was that questions that cast the use of force in terms of humanitarian objectives received higher support (56 percent) than those that linked the use of force to internal political change (34 percent).[7] Part of the problem in the Bosnia case was that policymakers could not separate these objectives. Thus the Bosnia case, while not as strictly reactive and phobic as the casualty-aversion thesis depicts, does speak to the constraints that are there.

The data from Kosovo are especially interesting in this regard. While by no means prepared to give overwhelming support to intervention in Kosovo, the public was much more inclined to support the use of force, *including ground troops and despite possible casualties*, than the Clinton administration assumed. Figure 2 shows that support for air strikes averaged about 57 percent and stayed fairly steady despite the ups and downs of the war effort and the media coverage. Even as far back as October 1998, an NBC/Wall Street Journal poll found 47 percent in favor of air strikes compared with 40 percent opposed. It also is important to note that although air strikes pose fewer risks to U.S. military personnel than do ground campaigns, the public expected some U.S. casualties; for example, the same April 6 CBS/New York Times poll that found 58 percent support for air strikes also found 84 percent of respondents expecting casualties.

Table 4 shows more ambivalence for ground troops, but in my view the extent of support is what is most significant. Initial support is low (March 25, 30), increases fairly quickly

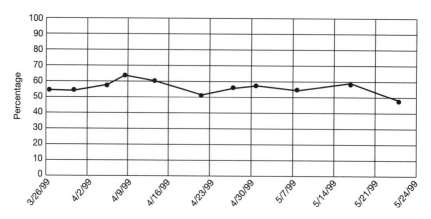

*Figure 2* U.S. Public Support for Air Strikes in Kosovo

*Table 4* U.S. Public Support for Ground Troops in Kosovo

| 1999 Polls | Support | Oppose |
|---|---|---|
| Gallup, 3/25 | 31% | 65% |
| Gallup, 3/30 | 39% | 57% |
| ABC/Washington Post, 4/5 | 55% | 41% |
| ABC/Washington Post, 4/6 | 57% | 39% |
| CBS/New York Times, 4/6 | 46% | 48% |
| Gallup, 4/7 | 47% | 47% |
| ABC/Washington Post, 4/8 | 57% | 39% |
| Harris, 4/8 | 62% | 31% |
| Gallup, 4/13 | 52% | 45% |
| Gallup, 4/16 | 41% | 53% |
| Gallup, 4/26 | 40% | 56% |
| ABC/Washington Post, 5/16 | 52% | 46% |
| **Average** | **48.2%** | **47.2%** |

(April 5–13), then declines (April 16, 26) before going back up (May 16). It should be no surprise that initial support was so low given that President Clinton was telling the American people that ground troops were not necessary and indeed not even "on the table." The fact that support increased as much as it did in early to mid-April thus seems significant. Not only was there no presidential cue effect to provide a bump up in approval, but the president was actually advancing a different option. We then see some bouncing around in late April and into mid-May, reflecting uncertainty and concern but still at levels of support that would have been a base on which to build had the administration decided to send ground troops. We also see a slight plurality in favor of ground troops in the overall average.

In addition to the noncasualty phobia that can be inferred from the ground troops data, Table 5 presents answers to some questions that asked directly about this issue. Here too my expectation is that the relative significance of these numbers is greater than their absolute levels. To be sure, they do not show levels of support as high as those during the Gulf War, but this is to be expected since even the strongest supporters of the Kosovo war would not compare its stakes to those of the Gulf War. Still, we see more support for the use of ground troops than opposition to it in four of the five polls.

*Table 5* U.S. Public Concern over Casualties in Kosovo

| Questions Asked of Respondents | 1999 Polls | Support | Oppose |
|---|---|---|---|
| Is the war worth the loss of some American soldiers' lives to help bring peace to Kosovo? | ABC/Washington Post. 4/5–6 | 45% | 52% |
| Is it worth having a few American casualties in a limited military action? | Gallup, 4/6 | 50% | 42% |
| Is it worth risking American soldiers' lives to bring peace to Kosovo? | Harris, 4/8 | 53% | 41% |
| Is it worth risking American soldiers' lives to demonstrate that Serbia should not get away with killing and forcing people from their homes? | Los Angeles Times, late March | 54% | – |
| If there was a ground war and up to 250 Americans were killed, would the war still be a right decision? | PIPA, 4/13–17 | 60% | 33% |

This is not to say that the U.S. public will ever be eager to use force and risk casualties. But it is to say that there is no enduring Somalia syndrome among the public.[8] Indeed, public opinion is more deliberative and less reactive than often depicted. Despite the low levels of information the public has, and despite the low levels of attention it pays to foreign affairs, the American public comes across as "pretty prudent" in its judgments about when, where, and why to use military force.

## Notes

1. Andrew F. Krepinevich, Jr., *The Army and Vietnam* (Baltimore: Johns Hopkins University Press, 1986), 270.
2. Bruce W. Jentleson, "The Pretty Prudent Public: Post Post-Vietnam American Opinion on the Use of Military Force," *International Studies Quarterly* 36 (March 1992): 49–74.
3. Exceptions were cases such as Grenada in 1983 and Panama in 1989 in which the high support in polls taken after the invasions reflected the "halo effect" of success. No pre-polling was done for Grenada; for Panama pre-polls showed only 32 percent support.
4. Jentleson, "Pretty Prudent Public," 68.
5. Bruce W. Jentleson and Rebecca L. Britton, "Still Pretty Prudent: Post-Cold War American Public Opinion on the Use of Military Force," *Journal of Conflict Resolution* 42 (August 1998): 395–417.
6. James Burk, "Public Support for Peacekeeping in Lebanon and Somalia: Assessing the Casualty Hypothesis," *Political Science Quarterly* 114, no. 1 (1999): 53–78; Peter Feaver and Christopher Gelpi, "The Civil-Military Gap and the Use of Force" (paper presented at the Triangle Institute for Security Studies [TISS] conference, Chapel Hill, N.C., July 1999).
7. Public opinion's flexibility to framing is not infinitely elastic, however. President Ronald Reagan, his "Great Communicator" skills notwithstanding, tried this on Nicaragua but never could persuade the public to see the conflict as other than an internal political one, and so support stayed consistently low.
8. See also the findings in the study by the Triangle Institute for Security Studies (Duke-UNC Chapel Hill), as discussed in Peter D. Feaver and Christopher Gelpi, "A Look at Casualty Aversion," *Washington Post*, November 7, 1999, B3.

# 7.4   The Responsibility to Protect: Report of the International Commission on Intervention and State Sovereignty

Synopsis

*The Responsibility to Protect: Core Principles*

**(1)  Basic Principles**

A.  State sovereignty implies responsibility, and the primary responsibility for the protection of its people lies with the state itself.

B.  Where a population is suffering serious harm, as a result of internal war, insurgency, repression or state failure, and the state in question is unwilling or unable to halt or avert it, the principle of non-intervention yields to the international responsibility to protect.

**(2)  Foundations**

The foundations of the responsibility to protect, as a guiding principle for the international community of states, lie in:

A.  obligations inherent in the concept of sovereignty;

B.  the responsibility of the Security Council, under Article 24 of the UN Charter, for the maintenance of international peace and security;

C.  specific legal obligations under human rights and human protection declarations, covenants and treaties, international humanitarian law and national law;

D.  the developing practice of states, regional organizations and the Security Council itself.

**(3)  Elements**

The responsibility to protect embraces three specific responsibilities:

A.  **The responsibility to prevent:** to address both the root causes and direct causes of internal conflict and other man-made crises putting populations at risk.

B.  **The responsibility to react:** to respond to situations of compelling human need with appropriate measures, which may include coercive measures like sanctions and international prosecution, and in extreme cases military intervention.

C.  **The responsibility to rebuild:** to provide, particularly after a military intervention, full assistance with recovery, reconstruction and reconciliation, addressing the causes of the harm the intervention was designed to halt or avert.

**(4)  Priorities**

A.  **Prevention is the single most important dimension of the responsibility to protect:** prevention options should always be exhausted before intervention is contemplated, and more commitment and resources must be devoted to it.

B.  The exercise of the responsibility to both prevent and react should always involve less intrusive and coercive measures being considered before more coercive and intrusive ones are applied.

*The Responsibility to Protect: Principles for Military Intervention*

**(1)  The Just Cause Threshold**

Military intervention for human protection purposes is an exceptional and extraordinary measure. To be warranted, there must be serious and irreparable harm occurring to human beings, or imminently likely to occur, of the following kind:

A. **large scale loss of life,** actual or apprehended, with genocidal intent or not, which is the product either of deliberate state action, or state neglect or inability to act, or a failed state situation; or

B. **large scale 'ethnic cleansing',** actual or apprehended, whether carried out by killing, forced expulsion, acts of terror or rape.

## (2) The Precautionary Principles

A. **Right intention:** The primary purpose of the intervention, whatever other motives intervening states may have, must be to halt or avert human suffering. Right intention is better assured with multilateral operations, clearly supported by regional opinion and the victims concerned.

B. **Last resort:** Military intervention can only be justified when every non-military option for the prevention or peaceful resolution of the crisis has been explored, with reasonable grounds for believing lesser measures would not have succeeded.

C. **Proportional means:** The scale, duration and intensity of the planned military intervention should be the minimum necessary to secure the defined human protection objective.

D. **Reasonable prospects:** There must be a reasonable chance of success in halting or averting the suffering which has justified the intervention, with the consequences of action not likely to be worse than the consequences of inaction.

## (3) Right Authority

A. There is no better or more appropriate body than the United Nations Security Council to authorize military intervention for human protection purposes. The task is not to find alternatives to the Security Council as a source of authority, but to make the Security Council work better than it has.

B. Security Council authorization should in all cases be sought prior to any military intervention action being carried out. Those calling for an intervention should formally request such authorization, or have the Council raise the matter on its own initiative, or have the Secretary-General raise it under Article 99 of the UN Charter.

C. The Security Council should deal promptly with any request for authority to intervene where there are allegations of large scale loss of human life or ethnic cleansing. It should in this context seek adequate verification of facts or conditions on the ground that might support a military intervention.

D. The Permanent Five members of the Security Council should agree not to apply their veto power, in matters where their vital state interests are not involved, to obstruct the passage of resolutions authorizing military intervention for human protection purposes for which there is otherwise majority support.

E. If the Security Council rejects a proposal or fails to deal with it in a reasonable time, alternative options are:

I. consideration of the matter by the General Assembly in Emergency Special Session under the "Uniting for Peace" procedure; and
II. action within area of jurisdiction by regional or sub-regional organizations under Chapter VIII of the Charter, subject to their seeking subsequent authorization from the Security Council.

F. The Security Council should take into account in all its deliberations that, if it fails to discharge its responsibility to protect in conscience-shocking situations crying out for action, concerned states may not rule out other means to meet the gravity and urgency of that situation—and that the stature and credibility of the United Nations may suffer thereby.

## (4) Operational Principles

A. Clear objectives; clear and unambiguous mandate at all times; and resources to match.

B.  Common military approach among involved partners; unity of command; clear and unequivocal communications and chain of command.

C.  Acceptance of limitations, incrementalism and gradualism in the application of force, the objective being protection of a population, not defeat of a state.

D.  Rules of engagement which fit the operational concept; are precise; reflect the principle of proportionality; and involve total adherence to international humanitarian law.

E.  Acceptance that force protection cannot become the principal objective.

F.  Maximum possible coordination with humanitarian organizations.

## 1.  The Policy Challenge

### *The Intervention Dilemma*

1.1  "Humanitarian intervention" has been controversial both when it happens, and when it has failed to happen. Rwanda in 1994 laid bare the full horror of inaction. The United Nations (UN) Secretariat and some permanent members of the Security Council knew that officials connected to the then government were planning genocide; UN forces were present, though not in sufficient number at the outset; and credible strategies were available to prevent, or at least greatly mitigate, the slaughter which followed. But the Security Council refused to take the necessary action. That was a failure of international will—of civic courage—at the highest level. Its consequence was not merely a humanitarian catastrophe for Rwanda: the genocide destabilized the entire Great Lakes region and continues to do so. In the aftermath, many African peoples concluded that, for all the rhetoric about the universality of human rights, some human lives end up mattering a great deal less to the international community than others.

1.2  Kosovo—where intervention *did* take place in 1999—concentrated attention on all the other sides of the argument. The operation raised major questions about the legitimacy of military intervention in a sovereign state. Was the cause just: were the human rights abuses committed or threatened by the Belgrade authorities sufficiently serious to warrant outside involvement? Did those seeking secession manipulate external intervention to advance their political purposes? Were all peaceful means of resolving the conflict fully explored? Did the intervention receive appropriate authority? How could the bypassing and marginalization of the UN system, by "a coalition of the willing" acting without Security Council approval, possibly be justified? Did the way in which the intervention was carried out in fact worsen the very human rights situation it was trying to rectify? Or—against all this—was it the case that had the North Atlantic Treaty Organization (NATO) not intervened, Kosovo would have been at best the site of an ongoing, bloody and destabilizing civil war, and at worst the occasion for genocidal slaughter like that which occurred in Bosnia four years earlier?

1.3  The Bosnian case—in particular the failure by the United Nations and others to prevent the massacre of thousands of civilians seeking shelter in UN "safe areas" in Srebrenica in 1995—is another which has had a major impact on the contemporary policy debate about intervention for human protection purposes. It raises the principle that intervention amounts to a promise to people in need: a promise cruelly betrayed. Yet another was the failure and ultimate withdrawal of the UN peace operations in Somalia in 1992–93, when an international intervention to save lives and restore order was destroyed by flawed planning, poor execution, and an excessive dependence on military force.

1.4  These four cases occurred at a time when there were heightened expectations for effective collective action following the end of the Cold War. All four of them—Rwanda, Kosovo, Bosnia and Somalia—have had a profound effect on how the problem of intervention is viewed, analyzed and characterized.

1.5   The basic lines in the contemporary policy debate, one constantly being re-engaged at UN headquarters in New York and in capitals around the world, have been clearly enough drawn. For some, the international community is not intervening enough; for others it is intervening much too often. For some, the only real issue is in ensuring that coercive interventions are effective; for others, questions about legality, process and the possible misuse of precedent loom much larger. For some, the new interventions herald a new world in which human rights trumps state sovereignty; for others, it ushers in a world in which big powers ride roughshod over the smaller ones, manipulating the rhetoric of humanitarianism and human rights. The controversy has laid bare basic divisions within the international community. In the interest of all those victims who suffer and die when leadership and institutions fail, it is crucial that these divisions be resolved.

1.6   In an address to the 54th session of the UN General Assembly in September 1999, Secretary-General Kofi Annan reflected upon "the prospects for human security and intervention in the next century." He recalled the failures of the Security Council to act in Rwanda and Kosovo, and challenged the member states of the UN to "find common ground in upholding the principles of the Charter, and acting in defence of our common humanity." The Secretary-General warned that "If the collective conscience of humanity . . . cannot find in the United Nations its greatest tribune, there is a grave danger that it will look elsewhere for peace and for justice." In his Millennium Report to the General Assembly a year later, he restated the dilemma, and repeated the challenge:

> . . . if humanitarian intervention is, indeed, an unacceptable assault on sovereignty, how should we respond to a Rwanda, to a Srebrenica—to gross and systematic violations of human rights that offend every precept of our common humanity?

1.7   In September 2000, the Government of Canada responded to the Secretary-General's challenge by announcing the establishment of this independent International Commission on Intervention and State Sovereignty (ICISS). Our mandate was generally to build a broader understanding of the problem of reconciling intervention for human protection purposes and sovereignty; more specifically, it was to try to develop a global political consensus on how to move from polemics— and often paralysis—towards action within the international system, particularly through the United Nations. The membership of the Commission was intended to fairly reflect developed and developing country perspectives, and to ensure that we represented between us a wide range of geographical backgrounds, viewpoints, and experiences—with opinions, at least at the outset, reflecting the main lines of the current international debate. If we could produce consensus among ourselves, there was at least a chance that we might be able to encourage it in the wider international community.

1.8   The Commission met for the first time on 5–6 November 2000, in Ottawa. A year-long strategy for carrying out our mandate was there mapped out, with agreement that our work process should be transparent, inclusive, and global. The Government of Canada supported the establishment of a research directorate, and with assistance from a number of other governments and major foundations, sponsored and organized a series of regional roundtables and national consultations intended to expose the Commission to a wide and diverse range of views, while at the same time helping to inform public opinion about our work and objectives.

Particular emphasis was placed on the need to ensure that views of affected populations were heard and taken into account, in addition to the views of governments, intergovernmental and non-governmental organizations (NGOs), and civil society representatives.

1.9    The Commission was strongly committed from the outset to consulting as widely as possible around the world, including in the countries of all five permanent members of the Security Council. Over the course of a year, accordingly, roundtable meetings' or consultations were conducted in Beijing, Cairo, Geneva, London, Maputo, New Delhi, New York, Ottawa, Paris, St Petersburg, Santiago and Washington. The discussions at those meetings were invariably rich and rewarding; they are summarized in the supplementary volume accompanying this report. In addition, individual Commissioners and members of the research team attended a large number of conferences and seminars—often by special invitation or in a representative capacity. The Commission has also made a particular effort to consult a broad range of academic thinking and expertise; much of this analysis and advice is embodied in the research papers and bibliography contained in the supplementary volume.

## The Changing International Environment

1.10   The issues and preoccupations of the 21$^{st}$ century present new and often fundamentally different types of challenges from those that faced the world in 1945, when the United Nations was founded. As new realities and challenges have emerged, so too have new expectations for action and new standards of conduct in national and international affairs. Since, for example, the terrorist attacks of 11 September 2001 on the World Trade Center and Pentagon, it has become evident that the war against terrorism the world must now fight—one with no contested frontiers and a largely invisible enemy—is one like no other war before it.

1.11   Many new international institutions have been created to meet these changed circumstances. In key respects, however, the mandates and capacity of international institutions have not kept pace with international needs or modern expectations. Above all, the issue of international intervention for human protection purposes is a clear and compelling example of concerted action urgently being needed to bring international norms and institutions in line with international needs and expectations.

1.12   The current debate on intervention for human protection purposes is itself both a product and a reflection of how much has changed since the UN was established. The current debate takes place in the context of a broadly expanded range of state, non-state, and institutional actors, and increasingly evident interaction and interdependence among them. It is a debate that reflects new sets of issues and new types of concerns. It is a debate that is being conducted within the framework of new standards of conduct for states and individuals, and in a context of greatly increased expectations for action. And it is a debate that takes place within an institutional framework that since the end of the Cold War has held out the prospect of effective joint international action to address issues of peace, security, human rights and sustainable development on a global scale.

### New Actors

1.13   With new actors—not least new states, with the UN growing from 51 member states in 1945 to 189 today—has come a wide range of new voices, perspectives, interests, experiences and aspirations. Together, these new international actors have added both depth and texture to the increasingly rich tapestry of international society and important institutional credibility and practical expertise to the wider debate.

1.14 Prominent among the range of important new actors are a number of institutional actors and mechanisms, especially in the areas of human rights and human security. They have included, among others, the UN High Commissioner for Human Rights and the International Criminal Tribunal for the former Yugoslavia, both created in 1993, and its sister tribunals for Rwanda established in 1994 and Sierra Leone in 2001. The International Criminal Court, whose creation was decided in 1998, will begin operation when 60 countries have ratified its Statute. In addition to the new institutions, established ones such as the UN High Commissioner for Refugees, and the ICRC and International Federation of Red Cross and Red Crescent Societies, have been ever more active.

1.15 Nearly as significant has been the emergence, of many new non-state actors in international affairs—including especially a large number of NGOs dealing with global matters; a growing number of media and academic institutions with world-wide reach; and an increasingly diverse array of armed non-state actors ranging from national and international terrorists to traditional rebel movements and various organized criminal groupings. These new non-state actors, good or bad, have forced the debate about intervention for human protection purposes to be conducted in front of a broader public, while at the same time adding new elements to the agenda.

**New Security Issues**

1.16 The current debate about intervention for human protection purposes takes place in a context not just of new actors, but also of new sets of issues. The most marked security phenomenon since the end of the Cold War has been the proliferation of armed conflict within states. In most cases these conflicts have centred on demands for greater political rights and other political objectives, demands that were in many cases forcibly suppressed during the Cold War. Gone with the end of the Cold War was the artificial and often very brutal check which Cold War politics imposed on the political development of many states and societies—especially in the developing world and in the former Eastern Bloc. In many states, the result of the end of the Cold War has been a new emphasis on democratization, human rights and good governance. But in too many others, the result has been internal war or civil conflict—more often than not with ugly political and humanitarian repercussions.

1.17 In other cases, conflict has been directed towards the capture of resources and towards plunder. The weakness of state structures and institutions in many countries has heightened the challenges and risks of nation building, and sometimes tempted armed groups to try to seize and themselves exploit valuable assets such as diamonds, timber and other natural resources, not to mention the raw materials of drug production.

1.18 These internal conflicts are made more complex and lethal by modern technology and communications, and in particular by the proliferation of cheap, highly destructive weapons which find their way into the hands, among others, of child soldiers. Many occur in desperately poor societies, or societies where there is a single valuable commodity—like oil or diamonds—which rapidly becomes the fuel which sustains a full-time war economy. In these places, the state's monopoly over the means of violence is lost, and violence becomes a way of life with catastrophic consequences for civilians caught in the crossfire.

1.19 An unhappy trend of contemporary conflict has been the increased vulnerability of civilians, often involving their deliberate targeting. Sometimes the permanent displacement of civilian populations has been a primary objective of the conflict; there has also been increasing concern about the deliberate use of systematic rape to provoke exclusion from a group. Efforts to suppress armed (and sometimes unarmed) dissent have in too many cases led to excessive and disproportionate actions by governments, producing in some cases excessive and unwarranted suffering on the part of civilian populations. In a few cases, regimes have launched campaigns of terror on their own populations, sometimes in the name of an ideology; sometimes spurred on by racial, religious or ethnic hatred; and sometimes purely for personal gain or plunder. In other cases they have supported or abetted terror campaigns aimed at other countries which have resulted in major destruction and loss of life.

1.20  Intra-state warfare is often viewed, in the prosperous West, simply as a set of discrete and unrelated crises occurring in distant and unimportant regions. In reality, what is happening is a convulsive process of state fragmentation and state formation that is transforming the international order itself. Moreover, the rich world is deeply implicated in the process. Civil conflicts are fuelled by arms and monetary transfers that originate in the developed world, and their destabilizing effects are felt in the developed world in everything from globally interconnected terrorism to refugee flows, the export of drugs, the spread of infectious disease and organized crime.

1.21  These considerations reinforce the Commission's view that human security is indeed indivisible. There is no longer such a thing as a humanitarian catastrophe occurring "in a faraway country of which we know little." On 11 September 2001 global terrorism, with its roots in complex conflicts in distant lands, struck the US homeland: impregnable lines of continental defence proved an illusion even for the world's most powerful state. At the same time, around 40 per cent of the victims of the World Trade Center attacks were non-Americans, from some 80 countries. In an interdependent world, in which security depends on a framework of stable sovereign entities, the existence of fragile states, failing states, states who through weakness or ill-will harbour those dangerous to others, or states that can only maintain internal order by means of gross human rights violations, can constitute a risk to people everywhere.

1.22  All this presents the international community with acute dilemmas. If it stays disengaged, there is the risk of becoming complicit bystanders in massacre, ethnic cleansing, and even genocide. If the international community intervenes, it may or may not be able to mitigate such abuses. But even when it does, intervention sometimes means taking sides in intra-state conflicts. Once it does so, the international community may only be aiding in the further fragmentation of the state system. Interventions in the Balkans did manage to reduce the civilian death toll, but it has yet to produce a stable state order in the region. As both the Kosovo and Bosnian interventions show, even when the goal of international action is, as it should be, protecting ordinary human beings from gross and systematic abuse, it can be difficult to avoid doing rather more harm than good.

1.23  Building a stable order after intervention for human protection purposes remains an equally great challenge. Finding a consensus about intervention is not simply a matter of deciding who should authorize it and when it is legitimate to undertake. It is also a matter of figuring out how to do it so that decent objectives are not tarnished by inappropriate means. As is widely recognized, UN peacekeeping strategies, crafted for an era of war between states and designed to monitor and reinforce ceasefires agreed between belligerents, may no longer be suitable to protect civilians caught in the middle of bloody struggles between states and insurgents. The challenge in this context is to find tactics and strategies of military intervention that fill the current gulf between outdated concepts of peacekeeping and full-scale military operations that may have deleterious impacts on civilians.

1.24 There is a further challenge: crafting responses that are consistent. Thanks to modern media, some humanitarian crises receive a surfeit of attention, while others languish in indifference and neglect. Some crises are exaggerated by media coverage and ill-considered calls for action skew the response of the international community in an inconsistent and undisciplined manner. Yet perfect consistency is not always possible: the sheer number of crises with serious humanitarian dimensions precludes an effective response in each case. Moreover, there are some cases where international action is precluded by the opposition of a Permanent Five member or other major power. But can the fact that effective international action is not always possible in every instance of major humanitarian catastrophe ever be an excuse for inaction where effective responses are possible?

**New Demands and Expectations**

1.25 The current debate about intervention for human protection purposes also takes place in a historical, political and legal context of evolving international standards of conduct for states and individuals, including the development of new and stronger norms and mechanisms for the protection of human rights. Human rights have now become a mainstream part of international law, and respect for human rights a central subject and responsibility of international relations. Some key milestones in this progression have been the Universal Declaration of Human Rights; the four Geneva Conventions and the two Additional Protocols on international humanitarian law in armed conflict; the 1948 Convention on the Prevention and Punishment of the Crime of Genocide; the two 1966 Covenants relating to civil, political, social, economic and cultural rights; and the adoption in 1998 of the statute for the establishment of an International Criminal Court. Even though in some cases imperfectly implemented, these agreements and mechanisms have significantly changed expectations at all levels about what is and what is not acceptable conduct by states and other actors.

1.26 The universal jurisdiction established in the Geneva Conventions and Additional Protocols (as well as the Convention Against Torture) means any state party in which a person accused of the crimes listed in them is found can bring that person to trial. Universal jurisdiction is also available under customary international law, and associated state legislation, for genocide and crimes against humanity. The recent Pinochet case in the UK and the conviction in Belgium for complicity in genocide of Rwandan nuns are an indication that the universal jurisdiction of these instruments is starting to be taken very seriously.

1.27 The change in law and in legal norms has been accompanied by the establishment, as has been noted, of a broad range of new international institutions and non-governmental organizations, concerned to monitor and promote the implementation worldwide of human rights and international humanitarian law—with the result that new expectations for conduct are increasingly accompanied by new expectations for corrective action.

1.28 The concept of human security—including concern for human rights, but broader than that in its scope—has also become an increasingly important element in international law and international relations, increasingly providing a conceptual framework for international action. Although the issue is far from uncontroversial, the concept of security is now increasingly recognized to extend to people as well as to states. It is certainly becoming increasingly clear that the human impact of international actions cannot be regarded as collateral to other actions, but must be a central preoccupation for all concerned. Whether universally popular or not, there is growing recognition worldwide that the protection of human security, including human rights and human dignity, must be one of the fundamental objectives of modern international institutions.

1.29 In considering changing expectations and conduct, nationally and internationally, it is impossible to ignore here the impact of globalization and technology. The revolution in information technology has made global communications instantaneous and provided unprecedented access to information worldwide. The result has been an enormously heightened awareness of conflicts wherever they may be occurring, combined with immediate and often very compelling visual images of the resultant suffering on television and in other mass media. In September 2001 the world suffered and grieved with Americans. Equally, killing and conflict occurring not only in major capitals but in distant places around the world has been brought right into the homes and living rooms of people all over the world. In a number of cases, popular concern over what has been seen has put political pressure on governments to respond. For many of these governments, it has created a domestic political cost for inaction and indifference.

**New Opportunities for Common Action**

1.30 A critically important contextual dimension of the current debate on intervention for human protection purposes is the new opportunity and capacity for common action that have resulted from the end of the Cold War. For perhaps the first time since the UN was established, there is now a genuine prospect of the Security Council fulfilling the role envisioned for it in the UN Charter. Despite some notable setbacks, the capacity for common action by the Security Council was shown during the 1990s to be real, with the authorization by the Council of nearly 40 peacekeeping or peace enforcement operations over the last decade.

1.31 Closely allied to this new awareness of world conditions and new visibility for human suffering has been the impact of globalization in intensifying economic interdependence between states. Globalization has led to closer ties at all levels and a pronounced trend towards multilateral cooperation. In the context of the debate surrounding the issue of intervention for human protection purposes, it is clear that the realities of globalization and growing interdependency have often been important factors in prompting neighbouring states and others to become engaged positively both in promoting prevention, and also in calling for intervention in situations that seem to be spiralling out of control.

*The Implications for State Sovereignty*

1.32 In a dangerous world marked by overwhelming inequalities of power and resources, sovereignty is for many states their best—and sometimes seemingly their only—line of defence. But sovereignty is more than just a functional principle of international relations. For many states and peoples, it is also a recognition of their equal worth and dignity, a protection of their unique identities and their national freedom, and an affirmation of their right to shape and determine their own destiny. In recognition of this, the principle that all states are equally sovereign under international law was established as a cornerstone of the UN Charter (Article 2.1).

1.33 However, for all the reasons mentioned already, the conditions under which sovereignty is exercised—and intervention is practised—have changed dramatically since 1945. Many new states have emerged and are still in the process of consolidating their identity. Evolving international law has set many constraints on what states can do, and not only in the realm of human rights. The emerging concept of human security has created additional demands and expectations in relation to the way states treat their own people. And many new actors are playing international roles previously more or less the exclusive preserve of states.

1.34    All that said, sovereignty does still matter. It is strongly arguable that effective and legitimate states remain the best way to ensure that the benefits of the internationalization of trade, investment, technology and communication will be equitably shared. Those states which can call upon strong regional alliances, internal peace, and a strong and independent civil society, seem clearly best placed to benefit from globalization. They will also be likely to be those most respectful of human rights. And in security terms, a cohesive and peaceful international system is far more likely to be achieved through the cooperation of effective states, confident of their place in the world, than in an environment of fragile, collapsed, fragmenting or generally chaotic state entities.

1.35    The defence of state sovereignty, by even its strongest supporters, does not include any claim of the unlimited power of a state to do what it wants to its own people. The Commission heard no such claim at any stage during our worldwide consultations. It is acknowledged that sovereignty implies a dual responsibility: externally— to respect the sovereignty of other states, and internally, to respect the dignity and basic rights of all the people within the state. In international human rights covenants, in UN practice, and in state practice itself, sovereignty is now understood as embracing this dual responsibility. Sovereignty as responsibility has become the minimum content of good international citizenship.

1.36    This modern understanding of the meaning of sovereignty is of central importance in the Commission's approach to the question of intervention for human protection purposes, and in particular in the development of our core theme, "the responsibility to protect."

## The Meaning of Intervention

### Scope of the Concept

1.37    Part of the controversy over "intervention" derives from the potential width of activities this term can cover, up to and including military intervention. Some would regard any application of pressure to a state as being intervention, and would include in this conditional support programmes by major international financial institutions whose recipients often feel they have no choice but to accept. Some others would regard almost any non-consensual interference in the internal affairs of another state as being intervention—including the delivery of emergency relief assistance to a section of a country's population in need. Others again would regard any kind of outright coercive actions—not just military action but actual or threatened political and economic sanctions, blockades, diplomatic and military threats, and international criminal prosecutions—as all being included in the term. Yet others would confine its use to military force.

1.38    The kind of intervention with which we are concerned in this report is action taken against a state or its leaders, without its or their consent, for purposes which are claimed to be humanitarian or protective. By far the most controversial form of such intervention is military, and a great part of our report necessarily focuses on that. But we are also very much concerned with alternatives to military action, including all forms of preventive measures, and coercive intervention

measures—sanctions and criminal prosecutions—falling short of military intervention. Such coercive measures are discussed in this report in two contexts: their
threatened use as a preventive measure, designed to avoid the need for military
intervention arising; and their actual use as a reactive measure, but as an alternative
to military force.

**"Humanitarian" Intervention?**

1.39 The Commission recognizes the long history, and continuing wide and popular
usage, of the phrase "humanitarian intervention," and also its descriptive usefulness in clearly focusing attention on one particular category of interventions—
namely, those undertaken for the stated purpose of protecting or assisting people at
risk. But we have made a deliberate decision not to adopt this terminology, preferring to refer either to "intervention," or as appropriate "military intervention," for
human protection purposes.

1.40 We have responded in this respect to the very strong opposition expressed by
humanitarian agencies, humanitarian organizations and humanitarian workers
towards any militarization of the word "humanitarian": whatever the motives of
those engaging in the intervention, it is anathema for the humanitarian relief and
assistance sector to have this word appropriated to describe any kind of military
action. The Commission has also been responsive to the suggestion in some
political quarters that use in this context of an inherently approving word like
"humanitarian" tends to prejudge the very question in issue—that is, whether the
intervention is in fact defensible.

1.41 We have taken the view from the outset that there is some virtue in anything which
may encourage people to look again, with fresh eyes, at the real issues involved in
the sovereignty–intervention debate. Beyond the question of "humanitarian intervention" terminology, there is a rather larger language change, and associated
reconceptualization of the issues, which the Commission has also felt it helpful to
embrace.

## 2.  A New Approach: "The Responsibility to Protect"

2.1   Millions of human beings remain at the mercy of civil wars, insurgencies, state
repression and state collapse. This is a stark and undeniable reality, and it is at the
heart of all the issues with which this Commission has been wrestling. What is at
stake here is not making the world safe for big powers, or trampling over the sovereign rights of small ones, but delivering practical protection for ordinary people, at
risk of their lives, because their states are unwilling or unable to protect them.

2.2   But all this is easier said than done. There have been as many failures as successes,
perhaps more, in the international protective record in recent years. There are
continuing fears about a "right to intervene" being formally acknowledged. If
intervention for human protection purposes is to be accepted, including the possibility of military action, it remains imperative that the international community
develop consistent, credible and enforceable standards to guide state and intergovernmental practice. The experience and aftermath of Somalia, Rwanda, Srebrenica and Kosovo, as well as interventions and non-interventions in a number of
other places, have provided a clear indication that the tools, devices and thinking
of international relations need now to be comprehensively reassessed, in order to
meet the foreseeable needs of the 21st century.

2.3   Any new approach to intervention on human protection grounds needs to meet at
least four basic objectives:

- to establish clearer rules, procedures and criteria for determining whether, when and how to intervene;
- to establish the legitimacy of military intervention when necessary and after all other approaches have failed;
- to ensure that military intervention, when it occurs, is carried out only for the purposes proposed, is effective, and is undertaken with proper concern to minimize the human costs and institutional damage that will result; and
- to help eliminate, where possible, the causes of conflict while enhancing the prospects for durable and sustainable peace.

2.4    It is important that language—and the concepts which lie behind particular choices of words—do not become a barrier to dealing with the real issues involved. Just as the Commission found that the expression "humanitarian intervention" did not help to carry the debate forward, so too do we believe that the language of past debates arguing for or against a "right to intervene" by one state on the territory of another state is outdated and unhelpful. We prefer to talk not of a "right to intervene" but of a "responsibility to protect."

2.5    Changing the language of the debate, while it can remove a barrier to effective action, does not, of course, change the substantive issues which have to be addressed. There still remain to be argued all the moral, legal, political and operational questions—about need, authority, will and capacity respectively—which have themselves been so difficult and divisive. But if people are prepared to look at all these issues from the new perspective that we propose, it may just make finding agreed answers that much easier.

2.6    In the remainder of this chapter we seek to make a principled, as well as a practical and political, case for conceptualizing the intervention issue in terms of a responsibility to protect. The building blocks of the argument are first, the principles inherent in the concept of sovereignty; and secondly, the impact of emerging principles of human rights and human security, and changing state and intergovernmental practice.

## The Meaning of Sovereignty

### The Norm of Non-Intervention

2.7    Sovereignty has come to signify, in the Westphalian concept, the legal identity of a state in international law. It is a concept which provides order, stability and predictability in international relations since sovereign states are regarded as equal, regardless of comparative size or wealth. The principle of sovereign equality of states is enshrined in Article 2.1 of the UN Charter. Internally, sovereignty signifies the capacity to make authoritative decisions with regard to the people and resources within the territory of the state. Generally, however, the authority of the state is not regarded as absolute, but constrained and regulated internally by constitutional power sharing arrangements.

2.8    A condition of any one state's sovereignty is a corresponding obligation to respect every other state's sovereignty: the norm of non-intervention is enshrined in Article 2.7 of the UN Charter. A sovereign state is empowered in international law to exercise exclusive and total jurisdiction within its territorial borders. Other states have the corresponding duty not to intervene in the internal affairs of a sovereign state. If that duty is violated, the victim state has the further right to defend its territorial integrity and political independence. In the era of decolonization, the sovereign equality of states and the correlative norm of nonintervention received its most emphatic affirmation from the newly independent states.

2.9    At the same time, while intervention for human protection purposes was extremely rare, during the Cold War years state practice reflected the unwillingness of many countries to give up the use of intervention for political or other purposes as an instrument of policy. Leaders on both sides of the ideological divide intervened in support of friendly leaders against local populations, while also supporting rebel movements and other opposition causes in states to which they were ideologically opposed. None were prepared to rule out *a priori* the use of force in another country in order to rescue nationals who were trapped and threatened there.

2.10   The established and universally acknowledged right to self-defence, embodied in Article 51 of the UN Charter, was sometimes extended to include the right to launch punitive raids into neighbouring countries that had shown themselves unwilling or unable to stop their territory from being used as a launching pad for cross-border armed raids or terrorist attacks. But all that said, the many examples of intervention in actual state practice throughout the 20th century did not lead to an abandonment of the norm of non-intervention.

**The Organizing Principle of the UN System**

2.11   Membership of the United Nations was the final symbol of independent sovereign statehood and thus the seal of acceptance into the community of nations. The UN also became the principal international forum for collaborative action in the shared pursuit of the three goals of state building, nation building and economic development. The UN was therefore the main arena for the jealous protection, not the casual abrogation, of state sovereignty.

2.12   The UN is an organization dedicated to the maintenance of international peace and security on the basis of protecting the territorial integrity, political independence and national sovereignty of its member states. But the overwhelming majority of today's armed conflicts are internal, not inter-state. Moreover, the proportion of civilians killed in them increased from about one in ten at the start of the 20th century to around nine in ten by its close. This has presented the organization with a major difficulty: how to reconcile its foundational principles of member states' sovereignty and the accompanying primary mandate to maintain international peace and security ("to save succeeding generations from the scourge of war")—with the equally compelling mission to promote the interests and welfare of people within those states ("We the peoples of the United Nations").

2.13   The Secretary-General has discussed the dilemma in the conceptual language of two notions of sovereignty, one vesting in the state, the second in the people and in individuals. His approach reflects the ever-increasing commitment around the world to democratic government (of, by and for the people) and greater popular freedoms. The second notion of sovereignty to which he refers should not be seen as any kind of challenge to the traditional notion of state sovereignty. Rather it is a way of saying that the more traditional notion of state sovereignty should be able comfortably to embrace the goal of greater self-empowerment and freedom for people, both individually and collectively.

**Sovereignty as Responsibility**

2.14   The Charter of the UN is itself an example of an international obligation voluntarily accepted by member states. On the one hand, in granting membership of the UN, the international community welcomes the signatory state as a responsible member of the community of nations. On the other hand, the state itself, in signing the Charter, accepts the responsibilities of membership flowing from that signature. There is no transfer or dilution of state sovereignty. But there is a necessary re-characterization involved: from *sovereignty as control* to *sovereignty as responsibility* in both internal functions and external duties.

2.15 Thinking of sovereignty as responsibility, in a way that is being increasingly recognized in state practice, has a threefold significance. First, it implies that the state authorities are responsible for the functions of protecting the safety and lives of citizens and promotion of their welfare. Secondly, it suggests that the national political authorities are responsible to the citizens internally and to the international community through the UN. And thirdly, it means that the agents of state are responsible for their actions; that is to say, they are accountable for their acts of commission and omission. The case for thinking of sovereignty in these terms is strengthened by the ever-increasing impact of international human rights norms, and the increasing impact in international discourse of the concept of human security.

## Human Rights, Human Security and Emerging Practice

### Human Rights

2.16 The adoption of new standards of conduct for states in the protection and advancement of international human rights has been one of the great achievements of the post-World War II era. Article 1.3 of its founding 1945 Charter committed the UN to "promoting and encouraging respect for human rights and for fundamental freedoms for all without distinction as to race, sex, language or religion." The Universal Declaration of Human Rights (1948) embodies the moral code, political consensus and legal synthesis of human rights. The simplicity of the Declaration's language belies the passion of conviction underpinning it. Its elegance has been the font of inspiration down the decades; its provisions comprise the vocabulary of complaint. The two Covenants of 1966, on civil–political and social–economic–cultural rights, affirm and proclaim the human rights norm as a fundamental principle of international relations and add force and specificity to the Universal Declaration.

2.17 Together the Universal Declaration and the two Covenants mapped out the international human rights agenda, established the benchmark for state conduct, inspired provisions in many national laws and international conventions, and led to the creation of long-term national infrastructures for the protection and promotion of human rights. They are important milestones in the transition from a culture of violence to a more enlightened culture of peace.

2.18 What has been gradually emerging is a parallel transition from a culture of sovereign impunity to a culture of national and international accountability. International organizations, civil society activists and NGOs use the international human rights norms and instruments as the concrete point of reference against which to judge state conduct. Between them, the UN and NGOs have achieved many successes. National laws and international instruments have been improved, a number of political prisoners have been freed and some victims of abuse have been compensated. The most recent advances in international human rights have been in the further development of international humanitarian law, for example in the Ottawa Convention on landmines which subordinated military calculations to humanitarian concerns about a weapon that cannot distinguish a soldier from a child, and in the Rome Statute establishing the International Criminal Court.

2.19 Just as the substance of human rights law is coming increasingly closer to realizing the notion of universal justice—justice without borders—so too is the process. Not only have new international criminal tribunals been specially created to deal with crimes against humanity committed in the Balkans, Rwanda and Sierra Leone; and not only is an International Criminal Court about to be established to try such crimes wherever and whenever committed in the future; but the universal jurisdiction which now exists under a number of treaties, like the Geneva Conventions, and which enables any state party to try anyone accused of the crimes in question, is now beginning to be seriously applied.

2.20 The significance of these developments in establishing new standards of behaviour, and new means of enforcing those standards, is unquestionable. But the key to the effective observance of human rights remains, as it always has been, national law and practice: the frontline defence of the rule of law is best conducted by the judicial systems of sovereign states, which should be independent, professional and properly resourced. It is only when national systems of justice either cannot or will not act to judge crimes against humanity that universal jurisdiction and other international options should come into play.

**Human Security**

2.21 The meaning and scope of security have become much broader since the UN Charter was signed in 1945. Human security means the security of people—their physical safety, their economic and social well-being, respect for their dignity and worth as human beings, and the protection of their human rights and fundamental freedoms. The growing recognition worldwide that concepts of security must include people as well as states has marked an important shift in international thinking during the past decade. Secretary-General Kofi Annan himself put the issue of human security at the centre of the current debate, when in his statement to the 54th session of the General Assembly he made clear his intention to "address the prospects for human security and intervention in the next century."

2.22 This Commission certainly accepts that issues of sovereignty and intervention are not just matters affecting the rights or prerogatives of states, but that they deeply affect and involve individual human beings in fundamental ways. One of the virtues of expressing the key issue in this debate as "the responsibility to protect" is that it focuses attention where it should be most concentrated, on the human needs of those seeking protection or assistance. The emphasis in the security debate shifts, with this focus, from territorial security, and security through armaments, to security through human development with access to food and employment, and to environmental security. The fundamental components of human security—the security of *people* against threats to life, health, livelihood, personal safety and human dignity—can be put at risk by external aggression, but also by factors within a country, including "security" forces. Being wedded still to too narrow a concept of "national security" may be one reason why many governments spend more to protect their citizens against undefined external military attack than to guard them against the omnipresent enemies of good health and other real threats to human security on a daily basis.

2.23 The traditional, narrow perception of security leaves out the most elementary and legitimate concerns of ordinary people regarding security in their daily lives. It also diverts enormous amounts of national wealth and human resources into armaments and armed forces, while countries fail to protect their citizens from chronic insecurities of hunger, disease, inadequate shelter, crime, unemployment, social conflict and environmental hazard. When rape is used as an instrument of war and ethnic cleansing, when thousands are killed by floods resulting from a ravaged countryside and when citizens are killed by their own security forces, then it is just insufficient to think of security in terms of national or territorial security alone. The concept of human security can and does embrace such diverse circumstances.

**Emerging Practice**

2.24 The debate on military intervention for human protection purposes was ignited in the international community essentially because of the critical gap between, on the one hand, the needs and distress being felt, and seen to be felt, in the real world, and on the other hand the codified instruments and modalities for managing world order. There has been a parallel gap, no less critical, between the codified best practice of international behaviour as articulated in the UN Charter and actual state practice as it has evolved in the 56 years since the Charter was signed. While there is not yet a sufficiently strong basis to claim the emergence of a new principle of customary international law, growing state and regional organization practice as well as Security Council precedent suggest an emerging guiding principle— which in the Commission's view could properly be termed "the responsibility to protect."

2.25 The emerging principle in question is that intervention for human protection purposes, including military intervention in extreme cases, is supportable when major harm to civilians is occurring or imminently apprehended, and the state in question is unable or unwilling to end the harm, or is itself the perpetrator. The Security Council itself has been increasingly prepared in recent years to act on this basis, most obviously in Somalia, defining what was essentially an internal situation as constituting a threat to international peace and security such as to justify enforcement action under Chapter VII of the UN Charter. This is also the basis on which the interventions by the Economic Community of West African States (ECOWAS) in Liberia and Sierra Leone were essentially justified by the interveners, as was the intervention mounted without Security Council authorization by NATO allies in Kosovo.

2.26 The notion that there is an emerging guiding principle in favour of military intervention for human protection purposes is also supported by a wide variety of legal sources—including sources that exist independently of any duties, responsibilities or authority that may be derived from Chapter VII of the UN Charter. These legal foundations include fundamental natural law principles; the human rights provisions of the UN Charter; the Universal Declaration of Human Rights together with the Genocide Convention; the Geneva Conventions and Additional Protocols on international humanitarian law; the statute of the International Criminal Court; and a number of other international human rights and human protection agreements and covenants.

2.27 Based on our reading of state practice, Security Council precedent, established norms, emerging guiding principles, and evolving customary international law, the Commission believes that the Charter's strong bias against military intervention is not to be regarded as absolute when decisive action is required on human protection grounds. The degree of legitimacy accorded to intervention will usually turn on the answers to such questions as the purpose, the means, the exhaustion of other avenues of redress against grievances, the proportionality of the riposte to the initiating provocation, and the agency of authorization. These are all questions that will recur: for present purposes the point is simply that there is a large and accumulating body of law and practice which supports the notion that, whatever form the exercise of that responsibility may properly take, members of the broad community of states do have a responsibility to protect both their own citizens and those of other states as well.

*Shifting the Terms of the Debate*

2.28 The traditional language of the sovereignty–intervention debate—in terms of "the right of humanitarian intervention" or the "right to intervene"—is unhelpful in at least three key respects. First, it necessarily focuses attention on the claims, rights and prerogatives of the potentially intervening states much more so than on the urgent needs of the potential beneficiaries of the action. Secondly, by focusing narrowly on the act of intervention, the traditional language does not adequately take into account the need for either prior reventive effort or subsequent follow-up assistance, both of which have been too often neglected in practice. And thirdly, although this point should not be overstated, the familiar language does effectively operate to trump sovereignty with intervention at the outset of the debate: it loads the dice in favour of intervention before the argument has even begun, by tending to label and delegitimize dissent as anti-humanitarian.

2.29 The Commission is of the view that the debate about intervention for human protection purposes should focus not on "the right to intervene" but on "the responsibility to protect." The proposed change in terminology is also a change in perspective, reversing the perceptions inherent in the traditional language, and adding some additional ones:

- First, the responsibility to protect implies an evaluation of the issues from the point of view of those seeking or needing support, rather than those who may be considering intervention. Our preferred terminology refocuses the international searchlight back where it should always be: on the duty to protect communities from mass killing, women from systematic rape and children from starvation.

- Secondly, the responsibility to protect acknowledges that the primary responsibility in this regard rests with the state concerned, and that it is only if the state is unable or unwilling to fulfill this responsibility, or is itself the perpetrator, that it becomes the responsibility of the international community to act in its place. In many cases, the state will seek to acquit its responsibility in full and active partnership with representatives of the international community. Thus the "responsibility to protect" is more of a linking concept that bridges the divide between intervention and sovereignty; the language of the "right or duty to intervene" is intrinsically more confrontational.

- Thirdly, the responsibility to protect means not just the "responsibility to react," but the "responsibility to prevent" and the "responsibility to rebuild" as well. It directs our attention to the costs and results of action versus no action, and provides conceptual, normative and operational linkages between assistance, intervention and reconstruction.

2.30 The Commission believes that responsibility to protect resides first and foremost with the state whose people are directly affected. This fact reflects not only international law and the modern state system, but also the practical realities of who is best placed to make a positive difference. The domestic authority is best placed to take action to prevent problems from turning into potential conflicts. When problems arise the domestic authority is also best placed to understand them and to deal with them. When solutions are needed, it is the citizens of a particular state who have the greatest interest and the largest stake in the success of those solutions, in ensuring that the domestic authorities are fully accountable for their actions or inactions in addressing these problems, and in helping to ensure that past problems are not allowed to recur.

2.31 While the state whose people are directly affected has the default responsibility to protect, a residual responsibility also lies with the broader community of states.

This fallback responsibility is activated when a particular state is clearly either unwilling or unable to fulfill its responsibility to protect or is itself the actual perpetrator of crimes or atrocities; or where people living outside a particular state are directly threatened by actions taking place there. This responsibility also requires that in some circumstances action must be taken by the broader community of states to support populations that are in jeopardy or under serious threat.

2.32 The substance of the responsibility to protect is the provision of life-supporting protection and assistance to populations at risk. This responsibility has three integral and essential components: not just the responsibility to *react* to an actual or apprehended human catastrophe, but the responsibility to *prevent* it, and the responsibility to *rebuild* after the event. Each of these will be dealt with in detail in chapters of this report. But it is important to emphasize from the start that action in support of the responsibility to protect necessarily involves and calls for a broad range and wide variety of assistance actions and responses. These actions may include both long and short-term measures to help prevent human security-threatening situations from occurring, intensifying, spreading, or persisting; and rebuilding support to help prevent them from recurring; as well as, at least in extreme cases, military intervention to protect at-risk civilians from harm.

2.33 Changing the terms of the debate from "right to intervene" to "responsibility to protect" helps to shift the focus of discussion where it belongs—on the requirements of those who need or seek assistance. But while this is an important and necessary step, it does not by itself, as we have already acknowledged, resolve the difficult questions relating to the circumstances in which the responsibility to protect should be exercised—questions of legitimacy, authority, operational effectiveness and political will. These issues are fully addressed in subsequent chapters. While the Commission does not purport to try to resolve all of these difficult issues now and forever, our approach will hopefully generate innovative thinking on ways of achieving and sustaining effective and appropriate action.

# 8

# The Prevention of Genocide

Ever since the term "genocide" was first coined by Raphael Lemkin in 1944, there has been much more talk about the prevention of genocide than action. Indeed, there have been few, for example, Secretaries-General of the United Nations, Presidents of the United States, or Prime Ministers of the United Kingdom who have not issued broadsides asserting that genocide must be prevented. And yet, all one needs to do is examine a short and incomplete list of the genocides that have been perpetrated over the past 50 years or so to see that talk has lorded over action almost every single time: the genocide of the Bangladeshis in East Pakistan (1971), the Khmer Rouge perpetrated genocide of their fellow Cambodians (1975–1979), the Iraqi gassing of the Kurds in northern Iraq (1988), the 1994 Rwandan genocide, the genocide of 7,000 to 8,000 Muslim boys and men of Srebrenica in 1995, and the ongoing genocide of black Africans in Darfur, Sudan since 2003.

One of the many grave errors that the international community has made repeatedly in regard to the prevention of genocide is that it has waited until a crisis has been definitively designated a "genocide" *before* it has taken action to attempt to ameliorate the problem. Thus, instead of acting early on to resolve a conflict (or ever-increasing but sporadic violence) *via* conflict resolution programs and diplomatic forays, members of the international community have waited, time and again, to see how a conflict is going to play out. Playing such a "wait and see" game plays directly into the hands of the perpetrators by allowing the killers just that much more time to carry out their murderous plans. When the mass murder has reached that point, prevention is no longer needed; rather, the situation calls for intervention, and intervention means that the international community must find nations willing to commit troops to a highly dangerous situation, locate the funding to cover the costs of transporting and equipping troops, and providing vehicles and planes and the resources to keep them in operation—all of which is extremely costly in a variety of ways. And that does not take into consideration the thorny issue of entering the sovereign territory of another nation, one that may argue that the international community is interfering in its "internal affairs" and will suffer the consequences for doing so.

Many public figures, including a number of Secretaries-General of the United Nations (for example, Boutros Boutros Ghali and Kofi Annan), have claimed, over and over again, that prevention is cheaper and safer than intervention, but the international community has not seemed to have learned that lesson—in actuality, it does not seem to want to learn it. That is more than a little unfortunate, for so long as that mentality remains in place there is little hope that the world will move from reacting slowly and inadequately to mass killing and genocide, to attempting to stave it off before it begins.

In his article "Early Warning," genocide scholar Gregory H. Stanton provides a succinct summary of the key arguments relating to the issue of early warning to stop the possibility of genocide, focusing on who should be warned, how warning should be conveyed, and how successful early warning strategies can be. His most important point, perhaps, is his last, as he argues that "early warning is meaningless without early response"—which takes the issue onto a wholly new plane.

Helen Fein, one of the earliest pioneers of genocide studies, uses the case of the 1994 genocide in Rwanda to examine the issue of the prevention of genocide in her article "The Three P's of Genocide Prevention: With Application to a Genocide Foretold—Rwanda." She asserts that there are three questions ("the three p's") that are critical to address when considering the prevention of genocide: "Is it our problem?"; "Is it not only prudent but in our interest to do so?"; and "Is it really possible to detect genocide?" Upon answering those questions, she applies herself to attempting to ascertain whether it was possible for the international community to have prevented the 1994 Rwandan genocide that resulted in the murder of between 800,000 and one million people in 100 days between April and July 1994. She concludes with a short discussion of the potential for and the impediments to the prevention of genocide.

The section concludes with a powerful and thought-provoking interview with General Romeo Dallaire about his experiences as force commander of the UN Assistance Mission for Rwanda (UNAMIR) prior to and during the 1994 Rwandan genocide. As he makes crystal clear, he believes that if the UN had heeded his warnings and requests, the genocide, at least to a large extent, would have been avoided. Instead, on a weak mandate (Chapter VI), he and his troops were largely forced to sit by and watch as hundreds of thousands of people were slaughtered in cold blood. It is a story of shameful and unconscionable *realpolitik* and inaction by the United Nations and the United States, the latter of which not only refused to support an intervention but lobbied intensely against one.

# 8.1   Gregory H. Stanton, "Early Warning"

The genocides in Rwanda (in 1994) and in Bosnia (during the period between 1992 and 1995) were alarming evidence of the failure of the United Nations (UN) Security Council and its member states to prevent genocides and other crimes against humanity. Studies by the UN Commissions of Inquiry concluded that reform in four areas is needed to prevent such crimes: institutions for early warning, programs for prevention, capacity for rapid response, and courts for punishment. Willingness to use these institutions on the part of political leaders is necessary to render reform measures effective. Public pressure is needed to motivate leaders to act.

One of the most common false assumptions about genocide is that it is the result of conflict—the resolution of which would be a preventive to genocide. Most genocide does not result from conflict. Genocide is one-sided mass murder. Empirical research by Helen Fein, Matthew Krain, Barbara Harff, Benjamin Valentino, and others has shown that genocide is most often committed by elites that are attempting to stay in power in the face of perceived threats to their dominance. Fein and Harff have found that six factors enhance the likelihood of genocide: prior genocide in the same polity, autocracy, ethnic minority rule, political upheaval during war or revolution, exclusionary ideology, and closure of borders to international trade.

Wishing to complement these statistical models, Gregory H. Stanton has devised a developmental model of the stages of genocide. The eight stages of genocide are classification ("us vs. them"), symbolization, dehumanization, organization (the formation of hate groups), polarization, preparation (the identification, expropriation, rounding up, and transportation of victims), extermination, and denial. Stanton's model is designed so that policy makers can recognize early warning signs and implement specific countermeasures to prevent genocide.

Who should be warned of the likelihood of impending genocide? Members of the victim group should surely come first, so that they can prepare to flee or defend themselves. Others who should receive this warning are political moderates, the members of religious and human rights groups, and the members of antigovernment opposition forces (who would be likely to oppose the impending genocide). If the government is not party to an impending genocide, it should be called upon to intervene and to protect its citizens. (This approach has halted ethnic and religious massacres in Kalimantan, Sulawesi, and the Moluccas [all part of Indonesia], and in Nigeria.) But because most genocides are committed by governments (either directly or indirectly through militias), regional and international leaders must be warned as well—with the idea that they will be able to bring pressure to bear on the government planning the genocide. In democracies, leaders seldom act without the stimulus of public pressure, so early warning must get through to the media and groups that can organize campaigns for action.

How early must warning come if it is to trigger action that will contribute to the prevention of genocide? The answer depends on the action that is being sought. In the context of long-term efforts to prevent genocide, the warning should be given as early as possible. Because structural factors such as totalitarian or autocratic government and minority rule correlate substantially with the incidence of genocide, long-term policies for genocide prevention should promote democracy, freedom and pluralist tolerance. Rudy Rummel's meticulously documented conclusion that democracies do not commit genocide against their own enfranchised populations has often been challenged, but never refuted. The protection of democracies requires that, in the face of threats by extremist, military, or totalitarian movements to overthrow those democracies, the warning be communicated as early as possible.

Freedom House, which tracks information pertaining to the relative freedoms of many countries and publishes an annual report on the subject, in its 2003 report counted 121 electoral democracies out of the 192 countries it evaluated (leaving 71 nondemocracies). Ted Robert Gurr has pointed out that periods of transition (from autocratic governments to democratic ones) can be particularly dangerous periods—at which times minority elites attempt to hold onto their power and are sometimes willing to commit mass murder to do so. The foreign policies of other nations should promote the peaceful transition to democracy, but must avoid the enunciation of mortal threats that would set off the undertaking of genocide by elites determined to maintain their power.

Rwanda was a case in which early warning failed. In 1992 the Belgian Ambassador to Rwanda warned the Belgian government that Hutu Power advocates were "planning the extermination of the Tutsi of Rwanda." In April 1993 the UN Special Rapporteur on Summary, Arbitrary, and Extrajudicial Executions issued a statement that the massacres of Tutsi in Rwanda already constituted genocide. General Roméo Dallaire, Commander of the UN Assistance Mission in Rwanda, in a cable sent on January 11, 1994, warned the UN Department of Peacekeeping Operations, headed by Kofi Annan, of the plan of extremist Hutu to exterminate Tutsis. The UN denied Dallaire permission to confiscate the cache of 500,000 machetes that had been shipped to Rwanda for the Hutu militias (the existence of which had come to his attention). Both early and late warnings of the Rwandan genocide were ignored by UN and other policy makers who denied the facts, who resisted calling the genocide by its proper name, and who refused to consider options for intervention—and who refused to risk the lives of any of their own soldiers. Instead they withdrew 2,000 UN Assistance Mission for Rwanda (UNAMIR) troops and sacrificed the lives of over 500,000 defenseless Rwandans.

There had been a similar failure of early warning in Cambodia in 1975, at which time reporters and diplomats were predicting a Khmer Rouge bloodbath. Political leftists in other countries refused to believe the warnings, and denied the mass killing while it was underway. Worn out by the wars in Indochina, the United States and western European nations were unwilling to intervene to overthrow the murderous Khmer Rouge. The UN General Assembly even condemned Vietnam for its intervention.

Instances of early warning that were successful in generating courses of action to prevent or frustrate genocidal massacres and the commission of crimes against humanity include Macedonia (in 1992 and 2001, when several hundred UN peacekeepers prevented the Balkan wars from widening); East Timor (in 1999, when, after East Timor had voted for independence, coordinated warnings coming from human rights groups and the intervention of Australian troops brought to a halt the massacre of East Timorese by Indonesian troops and militias); and Côte d'Ivoire (in 2002, when warnings by the Belgian organization *Prévention Génocides*, followed by French military and diplomatic intervention, helped to avert massacres).

What steps have been taken to develop early warning systems? The early warning of threats to national interests has long been a job of the intelligence agencies that inform government policy makers. Threats of genocide were added to that task by the U.S. Central Intelligence Agency (CIA) in 1994, when that organization inaugurated its "State Failure Task Force," whose mission includes the analysis of factors that predispose states to genocide. Efforts to develop systems of early warning on the part of think tanks and university officers have also been funded by governments—in the United Kingdom, the Netherlands, Denmark, Sweden, and Germany.

At the UN, the Framework for Coordination was established within the Department of Political Affairs to convene high-level planners from UN departments and agencies to discuss and plan responses to crises that are judged to be capable of generating genocical aggression. On April 7, 2004, Annan announced that he would appoint a Special Adviser on the Prevention of Genocide. In July Juan Mendez was named to the post.

Nongovernmental organizations (NGOs) and university-based organizations in Europe and the United States have also focused on early warning—notably the International Crisis Group, the Forum on Early Warning and Early Response (FEWER), Genocide Watch, and the International Campaign to End Genocide (a global coalition of organizations dedicated to preventing genocide).

Early warning is meaningless without early response. But early warning is the necessary first step toward prevention.

## Bibliography

Fein, Helen (1993). "Accounting for Genocide after 1945: Theories and Some Findings." *International Journal on Group Rights* 1(1):79–106.

Gurr, Ted Robert (2000). *Peoples Versus States: Minorities at Risk in the New Century*. Washington, D.C.: U.S. Institute of Peace Press.

Harff, Barbara (1998). "Early Warning of Humanitarian Crises: Sequential Models and the Role of Accelerators." In *Preventive Measures: Building Risk Assessment and Crisis Early Warning Systems*, ed. L. Davies and Ted Robert Gurr. Lanham, Md.: Rowman & Littlefield.

Harff, Barbara (2003). "No Lessons Learned from the Holocaust? Assessing Risks of Genocide and Political Mass Murder since 1955." *American Political Science Review* (February) 97(1):57–73.

Krain, Matthew (1997). "State-Sponsored Mass Murder: The Onset and Severity of Genocides and Politicides." *Journal of Conflict Resolution* 41:331–360.

Rummel, Rudolph J. (1995). "Democracy, Power, Genocide, and Mass Murder." *Journal of Conflict Resolution* 39:3–26.

Stanton, Gregory H. (2004). "Could the Rwandan Genocide Have Been Prevented?" *Journal of Genocide Research* 6(2):211–228.

Valentino, Benjamin A. (2004). *Final Solutions: Mass Killing and Genocide in the Twentieth Century*. Ithaca, N.Y.: Cornell University Press.

## 8.2    Helen Fein, "The Three P's of Genocide Prevention: With Application to a Genocide Foretold—Rwanda"

### Introduction

Neal Riemer has asked, "Can we develop a far-sighted, coherent, and effective policy of prudent prevention of genocide?" I shall make a case that this depends on positive answers to three questions: (1) Is it our problem? (2) Is it not only prudent but in our interest to do so? and (3) Is it really possible to detect genocide? And can one demonstrate how to employ a paradigm to organize intelligence on the ground to anticipate genocide? In this essay, I will show that there are positive answers to all three questions. I will also show the high cost of tolerating genocide (especially as compared to prevention) both in terms of geopolitical strategy and economic rationality.

First, there is the preliminary question: "Who are we?" By "we," the "international community" (usually an oxymoron) is often implied. Rather than assuming such an entity, let us look at how we as citizens of the United States cope with threats as a community, nation, and state. Let us also assume that the obligations we accept for ourselves apply to other states with similar responsibilities. However, other states' responsibilities in particular situations may be greater or lesser than ours, depending on their access to the situation in question, their resources, their interest, and their influence.

No one doubts that when we set out to do so, we can (and have) developed warning systems or indicators for earthquakes, fire, floods, hunger, pollution and weather trends (i.e., global warming). In the case of man-made disasters, we have developed codes, devices, and regimens for prevention and containment of such threats: building codes, dikes, food banks, pollution standards. Few planners in developed countries deny that there is a responsibility to prevent and contain such threats and to cooperate with other states to do so, although there is disagreement on methods and priorities. Nor do the most conservative parties deny humanitarian responsibility for relief of hunger and humanitarian disasters today.

Genocide is a prime target for prevention because it is a man-made, not a natural, disaster. It can be forecast because we know the warning signs; and it could be stopped—if it were not prevented—if we learned to recognize it promptly, discriminating it from warfare. Genocide is a calculated and rational crime of state (or pretenders to the state) and their calculus of costs and benefit can be altered. Their first question is "will we get away with it?"

Until now, the answer has been yes, most of the time. A few cases of genocide have led to interstate wars or upsets by an invading army with state losses of land or regime control (in Rwanda 1994, Cambodia 1979, Uganda 1979, and Pakistan 1971) but not before there was a terrible toll in victims. As Leo Kuper said over a decade ago, "The sovereign territorial state claims, as an integral part of its sovereignty, the right to commit genocide, or engage in genocidal massacres, against peoples under its rule, and . . . the United Nations, for all practical purposes, defends this right."[1] In 1998, the UN did not so much defend the right—it acknowledged war crimes and crimes against humanity and set up tribunals for judgment in the cases of the former Yugoslavia and Rwanda—but it scarcely recognizes genocide and gross violations of human rights in process. Such crimes are distanced by framing them with a neutral label that avoids perception of the criminal causes of such events: refugee or humanitarian crises, complex humanitarian emergencies; or civil wars and internal or ethnic conflict, implying there are two equally culpable parties. This serves to obscure both cause and perpetrator; thus, there is no crime, such as genocide, requiring international attention.

## Is it Our Problem?

But states argue (usually out of hearing) that it is not their problem, despite the fact that they are signatories of the UN Genocide Convention. Often, states distinguish their national interest from international obligations, putting short-range or narrow economic interests above their own long-term interests. To argue my case that the prevention of genocide is in our national interest because of its effect, when undeterred, on international security and economy, let us take the narrowest assumption. That is, as U.S. citizens—even if we take a simple view of our own interests as a community, a nation, and a state as the most minimal consensus—it can be shown that genocide, expanding and undeterred, is an impediment to our international goals and to our vision of ourselves in the world. This vision, or ideal of what kind of world we stand for, is itself an element of our collective identity—an ideal or bond among us, reiterating what kind of people we are, and a vision that may stir other peoples to identify with us.

Further, the prevention of genocide affects goals for international and regional security. It is an imperative for the prevention of further war, destabilization and regional crises, and massive refugee flows. Besides generating wars, genocide and gross violations of human rights often trigger the exodus of great numbers of refugees, sometimes called "people bombing." When they succeed in getting rid of an unwanted group—massacres are the quickest means to propel flight—*genocidaires* (a French term I will continue using as it has no English equivalent) externalize the cost of maintaining the unwanted on neighboring states and the world community. Refugees often create environmental degradation and public health and food emergencies in the states to which they flee. In addition, the states they flee (often poor to begin) may degenerate developmentally as state resources, infrastructure, and the economy are destroyed—land eroding and food declining if crops are not planted.

Studies show that the overwhelming majority of the world's refugees are created by states committing genocide and gross violations of human rights.[2] If we were to reframe the worldwide refugee problem as we frame programs of domestic assistance, we would label it a crisis of forced homelessness and dependency: 13.6 million refugees and 16.2 to 18.7 million internally displaced at last count.[3]

Further, refugees sometimes impose costs on their host country of social destabilization, competing in the labor market, raising prices, and raising natives' perception of their relative deprivation. The role of refugee has also been exploited by armed forces who have committed genocide and other crimes. In some instances (i.e., Cambodia and Rwanda), international humanitarian relief has been used by criminal organizations such as the Khmer Rouge and the *Interhamwe*. Such refugees are not always innocent victims but may have been perpetrators or become warriors to regain their motherland, committing crimes against others.

## Is it Prudent to Prevent Genocide?

Although there is widespread support for humanitarian assistance for victims of war and genocide, it is often assumed that we cannot afford to intervene because the cost of intervention is too high. But prevention in genocide, as in public health, is cheaper than response to an outbreak or epidemic. The cost of a short-term UN peace-enforcement action in Rwanda has been estimated at $100 million, whereas international assistance to Rwanda from April 1994 to December 1995 was over $2 billion—a 20:1 ratio for the cost of assistance to that of prevention.[4] The cost to the United States alone in Rwanda from April to November 1994 was eight times the estimated cost of its assessment for a peace-keeping force (which it rejected because of costs) in April 1994.[5] A comprehensive recent analysis, which assumed the need for a more long-term intervention in Rwanda beginning in

March 1994, estimated that the maximal cost would have been \$1.3 billion over three years compared with the actual direct costs to the international community and states for Rwanda of \$4.5 billion from April 1994 through 1996 for humanitarian relief, economic and military costs, without including costs to NGOs and the cost of the International Criminal Tribunal for Rwanda—\$332.55 million for 1996 alone.[6] If the cost of the Tribunal is added to other direct costs, making the total expenditures \$4.9 billion, the ratio of the cost of prevention to that of assistance and related costs is 1:3.8. So we are talking about cost ratios of 4 to 1 to 20 to 1 in favor of prevention, depending on the assumptions of force level and longevity and the completeness of expenditure aggregation. Brown and Rosecrance note that their estimate of the cost of a preventive force is an overestimate and conclude that "At the very least, preventive action in Rwanda could have saved \$3.2 billion" and observe that the postgenocide expenditures have "done nothing to solve the problems that caused it [the genocide] or prevent another outbreak of violence. Thus, the question is not only how much could have been saved, but how much might still have to be paid in the future."[7] The United States alone has spent \$1.23 billion for humanitarian assistance to the Great Lakes countries and the International Criminal Tribunal for Rwanda since 1994.[8] And the meter is still ticking.

These figures do not take into account the economic costs to perpetrators and victims. Rwanda, which had climbed between 1976 and 1990 from the seventh to the nineteenth place from the bottom among least-developed countries, descended to become the second poorest country on earth in 1997.[9]

## Is Democracy the Answer?

One question is outstanding: How do we anticipate potential genocides, and when should we intervene? Is democracy the answer, as some argue? Nondemocratic regimes are much more likely to engage in external wars and to practice genocide, but genocide almost always occurs during internal wars—and sometimes precipitates wars with neighbors.[10] The democratic peace thesis has been qualified by comparative research[11] and does not extend to internal war. Further, I found that in 1987, about one third to one half of the states with the worst violations of life-integrity directed at ethnic groups were democracies—depending on whose index and criteria were used.[12] Although this does not imply that half of democracies were gross violators (further discussed later), it makes us aware that democracies, including democracies in existence for fifty years, can and do tolerate pogroms and race riots—genocidal massacres—and gross human rights violations.

Developing mature democracies is an oxymoron; we need to remember that the United States protected slavery for seventy-five years after the formation of the union and did not mandate protection of the franchise for all until a full one hundred years after the abolition of slavery (the Civil Rights Act of 1965). The gap between what democracy promises and how democracies act can be better understood by deconstructing democracy as a goal, a set of institutional norms, and a process. At best, the international community can instigate processes that may lead to transformative steps toward democracy. Institutional norms of liberal democracy assume inclusion of all as equals regardless of gender, ethnicity, and race. They guarantee (a) free elections for representation, (b) civil liberties, and (c) rule of law. But the Achilles' heel of democratization is often the lack of agreement on who is to be included; who are "we, the people"?—a problem intensified in divided or plural societies.[13]

Regimes in divided societies in transition to democracy (e.g., Rwanda and Bosnia) are prone to the rise of ethnic entrepreneurs from groups whose domination appears threatened by power-sharing arrangements; democratization can enhance their power and fuel human rights violations.[14] Democratization in the former Yugoslavia reinforced processes that led to schism and genocide and in Rwanda led to polarizing processes among the Hutu elite, who precipitated genocide.[15] In other societies, when authoritarian regimes falter and there is a popular, democratic, nonviolent revolt, the military, security personnel, and criminal gangs may divert crowds representing the mainstream with antiminority violence, such as in Indonesia in 1998, where Chinese women were systematically raped and Chinese property burned. Division of states during decolonization and the breakdown of empires and multinational states often instigates groups to get resources and land by "ethnic cleansing" and expulsion. Democratic states with Westminster-type systems may also provoke ethnic polarization and exclusion, leading to rebellion and state massacres in retaliation, as in Sri Lanka.[16]

States in the middle—partly free states with some democratic forms—were in 1987 actually more prone than unfree states to practice gross violations of life-integrity.[17] This seems to be best explained by the fact that some freedom enables deprived classes and groups to challenge elites, provoking threatened elites to retaliate violently in order to repress opposition. Yet states that had protected some civil liberties were less apt to be violators than states that protected some political rights without protecting civil liberties. This suggests that institutionalizing civil liberties and the rule of law would be a better strategy for the protection of human rights in new democracies than merely imposing elections.

To prevent genocide and advance human rights and democracy, we need to focus both on security to protect lives and transformative steps toward an inclusive regime. However, the present international emphasis is almost exclusively on multiparty elections which the international community uses to legitimate governments, even when these are neither free nor fair, as in Cambodia in 1998,[18] or when free elections serve to legitimate ethnic cleansing by electing ethnic nationalist parties that prevent the return of refugees to their homes, as in Bosnia in 1998.

Security involves guaranteeing the inviolability of life and personal property by reform of police, army, and justice systems, and implementing the rule of law while annulling the culture of impunity. Transformative steps might include eliminating ethnic registration cards and distinctive regional signs labelling people, instituting trials or truth commissions to sanction past offenders, protecting civil liberties as far as possible while remaining consistent with security (civil liberties may need to be restricted to prevent the dissemination of hate propaganda, denial of past genocide, and incitement to violence), fostering local cooperation across ethnic lines with the incentive of foreign aid, integrating schools (where necessary and practicable), and instituting political parties in such a way as to open up alternatives other than group domination before elections.

If parties are based on ethnic groups, elections themselves may further polarize these groups and provide incentives to use illegitimate means to repress the opposition. There are, however, structural models to prevent this.[19] In some situations, where it is unlikely that two groups will accept representation in one polity, the international community should push for separation through nonviolent means, such as mediation.

## How Can We Anticipate and Deter Genocide?

To anticipate and deter genocide, we need to focus directly on protecting both individuals and groups against gross violations of life-integrity by using intelligence analysis, historical interpretation, monitoring, and warning systems. Past research shows us which states are most likely to be violators and which groups are most likely to be "minorities at risk,"[20] assuming that genocide is triggered by group conflict (which is true in most but not all cases). Anticipation demands a more specific analysis of conditions, contexts, and processes that are most likely to lead to genocide, taking into account that there is no single model of genocide. For example, neither the Holocaust nor another genocide is typical of all genocides. Some persons question whether "genocide" is more than rhetoric or a value judgment. Although scholars have distinguished several types of genocide—ideological, retributive, developmental, and despotic[21]—some underlying observable characteristics are the same. These are specified in my paradigm for detecting and tracing genocide:

1. There was a sustained attack or continuity of attacks by the perpetrator to physically destroy group members.
2. The perpetrator was a collective or organized actor or commander of organized actors.
3. Victims were selected because they were members of a collectivity.
4. The victims were defenseless or were killed regardless of whether they surrendered or resisted.
5. The destruction of group members was undertaken with intent to kill, and murder was sanctioned by the perpetrator.[22]

The first criteria includes indirect means of destroying a group (criminalized in the UN Genocide Convention in Article 2 b & c), including "genocide by attrition"—imposed starvation, poisoning of air and water, and consequent disease and death[23]—and systematic rape and sexual violence.

## Forecasting and Prevention of Genocide: The Case of Rwanda

Before 1994, several studies enabled us to forecast (using different methods) what kind of regimes, conflicts and processes may precipitate genocide. I shall illustrate this with the case of Rwanda.

When we look at the most prevalent condition preceding genocide, however, we find that ethnic stratification—systems in which one group is excluded from power and participation because of their ethnoclass—is most likely to promote group rebellion, which, in turn, provokes genocidal response from the dominant ethnoclass. Rwanda exemplifies a variation of this process.

What would early warning and response be? Although we can trace the historical processes back for thirty years, I shall show that we could discern the processes and steps leading to the genocide in the four years preceding it (mid-term detection) and the next-to-final stage of preparation in the year preceding it, in which the process might be braked abruptly. Such a time sequence—preceding political generation, present regime/crisis, and pregenocidal preparation—seems to work in my mental experiments in surveying other genocides. For prudent prevention, intervening in the middle stage would be optimal.

I shall show how this might have worked in Rwanda, drawing on both my inductively and historically based theory and that of Barbara Harff, who derives findings from an empirical cross-tabulation of post-1945 genocides.[24] Comparing warning signs derived from theories presented at a conference in 1993, I showed much consensus between us (see Tables 6 and 7). Both Harff and I largely agree on underlying conditions (Table 7); the exclusion of the Other (group to be victimized) from the universe of obligation of the dominant group,[25] a challenge to the solidarity and legitimacy underlying the polity, a crisis or opportunity related to the victim, and the lack of external checks on the power of the perpetrator, as manifested by either encouragement and toleration by patrons and allies of the perpetrator's use of violence or by empty threats against the perpetrator.

Gurr and Harff have gone on to explore "instigators"—immediate warning signs.[26] Harff and Gurr, Fein, and Kuper also view ethnic stratification and the struggle for power in plural societies as a breeding ground for genocide.[27]

*Table 6* Processes Leading Toward Genocide/Politicide
(potential checks/interventions in this table written in **bold italics**)

| $g^1$ *(Past Generations)* | $g^2$ *(Present Generations)* | *Precipating Events* |
|---|---|---|
| Abrupt breakdown<br>Change in regime or decline in state | STATE: Nondemocratic weak state Transfer of power/breakdown | WAR with other states or within state<br><br>**STATE CONSOLIDATION OF FORCES OF VIOLENCE** |
| Despotism | **ENFORCEMENT OF CIVIL LIBERTIES:**<br>**absent or discriminatory**<br>**GROSS VIOLATION OF HUMAN RIGHTS**<br>*HRNGO monitoring With-hold aid*<br>*Strengthen civil society* | **ESCALATION**<br>**GROSS VIOLATIONS OF HUMAN RIGHTS** |
| History of genocide, pogroms, or communal violence | ETHNIC HIERARCHY: Political exclusion, discrimin-ation, and severe inequality<br>*Advise depolarizing struc-tures International disinvestment*<br>*Sanctions* | ETHNIC/CLASS MOBILIZATION<br><br>**REBELLION OR POLITICAL CHALLENGE** (fear of elite los-ing control) |
| Isolation of indigenous peoples from dominant group related to urban/rural split and undeveloped land | POLITICAL ECONOMY: Con-flict over land use triggered by economic development in regions inhabited by indigenous peoples<br>*Require human rights and environmental impact reports*<br>*Withhold aid*<br>*Lobby multinationals*<br>*Develop competing uses to protect indigenous peoples* | |
| Explicit or implicit racism | VICTIM PERCEIVED AS, OR IS, CHALLENGER<br>*Assist nonviolent challengers through international aid/local NGOs*<br>*Increase visibility*<br>IDEOLOGY:<br>Growth of hate movements Exclusive nationalist, racist, Marxist-Leninist, or fascist, par-ties rising<br>*Monitor local press reports of refugees, NGOs, etc.*<br>*Denial of recognition*<br>*Strengthen domestic opposition*<br>*Diplomatic warnings* | JUSTIFICATION OF ANNIHI-LATION OF VICTIM<br><br><br>**CONQUEST OF STATE** |

*(Continued overleaf)*

*Table 6* Continued

| $g^1$ *(Past Generations)* | $g^2$ *(Present Generations)* | *Precipating Events* |
|---|---|---|
| | **EXTERNAL CONTROL:** Protected by international or regional hegemonic state (versus checked by such state) **Bans on military sales and transfers International/ regional sanctions Third-party warnings to patron states** | **IMMUNITY NO CHECKS BY PATRONS OR ALLIES** |

## Modern Times—The Past Generation: 1960–1990 (Table 6, Column 1)

Looking at the precedents of genocide as a historical process in Rwanda (Table 6), we observe that the past generation experienced the reversal of political fortunes of Hutu and Tutsi—viewed as ethnoclasses with differing access to power (although the economic status of ordinary Hutu and Tutsi did not differ much,[28]—in the few years before decolonization). The ranking and status of both groups, which previously had many overlapping bonds (e.g., clientage, loyalty to the king), was fixed by the Belgian colonizers, who had co-opted the Tutsis (about 14 percent of the population) as administrators and soldiers and prevented individual mobility between groups by imposing identity as an administrative classification with identity cards. The Belgian colonizers, who had established the myth of Tutsi racial superiority, switched sides in the years before decolonization and began to support the Hutus as an emerging political force. The new Hutu leaders developed a "Rwandese ideology" based on race, and colonial authorities began replacing Tutsi chiefs with Hutu chiefs. "These immediately organized the persecution of the Tutsi on the hills they now controlled, which started a mass exodus of refugees abroad, which eventually took some 130,000 Rwandese Tutsi to the Belgian Congo, Burundi, Tanganyika and Uganda by late 1963."[29] Genocidal massacres of the Tutsi—at first spontaneous and later government-organized, in response to incidents of Tutsi violence—propelled their flight. A report of the UN (which had previously called for group reconciliation) in 1961 concluded that "the developments of these last eighteen months have brought about the racial dictatorship of the one party ... An oppressive system has been replaced by another one.... It is quite possible that some day we will witness violent reactions on the part of the Tutsi."[30] Tutsis were subject to quotas in public employment and schools and virtually excluded from the government and the army. The invasion by some Tutsi exiles in 1963 not only provoked government slaughter of an estimated 10,000 Tutsis but the execution of all surviving Tutsi politicians in Rwanda.[31]

The mirror image of this may be seen in Burundi, the other state created from the Belgian Congo, in which the dominant Tutsi elite committed assassinations and genocide against Hutus in 1965 and 1972, after attacks by Hutu rebels.[32]

## Early-Warning Time: 1990–July 1993 (Table 6, Column 2)

Rwanda was ruled by military dictatorships between 1962 and 1991 and became a one-party state under President (former General) Habyarimana in 1973. The World Bank and other aid donors, who contributed 70 percent of public investment between 1982–1987, believed Rwanda to be a model developing country and overlooked the evidence of institutionalized inequality and racism.[33] However, the economic and social stability of Rwanda declined

*Table 7* Comparison of Fein and Harff Explanations of Genocide/Politicide (1994)

| Fein Theory | Harff Model | Agree? |
| --- | --- | --- |
| *I. Necessary Preconditions* | | |
| No check on power | State reliance on coercion vs. democratic experience | Yes |
| Solidarity/legitimacy, conflict/challenge based on ethnoclass exclusion | Intergroup stratification | Yes |
| Moral exclusion leading to justification of annihiliation; definition of group "outside of the universe of obligation of the perpetrator" | Intervening condition: "Commitment to an ideology that excludes categories of people . . . from the universe of obligation" | Yes |
| | Degree of stability in the multipolar system | Lack of agreement |
| Past experience of genocide rewarded | Lack of consistent collective . . . responses to ethnic strife and/or humanitarian crises | Yes |
| *II. Intervening Conditions* | | |
| | Fragmentation of the governing elite | Lack of agreement |
| State consolidation of forces of violence | Indicated by lack of restraints on state security agencies | Yes |
| Ideology | Ideology | Yes |
| | Charismatic leadership | Lack of agreement |
| | Economic hardship that results in increased differential treatment | Lack of agreement |
| *III. Precipitating or Accelerating Events* | | |
| Crisis or opportunity | Political upheaval (background condition) | Yes |
| 1. War | | |
| 2. Development in regions of indigenous peoples | Victims in the way of development | Yes |
| Patrons' tolerance (no checks by patrons or allies) | Empty threats of external involvement | Yes |
| | Increase in external support for targeted groups | Disagree |
| Ethnic/class mobilization and rebellion or political challenge | Occurrence of clashes between regime supporters and targeted groups | Yes |
| Political exclusion and discrimination | New discriminatory or restrictive policies | Yes |
| Escalation of gross violations of human rights/life-integrity violations | Rapid increase in frequency and severity of life-integrity violations | Yes |

gravely beginning in 1985 and continued through the 1990s because of a drop in international commodity prices. The situation was aggravated by a decline in food production, increased reliance on foreign loans, and an increase in military spending.[34] This led to greater competition among elites for the foreign aid needed to maintain the style of life to which they had been accustomed, as well as to general hopelessness about the future.[35]

The political crisis in Rwanda began with the 1990 invasion by the Rwandan Patriotic Front (RPF), led by Tutsi exiles and their children trained in Uganda. Although these Rwandans had been very active in the National Resistance Army (NRA) of Uganda, which led to the victory of President Museveni in 1986, internal pressures against the Rwandans in Uganda led them to call for the "Right of Return" at a World Congress of Rwandese refugees in 1988. France, Belgium, and Zaire sent troops to aid the government of Rwanda. The French viewed the RPF invasion as part of the worldwide "Anglo-Saxon" or anglophone conspiracy against francophones.[36] "This is how Paris found itself backing an ailing dictatorship in a tiny distant country producing only bananas and a declining coffee crop without even asking for political reform as a price for its support. This blind commitment was to have catastrophic consequences because, as the situation radicalised, the Rwandese leadership kept believing that *no matter what it did*, French support would always be forthcoming."[37]

Responding to domestic critics, President Habyarimana promised democratic multiparty elections in 1991 in Rwanda and an end to ethnic identity cards. This led to the formation of several parties including an openly racist Hutu party: the Coalition for the Defense of the Republic (CDR). Human rights organizations and a very partisan-free press also emerged.

Both the war and the economic crisis (fed by increased government spending, which produced inflation and currency depreciation) instigated opposition parties to agree to meet with the RPF, leading to the Arusha negotiations. The Arusha Accords, concluded in August 1993, authorized the return of Tutsi refugees and sharing of power with them in a transitional government prior to elections. The refugees, now 500,000, would add one to every 13.6 Rwandans in the most densely populated country in Africa. This was a portent of more intense competition for resources and power in the future—a key to foreign aid, franchises, and government preferences.

Warning signs during this period of crisis and political transition include an escalating series of gross violations of human rights. Between 1990 and 1993, government officials organized anti-Tutsi massacres on at least six occasions in response to the RPF victories, false allegations of a local Tutsi rising and plans for massacre, and the Arusha agreement. Each incident took the lives of 30 to 300 persons.[38] In a press conference in Brussels in October 1992, Professor Reyntjens revealed the existence of a "Xero Network," or death squad, of soldiers and militiamen on the Latin American model that included the prime movers, relatives, and agents of the Habyarimana regime.[39]

In 1993, Hutu parties and factions began organizing massacres. The *Interhamwe* (literally "those who work together"), the youth movement of the government party, *Mouvement Revolutionnaire National pour le Developpement et la Democratie* (MRND[D]), organized massacres in March and August of 1993. Leaders of the *Interhamwe* later organized the 1994 genocide. The RPF also killed eight civil servants and nine of their relatives in Ruhengeri in February 1993. "It seems that the victims were shot simply in reprisal for the recent massacres."[40]

The violence stopped when a monitoring mission, the International Commission on Human Rights, came to Rwanda on January 7, 1993 to investigate. It was renewed when the Commission left later that month, attesting to the control of the *bourgmestres* (local officials) of the communes, who openly decreed when to stop violence and when to start it.[41] Thus, there was a repertoire of collective violence authorized by the government, sometimes termed "collective work obligations." Although the Commission used the term "genocide" to describe the situation between 1990 and 1992, it later withdrew the term. However, the term was repeated in a report by the UN Commission on Human Rights a few months later.

Yet some moderate Hutu or opposition parties in Rwanda were initially willing to work with the RPF, whose own training was in the Ugandan movement and government of President Museveni. Although Museveni professed antitribal values, the actuality of his politics led the RPF to believe that they could co-opt other groups without giving up domination by a Tutsi core.[42] Distrust of the other groups, rumors, and myths on all sides reinforced the volatility of the political situation.

What potential checks were there during this period? The French were not only the biggest donors, but their army was in charge of counterinsurgency in Rwanda. Arms suppliers could have cut off sales and military aid, and allies—principally France—could have made support contingent upon speedy implementation of the Arusha Accords, suppression of internal forces using and threatening violence, and prosecution of government officials and private citizens fomenting ethnic violence. Donor countries played a large role in Rwanda, as foreign aid constituted 22 percent of the government's budget in 1991.[43]

Donors viewed Rwanda as a prime example of successful administration of development assistance.[44] The United States did not stress and France did not include human rights conditionality in their aid policies, and the donors who did—Belgium, Canada, and Switzerland—had less influence. The donors did not apply human rights conditionality for two reasons. Rwanda was known for its effective local administration (which also organized genocidal massacres) and its ability to absorb money. But the more fundamental reason was the donors' emphasis on democratization. "Project feasibility helps to explain the continued inflow from two traditional donors, France and Belgium.... Support for democratization and the related peace process implied continuous economic and diplomatic engagement in Rwanda. From this perspective, the threat of ultimately imposing sanctions by withdrawing aid—as western human rights organizations called for in 1992–93—was counterproductive. Donors thus became hostage to their own policies."[45]

There were some differences among donors. France was committed to President Habyarimana because of its francophone foreign policy and continued to aid the government even after the genocide started. The United States and Germany suspended their aid programs in 1994, and most of European Union aid was put on hold at that time.

Another positive step foreign donors could have taken to make genocide less possible was not implemented. This was the replacement of the Rwandan ethnic identity cards with new cards with no mention of ethnicity. Identification is a critical step in tracking potential victims.[46] In fact, the Rwandan cards were used as screening devices in the genocide of 1994, for neither name nor visage are reliable markers of identity in Rwanda. Two United States Agency for International Development (USAID) consultants, Alison Des Forges and Catherine Newbury, recommended in 1991 that USAID support the compilation of new cards and neutral birth records in the communes, but this was not done.[47]

### Crisis-Warning Time: August 1993–April 1994 (Table 6, Column 3)
The concessions the government made in Arusha incited the President's former supporters, the *akazi*, to organize extralegal action against him by organizing an extremist media and distributing arms to paramilitary forces.

The Arusha agreements provided for a Broad-Based Transitional Government (BBTG), with portfolios precisely allocated to contending parties within Rwanda and the RPF. Had a BBTG ever been implemented, it probably would have been paralyzed. In addition, the parties now controlling the distribution of incoming foreign exchange and state corporations might have lost control. Many key people within Rwanda might become losers.

After the accord was concluded, the RPF observed a truce and the UN agreed to send in a military monitoring force for peacekeeping, the UN Assistance Mission to Rwanda (UNAMIR), which arrived in October 1993. The army of Rwanda and the RPF were to be integrated into a force of 20,000, which would result in the unemployment of many former soldiers, who would be without a source for their agreed compensation.[48] But the President stalled, and the Agreements, which were supposed to be implemented in February with the installation of the BBTG, were never enforced.

According to Prunier, "the notion of a 'big clean-up,' a 'final solution to the ethnic problem,' had begun to circulate in late 1992."[49] The extremists' calculation of success was reinforced by the anti-Tutsi pogroms conducted by Hutus and the army massacres of Hutus in Burundi, together killing 50,000 ("roughly 60% Tutsi and 40% Hutu") after Burundi's army overthrew the first elected President—a Hutu—in October 1993 with no international intervention.[50] "To the fear of losing one's privileges (rational level) they [radical Hutu groups] added the fear of losing one's life (visceral level) and the fear of losing control of one's world (mythical level)."[51] The moderates lost confidence or were assassinated, and extremists consolidated their hold.

In July 1993, the CDR seized the opportunity to indoctrinate a wider public with its goals and opened a radical racist radio station (government licensed), Radio Television Libre des Mille Collines (RTLMC), which later broadcast injunctions to kill. RTLMC had an inestimable impact as a mobilizing tool and organizational instrument, conveying general and specific orders.

One step the international community could have taken in 1993 would have been to press the Rwandan government to de-license RTLMC, the hate radio, and/or suppress it directly. Broadcasting intervention (used later in Bosnia) is a cheap way to prevent the dissemination of messages to kill and is consonant with the Genocide Convention, which criminalizes "direct and public incitement to commit genocide" (Art. 3), as well as the International Covenant on Civil and Political Rights, which states that "any advocacy of national, racial, or religious hatred that constitutes incitement to discrimination, hostility or violence should be prohibited by law."[52] However, jamming was rejected by the United States.[53]

## Warnings Ignored

There were several warnings and many signs of a conspiracy to commit genocide. General Romeo Dallaire, the UNAMIR commander, had received warnings beginning in December 1993. He cabled UN headquarters on January 11, 1994 to report that a key informant had told him plans were being made to massacre 800,000 Tutsi—the whole group—and thousands of Hutus who might oppose the genocidal plot. The planners were compiling lists, training the *interhamwe* to kill, and storing arms.[54] Their plan was to incite a civil war and massacre the Belgian troops, the core element of the UNAMIR force, provoking them to withdraw. Dallaire asked permission to raid weapons caches and help the informant, a former member of the Rwandan President's security staff, escape with his family from Rwanda. The fax reached the then Under-Secretary-General for Peacekeeping Operations, Kofi Annan, who refused, saying that the "operation contemplated" was not within the peacekeeping mandate, and that Dallaire should inform the Rwandan President and the Ambassadors to Rwanda from Belgium, France, and the United States. In 1997, Kofi Annan refused to let Dallaire testify before a Belgian Senate investigatory commission, saying that he did not believe waiving the diplomatic immunity of past and present UN officials was "in the interest of the Organization."[55]

Belgian diplomats and intelligence, the diplomatic corps in Kigali, a Catholic bishop, and others noted what was going on.[56] Des Forges notes that in January 1994, "an analyst of the US Central Intelligence Agency knew enough to predict that as many as half a million persons might die in case of renewed conflict," but his prediction was not credited and was buried in agency files.[57] RTLMC broadcast hate propaganda with incitements to kill Tutsis. *Interhamwe* militias organized mob demonstrations in Kigali, killing dozens of people; some moderate politicians were also slain, and even diplomats received death threats.

In early April, both the European Union and the Rwandan President's African colleagues pressed President Habyarimana to implement the Arusha Accords; Returning from a meeting of African heads of state at Dar Es Salaam on April 6, President Habyarimana responded positively to a request for a lift from his neighbor, the President of Burundi. The plane was shot down by missiles in Kigali airport, killing all aboard, which served as a trigger for the genocide to follow. The men who downed the plane have never been definitively identified; all kinds of plotters have been alleged—French, Belgians, white mercenaries, the RPF, and the *genocidaires* themselves.[58]

The scenario developed as General Dallaire's informant had described in January: the Belgian troops were targetted (ten murdered), withdrawn by Belgium, disarming UNAMIR, and the UNAMIR troops stayed in their barracks (except for taking out the Europeans) before they were withdrawn by the UN. The UNAMIR force, sent in to help carry out the Arusha Accords, was underfunded and undermanned by the UN out of concern for economy. However, General Dallaire has stated that had he been equipped with a well-armed force of 5,000 members committed to a peace-enforcement mission (under Article 7 of the UN Charter), the massacres could have been stopped.[59]

Des Forges observes that there was nothing inevitable about the way the genocide unrolled; it depended on co-opting the local authorities to mobilize people to do the dirty work of killing. "The genocide was not a killing machine that rolled inexorably forward but rather a campaign to which participants were recruited over time by the use of threat and incentives."[60]

The UN Security Council (UNSC) and the Secretary-General failed to respond. Not only did the UNSC fail to respond, it never challenged the legitimacy of the representative of Rwanda on the UNSC at the time, and key members avoided calling the genocide a genocide, preferring neutral frameworks that implied no responsibility: tribal killings, ethnic conflict, chaos, a failed state.

Both France and the United States as UNSC members can be faulted. "Rwanda became the first application of President Clinton's admonition in an address to the United Nations on September 27, 1993, that the UN must learn 'when to say no.' "[61] Responding to its perceived defeat in Somalia (the causes of which were never properly analyzed), the U.S. President in May 1994 decreed Presidential Decision Directive 25 (PPD-25), which decrees sixteen stringent conditions that the United States would consider before sanctioning and engaging in any intervention. The administration reinforced its defense by refusing to recognize the events in Rwanda as genocide, telling officials to talk of "acts of genocide" if they must use the g-word.[62]

The French intervention in June and the RPF victory (some believe the intervention was to allow the *genocidaires* to escape) precluded further international dithering over what was to be done, provoked on April 29 by the UN Secretary-General, who had had a change of heart and confessed his failure.

### Consequences and Aftermath of Genocide in Rwanda

The immediate consequences of the genocide were that about 500,000 Tutsi were killed, 10,000 to 30,000 Hutus (also targetted by the *genocidaires*) were killed, and a substantial number of Tutsi women were raped, tortured and sexually mutilated. These events led to high personal and social trauma stemming from the deaths, degradation, and destruction of families, and the disadvantages of being women in a patriarchal culture.[63]

The RPF was found to have committed massacres during the genocide and war, perhaps killing 25,000 to 45,000, and afterward, apparently provoked by vengeance against suspected killers of Tutsis, collective reprisals against Hutus. These massacres may have been tolerated (if not calculated) for social control through terror.[64]

The subsequent flight of over 1,500,000 Hutu to refugee camps in Zaire and Tanzania included many perpetrators (who were to use the other Hutus as hostages). These camps, in turn, were run by the *genocidaires*. When the UN High Commissioner of Refugees requested assistance to disarm the refugees and exclude armed men from the camps, he did not get it. The growth, expense, and political implications of such refugees are well known. In Zaire, the *genocidaires* activated conflicts against peoples of Tutsi origin, destabilizing the country. The security implications for Rwanda and the intermittent massacres perpetrated by forces of the *genocidaires* at the border were among the factors that led the army of Rwanda to help Laurent Kabila overthrow the government of Mobutu and perpetrate genocidal massacres against those refugees who had been driven east, away from Rwandan borders. The UN, now led by Secretary-General Kofi Annan, first withdrew one team of investigators, complying with Kabila's demands, and finally withdrew its last team, in response to obstruction: the Security Council took no action after being given evidence that both the government of the Congo and of Rwanda were responsible.[65]

The government of Rwanda is confronted with a continuing external security problem— raids by remnants of the *interhamwe* from across the western border and massacres of Rwandans—and internal security and human rights problems. The latter results first from keeping over 100,000 persons, most not charged, under detention because of their alleged role in the genocide, and second, from the impossibility of giving them a fair trial, given the lack of resources of the Rwandan judicial system and the impossibility of releasing them. Ethnic mistrust and fear has been reinforced by memories of the genocide, border raids, assassination of witnesses in trials, the return of Tutsi and Hutu refugees from neighboring countries, false charges of genocide stemming from competition for land, and the unrepresentative character of the government, termed an "ethnocracy" by some.

Thus, this rare case of victory by representatives of the victim group demonstrates what a pyrrhic victory this is. The memory of genocide is used as political capital by the RPF-dominated government, which denies the massacres and gross violations of human rights that have taken place since that time. Conversely, Hutus often deny or justify the genocide and focus on their grievances, "using the RPF human rights violations as a kind of moral ransom money to redeem the horrors of April–June 1994."[66] This threatens both the stability and legitimacy of the government and reinforces the possibility of chronic civil war (as in Burundi) and renewed genocide.

The regional consequences still continue to evolve. It appears now that the government of Rwanda has turned against the rule of Laurent Kabila in Zaire for failing to guarantee security on Rwanda's western border and is supporting a rebel force, while Kabila's regime is alleged to have rounded up Tutsis in the capital. The dynamic of ethnic genocide and repression, rebellion, reprisals and transnational intervention continues.

## Conclusion: The Potential for and Impediments to Prevention

My analysis has shown that preventing genocide is our problem, that it is in the interest of the United States to curb it, and that it is prudent to do so, given the human, geopolitical, and economic consequences of tolerating genocide without intervention. This analysis has also shown that genocide cannot only be detected in process but can be anticipated.

This was demonstrated by examining the development and consequences of genocide in Rwanda (April 1994), a genocide that was both forseen and flagged. Not only were there many signs of impending genocide, but a warning was given to the UN in January 1994 based on insider information. The UN, however, did not heed the recommendations of its UNAMIR commander, General Dallaire, to intervene preemptively. This genocide has fueled a continuing latent internal conflict in Rwanda and a regional crisis in the Great Lakes, as both ethnic conflicts and interventions have become transnational: civil war and rebellion in Congo; genocidal massacres in 1997 in Zaire/Congo; massacres in Rwanda and Burundi by antigovernment groups drawn from the disaffected Hutus, and army massacres in response; grave violations of human rights in all countries; low legitimacy and high distrust among citizens of all countries; and massive flows of refugees (1994–1998) with resettlement of older refugee cohorts, leading to economic rivalry that is sometimes masked by false accusation.

There is general suspicion and distrust in Rwanda.[67] At this point, talk of reconciliation and conflict resolution by outsiders has become simply a sign of western palliatives and an inability to understand what it is like for former victims and perpetrators to co-exist in a postgenocidal society.

For the bystanders in the world community, the moral, political, and economic costs have been great. Humanitarian aid (and costs of the International Tribunal) for Rwanda have exceeded the cost of an intervention by estimates of 4:1 to 20:1 (depending on assumptions about the force level and longevity of an intervention). For the United States, which has spent $1.23 billion in the Great Lakes since 1994, and probably $877.2 million of that amount for Rwanda and its refugees alone, expenditures have been three to eight times what it would have spent for an intervention. Rather than asking, "Can we afford to prevent genocide?" the question should be, "Can we afford not to prevent genocide?" Further, what would prevention imply?

To be effective, a U.S. early warning-early response program to deter genocide must be consistent with a more general human rights policy, focussing on enforcement of sanctions against violators of life-integrity: torture, calculated executions or "disappearances," massacres, and imposition of life-threatening conditions on a group. Consistency is necessary for two reasons: (1) genocide is usually preceded by other life-integrity violations; and (2) we cannot predict the degree of escalation—whether the perpetrators will proceed from calculated execution to genocidal massacres to genocide. My research has shown that life-integrity violations are highly related; perpetrators of group massacre are also perpetrators of "disappearances," extrajudicial executions, and torture.[68] States both escalate and de-escalate on the scale of the violations, but gross violators seldom give up these practices unless there is a substantive change in regime.

Further, U.S. law since 1961 requires that we not give economic assistance to gross violators of human rights (unless it helps needy people) nor military assistance unless U.S. security interests are affected. These loopholes have been widely exploited. But if it were shown that such practices make genocide more likely and endanger both international and regional security, the evasion of these laws might be more difficult.

Holly Burkhalter (Physicians for Human Rights) proposed (in testimony before the House of Representatives Subcommittee on Human Rights and International Relations on May 5, 1998) a series of steps the United States could take immediately "to develop a 'Genocide Prevention and Response' policy initiative": the President should declare that prevention and suppression of genocide is a vital U.S. interest, should replace Presidential Decision Directive 25 (re: U.S. guidelines for participation and support of multilateral peacekeeping) with another directive that supports UN-sanctioned military operations, and should appoint a senior official to direct intelligence gathering and analysis for the purpose of protecting vulnerable communities. Further, the United States should stop the flow of weapons and military aid to the perpetrators, respond quickly to early warnings of genocide in the making, condemn actions that foment ethnic hatred, use nonhumanitarian foreign aid to pressure governments, deny visas to and seize assets of genocide-provoking individuals, stop the broadcasting of incitements to kill and injure minorities directly and indirectly—jamming the airwaves if necessary—before genocide occurs. She proposed other steps to stop genocide in progress and showed the application of these to Rwanda. This is a good beginning for consideration of what is needed institutionally and tactically to prevent genocide in the future. But to authorize this requires sustained commitment on the highest level. At present, we see intermittent commitment and sustained focus on impediments.

One impediment to a proactive policy is frequently raised: the ghost of American defeat and withdrawal in Somalia and Vietnam. These signify the fear of failure, national shame, and embarrassment. But neither of these interventions has been analyzed to evaluate (1) whether the proposed intervention and these earlier situations are good analogies, and (2) the cause of earlier perceived failures—the decision to intervene or the goals, strategy, and tactics of intervention (including the lack of coordination with other allies).[69]

We are continually misled by false metaphors. But Vietnam was not Munich, Bosnia was not Vietnam, and Rwanda was not Somalia. First, on an analytic level, we are misled by lumping together diverse situations which may legitimately call for different responses. The responsibility under international law to prevent genocide is clear, but it is not clear that it would be deemed right, permissible, or wise to intervene or aid intervenors in the case of civil war and failed states. Interventions to prevent genocide or liberate people who are victims of gross violations of human rights and humanitarian disasters (such as slavery and starvation) are often considered legitimate humanitarian interventions, but interventions to change the form of government are not considered legitimate under international law.[70]

The argument for early warning and early response based on cost and interests may be countered by another assumption: there is an economy based on money and an economy based on blood. U.S. citizens, it is said, will not bear the costs of losing "their boys" in foreign lands that do not threaten the United States. The fact that ours is a volunteer army does not seem to enter into the reasoning of such critics. They say that our soldiers do not enlist in order to be killed. If the fear of domestic reaction is a potent political argument against such interventions by democracies (not only in the United States), an international rapid reaction force based on volunteers who know the risk could answer this objection.

Yet, many consider this an impossible innovation because of the entrenched political hostility to international institutions in the United States; institutions—including the International Criminal Court proposed in July 1998—said to undermine American sovereignty. However, recent analyses of public opinion and elite opinion show that the American public accepts global responsibilities and does not want to go it alone.[71] These authors conclude:

> A significant gap exists between the US foreign policy community's perceptions of public attitudes and the results of polls that ask Americans what role the US should play in the world. . . . The majority of Americans supports a foreign policy of broad global engagement, provided that the US is not playing the role of dominant world leader (or "world policeman") and is contributing its "fair share" to multilateral efforts to resolve international problems. . . . Contrary to policy practitioners' view that the public wants US foreign policy tied to a narrow concept of US national interests, a strong majority of Americans supports a foreign policy that takes into account global and humanitarian concerns.[72]

Two thirds to nine out of ten Americans polled believed that it would be better to address problems requiring military force through the UN rather than have the United States act on its own, and 69 to 79 percent agreed that the United States should work with the UN "to maintain peace, protect human rights and promote economic development"—the differences in percentages reflect whether the question is put negatively or positively.[73]

Questions regarding genocide were also raised. Sixty-five percent of Americans polled in 1994 said that the UN, including the United States, should always or in most cases intervene with whatever force is necessary to stop acts of genocide; 80 percent said they would favor intervention in Bosnia or Rwanda if a UN commission determined that genocide was occurring. "This moral conviction was strong in focus groups. 'I think any reason for deciding whether someone lives or dies because of culture or race . . . or religion is wrong' said a Kalamazoo man in spring 1995. 'If Bosnia was an issue of . . . territory, then maybe you should just let them fight it out. But . . . genocide is wrong and when that is occurring, something needs to be done to stop it.' "[74]

Further, the Americans polled favored more robust peacekeeping and were not deterred by fear of some deaths. Contrary to elite and media perceptions, the majority of Americans favored increased involvement in Somalia after the firefight in 1995 rather than withdrawal.[75]

This implies that a strong and articulate U.S. President could rally Americans to back a policy preventing genocide that would require international cooperation, including (but not limited to) intervention. Such a rationale must go beyond the earlier ideological splits over intervention versus non-intervention that reflected ideological divisions between 1945 and 1990. Just as the conflicts that tear countries apart today cannot be explained by Cold War ideology, the means of their resolution cannot be evaluated by Cold War standards.

Besides pragmatism (needed to calculate the efficacy of proposed strategies), we need a practical idealism on the part of leaders that takes into account the fact that the majority of United States citizens do want to prevent genocide. Plans for changed American response and visions of a changed UN response (first proposed by Kuper 1985) require (1) that the United States abandon PDD 25 (which restricts American authorization and participation in multi-lateral peacekeeping) and (2) an investigation of why the United States did not respond in Rwanda in 1994.[76]

In order to pursue a proactive policy to prevent genocide, we need not only institutional change but direct communication with the American people. We need a political leadership ready to talk in Akron, Boston, Chicago, and San Diego about our responsibilities to prevent genocide, rather than just in Kigali. Recent war crimes and crimes against humanity (which may include genocide) in Kosovo and East Timor in 1999 indicate that this will be a persisting problem unless we pursue a policy of prevention.

## Notes

1. Leo Kuper, *Genocide: Its Political Use in the Twentieth Century* (New Haven, CT: Yale University Press, 1981), p. 161.

2. Helen Fein, ed., *The Prevention of Genocide: Rwanda and Yugoslavia Reconsidered* (New York: Institute for the Study of Genocide, November 1994), p. 13.

3. United States Committee on Refugees, *1998 World Refugee Survey* (Washington, D.C.: USCR, 1998), pp. 4–6.

4. John Eriksson, *The International Response to Conflict and Genocide: Lessons from the Rwanda Experience, Synthesis Report.* (Copenhagen: Joint Evaluation of Emergency Assistance to Rwanda, 1996), p. 34.

5. Milton Leitenberg, "US and UN Actions Escalate Genocide and Increase Costs in Rwanda," in *The Prevention of Genocide: Rwanda and Yugoslavia Reconsidered*, ed. Helen Fein, pp. 41–42.

6. Michael Brown and Richard Rosecrance, eds., *The Cost of Conflict: Prevention and Cure in the Global Arena*, Report to the Carnegie Commission on Preventing Deadly Conflict (Washington, D.C.: Carnegie Commission, 1998), p. 77.

7. Ibid., pp. 80–81.

8. U.S. State Department, *Memoranda and Conversations with Simon Whittemore*, Coordinator for Great Lakes Affairs, Bureau of Population, Refugees and Migration, and Tom Warrick, War Crimes Investigation Unit (Washington, D.C.: Government Printing Office, August 1998).

9. Gerard Prunier, *The Rwanda Crisis: History of a Genocide* (New York: Columbia University Press, 1995), p. 78; United States Committee on Refugees, *Life after Death: Suspicion and Reintegration in Post-Genocide Rwanda* (Washington, D.C.: USCR, February 1998), p. 6.

10. Helen Fein, "Accounting for Genocide after 1945: Theories and Some Findings," *Journal of Group Rights* (1993): 79–106.

11. Miriam Fendius Elman, *Paths to Peace: Is Democracy the Answer?* CSIA Studies in International Security (Cambridge, MA: MIT Press, 1997).

12. Helen Fein, *Lives at Risk: A Study of Life Integrity Violations in 50 States in 1987, Based on the Amnesty International 1988 Report* (New York: Institute for the Study of Genocide, 1990).

13. Larry Diamond and Marc F. Plattner, eds., *Nationalism, Ethnic Conflict, and Democracy* (Baltimore: Johns Hopkins Press, 1994), pp. xiii–xxii.

14. Steven L. Burg, "Ethnic Nationalism, Breakdown, and Genocide in Yugoslavia," in Helen Fein, ed., *The Prevention of Genocide: Rwanda and Yugoslavia Reconsidered* (New York: Institute for the Study of Genocide, 1994); Helen Fein, *The Prevention of Genocide, op. cit.*; Joint Evaluation of Emergency Assistance to Rwanda, *The International Response to Conflict and Genocide: Lessons from the Rwanda Experience*, 5 vols. (Copenhagen: Steering Committee of the Joint Evaluation of Emergency Assistance to Rwanda, 1996), pp. 2, 76.

15. Arthur J. Klinghoffer, "Democratization and Genocide: A Rwandan Case Study," paper presented at the Human Symposium on Democratization and Human Rights, Binghamton University, State University of New York, September 1998.

16. Donald Horowitz, *Ethnic Groups in Conflict* (Berkeley: University of California Press, 1985); Helen Fein, "Accounting for Genocide after 1945."

17. Helen Fein, "More Murder in the Middle: Life-Integrity Violations and Democracy in the World, 1987," *Human Rights Quarterly* 17, No. 1 (February 1995); 170–191.

18. Tina Rosenberg, "Hun Sen Stages an Election," *New York Times Magazine*, August 30, 1998, pp. 20–29.

19. Horowitz, *Ethnic Groups in Conflict.*

20. Ted R. Gurr et al., *Minorities at Risk: A Global View of Ethnopolitical Conflict* (Washington, D.C.: United States Institute for Peace Press, 1993). See also website: bsos.umd.edu/cid/mar for current data.

21. Helen Fein, *Genocide: A Sociological Perspective* (London: Sage, 1993), pp. 28–31.

22. Ibid., pp. 25–26.

23. Elaborated in Helen Fein, "Genocide by Attrition, 1939–1993—The Warsaw Ghetto, Cambodia, and Sudan: Links between Human Rights, Health, and Mass Death," *Health and Human Rights* 2, No. 2 (1997); 10–45.

24. Helen Fein, "Tools and Alarms: Uses of Models for Explanation and Anticipation," *Journal of Ethno-Development* (July 1994); 31–35; Barbara Harff, "A Theoretical Model of Genocides and Politicides," *Journal of Ethno-Development* 4, No. 4 (July 1994); 31–35.

25. Helen Fein, *Accounting for Genocide: National Responses and Jewish Victimization During the Holocaust* (New York: Free Press, 1979), Chapter 1.

26. Ted R. Gurr and Barbara Harff, *Early Warning of Communal Conflicts and Humanitarian Crises* (New York: United Nations University Press, 1995).

27. Barbara Harff and Ted R. Gurr, "Victims of the State: Genocides, Politicides and Group Repression since 1945," *International Review of Victimology* (1989), 23–24; Fein, *The Prevention of Genocide*, "Accounting for Genocide After 1945," *Genocide: A Sociological Perspective*, Helen Fein, "Scenarios of Genocide: Models of Genocide and Critical Responses," in *The Book of the International Conference on Holocaust and Genocide: Towards Understanding, Intervention, and Prevention of Genocide*, vol. 2, eds. I. Charny and S. Davidson (Boulder, CO: Westview Press, 1984), pp. 3–31; Kuper, *Genocide: Its Political Use in the Twentieth Century*, and Leo Kuper, *The Pity of It All* (Minneapolis: University of Minnesota Press, 1977).

28. Prunier, *The Rwanda Crisis: History of a Genocide*, p. 50.

29. Ibid., p. 51.

30. Ibid., p. 53.

31. Ibid., p. 56.

32. Kuper, *Genocide: Its Political Use in the Twentieth Century*, pp. 62–63.

33. Peter Uvin, *Aiding Violence: The Development Enterprise in Rwanda* (West Hartford, CT: Kumarian Press, 1998), pp. 40–46.

34. Ibid., pp. 52–57.

35. Prunier, *The Rwanda Crisis: History of a Genocide*, p. 84.

36. Ibid., pp. 104–107.

37. Ibid., p. 107.

38. Ibid., pp. 136–137, 162.

39. Ibid., p. 168.

40. Ibid., p. 175.

41. Ibid., p. 173.

42. Ibid., pp. 151–159.

43. Ibid., p. 79.

44. Joint Evaluation of Emergency Assistance to Rwanda, *International Response to Conflict and Genocide*, Vol. 2, p. 37; Uvin, *Aiding Violence: The Development Enterprise in Rwanda.*

45. Joint Evaluation of Emergency Assistance to Rwanda, *International Response to Conflict and Genocide*, Vol. 2, p. 32.

46. Raoul Hilberg, *The Destruction of the European Jews* (Chicago: Quadrangle Press, 1963); Fein, *Accounting for Genocide.*

47. Alison Des Forges, quoted in Fein, *The Prevention of Genocide*, p. 26.

48. Prunier, *The Rwandan Crisis: History of a Genocide*, p. 193.

49. Ibid., p. 200.

50. Ibid., p. 199.

51. Ibid., p. 200.

52. Jamie Metzl, "Information Intervention," *Foreign Affairs* 76, No. 6 (November–December 1997), 15–21.

53. Alison Des Forges, *The Killing Campaign: The 1994 Genocide in Rwanda* (New York: Human Rights Watch, 1998), p. 20.

54. Charles Truehart, "UN Alerted to Plans for Rwanda Bloodbath," *Washington Post*, September 25, 1997; *New York Times*, January 28, 1998 [McKinley]; Philip Gourevitch, "The Genocide Fax," *New Yorker*, May 11, 1998, pp. 42–45.

55. Gourevitch, "The Genocide Fax," pp. 43–44.

56. Des Forges, *The Killing Campaign*, p. 22; Joint Evaluation of Emergency Assistance to Rwanda, *International Response to Conflict and Genocide*, Vol. 2, p. 38.

57. Ibid., pp. 15–16.

58. Prunier, *The Rwanda Crisis: History of a Genocide*, pp. 213–229.

59. *New York Times*, January 28, 1998 [McKinley]; Carnegie Commission on Preventing Deadly Conflict, *Preventing Deadly Conflict*, Final Report (New York: Carnegie Corporation, 1997), p. 6.

60. Des Forges, *The Killing Campaign*, p. 5.

61. Milton Leitenberg, "US and UN Actions Escalate Genocide and Increase Costs in Rwanda," in Helen Fein, ed., *The Prevention of Genocide*, p. 37.

62. *New York Times*, June 10, 1994.

63. Prunier, *The Rwanda Crisis: History of a Genocide*, pp. 261–265; Human Rights Watch/Africa, *Shattered Lives: Sexual Violence during the Rwandan Genocide and Its Aftermath* (New York: Human Rights Watch, 1996); and Alison Des Forges, *"Leave None to Tell the Story": Genocide in Rwanda* (New York/Paris: Human Rights Watch/International Federation of Human Rights, 1999), pp. 15–16.

64. Gerard Prunier, *The Rwanda Crisis: History of a Genocide*, with a new chapter. (London: Hurst & Co., 1997), pp. 359–362; Des Forges, *The Killing Campaign: The 1994 Genocide in Rwanda*, p. 22; Des Forges, *"Leave None to Tell the Story,"* pp. 16, 702–722.

65. *New York Times*, July 29, 1998 [Crossette], April 16, 1998 [Crossette], July 11, 1997, July 2, 1997 [Crossette], June 8, 1997, June 1, 1997 [McNeil], May 28, 1997 [Crossette], May 27, 1997 [McNeil], May 15, 1997 [McNeil].

66. Prunier, *The Rwanda Crisis: History of a Genocide*, with a new chapter, p. 372.

67. United States Committee on Refugees, *Life After Death: Suspicion and Reintegration in Post-Genocide Rwanda* (Washington, D.C.: USCR, February 1998).

68. Helen Fein, "More Murder in the Middle," pp. 174–175, 186.

69. Tom J. Farer, "Intervention in Unnatural Humanitarian Emergencies: Lessons for the First Phase," *Human Rights Quarterly* 18, No. 1 (February 1996): 1–22.

70. Michael Walzer, *Just and Unjust Wars: A Moral Argument with Historical Illustrations* (New York: Basic Books, 1977); Richard B. Lillich, *Humanitarian Intervention and the United Nations* (Charlottesville: University of Virginia Press, 1973).

71. Steven Kull, I. M. Destler, and Clay Ramsay, *The Foreign Policy Gap: How Policymakers Misread the Public* (College Park: Center for International and Security Studies at the University of Maryland, October 1997).

72. Ibid., p. iii.

73.  Ibid., pp. 27, 36.
74.  Ibid., pp. 78–79.
75.  Ibid., pp. 80–81, 91–93.
76.  Holly Burkhalter, "US Failure in Rwanda—And How to Prevent Future Genocides," *Institute for the Study of Genocide Newsletter*, No. 21 (Summer/Fall 1998).

# 8.3    Interview: General Romeo Dallaire

**Were you excited about [being assigned to command the U.N. troops in Rwanda]?**
As I write in my book at times, I'm wondering whether or not I was salivating for this command. Imagine you are a fireman or a fire chief who spent his whole career in prevention, you'd say, "Well he did a good job, there was no fires." But imagine retiring without having gone to put out one fire, or a dentist who never pulled a tooth. We had just finished forty-five years of peace time soldiering in northwest Europe . . . and that had just all crashed, because of the end of the Cold War. . . . I had generals senior to me who retired without going into conflict, [or] coming close to it even. . . . And then all of a sudden this mission appears. . . . It was like God had given me finally a real challenge for my skills. I just lapped it up. I couldn't get enough of it. And of course when you do get it and so many of your colleagues don't, it creates jealousy and things like that. But also what it does is, there are so few commands like that, you're just not allowed to fail. . . .

**Can you describe the U.N. Department of [Peacekeeping] Operations, DPKO? What was your impression when you went there?**
Up until the mid-80s . . . it was a very small operation; there were only six officers there. It was of no great influence in any of the decision-making. However, with the end of the Cold War and the "new world disorder," the demand for more missions moves exponentially from a couple to sixteen, seventeen, eighteen, in less than a year. . . .

By the time I arrived there in the summer of '93 [it was] a pretty smooth-running operation, inasmuch as it could handle the volume and the complexities of the problems. There was a good attitude; the atmosphere was positive . . . But the whole organization was scrunched into small areas where people were literally sitting on printers because they didn't have enough room to print; they had to move furniture to do it. . . . We had a corner of a conference room with a couple of boxes and we were thrown out whenever there was a conference. We didn't have a dedicated phone, had absolutely no dedicated secretarial staff at all. We were starting, literally, from scratch.

**Kofi Annan. His job was?**
Kofi Annan was the U.N. under-secretary general for peacekeeping operations. He had the responsibilities in regards to the mounting and operation of peacekeeping missions around the world. You had Kofi Annan, the head; you had Iqbal Riza, a solid functionary within the U.N. as his chief of staff, who really ran the day-to-day things; and then you had Maurice [Baril, the military adviser]. They operated in a "triumvirate," what I call it anyway. These three were the heart of DPKO and decisions were [made] very much together. They worked in synergy.

**As you began planning and you had your corner of the conference room, there's a lot else going on in the world. . . . What was the message you got about where your mission fit within the grand scheme of what [the U.N.] had to deal with?**
. . . The Yugoslavian situation was very complex at the time—this is before Dayton and all

that stuff—just trying to stop the ethnic cleansing, with a small force and missing equipment. Somalia had blown up with the departure of the Americans. Cambodia had been a success but was becoming administratively complex to handle. Haiti had just taken off. . . . It wasn't a time where you felt that the concept of "peacekeeping" was having success. In fact, it was a time when you started to question whether or not this concept actually works anymore. Does it fit any of these missions that are going on?

And this one was to be just an outright straight classic Chapter VI* [peacekeeping mission]. With the peace agreement both sides want you there; we can do it on the cheap, very little resources required. And you got a sponsor. The French were keen, particularly on getting it going so, you know, let's go for it.

**On the 8th of August you get a phone call from Brent Beardsley saying that something had happened in Arusha. What had happened?**
What had happened is, unexpectedly, the peace agreement was signed. They had had problems with determining the prime minister of the interim government until the peace agreement's broad-based transitional government would come into place. . . . To everybody's surprise, all of a sudden, bingo! A lot of this stuff was resolved and they signed the agreement and we had a mandate—that is to say we had a mandate to look into that agreement and assess whether or not a U.N. mission would be plausible.

**So you went to Rwanda on a tactical mission?**
That's right. We left on the 17th of August, spent two weeks there. The tactical mission was to provide all facets of a possible mission and what would be the problems, what would be the solutions, what would be the concept of operations, generally speaking. How much is it going to cost? . . .

**What were your first impressions of Rwanda?**
What a phenomenal experience. You know the first breath of air of Africa—it felt like you were in another continent—you were, you were—and it was different. My skin, my senses felt that it was very significantly different, and as such you had to suck it in by the pores. . . .

It was incredible, just the adrenaline and the fact that what you were doing was going to provide the guidance for very senior people to decide whether or not these people would be helped or not in their path towards peace. I felt that as a very significant dimension of my responsibility. I mean, you were actually going to help them bring this about, because they couldn't do it on their own because of frictions and other reasons of that nature. And so the weight of that was real. The excitement of it was real. . . . [And I] felt a little nervousness, of course, first shaking hands with those leaders and starting up the mission.

**You met a range of people there from different political parties in Rwanda?**
Mostly [from] the moderate side of the house. It took to the last day of the two weeks to meet with the president, which was a very annoying sign. We never got to meet . . . the hard-line extremists. We had a good feel for the military on both sides, what they had been doing and what they were structured and equipped. . . . The sense was that the political stuff was uncertain, and they really wanted us there soon. They wanted us there by the 10th of September, thirty-seven days after signing. . . . And so there was a sense of urgency that was passed on to me constantly. And my report reflected that this is not a mission that has six months to build up or a year to sustain itself. This outfit had to be on the ground yesterday. Instilling that sense of urgency in the documents and so on was not a problem. Some of the staffs in New York acknowledged it but the system in regards to supporting it, providing people,

providing resources, authorities and so on simply was not up to the task. . . . It couldn't react to the sense of urgency because it didn't have the tools. . . .

**What were your impressions of the military sides?**
The RPF already looked quite disciplined and well structured, living in the bush in the North. Excellent physical condition. Weapons well maintained. Clothes clean and very businesslike.

On the government side, you could discern a difference between elite units, such as the presidential guard and the commandos, and your general run-of-the-mill units who had been, essentially, augmented by recruits nearly pressed into service during the previous three years of war. There was not that same commitment in that your run-of-the-mill soldiers, they didn't have good medical care or support. A lot of them suffered from malaria, and there wasn't this total sense of pride in the defense of the mission against these rebels except, again, when you hit those elite U.N. units. There you found equivalent to the RPF, and sometimes exceeding.

**When you met with the [diplomatic] community, what was the message that they were putting out? Were they saying to you, "Look, this country is in trouble" or did they feel that the Arusha peace accord was a big step forwards, that in general the road was leading towards peace?**
[They hadn't] expressed to us the fact that the extremists had signed under duress. You didn't get that solid clear feeling. What you did get, however, from the ambassadors and military attaches was "get your bodies here fast so we can take advantage of this moment, and if you don't it's going to turn complex again." . . .

I think when I left . . . I was quite optimistic. I was sure it needed a mission, was sure it was a Chapter VI. I would have preferred a bigger force but I was ready to do a minimum viable force. I felt that with timely interventions and support we'd be able to crack this thing.

**During the two-week tactical mission, did you feel that not only you but the commitment of the West was being evaluated by the extremists?**
I think all sides were doing that inasmuch as they knew the West was the entity that could intervene or provide the capabilities. They also knew that the West was absolutely overstretched in a number of operations, not the least of which was the whole Yugoslavian campaign. I felt that there was also an assessment going on as to whether or not the white western world or the developed world would, in fact, be keen at all in coming. . . . Whether they would, in fact, just let it ride and maybe throw some money at it. In that sense I think strategically they were being quite astute. Not being that astute, I was wrapped up too much in the operation and a lot of tactical stuff, and so I don't think I picked up enough on that side of the house and how they were going to play their cards for the future. . . .

**Do you think now, knowing what we all know now, that at the time of your first visit the genocide was being planned?**
You've asked a very perspicacious question, because the essence of your question is, "Do you believe the genocide was planned?" . . . There was an operation being planned. Whether it was clear as a genocide, whether they actually even articulated the term—I think it was eliminating that moderate political side. There was no doubt. The killing of the others, and the continued killing of the others could have been just as fortuitous because they had a structure in place, as it could have been deliberate. But the question that I keep asking myself, as I do in my book, is why did it take so long for the Rawandan Patriotic Front (RPF) to stop it? Why three and a half months? . . .

**After the technical mission, you write a report, you came back to New York and what happens then?**

We produced a report which has to be put in U.N.-ese and all that good stuff. So that takes a couple of weeks. As we're doing that I'm lobbying in different countries with the representatives in regards to the mission. I was told to do that because nobody was supporting it apart from the Belgiques, who were prepared to send in a small capability, and the French, who wanted people to come in. Nobody was interested; they were peacekeeping'd out. So a lot of time was spent on that, then a lot of time in interpreting my report into a format report that goes from the DPKO and Kofi Annan to the secretary-general, who then goes through it . . . and modifies it with the inputs of the political department [and the] humanitarian department. And then it's presented to the Security Council, who then deliberate on it and then take a decision whether or not that mission goes or no goes. . . .

They pretty well agreed to what I had planned, but they reduced a lot of the stuff I felt we had to do in support of the mission . . . which created enormous problems on the ground. . . . A lot of the emphasis of people looking at the report was on getting that thing to be a lowest cost possible and get out of there as fast as you can. . . .

**You said during this period, with all the restrictions you wondered whether you wanted the job too much.**

Yeah. Well as I say in the book, my enthusiasm for making this work got to the point that I had to sit back and assess whether or not I was taking too many risks, whether or not I was prepared to cut too many corners. I wanted that command, and I wanted it to be a successful exercise, so I had to sit back and go through all these parameters that were all pointing in a wrong direction and saying, "Am I right, am I being ethical? Is this morally correct to take all these risks and to have the mission created and me commanding it? Or should I pull the plug on it?" Ultimately, I felt we could do it. But that [was] bravado, I think. Nothing was going to stop me.

**When you got to Rwanda you decided to have a welcoming ceremony, raise the U.N. flag. Why did you do that?**

I did that barely after hitting the ground. I felt it absolutely essential that we plant the U.N. flag in Rwanda and plant it in a place of significance to show all the political entities, all the signees of the agreement and the Rwandans . . . that the international community were here and we're here to stay and we're going to be doing our job. . . .

The place where I wanted to make the most impact, because of the few forces that I had, was in the demilitarized zone. So I made a ceremony, invited both parties . . . [to] a beautiful little village on the top of a hill, a magnificent view of the area, and where a number of other negotiated components of the peace agreement were signed. I wanted to do it right there, right in the heart of the DMZ. And so with less than 60 troops, mostly the Tunisians . . . we made a ceremony, and the significance of it in security and so on became more and more evident as the big wheels from the government side started to arrive and then the big wheels from the RPF started to arrive, with the arms they brought and us trying to keep a certain control. It became just a mob festival after the few moments of formal recognition and speeches. But it was a great moment. . . .

And then that evening, during the night at five sites just south of the DMZ in the northwest of Rwanda, were massacres done with a total of about 40 people who were killed. In five different sites, co-coordinated. As the next morning the word started coming to us, and as we looked into it, it seemed so fishy. I personally even went up to one of the sites and the whole atmosphere there was trying to blame the RPF for this.

But for the RPF to go and kill in these five sites families of members of the National Revolutionary Movement for Development (MRND) party meant they had to go through about ten kilometers of DMZ in fairly mountainous bamboo forest to come and wipe out these five families, and then pull back. It made absolutely no sense. There was no advantage in any way, shape or form for the RPF to do that. On the contrary, it would have changed the attitude of how we saw the RPF and its movement and what it was trying to do as an attempt for peace. And so because it was so illogical, and because [there] was no proof of any consequence, it all pointed to the extremists having set up that scenario to ultimately discredit the RPF.

But the investigation never ended. I didn't have the investigating capabilities. I didn't have the legal support. So although we were leading the investigation and had all parties part of it, ultimately there was no resolution. And the extremists used that as a demonstration that we may be less than objective and transparent in regards to both parties.

In fact, on the second day of the genocide when the interim government of the extremists was established, they raised that [incident]. They said, "You U.N. guys are supporting the RPF. Look what you did on the 18th [of] November and the botched investigation." It was one of those creeping components that was well used throughout the propaganda exercise by the extremists and their radio station to try to discredit us as we kept moving ahead.

**Talk about the feel of the place in November as this was going on.**
It started to come clearer that this was not going to be a classic Chapter VI, where both sides had been totally committed to the peace agreement and didn't want to fight anymore. Rumors in regards to the extremists having signed under duress started to come out. The presence of the militias or, let's put it this way, the youth movements . . . were become more vociferous and more brazen. . . . The tone of what was happening was shifting from evident goodwill to an atmosphere that was less than stable, or less than solid. We were starting to get a whiff of the complexities that might be ahead. . . .

**By New Year's Eve, what was going through your mind, looking ahead?**
. . . A sort of gloom came in. We weren't going anywhere with increasing the capability of the mission. I was spending 70%—at least—of my time fighting for batteries and flash lights, just the most simple of requirements. Even just furniture, chairs and tables. I had officers still working off the floor at that time, a couple of months into the mission. . . . We had been going flat out, but we seemed at that point to be simply running in place, and there was nothing that was going to leap us ahead. There would not be a breakthrough, or didn't seem to be one, politically. There was certainly none militarily. There was no troop movements to Kigali. And so there was an atmosphere that things were starting to close in, that we might be more limited than I had ever imagined. . . .

Plus the fact that the political dimension was now degenerating, or was now becoming the major impasse. The hardliners were becoming more hard-line than expected. We were already getting all these stories about a third force, squadrons of killers, both political and military, or paramilitary, that was around. But we couldn't confirm anything. We were just getting all that as rumors, innuendoes and we couldn't crosscheck the damn stuff, because I was not allowed to have an intelligence capability.

. . . [As a] Chapter VI peace keeping [mission, our mandate included] just self defense and responding to what either side are telling us in our patrolling. I had no intelligence capability, officially. . . . I could not conduct any covert operations. I could not conduct hard intelligence gathering on either side, in the classic sense. I was totally dependent on the good will of both sides, and my ability to monitor. That was it. The ability to monitor is not necessarily always the most effective intelligence gathering; you do need other operations. You need even signals intelligence, the phones, the radios, all that kind of stuff.

So although there was lots of rumors of this third force and the extremists and the militias and stuff like that, we still couldn't get our hands onto something that I could [use as] tangible proof . . . until the 11th of January when an informant [established contact] through one of the moderate politicals. He was within the higher structures of the MNRD party, which was the single party for so many years, which was the hard line party of the president, which ultimately was one of the extremist parties . . .

[He told us that] he simply wasn't going to continue to work in that atmosphere. That they were undermining the whole [peace] process and were ultimately planning the evillest of deeds: attacking not only Tutsis, but also the whole attitude or philosophy of reconciliation between the two different ethnic groups that had been going on for a while, and as such decapitate all the moderate Hutu leaders also.

And so we covertly had meetings with him. I was able to . . . confirm that there were arms [caches]. The quality of the information and the correlation at that point within that very short time was way solid enough for me to take action. . . . If I could destabilize any of the hidden covert planning and operations that was trying to destroy the peace agreement, if I could get at the extremists and prove to them that I was onto them, and that not only was I onto them, I was taking action to curtail their operations, then I would regain the initiative. And then I would be calling the shots with them still trying to react to what I'm doing. And as such would be far more difficult for them to plan in more earnest. . . .

**So you sent a fax to General Baril. Why him?**
In normal procedures the force commander, who is the number two, doesn't send operational or new actions that are going to be taken directly to the military adviser to the secretary general. In this case [Maurice Baril] was a very good friend, and still is. [He was a] Canadian who had been there already for a year. . . . The workings with [U.N. Special Representative for Rwanda] Jacques Roger Booh-Booh had become very strained. I attended all these political meetings. Nothing was moving. And he wasn't moving. I mean, he was bringing nothing to the table. And although he had discussions, the discussions were of no depth. . . . He had not taken charge of the mission. He had not held one staff meeting with his principle subordinates of which I was one. And when we finally had one it ended up in catastrophe because he didn't want this arguing and discussing and having to take a decision.

So when I got that information [from the informant], it was late at night and [Booh-Booh] wasn't keen on being disturbed. [He had a] sort of, not regal but nearly sort of presidential attitude which both sides kept telling me, "We don't need this guy from outside with all this pomp and ceremony." So I sent it directly, because it was a military operation, to [U.N. Military Adviser General Baril]. Now that is not the formal way of doing it. But I sent it to him because I needed him to move it fast in the U.N. headquarters and I would inform Booh-Booh in the morning, and if he didn't like it then he could stop it right then and there. But in the interim I needed their confirmation that I was doing this operation so that I could continue planning. I had a 36-hour window there. That is to say we got the information on the night of the 11th. So we would need the next day for the troops to be all briefed up to plan and the following morning, just before daybreak, we would launch the operation. . . .

**You sent the fax off and you signed it –**
I signed it with the motto of the high school I was in, which in French is "peux ce que veux," meaning "you can do what you want," I suppose. I also added the motto of the brigade that I commanded, "allons-y," which means, "let's go." And Maurice is very conscious of that. It just flowed at the end of it. You don't normally do that in formal stuff, but I did it because I was so convinced and so committed to getting this operation going, and elated that we were actually going to crack this terrible uncertainty of what this third force was, and that we had

all the potential of wrestling the initiative away from the extremists. I sent it and I went to bed, and probably slept one of the best nights I had because I felt that finally we were going to take a certain level of control that would permit us to do so much more, politically and militarily, security wise.

**Then you woke up.**
I woke up and this cable came in, signed by Kofi Annan in his normal staff responsibilities that essentially said cease and desist. Conduct no such operations. It's out of your mandate. On top of that, in the proper process of a Chapter VI, you will inform the ex-belligerent of the shortcomings that we notice and make it quite clear that he's got to rectify these shortcomings within a very short time frame, or else we will be in a position to have to review the mission, and ultimately their commitment to the peace agreement.

**Your fax now is often referred to as the "genocide fax," and understood to mean that you were warning of the genocide.**
That's a bit erroneous inasmuch as it's a fax to say that they were planning to conduct huge massacres, or massacres on a larger scale. Now you're going to say, "Well, wait a minute. What's a massacre? And what's large? And when does a massacre end and when does genocide start?" Well . . . we then expected that there would be killings on a large scale and it could in fact take the nature of the ethnic cleansing. That we knew from Yugoslavia. . . . In fact, I couldn't even fathom the term "genocide." . . .

**You were not warning of an impending genocide?**
No, no, no. I was warning that there would be significant killings and massacres that would destabilize the whole political process, and that in fact we would ultimately not have a mandate anymore, because it would be totally destroyed by the extremists' actions. . . .

**So when you got the reply in the morning, how did you feel then?**
Well, being a French Canadian, I was quite expressive. I was swearing to beat the band. I was mad, nearly beyond self-control. I couldn't believe what I got. In fact, the first emotion was like, "This is treason. My superiors have turned against me. They have not grasped what was going on." . . .

**Your instructions from New York were to brief the government, but also brief the foreign ambassadors. I asked U.S. Ambassador Rawson about his meeting with you and I've seen a summary of the cable that he sent back to Washington describing it. And his memory of the way that you described the threat was that it wasn't that urgent. I'm just wondering after these discussions from New York, when you were briefing ambassadors, how did you characterize your sense of the threat? Were you as fired up as you were the night before? Did you feel like you had to sort of toe the line?**
. . . I don't know if I was less forceful than before, but I will say that the winds had been taken out of my sail. And with Booh-Booh around, who often minimized things, it may have come across without the same forcefulness. That's quite possible. . . . But it was the same information I had sent to New York. I sent exactly the same words. Whether he grasped that as being significant or not depends on [him]. . . .

**Over the next month or so, you requested authority to do other [operations].**
Oh my, yes. A number of times. Ultimately they did permit us to conduct operations, but at arms length. Really at arms length. . . . The aim was to keep us as far as possible from the operation and let the local gendarmerie—that had some very good people in it, but was infiltrated by the hardliners and extremists . . .—do it. . . .

**You describe in your book that you felt like your hands were being tied.**

Yes. . . . There was a sense that I was getting that maybe my assessments were not being taken at full value, and that because of that the instructions I were getting were very technically restrictive. They didn't want me to conduct any of these operations without fully informing them in advance, so they would look at the operation, make their assessment and then I could then start the operation . . . I was not to move unless I got specific authority on specific operations from them, and their outfit was like a sieve. So the Rwandan ambassador was sitting on the Security Council and there were all kinds of different interplays that go on in that very complex building. So telling them in advance what I was going to do and giving them the opportunity to assess it meant that there was a strong, strong chance that the information would get to the extremists [in Rwanda]. . . .

**Let's talk about your visit to Kigali in February when you met with [RPF Commander Paul] Kagame. . . .**

. . . By the time we're into February . . . the extremists are getting stronger and more brazen, because remember by then we've got assassinations going on and we've got huge riots, because the government is not paying anybody anymore. . . . [Kagame] expressed to me clearly that we were moving to a point that something would have to be done. He said one of the two of us—that is, [the RPF] or the government—was going to have to win this thing. . . . It wasn't very veiled as an expression of use of force. . . . This was not an insignificant statement . . . and from what I know of him, he didn't talk for nothing. . . . There was no doubt that he was expressing what was going on in the entrails of the decision making of the RPF.

. . . Interestingly Kagame's threat [of the imminent use of force] . . . waned very, very rapidly in the end of February, early March. In fact, we entered a phase where even the hardliners were being much more flexible. There was more of a discussion going on in the political negotiations . . ., an atmosphere of maybe working out a deal. There was movement going on, and that's why in March, I finally took a couple weeks of leave. . . . I went to New York, and my desire in New York was to clean up a whole bunch of problems, because I was still ineffective on the ground. I had received finally the Ghanaians who had arrived in February, which were the last of the forces to come in, but there was no equipment. . . . I was coming in to browbeat and to get that, so that the force could do the job on the ground, and also to ask more resources. . . .

The way I was received was attentive and so on, but they were continuously being pulled away from discussions because of phone calls from other missions. Higher priority problems. . . . However, I felt that they were genuinely trying to do their best to help me, within the context of all these other missions and priorities, who also were suffering from all kinds of problems. They knew that the situation was tense, that the situation could explode if we were not advancing the political process. They were conscious that this could not continue, [but] they really had nothing to offer me. On the contrary, they hoped that maybe I could go to the field operations divisions, the gang who receive our demands for resources, and who process them in New York for contracting and so on, that I might be able to go and encourage them. . . .

**And then you go back to Rwanda. You say in the book that the entire political landscape has changed.**

. . . What happened is that the president threw a curve in the whole [peace] process and insisted that to make this thing really ultimately work it had to be all-inclusive, including the overt, extremist, super-rightwing Coalition for the Defense of the Republic (CDI) party and the Muslim party, which was sort of in-between. The CDI party had refused to sign [the peace agreement] in Arusha, and so they were left out. They had refused to sign that they were going to follow an ethical process of bringing about the peace agreement and ultimately the new government. . . . I couldn't believe that [the president] had convinced all the players, including Booh-Booh, that that was the solution. . . .

It was to me the most illogical position to take and what they did by doing that is they shifted the pressure away from Habyarimana . . . and his guys to find a solution . . . onto the RPF. A whole international community shifted and said, "You RPF are the ones who are preventing this peace agreement from happening. And you have to demonstrate enormous flexibility, including accepting an overt, hard-line anti-Tutsi party." By doing that they were putting the RPF in an impossible situation. . . . How could they accept the inclusion of that party who had refused to sign, which meant that they were going against the original agreement of Arusha, and accept them into the peace process? A brilliant strategic move on the hardliners had been presented and had been sold hook, line and sinker to . . . the U.N., Boutros Boutros-Ghali and everybody else. . . .

The RPF would be blamed for this impasse. RPF would then be accused of not permitting the peace agreement to go on, and then would have created in the RPF a political hemorrhaging, inasmuch as "What do we do now?" That way, in my opinion, would have forced the hand of the RPF, by the nature of what they are, to take offensive action because that was the only solution, and so the extremists could then blame the destruction of the peace agreement on the RPF.

**You went to see Kagame and he said, "How could this have happened?" And he spoke about impending cataclysm. Tell us what he told you.**
. . . Kagame called me up and I went to [meet him]. And he was beside himself. He made it very, very clear that we were moving towards a catastrophic, cataclysmic scenario and that the RPF were in an impossible position. I didn't need him to tell me that because I had smelled that the minute they had told me about the CDI. And I could not convince anybody, certainly not Booh-Booh. . . . that they were taking the wrong road and that they were putting the RPF in an even more intransigent position. And, in fact, forcing them away from negotiating table.

**What did you say to Kagame when he said, "We're facing cataclysm?"**
Jeez, I can't remember. . . . I know I left there with a great sense of doom, but also of deep-seeded anger. I was angry at the RPF for having been intransigent throughout this and not demonstrating more willingness to maneuver. I was mad at the moderates and the Hutu parties who were not merely looking ultimately at the betterment of the overall process. . . . [I had a] high level of strategic respect for the extremists because they had finally found a way to take the pressure off them for the impasse and shifted it to the side that had been so strongly supported throughout. . . . All of a sudden the RPF are the real bad guys and the extremists—Habyarimana and [his party]—are seen to be reconciliatory and inclusive and wanting to bring a new initiative. It was the most idiotic scenario you could imagine, and it is no wonder that the situation blew up, and it is no wonder why still today I can give you ten options of who shot down that damned plane. . . . The hardliners, extremists felt that Habyarimana had given up the ghost in Arusha and was coming back with an impossible moderate position at that point.

**It could have been RPF.**
Could be RPF. Could be mercenaries at the [behest of] another group. They may be ultra-extremists. It is not crystal clear. And when you look at the events afterwards, it behooves you to be pondering who was gaining from the shooting down of a presidential plane and who was gaining from the actions thereafter. It's an incredible enigma, but there was no doubt in my mind that the international community, which was guarding the whole god

damned lot of them, had been sucked in. And they had precipitated a very complex scenario. . . .

**So on the day the president's plane was shot down, April 6th, where were you and what was the atmosphere then? Did you have a sense that something might happen?**
On the evening of the 6th I was in my residence there with Brent Beardsley, my executive assistant, and the aide-de-camp (ADC) and a driver, and we were working on some administrative directives . . . At 8:30 the first phone call came in, saying that there had been a big explosion in Kinumbi camp, which is just at the end of the runway of the Kigali airfield, and saying that it looked like an ammunition dump that had exploded. . . . Soon after that the call came in and said, no, the presidential plane had crashed. . . .

And then there were phone calls from the prime minister, who confirmed that it was the presidential plane, and asking me for advice and what's going to happen now and the security situation. She wanted things to stay calm, in the capital particularly. And then a couple of other calls where she was saying she couldn't get in touch with many of her moderate cabinet colleagues, but more significantly all the hard-line members of the cabinet had disappeared, every one of them. They had all of a sudden vanished. While the moderate ones, she was getting various reports of them hiding or still there. But it was very difficult to get anybody together at that time.

**What did you do then?**
. . . The liaison officer called me and said that there was a crisis meeting being held at the army headquarters and they would very much want me to attend to assist. . . . I took off with Brent Beardsley and my ADC and we went to army headquarters, and it was very quiet at that point and nothing much going on in the city. We attended the session with Colonel Bagosora who was the executive assistant or chef de cabinet of the Minister of National Defense. He's a retired colonel and a hardline person, in fact considered even more than hardline. He was chairing the meeting. . . . We had a number of exchanges explaining what I could do, what they wanted to do, dominated by the fact that I continued to insist that they should immediately get the Prime Minister Agathe to come to the fore and be the political leader so that it'd be clear that this thing is not a military initiative one way or the other. And continuously Bagosora, acquiesced by the other senior officers there, kept saying that she is of no use and she never was able to garner her cabinet anyways. She was ineffective and not representative of the government, and that's why they, the military, were going to hold the fort for the shortest time possible and find the political structure that will come out of this and hand over to them.

**Did you believe him?**
Well at the time, I had no immediate feel that I was in the face of a coup d'etat. . . . However their not acknowledging Agathe was that sort of signal to say, "Wait a minute, this is not necessarily as clear as it would seem. Bagosora was known to be a hardliner," and so on. Immediately you started to ponder, what was the aim of this exercise? . . .

I told Booh-Booh of my plan of action, which was to protect Agathe and get her to a radio station or some means of communicating with the population, so that she could express you know a calm to them. Because I was smelling more or more . . . that maybe this is not as clear as what we might think in regards to them simply trying to keep control of the situation. I was still not pondering coup d'etat as such, I was just [wondering] were they trying to maneuver and what did they consider to be the political process? And so I said, one thing for sure we gotta keep Agathe protected. . . .

**When you called New York what was the message that you got back?**

. . . Mr. Riza was very clear in that I was to stick to my classic Chapter VI mandate, that I was not an intervention force and that the rules of engagement were to be strictly self defense, and nothing more. There was a concern that we could get drawn into this exercise, and you can still see that paranoia of Somalia coming back, you know, "Just stay where you are, you are not in authority to intervene."

Now, in this U.N. stuff, the commander, although he has troops, they don't really belong to him. They're loaned by the country to the U.N. to be used, but each of these countries provide a contingent commander, a senior guy who communicates directly back to his capital. And so the contingents were over the course of the day getting more and more communications with their international capitals, who were becoming more and more restrictive in what they wanted their guys to do because the risk was too high, and the situation was too confused. And so we entered this arena where I had troops but I didn't have troops and how much of them could I use, and to what avail? And as the day wore on it proved that there were a bunch of the troops that were absolutely useless and they were going to do absolutely nothing. . . .

[I was also] trying to get the political meeting at nine o'clock at the American ambassador's residence sorted out, only to find out that the ambassadors couldn't make it there because there were more and more road blocks coming up and they were concerned about their security. . . . So the political process [was] going nowhere, and so we've got no data on what's happening. It made it only that much more significant that I had to go to where the source was . . . in order to get the sense of how much that side was going to try to stop this hemorrhage and go back to the Arusha agreement and to the rules of the weapons-secure area.

**And that was where? You were talking to people, the crisis committee, down in the camp?**

Well you see, there was no crisis committee as yet structured formally by that time, and I'm talking about 9:30 in the morning. What I'm talking about is Bagosora and [Augustin] Ndindiliyimana, the chief of staff of the gendarmerie and the other officers. Agathe was getting all the protection she needed, at least what we expected was needed. We ended up by having twenty-five troops there on the ground of different nationalities. With that sort of in hand, my job now is to go get ahold of Bagosora and say, "Okay, what's going on now, what is the situation?"

Meanwhile I had sent my deputy to the RPF battalion to keep them calm, because the last thing I needed was them to punch out and then we'd have altercations between the two forces, and then I wouldn't have a mandate. If one side was overflowing and the other side was being restrained, I could still negotiate to stop this hemorrhage and to re-establish the rules of the Arusha agreement. But if the other gang leapt in then I got both belligerents going at each other, my mandate then is nonexistent any more, Chapter VI. And then my mandate is Chapter VII [which is] to be an intervention force, pull out, which is the option in such circumstances, or attempt to negotiate ceasefires or truces. . . .

We made our way to the Ministry of Defense [thinking that Bagosora might be there, but] and nobody was there. I said, "Well maybe they're right back to where they were last night in the army headquarters." . . . [So we] went to the main gate of the Kigali camp where the headquarters was, and that was armed to the teeth. . . . They were there with the armoured vehicles in a very strong defensive position. The major went out to see if Bagosora[‡] and the guys were there; in a very short time, he came back and said, "No, they're not there, they're at the École Supérieure Militaire (ASM) with all the commanders." So we just turned and went towards the ASM.

At the secondary gate of the camp as we're driving by I saw two soldiers in the Belgian uniform lying on the ground about fifty odd meters inside, inside the camp, and I told the guy to stop, I said, "These are some of my guys." . . . I had already by then information that a number of my troops were unaccounted for, that I had Belgian soldiers already held up at the airport. I had a bunch of people that I didn't know what their state was in by the time I left. So that made me conscious of the fact that, "Hey, maybe they're not just held captive or something. I might be taking casualties." And that is the major shift in the whole operation at that point.

So by the time I'm objecting we're already at the ASM; it's only a hundred meters or so away; and at that point, the shock had turned into a rapid assessment of, what the hell am I going to do now? And in fact what it made me realize is that I had the bulk of my force, and also the civilians, in a very vulnerable position. I had over three hundred officers with no weapons or anything spread around the RGF side in particular for the security of the implementation of the peace agreement. . . .

**You wrote in your book that a commander spends his career training for moments like this.**
Yes, yes. Having been in the army at peace for so many years, I mean in the Cold War, but at peace, you rarely get really tested. You're sort of like a fireman who hasn't really gone to a fire but has spent his life in prevention. And so you don't really know even with the strong training you get that when you're actually in that operation to what extent all that training will come to the fore so that you take the right operational, tactical decisions at the time. And so, thirty years of military training to me, was to give us that ability to take instinctive decisions, and the right instinctive decisions, and not necessarily having to go through a pondered assessment of all the factors. . . . If you have war experience all the better but if you don't at least you are to be capable of taking those instinctive decisions, and the right ones. And so your whole life is dependent maybe on those nanoseconds of taking that right decisions, because it's life and death of people in these scenarios. And that's where I was [as I was] moving to the ASM. Also, I saw my soldiers there, who told me that the Belgians are being beaten up.

I was already saying, "I can't get those guys out of there, I just don't have the forces or the deployment capability. . . . I can't take these bastards on." I was already, not mellow in that decision, but already conscious that to do anything for them and for the others I had to negotiate. That's what I had to do. As long as I could keep the RPF under control and they don't bust out, then it was a matter of negotiating to put the clamps on those government forces and to stop that hemorrhaging right then and there, and then we could move back to the peace agreement. That was still in my mind, and that was dominating my mind, except I had this tinge, this gut feel of uneasiness that with the political process not having worked out, are we facing a coup d'etat here? And what are the ramifications of this coup d'etat, with guys like Bagosora running the show? And so because everything's so close, and I wanted to get at the source of what the hell is going on, I went directly into the large ampitheater and busted into the meeting that Bagosora was running.

The essence of what I said was one, my condolences at their losses, but two, get a grip of your units which seemed to be overflowing outside of their garrisons against the rules of Arusha. And [three,] I'm staying. I don't know whether or not at that point they had specifically taken those Belgians to kill them—remember by February, there had been planned ambushes, and Jean Pierre [the informant] had told us that they were trying to set up to wipe out a dozen or so or ten Belgians in order to break the back of our mission, because if the Belgians pulled out I had no real substantive capability to sustain myself, and that the international community would pull us all out. These guys knew about Mogadishu also, and so what I was making clear to them was, I'm staying. . . .

What came clear during the day was that Bagosora was very much in command, with Ndindiliyimana in support of him; and that the negotiations to try to curtail the units—which were mostly presidential guard and a few others—and get them back in their garrisons was not working. I was getting nowhere with them in getting my troops out because they made it quite clear that the camp was in riot, that their own officers had already been beaten up, and that there was no way, no one's getting in there, but they were still negotiating to get the Belgians out. So that went through the afternoon. Negotiations with the RPF broke down. The RPF then punched out by the late afternoon, and by that time, with the RPF punching out, my mandate had just ended.

However, there was no damn way that I was going to pull out of there, because I felt that maybe we might still be able to stop this because we've only got a few units in Kigali doing this, the rest of the country was quite calm. . . . And so we had a crisis meeting which was led by moderates but had ex-hardliners in it . . . We had another meeting that evening with the new interim chief of staff who was a known moderate from the South, and a good guy. . . . But I was still being stalled on where the hell my Belgians were. And so I made it quite clear that this meeting will never end until I have access to those Belgian soldiers, and by then we were still uncertain how many there were—thirteen, eleven, ten. . . . And then finally a phone call, after insistence, came, and said that they are all at the hospital at the morgue. . . .

And so I said, "Right, let's go." The morgue was a little shack, a bit of an L-shaped small shack, and there was a twenty-five watt bulb at best, and there in the corner of the L-shape was this pile of potato bags. Just looked like a pile of potato—Big, huge potato bags. As we got closer, we saw that they were bodies. And they had just been piled up, some face down, others face up, just sprawled there in a heap. . . . Some of them were half-garbed, others still had their uniforms on. There wasn't much blood. . . . You could see bullet holes and some cuts, but they were not, from what we could see there, significantly mutilated.

I had my ADC take pictures. I ordered them to sort out the bodies and clean them and prepare them, and [told them that] the next morning we'll have Belgian troops coming to get them, and then I just stormed away, through more bodies. . . . It started to sink in, the fact that I had lost troops in my command but it didn't waver in any way, shape or form my assessment that there was absolutely no way that I could have mustered even the Belgians into a cohesive force to be able to take on that camp and find those guys and save them. It was not going to happen. That is an interesting point of contention because when people say, "Well you should have stopped everything and go take care of those Belgian soldiers and to hell with the rest of the program," others would say that we—you know, white professional soldiers—can still totally overwhelm black soldiers, even the best of trained soldiers with merely their presence and a bit of shooting and stuff like that.

**And some say that the Belgians shouldn't have turned over their weapons.**
Well, they shouldn't have done that, absolutely . . . [but] what was happening is that the extremist military would arrive with a truck full of people in a sort of a scenario of changing the guards. They would simply approach my soldiers, and although they were on alert they approached the soldiers and simply beat them up and took their weapons away, before they could even react. . . . The procedures that were being used by the extremists were the normal routine procedures, except they brought in more people; and for the guards having more people come would have made sense because they were just increasing the number of security. They were all caught off guard and they simply either were beaten up and taken away or their weapons taken away and they were told to get lost. . . .

[As a commander], you have to take instinctive decisions in nano-seconds that will influence thousands or hundreds of thousands and you hope that what you've been building up over the years through ethical and moral references and command experiences and leadership that when you have to take that one instantaneous decision, you're taking the right one. And I've never doubted that that morning I took the right decision. . . . There was no way to get those guys out of there without risking the mission, the people and an enormous number of other casualties and potentially falling right into the trap that those bastards wanted me to, [to] become a belligerent and have to be totally pulled out. Because the nations would not want to sustain those casualties and become the third belligerent and then the whole lot of us would have been out. No way. I would not be able to live with the moral[ly] corrupt decision of packing up and leaving.

**The net result is that Belgium decides to pull out its troops. Obviously your own troops now know that they are potentially vulnerable and your best forces, best contingent leaves.**

. . . The situation was of course catastrophic for Belgium, having ten soldiers slaughtered like that at the start of the war. The government over the next couple of days attempted to argue for reinforcements; they did. Willy Claes did say, "We've got to reinforce," and did ask around for reinforcements to be committed there, but by the 12th, which is a few days down the road, nobody had any interest in coming to Rwanda, they didn't give a damn. They didn't want to take the risks, they were not going into another African escapade that could degenerate like Somalia. It's at that point, to the [best of my knowledge] that the government said, "No, that's it, we're pulling out."

. . . Losing the Belgians, although a major force in the mission, to me didn't give me the authority to close down the mission. That's why I'd said that earlier on at the meeting with all the commanders, "I'm staying." So if they were implementing their plan to scare us off by killing Belgians, right from the start I wasn't buying it. . . . I still felt that I could hold the fort and do something. But what then happened is the Belgians then went around and argued with all the other nations that if we didn't pull out, the Africans being what they are, the Belgians knowing the African mentality so well, is that when Africans have a major loss they go berserk. And when they go berserk they'll kill anything. . . . They convinced everybody else that if they didn't pull their troops out they'd all be slaughtered.

Well, the shit hit the fan then because the bulk of my forces then stopped doing anything, retreated into their trenches, and were going to do nothing to help stop this tidal wave that is starting to build up. And on the contrary . . . they're sitting ducks there, taking casualties, and they're eating up what I have left of rations. I simply said [to the U.N.], "Right, you're not going to increase me, here are the options of reduction." . . . Ultimately the minimum left on the ground would be about two hundred and seventy to stay alive, stay there, to keep reporting, negotiating ceasefires and ultimately hopefully being the foot on the ground for a reinforcement that ultimately would come in. . . .

**Let me talk to you about the April U.N. Security Council maneuver and how it looked from your perspective. Boutros-Ghali had put forward the options for the withdrawal—a cable came, and you were awakened at 4:30 [AM].**

Yes. It's a cable that essentially is saying that there is no option for reinforcement, and that the options that are being studied are options of withdrawal or reduction of the force. It also indicates that although some countries—the British, the French—were inclined to [keep] a smaller force for a short period of time to see if there's any good will, the Americans come down categorically and say, "No, there's no way there's going to be a cease fire, so let's pull everybody out and get out of that quagmire and then see what happens afterwards."

. . . The Security Council was already of a mindset that for political reasons, we should leave somebody on the ground, but they were certainly tending more and more to pulling out and following the lead of the Belgians and certainly the Americans. So it was a significant shift; forget any idea that somebody's going to come and help you Dallaire, or that your forces were going to actually do something positive. . . . So that scenario brought an enormous gloom. I remember Maurice Baril sending me a code cable not long after, but because I was up north with the RPF, Brent Beardsley took the phone call and Maurice said, "Tell Dallaire that there is no cavalry coming over the hill. None." . . .

As we got closer to the Security Council becoming far more involved with the process . . . Boutros-Ghali was being lobbied also extensively, and one of the options that came forward was that the whole outfit be pulled out. In fact I did get orders to pull out completely lock, stock and barrel from Boutros-Ghali and I said, "No way, I refuse to abandon the mission and turn tail and run while the bodies were piling up all over the god damn place."

When I got that order, I went to [my deputy, the Ghanaian General Henry Anyidoho.] . . . I said, "Henry, they want us out. We've failed in the mission, we've failed in attempting to convince, we've failed the Rwandans. We are going to run and cut the losses, that's what they want us to do. What do you think about this?"

And Henry responded and he said—now remember he had a large force there, he had over eight hundred troops, and he took it upon himself without consulting, as yet, his government and he said, "We've not failed and we're not going to leave. We should stay." And that was all I needed because by Henry saying that, that meant that I would still have troops on the ground —which were good troops, not well equipped but good troops. . . . His support was exactly the depth that I needed to give me just that much more oomph to decide, yeah, that's it. So I stood up and I said, "Henry, we're staying, we're not going to run, we're not going to abandon the mission, and we will not be held in history as being accountable for the abandonment of the Rwandan people." It was just morally corrupt to do that. And that's when I went back and told them to go to hell, or words to that effect.

When the order came to start withdrawing down to the lowest level . . . to 270, well then I implemented a withdrawal plan. . . . We were able to stop the withdrawal of the Ghanaians and to keep about 450 on the ground.

**What could you possibly do with such a small number of troops?**
I didn't see myself being able to protect a whole bunch of people, although we already had over 20,000 in our sites, so there was no way that I could abandon them. I needed some protection for those sites, or to consolidate those sites in one way or another. I also needed the transport capability, for if we were able to keep a life line going I could bring food and fuel and medicine, not only for my troops but for those people. . . .

**How did you find out the prime minister had been killed?**
Well, I was at the defense ministry after the morning meetings and, because none of those leaders were there, and I had discussed with the headquarters things that were going on, there was still this situation that hadn't been clarified.

And so I was directed that they're not at the UNDP [U.N. Development Program] office, but at the UNDP compound where people were living, and that was just down the street. So I went with my ADC and we walked not very far—again, it's within two hundred meters—and pounded on the gate, which was a light blue painted steel. The gate opened and to my surprise there was a man standing there with a U.N. vehicle right behind him. And I said "What are you doing here?" And he said "I received information and I came here in regards to the compound, the VVIP, and also simply coming in to assist or look at the situation."

I don't know how those instructions and stuff got to him, but he ended up there. He was a Senegalese officer, Captain Mbaye Diagne that was used a lot in passing information from one side to another. He had been behind the government lines for his work with a team of observers inside the city, and had been noticed by his courage already. I mean this guy would do things that other guys wouldn't do, and so he would take on missions that other guys would not necessarily look at. . . .

They showed me where the killings had happened. . . . [The prime minister] and her husband were killed but the children had been hidden and the extremists hadn't been able to find them . . . I said that I would try to get an APC to them as fast as possible so that they could evacuate the children and move them to a safe place. . . .

The UNDP staff, permanent staff, and some locals were living in this compound. There were about five, six houses all connected in the compound with a fairly decent yard, all walled in, with the back wall being the wall adjacent to the residence of the prime minister. She had jumped by a ladder over the wall with her husband and children to run from the assault that had been done on the Belgian troops earlier that morning. And, again, what's also surprising is that none of the Belgians followed her. There job was to protect her, and so she sort of escaped but none of the Belgians moved with her in protection at all. And certainly none of the Rwandan gendarmerie or military did either. . . . The people there, the UNDP people, had protected her and had hidden her and the children and her husband and all that, but later on that morning, in the second round, the extremists pounded in over the wall and found her and her husband. You could still see in the house where they had thrown a grenade. There was damage inside the big living room there, and there was blood-spots outside where they had been killed. And these same UNDP people had protected these children and hidden them. And Diagne appeared in this same scenario and participated in that. It was never really clear exactly how he did it or anything, with everything else going on, but he was participatory in this exercise. . . .

**I've heard a lot of stories about what Mbaye did. What did you know about his rescue missions, beyond the prime minister's children, during that month of April to May?**
He was part of that particular group of U.N. Military Observers, unarmed, that . . . on their own initiative would go to places where they were told people might be hidden, and they would get them out and bring them to either the Hotel Mille Collines or another safe place that we had. Diagne was one of those leaders in that. He was courageous and risk-taking. And there were a few other guys that were all the same. . . .

**Were they operating beyond the mandate?**
I had no mandate. U.N. had not given me it. I got orders on the 22nd of April, which is already over two weeks into the civil war and the genocide. But during that whole time there was no formal mandate. In fact they were trying to pull me out. And so we were operating by what we felt was right and what we could do, and it was under my instructions of what we can do that we used whatever forces that were willing to do things. . . .

I lost control of many of the U.N. observers around the country because a lot of them simply took off into the neighboring countries. . . . These guys didn't move. This heart of observers, the gang that stayed at the Mille Collines, Diagne was one of them—there were about fifteen of them—they stayed and they operated. Others did some. Others were observers in specific points. But apart from that the bulk of the force had been rendered inept in what it could do.

. . . These groups were responding to local demands, but then, pretty fast, within days of the start of this and the evacuation of the expatriates—all these white people, businessmen, abandoning the nannies who had raised their kids for years, with bags full of (certainly not) clothes, even bringing their dogs on the aircraft, [which is] against the rules. Running to the goddamn aircraft; running to the trucks to save their bums, and abandoning the ones who had been loyal to them for so many years . . . and a lot of them were Tutsis too. So we started to get these calls from New York . . . from here, there and everywhere, for us to go and save such and such. . . .

**You mean specific people.**
Absolutely, yeah. . . . Now there was probably remorse while they were sitting in Paris drinking their wine, so they got through channels to try and get us to save them, to pull them out. Other ones were very honest requests; like we saved a whole bunch of nuns from different religious orders. . . . Some of them were NGOs that were very worried about their local staff because that's all they had on the ground. But a lot of them were also friends of people of influence and power who could put the squeeze on the U.N. who

could put the squeeze on me to go get them. So we were getting, both verbally and in writing, requests like from [Riza] and the like, to send guys to go find these people and try to save them. . . .

These guys were often unarmed, running through barriers, and then having to pick up these people and hide them in the vehicles to bring them through, because if the extremists found in any of our U.N. vehicles people like Tutsis and so on that we were protecting, then that was it. Every vehicle would be searched and all my people would be at risk. The risk was worth it to try to save people, but it became so abusive. I mean, Brent was managing at one time over 600 people on a list of special requests to help, and I got to the point that I told [them] in New York, "That's it. My people are being burned out and risking their lives, and sometimes nobody's there." It became a real difficult ethical problem for me. Why am I saving them more than anybody else, and why am I risking the lives of my observers and my staff to get them out more than anybody else? And so I entered into a debate about whether or not it was right.

We also had another dimension that all of a sudden came into this: the extremists had caught on to this, that we were at least going around and looking for people. And so what they would do was they'd go to places where they suspected had Tutsis or people hiding, and they would come in and tell people there, "This is the U.N., we're here to save you," and all this kind of stuff. And people would climb out of the sewers or out of the ceilings and they'd slaughter them. That was the case, in fact, for the family of Kagame himself, who had put in a request for us to go [help them]. The guys went there, nobody was there. But they were seen going there. And so they came back and I said "Well, try again the next day," because we did attempt that, too often. And when they came the next day they were all slaughtered, all lying on the ground slaughtered in the house. So it started to get like, "Hey, are we helping people or are we guaranteeing them being slaughtered?" . . .

### How did you receive word of Captain Diagne's death and what happened?

I can't remember specifically [how I heard]. Diagne was so well known because he had done so many of these rescue missions and he had also been delivering written correspondence between the Mille Collines hotel and . . . the headquarters. . . . He was bringing some information across and he was stopped at a barrier . . . and while he was there, stopped, a very large mortar round landed beside the vehicle, and of course destroyed the vehicle and killed Diagne instantly, as best we could determine. By the time we were able to get there and evacuate him he was dead. But some of the correspondence had his blood on it. The correspondence made it through—he didn't. . . .

### There was a ceremony at the airport for Diagne's body being taken out? I heard that you helped carry the coffin to the plane.

Yes. We didn't have a coffin. . . . We didn't even have body bags. We took sheeting that is used for the internally displaced and refugees, to put on their huts to protect them from the rain, and that's all we had. So we had a ceremony inside the airfield terminal, and then we carried the stretcher with this light blue covered body into the Hercules aircraft. . . . It was a very, very low point. [He was] an incredibly courageous individual amongst others who were strong and courageous, but he seemed to be untouchable. . . . It was a low point.

What did, however, keep us going was the fact that the Canadian Hercules aircraft . . . were assigned so that if we did get injured, or any of my troops got injured, they'd have a chance of surviving. I had no medical capabilities, and so we could get them back to Nairobi fast enough to save them. And that became a very, very significant factor in the continued courage of the troops. . . . The sound of the engines of the Hercules became the lifeline. And without those Hercules I would have had to close down the whole damn outfit because there was nothing else coming—nobody else. . . .

**Tell me about Philippe Gaillard.**

Now there is an absolute guardian angel of the world community, I think the purest of what one expects the Red Cross to be: courageous, determined, gutsy, brash, an intimate leader, very close to his troops, to his people, will not back down, argumentative, pig-headed, but the heart of an angel. Humanity for him is all humans.

**You two have a bond.**

. . . When the war started he was a pillar. Everybody ran except him and his small band that not only stayed but established that ad hoc hospital, and that continued to face down the extremists who were trying to get into the hospital to kill the injured Tutsis. . . . Philippe Gaillard, who's not very tall—He's a very slight man, skinny, not muscular but wiry, and he would face these guys down. And they'd back off. . . .

Ultimately he lost something like 56 nationals who worked for the Red Cross. The old ambulances would be stopped and the extremists would simply kill the drivers or the assistant there from the Red Cross and then just pull out the injured out of the ambulances and just kill them right there on the spot. So he was taking several casualties, yet they never wavered. . . .

Philippe maintained an energetic but controlled rage. He was determined to do it. And right from the early moments of the war, when it was evident that he was staying, our personal communication took a much stronger bearing. I became very concerned about them and their situation.

And so I asked him to join my net of our communications and to listen in all the time, so he can keep abreast of what's going on, and to intervene whenever he felt he had to or he needed stuff. Pretty well every night we'd do a radio check, just the two of us, saying, "Are you there?" "Yeah." He became a reference for me, of staying and of determination. . . .

**I noticed in your book you talked about a meeting [where Gaillard was asked] how many people did he think had been killed so far, and Gaillard said something like over 200,000. This was May. And as Gaillard told the story, you said, "Philippe, that's an exaggeration. It's nowhere near that high." Do you remember that?**

Yes. At the start we knew it was massive, but there was no easy instrument of computing that. And although there was massive killings, the scale was difficult to comprehend. But my assessment was dead wrong. Gaillard had better data on what was going on. . . .

But what later on became worse is the fact that the impression I was getting from New York . . . was that a lot of them thought, or argued that the bulk of the killing had been done. And, in fact, by then we had come to grips with the scale and the killing was still going flat out. There may have been two or three hundred thousand killed, but ultimately they were way into the six, seven, eight, hundred thousand scale of people being killed. Some people say an intervention would have been useless because they were all dead. They weren't all dead. They were still being killed and slaughtered by the thousands and thousands. And so that became a point of contention. And the argument was ridiculous. It's just like the argument around the term "genocide." I mean it's a useless argument. Human beings are being killed in the thousands, it could be in the hundreds of thousands. You don't need the term "genocide" to decide to help other human beings. In fact, once they finally agreed to using the term genocide it did absolutely nothing, it changed nobody's perspective in any way, shape or form that brought any result on the field. On the contrary, the arguments were that the killing was over now, so is the deployment really so essential?

That whole exercise of numbers became a great perversion, because ultimately you don't need four thousand bodies to say that we've got a real problem. And the proof of that is that how many people died in that market in Sarajevo? Sixty? The whole damn world got really concerned, and the western world mobilized everybody they could to respond to that. . . . It was just an absolute perverse exercise of developed nations using excuses of sovereignty and nationalism and involvement and self-interest, to argue the way around one of the most fundamental premises: Are these people human? Do you have a capability? Then why aren't you doing something? Why is it that the black Africans sitting there being slaughtered by the thousands get nothing? Why is it when a bunch of white Europeans get slaughtered in Yugoslavia you can't put enough capability in there?

There were more people killed, injured, internally displaced and refugeed in less than a hundred days in Rwanda than the whole of the Yugoslavian six or seven years of problems. I couldn't keep nor reinforce my small force, even feed it, and they were pouring tens of thousands of troops into Yugoslavia and billions of dollars of aid, and they're still doing it. . . .

**[During the killing] where were you living and what was your routine like? Did you shave everyday? Did you try to make sure you were well dressed in your uniform and cleaning it up everyday? How did you try to keep a routine in that kind of chaos?**
. . . I'd had "prayers" at 7:30 in the morning.

**Prayers are what?**
Prayers is when I bring all the staff together and I do that twice a day, morning at 7:30, and in the evening, I think it was around 6:30. In the morning I'd get the intelligence briefing of what we knew that happened that night from wherever, and then we'd go over things that we had to do for that day. And then my staff and supporting commanders would tell me where they're at and what their needs are. Then the one in the evening was a review of what had gone on during that day and then the anticipation of the next days coming down the road, plus more on the higher plane discussions, which is not just what's coming out tomorrow, but what's coming down the road. . . .

There was a lot of feedback provided voluntarily by the media because of our very open scenario—I wasn't restricting them from anywhere. The odd meeting I'd have of course with my inner staff, but I mean outside of that they could go and we'd support where they'd want to go. They would come in to the headquarters area, the operation center, and they'd look at the map to bring themselves up to scratch, and then they'd say, "No, here's something that I saw there." Or, "No, there's another refugee camp here." We got a lot of the data from them. . . . And then in return my ops officers told them what was being planned and where I'm at with negotiation and stuff like that. . . .

**And you needed [the media] to help get your story out.**
Yes, in fact it became quite clear within the second week that the idea of reinforcement was being destroyed left, right and center. I mean from the Belgians who were pulling out telling Boutros-Ghali to get the whole damn lot of us out, through to in fact the Security Council discussions that barely touched on reinforcement. . . . There was nothing positive coming. Absolutely nothing positive coming to us except more and more people worried about their troops, worried about people they know and trying to get as far away as they could from Rwanda. Except the media. They were in a totally different mode. . . .

It became clear that the only weapon I had left between me and the whole rest of the world were the media. And a weapon that was not for me to manipulate because I didn't have to do that. What I did is facilitate. They were there. They were looking for those stories. They wanted to bring out the guts, the gore and the evil and the continuum of this terrible civil war and genocide and I just made whatever I could available to them. . . . There was no way that people could turn around and say, "We didn't know, we didn't see it, we couldn't understand it." Because the stuff was being plastered as much as it could. However, it is interesting that ABC, CBS and NBC in the United States put more air time to Tanya Harding trying to kneecap her competition than they did to the genocide, all going on at the same time. . . .

**Let me talk to you about the RPF's intentions in April. You write in your book that Kagame made it very clear that he wouldn't support a U.N. intervention.**
Absolutely. . . . Kagame or the RPF did not recognize that interim government that was set up by the extremists. They did not want in any way shape or form to give credence to that outfit. So they did not want to negotiate with them, because once they negotiated with them it would give them credence. . . . Secondly, Kagame continued to argue that any troops pulled off the line on the government side would be used to exacerbate the killing scenario. . . . Thirdly, Kagame's aim, as he stated, was to stop the killing behind the government lines. The only way he saw he was able to do it was conducting an outright civil war, or war between his army and the government army. Winning on the ground would permit him to be able to stop the killing. . . .

Kagame did not want an outside force that would stop his advance and potentially enter into negotiation; that would mean that while we're negotiating killings could continue to happen behind the other line. And so to me he was continuing a strategic aim of more and more taking ground. . . . They made it quite clear. Not only did they not want an intervention force, but they would take action if such an option was presented. . . .

Now there could have been, in behind all that, a plan to actually take over the whole country . . . and reconstitute a responsible government in which the Tutsis would have a responsible position and so on. . . . Did he want to take the whole country? Well, that was not evident. But it did come evident a little later on, because at one point he had a very defensible line . . . that went north-south and essentially divided the country in nearly two. . . .

**He told you that if the U.N. or any other outside intervention force came in to directly intervene in the war that the RPF would fight that.**
Yes, it would consider it as a force of belligerence, and as such it was totally unacceptable to them and yes they would take them on.

**Tony Lake—when I mentioned that you'd written about this in your book, he said "Well, this is kind of difficult to say, but maybe the best thing to do really was to just let these guys fight it out. The best way to end the genocide was to not intervene and to let the RPF win the war."**
Well, that's certainly consistent with what they actually did. . . . To say that the best thing was to do was to let them fight it out, is actually condoning the government forces in doing not only the fighting on the line, but continuing to let happen the killing and slaughtering behind the line. But ultimately that's what the Americans were aiming for. They didn't want to get involved. And so that's exactly what happened. They fought it out and one side lost and 800,000 people were slaughtered. . . .

**How do you feel now when you hear U.S. senior officials—Clinton, Albright, others—talk about Rwanda? Of course Clinton went and apologized –**
He didn't apologize.

**Well, it was couched as an apology.**
No, no. He went to reinforce the blackmail on the Rwandans. . . . When he was there in '98, he said, "Oh, I didn't know. We didn't realize." I've got all those quotes and stuff, which are outright lies. They knew, it was there as information, and it is evident that that information was either at his level or stopped within the structures. But the Americans knew what was going on inside there, and [it's awful] to go and excuse yourself—the Belgians did the same thing—in front of these people. The Americans scuttled any initiative to bring about a force to be able to save hundreds of thousands. How can they look at this guy and accept an apology?

But worse than that is that the Rwandans need American money. They need Belgian money to reconstitute themselves. What option do they have regarding Clinton coming in there and trying to excuse himself? Throw him out? No. Embarrass him? They gave him a bit of a hard time, but that was insignificant to what was deserved. These great leaders who go to these countries and ask for excuses, that's sort of like trying to get rid of the blood on their hands. Really what they're doing is imposing that on those people, blackmailing them to accept these apologies, so that it satisfies the people back home that we brought closure. "I went there and in humble statements I demonstrated that we had failed and that we are sorry about it." Bullshit. I have no time for any such actions. There is no respect of the people. I mean it's crass to actually be able to go there and say that. . . .

**Could something like this happen again?**
In my pessimistic mood, I'd like to use the example of Diane Fossey and the mountain gorillas in the northwest of Rwanda. I have this terrible feeling that if some outfit wanted to go and slaughter those 300-odd gorillas, that today people would react with far more consternation than they would if they started killing thousands of black Africans, Rwandans, in the same country.

I do not believe that the developed world actually considers Africans, particularly South Saharan Africans, as being total humans. I still feel that they consider them as children, as reactive to extreme emotions, and that sooner or later even the more developed ones you'll have a coup d'etat or something else and they'll go into [mass killings]. Now there's enough examples to prove that, I'm afraid. However, what I find sad is that it's sort of stated as an excuse to not get involved. It's sort of habit. . . .

**Let me ask you about a meeting you had with Kagame. He had asked you why you didn't do more. Do you remember that?**
. . . The mainstream argument was that [my] forces were simply not capable of conducting any of those operations. . . . They didn't have the resources, they were not structured for that, and our countries did not mandate them to do that, because within twenty-four hours, countries were already telling the troops not to do anything.

But that question being asked by Kagame does not surprise me, because it is the same type of question he asked of the moderates. Why didn't you do something, why didn't you react, why didn't you build a force to do something? The moderates would say, "Listen, we don't have loyal units; they're all infiltrated and on top of that our families are exposed to being slaughtered and killed also." Kagame would refuse those arguments; of course his family was safe somewhere else. Elements of his extended family were in Kigali, but he was working from a very secure base. . . .

So the question it doesn't surprise me that it was asked at the time, sure, but the fundamental premise was—is—those soldiers, one, didn't have the capabilities, two, did not have the mandate and, three, were being restrained from doing anything by their own nations. And so I did not have the capability of ordering them to conduct offensive operations.

The other thing is the only ones who could conduct it in any significant way were the Belgians. The Ghanaians could have done it, but they were limited. They had no transport or anything like that and they had next to no ammunition. We had no defensive stores, I had no secure base like he had in the North and those were the premises under which I took those decisions.

**In his interview, Gaillard applauded Captain Mbaye Daigne and other people, but he said if you really want to save people masses of people you have to deal with the people who want to kill them.**
Absolutely, absolutely. Take 'em head on, break their back, wrest the initiative from them, keep them off balance. . . . But you don't do it with the concepts of diplomacy, the concepts of neutrality and impartiality that exist today.

**Talk about your meeting with the Interahamwe.**

. . . I had to crack the nut of the militias, because it was evident they were dancing to a different drum. And so I asked Bagosora, I said listen, let me meet these guys, let me negotiate with them, because he was doing it, or the chief of staff of the army was doing it and I kept getting it second hand or third hand. I said, "I'll meet with them and we'll talk face to face and then we'll sort this out, hopefully."

So Bagosora established a couple of these meetings, but the first one was in the Diplomat Hotel that had been partially bombed out, that was used as the extremist headquarters in Kigali. . . . Bagosora brought me and there were these three guys, three Rwandans, one tall, one medium and one smaller who stood up when I entered. Bagosora introduced them and as I was looking at them and shaking their hands I noticed some blood spots still on them. And all of a sudden they disappeared from being human. All of a sudden something happened that turned them into non-human things.

I was not talking with humans, I literally was talking with evil, personified, maybe in those bodies and in those eyes. But they weren't human. And what was coming out of their mouths wasn't human. They were so proud of now being into discussions with the general from the U.N., and that gave them great personal prestige, and they were [elated at] this situation that they found themselves in. But everything that was coming out was not words of a human negotiating or discussing, it was evil blurting out their positions and their arguments. I didn't see humans anymore, I was totally overcome by the evil. These three guys just brought it into reality, brought evil into reality and by my religious background, the only way I could qualify that was being the devil. That son of a bitch had come on earth, in that paradise, and literally taken over. And these three guys were the right hand people of Lucifer himself, Bagosora. And I couldn't shake that.

. . . My instinctive reaction had me starting to pull my pistol, because I was facing evil. I wasn't facing humans I was facing something that had to be destroyed. . . . It even became a very difficult ethical problem. Do I actually negotiate with the devil to save people? Or do I wipe it out, shoot the bastards right there? I haven't answered that question yet. What if I'd killed them? Objectively their structure was such that if I'd wiped out these three guys the structure would have sustained itself and then I would have put the whole lot of us in guaranteed danger of being wiped out. But for a long time I felt that I wouldn't have been killing humans, I would have been actually destroying the devil.

**Can you talk about the personal impact that all of this has had on you?**

Like veterans of other wars and other conflicts . . . you are affected by not only what you've experienced, but as a commander even more you're affected by the decisions you took, or didn't take, and as such have a significant level of guilt, of responsibility, particularly when the whole scenario has failed. I came back with and still live with this enormous guilt. I was the commander, my mission failed and hundreds of thousands of people died. I can't find any solace in statements like I did my best. . . . A commander can't use that as a reference in any operation. He succeeds or he fails and then he stands by to be held accountable. My mission failed and that's that.

. . . The old theory of "you work hard and with time you forget" is a false statement. What you do is you remember the stuff in digitally clear slow motion. It's a matter of how you handle it, and how intrusive it is and what sort of prostheses you have that prevent you from falling into these bubbles of terrible depression, losing your objectivity totally and moving you even to suicide. . . . You want to hide, you don't want to see people, and you find solace in all of a sudden being in that bubble, even when that bubble is leading you to try to kill yourself. In fact, there's enormous solace because the pain of killing yourself is nothing compared to the pain of living with this, and it's only by flukes and by chances that some of us don't actually do it. My suicidal attempts were based on booze. I starting falling into these depressions, and I'd just drink and drink and then I'd cut myself or try to jump off things, but more often than not that was totally ineffective because I was pissed to the gills. It's only that and people checking up on me that prevented me from killing myself. . . . I'm not the man I was, and never will become [him again], but hopefully with some drugs or medication that I take, just like someone who's got diabetes takes insulin, to keep me stable . . .—that will be my life.

**Given everything, are you glad you took the job?**
Absolutely. Never ever a doubt. My whole life was to command, . . . to be given missions, to accomplish missions—of course accomplish them with the minimum amount of casualties or destruction, and with success. I've never ever even pondered that if the opportunity was given to me again would I do it, even knowing what's going on, because I'd say to myself I'm sure I will be able to change it. . . .

**Gaillard, and others who respect you, thought you've taken too much on yourself, too much responsibility.**
. . . I don't think so. I cannot argue that I did the best I can, and yet all those 800,000 or so were killed, three million were displaced or injured or refugeed. I cannot find solace nor logic in saying I did the best I can, now I have to carry on.

Rwanda will never ever leave me. It's in the pores of my body. My soul is in those hills, my spirit is with the spirits of all those people who were slaughtered and killed that I know of, and many that I didn't know. . . . Fifty to sixty thousand people walking in the rain and the mud to escape being killed, and seeing a person there beside the road dying. We saw lots of them dying. And lots of those eyes still haunt me, angry eyes or innocent eyes, no laughing eyes. But the worst eyes that haunt me are the eyes of those people who were totally bewildered. They're looking at me with my blue beret and they're saying, "What in the hell happened? We were moving towards peace. You were there as the guarantor"—their interpretation—"of the mandate. How come I'm dying here?" Those eyes dominated and they're absolutely right. How come I failed? How come my mission failed? How come as the commander who has the total responsibility—We learn that, it's ingrained in us, because when we take responsibility it means the responsibility of life and death, of humans that we love. . . .

There is no "I'm sort of pregnant." You are or you aren't. And in command there is no "sort of in command." . . . My failings, my inabilities, not taking advantage, lack of skills—all of it is there. What could I have done better, well, we can discuss that for hours. But there's one thing for damn sure: I was in the field, I commanded, I did not convince, I lost soldiers and 800,000 people died. And there's no way of taking that away. . . .

## Notes

*   A Chapter VI peacekeeping mission empowers the U.N. to step in and help put an end to hostilities through diplomacy and without the use of force. In contrast, a Chapter VII U.N. mission allows for coercive measures to be taken—from imposing economic sanctions to sending in troops and tanks.
‡   While Dallaire was looking for Bagosora, the prime minister's house was stormed by Rwandan troops. The U.N. soldiers sent to protect her radioed back for instructions, and were told to adhere to the peacekeeping mandate, offer protection to the prime minister but not to use force. The prime minister fled to a neighbor's house, where she was later killed; the U.N. soldiers surrendered their weapons and were taken hostage by the Rwandans. The African U.N. soldiers were soon released, and the ten Belgian peacekeepers were taken away.

# 9

# Intervention

While the international community and individual states are almost lackadaisical when it comes to preventing genocide, they are, more often than not, tentative, nervous, and unwilling to commit to strong, timely, and effective interventions once massive crimes against humanity and/or genocide have broken out. The latter situation is due to a host of reasons, but primarily can be put down to *realpolitik*, a lack of real care about others living in far off lands, and a lack of political will. With regard to *realpolitik*, a nation may not perceive an intervention as being in its national interest. That is, certain interventions may be directed at a country with which it is allied (or with which it has economic linkages), and thus supporting the intervention may be perceived as counter to its own interests. Or, a state committing egregious human rights violations may be of no significance at all to another state, and thus the latter state's leadership may see no purpose in committing troops or resources (monetary or otherwise) to help support an intervention.

Concomitantly, there is often great hesitation by the UN or individual nations to conduct an intervention to halt crimes against humanity and/or genocide when the targeted nation is averse to such an intervention. That is, the UN and individual nations are, more often than not, wary of entering a sovereign state's territory against its will and in contravention of the principle of sovereignty.

When an intervention to attempt to halt massive crimes against humanity, ethnic cleansing, or genocide is undertaken, for example, by the United Nations, it is essential to provide a force with a Chapter VII, or peace enforcement, mandate (which allows the force to confront and, if necessary, engage in battle with the perpetrators who are attacking innocents), versus a Chapter VI, or peacekeeping, mandate (which only allows a force to use force when it is attacked, thus doing little to no good for the innocent on the ground whose lives are threatened). When killers are roving across a country committing mass murder and mass rape (and, possibly, at one and the same time, engaging in warfare), it is virtually impossible for an interventionary force on a Chapter VI mandate to protect itself or the innocents under attack. The truth of this matter was evident during the 1994 Rwandan genocide, when the United Nations Assistance Mission for Rwanda (UNAMIR) was on a Chapter VI mandate, and, more recently, it has been evident in Darfur, Sudan, where African Union troops have been shackled to a Chapter VI mandate and thus unable to halt Government of Sudan and *Janjaweed* attacks against the villages of black Africans and internally displaced persons (IDP) camps.

No intervention is simple, cheap, easy, or devoid of potential danger, and for these reasons, among others, most nations are skeptical about engaging in interventions, either alone or in conjunction with the United Nations. Interventions involve massive amounts of planning, personnel, and resources, not to mention the potential for creating an even more complicated and costly conflict. The logistics alone in transporting personnel and *materiél* to the locale of the conflict is, in and of itself, extremely time-consuming and costly. And that does not even take into account the time and cost it takes to establish the mission on the ground (e.g., locating and/or erecting buildings and compounds, establishing communication centers, housing and safeguarding troops, weapons, equipment, and so on).

With any intervention, there is a wide range of actions that can be taken, from the imposition of different types of sanctions to the establishment of no fly zones or safe areas. The latter is achievable, but only if there is the political will and sustained support for such an effort. If such political will and support are not forthcoming, then the attempt to establish a safe area can result in an unmitigated disaster, as was evident in the former Yugoslavia in the mid-1990s. Interventionary actions can also range from the bombing of strategic sites in conjunction with a strong on-the-ground peace enforcement effort, or solely the latter when the bombing of an area of conflict is not feasible (such as during the 1994 Rwandan genocide).

The costs of any intervention can be, and generally are, enormous. First and foremost, intervention involves the potential and actual loss of lives of troops. Second, an intervention that goes poorly, involves the loss of even a small number of a nation's troops, and/or becomes prolonged due to one reason or another, could become highly unpopular at home, and result in political costs, including the plummeting of a leader's popularity and/or losses at the election booth. Any intervention is complicated for it not only involves trying to save the lives of innocents but quelling the violence of those intent on creating havoc and mass murder at all costs. Genocide carried out under the cover of war makes an intervention just that much more complicated. There is also the possibility that adjacent nations to a country and/or its allies may enter the fray or interfere in a way that makes the task at hand more difficult or dangerous. Likewise, there is always the potential for massive numbers of people either being forced from their homes or fleeing out of sheer fear, thus creating huge IDP camps or cross-border refugee camps where people must be cared for (provided with food, water, housing, and protection). Even those interventions with a Chapter VII mandate may face situations where the force is outgunned and outmanned.

In the first article ("Policies of Militarized Humanitarian Intervention") in this section, Thomas Weiss and Cindy Collins provide a solid overview of the complicated nature of interventions. They discuss, for example, the sticky question surrounding the decision to intervene or not; the major role the UN Security Council plays in this matter (and particularly the Permanent Five members—the United States, the United Kingdom, France, Russia, and China—who hold veto power, where a single veto can cancel a potential intervention); the motives that move individual nations to support and/or take part in an intervention or not; phases of an intervention; and trends in "militarized intervention."

In "Economic Sanctions and Genocide: Too Little, Too Late, and Sometimes Too Much," George A. Lopez discusses a host of key issues regarding the efficacy of sanctions in relation to preventing a potential genocide. He succinctly examines the issues surrounding the 1994 Rwandan genocide and the Yugoslav crisis in the 1990s. He also raises the question as to whether the imposition of sanctions can be genocidal by examining the sanctions imposed on Saddam Hussein's regime in Iraq. Finally, in discussing the future of sanctions dealing with genocide, he examines the potential of financial sanctions, arms embargoes, and travel and international participation bans.

Francis Kofi Abiew provides a succinct overview of the controversial intervention by India during the course of the Bangladesh genocide in "The East Pakistan (Bangladesh) Intervention of 1971." In addition to providing historical background *vis-à-vis* India's and Pakistan's strained relationship after the 1947 partitioning of India and the subsequent birth of Pakistan, he provides information about the cause and extent of the atrocities perpetrated in East Pakistan, India's rationale for conducting the intervention, and the uproar that erupted over India's intervention.

Next in "Vietnam's Intervention in Cambodia (Kampuchea), 1978," Abiew discusses Vietnam's highly controversial intervention in Kampuchea during the course of the Khmer Rouge's genocide (1975–1979) perpetrated against their fellow Cambodians. He succinctly discusses the background of the Cambodian genocide, the UN Security Council debate that ensued following the intervention, and the controversy that surrounds the intervention to this day.

"Against the Grain: The East Timor Intervention," by James Cotton, presents a detailed account of the unique Australian-led 1999 intervention in East Timor in an attempt to stanch ongoing human rights abuses that many feared could escalate into genocide. Among the numerous issues discussed are: precedents for intervention in Asia; the background and rationale behind the intervention; the role of different actors (including but not limited to the United Nations, Australia, and the United States); and lessons learned from the intervention in East Timor.

In "Reflections on the Legality and Legitimacy of NATO'S Intervention in Kosovo," Nicholas J. Wheeler discusses the highly controversial 1999 NATO intervention in Kosovo. The intervention was undertaken *without* the imprimatur of the United Nations, and was largely carried out *via* bombing, with no ground support. The result, ironically, was that hundreds of thousands of Kosovar Albanians were forced from their homes by the Serbs, which was the Serbs' original intention. Ultimately, though, the victors claim, nearly one million of Kosovo's displaced persons returned to Kosovo and Slobodan Milosevic was forced out. Among the questions that have arisen about the intervention are: Was the intervention legitimate? What impact did the intervention have on the role of the UN in regard to its role in maintaining world peace? And could the intervention lead to other such interventions, where a regional organization, a group of nations, or a single nation decides to carry out its own intervention without consulting or gaining the imprimatur of the United Nations? Wheeler discusses many of the aforementioned issues, as well as the contested legality of humanitarian intervention, NATO's justification for its use of force in Kosovo, and whether or not "a new solidarism norm of international intervention" has evolved among members of the international community.

## 9.1   Thomas G. Weiss and Cindy Collins, "Policies of Militarized Humanitarian Intervention"

*War is not neat. It's not tidy. It's a mess.*

—Admiral William Crowe, 1990

Humanitarian assistance alone cannot provide adequate protection to noncombatants who are specifically targeted by belligerents. Deployment of multinational military forces may be required to protect humanitarian activities, facilitate the delivery of emergency assistance, and insulate and protect a given geographical area or people from the effects of armed conflict and violence. As Sadako Ogata, the U.N. High Commissioner for Refugees, has argued:

> The threat of force, and the will to use it, becomes indispensable where consensual arrangements have no chance of success. Enforcement is a critical issue. It may complicate the arduous efforts of conflict mediators. It may undermine neutrality and engender risks for impartial humanitarian action, but are strict neutrality and effective protection not often incompatible? Humanitarian responses should serve first of all the protection of people.[1]

A military intervention, if it occurs, is the product of political negotiations among the Security Council's five permanent members (P-5), member states of regional security organizations such as NATO or the Organization of African Unity (OAU), states participating in a "coalition of the willing," or a single state's political and military elites. After a decision is reached to intervene, a second political process begins to ensure a commitment from United Nations member states to provide necessary resources and personnel. Success in the first political process does not ensure success in the second. For example, in 1994 the Security Council unanimously decided that 5,500 peacekeepers were urgently needed in Rwanda; it took six months for the member states to provide troops, even though 19 governments had pledged to keep some 30,000 troops on a stand-by basis for U.N. peacekeeping.

Unlike humanitarian agencies that respond to humanitarian crises with standard, predictable policy responses, the U.N. Security Council, regional organizations, and individual states determine on a case-by-case basis whether there will be a militarized intervention and what the character of that intervention will be. This chapter explores factors that determine whether an intervention is approved and the challenges of implementing policies. It also describes changes in the character of humanitarian interventions during the first post–Cold War decade, the 1990s.

## The Decision to Intervene

U.N. Charter provisions on the maintenance of international peace and security are the basis of peacekeeping and enforcement operations through the U.N. Security Council (UNSC). The UNSC is the primary forum and authority for discussing the political aspects of a potential intervention. Through its resolutions the council establishes a peace support operation, designs its mandates (including all required revisions and extensions thereto), and authorizes the deployment of troops as well as any subsequent increase or reduction in troop strength as the situation demands.

### Security Council Decisionmaking

Game theory and liberal institutionalism provide two theoretical frameworks for understanding Security Council decisionmaking. Game theory maintains that the P-5 members are rational, power-seeking actors with complete and perfect information, who are involved in a process of negotiation with other members. In the words of P. Terrence Hopmann, the members are in a "situation of interdependent decisionmaking, where each must make decisions and where the outcome for the parties is not exclusively under their own control, but is a result of their joint decisions."[2] Decisions to mandate a particular peace operation must not contradict the perceived interests of each member. Using the concept of "nested games," one can show how a P-5 member may use the threat of its veto of a peace operation desired by others to achieve its gains in another arena—for example, in World Trade Organization (WTO) negotiations. The behavior of China on the Security Council provides the most transparent example of a bargaining party exchanging votes for payoffs. In November 1990—one day after China abstained on Resolution 678, which authorized the use of force against Iraq—the Bush administration invited the Chinese foreign minister to Washington. This was the first high-level exchange since the Tiananmen Square massacre. Four days later, Washington helpfully abstained on a World Bank vote allocating, for the first time since Tiananmen, an international development loan to China for purposes other than "basic human needs."[3] In contrast, NATO's sidestepping of U.N. approval in the Kosovo crisis diminished the ability of China as well as Russia, which rejected NATO intervention, to veto intervention or to gain in another arena in exchange for an abstaining vote.

A primary criticism of the game theory model for Security Council decisionmaking is that it is contextually insensitive to the influence of institutional rules, procedures, and norms that assist in redefining or expanding interests and stimulating new ideas. Game theory focuses primarily upon given preferences and perceptions without asking about their origins.

In contrast, liberal institutionalism argues that environment and organizational structures mediate between narrowly defined interests and behavior and can influence and even transform actors' conceptions of what constitutes vital interests. A hypothesis generated by such a model would maintain that if each permanent member has no substantial reason to reject a U.N. intervention, then the decision to issue a mandate may be governed by a feeling of obligation to the more idealized notion of collective responsibility outlined in the U.N. Charter.

A link between game theory and institutionalism is the dependency of actors on information concerning the conflict (the reduction of uncertainty) and the probabilities of successfully meeting the objectives outlined in a proposed mandate (the measure of risk and cost). Whether one explains Security Council deliberations as negotiations among autonomous, rational actors pursuing individual national interests or as a collective response by institutionally conditioned representatives of a public good called "international peace and security," the sources and the credibility of information, as well as the privilege given certain data over others, influence both the issue of a mandate and its content.

The case of Rwanda illustrates the need for future investigation into information pathways and processing. Shortly before the genocide began, the U.N. secretariat received varied information from two sources: The U.N. Special Representative of the Secretary-General (SRSG) to Rwanda cabled that there was tension in Kigali. On the same day, the commanding officer of the United Nations Assistance Mission for Rwanda (UNAMIR) sent a cable describing a reign of terror permeating the city. The secretary-general accepted the first interpretation of activities, and the wave of genocide commenced less than one month later.[4] One possible explanation for the primacy given one cable over the other is cognitive bias: That is, decisionmakers tend to look for information that supports what they would like to see happen, in view of their personal and professional interests.

The procedures by which humanitarian crises are placed on the agenda of the Security Council also partially explain why certain crises are not addressed immediately or are never addressed. The Security Council can manipulate the presentation of events: The provisional agenda for the Security Council's consideration is drawn up by the secretary-general and approved by the president of the council. Titles of items on the agenda can be altered so as to be less objectionable to particular P-5 members and potentially less demanding of Security Council action. As described by Sydney Bailey, the most noted authority on U.N. Security Council procedures: "In addition to proposals to vary the wording of items, which are usually adopted without a vote, the Council has voted on motions to include an item in, or delete an item from, the agenda; to include an item in the agenda but to postpone consideration; to add an item not included in the Provisional Agenda; to confirm or change the order of items; to combine two or more items; and to adopt or reject the Provisional Agenda as a whole."[5]

## Regional Organizations and Coalitions of the Willing

As will be discussed later in this chapter, the Security Council became more reluctant to authorize new U.N. peace support operations as the 1990s drew to a close. Usually under the auspices of the United Nations, regional organizations (such as NATO and the OAU security group) and ad hoc coalitions of individual states with an interest in a conflict's outcome (also referred to as "coalitions of the willing") became the operational commanders and financiers for peace support operations requiring force.

Distinctions must be noted between U.N. peacekeeping forces and multinational forces authorized by the Security Council. U.N. peacekeeping operations are under the direct operational control of the United Nations, although each national contingent follows the command of its own national commanders. Such operations are established after there is a demonstrated commitment to peace by the warring parties. The cost of a U.N. peacekeeping operation is shared among all U.N. member states. Peace support operations conducted by a regional organization or coalition of the willing are under the operational control of a lead nation, do not require a demonstrated commitment to peace by the parties, and are undertaken at the cost of those states carrying out the operation. The Security Council may yield to other parties in the conduct of peace support operations because of its reluctance to be involved in messy, costly crises or because of dissent in the form of a veto (for example, Kosovo).

Chapter VIII of the U.N. Charter allows for regional arrangements deemed necessary to restore stability. Incentives for regional involvement are strong. The flow of refugees into neighboring countries is usually economically unsettling and can bring about or exacerbate social unrest. Wars disrupt normal patterns of trade, which might be distorted further if economic sanctions are imposed. Personal contacts among regional leaders are usually intense, if not always warm. Shortcomings of regional collective action include the fact that regional blocs of power and influence routinely require a regional hegemonic power to lead a collective response to political and social instability and to humanitarian needs.

The North Atlantic Treaty Organization has proven a viable alternative to the UNSC as a forum for initiating peace support operations, although its mission statement restricts NATO's actions to the enhancement of security and stability among its 19 members and through the Euro-Atlantic area.

Since the end of the Cold War, NATO has been restructured to adapt to peacekeeping and crisis management tasks undertaken in cooperation with countries that are not members of the alliance as well as with IGOs. Although humanitarian intervention in the former Yugoslavia has benefited from NATO's restructuring, the alliance's internal adaptation is guided primarily by the fundamental objectives of ensuring its military effectiveness, preserving the transatlantic link, and increasing security burden-sharing among NATO members. Humanitarian intervention is, in a sense, a way for NATO to fine-tune its internal adaptations and evolving command structure. NATO is striving for flexibility in its ability to generate forces to conduct a full range of alliance missions and to operate seamlessly in multinational and joint formations.

African peacekeeping increased in the latter half of the 1990s because of the growing unwillingness of external powers to expose their forces to uncontrollable violence in places like Somalia, Rwanda, and Sierra Leone. In lieu of non-African forces directly engaging in African crises, Western funding has been increased to West and Central African troop-contributing countries. The United States established the African Crisis Response Initiative (ACRI) in late 1996 to organize and train an African peacekeeping team. Congress allocated $35 million for ACRI's start-up costs. The initial training focuses on the development of soldier skills for peacekeeping, working with refugees and humanitarian organizations, and observing human rights.

Unlike NATO's peace support operations or coalitions of the willing, such as the Australian-led intervention in East Timor in late 1999, African peacekeeping suffers from the deep involvement of troop-contributing countries in the hostilities, on one side of the conflict or the other. Decisions to intervene may be based upon a contributing country's political objectives or opportunity for economic gain. Traditional humanitarian principles of impartiality or neutrality may be totally absent.

### State Decisionmaking

The perspectives of traditional realists and structural institutionalists can provide interpretations of why states decide to contribute material and troops. A traditional realist approach argues that a state participates when it is in its perceived national interest to do so. The state is seen as a rational, autonomous, and unitary actor capable of behaving strategically out of self-interest, regardless of bureaucratic restraints or the preferences of civil society. In contrast, structural institutionalism argues that barriers in structures and processes may prevent or may facilitate state participation even if dominant political elites hold an opposing view. A research design following a structural-institutionalist approach would examine in a systematic manner the organization of the military, peace operations funding, the political system, the organization of the state, and the state's position in the international system.[6] The organization of a state's military is a critical factor. Is the military conscripted, and are there special forces trained for low-conflict environments? Is there interservice competition? Do promotion procedures provide an incentive to the military for involvement in peace operations? Are existing military doctrine and training conducive to peace operations? To what extent do military elites influence or control foreign policy?

Organization in a national capital identifies which agency will bear the cost of participation, and decides whether the reimbursement from the United Nations adequately offsets the cost of participation. Organization of the state identifies the internal state apparatus responsible for peace-keeping and decisionmaking, and for the operationalization of executive strategies. Organization of the political system identifies the influence exerted on state decisionmaking by the structure of representation, electoral practices, networks of organized political parties, and NGOs' advising and pressuring of governments to support peace operations.

## Phases of Intervention

Decisions to intervene tend to follow a series of relatively predictable phases—from neutral, purely humanitarian operations guided primarily by the mission statements and mandates of U.N. agencies, through Chapter VI efforts at resolution by peaceful means, and if necessary, the use of force under Chapter VII of the U.N. Charter.

During the first phase, certain NGOs and U.N. organizations operate within a country with the consent of its government (if one exists), providing food, shelter, water, and medicine to victims of natural disasters, growing political instability, and forced displacement of communities. When violence escalates, other NGOs and U.N. agencies are called upon by their constituents and governing bodies to deploy relief personnel to the area. Attempts at the pacific settlement of disputes, as outlined in Chapter VI of the U.N. Charter, may run in tandem with humanitarian action. Consent by the government to the presence of humanitarian personnel generally has been negotiated, although often heavily conditioned. If a ceasefire or other agreement has been negotiated, U.N. peacekeepers also may be deployed to the area to monitor compliance.

However, if consent to assist the most vulnerable is not forthcoming or is so heavily conditioned that humanitarian assistance cannot be administered without tilting the political balance in favor of one of the belligerents, humanitarians then consider whether to withdraw or limit operations as the Security Council contemplates more forceful measures. If the lives of humanitarian personnel and peacekeepers are targeted, the Security Council may move from Chapter VI to Chapter VII. A stream of decisionmaking takes place at various levels and within various institutions as violence escalates and populations are put at greater risk or begin migrating to unstable neighboring areas or countries. Development NGOs must decide when to ask for relief assistance; relief personnel must decide when to ask for diplomatic and peacekeeping assistance; and the Security Council must determine how and at what point it becomes necessary to move toward force and away from traditional diplomacy, impartiality, and political neutrality. Additional questions follow: What tools of Chapter VII should be employed—such as economic, communications, and diplomatic sanctions and the use of force by land, sea, and air—and how will they affect relief efforts and personnel? Should the level of force be proportional to the force exerted by the warring parties upon noncombatants? Or is it better to dismiss caution and overwhelm belligerents?

Economic sanctions and overwhelming air campaigns, used as tools of intervention, have been widely criticized by humanitarians. Chapter VII allows for economic sanctions against the accused. The logic of economic sanctions is that they create pain and suffering in the lowest strata of society, which within time will percolate upward to the governing authority and bring about policy changes or perhaps a change in regime. Economic sanctions often are applied in knee-jerk reaction, regardless of the fact that authoritarian regimes are not accountable to civil society and are not affected by the pain and suffering of noncombatants. Indeed, there is little evidence to suggest that civilian pain leads to political gain. In the words of Boutros Boutros-Ghali: "Sanctions, as is generally recognized, are a blunt instrument. They raise the ethical question of whether suffering inflicted on vulnerable groups in the target country is a legitimate means of exerting pressure on political leaders whose behaviour is unlikely to be affected by the plight of their subjects."[7] Moreover, repressive governments may even be strengthened by sanctions because they can mobilize local support to counteract targeting by outsiders—a kind of "martyr" or "rally-around-the-flag" effect that plucks the most shrill nationalist chords. To counter the effects of economic sanctions on the most vulnerable populations, humanitarian agencies are then called upon to increase assistance. The effects of sanctions and humanitarian assistance in many ways cancel each other out, and at a high price. Economic sanctions—in Iraq and Haiti, for example—hurt most those whom the international community was supposedly trying to help (women, children, the sick, and the elderly) and left targeted regimes and elites ensconced in power.[8]

The diplomacy and subsequent military action approved by the Security Council were decisive in reversing Iraqi aggression against Kuwait and Iraq's own Kurdish population. But the combination of previous and ongoing economic sanctions against Iraq from 1989 and into the twenty-first century has yielded immense suffering among Iraqis. U.N. Security Council Resolution 661 was the first of numerous calls for economic sanctions against Iraq. Although food and medicine earmarked for humanitarian efforts were exempted, the process by which shipments must be inspected before entry into Iraq created a critical lag in the delivery of relief supplies and aggravated human suffering.

Economic sanctions also create hardships for nondisplaced locals whose livelihood is hindered or completely eliminated by the consequences of sanctions. For example, sanctions against Serbia in the Bosnian crisis affected the ability of host families caring for roughly 95 percent of incoming refugees from Bosnia and Croatia to support themselves. One study concluded that "90 percent of the resident Serbian population . . . was unable to meet basic food needs."[9] By the time the Dayton Accords were signed in 1995, Serbia had received some 550,000 refugees, including 250,000 Bosnian Serbs who had fled the war in Bosnia-Herzegovina in 1992 and 300,000 Croat Serbs who had escaped the conflict in Croatia in 1991 and 1995. Thousands more Kosovar Serbs and gypsies became the responsibility of the Yugoslav government in 1999.

Air campaigns are similarly indiscriminate and therefore tend to be ineffective. Overwhelming air bombardments, such as those on Baghdad in 1991 and on Belgrade in 1999, are undertaken because they present a relatively low risk of mortality in comparison with peace-keeping forces. "Surgical strikes" is the term frequently used to describe the military's intent to directly target and hit military-related sites during militarized humanitarian missions. During the Gulf Crisis, the term was used widely by the media as television screens showed real-time film footage of U.S. missiles going through the front doors of the Iraqi military command. However, the visuals misled the public into believing that massive high-tech weaponry was infallible and could discriminate between combatants and noncombatants. The bombing of a Baghdad air raid shelter and the subsequent deaths of hundreds of Iraqi women and children who had sought safety there was not given much coverage by the media.

However, the NATO air campaign against Serbia in 1999 confirmed to many that coercive diplomacy in the form of an overwhelming air campaign may be the only alternative to halting massive violations of human rights. This campaign was described by many as the first "humanitarian war."[10]

The case studies provide examples in which there was ambiguity within and between mandates over when to move from diplomacy to force. From the beginning of Chapter VII action in the Bosnian crisis, proportionality of force was the strategy. Its ineffectiveness was obvious and left uncorrected until the Croatian offensive and NATO attacks in August 1995. Within four months of the use of overwhelming force by a Croatian-Bosnian alliance and NATO air strikes, a peace agreement was signed. Many argue that the years of diplomatic negotiations produced nothing but borrowed time for war criminals and unnecessary loss of life. As one close collaborator of the U.N. secretary-general put it, "It is extremely difficult to make war and peace with the same people on the same territory at the same time."[11]

A distinction must be made, however, between the use of force and the display of force, Somalia being a striking example of the latter. The display of force in that country was overwhelming, particularly initially; but the use of force was at first constrained and later underwhelming (total withdrawal), when it became clear that 25,000 soldiers could not capture one warlord and that outside soldiers would have to be casualties in order to bring about stability in the failed state. "Mission creep" is a catchphrase used by the military to describe unwanted divergence from an operation's original mandate. Critics of military performance and fecklessness argue that the armed forces do not understand the difference between mission creep and flexibility. Cynics argue that military reluctance to incur casualties—the so-called Somalia syndrome—has led to "mission cringe."

At present, movement from Chapter VI to Chapter VII—and frequently, back again—often introduces contradictory actions that can cancel each other out or even inflate the degree of suffering among noncombatants. Mandates and strategies are further complicated when Chapter VI and Chapter VII actions are used simultaneously (as in the former Yugoslavia) or alternated (as in Rwanda). Chapter VI is theoretically impartial and neutral; Chapter VII makes a highly political statement regarding which belligerent is at fault and must be brought back into line by concentrated and coercive actions of the international community—first by sanctions, and if sanctions are ineffective, then by military force. Humanitarian practitioners also have failed to integrate into their operational philosophies the basic incompatibility between their traditional operational principles (impartiality and neutrality) and the requirements of working in a war zone where Chapter VII actions are in effect. Chapter VII is anything but impartial and neutral. It is the only instance in the world organization's constitution in which finger-pointing is condoned and blame is attached to decisions. To try to preserve a traditional humanitarian stance within a Chapter VII operation is to force what is definitely a square peg into a round hole.

Mandate ambiguity is understandable, given that the Security Council's P-5 members attempt to negotiate a resolution that is politically agreeable among themselves, and not necessarily one that is operationally or tactically feasible. This is one reason why P-5 discussions regarding an intervention are held behind closed doors and are not recorded.

Undeniably, there is an inherent contradiction in the Security Council's acting as manager of international security. Ongoing strains between legitimacy and efficiency reflect a general tension between absolute duties and relative interests. The paradox is that to find legitimacy, "military intervention must be based on universal principles, while its implementation depends on a particular constellation of power and interests."[12]

In sum, powerful state interests are negotiated during discussions of whether to intervene. The compromises and constraints woven into the decision emerge in the mandate's architecture. The resulting ambiguity in mandate, in turn, is reflected in confusion in the field and ineffective protection of noncombatants. Mandate ambiguity is less likely to be found in operations led by a single state or regional organization with strong objectives. The protection of Kurds in northern Iraq, an effort led by the United States in Operation Provide Comfort; the stabilization of the crisis in Rwanda, led by France in Opération Turquoise; and NATO's bombing of Serbia in 1999 are three examples of clear intent, coordinated implementation, and commitment of adequate military means. In northern Iraq and Kosovo, in particular, the willingness to maintain a secure environment for the Kurds and Kosovars, respectively, was present and remains today with NATO air power poised to respond in both cases as it has in the past.

## Recent Trends in Militarized Humanitarian Intervention

An upsurge in the frequency of U.N. peace support operations immediately followed the end of the Cold War (three operations commenced within a two-month period in 1992); peaked in 1993, in terms of the number of peacekeepers deployed (78,744), and in 1994, in terms of U.N. peacekeeping expenditures ($3.5 billion). By the decade's end, the operational command and execution of peace support operations had shifted more toward regional organizations—a shift that is supported by Article VIII of the U.N. Charter and by U.N. critics who charge that the United Nations is not operationally or politically capable of mounting an unambiguous, consistent, and successful intervention campaign. A comparison of U.N. peacekeeping troop contributions between 1993 and 1999 illustrates the diminished U.N. military presence.[13]

The decline in U.N.-led militarized operations is attributable to real and perceived failures during the early to mid-1990s. Operational planners relied on Security Council mandates and state policymakers to provide a conceptual framework for understanding the material and personnel requirements for a peace support operation. The humanitarian interventions of the early 1990s took place largely without conceptual guidance, clear and feasible mandates, flexible rules of engagement, or explicit definitions of the conditions under which missions would be terminated. In the absence of conceptual mooring and the presence of increasingly violent and complicated conflicts, operational institutions and personnel struggled with designing practical plans for constantly changing environments of which they had very little knowledge and experience; coordinating among multinational contingents, key humanitarian agencies and relief personnel; and resolving command and control issues.

Along with political elites, military commanders from major powers have lost confidence in the ability of the United Nations to lead a multinational effort in a potentially volatile environment. As the success of recent NATO actions has demonstrated, alternative force structures, such as NATO or a coalition of interested states, may be preferable, leaving U.N.-led force structures to conduct only those operations with a low risk of escalation in violence. The most consistent recommendation from peacekeeping observers is that the United Nations concentrate on improving its real capabilities—essentially, activities closer to Chapter VI than to Chapter VII. It should focus its energy on developing "peace packages" comprising peacemaking, peacekeeping, and peace-building activities in the context of nonviolent, consent-based operations. Some believe that the United Nations should attempt to regain the trust of states by building a portfolio of successes in low-risk environments. In this scenario, the organization would reinforce existing low-risk instruments for peace, such as observer missions. All of these recommendations, of course, are based on relatively untested assumptions about what ails the U.N. system and begin with the belief that there is a strong association between structural problems at U.N. headquarters and performance in the field.

Field-level problems highlight the inadequacies of political decisions and planning strategies. Common implementation problems of the early to mid-1990s can be found in military after-action reports and in case studies that emphasize a host of tactical issues.

In northern Iraq, implementation efforts were constrained by the hostility of the Iraqi government toward the Kurds, the isolated terrain, the weakness of the United Nations, and the absence of alternatives for the Kurds, who could neither return home nor remain permanently in camps. Additional constraints were the pace of U.N. mobilization, the narrowness of NGO mandates, and the difficulty of protecting relief personnel. Although the United Nations could improve its procurement and deployment mechanisms and supply greater protection to NGOs in the field, it can do little to ensure the long-term viability of the politically fragmented Kurdish population. There can be no exit strategy from the safe havens in northern Iraq.

After-action reports from the crisis in Somalia highlight the first experiences of U.S. military forces in true cooperation with nonstate actors. The U.S. military did not understand U.N., NGO, or ICRC mandates, due to its lack of formal training in civilian resources and organizational mandates. As time passed and experience accumulated in military-NGO cooperation, learning occurred.

Positive and negative experiences of military and humanitarian collaboration in Rwanda were reported by various NGOs and U.N. agencies. There were three joint military-humanitarian phases: the multilateral peacekeeping forces of UNAMIR during the worst wave of genocide; the French unilateral security action and the U.S. Support Hope humanitarian action; and the national military contingents involved in humanitarian activities under UNHCR invitation and direction. The designated functions of military units during the Rwandan crisis were to provide a secure environment for humanitarian activities, to assist humanitarians, and to carry out various relief activities on their own.

Because UNAMIR troops did not have the mandate to use force except in self-defense, they were unable to provide a secure environment for victims and humanitarian personnel—a task in which military contingents supposedly have a comparative advantage. Only French troops in Opération Turquoise proved capable of fostering a secure environment, but not without heavy criticism from French NGOs that viewed the military's show of force as undermining their ability to deal with all victims impartially. Even after the humanitarian emergency had stabilized, more humanitarian organizations had arrived on the scene, and troop operations had wound down, some NGOs maintained their distance from military units performing strictly humanitarian activities. Dutch NGOs, such as MSF-Holland, which were thankful for Dutch military transport to Goma, nevertheless maintained the view that the presence of the military compromised their organizations' humanitarian mandate. Many others, however, praised the professional working relationship between the military and humanitarians. Irish soldiers made the task easier by wearing T-shirts and carrying no weapons while assisting NGOs; the Irish government, unlike wealthier countries, also provided its military personnel at no cost to the relief organizations. The cost of UNAMIR was $162 million. The official figure for Opération Turquoise is about $200 million, and that for Operation Support Hope, about $135 million, although unofficial tallies are much higher—some, four or five times greater.[14]

The positive aspects of military-humanitarian collaboration in Rwanda included the military's financial, technical, and logistical capacity; its "can-do" approach; its ability to attract media and public attention to human tragedy; and its focus on evaluation of performance once tasks were completed. On the negative side, military units were less willing than humanitarians to take risks (the Japanese troops, for example, refused to work inside refugee camps for security reasons, and some U.S. troops were not allowed to leave the Kigali airport); contingency planning did not occur until the last moment; and the timetable of military involvement was problematic (humanitarian personnel were reluctant to form working relationships with military units not scheduled to remain in the area for long). Perhaps the clearest lesson concerned physical protection: Here, unilateral action was more effective than action under U.N. command and control.

The failures of past interventions have made the international humanitarian system more cautious. The chronology of events, and the tools used by international humanitarian actors in the crisis in East Timor in late 1999 may be indicative of a new pattern of crisis escalation and third-party interventions that could continue in the twenty-first century.

Indonesia used its military might to integrate East Timor as an Indonesian province in 1975. With the diplomatic help of the United Nations, on May 5, 1999, Indonesia and Portugal (a former administrator of East Timor) agreed to allow the East Timorese to vote on whether to accept special autonomy within Indonesia or to seek complete independence. The "popular consultation" with the East Timorese required, first, the registration of voters, followed by the actual vote. On August 30, 1999, some 98 percent of registered voters went to the polls and decided by a margin of 21.5 percent to 78.5 percent to seek complete independence. Following is a chronology of the massive humanitarian and human rights abuses conducted by pro-autonomy militias against the pro-independence population and the corresponding responses by the international humanitarian system.

In 1975, Indonesian troops landed in East Timor and declared it the 27th province of Indonesia. The U.N. Security Council and General Assembly call for Indonesia to withdraw and to respect East Timor's territorial integrity and the inalienable right of its people to self-determination. From 1975 to 1999, the East Timorese independence movement received no assistance from the international system except for informal consultations in which diplomatic pressure was the only tool of persuasion. Not until April 1998 did the U.N. Commission on Human Rights publicly note its deep concern over reports of human rights violations in East Timor. In December 1998, the U.N. secretary-general issued a public statement underlining the need for stability and peace in the territory.

Indonesian president Bacharuddin Habibie indicated in a public statement in January 1999 that his government might be prepared to consider independence for East Timor. Diplomatic talks among the parties followed in New York. Indonesia accepted sole responsibility for the protection of East Timorese throughout the process leading to a popular consultation. The May 5 agreements, which called for a popular consultation, were followed two days later by Security Council Resolution 1236, which stressed the Indonesian government's responsibility for ensuring the safety and security of international staff and observers. Resolution 1246 of June established the U.N. Administrative Mission in East Timor (UNAMET), an international group of 900 U.N. staff members, including 270 unarmed civilian police, who would carry out duties related to the popular consultation. UNAMET also employed 4,000 locals during its stay.

From January to August 30, 1999, intimidation and violence against pro-independence supporters increased dramatically. Indonesian military, police, and militia forces became engaged in a campaign of terror. A pattern of massive involuntary displacement began. Reports of killings in pro-independence villages increased. Serious militia attacks occurred on the UNAMET regional office and a humanitarian convoy accompanied by a UNAMET humanitarian affairs officer and a local representative of the UNHCR.

The only international responses to clear indications of humanitarian and human rights abuses were statements by the Security Council, demanding an immediate halt to the violence; by the U.N. secretary-general, who made public the continued challenge to security by armed civilian groups most probably trained by the Indonesian military, and the urgent problem of internal displacement; and by humanitarian and human rights agencies, asking the Indonesian authorities to make good on their pledge to investigate attacks and bring justice to those responsible. UNAMET's call for the removal of Indonesian army officers who were associated with militia activities could not be backed by force.

One week before the popular vote, the Security Council was briefed on the unsettling security situation in East Timor. However, the Security Council and the West were preoccupied with Kosovo, and the council's only response was to issue a statement expressing strong concern. The unarmed UNAMET civilian police requested additional security measures and received verbal assurances from Indonesia that it would protect voters.

On voting day, seven polling stations were temporarily shut down due to violence, and a local U.N. staff member was fatally stabbed. Two days after the vote, militia members attacked pro-independence supporters outside the UNAMET compound. UNAMET headquarters soon became a refuge for frightened journalists and several hundred IDPs. The response of the Security Council and the secretary-general was to produce statements urging the Indonesian authorities to exercise their responsibility to the people. The murders of more local UNAMET staff members followed.

When the votes were tallied and independence was declared to the people's choice, a militia rampage began. The U.N. High Commissioner of Human Rights begged the Security Council to deploy international or regional forces. The secretary-general initiated high-level talks with governments that might have an interest in mounting and supporting an international force and with the Indonesian government to obtain the latter's consent to an international presence.

While talks were in progress, militiamen attacked the compound of the International Committee of the Red Cross. The U.N. began its withdrawal of UNAMET personnel, in whose defense the secretary-general remarked that the "situation has clearly got far beyond what a small mission, which was sent to organize the popular vote and never equipped or mandated to enforce law and order, can possibly be expected to cope with."[15]

By the time President Habibie agreed to accept international assistance to restore peace and security in East Timor (September 12, 1999) and the Security Council voted to set up a multinational force acting under Chapter VII of the U.N. Charter (Resolution 1264, September 15, 1999) to be led by Australia, the humanitarian disaster in East Timor was of catastrophic proportions. Nearly two-thirds of the population had fled their homes and were dependent upon humanitarian assistance. The estimate of funds needed to care for the IDPs over a six-month period was $135.5 million; the World Food Programme estimated that 740,000 East Timorese would require food aid for that period. Before the escalation in violence following the vote, the UNHCR had organized aid convoys only for an estimated 60,000 IDPs. The threat of malaria also was of great concern as the rainy season was soon to commence and there was a lack of medical supplies and personnel due to the intimidation of relief workers by militia forces and common criminals. IDPs who had fled to the countryside could not be reached due to lack of security.

The limits of U.N. protection are clear in this case. The United Nations has no standing military force or assets. It cannot deploy troops or equipment rapidly. Months may pass before the secretary-general can persuade governments to contribute personnel and material. No government was willing to offer troops for an early U.N. intervention, especially without the consent of Indonesia, which ironically and tragically was responsible for the emergency. The U.N. budget is extremely limited and requires a coalition of the willing to assume responsibility for their own costs in exchange for the freedom to exercise control within another government's territory under the authority and legitimacy of the United Nations. While the U.N. secretary-general and member states work the phones, humanitarian and human rights personnel must work the field without any meaningful form of protection for themselves or those who they are trying to assist.

Given the above scenario, vulnerable populations are completely dependent upon their own forms of self-defense for protection and upon the international humanitarian system for food, health care, and shelter. Justice comes only after the conflict is over, if at all. In the case of East Timor, the Commission on Human Rights has requested that the secretary-general establish a committee to investigate human rights violations throughout the territory.

In the early 1990s, it was widely thought that the media could influence the Security Council and member states to act quickly and responsibly. Those heady days of optimism are past, although the media remains a factor in accelerating certain decisionmaking processes. In the early 1990s, some thought that a U.N. standing army could be created that would respond to humanitarian crises before the numbers of refugees, IDPs, dead, and dying mounted, and that the further development of early warning systems would increase the speed with which a protection force could be deployed. These ideas appear to be mistaken. To all indications, there is already an abundance of early warnings, and no one is caught off guard by the outbreak of humanitarian and human rights catastrophes; yet the speed of organized responses has not accelerated.

It has become increasingly clear that protection is extremely problematic in most humanitarian crises. If the international system of states cannot effectively provide protection to vulnerable populations suffering from extreme humanitarian and human rights abuses, then NGOs, commonly referred to as members of international civil society, must work harder before protection becomes necessary.

The challenge, thus, is what has commonly been referred to as "development education." This is a task of NGOs that is distinct from their assistance and protection efforts in war zones but that may in fact be more critical in the long run, helping alter attitudes and preferences in order to attack silent emergencies. This book is focused almost exclusively on the targets of operational NGOs (the victims of war); but the targets of educational and advocacy NGOs (their contributors, the public, and national decisionmakers) are just as important. Educational NGOs seek primarily to influence citizens, whose voices are then registered through public opinion and bear fruit in the form of additional resources for NGOs' activities as well as for new policies, better decisions, and on occasion, enhanced international regimes. Educational NGOs often play a leading role in promoting the various "days," "years," and "decades" that the U.N. system regularly proclaims. Nongovernmental organizations can reinforce the norms promoted by intergovernmental organizations through public education campaigns, which in turn can help hold states accountable to their international commitments.

Western operational NGOs are under growing pressure from their Third World partners to educate contributors and Western publics about the origins of poverty and violence. Without such efforts, one commentator remarked that "conventional NGO project activities are manifestly 'finger-in-the-dike' responses to problems that require nothing short of worldwide and whole-hearted government commitment to combat."[16] Operational activities are supported by the education of populations and the mobilization of public opinion in favor of more equitable global distribution of power and resources.

Nongovernmental organizations focusing exclusively on education in their own countries without overseas activities within at least some internal conflicts are not numerous, but they exist. The most effective educators are those with credibility, knowledge, and convictions gained from substantial operational experience or from firsthand experience with war-torn societies. Examples are Oxfam and Save the Children, whose efforts in development education are linked to the origins of poverty and injustice as well as to specific campaigns for dealing with the victims of wars like those in Bosnia and Somalia. Many NGOs have moved away from an exclusive concern with projects and toward a focus on preventing the need for relief projects in the first place through the promotion of structural change and avoidance of violent conflict. The shift is toward educating the public about its attitudes and the necessity for systemic change, and away from a preoccupation with relief. Two observers summarize the logic behind this shift, in the context of their negative views about the World Bank and the IMF: "Many of the causes of under-development lie in the political and economic structures of an unequal world . . . and in the misguided policies of governments and the multilateral institutions (such as the World Bank and IMF) which they control. It is extremely difficult, if not impossible, to address these issues in the context of the traditional NGO project."[17]

Linked to education are the related activities of NGOs working primarily in the corridors of governments and intergovernmental organizations, where international responses to internal conflicts are shaped. These advocates pursue discussions with national delegates and staff members of international secretariats in order to influence international public policy. "Lobbying" is perhaps an accurate image but an inaccurate description, because by definition *lobbying* applies only to efforts to influence legislators. In seeking to inform or alter the policies of governments as well as of governmental, intergovernmental, and nongovernmental agencies, advocacy NGOs seek to influence a wide variety of policymakers and not simply parliamentarians. Prominent examples in the humanitarian arena in the United States include the Lawyers' Committee for Human Rights, Refugees International, and the U.S. Committee for Refugees. In spite of the pertinence of advocacy NGOs, they are not numerous and have the greatest difficulty in raising funds.

A great deal of NGO advocacy in the past has been directed *against* the official policies of governments and U.N. organizations. Recently, however, many nongovernmental organizations have moved toward institutionalizing a full-fledged partnership with U.N. member states. Historically, NGOs have had some responsibility for the implementation of treaties drafted mainly by representatives of states. But now these NGOs aspire to more direct involvement in the drafting of language and in the political processes resulting in treaties. When governments or international institutions are trying to shape their responses to humanitarian emergencies in war zones, NGO views can be influential, as responses in northern Iraq, Somalia, Rwanda, Haiti, Bosnia, Kosovo, and Timor suggest. Both through formal statements in U.N. forums and informational negotiations with international civil servants and members of national delegations, advocacy NGOs seek to ensure that their views and those of their constituencies are reflected in international texts and decisions. Some offer research and drafting skills and provide scientific or polling data to support their positions. Firsthand reports and testimonies from NGO field staff also are powerful tools for influencing parliamentary committees.

## Conclusion

Complex emergencies will continue because no viable and politically acceptable solutions have been found to deal with resource scarcity, political manipulations, and adaptive measures (of which conflict is one) of economically marginalized societies incapable of competing in the world market. Moreover, decreases in private investment and development assistance leave international crisis management as the sole predictable source of external material inputs and worldwide attention—providing marginalized groups an incentive to initiate or perpetuate civil wars and other internal conflicts. Conflicts may also continue because they are profitable for certain merchants and justify the maintenance of troop levels and military budgets. There have been dramatic increases in sales of weapons from developed to developing or politically unstable countries since 1989 (for example, 41 percent of 1993 U.S. arms exports went to non-democratic regimes). Some countries justify their military expenditures by the need to develop and train for peacekeeping responses. In such an environment, the economic immigrants who are refused visas and work permits today may very well be tomorrow's refugees who are refused asylum.

Long-term development assistance, although it may appear to be the answer to many ills, is not a panacea for humanitarian problems. Although more often than not economically satisfied countries have buffers to prevent them from imploding, not all geographic areas are good candidates for sustainable development; in some locales, the environment is not sufficiently life-sustaining. Many people are affected by chronic famine resulting from the infertility of the soil and inhospitable climatic conditions, and the investment of funds in unsustainable land is inappropriate.

In some developing countries, remittances sent home by relatives working abroad are as important a source of foreign exchange as is foreign aid. As immigration laws tighten in response to domestic factors such as limited resources, social unrest, and nationalist sentiments, remittances drop and survival mechanisms kick in, including violence and crime. Demands for international humanitarian assistance are therefore expected to rise. The break-down of states and increase in humanitarian need are also rooted in privatization trends. Weak states can no longer depend upon state-to-state cooperation as a source of legitimacy. Legitimacy now frequently rests on a state's ability to provide social services. Without social services, local military forces become the preferred vehicle for confiscation and redistribution of resources.

In sum, actors following and affecting world politics know that crises will appear, whether they are prepared to address them or not. Meanwhile, changes may be occurring that will shape future possibilities for intervention. A hint at possibly desirable changes arose during the opening ceremony of the final U.N. General Assembly of the twentieth century. One of the U.N. secretary-general's more pleasurable ceremonial tasks is to open this assembly; but the secretary-general's September 1999 speech was anything but routine. The focus was on glob-alization and humanitarian intervention; but the latter touched a raw nerve, especially among representatives of developing countries. Secretary-General Kofi Annan's predecessor, Boutros Boutros-Ghali, had been indirect in pointing out, "The time of absolute and exclusive sover-eignty, however, has passed; its theory was never matched by reality."[18] Annan's language was far more direct and concrete, as he announced, "States bent on criminal behaviour [should] know that frontiers are not the absolute defence . . ., that massive and systematic violations of human rights—wherever they may take place—should not be allowed to stand."[19]

Moreover, Annan expressed the heretical view that effectively addressing abuses is more important than U.N. aggrandizement. Although he did not endorse the use of force by NATO without Security Council authorization, he stressed the importance of not standing idly by when faced with the kind of atrocities that Serbs were committing in Kosovo. In addressing "those for whom the greatest threat to the future of international order is the use of force in the absence of a Security Council mandate," the secretary-general brought up the events in Rwanda. If there had been a coalition of the willing that did not receive a council imprimatur, "should such a coalition have stood aside and allowed the horror to unfold?" In posing this rhetorical question, Annan clearly was speaking not as a bureaucrat protecting his organizational turf at all costs but as an idealist.

Why does the topic of this book, humanitarian intervention, remain so controversial? The secretary-general's speech raised hackles because a revolution is taking place in the justification for intervention: A lower threshold for the entry of international military forces into international conflicts is gaining wider acceptance, although it has not yet been canonized.

The past decade has witnessed a dramatic increase in the weight assigned humanitarian values as acceptable justification for diplomatic and military action. "In the 1990s," wrote Adam Roberts, "humanitarian issues have played a historically unprecedented role in inter-national politics."[20] On the dramatic example of the military campaign in Kosovo, Michael Ignatieff noted that "its legitimacy [depends] on what fifty years of human rights has done to our moral instincts, weakening the presumption in favor of state sovereignty, strengthening the presumption in favor of intervention when massacre and deportation become state policy."[21]

There is a persistent tendency in the discourse of international relations to juxtapose ideals with Reälpolitik. Despite the dramatic growth in the numbers and significance of trans-national actors, the principal locus of political decisions in response to the push and pull of humanitarian values is still the state. There is no compelling evidence that the state's role has been transcended within international relations in general or humanitarian affairs in particu-lar. The point is not to establish a "space of victimhood"[22] against the state but rather to get state authorities to take seriously their obligations to the individuals living within their jurisdiction. This book ultimately does not challenge the concept that states act on the basis of power and material interests, but it does show the extent to which humanitarian values have shaped perceptions of state interests among intervening states.

There is no escape from moral reasoning in international politics; but David Rieff was correct when he wrote, "Our moral ambitions have been revealed as being larger than our political, military, or even cognitive means."[23] Greater attention to humanitarian values from policymakers and practitioners has not of course brought utopia, but it has made the world a somewhat more livable place. It is inconceivable, for instance, that a responsible Western leader could have made the same argument about Kosovo that Neville Chamberlain made about Czechoslovakia. Although vigorous action was too slow in East Timor, at least the outcry over Indonesia's military and militia atrocities was immediate; and enough arms were twisted in Djakarta to permit the deployment of the Australia-led force, which was followed by the first full-fledged experiment with U.N. trusteeship.

Humanitarian values have become more central to the definition of vital interests as well as more central to the worries of thugs and war criminals. Notwithstanding the remarkably mixed record of humanitarian intervention in the 1990s, the eternal policy challenge in an eternally imperfect world is to reduce the discrepancy between rhetoric and reality. The humanitarian glass is nine-tenths empty, but perhaps readers of this volume will live to see the day when it will be half full.

## Notes

1. Sadako Ogata, "Statement to a Conference on Humanitarian Response and the Prevention of Deadly Conflict, Convened By the Carnegie Commission on the Prevention of Deadly Conflict and UNHCR," Geneva, February 1997.
2. P. Terrence Hopmann, *The Negotiation Process and the Resolution of International Conflict* (Columbia, S.C.: University of South Carolina Press, 1996), p. 26.
3. Bruce Russet, Barry O'Neill, and James Sutterlin, "Breaking the Security Council Restructuring Logjam," *Global Governance* 2, no. 1 (1996):65–80.
4. Joint Evaluation of Emergency Assistance to Rwanda, *The International Response to Conflict and Genocide: Lessons from the Rwanda Experience* (Copenhagen: Steering Committee of the Joint Evaluation of Emergency Assistance to Rwanda, March 1996).
5. Sydney D. Bailey, *The Procedure of the UN Security Council* (Oxford: Clarendon Press, 1988), p. 51.
6. Cindy Collins and Thomas G. Weiss, *An Overview and Assessment of 1989–1996 Peace Operations Publications*, Occasional Paper no. 28 (Providence, R.I.: Brown University, Thomas J. Watson Jr. Institute for International Studies, 1997), pp. 78–79.
7. Boutros Boutros-Ghali, *Supplement to an Agenda for Peace: Position Paper of the Secretary-General on the Occasion of the Fiftieth Anniversary of the United Nations* (New York: United Nations, 1995), par. 70.
8. See Thomas G. Weiss, David Cortright, George A. Lopez, and Larry Minear, eds., *Political Gain and Civilian Pain: The Humanitarian Impact of Economic Sanctions* (Boulder: Rowman & Littlefield, 1997).
9. Larry Minear, Jeffrey Clark, Roberta Cohen, Dennis Gallaghan, and Thomas G. Weiss, *Humanitarian Action in the Former Yugoslavia: The U.N.'s Role, 1991–1993*, Occasional Paper no. 18 (Providence, R.I.: Brown University, Thomas J. Watson Jr. Institute for International Studies, 1994), p. 13.
10. Adam Roberts, "NATO's 'Humanitarian War' over Kosovo," *Survival* 41, no. 3 (1999):102–123.
11. Shashi Tharoor, "The Changing Face of Peace-Keeping and Peace-Enforcement," speech presented at the International Institute for Strategic Studies meeting in Vienna, Austria, September 9, 1995, p. 10.
12. Pierre Hassner, "Beyond Nationalism and Internationalism," *Survival* 35, no. 2 (Summer 1993):61.
13. Council for a Livable World, "U.N. Peacekeeping," available at www.clw.org/pub/clw/un/troops0499.htm, April 1, 1999.
14. Larry Minear and Philippe Guillot, *Soldiers to the Rescue: Humanitarian Lessons from Rwanda* (Paris: OECD, 1996).

15. United Nations, "East Timor," available at www.un.org/peace/etimor, August 4, 1999.
16. John Clark, "Policy Influence, Lobbying, and Advocacy," in Michael Edwards and David Hulme, eds., *Making a Difference: NGOs and Development in a Changing World* (London: Earthscan, 1992), p. 199.
17. Michael Edwards and David Hulme, "Introduction," in ibid., p. 20.
18. Boutros Boutros-Ghali, *An Agenda for Peace* (New York: United Nations, 1992), para. 17.
19. Secretary-General's Speech to the 54th Session of the General Assembly, September 20, 1999.
20. Adam Roberts, "The Role of Humanitarian Issues in International Politics in the 1990s," *International Review of the Red Cross* 81, no. 833 (March 1999):19.
21. Michael Ignatieff, "Human Rights: The Midlife Crisis," *New York Review of Books* 46, no. 9 (20 May 1999):58.
22. François Debrix, "Deterritorialised Territories, Borderless Borders: The New Geography of International Medical Assistance," *Third World Quarterly* 19, no. 5 (1998):827–846.
23. David Rieff, "A New Age of Liberal Imperialism?" *World Policy Journal* 16, no. 2 (Summer 1999):3.

# 9.2   George A. Lopez, "Economic Sanctions and Genocide: Too Little, Too Late, and Sometimes Too Much"

## Introduction

Economic sanctions have become a common feature of multilateral, regional, and big-power foreign policy in the 1990s.[1] After invoking their sanctions power in only two cases during the UN's first forty-five years (Rhodesia, 1966; South Africa, 1977), the UN Security Council has imposed sanctions, both comprehensive and partial, eleven times during this decade. The cases include sanctions against Iraq (UN, 1990), the former Yugoslavia (UN and Organization for Security and Cooperation in Europe [OSCE], 1991), Libya (UN, 1992, 1993), Somalia (UN and Organization of African Unity [OAU] 1992), Liberia (UN, 1992), Haiti (Organization of American States [OAS], 1991; UN, 1993), Union for the Total Independence of Angola (UNITA) faction in Angola (UN, 1993), Rwanda (UN, 1994), the Khmer Rouge (UN, 1995), Burundi (OAU, 1996), Sierra Leone (UN and OAU, 1997). Parallel to these actions, unilateral sanction, often imposed by the United States, were imposed more than three dozen times.[2]

In many of the Security Council cases, the rationale for sanctions has been the need to respond to the occurrence of massive abuse of human rights or the potential for such abuse during brutal internal wars. Although the language of Security Council resolutions does not use the term "genocide" itself, it is fair to state that in at least two instances—that of Rwanda and the former Yugoslavia (and later, by extension, the Bosnian Serbs)—and with an eye toward such occurrences in the recent past (sanctions against the Khmer Rouge), the council has consciously used sanctions to reduce the means by which a national group can pursue genocide. A related course of action designed to thwart mass killing was pursued by the OAU's economic sanctions and border closing of Burundi in July, 1996.[3] Although these comprise a very small set of cases from which to judge, it is not an implausible claim that an international consensus exists about economic sanctions as a legitimate and effective instrument for deterring the potential for genocide, for limiting genocide as it unfolds, and for punishing a genocidal set of actors after the fact of the crime.

Yet an examination of the outcome of multilateral sanctions may lead to a somewhat different conclusion: that sanctions, not unlike other measures of international diplomacy or coercion, do little to deter genocide when it is in the offing and are ineffective at halting it when it is occurring. In this article I first present whatever plausible notions may exist for considering some particular types of sanctions as a deterrent to genocide. Next, I briefly scrutinize the cases of Rwanda and the former Yugoslavia, where sanctions were imposed as a means of condemning genocide or near-genocidal conditions. I then address the concern of some analysts and activists that sanctions against Iraq by the mid-1990s actually caused genocide. Finally, I raise the most current topic of investigation and inspiration to sanctions specialists, that of targeted "smart" sanctions as a near-future device for stifling genocidal elites.

## Can Sanctions Effectively Protect Populations Against Genocide?

To consider how sanctions might be an effective policy for protecting a population from genocide or for enhancing human rights in a nation on the brink of genocide, we must examine, albeit briefly, (1) what we know about the ways in which persons who may be targets of genocide and their human rights come to be protected and improved in any society, and (2) what we know about the effectiveness of sanctions generally.

Regarding the first point, because there are a number of different types of rights-abusive and genocide-prone regimes that might be targeted for sanctions, "improvement" can take on very different meanings. For example, in nations where brutal treatment of citizens by their government has sparked international concern, rights improvement clearly means ending the terror of the state against its own people. In such cases, sanctions may play a role by (1) denying repressive leaders the resources (often arms), they need to continue their repressive policies, or by (2) changing the internal paradigm of repressive leaders, so that they perceive sanctions as creating both declining gains and increasing (and now unacceptable) costs for their rights-abusive behavior. This is what appears to have led to the reasonable claim that in the cases of Rhodesia and South Africa, the pressure of sanctions played a major role in the devolution of power-holding to black majority rule.[4]

In nations where a general system of oppression or repression reigns, it is clear that changes in the basic structural conditions of the political and economic orders that serve to protect groups at risk are required to enhance and protect human beings and their rights. Among necessary conditions are: police and military institutions that are guided by civilian oversight and, like the civilian government itself, are disciplined by the rule of law; a functioning constitution; an independent and functional judiciary system; and the existence of a degree of social peace characterized by the absence of largescale crime or political violence. Further, it is generally the case that political and civil rights are more protected in societies with thriving economies, whereas rights are more restricted in situations of economic crisis.

Such structural conditions develop very gradually, and are the result of more slowly evolving "democratizing" and "rights-protective" processes. Because they are slow to develop, especially in societies with a history of repression, they are less likely to emerge as the short-term result of external factors, such as a sanctions policy. On the positive side, however, sanctions can have, albeit indirectly, a major impact on the emergence of these trends, either by depriving the repressive regime of resources used to stifle such development, or by enhancing the prospect that the rights-conscious and democratic-minded groups will have a greater voice in the society. Sanctions may therefore help create an equalization of power between a government and an opposition that would result (in some situations) in the enhancement and protection of human rights. Sanctions—in their purpose and design—are meant to counteract some of the proximate conditions needed for genocide to emerge.

Although sanctions are frequently called upon to achieve purposes such as advancing human rights or stifling mass murder, many analysts doubt their effectiveness. The available evidence confirms that sanctions by themselves are seldom able to achieve either substantive political changes or the replacement of the leadership in a targeted regime. According to the major empirical study in the field, conducted by the Institute for International Economics (IIE), "sanctions are seldom effective in impairing the military potential of an important power, or in bringing about major changes in the policy of the target country."[5] If the goal is rolling back military aggression, impairing the military capability of an adversary, or forcing a change in the leadership of a regime, sanctions alone are unlikely to be effective. These realities led the United States General Accounting Office to conclude that "the primary goal of sanctions is usually the most difficult to achieve."[6]

Yet these conventional assumptions may be too pessimistic. Sanctions may be ineffective at times, not because of the inherent limitations in the instrument but because of flaws in implementation and enforcement. In Haiti, for example, sanctions alone did not succeed in restoring President Jean Bertrand Aristide, but this was due in large part to the flawed nature of the Governors Island Agreement (which lifted sanctions before Aristide's actual return) and the inept and inconsistent implementation of sanctions. Claudette Werleigh, former minister of the Aristide government, has argued that sanctions against Haiti could have been much more effective if they had been properly enforced.[7]

The case of South Africa is particularly controversial. Most analyses published before 1992, including the IIE study, judged the sanctions against apartheid as ineffective. At the time such assessments seemed reasonable, since more than two decades of economic pressure and diplomatic isolation had failed to dislodge the apartheid system. Nonetheless, financial pressures on the Pretoria government eventually had a significant impact on economic and political dynamics within South Africa, and contributed to the sweeping political transformation that brought Nelson Mandela and the African National Congress to power in 1994. From this perspective, sanctions against the apartheid regime could be judged a partial success, albeit an indirect and slow one. Compared to the human costs and rights abuse of civil war as a means of ending apartheid, sanctions were a major success.

Yet evidence can also give a more negative direction to our assessment. As was the case in the former Yugoslavia, and also in Iraq, sanctions may also play a major role in the further deterioration of the human rights situation in a target nation, thus creating a favorable climate for genocide. In rights-abusive nations, the leaders of the target government may, in fact, increase their repression of opponents and others as a "justifiable action" in light of the economic hardship caused by sanctions. In addition, the impact of sanctions on the economic and social infrastructure of a target nation can cause a serious decline in the "second order" rights of the people of that country. Those most abused in this situation are likely to be the most vulnerable: women, children, and those heavily dependent on the societal "safety net" that is often provided by international agencies.

The conventional assumption about sanctions is that economic hardship is directly proportional to political change. The greater the economic pain caused by sanctions, the higher the probability of political compliance. This conventional view is mostly based on the assumption that the population in the target state will redirect the pain of sanctions onto political leaders and force a change in policy. But this mechanism requires that (1) some level of democratic or popular influence of the citizenry on the elites operates in the society, and that (2) time is on the side of the sanctioners, as historically sanctions require nearly three years to achieve their objectives. Analysts are quick to point out, however, that the greatest economic impact of sanctions occurs in the first year, after which effectiveness declines as target states adapt to new conditions.[8] And finally, as I will discuss in the last section of this article, one of the most important empirical findings about the effectiveness of sanctions concerns the use of financial restrictions. According to the IIE report, financial sanctions have a higher political success rate (41 percent) than do the more widely imposed general trade sanctions (25 percent).[9]

At times, economic sanctions may actually strengthen a targeted regime by generating a "rally-around-the-flag" effect. Rather than causing political disintegration, sanctions may evoke nationalist sentiments and generate autarky in the target country. In some cases, sanctions may enrich and enhance the power of elites who respond to sanctions by organizing and profiting from smuggling and illicit trade activities. In Haiti, critics charged that military and business elites close to the military regime of Raoul Cedras controlled the black market trading of oil and other vital commodities. In former Yugoslavia, hard-line militia groups used their control of check points and transportation routes to enrich themselves and consolidate political power. In this later case, the means of control necessary to undertake genocide are reinforced, however inadvertently, by sanctions. And the reality of sanctions is used by the elite as a nationalist rallying cry, permitting a leader to further augment whatever ideological or nationalist underpinning the momentum to genocide may already have.

In contrast, the principle intention of imposing sanctions against a rights-violating regime is the generation of an "internal opposition effect." In this situation, sanctions have the effect of empowering internal political forces, thus rendering them more effective in their opposition to a regime's objectionable policies.[10] As the U.S. General Accounting Office has observed, "if the targeted country has a domestic opposition to the policies of the government in power, sanctions can strengthen this opposition and improve the likelihood of a positive political response to the sanctions."[11] In the case of South Africa, the opposition African National Congress actively encouraged stronger international sanctions and gained moral and political support from the solidarity thus expressed by the world community. In South Africa, external sanctions combined with the internal resistance campaign of the United Democratic Front to create political turmoil and economic uncertainty, which prompted foreign investors to deny long-term credit in the mid-1980s. This led sectors of the white business community to lobby for changes in the apartheid system and to urge dialogue with Nelson Mandela.[12]

Although a "blood bath" had been predicted by many as the only way in which majority black rule would come to South Africa, sanctions played an essential role in leading those who ruled under the apartheid system to a set of choices that prevented this. Sanctions also served as a proactive strategy that blacks could support as an alternative to such direct violence as a means of changing the regime. In this sense, it is not inaccurate to claim that sanctions were an effective means of preventing such massive violence, which would have bordered on, if it did not actually become, a genocide of blacks, of whites, or of each, in South Africa. Unfortunately, circumstances—the pace of events and the inability of sanctions on their own, or in conjunction with other policies, to prevent genocide, or stifle it as it unfolded—were different in the cases of Rwanda and the former Yugoslavia.

## The Rwandan Case

The series of events that led to the genocide in Rwanda was not without its warning signs. Those who knew the region well, and who would have seen in the plane crash killing President Juvenal Habyarimana the beginning of a major series of events, may not have been surprised by *what* occurred—that is, the political murdering of Tutsis (and moderate Hutus) by Hutus—but the scale of the slaughter, *how* it unfolded, and its rapidity were certainly shocking.[13]

A UN "concern" about tensions in Rwanda had developed in the form of the creation of the UN Assistance Mission for Rwanda (UNAMIR), which was created by Security Council Resolution 872, passed in 1993. This resolution was to give the UN a presence in the region and was meant to serve as a support of and cease-fire monitoring mechanism for the Arusha Accords, signed by the nations of the region that year. Perhaps now, in full hindsight, one might wonder why the Security Council did not attempt to further bolster the peace process through an arms embargo against all major factional and state actors when it created UNAMIR. Such an action might have stifled a bit of the violence, or might have made government forces less bold.

Yet the harsh truth may be that so much propaganda had already been broadcast throughout Rwanda that fueled the genocidal urge, and so much of the killing was "up-close" in the form of machete murders or killings by machine gun or rifle over the short span of April to June 1994, that no international mechanism such as sanctions would be an effective response to such mass killing. Acting under the "threat to peace" rubric provided by Chapter VII of the UN Charter, the Security Council actions regarding the Rwandan crisis commenced with the adoption of Resolution 918 on May 17, 1994. In this resolution, the council imposed a mandatory embargo on the supply or sale to Rwanda of arms and all related material, including military vehicles, equipment, and spare parts, as well as a ban on weapons and ammunition, and the supply of police and paramilitary equipment and spare parts. The council considered both UNAMIR, a relatively weak presence on the scene for stifling genocide, and especially Resolution 918 as actions responding to the genocide in its own terms, and also as supportive of the diplomatic, political, and humanitarian efforts existing in the region under the auspices of the OAU and the special regional facilitator of Tanzania.

In early 1995, the Council recognized that the free flow of arms in this genocide, which had already claimed more than 750,000 ethnic Tutsi and 50,000 moderate Hutus, had to be halted. Thus, through Resolution 997, it "called upon" the neighboring states of Rwanda to make special efforts in this regard. Later that same year, in Resolution 1005, the Council approved the importation and use of explosives and related devices for the sole purpose of supporting humanitarian demining efforts underway in Rwanda. But by this time, the incredible damage of genocide had already been done. Worse yet, many acknowledged that the arms embargo was generally unenforceable when various factions in front-line, border states had so much to gain economically and politically by violating it.

The Rwandan genocide illustrates the ineffectiveness of instruments like economic sanctions when the policy goal is to end mass murder in a short period of time. Economic sanctions can clearly deprive a regime of the tools of genocide, most especially weapons that may be used in such undertakings. But for this outcome, sanctions must be imposed during the time period when emotions, propaganda, and mobilization—but not killing—are running high. Such sanctions must also be subject to intense monitoring. That sanctions should also be bolstered by other forms of pressures and incentives aimed at genocide prevention is a necessity as well. By March of 1994, however, all the elements for genocide were in place in Rwanda. The small size and diffuse character of the regional peacekeeping mandate of UNAMIR meant that neither that mission nor UN sanctions were going to alter the course of the gruesome events that would unfold in the next three months.

## Sanctions and the Yugoslav War

The genocide of Bosnian Muslims during the Yugoslav war through the Serbian policy of ethnic cleansing proved an embarrassment to UN peacekeeping functions, as in varying ways the UN force was either unable or unwilling to halt what obviously were direct Serbian attacks on reasonably defenseless Bosnians. If UN protective forces on the ground during the war were meant to be a first-line order of defense of innocent civilians, then sanctions were meant to be a second order strategy, whereby the parties assumed to be perpetrating the atrocities—first the Serbs of Yugoslavia-Montenegro and then the Bosnian Serbs—would be deprived of arms for continuing the killing and economic resources that would support the general war effort.[14]

With Security Council Resolution 713 of September, 1991, which imposed an arms embargo on the entire region, the UN began its extensive involvement in the conflicts in the former Yugoslavia.[15] The Council confirmed its intention that the embargo apply to all parts of the former Yugoslavia in Resolution 727, passed in January, 1992, the same month in which the European Community (EC) recognized Slovenia and Croatia as independent states. The conditions for lifting the arms embargo were more than ambiguous, with the embargo not formally lifted until November 22, 1995, when the Security Council passed Resolution 1021 in response to the Dayton Accords peace agreement signed by the warring factions.

Although intended to prevent or at least limit the fighting in the region, the arms embargo, in fact, effectively helped set the balance of military power in favor of the Serbs, and to some extent the Croats, who were both better armed than the Bosnian Muslims. Due to the nature of the former Yugoslav federation, individual republics did not maintain active military forces, or even police. Serbia controlled the army of the former Yugoslavia (JNA) although many of the troops came from Bosnia. Both Croatia and Bosnia, but especially the latter, were short of arms, training, and seasoned soldiers.

Precipitated by an attack that killed up to 22 people waiting in a bread line in Sarajevo, the UN Security Council imposed comprehensive international sanctions against the Federal Republic of Yugoslavia in May, 1992. The UN's involvement followed the EC and US withdrawal of economic and financial aid to the region in May and June of 1991, in an attempt to prevent the disintegration of the former Yugoslavia. The EC had also imposed trade sanctions against the entire region after fighting broke out in Slovenia and Croatia in July, 1991. With the UN's action in May, the EC lifted its trade embargo on all of the republics *except* the Federal Republic of Yugoslavia (FRY).

On May 15, 1992, the Security Council passed Resolution 752, a unanimous request that the FRY end its military interference, withdraw the JNA, and disband and disarm the irregular forces operating in Bosnia-Herzegovina. This resolution provided the foundation for all subsequent sanctions resolutions. Two weeks later, in Resolution 757, passed on May 30, 1992, the Council imposed comprehensive sanctions against the FRY, including a boycott on all exports and imports of goods and services from FRY, the interdiction of air traffic and related services, a ban on all financial transactions, the reduction of staff at diplomatic missions, a ban on FRY's representation at sport and cultural events, the suspension of scientific and technical cooperation and cultural exchanges, and a provision that no legal claims could result from the consequences of implementing sanctions. In this resolution, the Security Council did not prohibit the transshipment of goods through the FRY, mainly in deference to the economic strain this would put on neighboring economies, especially Bulgaria and Rumania.

Partly because of numerous violations of sanctions through these porous borders, the sanctions reportedly were having little effect six months later. Thus, on November 16, 1992, the Security Council passed Resolution 787, tightening the sanctions by prohibiting transshipment of certain strategic items, such as crude oil and petroleum products, iron, steel, chemicals, and energy-related products through the FRY unless specifically authorized by the Security Council. On April 17, 1993, almost one year after their imposition, Resolution 820 confirmed, partly restructured, and tightened the earlier sanctions. Specifically, they strengthened the sanctions' monitoring and control mechanisms through the Sanctions Monitoring System (SAMS) and permitted Bosnia and Croatia to move goods on and to their respective territories. These sanctions were thus aimed directly at the Bosnian Serbs and at Belgrade, as the council considered these parties the aggressors in a war of ethnic cleansing in Bosnia during which other measures of international opinion or invoking international law had failed to halt the large-scale killing.

After many months of pressure from the council, in August 1994, President Milosevic finally agreed to enforce an embargo on the Bosnian Serbs after they again rejected a United States-backed peace plan. By this time, Serbs occupied almost 70 percent of Bosnia as well as a large section of Croatia. The full sanctions package against the FRY had been in place for almost a year and a half and had firmly taken hold. The FRY economy had nearly collapsed in late 1993, and although stabilizing somewhat since internal economic reforms in January 1994, its gains were tentative. Milosevic had seemingly had a "change of heart" and had begun to work with the international community to establish peace in the region. But as was already suspected, he and the Bosnian Serb leader Radovan Karadzic had been able to take 70 percent of the territory within Bosnia-Herzegovina, and had displaced over 250,000 Muslims, with tens of thousands more killed in the war and ethnic cleansing operations.

In September 1994, when Security Council Resolution 942 extended the UN sanctions to Bosnian-Serb territory in eastern Bosnia bordering Serbia, Milosevic, who was now anxious for peace, permitted UN observers to monitor the border and verify his compliance with the blockade. Because of the debilitating impact of the sanctions on the Serb economy, most international observers credit the sanctions with bringing about these changes in Milosevic's policies. However, a number of questions still remain about the actual impact of the sanctions in light of the pre-existing conditions in the country and its continuing economic policies.

Clearly, at the very least, the sanctions accelerated and intensified the economic and social crises within the FRY and increased the costs to the Belgrade government of its unqualified support for the Bosnian-Serb's war effort. But sanctions were simply not very effective in changing the character or volume of the killing "on the ground" in Bosnia, particularly by the Bosnian Serbs, who came rather unwillingly both to the peace table and to affirm its results in the Dayton Accords. Unlike the case of Rwanda, where the genocide occurred so quickly that any international action, especially multilateral sanctions, seemed doomed from the start, sanctions in the FRY were imposed and refined in response to the changing conditions of the war and coexisted with the deployment of the UN peacekeeping mission troops called the UN Protection Force (UNPROFOR). But like that force, sanctions involved too little coercion and always seemed to lag behind the horrors that were being perpetrated against civilians in this brutal war.

## Iraq's Ordeal: Can Sanctions Be Genocidal?

As if it were not a sufficient concern that sanctions fail to prevent or curtail genocide, the open-ended and continually devastating nature of the comprehensive economic sanctions imposed on Iraq in August of 1990 in Security Council Resolution 661 (and then reconstituted and amplified in the Gulf War ceasefire Resolution 687) have been claimed by a number of activists and analysts alike to be so harsh that they comprise a genocide against the Iraqi people.[16] In attempting to end Iraqi aggression against Kuwait, and then as a means of controlling the Iraqi development of weapons of mass destruction, the economic sanctions imposed by the UN were not intended to produce such loss of life and debilitation of the quality of life on Iraqi society or to generate, even as a rhetorical claim, the possibility of genocide. Can sanctions have such an effect?

Because of concern about the humanitarian consequences of sanctions in Iraq, no humanitarian situation in the world has been more intensely studied in recent years than the crisis in Iraq resulting from the Gulf War and more than eight years of UN sanctions. By 1990 more than a dozen major studies had been conducted on the impact of the war and sanctions, including reports from the UN Secretariat, UNICEF, the World Health Organization, the UN Food and Agriculture Organization (FAO), the Harvard study team, the Center for Economic and Social Rights in New York, and Greenpeace. A December 1995 report in *The Lancet*, the journal of the British Medical Association, drawing from a study of the food and nutritional situation by FAO, claimed that sanctions against Baghdad had been responsible for the deaths of 567,000 Iraqi children since the end of the Gulf War.[17] Release of the FAO study and *The Lancet* report generated considerable publicity. A *New York Times* article in December 1995 flatly declared, "Iraq Sanctions Kill Children."[18] A feature segment on the widely viewed CBS television program "60 Minutes" also depicted sanctions as a murderous assault on children.[19] Critics have called the UN sanctions a "massive violation of human rights" and have described the situation in catastrophic terms: "More Iraqi children have died as a result of sanctions than the combined total of two atomic bombs on Japan and the recent scourge of ethnic cleansing in former Yugoslavia."[20] This is the type of data that generates claims of genocide.[21]

That the people of Iraq have suffered grievously since the Gulf War is undeniable, but the scale of the crisis is uncertain, as is the assertion that sanctions have been the primary cause of

Iraq's ordeal. Even more doubtful is the charge that responsibility for the humanitarian suffering lies exclusively or primarily with Western governments and the UN Security Council. The eight-year war that Iraq fought with Iran imposed a heavy burden on Iraq, leaving more than 100,000 soldiers dead, a foreign debt of nearly $100 billion, foreign currencies depleted, and widespread labor force and economic disruptions. These effects were compounded by the Gulf War, especially by the allied air bombardment. More than 90,000 tons of explosives rained down on Iraq during the Gulf War, much of it targeted on the country's economic infrastructure. Allied air commanders went to great lengths to avoid the bombing of civilian neighborhoods, striking instead industrial and communications facilities that were deemed essential to Iraq's military capability. The bombing destroyed industrial complexes, oil refineries, sewage pumping stations, telecommunications facilities, roads, railroads, and dozens of bridges. Eighteen of Iraq's twenty power-generating plants were destroyed or incapacitated in the first days of the war, reducing electricity generation to just 4 percent of prewar levels.[22] In total, the bombing campaign caused an estimated $232 billion worth of damage to Iraq's economy.[23]

Ironically, although allied commanders sought to avoid civilian casualties in the air war, the destruction of Iraq's electrical generating capacity and industrial infrastructure may have had an impact equivalent to that of bombing residential neighborhoods. The crippling of Iraq's electrical and water supply systems had a devastating effect on the country's population and created conditions that led to disease, suffering, and death *after* the war. A report issued immediately after the war by UN Undersecretary General Martti Ahtisaari described "near apocalyptic destruction" in Iraq. The report asserted that Iraq had been "relegated to a preindustrial age" in which "most means of modern life support have been destroyed or rendered tenuous."[24] Reports from UNICEF and FAO in June and July 1991 warned of rising malnutrition and disease rates, especially among children.[25] Thus, it is not out of the realm of possibility to suggest that massive attacks on civilians, which is at least the equivalent of mass murder, began indirectly during the Gulf War but had a fuller impact in the form of disease and death long after the bombs were silent.

Unquestionably, this situation has left such a fragile social, medical, physical, and economic infrastructure that the comprehensive and tightly enforced UN sanctions have compounded and intensified these diverse hardships resulting from the war. The cumulative impacts of sanctions and the war have been simply overwhelming. Health and mortality statistics from Iraq during this decade have been shocking. Typhoid incidence jumped from eleven per 100,000 in 1990 to 142 per 100,000 in 1994.[26] Cholera, scarcely detected in the 1980s, jumped to near epidemic levels after the Gulf War. Malnourishment among children has risen sharply as well. The percentage of underweight children under five rose from 7 percent in 1991 to 29 percent in 1995. Rates of stunting and wasting among children jumped 230 percent and 400 percent, respectively, during the same period.[27] Most disastrous of all has been the reported increase in the rate of infant and under-five-years mortality. There has been much debate about the accurate number of child deaths and how to assess such deaths accurately. Those who often refer to sanctions as constituting a genocide against the Iraqi people cite child deaths under five years of age from 1990 to 1998 at about the 600,000 mark, with the total population deaths attributable to sanctions being more than 1 million. This author agrees with lower estimates that would place the former figure at about 230,000.[28]

These are truly horrifying figures, reflecting an unspeakable human tragedy. They show beyond doubt that the Gulf War and continuing sanctions have had a devastating impact on the Iraqi people. Whether these results constitute genocide in any traditional sense may be a matter of judgment, but they are certainly not what sanctions were intended to produce as conceived of by past and current UN officials.

## The Future of Sanctions in Dealing with Genocide

Without question, sanctions have been too little and too late in dealing with genocide and near-genocidal occurrences in recent international affairs. It also is the case that rapid injection of military forces to prevent genocide has seldom been an effective option. What, then, will the international community seek in a mechanism like sanctions when faced with such situations? Or, what adaptations in what now comprises economic sanctions policy might be developed to contribute more to the global capacity to prevent or stifle genocide? Among the improvements and alternatives attracting the widest attention within the UN community has been the concept of "smart sanctions."

As discussed by both UN practitioners and sanctions scholars, smart sanctions include *targeted financial measures*, including asset freezes, more comprehensive approaches to *arms embargoes*, and *restrictive international travel and participation bans*. Although arms embargoes are often the first sanctions imposed during a genocidal crisis, the case evidence suggests that little effort has been made to monitor or enforce these measures, and inadequate attention has been devoted to improving their design and implementation. Even less attention has been devoted to travel bans and the denial of participation in international activities, despite the fact that such sanctions have been imposed with increasing frequency in recent years.

Although smart sanctions are not a magic bullet for dealing with violators of general international law, this array of sanctions, when strategically combined, may prove to be a more effective tool than general trade sanctions, especially because of their rapid impact on decisional elites. With just a glance at their own central bank computers, leaders will find that the international reaction to their massive extermination of a foe has been the blocking of all state and personal bank accounts. Since the UN community is experiencing "sanctions fatigue" from dealing with the terrible human costs associated with sanctions in Iraq and the seemingly ineffective use of sanctions in Rwanda and elsewhere, smart sanctions may soon be the only politically viable economic measure the Council invokes.

## Financial Sanctions

The centerpiece of any serious targeted sanctions effort lies in the imposition of elite-targeted, financial sanctions. In March 1998, and again at the 1999 meetings at Interlaken, Switzerland, progress was made on formulating the contours of policies that would control the flow of assets and link international institutions in enforcing such controls.

Analysts and practitioners agree that much of the work that needs to be undertaken to bring financial sanctions to reality is of a technical, legal, and administrative kind, with more work to be done to clarify the language, technical, and (in some cases) legal distinctions that exist among various types of financial options. For example, more precision about and differences regarding such terms and processes as blocking assets and freezing assets is needed, as is more clarity regarding the diverse legal standing of these actions in different nations.

Some newer trends of the last decade, notably the increased speed of money made possible by both increased currency convertibility in the post-1989 era and the computerization of international banking technology, may pose particular difficulties for full implementation of targeted financial sanctions. Moreover, the presence of an international money-laundering industry and the related existence of various "safe havens," such as the Cayman Islands, may make it easier to hide money than to find it.

Despite such concerns and cautions, asset control and constraint may be a powerful financial sanction not yet fully utilized. But a substantial agenda of what yet needs to be further investigated exists. The most pressing concern is that the diplomatic and scholarly communities need a shared lexicon, both of the distinctive options that exist for financial sanctions and of what the Security Council might, in fact, choose to impose. In too many nations at this moment, the differences between such terms as "blocking," and "freezing"; "monetary" and "financial"; "assets" and "holdings," to name a few, have very different economic, banking, and legal meanings. So too, from a policy and international law perspective does the difference between targeting public funds and the private accounts of individuals.

Thus, in light of the major differences that exist in national legal control of banks, governments need to develop legislation that synchronizes control and action policies, in order to make any Security Council action effective. Further, it is widely acknowledged that the success of financial sanctions is tied to the speed and discretion with which they can be applied. That such sanctions can now only be imposed after open, and sometimes lengthy, political debate becomes self-defeating. How this fundamental dilemma can be overcome is unclear, but the problem is not insurmountable.

The benefit of such financial tools *vis-à-vis* the genocidal state is that such constraints may deprive leaders of the resources that provide their arms or that guarantee their ability to reward supporters. In particular, many analysts hope that targeting elite assets would cut deeply into the ability of such elites to purchase arms.

## Arms Embargoes

Arms embargoes have been rather prominent in sanctions episodes of the past decade, most obviously in cases where the parties are engaged in violent conflict. Arms embargoes are considered by most states to be an important mechanism for accomplishing the dual goals of reducing the real (or potential) level of violence involved in a dispute, and refraining from contributing to the harm embargoes cause civilians. The UN's seriousness with regard to fulfilling this mandate is manifest in a number of ways, but none may be more apparent than the imposition of arms sanctions by the Security Council, in three instances in the 1990s, against subnational entities (UNITA, Khmer Rouge, Bosnian Serbs) in order to halt the progress of civil war and genocidal violence. Certainly in the latter case it failed miserably.

Despite the Council's positive contribution of general support for arms embargoes, sanctions on the international exchange of weapons, ammunition, arms replacement parts, technical advisors, and even of soldiers themselves, continue to pose unique challenges to the UN system. Among the most prominent difficulties encountered in imposing effective arms embargoes are that they require a very high level of national cooperation in transparency, public identification of national violators, and ongoing monitoring. In addition, because of the great economic benefits that accrue to trading states from international arms sales, arms exporters and their resident businesses often consider themselves uncompensated third parties (in an Article 51 sense) who are very negatively affected by Council arms sanctions. Under these conditions, incentives to support the embargoes through self-restraint and other policies are nonexistent.

At least two important actions might be undertaken to strengthen the effectiveness of arms embargoes. Each of these requires additional research and more detailed consideration of implementation strategies by member states of the UN Security Council. First, arms embargoes must be adopted with more tightly crafted specifications regarding the items banned, monitoring compliance of states, interdiction authority, and the specific consequences that ensue if a member state violates the embargo. Secondly, the specific criteria for the removal of an arms embargo must be articulated in the resolution that imposes it. Certain earlier bans on arms were insensitive to real changes in the behavior of targeted groups over time. This has compounded the problem of lack of compliance, as exporters see little resolve to bring closure on events and UN actions even when conditions in a locale have changed.

## Travel and International Participation Bans

Historically, the Security Council has imposed two types of travel bans: restriction in air travel to and from a targeted state, and restrictions on the travel of targeted individuals. With the latter, individuals may not be "elites" in any economic or political decision-making sense but may be national representatives to international athletic competitions or belong to cultural/entertainment groups. Denial of freedom to participate in international meetings or events brings much of the second travel ban into being.

Certainly such bans by themselves are not expected to provide quick compliance with UN demands. But more than any other form of smart sanctions, these constraining devices have been underinvestigated and their coercive potential has not been fully maximized. In particular, nations such as South Africa, which have suffered under such bans in the past—especially the international sports and cultural restraints—have noted the sense of psychological isolation, the denial of legitimacy, and damaged national pride that accompany such bans. Such realities can take their toll. Travel bans, especially, can move quickly from being matters of inconvenience to matters effecting the economic and diplomatic business of a nation. And in situations of genocide, they can be clear and direct *personal* condemnations of individuals on the basis of their actions.

Although easier to enforce than arms embargoes, travel and participation bans are not without controversy. Among other areas for future research and policy formulation, model Security Council resolutions must fully and appropriately sketch what a travel ban means in operational form for airlines and other forms of transportation. Moreover, a research agenda should also rank highly the need for increased monitoring of travel bans and, often, the need for special sanctions assistance missions, which often comprise customs officers from member countries.

## The Future Agenda

Financial mechanisms, arms embargoes, and travel and participation bans are each underutilized as components of a targeted sanctions policy, and may be undervalued due to a lack of full understanding of their efficacy, especially when employed in tandem. More than general trade sanctions, these tools will increase the likelihood that the UN can sting genocidal leaders quickly and *may* force them to dramatically reconsider, if not actually change, their policies.

Although a general air of optimism about smart sanctions prevails among UN members, three issues are now posed—comprising the near-term research and design agenda—that must be addressed if thinking about targeted or smart sanctions is to progress to viable Security Council action in thwarting those bent on genocide. First, nations must recognize that smart sanctions will succeed only if they are part of a strategic design of negotiation and diplomacy with the targeted state. As has often been the case with trade embargoes, when sanctions become *the* policy, they seldom produce the desired results. Secondly, no targeted sanctions approach can succeed without a firm commitment to monitoring, both in the "control of borders" enforcement sense, and in terms of assessing the humanitarian impact of such measures. Finally, UN and member-state technical means of implementation and enforcement are even more critical in these areas than they have been in trade sanctions. But wide variation in institutional capabilities, practices, and preferences means that increased cooperation among members regarding these variations is a must if smart sanctions are to be imposed.

The UN system generally, and the Security Council in particular, face a number of challenges in dealing with members that verge on becoming genocidal states. As these entities often are classified as such because of violent internal conflicts, focused, targeted sanctions have a certain appeal as a means of withdrawing resources from elites bent on genocide. But general trade-based sanctions have produced more state fatigue among Security Council members than they have produced desired results in the target state. And some sanctions cases, as in Council sanctions against Iraq, have been mired in controversy and tragedy because of their adverse impact on the innocent—an impact that some would even label genocide. For these reasons, the time is now ripe for developing a smarter, more targeted sanctions policy than now exists.

## Notes

1. Although he is not a coauthor of this particular chapter, many of the insights in this essay derive from my work with David Cortright over the past eight years. Thus his contribution here is gratefully noted.

2. For a discussion of the rationale behind the increase in use of United Nations sanctions, see George A. Lopez and David Cortright, "The Sanctions Era: An Alternative to Military Intervention," *The Fletcher Forum on World Affairs* 19, No. 2 (Summer/Fall 1995): 65–86. For insights into unilateral sanctions and U.S. sanctions policy in particular, see Richard Haass, *Economic Sanctions and American Diplomacy* (New York: Council on Foreign Relations, 1998).

3. For a discussion of the Burundi case, see Eric Hoskins and Samantha Nutt, "The Humanitarian Impact of Economic Sanctions on Burundi," The Thomas J. Watson Institute for International Studies, Occasional Paper #29, Brown University, 1997.

4. For a more far-reaching discussion of the role of sanctions in enhancing human rights, see George A. Lopez and David Cortright, "Economic Sanctions and Human Rights: Part of the Solution or Part of the Problem?" *The International Journal of Human Rights* 1, No. 2 (May 1997): 1–25.

5. Gary C. Hufbauer, Jeffery J. Schott, and Kimberly Ann Elliott, *Economic Sanctions Reconsidered: History and Current Policy*, 2d ed. (Washington, DC: Institute for International Economics, 1990).

6. U.S. General Accounting Office. "Economic Sanctions: Effectiveness as Tools of Foreign Policy," report prepared for the Chairman, Committee on Foreign Relations, U.S. Senate, 102nd Cong., 2d sess., 1992, p. 11.

7. See Claudette Antoine Werleigh, "The Use of Sanctions in Haiti: Assessing the Economic Realities," in David Cortwright and George A. Lopez, eds., *Economic Sanctions: Panacea or Peacebuilding in a Post-Cold War World?* (Boulder, CO: Westview Press, 1995), pp. 161–172.

8. Miroslav Nincic and Peter Wallensteen, eds., *Dilemmas of Economic Coercion: Sanctions and World Politics* (New York: Praeger, 1983), p. 109.

9. Hufbauer et al., *Economic Sanctions Reconsidered*, 63ff.

10. Ivan Eland, "Economic Sanctions as Tools," in *Economic Sanctions: Panacea or Peacebuilding in a Post-Cold War World?*, pp. 32–33.

11. U.S. General Accounting Office, "International Trade: Issues Regarding Imposition of an Oil Embargo Against Nigeria," report prepared for the Chairman, Subcommittee on Africa, Committee on Foreign Affairs, U.S. House of Representatives, 103rd Cong., 2d. sess., November 1994, GAO/GGD-95–24, p. 12.

12. See Jennifer Davis, "Sanctions and Apartheid: The Economic Challenge to Discrimination," in *Economic Sanctions: Panacea or Peacebuilding in a Post-Cold War World?*, 173–186.

13. Scott R. Feil. "Preventing Genocide, How the Early Use of Force Might Have Succeeded in Rwanda," Report to the Carnegie Commission on Preventing Deadly Conflict (New York: Carnegie Corporation, 1998).

14. For two accounts of the impact and effectiveness of the UN sanctions on the former Yugoslavia, see Susan L. Woodward, "The Use of Sanctions in Former Yugoslavia: Misunderstanding Political Realities," Economic Sanctions: Panacea or Peacebuilding in a Post-Cold War World?, pp. 141–152; and Julia Devin and Jaleh Dashti-Gibson, "Sanctions in the Former Yugoslavia: Convoluted Goals and Complicated Consequences," in Thomas Weiss et al., eds., *Political Gain and Civilian Pain* (Lanham, MD: Rowman & Littlefield, 1997), pp. 149–198.

15. For a detailed treatment of the various sanctions imposed against the Yugoslav parties, and especially their humanitarian and economic impact, see Julia Devin and Jaleh Dashti-Gibson, "Sanctions in

the Former Yugoslavia: Convoluted Goals and Complicated Consequences," in *Political Gain and Civilian Pain*, pp. 149–188.

16. The primary activist group involved in challenging the sanctions against Iraq with these concerns and claims has been the Voices from the Wilderness campaign, whose members also engaged in acts of civil disobedience in protest of U.S. maintenance of restrictions of certain medical goods. These acts primarily entailed "violating" the sanctions by entering Iraq to deliver such goods without an embargo exemption as issued by the U.S. Treasury Department.

17. Sarah Zaidi and Mary C. Smith-Fazi, "Health of Baghdad's Children," *The Lancet* 346, No. 8988 (December 2, 1995): 1485. See also the editorial in the same issue, "Health Effects of Sanctions on Iraq," p. 1439.

18. See Barbara Crossette, "Iraq Sanctions Kill Children, UN Reports," *New York Times*, December 1, 1995, p. A6.

19. CBS Television, "60 Minutes," May 12, 1996.

20. Center for Economic and Social Rights, *UN Sanctioned Suffering: A Human Rights Assessment of United Nations Sanctions on Iraq* (New York: Center for Economic and Social Rights, May 1996), p. 1.

21. For an extensive discussion of the humanitarian impact of sanctions in Iraq and the various controversies surrounding the data that assess this, see Eric Hoskins, "The Humanitarian Impacts of Economic Sanctions and War in Iraq," in Weiss et al., *Political Pain and Civilian Pain*, pp. 91–148; David Cortright and George A. Lopez, "Sanctions and Contending Views of Justice: The Problematic Case of Iraq," *Journal of International Affairs* 52, No. 2 (Spring 1999): 33–53; and David Cortright and George A. Lopez, "Trouble in the Gulf: Pain and Promise," *The Bulletin of the Atomic Scientists* 54, No. 3 (May/June 1998): 39–43.

22. Harvard Study Team, "The Effect of the Gulf Crisis on the Children of Iraq," *New England Journal of Medicine* 325, No. 13 (1991): 977–980.

23. Abbas Alnasrawi, "Does Iraq Have an Economic Future?" *Middle East Executive Reports*, 19, No. 3 (March 1996): 8–18.

24. United Nations, *Report to the Secretary General on Humanitarian Needs in Kuwait and Iraq in the Immediate Post-Crisis Environment by a Mission to the Area Led by Mr. Martti Ahtisaari, Undersecretary General for Administration and Management, Dated 20 March 1991* (New York, 1991).

25. Hoskins, "Humanitarian Impact," in *Political Gain*, p. 30.

26. Ibid., Fig. 5.

27. Food and Agriculture Organization (FAO), *Evaluation of Food and Nutrition Situation, Iraq* (Rome: FAO, October 3, 1997), p. 1.

28. This data controversy is addressed in George A. Lopez and David Cortright, "Trouble in the Gulf: Pain and Promise," *The Bulletin of the Atomic Scientists* 54, No. 3 (May/June 1998): 39–43; and George A. Lopez "The Sanctions Dilemma: Hype Doesn't Help," *Commonweal*, September 11, 1998, pp. 10–12.

# 9.3  Francis Kofi Abiew, "The East Pakistan (Bangladesh) Intervention of 1971"

The Indian intervention in East Pakistan which resulted in creation of the independent state of Bangladesh provides an instance of humanitarian intervention. The origins of this intervention could be traced back to the partition of India in 1947 as a result of which Pakistan came into being, composed of two different parts geographically separated by a distance of over 1,000 miles. It was also divided by ethnic, cultural and linguistic differences. The two common factors, namely Islam and alienation from India, which held these parts together, were, however, not sufficient to ensure stability.[1] By the late 1960s political and economic domination of East Pakistan by West Pakistan had resulted in increasing political discontent.

The Pakistani general elections of December 1970 resulted in an overwhelming victory for Sheikh Mujibur Rahman's East Pakistani Awami League party, which campaigned for political and economic autonomy.[2] Following results of the elections, there were simmering fears in West Pakistan, given the demand for autonomy and the possibility of being ruled by the Awami League Party. The National Assembly having been postponed indefinitely,[3] the situation degenerated into mass demonstrations with the East Bengalis clamouring for total independence. With no possibility of peaceful settlement of the political impasse in sight, the Pakistani army moved into Dacca on March 25, 1971, unleashing a reign of terror. There were reported cases of mass murders and other human rights atrocities committed by the Pakistani army.[4] The Report of the International Commission of Jurists observed:

> The principal features of this ruthless oppression were the indiscriminate killing of civilians, including women and children and the poorest and weakest members of the community; the attempt to exterminate or drive out of the country a large part of the Hindu population; the arrest, torture and killing of Awami League activists, students, professional and business men and other potential leaders . . .; the raping of women; the destruction of villages and towns; and the looting of property. All this was done in a scale which is difficult to comprehend.[5]

The result of these atrocities saw the death of at least one million people and the influx of over ten million people seeking refuge in India.[6] These flow of refugees put severe strains on India's economy. The refugee situation thus made it impossible for India to remain indifferent to the conflict. Prior to the intervention, the Indian Prime Minister had appealed to other states and, in vain, to the UN to do something about the situation in which "the general and systematic nature of inhuman treatment inflicted on the Bangladesh population was evidence of a crime against humanity".[7] But no international action was taken. Relations between India and Pakistan deteriorated, erupting into a full-scale war on December 3, 1971—a war that lasted 12 days and ended with the surrender of the Pakistani Army.[8] In the aftermath of the intervention, political prisoners were released, refugees returned to East Pakistan and finally, Bangladesh was established as a new independent state.

Adducing reasons for its intervention, India claimed it had reacted to the aggression committed by Pakistan, in effect, that it was the lawful exercise of the right of self-defence. It also claimed the action was necessary for the protection of Bengalis from gross and persistent violations of human rights by the Pakistani army, whilst at the same time addressing the problem of over 10 million Bengali refugees that crossed into its territory. India's representative at the Security Council stated that

> [r]efugees were a reality. Genocide and oppression were a reality. The extinction of all civil rights was a reality. Provocation and aggression of various kinds by Pakistan from 25 March onwards were a reality. Bangladesh itself was a reality, as was its recognition by India. The [Security] Council was nowhere near reality.[9]

Elsewhere, the Indian representative again notes "that we have on this particular occasion absolutely nothing but the purest of intentions: to rescue the people of East Bengal from what they are suffering".[10] Thus, in India's opinion, its presence was necessary to put a stop to the atrocities and to prevent further massacres.

India's point of view was supported by the Soviet Union. It pointed to Pakistan's attack on India as an invasion of India's territorial integrity. It also drew attention to the refugee situation as having created security problems for India, but emphasized the fact that the main causes of the conflict were the "inhuman acts of oppression and terrorism" perpetrated in East Bengal by Pakistan, and that a ceasefire was only possible after Pakistani atrocities had come to an end.[11] Other states belonging to the Eastern bloc—i.e. Czechoslovakia, Poland,

Hungary, Bulgaria, Mongolia, and also Bhutan, sided with India's point of view emphasizing the severe breaches of human rights and the atrocities committed by Pakistan.[12]

Some states reacted negatively to the intervention. Pakistan, China, and the United States accused India of aggression and argued that India had no right to intervene in Pakistan's treatment of the East Pakistani population.[13] In the Security Council, Saudi Arabia, Argentina, and Tunisia variously opposed the intervention by condemning "aid given by one state to secessionist movements in another", "secession, subversion and interference in the internal affairs of a State", and "intervention by a third party in the internal affairs of a State".[14] In the General Assembly, most delegates referred to the situation in East Pakistan as an internal one, asserting that India had to respect Pakistan's sovereignty and territorial integrity.[15]

The validity of India's intervention has been the subject of considerable debate. First, the purported justification for the Indian action, in part, was on the basis of self-defence. This was a direct response to the earlier preemptive air strike launched by Pakistan. India's action therefore can be explained by her being a victim of a full scale war initiated by Pakistan and used proportionate force in reacting to the aggression. Thus, in principle, the right of self-defence was involved and claimed.

Secondly, the Indian action can be justified on the basis of humanitarian intervention. Tesón for instance characterizes it partly, as one of rendering foreign assistance to a people struggling for their right to self determination—a collective human right, and secondly, as intervention with the objective of ending acts of genocide, that is, humanitarian intervention proper. For him, the strength of India's claim to legality is that these two aspects of humanitarian intervention are present in the Indian example.[16] Majority of writers have echoed a viewpoint somewhat similar to the conclusions of the East Pakistan Staff Study which stated:

> In our view the circumstances were wholly exceptional; it was becoming more and more urgent to find a solution, both for humanitarian reasons and because the refugee burden which India was bearing had become intolerable with no solution in sight. Events having been allowed to reach this point, it is difficult to see what other choice India could have made.
>
> It must be emphasized that humanitarian intervention is not the ground of justification which India has herself put forward. As we have seen, India claimed to have acted first in self-defense, and secondly, in giving support to the new government of Bangladesh which she recognized when hostilities began. We have given our reasons for not accepting the validity of these claims. If India had wished to justify her action on the principle of humanitarian intervention she should have first made a preemptory demand to Pakistan insisting that positive action be taken to rectify the violations of human rights. As far as we are aware no such demand was made.
>
> In conclusion, therefore, we consider that India's armed intervention would have been justified if she had acted under the doctrine of humanitarian intervention, and further that India would have been entitled to act unilaterally under this doctrine in view of the growing and intolerable burden which the refugees were casting upon India and in view of the inability of international organizations to take any effective action to bring to an end the massive violations of human rights in East Pakistan which were causing the flow of refugees. We also consider that the degree of force used was no greater than was necessary in order to bring to an end these violations of human rights.[17]

Contrary to the East Pakistan Staff Study and comments to a similar effect by some writers however, India did invoke humanitarian reasons for her action in East Pakistan. India's representative in the General Assembly had stated that

> the reaction of the people of India to the massive killing of unarmed people by military force has been intense and sustained . . . There is intense sorrow and shock and horror at the reign of terror that has been let loose. The common bonds of race, religion, culture, history and geography of the

people of East Pakistan with the neighbouring Indian state of West Bengal contribute powerfully to the feelings of the Indian people.[18]

Indeed, many commentators, citing the widespread slaughter of East Bengalis by the West Pakistani army, have considered this intervention to be a leading case of humanitarian intervention.[19] Others, however, have taken a sceptical view of the Indian action and considered it to be unlawful.[20] Comments have been made to the effect that more importantly, the operation was a strategic one undertaken by a partisan actor. India was interested politically in the secession of East Pakistan. It thus seized the opportunity to curtail Pakistan's power and to diminish the territory of its political and military rival.[21] It is probable that taking into consideration the overall political dynamics for control of the region, it was in India's interest to take some form of action to cause the break-up of Pakistan and thus reduce the threat posed by its neighbour. If that happened, then predictably India would have emerged as a dominant power in the region.

However, if one brings into focus the entirety of the crisis, there was no doubt that given the massive scale on which human rights were being violated, India's action could be looked upon as intervention to stop the human rights atrocities that were being perpetrated.[22] India's "various motives converged on a single course of action that was also the course of action called for by the Bengalis".[23] As Sornarajah argues, "the existence of self-interest should not affect the legality of humanitarian intervention. Therefore, at least on occasions where political expediency coincides with the existence of humanitarian grounds for intervention, human rights may be protected".[24] The Bengali people welcomed the intervention which not only freed them from the massive scale of repression but also enabled them to obtain their independence—the creation of Bangladesh, which was quickly recognized by the UN and subsequently admitted to that body.

Another possible basis for justification of India's action relates to the UN's inability to deal with the situation over the period in which these massacres were going on.[25] There was no doubt that the massacres were a matter of international interest, yet no action was taken.[26] India interested itself in the situation and went to the rescue, withdrawing its forces promptly. The fact that the UN did not condemn the intervention could also be interpreted as an implied recognition of the doctrine. Given the extraordinary circumstances in East Pakistan, which some writers view as being of genocidal proportions, this case fits into the category of acts 'shocking the conscience of mankind' for which intervention to redress the situation was necessary.[27] Despite the self-interested nature of the Indian action, this intervention nevertheless, ultimately achieved the task of protecting human rights and was not condemned by the Security Council.[28]

## Notes

1. For details of events leading to the breakup of Pakistan and comments on the Indian intervention in East Pakistan see for example, International Commission of Jurists, *The Events in East Pakistan, 1971* (Geneva, 1972); Nanda, "A Critique of the United Nations Inaction in the Bangladesh Crisis" (1972) 49 *Denver Law Journal* 53; Tesón, *supra*, note 3 at 179–188.
2. International Commission of Jurists, *ibid.*, at 12.
3. *Ibid.* at 13–14.
4. *Ibid.* 24–27.
5. *Ibid.*, at 26–27.
6. The precise number of refugees is in dispute. Whilst the Pakistani government claimed there were no more than 2 million people, the Indian government claimed otherwise. What is certain is that this influx of people put a severe strain on India's economy. See, Tesón, *supra*, note 3 at 182.
7. Quoted in Verwey, *supra*, note 2 at 401.
8. International Commission of Jurists, *supra*, note 143 at 43–44.

9. See, *UN Monthly Chronicle*, January 1972, at 25.

10. Statement of Ambassador Sen to the UN Security Council, UN Doc.s/PV. 1606, 86(1971). Cited in Franck & Rodley, "The Law, The United Nations and Bangla Desh" (1972) *2 Israel Yearbook on Human Rights* 142 at 164. Some writers claim India did not invoke humanitarian considerations as a reason for intervention. Others note that it did not claim the doctrine as her main line of defence. See for example, Hassan, *supra*, note 2 at 884 footnote 167; Akehurst in Bull ed., *supra*, note 26 at 96; Ronzitti, *supra*, note 2 at 96. But as Tesón correctly observes, whether India invoked it or not is not important. The significant thing to note is the totality of the circumstances which called for intervention on grounds of humanity. Tesón, *supra*, note 3 at 186.

11. 26 UN SCOR, 1606th meeting, 4 December 1971, paras 253, 267, 268, 270, 271. Cited in Ronzitti, *supra*, note 2 at 97.

12. 26 UN GAOR, Plen. meetings, 2003rd meeting, 7 December 1971, paras 38–39, 43, 145, 206, 326, 377, 416. Cited in *ibid.*

13. *Supra*, note 151 at 5, 7–8, 10–11.

14. *Ibid.*, at 32, 37.

15. *Ibid.*, at 90. The delegate from Ghana, for example, declared that once one permitted oneself the higher wisdom of telling another Member State what it should do with regard to arranging its own political affairs, one opened a Pandora's box. *Ibid.*

16. See Tesón, 2nd ed., *supra*, note 3 at 206–207. But see Clark and Beck, *International Law and the Use of Force: Beyond the UN Charter Paradigm* (London: Routledge, 1993) at 119 (rejecting Tesón's argument and making a case for taking into account India's motives in a legal assessment of this intervention).

17. East Pakistan Staff Study, The Review, International Committee of Jurists, No. 8, 1972, at 62. Quoted in Behuniak, *supra*, note 3 at 176–177.

18. See, 26 UN GAOR 2002th, UN Doc. A/PV 2002 (1971), at 14. Quoted in Tesón, 2nd. ed., *supra*, note 3 at 207, footnote 187. See also footnote 153.

19. See for instance, Ronzitti, *supra*, note 2 at 95. Fonteyne holds the opinion that ". . . the Bangladesh situation probably constitutes the clearest case of forceful individual humanitarian intervention in this century". Fonteyne, *supra*, note 3 at 204. Walzer supports this intervention as humanitarian by arguing "it was a rescue, strictly and narrowly defined". Walzer, *supra*, note 34 at 105.

20. See for example, *supra*, note 18; Brownlie, "Thoughts on Kind-Hearted Gunmen" in Lillich ed. *supra*, note 2 at 139. Frank and Rodley have commented: "[T]he Bangladesh case . . . does not constitute the basis for a definable, workable, or desirable new rule of law which, in the future, would make certain kinds of unilateral military interventions permissible". Frank and Rodley, "After Bangladesh: The Law of Humanitarian Intervention by Military Force" (1973) 67 *American Journal of International Law* 275 at 276.

21. See, Verwey, *supra*, note 2 at 402; Bazyler, *supra*, note 3 at 589.

22. Tesón points out this action could also be viewed as rendering foreign assistance to a people engaged in a struggle for their right to self-determination, which is a collective human right. However, he notes that it is not necessary to draw those distinctions since claims of self-determination and human rights violations both converge in this example. Tesón, *supra*, note 3 at 185.

23. Walzer, *supra*, note 34 at 105.

24. *Supra*, note 127 at 70.

25. According to Nanda "there was no doubt regarding the nature or extent of the Pakistani military's atrocities . . . [T]he United Nation's inaction . . . is equally well documented". Nanda, *supra*, note 92 at 319.

26. The International Commission of Jurists suggested that the Security Council, inter alia, could have investigated the allegations of atrocities being committed prior to the Indian attack under the authority of Article 34 of the Charter. Further, it found that had the Security Council investigated, it would have discovered a "threat to the peace" in accordance with Article 39. In conclusion, it pointed out that the Council had an array of measures it could have taken to stop the carnage, from recommending dispute resolution methods under Article 36 to using force under Article 42. International Commission of Jurists, *supra*, note 144 at 488–489.

27. Tesón, after studying this case, states the action ". . . directed toward rescuing the Bengalis from the genocide attempted by Pakistan, is an almost perfect example of humanitarian intervention". Tesón, *supra*, note 3 at 185. See also Reisman, comment in "Conference Proceedings" Lillich ed., *supra*,

note 2 at 17–18; Farer, "Humanitarian Intervention: The View from Charlottesville" in *ibid.*, at 149–157; Nawaz, "Bangla-Desh and International Law" (1971) 11 *Indian Journal of International Law* 459

28. Sornarajah maintains that "the absence of condemnation of the Indian intervention by the international community amounts to a condonation of intervention" to prevent mass atrocities against the Bengalis. *Supra*, note 127 at 73.

## 9.4 Francis Kofi Abiew, "Vietnam's intervention in Cambodia (Kampuchea), 1978"

The Vietnamese intervention in Cambodia offers another illustration of the use of force for the protection of human rights. In April 1975, the Khmer Rouge forces of Pol Pot took over power from the Republican government.[1] Soon thereafter it embarked upon a programme of total reorganization of the country. In the process of this reorganization, massive violations of human rights by the regime against its own citizens took place.[2] There were reported cases of starvation, torture, mass killings and deportations. In a three year period, an estimated number of over 2 million (out of a total population of 7 million) were reported dead through starvation, disease and slaughter.[3] The enormity of the human rights violations in Kampuchea at the time has been described as of genocidal proportions.[4]

Despite the international community's expression of outrage at the human rights atrocities, no effective measures were taken to stop what was happening in Kampuchea.[5] In December 1978, Vietnamese troops and the Kampuchean United Front for National Salvation (made up of Cambodian refugees in Vietnam) invaded Kampuchea and overthrew the Pol Pot regime, installing a Vietnamese-supported government.[6]

In the UN Security Council debate following the intervention, Vietnam set out its rationale for undertaking military action against Cambodia. Its official position was that the Kampuchean affair comprised two distinct conflicts: first, the conflict between Vietnam and Kampuchea; and second, the civil war in Kampuchea. Vietnam had become involved in the former conflict only after prior Kampuchean aggression. Thus, its use of force had been undertaken only in self-defence. Regarding the latter, its cause originated from the inhuman conditions which the citizens of Kampuchea were being subjected to by their government. The civil war was fought by the Kampuchean people themselves who eventually overthrew the inhumane Pol Pot regime.[7]

In the Security Council, the Soviet Union, Cuba, Czechoslovakia, the German Democratic Republic, Hungary, Mongolia, Poland, and Bulgaria supported the Vietnamese position. These states pointed to the inhumane conditions in which the Cambodian people were being held and stated that the Pol Pot regime had been overthrown solely by the United Front for National Salvation.[8]

Other members of the Security Council challenged these representations. China did not comment on the inhumane conditions in which the Kampuchean population were being held. Given the perennial tensions between China and Vietnam, China declared Vietnam had committed aggression against Kampuchea, thus violating that country's political and territorial sovereignty. The United Front, it contended, was nothing but a puppet organization created and run by Vietnam.[9] China, of course, had been a supporter of the Khmer Rouge. However, it is also worth mentioning that those states that supported Vietnam's action were opposed to the Khmer Rouge regime. The Non-Aligned countries held Vietnam responsible for violating Kampuchea's territorial integrity. They did not explicitly condemn Vietnam but asked for its withdrawal from Kampuchea. Most of these states did not raise the issue of human rights violations, except Bolivia, Nigeria and Singapore which mentioned the issue. They were, however, of the view that such human rights violations did not justify intervention by a third state.[10] Some Western States also condemned the Vietnamese action. The United States, however, did not declare it is prohibited to use force against a government that committed grave breaches of human rights within its territory. The Security Council, however, was unable to adopt any resolution.[11] At its 34th session, the General Assembly adopted a number of resolutions censuring "foreign intervention" in Kampuchea and called for the withdrawal of foreign forces from that country.[12] On the whole, it seems to be the case that international reaction to this case was shaped by the bitter Cold War rivalries rather than any concern for human rights atrocities prevalent before the Vietnamese intervention.

It has been observed that Vietnam had other motives. It harboured territorial ambitions over Kampuchea and seized the opportunity, given the situation, to invade Kampuchea and install a puppet government.[13] Added to this is the fact that over a decade after the invasion Vietnamese troops and advisors were still present on Kampuchean soil.[14] Although it is worth mentioning that in February 1979, Vietnam had signed a Treaty of Friendship with the government of the new People's Republic of Kampuchea, formed in early January. That treaty of Friendship provided the legal basis for the acknowledged presence of Vietnamese troops inside Kampuchea until their declared withdrawal.[15] The danger here, as Thomas comments, is that while interventions may relieve the immediate reign of terror or the persecution of a particular group, they can also end up in the substitution of one oppressor by another. Alternatively, they may create new uncertainties and dangers springing from a different geopolitical configuration.[16] Kampucheans freed from the terror of the Pol Pot regime, for example, found themselves dependent on Vietnam on the one hand, with the added threat of the Khmer Rouge, supported by the West, on the Thai border on the other.[17]

The purported basis for the Vietnamese intervention was self-defense. Cambodian aggression against Vietnam supported a proportionate response aimed at neutralizing Cambodian forces along Vietnam's border. What is less clear, according to one analyst, is whether Vietnam's response justified seizure of the capital, installation of a puppet regime, and the presence of Vietnamese troops in Cambodia, although it could be argued that despite the superiority of its forces, Vietnam believed the overthrow of the Pol Pot regime was the only option left in eliminating the Cambodian threat.[18]

A possible basis for justifying this intervention on humanitarian grounds was the existence of large scale atrocities. The Pol Pot regime had killed between one-quarter to one-third of the Cambodian population, and by so doing had lost the legal right to govern the Cambodian people. The justification for a humanitarian intervention thus existed, at least initially, when Vietnam undertook its military action against Cambodia.[19] As Wolf suggests, the international community's negative reaction to this case "does not constitute a negation of the doctrine of humanitarian intervention" since cold war rivalries shaped opinion either in favour or against the Vietnamese intervention. Viewed in this light, strict issues of legality thus played only a minor role in international reaction to the intervention.[20]

On the basis of the facts noted, it is difficult to discern whether in fact, the objective of the Vietnamese was merely humanitarian.[21] There is no doubt, however, that the Kampuchean case was "a perfect candidate for humanitarian intervention"[22] given the massive scale of human rights violations. The failure of the international community, including the UN, to find a diplomatic solution or to take any concrete measures of response, left the Vietnamese course of action as the viable option and the immediate solution to end the atrocities that were being committed.

## Notes

1. The genesis of the Cambodian calamity was a result of the Vietnam-Indochinese conflict. Cambodia escaped the conflict in the 1960s but became involved in it in the 1970s. In early 1970, Lon Nol forces deposed Norodom Sihanouk's regime, which had attempted to keep its neutrality in the

Indochinese conflict. Consequently, a civil war began between the American-backed Khmer republican forces and the Khmer Rouge communists supported by North Vietnam and China. Bazyler, *supra*, note 3 at 551.

2. See, Ronzitti, *supra*, note 2 at 98.

3. See, Bazyler, *supra*, note 3 at 551.

4. The Chairman of the UN Human Rights Subcommission described it as "the most serious to have occurred anywhere since Nazism". Quoted in *ibid.* at 552.

5. Ronzitti remarks that the UN failed to do anything but pass resolutions. In 1978, the US Senate hearings on the Cambodian situation condemned the government for committing human rights atrocities against its own citizens. During the Senate hearings, Senator George McGovern called for the use of force to restore human rights in that country. He said: "I am wondering under those circumstances if any thought is being given, either by our Government or at the United Nations or anywhere in the international community of sending in a force to knock this Government out of power, just on humanitarian grounds". See Indochina: Hearings before the Subcommittee on East-Asian and Pacific Affairs of the Senate Committee on Foreign Relations, 95th Congress, 2d Sess. (1978). Quoted in Ronzitti, *supra*, note 2 at 98.

6. Ronzitti, *ibid.*, at 98–99.

7. *Ibid.*

8. See *ibid.*, at 99–101 and the footnotes cited therein.

9. *ibid.*

10. *ibid.*

11. *ibid.*

12. See, *ibid.*, at 101.

13. Bazyler, *supra*, note 3 at 608.

14. *ibid.* at 609. It has been claimed that the troops departed in early 1993.

15. Leifer, "Vietnam's Intervention in Kampuchea: The Right of State v. The Right of People" in Forbes & Hoffman eds., *supra*, note 6 at 145.

16. Thomas, "The Pragmatic Case Against Intervention" in Forbes & Hoffman eds., *supra*, note 6 at 94.

17. *ibid.*

18. *Supra*, note 197 at 104.

19. Bazyler, *supra*, note 3 at 608. See however, 610 (arguing even though the invasion did result in the ouster of one of the most ruthless regimes in the post-World War II period, it cannot be justified on humanitarian grounds since Vietnam harboured other motives).

20. Wolf, *supra*, note 199 at 352.

21. Leifer, in his analysis of the Kampuchean situation concludes that the motivation for intervention should ideally have been humanitarian. But in this particular case, intervention "was governed by strategic priorities and the international responses to that intervention by the corresponding priorities of interested parties". See Leifer, *supra*, note 219 at 155.

22. *ibid.*

# 9.5   James Cotton, "Against the Grain: The East Timor Intervention"

The principle of non-interference is an integral part of the 'Asian Way'. Countries of the region have doggedly opposed any suggestion that state sovereignty should be softened by a new doctrine of 'humanitarian intervention'. The participation of some of these countries in the 1999 intervention in East Timor—an action sanctioned by the United Nations for specifically humanitarian purposes—was thus out of character. But this departure, far from reflecting a re-evaluation of the doctrine, was a consequence of specific historical and political factors. Most important of these was the fact that the UN had never accepted the Indonesian incorporation of the territory as legitimate. Once the United States adopted a more critical attitude, after Australia pressured Indonesia to test local opinion on East Timor's future, the internationalisation of the issue became inevitable. In the aftermath of the post-ballot militia violence, Indonesia's uncertain transitional leadership could not resist calls for an intervention by peacekeepers. There are certainly lessons in the East Timor case for coalition operations and other interventions in the region. But the actions of the Australia-led coalition do not indicate a wider regional acceptance of the norm of humanitarian intervention.

## Precedents for Intervention in Asia

And yet, in a different sense, Asia is the continent of intervention. The United Nations-sponsored intervention in East Timor in 1999, no less than Indonesia's initial invasion in 1975, should be seen in this light. Since 1945, there has been a series of interventions in Asia that have had a lasting impact on the societies directly affected, as well as on regional relations. Asian and Pacific countries were significant participants in the Korean and Vietnam Wars.[1] The territory of Irian Jaya (West Papua) was acquired by Indonesia in 1963 after Indonesian guerrilla operations had undermined the resolve of the Netherlands to hold the territory. The consequences of Soviet intervention in Afghanistan are still a major source of regional instability. India's intervention in East Pakistan in 1971 facilitated the birth of Asia's fourth most populous nation, Bangladesh. In addition to its annexation of Portuguese Goa, India has also intervened in the Maldives and with somewhat less success in Sri Lanka. Vietnam's displacement of the Khmer Rouge regime in Kampuchea/Cambodia in 1978 exhibits some parallels with Indian action in Bangladesh. Later, under UN auspices, the political system of Cambodia was fundamentally re-engineered in 1992–93. Throughout the intervention in Cambodia, moreover, the Association of South-east Asian Nations (ASEAN) countries were prominent players. The first Jakarta Informal Meeting of July 1988 was the initial step in ASEAN attempts to secure cooperation between the Cambodian factions. With the establishment of the UN Transitional Authority in Cambodia (UNTAC), ASEAN countries, including Indonesia, Malaysia and the Philippines, were major contributors to the military component of the mission. Finally, the Russian Federation intervened in forcibly policing the internal borders of Tajikistan.

But if Asia is the continent of intervention, none of these interventions can be described as having been initiated in defence of humanitarian norms. Whether or not it quite merits the label of 'intervention', the Korean case was sanctioned by the UN Security Council's resolutions that referred to the obligation of the international community 'to repel armed attack'. The Indonesian action in Irian Jaya was defended as the final act in the decolonisation of the Dutch East Indies. Neither the Vietnam nor the Bangladesh cases were sanctioned by international agreement, and the Afghanistan War was fought in the teeth of international opposition. Though grave humanitarian issues (including the cost of supporting as many as 10 million refugees on Indian soil) featured prominently in the rationale initially offered by India for its conduct in Bangladesh, the Indian justification rested ultimately on claims of self-defence. India's action was not performed in concert with others, and censure in the United Nations Security Council was avoided only through the exercise of a Soviet veto. Moreover, the fact that this crisis also represented an opportunity to dismember long-time rival Pakistan cannot be ignored. Vietnam's actions in Cambodia were largely applauded for their humanitarian consequences, and those consequences figured in Vietnam's subsequent justification for its actions. However, at the time self-defence was advanced as the rationale (and not without good reason). The UN intervention in Cambodia was ultimately legitimised by the fact (or fiction) that UNTAC was acting as legatee for the Cambodian Supreme National Council, whose objective was national political reconciliation. A subordinate aspect of the exercise was to resettle around 360,000 Cambodian refugees present in Thailand. Russia polices the Tajik border in pursuit of Moscow's own security end. In short, humanitarian issues were at best ancillary objectives in all these interventions (and some were, in fact, the actual cause of additional human suffering).

If the practice of intervention in Asia has not been in pursuit of humanitarian ends, the theory too has had very few influential supporters in the region. Any suggestion that international standards or obligations might lead to censure or sanction, let alone interference in domestic affairs, is stoutly resisted. Thus, the Bangkok Declaration of April 1993 was framed by Asian nations specifically to limit the applicability of the Universal Declaration on Human Rights and its covenants to the domestic circumstances of the declaration's signatories. Humanitarian problems were not to be considered grounds for infringing the political sovereignty of nation states. In matters of security, this resistance is overt. Since its inception in 1967, ASEAN has been committed to the principles of non-interference and consensus.[2] In 1997, ASEAN admitted Myanmar, despite the very poor humanitarian and human rights record of its government, and in the face of international condemnation of Myanmar's refusal to accept the results of the democratic elections of May 1990.[3] Attempts to modify the principle of non-interference, following the organisation's poor performance during the regional financial crisis and in response to new transnational issues (including environmental threats, piracy and drug trafficking) have not been successful, even though some ASEAN leaders and policy intellectuals have been candid enough to concede that the organisation courted 'irrelevance' if it did not respond to its perceived shortcomings.[4] China is even more opposed to the principle of intervention. According to Beijing, humanitarian intervention should have UN Security Council sanction as well as the approval of the countries concerned, and, in the words of an authoritative Chinese analyst, 'the principle of non-intervention must be further strengthened not weakened'.[5] Consequently, provisions for intervention are prominent neither in the equipment and training nor in the doctrine of most Asian military forces. The exceptions are South Korea, and to some extent (having been significant providers of various forces to UN operations) Bangladesh, Pakistan and India. Japan also has a commitment to humanitarian intervention, though under special constitutional constraints.

Indonesia's original East Timor intervention of 1975 is not inconsistent with the regional pattern of justifying such actions in terms of self-defence. The ostensible grounds for Indonesia's invasion were provided by an appeal by opponents of *Fretilin* (*Frente Revolucionária de Timor-Leste Independente*) for integration with Indonesia. *Fretilin*, after victory in a brief civil conflict, had declared independence on 28 November 1975, Indonesian-led forces having by that stage occupied a number of border regions.[6] Following the Indonesian invasion proper, begun on 7 December, the petitioners of the previous year were marshalled for a meeting of a 'Regional Popular Assembly' which, on 31 May 1976, requested Indonesia to accept integration. The Indonesian case for acquisition of the territory was never clearly stated, but rested on putative historical ties, shared cross-border cultural affinities, and suggestions that any other course would produce an impoverished and unsustainable state.[7] There is some evidence that India's annexation of the Portuguese enclave of Goa had provided a precedent. Indonesian spokesmen also claimed that the influx of refugees into West Timor from late August 1975 was a burden for Indonesia, however, danger to the Indonesian state from the putative radicalism of the East Timorese political leadership was the main theme of Jakarta's justification, both at the time and later.

A preliminary analysis would suggest that the East Timor intervention of 1999 marks a departure for the region. Firstly, the humanitarian issue was the chief rationale offered for the deployment of INTERFET (International Forces in East Timor). Indeed, it could be argued that, without the systematic and wanton abuses visited on the population of East Timor immediately following the UN-conducted ballot of 30 August 1999, international opinion would not have been sufficiently mobilised to make the intervention possible.[8] Secondly, regional countries were prominent in the 'coalition of the willing' mobilised to provide personnel for the intervention. The commander of the military component of the successor to INTERFET, UNTAET (United Nations Transitional Administration in East Timor), was an officer from the Philippines, who was replaced after the completion of his tour by a colleague from Thailand. Perhaps most remarkable was China's contribution to UNTAET of civilian police. But upon examination, the Timor case is profoundly ambiguous, with humanitarian questions at best serving as a trigger for addressing international and regional issues of longer standing. If humanitarian abuses had been of primary importance at that time, intervention would surely have occurred in 1975 or 1976, and the original invasion would have been roundly condemned in the neighbourhood. The terror and dislocation experienced by the population in 1999, though horrible, were much less than their sufferings in the later 1970s.

## The East Timor Intervention

The grounds for and background to the East Timor intervention illustrate its exceptional character. UNSC Resolution 1264 of 15 September 1999 authorised the commitment of a multinational force to East Timor. The resolution noted the 'worsening humanitarian situation in East Timor' and expressed concern at 'reports indicating that systematic, widespread and flagrant violations of international humanitarian and human rights law have been committed'. It also underlined the need to punish those responsible for such violations as may subsequently be verified.[9]

Humanitarian assistance, while needed urgently, would be provided only in the context of a transfer of sovereignty and in light of Indonesia's invitation. In turn, the ballot organised by the United Nations Mission in East Timor (UNAMET) was framed by the agreement between the UN, Portugal and Indonesia, signed on 5 May, that explicitly set aside the positions taken by the parties on the status of East Timor. Throughout 1999, the uncertain political status of East Timor was thus an irreducible element in the UN position. Without this uncertain status, international intervention on the putative territory of the world's fourth-largest nation would not have been contemplated.

All the UN operations in East Timor have been coalition operations with a significant regional component. UNAMET contained many personnel from the neighbourhood. While Australian logistics and personnel were crucial, the 321-strong police and military component also included members from Bangladesh, Japan, Malaysia, Nepal, New Zealand, Pakistan, the Philippines, South Korea, the Russian Federation and Thailand, as well as others from beyond the Asia-Pacific. Australian personnel comprised the core of INTERFET, but regional states also contributed, with Thai Major-General Songkitti Jaggabatara serving as deputy-commander, 1,580 Thai military personnel comprising the second-largest element, and support provided by forces from the Philippines, Singapore and Malaysia.[10] With the advent of UNTAET, the first commander of the military component was Lieutenant-General Jaime de los Santos of the Philippines, his position being taken by Lieutenant-General Boonsran Niumpradit of Thailand in July 2000. As of late 2000, the UNTAET military and civilian police component included personnel from Bangladesh, China, Malaysia, Nepal, New Zealand, Singapore, Sri Lanka, Thailand and a substantial number from Australia.

From this roll-call it might be supposed that countries in the region are committed to peacekeeping operations as a matter both of doctrine and of force characteristics. It is certainly the case that some South-east Asian countries have been prominent in peacekeeping missions. Malaysia, for example, has taken part in 18 such exercises prior to the Timor crisis (including UNTAC, UNOSOM II and UNPROFOR). However, the strategic reality is that as most of these countries have been preoccupied with internal threats, their forces, though numerous, have been trained and configured to operate close to home and thus with supplies and support to hand.[11] These priorities are reflected in the White Papers of the various nations.[12] Malaysia devotes more attention to this issue than any of its neighbours, though it should be noted that its published guidelines on commitments to peacekeeping operations require acceptance by all disputing parties and impartiality from intervening forces.[13]

An exception to this generalisation is South Korea. The Republic of Korea presently regards participation in UN peacekeeping operations as both a duty and a source of useful experience.[14] Korea's participation in the East Timor intervention, although unexpected in Korean military circles, was consistent with the nation's force structure and doctrine. The decision to contribute to INTERFET, announced by President Kim Dae Jung at the Auckland Asia-Pacific Economic Cooperation (APEC) meeting on 13 September, was a major step forward in assembling the 'coalition of the willing' with Asian participation.

Still, without Australia's role as the lead nation in the coalition, INTERFET would not have proceeded. As early as March 1999, the Australian Defence Force (ADF) moved an additional brigade of troops to Darwin and readied further elements for regional deployment at short notice. Staff officers in the ADF formed a planning team to work on possible East Timor scenarios, with June exercises simulating a possible landing on the territory. According to press reports, Australian special forces landed covertly in mid-1999 to scout possible landing sites.[15] At this time, interception of TNI (*Tentara Nasional Indonesia*—Indonesian Military Forces) communications by Australian signals intelligence clearly demonstrated high-level Indonesian military support for the East Timorese militias.[16] The ADF had to assume that if an intervention became necessary, it could be into a hostile environment. At first it was expected that Australia's contribution would be around 1,500 troops plus logistics, but this number was increased, by stages, to 4,500 as the urgency of the commitment increased and as the misgivings of potential regional partners became more evident.

Initially, there was great reluctance on the part of Australia's potential coalition partners to an intervention. The United States cited other commitments and the ASEAN countries had no wish to offend Indonesia, irrespective of the humanitarian crisis on their doorstep. President B. J. Habibie hinted that an invitation might be extended to such a force if the disorder could not be contained, but was adamant that a unilateral action by Australia would be considered warlike. A full UN peacekeeping operation would take months to arrange and even the UN legitimation required for an international force was delayed by the slow processes of the organisation. As the potential leader of a 'coalition of the willing', Australia's delegates set out for the APEC conference in Auckland scheduled for 12–13 September with no assurance that there would be any resolution to the problem. There was talk in Australia of a crisis in the alliance relationship as a result of an apparent lack of US engagement.

In the event, Indonesia, weakened by the financial crisis and thus dependent upon international aid donors, and in the hands of an uncertain transitional political leadership, authorised an intervention. The United States applied diplomatic pressure and promised vital logistics support, and then a number of ASEAN countries joined the coalition. However, if the key players had not, fortuitously, been committed to the APEC meeting at that very time, the operation might have been delayed further or not even have occurred. And if the territory concerned had not been East Timor, Australia would not have assumed the leadership role.

## The UN and East Timor

The central theme in the history of the East Timor conflict is Indonesia's consistent rejection of international norms and opinion. In this policy, Jakarta was abetted by the determination of regional and other states to ignore what was by all accounts a human-rights disaster. The belated recognition of these aspects of the conflict lies behind the action of many states in 1999.

Indonesia acquired East Timor by military conquest, starting in October 1975 and largely accomplished by late 1978. Indonesia's conduct was in violation of important principles and conventions in international law, a fact the UN could never thereafter completely ignore. The

aggressive use of armed forces against the population of another state or territory is specifically proscribed by the UN Charter (as well as by other international instruments prohibiting
the use of force). The right of self-determination is both a recognised feature of international
law and major operating principle of the various organs of the United Nations. However,
while decolonisation has been pursued single-mindedly by the UN, secessionist movements
within already decolonised states have not generally received recognition. Indonesia itself was
a beneficiary of the principle of the non-recognition of secessionist movements, in that
Jakarta could claim Irian Jaya as an integral part of its territory on the grounds that it had
been part of the Dutch East Indies. East Timor, however, had never been part of the Dutch
empire had been recognised as a colonial territory by the UN (despite non-acknowledgement
by Portugal) and had never been previously claimed by Indonesia. Indeed, in a letter of
17 June 1974 to the East Timorese resistance leader José Ramos-Horta, the then Indonesian
Foreign Minister Adam Malik explicitly acknowledged that 'the independence of every country is the right of every nation, with no exception for the people in Timor'.[17] There are also
grounds for holding Indonesia guilty of serious humanitarian and human rights abuses.[18]
Census and other data, as well as the statements of some of the principals concerned, indicate
that between 100,000–200,000 of the inhabitants of East Timor died in the years after 1975.

The extent of the UN's commitment to East Timor is undoubtedly a function of its long
association with the territory. This association includes the fact that demands for self-
determination were for so long denied, and also the fact that East Timor's present parlous
condition is a consequence of the revenge taken after a UN-sponsored ballot demonstrated
the extent of popular opinion in favour of independence.

While the Indonesian invasion was still under way, the UN Security Council called for an
immediate Indonesian withdrawal and for 'all States to respect the territorial integrity of East
Timor as well as the inalienable right of its people to self-determination'.[19] The Security
Council restated its position in almost identical terms on 22 April 1976. While this was the
last occasion for some time on which the Security Council considered the East Timor issue, it
was a matter that the General Assembly debated annually until 1982. Although General
Assembly majorities diminished over that period, on each occasion the resulting resolution
affirmed the right of the East Timorese to self-determination.[20] Though some 22 member
states signified in one form or another that they accepted Indonesia's sovereignty over the
territory, most did not.

As long as Indonesia remained the key state of the region, and was in the hands of a
leadership determined to retain the territory, little movement could be expected. However, the
Asian financial crisis of 1997 exposed the regime's weakness. Jakarta's urgent requirement
for emergency help from the International Monetary Fund (IMF) opened the way for external
leverage to be applied. Under international pressure, and now in the hands of a transitional
political leadership of doubtful credibility, Jakarta turned to the UN to negotiate new
arrangements for the increasingly restive territory. Once its political future passed to the
forefront of the UN agenda, history could no longer be ignored.

## Regional Indifference

In any event, the United Nations could not rely upon any regional organisation to assume
responsibility for the problem. Since its inception, an important focus of ASEAN has been on
security, and the formation of the ASEAN Regional Forum (ARF) has institutionalised
region-wide security dialogue. Yet neither ASEAN nor the ARF took an active interest in the
East Timor issue.

In fact, the East Timor case illustrates the major deficiency of regional organisations acting
in such a role: as they generally include interested parties, they cannot act impartially. Aside
from Singapore's abstention at the UN General Assembly votes on Timor in 1975 and 1976,

the then ASEAN member countries always voted with Indonesia on this issue. China and Vietnam—not yet an ASEAN member—were among Indonesia's sternest critics. Japan and India, on the other hand, accepted the Indonesian position.

East Timor became the subject of renewed international attention following the 12 November 1991 Santa Cruz incident, in which 271 unarmed East Timorese civilians were killed and 382 wounded by the Indonesian army during a demonstration in Dili, and about 250 people subsequently disappeared as Jakarta's forces pursued the organisers. Yet even in this changed environment, the Philippines, Thailand and Malaysia all took steps to obstruct East Timorese pro-independence meetings and gatherings on their territory.[21] The 'Asia-Pacific Conference on East Timor' of May–June 1994 saw the Philippines, in response to pressure from Jakarta, impose entry bans on a number of participants and endeavour to have the meeting excluded from the grounds of the University of the Philippines. A meeting in July of the same year in Bangkok of the South-east Asian Human Rights Network devoted to the East Timor issue was similarly discouraged. The second 'Asia-Pacific Conference on East Timor' convened in Kuala Lumpur in November 1996 was broken up by the youth wing of the ruling United Malays National Organisation (UMNO), with police arresting some 66 local activists and journalists.

## Australia and the US

If Asian countries ignored the plight of the East Timorese, the stand taken by those states generally predisposed to defend humanitarian standards was no more helpful. Both the United States and Australia had advance warning of the original invasion, but did nothing to prevent it, and took steps subsequently to deflect criticism from Jakarta for its policies. Only much later were there any second thoughts, prompted by the Santa Cruz killings and their aftermath. US withdrawal of International Military Education and Training (IMET) funding for cooperation with Indonesia in 1993 was a major blow for the Suharto regime, and US NGOs and writers have kept the issue before the attention of the global public throughout the 1990s. Nevertheless, without US support, the annexation would not have taken place, and without US materiel, the war against the Timorese resistance forces of *Falintil (Forças Armadas de Libertação de Timor Leste Independente)* would not have been successful. On his visit to Jakarta with President Gerald Ford on 5–6 December 1975, then US Secretary of State Henry Kissinger was informed of Indonesia's invasion plans; deliveries of more than US$1 billion of arms, including counter-insurgency aircraft and other specialist items, gave Indonesian forces the upper hand from 1978. In the UN, the United States deliberately obstructed censure of Indonesia.[22]

Australian policy paralleled that of the United States.[23] Prime Minister Gough Whitlam, despite having access to information that Indonesia had launched a programme to destabilise East Timor in advance of an actual invasion, encouraged President Suharto in 1974–75 to think that Australia would find integration acceptable.[24] For a brief period under Whitlam's successor, Malcolm Fraser, a more critical approach was taken, but from December 1978, Australia acknowledged East Timor as a province of Indonesia. Australia was the only nation to enter an international legal instrument positively affirming Indonesian sovereignty, the February 1991 Timor Gap 'Zone of Cooperation' agreement. The object of this arrangement was to regulate the extraction of hydrocarbons from the basin between the two countries. The Timor Gap Agreement was the subject of a case before the International Court of Justice, brought by Portugal on the grounds that Australia, in negotiating with Indonesia, had denied Portugal's status as the administering power under international law, and therefore also had ignored the right of the population to self-determination.[25]

Meanwhile, Australia had embarked on a major programme of defence cooperation with Indonesia, including training the very forces in whose care East Timor was placed. This cooperation was codified in the December 1995 Australia–Indonesia Agreement on Maintaining Security. The avowed policy of the Australian government was to pursue 'engagement' with Asian nations, and Indonesia was regarded as the key power.[26]

The reassessment of the East Timor issue by the governments of the United States and Australia was undoubtedly fuelled by the regional financial crisis and its fallout in the form of the collapse of the Suharto regime. Even so, as late as December 1998, the Australian prime minister could still express the view that he would prefer to see East Timor remain part of Indonesia, albeit within a framework of local autonomy. Australia's role as leader of the INTERFET coalition, its support by the US, the participation of major ASEAN countries and its endorsement by the UN therefore all represent at least partial reversals of previous positions. In the case of Australia in particular, a growing awareness of the bad faith of the past has touched the national conscience and is perhaps the key to an otherwise surprising and radical policy innovation.

## Lessons of East Timor

If the East Timor intervention was, in Asian terms, uncharacteristic, there are nevertheless other protracted conflicts in the neighbourhood that may yet require some form of international action. These include religious and ethnic separatism in Myanmar and the Philippines, where failures in state capacity may force external players to assume a role. Elsewhere in Indonesia, notably in Maluku, Aceh and Irian Jaya, it is clear that Jakarta has neither the means nor the will to resolve conflicts that threaten the very integrity of the state. Further, a collapse of the regime in North Korea may generate a humanitarian and security threat beyond the capabilities of South Korea alone. State failure is a possibility in Laos, Nepal, Pakistan and Sri Lanka, and is a present reality in Afghanistan. Thus, however unique its circumstances, the East Timor case does offer some lessons for the future.

## Election Security

Perhaps the clearest lesson is that Indonesia should not have been entrusted with the maintenance of security during and after the UNAMET ballot. Throughout the ballot period, the pro-Indonesia militias were armed and directed by Indonesian military personnel who planned the post-ballot mayhem. Quite apart from the fact that Indonesia and the Indonesian security forces were interested parties in every sense, the actual security arrangements were flawed and ambiguous. The police alone were entrusted with keeping order, which allowed the numerous army personnel on the scene an excuse for inaction. UNAMET contained both a military and a police component, but they served in an advisory capacity only (though sometimes at the risk of their lives).

This is not to say that alternative security arrangements would have been easy to organise, but simply that they were not attempted. From the outset, critics argued that an international force with direct responsibility for security was needed.[27] But this demand was rejected by Jakarta as inappropriate and, indeed, Indonesia would not have been a party at all to a balloting process under which security was an international responsibility. Despite ordering two delays in the process and repeatedly criticising the partiality and ineffectiveness of Indonesian security efforts, the UN Secretary-General in his reports to the Security Council never found the situation to have deteriorated so badly as to warrant the withdrawal of UNAMET. Consequently, quite apart from the fact that there was insufficient time—in light of the normal pace of UN proceedings—to bring the Security Council to the point of debating the issue, it is unlikely that a majority could have been mustered for any modification to the UN role. In any event, a Chinese veto would have been likely.

The timing of the ballot can also be questioned. Australia, Portugal and other parties encouraged Habibie in his initiative to resolve East Timor's status in the knowledge that he was an interim leader with an uncertain mandate. Waiting for the outcome of Indonesia's 1999 elections might have been a better policy. However, the front-runner in the contest, Megawati Sukarnoputri, was opposed to relinquishing control of the territory. And once Habibie announced his intention to address the Timor issue, a delay might well have prompted the violence that was the result in September.

The lesson here has become a commonplace, namely, that a swift response to humanitarian crises is required, and that global institutions are not yet adequate to this requirement. The potential for discord during and immediately after a ballot process is heightened if the results can be interpreted as zero-sum. In the East Timor case, integration and independence were mutually exclusive outcomes. Further, neither interested parties nor their surrogates should have a role in the maintenance of security during a popular ballot in a disputed political entity. Whether such a ballot should be aborted altogether in the absence of a neutral security force must, perforce, remain a matter of judgement.

## Logistics

Operation *Stabilise*, the initial task of INTERFET, constituted a major test of the Australian military, its equipment and its systems. These performed surprisingly well, given the urgency of the operation. The leasing of a high-speed double-hulled lightweight vessel by the Royal Australian Navy in 1999 allowed for the rapid transportation of the three committed battalion groups. The deployment of infantry who then were able to patrol intensively was a crucial element in this success, though a shortage of interpreters hampered some operations.

Most noteworthy was the fact that, as the INTERFET commander, Major-General Peter Cosgrove candidly observed, 'the Australian logistics contingents supported the whole [INTERFET] force—well above design capacity.'[28] It was little short of miraculous that the Australian logistics system successfully supported the entire INTERFET operation in its initial phase. The coalition leader had to be prepared to provide whatever support was necessary for the force components. This included not only food and shelter but also, on occasion, munitions, communications facilities and transport. This is consistent with what is known of other coalition operations, notably those led by the US.[29] The difference in the East Timor case was that Australia did not have extensive experience of working with some of the military partners involved. Further, the supply of materials and equipment did not even remotely resemble the munificence associated with the world's only superpower.[30] It should be noted that the INTERFET force took from 21 September, when the initial landings were made at Dili, to 16 November, when they appeared in the Ocüssi enclave, to occupy the territory. They faced little organised opposition, took no fatalities, and killed only a handful of militia members. In retrospect, the deployment may appear to have been excessively cautious. Yet the reality is that logistics systems were fully stretched to deliver this result. If elements of the Indonesian military had opposed it, even surreptitiously, the operation would have run into severe difficulties.

This last point is not insignificant. Despite the UN mandate and Indonesia's formal assent, it was never absolutely clear whether the Indonesian military would unite in its cooperation with the international force. There was even the possibility of outright conflict, perhaps in the context of the overthrow or replacement of the political leadership responsible for the agreement. When deploying the forces, the INTERFET command had to have the demonstrated capability to protect it from any possible attack. Once the troops were in place, the commander needed to have on hand whatever systems might be required to deal with antagonists. Consequently, the INTERFET force, though charged with peacekeeping duties, had to be protected by advanced air and sea units, and its commander needed heavy armour and artillery for rapid deployment. This is a lesson both for coalition operations, where such protection may well be needed again, but also for states that consider current training and equipment for peacekeeping operations appropriate and sufficient for conditions in the twenty-first century.

Unlike some other peacekeeping operations, INTERFET found itself in a theatre without civil power, putative or otherwise. The operation was clearly opposed by militia elements, yet even their identification was a problem, as was what to do with them if they were detained. East Timor was not so much a failed state as a territory from which the attributes of the state had been removed. INTERFET was given all the necessary powers to deal with any issue; however, despite some creative measures in the dispensing of justice and in the maintenance of public order, this essentially military instrument was not always equal to every task. The relative success of this intervention in a non-state was due to widespread popular acceptance, which cannot be always assumed.

In all, the Australian commitment to East Timor in the 12 months from September 1999 cost in excess of US$550m and while Australian participation in UNTAET is partly defrayed by UN peacekeeping funds, significant costs of the same order are expected in 2000–2001. Without Australian preparedness to undertake this commitment, the coalition would never have been assembled or its forces deployed. Further, it is well-known in Australia that this commitment is only the start of what may prove a long story. Australian military forces are likely to be deployed, in one form or another, in East Timor even beyond independence, and Australian aid (not to mention revenues foregone when East Timor is given, as is expected, a larger share of the oil revenues from the Timor Gap) will need to flow for years to come.[31] Australian policy-makers are well aware of the need to avoid having yet another weak and fragile state in what is already a difficult neighbourhood.

In short, if coalition operations are to become a regular adjunct to, or even replacement for, conventional peacekeeping forces, coalition leaders (who will not always be the US) must be prepared to move, provision and protect many of their partners. Once again, the East Timor case is exceptional by virtue of the fact that Australia was prepared to act as coalition leader and possessed the necessary capability.

## Beyond Peacekeeping

The experience of the UN in building the political and civil infrastructure in the territory has been far from positive. Some critics have suggested that the organisation is unsuited to such work and that if a similar task is required elsewhere in the future, other agencies should be found to perform it.[32]

The closest analogy for the UN intervention in East Timor is the role of UNTAC in Cambodia, which might suggest that this experience constitutes something of a regional precedent.[33] However, UNTAC's role was to reconstitute political authority in the country through the convening of national elections. UNTAC's military forces were given the mission to ensure security during the preparations for the ballot. In practice, however, the Khmer Rouge remained hostile to the peace process, and the officials of Hun Sen's State of Cambodia did not always comply with the directives they received from UNTAC. In addition, all the factions retained their separate political status.[34] By contrast, the United Nations in East Timor is both state and state builder. Though East Timor also has its political factions, there are no political or administrative structures beyond or outside those engineered by UNTAET. Moreover, the CNRT (*Conselho Nacional Da Resistência Timorense*), which incorporates most of the political factions, agreed initially to set aside the rudimentary local administration that was instituted when the population moved back to their home areas once the militia violence had subsided.

As a result of the Kosovo and East Timor experiences, the latest generation of peacekeeping activities have broadened far beyond those envisaged by the originators of the practice.[35]

UN peace-builders now bring not only police, but also laws and courts; not only administrators, but administrative structures and tribunals; indeed, almost all the requisites of a modern state except modern citizens. The military element, central to the original conception of peacekeeping, must now share the stage with other, perhaps more prominent and prestigious, components. But if the inhabitants and their élites, or a significant number of either, fail to behave as modern citizens, not only is the entire intervention placed at risk, but those military forces integral to the exercise may be called to discipline or control recalcitrant members of the body politic. This outcome was narrowly avoided by UNTAC in Cambodia. It is the present predicament of the intervention force in Kosovo. Whether the same predicament will be a feature of the UNTAET experiment remains to be seen.

## Conclusions

In retrospect, the fact that Indonesian sovereignty over East Timor was never accepted by the United Nations, and that Australia, for complex domestic and historical reasons, was prepared to end of policy of engagement with Jakarta that it had pursued for almost a generation, is a concurrence of circumstances unlikely to be repeated elsewhere in the Asia-Pacific. Australia's interest in East Timor was an anomaly, and no other nation in the region looks like a viable candidate for leading future humanitarian interventions in the territories of failing states. There is little evidence that the East Timor experience has influenced the regional security perspective. Tellingly, in the Chairman's Statement concluding the Sixth ASEAN Regional Forum meeting—at a time when disorder was threatening the most important UN operation in South-east Asia since UNTAC—East Timor did not rate a mention. The most serious security issue besetting South-east Asia's most populous and powerful nation has done little to disturb the Asian resistance to humanitarian encroachment on state sovereignty.

## Notes

1. In the former, the Philippines and Thailand, as well as Australia and New Zealand; in the latter, the Philippines, Thailand, South Korea, Australia and New Zealand.
2. Kusuma Snitwongse, 'Thirty years of ASEAN: achievements through political cooperation', *The Pacific Review*, vol. 11, no. 2, 1998, pp. 184–94.
3. John Funston, 'ASEAN: Out of its Depth?', *Contemporary Southeast Asia*, vol. 20, no. 1, 1998, pp. 22–37.
4. Jusuf Wanandi, 'Asean's future at stake', *The Straits Times* (Singapore), 9 August 2000.
5. Linbo Jin, 'The Principle of Non-Intervention in the Asia Pacific Region: A Chinese Perspective', in David Dickens and Guy Wilson-Roberts (eds.) *Non-Intervention and State Sovereignty in the Asia-Pacific* (Wellington: Centre for Strategic Studies, 2000), p. 56.
6. Peter Carey, 'Historical Introduction', in Peter Carey and Steve Cox, *Generations of Resistance: East Timor* (London: Cassell, 1995), pp. 9–55; James S. Dunn, *Timor: A People Betrayed* (Milton, Queensland: Jacaranda Press, 1983); Geoffrey C. Gunn, *Timor Loro Sae: 500 years* (Macau: Livros do Oriente, 2000); Jill Jolliffe, *East Timor: Nationalism and Colonialism* (St Lucia: University of Queensland Press, 1978).
7. Heike Krieger (ed.), *East Timor and the International Community: Basic Documents* (Cambridge: Cambridge University Press, 1997), pp. 60–3.
8. Leonard C. Sebastian and Anthony L. Smith, 'The East Timor Crisis: A Test Case for Humanitarian Intervention', *Southeast Asian Affairs 2000* (Singapore: ISEAS, 2000), pp. 64–86.
9. INTERFET, http://203.46.183.231/easttimor/; James Cotton, 'The Emergence of an Independent East Timor: National and Regional Challenges', *Contemporary Southeast Asia*, vol. 22, no. 1, 2000, pp. 1–22.
10. Alan Dupont, 'ASEAN's Response to the East Timor Crisis', *Australian Journal of International Affairs*, vol. 54, no. 2, 2000, pp. 163–170
11. Joon-Num Mak, 'The Security Environment in Southeast Asia', in Desmond Ball (ed.) *Maintaining*

*the Strategic Edge: The Defence of Australia in 2015* (Canberra: Strategic and Defence Studies Centre, 1999), pp. 102, 108.

12. Department of National Defense, Republic of the Philippines, *In Defense of the Philippines. 1998 Defense Policy Paper* (Manila: Department of National Defense, 1998); Ministry of Defence, Thailand, *The Defence of Thailand 1996* (Bangkok: Ministry of Defence/Strategic Research Institute, 1996), p. 31.

13. Ministry of Defence, Malaysia, *Towards Defence Self-Reliance* (Kuala Lumpur: Ministry of Defence, 1997), p. 71.

14. Ministry of National Defense, Republic of Korea, *Defense White Paper 1998* (Seoul: Ministry of National Defense, 1999), p. 149. Prior to the East Timor commitment, the most numerous Korean contingents served in Somalia (UNOSOM II) and in Angola (UNAVEM III). From 1995 South Korea has kept one infantry battalion and an engineering company, as well as other support forces, earmarked for service under the UN.

15. *Sydney Morning Herald* (Sydney), 11 October 1999.

16. Peter Bartu, 'The Militia, the Military, and the People of Bobonaro District', *Bulletin of Concerned Asian Scholars*, vol. 32, no. 1–2, 2000, pp. 35–42.

17. Jill Jolliffe, *East Timor: Nationalism and Colonialism* (St Lucia: University of Queensland Press, 1978), p. 66.

18. Garth Nettheim, 'International Law and international politics', in Catholic Institute for International Relations and International Platform of Jurists for East Timor, *International Law and the Question of East Timor* (London: CIIR/IPJET, 1995), pp. 181–204.

19. Heike Krieger (ed.), *East Timor and the International Community: Basic Documents* (Cambridge: Cambridge University Press, 1997) p. 53.

20. José Ramos-Horta, *Funu: The Unfinished Saga of East Timor* (Lawrenceville: The Red Sea Press, 1987). The issue was then devolved to the Secretary-General under his 'Good Offices' powers. East Timor never disappeared from the UN agenda; human-rights abuses and the frustration of seeking self-determination were regularly discussed. UN attentions were rekindled by the Santa Cruz incident of November 1991. Indonesia's actions were the subject of a particularly damning report by Bacre Waly Ndiaye, the Special Rapporteur on extrajudicial, summary or arbitrary executions. See Heike Krieger, *East Timor and the International Community: Basic Documents*, pp. 261–3. Aid donors, including the Netherlands and Canada, withdrew their support, and the international media turned its attention to other forms of malfeasance by the Suharto regime. The UN arranged meetings abroad of various East Timorese to encourage reconciliation. In this context, José Ramos-Horta met Indonesian Foreign Minister Ali Alatas for the first time at the UN in 1995.

21. José Ramos-Horta, *Funu: The Unfinished Saga of East Timor* (Lawrenceville: The Red Sea Press, 1987); Sonny Inbaraj, *East Timor: Blood and Tears in ASEAN* (Chiangmai: Silkworm Books, 1995).

22. Daniel P. Moynihan, *A Dangerous Place* (Boston: Little Brown, 1978), p. 247; Carmel Budiardjo and Liem Soei Liong, *The War Against East Timor* (London: Zed Books, 1984), pp. 8–10; John Taylor, *Indonesia's Forgotten War: The Hidden History of East Timor* (London: Zed Books, 1991) pp. 84, 134; Allan Nairn, 'U.S. Support for the Indonesian Military. Congressional Testimony', *Bulletin of Concerned Asian Scholars*, vol. 32, no. 1–2, 2000, pp. 43–48.

23. James Cotton, 'East Timor and Australia—Twenty-five years of the policy debate', in James Cotton (ed.) *East Timor and Australia* (Canberra: Australian Defence Studies Centre/Australian Institute of International Affairs, 1999), pp. 1–20.

24. Desmond Ball and Hamish McDonald, *Death in Balibo, Lies in Canberra* (Sydney: Allen & Unwin, 2000); Department of Foreign Affairs and Trade, *Australia and the Indonesian Incorporation of Portuguese Timor 1974–1976*, Wendy Way (ed.) (Melbourne: Melbourne University Press, 2000).

25. Christine M. Chinkin, 'East Timor Moves to the World Court', *European Journal of International Law*, vol. 4, no. 2, 1993, pp. 206–22; Heike Krieger (ed.), *East Timor and the International Community: Basic Documents*, pp. 399–406; Thomas D. Grant, 'East Timor, the U.N. system, and enforcing non-recognition in international law', *Vanderbilt Journal of Transnational Law*, vol. 33, no. 2, 2000, pp. 273–97.

26. James Cotton and John Ravenhill (eds.), *Seeking Asian Engagement. Australia in World Affairs 1991–95* (Melbourne: Oxford University Press, 1997) pp. 1–16.

27. Lansell Taudevin, *East Timor: Too Little Too Late* (Sydney: Duffy & Snellgrove, 1999); William Maley, 'The UN and East Timor', *Pacifica Review*, vol. 12, no. 1, 2000, pp. 63–76.

28. Ian Bostock, 'By the Book. East Timor: An Operational Evaluation', *Jane's Defence Weekly*, 3 May 2000; p. 27; Sue Smith, 'A Handmaidens Tale: An Alternative View of the Logistic Lessons Learned from INTERFET' (Canberra: Australian Defence Studies Centre, unpublished paper, 2000).

29. Patrick Walsh, *Military Coalition Building: A Structural and Normative Assessment of Coalition Architecture* (Ann Arbor: UMI, 1999).

30. Estimates of how much coalition operations added to the overall cost of INTERFET vary but a sum of A\$20 million is probably conservative. *The Canberra Times* (Canberra), 13 May 2000.

31. Geoffrey A. McKee, 'A New Timor Gap', *Inside Indonesia*, 62 (April–June, 2000), pp. 18–20.

32. Jarat Chopra, 'The UN's Kingdom of East Timor', *Survival*, vol. 42, no. 3, 2000, pp. 27–39, James Traub, 'Inventing East Timor', *Foreign Affairs*, vol. 79, no. 4, 2000, pp. 74–89.

33. Sue Downey, 'The United Nations in East Timor: Comparisons with Cambodia', in Damien Kingsbury (ed.) *Guns and ballot boxes. East Timor's vote for independence* (Clayton; Monash Asia Institute, 2000), pp. 117–134.

34. Sorpong Peou, *Intervention and Change in Cambodia: Towards Democracy?* (Singapore: ISEAS, 2000), pp. 247–86.

35. Jarat Chopra, *Peace-Maintenance: The Evolution of International Political Authority* (London: Routledge, 1999); Tonya Langford, 'Things Fall Apart: State Failure and the Politics of Intervention', *International Studies Review*, vol. 1, no. 1, 1999, pp. 59–79; William Shawcross, *Deliver us from Evil. Warlords & Peacekeepers in a World of Endless Conflict* (London: Bloomsbury, 2000) pp. 362–75.

## 9.6    Nicholas J. Wheeler, "Reflections on the Legality and Legitimacy of NATO's Intervention in Kosovo"

> If, in those dark days and hours leading up to the genocide [in Rwanda], a coalition of States had been prepared to act in defence of the Tutsi population, but did not receive prompt Council authorisation, should such a coalition have stood aside and allowed the horror to unfold?[1]

This provocative challenge, issued by the UN Secretary-General to the General Assembly during its 54th session in September 1999, encapsulates the conflict between legality and legitimacy posed by NATO's military intervention in Kosovo earlier in March. On the one hand, the leading governments prosecuting the war, primarily the United States and the United Kingdom—lacked a firm basis in UN Charter law for bombing the Federal Republic of Yugoslavia (FRY). On the other, the Security Council was unanimous that the FRY was committing gross and systematic violations of human rights against the Albanian minority in Kosovo; that these constituted a threat to 'international peace and security'; and that the Security Council had demanded a cessation of the violence in three successive resolutions adopted under Chapter VII. However, owing to the threat of a Russian and Chinese veto, the Security Council was unable to authorise NATO to take military action against the FRY. Consequently, the question in the Kosovo case was not the hypothetical one posed by the Secretary-General in relation to the Rwandan genocide, since NATO in 1999 had been prepared to use force to end the atrocities in Kosovo with or without Council authorisation.

This contribution considers whether NATO's action in Kosovo represents a watershed in the development of a new norm of humanitarian intervention, and how far this is to be welcomed or feared in a society of states built on the principles of sovereignty, non-intervention and non-use of force. Does NATO's attempt at promoting justice in Kosovo signal the arrival of a doctrine of humanitarian intervention that will protect civilians who are being terrorised by their governments, or has it set a dangerous precedent that places in jeopardy the foundations of international order?

In exploring these questions, I identify three models for thinking about the legality and legitimacy of humanitarian intervention: the *posse*, the *vigilante* and the *norm entrepreneur*.[2] The idea of the posse is taken from the 'wild west' and refers to a situation where the sheriff calls upon the assistance of a group of citizens in the task of law-enforcement.[3] These individuals are given a warrant to use force from the sheriff. By analogy, the Security Council is accorded 'primary responsibility' in Article 24 of the Charter for the maintenance of 'international peace and security', and its authority under Chapter VII to authorise the use of force in defence of this purpose constitutes the Council as a posse at the global level. The response of the Security Council to the humanitarian crises in Somalia and Bosnia fits this model because the Council defined these emergencies as a threat to international security and explicitly authorised member-states under Chapter VII to use 'all necessary means' to enforce global humanitarian norms.

NATO's intervention in Kosovo does not conform to the posse model because the lack of unanimity among the permanent members led to a situation where the Alliance could not secure a warrant for military action. At this point, NATO was confronted with three possibilities. First, it could have argued that the plight of the Kosovo Albanians was so appalling as to justify intervention on moral grounds, but that it recognised that its action was an illegal one because there is no general right of humanitarian intervention under customary international law. Second, NATO governments could have defended their action on the grounds that there is a legal basis for the use of force in both treaty and customary international law. This is where the idea of an international equivalent to the vigilante comes in. The term vigilante developed in the United States in the nineteenth century and explains the actions of those private individuals who enforced the law in the absence or breakdown of officially constituted legal bodies. The key point about vigilantes is that they claim to be enforcing existing law on behalf of society; they do not advance new norms nor do they try to create new law.[4] Similarly, Alliance governments claimed (as have vigilantes in domestic societies) to be acting with the authority of the law, though no UN body authorised NATO to use military force in Kosovo.

Categorising NATO's action in Kosovo in terms of a vigilante model is at first sight appealing. The Security Council as the legally constituted law enforcement body failed to act to enforce its demands in earlier resolutions, and so NATO stepped in by claiming a legal right of humanitarian intervention. This view suited Alliance governments who wanted to argue that their action did not break international law and upheld internationally agreed standards of human rights. I argue here that this vigilante defence of NATO's action is unsustainable because there was no basis in existing law for NATO's action. The alternative interpretation of NATO's action proposed below is that members of the Alliance, notably the Blair government, were advancing a new norm of humanitarian intervention without express Security Council authorisation (I will call this 'unilateral humanitarian intervention' to distinguish it from Security Council authorised intervention).

Martha Finnemore and Kathryn Sikkink argue that the development of new norms depends crucially upon particular states acting as 'norm entrepreneurs' who attempt to convince other states to adopt the norm or norms concerned.[5] In the Kosovo case, NATO governments refused to acknowledge that they were challenging existing Charter norms concerning the prohibition on the use of force, and so they never acted as full-blown norm entrepreneurs. But the argument invoked by the British Government, in particular, in defence of NATO's bombing of the FRY, was unprecedented and raises the question of how far NATO's breach of Charter law was legitimated by other states. Finnemore and Sikkink argue that new norms emerge through a process of contestation as advocates of a new norm try to persuade a critical mass of followers that their action should not be viewed as norm-breaking behaviour. If norm entrepreneurs succeed in gaining a significant group of supporters, then a 'norm cascade' takes place as the new standard of behaviour more quickly becomes internalised. Finnemore and Sikkink consider that a fruitful area for research is to investigate how norm creation leads to new laws, and with this idea in mind, this contribution considers how far NATO's action in Kosovo sets a precedent for a new rule of customary international law supporting the legality of unilateral humanitarian intervention.

## The Contested Legality of Humanitarian Intervention

The contention that there already exists a legal right of humanitarian intervention rests on two foundations: first, on an interpretation of UN Charter provisions relating to the protection of human rights, and second, on customary international law. These foundations were stressed by a minority of international lawyers during the Cold War, and their proposition is that the promotion of human rights ranks alongside peace and security in the hierarchy of UN Charter principles. Here, they point to the language in the preamble to the UN Charter and Articles 1(3), 55, and 56 which impose a legal obligation on member-states to cooperate in promoting human rights.

According to Fernando Teson, the 'promotion of human rights is as important a purpose in the Charter as is the control of international conflict.'[6] Consequently he argues that the Security Council has a legal right to authorise humanitarian intervention irrespective of whether it has found a threat to 'international peace and security' under Chapter VII. Some jurists go even further and assert that if the Security Council fails to take remedial action in cases of massive human rights abuses, then individual states should act as armed vigilantes and take the enforcement of the human rights provisions of the Charter into their own hands. Michael Reisman and Myers McDougal claim that were this not the case, 'it would be suicidally destructive of the explicit purposes for which the United Nations was established'.[7] In response to the argument that unilateral humanitarian intervention violates the legal ban on the use of force in Article 2(4), they reply:

> Since a humanitarian intervention seeks neither a territorial change nor a challenge to the political independence of the state involved and is not only not inconsistent with the purposes of the United Nations but is rather in conformity with the most fundamental peremptory norms of the Charter, it is a distortion to argue that it is precluded by Article 2(4).[8]

Set against such views, the majority of international lawyers have been labelled 'restrictionists' because they restrict the legal right to use force under the Charter to the purposes of self-defence. They contend, in Rosalyn Higgins's words, 'that the Charter *could* have allowed for sanctions for gross human-rights violations, but deliberately did not do so'.[9] Consequently, restrictionists assert that there are only two legally recognised exceptions to the general ban on the use of force in Article 2(4): the right of individual and collective self-defence under Article 51 and Security Council enforcement action under Chapter VII of the Charter. The restrictionist case is buttressed by an appeal to customary international law. Article 38 of the statute of the International Court of Justice refers to this 'as evidence of a general practice accepted as law'. Customary law is different from treaty law because it is not created by written agreements between states that sets down the rules to regulate their interactions in a specific area.[10] It is not enough that states actually engage in the practice that is claimed to have the status of customary law; they must also justify the practice as being legally permitted. This subjective element is referred to by lawyers as *opinio juris* and is essential in identifying which norms of behaviour have become the customary rules that become legally binding upon states.

Restrictionists argue that state practice and *opinio juris* since 1945 does not support a legal right of unilateral humanitarian intervention. Here they point to the following: General Assembly standards on non-intervention, such as the 1965 Declaration on the Inadmissibility of Intervention that denied legal recognition to intervention 'for any reason whatever'; the 1970 Declaration on Principles of International Law concerning Friendly Relations and Cooperation that confirmed that '[n]o State or group of states has the right to intervene . . . in the internal or external affairs of any other State'; and the 1987 Declaration on the Enhancement of the Effectiveness of the Principle of Refraining from the Threat or Use of Force in International Relations which stated that 'no consideration of whatever nature may be invoked to warrant resorting to the threat or use of force in violation of the Charter'.[11] The International Court of Justice in the *Nicaragua* judgment considered the question of whether there were legal exceptions to the non-intervention rule, and its judgment was that this 'would involve a fundamental modification of the customary law principle of non-intervention' for which there was no support in state practice.[12]

The concept of *jus cogens* denotes 'a norm accepted and recognized by the international community of States as a whole as a norm from which no derogation is permitted and which can be modified only by a subsequent norm of general international law having the same character'.[13] 'Counter-restrictionists' deny that the prohibition on the use of force is *jus cogens*. They claim that there is custom from the pre-Charter and post-Charter period supporting a norm of unilateral humanitarian intervention. Lawyers date its origins to the seventeenth-century Dutch international lawyer Hugo Grotius, who considered that the rights of the sovereign could be limited by principles of humanity.[14] The norm was the subject of debate among international lawyers during the eighteenth century, but it was not pressed into service by states until the early nineteenth century. The 1827 intervention by Britain, France and Russia to protect Greek Christians from the oppressive rule of Turkey set the pattern for subsequent interventions in the Ottoman Empire. In language that was little different from that used by NATO to justify its use of force against the Milosevic regime, the intervening states claimed that their action was required 'no less by sentiments of humanity, than by interests for the tranquillity of Europe'.[15]

The importance of this discussion is that if a doctrine of unilateral humanitarian intervention is part of customary international law, then we should expect to see states employing it as justification and having it validated in cases where the doctrine could be plausibly invoked. However, in the three Cold War cases where a government was carrying out the mass murder of its citizens, and where there was intervention by a neighbouring state that ended the oppression, none of the intervening states—with the partial exception of India— justified the use of force on humanitarian grounds. These cases were India's intervention in East Pakistan in 1971; Vietnam's intervention in Cambodia in 1978; and Tanzania's intervention in Uganda in 1979. The international response varied from case to case depending upon Cold War geopolitics and the particular context surrounding the use of force. Vietnam suffered the greatest condemnation and sanctioning for its overthrow of the Pol Pot regime, while Tanzania's action in removing Idi Amin was treated the most leniently, but in none of these cases was there *opinio juris* supporting a legal right of humanitarian intervention.[16]

The formation of new custom requires both state practice and *opinio juris* but it would be wrong to think that non-compliance with a rule means that it has lost its legally binding character. Rosalyn Higgins gives the example of the international prohibition on torture which continues, despite widespread non-compliance on the part of states, to be a legally binding rule of customary international law 'because *opinio juris* as to its normative status continues to exist'.[17] New custom requires states to raise novel claims that by definition cannot be contained in the existing law and this means that such claims are always open to the rejoinder that they are deviant and unlawful. On the other hand, the advocacy of new norms by a state or group of states might lead, as argued above, to a 'norm cascade'.

If we accept that there was no custom supporting a right of unilateral humanitarian intervention in Cold War international society, two questions arise. How should the reluctance of states to embrace this doctrine be explained? And how far do the reasons for this reluctance persist at the end of the Cold War?

Objections to the doctrine of humanitarian intervention usually boil down to two themes: the conflict between order and justice, and the problem of abuse. Humanitarian intervention, according to theorists of international society like Hedley Bull, exposes the conflict between order and justice at its starkest because to recognise such a legal right would 'jeopardise the rules of sovereignty and non-intervention' in a world where there is no consensus on what moral principles should govern the practice of humanitarian intervention.[18] Bull dubbed the view that order had to be prioritised over justice as the 'pluralist' conception of international society, in which states are only able to agree on a minimum ethic of coexistence. He contrasted this with the 'solidarist' conception where there is sufficient consensus on basic values to create a 'solidarity . . . of the states comprising international society, with respect to the enforcement of the law'.[19] Bull argued that a solidarist society of states is one in which a right of humanitarian intervention is bestowed upon individual states who act as agents of the world common good, but maintained that the lack of solidarity on standards of justice and morality had wisely led states to eschew such solidarist ambitions. The pluralist concern is that if a right of humanitarian intervention is conceded to individual states, the door will be opened for powerful states to act on their own particular moral preferences, thereby weakening the restraints on the use of force in the society of states.

The second objection to humanitarian intervention is that such a doctrine is open to abuse. The problem of abuse only arises in a context where humanitarian justifications for the use of force have secured an important measure of collective legitimation on the part of the society of states. The concern is that by permitting a further exception to the general ban on the use of force in Article 2(4) of the UN Charter, states will be free to abuse this new legal right by claiming humanitarian justifications to cover the use of force motivated by selfish interests. The international lawyer Ian Brownlie (who represented the FRY when it tried unsuccessfully in April 1999 to persuade the International Court of Justice (ICJ) to hear its case that NATO's bombing was illegal) relates the problem of abuse specifically to the idea of vigilante action. He writes:

> Whatever special cases one can point to, a rule allowing humanitarian intervention, as opposed to a discretion in the United Nations to act through the appropriate organs, is a general license to vigilantes and opportunists to resort to hegemonial intervention.[20]

Some lawyers, who are critical of legalising humanitarian intervention because of the fear that such a rule will be abused, recognise that humanitarian intervention might be morally required in exceptional cases. Writing in 1974, Thomas Franck and Nigel Rodley argued that humanitarian intervention 'belongs in the realm not of law but of moral choice, which nations, like individuals must sometimes make'.[21] States might admit that their action is unlawful but seek to legitimate this on the grounds that it is the only means to prevent or stop genocide, mass murder and ethnic cleansing. A recent report by the Danish Institute of International Affairs on *Humanitarian Intervention: Legal and Political Aspects*, commissioned by the Danish Government, recommended adopting this policy, concluding that 'in extreme cases, humanitarian intervention may be necessary and justified on moral and political grounds even if an authorisation from the UN Security Council cannot be obtained'.[22]

Humanitarian intervention without Security Council authorisation is certainly morally preferable to the alternative of inaction in cases of extreme human rights abuses, but the Danish Institute's recommendation is unsatisfactory for two reasons. First, there is the danger that others might decide to treat the law in an equally cavalier manner in other cases, thereby fatally eroding the fabric of international law. It is an inherently flawed international legal order that expects law-abiding states to break the law in order to uphold minimum standards of humanity.[23] A second problem with the Danish Institute's position is that since it contains within it the potential to develop into a modification of existing Charter norms, why not go the whole way and argue for such a legal exception to be incorporated into international law from the outset? Surely rather than states arguing that humanitarian intervention is morally but not legally permitted, the better strategy for law-abiding states is to take the unprecedented step in post-1945 international society of invoking a new legal right of humanitarian intervention as an exception to Article 2(4) in the expectation that advocacy of a new norm will trigger a 'norm cascade', leading to a modification of customary international law. The next section asks how far the justifications employed by NATO governments for their use of force in Kosovo marked such a turning point.

## NATO's Justification for its Use of Force in Kosovo

At the request of Russia, the Security Council met on 24 March 1999 to debate NATO's action and Ambassador Lavrov opened proceedings by accusing NATO of violating the UN Charter. He argued that there was no basis in the accepted rules of international law to justify such a unilateral use of force. Russia did not defend the FRY's violations of international humanitarian law, but asserted it is only 'possible to combat violations of the law . . . with clean hands and only on the solid basis of the law'.[24] Russia was supported by Belarus, Namibia and China. They pressed the point that it was only the Security Council that had the authority to sanction military enforcement action in defence of its resolutions. India, which had asked to participate in the Security Council's deliberations, supported this position, arguing that 'No country, group of countries or regional arrangement, no matter how powerful, can arrogate to itself the right to take arbitrary and unilateral military action against others'.[25]

Set against this view, NATO governments argued that their action was both legal and morally justified because it was aimed at 'averting a humanitarian catastrophe', and hence was in conformity with Security Council Resolutions 1199 and 1203, which had demanded Serbian forces to stop their violations of human rights in Kosovo. The following reveal the legal and moral arguments justifying NATO's position. The Canadian Ambassador, for example, claimed that '[h]umanitarian considerations underpin our action. We cannot simply stand by while innocents are murdered, an entire population is displaced, villages are burned.'[26] The Netherlands Ambassador acknowledged that his government would always prefer to base action on a specific Security Council resolution when taking up arms to defend human rights; but if 'due to one or two permanent members' rigid interpretation of the concept of domestic jurisdiction, such a resolution is not attainable, we cannot sit back and simply let the humanitarian catastrophe occur'. Rather, 'we will act on the legal basis we have available, and what we have available in this case is more than adequate'.[27] Unfortunately, the Netherlands Ambassador did not specify what this legal basis was.

It is to the United Kingdom Government that we have to look to find a legal defence of NATO's action. The Blair government had taken the lead in late 1998 in arguing within the alliance that there was indeed a legal basis for NATO to use force against the FRY even without explicit Security Council authorisation. This reasoning was set out in a Foreign and Commonwealth Office paper circulated to NATO capitals in October 1998. The key sections are as follows:

> A UNSCR [Security Council Resolution] would give a clear legal base for NATO action, as well as being politically desirable. . . . But force can also be justified on the grounds of overwhelming humanitarian necessity without a UNSCR. The following criteria would need to be applied:
>
> (a) that there is convincing evidence, generally accepted by the international community as a whole, of extreme humanitarian distress on a large scale, requiring immediate and urgent relief.

(b) that it is objectively clear that there is no practicable alternative to the use of force if lives are to be saved.

(c) that the proposed use of force is necessary and proportionate to the aim (the relief of humanitarian need) and is strictly limited in time and scope to this aim.[28]

This paper echoes the views expressed by Anthony Aust, Legal Counsellor to the Foreign Office, when he defended the legality of the 'safe havens' in northern Iraq before the House of Commons Foreign Affairs Select Committee in late 1992.[29] British ministers were quick to invoke this case in late 1998 as a precedent supporting the legality of NATO's threat to use force against the FRY. The government's evolving legal position was publicly set out by Baroness Symons, Minister of State at the Foreign Office, in a written answer to Lord Kennet on 16 November 1998:

> There is no general doctrine of humanitarian necessity in international law. Cases have nevertheless arisen (as in northern Iraq in 1991) when, in the light of all the circumstances, a limited use of force was justifiable in support of purposes laid down by the Security Council but without the Council's express authorisation when that was the only means to avert an immediate and overwhelming humanitarian catastrophe.[30]

At no point during the Security Council debates in March 1999 did NATO governments try to advance the argument that the bombing of the FRY was illegal but morally justified. Rather, they emphasised that their action had the backing of international law. British Foreign Secretary, Robin Cook, appearing before the House of Commons Foreign Affairs Committee in April 1999 was pressed by Diane Abbot MP on the legal grounds for NATO's action in Kosovo. He replied: '[t]he legal basis for our action is that the international community [*sic*] states do have the right to use force in the case of overwhelming humanitarian necessity'.[31] To sustain this line of legal argument, it would have to be shown that there is existing customary law supporting such a right. However, there are two main reasons for rejecting the United Kingdom Government's claim that the case of the 'safe havens' in northern Iraq establishes such a precedent.

First, the justification employed by Baroness Symons in November 1998 was not in fact the one invoked by Western governments to defend the intervention in northern Iraq. Rather, the argument in April 1991 was that Resolution 688, which had not been adopted under Chapter VII, provided sufficient legal authority by *itself* to justify the creation of the safe havens and 'no-fly' zones. In the case of Kosovo, the existing Security Council resolutions adopted under Chapter VII were not claimed to constitute express Council authorisation; rather, they were adduced as evidence that the society of states recognised an 'overwhelming humanitarian necessity' to act.

The second reason for challenging the view that northern Iraq in 1991 established a precedent is that there has been no *opinio juris* supporting it. As discussed above in relation to the judgment of the International Court of Justice in the Nicaragua case, new custom requires states to withdraw their existing *opinio juris*. The international silence that greeted the allies' action in northern Iraq should not be interpreted as evidence that the society of states viewed these actions as permitted by international law. Acquiescence does not count as acceptance in principle of a new rule of customary international law.

Consequently, the defence of NATO's action over Kosovo in terms of the vigilante model is unsustainable because it exaggerates how far the alliance was acting in accordance with international law. Whatever Alliance governments might say to the contrary, their justifications for the use of force in Kosovo lead to the conclusion that NATO was not so much taking existing law into its own hands as establishing a normative precedent that might itself become the basis of new law.

## A New Solidarist norm of Humanitarian Intervention?

Two days after the NATO bombing began, Russia tabled with Belarus and India a draft resolution condemning NATO's action as a breach of Articles 2(4), 24 and 53 of the Charter and demanded a cessation of hostilities. States routinely invoke Article 2(4) when they want to criticise the use of force by other states, but the claim that NATO was violating Articles 24 and 53 took the debate over the legitimate use of force into new territory. As noted earlier, Article 24 refers to the 'primary responsibility' of the Security Council 'for the maintenance of international peace and security', with UN member-states agreeing that 'in carrying out its duties under this responsibility the Security Council acts on their behalf'.[32] Under Article 53 of the Charter, the Security Council is empowered to 'utilise . . . regional arrangements or agencies for enforcement action', but the Charter is explicit that this can only take place with authorisation by the Security Council. Consequently, NATO is charged with usurping the Security Council's 'primary responsibility', with the Russian Ambassador arguing that '[w]hat is in the balance now is the question of law and lawlessness. It is a question of either reaffirming the commitment of one's country and people to the basic principles and values of the United Nations Charter, or tolerating a situation in which gross force dictates realpolitik.'[33]

In response to these charges, three of the NATO states on the Security Council robustly defended 'Operation Allied Force'. The US, Netherlands and Canada rejected the charge that they were acting outside UN Charter norms, justifying their actions as being in conformity with existing Council resolutions and necessary to prevent a humanitarian catastrophe. The US argued that NATO's action was not in violation of the Charter because this did 'not sanction armed assaults upon ethnic groups, or imply that the international community should turn a blind eye to a growing humanitarian disaster'.[34] Canada stressed the international legitimacy behind NATO's actions, arguing that supporting the draft resolution would place states 'outside the international consensus, which holds that the time has come to stop the continuing violence' by the FRY against the Kosovars.[35]

When the draft resolution was put to the vote, it was defeated by 12 votes to three (Russia, China and Namibia). Speaking after the vote, the British Government argued that Security Council resolutions 1199 and 1203 determined that Milosevic's policies had 'caused the threat to peace and security in the region', and that 'military intervention is justified as an exceptional measure to prevent an overwhelming humanitarian catastrophe'.[36] This was endorsed by the French Government which argued that the 'actions decided upon respond to Belgrade's violation of its international obligations under the resolutions which the Security Council has adopted under Chapter VII of the United Nations Charter'.[37]

The legal and moral position taken by NATO governments in the Security Council debate on 26 March is not surprising, but what has to be explained is how six non-Western states came to vote with Slovenia in comprehensively defeating a Russian draft resolution condemning NATO's bombing. Nigel White argues that 'lack of condemnation by the Security Council cannot be seen as an authorisation to use force',[38] but while this is correct, the more pertinent question is whether this vote constitutes a new practice and *opinio juris* in support of a right of unilateral humanitarian intervention. The first point to make here is that of the six non-Western states on the Council which rejected the draft resolution, only three chose to make statements. The Bahrain government reiterated the standard NATO argument that the humanitarian catastrophe taking place inside Kosovo justified NATO's action, and that support for the draft resolution would encourage the Milosevic regime to continue its policy of ethnic cleansing.[39] The Malaysian Government regretted that owing to irreconcilable differences within the Security Council, it had 'been necessary for measures to be taken outside of the Council'.[40] Although this was hardly a ringing endorsement of NATO's action, the Malaysian Government is a staunch defender of the non-intervention rule, and the fact that it was prepared to publicly legitimate an action that bypassed the Security Council is highly significant. The position it took over Kosovo probably reflected the fact that NATO's intervention was in defence of Moslems. The Argentine Government was even stronger in its support for NATO's action, stating that rejection of the draft resolution was based on contributing to efforts to stop the massive violations of human rights in Kosovo. Indeed, the Argentinean Ambassador argued that the obligation to protect human rights and fulfil 'the legal norms of international humanitarian law and human rights is a response to the universally recognised and accepted values and commitments'.[41] The implication of this was that in exceptional circumstances—such as those prevailing in Kosovo—states have a right to use force to put an end to human rights violations even without express Security Council authorisation. One important explanation for Argentina's public support of NATO's action is that its growing commitment to democratic values at home was being reflected in a commitment to defend human rights internationally. Gambia and Gabon did not participate in the debate and Brazil, which had strongly opposed any use of force by NATO without Security Council authority in earlier debates, also remained silent.

The approval given to NATO's action by the Slovenian Government was less surprising than that given by the Argentine and Malaysian Governments. The Slovenian Ambassador, as it happened a former professor of international law, argued that while his government would have preferred direct Security Council authorisation, 'the Security Council has the primary but not exclusive responsibility for the maintenance of international peace and security'. This argument represented an imaginative response to the Russian charge that NATO was acting contrary to Article 24 of the Charter since the Slovenian Ambassador considered that 'all the Council members have to think hard about what needs to be done to ensure the Council's authority and to make its primary responsibility as real as the Charter requires'.[42] According to this view Russia and China were in breach of Article 24 because the threat of their vetoes had prevented the Security Council from exercising its 'primary responsibility for the maintenance of international peace and security'.

The various justifications for NATO's action proffered by members of the Security Council during the debate on 26 March were rejected by the sponsors of the draft resolution and their supporters. For example, the Indian representative stated that NATO 'believes itself to be above the law. We find this deeply uncomfortable.' Indeed, India challenged the international legitimacy of NATO's action by arguing that the 'international community can hardly be said to have endorsed their actions when already representatives of half of humanity have said that they do not agree with what they have done'.[43]

These arguments and counter-arguments raise the question: how many states have to validate a new practice before a 'norm cascade' takes place and a new rule of customary international law develops? The 26 March vote in the Security Council was historic because for the first time, since the founding of the Charter, seven members either legitimated or acquiesced in the use of force justified on humanitarian grounds in a context where there was no express Council authorisation. NATO's action was also endorsed beyond the Security Council by the European Union (though there was significant domestic opposition in states such as Germany, Greece and Italy), by the Organisation of Islamic states (which, like Malaysia, welcomed an action that might save Moslems), and by the Organisation of American States, which issued a statement regretting the action, but not condemning it.

NATO's justification for its use of force in Kosovo was that it expressed the collective will of the society of states as embodied in Security Council resolutions. The Security Council vote lends some support to this proposition, but it is unwise to read too much into what was effectively a 7–3 vote where only three of the seven spoke in support of NATO's action, and a variety of factors came into play, as well as the particular issues relating to Kosovo. NATO could have attempted to strengthen its claim to be acting on behalf of the 'international community' by another route, namely placing the issue before the General Assembly. Nigel White argues that the General Assembly has legal competence under the Charter to recommend military measures when the Security Council is unable to exercise its 'primary responsibility for maintaining international peace and security', and that the 1950 'Uniting for Peace' Resolution could have been invoked for this purpose. Adopted at the height of the Cold War, this Resolution was a way of bypassing the Soviet veto in the Security Council.[44]

NATO could have placed a draft resolution before the Security Council authorising it to use force against the FRY in the event that the Milosevic regime continued to fail to comply with Council resolutions. At this point, a Russian and Chinese veto would have publicly exposed these states as the ones opposing intervention to end the atrocities. Even if Russia and China had cast their vetoes, NATO would then have been able to put a procedural resolution forward requesting that the matter be transferred to the General Assembly under the 'Uniting for Peace' resolution (the right of the veto does not exist in relation to procedural resolutions). This possibility leads White to argue that had NATO 'won both a procedural vote in the Security Council and a substantive vote in the General Assembly [requiring a two-thirds majority of the Assembly], NATO then would have had a sound legal basis upon which to launch its air strikes'.[45]

NATO governments did not go down the Uniting for Peace road because they could not guarantee securing the two-thirds majority to pass a resolution recommending military action. Western governments were not even prepared to risk putting a draft resolution before the Security Council authorising the use of force, and this is a body that they can be much more confident about controlling than the General Assembly. Requiring a two-thirds majority in the General Assembly for humanitarian intervention in cases where the Security Council has found a threat to the peace but is unable to act because the use of the veto establishes a high threshold of legitimacy, and it would certainly minimise the risks that states would abuse this right. However, the problem with this prescription is that it makes state practice the acid-test of legitimacy. Indeed, making Assembly approval a precondition for intervention poses the same question that Kofi Anan addressed to the General Assembly in September 1999: should a group of states stand aside if they cannot secure the necessary votes in the General Assembly in cases where massive and systematic abuses of human rights are taking place? If we think back to the cases of the 1970s, had India, Vietnam and Tanzania in the 1970s relied on General Assembly resolutions to legitimise their interventions, the victims of state terror in East Pakistan, Cambodia and Uganda would have been left to their fate. In the cases of East Pakistan and Cambodia, India and Vietnam's non-humanitarian reasons for intervening did not contradict a positive humanitarian outcome, but in both cases, especially the Cambodian one, the General Assembly failed to legitimate the action as a humanitarian exception to the rules of the society of states.[46]

## A Historical Watershed?

The experience of the 1990s suggests that the Security Council is too weak to enforce minimum standards of common humanity. In 1991, it was divided over the use of force to protect the Kurds; at the end of the decade, it was unable to issue NATO with a warrant for its use of force in Kosovo. Given the volatile domestic situation in Russia, and the heightened sensitivity of Russia and China to actions that erode the sovereignty rule, it is highly unlikely that the permanent members of the Security Council will become a humanitarian coalition of the willing in future cases of gross human rights abuses. The limited prospects of the Security Council acting as a global posse means that the enforcement of global human rights standards depends upon particular states acting on behalf of the society of states. The problem, as Brown puts it, is '[u]nder what circumstances is enforcement action to be seen as the action of "international society" and not simply the individual states who take it?'.[47]

The standard pluralist objection to humanitarian intervention, in Hedley Bull's words, is that 'states or groups of states that set themselves up as the authoritative judges of the world common good ... are in fact a menace to international order'.[48] However, as Bull also recognised, intervention which 'expresses the collective will of the society of states' may be carried out without challenging order.[49] The challenge taken up by solidarist international society theory is to find ways of making unilateral humanitarian intervention an expression of the collective will of the society of states, and not a fundamental threat to its ordering principles. In developing the norms to regulate a practice of unilateral humanitarian intervention, the moral imperative to end the mass slaughter of civilians must not be subordinated to the requirement that intervention always be authorised by the UN Security Council or General Assembly. These bodies are important in securing collective legitimation for unilateral humanitarian intervention, but they cannot be allowed a veto on whether gross violations of human rights are ended in cases like Rwanda and Kosovo.

States that decide to use force to end atrocities without express UN authorisation, either from the Security Council or the General Assembly, must justify their actions on the basis of criteria that they would applaud others invoking in similar circumstances. They should justify their actions in terms of a new legal right of humanitarian intervention in customary international law in the hope that this will trigger a 'norm cascade' in the society of states. There will be opposition to a new norm from powerful governments like Russia, China and India, but future norm entrepreneurs should seek as wide a base of legitimation as possible among domestic publics, media, other governments, human rights NGOs and wider world public opinion.

The need for legitimation is a powerful constraining force on state actions, and if governments are unable to make a plausible defence of their use of force as humanitarian, then international society and wider transnational global civil society should mobilise moral censure and economic sanctions against these states as a deterrent to others. Considerations of power and interest will clearly influence the level of sanctioning in particular cases, and if the most powerful states abused such a norm, there are clear constraints on the level of pressure that can be brought to bear on these governments. However, what is crucial is that even the most powerful governments do not want to be exposed as hypocrites. And once a state has legitimated its action as humanitarian, its subsequent actions will be constrained by the need to remain true to the humanitarian purposes that it claimed motivated its action.

What is required in the aftermath of the Kosovo intervention is that the society of states begin a genuine dialogue on the criteria that justify states using force for humanitarian purposes in cases where the Security Council is unable to act because of the power of the veto. Governments committed to the defence of human rights should take the lead in initiating this dialogue, and what is needed is a commitment by governments to the idea that in exceptional cases the slaughter of civilians might be so appalling as to legitimate the use of force to enforce minimum standards of common humanity. It might be argued that such a modification of Charter norms is not possible in a General Assembly dominated by non-democratic regimes which are jealous of their sovereign prerogatives. One way of testing this would be for Western states to respond more urgently to the challenge raised by many southern states that the ideology of humanitarianism propounded by Western governments since the end of the Cold War masks the continuing political and economic hegemony of Western states, and the violence required to sustain it.

Creating a new norm that enables humanitarian intervention is no guarantee that it will take place when it is desperately needed, as in Rwanda in 1994.[50] The positive interpretation of NATO's action in Kosovo is that the moral claims raised in defence of Kosovo Albanians will make it very difficult for the Alliance to look on with indifference the next time genocide, mass murder or ethnic cleansing occurs in Europe or elsewhere. The problem with this argument is that it overlooks the fact that the humanitarian impulse to act in Kosovo was joined by the belief that NATO had important security interests at stake in the region, and that the credibility of the Alliance was on the line if it did not stand up to Milosevic. This combination of humanitarian emergency and hard-headed security interests is unlikely to confront the Alliance outside the Balkans, and this suggests that Kosovo does not mark the beginning of an era in which NATO will act as a global enforcer of humanitarian norms.

The Kosovo case is further limited as a legal precedent because it could only plausibly be invoked by other states in a context where the Security Council has already adopted Chapter VII resolutions identifying a government's human rights abuses as creating a threat to 'international peace and security', and where the threat or use of the veto has prevented the Council from authorising the use of force. Having watched NATO governments defend their military action in Kosovo by appealing to resolutions adopted under Chapter VII, it is likely that Russia and China will be considerably more cautious about passing such resolutions in the future.

NATO's intervention in Kosovo did secure widespread approval in the society of states, but where there is only one case in support of a new rule, states can easily nullify it by acting against the rule in future instances.[51] Consequently, given the record of state practice against a norm of unilateral humanitarian intervention in the post-1945 period, it will require additional cases where practice and *opinio juris* support this norm before a judgment can be made as to how far Kosovo marks a turning point in legitimising the practice of unilateral humanitarian intervention.

## Notes

1. Secretary's General Annual Report to the General Assembly, Press Release SG/SM7136 GA/9596, http://srch 1.un.org:80/plweb-cgi/fastweb, 20 Sept. 1999
2. See Nicholas J. Wheeler, 'Humanitarian Vigilantes or Legal Entrepreneurs: Enforcing Human Rights in International Society', which will appear in a special issue of *Critical Review of International Social and Political Philosophy* (forthcoming, 2000), edited by Peter Jones and Simon Caney.
3. The idea of the posse is developed by Chris Brown in his 'The Artificial Person of International Society' (unpublished paper, supplied by the author, pp. 11–12).
4. Ibid., p. 12.
5. Martha Finnemore and Kathryn Sikkink, 'International Norm Dynamics and Political Change', *International Organization*, Vol.2, No.4 (1998), p. 895.
6. Fernando Teson, *Humanitarian Intervention: An Inquiry into Law and Morality* (Dobbs Ferry, NY: Transnational Publishers, 1988), p.131.
7. Quoted in A.C. Arend and R.J. Beck, *International Law and the Use of Force: Beyond the UN Charter Paradigm* (London: Routledge, 1993), p.133.
8. Quoted in Arend and Beck, *International Law and the Use of Force*, p.134.
9. Rosalyn Higgins, *Problems and Process: International Law and How We Use It* (Oxford: Clarendon Press, 1994), p.255.
10. Arend and Beck (note 8), p.6.
11. These examples are cited by Marc Weller in 'Access to Victims: Reconceiving The Right To "Intervene" ', in Wybo P. Heere, *International Law and The Hague's 750th Anniversary* (Leiden: A.W. Sijthoff, 1972), p.334.
12. Quoted in ibid., p.334. See also Michael Byers, *Custom, Power and the Power of Rules: International Relations and Customary International Law* (Cambridge: Cambridge University Press, 1999), p.184.
13. This definition from the 1969 Vienna convention on the Law and Treaties is quoted in Byers, ibid., p.183.
14. This is discussed in Francis Kofi Abiew, *The Evolution of the Doctrine and Practice of Humanitarian Intervention* (The Hague: Kluwer Law International, 1999), p.35.
15. Ibid., p.49.
16. These cases are discussed in detail in Nicholas J. Wheeler, *Saving Strangers: Humanitarian Intervention in International Society* (Oxford: Oxford University Press, 2000).
17. Higgins (note 9), p.22.

18. Hedley Bull, 'Conclusion' in Hedley Bull (ed.), *Intervention in World Politics* (Oxford: Oxford University Press, 1984), p.193.

19. Hedley Bull, 'The Grotian Conception of International Society' in Martin Wight and Herbert Butterfield (eds) *Diplomatic Investigations: Essays in the Theory of International Politics* (London: Allen and Unwin, 1966), pp.51–73.

20. Ian Brownlie, 'Thoughts on Kind-Hearted Gunmen', in Richard Lillich (ed.), *Humanitarian Intervention and the United Nations* (Charlottesville, Va.: University Press of Virginia, 1973), pp.147–8.

21. Thomas Franck and Nigel Rodley, 'After Bangladesh: The Law of Humanitarian Intervention by Force', *American Journal of International Law*, Vol.67 (1973), p.304.

22. See *Humanitarian Intervention: Legal and Political Aspects* (Danish Institute of International Affairs, 1999), p.128.

23. See Wil Verwey, 'Humanitarian Intervention in the 1990s and Beyond: an International Law Perspective' in Jan N. Pieterse (ed.), *World Orders in the Making: Humanitarian Intervention and Beyond* (London: Macmillan, 1998), p.200.

24. S/PV.3988, 24 March 1999, p.3.

25. Ibid., p.15.

26. Ibid., p.6.

27. Ibid., p.8.

28. Quoted in Adam Roberts, 'NATO's "Humanitarian War" over Kosovo', *Survival*, Vol.41, No.3 (1999), p.106.

29. See FCO text quoted in *The British Yearbook of International Law 1992* (Oxford: Clarendon Press, 1993), pp.827–8.

30. Baroness Symons of Vernham Dean, written answer to Lord Kennet, *Hansard*, 16 November, 1998, col. WA 140.

31. Robin Cook's statement is quoted in N.D. White, 'The Legality of Bombing in the Name of Humanity', paper presented at the 1999 BISA conference held at the University of Manchester, 20–2 Dec. 1999, p.7.

32. Charter of the United Nations, Article 24.

33. S/PV.3989, 26 March, 1999, p.6.

34. Ibid., p.5.

35. Ibid., p.3.

36. Ibid., p.7.

37. Ibid., p.7.

38. White (note 31), p.6.

39. S/PV, 3989, 26 March, 1999, p.9.

40. Ibid., p.9.

41. Ibid., p.7.

42. Ibid., p.4.

43. Ibid., p.16.

44. White (note 31), pp.10–11.

45. Ibid., p.14.

46. See *Saving Strangers* (note 16), Chapters 2, 3 and 4.

47. Brown (note 3), pp.11–12.

48. Hedley Bull, *Justice in International Relations* (Hagey Lectures, University of Waterloo, 1983), p.14.

49. Bull (note 18), p.195.

50. Henry Shue, 'Let Whatever is Smouldering Erupt? Conditional Sovereignty, Reviewable Intervention and Rwanda 1994' in Albert J. Paolini, Anthony P. Jarvis and Christian Reus-Smit, *Between Sovereignty and Global Governance: the United Nations, the State and Civil Society* (London: Macmillan, 1998), p.77.

51. Byers (note 12), p.159.

# Part V

*Prosecution of Crimes against Humanity and Genocide*

# 10

## Setting a Precedent
### The Nuremberg Trials

At the end of World War II, between October 18, 1945 and October 1, 1946, the International Military Tribunal (IMT) was established for the purpose of trying twenty-two major Nazis, pursuant to the following counts: Crimes Against Peace; War Crimes; Crimes Against Humanity; and (the chief indictment) Conspiring to Commit any of the foregoing in a "Common Plan." The IMT sat at the Palace of Justice, in the German city of Nuremberg.

The trials were established as a result of decisions taken over a lengthy period during the war itself, and were ultimately endorsed and carried out by all the major Allied powers fighting to defeat Nazism: Britain, France, the United States, and the Soviet Union. The idea of bringing the leading Nazis before the bar of international justice had evolved over time, and, as Howard Ball shows in his article "The Path to Nuremberg," there was some debate over what should be done with the major Nazi leaders right up to the spring of 1945. Once the decision was made to proceed, however, the IMT developed a momentum of its own, after which it was viewed as the most appropriate vehicle for dealing with those who were held to be responsible for the outbreak of the war and all the death and damage it had caused.

The trials were to set the tone for all subsequent war crimes trials down to the present day, though the major emphasis of the IMT lay in a concern to bring to justice those who had upset the international order by waging aggressive war—not those who had necessarily committed crimes against humanity and certainly not genocide, which had not even been deemed an international crime at this stage.

A general understanding since the trials is that the IMT was set up to sit in judgment on the Holocaust, but that was not the case. Owing to the shocking revelations and film footage that came to light during the trial, the original aims of the IMT, as they pertained to the criminal act of waging aggressive war, were somewhat submerged into a more general revulsion at the Nazis' actions against their captive populations (and in particular, the Jews). Hence, while the perpetration of the Holocaust itself was not on trial, revelations about the horrors of Nazi mass murder served to confirm for people living in the Allied countries why the struggle against the Nazis had been too important to lose—and why those deemed responsible for it should be brought to trial and, if found guilty, be punished accordingly.

As Ball shows, the issues surrounding the IMT were many, not the least of which was the question of just what should be on trial. By the time the court sat for the first time, it was universally recognized by all concerned that it would have to be seen as more than simply a trial sitting in judgment on the Nazi persecution of the Jews. Nothing was seen in the first instance as being more criminal than the foisting of aggressive war upon a world which had previously been clearly committed to avoiding it.

When the Tribunal (comprised of two judges each from Britain, France, the United States, and the Soviet Union) handed down its decisions, there were few surprises. Six of the accused were found guilty on all four counts, and sentenced to hang; another six were similarly sentenced after having been found guilty of some of the counts. Seven were given prison terms of various lengths and three were acquitted.

Twelve subsequent trials were held between 1946 and 1949. These trials considered the fates of the SS as a criminal organization, Nazi physicians who had conducted medical experiments against prisoners, commandants of Nazi concentration camps, leaders of major business enterprises, and other similar charges. One hundred seventy-seven persons were convicted of various criminal acts, and were sentenced either to death or to prison terms.

The Charter of the Nuremberg Trials was unprecedented in international law, and it was a crucial step on the road to a universal anti-genocide, anti-crimes against humanity, and anti-war crimes regime that would be binding upon all. It served as the major springboard for a number of international agreements to follow, the first of which was the United Nations Convention on the Prevention and Punishment of the Crime of Genocide (UNCG), in 1948. The development of a jurisprudence covering genocide and crimes against humanity would see its crowning moment in 2002, with the establishment of the International Criminal Court (ICC) in The Hague. The IMT was, therefore, the great precedent in the creation of international case-law that would ultimately relate to the prevention and punishment of the crime of genocide, a word which had only recently (in 1944) been coined by Raphael Lemkin and which was not, at the time of the IMT, yet in general currency.

The IMT was path breaking in another sense, too: it established what became known as the "Nuremberg Principles," according to which every person is considered to be responsible for his or her own actions, and that, as a result, no one stands above international law. The notion of "following superior orders," which many of the Nazi defendants attempted to use as their key defense position during the trials, became nullified by these principles.

The Nuremberg Principles, in summary form, read as follows: (I) any person who commits a crime under international law is responsible for the act, and liable to punishment; (II) where there is no set punishment for the act committed, it does not negate its criminality; (III) being a Head of State or a government official does not absolve a person from the responsibility of having committed a criminal act, if the act committed is criminal within international law; (IV) "following superior orders" is not a valid or legitimate defense, provided a moral choice was available to the person committing the criminal act; (V) a fair trial should be made available as a matter of right to anyone accused of committing a crime under international law; (VI) the crimes for which a person may be indicted are: (a) crimes against peace; (b) war crimes; and (c) crimes against humanity; and (VII) complicity in the commission of any of the above-mentioned crimes is itself considered a criminal act under international law. The Nuremberg Principles have since been incorporated into a number of other multilateral treaties, most notably that which established the International Criminal Court in 2002.

Although the IMT carried within it numerous legal-ethical problems—not the least of which was the allegation from its detractors that it was nothing but a "victors' court" devoid of neutrality or impartiality—its appearance marked an important intellectual and practical step on the road to creating a human rights regime enshrined in law.

# 10.1   Howard Ball, "The Path to Nuremberg: 1944–1945"

There is a common wisdom about Allied punishment of Nazi leaders after the war ended. Because of the brutal actions taken by Nazi Germany against belligerents, prisoners of war, civilians in occupied nations, and especially targeted-for-extermination *untermenschen* such as Jews, Gypsies, Poles, and Russians, the victors would quickly create an ad hoc international criminal justice tribunal to bring to trial and punish the Nazis found guilty of waging aggressive war, war crimes, crimes against humanity, and genocide. In actuality, the decision to try the major Nazi leaders in a courtroom was finally reached only after the war in Europe ended in May 1945.

Although it is correct to say that the "punishment of war criminals came to be regarded among the most urgent problems to be solved after the war,"[1] it is somewhat misleading because of what it leaves out. Until the spring of 1945, to the British and the Americans, "punishment" of Nazis for war crimes meant *summary execution after capture—without a trial.* Ironically as early as November 1942, it was the Russians who suggested and continually pushed for the establishment of a postwar tribunal.[2] As late as the winter of 1945, the British and Americans were in agreement on a plan that called for summary execution, and these two nations fruitlessly tried to convince the Russians to go along.

For the Allies, until May 1945, the promised "stern justice" for the Nazi war criminals was not spelled out. There were essentially two choices: judicial proceedings (like those enumerated in the Versailles Treaty) or executive action. The British were strongly in favor of executive action, that is, summary executions of Nazi leaders without trial. An aide-mémoire from Great Britain, sent to Roosevelt on April 23, 1945, stated Churchill's views:

> [His Majesty's Government is] deeply impressed with the dangers and difficulties of this course [judicial proceedings], and they think that execution without trial is the preferable course. [A trial] would be exceedingly long and elaborate, [many of the Nazis' deeds] are not war crimes in the ordinary sense, nor is it at all clear that they can properly be described as crimes under international law.[3]

In the United States, no fewer than seven federal agencies were working on plans for a defeated postwar Germany (the Departments of State, War, Navy, Treasury, and Justice; the Office of Strategic Services; and the White House staff). The most influential person through early 1945 was "the president's old friend,"[4] Secretary of the Treasury Henry Morganthau, Jr. (whose father, as U.S. ambassador to the Ottoman Empire, had observed firsthand the Turkish genocide of the Armenians in 1915). Roosevelt asked Secretary of War Henry Stimson and Secretary of State Cordell Hull to prepare recommendations as to how the Nazi leaders should be punished after the war, but Morganthau also gave the president his thoughts and a plan. Morganthau, a member of one of New York's old Jewish families,[5] agreed with the British and recommended a "tough peace" for Germany. On his return from a visit to France in the summer of 1944, he quickly prepared and sent to Roosevelt a vengeful plan in opposition to a War Department plan that he thought would "coddle the defeated Nazis."[6]

Morganthau called for the deindustrialization of the Ruhr and Saar Valleys and for Germany to be turned "into a country primarily agricultural and pastoral."[7] He also called for the use of German POWs to rebuild Europe, the banishment of all SS storm troopers and their families from Germany to "remote places,"[8] and the distribution to the advancing Allied armies of a list of 2,500 top Nazi war criminals–generals, admirals, party leaders, gestapos, and industrialists–to be shot upon capture.[9]

Churchill approved Morganthau's plan, as did Roosevelt, and the two leaders sought to convince the Russians to accept it. But there were Americans in the Roosevelt administration, in particular Stimson and his assistant secretary, John McCloy (with behind-the-scenes support from U.S. Supreme Court Justice Felix Frankfurter, a friend of Stimson's and McCloy's mentor), along with Hull and the Army Judge Advocate Group, who were dead set against the tough summary justice plan–the Old Testament's "eye for an eye" punishment.[10] However, through December 1944, the Morganthau plan was on "the front burner."[11]

Stimson and Hull had always believed that some kind of international judicial proceeding for the punishment of the Nazi leaders was required. The task of developing such a plan was given, in September 1944, to a Jewish lawyer in the War Department's three-man Special Project Branch, Lieutenant Colonel Murray Bernays. He addressed the problem of punishment by asking two questions: how to punish Nazi leaders for prewar crimes against German Jews and others, and how to deal with the millions of Germans who were members of the SS, the gestapo, and other Nazi organizations responsible for the murder of millions of persons during the war.[12]

His answer was one found in American and British jurisprudence: the law of criminal conspiracy. (He noted some precedents: the Smith Act in America, passed in 1938, and the British India Act of 1836.[13]) Nevertheless, a big problem existed for Bernays and the Americans if this plan were adopted: Conspiracy was essentially an American and British concept. It did not exist in French, Russian, and German jurisprudence or in their criminal law.[14]

If a Nazi organization–political, military, or police–"contemplate[d] illegal methods or illegal ends," each member of the organization was liable for the acts of all other knowing members. Collective criminality, the crime of membership, was at the core of the Bernays plan. As developed by the international military tribunal (IMT) at Nuremberg, there were five questions that had to asked by prosecutors before indicting a detainee:

1.  Did the Nazi organization have a common plan of criminal action?
2.  Was a group's actions criminal?
3.  Was a person's membership in such a group voluntary?
4.  Was a person's membership a knowing one, that is, did the person have some knowledge of the criminal aims of the organization?
5.  Was there evidence that the person was such a member and that he or she acted to achieve the organization's criminal goals?[15]

The strategy was to indict and try the Nazi leaders for conspiring to commit criminal acts; charge them with committing the actual violations themselves; then quickly try other low-ranking Nazi war criminals under this "guilt by knowing association" charge inherent in the criminal conspiracy-criminal organization strategy.

Within weeks, Bernays devised a plan that would be implemented at the IMT at Nuremberg. From the time Hitler came to power in 1933, reasoned Bernays, the Nazi dictatorship had been a gigantic criminal conspiracy to wage aggressive war and to commit war crimes and crimes against humanity.

> The whole movement had been a deliberate, concerted effort to arm for war, forcibly seize the lands of other nations, steal their wealth, enslave and exploit their populations, and exterminate the . . . Jews of Europe.[16]

Bernays sent the plan to Stimson, and in the fall of 1944, the secretary of war began lobbying for its adoption, rather than the vindicative Morganthau plan. It was, until January 1945, a "mission impossible." Most of Roosevelt's advisers were against the Bernays plan; instead of indictments and trials for conspiracy, there was comfort in the security of Morganthau's summary execution proposal. There was little chance that Roosevelt would opt for the War Department proposal for dealing with Nazi war criminals.

The turning point came in January 1945, when Americans woke up to read and hear about German atrocities committed against American soldiers who had surrendered at a place in Belgium called Malmédy. During the December 1944 battle of the Bulge (a futile German effort to breech the Allied forces in Belgium and turn the war around), over seventy Americans were captured by the finatical Waffen SS First Panzer Division, tied up, machine-gunned to death, and buried under the snow in the Malmédy battlefield. The "emotional impact in America was unbelievable."[17] Stimson quickly argued that Malmédy was not an isolated war crime: it was part of a general Nazi plan to wage a brutal, criminal war against military and civilians alike. The tragedy at Malmédy violated the Geneva Accords regarding the treatment of prisoners of war. Malmédy was a small part of a "purposeful and systematic conspiracy to achieve domination of other nations and peoples by deliberate violations of the rules of war as they have been accepted and adhered to by the nations of the world."[18]

In a joint memorandum sent to Roosevelt by Stimson and Hull on January 22, 1945, they forcefully restated their views:

> While [executive action] has the advantage of a sure and swift disposition, it would be violative of the most fundamental principles of justice, common to all the United Nations. This would encourage the Germans to turn these criminals into martyrs and, in any event, only a few individuals could be reached in this way. Consequently [although there are serious legal difficulties involved in a judicial proceeding], we think that the just and effective solution lies in the use of the judicial method. Condemnation of these criminals after a trial, moreover, would command maximum public support in our own times and receive the respect of history. The use of the judicial method will, in addition, make available for all mankind to study in future years an authentic record of Nazi crimes and criminality.[19]

Roosevelt was finally persuaded by their arguments and took the Bernays plan with him for his meeting at Yalta in February 1945 with Churchill and Stalin. Bernays's plan met stiff resistance from the British. Churchill still insisted on a Morganthau-type plan that would summarily execute the top Nazi political and military leaders. In April 1945, he was still calling for death without trial for the Nazi leaders.[20] (France, a late participant in these conversations, agreed with Russia and the United States on the necessity of war crimes trials.)

However, in late April 1945, the British and American armies came across the concentration camps at Belsen, Buchenwald, and Dachau, and the Russian armies discovered the killing center at Auschwitz. The shock of discovering the Holocaust moved the Allies to adopt a postwar plan that would show the world the horrors of a bureaucratically planned and implemented genocide of unimaginable magnitude. In May 1945, the plan was finally, though grudgingly, accepted by Great Britain,[21] and the Allied quartet prepared to ask the recently formed United Nations to adopt the plan at its first meeting in San Francisco, California, later that summer.

At this time, another problem surfaced. It was "the most nettlesome one that would face the judges."[22] And it is still controversial more than fifty years after Nuremberg: the "victors' justice" label placed on the work of the Nuremberg tribunal.[23]

The Roman adage *nullum crimen et nulla poena sine lege,* "no crime and no punishment without law," was a criticism heard by the jurists who drafted and the prosecutors and judges who were involved in the trial of the major Nazi war criminals at Nuremberg. German actions, however horrible and violative of the basic values of civilized communities, were committed in the absence of a specific set of international criminal laws. Furthermore, other than the *schmachparagraphen* of the 1919 Versailles Treaty, which were never enforced by the Allies, there was a near total absence in international law of punishment meted out to violators of the norms, nor were there any guides as to who would determine the verdict and pronounce sentence on those found guilty of violating international criminal law.

The criticism of the Bernays plan was that it *had* to lead, *after the fact*, to the establishment of a set of specific international criminal laws. These newly crafted criminal laws would be used, ex post facto, to indict and then punish the defeated Nazi leaders. Underscoring this controversial issue, Göring wrote on the front of his indictment (issued in late October 1945): "The victor will always be the judge and the vanquished the accused."[24]

However, Justice Robert H. Jackson, America's chief prosecutor, responded to the ex post facto criticism of the trial in a manner that reflected the views of all who participated when he said: "Let's not be derailed by legal hair-splitters. Aren't murder, torture, and enslavement crimes recognized by all civilized people? What we propose is to punish acts which have been regarded as criminal since the time of Cain and have been so written in every civilized code."[25] In effect, Jackson was applying the Martens clause in the 1907 Hague Convention to justify the jurisdiction and justiciability of the Nuremberg tribunal.

## The London Charter: August 1945

In June 1945, the legal representatives of the four victorious Allies met in London to establish guidelines and procedures for the international military trial of the major Nazi war criminals.[26] Representing the United States was its chief prosecutor, Justice Robert H. Jackson, on leave from the U.S. Supreme Court. Great Britain had its attorney general, Sir David Maxwell-Fyfe, heading the delegation. Russia's representative was its chief prosecutor, Lieutenant General Roman Rudenko, assisted by Major General of Jurisprudence Ion Timifeevich Nikitchenko. The French delegation was led by Robert Falco.

There would be an international criminal tribunal created to try all Nazis charged with war crimes that went beyond the territory of a single occupied nation. (Many thousands of Nazis were put on trial in Polish courts.) There were more than six weeks of discussions and debates over jurisdiction of the international tribunal, trial procedures, and the nature of the indictments against the Nazis.

These were complex negotiations, because the Russians and the French followed Continental criminal procedures, where judges play a major inquisitorial role in the trial itself and lawyers have only a limited role in the criminal proceedings; the Americans and the British followed the adversarial criminal justice process, where prosecutors and defense attorneys engage in examination and cross-examination of witnesses in an effort to find the truth. The two systems were quite different, and some Allied jurists were clearly uncomfortable. Telford Taylor, one of the young American assistant prosecutors at Nuremberg, remembers the Russian prosecutor Nikitchenko asking: "What is meant in the English by 'cross-examine?' "[27]

Compromises were developed in the trial procedures so that the four Allies could comfortably and effectively prosecute the defendants. Included in the negotiations was the question of who would be brought to Nuremberg to stand trial. In the end, twenty-two were tried, including one, Martin Bormann, in absentia. These were some of the major leaders of Nazi Germany who had survived the war, had been captured, and, unlike Hitler, Heinrich Himmler (who ran the extermination programs), and Joseph Goebbels (Nazi minister of propaganda), had not committed suicide. One of the major Nazi leaders arrested and brought to Nuremberg to stand trial was Robert Ley, the head of labor in the Nazi dictatorship. In late October 1945, after he was indicted, he took his own life in his prison cell.[28] Gustav Krupp, head of Germany's leading industrial and arms maker, escaped trial before the IMT because of his mental deterioration. His son, Alfred Krupp, was subsequently tried and convicted in a U.S. sector court. The defendant list follows, showing the charges against them and the judgment of the IMT. Most of them had been captured and detained in military prisons by the advancing American forces. All were flown to Nuremberg in late summer 1945 to await the beginning of the IMT's actions, scheduled to start in November 1945.

| Name/Position | Counts* | Verdict† |
|---|---|---|
| **Generals and Admirals from the German General Staff** | | |
| General Jodl, former chief of staff, Wehrmacht | 1–4 | D |
| General Keitel, chief of staff, Wehrmacht | 1–4 | D |
| Admiral Raeder, former commander, Navy | 2, 4 | L |
| Admiral Doenitz, commander, Navy | 2, 3 | 10 |
| **Nazi Party and Government Leaders** | | |
| Göring, Reichsmarshall | 1–4 | D |
| Bormann, Nazi Party leader | 3, 4 | D |
| Frank, governor, occupied territory, Poland | 2, 4 | D |
| Frick, governor, Bohemia-Moravia | 1–4 | D |
| von Ribbentrop, foreign minister | 1–4 | D |
| Rosenberg, head, occupied territories | 1–4 | D |
| Seyss-Inquart, head, occupied Netherlands | 1–4 | D |
| Hess, Nazi Party leader, deputy to Hitler | 1, 2 | L |
| Neurath, minister, foreign affairs | 1–4 | 15 |
| von Papen, vice-chancellor, Nazi government | 1, 2 | A |
| von Schirach, head, Hitler Youth | 4 | 20 |
| Streicher, publisher, *Der Sturmer* | 4 | D |
| Fritzsche, head, Radio Division, Ministry of Propaganda | 1, 2 | A |
| Sauckel, head, labor mobilization | 2, 4 | D |
| **Bankers and Industrialists** | | |
| Funk, president, Reichsbank | 2, 4 | L |
| Speer, minister, armaments and war production | 3, 4 | 20 |
| Schacht, minister, economics | 1, 2 | A |
| **Secret Police** | | |
| Kaltenbrunner, head, Reich Central Security Office‡ | 3, 4 | D |

*1: planning and conspiring to wage aggressive war, a crime against the peace; 2: waging aggressive war; 3: war crimes; 4: crimes against humanity.

†D: death; L: life imprisonment; A: acquitted; 10, 15, 20: years of imprisonment

‡This agency included the gestapo, or *Geheime Staatspolizei*, the secret state police established in 1933 to interrogate, torture, and kill "enemies" of the Reich; and the SD, or *Sicherheitsdienst*, the security and intelligence service.

On August 8, 1945, the London agreement was signed by the four Allied legal representatives. Immediately, it became the basis for the international war crimes trials of Nazi and Japanese leaders, as well as the foundation for subsequent actions by the international community in the area of international law.

The agreement consisted of seven general articles and an important annex: the Charter of the International Military Tribunal, which contained seven parts and thirty articles. After describing how the IMT was to be constituted (four members, each with an alternate, representing the four Allies: Russia, the United States, Great Britain, and France), the core of the IMT's jurisdiction was laid out in Article VI:

[The IMT] shall have the power to try and punish persons who, acting in the interests of the European Axis countries, whether as individuals or as members of organizations, committed any of the following crimes [which fall under the jurisdiction of the IMT and] for which there shall be individual responsibility:

(a) *Crimes against peace:* namely, planning, preparation, initiation or waging a war of aggression, or a war in violation of international treaties, agreements or assurances, or participation in a common plan or conspiracy for the accomplishment of any of the foregoing.

(b) *War crimes:* namely, violations of the laws or customs of war. Such violations shall include, but not be limited to, murder, ill-treatment or deportation to slave labor or for any other purpose of civilian population of or in occupied territory, murder or ill-treatment of prisoners of war or persons on the seas, killing of hostages, plunder of public or private property, wanton destruction of cities, towns, or villages, or devastation not justified by military necessity.

(c) *Crimes against humanity:* namely, murder, extermination, enslavement, deportation, and other inhumane acts committed against any civilian populations, before or during the war; or persecution on political, racial, or religious grounds in execution of or in connection with any crime within the jurisdiction of the tribunal, whether or not in violation of the domestic law of the country where perpetrated.

Article VII rejected the sovereign immunity, "head of State" defense, and Article VIII stated that "the fact that a defendant acted pursuant to [an] order of his Government or of a superior shall not free him from responsibility, but may be considered in mitigation of punishment if the Tribunal determines that justice so requires."

The concept of criminal conspiracy was embedded in Articles IX and X: "At the trial of any individual member of any group or organization the Tribunal may declare (in connection with any act of which the individual may be convicted) that the group or organization of which the individual was a member was a criminal organization." Once the IMT declared a Nazi organization criminal, at any subsequent trial of individual members of that organization, "the criminal nature of the group or organization is considered proved and shall not be questioned."

The four nations' chief prosecutors (and staff) were responsible for investigations, collection of data, examination of all witnesses, preparation and lodging of indictments against the Nazi defendants, and prosecution of the defendants. The defendants were promised, in Article IV, a fair trial, which meant the right to conduct their own defense or to have the assistance of counsel (half of the defense attorneys selected by the defendants had been members of the Nazi Party); to have full particulars of the charges, including documents, enumerated in their indictments; and to present evidence at trial "in support of [their] defense, and to cross-examine any witnesses called by the prosecution."

Article XXIV laid out the process followed by the IMT: the reading of the indictment, followed by the plea (guilty or not guilty) of each defendant; prosecutors' opening statements; tribunal determination of admissibility of evidence submitted by prosecution and defense; witnesses for prosecution; cross-examination; witnesses for defense; cross-examination; rebutting evidence; tribunal questioning of witnesses and defendants (allowable at any time); defense addresses to the tribunal; prosecution addresses to the tribunal; defendant statements to the tribunal; delivering of judgment and pronouncement of sentence.

The IMT's judgment "shall be final and not subject to review" (Article XXVI). Finally, upon conviction, imposition of the death sentence "or such other punishment as shall be determined by it to be just" was declared a basic "right" of the IMT (Article XXVII).

## The International Military Tribunal at Nuremberg: 1945–1946

The IMTs at Nuremberg and Tokyo took place in the months immediately following the conclusion of hostilities and the unconditional surrender of Nazi Germany and Japan. The IMT at Nuremberg was precedent setting; it was history's first international criminal tribunal. The purpose of the trial was evident: punish those major figures in the defeated nations who were responsible for war crimes and the mass extermination of millions of civilians and prisoners of war. Inherent was the belief that "superior orders," "acts of state," and "sovereign immunity" were not defenses and that the concept of "individual responsibility" was the prominent characteristic of the post-World War II trials.

The trial was also a lesson for future military rulers. Newly written and internationally agreed-upon (in the UN in 1946 and 1948, and in Geneva in 1949) international criminal laws became part of international law. The international community's willingness to create an ad hoc (and afterward, as contemplated in 1946, a permanent) international criminal court to try and punish those found guilty of war crimes or genocide was another key outcome of Nuremberg.

There were 403 open sessions of the IMT at Nuremberg between November 1945 and October 1946. Thirty-three witnesses were called by the prosecution, and sixty-one witnesses for the defendants appeared in court. There were an additional 143 written depositions presented to the tribunal by defense counsel. Due to the ingenuity of IBM engineers, working feverishly in the United States in the months preceding the opening of the trial, there was simultaneous translation of the proceedings into four languages: German, French, Russian, and English.[29]

There were gaffes and clashes among the four Allies at Nuremberg. With hundreds of staff, including military personnel, lawyers, translators, researchers, investigators, and secretaries, there was bound to be some friction and jealousy. The Americans were the most populous group at the IMT, with over 700 persons. (The next largest Allied staff was the British group, numbering about 170.) The Americans' salaries were seen as outrageously high compared with the salaries of other Allied personnel working in Nuremberg. An American lawyer (and many hundreds of them moved between Nuremberg and the United States) received a salary of over $7,000. The president of the tribunal, Great Britain's Sir Geoffrey Lawrence, received about $2,800 annually, "roughly at the level of an American translator."[30]

The prosecution presented its case against the twenty-two defendants from November 1945 to March 1946, followed by defense arguments from March to July 1946. In July, the defense summarized its case, followed by the prosecution's closing arguments.

In July and part of August 1946, the tribunal heard arguments by the prosecution charging seven Nazi organizations with criminal conspiracy: Nazi Party leaders; the Reich cabinet; Nazi government ministers; the SS; the gestapo; the SD; the Sturmabteilung (SA), the storm troopers; and the military high command, consisting of German army, navy, and air force commanders in chief, both former chiefs and those in command at war's end.[31]

In August 1946, there were fifteen-minute statements by each defendant to the tribunal. The tribunal adjourned for deliberation in September 1946, and on September 30–October 1, 1946, it rendered its judgments in open court.

At the start of the trial, in November 1945, defense counsel jointly objected to the core juristic foundations of the IMT itself. This plea was summarily rejected by the tribunal, and the trial began.

Justice Jackson made the opening remarks for the combined prosecution team, thus beginning the first international war crimes tribunal. His words have remained benchmark values for those who seek to bring to justice persons who have violated the laws of war and the conscience of the international community.

> The wrongs which we seek to condemn and punish have been so calculated, so malignant, and so devastating that civilization cannot tolerate their being ignored because it cannot survive their being repeated. That four great nations, flushed with victory and stung with injury, stay the hand of vengeance and voluntarily submit their captive enemies to the judgment of the law is one of the most significant tributes that power has ever paid to reason . . . Either the victors must judge the vanquished, or we must leave the defeated to judge themselves. After the First World War, we saw the futility of the latter course.

Over the next few days, the four Allies took turns reading the general indictment against the defendants. There were four counts in the indictment. Counts one and two—planning, conspiring, and carrying out an aggressive war, that is, conspiring to commit "crimes against the peace"—were presented to the tribunal by the Americans and the British. Jackson presented the charge that twelve of the defendants were involved in the development of the common plan or conspiracy to wage aggressive war, in violation of the 1928 Kellogg-Briand Treaty signed by Germany and sixty-odd nations, and Sir Hartley Shawcross charged most of the defendants with the actual waging of aggressive war.

The French presented the third count of the indictment, maintaining that thirteen defendants had committed a variety of war crimes in violation of the Hague and Geneva treaties. These war crimes—such as massive use of slave labor, Luftwaffe medical experiments with human brains, the wanton killing of captured Allied aircrews and prisoners who tried to escape, the looting of art treasures, the killing of civilian hostages in the occupied territories of Europe—said the French prosecutor, "spring from a crime against the spirit, [one] which denied all spiritual, rational, and moral values by which nations have tried, for thousands of years, to improve the human condition."[32]

The Russian prosecutor, Rudenko, presented the final count, claiming that seventeen of the defendants had committed "crimes against persons and humanity" in occupied Europe "and against Slav countries first of all." Millions of civilians, he stated, "were subjected to merciless persecutions, atrocities, and mass extermination."[33]

Over the course of five months, the prosecution presented the case against the defendants, using over 2,500 Nazi documents from among the more than 1,700 tons of documents, records, photographs, and movies seized by the Allies. By September 1945, there were thirteen Allied document collection centers operating in Germany and Austria, where all documents were "cataloged, photographed, translated into English, and given a unique document number."[34] These documents were also used by prosecutors in the trials of thousands of lesser Nazis in the four occupation zones controlled by the French, Russians, British, and Americans in the years following the IMT at Nuremberg.

In addition to the showpiece trial of the major Nazi leaders at Nuremberg, in the four Allied occupation zones, controlled by the Americans, Russians, British, and French, trials of thousands of Nazis took place during and after the conclusion of the IMT at Nuremberg. By 1950, in the American zone, 570 Nazis had been confined and 185 indictments had been handed down. American civilians, both judges and lawyers, were brought to Germany to form six three-judge tribunals to hear twelve sets of cases against these lower-tier Nazi leaders. In the end, 177 were tried and 142 were convicted (with twenty-five executed after trial).

The twelve separate trials in the American sector included the doctors' trial, in which doctors were charged with conducting medical experiments on Jews and others; the jurists' trial, in which fourteen Nazi judges were charged with participating in the enforcement of Nazi edicts; the I. G. Farben trial, in which twenty-three German industrialists were charged with exploiting slave labor; the Krupp trial, in which twelve leaders of the arms manufacturing firm were charged with using slave labor and POWs in its factories; the hostages' trial; the *Einsatzgruppen* trial, in which twenty-two members of the SS were tried and convicted for their role in the extermination of Jews and others; and the SS Office for Race and Resettlement trial, in which fourteen SS members were charged with mass extermination of Jews and others at the killing centers.

In addition, British military courts heard almost 1,000 cases involving war crimes, with about 700 Nazis convicted and 230 sentenced to death. French military tribunals tried over 2,100 Nazis, with over 1,700 convicted and 104 sentenced to death. German courts conducted over 2,100 trials. About 900 of the Nazi defendants (or 40 percent) were *acquitted* in these courts (and only four were sentenced to death). There are no records of the number of Nazis tried, convicted, and executed in the Soviet zone military tribunals. (Other trials took place in Poland and the Netherlands.) Between 1947 and 1953, the British, French, and Americans tried 10,400 accused Nazi war criminals, and 5,025 were convicted and sentenced, including 506 who were sentenced to die by hanging.[35]

Beginning on March 8, 1946, for a second time, the Nazi defense attorneys tried to counter the mass of evidence presented by the prosecution. It was an impossible task, given the enormous volume of Nazi documents used to show, in their own words, how the defendants had planned, conspired, and acted to wage aggressive war and commit war crimes and crimes against humanity. The German lawyers, many of whom were former Nazi Party members themselves, were given great latitude, but given the evidence amassed against the defendants and given their lack of experience with adversarial criminal proceedings, they did not fare well. The witnesses and depositions introduced on behalf of the Nazi defendants tried to present mitigating and extenuating explanations for some of the accusations, but they did not stand up well to prosecutorial cross-examination.

Challenges to the tribunal's jurisdiction having been set aside on the first day, the defense argued the *Führerprinzip*, that is, that Hitler was responsible for all the crimes. All the defendants had done, as "good, loyal Germans," was show obedience to their leader by following his orders.[36] Beyond this defense, shot down in cross-examination by the prosecutors (who demonstrated the defendants' complicity in these crimes), the defense tried to explain, for example, that the Luftwaffe had flown defensive sorties only; that the invasion of the Netherlands and Norway and the alleged war crimes of the Wehrmacht had been acts of "military necessity"; that the defendants, especially the military leaders, had merely been following the orders of their superiors; and that the navy captains had always followed the customs and laws of sea warfare (in Admiral Doenitz's case, using a deposition from U.S. Admiral Chester Nimitz stating that German U-boat actions during the war had been no different from the actions of American submariners). Russian POWs had been treated differently from other Allied prisoners, the defense argued, because Russia had not signed the 1929 Geneva Accord on the treatment of prisoners of war.

For contemporary observers, it was ludicrous to argue, for example, that the Hitler Youth, which prepared young German males for war, was analogous to America's Boy Scouts. Allied prosecutors quickly pointed out, in cross-examination, that the Hitler Youth was a training ground for the Wehrmacht; that the Hitler Youth were kept busy with small-caliber weapons training and glider piloting; and that von Schirach, head of the organization, had an agreement with SS leader Heinrich Himmler that those Hitler Youth "who meet SS standards would be considered as the primary source of replacements for the SS."[37]

Equally comical amidst the tragedy of the trial was Göring's argument that his massive looting of the art treasures of occupied Europe was done to protect the art and to open a massive people's art museum after the war. And so on. Even before the defense concluded their arguments, four American lawyers on Jackson's staff, including Herbert Wechsler and James Rowe (who were to become highly respected figures in U.S. jurisprudence and politics) began drafting guilty verdicts for the tribunal to use in reaching its final judgments.[38]

Justice Jackson began his closing arguments after the defense rested with an apt quote from Shakespeare.

These defendants now ask the tribunal to say that they are not guilty of planning, executing, or conspiring to commit this long list of crimes and wrongs. They stand before the record of this trial as blood-stained Gloucester stood by the body of his slain king. He begged of the widow, as they beg of you: "Say I slew them not." And the Queen replied, "Then say they are not slain. But dead they are. . . ." If you were to say of these men that they are not guilty, it would be as true to say that there has been no war, there are no slain, there has been no crime.[39]

In the face of damning "tested evidence" showing the defendants' participation in waging aggressive war and committing war crimes and crimes against humanity, Jackson ridiculed the "flimsy excuses" offered by way of defense. The British prosecutor maintained that the mass of evidence presented by the prosecution—not successfully rebutted by the defense—

clearly showed that the defendants were guilty of "crimes so frightful that the imagination staggers and reels back."[40]

The judgment of the tribunal was announced on September 30 and October 1, 1946. Read over the two days, the lengthy judgment noted the importance of the documents introduced by the prosecution. "The case against the defendants rests in a large measure on documents of their own making, the authenticity of which has not been challenged except in one or two cases." The tribunal next carefully considered the four charges against the defendants: planning and waging aggressive wars and committing war crimes and crimes against humanity.

Were the first two charges violations of international treaties promulgated in 1899, 1907, 1919, 1925, 1928, and 1929 and signed by Germany? The tribunal noted that the actions taken by the Nazi government since 1937 were both illegal and criminal "crimes against the peace." The defense's use of the ex post facto "no punishment without law" maxim, the judges concluded, "has no application to the present facts." Hitler, the judges determined, "could not make aggressive war by himself. He had to have the cooperation of statesmen, military leaders, diplomats, and businessmen." By supporting the Nazi dictator, "they made themselves parties to the plan."

Regarding the third charge in the indictment, commission of war crimes in violation of international treaties signed in 1907 and 1929, the tribunal concluded that the "evidence has been overwhelming in its volume and its detail" that the Nazis committed war crimes "on a vast scale never before seen in the history of war." These war crimes included the murder and ill treatment of POWs, civilian populations, and slave laborers.

Finally, the tribunal took judicial notice of the mass of data that illuminated the Nazis' "crimes against humanity," especially their persecution of European Jewry, where, the tribunal noted, the Nazi "record of consistent and systematic inhumanity [was] on the greatest scale."

The IMT judges then ruled that four of the seven Nazi groups charged by the prosecution with being "criminal organizations" were criminal: the Nazi Party leadership, the gestapo, the SS, and the SD. The three others—the military high command, the Reich cabinet, and the SA—were not. The tribunal noted that individual members of Hitler's cabinet and military would be tried by the Allies. The SA, the brown shirts, were "ruffians and bullies," but since the group was in disfavor by 1935, it was not involved in planning or conspiring to wage war and did not, as a group, engage in war crimes or crimes against humanity; thus it could not be labeled a criminal organization.

The tribunal then came to the question of guilt or innocence of the twenty-two defendants. It found nineteen of them guilty of some or all of the charges leveled against them. The other three were acquitted because of a two-to-two deadlock among the judges; conviction required three judges to vote guilty. Finally, each defendant was brought before the tribunal to hear the sentence read by the chief judge. Twelve were sentenced to death by hanging, three received life imprisonment, and four were sentenced to prison terms ranging from ten to twenty years. The death sentences were carried out within fifteen days of the tribunal's pronouncements. (Just before his scheduled execution, Hermann Göring committed suicide by taking cyanide.)

The Russian judge announced three dissents from the decisions of the IMT: the not-guilty verdicts for Schacht, von Papen, and Fritzsche; the judgment that the military high command and the Reich cabinet were not criminal groups; and the sentencing of Hess to life imprisonment, arguing that he should have been executed along with the others.

The tribunal completed its work on October 1, 1946, and adjourned. By then, trials of other Nazis were beginning in the four Allied occupation zones of Germany. And in Tokyo, Japan, that IMT was in the middle of hearing criminal cases against twenty-eight Japanese leaders, most of them military.

Both IMTs were ad hoc international courts created by the victors to try their defeated enemies and punish the guilty. The victorious participants in both trials had to address the charge, voiced by jurists from both victorious and defeated nations, that the tribunals were ex post facto "victors' justice." One response to this criticism was the argument for the creation of a permanent international criminal court composed of jurists from states that were party to the treaty creating the international criminal tribunal, with authority to hear cases involving grave violations of the Nuremberg principles.

The unfulfilled legacy of Nuremberg has been the creation of such a permanent tribunal. Nuremberg crafted principles that the international community agreed on; individual rights, individual responsibility for war crimes, and international criminal laws of war were the major outcomes of Nuremberg. The world community was beginning to discuss the creation of such a tribunal when the cold war began just months after the IMT at Nuremberg ended. The discussions would not be revived for another forty years.

There have been over 100 revolutionary and regional wars since 1945. As an upcoming chapter notes, war crimes, crimes against humanity, and genocide occurred in many of these conflicts, but without a permanent international tribunal to hear charges against those accused of violating international criminal laws, and without a worldwide sense of outrage to lead to another ad hoc international tribunal, the perpetrators have gone unpunished. Until the 1990s, no international criminal tribunals were convened other than those at Nuremberg and Tokyo.

The August 1945 London Charter also became the jurisprudential foundation for the trial presented by the eleven victorious Allies against the leaders of Japan before the IMT of the Far East. However, the Tokyo war crimes tribunal was in many ways very different from and much more controversial than the European IMT.

## Notes

1. Bassiouni and Nanda, *Treatise*, p. 583.
2. Telford Taylor, *The Anatomy of the Nuremberg Trials: A Personal Memoir* (New York: A. A. Knopf, 1992), p. 28.
3. Quoted in Richard H. Minear, *Victors' Justice: The Tokyo War Crimes Trial* (Princeton, N.J.: Princeton University Press, 1971), pp. 8–9.
4. Persico, *Nuremberg*, p. 15.
5. Ibid.
6. Bradley F. Smith, *The Road to Nuremberg* (New York: Basic Books, 1981), pp. 20–21.
7. Taylor, *Anatomy*, p. 31.
8. Persico, *Nuremberg*, p. 15.
9. Smith, *Road to Nuremberg*, p. 22.
10. Ibid., pp. 45, 28ff.
11. Ibid., p. 76.
12. Taylor, *Anatomy*, pp. 35–36.
13. Smith, *Road to Nuremberg*, p. 51ff.; Taylor, *Anatomy*, p. 36ff.
14. Persico, *Nuremberg*, p. 18.
15. United Nations War Crimes Commission, *Law Reports of Trials of War Criminals: Four Genocide Trials* (New York: Fertig, 1992), p. 45.
16. Persico, *Nuremberg*, p. 17.
17. Smith, *Road to Nuremberg*, p. 114. After the war, in a trial held in the American sector of Germany, seventy-seven Waffen SS soldiers were convicted of the murders of the American military prisoners; forty-three were hung for their crimes. Persico, *Nuremberg*, p. 332.
18. Quoted in Smith, *Road to Nuremberg*, p. 116.
19. Quoted in Minear, *Victors' Justice*, pp. 9–10.
20. Smith, *Road to Nuremberg*, p. 152ff.
21. Samuel I. Rosenman, Roosevelt's special envoy to the British, noted that in 1947, Churchill told him:

"I think the President was right [about conducting a trial] and I was wrong." Samuel I. Rosenman, *Working with Roosevelt* (New York: Harper, 1952), p. 545.

22. Persico, *Nuremberg*, p. 78.
23. See, for example, Minear, *Victors' Justice*.
24. Quoted in Persico, *Nuremberg*, p. 83.
25. Quoted ibid., pp. 33–34. In a note to Roosevelt that touched on this issue of victors' justice, Jackson wrote: "We can save ourselves from those pitfalls if our test of what legally is crime gives recognition to those things which fundamentally outraged the conscience of the American people and brought them finally to the conviction that their own liberty and civilization could not persist in the same world with the Nazi power. . . . I believe that these instincts of the American people were right and that they should guide us as the fundamental tests of criminality." Quoted in Minear, *Victors' Justice*, p. 16.
26. See Viscount Maugham, *U.N.O. and War Crimes* (Westport, Conn.: Greenwood Press, 1975), p. 17.
27. Quoted in Taylor, *Anatomy*, p. 59.
28. Gilbert, *Nuremberg Diary*, pp. 7, 37.
29. Persico, *Nuremberg*, p. 27.
30. Ibid., p. 176.
31. United States Holocaust Memorial Museum, *In Pursuit of Justice: Examining the Evidence of the Holocaust* (Washington, D.C.: U.S. Holocaust Memorial Council, 1996), pp. 237, 253, 254.
32. Quoted in Gilbert, *Nuremberg Diary*, p. 123.
33. Quoted in ibid., p. 135.
34. U.S. Holocaust Memorial Museum, *Historical Atlas*, p. 31.
35. Campbell, *Experience of World War II*, p. 217.
36. See Gilbert, *Nuremberg Diary*, pp. 148ff, 407ff.
37. Quoted in ibid., p. 351.
38. Persico, *Nuremberg*, p. 329.
39. Quoted in ibid., p. 365.
40. Quoted in Gilbert, *Nuremberg Diary*, pp. 415, 420.

# 11

# The International Criminal Tribunal for the Former Yugoslavia

As communism collapsed throughout eastern Europe between 1989 and 1991, secessionist ethnonationalists throughout the various republics comprising Yugoslavia began to rear their heads. Several among the six republics of the Yugoslav Federation began to grow restive, and in 1991 Slovenia, Croatia, and Macedonia seceded. Serbia, Yugoslavia's dominant republic, responded by intensifying its attempts to retain a "Greater Serbia" out of what remained, while Croatia also aimed to enlarge its territory by including all ethnic Croats within the new Croat state. Both republics had their eyes on Bosnia-Herzegovina; indeed, both sought to achieve their own homogeneous state, and the latter effort resulted in mass killing and the expulsion of minorities. For three years (1992–1995), unrestrained violence raged in the territory of what had been Yugoslavia. The war for the partition of Bosnia was fought so ferociously that it became a three-way war of atrocities and counter-atrocities, involving Serbs (from Bosnia and Serbia), Croats (from Bosnia and Croatia), and Bosnian Muslims (Bosniaks). This vicious warfare resulted in the death of up to 250,000 civilians and the worst massacre in Europe since the end of World War II, namely the Serbs' mass murder of between 7,000 and 8,000 Bosnian Muslim men and boys at Srebrenica in July 1995. The fighting lasted for over three years, until, in November 1995, a settlement was negotiated through the US-sponsored and UN-supported Dayton Agreement (November 21, 1995). In effect this treaty, which was to be supervised by NATO, segmented Bosnia into three ethnic enclaves.

Then, in the aftermath of Serbia's failed wars to retain Slovenia and Croatia, and the drawn-out and bloody conflict in Bosnia-Herzegovina, it was hoped by many that Serbia's nationalist regime, led by Slobodan Milosevic, would settle down and rejoin the world of peaceable nations. In March 1998, however, violence once more erupted, this time in Serbia itself—or, more specifically, in its southern territory of Kosovo. The long-term ethnic and religious animosity between minority Serbs and majority Kosovar Albanians in the province led to the establishment of a self-defense organization, the Kosovo Liberation Army (KLA), which engaged in terrorist activities in order to attract international attention to their cause and at the same time intimidate Serbs in the province to flee Kosovo. Serbian responses took a military form, with widespread killings of Kosovar civilians taking place—particularly, though not exclusively, in areas well-known as KLA strongholds, such as the Drenica Valley. Increasingly, the United States and its European allies saw a need to intervene before this state-initiated killing got totally out of hand: the result was the decision by NATO, after many serious attempts at negotiation, to commence military action against Serbia in March 1999. The hope was that this would coerce Milosevic into halting the attacks against the Kosovars, but the opposite took place: rather than succumbing, Milosevic took the chance afforded by

NATO's intervention to attempt to "ethnically cleanse" Kosovo of Albanians. During Serbia's war with NATO, an estimated 1.3 million Kosovars were forcibly driven from their homes, and some 800,000 were physically expelled from Kosovo. Thousands were killed, raped, and maimed in the process. This expulsion was only halted through extensive NATO bombing of Serbia and exhaustive diplomatic activity in the major European capitals (as well as Washington and New York).

In response to the extreme violence inflicted on civilians in the wars of Yugoslav disintegration between 1991 and 1999, the United Nations Security Council established the International Criminal Tribunal for the Former Yugoslavia, or ICTY, by UNSC Resolution 827 on May 25, 1993. It was resolved that this would be a special *ad hoc* court specifically designed to try those charged with three types of offenses, namely, grave breaches of those sections of the 1949 Geneva Conventions relating to war crimes; crimes against humanity; and genocide. The crime of genocide was introduced because of the specific kind of mass killings of ethnic groups that took place during these wars, in concentration camps, rape camps, through the mass murder of civilians, and through the brutal practices associated with forced deportations and "ethnic cleansing."

The ICTY is located in The Hague, in the Netherlands; its essential purpose is to render justice to the victims, to deter further crimes, and to contribute to the restoration of peace by holding accountable those found responsible for serious violations of international humanitarian law. The tribunal's judges and officials are drawn from a pool of prominent international jurists. Those tried at the ICTY are drawn from all four of the major ethnicities involved in the war: Serbs, Croats, Bosnian Muslims (Bosniaks), and Kosovar Albanians. The accused, it is alleged by court indictments, have been tried on a wide variety of charges (some of which are not directly related to genocide or genocidal violence). By far, the majority of those indicted have been Serbs, both from Serbia and from the ethnic Serb entity in Bosnia-Herzegovina, Republika Srpska.

At the outset, the ICTY suffered setbacks, both budgetary and administrative: costs outpaced the income of the court; reviewing evidence in preparation for each trial proved time-consuming; and each trial got bogged down in repeated postponements or recesses. Most troublesome was the process of locating and detaining the indicted themselves, whose arrests frequently depended on the cooperation of the governments of Bosnia-Herzegovina, Croatia, and, particularly, Serbia, the latter of which shielded not only its own nationals but those from Republika Srpska. The court has no marshals with the power to arrest indictees in the aforementioned countries, meaning that some of the indicted are still living in hiding, or (less likely) are living in the open, albeit out of reach of the tribunal.

Despite these obstacles, the court has managed to try suspected criminals from all combatant nationalities and to convict both high- and low-ranking criminals, particularly those associated with the war in Bosnia. The ICTY's most notable indictment and trial to date was that of Slobodan Milosevic, the former President of Serbia. He was the first head of state ever accused and tried for genocide, an unprecedented step in judicial history. (The trial did not conclude with a verdict, however, as Milosevic died of a heart attack in 2006, while in custody during the trial.) It is anticipated that the ICTY will have completed the trial process of all those indicted by the end of 2009, with all appeals completed by the end of 2010. This might, however, be extended should currently pending warrants be met by the arrest of leading indictees yet to be apprehended, such as Bosnian Serb General Ratko Mladic.

Payam Akhavan and Mora Johnson, in their article "International Criminal Tribunal for the Former Yugoslavia," present a highly detailed analysis of how the ICTY works in practice, showing its breadth as well as its limitations, and pointing out how the tribunal has added to the case-law of genocide prosecutions. That this has happened is all to the good, as it provides the necessary precedents upon which future prosecutions will rely; given this, Akhavan and Johnson reveal that the ICTY is in reality a body that has enabled anti-genocide and human rights law to evolve beyond what it was prior to the tribunal's establishment. With this in mind, they show how the ICTY paved the way for a similar *ad hoc* tribunal governing the massive human rights abuses that were perpetrated in Rwanda in 1994, and for the signing of the Rome Statute (1998) that led to the introduction of the International Criminal Court in 2002.

The second reading in this section is a press release from the ICTY itself, summarizing the decision of the trial chamber in the case of the Serbian general Radislav Krstic ("Radislav Krstic Becomes the First Person to be Convicted of Genocide at the ICTY and Is Sentenced to 46 Years Imprisonment"). In this document can be seen something of the legal processes undertaken by the tribunal in seeking transparent justice. The decision handed down here is a clear summary of the background to the indictment, the nature of the charges against Krstic, and the nature of the witness statements that resulted in his being the first person to be convicted of genocide at the ICTY. As a statement, it says much about the assumptions that underlay the operation of the tribunal, and in this sense it is a valuable document worthy of consideration by students of genocide.

# 11.1   Payam Akhavan and Mora Johnson, "International Criminal Tribunal for the Former Yugoslavia"

The establishment of the International Criminal Tribunal for the Former Yugoslavia (ICTY) by the United Nations Security Council in 1993 is one of the most significant contemporary developments for the prevention and punishment of crimes against humanity and genocide. Born out of the horrors of ethnic cleansing in the former Yugoslavia, the ICTY successfully prosecuted perpetrators irrespective of rank and official status, and became the first tribunal to prosecute a sitting head of state, Slobodan Milosevic. Against a long-standing culture of impunity that countenanced the likes of Pol Pot, Idi Amin, and Mengistu, it represented a revolutionary precedent that led to the acceptance and proliferation of other international and mixed courts, national trials, and other accountability mechanisms. As a central element of post-conflict peace-building in former Yugoslavia, it also challenged the conventional wisdom of political "realists," who held that accountability and peace are incompatible. Furthermore, ICTY jurisprudence made significant contributions to the law of crimes against humanity and genocide.

## Creation of the ICTY

The unfolding of the atrocities in former Yugoslavia coincided with the end of the cold war and the consequent transformation of international relations. In the new political dispensation, the Soviet-era paralysis of the United Nations was increasingly replaced by cooperation between the five permanent members of the UN Security Council and unprecedented recourse to enforcement measures under Chapter VII of the UN Charter, especially in response to Iraq's invasion of Kuwait in 1990. Equally important was the rapid emergence of democratic governments in Eastern Europe, Latin America, and elsewhere in the world, giving human rights an unprecedented prominence.

In 1992 the Security Council took the unprecedented step of creating a Commission of Experts to investigate humanitarian law violations in the former Yugoslavia. On May 25, 1993, the Council unanimously adopted Resolution 827, pursuant to which it established the ICTY. The Tribunal was created under Chapter VII, which authorizes the Security Council to take enforcement measures binding on all member states of the UN. This was an unprecedented use of Chapter VII enforcement powers, and it directly linked accountability for humanitarian law violations with the maintenance of peace and security. This approach was necessary because Yugoslavia was unwilling to consent to an international criminal jurisdiction, because a treaty mechanism was too time-consuming in view of the need for expeditious action, and because the primary objective of the armed conflict was ethnic cleansing and other atrocities committed against civilians.

The ICTY Statute is a relatively complex instrument that had to express developments in contemporary international humanitarian law that had evolved over the half-century since the Nuremberg trials. It also had to elaborate the composition and powers of a unique independent judicial organ created by the Security Council. Under the statute, the subject-matter jurisdiction of the ICTY is based on norms that had been fully established as a part of customary international law. Articles 2 and 3 of the statute define war crimes, including violations of the 1949 Geneva Conventions and the 1907 Hague Regulations respectively. Article 4 reproduces the definition of genocide as contained in the 1948 Genocide Convention, and Article 5 defines crimes against humanity based on the Charter of the International Military Tribunal at Nuremberg. Article 7(1) defines the basis for the attribution of individual criminal responsibility, encompassing persons who "planned, instigated, ordered, committed or otherwise aided and abetted in the planning, preparation or execution of a crime" recognized under the statute. Article 7(2) expressly rejects any form of immunity for international crimes, stipulating that "[t]he official position of any accused person, whether as Head of State or Government or as a responsible Government official, shall not relieve such person of criminal responsibility nor mitigate punishment." Furthermore, Article 7(3) codifies the doctrine of command responsibility, providing that crimes committed by subordinates may be attributed to their superior "if he knew or had reason to know that the subordinate was about to commit such acts or had done so and the superior failed to take the necessary and reasonable measures to prevent such acts or to punish the perpetrators thereof." Conversely, Article 7(4) provides that superior orders shall not relieve a subordinate of criminal responsibility, though it may be considered in mitigation of punishment.

Article 8 restricts the jurisdiction of the ICTY to the territory of the former Yugoslavia, and limits the ICTY to consideration of crimes beginning on January 1, 1991, coinciding with the early stages of Yugoslavia's disintegration. There is however, no outer temporal limit to jurisdiction. Article 9 provides that the ICTY and national courts enjoy concurrent jurisdiction, but that the ICTY shall have primacy, it can request national courts to defer investigations and prosecutions to the ICTY. Article 10 provides, however, that the principle of double jeopardy must also be respected, which means that a person may not be tried before the ICTY for crimes already tried before a national court, unless the earlier proceedings were not impartial or independent, or were designed to shield the accused from criminal responsibility, or otherwise not diligently prosecuted.

The ICTY was initially composed of a prosecutor, the registry, three trial chambers with three judges each, and an appeals chamber with five judges that also serves the International Criminal Tribunal for Rwanda (ICTR). Since its early days, additional judges have been added to the tribunal. Unlike the Nuremberg Tribunal, the ICTY cannot rely on an army of occupation to conduct the investigation or to apprehend accused persons. Thus, Article 29 provides that UN member states are under an obligation to render judicial cooperation to the ICTY. Specifically, they are obliged to "comply without undue delay with any request for assistance or an order issued by a Trial Chamber" in matters such as the identification and location of persons, the taking of testimony and the production of evidence, the service of documents, the arrest or detention of persons, and the surrender or the transfer of an accused to the

ICTY. Such extensive powers derive from the binding character of Chapter VII enforcement measures, and are unprecedented in the history of international tribunals.

The ICTY was created by the Security Council, which also prepared a list of potential judges. The judges were then elected by the UN General Assembly. Furthermore, the General Assembly is responsible for reviewing and approving the ICTY's budget. Although the ICTY is a subsidiary judicial organ of the Security Council, the Council has no power to interfere in judicial matters such as prosecutorial decisions or trials. The ICTY Statute and its rules of procedure and evidence contain numerous procedural safeguards to ensure the independence and impartiality of the tribunal, and to guarantee the rights of the accused to a fair trial.

The first chief prosecutor, South African Constitutional Court judge Richard Goldstone, was appointed in July 1994. In the early days, the Office of the Prosecutor (OTP) was under-staffed and inexperienced; investigators and prosecutors who were familiar only with domestic law enforcement wasted scarce resources investigating low-ranking perpetrators for the direct commission of crimes such as murder, rather than focusing on leadership targets.

During Judge Goldstone's tenure, the ICTY's prospects for arrest were meager because the war was still raging, and even after the conclusion of a peace agreement, the prosecutor had to rely on reluctant peacekeeping forces or local police to arrest and surrender indictees. In contrast with the Nazi leaders who were put on trial at Nuremberg, the first defendant before the ICTY was a low-ranking Bosnian Serb, Dusko Tadić, who was captured haphazardly while visiting relations in Germany. He was accused of torturing and killing civilians at detention camps in Bosnia's Prijedor region. Although he was a relatively low-profile defendant, his trial created the image of a court in action.

In 1996 Judge Goldstone stepped down and a Canadian appellate judge, Louise Arbour, was appointed as the new ICTY prosecutor. Her emphasis was on increasing the overall professional standards and effectiveness of the prosecutor's office. Her major accomplishment was in enhancing international cooperation in obtaining intelligence and executing arrest warrants, particularly with NATO countries. Although peacekeeping forces in the former Yugoslavia were initially reluctant to make arrests, it soon became clear that the leaders responsible for inciting ethnic hatred and violence were an impediment to post-conflict peace- and nation-building. UN peacekeepers began arresting indictees, and the ICTY's fortunes were dramatically changed. The first such arrest was that of Slavko Dokmanović, the mayor of Vukovar during the war, and it was affected by Polish peacekeepers belonging to the UN Transitional Authority in Eastern Slavonia, a Serb-controlled region of Croatia. With the arrest of more and more defendants, Arbour streamlined the work of the prosecutor's office, dropped several indictments against low-ranking perpetrators, and increasingly focused on the "big fish."

The pressure to indict the biggest "fish" of all, Slobodan Milosevic, became particularly intense, and on May 27, 1999, Arbour made public the indictment of Milosevic and four other senior officials for crimes against humanity and war crimes in Kosovo, both in relation to mass expulsions and massacres in certain locales. This move was initially controversial. Some viewed the indictment as an obstacle to a deal with Milosevic, while others criticized the appearance that the ICTY was unduly influenced by NATO countries.

Following intense international pressure, the Serbian government arrested Milosevic and surrendered him to the ICTY in June 2000. In October 2000, Milosevic was indicated for atrocities committed in Bosnia and Croatia. His historic trial began in 2002, consummating the ICTY's remarkable emergence from obscurity. Arbour resigned as prosecutor in 1999, to be replaced by Carla Del Ponte, a Swiss prosecutor renowned at home for prosecuting mobsters. Del Ponte focused heavily on the Milosevic case and on securing the arrest of other indicted leaders, from both Serbia and Croatia.

By 2003, the final wave of indictments was issued for atrocities committed in the Kosovo conflict. Many were against Serb military officers, but some were also issued against high-ranking members of the Kosovo Liberation Army for atrocities committed against ethnic Serbs in Kosovo. With the success of the ICTY and the mounting costs of time-consuming international trials, the Security Council called upon the prosecutor to complete all investigations by the end of 2004 and for the ICTY to complete trials by the end of 2008. The Council also approved the establishment of war crimes trial chambers in Bosnia and Herzegovina for the prosecution of lower-ranking defendants, in order to alleviate the ICTY's burden. As of early 2004, the ICTY prosecutor was not only responsible for trials of crimes committed in the former Yugoslavia, but also for the International Criminal Tribunal for Rwanda. In August 2003, the Security Council decided that the two spheres of responsibility should be split, and appointed a separate prosecutor for the ICTR.

## Jurisprudence and Legal Developments

The jurisprudence of the ICTY has made significant contributions to international law, particularly in honing the definition of crimes against humanity and genocide. In an effort to effectively use its limited resources, ICTY trials were focused on the most serious crimes and on those most responsible for committing them. In practice, this focus was on crimes committed in execution of the ethnic cleansing campaign that amounted to crimes against humanity and, in certain important aspects, genocide. In order to ensure an appearance of impartiality, there were indictments not only against ethnic Serbs, but also against ethnic Croats, Muslims, and Kosovar Albanians. Furthermore, while focusing on those in leadership positions, certain prosecutions focused on issues of particular importance, such as the systematic use of rape as a weapon of war, and the destruction of cultural property. This prosecutorial strategy influenced and shaped the jurisprudence of the ICTY.

## Jurisdiction

The first ICTY trial was the case of *Prosecutor v. Dusko Tadić*. This trial involved significant pronouncements on international humanitarian law, but the case is best known for its jurisprudence on the jurisdiction of the ICTY. Tadić challenged the legality of the ICTY's establishment, both on the grounds that it was beyond the powers of the UN Security Council, and because it was not a court established by law, insofar as the Council was not a legislative body. Appeals chamber president Antonio Cassese heard these arguments, and held that the establishment of a judicial organ was a valid exercise of the powers of the Security Council, in accordance with Chapter VII of the Charter of the United Nations. He also found that the ICTY was duly established by law in the international context because its standards conformed with the rule of law, there being no analogue to a legislature in the UN system. The appeals chamber also rejected challenges to the primacy of ICTY over national courts, based on the overriding interest of the international community in the repression of serious humanitarian law violations.

## Enforcement Powers

The leading case dealing with the ICTY's enforcement powers and the corresponding obligation of states to render judicial assistance is *Prosecutor v. Blaškić*. The case revolves around the refusal of the Croatian government to comply with orders for the production of evidence issued by an ICTY Trial Chamber. The Appeals Chamber held that Article 29 of the ICTY Statute obliged states to comply with ICTY orders, and that Chapter VII of the UN Charter was sufficient to assert the authority of ICTY to issue such orders. The Appeals Chamber also held that the failure of a state to comply with orders of the court could result in a charge of non-compliance against the state (or its agent), which could then be turned over to the UN Security Council for further action.

## Arrest Powers

The arrest powers of the ICTY are found in Articles 19, 20, and 29 of the tribunal's statute, and in Rules 54 through 59 of the rules of procedure and evidence. Rule 55 obligates states to execute arrest warrants. The most significant cases on arrest powers were *Prosecutor v. Slavko Dokmanović* and *Prosecutor v. Dragan Nikolić*, respectively. In both cases, the defendants alleged that they had been arrested through either abduction or duplicity (in legal terms, the charge is called "irregular rendition"). The defendants argued that the nature of their arrests should preclude the ICTY from exercizing jurisdiction over them.

At least one of the arrests had, in fact, involved subterfuge. In Dokmanović's case, he was arrested after having been tricked getting into a vehicle that he thought was going to take him to a meeting. In this case, the trial chamber made a distinction between "luring" and "forcible abduction," and held that the former (which is what was done to Dokmanović) was acceptable, whereas the latter might provide grounds for a dismissal in future cases. Dokmanović was not permitted to appeal this decision. (Dokmanović's trial was later terminated because the defendant committed suicide).

Nikolić, whose motion was heard six years after Dokmanović's, was subject to a much more straightforward adbuction by "persons unknown" from the territory of the Federal Republic of Yugoslavia, and subsequently turned over to the ICTY. He based his appeal against his arrest on the grounds that the sovereignty of the Federal Republic of Yugoslavia was violated by his abduction, and that his rights were violated in a manner sufficiently serious to warrant discontinuance of proceedings. The Appeals Chamber held that state sovereignty does not generally outweigh the interests of bringing to justice a person accused of a universally condemned crime, especially when the state itself does not protest. Moreover, it found that, given the exceptional gravity of the crimes for which Nikolić was accused, a human rights violation perpetrated during his arrest must be very serious to justify discontinuance of proceedings.

## Crimes Against Humanity

The definition of crimes against humanity found in Article 5 of the ICTY Statute is based on the Nuremberg Charter, but it incorporates enumerated acts such as imprisonment, torture, and rape, which were not included in the charter. Furthermore, while the Charter required that crimes against humanity be linked to an international armed conflict, the ICTY Statute also includes internal armed conflicts. This issue came up in the *Tadić* case. The defendant maintained that prosecution of crimes against humanity in the former Yugoslavia deviated from customary international law because the conflict was not international in character, as required by the Nuremberg Charter. Being that there was no existing law extending jurisdiction to the ICTY, the defense argued, there could be no legitimate charge of criminal action. The Appeals Chamber rejected this submission, however, commenting that customary law had evolved in the years since Nuremberg, and stating that the need for a connection to international armed conflict was no longer required. In fact, it argued that customary law might recognize crimes against humanity in the absence of any conflict at all.

This precedent helped persuade the drafters of the Rome Statute of the International Criminal Court to omit a requirement of a connection with armed conflict in the definition of crimes against humanity under its Article 7. Thus, under contemporary international law, atrocities committed outside the context of armed conflict also qualify as crimes against humanity, and this has resulted in a significant expansion of the protection afforded by this norm.

According to the ICTY, a crime against humanity is committed when an enumerated offence is committed as part of a widespread or systematic attack directed against a civilian population. ICTY jurisprudence has elaborated upon what is meant by a "widespread or systematic" attack. In *Tadić*, the Trial Chamber held that this requirement is inferred from the term "population," which indicates a significantly numerous victim group. While it does not necessitate that the entire population of a given state must be targeted, it does refer to collective crimes rather than single or isolated acts.

A finding either that the acts were committed on a large scale (widespread), or were repeatedly carried out pursuant to a pattern or plan (systematic), is sufficient to meet the requirement that they be committed against a population. It is the large number of victims, the exceptional gravity of the acts, and their commission as part of a deliberate attack against a civilian population, which elevate the acts from ordinary domestic crimes such as murder to crimes against humanity, and thus a matter of collective international concern. ICTY jurisprudence has also expanded the definition of potential victim groups vulnerable to crimes against humanity. This is done through its interpretation of the requirement that attacks must be "directed against any civilian population." In the Vukovar Kupreškić cases, the ICTY held that the definition of "civilian" is sufficiently broad to include prisoners of war or other non-combatants.

ICTY jurisprudence has also affirmed that crimes against humanity may be committed by people who are not agents of any state, thus broadening the ambit of possible perpetrators to include insurgents and terrorists. This definition was adopted in Article 7 of the Rome Statute, which requires that an attack be "pursuant to or in furtherance of a State or organizational policy."

Crimes against humanity also require a so-called mental element, which has to do with the intent of the perpetrators. For an act to be termed a crime against humanity, the perpetrator must not only meet the requisite criminal intent of the offence, but he must also have knowledge, constructive or actual, of the widespread or systematic attack on a civilian population. This requirement ensures that the crime is committed as part of a mass atrocity, and not a random crime that is unconnected to the policy of attacking civilians. ICTY jurisprudence has held that this requirement does not necessitate that the accused know all the precise details of the policy or even be identified with the principle perpetrators, but merely that he be aware of the risk that his act forms part of the attack.

ICTY jurisprudence has also developed definitions of the enumerated offences included under the rubric of crimes against humanity. These include extermination, enslavement, forced deportation, arbitrary imprisonment, torture, rape, persecution on political, racial, or religious grounds, and other inhumane acts. In addition, it has further sharpened the definition of genocide itself.

The definition of the crime of extermination was developed in the *Krstić* case, wherein the Trial Chamber noted that extermination was a crime very similar to genocide because it involves mass killings. Unlike genocide, however, extermination "may be retained when the crime is directed against an entire group of individuals even though no discriminatory intent nor intention to destroy the group as such on national, ethnical, racial or religious grounds" is present. Nonetheless, the crime had to be directed against a particular, targeted population, and there must have been a calculated intent to destroy a significant number of that targeted group's members. In one of the Foča rape cases, *Prosecutor v. Kunarac et al*, the Trial Chamber similarly contributed to the definition of the elements that make up the crime of enslavement. It held, that the criminal act consisted of assuming the right of ownership over another human being, and that the mental element of the crime consisted of intentionally exercising the powers of ownership. This included restricting the victim's autonomy, curtailing his freedom of choice and movement. The victim is not permitted consent or the exercise of free will. This curtailment of the victim's autonomy can be achieved in many ways.

Threats, captivity, physical coercion, and deception, are but four such ways. Even psychological pressure is recognized as a means of enslavement. Enslavement also entails exploitation, sometimes (but not necessarily always) involving financial or other types of gain for the perpetrator. Forced labor is an element of enslavement, even if the victim is nominally remunerated for his or her efforts. Important to note is that simple imprisonment, without exploitation, can not constitute enslavement.

The ICTY Statute lists deportation as a crime against humanity, but goes on to specify that such deportation must be achieved under coercion. According to the statute, deportation is the "forced displacement of the persons concerned by expulsion or other coercive acts from the area in which they are lawfully present, without grounds permitted under international law." In the *Krstić* case, deportation was distinguished from forcible transfer. Deportation requires a population transfer beyond state borders, whereas forcible transfer involves internal population displacements. Both types of forced population movements were nonetheless recognized as crimes against humanity under customary law. The Trial Chamber in *Krstić* found that deportations or forcible transfers must be compulsory. In other words, they must be driven by force or threats or coercion which go beyond a fear of discrimination, and that there be no lawful reason for ordering the transfer, such as for the protection of the population from hostilities.

An ICTY Trial Chamber first defined imprisonment as a crime against humanity in *Prosecutor v. Dario Kordić* and in *Prosecutor v. Mario Čerkez*. However, such imprisonment must be arbitrary, without the due process of law. Further, it must be directed at a civilian population, and the imprisonment must be part of a larger, systematic attack on that population. ICTY jurisprudence also redressed a long-standing omission in humanitarian law, because prior to its rulings, a clear, explicit definition of torture had yet to be formulated. The leading ICTY case on torture is *Prosecutor v. Anto Furundžija*, as elaborated by *Prosecutor v. Kunarac et al.* In the *Furundžija* case, the Trial Chamber borrowed legal concepts from the human rights law of torture. Ultimately, the Trial Chamber determined that torture:

(i)   consists of the infliction, by act or omission, of severe pain or suffering, whether physical or mental; in addition
(ii)  this act or omission must be intentional;
(iii) it must aim at obtaining information or a confession, or at punishing, intimidating, humiliating or coercing the victim or a third person, or at discriminating, on any ground, against the victim or a third person;
(iv)  it must be linked to an armed conflict;
(v)   at least one of the persons involved in the torture process must be a public official or must at any rate act in a non-private capacity, e.g. as a de facto organ of a state or any other authority-wielding entity.

When the ICTY was established, there was also no clear definition for rape under humanitarian or indeed, customary international law. Thus, the ICTY was required to define it more precisely when difficult cases came up. Borrowing from legal systems around the world, the Trial Chamber in *Furundžija* held that rape is the coerced sexual penetration of a victim (vaginally or anally), whether by the perpetrator's penis or by some other object, or the penetration of the victim's mouth by the perpetrator's penis. Coercion could involve force or the threat of force, and the coercion might be imposed on the victim or on a third party. The Trial Chamber added that

[I]nternational criminal rules punish not only rape but also any serious sexual assault falling short of actual penetration. It would seem that the prohibition embraces all serious abuses of a sexual nature inflicted upon the physical and moral integrity of a person by means of coercion, threat of force or intimidation in a way that is degrading and humiliating for the victim's dignity. As both these categories of acts are criminalised in international law, the distinction between them is one that is primarily material for the purposes of sentencing.

In a later case, *Prosecutor v. Kunarac et al.*, an ICTY Trial Chamber expanded the second element of the crime to encompass situations in which the threshold of force may not be met, but where consent is not freely given as a result of the complainant's free will. In *Prosecutor v. Kupreškić*, the ICTY drew on Nuremberg jurisprudence to clarify the definition of persecution, and set out its conclusions in the *Prosecutor v. Tadić* judgment. It defined persecution as a form of discrimination on the grounds of race, religion, or political opinion that is intended to be, and results in, an infringement of an individual's fundamental rights. In *Prosecutor v. Kupreškić*, the court determined what actions or omissions could amount to persecution. Drawing on various human rights instruments, the Trial Chamber defined persecution as

> [T]he gross or blatant denial, on discriminatory grounds, of a fundamental right, laid down in international customary or treaty law, reaching the same level of gravity as the other acts prohibited in Article 5. In determining whether particular acts constitute persecution, the Trial Chamber wishes to reiterate that acts of persecution must be evaluated not in isolation but in context, by looking at their cumulative effect. Although individual acts may not be inhumane, their overall consequences must offend humanity in such a way that they may be termed "inhumane". This delimitation also suffices to satisfy the principle of legality, as inhumane acts are clearly proscribed by the Statute. . . . In sum, a charge of persecution must contain the following elements:
>
> (a) those elements required for all crimes against humanity under the Statute;
> (b) a gross or blatant denial of a fundamental right reaching the same level of gravity as the other acts prohibited under Article 5;
> (c) discriminatory grounds.

## Room for Further Evolution

The ICTY included a non-specific category of offenses, styled "other inhumane acts" as residual provision that allows for the inclusion by analogy of inhumane acts not enumerated. This was done to ensure that acts of similar gravity do not go unpunished simply because they are not expressly contemplated. This however, raises problems of legal principle. The concept of *nullem crimen sine lege* requires that there can be no crime if no law exists prohibiting an act. This, in turn, requires that crimes be exhaustively defined in order to be prosecutable. The Trial Chamber in *Prosecutor v. Kupreškić* discussed this problem and noted that, by drawing on various provisions of international human rights law, such as the Universal Declaration of Human Rights and the two UN Covenants for Human Rights,

> it is possible to identify a set of basic rights appertaining to human beings, the infringement of which may amount, depending on the accompanying circumstances, to a crime against humanity. Thus, for example, serious forms of cruel or degrading treatment of persons belonging to a particular ethnic, religious, political or racial group, or serious widespread or systematic manifestations of cruel or humiliating or degrading treatment with a discriminatory or persecutory intent no doubt amount to crimes against humanity.

Once the legal parameters for determining the content of the category of "inhumane acts" are identified, the trial chamber held, resort may be had to comparing their similarity to other crimes against humanity to determine if they are of comparable gravity.

## Genocide

The definition of *genocide* in the ICTY Statute is identical to that in the Genocide Convention. Of great significance in determining that an act of genocide has been committed in the mental element of the crime. This requires a finding of a special intent, in which the perpetrator desires to bring about the outcome of destroying, in whole or in part, a national, ethnical, racial or religious group, in addition to the criminal intent required by the enumerated offence. ICTY jurisprudence has elaborated on the threshold of the special intent that must be demonstrated in a charge of genocide. Two particularly noteworthy cases are the *Prosecutor v. Goran Jelisić* case and *Prosecutor v. Radislav* appeal. Goran Jelisić was a detention camp leader who styled himself a "Serbian Adolf" and who had "gone to Brčko to kill Muslims." Despite compelling evidence of genocidal intent, the Trial Chamber acquitted Jelisić of genocide on the grounds that

> the acts of Goran Jelisić are not the physical expression of an affirmed resolve to destroy in whole or in part a group as such. All things considered, the Prosecutor has not established beyond all reasonable doubt that genocide was committed in Brcko during the period covered by the indictment. Furthermore, the behavior of the accused appears to indicate that, although he obviously singled out Muslims, he killed arbitrarily rather than with the clear intention to destroy a group.

The Trial Chamber seemed to create an extremely high threshold for an individual committing genocide, because it is not satisfied even if the defendant was clearly driven to kill and did kill large numbers of a particular religious group. However, the Appeals Chamber held that the Trial Chamber had erred in terminating the trial on the genocide count, and that a reasonable trier of fact may have found Jelisić guilty of genocide on the evidence presented. It noted that occasional displays of randomness in the killings are not sufficient to negate the inference of intent evidenced by a relentless campaign to destroy the group. Notwithstanding this conclusion, the Appeals Chamber declined to remand the matter back to trial for a proper hearing on the genocide count, on the ground of public interest. Jelisić had pleaded guilty to crimes against humanity and war crimes for the same murders and was already sentenced to forty years' imprisonment, a probable life sentence. Judge Wald's partial dissent suggested that the decision may have reflected the view that convicting such a low level offender of genocide would diminish this "crime of crimes" and create a problematic precedent.

The Krstić appeal also explored the evidentiary threshold for the special intent of genocide, along with elaborating on the definition of aiding and abetting genocide. Major-General Krstić was charged with genocide for his part in the perpetration of the Srebrenica massacre, in which about seven thousand Bosnian Muslim men from the Srebrenica enclave were systematically separated from the rest of the population, transported to remote areas, and executed over the course of several days. The Appeals Chamber overturned the verdict and substituted a conviction of aiding and abeting genocide, an offence not taken from the genocide provisions of the Statute, but rather from the article providing individual criminal responsibility for persons participating in the commission of crimes under the Statute. The genocide conviction of Krstić, the chamber noted, rested on circumstantial evidence that could only demonstrate that the accused had knowledge of the killings and was aware of the intent of others to commit genocide. The Appeals Chamber held that this evidence could not be used to infer that Krstić possessed a genocidal intent, and thus he should not have been convicted as a principal perpetrator. Nonetheless, the Chamber held that his knowledge of the killings, and his allowing the use of personnel under his command, did meet the threshold of aiding and abetting genocide, a lesser offense.

The elements of genocide require that a national, ethnical, racial or religious group be targeted for destruction. The Trial Chamber in *Krstić* considered the definition of *group*, and found that what constitutes a group is a subjective and contextual determination, one criterion being the stigmatization of the group by the perpetrators. The *Krstić* trial judgement, supplemented by the Appeals Chamber, also considered the definition of *part of a group* in the requisite intention "to destroy in whole or in part." It held that genocide could be perpetrated against a highly localized *part of a group*, as exemplified by the Muslim population of Srebrenica, which formed part of the protected group of all Bosnian Muslims. On this question, the Chamber held,

> the killing of all members of the part of a group located within a small geographical area, although resulting in a lesser number of victims, would qualify as genocide if carried out with the intent to destroy the part of the group as such located in this small geographical area.

The Appeals Chamber affirmed that the "part" must be "substantial," as "[t]he aim of the Genocide Convention is to prevent the intentional destruction of entire human groups, [thus] the part targeted must be significant enough to have an impact "on the group as a whole." But beyond considerations of numeric importance, if a specific part of a group were essential to the survival of the group, the Chamber held that such a part could be found to be substantial, and thus meet the definition of *part of a group*. The Appeals Chamber noted that the population of the Bosnian Muslims of Srebrenica was crucial to their continued presence in the region, and indeed, their fate would be "emblematic of that of all Bosnian Muslims."

The case against Krstić also considered whether the killing of only the men of Srebrenica could be held to manifest an intention to destroy a part of the protected group, the Muslims of Bosnia. The Trial Chamber noted that the massacre of the men of Srebrenica was being perpetrated at the same time that the remainder of the Muslim population was being ethnically cleansed out of Srebrenica. It concluded that the community's physical survival was jeopardized by these atrocities and, therefore, these acts together could properly be held to constitute the intent to destroy part of group:

> The Bosnian Serb forces could not have failed to know, by the time they decided to kill all the men, that this selective destruction of the group would have a lasting impact upon the entire group. Their death precluded any effective attempt by the Bosnian Muslims to recapture the territory. Furthermore, the Bosnian Serb forces had to be aware of the catastrophic impact that the disappearance of two or three generations of men would have on the survival of a traditionally patriarchal society, an impact the Chamber has previously described in detail. The Bosnian Serb forces knew, by the time they decided to kill all of the military aged men, that the combination of those killings with the forcible transfer of the women, children and elderly would inevitably result in the physical disappearance of the Bosnian Muslim population at Srebrenica.

The material element of genocide requires that one or more acts be committed which are enumerated in the definition, namely, killing members of the group; causing serious bodily or mental harm to members of the group; deliberately inflicting on the group conditions of life calculated to bring about its physical destruction in whole or in part; imposing measures intended to prevent births within the group; or forcibly transferring children of the group to another group. On several occasions, the ICTY has considered whether ethnic cleansing alone—that is, the forcible expulsion of the members of a protected group—meets the material threshold of genocide. The appeal in the *Krstić* case confirmed that forcible transfer in and of itself does not constitute a genocidal act. However, it may be relied upon, with evidence of enumerated acts targeting the group, to infer a genocidal intent.

According to the findings of the ICTY, for a charge of genocide to be apt, the killing or causing of serious bodily or mental harm to members of a group must be intentional, but they need not be premeditated. The ICTY has also held that, with regard to causing bodily or mental harm, the harm need not be permanent and irremediable harm, but it must result in a "grave and long-term disadvantage to a person's ability to lead a normal and constructive life." Such acts could include cruel treatment, torture, rape, and deportation, or, for example, the agony suffered by individuals who survive mass executions.

From its modest beginnings, the ICTY has become an essential element of post-conflict peace-building in the former Yugoslavia. The link between prosecution of leaders responsible for incitement to ethnic hatred and violence, and the emergence of democratic multiethnic institutions that can secure a lasting peace has become increasingly apparent. Beyond abstract human rights considerations, international criminal justice has become an element of enlightened realpolitik. The initially haphazard ICTY precedent was an important catalyst for the resumption of efforts after the Nuremberg Judgement to establish an international criminal justice system. It prepared the path for the ICTR, the Special Court of Sierra Leone and other hybrid tribunals, and encouraged national courts to prosecute international crimes. Most significantly, it expedited and informed the deliberations leading to the adoption of the Rome Statute for the ICC in 1998. Thus, beyond the former Yugoslavia, the ICTY has introduced an accountability paradigm into the mainstream of international relations, challenged a hitherto entrenched culture of impunity, and helped alter the boundaries of power and legitimacy.

## Bibliography

Akhavan, Payam (2001). "Beyond Impunity: Can International Criminal Justice Prevent Future Atrocities?" *American Journal of International Law* 95:7.

Arbour, Louise (1999). "The Prosecution of International Crimes: Prospects and Pitfalls." *Washington University Journal of Law and Policy* 1:13–25.

Askin, Kelly D. (1999). "Sexual Violence in Decisions and Indictments of the Yugoslav and Rwandan Tribunals: Current Status." *American Journal of International Law* 93:97.

Boas, Gideon (2003). *International Criminal Law Developments in the Case Law of the ICTY.* The Hague: Martinus Nijhoff Publishers.

Burg, Steven L., and Paul S. Schrop (1999). *The War in Bosnia and Herzegovina.* Armonk, N.Y.: M. E. Sharpe.

Hagan, John (2002). *Justice in the Balkans.* Chicago: University of Chicago Press.

Ignatieff, Michael (1994). *Blood and Belonging: Journeys into the New Nationalism.* New York: Penguin Books.

Kalinauskas, Mikas (2002). "The Use of International Military Force in Arresting War Criminals: The Lessons of the International Criminal Tribunal for the Former Yugoslavia." *Kansas Law Review* 50(383).

Kerr, Rachel (2004). *The International Criminal Tribunal for the Former Yugoslavia: An Exercise in Law, Politics, and Diplomacy.* Oxford: Oxford University Press.

Lamb, Susan (1999). "The Powers of Arrest of the International Criminal Tribunal for the Former Yugoslavia." *The British Yearbook of International Law* 70(165).

McDonald, Gabrielle Kirk, ed. (2001). *Essays on ICTY Procedure and Evidence in Honour of Gabrielle Kirk McDonald.* The Hague: Kluwer Law International.

Mettraux, Guenael (2002). "Crimes Against Humanity in the Jurisprudence of the International Criminal Tribunals for the Former Yugoslavia and for Rwanda. *Harvard International Law Journal* 43(237).

Morris, Virginia, and Michael P. Scharf (1995). *Insider's Guide to the International Criminal Tribunal for the Former Yugoslavia.* Irvington-on-Hudson, N.Y.: Transnational Publishers.

Ramet, Sabrina P. (2002). *Balkan Babel,* 4th edition. Boulder, Colo.: Westview Press.

Schabas, William A. (2003). "Mens Rea and the International Criminal Tribunal for the Former Yugoslavia." *New England Law Review* 37(1015).

Wald, Patricia (2001). "The International Criminal Tribunal for the Former Yugoslavia Comes of Age: Some Observations on Day-To-Day Dilemmas of an International Court." *Washington University Journal of Law and Policy* 5(87).

Williams, Paul R., and Michael P. Scharf (2002). *Peace with Justice? War Crimes and Accountability in the Former Yugoslavia.* Lanham, Md.: Rowman & Littlefield.

Zimmerman, Warren (1996). *Origins of a Catastrophe.* Toronto: Random House.

## 11.2   "Radislav Krstic Becomes the First Person to Be Convicted of Genocide at the ICTY and Is Sentenced to 46 Years Imprisonment."

Today 2 August 2001, Trial Chamber I of the International Criminal Tribunal for the former Yugoslavia, composed of Judges Rodrigues (Presiding), Riad and Wald, rendered its Judgement in The Prosecutor v. Radislav Krstic. The Trial Chamber stated that it was "convinced beyond any reasonable doubt that a crime of genocide was committed in Srebrenica" and that General Radislav Krstic is guilty of genocide. Please find below the summary of the Sentencing Judgement of Trial Chamber I, read out by Presiding Judge Almiro Rodrigues at today's Judgement hearing.

### Introduction

"May justice be done lest the world perish" said Hegel. The Trial Chamber is doing its duty in meting out justice and, in this way, hopes to have contributed to creating a better world."

The Trial Chamber is rendering its Judgement today in the Prosecutor's case against General Krstic who stands accused of genocide, complicity to commit genocide, persecution, extermination, murder and forced transfer or deportation and of crimes committed between July and November 1995 following the attack of the Serbian forces on the town of Srebrenica. At the time the attack was launched, General Krstic was the deputy commander of the Drina Corps, one of the corps which constitute the army of Republika Srpska, often known as the VRS. The exact date General Krstic became the Drina Corps commander has been the subject of professional, courteous but, at times, particularly acrimonious debates between the parties. I will return to this point.

I wish to make several preliminary comments.

First, I wish to point out that throughout the trial the debates proceeded smoothly and the parties conducted themselves in an exemplary manner. In this case, both the Prosecution and Defence demonstrated in the most striking fashion that co-operation and confrontation need not be mutually exclusive. The arguments were always correct and, in particular, were of the highest quality. The final arguments were presentations of excellent legal and factual summaries of the respective positions of the Prosecution and the Defence. I wish to extend my appreciation to all counsel and their teams for the work they have done and the atmosphere in which it was carried out.

I wish to pay tribute to the work of the Office of the Prosecutor in the broadest sense and, in particular, to Mr. Jean-René Ruez, the former team leader in the Office of the Prosecutor. I also have in mind everyone working for the Prosecution and the Defence who travelled on-site: the experts and their assistants, the investigators, technicians, soldiers, security officers and also all those who saw, smelled, touched, exhumed, washed, autopsied, and analysed. It is not difficult to imagine how much patience, perseverance and devotion was required to perform this thankless but indispensable task.

I also wish to thank everyone who offered us their unstinting assistance, frequently after normal working hours.

I also wish to thank the staff of the Detention Unit and the Serbian and Dutch physicians and surgeons who shared their experience with us so that the accused would receive the treatment required for his medical condition.

Lastly, I wish to underscore the work of the military analysts and experts, Mr. Richard Butler and General Dannatt for the Prosecutor and General Radinovic for the Defence.

All this work made it possible to hear 128 witnesses, two of whom were called by the Trial

Chamber. In all, more than eleven hundred exhibits (some several hundred pages long) were admitted during the proceedings.

I will move quickly over the details of the proceedings which appear in the annex to the Judgement. I will note only that because of General Krstic's medical condition, the trial was interrupted for several weeks at the start of the year. Nonetheless, as you know, the Trial Chamber's work did not stop since it was hearing two cases at the same time.

I now come to the reason for this hearing, pronouncing of the judgement in the case The Prosecutor against Radislav Krstic. I do not intend to read out the entire written Judgement but to present a summary thereof so that you, General Krstic, and the public will know essentially the reasons why the Trial Chamber reached the conclusions it has reached. I wish to point out that the only authoritative text is the written Judgement which will be available after this hearing and nothing I am going to say can be seen as modifying that Judgement in any way.

General Krstic, the crimes of which you stand accused are based on the events which occurred following the attack of the Serbian forces on the town of Srebrenica in July 1995. Srebrenica—the name of a town which has become synonymous with the conflict which devastated the former Yugoslavia. It is a name which immediately calls to mind thousands of people subjected to siege, famine and deprivation of everything—even water and time to breathe. The name of an enclave which the United Nations declared a safe area and which fell almost without a shot being fired. Srebrenica—a name which conjures up images one would prefer not to see: women, children and old people forced to climb into buses leaving for destinations unknown; men separated from their families, stripped of their belongings, men fleeing, men taken prisoner, men never to be seen again, men who would be found—but not always—dead, corpses piled up in mass graves; corpses with their hands tied or their eyes blind-folded—frequently; dismembered corpses as well; unidentified corpses . . . corpses.

Srebrenica is also a name for a post-traumatic syndrome, the syndrome displayed by the women, children and old people who did not die and who, ever since July 1995, six years now, still have no news of their husbands and sons, fathers, brothers, uncles, grandfathers. Thousands of amputated lives six years later, robbed of the affection and love of their kin now reduced to ghosts who return to haunt them day after day, night after night.

The Trial Chamber was presented with a great deal of evidence which could be called impressive.

Because of the violence of the crimes, the almost unbearable images put before it, and the pain to which the victims gave voice in their testimony, the Trial Chamber needed to be particularly vigilant so that it could take the necessary distance for carrying out its work of justice with the requisite calm and as objectively as possible. During its meticulous analysis of inter alia all the evidence, testimony, exhibits, it was especially attentive to the need to ensure that the evidence it had made it possible to verify whether crimes had been committed. It carried out a scrupulous examination of all these in order to decide on which or any of the criminal characterisations the Prosecutor set out in her indictment a conviction could be entered. Lastly and above all, the Trial Chamber carefully weighed whether one or several of the crimes could be ascribed to General Krstic.

Essentially, the Trial Chamber is responding to three questions: what are the facts, which are the crimes that were committed, can General Krstic be held responsible for any of these crimes? I will now present a summary of the conclusions the Trial Chamber reached in respect of these three questions.

## I—What are the Facts?

### Transfer of Women, Children and Old People
The attack of the Serbian forces on the Srebrenica enclave followed several months, actually several years, of confrontation. Srebrenica is located in a part of eastern Bosnia, central

Podrinje, which was of particular interest to both parties involved. To the Bosnian Muslims because the town was predominantly Muslim before the conflict; because it is located between Tuzla to the north and Zepa to the south both of which were under Muslim control; because the fall of Srebrenica could have extremely negative consequences for Sarajevo under siege at the time. To the Bosnian Serbs because the region known as central Podrinje was in that part of Bosnia bordering Serbia and because it was important to establish the continuity, in Bosnia like in neighbouring Serbia, of the territories under Serbian control; and, of course, for the opposite reasons of those of the Bosnian Muslims.

In 1992–1993, there were many clashes between the Serbs and the Bosnian Muslims for control of the region. After several successful operations, the ABiH (the Bosnian Muslim army) was confronted with a counter-offensive mounted by the VRS (the Bosnian Serb army) which finally reduced the enclave to about 150 km². In March 1993, siege was laid to Srebrenica and part of the population was transferred.

On 16 April 1993, the United Nations Security Council declared Srebrenica a "safe area" and an agreement signed by the parties turned it into a demilitarised zone to which an UNPROFOR contingent was dispatched. However, the parties did not agree on the definition and interpretation of the notion of demilitarised zone. In particular, the Bosnian Muslims considered that only the town of Srebrenica itself was demilitarised and the ABiH sent weapons and munitions to the enclave.

Still, the situation remained relatively stable until January 1995 when the Bosnian Serbs adopted a more hard-line position, in particular, in respect of the supply of humanitarian aid.

On 8 March 1995, the President of the Bosnian Serbs, Radovan Karadzic, issued the order under the name of "Directive 7" to separate the enclaves of Srebrenica and Zepa. In respect of what concerned the Drina Corps in particular, President Karadzic wrote "By well thought out combat operations, create an unbearable situation of total insecurity with no hope of further survival or life for the inhabitants of Srebrenica and Zepa."

On the basis of this directive, on 31 March 1995, General Ratko Mladic also issued a directive which he sent inter alia to the Drina Corps. The Directive organised a large-scale attack known as "Sadejstvo-95" whose objective was to defend the territory of Republika Srpska on all fronts and, in particular, to avoid, and I quote, "at any cost" the lifting of the siege of Sarajevo. General Mladic foresaw that whatever the result of the events and the escalation of the conflict, UNPROFOR land forces and NATO forces would probably not be engaged, except in those cases when they come under direct physical threat. During the operation, he stated that the forces of the Republika Srpska army would collaborate in strategic camouflage and improvement of the tactical position by carrying out, among others, active combat operations (. . .) around the Srebrenica, Zepa and Gorazde enclaves.

In the spring of 1995, the situation in Sarajevo deteriorated significantly. Humanitarian convoys were obstructed and sometimes blocked. Even the Dutch UNPROFOR contingent could not effect its normal troop rotation. Some of the observation posts reported a significant reinforcement of the nearby Serbian positions. The humanitarian situation became catastrophic. The 28th ABiH Division, that is, the Bosnian Muslim army in the Srebrenica enclave, asked that the blockade be lifted. Harassment operations were launched against the Serbian positions. This is known as "Operation Skakavac" and, apparently, crimes were committed while it was being carried out, in particular in the Serbian village of Visjnica on 26 June 1995. At the same time, the Bosnian Serb army was on the move. On 31 May 1995, it captured one of the UNPROFOR observation posts.

On 2 July 1995, the Drina Corps commander, General Zivanovic signed the orders for a planned attack on Srebrenica. On 6 July the attack was launched from south of the enclave. Thousands of Bosnian Muslims fled to the town. The Bosnian Serb forces encountered no resistance. On 9 July, President Karadzic decided that, under the prevailing conditions, the town was to be taken. On 10 July, the panicked Bosnian Muslim population began to flee toward the United Nations facilities in the town (Bravo company) or out of the town towards the north, on the Bratunac road, to Potocari. The commander of the Dutch Battalion often called Dutchbat, asked for air support but did not receive it.

On 11 July, General Mladic, Chief-of-Staff of the Bosnian Serb army, along with General Zivanovic, General Krstic and many other VRS officers, made a triumphant entry into a Srebrenica deserted by its inhabitants.

By the evening of 11 July, Srebrenica was a dead town in the hands of the Bosnian Serb forces.

The inhabitants of Srebrenica and the refugees there fled en masse to the United Nations base in Potocari. The Bosnian Serb forces would soon learn that there were very few men in the milling crowd gathering around the UNPROFOR camp. In Potocari there were mostly women, children and old people.

There were very few men in Potocari because, even though one cannot know for sure who gave the orders or organised the departures, they took a different route. Whether members of the 28th Division or not, they assembled in the little villages of Jaglici and Susnjari north-west of Srebrenica and decided to flee through the woods towards Tuzla much further to the north in territory under Bosnian Muslim control. About ten to fifteen thousand men formed a column several kilometres long and left on foot through the woods.

However, General Mladic did not yet know that when, on 11 July, he called the Dutchbat commander Colonel Karremans to a meeting at the Hotel Fontana in Bratunac. Along with General Mladic were many VRS officers, including General Zivanovic, but not General Krstic. At 20.00 hours on 11 July, General Mladic asked Colonel Karremans whether UNPROFOR could organise the transport of the population. He also asked him to return with a representative of the population of Srebrenica. The second meeting was held in the same hotel on that same day. It was about 23.00 hours. General Mladic was in attendance with General Krstic but without General Zivanovic. Colonel Karremans came with a teacher, Mr. Mandzic, who represented the population. This time, General Mladic's tone and attitude were much harder. Through the open window came the sounds of a pig being slaughtered. General Mladic had the signboard of the Srebrenica town hall which had been removed from the building placed on the table. The Dutchbat commander said that there were about 15–20,000 refugees and that the humanitarian situation was distressing. General Mladic raised his voice and became threatening. He said that he would organise the transport of the population and demanded that the ABiH lay down its weapons. He also demanded that Mr. Mandzic make sure that this was done although Mr. Mandzic tried, in vain, to explain that he had no power to do so. The answer fell and it was final: that's your problem; bring in the people who can ensure that the weapons are laid down and save your people from destruction.

Another meeting was scheduled for the following day. It began around 10.00 on 12 July. General Mladic was still there with General Krstic beside him. Colonel Popovic, to whom we will return later, was also there. The Dutchbat representatives returned with Mr. Mandzic and two other "civilian representatives", Mrs. Omanovic, an economist, and Mr. Nuhanovic, a businessman. General Mladic again insisted that the condition for the survival of the Bosnian Muslims of Srebrenica was that they lay down their weapons. He said that he would supply the buses to transport the population but that the fuel would have to be provided by UNPROFOR. Everyone understood that the Bosnian Muslims were to leave the enclave. Last, General Mladic said that all the men in Potocari would be separated in order to identify any possible war criminals.

At around noon on 12 July, General Krstic gave a filmed interview to a journalist from Serbia. This took place right next to the United Nations base in Potocari. Behind him, passing trucks could be seen. Buses as well. These were the buses the women, children and old people would get into. The video the journalist made shows resigned people. The men are being separated from the women. Here and there one sees bags, bundles, a few belongings. Further away, a larger pile. The Trial Chamber would learn that these were the belongings of the men who had come to seek refuge in Potocari and who had been ordered to leave them there. The Trial Chamber knows that the belongings were subsequently burned by the Serbian forces.

How did the situation appear to the Bosnian Muslims who had sought refuge in Potocari? It was extremely serious. One needs to remember the shelling, including the shelling of the United Nations base in Srebrenica. One needs to imagine thousands of people crowded into a few buildings without water or food other than a few pieces of candy thrown in by General Mladic in front of the cameras and, we were told, taken back once the cameras had left. One must imagine the heat. One must picture the dozens of soldiers and Serbian armed men coming and going shouting out discriminatory insults. One must see the houses set on fire, the night falling and the rising screams. The witnesses described to the Trial Chamber the prevailing atmosphere of terror, the rapes and murders and the mistreatment so pervasive that some of the refugees committed suicide or attempted to do so.

In the evening of 13 July, all the women, children and old people were transferred. The Trial Chamber concludes that for legal reasons which it explains in its Judgement, there was no expulsion. There was, however, a forced transfer of the women, children and old people of Srebrenica. The men were systematically separated and were forced to leave behind their meagre possessions, leave behind even their identify papers. They were taken to a white house several metres from the United Nations base. They were beaten. Some were taken behind the house and killed. The survivors were taken away to various detention locations, including Bratunac. Those who were able to get on the buses were stopped right before leaving the territory under VRS control and driven to other detention locations (bus, school, hangar. . . .).

During that time, the column, with most of the 28th Division armed forces at the head, tried to go through the forest and cross the east-west Bratunac-Konjevic Polje road. There were about ten to fifteen thousand men in the column. About one-third was able to get through, including 3,000 men of the 28th Division. The first of these arrived in Bosnian Muslim controlled territory on 16 July. The others, subjected to shelling and automatic weapons fire, were captured or surrendered, sometimes to the so-called UNPROFOR soldiers who were, in fact, none other than members of the Serbian forces using equipment stolen from Dutchbat. Some of these were killed immediately. Most were taken to collection centres, like a meadow in Sandici or a football field in Nova Kasaba. A last group would be luckier because when they came into contact with the Serbian forces, negotiations were initiated and they would, finally, be able to go to territory under Bosnian Muslim control.

In all, 7 to 8,000 men were captured by the Serbian forces. Almost all of them were killed. Only very few survived and some of them testified before the Trial Chamber and described the horror of the mass executions which they miraculously escaped.

### The Mass Executions Began on 13 July

Some of the executions involved only a few individuals, like the one in Jadar on the morning of 13 July. In the afternoon of 13 July, there was another execution at a relatively isolated place, the Cerska Valley. 150 bodies would be exhumed there on which 50 metal ties would be found, some of them still wrapped around the victims' wrists. Late in the afternoon, the Serbian forces indulged in a real killing spree. A large number of Bosnian Muslims, about 1,000–1,500, were assembled in a warehouse in Kravica. The soldiers opened fire and lobbed in grenades. Those who tried to escape were killed immediately. The next day, the Serbian forces called out to any survivors. Some of those who responded were forced to sing Serbian songs and then executed. A large machine came to carry away the bodies and, in so doing, ripped off part of the warehouse doorframe. The experts would find traces of hair, blood and human tissue on the floor and walls.

On 13 and 14 July, there were executions in Tisca also, that is, the place where the buses were to stop so that the Serbian forces could verify whether there were still men on board, and if so, to force them to get off. They were then taken to a school and, after their hands were tied, to a field where they were executed.

On 14 July, a thousand Bosnian Muslims were assembled in the Grbavci school (Orahovac) gymnasium. Their eyes were blindfolded and they were taken by truck to a field where they were executed. Machines were already digging up the ground before the executions had been completed.

There were other executions from 14 to 16 July. A group of 1,500–2,000 Bosnian Muslims was being detained at the Petkovci school. They were taken to an execution site next to an artificial lake, the Petkovci dam. Their hands were tied and they were barefoot. They were executed with automatic weapons.

This would also be the fate of 1,000 to 1,200 men at the Branjevo military farm. The Trial Chamber heard the testimony of a former VRS soldier convicted by the Tribunal for his participation in that execution—Mr. Drazen Erdemovic. The Bosnian Muslim men were brought in by truck, many with their hands tied, some wearing blindfolds. All but one were dressed in civilian clothing. The execution squad fired over and over again until, as Mr. Erdemovic said, their fingers hurt. Immediately afterwards, the soldiers went to Pilica. Several hundred Bosnian Muslims were locked up in the village cultural centre, the Pilica Dom. Mr. Erdemovic and several others refused to participate any further in the executions and sat down in the café across from the cultural centre from where they could hear the shots and explosions. There would be no survivors. When the investigators forced open the door to the cultural centre, they discovered clear traces of the massacre and the conditions in which it had been perpetrated: bullet marks, traces of explosives, blood stains, bits of human remains, everywhere, high up on the walls and even under the stage of the theatre. And a single forgotten identity document belonging to a Bosnian Muslim. The cultural centre is located on the side of the main road crossing the village at the point where buses stop. In front of the cultural centre today stands a memorial in honour of the . . . Serbian heroes who died for the Serbian cause. There were other executions as well, in particular, in Kozluk and Nezuk. The last mass execution appears to have been on 19 July 1995.

In all, the experts estimate that between seven and eight thousand Bosnian Muslim men were executed between 13 and 19 July 1995.

Despite the efforts which have been made, very few mortal remains have been found. Why? Because in the fall of 1995 measures were taken in order to attempt to cover up the scale of the crimes.

The proof of what happened can be seen, in particular, in the aerial photographs provided to the Prosecutor. These photographs have made it possible: to identify the number of mass grave sites at the time the executions were carried out; and to note that other sites appeared after September 1995. The work of the experts has also made it possible to confirm the data by comparing the older mass graves with the more recent ones since the latter are always located in regions with more difficult access than those of the first group. No particular care was taken when the bodies were moved and it has not been uncommon to find bodies with missing limbs. There can therefore be no doubt about the deliberate desire to conceal the existence of mass graves and therefore the mass executions of civilians or persons no longer fit for combat.

## II—Which are the Crimes that were Committed?

The Prosecutor has characterised all the crimes and has charged General Krstic with: genocide (or complicity therein); persecution by means of murder, cruel treatment, acts of terror, destruction of personal property and forced transfer; extermination; murders within the meaning of Article 5 of the Statute; murders within the meaning of Article 3 of the Statute; deportation or the inhumane act of forced transfer.

In its Judgement, the Trial Chamber responds to all these points and concludes by applying the case-law of the Appeals Chamber in respect of cumulative charges. It is clear that the principal question which arose was whether genocide was committed against, in the Prosecutor's words, "a part of the Bosnian Muslim people as a national, ethnical, or religious group".

The notion of genocide is itself a recent one. It appeared for the first time in the Second World War and was codified in December 1948 in the Convention on the Prevention and Punishment of the Crime of Genocide which came into force on 12 January 1951. Article 5 of the Statute of the Tribunal, "Genocide", repeats the definition of the Convention word for word. I quote: "genocide means any of the following acts committed with intent to destroy, in whole or in part, a national, ethnical, racial or religious group, as such." Among the acts of genocide are killing members of the group and causing serious bodily or mental harm to members of the group.

There is little case-law on genocide. While the International Criminal Tribunal for Rwanda has rendered several decisions on this point, the case-law of our Tribunal on the subject is almost non-existent.

In this case, the fact that serious bodily or mental harm was inflicted on the Bosnian Muslims or that they were murdered has not been disputed. The Trial Chamber considers that one also cannot dispute the fact that the victims were chosen because of their membership in a national group, that is, precisely because they were Bosnian Muslims. However, can one claim that there was a will or intent to destroy, in whole or in part, a group as such protected by the Convention?

The Defence submitted that there was not and expressed this opinion exhaustively and most clearly both in its written submissions and final arguments. I will present a very brief, and therefore incomplete, summary of its arguments.

The Defence does not dispute the fact that the Serbian forces attacked Srebrenica's Bosnian Muslim population of fighting age. It claims, however, that precisely for this reason, one cannot speak of genocide, despite the scale of the murders committed. It points out first that the women, children and old people were transferred and not killed. It goes on to state that a part of the column, as I mentioned a few minutes ago, was able to pass into territory under Bosnian Muslim control after negotiations had taken place. According to the Defence, it cannot even be claimed that all the Bosnian Muslim men of fighting age were targeted. Lastly, and in any case, the Defence sets out that the intent to destroy all the Bosnian Muslim men of fighting age cannot be interpreted as the intent to destroy, in whole or in part, a group as such, within the meaning of Article 4 of the Statute.

The Trial Chamber does not share this view.

The Trial Chamber observes that although Bosnian Muslim men from Srebrenica were able to escape the hands of the Serbian forces after the fall of the enclave, this was due to chance or the Serbian forces' inability to prevent the passage of the end of the column into territory under Bosnian Muslim control given the operations in which it was engaged elsewhere. In other words, the Serbian forces really had no other choice at the time than to allow the rest of the column to pass. Subject only to the reservation which we have just stated, the executions were carried out on such a mass scale that the men from Srebrenica of fighting age were annihilated.

The Trial Chamber points out that the decision to kill all the Bosnian Muslim men of fighting age was taken after the decision to transfer the women, children and old people. For this reason, the Serbian forces had to realise the impact such a decision would have on the group's survival.

The Trial Chamber is not stating, nor does it wish to suggest, that a plan to commit genocide existed prior to the attack on Srebrenica or even right before the city fell. However, according to the Appeals Chamber decision in the Jelisic case, a plan of genocide need not have been formed. Nor is it indispensable that, should such a plan exist, some time must pass between its conception and its implementation.

What we are asserting here, on the basis of all the evidence presented to us, is that a decision was first taken to carry out "ethnic cleansing" of the Srebrenica enclave. Moreover, it is not unreasonable to note that the men could be separated from the women, children and old people. Furthermore, the men taken prisoner could subsequently serve as a "bargaining chip" as was frequently the case throughout the conflict in the former Yugoslavia. What was important at that time was to drive out all the Bosnian Muslims from the enclave, including the women, children and old people.

However, for reasons the Trial Chamber has been unable to clarify, the decision was then taken to kill all the men of fighting age. The result was inevitable: the destruction of the Bosnian Muslim population in Srebrenica. At issue is not only the commission of murders for political, racial or religious reasons, which already constitutes a crime of persecution. At issue is not only extermination of the Bosnian Muslim men of fighting age alone. At issue is the deliberate decision to kill the men, a decision taken with complete awareness of the impact the murders would inevitably have on the entire group. By deciding to kill all the men of Srebrenica of fighting age, a decision was taken to make it impossible for the Bosnian Muslim people of Srebrenica to survive.

Stated otherwise, what was ethnic cleansing became genocide.

The Trial Chamber is also convinced beyond any reasonable doubt that a crime of genocide was committed in Srebrenica.

Finally, for the reasons set forth in detail in its Judgement, the Trial Chamber considers that the following crimes were committed: genocide, persecution, extermination, murder within the meaning of Article 3 of the Statute; murder within the meaning of Article 5; and the forced transfer of Bosnian Muslims.

In light of the rules applicable to cumulative charging, only the crimes of genocide, persecution and murder within the meaning of Article 3 of the Statute have been retained.

## III—Is General Krstic Guilty of Any of these Crimes?

The final question which the Trial Chamber must answer is whether General Krstic can be held guilty of these crimes. The Prosecution claims that he can; the Defence claims that he cannot. In order to establish the possible responsibility of General Krstic for these crimes, the Trial Chamber took account of his position as Deputy Commander and then Commander of the Drina Corps at the time these crimes were committed. The Drina Corps, as I have already said, had authority over the entire area in which the crimes took place. For this reason, the Trial Chamber first reviewed what in the evidence presented by the parties would make it possible to establish whether or not the Drina Corps forces were involved in the crimes. This review allowed the Trial Chamber to conclude beyond any reasonable doubt that the Drina Corps forces participated in, if not all the crimes, at least some of them.

However, it appeared also that other forces played a role, and sometimes a decisive one at that, in what happened and, in particular, in the capture of the Bosnian Muslims and the executions. The Judgement thus makes it clear that the following were involved in these crimes:

- the forces of the Ministry of the Interior, more commonly known as the MUP;
- forces answering in principle to the Main Staff and, in particular: the 65th motorised protection regiment; or the 10th sabotage detachment of which Mr. Erdemovic was a member;
- the military police forces;
- other armed forces which probably included civilians or reservists who had taken up arms.

However, the evidence also leads to the conclusion that all these forces acted in a co-ordinated manner and were organised for the same objective. The presence of General Mladic in Srebrenica and Potocari was mentioned on several occasions. At the time, General Mladic was the Chief-of-Staff of the General Staff of the armed forces of Republika Srpska, that is, the number 2 man in the military hierarchy right below President Karadzic. The Trial Chamber then sought to verify General Krstic's role at the time of the crimes and, in particular, any role he may have played in their commission.

I will sketch out the positions taken by the Prosecution and the Defence.

The Prosecution claims that General Krstic was the Deputy Commander of the Drina Corps at the time the attack on Srebrenica was launched. As such, he was involved in the organisation of the troops who took part in the attack. General Krstic assumed command of the Corps by the evening of 13 July 1995 at the latest. According to the Prosecutor, he is thus responsible for all the crimes committed on the territory of the Drina Corps by virtue of Article 7(1) of the Statute, that is, individually responsible. However, the Prosecutor claims that General Krstic is also responsible as a commander by virtue of Article 7(3) of the Statute.

The Defence contends that General Krstic was a professional officer trained in the JNA and was well aware of the rules applicable to armed conflicts. The Defence never disputed that General Krstic was alongside General Mladic when the town of Srebrenica fell, that he was present at two of the three meetings at the Hotel Fontana, that General Krstic was successively the Deputy Commander and then the Commander of the Drina Corps, a corps whose territorial jurisdiction covered all the territory on which the crimes occurred.

It points out however that General Krstic in no manner committed any crime himself and claims that he cannot be held responsible as a superior either. First, the attack on Srebrenica in which he participated was not unlawful as such. However, according to the Defence, General Krstic became the Commander of the Drina Corps only on 20 July 1995 and learned of the mass executions of Bosnian Muslims in Srebrenica only after that date. He had in fact been tasked by General Mladic to carry out the attack on Zepa on 13 July at the latest. The Defence goes on to claim that General Krstic therefore had to change the position of his forward command post and found himself isolated in respect of the communications he was receiving. Lastly, the Defence asserts that General Krstic had no involvement whatsoever in the digging up and reburial of the bodies.

The Trial Chamber has carefully reviewed all the arguments. It has conducted a scrupulous examination of all the exhibits in the case-file as well as the testimony whether of United Nations staff or victims. The Trial Chamber has meticulously weighed the information provided by the radio taps. In this respect, I recall that the Trial Chamber did not admit the recording in which a voice alleged to be that of K. is heard saying: kill them all! I emphasise this point because it might have appeared that this exhibit was part of the case-file whereas it has NOT been admitted and is not an exhibit. However, the Trial Chamber did admit many other recordings some of which are the subject of a detailed analysis in the Judgement. Lastly, the Trial Chamber analysed the reports of the military experts submitted both by the Prosecution and the Defence. And there is no possible doubt.

When you entered Srebrenica with General Mladic on 11 July 1995, General Krstic, you found a deserted town. You thus knew that the population had fled. You were the Deputy Commander of the Drina Corps and your commander, General Zivanovic was there along with many other VRS officers.

Assuming that you did not already know, you must have wondered where the population had gone. Because, according to your own statements, your objective was to separate Srebrenica from Zepa and to reduce the enclave to its urban area. It was therefore essential for you to know where at least the forces of the 28th Division might be since they were not there.

You were not at the first meeting in the Hotel Fontana in Bratunac on the evening of 11 July around 20.00 hours. But you were present at the second meeting around 23.00 hours. You say that you did not hear the scream of the pig being killed at that moment. But because you were sitting right next to General Mladic, you heard him speak in an arrogant and threatening voice both to the Dutchbat commander and the "representative" of the Bosnian Muslim population of Srebrenica who was there. You saw when General Mladic had the signboard which had been removed from the Srebrenica town hall put on the table. You heard General Mladic asking the Bosnian Muslim armed forces to surrender and the Dutchbat commander to organise the transfer of the women, children and old people from Potocari. You were there, General Krstic, on 12 July around 10.00 hours when General Mladic told the UNPROFOR officers that the forces of the VRS were going to organise the transfer but that UNPROFOR would have to provide the necessary fuel. You heard General Mladic's tone of voice, even more menacing than the day before, when he spoke to the people who you knew were acting as representatives of the Bosnian Muslim community of Srebrenica. You gave orders for buses and other transport to come to Potocari quickly. You knew, at least by early morning on 12 July, that a large column of Bosnian Muslims was trying to cross the Bratunac-Konjevic Polje road. In any case, you knew that the column was moving north and therefore represented no danger for the rest of your operations in the other United Nations safe area which you were preparing to attack. You were in Potocari giving an interview when the first buses arrived. You were there when they began to separate the men from the women, children and old people. You could not not have seen their physical condition. You could not not have heard the screams of the men who were taken to the building called the White House as they were being beaten.

In accordance with the orders you received from General Mladic, on 13 July, you focused on the preparations for the attack on Zepa. But you received information on a regular basis. You knew that when the buses arrived at the border of the area under Bosnian Muslim control, Drina Corps soldiers were making the men seeking refuge there get off. On 13 July in the evening, you knew that thousands of men from the column had been captured. On the evening of 13 July, I repeat—13 July—you took command of the Drina Corps and signed your first order as the corps commander around 20.30 hours. On 14 July, you launched the attack on Zepa. Nonetheless, you remained perfectly well informed of what was going on in the area to the north of the town of Srebrenica. In the night of 14–15 July, troops from the Zvornik Brigade (one of the Drina Corps brigades) moved up from Zepa towards Srebrenica and you knew why they were doing that. On 15 July in the morning, the security chief of the Main Staff called you and asked for your help in dealing with "3,500 packages". You knew exactly what was meant by "packages", General Krstic—Bosnian Muslims who were to be executed. You expressed your displeasure. That same officer told you that the MUP forces, the Interior Ministry police, did not want (no longer wanted) to do it. You said you would see what you could do. On 16 July, some of your subordinates, men from the Bratunac Brigade, participated in the mass executions at the Branjevo military farm. On 16 July, the security chief of the Drina Corps whose commander you were, continued to keep you informed about the situation. You asserted to the Trial Chamber that, subsequently, you wanted to take measures against that officer, but out of fear of reprisals against yourself or, more specifically against your family, you decided not to. The Trial Chamber, however, found nothing to confirm your assertions. Not a single soldier of the Drina Corps was punished for the murder of one or several Bosnian Muslims. On the contrary. Nothing makes it possible to establish that you participated in the activities designed to conceal the massacres and, to this end, in the operations of digging up and reburial of the corpses. But how could anyone think that you would not have known about work requiring the use of such large machines? In any case, General Krstic, you were seen being congratulated for the action you took in Srebrenica. You were seen right next to General Mladic when in December 1995 a ceremony was organised for the Drina Corps. Finally, General Krstic, you supported General Mladic against President Karadzic when he tried to remove General Mladic.

GENERAL KRSTIC, PLEASE RISE.

The Trial Chamber does not dispute that you are a professional soldier who loves his work. The Trial Chamber can accept that you would not of your own accord have taken the decision to execute thousands of civilians and disarmed persons. Someone else probably decided to order the execution of all the men of fighting age.

Nonetheless, you are still guilty, General Krstic.

You are guilty of having knowingly participated in the organised forced transfer of the women, children and old people in Srebrenica at the time of the attack on 6 July 1995 against the United Nations safe area.

You are guilty of the murder of thousands of Bosnian Muslims between 10 and 19 July 1995, whether these be murders committed sporadically in Potocari or murders planned in the form of mass executions. You are guilty of the incredible suffering of the Bosnian Muslims whether these be the ones in Potocari or survivors of the executions. You are guilty of the persecution suffered by the Bosnian Muslims of Srebrenica. Knowing that the women, children and old people of Srebrenica had been transferred, you are guilty of having agreed to the plan to conduct mass executions of all the men of fighting age. You are therefore guilty of genocide, General Krstic.

In order to determine the penalty you deserve, we have, of course, taken into account the extreme gravity of the crime. Still, we also wished to show that, in respect of the crimes committed on the territory of the former Yugoslavia, there are certainly people whose individual responsibility is much greater than your own.

At this point I wish to make a personal observation. Kant has said that if justice is ignored, life on this earth has no value.

I believe it is essential to make a distinction between what might be collective responsibility and individual responsibility. The Tribunal has not been established to deal with the possibility of collective responsibility. What is of interest to me in each of the trials in which I have sat in this court is to verify whether the evidence presented before it makes it possible to find an accused guilty. I seek to judge an accused. I do not judge a people. Yes, in the former Yugoslavia there were attacks against civilian populations. Yes, there were massacres and there was persecution. Yes, some of these crimes were committed by Serbian forces. However, to paraphrase a great humanist, I consider that to associate this evil with Serbian identity would be an insult to the Serbian people and would betray the concept of civil society. But it would be just as monstrous not to attach any name to this evil because that could be an offence to the Serbs.

In July 1995, General Krstic, you agreed to evil.

This is why the Trial Chamber convicts you today and sentences you to 46 years in prison.

The court stands adjourned.

# 12

# The International Criminal Tribunal for Rwanda

Between April and July 1994, a genocide was perpetrated in Rwanda against Tutsis and liberal democratic ("moderate") Hutus by the extremist Hutu Power regime of the *Mouvement Révolutionnaire Nationale pour le Développement* (National Revolutionary Movement for Development, or MRND). In a 100-day period, between 500,000 and one million people—primarily Tutsis but also moderate Hutus—were slaughtered.

During the German and Belgian colonial periods in what would become Rwanda (1880s to 1961), Hutus and Tutsis were identified as distinctly different peoples. During this colonial period, the Tutsis were accorded a higher social status than the majority Hutus, who were perceived as belonging to a lower socio-economic order. The end of colonial rule overturned this ranking of peoples, with the Hutus (with the connivance of the former Belgian colonizers) claiming majority rights politically. This triggered periodic outbursts of escalating violence in 1959, 1962, and 1973. In the early 1990s, the MRND laid extensive and somewhat transparent plans to carry out a campaign of extermination of the Tutsis and their Hutu political allies. The blueprint included an intense propaganda campaign broadcast over *Radio-Télévision Libre des Mille Collines* (RTLM), and the creation of killing units, the *Interahamwe* and the *Impuzamugambi* militias, together with the ethnic politicization of the Rwandan armed forces. The trigger leading to the initiation of the genocide was the murder of President Juvenal Habyarimana on April 6, 1994, after an airplane in which he was traveling was shot down by a missile as it approached the Kigali airport in Rwanda. The death of Habyarimana acted as a tocsin for radical Hutus across the country to commence the long-planned operation to completely eliminate the Tutsi population of Rwanda.

A distinguishing characteristic of the killings was the manner in which they were carried out. Most victims were butchered with hand-held agricultural tools, particularly machetes, as well as nail-studded clubs which had only one possible function. Moreover, the government exhorted *every* Hutu to kill Tutsis, wherever they could be found. As mass murder thereby became a civic virtue, neighbor killed neighbor, and even family members killed each other (where there were Tutsis or moderate Hutus in the family). What was striking was the efficiency of the *génocidaires*; there was little doubt that this was a *bona fide* case of genocide.

It also became clear from an early date that only outside intervention could stop the process of genocidal killing, but such help never materialized. Among those unwilling to intervene was the United Nations Security Council. It failed totally to prevent the genocide, and further failed to stop the killing once it had begun. The UN Security Council even went so far as to reduce by nine-tenths the small peacekeeping force already in Rwanda, UNAMIR (United Nations Assistance Mission for Rwanda) under the command of Canadian General Romeo Dallaire. Within days of the onset of the genocide, the UN also oversaw the evacuation of all whites from the country. Were it not for the intervention of a Tutsi rebel force invading from Uganda, the Rwandan Patriotic Front, the genocide might have been total.

Only the eventual return of a sizable population of Tutsi refugees from Uganda, Burundi, and those who had fled to the Congo and elsewhere enabled a reconstituted Rwandan Tutsi population to be established. Up to 90 percent of the pre-genocide Rwandan Tutsi population—by some accounts, numbering one million, by others, 800,000 to 900,000, and still others 500,000—were slaughtered.

The question of how to begin the process of creating a new Rwanda on the ruins of the old became centered on the issues of justice and reconciliation, and, while trials have been held within Rwanda itself in two primary judicial formats (the national courts and the system of localized justice known as *gacaca*), it was the creation of the International Criminal Tribunal for Rwanda (ICTR) that garnered the most interest around the world. The ICTR was established by the United Nations Security Council on November 9, 1994, and is located in Arusha, Tanzania. Like its judicial sibling, the International Criminal Tribunal for the Former Yugoslavia (ICTY), the ICTR is comprised of a tribunal of eminent judges from a wide range of countries, and is truly international in scope. It possesses an open and transparent appeals procedure, which has been successful on a number of occasions in hearing appeals and upholding or reducing sentences where appropriate; it has, moreover, handed down the maximum penalty permitted by the United Nations—life imprisonment—on numerous occasions. Those sentenced to any term of imprisonment are required to serve their sentences in African jails; the one exception to this involved the Belgian-born journalist Georges Ruggiu, who was permitted to serve out his sentence in Europe owing to the fact that he was of European, and not African, origin.

A criticism of the ICTR is that it is a tribunal which only seeks to hear cases against those considered politically important within the overall scope of the Rwandan genocide—the "big fish," as the conventional wisdom runs. While the leaders and most of the visible supporters of the Hutu Power regime are thus incarcerated in sanitary conditions, are well-fed, and have the full panoply of Western justice with which to mount their defense, their victims back in Rwanda have in many cases been left destitute, irreparably scarred and/or wounded, and, in the case of many, if not most, rape victims, facing a death sentence through having contracted HIV/AIDS at the time of their ordeal. Of those "lesser fish," who simply followed blindly the orders of those above them, post-genocide Rwandan justice has often taken a less formalized appearance, with faster trials, or, all too frequently, no trials at all. There are many cases where indicted prisoners in the national system have simply been released in order to alleviate the immense overcrowding in Rwanda's jails.

The ICTR's first trial began in January 1997, with the case of the former mayor of the town of Taba, Jean-Paul Akayesu. By 1998 this had resulted in the first successful prosecution, in an international court, specifically for the crime of genocide. Beyond this monumental ruling, the judgment on this occasion also extended genocide case-law by ruling that rape could henceforth be considered within a general legal framework of crimes against humanity and genocide. In fact, as the Press Release entitled "Historic Judgment Finds Akayesu Guilty of Genocide" issued by the ICTR shows, the judgment against Akayesu was notable in its uniqueness up to that point. It is important to realize, as the Press Release makes clear, that the ICTR did not find Akayesu guilty on all charges for which he was arraigned; this underscores the tribunal's perception of itself as a transparent and fair chamber that respects evidence and weighs all sides of a legal argument.

Another important precedent established by the ICTR came as a result of the trial of former Rwandan Prime Minister Jean Kambanda. In pleading guilty to the crime of genocide, Kambanda was not only the first person so accused to do so in any international setting; he was also the first head of government (though not head of state) to be convicted for this crime. This sent a clear warning to the leaders of rogue regimes throughout the world that a new legal culture had come into existence that—ostensibly—would not permit impunity where genocide, crimes against humanity, and war crimes were concerned.

For all this, it could be said that, generally speaking, progress in securing judicial verdicts has been slow. The tribunal has handed down judgments on fewer than forty of the accused since its inception, and by its Security Council mandate the ICTR is scheduled to have completed all of its major investigations by the end of 2008. It is, further, scheduled to be wound up *in toto* by the end of 2010.

Some of the points of critique surrounding the ICTR are identified and explored in "The International Criminal Tribunal for Rwanda" by Peter Uvin and Charles Mironko. They show, in a few well-chosen words, that the tribunal has both positive and negative points that have rendered it a mixed blessing in the post-genocide environment. Their article offers more than this, however; they also show how the ICTR has been viewed within Rwanda itself, and in doing so, they perform a valuable service by pointing out the variegated nature of post-genocide Rwandan opinion.

The article by Uvin and Mironko is to be contrasted with that of Howard Ball ("Formation of the ICTR"), who—while also pointing out the criticisms of the tribunal voiced from within Rwanda—explains more clearly the objections of the post-genocide Rwandan government to the formation of the ICTR, and shows the response by the United Nations to the Rwandan concerns. He also considers the degree to which the ICTR might well have been created as a "weak sister" to the ICTY, and addresses the question of why this should be so. Finally, Ball shows the manner in which the first trials began, once again reinforcing the notion that the ICTR was established as a tribunal for the "big fish."

On the other hand, in their article "International Criminal Tribunal for Rwanda," Michelle S. Lyon and Mark A. Drumbl provide a somewhat straightforward account of the origin, goals, structure, and functioning of the ICTR. Their article is replete with solid data regarding the essentials of the tribunal, employing a highly readable narrative style. Importantly, they also look into the question of what the trials represent for post-genocide Rwandan society, and they offer the suggestion that before it is wound up the ICTR might find itself relocated to Kigali, Rwanda; what this would signify for reconciliation is of course a matter for speculation, though Lyon and Drumbl conclude with the thought that such a move should serve to strengthen Rwanda's judicial system in the future.

This section concludes with an official statement—"Historic Judgement Finds Akayesu Guilty of Genocide"—issued by the International Criminal Tribunal for Rwanda regarding the first-ever judgment by an international court for the crime of genocide. The statement spells out the case against Jean-Paul Akayesu, the former Bourgmestre (mayor) of Taba, how the court came to its decision, and why and how the trial resulted in the first definition of rape in international law.

# 12.1    Peter Uvin and Charles Mironko, "The International Criminal Tribunal for Rwanda"

The ICTR—whose full name is the International Criminal Tribunal for the Prosecution of Persons Responsible for Genocide and Other Serious Violations of International Humanitarian Law Committed in the Territory of Rwanda and Rwandan Citizens Responsible for

Genocide and Other Such Violations Committed in the Territory of Neighboring States Between 1 January 1994 and 31 December 1994—is the product of the international community; it is fully managed and funded by it and exists to no small extent over the objections of the government of Rwanda.

The language of the 1994 UN Security Council Resolution 955 authorizing the ICTR refers to its aim "to contribute to the process of national reconciliation and to the restoration and maintenance of peace, . . . contribute to ensuring that such violations are halted and effectively redressed, . . . strengthen the courts and judicial system of Rwanda, having regard in particular to the necessity for those courts to deal with large numbers of suspects." However, the ICTR's prime function is widely perceived to be the reaffirmation of the international community's own morality. The ICTR is not a form of deterrence—it will take a lot more than nine persons convicted in eight years to deter future bloodshed in the region—nor does it impact on dynamics of reconciliation or lighten the burden on the Rwandan justice system. Rather, it is about symbolic politics: we, the international community, *do* care about Rwanda, *are* outraged by it, and solemnly pledge to show our disapproval. This move was necessary in the light of the total inaction of that same community during the genocide, which was widely perceived as shameful.

The record of the ICTR is mixed. Legally, some of its work was groundbreaking. The court's 1998 verdict of Jean-Paul Akayesu was the first-ever conviction by an international court for the crime of genocide. In 1999, the first confession of genocide was registered, by Jean Kambanda, Rwanda's interim prime minister. In addition, for the first time, an individual was convicted of rape as a crime against humanity. On the negative side, the ICTR is mainly famous for its bureaucratic inefficiency and political infighting (partly changed now) and the slowness of its work. Indeed, in more than seven years, the tribunal has produced remarkably little: by early 2002, with 800 employees and after having spent approximately U.S.$540 million, it had handed down eight convictions and one acquittal, with seven trials for seventeen accused in progress, two appeals pending, and fifty-five suspects in the tribunal's custody.[1] In addition, the ICTR is seen as having caved in to the government of Rwanda in the case of one defendant who was dismissed on a technicality. Under heavy pressure from the government of Rwanda, the same person was subsequently reindicted!

What is the impact of the ICTR inside Rwanda? For various reasons, the government of Rwanda maintains a negative attitude toward the ICTR. Many in the government argue that the ICTR is a hypocritical show with too much gentleness for the killers: the conditions of detention are too comfortable; the death penalty—which exists in Rwandan domestic law—is absent; and there are too many judicial niceties and lengthy procedures and too little progress in detaining the known suspects. These criticisms resonate emotionally among many Rwandans. There is a deep, widespread, and understandable feeling of a dramatic imbalance between the extreme evil of the genocide and the refined judicial treatment afforded the detained leaders of the genocide.[2]

Behind these arguments, however, there may be another, deeper set of political issues that explain the government's adversarial stance to the ICTR. Fundamentally, the government does not share the international community's desire to atone for its sins, nor does it like any process that it cannot control.[3] Indeed, the government, as one might expect from a militaristic movement that had to fight genocide in a context of international indifference, has no sympathy for the international community's desire to reaffirm its morality. Rather, it cares about the establishment of its own power, stability, and control. The ICTR runs against both these political realities, and consequently the government is at best neutral or indifferent, and at worst hostile to the ICTR. Its hostility is tempered only by a sense that outright refusal to collaborate might create a serious backlash from the international community and by the fact that the constant negotiations allow it to possibly reap more political advantages than a total cutoff of relations.[4]

What is the opinion of the population at large about the ICTR? There are, as always in deeply divided societies such as Rwanda, many different and often contradictory strands of perception and interpretation. Parts of the population—especially those who are Tutsi, urban, and close to the government—share the government's disdain and cynicism about the ICTR.[5] Smaller groups, especially in human rights circles, share the international community's vision of justice, although they too resent the few results produced so far. The largest part of the population, however,' has little or no opinion on the matter, largely because it has little or no knowledge of the ICTR. The main sentiment in Rwanda regarding the ICTR may well be massive ignorance: ordinary people know or understand next to nothing about the tribunal's work, proceedings, or results.[6]

The international press hardly covers the ICTR. For years, the ICTR had a very limited website that only recently improved. Two websites managed by international nongovernmental organizations (NGOs) publish excellent analyses and information on the ICTR's work.[7] But, as almost no Rwandans have access to the Internet, this basically serves only foreigners. One human rights NGO, LIPRODHOR, publishes a newsletter (*Le Verdict*, in French) with some information about the ICTR. Only a handful of Rwandan scholars study the proceedings of the tribunal. The ICTR created an outreach project in 1998 and an Information and Documentation Center in Rwanda only in 2000.[8] Recently, a U.S.-funded NGO, Internews, began an information campaign inside Rwanda, showing documentary films on the ICTR in the countryside and promoting debates afterwards.[9] These initiatives are commendable but marginal.

There exists still another strand of opinion about the ICTR among certain parts of the population. In this view, the ICTR is a blatantly biased and evil institution, for the opposite reason from the one described above. It is seen as de facto, if not by design, supporting the current government by neglecting its crimes, by a priori accepting the existence of the genocide, by allowing shoddy legal procedures, by submitting too much to the pressures of the Rwandan government, by refusing to indict President Kagame and other Rwandan Patriotic Front (RPF) members, and so forth. In short, in this opinion, the ICTR is a deliberate farce that maintains an oppressive regime and silences the violence of which the Hutu were victims.[10] This vociferously articulated position is held mainly by people living outside of Rwanda, but there is no reason to assume that it is not shared by at least part of the population.

This is clearly an extremist position, often associated with genocide denial. However, without wishing to minimize the prominence and extreme gravity of the genocide, the ICTR and domestic trials have combined to create an impression that the only violence worth looking at is that of the genocide. This has precluded further contextualization of the genocide or investigation of the human rights violations committed by the RPF before, during, and after the genocide. The one-dimensional focus on genocide over the past decade thus reinforces the notion, like in old Hollywood westerns, that all evil is associated with one type of people and all goodness, implicitly or explicitly, with another. Those now in power, have clearly benefited from this situation.

## Notes

1. Mary Kimani, "Expensive Justice: Cost of Running the Rwanda Tribunal," *Internews* (Kigali) 9 April 2002, available online at www.internews.org/activities/ICTR_reports/ICTR_reports.htm.
2. Aloysius Habimana, "What Does 'International Justice' Look Like in Post-Genocide Rwanda?" *Human Rights Forum* (spring 2000): 14, 21.
3. Helena Cobban, "The Legacies of Collective Violence: The Rwandan Genocide and the Limits of Law," *Boston Review* 27, no. 2 (April–May 2002): 6.
4. See the interview with Martin Ngoga, government of Rwanda representative to the ICTR, in Eugene Habiyambere, "Interview with Martin Ngoga," *Judicial Diplomacy* (August 2000): 1–4.

5.  André Sibomana, *Hope for Rwanda* (London: Pluto Press, 1997), p. 110. Also based on informal interviews done by, and personal communication of, Charles Mironko, May–June 1999, July–September 2001.

6.  Elizabeth Neuffer, *The Keys to My Neighbor's House: Seeking Justice in Bosnia and Rwanda* (New York: Picador, 2001), pp. 371–373.

7.  *Hirondelle* at www.hirondelle.org/ and *Diplomatie Judiciaire* at www. diplomatiejudiciaire.com.

8.  Kingsley C. Moghalu, "Image and Reality of War Crimes Justice: External Perceptions of the International Criminal Tribunal for Rwanda," *Fletcher Forum of International Affairs* (June 2002), footnote 3.

9.  See http://www.internews.org.

10. Thierry Cruvelier, "Explosive Leak or Wet Firecracker?" *Diplomatie Judiciaire* (9 May 2000), available online at http://www.diplomatiejudiciaire. com/UK/Tpiruk/TPIRUK14.htm.

## 12.2    Howard Ball, "Formation of the ICTR"

For reasons associated with realpolitik, the major world powers and the international community did nothing to prevent the genocide. Although the general of UN forces in Rwanda had presented an action scenario that he believed would constrain the Hutu from committing genocide, his suggestions were rejected by the Security Council. Only after the magnitude of the genocide was revealed to the international community did the UN take any action.

In the summer of 1994, the UN sent a special rapporteur for Rwanda, Rene Degni-Segui, and then appointed a commission of experts to visit Rwanda and report back to the Security Council. In the fall of 1994, after visiting the genocide-ravished country and seeing mounds of dead bodies gnawed at by dogs and other animals, both the rapporteur and the commission reported finding clear evidence of genocide and crimes against humanity. Their recommendations called for the creation of an international criminal tribunal to hear cases and pronounce sentence on those found guilty of conspiring and/or committing these crimes.

Based on these recommendations and the request of the new government in Kigali, the International Criminal Tribunal, Rwanda (ICTR) was proposed by the UN Security Council in November 1994 (one year after the ICTY was established). The ICTR became the world's first "genocide court,"[1] with jurisdiction over crimes of genocide, other crimes against humanity, and actions in violation of Article III of the 1949 Geneva Conventions.[2] (Although some Bosnian Serbs had been indicted because they ordered genocidal acts by their subordinates, most of the ICTY charges were war crimes allegations.) On December 18, 1994, the Security Council passed Resolution 955 establishing the ICTR. Its charge was to

> prosecute persons responsible for genocide and other serious violations of international humanitarian law committed in the territory of Rwanda and Rwandan citizens responsible for genocide and other such violations committed in the territory of neighbouring states between January 1st 1994 and December 31, 1994.

Another UN Security Council resolution, dated February 22, 1995, established the seat of the ICTR in Arusha, Tanzania. (A suboffice of the ICTR was established in Kigali, Rwanda.) The ICTR was not located in Rwanda to avoid the appearance of "victors' justice" by the new Tutsi-led Rwandan government.[3]

The initial trials of indicted defendants took place almost two years later, when Jean Paul Akayesu, a Hutu *bourgmestre*, was escorted into Trial Chamber One on January 9, 1997, to answer charges that he had committed genocide and other crimes against humanity.

## Rwandan Opposition to Resolution 955

Ironically, the Rwandan delegation to the UN, sitting on the Security Council when the resolution proposing the ICTR was adopted on November 8, 1994, cast the sole vote against its creation. Even though they had requested the UN to respond to the genocide with the creation of an ad hoc criminal tribunal, Rwandan officials were sufficiently aroused by the perceived weaknesses of the tribunal to cast the sole negative vote.

There were several reasons for their vote. First, Rwanda objected to the time frame for ICTR prosecutions, January 1–December 31, 1994. Their argument was that the Hutu Power organizational planning for the genocide had begun in 1990 and that the UN resolution would not enable the ICTR to address those involved prior to 1994. Second, the statute gave the ICTR jurisdiction over "natural persons"; therefore, cases against groups, whether public or private, could not be instituted.

They also objected to the poor staffing of the ICTR. The ICTR statute "provided for so little personnel, both judicial and prosecutorial, that the ICTR could not possibly be expected to fulfill the monumental task set before it. Not only was the total number of judges very small (six trial judges and five appellate judges), but the appellate judges were to be shared with the ICTY. Moreover, the ICTR and ICTY were to share one prosecutor."[4]

Finally, Rwanda objected to the absence of the death penalty as a punishment for genocide. This, they argued, could lead to the Hutu leaders tried in the ICTR receiving prison terms while their subordinates in the provinces and communes, the men who had carried out the genocide, faced the death penalty if found guilty in Rwandan national courts.[5]

In a formal position paper to the UN entitled *The Position of the Government of the Republic of Rwanda on the International Criminal Tribunal for Rwanda (ICTR)*, the government enumerated its concerns about the international tribunal. It had "grave misgivings" about the structure and the functioning of the ICTR. In particular, the report focused on the following:

- The poor organization of the ICTR; for example, "the current prosecutor has centralized all decision making in the Hague. . . . Yugoslavia is the prime focus of the prosecutor's attention."
- The personnel problems of the ICTR, involving reporting lines and the competence of ICTR staff.
- The prosecution and investigation strategy; for example, "the office of the prosecutor has been the weakest link in the chain of organs that constitute the tribunal. . . . [The prosecutors] have never determined policy as to whom the tribunal should pursue. They have never indicated the kind of cases they wish to prosecute before the tribunal and those they expect to be tried by national courts. . . . They proceed on an *ad hoc* basis." Although some major defendants were still at large when the report was issued, the Rwandan government noted that "the Prosecutor has indicated both to her staff and to officials in the Ministry of Justice of the Republic of Rwanda that she does not in the foreseeable future plan to issue any new indictments and plans from now onwards to concentrate only on the prosecution of suspects who have so far been indicted."
- The ICTR conduct of investigations, which left "a lot to be desired." There had been no investigations of the regions "where some of the worst atrocities took place." When they did visit the areas, the investigators were "discourteous"; they traveled in brightly marked UN vehicles, "clearly aggravating risks to the security of the potential witnesses."
- The prosecutor's interpretation of the ICTR mandate, which was "regrettab[ly] misconc[eived]. "She is on record . . . as saying that her objective is to render 'deluxe justice.' . . . Her actions are at variance with the spirit of Resolution 995 which seeks to

promote national reconciliation and maintenance of peace in Rwanda by bringing to justice the perpetrators of genocide and other serious violations of international humanitarian law."

- The attitude of the Prosecutor's Office toward the Rwandan government and people, which was disgraceful. There was no sensitivity toward the survivors of the genocide; "on the contrary, personnel of the tribunal, specifically the prosecutor's office, have behaved with hostility, arrogance, and insensitivity that is difficult to explain."

The concluding segment contained the Rwandan recommendations for changing the ICTR. Kigali called for

an independent Prosecutor for the Rwandan tribunal;
moving the ICTR to Kigali, Rwanda;
strengthening the powers of the prosecutorial staff of the ICTR;
recruiting more qualified personnel for the ICTR; and, improving cooperative actions with the Rwandan government and legal authorities.[6]

These Rwandan recommendations have not been acted on by the Security Council, and the ICTR has functioned in accord with Resolution 955 since 1995.

As finally adopted, Resolution 955's annex spelled out the scope of the ICTR. Persons "responsible for serious violations of international humanitarian law [genocide and crimes against humanity, along with violations of Article III of the 1949 Geneva Convention] committed in the territory of Rwanda . . . between January 1 and December 31, 1994," were the sole targets of the ICTR prosecutors. The ICTR's jurisdiction extended to "natural persons" only, underscoring the principle of individual criminal responsibility that had emerged from the Nuremberg and Tokyo trials.

The organization of the ICTR mirrored that of the ICTY: the Chambers, the Prosecutor's Office, and the Registry. There was only one prosecutor for both ad hoc criminal courts, although deputy prosecutors were assigned to the two tribunals. In Arusha and Kigali, again mirroring the ICTY process, the prosecutor investigated charges and drew up indictments that were presented to the Chambers for approval by a judge. "If satisfied that a prima facie case has been established by the prosecutor, he or she shall confirm the indictment. If not so satisfied, the indictment shall be dismissed." After the indictment was confirmed, the ICTR issued "orders and warrants for the arrest, detention, surrender and transfer of persons . . . as may be required for the conduct of the trial."

The ICTR was responsible for conducting expeditious but fair and public trials of the defendants; Article XX, Rights of the Accused, laid out the protections that had to be accorded each defendant. Article XXI required the ICTR to protect victims and witnesses from harassment, including "the conduct of in camera proceedings and the protection of the victim's families." Judgment was by majority of the three-judge panel, and if found guilty, defendants faced penalties that "shall be limited to imprisonment." Final appeals were directed to the ICTR's Appeals Chamber, consisting of five ICTR judges.[7] UN member states were encouraged to cooperate with the ICTR regarding extradition of those indicted and with regard to human and other vitally needed resources.

## The ICTR: A Weak Sister to the ICTY?

One writer noted that the ICTR "always seemed a shadow of its sister in the Hague, beset from its inception by a host of problems. [These difficulties involved] a lack of personnel, facilities for the trials, money mismanagement, and cronyism."[8]

Another huge problem was the location of the ICTR itself. The feeling in the UN Security

Council was that the trials should take place in Africa, and after some discussion, the council selected Arusha, Tanzania (a city of 140,000 people), for largely symbolic and political reasons: it was the host city to the RPF–Rwanda government peace conferences and other African states' meetings. But the city is hard to get to. As the registrar for the ICTR, Agwu Ukiwe Okali, understated, Arusha is not a "global media station." Furthermore, "phone service, especially overseas, is spotty at best."[9]

Sara Darehshori, an ICTR prosecutor on loan from her law firm in New York City, was co-counsel in the trial of Jean-Paul Akayesu. Upon her arrival in Kigali, she found that the office she shared with about a dozen Dutch policemen

> lacked the most basic amenities. We created makeshift desks by removing doors from their hinges and placing them on crates. We fought over garbage cans, which we used as chairs. The one telephone line was erratic. [Although after three months we received] real desks and chairs, . . . we still didn't have pens, paper, or a dependable copy machine.[10]

Another deputy prosecutor from the United States, Brenda Sue Thornton, complained to the tribunal that trial transcripts of testimony given in October and November 1997 had not yet been received by either set of lawyers in the Clement Rayishema case as of mid-February 1998. She was informed by the Registry that the delay occurred because transcribing companies in Canada, the United States, and France were being used by the ICTR because of a "lack of staff."[11]

The existing infrastructure in Arusha was "not equipped to handle the technical needs of a staff that has now grown to 400 here and in Kigali." As a consequence of the city's remoteness and lack of amenities, the circumstances of the ICTR staff are "very difficult," said Alessandro Caldarone, the ICTR administrator responsible for the detention cells.[12] In May 1998, Registrar Okali told the UN that the ICTR needed "investigators, administrators, bilingual lawyers, interpreters, and court stenographers. . . . [Also needed were computers and computer experts, because] you can't just run down the street [in Arusha or Kigali] and buy computer parts." The ICTR had great difficulty finding these human resources. As Okali stated, "Arusha is four hours by road from Nairobi, Kenya, the nearest large international center. . . . In Arusha there is not even a cafeteria," he lamented.[13]

In spite of these difficulties—financial, human, and geographic—by the summer of 1998 the ICTR had indicted thirty-six individuals, with thirty-one of them in custody in Arusha detention cells. Most of those indicted were seized at the displaced persons camps in Zaire. Also, a number of nations, including Belgium, Cameroon, Zambia, and Kenya, turned people over to the ICTR.

In the United States, which passed domestic legislation in February 1996 to cooperate with the ICTR on the extradition of indicted persons, the government arrested a man on September 26, 1996, at the tribunal's request. He was a seventy-three-year-old Hutu religious leader, the former president of the Seventh Day Adventist Church in Rwanda, Elizaphan Ntakirutimana. He hired Ramsey Clark, former U.S. attorney general, as defense counsel. (Clark was also serving as Karadzic's defense attorney in civil proceedings in U.S. federal court.) He unsuccessfully appealed his extradition from the United States to the ICTR. On August 5, 1998, United States District Court Judge John Rainey ordered the pastor "to be turned over to an international war crimes tribunal on the charge of genocide."[14] However, as of the end of 1998, Ntakirutimana was still in a Texas prison fighting extradition in the federal courts.

By mid-1998, the ICTR was conducting four trials, with others scheduled following this initial quartet of defendants. Unlike the ICTY, the defendants in Rwanda "include some of the highest-ranking officials [Jean Kambanda, the prime minister; Pauline Nyiramasuhuko, minister of family and social welfare;[15] and Colonel Theoneste Bagosora, head of the FAR during the genocide of the Hutu-dominated government whose officers and allied militia reportedly carried out the massacres, mainly of ethnic Tutsi, over three months in 1994."[16]

Because of poor funding and a perennial lack of staff, it took the ICTR over two years before the first indictments received from the prosecutor were approved by the judges. On December 15, 1995, the ICTR issued its first warrants for the arrest of eight men accused of genocide and crimes against humanity.[17] Legal proceedings opened against the first three men in May 1996, when their pleas were entered. The three were Georges Rutaganda, a radio station owner and a top official in the *interahamwe*; Jean-Paul Akayesu, a former *bourgmestre* of the Taba commune; and Clement Kayishema, a former prefect. The ICTR charged them with commission of genocide, crimes against humanity, and murder. All three pled not guilty. Immediately after the charges were read and the pleas entered, the court adjourned until December 1996, when the first trial began.

Rutaganda was one of the owners of Radio Television Libre de Mille Collins, which continually broadcast scurrilous attacks on the Tutsi and orders to kill them. He was also the second vice president of the National Committee of the *interahamwe*. The ICTR charged him with eight counts of genocide, crimes against humanity, and violations of Article III, carried out in the provinces of Kigali and Gitarama. He was arrested in Zambia in October 1995 and extradited to Arusha to stand trial. His trial began March 18, 1997, and as of the end of 1998, there had still been no judgment from the tribunal.

Kayishema was the prefect of Kibuye province and was charged with genocide. It was alleged that he and other Hutu leaders rounded up Tutsi and placed them in the local Catholic churches, which the Hutu claimed were "safe havens," and other public arenas. Then they executed the huddled, terrified Tutsi with machetes. Finally, the churches were burned to the ground with the Tutsi inside. He was arrested in Kenya in September 1996 and brought to Arusha. His trial began on April 11, 1997, and as of the end of 1998 was still ongoing. There were fifty-two witnesses for the prosecution and over 400 documents and depositions; all placed him at the center of the genocide, ordering the killings and taking part in them. One witness, NN, told the tribunal how Kayishema had murdered a baby: " 'He took the baby, and then grabbed hold of one leg, giving the other to another soldier. Then he took a sword and cut the child in two vertically. Then he threw it to the ground.' "[18]

Akayesu, who had been extradited from Zambia on May 26, 1996, was also charged with genocide and crimes against humanity. The indictment alleged that he had encouraged the murder of Tutsi, directly ordered the killing of several persons near his office, and personally supervised the interrogation, beating, and execution of local residents of his commune.

## Notes

1. Kingsley Chiedu Moghalu, "A Shared Duty to Justice," *Legal Times*, August 17, 1998, p. 29.
2. Article III deals with the treatment of prisoners of war, prohibiting "willful killing, torture, or inhuman treatment, including biological experiments, willfully causing great suffering or serious injury to body or health, . . . or willfully depriving a prisoner of war of the rights of fair and regular trial."
3. Vantage Conference, 1997, "Post-Conflict Justice: The Role of the International Community," Stanley Foundation, Queenstown, Md., 1997, p. 19.
4. Morris, "Case of Rwanda," pp. 1–5.
5. See, generally, "Open Letter Regarding the Need to Expand the Jurisdiction of the International Tribunal for Rwanda," Attorneys without Borders, May 18, 1995, pp. 1–2.
6. *Position of the Government of the Republic of Rwanda on the ICTR*, April 21, 1998, pp. 1–9.
7. See UN Security Council Resolution 955 (1994), S/RES/955, adopted on November 8, 1994.
8. Steven Lee Myers, "In East Africa, Panel Tackles War Crimes, and Its Own Misdemeanors," *New York Times*, September 14, 1997, p. A6.
9. UN press release, March 25, 1998, p. 1.

10. Sara Darehshori, "Inching toward Justice in Rwanda," *New York Times*, September 8, 1998.
11. *Ubutabera*, no. 30 (February 16, 1998), pp. 7–8.
12. Myers, "In East Africa," p. A6.
13. Barbara Crossette, "UN Told a Tribunal Needs Help," *New York Times*, May 23, 1998, p. A8.
14. Moghalu, "Shared Duty," p. 29. The pastor was charged with ordering the death of hundreds of frightened Tutsi who had sought safe haven in his church. He had offered them refuge, and after the Tutsi were inside, he brought a truckload of *interahamwe* to the church and ordered them to begin the killings. AP, "Rwandan Pastor Arrested, Charged with Genocide," September 28, 1996.
15. She is the first woman to be indicted by a war crimes tribunal.
16. Myers, "In East Africa," p. A6.
17. UN press release/L2841, December 15, 1995, p. 1.
18. Quoted in *Ubutabera*, no. 32 (March 16, 1998), p. 12.

## 12.3 Michelle S. Lyon and Mark A. Drumbl, "International Criminal Tribunal for Rwanda"

The United Nations (UN) Security Council created the International Criminal Tribunal for Rwanda (ICTR) in November 1994 to investigate and, when an apparent case exists, prosecute a select number of political, military, and civic officials for their involvement in the Rwandan genocide that took place from April to July 1994. An estimated 500,000 Rwandans, overwhelmingly Tutsi, were killed during this period.

The ICTR plays an important, albeit not exclusive, role in promoting accountability for perpetrators of genocide. The Rwandan government, for its part, has incapacitated more than 80,000 suspects and provisionally released another 30,000. It intends to prosecute these individuals through national trials or traditional dispute resolution (*gacaca*). Approximately 6,500 people have thus far been convicted of genocide-related offenses in Rwandan national courts. A handful of perpetrators have been prosecuted in foreign countries, such as Belgium and Switzerland.

The ICTR is a temporary, or ad hoc, institution that will close down once it completes its work. The initial thinking was that the ICTR would complete its investigative and trial work by 2008, to be followed by the resolution of outstanding appeals. It is unclear whether 2008 remains a realistic end-point.

ICTR judgments clarify important aspects of international law regarding genocide and crimes against humanity. In this regard, they establish a strong foundation for the permanent International Criminal Court (ICC), which came into effect in 2002. ICTR experiences have informed and inspired other ad hoc tribunals to involve the international community in the prosecution of systemic human rights abuses, such as the Special Court for Sierra Leone, the hybrid international/national tribunals in East Timor and extraordinary chambers contemplated for Cambodia. Moreover, the ICTR has helped authenticate a historical record of the violence in Rwanda, has decreed that the violence constituted genocide, has educated the international community, and has offered some vindication for victims. That said, the ICTR also has been subject to criticism for its distance—both physically and psychologically—from Rwanda, the length of its proceedings, the small number of accused in its docket, the mistreatment of witnesses in sexual assault cases, and allegations of financial irregularities involving defense counsel and investigators.

### Creation of the ICTR

The Security Council, acting under Chapter VII of the UN Charter, created the ICTR by virtue of Resolution 955, adopted on November 8, 1994. Ironically, the only member of the

Security Council not to support Resolution 955 was Rwanda, although Rwanda had previously requested that the international community establish a tribunal. Rwanda objected to the limited temporal jurisdiction of the ICTR and the fact the ICTR could not issue the death penalty. On February 22, 1995, the Security Council resolved that the ICTR would be based in Arusha, a city in northern Tanzania. This, too, was of concern to the Rwandan government, as it wished the tribunal to be sited in Rwanda itself.

In Resolution 955 the Security Council recognized reports that "genocide and other systematic, widespread, and flagrant violations of international humanitarian law have been committed in Rwanda." The Security Council determined that this situation rose to the level of a threat to international peace and security. It also affirmed its intention to put an end to these violations and "to take effective measures to bring to justice the persons who are responsible for them."

The ICTR is governed by its statute, which is annexed to Resolution 955. Details regarding the process of ICTR trials and appeals are set out in the ICTR Rules of Procedure and Evidence. These rules were adopted separately by the ICTR judges and have been amended several times since their inception.

## Goals

In creating the ICTR, the Security Council affirmed its conviction that the prosecution of persons responsible for serious violations of international humanitarian law in Rwanda would promote a number of goals. The Security Council identified these as: (1) bringing to justice those responsible for genocide in Rwanda; (2) contributing to the process of national reconciliation; (3) restoring and maintaining peace in Rwanda and the Great Lakes region of Africa generally; and (4) halting future violations and effectively redressing those violations that have been committed. On a broader level, the Security Council also intended to signal that the international community would not tolerate crimes of genocide—architects of such violence would incur responsibility instead of benefiting from impunity.

In order for the ICTR to fulfill its mandate, the Security Council exhorted that it should receive the assistance of all states. Article 28 of the statute requires states to cooperate with the ICTR in its investigations and prosecutions if a request for assistance or order is issued. Many suspects indicted by the ICTR have been arrested in a variety of African and European countries and been transferred to the ICTR, demonstrating the respect and support foreign national governments exhibit toward the ICTR.

## Jurisdiction

Article 1 of the statute provides that the ICTR has the power to prosecute persons responsible for serious violations of international humanitarian law committed in the territory of Rwanda between January 1, 1994, and December 31, 1994, as well as Rwandan citizens responsible for violations committed in the territory of neighboring states. The jurisdiction of the ICTR is thus circumscribed by territory, citizenship, and time.

The ICTR prosecutes three categories of crimes: genocide (Article 2), crimes against humanity (Article 3), and war crimes (Article 4). The ICTR has issued convictions for each of these crimes.

Article 2 defines genocide in standard fashion: as one of a number of acts committed with the intent to destroy, in whole or in part, a national, ethnical, racial, or religious group. According to Article 2(2), the enumerated acts are: (a) killing members of the group; (b) causing serious bodily or mental harm to members of the group; (c) deliberately inflicting on the group conditions of life calculated to bring about its physical destruction in whole or in part; (d) imposing measures intended to prevent births within the group; and (e) forcibly transferring children of the group to another group. The ICTR has jurisdiction to prosecute genocide, conspiracy to commit genocide, direct and public incitement to commit genocide, attempt to commit genocide, and complicity in genocide (Article 2[3]).

Article 3 defines crimes against humanity as certain crimes when committed as part of a widespread or systematic attack against any civilian population on national, political, ethnic, racial, or religious grounds. Specified crimes include murder; extermination; enslavement; deportation; imprisonment; torture; rape; and political, racial, or religious persecution.

The ICTR has jurisdiction only over individuals (Article 5). Persons incur criminal responsibility if they planned, instigated, ordered, committed, or otherwise aided and abetted in the planning, preparation, or execution of a crime (Article 6[1]). The statute eliminates official immunity, stipulating that the position of any accused person (even a head of state) does not relieve that person of criminal prosecution or mitigate punishment (Article 6[2]). One of the first convictions issued by the ICTR involved Jean Kambanda, the prime minister of Rwanda at the time of the genocide. The fact that the crime was committed "by a subordinate does not relieve his or her superior of criminal responsibility if he or she knew or had reason to know that the subordinate was about to commit such acts or had done so and the superior failed to take the necessary and reasonable measures to prevent such acts or to punish the perpetrators thereof" (Article 6[3]). If a crime was carried out by a subordinate in the chain of command because that subordinate was so ordered, the subordinate is not relieved of individual criminal responsibility, although that fact can be considered in mitigation of punishment.

The ICTR shares concurrent jurisdiction with national courts (Article 8[1]). However, the ICTR can exert primacy over the national courts of all states, including those of Rwanda (Article 8[2]), at any stage of the procedure. The primacy of the ICTR also is buttressed by the overall effect of Article 9 of the statute. This provides, on the one hand, that no person shall be tried before a national court for acts for which he or she has already been tried by the ICTR, but, on the other hand, a person who has been tried before a national court for acts constituting serious violations of international humanitarian law may be subsequently tried by the ICTR if one of two conditions applies. These are: (a) the act for which he was tried was characterized as an ordinary crime; or (b) the national court proceedings were not impartial or independent, were designed to shield the accused from international criminal responsibility, or were not diligently prosecuted.

## Structure

The ICTR is composed of three units: Judicial Chambers, the Prosecutor's Office, and the Registry. The ICTR has three Trial Chambers and one Appeals Chamber (Article 10). The Trial Chambers handle the actual trials of the accused and pretrial procedural matters. The Appeals Chamber hears appeals from decisions of the Trial Chambers. Appeals may involve judgments (guilt or innocence) or sentence (the punishment imposed on a convicted person). The Office of the Prosecutor is in charge of investigations and prosecutions. The Registry is responsible for providing overall judicial and administrative support to the chambers and the prosecutor.

The structure of the ICTR is intertwined with that of the International Criminal Tribunal for the Former Yugoslavia (ICTY), which was created in 1993 and to some extent served as a precedent for the ICTR. Although both tribunals operate separate Trial Chambers (the ICTY in The Hague [Netherlands], the ICTR in Arusha), they share common judges in their Appeals Chambers (located in The Hague, although these judges sometimes sit in Arusha as well). Until September 2003 the two tribunals also shared a single chief prosecutor, Carla Del Ponte of Switzerland. That changed when the UN Security Council appointed Hassan Jallow from Gambia as ICTR Chief Prosecutor, with Del Ponte remaining as ICTY Chief Prosecutor.

The three Trial Chambers and the Appeals Chamber are composed of judges elected by the UN General Assembly. The Security Council proposes candidates for election based on a list of nominees submitted by member states. Nominations must ensure adequate representation of the principal legal systems of the world. ICTR judges are elected for a term of four years, and are eligible for reelection. Judges "shall be persons of high moral character, impartiality and integrity who possess the qualifications required in their respective countries for appointment to the highest judicial offices" (Article 12). They are to be experienced in criminal law and international law, including international humanitarian law and human rights law.

The full ICTR consists of sixteen permanent judges, no two of whom may be nationals of the same state. This total breaks down as follows: three judges in each of the three Trial Chambers and seven judges in the Appeals Chamber. Five judges of the Appeals Chamber hear each appeal. There also is an option of adding a number of *ad litem* (temporary) judges owing to the workload of the ICTR at any point in time. The permanent judges elect a president from among themselves.

The Office of the Prosecutor acts independently to investigate crimes, prepare charges, and prosecute accused persons. The prosecutor does not receive instructions from any government or from any other source. However, the prosecutor may initiate investigations based on information obtained from governments, UN entities, and both intergovernmental and nongovernmental organizations.

The Registry is responsible for the ICTR's overall administration and management. It is headed by the registrar, who provides judicial and legal support services for the work of the judicial chambers and the prosecution and also serves as the ICTR's channel of communication. The ICTR's working languages are English and French (Article 31).

## Trial and Appeal Processes

The trial process begins when the prosecutor investigates allegations against an individual. In this investigative process, the prosecutor has the power to question suspects, victims, and witnesses. The prosecutor may also collect evidence and conduct onsite investigations. If the Prosecutor determines that a prima facie (in other words, apparent) case exists, he or she is to prepare an indictment. It is at this point that a suspect becomes an accused. The indictment contains a concise statement of the facts and the crime(s) alleged against the accused. The indictment then is sent to a judge of the Trial Chamber for review. If this judge is satisfied that a prima facie case has in fact been established by the prosecutor, he shall confirm the indictment (Article 18). If the judge is not satisfied, he is to dismiss the indictment. Once the indictment is confirmed, the judge may, at the request of the prosecutor, "issue such orders and warrants for the arrest, detention, surrender or transfer of persons, and any other orders as may be required for the conduct of the trial" (Article 18[2]).

A person under confirmed indictment can be taken into the custody of the ICTR. That person is then immediately to be informed of the charges. The accused then enters a plea— guilty or not guilty—and, in the event of a not guilty plea, the trial begins thereafter. Details of the trial proceedings are regulated by Rules of Procedure and Evidence.

Hearings are in public unless exceptional circumstances arise, for instance, when witnesses need to be protected. Testifying in a closed session can provide such protection. Of more than eight hundred witnesses who have testified in ICTR proceedings as of 2004, the majority have required protective measures that permit them to testify anonymously and thereby be safe-guarded from reprisals. The ICTR also has established a sophisticated witness protection program.

Accused persons are entitled to procedural rights. Some of these—such as the right to counsel—arise as soon as an individual is a suspect. At trial, an accused is presumed innocent until proven guilty. An accused person also is entitled to the rights set out in Article 20(4) of the statute. These include protection against self-incrimination, as well as rights to be tried without undue delay, to be informed of the charges, to examine witnesses, and to an interpreter. Moreover, accused are free to retain counsel of their own choice. If an accused person is unable to afford counsel, the ICTR is to assign counsel to that person. In such a situation, which frequently has arisen at the ICTR, the accused person can choose from a list of qualified counsel. These legal services are without charge to the accused. The ICTR Appeals Chamber, however, has ruled that the right of an indigent person to be represented by a lawyer free of charge does not imply the right to select counsel (*Prosecutor v. Akayesu*, Appeal Judgment, 2001, para. 61).

After the trial has concluded, the Trial Chamber pronounces judgment. The judges are triers of fact and law; there are no juries. At the same time, the judges impose sentences and penalties. This differs from the procedure in a number of national legal systems, such as the United States, where the sentencing stage begins as a separate process following the issuance of a guilty verdict. However, this tracks the process that obtains in many civil law countries. Judgment is by a majority of judges and delivered in public. The majority provides a reasoned written opinion. Dissenting judges may provide their own opinion.

The accused has a right to appeal the judgment and the sentence. The prosecutor also can appeal (this also runs counter to the national practice in some states, e.g., the United States, but reflects national practices in many civil law countries and some common law countries such as Canada). However, the Appeals Chamber is empowered only to hear appeals that stem from an error on a question of law that invalidates the decision, or an error of fact that has occasioned a miscarriage of justice. The Appeals Chamber may affirm, reverse, or revise Trial Chambers decisions.

Article 25 of the statute permits an exceptional measure called a *review proceeding*. This is permitted in instances in which "a new fact has been discovered which was not known at the time of the proceedings before the Trial Chambers or the Appeals Chamber and which could have been a decisive factor in reaching the decision" (Article 25). In such a situation, a convicted person or the prosecutor may submit an application for the judgment to be reviewed.

Article 25 has been successfully invoked by the prosecutor in the case of Jean-Bosco Barayagwiza, the former director of political affairs in the Rwandan Ministry of Foreign Affairs eventually convicted of genocide. Barayagwiza helped set up a radio station whose purpose was to incite anti-Tutsi violence. On November 3, 1999, the Appeals Chamber had quashed the indictment against Barayagwiza and ordered him released owing to the lengthy delays that had occurred during the process of his being brought to justice, which were found to have violated his human rights. One and a half years had elapsed from the time of Barayagwiza's arrest to the time of his actually being charged, and additional delays had subsequently occurred at the pretrial stage. The former prosecutor, Carla Del Ponte, then filed an Article 25 application with the Appeals Chamber for the review of the prior decision to free Barayagwiza. On March 31, 2000, the Appeals Chamber unanimously overturned its previous decision to quash Barayagwiza's indictment (*Prosecutor v. Barayagwiza*, Appeals Chamber, 2000). It found that, although Barayagwiza's rights had been infringed, "new facts" presented to the ICTR for the first time during the request for review diminished the gravity of any rights infringement. For example, it was found that the actual period of pretrial delay was much shorter than previously believed; it was also found that some of the delays faced by Barayagwiza were not the responsibility of the prosecutor. Because of this diminished gravity, the ICTR characterized its previous decision to release Barayagwiza as "disproportionate." Basing itself in "the wholly exceptional circumstances of the case," and the "possible miscarriage of justice" that would arise by releasing Barayagwiza, the ICTR set aside its prior release (*Prosecutor v. Barayagwiza*, Appeals Chamber, 2000, para. 65).

## Sentencing

Article 23 limits the punishment that the ICTR can impose to imprisonment. The Trial Chambers do have considerable discretion as to the length of the period of imprisonment. The ICTR has issued a number of life sentences and sentences in the ten to thirty-five-year range. The practice of the ICTR reveals that genocide is sentenced more severely than crimes against humanity or war crimes, even though there is no formalized hierarchy among the various crimes the statute ascribes to the jurisdiction of the ICTR. This comports with the notion, evoked judicially by the ICTR, that genocide is the "crime of crimes" (*Prosecutor v. Serushago*, Sentence, 1999, para. 15; Schabas, 2000, p. 9). Other factors that affect sentencing include the accused's seniority in the command structure, remorse and cooperation, age of the accused and of the victims, and the sheer inhumanity of the crime. In addition to imprisonment, the ICTR "may order the return of any property and proceeds acquired by criminal conduct, including by means of duress, to their rightful owners" (Article 23[3]). In practice, this option has not been utilized.

Convicted persons serve their sentences either in Rwanda or in countries that have made agreements with the ICTR to enforce such sentences. Mali, Benin, and Swaziland have signed such agreements.

## Budget and Staff

From 2002 to 2003 the UN General Assembly appropriated $177,739,400 (U.S.) for the ICTR. Approximately 800 individuals representing 80 nationalities work for the ICTR.

## History of Prosecutions

The ICTR issued its first indictment in late 1995. By early 2004 it had issued approximately seventy indictments, and more than fifty-five indicted individuals were in the custody of the ICTR, either on trial, awaiting trial, or pending appeal.

As of early 2004, the ICTR had convicted twelve individuals, including a number of very senior members of the Rwandan government, civil society, and clergy. Convicted individuals include Jean Kambanda, the Prime Minister of Rwanda during the genocide; Jean-Paul Akayesu and Juvenal Kajelijeli, both local mayors; Georges Rutaganda, a militia leader; Elizaphan Ntakirutimana, a Seventh-Day Adventist pastor, and Georges Ruggiu, a Belgian-born radio journalist whose broadcasts encouraged the setting up of roadblocks and congratulated those who massacred Tutsi at these roadblocks.

Kambanda is the first head of state to have been convicted of genocide, establishing that international criminal law could apply to the highest authorities. On October 19, 2000, the Appeals Chamber unanimously dismissed Jean Kambanda's appeal against conviction and sentence (*Prosecutor v. Kambanda*, Appeals Chamber, 2000). Kambanda had previously pleaded guilty to six counts of genocide and crimes against humanity (although he subsequently sought to challenge his own guilty plea and demanded a trial), and had been sentenced to life imprisonment by the Trial Chamber on September 4, 1998. As to conviction, Kambanda had argued that his initial guilty plea should be quashed as he allegedly had not been represented by a lawyer of his own choosing, he had been detained in oppressive conditions, and the Trial Chamber had failed to determine that the guilty plea was voluntary, informed, and unequivocal. The Appeals Chamber rejected all of these arguments. In so doing, it drew heavily from its prior decisions in matters involving appeals from the ICTY Trial Chamber, thereby promoting principles of consistency and precedent. As to sentence, the Appeals Chamber dismissed Kambanda's allegations of excessiveness. Although Kambanda's cooperation with the prosecutor was found to be a mitigating factor to be taken into consideration, the "intrinsic gravity" of the crimes and the position of authority

Kambanda occupied in Rwanda outweighed any considerations of leniency and justified the imposition of a life sentence (*Prosecutor v. Kambanda*, Appeals Chamber, 2000, paras. 119, 126).

Not all prosecuted individuals are convicted. The ICTR issued its first acquittal in the matter of Ignace Bagilishema, the *bourgmestre* (mayor) of the Mabanza commune, who was accused of seven counts of genocide, crimes against humanity, and war crimes related to the murder of thousands of Tutsi in the Kibuye prefecture (*Prosecutor v. Bagilishema*, Appeals Chamber, 2002). The Trial Chamber held that the prosecutor failed to prove beyond a reasonable doubt that Bagilishema had committed the alleged atrocities. It concluded that the testimony of prosecution witnesses was riddled with inconsistencies and contradictions and thereby failed to establish Bagilishema's individual criminal responsibility (*Prosecutor v. Bagilishema*, Trial Chamber, 2001). The *Bagilishema* case demonstrates the ICTR's attentiveness to matters of due process and procedural rights, although the acquittal triggered controversy in Rwanda.

Many ministers of the genocidal regime are in ICTR custody, along with senior military commanders, bureaucrats, corporate leaders, clergy, journalists, popular culture icons, and intellectuals. Many of these individuals are being tried jointly. Joined proceedings involve two or more defendants, among whom there is a nexus justifying their being tried together.

For example, on December 3, 2003 the ICTR Trial Chamber issued convictions in the "media case." The media case explores the role, responsibility, and liability of the media in inciting genocide. This case represents the first time since Julius Streicher, the Nazi publisher of the anti-Semitic weekly *Der Stürmer*, appeared before the Nuremberg Tribunal that a group of leading journalists have been similarly charged. Convicted by the ICTR of inciting genocide through the media are Hassan Ngeze (editor of the extremist *Kangura* newspaper), Ferdinand Nahimana (former director of Radio-Télévision Libre des Mille Collines (RTLM), the national broadcaster), and Jean-Bosco Barayagwiza (politician and board member of the RTLM). Ngeze and Nahimana were sentenced to life imprisonment and Barayagwiza to a term of thirty-five years. In its judgment, the ICTR Trial Chamber underscored that "[t]he power of the media to create and destroy fundamental human values comes with great responsibility. Those who control such media are accountable for its consequences." The media case unpacks the interface between international criminal law and freedom of expression. The defense vigorously argued that the impugned communications constituted speech protected by the international right to freedom of expression. The ICTR disagreed. It distinguished "discussion of ethnic consciousness" from "the promotion of ethnic hatred." While the former is protected speech, the latter is not. On the facts, it was found that the exhortations to incite genocide constituted the promotion of ethnic hatred and, hence, unprotected speech.

The prosecutor is charging political leaders jointly in three separate groups. The "Butare group," which consists of six accused, includes Pauline Nyirama-suhuko, the former Minister for Family and Women's Affairs and the first woman to be indicted by an international criminal tribunal (among the charges she faces is inciting rape). Butare is a city in southern Rwanda and the seat of the national university. The second group, known as the Government I group, involves four ministers from the genocidal government, including Edouard Karemera, former Minister of the Interior, and André Rwamakuba, former Minister of Education. The third group, Government II, includes four other ministers from the genocidal government. All defendants in the Government I and II groups face charges of genocide and crimes against humanity based on theories of individual criminal responsibility that include conspiracy and direct and public incitement to commit genocide.

The military trial involves Colonel Théoneste Bagosora, the Director of the Cabinet in the Ministry of Defense, and a number of senior military officials. It examines how the genocide allegedly was planned and implemented at the highest levels of the Rwandan army. Bagosora is alleged to be the military mastermind of the genocide.

Former prosecutor Del Ponte had affirmed an interest in investigating allegations of crimes committed by Tutsi armed forces (the RPA). This is a matter of considerable controversy for the Rwandan government. Thus far, no indictments have been issued against the RPA, notwithstanding allegations that it massacred up to thirty thousand Hutu civilians when it wrested control of the Rwandan state from its genocidal government in 1994.

## Contribution to Legal and Political Issues Concerning Genocide

The ICTR shows that those responsible for mass violence can face their day in court. In this sense, the ICTR helps promote accountability for human rights abuses and combat the impunity that, historically, often has inured to the benefit of those who perpetrate such abuses.

However, the ICTR—and legal responses to mass violence more generally—cannot create a culture of human rights on its own. Democratization, power-sharing, social equity, and economic opportunity each are central to transitional justice. Moreover, although the law can promote some justice after tragedy has occurred, it is important to devote resources prospectively to prevent genocide in the first place. In this sense, by creating the ICTR the international community only addressed part of the obligation announced by the 1948 UN Genocide Convention, namely the prevention and punishment of genocide.

For many Rwandans, the international community's response to and effort in preventing the genocide is questionable at best. The international community was not willing to meaningfully invest in armed intervention that may have prevented, or at least mitigated, genocide in Rwanda in the first place. Various independent reports and studies have found the UN (as well as many states) responsible for failing to prevent or end the Rwandan genocide.

The ICTR's most significant contribution is to the development of international criminal law. Its decisions build a jurisprudence that informs the work of other international criminal tribunals, such as the ICTY, other temporary institutions, and prospectively the permanent ICC. National courts in a number of countries have also relied on ICTR decisions when these courts have been called on to adjudicate human rights cases.

Several of the ICTR's decisions highlight these contributions. One of these is the Trial Chamber's ground-breaking 1998 judgment in the *Akayesu* case (subsequently affirmed on appeal), which provided judicial notice that the Rwandan violence was organized, planned, ethnically motivated, and undertaken with the intent to wipe out the Tutsi (the latter element being a prerequisite to genocide). The *Akayesu* judgment marked the first time that an international tribunal ruled that rape and other forms of systematic sexual violence could constitute genocide. Moreover, it provided a progressive definition of rape. Another important example is the Trial and Appeals Chamber's conviction of Clément Kayishema, a former local governmental official, and Obed Ruzindana, a businessman, jointly of genocide and crimes against humanity, and its sentencing them to life imprisonment and twenty-five years imprisonment, respectively, clarifying the law regarding the requirement of the "mental element" (proof of malevolent intent) in the establishment of the crime of genocide, and the type of circumstantial evidence that could establish that mental element (*Prosecutor v. Kayishema*, Appeals Chamber, 2001).

Also significantly, the notion of command responsibility was squarely addressed and expanded in the case of Alfred Musema, the director of a tea factory. Along with other convictions for crimes for which he was directly responsible, Musema was held liable for the acts carried out by the employees of his factory over whom he was found to have legal control, an important extension of the doctrine of superior responsibility outside the military context and into the context of a civilian workplace (*Prosecutor v. Musema*, Trial Chamber, 2000, paras. 141–148). In the *Musema* case, the ICTR also provided interpretive guidance as to what sorts of attacks could constitute crimes against humanity.

## Contribution to Postgenocide Rwanda

There is cause to be more circumspect regarding the contribution of the ICTR to postgenocide Rwanda. Many Rwandans are poorly informed of the work of the ICTR. Moreover, many of those aware of the work of the ICTR remain skeptical of the process and results. The justice resulting from the operation of the ICTR is distant from the lives of Rwandans and may inure more to the benefit of the international community than to victims, positive kinds of transition, and justice in Rwanda itself. This provides a valuable lesson: In order for international legal institutions to play catalytic roles, it is best if they resonate with lives lived locally. This signals a need for such institutions to work in harmony with local practices. Moreover, there also is reason to suspect that for many afflicted populations justice may mean something quite different than the narrow retributive justice flowing from criminal trials. In this vein, it is important for international legal interventions to adumbrate a multilayered notion of justice that actively contemplates restorative, indigenous, truth-seeking, and reparative methodologies.

There is evidence the international community is moving toward this pluralist direction, both in terms of the work of the ICTR and also the construction of recent justice initiatives that are more polycentric in focus. There is an emphasis on institutional reform that could make the work of the ICTR more relevant to Rwandans. The ICTR has, in conjunction with Rwandan nongovernmental organizations, launched a victim-oriented restitutionary justice program to provide psychological counseling, physical rehabilitation, reintegration assistance, and legal guidance to genocide survivors. There also is a possibility—as of 2004 unrealized—of locating ICTR proceedings in Kigali, where the ICTR has opened an information center. Such a relocation would invest financial resources and infrastructure into Rwanda itself and thereby facilitate one of the unattained goals of Resolution 955, namely to "strengthen the courts and judicial system of Rwanda" (Resolution 955, 1994, Preamble).

## Bibliography

Alvarez, Jose (1999) "Crimes of State/Crimes of Hate Lessons from Rwanda." *Yale Journal of International Law* 24:365–484.

Arbour, Louise (2000). "The International Tribunals and Serious Violations of International Humanitarian in the Former Yugoslavia and Rwanda." *McGill Law Journal* 46(1):195–201.

Bassiouni, Cherif, ed. (1991). *International Criminal Law* 2nd edition. New York: Transnational Publishers.

Des Forges, Alison (1999). *Leave None to Tell the Story Genocide in Rwanda.* New York: Human Rights Watch.

Drumbl, Mark A. (2000). "Punishment, Postgenocide: From Guilt to Shame to Civis in Rwanda." *New York State University Law Review* 75(5):1221–1326.

Drumbl, Mark A., and Kenneth S. Gallant (2002). "Sentencing Policies and Practices in the International Criminal Tribunals." *Federal Sentencing Reporter* 15(2):140–144.

International Criminal Tribunal for Rwanda. "ICTR Rules of Procedure and Evidence." Available from http//www.ictr.org/ENGLISH/rules/index.htm.

International Criminal Tribunal for Rwanda. "Statute of the International Criminal Tribunal for Rwanda." Available from http://www.ictr.org/ENGLISH/basicdocs/statute.html.

Morris, Madeline (1997). "The Trials of Concurrent Jurisdiction: The Case of Rwanda." *Duke Journal of Comparative and International Law* 7(2):349–374.

Morris, Virginia, and Michael P. Scharf (1998). *The International Criminal Tribunal for Rwanda.* New York: Transnational Publishers.

*Prosecutor v. Akayesu.* Case No. ICTR-96-4, Appeals Chamber (2001).

*Prosecutor v. Bagilishema.* Case No. ICTR-95-1A-T, Trial Chamber (2001); Case No. ICTR-95-1A-A, Appeals Chamber (2002).

*Prosecutor v. Barayagwiza.* Case No. ICTR-97-19-AR72, Appeals Chamber (2000).

*Prosecutor v. Kambanda.* Case No. ICTR 97-23-A, Appeals Chamber (2000).

*Prosecutor v. Kayishema.* Case No. ICTR-95-1-A, Appeals Chamber (2001).

*Prosecutor v. Musema.* Case No. ICTR-96-13, Trial Chamber (2000).

*Prosecutor v. Serushago.* Case No. ICTR-98-39-S, Sentence (1999).

Sarkin, Jeremy (2001). "The Tension between Justice and Reconciliation in Rwanda: Politics, Human Rights, Due Process and the Role of the Gacaca Courts in Dealing with the Genocide." *Journal of African Law* 45(2):143–172.

Schabas, William (2002). *Genocide in International Law.* Cambridge: Cambridge University Press.

Schabas, William (2000). "Hate Speech in Rwanda: The Road to Genocide." *McGill Law Journal* 46(1):141–171.

United Nations Security Council (1994). "United Nations Security Council Resolution 955, Adopted by the Security Council at Its 3,453rd Meeting, on November 8, 1994." UN Document S/RES/955.

Uvin, Peter, and Charles Mironko (2003). "Western and Local Approaches to Justice in Rwanda." *Global Governance* 9(2):219–231.

# 12.4    "Historic Judgement Finds Akayesu Guilty of Genocide"

ICTR/INFO-9-2-138 Arusha, 2 September 1998

*"Despite the indisputable atrociousness of the crimes and the emotions evoked in the international community, the judges have examined the facts adduced in a most dispassionate manner, bearing in mind that the accused is presumed innocent".*

With these words among others, the International Criminal Tribunal for Rwanda, in the first-ever judgement by an international court for the crime of genocide, today found "Jean-Paul Akayesu guilty of Genocide and Crimes Against Humanity".

Akayesu, former Bourgmestre (mayor) of Taba, was indicted on 15 counts of Genocide, Crimes Against Humanity, and Violations of Article 3 Common to the Geneva Conventions and Additional Protocol II Thereto. In its judgement, Trial Chamber I Judges Laïty Kama (Senegal), presiding, Lennart Aspegren (Sweden) and Navanethem Pillay (South Africa) unanimously found Akayesu guilty of nine out of the 15 counts on which he was charged, and not guilty of six counts in his indictment. The former Rwandan official had pleaded not guilty, to all 15 counts.

Specifically, he was found guilty of Genocide, Direct and Public Incitement to Commit Genocide, and Crimes against Humanity (Extermination, Murder, Torture, Rape, and Other Inhumane Acts). But the Tribunal also held that he was not guilty of the crimes of Complicity in Genocide and Violations of Article 3 common to the Geneva Conventions (Murder and Cruel Treatment) and of Article 4(2)(e) of Additional Protocol II (Outrage upon personal dignity, in particular Rape, Degrading and Humiliating Treatment and Indecent Assault).

## Genocide Interpreted

In this precedent-setting case in which Genocide, as defined in the Convention for the Prevention and Punishment of the Crime of Genocide (1948) was interpreted for the first time by an international tribunal, the Rwanda Tribunal recalled that Genocide means, as described in the Convention, "the act of committing certain crimes, including the killing of members of the group or causing serious physical or mental harm to members of the group with the intent to destroy, in whole or in part, a national, racial or religious group, as such", The Chamber stated: "there was an intention to wipe out the Tutsi group in its entirety, since even newborn babies were not spared".

Examining the fact that a civil war raged in Rwanda between the RAF (Rwandan Armed Forces) and the RPF (Rwanda Patriotic Front) at the time the genocide occurred, the Trial Chamber concluded that this fact cannot serve as mitigating circumstances for the genocide. Furthermore, the court found that the genocide was not organized only by members of the RAF, but also by the political leaders of the "Hutu-power" persuasion, and it was executed essentially by civilians including the armed militia and even ordinary citizens. Above all, the court concluded, the majority of the Tutsi victims were non-combatants, including women and children.

## Akayesu Was Individually Responsible

In finding Akayesu guilty on nine counts of his indictment, Trial Chamber I firmly established the individual responsibility of the accused for the crimes. While Akayesu conceded during his trial that massacres aimed mainly at Tutsis took place in Taba commune in 1994, the Defence argued that he was helpless to prevent the commission of such acts because the effective power in the commune lay with the Interhamwe and, as soon as the massacres began, Akayesu was stripped of all authority and lacked the means to stop the killings. The Chamber found, to the contrary, that Akayesu, in his capacity as bourgmestre, was responsible for maintaining law and public order in the commune of Taba and that he had effective authority over the communal police. Akayesu had admitted during his trial that the inhabitants of Taba respected him and followed his orders.

He initially tried to stop the killings of Tutsis, but later stopped trying to maintain law and order. The accused was subsequently present during the killings and sometimes gave orders himself for bodily or mental harm to be caused to certain Tutsi, and endorsed and even ordered the killing of several Tutsi.

In addition to the criminal responsibility that attaches from committing or participating in the commission of any of the crimes under the Tribunal's jurisdiction, Article 6(3) of the Statute of the Rwanda Tribunal provides that a superior is criminally responsible for the acts of subordinates if the superior knew or had reason to know that the subordinate was about to commit such acts or had actually done so and yet failed to prevent or punish such acts.

The court found that Akayesu also incited genocide by leading and addressing a public gathering in Taba on 19 April 1994, during which he urged the population to unite and in order to eliminate what he referred to as the sole enemy: the accomplices of the "Inkotanyi"— a derogatory reference to Tutsis which was understood to be a call to kill the Tutsis in general. The Chamber defined the crime of direct and public incitement to genocide mainly on the basis of Article 91 of the Rwandan Penal Code, as directly provoking another to commit genocide through speeches at public gatherings, or through the sale or dissemination of written or audiovisual communication, and considered the crime to have been committed whether or not such public incitement was successful.

## Rape Defined in International Law

Trial Chamber I also defined the crime of rape, for which there is no commonly accepted definition in international law. "The Chamber defines rape as a physical invasion of a sexual nature, committed on a person under circumstances which are coercive. Sexual violence is not limited to physical invasion of the human body and may include acts which do not involve penetration or even physical contact" the court elaborated. It noted that coercive circumstance did not need to be evidenced by a show of physical force. "Threats, intimidation, extortion and other forms of duress which prey on fear or desperation could be coercion".

Numerous Tutsi women seeking refuge at the Taba communal office from the massacres were systematically raped and regularly subjected to multiple acts of sexual violence by armed local militia. As one female victim put it during her testimony in the Akayesu trial, "each time you met assailants, they raped you". Akayesu encouraged these acts by his attitude and utterances, the Trial Chamber found. One witness testified that Akayesu addressed the Inter-hamwe militia who were raping female victims thus: "never ask me again what a Tutsi woman tastes like".

In its judgement, the Trial Chamber underscored the fact that rape and sexual violence also constitute genocide in the same way as any other act as long as they were committed with intent to destroy a particular group targeted as such. The court held that sexual violence was an "integral" part of the process of destruction of the Tutsi ethnic group. "The rape of Tutsi women was systematic and was perpetrated against all Tutsi women and solely against them", the Chamber concluded. Furthermore, these rapes were accompanied by a proven intent to kill their victims. At least 2,000 Tutsis were killed in Taba between 7 April and the end of June 1994, while Akayesu held office as bourgmestre.

## Violation of Geneva Conventions: Insufficient Proof

With respect to the charges of Violations of Article 3 common to the Geneva Conventions of 1949 and Additional Protocol II thereto, the Chamber concluded that a non-international armed conflict in Rwanda in 1994, and that this conflict was well within the provisions of these laws. However, it found that the Prosecution had failed to show beyond reasonable doubt that Akayesu was a member of the armed forces and that he had the authority to support and carry out the war effort.

## Jean-Paul Akayesu

Jean-Paul Akayesu was born in 1953. Prior to becoming the bourgmestre of Taba commune in the Gitarama prefecture of Rwanda, he was a school teacher and school inspector. He entered politics and the Mouvement Democratique Republicain (MDR) in 1991, and became Chairman of the local wing of the MDR in Taba. In April 1993 he was elected bourgmestre of Taba, and held that position until June 1994 when he fled Rwanda.

Akayesu was arrested in Zambia on 10 October 1995, indicted by the Tribunal on 16 February 1996, and transferred from Zambia to Arusha on 26 May 1996, where he was detained at the Tribunal's detention facility. His trial began on 9 January 1997. On 17 June 1997, Trial Chamber I permitted the Prosecutor to amend his indictment to include charges of sexual crimes. He is married with five children.

# 13

# Trials in National Courts

The biggest post-genocide problem for Rwanda has been the issue of justice and reconciliation. The former is of crisis proportions, as too many Hutus were involved in the killings to bring to trial in traditional, or "classical," courts, as they are referred to in Rwanda. While a handful of senior officials have been indicted and convicted at the International Criminal Tribunal for Rwanda (ICTR), the vast majority of Hutu killers have been facing hearings in the context of a local village assembly, a form of justice known as *gacaca* (see below). Those higher up in the killing machinery who have not been sent for trial at the ICTR in Arusha have been (and continue to be) tried in the national courts of Rwanda.

The aftermath of the genocide saw approximately 130,000 alleged *génocidaires* incarcerated in Rwandan prisons across the country. Those who were suspected of having planned and directed the genocide, who were termed Category One prisoners, were to be tried at the ICTR or in national courts within Rwanda. That said, some estimates held that if regular courts tried all the cases under consideration it would take between 60 and 200 years to complete the trial process. That was true not only due to the large number of defendants incarcerated in the horrifically over-crowded, filthy, and disease-ridden prisons, but also to the fact that during the course of the genocide the judicial system of Rwanda had been destroyed as most of the prosecutors, defense attorneys, and judges had been killed. Of equal concern was the prospect that many of those imprisoned were possibly innocent. Also to be taken into account was the enormous cost of feeding, clothing, and guarding such an overwhelming number of prisoners; such a cost, it was felt, was bound to tax Rwanda's already overwhelmed social system.

By way of illustration, in August 2003, the Rwandan Ministry of Justice announced that slightly over six thousand of the 130,000 prisoners arrested for the genocide had by that stage been sentenced in the national courts; of these, seven hundred had been sentenced to death, and at least up to eighty executions had taken place. It is the slowness of this approach to Western-style forms of justice that has led to the horrible conditions of overcrowding and disease in Rwanda's jails, with little immediate hope for prisoners seeking to have their cases heard.

Another way had to be found if justice—in any form—was to be achieved. Rwanda's problems stemmed from the genocide, to be sure, but the crisis inherent in the quest for post-genocide justice was equally problematical; there could be no reconciliation without judicial closure. All too frequently, in order to ease conditions and alleviate the immense overcrowding in Rwanda's jails, prisoners were simply released without any further ado. Thus, in February 2007, thousands of detainees suspected of genocide were released. After having languished in Rwandan prisons since the mid-1990s, they were herded onto transports provided by the state and returned, often to their home districts where the original crimes with which they had been charged took place in 1994. All told, some nine thousand were released in this single two-day operation (http://news. bbc.co.uk/2/hi/africa/6376979.stm).

If release was one way to achieve closure—and it was, it must be said, far from satisfactory in the eyes of many, particularly the survivors—another means was through the introduction, in March 2001, of the process of an indigenous form of dispute resolution, known as *gacaca*. The term *gacaca* (pronounced "ga-cha-cha") is derived from the Kinyarwarda word *guacaca*, meaning grass; hence, *gacaca* literally means "justice on the grass." This is explained through the practice of these sessions taking place, during the precolonial period, out in the open, frequently on grass in the literal sense. Traditionally, the *gacaca* system was used in villages all across Rwanda to settle family disputes, disputes among neighbors, conflicts over land, trade, and the like. The local *gacaca* would meet in the village, and a group of elders would make a decision based on the merits of each person's argument.

Significantly, the goals of the new *gacaca* system were many; indeed, *gacaca* was not put in place solely for the purpose of punishing the guilty. It was, rather, intended as a way for the victims to tell their stories; to allow the victims to discover how and where their family members and friends had been killed and/or were buried; to allow perpetrators to confess and ask for forgiveness; and to help bring about reconciliation for the nation's peoples (perpetrators, victims, and survivors, alike).

Initially, attendance at the *gacacas* was optional, but when extremely large numbers of people failed to attend the hearings, the government made it mandatory for all individuals eighteen years of age and older to attend. The rationale was that *gacacas* are to constitute a participatory type of justice in which the hearings are conducted by, in front of, and for the local people in the very area where the crimes were alleged to have taken place. In each city, town, and village, *gacacas* are held on a specific day of the week. On the day of *gacaca*, all government offices (with the exception of the police), businesses, and schools are closed from 8:00 am to 1:00 pm so that all individuals can attend and not claim that they have other draws on their time. *Gacacas* are led by "Persons of Integrity," or those individuals who have been selected by the local people based on that person's known honesty. He or she, of course, cannot have taken part in the genocide in any way whatsoever. Those selected as Persons of Integrity have been provided with the rudiments of state law through a number of government-run workshops, though in most areas these have been very short, and restricted to a single session.

Neither the perpetrators nor the victims are represented by lawyers, but each is allowed to speak. The Persons of Integrity are allowed to ask questions of each and, if need be, to adjourn a hearing in order to obtain additional information or to call in additional witnesses. All alleged perpetrators—except for Category One prisoners—are allowed to be tried by *gacacas*. Those perpetrators who confess their crimes in public at *gacaca* hearings and ask for forgiveness in a genuine way can have their sentences cut in half. Those who do not confess or are not genuine in asking forgiveness are sent back to prison to complete their full sentence. If it is discovered that an individual has failed to provide a full confession, he or she can, and usually is, given a lengthier sentence than had already been handed down. *Gacaca* courts may only impose custodial sentences, not capital punishment.

Ultimately, the express purposes of the *gacaca* courts are: (1) the reconstruction and recounting of what actually took place during the genocide (who, what, where, and how); (2) providing victims with the opportunity to see the perpetrators who harmed and killed their loved ones being held accountable for their crimes, thus ending a culture of impunity; (3) speeding up the process of hearing the cases of the alleged perpetrators; (4) freeing the innocent from prison; (5) removing the burden on the national system of courts and thus allowing them to concentrate on trying those who planned and led the genocide; and (6) working towards the reconciliation of all Rwandans. To date, more than 60,000 prisoners—both *génocidaires* and those suspected of having been so—have been released under the *gacaca* system.

*Gacaca* is not without its critics and drawbacks. Some believe that allowing perpetrators to have their sentences cut in half for confessing and asking for forgiveness is unconscionable in light of their crimes. Others consider that the perpetrators will ask for forgiveness regardless of whether or not they are truly contrite. Some worry that even those who are not guilty of taking part in the genocide, but have been accused of doing so, will falsely admit their guilt in order to get out of prison faster than they would have normally. Yet others are concerned by the lack of education of the Persons of Integrity, as well as a lack of adequate training for the job they have to perform. Still, *gacaca* is an innovation implemented by the Rwandan government in an ostensible attempt to be as fair as possible to as many people as possible within Rwandan society, and to bring about reconciliation in the still damaged country.

In a few short words, Jennifer Balint (in her article "National Trials in Rwanda") conveys something of the background and operation of the national justice system in Rwanda, as it seeks to bring the perpetrators of the genocide to account. As she points out, the legislation behind such trials was located in a new law, Organic Law No. 08/96 (August 30, 1996). Interestingly, this takes as its starting point offenses committed since October 1, 1990; here we see a contrast with the ICTR, which is much narrower in terms of time frame (January 1, 1994 to December 31, 1994). Because Balint's article predates the introduction of the *gacaca* law (March 2001), she makes no mention of it here (which necessitates the explanation above). Had *gacaca* been introduced at the time of her writing, we should certainly have seen comment on this additional element of post-genocide national law. As it is, Balint's article shows clearly the limitations and weaknesses facing Rwandan national justice at the time she was writing, and—without recognizing it—her final words presage ideally the introduction of the new system of justice that was introduced just two years later.

# 13.1   Jennifer Balint, "National Trials in Rwanda"

These are trials established to provide legal redress for the approximately 500,000–800,000 civilians (mainly Tutsis) killed by the Hutu government and their accomplices during April–July 1994. These legal proceedings are being held concurrently; the first convened by the Rwandan government in Rwanda, the second by the United Nations in Arusha, Tanzania.

## National Trials in Rwanda

The first trials began on December 27, 1996. They were established by a new law, Organic Law No. 08/96 (August 30, 1996). The trials are held in different provinces throughout Rwanda, they are public, and are broadcast on national radio. There was debate in post-genocide Rwanda as to whether the trials should be conducted by the courts which existed prior to 1994, or whether a new court should be established to deal only with the genocide. The decision was taken to create specialized chambers within the existing structure, namely, chambers which would be established in the Court of First Instance, the court with civil and criminal jurisdiction over the provinces (prefectures) of Rwanda. The specialized chambers would not have jurisdiction over crimes of military personnel and public officials ordinarily subject to the criminal jurisdiction of other tribunals. Military offenders would be tried by a specialized chamber of the military courts. The new legislation is designed to work in conjunction with the Rwandan Penal Code and Code of Criminal Procedure, although it does take precedence. As such, the national trials are a hybrid, born of old and new, specifically developed to address the genocide of 1994.

Organic Law 08/96 was established for "the organisation of prosecutions for offenses constituting the crime of genocide or crimes against humanity committed since 1 October 1990." Key aspects of Organic Law 08/96 include:

- Alleged offenders are classified into four categories of participation (Article 2). Category One includes the "planners, organisers, instigators, supervisors and leaders of the crime of genocide or of a crime against humanity," "persons who acted in positions of authority," "notorious murderers," and "persons who committed acts of sexual torture." Category Two includes "perpetrators, conspirators or, accomplices of intentional homicide or serious assault . . . causing death." Category Three includes "persons . . . guilty of other serious assaults against the person." Category Four includes "persons who committed offenses against property."
- A plea-bargain mechanism through explicit confession, which enables all but those in Category One to a possible reduction in penalty, and purports to "encourage reconciliation" (Articles 5, 6, 9).
- Victims are entitled to initiate claims for civil damages within the context of the criminal trial, or to pursue this separately through civil jurisdiction (Articles 27–32).
- Victims can initiate a public criminal trial through written petition to the Public Prosecutor, or initiate a prosecution in their own capacity (Article 29).
- Limited appeal procedures for those convicted, less than those provided for in the Rwandan Code of Criminal Procedure.

Tension has existed between the national trials, conducted by the Rwandan government, and the International Criminal Tribunal for Rwanda (ICTR), conducted by the United Nations. Both sets of trials are addressing the same event: the 1994 genocide in Rwanda. Although a division of functions between the two sets of trials does exist—the ICTR is targeting the key perpetrators (the main officials), whereas the national criminal trials are targeting the "second rung" perpetrators, there is still somewhat of a strained relationship between them. One key problem has been that of punishment. The Rwandan national trials include the death penalty in punishment for those in Category One, whereas the ICTR, according to international law, does not. The situation thus is that the highest penalty that the key perpetrators (those tried at the ICTR) can receive is life imprisonment, while the highest penalty that the second-rung perpetrators (those tried in Rwandan national trials) can receive is the death penalty. Prosecutor-General, Simeon Rwagasore, commented in January 1998 that in the context of Rwanda, death sentences must be carried out "so that Rwandans understand the life of a person cannot be trampled on. Killers have been pardoned throughout Rwanda's history. Social and political conflicts have been settled using machetes and this has to change. One can always debate using the death penalty to serve as an example, but Rwanda is a unique case."

The first executions of Rwandans found guilty by the national trials were carried out on May 1, 1998, surrounded by much international protest. Protest has also focused on the fact that there are presently over 130,000 alleged perpetrators being held in Rwandan jails, in overcrowded and unsanitary conditions. Most of those in jail have been held there without charge since the genocide was committed. There is concern too as to the nature of the trials, that they are not being held according to "rule of law" legal procedure (for example, due to the lack of lawyers in Rwanda, it is rare that a suspect has legal representation, either during their interrogation or during their trial), and that the Rwandan legal system is illequipped to hold such trials. The central criticism has been that the trials are being used as a political tool by the new Rwandan government, as a tool of consolidation of power and further repression. This is reflected in the fact that there are no Hutu judges presiding over these trials, and that it appears that none of the Tutsi Rwandese Patriotic Front (RPF) members have been brought before the courts for crimes committed. These concerns in particular were raised by an Amnesty International Report, "Rwanda: Unfair Trials—Justice Denied," to which the government replied through the Ministry of Justice (May 8, 1997). In part it acknowledged these "shortcomings," and that "Judges and Prosecutors involved in the jurisdictions concerned have been working together to improve the functioning of a system of justice which is being rebuilt from scratch."

## International Trials

The International Criminal Tribunal for Rwanda (ICTR) was established by United Nations Security Council Resolution 955, on November 8, 1994. Its full name is the International Criminal Tribunal for the Prosecution of Persons Responsible for Genocide and Other Serious Violations of International Humanitarian Law Committed in the Territory of Rwanda and Rwandan Citizens Responsible for Genocide and other such Violations Committed in the Territory of Neighbouring States, between 1 January 1994 and 31 December 1994.

The ICTR was originally requested by the new government of Rwanda. It is located in the neighboring country of Tanzania, in the town of Arusha. The trials are public trials; the judges are appointed by the United Nations, from a variety of countries. It is integrally connected to the International Tribunal for the Former Yugoslavia (ICTY), which was established in May 1993. The two Tribunals are integrally linked, legally and politically. Not only do they share a Prosecutor, but without the ICTY, the ICTR would not have come into existence.

The ICTR Statute outlines that the ICTR is mandated to prosecute persons (Rwandan citizens) responsible for the following offenses (serious violations of international humanitarian law), committed in the territory of Rwanda 1 January 1994–31 December 1994: Genocide (Article 2, Statute ICTR); Crimes Against Humanity (Article 3, Statute ICTR); Violations of Article 3 common to the Geneva Conventions and of Additional Protocol II (Article 4, Statute ICTR). The ICTR consists of two Trial Chambers and an Appeals Chamber, the Prosecutor, and the Registry. Article 8 of the ICTR Statute grants the ICTR primacy over any national courts, although it acknowledges concurrent jurisdiction with national courts.

The ICTR has in many ways been seen as the "poor cousin" of the ICTY. Its location in an out-of-the-way place in Africa (contrasted with the ICTY location in the seat of international law, the Hague), has meant that it has experienced many organization problems, added to the fact that it has had fewer resources allocated to it. It has, however, in contrast to the ICTY, indicted and arrested a large number of suspects, and in that respect so far has a higher "success" rate than the ICTY. The first judgment and sentencing of the ICTR was delivered on 2 and 4 September 1998. Mr. Jean-Paul Akayesu, former mayor of Taba commune, was found guilty on 2 September of 9 out of 15 counts of genocide, crimes against humanity, and violations of common Article 3 of the Geneva Conventions. This case was hailed in much of the world press as the first conviction for genocide by an international court. The former prime minister of Rwanda, Mr. Jean Kambanda, after pleading guilty to six counts of genocide and crimes against humanity, was sentenced on 4 September 1998 to life imprisonment. These were the first convictions for genocide by an international court.

## References and Recommended Reading

Ferstman, Carla J. (1997). Domestic trials for genocide and crimes against humanity: The example of Rwanda. *African Journal of International and Comparative Law*, 9, 857–877.

Morris, Madeline H. (1997). The trials of concurrent jurisdiction: The case of Rwanda. *Duke Journal of Comparative & International Law*, 7(2), 349–374.

Schabas, William A. (1996). Justice, democracy, and impunity in post-geonocide Rwanda: Searching for solutions to impossible problems. *Criminal Law Forum*, 7(3), 523–560.

## Suplemental References

Gahima, Gerald (Rwandan Ministry of Justice). Rwanda: The Challenge of Justice in the Aftermath of Genocide. Presented at Justice in Cataclysm: Criminal Trials in the Wake of Mass Violence Conference, Brussels, Belgium, July 21, 1996.

Organic Lae on the Organization of Prsecutions for Offenses Constituting the Crime of Genocide or Crimes against Humanity, J.O., 1996, Year 35, No. 17, at 14 (Rwanda).

Statement Dated 28 September 1994 on the Question of Refugees and Security in Rwanda, U.N. SCOR, 49th Sess. Annex, at 2, U.N. Doc. S/1994?1114 (1994) (request by Rwanda for International Tribunal).

Statute of the International Criminal Tribunal for Rwanda, adopted at New York, Nov. 8, 1994, S.C. Res. 955, U.N. SCOR, 49th Sess, 3453 mtg. U.N. DOC, S/RES/955 (1994).

# 14

# The International Criminal Court (ICC)

The idea for the establishment of an international criminal court reaches back to the nineteenth century, when Gustav Moynier, one of the founders of the International Committee of the Red Cross, suggested the need for such a court to uphold the Geneva Convention of 1864. From then on, proposals for such a court were raised many times (for example, during the course of the Versailles Peace Conference of 1919, by the Committee of Jurists in 1920 under the auspices of the League of Nations, several times during World War II, and on numerous occasions in the post-World War II years). All of these were to no avail, usually falling short over such issues as national jurisdiction, sovereignty, and enforcement. It was not until the late 1980s and early to mid-1990s that actual headway was made in establishing such a court, the impetus being hastened by the genocidal atrocities that were being perpetrated, first, in the former Yugoslavia between 1991 and 1995, and then in Rwanda in 1994.

The International Criminal Court (ICC) was established officially by the United Nations on July 1, 2002, after sixty member states became parties to the Rome Statute of the International Criminal Court. Earlier, on July 17, 1998, an international agreement was signed in Rome, Italy, under the auspices of the United Nations General Assembly, authorizing "the establishment of an international criminal court." It had taken half a century of constant effort for human rights law to arrive at this point. Article IV of the United Nations Convention on the Prevention and Punishment of the Crime of Genocide (General Assembly Resolution 260 of December 9, 1948) referred to the establishment of "such an international penal tribunal as may have jurisdiction" for the purpose of trying cases of genocide, but no such universal tribunal existed until the Rome Statute authorized the creation of one.

At its fifty-second session, the UN General Assembly decided that a "Diplomatic Conference of Plenipotentiaries on the Establishment of an International Criminal Court" would take place in Rome between June 15 and June 17, 1998. During the conference, it was agreed that the key crimes the court would address would be genocide, crimes against humanity, and war crimes. (The crime of international aggression was considered, but shelved.) With the adoption of the Rome Statute, it was decided that the International Criminal Court would become operational after sixty of the signatory states had ratified their accession within their home legislatures. The latter was achieved in April 2002.

A number of states, wary as to the implications the court may hold for their sovereignty, held back from signing, but the one that garnered the most attention and criticism was the United States, which had not been one of the original signatories to the Rome Statute. A major objection voiced from Washington was that the way the Rome Statute was worded would leave U.S. officials and military personnel open to possibly being charged with war crimes and/or crimes against humanity, if not genocide, even though the United States might be engaged in a humanitarian action (which involved combat). Thus, in 1998, the United States voted against the Rome Statute. It was one of only seven nations to do so, the other six being China, Israel, Iraq, Libya, Qatar, and Yemen. Then, on December 31, 2000, U.S. President Bill Clinton signed the treaty, basically agreeing to support the creation of the ICC. On May 6, 2002, however, the Administration of U.S. President George W. Bush reneged, effectively withdrawing the United States from its accession to the treaty. The earlier justifications of national sovereignty, checks and balances, and national independence were once again cited: the argument put forth was that the United States would not submit its troops to prosecutors and judges whose jurisdiction it did not accept, with the alternative preference being that U.S. military personnel should only be answerable to their own superiors and to U.S. military law, not to the rulings of what was considered an unaccountable International Criminal Court.

Howard Ball provides a detailed treatment of the steps leading to the creation of the International Criminal Court, from the time the idea was first given serious consideration until its realization at the Rome meeting in 1998. In this extract ("Nuremberg's Legacy: Adoption of the Rome Statute"), he shows how the various preparatory committees meeting throughout the 1990s were given the dual tasks of establishing the form such a court would take, and drafting the precise proposals on which the states attending the formal establishment of the court would vote. As Ball points out, the process was laborious and fraught with diplomatic traps; often, it seemed, the whole proposal could collapse, or at least be watered down substantially. A number of issues remained unresolved for quite some time, none more so than the question of jurisdiction, the question of impunity, and the obligations placed on participating states. Yet, as Ball shows, these issues were ultimately sorted out in such a way that the contracting parties were satisfied that the ICC could proceed—despite the omission of several key players that would otherwise have been expected to play a part.

Critical concerns about the ICC continue to surface regarding such matters as the political biases of court members, the quality of due process, interference with national processes of reconciliation, and questions regarding jurisdiction. Unlike in earlier times, these have been resolved to a satisfactory standard, such that they have thus far not prevented the ICC from proceeding with its mandate. The ICC's position is that it acts as a court of last resort. It will not, for example, act if a case is already being investigated or prosecuted within a national judicial system, though this position can be overridden if such national proceedings are not considered to be genuinely based on transparent justice—for example, if formal proceedings were being undertaken within a national court system solely in order to shield an alleged perpetrator from criminal responsibility. The other key feature of the ICC is that it only tries those accused of the gravest breaches of international humanitarian law: that is, major violations under the Geneva Conventions, which prohibit, *inter alia*, willful killing, torture, rape, or inhuman treatment of protected persons, willfully causing great suffering or serious injury to body or health, and extensive destruction and appropriation of property not justified by military necessity and carried out unlawfully and wantonly. It is under these headings that the charges of genocide, war crimes, and crimes against humanity are to be located.

To date (2008), 104 nations, from all continents, have become signatories to the ICC, though there are some notable omissions, such as China, Egypt, Guatemala, Iraq, Israel, Libya, North Korea, Russia, Sudan, Syria, the United States, and Yemen. Investigations and proceedings have begun regarding gross human rights violations in Uganda, Democratic Republic of Congo, Central African Republic, and Sudan (pertaining, specifically, to the ongoing genocide in Darfur). While the hope is that the list will not grow, it is fully anticipated that the scope and range of ICC activities will be extended in the future owing to human rights abuses taking place in a variety of settings around the world.

# 14.1   Howard Ball, "Nuremberg's Legacy: Adoption of the Rome Statute"

Since the Nuremberg and Tokyo war crimes tribunals ended their work in 1948, "it's been a dream of international human rights advocates [to see created] a permanent world court that would try individuals for genocide, crimes against humanity, and crimes of war."[1] The unfinished legacy of those World War II ad hoc tribunals has been the creation of a permanent international criminal court (ICC) that could hear cases involving grave violations of the laws and customs of war—situations not addressed, for whatever reason, by national prosecutors.

Ironically, wrote T. R. Goldman in 1998, the "biggest impediment, say U.S. and international human rights groups, . . . is not rogue states like Libya, Nigeria, or Iraq [but the] government of the United States." Although President Bill Clinton was on record as supporting the creation of an ICC, the United States "has emerged as the main obstacle" to its creation.[2] The primary opposition to the Rome statute came from the Pentagon and some foreign policy planners in the White House.

## U.S. Military Antipathy toward UN Peacekeeping and the ICC

In the last two years of the George Bush administration (1989–1993), the United States "jumped into peace enforcement [in Somalia and the Persian Gulf] with gusto."[3] Although there was a quick, somewhat successful, end to the UN's military action against Iraq, the deaths of scores of American soldiers in Somalia a few years later led to almost instant disenchantment with U.S. involvement in Somalia and with UN peacekeeping missions generally. American foreign policy, known for its "particular mix of generosity, power, and multiple personalities,"[4] took a bold right turn after Somalia and after Bill Clinton was elected president in 1992, defeating Bush.

When Clinton entered the White House, he was confronted by a military hierarchy that had little regard for the deployment of American military personnel in "dangerous" UN peacekeeping efforts. There was also the "warrior culture" in the Pentagon that initially disdained Clinton, the first post-World War II president. They did not appreciate his critical comments about Vietnam and his successful effort to evade the draft during that bloody, controversial war. They certainly did not like his view of gays and lesbians in the military and successfully thwarted the commander in chief's effort to liberalize military values and regulations regarding homosexual personnel.

The Pentagon leaders also did all they could to dampen Clinton's enthusiasm for U.S. participation in multinational UN peacekeeping efforts. Chairman of the Joint Chiefs of Staff General Colin Powell said in September 1993:

> Notwithstanding all of the changes that have occurred in the world, notwithstanding the new emphasis on peacekeeping, peace enforcement, peace engagement, preventive diplomacy, we have a value system and a culture system within the armed forces of the U.S. We have this mission: *to fight and win the nation's wars.* . . . Because we are able to fight and win the nation's wars, because we are warriors, we are also uniquely able to do some of these new missions that are coming along, . . . but we never want to do it in such a way that we lose sight of the focus of why you have armed forces—to fight and win the nation's wars.[5]

Anthony Lake, who was in the Clinton White House at the time, supported Powell's view and announced the Clinton turnaround on such UN activities: "Let us be clear: peacekeeping is not at the center of our foreign and defense policy. Our armed forces' primary mission is not to conduct peace operations but to win wars."[6]

Powell and others in the Pentagon took particular umbrage at a 1993 proposal for the creation of a UN rapid reaction force (RRF), essentially a standing UN multination military force that would be used to carry out the Security Council's peacekeeping responsibilities.[7] A Clinton transition team on foreign policy had enthusiastically supported the creation of the RRF, with the U.S. military forming part of it, but given the harsh criticism by his military experts, Clinton bowed to pressure from the Pentagon and the extremely popular Powell, then chairman of the Joint Chiefs of Staff.

Powell quashed the idea of committing American forces to fight in an unknown war, in an as-yet-undetermined land, for an unknown cause, led by a non-American general. His unequivocal rejection of what he believed was an outlandish proposal had an immediate impact. Clinton's UN delegation informed the secretary-general that although the RRF was needed, the United States was rejecting the creation of one "at this time."

> The U.S. does not plan to earmark forces or to assign troops to the UN Security Council permanently under Article 43 of the UN Charter.[8] Given the immediate challenges facing UN peacekeeping, these options are impractical at this time.[9]

Clearly, the military planners were concerned that the essential mission of America's armed forces, "to fight and win our nation's wars," would be jeopardized by U.S. membership in an RRF. Powell in the Pentagon and Lake in the White House emphatically rejected the idea of American participation in an RRF.

The military's anger at the RRF concept was repeated when the idea of an ICC became a serious issue in the early 1990s. The Pentagon was unalterably opposed to any institution that would place the lives and liberty of American men and women in jeopardy because of allegations that they had committed war crimes. This singular view was impressed on Clinton many times before and during the Rome meeting of 161 UN member states to discuss the creation of a permanent ICC.

The president and Secretary of State Madeleine Albright took the high road on the issue, repeatedly speaking positively about the need for such an international criminal law tribunal. He did so in Rwanda, barely four months before the convening of delegates in Rome, Italy. However, the Pentagon hard-liners—who, an observer wrote, "conducted [U.S. foreign policy] with the same brontosaurian finesse in vetoing U.S. accession to the UN convention against landmines"[10]—along with the State Department's delegation to the Rome conference, played hardball before and during the deliberations. The Pentagon never budged from its position, and the delegation in Rome only infrequently moved from predetermined positions on key issues—positions that went against the overwhelming majority of the delegations in Rome.

On March 3, 1997, more than a year before the Rome conference, nine women—all U.S. senators, liberal and conservative, Republican and Democrat[11]—wrote a letter to President Clinton. They welcomed his support for the "establishment of a permanent international institution for the prosecution of those who have committed war crimes. . . . It is critical that the international community take action to assure that war criminals not be allowed to continue to elude justice" with impunity. They implored the president to "aggressively exercise leadership in the international community to ensure that [violators] are brought to justice."

It is not known whether Clinton answered the solons. However, it has become evident that his administration, as well as leading figures in the U.S. Senate (which must give its advice and consent before a treaty becomes law), has come down hard on the ICC as proposed by the UN. A year after the president received the letter from the nine senators, the *New York Times* ran a story that illuminated the Clinton administration's view of the proposed ICC.

The article, "Pentagon Battles Plans for International War Crimes Tribunal," appeared in April 1998, just a few months before the UN-sponsored Rome conference was scheduled to begin. The story noted that "while President Clinton and Secretary of State Madeleine K. Albright have endorsed the idea of an [ICC], they have given their blessing to the Pentagon to become the attack dog in the United States' campaign to create a court more to Washington's liking."[12] The military's greatest fear, if an ICC were created, was "frivolous prosecutions of commanders and ordinary soldiers that are politically motivated by opposition to U.S. military actions."[13]

Military leaders in the Pentagon, as was the case in their opposition to the UN's RRF, were taking aggressive steps, including lobbying U.S. allies and many other nations, to reject the proposed ICC. These "scare campaign" tactics included the following:

- Briefings of over 100 foreign military attachés from embassies in Washington, D.C., about the "potential menace" to their troops posed by the ICC.
- Distribution of a three-page memo stating that "the U.S. is committed to the successful establishment of a court. But we are also intent on avoiding the creation of the wrong kind of court." Further on, the memo warned other nations about the threat posed to their military forces—and to their political and military leaders—by an ICC that gave "independent prosecutors unbridled discretion to start investigations. . . . We strongly recommend that you take an active interest in the negotiations regarding an international criminal court."
- The dispatch of a team of senior Pentagon officers to London, Paris, Brussels, Rome, and Bonn, "impressing top military brass in each capital with the American arguments."

At about the same time, fifteen prominent lawyers, members of the Lawyers Committee for Human Rights (LCHR), wrote a letter to President Clinton.[14] They urged Clinton "to make certain that the United States leads the way in Rome for an independent ICC." They noted that "with only weeks until the nations of the world gather in Rome, the need for your leadership is more critical than ever."[15] Unfortunately for the LCHR, the president was already committed to a hard line on a score of critical, unresolved issues surrounding the birth of the ICC.

Essentially, the Pentagon's fear was that the ICC, as proposed by the UN drafting commission, could target for war crimes trials U.S. soldiers and their superiors, "particularly when they were acting as peacekeepers." Early on, the president was persuaded by the military that such a state of affairs must be rejected by the American delegation in Rome. Eric Schmitt's *New York Times* article concluded with a warning to the international community:

[T]he Pentagon has a key ally in the Senate, which must approve United States membership in the court. Senator Jesse Helms, the North Carolina Republican who heads the Senate Foreign Relations Committee, vowed last month that any international criminal court would be "dead on arrival" in the Senate unless Washington had veto power over it.[16]

During the Rome deliberations, a team of U.S. Senate Foreign Relations Committee members (the Subcommittee on International Operations) and staffers visited the conference, attending meetings and meeting delegates during their weeklong stay. At the end of their stay, they held a closed-door meeting with the American delegation. Marc Thiessen, a spokesperson for Helms, said that the group still "considers the ICC to be the most dangerous threat to national sovereignty since the League of Nations." American taxpayers, he concluded, "would not want to spend a single dollar for a Court that Washington does not support."[17] The head of the group, U.S. Senator Rod Grams (R-Minn.) told those in attendance that "this court is truly a monster, and it is a monster that must be slain."[18]

The message from the United States before the Rome deliberations even began in June 1998 was clarion: the United States would not support an ICC that could place Americans, civilian and military alike, in legal jeopardy. The message was like other messages the Clinton administration had sent to the UN since 1993.

## Molecular Movement toward Creation of the ICC: 1919–1998

The concept of a permanent ICC emerged in 1919 when the Allies crafted the Versailles Peace Treaty, signed reluctantly by Germany that year. One of the hundreds of articles in the treaty called for the creation of an international criminal tribunal to try Germans accused of committing war crimes in violation of the Hague Treaties of 1899 and 1907.[19] Given the unwillingness of the United States to implement that and other war crimes articles in the treaty (Articles 227–230), as well as the desire of the victorious Allies, "in the interest of regional stability and political agendas,"[20] to forgo its implementation, no international criminal tribunal was created.

These post-1919 events led one scholar to write that they "exemplified the sacrifice of justice on the altars of international and domestic politics of the Allies. . . . [The Allies] missed the opportunity to establish an international system of justice that would have functioned independently of political considerations to ensure uncompromised justice."[21] In 1926, a permanent ICC was again proposed in the League of Nations, but nothing came of it. During the interwar period, 1920–1937, nothing further was proposed by either the Allies or the League of Nations.

The horrors the world glimpsed at the end of the European (1939–1945) and Pacific (1937–1945) wars led the UN to reexamine the possibility of an ICC.[22] After the ad hoc Nuremberg and Tokyo war crimes trials ended, and with the adoption of the Convention on the Prevention and Punishment of the Crime of Genocide in 1948, there was renewed interest in the creation of a permanent ICC with jurisdiction over the actions of individuals that violated the Nuremberg Principles, the Genocide Convention, and the revised 1949 Geneva Protocols on the conduct of war on land and sea.

Article VI of the 1948 Genocide Convention was, in certain respects, a watershed section. It provided that persons charged with genocide "shall be tried by a competent tribunal of the State in the territory of which the act was committed *or by such international penal tribunal as may have jurisdiction.*" This language introduced the world community to the concept of *complementarity* in international law. A national authority has first crack at bringing to justice persons who commit war crimes, genocide, or crimes against humanity. Another consequence of the 1948 convention was the notion that crimes against humanity and genocide were so universally abominable that an offender could be tried in the domestic criminal court of any nation. The brutal actions were considered "crimes of *universal jurisdiction*, meaning that all who commit them can be tried in any court, even if the court has no connection with the crime." Complementarity and universal jurisdiction underscore the precedential point that if "national authorities are 'unwilling or unable' to carry out a genuine investigation and prosecution," then a regional or an international penal tribunal has jurisdiction to investigate and, if appropriate, to prosecute.[23]

The General Assembly, in the 1948 Convention, also invited the creation of a UN committee "to study the desirability and possibility of establishing an international judicial organ for the trial of persons charged with genocide." The UN mandated that the International Law Commission (ILC), a UN General Assembly body created to implement Article XIII of the UN Charter,[24] codify the Nuremberg Principles and prepare a draft statute for the establishment of a permanent ICC. Draft statutes were submitted in 1951 and 1953, but no further action was taken. In 1948, with the onset of the cold war between the United States and its allies and the Soviet Union and its "captive" socialist nations, interest in the creation of an ICC "ebbed because of the fear that a powerful court could be manipulated for political ends."[25]

With the collapse of the Soviet Union's "evil empire" in 1989, along with the "freedom" revolutions that took place across Eastern Europe, the idea of a permanent ICC was renewed. In that year, the Trinidad and Tobago delegate, speaking for a group of sixteen Caribbean and Latin American countries in the General Assembly, called for the establishment of an international court to prosecute international drug traffickers. On November 25, 1992, the General Assembly passed a resolution requesting the ILC to prepare a draft statute for a permanent ICC.

In 1993 and 1994, the UN Security Council created the ad hoc war crimes tribunals for the former Yugoslavia and Rwanda, respectively. Viewing the negatives of these ICTs—the slow start-up, the personnel problems, the management and financial inefficiencies, and the inordinate delays in getting to trial—as well as the positives—the eventual incarceration of some of those indicted, followed by trials and convictions of war criminals and those who committed genocide—many nations insisted that the UN encourage the creation of a permanent ICC.

In November 1994, the ILC presented a draft treaty to the UN General Assembly, and on December 9, 1994, that body created an ad hoc committee to review the seminal issues in the draft treaty. In 1995, the ad hoc committee recommended the establishment of a UN preparatory committee (PrepCom) that would hold a series of meetings to refine and redraft the ILC proposal.

PrepCom was established and given the task of examining the ILC work, making changes in the draft statute, and recommending further action by the UN on the question of the establishment of a permanent ICC. Its chairperson was Adriaan Bos (Netherlands). All member states of the UN were permitted to send delegates to the PrepCom sessions (as well as members of specialized agencies and members of the International Atomic Energy Agency).

There were six committee sessions between 1996 and early 1998, as well as a drafting committee meeting in the Netherlands in January 1998. To manage the complex issues associated with the establishment of an ICC, the PrepCom was divided into eight smaller working groups, including the Working Group on Definitions and Elements of Crimes, the Working Group on General Principles of International Law, the Working Group on Procedural Matters, the Working Group on International Cooperation and Judicial Assistance, and the Working Group on Penalties.

The first session was held in New York on March 25–April 12, 1996. The agenda focused on the jurisdiction of the ICC, definitions of the core crimes that would fall under its jurisdiction, trigger mechanisms (an extremely contentious issue then and now), and general principles of international criminal law. Alternative drafts of the ICC statute were the outcome of the meeting.

Between August 12 and 30, 1996, PrepCom, meeting again in New York, turned its attention to procedural questions, issues of fair trials and rights of defendants, organizational questions, and the relationship of the proposed ICC to the Security Council and to the UN. In December 1996, the General Assembly scheduled a diplomatic conference on the establishment of a permanent ICC, to be held in 1998. Italy immediately offered to host the meeting in Rome.

The third meeting of PrepCom, February 11–12, 1997, saw the delegates begin redrafting the ILC statute, which would be the basis of deliberations in Rome. They focused on the definitions of core crimes that fell under the new court's jurisdiction (genocide, war crimes, aggression, and crimes against humanity), as well as the general principles of international law and penalties for those found guilty of committing one or more of the core crimes. At this session, no fewer than six draft statutes were reviewed by the delegates.

A fourth meeting of PrepCom, held on August 4–15, 1997, examined the contentious "trigger mechanism," that is, the manner by which ICC proceedings would be initiated, and, equally contentious, the issue of "complementariness," that is, the relationship between the ICC and national jurisdiction. At the fifth meeting, held December 1–12, 1997, PrepCom continued discussions on international cooperation, extradition, and penalties and general principles of international criminal law. The sixth meeting, held in New York City on March 16–April 3, 1998, focused on preparation of the draft statute's text for consideration by the delegates in Rome.

After the sixth meeting, a draft statute was adopted and presented to Kofi Annan, the UN's new secretary-general. The draft statute was 167 pages long, with 13 parts, 116 articles, and 478 bracketed passages indicating words that were disputed by one or more states.[26] It was the foundation for the debates and bargaining at the Diplomatic Conference on the Establishment of an ICC. PrepCom had done a great deal of work since 1996: the ILC draft statute had contained only sixty articles, half the number contained in the final draft.[27]

## Participants at the Rome Conference on the Establishment of a Permanent ICC: June–July 1998

Of the 185 member states of the UN, 161 sent representatives to Rome for the conference, officially called the United Nations Diplomatic Conference of Plenipotentiaries on the Establishment of an International Criminal Court. There were 235 accredited NGOs in attendance at the Rome deliberations that began on June 15, 1998, and ended on July 17, 1998. These NGOs were all 'under one organizational roof: the Coalition for an Independent Criminal Court (CICC). Workers for the CICC were vital to the final actions of the conferees. The CICC continually lobbied for the strongest, most independent ICC that could be created. Additionally, the CICC served as the circulator of information to the delegates in Rome.

A list of some of the CICC groups illustrates the representational breadth of this important cohort, with its many hundreds of professional and volunteer workers who monitored every committee and subcommittee session during the four and a half weeks of deliberation:

American Bar Association
Amnesty International
Association Internationale de Droit Penal
Baha'i International Community
B'nai B'rith International
Carter Center
Center for the Development of International Law
Coordinating Board of Jewish Organizations
DePaul Institute for Human Rights
European Law Students Association
Equality NOW
FN-Forbundet
Global Policy Forum
Human Rights Watch
Instituto Superiore Internazionale de Scienze Criminali
International Commission of Jurists
International Human Rights Law Group
Lawyers Committee for Human Rights
No Peace without Justice

Parliamentarians for Global Action
Quaker UN Office
Transnational Radical Party
United Nations Association–USA
War and Peace Foundation
World Federalist Movement
World Order Models Project

As one observer in attendance at the Rome deliberations wrote:

> The Coalition . . . monitored all of the working committees of the Conference, and provided vital head counts of the countries that had declared themselves for or against the many contentious issues facing the delegations. Delegations from smaller countries lacked the personnel to keep in touch with the many simultaneous meetings. . . . In the end, the CICC also helped to strengthen the resolve of the "like-minded" countries to resist the pressure applied by the United States.[28]

These NGOs and their staffers were joined by the diplomatic plenipotentiaries from 161 nations. Fifty years after the Nuremberg and Tokyo trials ended, fifty years after the Genocide Convention and the Universal Declaration of Human Rights were adopted by the UN,[29] the 50th UN General Assembly placed on its agenda the establishment of a permanent ICC. However, the draft treaty that was the basis of the Rome sessions contained almost 500 disputed options that the delegates had to resolve. Further confounding the dynamics of the Rome conference were the concerns of the United States and other major powers about the emergent ICC. As the London *Economist* editorialized:

> After nearly four years of intense negotiations among some 120 countries, the effort to set up the world criminal court has run smack into the ambivalence that has always been felt by the world's biggest powers about international law: they are keen to have it apply to others in the name of world order, but loath to submit to restrictions on their own sovereignty.[30]

## Three Major Unresolved Issues

When the representatives arrived in Rome, there were three major questions left open by PrepCom for the delegates to answer: (1) What would be the relationship of the ICC and the UN Security Council? (2) Was there to be the creation of a truly independent Prosecutor's Office? and (3) What were the core crimes that made up the jurisdiction of the ICC? The "heart of the debate" before and during the Rome conference was "the scope of the UN's Security Council involvement in deciding whether or not the ICC takes up a particular case." Could a permanent member of the Security Council veto the ICC's ability to investigate and to prosecute war criminals?[31]

The PrepCom draft that the representatives brought with them to Rome had hundreds of options available for answering these difficult issues and others. For example, Section 23 (1) of the draft treaty stated that only states party to the treaty and the UN Security Council could refer "situations" to the prosecutor for investigation and prosecution. However, a fundamental option discussed in Rome was whether the Prosecutor's Office could or should institute proceedings on its own authority.

A number of states, especially the United States, fought against that option, fearing an overzealous, politically motivated prosecutor, but to no avail. Many delegations maintained that the draft treaty did have constraints on the prosecutor: impeachment, "complementariness," and Article 23 (3), stating that the Security Council had the power to prescribe the actions of the prosecutor in a situation that was "being handled" by the Security Council.

The "core crimes" jurisdiction of the ICC was generally accepted by the delegates: genocide, crimes against humanity, and substantive war crimes. Jurisdictional options presented in the draft treaty included wars of "aggression," terrorism, and treaty-based crimes.

Opposing the American positions on accountability, prosecutorial independence, and the relationship of the ICC to the Security Council were the great majority of the nations present. In the center of the opposition was a group of forty-two nations (ultimately over eighty nations were in the group) led by Great Britain, Canada, and Argentina, called the "Like-Minded Group."[32] This group of delegates, working with the 264 NGOs and human rights associations that were in Rome to observe and to lobby for a strong ICC, pushed for the selection of options for the final treaty that would create a truly independent ICC, free of Security Council (read U.S.) control.

Elisa Massimino, with LCHR–USA, said of her government's position: "[a veto power in the Security Council] would eviscerate the court's effectiveness." The NGOs and the human rights groups, especially those from the United States, saw Rome "as a classic opportunity for President Clinton to assert what they consider a moral prerogative: to craft a treaty which creates an ICC with enough safeguards to avoid frivolous pursuits, but enough independence to investigate the major powers, if it must."[33]

President Clinton, obviously overwhelmed by the ongoing investigation of his sex life by an aggressive independent prosecutor, and accepting the Pentagon's arguments about the weaknesses of the treaty, did not rise to the occasion.[34]

## U.S. Concerns

The problem faced by the national representatives and NGOs at the Rome conference was that the U.S. delegation, as a matter of principle and policy, was unwilling to compromise on its insistence of a veto power for the five permanent members of the Security Council. Since PrepCom began meeting in 1996, the U.S. position had been unvarying: actions of U.S. citizens, especially the U.S. military, "will always remain beyond the conceivable reach of such an [international criminal] court."[35] David Scheffer, head of the U.S. delegation, said, the "Security Council needs to be a very significant player in the operation of this court."[36] The major areas of concern for the Clinton administration were as follows:

1. *How cases come to the ICC.* The U.S. view was that there must be limits on prosecutorial powers. The ICC's ability to hear cases must be determined by the Security Council, either through referral or though a Security Council veto of proposed ICC action, and by states that refer cases to the ICC.
2. *National court versus ICC action.* The U.S. position on this issue was that "complementariness" must limit the scope of the ICC only to "grave" situations in which a nation's criminal justice system did not, could not, or would not take action against persons within its jurisdiction who were accused of genocide. The ICC could not substitute for a national prosecution of alleged war criminals.
3. *Definition of criminal procedures and guarantees for the protection of sovereign states.*[37] The U.S. position, expressed by its ambassador, was that the rights of governments that refused to cooperate with ICC investigations and trials had to be ensured by the Security Council. From the time deliberations surrounding the creation of an ICC became serious, Washington was and "remains strongly opposed to giving an international prosecutor the right to initiate cases."[38]

The U.S. delegation was also unwilling to compromise on its view that the ICC had substantive limitations on its jurisdiction. The Americans insisted, both before and during the Rome meetings, that the ICC, before it could begin an investigation, must secure the consent of any state that had an "interest" in the case. For one of the American delegates, the U.S.

unwillingness to compromise on this issue was America's "nuclear bomb" in the tense negotiations.[39]

This attitude of the Americans was not unusual. From its refusal to join the League of Nations in 1919 to the crises over U.S. membership in the UN (1945) and acceptance of the World Court's jurisdiction, the United States continually opted for the primacy of national sovereignty. It took four decades for the United States to ratify, with substantive reservations, the 1948 Genocide Convention. And just a few years prior to the Rome conference, the United States refused to sign a treaty banning the use of land mines that had been signed by over 100 other nations.[40]

The majority of delegations blocked efforts by the United States, France, and China to delay the creation of the ICC. Further, the majority added language that automatically extended the jurisdiction of the ICC to cover genocide, crimes against humanity, and war crimes. The polar view of the majority in Rome was that the American "position in the ICC negotiations would compromise the court's independence and credibility by politicizing the most crucial decisions—namely, determining which cases the ICC will be able to consider."[41]

The United States was not happy, for example, with the Singapore compromise proposal, proffered before the Rome conference even began. It proposed that the Security Council could opt to take action to delay or forestall ICC investigations and prosecutions. It would take the veto action of one of the five permanent members to halt the ICC's actions—if there was agreement from the other four and a majority vote of the entire Security Council. Prior to Rome, only Great Britain endorsed the proposal. There was also an American unwillingness to compromise on the role of the Prosecutor's Office, which the United States believed should be circumscribed and limited.

## U.S. Arguments against Ratification of the Rome Statute

The United States' concerns about the direction the conference was taking were both practical and legal, said Scheffer.

> On the practical side, no other nation matches the extent of U.S. overseas military commitments through alliances and special missions such as current peacekeeping commitments in the former Yugoslavia. . . . We don't have the luxury of not considering those factors. [On the legal side], the proposed treaty violates a fundamental principle of international law that a treaty cannot be applied to a state that is not a party to it.

With the withering away of the Soviet Empire in 1989, the United States was the world's only superpower, providing the bulk of finances and military personnel for the various peacekeeping actions of the UN. As Scheffer said in another sharp statement: "We constantly have troops serving abroad on humanitarian missions, rescue operations, or missions to destroy weapons of mass destruction. . . . Someone out there isn't going to like it, but we're the ones who do it. [And U.S. personnel must be protected from the possibility of politically inspired legal actions in the ICC.]"[42]

Because of their presence in Asia, Europe, the Middle East, and the Pacific, American personnel were potentially vulnerable to charges that they had committed grave crimes that fell under the ICC's jurisdiction. The bottom line for the Pentagon and hence for the United States was: "It is in our collective interest that the personnel of our militaries and civilian commands be able to fulfill their many legitimate responsibilities without *unjustified* exposure to criminal legal proceedings."[43]

Scheffer also focused on the principle of national sovereignty, an extremely powerful concept defended by most members of the House of Representatives and the Senate. He said, months before Rome, that "the . . . bedrock of international law [was the] threshold of [national] sovereignty."[46] For the Americans, the commitment to the vitality of national sovereignty, in the face of growing demands for international agencies that preempted national law, had to be firm and unyielding. If not, the United States would confront two choices: remain committed to treaties that involved U.S. forces (thereby subjecting them to the jurisdiction of the ICC), or pull its military troops out of these missions to avoid the possibility of a zealous prosecutor investigating and indicting U.S. military leaders for allegedly committing war crimes.

On June 17, 1998, Ambassador Bill Richardson presented the U.S. policy on the question of nation-state and international law to the assembled delegates and NGOs. It contained basic principles of American policy, as well as using the categorical word "must" six times in the following excerpt regarding the establishment of the ICC. His country's views remained seriously at odds with the views of almost all those in attendance:

> We *must* recognize the reality of the international system today. . . . [The ICC] will not act in a political vacuum. Experience teaches us that we *must* carefully distinguish between what looks good on paper and what works in the real world. . . . The ICC cannot stand alone. . . . The U.S. believes that the Security Council *must* play an important role in the work of a permanent court. . . . [Furthermore], the ICC *must* work in coordination, not in conflict, with states. The Court *must* complement national jurisdiction and encourage national state action wherever possible. . . . We *must* not turn the ICC—or its Prosecutor—into a human rights ombudsman, open to, and responsible for responding to, any and all complaints from any source. . . . An ICC will succeed only if governments draft a treaty that melds effectively the proper roles of individual states, their national judicial systems, the Security Council, and the UN itself. The U.S., which has been so instrumental in establishing [ad hoc] international tribunals from Nuremberg to Arusha, will continue to seek actively the achievement of this important objective.

The United States established, in statements such as the above, *de minimus* lines beyond which it would not go. In the end, although there was U.S. agreement on some changes to the language of the ICC treaty, especially the concept of complementarity, the delegation did not go beyond the line drawn by the Pentagon and the president.

## Domestic Woes for the President and U.S. Opposition to the ICC

Early in the PrepCom work on the ICC draft statute, on October 31, 1996, U.S. ambassador to the UN Bill Richardson spoke in the General Assembly. In the relatively brief speech, although supporting the concept of a permanent ICC, he warned the UN about his country's serious problems with the proposed ICC. The gravest concerns for the Americans were the "trigger mechanism" issue and the need for "checks and balances with respect to the powers and the decisions of a single Prosecutor."

> There are some who argue that the Security Council will politicize the work of the Court, that it will undermine the Court's independence. [Regarding the perception that] the Security Council is a political body, and its actions are therefore wholly suspect, . . . while individual governments and individual Tribunal staff are objective, non political, and reliable, [that is an incorrect view]. . . . The Security Council transcends the individual political views and agendas of each specific member. It is an institution with checks and balances and an essential, objective mission to fulfill. . . .

> There is also a need for checks and balances with respect to the decisions of a single Prosecutor, who in theory also could be influenced by *personal and political considerations*. If the Prosecutor has sole discretion to initiate investigations and file complaints—as some delegations have sought under the rubric of "inherent jurisdiction"—*the results could be more idiosyncratic, possibly even more political, than the decisions of the Security Council* [emphasis added].

Richardson's words about the ICC prosecutor possibly being "influenced by personal and political considerations" went to the heart of one set of American objections to the Rome statute. Michael Sharf's reactions to the ambassador's speech are appropriate: "There's a fear the ICC's prosecutor will become an independent counsel for the universe. The actions of Independent Prosecutor Kenneth Starr," he continued, have "fueled anxiety about an ICC prosecutor untrammeled by Security Council oversight."[45] The Clinton administration, in small part, continually pushed for Security Council control of the ICC's Prosecutor's Office because of its real fear of a prosecutor "running wild." This fear of an independent prosecutor intruding into the domestic life of a sovereign nation-state has been expressed throughout the twentieth century. It led the United States to reject the call for an international tribunal to bring the kaiser to justice after the First World War, to defeat President Wilson's efforts to get America to join the League of Nations, and to take four decades to ratify the Genocide Convention. In the Clinton administration, that "evil" person had a face and a name. The Clinton White House had a vision of an international Kenneth Starr.[46]

For the Americans, there was and remains a fundamental unwillingness to surrender national sovereignty to an international prosecutor with the ideological drive and political agenda of a Ken Starr. Therefore, in a basic way the ICC "must" be answerable to the world's major powers, the five permanent members of the Security Council (the United States, Russia, China, France, and Great Britain).

The Americans were accused by the other delegations of erecting a "serious roadblock" to consensus about the ICC. The American view, "that it must be able to veto any effort [by the Prosecutor's Office] to investigate and prosecute,"[47] was pronounced daily at the Rome deliberations, much to the anger and chagrin of a number of its allies as well as third-world delegations. Among the five permanent Security Council members, only Great Britain categorically rejected the American views. President Clinton and his representatives at Rome wanted "to see a court emerge, as long as it was a court they can control," said Richard Dicker, the spokesperson for Human Rights Watch, one of the NGOs present at the deliberations in Rome.[48]

Critics of the U.S. position on the ICC's jurisdiction and independence referred to it as a "neocolonial" policy. The United States was also seen as an uncomfortable member of a very small group of strange bedfellows that included Libya, Iraq, and China. Louise Arbour, the Canadian prosecutor for the Bosnian and Rwandan ICTs, along with the rest of her Canadian cohort, repeatedly called for the creation of an ICC "with considerable independent prosecutorial power. . . . [This independence] was crucial to the success of a permanent tribunal," she said. Furthermore,

> an organization should not be constructed on the assumption that it will be run by incompetent people, acting in bad faith, for improper purposes. It's better to equip the prosecution well but to keep him or her under some kind of institutional leash by some kind of impeachment process.[49]

Lloyd Axworthy, the Canadian foreign minister, admonished the United States about its hard-and-fast position on the relationship between the ICC and the Security Council. He said, "You need to have a court with teeth even if you have to sacrifice some participation."[50]

The Americans professed "dismay" over the extreme idealism of most of the supporters of an ICC that would give substantive powers to the prosecutor and have a broad-based jurisdiction. Said Scheffer, "That's unrealistic: these things (ICC) work when governments such as the U.S. use their clout to make it work."[51]

## The Rome Statute Emerges: Specifics

The PrepCom draft statute that the Rome deliberations were based on was 167 pages long; it was divided into 13 parts and contained 116 articles. Only 2 of the 13 part titles (3 and 8) were changed—very slightly—in the final draft of the ICC, approved by 120 nations at the end of the Rome conference in July 1998. The numbering of the articles also changed as a consequence of the deliberations, because articles were added; the final Rome statute contained 128 articles. The section headings for the 13 parts of the PrepCom draft suggest the agenda for those in working in Rome:

*Part 1. Establishment of the Court* (Articles 1–4), including general observations about its relationship with the UN.

*Part 2. Jurisdiction, Admissibility, and Applicable Law* (Articles 5–20). This part contained many options for the delegates to discuss and choose among, regarding controversial issues such as the ICC's jurisdiction, core crimes, the trigger mechanism, the role of the prosecutor, complementarity, and the law to be applied by the ICC in deciding cases.

*Part 3. General Principles of International Law* (Articles 21–34), called *General Principles of Criminal Law* in the final draft. Individual responsibility for genocide and other war crimes, recognized at Nuremberg, was a conceptual anchor in this part of the draft statute. Draft Article 23 (final treaty Article 25) held that such individuals were individually responsible and liable for punishment for their crimes. Article 31 (in both versions) laid out exceptions to individual responsibility: mental illness, intoxication, and threats to one's life.

*Part 4. Composition and Administration of the Court* (Articles 35–53). This part essentially replicated the composition and administration of the two ad hoc tribunals of the 1990s: Yugoslavia and Rwanda. Articles in this section, borrowing from the two ICTs, discussed the role and functions of the Presidency, the Appeals Chamber, the Office of the Prosecutor, and the Registry and the qualifications of ICC judges.

*Part 5. Investigation and Prosecution* (Articles 54–61). This section dealt with investigational and prosecutorial aspects of the international criminal justice process, including due process for those suspected of committing genocide and other crimes.

*Part 6. The Trial* (Articles 62–74). These articles addressed the various aspects of the trial proceedings, including the rights of the accused, the protection of witnesses and victims, and the issue of reparation for victims.

*Part 7. Penalties* (Articles 75–79). The segment limited punishment to imprisonment. The absence of the death penalty led to heated discussions in Rome.

*Part 8. Appeal and Review* (Articles 80–84), called *Appeal and Revision* in the final draft. This part addressed issues relating to the appeal and review of judicial decisions.

*Part 9. International Cooperation and Judicial Assistance* (Articles 85–92).

*Part 10. Enforcement* (Articles 93–101). States that were party to the treaty had to enforce the judgments of the ICC by providing, at their discretion, prison facilities for convicted defendants.

*Part 11. Assembly of States Parties* (Article 102) dealt with the oversight of the ICC divisions by states that ratified the Rome treaty.

*Part 12. Financing of the Court* (Articles 103–107).

*Part 13. Final Clauses* (Articles 108–116) created parameters for states to file reservations and amendments to the ICC statute, for review of the statute, and for its ratification and entry into force.

The Rome conference began with four days of speech making and public celebrations. The size of the national delegations ranged from one person (Nicaragua) to the fifty delegates representing the host nation, Italy. The five permanent members of the Security Council had large delegations: United States, forty; France, forty; Great Britain, twenty-one; China, fifteen; and Russia, eleven.

Divergent views were expressed by the delegates in the opening speeches, especially "concerning the relationship between the Court and the Security Council and the power of the Prosecutor to initiate investigations."[52] These were huge political decisions that had to be made if there was to be an ICC statute. Their difficulty made the Rome meeting a "lengthy, tense, and divided conference."[53] The delegates began tackling the major unresolved issues, which were intensely political in nature, and the politics of bargaining and compromise took place in the daily informal meetings in Rome.

There were, as one onlooker wrote, several levels of work at Rome. There were plenary sessions at the beginning and end of the convention. The Committee of the Whole, chaired by Canadian Phillipe Kirsch, delegated the work of revising the PrepCom draft treaty to eight smaller working groups. Once the deliberations began, given the time line for concluding the treaty drafting process, there were daily, lengthy sessions of the working groups, often as long as fifteen hours.

There were two types of daily meetings, an observer noted. The daily public work sessions consisted of delegates speaking for hours on end on the agenda items for that working group. There was no debate, just speeches translated into a number of languages by UN translators. The second type was referred to as "informals," the daily off-the-record meetings of "serious players" trying to resolve hotly debated differences on specific issues within the domain of that working group. The "real negotiations took place elsewhere, either bilaterally, or in delegations that met together, but outside the format of the Conference itself."[54]

On July 8, Kirsch addressed the group. He presented a set of ten basic questions that had to be answered if there was to be closure. Six of the unresolved issues involved the complex problem of defining the scope of "serious crimes," and the other four focused on the ICC's powers. The two most contentious issues remaining at the Rome conference were the questions of automatic jurisdiction of the ICC and whether the prosecutor would be an independent officer of the ICC.

The first set of questions dealt with the definition of "aggression," whether "treaty crimes" would be included in the treaty, and whether war crimes and genocide that occurred during internal armed strife fell within the jurisdiction of the statute. The four jurisdictional questions Kirsch raised were: What was the jurisdiction of the ICC? What were the trigger mechanisms (i.e., was there to be automatic jurisdiction)? Should the prosecutor be independent (i.e., with *propio motu* power [power on his own initiative])?[55] What was the role of the Security Council regarding jurisdiction and an independent prosecutor?

The U.S. delegation's response to the working agenda presented by Kirsch was quick and unchanged: the new court must not have automatic jurisdiction over cases involving war crimes and crimes against humanity. Automatic jurisdiction of the ICC should apply only to genocide, the U.S. statement concluded. States must give their consent before the ICC could proceed with an investigation involving other charges. The response on the part of the opposing delegations was to essentially write off the United States as a substantive participant in the negotiations. In exasperation, the associate counsel of Human Rights Watch said to reporters in Rome that "on some key issues of the court's jurisdiction [the U.S.] position is closer to that of Iraq and Pakistan than such close allies as Britain and Canada."[56] Kirsch did not include the U.S. position paper on these issues because it was "so indefensible."[57]

The head of the LCHR, Jelena Pejic, issued a statement maintaining that

> such U.S. inflexibility at this late date sharply increases the chances that the U.S. is simply going to be left behind by this conference. . . . The U.S. approach would create a court that the Pol Pots of the world could laugh at. The U.S. is in effect saying that you should ask Pol Pot's permission before you can bring him before the court. It would gut the court.[58]

Over the next week, these and other controversial questions were hammered out in the "informals." American delegates were in attendance in all of them, and their position was the losing one. In the last two days of the Rome conference, another tough speech by Scheffer and a potent rumor swept across the conference that further eroded the U.S. position on the issues and isolated the U.S. delegation. At a press conference on July 15, 1998, Scheffer said that the world stands "on the eve of the conference's conclusion without having found a solution. We fear that governments *whose nations make up at least two thirds of the world's population* will find the emerging text unacceptable. The world desperately needs this mechanism for international justice, but it must be a community, not a club" (emphasis added). The immediate response of the LCHR was one of "dismay." The head of the LCHR said:

> The U.S. is saying "our way or no way." It is making a thinly veiled threat to get what it wants in the ICC package "or else." We can just imagine what the "or else" might be. . . . President Clinton has not backed up his words [about the necessity of an ICC] with deeds at this conference. This Court is squarely in the U.S. national interest, but President Clinton is pandering to the lobby of fear.[59]

On July 16, 1998, the *International Herald Tribune* carried a story confirming a rumor that had spread like wildfire the previous day. The rumor "at the Conference was that the U.S. was threatening poor nations with a loss of aid and its NATO allies with the reduction of U.S. military support."[60] The *Tribune* story quoted "talking points" prepared for U.S. Secretary of Defense William Cohen, including the following: "If Germany succeeded in lobbying for 'universal jurisdiction' for the court, the U.S. might retaliate by removing its overseas troops, including those in Europe."[61]

The Rome conference required, for passage of the treaty, a two-thirds vote of the 161 delegations. The minimum number required was 107; in the end, 120 voted in favor of the draft treaty. On the final day of the Rome conference, July 17, 1998, the U.S. delegation requested a roll-call vote on the treaty. Three permanent Security Council members, Russia, France, and Great Britain, voted for the statute; the United States and China voted against it. Five other nations also opposed the treaty—Israel,[62] Libya, Iraq, Qatar, and Yemen—"leaving the U.S. in unfamiliar—and no doubt unwelcome—company."[63]

Some saw the U.S. negative vote as a strategic blunder as well. By not signing the Rome statute, "a largely nonbinding gesture," the United States could not participate in the follow-up meetings of PrepCom "in drafting procedural rules, defining elements of crimes, financing arrangements and other matters [including] the preliminary selection of a prosecutor and judges."[64]

The treaty is open for nations to sign until December 31, 2000. It will enter into force when ratified by at least sixty nations. By mid-September 1998, about sixty nations had signed the treaty, including France, Greece, the Netherlands, Spain, and Switzerland. Ratification comes after the initial signing of the document.

The week after the Rome conference ended, Michael Posner, the executive director of LCHR, gave a briefing in the U.S. State Department. He argued that supporting the ICC would lessen the need for U.S. forces to be sent to crises around the globe: "Once established, such a Court will deter gross abuses, such as genocide, that may otherwise require U.S. military involvement." Added Jerry Fowler, the LCHR's legislative counsel: "An effective Court also will deter the commission of war crimes against U.S. military personnel when they are deployed overseas. It will help break the impunity of those who commit genocide, crimes against humanity, and war crimes."[65]

## Part 2 of the Rome Statute: Addressing the Major Issues

Part 2 was the centrally important—and very controversial, from the U.S. perspective— "Jurisdiction, Admissibility, and Applicable Law" section of the Rome statute. It contained sixteen articless (5–20), some of which were included after some bitter clashes between the United States and the majority of states participating in the conference.

Article 5 focused on the threshold for ICC jurisdiction: The ICC "shall be limited to the most serious crimes of concern to the international community as a whole (genocide, war crimes, crimes against humanity, and the crime of aggression [when it was defined at a subsequent time, but no sooner than seven years after the Rome statute comes into force])." At least 73 percent of the nations participating in the discussion, sixty-four states, voted for automatic ICC jurisdiction for all three core crimes, whereas the United States and twenty others voted for automatic jurisdiction for crimes of genocide only, with an (extremely unlikely) "opt in" by an affected state for the other core crimes.

There was no disagreement on the definition of genocide. Article 6 was taken from the 1948 Genocide Convention. Article 7, "Crimes against Humanity," covered actions committed by either official or nongovernmental actors in either peacetime or time of armed conflict. Further, the article authorized the ICC to prosecute forcible transfers of population, severe deprivation of physical liberty, rape, sexual slavery, enforced prostitution, forced pregnancy, and persecution on political, racial, national, ethnic, cultural, religious, gender, or other grounds that are universally recognized as impermissible under international law. The language used to enumerate these core crimes was, to American delegates and others, too amorphous and general. Many of the criminal acts were ill defined. For example, the statute used such phrases as "mental harm" and "committing outrages on personal dignity."

Article 8 (1), agreed on by 80 percent of the nations voting (thirty-nine), stated that there was ICC jurisdiction "in particular, when" war crimes were committed as part of a plan or conspiracy. The losing position, argued by the United States and eight other nations, was that there should be ICC jurisdiction "only when" war crimes were committed as part of a plan or conspiracy. Article 8 (2) provided the ICC with jurisdiction over war crimes committed in both international and noninternational (internal) armed conflict.

Article 12 (1) provided for automatic jurisdiction by the ICC over all three core crimes. (To obtain French agreement to the Rome statute, a "transitional provision," Article 124, was added. It allowed a nation that was party to the treaty to "opt out" of court jurisdiction for alleged war crimes for a period of seven years following the "entry into force of the Statute for the Party concerned.") However, Article 12 (2) did not provide "universal jurisdiction" to accompany the automatic jurisdiction. Absent a referral by the Security Council, the ICC can take up a case *only* when submitted to it by a state party *or* initiated by the prosecutor when either the state on whose territory the crime was committed or the state of the accused's nationality is a state party or has accepted the ICC's jurisdiction over the crime on an ad hoc basis. (Article 12 [2] is a limitation on the ICC until all states are parties to the statute, thereby making it universal.)

There emerged, as a result, the Article 12 paradox. Even if the United States, for example, did not ratify the Rome statute, its military and civilian forces would be subject to ICC jurisdiction so long as the nation in which the alleged war crimes took place had ratified the statute and could not or would not try the American soldiers charged with war crimes or other crimes of universal jurisdiction. In contrast, the opt-out clause in Article 12 enabled nation-states that had committed war crimes and were party to the Rome statute not to be exposed to ICC jurisdiction, for at least seven years, and possibly for decades.

The controversial issue of whether the Prosecutor's Office had independent power was addressed in Article 15(1) of the Rome treaty. The U.S. position was convincingly rejected by 83 percent of the nations participating. By a vote of sixty-three to thirteen, the delegates adopted language that gave the prosecutor independent power to investigate and to initiate prosecutions. In addition, as noted in Article 13(b) and (c), cases could be referred to the Prosecutor's Office by the Security Council or by a state that was party to the treaty. To dampen concern on the part of some states about the discretionary powers of the prosecutor in initiating investigations, Articles 15(3)(4) and 18 were grafted onto this part of the statute. The former requires the prosecutor to obtain judicial approval by the Chambers at an early stage of the ICC actions. Article 18 enables an "interested party" to challenge the admissibility of a case at an early stage in the ICC proceedings.

The Singapore compromise, allowing the Security Council to defer a case for one year, was included in the final Rome statute as Article 16. It enabled the Security Council, when necessary for "peacekeeping" purposes, to halt ICC actions for one year: "No investigation or prosecution may be commenced or proceeded with under this statute for a period of 12 months after the Security Council, in a resolution adopted under Chapter VII of the Charter of the UN,[66] has requested the Court to that effect; the request may be renewed by the Council under the same conditions." Fifty-three nations opted for the one-year deferral; the United States and four other nations voted for the "unspecified number of years" deferral option.

## The ICC: Political Expediency over Justice?

In addition to the Pentagon, foreign policy personnel in the White House, and U.S. senators such as Jesse Helms,[67] there were others who harshly condemned the creation of the permanent ICC as an idealistic, utopian project that had no hope of being actualized in practice. Given the primacy of the nation-state system and the foreign policy agendas of major powers such as the United States, it was nonsense to think about an effective supernational criminal court.

There was "unwarranted enthusiasm for the ICC," wrote critics after the Rome meetings ended in July 1998.[68] The events that had transpired in Rome were an acknowledgment of the reality that the world is "facing moral and political challenges posed by the world of genocide and 'ethnic cleansing' in which we find ourselves." And law, wrote David Rieff, "cannot rescue us from situations from which politics and statecraft have failed to deliver us."[69]

The ICC was too weak—basically without universal jurisdiction, for example—to deal with internal civil wars and the accompanying genocide, but just strong enough to impinge on the sovereignty of individual states. The prosecutor's powers and the ICC's jurisdiction were limited in the treaty: there is no jurisdiction over genocide, crimes against humanity, and war crimes committed in an internal armed conflict by states that have not signed the treaty— unless a Pol Pot-type leader "opts in" to the Rome statute.

At bottom, the critics are pessimistic about human nature: world behavior has not changed since Nuremberg and Tokyo. Nations are lawless and understand only force, not the abstractions of international law. Hubert Vedrine, the French foreign minister, noted that the "world . . . isn't getting any stronger, with 25 regional conflicts involving 40 countries."[70] These wars, the majority of them internal conflicts, continue unabated as the world approaches the millennium, occasionally involving Security Council peacekeeping action in light of Article 24 of the UN Charter.

Criminals, they claim, are not deterred by international laws and customs of war. Armed force, as proposed by General Dallaire in Rwanda in January 1994, not law, can prevent genocide and other crimes against humanity. So long as there is the cruel Hobbesian state of nature, where life is short and brutish, these critics maintain that force is needed and an ICC-type of justice is doomed to failure. "Law proceeds out of civilizational change; it can never prefigure it."[71]

Yale Law School professor Ruth Wedgwood was another critic of an independent ICC. Although "we often set ourselves up as Alamo holdouts,[72] and are criticized as the indispensable country with indefensible positions," the U.S. position on the criticality of Security Council referral (and veto) power to the ICC was the correct stance. To "disregard the Security Council is unrealistic."[73]

UN Secretary-General Kofi Annan had a view light-years distant from that of the critics.[74] In his opening statement to the delegates in Rome, he said:

> There can be no global justice unless the worst of crimes—crimes against humanity—are subject to the law. In this age more than ever we recognize that the crime of genocide against one people truly is an assault on us all—a crime against humanity. The establishment of an ICC will ensure that humanity's response will be swift and will be just.[75]

"Justice" was the central concept for those supporting the creation of the ICC. Without the reality of perpetrators of horrible crimes being indicted, tried, and punished if found guilty— either by a national court of justice or by the ICC if domestic law is not enforced—hatred between groups will fester, and there will be no realistic peace and rapprochement in the community after the fighting ends. Said Sadako Ogata, the UN's High Commissioner for Refugees, "Is it fair and realistic to expect the survivors to forgive and to cooperate if there is not justice? In the absence of justice, private revenge may prevail, which will spread fear and undermine the possibility of reconciliation."[76]

"There is a delicate balance between peace and justice," a study group concluded. "Some degree of justice is increasingly a precondition of peace and reconciliation." If war criminals are immunized from prosecution, as was the case in Cambodia, that inaction "corrodes the fabric of society."[77] Richard Dicker, associate counsel for Human Rights Watch, said that "any notion of international peace and security at the end of the 20th Century that subordinates justice and bringing individuals accused of genocide . . . before the ICC for the sake of a peace agreement, is a violation of the permanent members' fiduciary duties."[78]

ICTY judge Gabrielle Kirk McDonald, one of the judges in the *Tadic* trial at the Hague and presently president of the ICTY Chambers, recently gave a speech to members of the U.S. Judge Advocate General's School in Charlottesville, Virginia. Part of her talk focused on what she called "the cycle of impunity."

> The twentieth century is best described as one of split personality: aspiration and actuality. The reality is that this century has been the bloodiest period in history. As improvements in communications and weapons technology have increased, the frequency and barbarity of systematic uses of fundamental rights have likewise escalated, yet little has been done to address such abuses. . . . In the prospect of an ICC lies the promise of universal justice.[79]

"*Impunity*," she said, "is not a new phenomenon. However, the crystallization of the cycle of impunity is very much a twentieth century concept: perpetrators of massive human rights violations[80] have often been supported, rather than held accountable, by the international community. . . . With few, but notable exceptions, there has been no reckoning for the great majority of mass violations of human rights throughout this century; perpetrators have either not been identified, or have not been required to account for their crimes. *The prevalence of such impunity has placed expediency above both principle and pragmatism*," she concluded. She closed her observations with a somber warning to the audience: "*there will be no lasting peace without justice.*"[81]

The Rome statute's preamble states, in part, that the world community is "conscious" of the "grave crimes" committed in war and in peace, and that it is "determined to put an end to *impunity* for the perpetrators of these crimes." Norman Dorsen, a civil liberties advocate and board member of the LCHR attending the Rome conference, fervently supported the preamble's concepts. He echoed the judge's concern about the evil of impunity for alleged war criminals: "the ICC treaty is an historic step toward ending impunity for serious human rights violations."[82]

After fifty years, the global community has finally structured a permanent international criminal court. There was, in the end, a great deal of unanimity on the fundamentals of a working ICC: jurisdiction, definition of the major crimes (genocide, crimes against humanity, and war crimes), an independent Prosecutor's Office to investigate possible "grave violations" of international law, and the ICC's relationship to the UN Security Council. In the end, only seven nations voted against the Rome statute's adoption.

A review of the activities, the bargaining, and the negotiations involving many of the 160 nations attending the Rome meeting shows a lessened reliance on the once-steel reality of nationalism and its corollary, realpolitik, national political expediency. Judge McDonald observed that because "the international community has clung passionately, politically, to the immovable rock of State sovereignty that keeps alive and keeps dominant archaic perceptions of warfare, the pace of the [international] law has been far slower than the pace of the war."[83]

However, at the Rome conference, nations opted to give the notion of international criminal justice some form of operational status. They did so by delegating a very small number of once-sovereign national rights and powers in the area of criminal justice to the new international creation, the ICC. However, given the principle of complementarity in the treaty, the nation-state still has the initial opportunity to try war criminals and others who have committed crimes against humanity or genocide. Only if such action does not take place can the ICC take jurisdiction to investigate and, if appropriate, charge the offender with violations of the human rights conventions.

The United States drew a *de minimus* line on this crucial issue, and in the end, the delegation did not cross it. Instead, isolated and with a small number of unusual "friends," it voted against the ICC and vowed to "actively oppose" its final ratification. This negative foreign policy of the United States (probably shared by most of the Security Council's permanent members), if "actively" implemented, can cause serious problems for the ICC. That tribunal needs international "marshals," i.e., law-enforcement personnel, to enforce its orders.

Persons indicted must be apprehended. Apprehension today is not what it was in Germany and Japan after their "unconditional" surrender in 1945. Fugitives seek refuge in "friendly" states, protected by their own forces and those of the host nation. If they are not tried in a national court for their alleged war crimes, and if they are not captured and brought to the Hague (selected as the permanent site of the ICC) to stand trial for grave war crimes, then the reputation—and power—of the ICC suffers immeasurably, and the alleged war criminals continue to act with impunity.

In the end, the success of the ICC depends on the willingness of powerful nation-states, chief among them the United States, to support and to assist the ICC in these matters. Initially, there must be a commitment in domestic policy and law to act against persons charged with committing these violent, universally condemned, actions. If a nation-state will not or cannot provide a fair trial for the defendant, ICC jurisdiction enables the independent prosecutor to initiate action in the Hague. If it is to succeed, the ICC must reflect a balancing of international idealism with the realpolitik of the nation-state system, epitomized by the United States' "multiple personalities" in the foreign policy arena.

## Notes

1. T. R. Goldman, "A World Apart? U.S. Stance on a New ICC Concerns Rights Groups," *Legal Times*, June 8, 1998, p. 1.
2. Ibid.
3. William J. Durch, "Keeping the Peace," in *UN Peacemaking, American Policy, and the Uncivil Wars of the 1990s*, ed. William J. Durch (New York: St. Martin's Press, 1996), p. 12.
4. Ibid.
5. Testimony before U.S. Congress, House Committee on Foreign Affairs, *U.S. Participation in UN Peacekeeping Activities*, 1993, pp. 31–59.
6. Anthony Lake, "The Limits of Peacekeeping," *New York Times*, February 6, 1994, p. D17.

7. In Article 24 of the UN Charter, which entered into force on October 24, 1945, the UN Security Council was given "primary responsibility for the maintenance of international peace and security." There emerged four types of peacekeeping activities since 1945: (1) traditional peacekeeping, with a UN force between the belligerents, often for decades; (2) multidimensional peacekeeping, which involves the presence of UN Blue Helmets between the belligerents and assistance in the implementation of peace accords, as in the former Yugoslavia after the Dayton Peace Treaty was signed; (3) humanitarian intervention by the UN to relieve the suffering of innocent civilians trapped in the midst of civil war; and (4) peace enforcement, the use of UN Blue Helmets to suppress conflict before war crimes, genocide, and crimes against humanity have an opportunity to occur. See Durch, "Keeping the Peace," pp. 3–7, passim.

8. Article 43 of the UN Charter calls for "all members of the UN . . . [to] undertake [and] to make available to the Security Council, on its call and in accordance with a special agreement or agreements, armed forces, assistance, and facilities, including rights of passage, necessary for the purpose of maintaining international peace and security."

9. Frank Wisner, statement before U.S. Congress, Senate Committee on Armed Forces, *International Peacekeeping and Peace Enforcement*, 1993, p. 69.

10. Ian Williams, "Criminal Neglect," *The Nation*, August 10, 1998.

11. The senators were Barbara Boxer (D-Calif.), Susan M. Collins (R-Me.), Dianne Feinstein (D-Calif.), Kay Bailey Hutchison (R-Tex.), Mary L. Landrieu (D-La.), Barbara A. Mikulski (D-Md.), Carol Mosely Braun (D-Ill.), Patty Murray (D-Wash.), and Olympia J. Snowe (R-Me.).

12. Eric Schmitt, "Pentagon Battles Plans for International War Crimes Tribunal, *New York Times*, April 14, 1998, p. 7.

13. Thomas Omestad, "The Brief for a World Court," *U.S. News and World Report*, October 6, 1997, p. 53.

14. Among the fifteen lawyers were former U.S. attorney general Benjamin R. Civiletti, former federal court of appeals judge A. Leon Higginbotham, Jr., American Civil Liberties Union leader Norman Dorsen, and others, including three former American Bar Association presidents.

15. Letter, Lawyers Committee for Human Rights (LCHR) to President William J. Clinton, May 15, 1998, published in *Media Alert*, May 15, 1998, p. 1.

16. Quoted in Schmitt, "Pentagon Battles Plans," p. A 7. In his March 26, 1998, letter to Secretary of State Albright, Helms rejected any ICC compromise that placed Americans in any prosecutorial jeopardy.

17. Quoted in Donald W. Jackson, "Creating a World Criminal Court Is Like Making Sausage—Except It Takes Longer," *Texas Observer*, June 30, 1998, pp. 7–8.

18. James Podgers, "War Crimes Court under Fire," 84 *American Bar Association Journal* 64 (September 1998).

19. Article 227 stated: "A special tribunal will be constituted to try the accused [Wilhelm II]. . . . [The special tribunal] will be composed of five judges, one appointed by each of the following Powers: namely, the United States of America, Great Britain, France, Italy, and Japan. . . . In its decision the tribunal will be guided by the highest motives of international policy, with a view to vindicating the solemn obligations of international undertakings and the validity of international morality. It will be its duty to fix the punishment which it considers should be imposed."

20. Barrett Prinz, "The Treaty of Versailles to Rwanda: How the International Community Deals with War Crimes," 6 *Tulane Journal of International and Comparative Law* 553 (spring 1998).

21. M. Cherif Bassiouni, "From Versailles to Rwanda in Seventy Five Years: The Need to Establish a Permanent International Criminal Court," *Harvard Human Rights Journal* 10:11, 20–21 (1997).

22. Also created was the International Court of Justice (ICJ), which was a dispute resolver in cases involving states party to the ICJ treaty, with their consent.

23. Kenneth Roth, "The Court the U.S. Does Not Want," *New York Review of Books*, November 10, 1998, p. 45.

24. The ILC was created to encourage the development of international law. Article XIII states that "the General Assembly shall initiate studies and make recommendations for the purpose of encouraging the progressive development of international law and its codification."

25. Omestad, "Brief for a World Court," p. 52.

26. Jackson, "Creating a World Criminal Court," p. 4.

27. An earlier draft by PrepCom contained ninety-nine articles.

28. Donald W. Jackson and Ralph G. Carter, "Public International Law and the Politics of Judicial Creation: The Permanent International Criminal Court and American Foreign Policy," paper presented at the 1998 American Political Science Association National Convention, Boston, August 30–September 3, 1998, p. 24.

29. The Genocide Convention was finally adopted by the United States, with reservations, in the late 1980s, four decades after it was ratified by the UN. The UN's Universal Declaration of Human Rights was adopted by the General Assembly in 1948 and contained thirty articles "which are mainly concerned with setting out traditional civil and political rights such as equality before the law, freedom from arbitrary rights and freedom of peaceful assembly." David Armstrong, Lorna Lloyd, and John Redmond, *From Versailles to Maastricht: International Organization in the Twentieth Century* (New York: St. Martin's Press, 1996), p. 265. Article 1 states: "All human beings are born free and equal in dignity and rights."

30. Editorial, "A New World Court," *Economist*, June 13–19, 1998, p. 16.

31. See Goldman, "A World Apart?" p. 16. Aryeh Neier wrote that the "most contentious issues" were the independence (or lack of independence) of the ICC and what would be the "trigger mechanisms" for launching an ICC investigation into possible war crimes, crimes against humanity, and/or genocide (*War Crimes: Brutality, Genocide, Terror, and the Struggle for Justice* [New York: Times Books, 1998], p. 257).

32. By the fourth week of the Rome conference, the number of nations in the "Like-Minded Group" had almost doubled, to eighty.

33. Quoted in Goldman, "A World Apart?" pp. 16, 17.

34. See, for example, John N. Broder and Don Van Netter, Jr., "Clinton and Starr, a Mutual Admonition Society," *New York Times*, September 20, 1998, pp. A1, 35.

35. Joe Stork, "The ICC in focus," *International Criminal Court* 3, no. 4 (1998): 1.

36. Quoted in Goldman, "A World Apart?" p. 16.

37. Barbara Crossette, "World Criminal Court Having a Painful Birth," *New York Times*, August 13, 1997, p. A7.

38. Barbara Crossette, "U.S. Budges at UN Talks on a Permanent War Crimes Tribunal," *New York Times*, March 18, 1998, p. A1.

39. Quoted in Stork, "ICC in Focus," p. 5.

40. See Jackson and Carter, "Public International Law," pp. 13–17, passim.

41. Stork, "ICC in Focus," p. 2.

42. Quoted in Alessandra Stanley, "U.S. Specifies Terms for War Crimes Court," *New York Times*, July 10, 1998, p. A1.

43. Podgers, "War Crimes Court under Fire," p. 65; emphasis added.

44. David Frum, "The International Criminal Court Must Die," *Weekly Standard*, August 10, 17, 1998, p. 27.

45. Quoted in Goldman, "A World Apart?" p. 17.

46. Kenneth Starr, a Republican lawyer who served as U.S. solicitor general during the Bush administration (1989–1992), was appointed by a panel of three federal judges to examine possible criminal actions of President and Mrs. Clinton involving, initially, land deals in Arkansas while he was governor. In December 1997, Starr was given approval by the federal panel and U.S. Attorney General Janet Reno to examine possible obstruction of justice, perjury, and abuse of power by President Clinton in his efforts to cover up a sexual affair he had with White House intern Monica Lewinsky.

47. Norman Dorsen and Morton H. Halperin, "Justice after Genocide," *Washington Post*, May 13, 1998, p. A17.

48. Quoted in Alessandra Stanley, "UN Conference to Consider Establishing Court for Crimes against Humanity," *New York Times*, June 15, 1998, p. A1.

49. Barbara Crossette, "UN Prosecutor Urges New Criminal Court," *New York Times*, December 9, 1997, p. A8.

50. Quoted in Goldman, "A World Apart?" p. 17.

51. Quoted in Stanley, "UN Conference," p. A1.

52. UN press release, *Daily Summary*, June 18, 1998, p. 1.

53. Alessandra Stanley, "U.S. Dissents but Accord is Reached on War-Crimes Court," *New York Times*, July 18, 1998, p. A7.
54. See Jackson, "Creating a World Criminal Court," p. 4.
55. See ibid., pp. 10–11.
56. Quoted in Stanley, "UN Conference," p. A1. Canadian Foreign Minister Lloyd Axworthy said to the reporter that the Clinton policy was "specious—an exercise in realpolitik."
57. Quoted in *Media Alert*, July 9, 1998, p. 1.
58. LCHR, "Lawyers Committee Labels U.S. Statement on ICC 'A Major Disappointment,' " *Media Alert*, July 9, 1998, p. 1.
59. LCHR, "Lawyers Committee Expresses Dismay at U.S. Statement," *Media Alert*, July 15, 1998, p. 1.
60. Jackson, "Creating a World Criminal Court," p. 19.
61. Quoted in ibid., p. 18.
62. Israel voted against the draft treaty because the omnibus war crimes definition in Article 8 (2) (b) (viii) included "the transfer, directly or indirectly, by the Occupying Power of parts of its own civilian population into the territory it occupies, or the deportation or transfer of all or parts of the population of the occupied territory within or outside this territory." The Israeli delegation viewed this as a pro-Palestine Liberation Organization (PLO) section.
63. Jackson and Carter, "Public International Law," p. 24.
64. Podgers, "War Crimes Court under Fire," p. 65.
65. LCHR, "Lawyers Committee Urges U.S. Government to Support ICC," *Media Alert*, July 21, 1998, p. 1.
66. Section VII is a critical definition of the role of the UN Security Council. Entitled "Action with Respect to Threats to the Peace, Breaches of the Peace, and Acts of Aggression," its thirteen articles (39–51) provide guidelines for the Security Council to take necessary steps to restore the peace, including the use of military force.
67. In April 1998, Helms, the chair of the Senate Foreign Relations Committee, sent Secretary of State Madeleine Albright a letter. In it, he said that any ICC treaty "without a clear U.S. veto" of an ICC investigation will be " 'dead on arrival' when it reaches the Foreign Relations Panel" (quoted in Goldman, "A World Apart?" p. 17).
68. David Rieff, "Court of Dreams," *New Republic*, September 7, 1998, p. 16.
69. Ibid.
70. Quoted in R. W. Apple, "Deep Concern in the World over Weakened Clinton," *New York Times*, September 25, 1998, p. A1.
71. Rieff, "Court of Dreams," pp. 16–17.
72. The United States, Russia, and China were among a handful of nations that did not ratify the Anti-Landmines Treaty of 1997.
73. Ruth Wedgwood, "The Pitfalls of Global Justice," *New York Times*, June 10, 1998, p. A24.
74. Annan was, in January 1994, an undersecretary at the UN, head of the Department of Peacekeeping Operations. He worked with the commanders of UN peacekeeping missions. It was Annan who received General Dallaire's warnings about Hutu extremist plans for a Tutsi genocide and the general's request for a few thousand more UN Blue Helmets. Dallaire argued, unsuccessfully, that with only 5,000 soldiers he could prevent the genocide he knew was about to occur in Rwanda. Annan rejected the proposal, as did the Security Council. The genocide began three months later, in April 1994.
75. Speech, Rome, Italy, June 15, 1998.
76. Speech, Rome, Italy, June 18, 1998.
77. "The UN Security Council and the ICC: How Should They Relate?" Stanley Foundation, Arden House, N.Y., February 20–22, 1998, p. 11.
78. Quoted in "Press Briefing of the NGO Coalition for an International Criminal Court," Lawyers Committee for Human Rights, New York, August 4, 1997, p. 5.
79. Gabrielle Kirk McDonald, "The Changing Nature of the Laws of War," 156 *Military Law Journal* 30, 32–33 (June 1998).
80. She noted that "scholars estimate that over 175 million non-combatants have been killed in episodes of mass killings in the twentieth century. A further 40 million combatants have died in conflicts. That is a total of over 210 million people, or one in every 25 persons alive

today—truly a figure that defies imagination" (McDonald, "Changing Nature of the Laws of War," p. 34).

81. McDonald, "Changing Nature of the Laws of War," p. 33; emphasis added.
82. Norman Dorsen, "The United States and the War Crimes Court: A Glass Half Full," *Lakeville, Florida Journal*, July 30, 1998, p. 1.
83. McDonald, "Changing Nature of the Laws of War," p. 51.

# *Part VI*

*Denial of Genocide*

# 15

# Denial of Genocide

The denial of genocide occurs both during and following the perpetration of the act. In most cases, perpetrators generally attempt either to hide their genocidal actions or, if confronted about the atrocities, deny them. This was certainly the case throughout the twentieth century, and it continues into the twenty-first century. In the twentieth century, the Ottoman Turks denied that they were massacring the Armenians; the Nazis set up a whole slew of subterfuges, including the "beautification" of Theresienstadt prior to the visit by the International Committee of the Red Cross (ICRC) during the summer of 1944; in the early 1990s the Serbs reintroduced the term "ethnic cleansing" (and this was picked up by the international community) so as not to admit they were committing mass murder and genocide; and today the Government of Sudan blames the "excesses" in Darfur on the *Janjaweed* (versus accepting responsibility for its genocidal policies).

That said, when scholars and others refer to the denial of genocide they generally mean that the perpetrators, their descendants, successor governments, and/or individuals who sense an affiliation with the perpetrators, all deny that a genocide was ever perpetrated in the first place. To this day, for example, the Turkish government denies that the Ottoman Turks committed genocide between 1915 and 1923 against the Armenians living in the Ottoman Empire. In fact, the Turkish government is so zealous in its denial of the facts that it is a crime to mention (or even allude to) the genocide in Turkey today. Furthermore, Turkish governments have repeatedly applied pressure on other nations to either prevent conferences to address the genocide of the Armenians or to officially acknowledge within their national bodies that the Armenian genocide was perpetrated by the Ottoman Turks. The Turkish government has also gone so far as providing tens, and probably hundreds, of thousands of dollars to various universities in the United States and elsewhere to establish endowed chairs in Turkish history, which basically serve as public relations outlets for the Turks in which denial of the Armenian genocide forms an important part

Various antisemitic groups in the United States, the United Kingdom, Canada, Australia, and Europe have, over the past thirty years or more, churned out massive quantities of denial literature regarding the Nazi Holocaust of the Jews. Such efforts form a huge underground industry—one that is slick in its production of materials and faux-scholarship. Such efforts include periodicals that have the appearance of scholarly journals with abstracts, footnotes, and the like, but are nothing more than hate-mongering initiatives that purposely obfuscate the facts and spew outright lies in an attempt to blot out the truth.

Over the past 25 years or so, various members of the Khmer Rouge leadership have denied the fact that they perpetrated genocidal destruction against their own people. Tens of thousands of pages of documentation (including photographs and first-person accounts) contradict such claims, and once the criminal tribunal now being formed in Phnom Penh to try crimes committed during the Pol Pot years is in operation, it too will provide documentation (including court transcripts) that counter the denials of the perpetrators.

Ever since the extremist Hutus who perpetrated the 1994 Rwandan genocide fled in the face of the advance of Rwandan Patriotic Front (RPF) troops, the extremists have denied that they carried out genocide. Instead, they argue that mass killings were a result of the war they (the Hutus) engaged in with the RPF. Despite the ample documentation that exists regarding all aspects of the genocide, the deniers persist in their denial. The extremists also accuse the RPF of having committed many of the atrocities as they made their way into Rwanda from Uganda. While certain massacres were committed by RPF troops—some of whom have been tried in Rwandan courts and been found guilty of such atrocities—the genocide was the sole work of the extremist Hutus.

In "A Classification of Denials of the Holocaust and Other Genocides," Israel W. Charny discusses why and how denials are undertaken, as well as how they can and need to be countered. Charny asserts, understandably, that denial is just one more tool of the *génocidaires* in their attempt to destroy in whole or in part a particular group of people. As a result of the actions of the deniers, scholars find themselves—in addition to conducting scholarship into various cases of genocide, the causes of genocide, ways to prevent it, and the most efficacious manner to intervene in an ongoing genocide—working to counter the false claims of killers and their supporters who, in a sense, are attempting to destroy the truth, and in doing so are destroying their victims a second time.

# 15.1   Israel W. Charny, "A Classification of Denials of the Holocaust and Other Genocides"

Gross denials of the Holocaust are increasing (see Kaye, 1997; Jacobs, 1999); a dramatic reflection of these was the notorious suit brought by David Irving against Deborah Lipstadt over her major work (Lipstadt, 1993) in London. These join the tradition of continuing denials of the Armenian Genocide (Charny, 1983; Smith, 1991; Smith *et al.*, 1995; Hovannisian, 1997), as well as recurrent denials of contemporary state-organized genocidal massacres, such as those in China, Sri Lanka, or Bosnia where genocidal massacres were flagrantly denied even as they were being accurately reported by world news media. Even years after a genocide, the fact that the everyday journalistic record of an event was replete with information doesn't stop the denier. See, for example, Kloian (1988) for an outstanding compilation of original *New York Times* reports of the Armenian Genocide in the period from 1915 which detail the day-to-day progress of the genocide, but these are totally ignored by a whole host of even bona fide academics as they go about denying the genocide.

There is an urgent need for a concerted battle against denials which will penetrate the inner mind-structures and propaganda techniques of the deniers so as to combat their explicit and implicit strategies more effectively. The battle against denials can no longer be limited to reproving again and again the evidential proofs of a genocide, although one also must not cease from continuing to marshal the historical data. Effective combating of denial will be possible only when based on a comprehensive model of different types of denial which successfully interprets the political purposes, cognitive structures and communication strategies of the various types of denial.

The following is a classification of different types of denial. An earlier classification from which several of the categories are drawn can be found in Charny (1991). The content analyses presented at that stage of work showed that, in addition to the denial of responsibility, denials are celebrations of destruction, renewed humiliations of survivors and all others who care about the destruction of life, attacks on the identity of the victim people, unabashed attempts to dominate the minds of people by dictatorial fiat and, metaphorically, "murders" of historical truth and collective memory.

The classification presented here addresses a broader coalition of deniers, which includes not only perpetrators and bigots, but many other people who are drawn to denials because they serve their self-interests in one or more ways. These include opportunistic self-serving, such as scholars who protect their positions by acquiescing to accept an institutional culture of denial, or those who seek to gain prominence or to campaign for funds for their denials such as on the Internet; or deniers who have been characterized as "innocent," who maintain a rosy clean picture of the world and themselves by not acknowledging the real extent of human evil; academic turf-battlers and others concerned obsessively with delimiting definitions of what is *really* genocide; others who want to reserve the concept of "true" genocide for one or more ethnic-national groups to the exclusion of other "competing" groups; and deniers who, individually and collectively, tire of preserving a genuine sense of tragedy and moral outrage about a genocidal event. The fact that most deniers are *not* manifest bigots is a reminder that there is never a shortage of plain, everyday or "ordinary men" (Browning, 1993) to commit genocide in the first place, and that most genocidaires have proven to be psychologically–psychiatrically "normal people" (see Charny (1982) for a summary of many of the findings on perpetrators of the Holocaust).

The present classification is offered as a heuristic framework for further analyses and researches by scholars rather than as a final or immutable framework. In the following classification, denials of the Holocaust and genocides are grouped into six major groups (Table 8 presents the complete classification).

## I. Malevolent Bigotry

### Denials by Perpetrators

Denials of ongoing genocidal events by perpetrator governments and/or perpetrators. The genocidaires, usually but not always governments, characteristically deny that they are engaging in mass killings. These denials even emanate from governments at the very time they are clearly committed to the murder of a targeted people, but there remain concerns about possible international reactions should the ongoing genocide be hurled more brazenly in the face of the world, plus the "practical consideration" that victims who have not yet been trapped should not know the full truth of what awaits them. A prototypal example where government was caught red-handed commanding a cover-up was reported out of Kosovo. After a Serbian troop and police attack on a Kosovo village led to the deaths of 45 Albanian civilians, government officials were overheard in phone conversations ordering a cover-up. "According to the monitored conversations . . . a high-ranking political figure in Belgrade and a senior commander of security operations in Kosovo sought to cover up what had taken place . . . The two discussed how to make the killings look like the result of a battle" (Smith, 1999). They also discussed whether they could lay the blame on an independent group by claiming that they had come into the region.

No less remarkable is the fact that such denials are generally "accepted" by other nations at least as a basis for maintaining that reports of the "alleged" killings are still inconclusive. Nazi Germany even created a concentration camp at Theriesenstadt that faked decent enough conditions to "pass" the inspection of the International Red Cross. The Nazis also excelled in a language of deception and sanitization of the horrors they were perpetrating. The Cambodian government raised an impenetrable "bamboo curtain" over information on what was happening in what later came to be known as "the killing fields." Though the world

*Table 8* A classification of denials of the Holocaust and other genocides

| | | |
|---|---|---|
| **I.** | | **Malevolent bigotry** |
| 1. | | *Denials by perpetrators* |
| | 1.01 | Denials of *ongoing* genocidal events by perpetrator governments and/or perpetrators |
| | 1.02 | Denials of *past* genocidal events by perpetrator governments and/or perpetrators |
| | 1.03 | Denials of genocide after the fact by perpetrators brought to trial |
| 2. | | *Denials by non-perpetrators in the traditions of fascism and bigotry* |
| | 2.01 | Denials by governments and government-sponsored bodies who continue the tradition of the perpetrator |
| | 2.02 | Denials by various fascists, neo-fascists and bigots |
| | 2.03 | Denials of perpetration of genocide by groups which are or have been victims of genocide, or groups which come under retaliatory attack for the genocide they committed, or groups which are manifestly weaker underdogs vis-a-vis a stronger power |

| | | |
|---|---|---|
| **II.** | | **Self-serving opportunism** |
| 3. | | *Denials in the service of personal or collective self-interest or power such as careerism, pragmatism, exhibitionism and* realpolitik |
| | 3.01 | Denials by governments which do *not* sympathize with or condone the genocide, but support denials for reasons of *realpolitik* |
| | 3.02 | Denials in the service of careerism, pragmatism, or *realpolitik* |
| | 3.03 | Denials in the service of self-styled display of oneself in a provocative or aggressive counterculture position<br>a. Scandalous denials to gain public prominence and exhibitionistic display, including for political reasons, or in jockeying for academic exclusivity, power or notoriety<br>b. Denials as provocation, negativism and being annoying to large numbers of people or established society |
| | 3.04 | Denials in conformity or failure to challenge the denialist positions of an employer, supervisor, other senior colleague, or an institutional climate |

| | | |
|---|---|---|
| **III.** | | **"Innocent denials" and/or "innocent disavowals of violence" which maintain views of oneself and/or one's people or society as just and not evil**<br>Note: It is extremely important to evaluate all apparently "innocent denials" for possible degrees of manipulation and lying as camouflages for denial infiltration—see entry 5 below |
| 4. | | *"Innocent denials" which deny knowledge or believability of a genocide* |
| | 4.01 | & Profiling deniers on two continuums of malevolence of denial and celebrations of violence |
| | 4.02 | Denials on a continuum from apparently or possibly "innocent" lack of knowledge and disbelief to more malevolent denial of available knowledge<br>a. Denials of the factual history of a genocide—including disinformation through denials of key facts which set a major tone of the event, whose discrediting casts a larger shadow of doubt on the total event even if it is not explicitly denied, e.g. claims there were no gas chambers in the Holocaust, or "questioning" of the validity of the Talaat telegrams, hence the central government's mandating the Armenian Genocide<br>b. The facts of the genocide are not necessarily denied, and may even be tacitly recognized or even given fuller lip-service recognition, but perhaps "innocently" they are contextualized, justified, relativized or otherwise deconstructed (see entry 7), e.g. there is nothing new about the Holocaust in the broad range of human history or the government took necessary steps to preserve order |
| | 4.03 | Denials on a continuum from apparently or possibly "innocent disavowals of violence" to more explicit innuendos and open celebration of the genocidal violence |
| | 4.04 | Need to maintain an innocent view of a people, society or of human life as a whole as just |
| | 4.05 | "Innocent denials" based on an extreme free speech position which supports the unqualified rights of deniers to present their views<br>a. Denials on a continuum from basically sincere beliefs in free speech and hearing all points of view to manipulative exploitation of the ideal of free speech in order to promote the propaganda of denial |

b. Denials under the guise of historical debates

5. *Manipulation and lying through seeming "innocent denials"*

a. Confusion, contradiction, and double talk where elements of acknowledgment of facts of a genocide and/or expression of regret over deaths are mixed, purposely, with dissimulated texts of "innocent denial" in order to weaken factual basis of a genocide

b. Manipulative dissimulation of seeming "innocent denial" in order to infiltrate the academic community with denial positions

**IV.** **"Definitionalism" or insistence on defining cases of mass murders as *not genocide***

6. *Denials on the basis of excluding cases from being defined as genocide*

6.01 Denials on the basis of pedantic obsessive academic disputes and hairsplitting about details of an event to a point that obscures the event as a reality, and/or banishes moral outrage and sensitivity to its infamy and tragedy

6.02 Denials based on insistence that a case of mass murder cannot be defined as *genocide* but "only" as another and in effect lesser category such as "accepted acts of war" or "government response to internal dissent"

a. Contextualizers—not really "genocide" but another type of event such as war, civil war, wartime starvation and disease, revolution, deportations and resettlement

b. Justifiers—not really "genocide" but a response in self-defense against attack or threat of attack such as counter-terrorism, subversion or rebellion, or retaliation against the above in counter-massacres

6.03 Denials on the basis of escapes into legal loopholes that the people murdered were citizens of the perpetrator state, or not all were of a single ethnicity or religion, or that they were "simply" political victims, hence the mass murders do not constitute *genocide*

7. *Denials on the basis of rationalization, minimization, relativization or other deconstruction of meaning*

7.01 Denials based on manipulation and/or minimization of statistics—not enough to be *genocide*

7.02 Denials justified by contrived arguments that not *all* members of a target group died or not all were intended victims, hence no *genocide* took place or was planned in the first place.

7.03 Relativizers and deconstructionists—mass deaths that took place, however unfortunate, and perhaps even genocide, are no different than countless historical events of mass murder and do not justify undue emphasis; the victims drew the suffering on themselves by their own aggression.

7.04 Tarnish the character of the victim population and stigmatize them as if to justify psychologically their deserving to be attacked

**V.** **Nationalistic hubris or self-involvement which justify exclusion of others**

8. *Denials of the significance of the genocide of another people*

8.01 Denials based on indifference to the fates of other victims

a. *Not Knowing*—not investing the effort to know the facts of the genocide of another people

b. *Not Caring*—not feeling emotional or spiritual involvement with the fate of another people

c. *Justifications of indifference* on the basis of being overly occupied with one's own people's problems

8.02 Denials accompanied by celebration of open antagonism in fulfillment of revenge to a past perpetrator who has now become the victim of genocide

8.03 Denials based on insistence on uniqueness or superordinate meaning of one people's genocide which is taken as a basis for exclusion or devaluation of another people's genocide

8.04 Denials deriving from disrespectful, harsh or radical overstatements of criticisms of claims of uniqueness, also legitimate criticisms of a victim people's policies including violations of the human rights of others, which result in minimization or irreverence for the genuine tragedy and significance of the victim people's original genocide

(*Continued Overleaf*)

*Table 8* Continued.

| VI. | Human shallowness—the dulling and depletion of a genuine sense of tragedy and moral outrage |
|---|---|
| 9. | *Denials deriving from routinization, desensitization or banalization of events of genocide* |
| 9.01 | Denials based on acceptance of genocide as a routine event in history or inevitable in human nature |
| 9.02 | Denials deriving from routinization of scholarship about genocide, or desensitization and boredom in response to repeated mention of event with a failure to maintain a deep moral concern |
| 9.03 | Denials deriving from trivialization of information about a genocide<br>a. A "one liner" in history books<br>b. Kitsch representations of suffering |
| 9.04 | Denials deriving from long-term cultural processes of routinization of memorials and depletion of meaning<br>a. Transformations of memorial events for genocide into essentially joyous family and community events (e.g. Passover celebration)<br>b. Soft core denials by way of sweetening the outcome, talking of survivors and not victims, happy endings—the triumph of survival, the reconstruction of one's people<br>c. "Souvenirs" of a genocide for the fetish of collection rather than out of memorial and commitment |

already knew the viciousness of the forced expulsion of a million residents from the capital city Phnom Penh, there were liberals and committed pacifists who called for honoring the basic good intentions of the agrarian regime in Cambodia. When the news of the forced evacuation of Phnom Penh in 1975 reached the West, especially following the reports by Sidney Schanberg to the *New York Times*, a stalwart pacifist organization, Fellowship of Reconciliation (FOR), published in its *Fellowship Magazine* an apologetic interpretation of the forced evacuation (Ferry, 1975). The author suggested that we in the West may be shocked by the loss of life, but that it behooved us to try to understand the different concepts of life and the naturalness of triage or selection of the fittest under duress which characterize a non-Western culture such as Cambodia. A readiness to attribute honorable meanings to genocidal killing, such as resistance to occupation or opposition to the encroachments of global capitalism, continues to characterize the rationalizations of what I call the *genocidal terrorism* of our era, e.g. the September 11 murders of thousands of civilians in New York and Washington or the waves of terrorist attacks including suicide bombers against Israel.

*Denials of past genocidal events by perpetrator governments and/or perpetrators.* Cynical Machiavellian governments which have committed genocidal massacres may calculatedly employ all means of the enormous power invested in government to destroy and rewrite the historical record. These denials occur not only while the murders are being committed but in the years that follow, and in the face of the sorrows and memories of the grieving survivors and a people's historical memory. A contemporary small-scale example of genocidal massacre and its denial was the denial by the Chinese government of the mass slaughter of an estimated 3,000 students in Tiananmen Square just days after the event (*Encyclopedia of Genocide*, 1999, p. 175). An almost ludicrous example of denial, except that this is a subject which admits no humor, is that until 1988 the Soviet Union denied responsibility for the 1941 Katyn Massacre of Polish officers in World War II; there developed the absurd situation that the seemingly outraged Nazi government which was accused by Russia of the Katyn killings self-righteously sought to prove its innocence of these charges while it ruthlessly continued with its own mass killings.

*Denials of genocide after the fact by perpetrators brought to trial.* Among the denials by perpetrators brought to trial are the following: denials of having personally executed killings [see for example, denials by a killer in Cambodia as analyzed by Hinton (1996)]; denials of one's individual responsibility for participation in the killings, or denial of intentional genocide, especially as not falling within the range of one's personal choices, e.g. "I was only following orders," and "I had to do what I was told or they would have killed me"; denials of having been associated with the genocide if perpetrated by others; denials of the deaths as genocidal killings by reframing the deaths to represent another kind of event such as casualties of wartime, an army's response to civilian resistance, or deaths as a result of inadvertent illness and malnutrition during wartime.

## Denials by Non-perpetrators in the Traditions of Fascism and Bigotry

Denials of bona fide genocides naturally attract fascists, such as neo-Nazis, virulent antisemites, "skinheads" and bigots of all kinds who hate other peoples and ethnicities, who utilize denials of genocide to celebrate violence and death to human life. Historically, the deniers of genocide, such as of the Holocaust, began years ago with what can be described simply as "sloppy" gross denials of the facts [summaries of recurring types of denials of the Holocaust can be found in Anti-Defamation League (1993), Kaye (1997), Kulka (1991) and Stern (1993)]. Examples of gross denials include claims that there was no Holocaust; there were no organized killings of the Jews: e.g. "Not a single German document has ever been found which even refers to an extermination program" (Mark Weber, in a publication by the Institute for Historical Review, a known neo-Nazi center in California for denials of the Holocaust, no date); the prisoners in Auschwitz dined to symphony music and there was an Olympic pool at Auschwitz [e.g. a headline in the *Toronto Sun* in a story on the trial of denier Ernest Zundel: "Auschwitz . . . had a pool and a dance floor"; there were no gas chambers: e.g. "The Jews are very foolish not to abandon the gas chamber theory while they still have time," said David Irving (cited by Anti-Defamation League, 1993, p 24)].

In other words, whatever gross nonsense one could invent in one's mind was introduced by the deniers with the bravado of the huckster politician who calculates that if you lie about anything long enough and loud enough there will be some people who believe you. Later, seeing that they were objects of derision and contempt, many of the deniers moved slowly but surely towards increasing degrees of control of their mind constructions to increasing sophistication in the packaging of their ideas. Some of the more sophisticated arguments used by the deniers are that there were deaths of the victims but that they were a result of wartime conditions that affect everybody, and/or that there were deaths but at the hands of lower levels of the government or military-police squads, or even by an antagonist population of civilians running wild; e.g. French denier Paul Rassinier said the SS was not responsible for the killings but rather the inmates' kapos to whom the SS entrusted the running of the camps, and British denier Richard Harwood and others claimed that the statistics of the dead were grossly exaggerated (see Kaye, 1997).

A more far-reaching type of argument that involves much greater daring, and in a sense reverts to some of the gross hucksterism except that it is presented in more sophisticated forms and is backed by pseudo-documentation, is that the *victims* were really the *victimizers*, and it was the victims who really did the genocidal killing, the exact opposite of what the conventional history of the genocide reports. Thus, the Turks claim that the Armenians massacred more than a million Turks and several communities in Turkey have actually erected memorials to the martyrs of the genocide of the Turks by the Armenians! Even the Jews have been accused of having been the aggressors against the Nazis, e.g. Harwood argued that Chaim Weizmann, a leader of international Jewry, who later was to be the first president of Israel, had "declared war" on Germany by world Jewry—words in a statement by

Weizmann on September 5, 1939 that the Jews would fight on the side of the democracies, and this is the reason Himmler and Hendrich introduced their policies of imprisoning Jews (cited by Kaye, 1997, p 17).

A still newer variation of denials is a kind of belated or grudging acknowledgment of the historical genocide accompanied by a variety of denials of aspects of that same genocide, so that the *configuration* is one where there is ostensibly historical fairness (after all, we acknowledge the genocide), but the prevailing symbolic effect of the statement is weighted towards the subsequent denial. Thus, German historian Ernst Nolte (1966, 1994) who became widely known for an invidious intellectual revisionism based on the contention that the Holocaust is "nothing much more" than a continuation of oft-repeated events in history, will briefly bemoan the death of the Jews, but then cite approvingly the "engineering consultation" by Leuchter which "proves" that there were no gassings and that the crematoria couldn't have handled as many bodies as reported, so there was no mass extermination program. By acknowledging the deaths of the Jews, he maintains the facade of a respectable historian when, in fact, he is mocking his readership with classic revisionist insults of the truth.

The continuing denial of the Armenian Genocide by the Turkish government is probably the outstanding and most persistent case of denial by non-perpetrators. The denials are made by government officials such as ambassadors or by government-sponsored organizations, e.g. the Assembly of Turkish American Associations [see McCarthy and McCarthy (1989) for a revisionist publication sponsored by the Assembly; and Charny and Fromer (1990a, 1998) for a study of the 69 academics who signed an advertisement promulgated by this organization in 1985], or the Turkish Institute [see Smith *et al.* (1995) for a dramatic exposé of the propaganda and coercive efforts of this institute in academia]. Denial of the Armenian Genocide has been accompanied by an incredible political process to gain the cooperation even of democratic governments like the US and Israel and of international bodies such as the UN.

Another example of denials by aggressor governments is Japan's long-time refusal to acknowledge the "rape of Nanking," or Japan's horrifying medical experiments on prisoners in Manchuria. In the wake of the Holocaust, the Western world in general, and the profession of medicine in respect of its own specific concerns about the integrity of its practitioners, was shocked by the vicious Nazi medical experiments on Jews in the concentration camps and the devotion of the results of these experiments, ostensibly to furthering science and medicine. But relatively few were aware that no less excruciatingly cruel experiments had been carried out initially on Chinese victims and later also on American, British and Australian POWs by the infamous Japanese Army Unit 731 in Manchuria, under the direction of Lt. Shiro Ishii. An endless supply of victims were infected with typhus, cholera, mustard gas, frozen piecemeal to death, staked out to experimental disease-carrying bombs and shells, subjected to vivisection, etc. (*Encyclopedia of Genocide*, 1999, p 413). From time to time, Japanese officials have made some apologies to the people of China and Korea for war crimes against their civilian populations, but the prevailing government and cultural modes continue to be mainly evasion and denial. For example, in an interview in 1994, then Justice Minister Shigeto Nagano, a former Japanese general, criticized another minister for expressing regret for "the pain suffered by people in Asia and neighboring countries," and for terming Japanese conquests "a war of aggression." Nagano said, "I believe that the Nanking Massacre and the rest is a fabrication" (Sanger, 1994).

A surprisingly unnoted form of denial issues from or about underdog peoples who themselves were or are the victims of genocide or human rights violations, but who also are perpetrators of genocide in their own right. The denial is as if the victims cannot be perpetrators, which is not true [see Robins (2002) for a study of the Great Rebellion in Upper Peru, today Bolivia, in 1780–82 where the victim native people were perpetrators of genocide]. Similarly a genocider may complain about a subsequent strike against them, as if it cancels the record of their genocidal actions. Thus, the spokesman for Taliban leader Mullah Mohammed

Omar told journalists in November 2001 (Associated Press, November 22, 2001) that the US was "killing daily our innocent people," and, therefore, "you should forget the September 11 attacks."

## II. Self-serving Opportunism

### Denials in the Service of Personal or Collective Self-interest or Power such as Careerism, Pragmatism, Exhibitionism and Realpolitik

Denials by non-perpetrators who are not bigots are the most widespread form of denials that one encounters. These denials by non-bigots are especially dangerous for civilization since they issue in many cases from seemingly well-intentioned people, and thereby are more capable of undermining societal foundations of historical truth and fair-mindedness. These are particularly perplexing when one seeks to understand what can be the motivations and rewards of the deniers, especially when one needs to account for denials by ostensibly peace-seeking people, including a considerable number of bona fide academics—who unfortunately are to be found in all Western countries (Charny, 1997, 2001; Des Pres, 1986).

Denials by non-perpetrators who are not bigots include governments which do not necessarily condone a genocide, but support denials for reasons of *realpolitik*. The denials also come from individuals whose major purpose and gratification is to be provocative or negativistic and/or to enjoy public prominence and notoriety through drawing public fire and attention to themselves as problematic people to be reckoned with. In some cases the deniers are jockeying for intellectual or academic exclusivity and power by creating for themselves high visibility. The failed suit brought by David Irving against Deborah Lipstadt, for example, seems to have been created by Irving to give him an opportunity to "win" even were he to lose, just as he "won" in the past when several times he was declared persona non grata in a number of countries. He also exploits his losses to engage in world-wide appeals for funds to antisemites and whoever else identifies with his battles against the "Holocaust-cultists." One text from Irving's Internet site in January 2000 reads: "David Irving needs your help to defend his career and reputation against the mudslide triggered by Professor Deborah Lipstadt and her Israeli paymasters." Irving seems to feel pride and to thrive on publicity as an arch spokesman of denials of the Holocaust even if he loses a formal legal case—except that this time he seems to have lost "big time" with the court's resounding condemnation of him as a denier and antisemite along with the enormous costs he has incurred.

There may be ostensibly upright citizens who identify themselves with the search for truth and justice, yet who join forces with the deniers and revisionists because of conscious and unconscious economic or political interests or other aspects of expanding their power that are served by their cooperation with those who have committed genocide and massacre. The concept that personal interests can lead many people who are not initially bigoted or violent even into participating in the actual commission of genocide is a critically important one. One dramatic rendition of this disturbing truth appeared in the television series, *Holocaust*, which was seen by hundreds of millions of viewers around the world in the late 1970s, in which a young German officer, also spurred on by his ambitious wife, becomes a devoted expert of persecuting Jews precisely because he wants to advance his career.

Much self-serving opportunism is, in fact, the regrettable acquiescence and conformity of people who do not feel impelled and capable of standing up to the prevailing position of their supervisors or to the climate of ideas in their institution or professional circle. Some years ago at Tel Aviv University, for example, a rector and president remained admiring supporters of Professor Bernard Lewis even *after* he was convicted in Paris of denial of the Armenian Genocide, and they were active in supporting his nomination for recognition by the Tel Aviv municipality (the nomination was defeated by a public outcry). In this kind of situation junior scholars facing promotion or other support from the university administration would need to think twice about their position on the Armenian Genocide, and it is obvious in life that many will go along with the comfortable position of not challenging the leadership of their institution or profession.

## III. "Innocent Denials" and/or "Innocent Disavowals of Violence" which Maintain Views of Oneself and/or One's People or Society as Just and not Evil

Not only are most deniers not perpetrators or bigots. It has become clear that there are many deniers—they may even be the statistical majority—who profess standards of human rights and historical justice and are not driven by any tangible rewards, and whose denials of a genocide may be seen as relatively "innocent."

The basic purpose of these denials is to maintain a world view, either of oneself, or of one's people, or of society as a whole, as basically just and not flagrantly evil (Lerner, 1980). Genocide is seen as unthinkable and unfathomable. As John Darley (1996) has written, "We are invited to adopt the view that the unimaginable is impossible; that the Holocaust never happened ... A grisly magic is attempted: the corpse is made to disappear from the coffin" (p 576). The purpose of such denials is to make it psychologically possible to continue living with hope and trust in the world in which we live and in mankind. The denial is rooted in a primitive inability to comprehend that humans can be so cruel, and the magnitude of the horror of genocide is left unfathomable, incomprehensible and unbelievable. An additional specific motivation for "innocent denials" is the tendency of members of a group, which was a perpetrator of genocide, to defend their people from being identified as vicious mass murderers.

In other words, many of the deniers are not committed propagandists or hate-mongers, they are not known to be in the pay or employ of a group that has a commitment to revise the history of a given genocide, and in many cases they do not have a record of prejudice and antagonism to the target people whose genocide is being denied. Denial is, after all, a common powerful mechanism in the human mind which is capable of numbing, avoiding, and blocking out awareness both of terrible events that have befallen oneself as a victim as well as awareness of terrible things done to others.

The concept of "innocent deniers" of known genocides was developed in the course of the study previously referred to (Charny and Fromer, 1990a, 1998) of "Middle-Eastern scholars" who were recruited to sign a prominent advertisement which appeared on May 19, 1985, in the *New York Times, Washington Post*, and elsewhere. Sponsored by a Turkish government association, the advertisement launched a new, remarkably insidious version of denial of the Armenian Genocide which has since been used repeatedly to "prove" that a significant number of major professionals in the field question the validity of the Armenian Genocide. In their responses to the study, many of the scholars emphasized their wishes to be seen as *good people*. Several of them conveyed that they felt rather ennobled by a sense of justice and fairness when they accepted at face value the denial of genocide by "a good people" like the Turks. They also expressed pride in their explicit efforts to contribute to a new reconciliation between the Armenians and the Turks. Not pressing claims of an Armenian Genocide could open a door to a new rapprochement, they suggested; it is useless to continue hating another people for a crime of so long ago, they insisted. In other words, unless one believes that all of these scholars are lying brazenly, which we believed they were not, many of their conscious intentions are indeed innocent. One can argue, as did an investigation by the Armenian Assembly of America (1987) and another study by Vyronis (1993), that in the case of many of those scholars there were likely implicit and explicit payoffs in their being able to continue their research connections and gain grants from Turkish sources; therefore, even if they themselves consciously are unaware of their corruption, they can hardly be thought of as entirely innocent. Still the correct conclusion has to be that some and probably even much of the denial seen in these scholars is not consciously malevolent or self-serving.

## Profiling Deniers on Two Continuums of Malevolence of Denial and Celebration of Violence

We need to explain the emotional satisfactions and rewards that are inherent in the adoption of denials of known genocides when these denials are not linked to any form of political, economic or personal power, or malevolent hatred or bigotry. To further explain the psychology of denials of genocide, I have proposed (Charny, 1993, 2000) a two-tier theory of the psychological motivations or gratifications that are being sought by those who deny a genocide.

The *first* tier refers to a *Continuum of Malevolence of Denial* or the extent to which the denier is or is not consciously aware of the facts of the genocide, hence is or is not malevolently—purposely, cynically—denying a known genocide. This continuum is defined as running from a position where the person denying the genocide really or largely does *not* know the facts to a position on the other side where there is full knowledge of the historical facts accompanied by brazen denial. There are countless deniers and revisionists who really believe the nonsense with which they have identified because it fits their system of thinking, values or way of looking at the world. Some have not bothered to learn facts that are within their cultural/information reach; there are psychological and ethical implications to their failure to know or to want to know, but factually they do not know. Sadly, I have periodically demonstrated to Israeli students their indifferent lack of knowledge of various genocides of other peoples, even as they are outraged at ignorance of the Holocaust today or at the time of the Holocaust. In a number of empirical studies, Charny and Fromer (1990b, 1990c, 1992) have also shown how some Israelis are prepared to do or approve evil to others in contexts where they believe they are helping others or doing their duty. Many revisionists are intensely bigoted people but who *really don't know the facts* of the genocide they have been taught to deny. They themselves repeat the refrain they have been given because it feels like a way of attacking people they hate. Reluctantly, we must recognize that theirs, too, is a degree of innocence of the facts. The most distressing "innocents" are the deniers who are actually "nice people," not consciously bigoted, who also really don't know the facts of the genocide, even mean well, and are drawn to believe in and become promoters of revisionist propaganda because they somehow feel good and self-righteous in adopting this position.

The *second* tier describes a *Continuum of Celebration of Violence* that refers to the extent to which the denier seeks through the denial of a given genocide implicitly to celebrate the past deaths of the victims, and/or to evoke favorable images of still future mass deaths—to the same victims or to other victims. There are revisionists who are virulent antisemites or anti-Armenian, or plain generic bigots and scoundrels who delight in jumping on the bandwagon of denial of the genocide of any victim group because it serves their basic authoritarian and reactionary attitudes and their wishes to vent violence on victims. Along with their denials, they express quite openly their frightening slogans and statements of intention and even plans to "send them back to the gas chambers," or "burn them." There is no doubt whatsoever that the denial of a past genocide is a device through which these people are not only humiliating the remnants of the victim people, in itself a form of further psychological victimization, but are exhorting people to engage in renewed massacre and genocide—of the same victim people or of others. However, there are also many deniers who do *not* adopt rabid bigoted positions, and in no way associate themselves with manifest exhortations to further violence, pogroms or genocide. In fact, as we have seen, there are many deniers and revisionists, especially among academic circles, who go to great lengths to emphasize that they mean no harm whatsoever, and that their wish to set the historical record straight about the false or exaggerated claim of a past genocide is to make it possible for people in question to live more peacefully.

Each person or group who denies a history of genocide can be characterized at appropriate points along each of the two continua. Such a theory of the psychology of the denial of genocide is compatible with the facts that when the genocides actually take place, the actual perpetrators, accomplices and bystanders to genocide also distribute themselves along similar continua of consciousness to unconsciousness of destructive actions. Some people make it clear in every possible way that they are happy to "kill the Jews," but there are countless others, in each real historical event of genocide, who are happy to participate without admitting it to themselves, even without admitting to themselves what they are actually doing in their respective small or large roles in the genocide.

### "Innocent Denials" Based on an Extreme Free Speech Position which Supports the Unqualified Rights of Deniers to Present Their Views

An insidious form of revisionism which can develop from a genuine espousal of the cardinal democratic value of free speech, but which can also be taken to extremes that allow totalitarianism to overpower democratic institutions, is the insistence that the revisionists should not be deined any and all public forums for lectures, publications or media promotion. A sad example of this distortion is an introduction to the work of a disreputable denier of the Holocaust, French Professor Robert Faurisson by outstanding linguist, Noam Chomsky (see Lipstadt, 1993; Vidal-Naquet, 1992).

An important variation on the appeals to the grand democratic principle of free speech is the call to the ostensible fairness of giving the "other point of view" a hearing. The obvious trap in these arguments is that such resort to valued aspects of democracy can be used to elevate any totalitarian and anti-democratic ideas, and even actual conspiratorial and demagogic movements, to "equals" with genuine diversity of opinion. Democracy can tolerate a wide range of controversy so long as there is no attempt to undermine the very structure of democratic society and the opportunity it gives for free speech, which is soon lost when democracy is destroyed. Several countries (e.g. Germany, France, Canada) have legislated that denials of the Holocaust and other known genocides are to be legally defined as incitements to violence and against the public welfare.

### Manipulation and Lying through Seeming "Innocent Denials"

It is also extremely important to evaluate all apparently "innocent denials" for possible degrees of manipulation and lying which are being used as camouflages for infiltrating denial positions into academia. For example, a common strategy is to appeal to have the "other side" of a "controversial issue" presented as the basis for gaining the permission of academic authorities to hold meetings on campus or to convince editors of college newspapers to present "all sides to a controversy." Under the guise of historical debate and appeals to a sense of fair play, the deniers insist on their right to present the "other point of view" when the truth is that they are using the principle of free speech to disguise their explicit propaganda [see the case of Bradley Smith who succeeded in placing many articles in college newspapers as reported and discussed in a Special Issue of *Internet on the Holocaust and Genocide* on denials of genocides (1993); also in Jacobs (1999)].

The basic strategy of manipulation and lying is not only a political one to gain entrance into formal structures in the community, but a calculated strategy to befuddle and confound the thinking of well-intentioned people by mixing elements of acknowledgment of the facts of a genocide and/or expression of regret over violence and deaths with various lies and denials which seriously weaken or cripple the factual basis of a genocide. The denials are often constructed to sow doubt, confusion and contradiction. A doubletalk is constructed of recognition of some of the facts of a genocide mixed, purposely, with texts of seemingly "innocent denials." Thus, the declaration that one regrets the deaths of so many Armenians may be coupled with statements that wartime conditions were prevailing and no fewer Turks and Kurds died than Armenians, and that they died at the hands of the warring Armenians. Making people believe that all sides were equally at fault is often the goal of deniers (although as noted they also can progress to reversing the roles, hence claims that the Armenians were the authors of the real genocide and not the Turks). David Irving trades on parts of his career as a legitimate and even impressive historian. His research achievements provided him with a platform for his incredible denials of the Holocaust such as his claim that the gas chambers at Auschwitz were built *after* the war to create a false image of Auschwitz as a death camp it never was! Other revisionists make calculated efforts to pretend to do genuine research to explore the historical record open-mindedly, and there are cases where such dissimulation is by academics who are on the actual payroll of a government or revisionist group [see the marvelous exposure by Smith *et al.* (1995)].

## IV. "Definitionalism" or Insistence on Defining Cases of Mass Murders as *Not Genocide*

To date, the most common way to attempt to refute charges of genocide is to argue for the inclusion of events of mass killing under the definitional rules of *wars*. Thus, the massive fire bombings of Dresden and Tokyo in World War II are defended as the proper pursuits of military actions and not genocide, and given that the bombings were initiated in contexts of combat against aggressors, there is generally a tendency to accept the claim that, even if exaggerated power was used in these bombings, they were "at most" war crimes and not *genocide* [see Markusen and Kopf (1995) for a powerful argument that these bombings of civilians *did* constitute genocide]. Similarly, the two nuclear bombings, first of Hiroshima and then of Nagasaki, are claimed to have been necessary steps to reduce Allied casualties, even though there are many critics who claim that the second bombing certainly was manifestly superfluous, and possibly both were. In other words, for some scholars, including the great pioneer of genocide studies, Leo Kuper, the nuclear bombings of Hiroshima and Nagasaki constituted genocidal acts or senseless mass killing of civilian populations.

The definition of genocide under law is, of course, anchored in the UN Convention on Genocide where genocide is defined as involving a willful attempt to eliminate the identified target people. Admittedly, the Convention refers to intent to destroy *in whole* or *in part*, and any number of purists have argued that unless the goal was to kill *all* of a given people, the event was not "really" genocide, or at the least it was a "lesser genocide." This has also served as a basis for flagrant denials, e.g. Turkish arguments that since the majority of Armenians living in Istanbul were not killed, it is proof that there was no intent to kill all Armenians (e.g. McCarthy and McCarthy, 1989); and for some that is to say that there was no true "genocide" of the Armenians. Nonetheless, despite a legal weakness issuing from the above phrasing, slowly but surely the majority of legal and social science authorities have defined genocide under the Convention as any significant calculated destruction of a target people—thus honoring more fully the meaning of *in part* in the original wording.

The UN Convention also does not include cases where the mass killing is of "political groups," such as a government's response to disturbing elements in its own country. Under this exclusion, for many years Stalin's extensive mass-murders of ethnic groups in the Soviet Union were not acknowledged by many people as genocide, and scholars had to "fight" their way back to proving the genocidal intent let alone extent of Stalin's murders. The UN's Whitaker Report in 1985 called for revision of the basic definition of genocide to be much more inclusive and to include "political genocide."

*Denials on the Basis of Excluding Cases from being Defined as Genocide*
Incredible energies have been expended by academicians on battles over competing definitions of *genocide*. Science and scholarship do require clarification and precision, and there is an intellectually honest basis to many of these efforts. But there are also many excursions into defining genocide which are revealed to be efforts to exclude one or more—sometimes almost all but one—events of mass murders from "qualifying" for the vaunted definitional identification of *genocide* (see Rosenbaum, 1996).

There are disputations that issue from a kind of academization-intellectualization which becomes an end of its own. It is fair to characterize some of these as reaching an obscene level of obsessive hairsplitting where the joy and/or power-seeking of what I have called "definitionalism" (Charny, 1994) or excessive involvement with splitting hairs and dotting *is* lead scholars to fight narcissistically over their definitional criteria to a point where one loses sight of the actual phenomenon under discussion. In these contexts, academic pride in effect banishes reverence or anger over the victims of genocide, and the academic turf war becomes an end in itself. One discerns a point where the hairsplitting clearly obscures the genocidal event as a reality and banishes moral outrage and sensitivity to the infamy of the event and its tragedy.

There are denials of genocide after the fact as not constituting *genocide* as such, but rather as events of taking mass lives that are to be included in some other category as an accepted act of war, either within the framework of legitimate military actions or at least within the boundaries of "inadvertent" destruction in the course of war, or as a legitimate governmental response to internal political dissent. The "contextualizers" attempt to say that such and such mass killing was not *really* "genocide," but another type of event such as war, civil war, wartime starvation and disease, revolution, deportations and resettlement. The "justifiers" go further and not only insist the event was not really "genocide," but they give the killings a credible explanation, that they were in response against attack or threat of attack such as counter-terrorism, subversion or rebellion, or retaliation against the above in counter-massacres, in effect self-defense [see Adalian (1992) for a classification of deniers as participants, apologists, rationalizers, revisionists, disinformers and distorters, and their use of three types of arguments: a denial thesis, revision thesis, and justification thesis].

There are also denials which are based on escapes into ostensible legal loopholes, beginning with the claim that all the victims were citizens of the perpetrator state, hence were "simply" political victims who cannot qualify as victims of *genocide* because technically political genocide was dropped from the original formulation of the UN Convention on Genocide. Similarly, those who argue that the UN Convention requires an intention to murder all or even part of a victim people, given a situation where all the victims are not of the same ethnicity or religion, or are "simply" bona fide political victims, the argument is made that no genocide has taken place. These disputations and definitional controversies take on appearances of legitimate intellectual-scholarly differences when they are basically contrived gimmicks and maneuvers, at times quite malicious, to get away with denying crimes of genocide.

*Denials on the Basis of Rationalization, Minimization, Relativization or other Deconstruction of Meaning*
One of the first devices of deniers is to attempt to downgrade a significance of a genocide by minimizing the statistics of the number of dead (Charny, 1999). On the one hand, it is as if the numbers will be reduced to a level below some mythical mathematical quantity where they can no longer qualify as genocide; on the other hand, it is as if discrediting the conventional statistics will discredit the very essence of the genocide. Thus, when a scholar of the Holocaust of the stature of Yehuda Bauer revised downwards the number of Jews killed at Auschwitz, the denial industry immediately celebrated such further "evidence" for their corrupt revisionism.

So too there are denials based on the often correct claims that not *all* members of a group were killed or were intended to be killed; hence, it is argued no true genocide was committed or even was attempted. Thus, as previously mentioned, an argument used by those who insist that only the Holocaust was a "true" genocide is that the Turks did not attempt to kill all the Armenians in Istanbul. In fact, it has been shown that there was an original roundup of Armenian political leaders and intelligentsia in Istanbul on April 24, 1915, which marked the onset of the Armenian Genocide, and that the Turks went on to murder thousands of additional Armenians in Istanbul later on, although they never reached the point of creating a total population transfer in that region. The fact is that neither were all Jews killed by the Nazis, not only because the Nazis did not get around to them all, but because there were various exceptions such as deals to allow some Jews to leave in return for trucks, and there are a variety of instances in which the ultimate annihilation of the Jews was postponed in various regions of Europe in response to the complex political interactions with local governments. Obviously, the definition of an obvious event of genocide of a large number of people should not be dependent on the degrees of efficiency and inefficiency or the timetables of the perpetrators for getting to victims.

Another device used by deniers which borders on a return to the sloppy or flagrant forms of racism is to attempt to stigmatize the victim group as unlikable, or say as provocative, rebellious and disloyal to a host nation, as if to justify, at least psychologically, their deserving to be attacked.

Over time the intellectual argumentation employed by deniers has become more and more sophisticated. The deniers attempt to employ various devices of rationalization and deconstruction of meaning that seek to avoid placing the deniers themselves in *obviously* bad lights as intellectual hooligans or bigots. Professor Bernard Lewis, for example, argued in formal written communications to the court in Paris—where he was successfully sued, convicted and fined for having been derelict of his responsibilities as a scholar—that he had revised his earlier writing about the holocaust of the Armenians based on new researches which he never cites even when challenged (Adalian, 1997; Charny, 1997, 2001).

Similarly, historical "reinterpretations" of the Holocaust were advanced in Germany by Professor Ernst Nolte and others in a thinly veiled but unfortunately clever maneuver to devalue the Holocaust, arguing that there was nothing new in human history about collective mass murder. Nolte, moreover, accompanies the above subtle denial with manifest adulation of Hitler as a great German, as well as citations of full-fledged known revisionists, but then too with periodic statements of regret over the deaths of the Jews. The total effect is one of masterful sophisticated denial, in which the central argument that there have always been mass murders and therefore the Holocaust is not uniquely new in itself is literally correct. Yet the meta-meaning is to relativize and deconstruct the Holocaust, let alone as noted to engage in various forms of partial denial of central facts of the Holocaust (Nolte, 1966, 1994; Charny, 1997, 2001).

What is common to all the labored redefinitions is that they seek to achieve the exclusion of some large number(s) of dead human bodies that have been murdered en masse from the universe of genocide. For a further discussion of "definitionalism" in the context of the legitimate and necessary functions of the process of definition in the workings of science, see Charny (1994) where a generic classification of genocide is presented which treats *all* cases of mass murder as genocide and then further defines specific different subcategories of genocides carefully according to their differential characteristics, so that differences between cases are not at all lost, but at the same time all cases of mass murder are honored as belonging to an overarching world of genocidal events.

## V. Nationalistic Hubris or Self-involvement which Justify Exclusion of Others

### Denials of the Significance of the Genocide of another People

This is an additional category to the classification of denial that is little recognized so that denial is also at work when people of any one ethnicity, including people and nations who themselves have suffered genocide at the hands of another persecutor and who would be expected to be champions of other victims, declare themselves indifferent to the fates of other people and their claims for historical justice.

There are many people and groups of people who have no interest in investing energy to concern themselves with the fates of others. These may be further divided into categories of *not knowing*—not investing the effort to know the facts of the genocide of another people; *not caring*—not feeling emotional or spiritual involvement with the fate of another people; and *justifications of indifference* on the basis of being overly occupied with one's own people's problems. As noted, I have found these phenomena among Israeli-Jewish students, many of whom simply do not know—have not invested the effort to know—the facts of the genocides of many different peoples including both major cases and lesser known cases of genocide; their responses were sadly reminiscent of the way much of the world was unknowing and indifferent to the Holocaust. In other cases, the indifference is, simply stated, as emotional indifference even in the face of full knowledge of an event. Of the different variations on not being responsive to the genocide of another people, the most "sensible" or understandable variation on the theme of indifference is when members of a people are beset by their own survival problems and are unable to devote energies to caring about others, although one still must question whether the choice of indifference is also an unwillingness to be concerned or involved with what happens to others.

Since history is full of tangled webs of many peoples persecuting one another, indifference to the fate of another people can also be out of open antagonism to the victims because these people have previously persecuted one's own people, e.g. indifference of Armenians towards the genocide of Kurds at the hands of Iraq and Turkey, Jews towards Ukrainian victims of Stalin's genocidal famine, or Jews towards Croatians and Moslems slaughtered by Serbs.

A curious and often unwitting contribution to denial of genocide derives from what seems to be anthropologically a natural and universal tendency and need to define the genocide or massacre of one's own people as unique; it then follows that one is inclined to begrudge the equal significance of another people's tragedy and perhaps to exclude another people's tragedy from qualifying for the same serious definition of "genocide" (Kuper, 1990). This same mechanism is periodically also adopted by some others who are not of the victim ethnic group but who choose to identify fervently with the cause of a given people as uniquely overriding all other cases of genocide.

### The Meta-meanings of Claims of Uniqueness of the Holocaust

I believe that it especially behooves all of us who are deeply identified with commemoration of the Holocaust to take a probing meta-analytic look at the meanings, implications and consequences of repeated categorical claims that a given genocide is so unfathomably unique that no other events of genocide can qualify for the same designation. I too am committed to eternal memorial of the Holocaust, recognition of its many unique elements, and even more, I believe, its archetypal meanings for the past, present and future. However, if the ways in which we analyze and categorize the Holocaust contribute to failures to define other events of genocidal murders as high crimes of genocide, or to any other degrees of delegitimizing or devaluing the other events, or if our argumentation on behalf of the uniqueness of the Holocaust becomes a justification of other events of mass murder as natural in the history of the human species, thus lending support to Nolte-like minimizations of the significance of other mass murders, we are duty bound to reexamine the ways in which we present the unique aspects of the Holocaust.

Along with many aspects of new and precedent-shattering depravity, including the Nazis' intense level of commitment and organization of societal resources and human will to the creation of death factories never before seen, the events of the Holocaust nonetheless resemble a variety of genocides of other peoples. They are also prototypes that can be easily exceeded in events of mass murder yet to come, perhaps some day even against entire planets (in what I have called *planeticide*) as we prepare for the continued unfolding of human life within the limitless mystery of the universe. As I have written in a book that collates oral histories of different peoples in a single volume and seeks to convey the orchestra of universal human suffering in genocide (Totten *et al.*, 1997), the Holocaust was a decidedly unique event which is superimposed on a pattern of genocidal killing long familiar in human history.

The insistence on uniqueness of the Holocaust may also add unwanted fuel to fires that claim the Jewish people place themselves above other peoples, and make themselves superior to others in an arrogant insistence on their specialness. Anthropological history teaches us that *many* peoples claim that they were chosen and/or better than others, including that they were chosen by divine force for a unique role. This mechanism of attributing special and even divine significance to one's people seems to be a collective defense mechanism to give a people a sense of security and a rallying point, and while the folklore around being a chosen people can be appreciated and even loved, humanistic people need to be careful not to reify such concepts which we know all too well are the backbone of every virulent pattern of dehumanization of others by whatever master race or power. No less a great scholar of genocide and humanist than Leo Kuper (1990, p 1) wrote in pain and anger of "the alienation of many major Jewish organizations from our work of prevention of genocide ... What I cannot understand is why the emphasis on the uniqueness of Jewish annihilation in the Holocaust cannot be combined with a heightened concern for the suffering of others?"

When one allows oneself wittingly or unwittingly to be drawn into over-valuations of the uniqueness of the Holocaust, or even into legitimate statements of the unique aspects of the Holocaust without paying attention to the metameanings that are implied and which will be perceived by others as claims of superiority over others, *one is engaging in denial of the tragedy and significance of others, and in this, unknowingly, we too end up joining no less than the larger body of revisionists.* I believe that we are the more true and devoted to the sanctity of the Holocaust when we transform memorial of the Holocaust into a clarion call to all humankind to seek justice and protection of all human life. I have little doubt that in doing so we also become more effective spokesmen of the memorial of the Holocaust.

Paradoxically, in the process of fighting back against claims of uniqueness or super-special meaning of a given genocide, there have been instances where the antagonistic responses have been rendered in such a hostile combative manner that, although quite likely inadvertently, they have minimized the extent of the genocide to which the grand claims were laid, and worse yet projected an air of irreverence and disrespect for the genuine significance of that genocide. And so the tables are once again turned, and in the battle against hubris and overspecialness of one people, there is a seesawing back to diminution of that people's significance or overelevation of another or other peoples.

## VI. Human Shallowness—the Dulling and Depletion of a Genuine Sense of Tragedy and Moral Outrage

### Denials Deriving from Routinization, Desensitization or Banalization of Events of Genocide

Finally, some comment on a culture-trend that seems inherent in human experience over time to desensitize and dull meanings of past events, even when these are enormous tragedies.

(Already back in the 1980s I recall a conference on genocide at a university where the assisting staff hung signs, "This Way to Genocide Banquet"!) Perhaps we are doomed to trivialization even of great events of hell, because history forever goes on to produce newer events of disaster, and one ends up living with the most recent memories, let alone the dread of what is coming next. Perhaps, too, existentially people naturally transform memorials into celebrations of being alive. In any case, the long-term maintenance of meaning and sanctity in memorials of genocide requires considerable attention and efforts.

## Conclusion: Planning Counterattacks of Denials

Coping with denial requires that one plan interventions and policies on the basis of understanding the specific mind constructions and dynamics of argumentations and language that one needs to overcome. Deeper understanding of the many different faces of denials of Holocaust and genocide is a necessary basis for formulating more effective campaigns for responding to the various revisionists.

Many revisionists are exploiting structures of democratic society, including the institutions of free speech and the inherent principles of political open-mindedness and respect for controversy, diversity, and complexity, but theirs is *not* a genuine exploration of history, nor do they honestly subscribe to what we really mean by free speech. The revisionist message is, after all, one of suppressing truth and rewriting history without reference to and in violation of reality. Their basic message is also a celebration of fascism and violence. I suggest that their calls of "Fire, Fire" in the crowded and vulnerable theaters of human life are fuel on the fires of prejudice, hatred and violence, and these are malignant forces that healthy democratic societies must control even at the expense of some tension with democratic values of free speech.

There are also other forms of denial which, though also facilitating bigotry and violence, are defined in more "innocent" forms, often even in conscious sincerity of the deniers that they are doing good and not out to harm anyone. These denials too must be fought vigorously and aggressively. In public and scholarly debates, I would not be polite or simply "scholarly" with such deniers, and I would attack their self-serving motives, lack of intellectual integrity, incitement of violence, celebration of power, and certainly their lack of humanity in throwing out statements in the faces of grieving relatives and descendants and surviving ethnic communities that the murdered people were not murdered. An important development in this direction which took place in the Spring of 1995 was the previously mentioned conviction of Professor Bernard Lewis in a French court for denials of the Armenian Genocide (Adalian, 1997).

As for scholars who pontificate or obsessively disqualify any event of mass murder from the definition of genocide, while I respect any intellectual differences, I protest their right to disqualify and dishonor peoples of other ethnicities. I would say that to rank genocides in importance is, symbolically, an echo of other despicable rankings of peoples from superior to inferior, from chosen peoples to rejected peoples; and that such hierarchical classifications continue, even if unknowingly, the very underlying illness of our human species of denying that we are intrinsically all one and the same in the face of the perplexity and unfathomable nature of our species' place in the mystery of cosmic interplanetary and intergalactic reality. The burnt offerings of any one people by another to the evil gods of genocide cannot be ranked in relative importance, even as at any given time a particular event, such as the Holocaust, so violates human sensibility that it becomes defined as an archetypal milestone of the sacrificing of human life.

Finally, I wish to propose the convening of a conference for the purpose of designing international, national, community, and individual strategies and tools for relentlessly counterattacking all forms of denial. Such a conference should include social psychology and communication specialists, public opinion pollsters, media and journalism experts and advertising professionals, human rights experts, attorneys, clinical psychologists and psychiatrists, educators, philosophers, theologians, and historians. Denials of genocides need to be fought by a variety of historical evidences, legal injunctions and protections, human rights standard-setting and watchdog agencies, and psychological information and public opinion programs which, all together, will press deniers back into corners in the public mind where they will be disrespected as vendors and advocates of ugly violences to human life, and will be seen to be both in violation of the law and in violation of decent people's norms.

## Bibliography

Adalian, Rouben (1992) "The Armenian Genocide: revisionism and denial," in Michael N. Dobkowski and Isidor Wallimann, eds, *Genocide in Our Time: An Annotated Bibliography with Analytical Introductions* (Ann Arbor, MI: Pierian Press), pp 85–106.

Adalian, Rouben (1997) "The ramifications in the United States of the 1995 French Court decision on the denial of the Armenian Genocide and Princeton University," *Revue du monde arménien modern et contemporain* (Paris: Societé des Etudes Arméniennes), Vol 3, pp 99–122.

Anti-Defamation League (1993) *Hitler's Apologists: The Anti-Semitic Propaganda of Holocaust "Revisionism,"* prepared by Marc Caplan (New York: Anti-Defamation League).

Armenian Assembly of America (1987) "US academicians and lobbying on the Armenian genocide resolution," *Journal of the Armenian Assembly*, Vol 14, No 1, pp 1, 6–8, 12.

Browning, Christopher (1993) *Ordinary Men: Reserve Police Batallion 101 and the Final Solution in Poland* (New York: Harper-Collins).

Charny, Israel W. (1982) *How Can We Commit the Unthinkable? Genocide: The Human Cancer* (Boulder, CO: Westview Press). Republished in Portuguese with a new Introduction and Bibliography as *Anatomia do Genocído: Uma Psicologia da Agress111o Humana* (Rio de Janeiro: Editora Rosa dos Tempos, 1998).

Charny, Israel W. (1983) "The Turks, Armenians and Jews," in Israel W. Charny and Shamai Davidson, eds, *The Book of the International Conference on the Holocaust and Genocide. Book One. The Conference Program and Crisis* (Tel Aviv: Institute of the International Conference on the Holocaust and Genocide), pp 269–315.

Charny, Israel W. (1991) "The psychology of denial of known genocides," in Israel W. Charny, ed., *Genocide: A Critical Bibliographic Review, Volume 2* (London: Mansell Publishing; New York: Facts on File), pp 3–37.

Charny, Israel W. (1993) " 'Innocent denials' of known genocides: a further contribution to a psychology of denial of genocide (revisionism)," *Internet on the Holocaust and Genocide*, Special Triple Issue 44–46 (September), *Denial of the Holocaust, Genocide and Contemporary Massacres*, pp 20–22.

Charny, Israel W. (1994) "Towards a generic definition of genocide," in George Andreopoulos, ed., *The Conceptual and Historical Dimensions of Genocide* (Philadelphia: University of Pennsylvania Press), pp 64–94. (Presented at the Yale University Law School Raphael Lemkin Symposium on Genocide, February 1991.)

Charny, Israel W. (1997) "L'intolérable perversion des universitaires négateurs du génocide Arménien ou de l'Holocauste," *Revue du monde arménien moderne et contemporain* (Paris: Societé des Etudes Arméniennes), Vol 3, pp 123–141 (French).

Charny, Israel W. (1999) "Templates for gross denial of a known genocide: a manual," in *Encyclopedia of Genocide* (see below), p 168.

Charny, Israel W. (2000) " 'Innocent denials' of known genocides: a further contribution to a psychology of known genocide (revisionism)," *Human Rights Review*, Vol 1, No 3, pp 15–39.

Charny, Israel W. (2001) "The psychological satisfaction of denials of the Holocaust or other genocides by non-extremists or bigots, and even by known scholars," *Idea—A Journal of Social Issues*, Vol 6, No 1. http://www.ideajournal.com/charny-denials.html.

Charny, Israel W. and Fromer, Daphna (1990a) "A follow-up of the sixty-nine scholars who signed an advertisement questioning the Armenian genocide," *Internet on the Holocaust and Genocide, Special Double Issue 25/26 on the Seventy-Fifth Anniversary of the Armenian Genocide*, April, pp 5–6. Brief report. Reprinted in *Journal of the Armenian Assembly of America*, 1990, Vol 17, No 1, p 5.

Charny, Israel W. and Fromer, Daphna (1990b) "A study of the readiness of Jewish/Israeli students in the health professions to authorize and execute involuntary mass euthanasia of 'severely handicapped' patients," *Holocaust and Genocide Studies*, Vol 5, No 3, pp 313–335.

Charny, Israel W. and Fromer, Daphna (1990c) "The readiness of health profession students to comply with a hypothetical program of 'forced migration' of a minority population," *American Journal of Orthopsychiatry*, Vol 60, No 4, pp 486–495.

Charny, Israel W. and Fromer, Daphna (1992) "A study of attitudes of viewers of the film 'Shoah' towards an incident of mass murder by Israeli soldiers (Kfar Kassem, 1956)," *Journal of Traumatic Stress*, Vol 5, No 2, pp 303–318.

Charny, Israel W. and Fromer, Daphna (1998) "Denying the Armenian genocide: patterns of thinking as defence-mechanisms," *Patterns of Prejudice*, Vol 32, No 1, pp 39–49.

Darley, John (1996) "Review," *Political Psychology*, Vol 17, No 3, pp 573–586.

Des Pres, Terrence (1986) "On governing narratives: the Turkish–Armenian case," *Yale Review*, Vol 75, No 4, pp 517–531.

*Encyclopedia of Genocide* (1999) (Santa Barbara, CA, Denver, CO, Oxford, UK: ABC-CLIO (2 volumes). Editor-in-Chief: Israel W. Charny. Forewords by Archbishop Desmond M. Tutu and Simon Wiesenthal. Associate Editors: Rouben P. Adalian, Steven L. Jacobs, Eric Markusen, Samuel Totten; Bibliographic Editor: Marc I. Sherman. See especially Section: Denials of genocide, pp 159–186.

Ferry, W. H. (1975) "The urban exodus in Cambodia: other possibilities," *Fellowship Magazine*, Vol 41, No 6, p 20.

Hinton, Alexander L. (1996) "Agents of death: explaining the Cambodian Genocide in terms of psycho-social dissonance," *American Anthropologist*, Vol 98, No 4, pp 818–826.

Hovannisian, Richard G. (1997) *Denial of the Armenian Genocide: With Some Comparisons to Holocaust Denial* (Sydney, Australia: Macquarie University, Centre for Comparative Genocide Studies, Pamphlet).

*Internet on the Holocaust and Genocide* (1993) "Denial of the Holocaust, genocide and contemporary massacres," Special Triple Issue 44–46 (September).

Jacobs, Steven L. (1999) "Holocaust/Shoah revisionists," in *Encyclopedia of Genocide, op. cit.*, pp 181–187.

Kaye, Ephraim (1997) *Desecraters of Memory: Confronting Holocaust Denial* (Jerusalem: Yad Vashem International School for Holocaust Studies).

Kloian, Richard, ed. (1988) *The Armenian Genocide, News Accounts from the American Press: 1915–1922*, 3rd edition (Richmond, CA: Armenian Genocide Resource Center).

Kulka, Erich (1991) "Denial of the Holocaust," in Israel W. Charny, ed., *Genocide: A Critical Bibliographic Review, Volume 2* (London: Mansell Publishing; New York: Facts on File), pp 38–62.

Kuper, Leo (1990) "An agonizing issue: the alienation of the unique," *Internet on the Holocaust and Genocide*, Issue 27, June 1990, Special Supplement, 2 pp.

Lerner, Melvin J. (1980) *The Belief in a Just World: A Fundamental Delusion* (New York: Plenum).

Lipstadt, Deborah (1993) *Denying the Holocaust: The Growing Assault on Truth and Memory* (New York: Free Press).

Markusen, Eric and Kopf, David (1995) *The Holocaust and Strategic Bombing: Genocide and Total War in the Twentieth Century* (Boulder, CO: Westview Press).

McCarthy, Justin and McCarthy, Carolyn (1989) *Turks and Armenians: A Manual on the Armenian Question* (Washington, DC: Assembly of Turkish Armenian Association).

Nolte, Ernst (1966) *Three Faces of Fascism: Action Française, Italian Fascism. National Socialism*, translated from the German by L. Vennewitz (New York: Holt, Rinehart & Winston).

Nolte, Ernst (1994) Interview of Professor Ernst Nolte in *Der Spiegel*, as presented in Hebrew translation in *Haaretz*, October 28, 1994 (translated from the Hebrew).

Robins, Nicholas A. (2002) *Genocide and Millennialism in Upper Peru: The Great Rebellion of 1780–1782* (Westport, CN: Greenwood Publishing).

Rosenbaum, Alan, ed. (1996) *Is the Holocaust Unique? Perspective on Comparative Genocide* (Boulder, CO: Westview Press).

Sanger, David L. (1994) "New Tokyo Minister calls 'Rape of Nanking' a fabrication," *New York Times International*, May 5, A9.

Smith, R. Jeffrey (1999) "A phone intercept links Belgrade to an order to kill 45 in Kosovo," *Washington Post Service* as reported in the *International Herald Tribune*, January 29.

Smith, Roger (1991) "Denial of the Armenian Genocide," in Israel W. Charny, ed., *Genocide: A Critical Bibliographic Review, Volume 2* (London: Mansell Publishing; New York: Facts on File), pp 63–85.

Smith, Roger W., Markusen, Eric and Lifton, Robert Jay (1995) "Professional ethics and denial of the Armenian Genocide," *Holocaust and Genocide Studies*, Vol 9, No 1, pp 1–22.

Stern, Kenneth S. (1993) *Holocaust Denial* (New York: American Jewish Committee).

Totten, Samuel, Parsons, William and Charny, Israel W., eds (1997) *Century of Genocide: Eyewitness Accounts and Critical Views* (New York: Garland Publishing Co.).

Vidal-Naquet, Pierre (1992) *Assassins of Memory: Essays on the Denial of the Holocaust* (New York: Columbia University Press).

Vyronis, S. Jr. (1993) *The Turkish State and History: Clio Meets the Grey Wolf*, 2nd edition (Thessalonika: Institute for Balkan Studies; New York: Aristide D. Caratzas).

# Permissions Acknowledgements

Abiew, Frances Kofi. "The East Pakistan (Bangladesh) Intervention of 1971" and "Vietnam's Intervention in Cambodia (Kampuchea), 1978" in The *Evolution of the Doctrine and Practice of Humanitarian Intervention* by Francis Kofi Abiew. The Hague: Kluwer Law International, 1999, pp. 113–120 and 127–131. Copyright © 1999 by Brill Academic Publishers. Reproduced with permission of Brill Academic Publishers in the format Textbook via Copyright Clearance Center.

Akhavan, Payam and Mora Johnson. "International Criminal Tribunal for the Former Yugoslavia" in *Encyclopedia of Genocide and Crimes Against Humanity, Vol. 3*, edited by Dinah Shelton, pp. 555–564. New York: Macmillan, 2005. Copyright ©2005 by Gale, a part of Cengage Learning, Inc. Reproduced with permission. www.cengage.com/permissions

Balint, Jennifer. "National Trials in Rwanda" in *Encyclopedia of Genocide, Vol. II*, edited by Israel W. Charny, pp. 557–559. Copyright © 1999 by ABC-CLIO Inc. Reproduced with permission of ABC-CLIO Inc. in the format Textbook via Copyright Clearance Center.

Ball, Howard. "The Path to Nuremberg," "Formation of the ICTR," and "Nuremberg's Legacy: Adoption of the Rome Statute" in *Prosecuting War Crimes and Genocide: The Twentieth-Century Experience*, pp. 44–61, 170–177, and 188–216. Lawrence: University of Kansas, 1999. Copyright © 1999 by the University Press of Kansas. Reprinted with permission of the publisher.

Bartrop, Paul and Samuel Totten. "The History of Genocide: An Overview" in *Teaching About Genocide: Issues, Approaches, and Resources*, edited by Samuel Totten, pp. 23–56. Greenwich, CT: Information Age Publishing, 2004. Copyright © 2004 by Information Age Publishing. Reproduced with permission of Information Age Publishing in the format Textbook via Copyright Clearance Center.

Bassouni, M. Cherif. "Realpolitik" (Originally entitled "Preface") in *State Sovereignty and International Criminal Law: Versailles to Rome*, pp. ix–xi. Ardsley, NY: Transnational Publishers, 2003. Copyright 2003 © by Transnational Publishers. Reproduced with permission of Brill Academic Publishers.

Bell-Fialkoff, Andrew. "A Typology of Cleansing" in *Ethnic Cleansing*, pp. 51–56. New York: St. Martin's, 1999. Copyright © 1999 by Andrew Bell-Fialkoff. Reproduced with permission of Palgrave Macmillan in the format Textbook via Copyright Clearance Center.

Bergsmo, Morten. "Intent" in *Encyclopedia of Genocide and Crimes Against Humanity, Vol. 3*, edited by Dinah Shelton, pp. 525–530. New York: Macmillan, 2005. Copyright © 2005 by Gale, a part of Cengage Learning, Inc. Reproduced by permission. www.cengage.com/permissions

Charny, Israel. "The Definition of Genocide" in *Genocide: A Critical Bibliographic*

*Review*, edited by Israel W. Charny, pp. 2–4. New York: Facts on File, 1988. Copyright © 1988 by Facts On File, Inc. Reproduced with permission of Facts On File, Inc in the format Textbook via Copyright Clearance Center.

Charny, Israel. "A Classification of the Denials of the Holocaust and Other Genocides," *Journal of Genocide Research* 5(1) (2003): 11–34. Reprinted by permission of the publisher, Taylor & Francis Ltd, http://www.informaworld.com.

Cotton, James. "Against the Grain: The East Timor Intervention," *Survival* 43(1) (Spring 2001): 127–142. (Published by the International Institute for Strategic Studies). Reprinted by permission of the publisher, Taylor & Francis Ltd, http://www.informaworld.com.

Fein, Helen. "Defining Genocide as a Sociological Concept" from "Genocide: A Sociological Concept" in *Current Sociology: The Journal of the International Association*, 38(1) (Spring 1990): 8–25. Copyright © 1990 by International Sociological Association/ISA. Reproduced with permission of Sage Publications Ltd.

Fein, Helen. "The Three P's of Genocide Prevention: With Application to a Genocide Foretold – Rwanda" in *Protection Against Genocide: Mission Impossible?*, edited by Neal Riemer, pp. 42–66. Westport, CT: Praeger, 2000. Copyright © 2000 by Neal Riemer. Reproduced with permission of Greenwood Publishing Group, Inc. Westport, CT.

Harff, Barbara. "The Etiology of Genocides" in *Genocide and the Modern Age: Etiology and Case Studies of Mass Death*, edited by Isidor Wallimann and Michael N. Dobkowski, pp. 41–59. Copyright © 1987 by Isidor Wallimann and Michael N. Dobkowski. Reproduced with permission of Greenwood Publishing Group, Inc. Westport, CT.

Harff, Barbara. "Recognizing Genocides and Politicides" in *Genocide Watch*, edited by Helen Fein, pp. 28–41. New Haven, CT: Yale University Press, 1992. Copyright © 1992 by Helen Fein. Reproduced with permission of Yale University Press.

Honig, Jan Willem. "Srebrenica" in *Encyclopedia of Genocide and Crimes Against Humanity, Vol. 2*, edited by Dinah Shelton, pp. 988–989. New York: Macmillan, 2005. Copyright © 2005 by Gale, a part of Cengage Learning, Inc. Reproduced by permission. www.cengage.com/permissions

Interview with Romeo Dallaire from the Frontline website for The Ghosts of Rwanda located at: http://www.pbs.org/wgbh/pages/frontline/shows/ghosts/interviews/dallaire/html. From Frontline WGBH Educational Foundation. Copyright © 2005 by WGBH/Boston. Reproduced with the permission of WGBH/Boston.

Jentleson, Bruce W. "The Dilemma of Political Will: How Fixed, How Malleable the Domestic Constraints?" in *Coercive Prevention: Normative, Political, and Policy Dilemmas*, pp. 24–28. Washington, D.C.: United States Institute of Peace, 2000. Reprinted with permission of the publisher.

Kiernan, Ben. "Twentieth Century Genocides: Underlying Ideological Themes from Armenia to East Timor" in *The Specter of Genocide: Mass Murder in Historical Perspective*, edited by Robert Gellately and Ben Kiernan, pp. 29–52. New York: Cambridge University Press, 2003. Copyright © by Cambridge University Press 2003. Reprinted with the permission of Cambridge University Press.

LeBlanc, Lawrence J. "Development of the Rule on Genocide" in *The United States and the Genocide Convention*, pp. 17–33. Copyright © 1991 by Duke University Press. All rights reserved. Used by permission of the publisher.

Levene, Mark. "Connecting Threads: Rwanda, the Holocaust, and the Pattern of Contemporary Genocide" in *Genocide: Essays Toward Understanding, Early – Warning and Prevention*, edited by Roger W. Smith. Williamsburg, VA: Association of Genocide Scholars, 1999. Copyright © 1999 by Mark Levene. Reproduced with permission of author.

Lopez, George A. "Economic Sanctions and Genocide: Too Little, Too Late, and Sometimes Too Much" in *Protection Against Genocide: Mission Impossible?*, edited by Neal Riemer, pp. 67–84. Westport, CT: Praeger, 2000. Copyright © 2000 by Neal Riemer. Reproduced with permission of Greenwood Publishing Group, Inc. Westport, CT.

Lyon, Michell S. and Mark A. Drumbl. "International Criminal Tribunal for Rwanda" in *Encyclopedia of Genocide and Crimes Against Humanity, Vol. 3*, edited by Dinah Shelton, pp. 547–555. New York: Macmillan, 2005. Copyright © 2005 by Gale, a part of Cengage Learning, Inc. Reproduced by permission. www.cengage.com/permissions

Mann, Michael. "Explaining Ethnic Cleansing" in *The Dark Side of Democracy: Explaining Ethnic Cleansing*, pp. 1–10. New York: Cambridge University Press, 2005. Copyright © by Michael Mann 2005. Reprinted with the permission of Cambridge University Press.

Maogoto, Jackson Nyamuya. "The Concept of Sovereignty and the Development of International Law" (Originally entitled "Introduction") in *State Sovereignty and International Criminal Law: Versailles to Rome*, pp. 1–5. Ardsley, NY: Transnational Publishers, 2003. Copyright 2003 © by Transnational Publishers. Reproduced with permission of Brill Academic Publishers.

Melson, Robert F. "The Armenian Genocide as Precursor and Prototype of Twentieth Century Genocide" in Is *the Holocaust Unique? Perspectives on Comparative Genocide*, edited by Alan S. Rosenbaum, pp. 87–99. Boulder, CO: Westview Press, 1998. Copyright © 1998 by Westview Press, A Member of Perseus Books, L.L.C. Reprinted with the permission of the publisher.

Niewyk, Donald. "Holocaust: Genocide of the Jews" in *Century of Genocide*, Second Edition, edited by Samuel Totten, William S. Parsons, and Israel Charny, pp. 127–140. New York: Routledge, 2004. Copyright © 2004 by Taylor & Francis Group LLC – Books. Reproduced with permission of Taylor & Francis Group LLC-Books in the format Textbook via Copyright Clearance Center.

Report of the International Commission on Intervention and State Sovereignty. Excerpts from *The Responsibility to Protect*. Synopsis (pp. XI–XIII), Chapter 1 ("The Policy Challenge", pp. 1–9) and Chapter 2 ("A New Approach: The Responsibility to Protect", pp. 11–18).

Schabas, William. "Crimes Against Humanity" in *Encyclopedia of Genocide and Crimes Against Humanity, Vol. 3*, edited by Dinah Shelton, pp. 209–216. New York: Macmillan, 2005. Copyright © 2005 by Gale, a part of Cengage Learning, Inc. Reproduced by permission. www.cengage.com/permissions

Semelin, Jacques. "Massacres" in *Encyclopedia of Genocide and Crimes Against Humanity, Vol. 3*, edited by Dinah Shelton, pp. 661–665. New York: Macmillan, 2005. Copyright © 2005 by Gale, a part of Cengage Learning, Inc. Reproduced by permission. www.cengage.com/permissions

Sharlach, Lisa. "State Rape: Sexual Violence as Genocide" in *Violence and Politics: Globalization's Paradox*, edited by Kenton Worcester, Sally Avery Bermanzohn, and Mark Ungar. New York: Routledge, 2002, pp. 107–123. Copyright © 2002 by Taylor & Francis Group LLC – Books. Reproduced with permission of Taylor & Francis Group LLC – Books in the format Textbook via Copyright Clearance Center.

Smith, Roger W. "Human Destructiveness and Politics: The Twentieth Century as an Age of Genocide" in *Genocide and the Modern Age: Etiology and Case Studies of Mass Death*, edited by Isidor Wallimann and Michael N. Dobkowski, pp. 23–27. Copyright © 1987 by Isidor Wallimann and Michael N. Dobkowski. Reproduced with permission of Greenwood Publishing Group, Inc. Westport, CT.

Smith, Roger W. "Scarcity and Genocide" in *On the Edge of Scarcity: Environment, Resources, Population, Sustainability and Conflict*, edited by Michael N. Dobkowski and Isidor Wallimann, pp. 138–148. Syracuse, NY: Syracuse University Press, 2002. Reproduced with permission of Syracuse University Press.

Stanton, Gregory. "Early Warning" in *Encyclopedia of Genocide and Crimes Against Humanity, Vol. 3*, edited by Dinah Shelton, pp. 271–273. New York: Macmillan, 2005. Copyright © 2005 by Gale, a part of Cengage Learning, Inc. Reproduced by permission. www.cengage.com/permissions

Stanton, Gregory. "The Eight Stages of Genocide" in http://www.genocidewatch.org/8stages.htm. Copyright © 1998 by Gregory H. Stanton. Reproduced with permission of the author.

Staub, Ervin. "The Origins of Genocide and Mass Killing: Core Concepts" in *The Roots of Evil: The Origins of Genocide and Other Group Violence*, pp. 13–28. New York: Cambridge University Press, 1989. Copyright © 1989 by Cambridge University Press. Reprinted with the permission of Cambridge University Press.

Totten, Samuel. "Genocide in Darfur" in *Century of Genocide: Critical Essays and Eyewitness Accounts*, edited by Samuel Totten and William S. Parsons. New York: Routledge, forthcoming. Copyright © 2009 by Routledge. Reproduced by permission of Routledge, Inc., a division of Informa plc.

Uvin, Peter and Charles Mironko. "The International Criminal Tribunal for Rwanda" in *Global Governance: A Review of Multilateralism and International Organizations*, 9(2): 219–222. Copyright © 2003 by Lynne Rienner Publishers, Inc. Used with permission of the publisher. Excerpted from "Western and Local Approaches to Justice in Rwanda" in *Global Governance* 9 (2003): 210–231.

Weiss, Thomas G. and Cindy Collins. "Policies of Militarized Humanitarian Intervention in *Humanitarian Challenges and Intervention*, pp. 159–182. Boulder, CO: Westview Press, 2000. Copyright © 2000 by Westview Press, A Member of the Perseus Books Group. Reprinted with permission of the publisher.

Wheeler, Nicholas J. "Reflections on the Legality and Legitimacy of NATO'S Intervention in Kosovo" in *The Kosovo Tragedy: The Human Rights Dimensions*, edited by Ken Booth. Copyright © 2001 Frank Cass Publishers, 2001. Reprinted with permission of Taylor and Francis Books, UK.

# Index

Abbot, Diane 415
Abdouffrag, Abdul 217
Abdul Hamid II, Sultan 138, 235
Aborigines, Australian 71, 137–8
Abu Shouk 205
Aché Indians, Paraguay 16, 147
Afghanistan
    Soviet destruction of 51, 52, 53
    US invasion xiv, 398
African Crisis Response Initiative (ACRI) 366
African National Congress 380
African Union (AU) 207, 218–19
African Union Mission in Sudan (AMIS) 207, 210
Agathe, Prime Minister 347
age, cleansing by 63
Ahtisaari, Martii 385
aid, withholding of 37
Akayesu, Jean-Paul 153, 182, 187
    trial 26, 464, 466, 468, 471, 472, 478, 480, 482–4,
        489
Akçura, Yusuf 243, 245, 247, 248
Albright, Madeleine K. 357, 494, 495
Alquen, Gunter d' 249
Amin, Idi 72, 117, 118, 129, 412
Amnesty International 205, 211
Amristar massacre 88
Annan, Kofi xiv, 219, 316, 318, 330, 332, 338–9, 341, 344,
        376, 418, 509
anticolonial rebellions 113
Anti-Defamation League 523
anti-Semitism 14, 101–2, 115, 161–2, 244
    see also Holocaust, Nazi
Anyidoho, General Henry 352
apartheid 81, 84, 380
APODETTI 116
Arbab, Mohammed Abdullah 223–6
Arbour, Louise 443, 503
Arendt, Hannah 91
Aristide, Jean Bertrand 380
Armenian genocide 3, 42, 68, 78–9, 90, 114, 122, 133,
        138–9, 215, 268
    Bosnian genocide and 241
    Holocaust vs 236–8
    Nigeria and 238–9, 240–1

as precursor and prototype of 20th-century genocide
    234–43
    Yugoslavia and 239–40
arms embargoes 386, 387
Army Judge Advocate Group 428
Arnold, George 214
Arusha Accords 186, 328, 329, 348
Aschersleben 178
ASEAN 398, 399, 401, 402–3, 404
ASEAN Regional Forum (ARF) 402
Asia-Pacific Conference on East Timor 403
Aspegren, Lennart 482
Assembly of Turkish American Associations 524
Atrocities Documentation Team (ADT) 205
Auschwitz-Birkenau death camp 9, 139, 158, 161, 163,
        171–3, 176, 177, 179, 245, 249, 250, 260, 265, 429,
        523, 529
Aust, Anthony 415
Australia–Indonesia Agreement on Maintaining
        Security 404
autogenocide 52, 96, 133, 149
Axis Rule in Occupied Europe 13–14
Axworthy, Lloyd 503

babies, cleansing through killing 63
Badri, Gabril Abdul Kareem 207
Bagilishema, Ignace, trial 479
Bagosora, Colonel Théoneste 347, 348, 349, 359, 471,
        479
Balkan Wars 114, 247
Ban Ki-moon 208, 211
Bangkok Declaration (1993) 399
Bangladesh
    genocide 115, 117, 138, 149
    state rape 182–4
Bangladesh intervention (1971) 390–3
Barayagwiza, Jean-Bosco 477, 479
barbarity 12
Barbie, Klaus 165
Baril, General Maurice 338, 343, 351
al Bashir, Omar 198, 199, 200, 204, 207–8, 216, 217
Beara, Colonel Ljubisa 193
Beardsley, Brent 339, 347
beggars, cleansing of 63

Belzec death camp 139, 158
Berbester Rebbe xv
Bergen-Belsen 178, 429
Bernays, Lieutenant Colonel Murray 428
Bernays plan 428–30
Bernstein, Eduard 115
Bhopal accident 49
Biafra 115, 117, 148–9, 150, 239, 241
Bialystok, pogrom 3
Bin Laden, Osama 199, 207, 217
biological methods of genocide 8–9
Birkenau death camp *see* Auschwitz-Birkenau death camp
*Black Book, The* 201, 203
Blair, Tony, government 414
*Blaškić* trial 444
Blum, Leon 265
*Blut und Boden* 250
Boder, David P. 166
Bolsheviks 66, 89
Booh-Booh, Jacques Roger 343, 344, 346, 347
Bormann, Martin 250, 430, 431
Borovcanin, Colonel Ljubomir 193
Bos, Adriaan 497
Bosnia-Herzegovina xiii, 57, 122, 151, 246
    state rape in 184–6
Boutros-Ghali, Boutros 316, 346, 351, 368, 376
British Medical Association 384
Brownback, Sam 205
Brownlie, Ian 413
Bruny Island people 137
Buchenwald 429
Burkhalter, Holly 333
Burundi 42, 111, 115, 116, 149
Bush, George H.W. 493
Bush, George W. 207, 214, 492
Butler, Richard 452

Caldarone, Alessandro 471
Cambodia xv, 42, 51, 91, 395–6
Carthage, destruction of 133, 135
Cassese, Antonio 28, 444
casualty phobia 293–7
categories of genocide xi–xii
Cathars 136
Catholic Church 163
Cayman Islands 386
Cedras, Roaul 381
Center for Economic and Social Rights i, New York 384
Central Intelligence Agency (CIA) 319
Ćerkez, Mario, trial 447
Cham Muslims 91
Chamberlain, Neville 377
Cheadle, Don 214
Chelmno death camp 139, 158
Chernobyl nuclear disaster 49, 87
Cherokee Indians 108–9
Cheyenne Indians, massacre of 133–4
Chingis-khan *see* Genghis Khan
Chmielnicki, Bogdan 136

Chomsky, Noam 528
Churchill, Winston 427, 429
Chvalkovsky, Czech Foreign Minister 264
Civil Rights Act (1965) 322
Claes, Willy 351
Clark, Ramsey 471
class cleansing 61
classification of genocide 38
classification stage 127
Clausewitz's formula 89
cleansing, typology of 60–3
Clinton, Bill 295, 296, 331, 357–8, 493, 494, 495, 500
    administration 495, 503
Clooney, George 214
Club of Rome doom project 109
CNRT 406
Coalition of International Justice (CIJ) 205
Cohen, William 506
Cold War 148–50, 292
collective terrorism 51
collective violence 50
collectivities 54
Columbus, Christopher 136
commentaries 28–9
Commission on the Responsibilities of the Authors of War and on Enforcement of Penalties 291
concentration camps ix, 9, 139–40
    *see also under names*
Congo 68
Congor, Yacoub 217
conquest, genocides of 118
Control Council Laq No. 10 80
Convention Against Torture and Other Cruel, Inhuman and Degrading Treatment or Punishment 83
Convention on the Non-Applicability of Statutory Limitations to War Crimes and Crimes Against Humanity 81
Convention on the Prevention and Punishment of the Crime of Genocide (UNCG) *see* Genocide Convention
Cook, Robin 415
Corzine, Jon 205
Cosgrove, Major-General Peter 405
coups 113
crimes against humanity 58–9, 78–86
    contextual elements 81–3
    genocide vs 86
    history of term 78–80
    prosecution of 85
    punishable acts 83–5
    statutory limitations 85
Croatia 57
Crusades 41, 43
Crystal Night pogrom *see* Kristallnacht
cultural genocide 7–8, 37, 45, 50, 145
culture 107
Czechoslovakia, invasion of 62

Dachau 429
Dafur, Sudan xiv
Daighne, Captain Mbaye 358

Dakoro, Saleh 217
Dallaire, General Roméo 318, 330, 331, 332, 338–60,
    463, 508
Damon, Matt 214
Dannatt, General 452
Dardama, Shiekha 224
Dardamo, Salih 225
Darehshori, Sara 471
Darfouri, Ibrahim 217
Darfur genocide 133, 134, 194–230
    2007–8 210–11
    Arab supremacism 198–200
    authoritarianism 200
    disagreement among scholars 211–13
    disenfranchisement 200–1
    extreme drought and desertification 198
    first-person accounts by survivor 215–26
    insecurity and bellicosity 201–2
    international community and 206–8
    peace talks 208–9
    reason for 197–8
    rebel attacks amd response by Government of Sudan
        202–6
    victims 196–7
Darfur Peace Agreement (DPA) 208, 209–10
Darré, Richard Walther 249
Dawai, Hamid 224
Dawai, Hasballa 224
Dayton Accords 194, 368, 382, 384
Deby, Mohammed Ahmed Mustafa, General 216
Declaration on Principles of International Law
    Concerning Friendly Relations and Cooperation
    412
Declaration on the Enhancement of the Effectiveness of
    the Principle of Refraining from the Threat or
    Use of Force in International Relations 412
Declaration on the Inadmissibility of Intervention
    411–12
definition of genocide 6–11, 11–14, 36–9, 44–55,
    146–8
definitionalism 529–31
Degni-Segui, Rene 468
dehumanization stage 127–8
Del Ponte, Carla 443, 475, 477, 480
Delimustafic, Alija 185
delusional rationality 88
Demjanjuk, John 85
democide 96
democracy
    ethnic cleansing and 65, 66
    prevention of genocide and 322–3
denial of genocide 517–18
    classification 518–35
    definitionalism 529–31
    human shallowness 533–4
    innocent denials 526–9
    innocent disavowels of violence 526–9
    malevolent bigotry 519–25
    nationalistic hubris 532–3
    self-serving opportunism 525–6
denial stage 128–9

deportation or incarceration societies 38
Des Forges, Alison 329, 330, 331
despotic genocide xii, 37
destruction-and-subjugation methods 89, 91
destruction-for-eradication 89–91
detection of genocide 72–6
Deutsch, Eberhard 19
developmental genocide xii, 37
Diagne, Captain Mbaye 352, 353, 354
Dicker, Richard 503, 509
disappearance method 89
Doenitz, Admiral 431, 435
Dokmanović, Slavko 443, 445
    trial 445
*dolus directus* 28
*dolus eventualis* 23
*dolus specialis* 23, 24
domestic genocides 38
Dorsen, Norman 509
Dresden bombing 52
Dreyfus affair 101
Drina Corps 459, 460, 461
Drost, Pieter N. 5
Dührin, Eugen 237
*Duško Sikirica et al.* case 25
Dyer, Reginald 88

East Pakistan *see* Bangladesh
East Timor 115, 116–17, 150, 251–4
East Timor Intervention 397–407
    precedents 398–400
    UN and 401–2
    regional indifference 402–3
    Australia and US 403–4
    logistics 405–6
    election security 404–5
ecocide 37, 71
economic cleansing 62
economic methods of genocide 8
economic sanctions 368, 378–90
    effectiveness 379–85
ECOSOC 16–17, 18
Edhie, Sarwo 252
Edict of Nantes 137
Egeland, Jan 205
Eichmann, Adolf 85, 163–4
*Einsatzgruppen* trial 434
El Salvador 75
Elhassan, Gaffar Mohamed 207
elite domination 109–10
Enabling Act 114, 119
enforced disappearance of persons 84
Epstein, Nechama 166–79
eradication 89–91
Erdemovic, Drazen 193, 457
Eser, Albin 29
*Eternal Forest, The* 250
ethnic cleansing xiii, 57–8, 61, 63–9, 83, 87, 90, 91, 151,
    181, 240, 440, 517
ethnicity, definition of 69–70
ethnocide 11, 37, 45, 96

ethnonationalism 66
ethnoreligious cleansing 61
etiology of genocides 108–20
EU Rapid Response Force 128
eugenics 244
evil 105–6
extent 48–51
extermination stage 128
external cleansing 62

Falco, Robert 430
*Falintil* 403
Farben, I/G. 434
Farrow, Mia 214
Faurisson, Robert 528
financial sanctions 386–7
Finta, Imre 85
Food and Agriculture Organization (FAO) (UN) 384
Ford, Gerald 403
Forum on Early Warning and Early Response (FEWER) 319
Fossey, Diane 358
Fowler, Jerry 506
Frank, Governor 431
Frankfurter, Felix 42
Fraser, Malcolm 403
Freedom House 318
French Revolution 89, 101
*Fretilin* 116, 252, 399
Freud, Sigmund 105
Frick, Governor 431
Fritzsche 431, 436
Funk 431
Furundžija, Anto, trial 447

*gacaca* 486–7
Gaddafi, Colonel 198
Gagovic, Dragan 186
Gaillard, Philippe 355, 358
game theory 364
gang of security disruptors (GPK) 252–3
gender, cleansing by 62
gendercide 96
Geneva Accords 429, 435
Geneva Conventions 287, 440, 442, 468, 484, 491
Genghis Khan 41, 136
genocidal killing 37
genocidal massacres 37, 47, 51, 88
genocidal pragmatism 244
genocidal societies 38
Genocide Convention xi, xii, xv, 4, 5, 11, 12, 13, 14–21, 23, 24, 25, 27–9, 30–3, 34, 35, 51, 52, 80–1, 86, 95, 96, 111, 134, 135, 137, 140, 142–3, 143–8, 154, 287, 321, 426
   basic elements 18–21
   definition 44–6, 58
   drafting 16–18
   need for 15–16
   on rape 181–2, 183
genocide early warning processes 39
Genocide Intervention Network 214

Genocide Watch 319
Germanification 114, 115
Germanization 44
goals 99–100, 107
Goebbels, Joseph 430
Gokalp, Ziya 248
Goldberg, Arthur 14
Goldstone, Richard 443
Göring, Hermann 158, 248, 430, 431, 435, 436
Governors Island Agreement 380
Gowon, General Yakubu 240
Grams, Rod 496
Great Rebellion in Upper Peru (1780–82) 524
Green, Theodore Francis 13
Greenpeace 384
Grotius, Hugo 412
Guatemalan Civil War 86
   debates surrounding 87–8
Guayaki (Aché) Indians 118, 119
guerrilla war 77
guilt societies 38
Gulf War 294, 384–5
Gypsies (Roma) 75, 114, 115, 244–5, 267, 270

Habibie, Bacharuddin J. 372, 373, 401, 405
Habyarimana, Juvénal 186, 187, 246, 251, 262, 326, 328, 329, 330–1, 346, 381, 463
Hague Conventions (1899, 1907) 78, 289, 430
   Martens clause 430
Hague Regulations 10, 11, 442
Hague Treaties (1899, 1907) 496
Hamidian Massacres 138
harassment societies 38
Harding, Tanya [sic], Tonya 356
Haron, Algali 225
Harwood, Richard 523
Hausa-Fulani Muslims 116, 239, 240
Helms, Jesse 13, 19, 495
Hendrich [sic], *see* Heydrich, Reinhard
Hereros, Namibia, slaughter of 77, 90, 118, 119–20, 133
Heydrich, Reinhard 158, 524
Hilal, Sheikh Musa 207
Himmler, Heinrich 158, 246, 249–50, 251, 430, 435, 524
Hiroshima, nuclear bombing of 52, 82, 529
history of genocide 135–55
Hitler, Adolf xv, 3, 6, 7, 19, 42, 44–5, 68, 71, 102–4, 114, 115, 117, 119, 157, 158–9, 162–5, 244–8, 250, 264, 430, 435, 436
   *Mein Kampf* 245, 249
Hitler Youth 435
HIV, deliberate transmission of 187, 188, 464
Hobbes, Thomas 105, 107
Hoess, Rudolf 246, 248, 249, 250, 431
Holmes, John 210
Holocaust, Nazi xi, 37, 64, 68, 87, 90, 108, 111, 114, 119, 138, 139, 157–80, 215
   Armenian genocide vs 236–8
   burden of history 161–2
   debates about 164–5
   eyewitness accounts of Jews 166–79
   lessons 165–6

modern-day perspective 165
participants and bystanders 160–1
perpetrators 15
policy and procedures 158
responses after 163–4
Rwanda and 258–84
survivor responses 162–3
victims 159–60
homosexuality 37
cleansing 62–3
Hitler and 244
Hoxha, Batisha 63–4
Hoxha, Izet 63–4
Huguenots 137
Hull, Cordell 427, 428, 429
Human Rights Watch 187, 205, 211, 503, 505, 509
human shallowness 533–4
humanitarian intervention 295
Hun Sen 406
Hungarian revolution 62
Hussein, Saddam 133, 207, 271, 294
Hutu Power 244
Hutus, Rwanda 38, 91, 115, 116, 138, 149, 152, 186, 187, 261

Ibos 116, 239, 240
ideological cleansing 61–2
ideological genocide xii, 37, 42–3
ideological massacres 47
Idris, Alamin 225
Ieng Sary 248
India 116
India Act (1836) (UK) 428
Indonesia 115
innocent denials of genocide 526–9
innocent disavowels of violence 526–9
Inquisition 43
institutional genocide 41
intent 22–30, 48–52, 146–7
interahamwe 187, 260
Inter-American Association for Democracy and Freedom 118
INTERFET (International Forces in East Timor) 399, 400, 401, 404, 405, 406
internal cleansing 62
International Campaign to End Genocide 319
international case law
on degree or quality of genocidal intent 23–7
International Commission of Jurists 5
International Commission on Human Rights 328
International Commission on Intervention and State Sovereignty, Report of 298–315
International Committee of the Red Cross (ICRC) 373, 491, 517
International Convention on the Suppression and Punishment of the Crime of Apartheid 81
International Court of Justice 11, 27, 86, 403, 412, 413, 415
International Covenant on Civil and Political Rights 330
International Criminal Court (ICC) 23, 34, 59, 78, 153, 154, 206, 211, 287, 290, 426, 491–3

International Criminal Tribunal for Rwanda (ICTR) 23, 26–7, 34, 59, 78, 82, 85, 153, 154, 182, 187, 213 287, 290, 442, 463–5, 465–7, 473–81, 485
budget and staff 478
contribution to postgenocide Rwanda 481
contribution to legal and political issues concerning genocide 480
creation 473–4
formation 468–72
goals 474
history of prosecutions 478–80
jurisdiction 474–5
sentencing 478
structure 475–6
trial and appeal processes 476–7
International Criminal Tribunal for the Former Yugoslavia (ICTY) 23–6, 34, 59, 78, 81, 82, 85, 153, 154, 184, 185, 186, 192, 287, 290, 439–51
arrest powers 445
creation 441–4
crimes against humanity 445–8
enforcement powers 444–5
jurisdiction 444
jurisprudence and legal developments 444
International Crisis Group 319
International Law Commission (UN) 23, 27–8, 82–5
International League for the Rights of Man 118
International Military Education and Training (IMET) funding 403
International Military Tribunal for the Far East (Tokyo) 289, 291–2, 436
International Monetary Fund 374, 402
International Red Cross 519
international treaty law
on degree or quality of genocidal intent 23
intervention 361–3
Iraq, US invasion xiv
Irving, David 518, 525, 529
Ishii, Lt. Shiro 524
Israel, creation of 162–3

Jackson, Justice Robert H. 430
Jackson, Robert H. 79, 80, 142, 430, 433, 435
Jaggabatara, Major-General Songkitti 400
Janjaweed 128, 133, 135, 194, 195–6, 197, 203–12, 215, 217–25, 517
Javits, Jacob 14
Jelisić, Goran 449
trial 23, 24, 25, 26, 28, 29–30, 449
Jenin "massacre" 86
Jewish self-ascription 60
Jews, destruction of 136
see also anti-Semitism; Holocaust, Nazi
Jodl, General 431
John XXIII, Pope 163
Johst 251

Kabila, Laurent 332
Kagame, Paul 345, 346, 354, 357, 358, 467
Kajelijeli, Juvenal 478
Kalimantan, Indonesia 318

Kaltenbrunner 248, 431
Kambanda, Jean 465, 471, 475, 478–9, 489
  trial 478, 479
Kampuchea 52, 75–7, 109, 119
Kampuchean United Front for National Salvation 395
Karadzic, Radovan 185, 193, 240, 246, 383, 454, 460, 461
Karemera, Edouard 479
Karremans, Colonel Thomas 455
Katson, Trisha 13, 14
Katyn massacre (1941) 86, 522
Kayishema, Clement 472, 480
  trial 26, 480
Keitel, General 431
Kellogg-Briand Treaty (1928) 434
Kennet, Lord 415
Khmer Rouge 43, 47, 52, 53–6, 76, 89, 100, 117, 122, 127,
    129, 133, 138, 149, 244–8, 250, 251, 318–19, 387,
    395, 406
Kim Dae Jung 401
Kirsch, Phillipe 505
Kishinev pogrom 88
Kissinger, Henry 403
Knights Templar 48
Koik, Arbab Abou 224
Kordić, Dario, trial 447, 448
Korean War 295
Kosovo Liberation Army (KLA) 439
Kosovo xiii–xiv, 57, 152
  ethnic cleansing xiv, 64
  state rape in 186
*Kristallnacht* 87, 157, 244
Kristof, Nicholas D. 214
Krstić, Major-General Radislav 193, 194, 441, 449–50,
    452–62
  trial 24–5, 26, 26, 28, 40, 449–50
Krupp, Alfred 430
Krupp, Gustav 430, 434
Kulak classes 66
Kuper, Leo 4, 529, 533
*Kupreškić* case 448
*Kunarac et al* case 446, 447, 448
Kurds, Iraqi massacre of 133, 138
Kuwait, Iraq aggression against 384

Lake, Anthony 357, 494
Lansing, Robert 78
Lassalle, Ferdinand 115
Lausanne, Treaty of 79
Lavrov, Ambassador 414
Lawrence, Sir Geoffrey 433
Lawyers Committee for Human Rights (LCHR) 375, 495
League of Nations 10, 79, 491, 496, 503
Lemkin, Raphael ix, x, xi, 3–4, 6–11, 11–15, 16, 20, 36,
    44–6, 54, 58, 71, 95, 135, 141–3, 144, 426
Lenin, Vladimir 89, 162
Lenk, Timur 41, 77
Leopold, King 78
Leuchter, Fred 524
Lewis, Bernard 525, 531
Ley, Robert 430
Liberty Lobby 14

libricide 96
linguicide 50
LIPRODHOR 467
Lipstadt, Deborah 518, 525
Lodge, Henry Cabot, Jr 13
Lon Nol regime 118
London Conference (1945) 79
Louis, XVI, King 78
Luxembourg, Rosa 115
lynchings 50

MacKinnon, Catharine 181
Maidanek death camp 9, 139, 158, 171, 172, 174–6
malevolent bigotry 519–25
Malik, Adam 402
Malmédy massacre 429
Mandela, Nelson 380, 381
Mandzic, Mr 455
Maoists 66
Marr, Wilhelm 238
Martens clause 78
Martin, James 13–14
Marx, Karl 115, 161
mass killing, origins of 97–107
massacres 59, 86–91
  destruction and subjugation 88–9
  local 87
  long-distance 87
material scarcity 122, 123–4, 125
Maxwell-Fyfe, Sir David 430
McCloy, John 428
McDonald, Gabrielle Kirk 509
McMahon, Brien 13
*Médicins Sans Frontières* 203
Melians, mass slaughter of 133
Melos massacre 135
mental illness, cleansing by 63, 90
microethnicity 69
Miedzyrzec ghetto 168–9
militarized humanitarian intervention 363–78
militias 75, 90
Milosevic, Slobodan xiv, 152, 185, 186, 193, 239, 246,
    271, 383, 384, 412, 416, 418, 419, 439, 440, 441,
    443
Minni Arkoy Minawi 209, 210
Missimino, Elisa 500
mission creep 369
"Mississippi appendectomies" x
Mladic, General Ratko 193, 248, 440, 454, 455, 460, 461
Mogadishu 295
Moluccas, Indonesia 318
Mongols 136
monolithic culture 101
monopolistic genocide 42
moral methods of genocide 8
Morganthau, Henry, Jr 427
motivation 102, 107
motive 107
Moynier, Gustav 491
MSF-Holland 371
multiple genocide 96

Mundurucú headhunters 104
murderous cleansing 64–8
Musema, Alfred 480
    trial 26–7, 480
Museveni, Yoweri 262, 267, 328, 329
Muslim Brotherhood 198, 199
Mussolini, Benito
    160
mutually-assured total nuclear destruction (MAD) 148
My Lai massacre, North Vietnam 16

Nagano, Sigeto 524
Nagasaki, atom-bombing of 36, 52, 82, 529
Nahimana, Ferdinand 479
Nanking Massacre 89, 524
Nasution, General 251, 263
nation, definition of 69–70
national case law 28
National Socialism 6
national upheavals, types 111–13
nationalism 101
Native American peoples 90
    see also under tribes
nationalistic hubris 532–3
NATO 151, 152, 193–4, 294, 364, 366
NATO intervention in Kosovo 409–20
    contested legality 411–14
    NATO's justification 414–18
Nazim, Dr 249
Ndindiliyimana, Augustin 348
needs 99–100, 107
Neurath, Konstantin von 431
Newbury, Catherine 329
Ngeze, Hassan 479
Niebuhr, Reinhold 106
Nigeria 42, 115, 116
    Armenian genocide and 238–9, 240–1
Nigerian Civil War 148–9
Nikitchenko, Ion Timifeevich 430
Nikolić, Dragan, trial 445
Nimeiri, Colonel Jaafar 198, 199, 202
Nimitz, Admiral Chester 435
Niumpradit, Lieutenant-General Boonsran 400
Nixon, Richard 13
Nolte, Ernst 524, 531
non-governmental organizations 79, 205, 319, 374, 375,
    467
norm entrepreneur model of humanitarian intervention
    410
North Atlantic Treaty Organization see NATO
Ntakirutimana, Elizaphan 471, 478
Ntaryamira, President 187
nuclear war 76–7
Nuhanovic, Mr 455
Nuon Chea 248
al Nur, Abdel Wahid Mohamed 209
Nuremberg Charter 79–80, 81, 82, 83, 84, 426
    Control Council Law No. 10 83, 84
Nuremberg International Military Tribunal 3, 12, 15, 20,
    59, 80, 85, 142, 287, 289, 291–2, 425–6, 427–37
Nuremberg Law 245

Nuremberg Principles 426
Nyiramasuhuko, Pauline 188, 471, 479

Obote, Milton 117, 262
Ogata, Sadako 363, 509
Okali, Agwu Ukiwe 471
old age, cleansing by 63
Omanovic, Mrs 455
Omar, Mullah Mohammed 524–5
omnicide 96
Operation Allied Force 416
Operation Barbarossa 159, 265, 267
Operation Skakavac 454
Operation Support Hope 371
Opération Turquoise 370, 371
Oradour-sur-Glane massacre 87
Organic Law No. 08/96 487–8
Organization of African Unity (OAU) 117, 364
organization stage 128
origins of genocide 97–107
    continuum of destruction 100
    coping and fulfilling needs and goals 99–100
    cultural-societal characteristics 100–2
    difficult life conditions 98
    groups as evil or good 106–7
    individual and the system 104–5
    leadership and followership 102–4
    psychological consequences 98–9
    role of bystanders 102
    role of motivation 102
    roots of evil 105–6
Ostojic, Velibor 185
Oswiecim death camp 9
Ottoman Empire 114, 235, 247, 260
Oumar, Condoleezza Mahjoub 219
Oxfam 218, 374

Pakistan 42, 115, 116
Pan-Turkism 235, 236
Papen, Franz von 431, 436
Papon, Maurice 85
paradigmatic cleansing 61
Paris Commune 62
Paris Peace Conference, Responsibilities Commission of
    79
Pasha, Enver 114, 235, 248
Pasha, Talaat 235, 248
Payne, Donald 205
Pejic, Jelena 505
Pell, Herbert C. 79
Pequots genocide 133
permissive societies 38
persecution as crime against humanity 84
personal goal theory 102
Philippines 75
philosophy of genocide 6–7
physical deformity, cleansing of 61
physical methods of genocide 9
Physicians for Human Rights 205
Pillay, Navanethem 482
Pitt, Brad 214

Pius XII, Pope 161
Plaszow camp 176
pluralistic society 101
pogroms 3, 50, 88
Pol Pot 36, 71–2, 89, 100, 109, 111, 117–18, 129, 149–50, 244–8, 250, 251, 396, 412
polarization stage 128
political cleansing 62
political methods of genocide 7
political scarcity 121–2
political will 293–7
politicide 47, 58, 71–2, 73–5, 96
Popovic, Colonel 455
Popular Arab Islamic Conference (PAIC) 199
Posner, Michael 506
posse model of humanitarian intervention 410
post-colonial genocides 115–17
post-coup genocides 117–18
post-Holocaust victim responses 162–3
post-revolutionary genocides 117–18
post-war, post-imperial genocides 114–15
Powell, Colin 205, 206, 211, 212, 213, 219–20, 493, 494
prediction, genocide 38, 39
preemptive cleansing 61
preparation stage 128
Preparatory Commission for the International Criminal Court (PCICC) 34
Prévention Génocides 319
prevention of genocide 124–6, 150–3, 153–4, 320–38
    anticipation and deterrence 323–4
    cost 321–2, 333
    democracy and 322–3
    early warning 317–19
primitivism 67
Prosecutor v. Alfred Musema 26–7, 480
Prosecutor v. Anto Furundžija 447
Prosecutor v. Bagilishema 479
Prosecutor v. Blaškić 444
Prosecutor v. Clément Kayishema and Obed Ruzindana 26
Prosecutor v. Dario Kordić 447, 448
Prosecutor v. Dragan Nikolić 445
Prosecutor v. Duško Sikirica et al. 25
Prosecutor v. Dusko Tadić 444, 445–6
Prosecutor v. Georges Anderson Nderubumwe Rutaganda 27
Prosecutor v. Goran Jelisić 23, 24, 25, 26, 28, 29–30, 449
Prosecutor v. Jean-Paul Akayesu 26
Prosecutor v. Kambanda 478, 479
Prosecutor v. Kayishema 480
Prosecutor v. Kunarac et al 446, 447, 448
Prosecutor v. Kupreškić 448
Prosecutor v. Mario Ćerkez 447
Prosecutor v. Milomir Stakić 25–6
Prosecutor v. Radislav Krstić 24–5, 26, 27, 28, 30, 449–50
Prosecutor v. Slavko Dokmanović 445
Prosper, Pierre 153, 212
prostitutes, cleansing of 63
Proxmire, William 11, 14
pseudoracial cleansing 61

psychological processes 107
psychological scarcity 121

race 243–4
    defining 244–5
race riots 50
racial cleansing 61
Radio-Télévision Libre des Mille Collines (RTLMC) 330
Raeder, Admiral 431
Rahman, Sheikh Mujibur 188, 391
Rainey, John 471
Ramos-Horta, José 402
rape 151, 447
    case studies 182–8
    as crime against humanity 84
    defined in international law 483–4
    as genocide 181–2
    state 180–92
Rassinier, Paul 523
Rawson, Ambassador 344
Rayishema, Clement 471
Reagan, Ronald, Administration 143
realpolitik 288–90
Red Cross 218, 219
Refugees International 375
religion 8, 243–4
religious cleansing 61, 62
responsibility to protect 287
retributive genocide xii, 37, 41
revolutions 113, 268
Reyntjens, Professor 328
Riad, Judge 452
Ribbentrop, Joachim von 431
Rice, Condoleezza 219, 220
Richardson, Bill 502
Riza, Iqbal 338, 348
Robespierre, Maximilien 78
Rodrigues, Judge Almiro 452
Rogers, Carl 106
Röhm, Ernst 248
Roman Empire 41
Rome Statute 29, 82, 83, 84, 85, 293, 493–510
Roosevelt, Franklin Delano 141, 427, 428, 429
Roosevelt, Theodore 161
Rosenberg, Alfred 7, 248, 431
Rousseau, Jean-Jacques 106
Rowe, James 435
Roy, Khamiss 225
Rubenstein, Richard L. xiii
Rudenko, Lieutenant General Roman 430, 434
Ruez, Jean-René 452
Ruggiu, Georges 464, 478
Rummel, R.J. 35
Rundstedt, Marshal von 6, 7
Russell tribunal 16
Russian civil war 62
Russo-Turkish War 247
Rutaganda, George Anderson Nderubumwe 472, 478
    trial 27

Ruzindana, Obed 480
   trial 26
Rwagasore, Simeon 488
Rwamakuba, André 479
Rwanda 152, 153
   economic sanctions 381–2, 386
   forecasting and prevention of genocide 324–32
   genocide xiv, 16, 122
      Holocaust vs 258–84
   state rape 186–8
   trials for genocide in 487–9
Rwandan Patriotic Front 464

Sabra and Shatila massacre, Lebanon 90
Sadjstvo 95 454
Saint Bartholomew 87–8
sanctions, economic 368, 378–90
   effectiveness 379–85
   on Rwanda 381–2, 386
   on Iraq 384–6
Sanctions Monitoring System (SAMS) 383
Santos, Lieutenant-General Jaime de los 400
Sarajevo, siege of xv
Sauckel, Fritz 431
Save Darfur Coalition 214
Save the Children 374
scarcity, genocide and 120–6
Schabas, William A. 28
Schacht, Hjalmar 431, 436
Schanberg, Sidney 522
Scheffer, David 500, 506
Schirach, Baldur von 431, 435
self-cleansing 62
self-serving opportunism 525–6
September 11, 2001 64–5, 82, 207, 522
Sèvres Treaty 79, 291
sexual preference, cleansing by 62–3
Seyss-Inquart, Artur von 431
Shaka 48
Shant, Adam Yacub 207
Sharf, Michael 503
Sharpesville demonstration, S. Africa 89
Shawcross, Sir Hartley 434
Sihanouk, Prince Norodom 117
Sikhs 116
Simeon Bar Kochba 136
Six-Day War 164
slavery 52–3, 60, 62
Slovenia 57
Smith Act (USA) 428
Smith, Bradley 528
Smith, H. Alexander 13
Sobibor death camp 139, 158
social cleansing 63
social methods of genocide 7
sociocide 50
sociological definition 54–5
Somalia syndrome 369
Son Sen 248
Soviet Gulag system 259
Spanish civil war 62

Spanish conquest of Mexico 123
Spartacus Revolt 159
Speer 431
Srebenica massacre xiii, 133, 134–5, 151, 192–4,
   453–62
SS Office for Race and Resettlement trial 434
St Bartholomew's Day massacre 137
stages of genocide 127–9, 317–18
Stakić, Milomir, trial 25–6
Stalin, Joseph 36, 37, 48, 54, 71, 87, 111, 139, 268, 429,
   529
STAND 214
Stanton, Gregory 35
Starr, Kenneth 503
state sovereignty 289, 290–3
Stimson, Henry 427, 428, 429
Stolen Generations 138
strategic cleansing 62
Streicher, Julius 85, 431, 479
subjugation, massacre and 88–9
Sudan 115
Sudanese Liberation Movement/Army (SLM/A) 203
Suharto, President 251, 263, 274, 403
   regime 118
Sukarno, President 117
Sukarnoputri, Megawati 405
Sulawesi, Indonesia 318
surgical strikes 368
survivor syndrome 162
symbolization stage 127
Symons, Baroness 415

Tadić, Dusko 443, 444
   trial 444, 445–6
Tadjdein, Battalion Commander 225
Taha, Ali Osman Mohamed 199, 200
Tamil Tigers 73
Tasmanian Aborigines 137
Taylor, Telford 430
techniques of genocide 7–9
temporary cleansing 63
territorial decline 247–8
territorial expansionism 245–7
Theresienstadt concentration camp/ghetto 179, 519
Thiessen, Marc 495
Thirty Years' War 137
Thornton, Brenda Sue 471
Thucydides 135
Tiananmen Square massacre 364, 522
Tilly, Charles 90
Timor Gap 'Zone of Cooperation' agreement 403
Tito, Marshal 239
tolerant societies 38
torture 48, 77, 83, 89, 105, 150
torture societies 38
Totten, Samuel 216, 222, 223
traditional-shame societies 38
Trail of Tears 108–9
travel and participation bans 386, 388
Treblinka death camp 85, 139, 158, 167, 169, 170–1
Trnopolje detention camp 184

Trotha, General Lothar von 77, 243
Trotsky, Leon 161
Truggernanna (Truganini) 137
Tudjman, Franco 239, 271
al Turabi, Hassan Abd 198–200
Turkification 114, 115
Turkish Institute 524
Tutsi, Rwanda, genocide by Hutus xiv, 38, 68, 90, 91, 116, 133, 134, 138, 149, 152, 186–7, 188, 261–2
Twa 268

UDT 116
Ukraine, manmade famine in 37, 54, 87, 123, 133, 138, 139, 215
UN ix, xi
    Ad Hoc Committee on Genocide 46
    General Assembly 80–1, 144
    Human Rights Commission 46
    role in defining genocide 14–15
    Secretariat 384
UN Administrative Mission in East Timor (UNAMET) 372–3, 400, 404
UN Assistance Mission to Rwanda (UNAMIR) 318, 329, 330, 331, 365, 371, 381, 382, 463
UN Commission of Inquiry into Darfur (COI) 206, 211
UN Department of Peacekeeping Operations (DPKO) 338
UN Protection Force (UNPROFOR) 151, 194, 384, 400, 454, 455, 456
UN Security Council xiv, 128, 152, 153, 206, 290, 364, 395, 398
    intervention decisionmaking 364–5
    regional organization and coalitions of the willing 165–6
    state decisionmaking 267
UN Security Council Resolutions 192, 194
    Resolution 661 384
    Resolution 678 364
    Resolution 687 384
    Resolution 688 415
    Resolution 713 382
    Resolution 727 382
    Resolution 752 383
    Resolution 757 383
    Resolution 827 442
    Resolution 872 381
    Resolution 918 382
    Resolution 942 384
    Resolution 955 466, 469–70
    Resolution 997 382
    Resolution 1021 382
    Resolutions 1199 and 1203 414, 416
    Resolution 1264 400
    Resolution 1564 206
UN Standing High Readiness Brigade 128
UN Transitional Authority in Cambodia (UNTAC) 398, 400, 406
UN War Crimes Commission 79
UNAMET 372–3, 400, 404
UNAMID 208

UNAMIR 318, 329, 330, 331, 365, 371, 381, 382, 463
UNCG see Genocide Convention
UNICEF 384
UNITA 387
United Nations see entries under UN
United States Holocaust Memorial Museum (USHMM) 205
Uniting for Peace Resolution 418
Universal Declaration of Human Rights (UN) 134, 146, 287
universal jurisdiction, principle of 85
UNOSOM II 400
UNPROFOR 151, 194, 384, 400, 454, 455, 456
UNTAC 398, 400, 406
UNTAET (UN Transitional Administration in East Timor) 400, 406
US Agency for International Aid (USAID) 205, 329
US Committee for Refugees 375
utilitarian genocide 41–2

vandalism 12
Vatican Commission for Religious Relations with the Jews 163
Vedrine, Hubert 508
Vendean population, massacre 89
Versailles Peace Conference (1919) 491
Versailles Treaty (1919) 291, 427, 429, 496
Vietnam War 52, 53, 117, 294
vigilante model of humanitarian intervention 410
Vlad the Dracul 63
Vraalsen, Tom 205

Wald, Judge 449, 452
Waldheim, Kurt 165
Wannsee conference 76
war 76–7
war against terrorism 64, 67
war vs genocide xii–xiii, 52–4, 110–11
wars of religion 43
Warsaw ghetto 9
Wasserman, Chaykele 176–8
Wax, Emily 214
Wechsler, Herbert 435
Wedgwood, Ruth 508
Weizmann, Chaim 523, 524
Werleigh, Claudette 380
Westphalia, Peace of 290
Westphalia, Treaty of 287, 288
Whitaker Report (1985) 529
Whitaker, Ben 5, 37
Whitlam, Gough 403
Wiesel, Elie ix
Williams, George Washington 78
Wilson, President 503
witches, burning of 63
women as victims and perpetrators 53
World Bank 326, 364, 374
World Council of Churches 71
World Health Organization (WHO) 384
World Trade Organization (WTO) 364
World War I xii, xiii, 162, 247, 291

Young Turks 68, 114, 138, 235, 237, 241, 245, 247,
    248, 249
Yugoslavia
    Armenian genocide vs 239–40, 241
    sanctions 382–4
    *see also* Bosnia-Herzegovina

Yuki Indians, California, genocide of
    133

Zionism 14, 162, 237
Zivanovic, General 454, 455
Zundel, Ernest 523